THE IRWIN SERIES IN ECONOMICS

CONSULTING EDITOR

LLOYD G. REYNOLDS
YALE UNIVERSITY

BOOKS IN THE IRWIN SERIES IN ECONOMICS

Economics A General Introduction

A General Introduction

REVISED EDITION—1966

Sterling Professor of Economics and Director, Economic Growth Center, Yale University

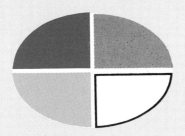

HOMEWOOD, ILLINOIS

Economics

LLOYD G. REYNOLDS

RICHARD D. IRWIN, INC.

Revised Edition
First printing, March, 1966
Second printing, January, 1967
Third printing, August, 1967

Library of Congress Catalog Card No. 66–14544

PRINTED IN THE UNITED STATES OF AMERICA

for Mary

Preface to the Revised Edition

It is naturally gratifying that the earlier edition of this book has been found teachable and readable at so many places. But in a first effort there is always a gap between intent and accomplishment. I have benefited by comments from scores of teachers and students, whose suggestions are reflected in this thorough revision.

It is difficult to organize a text to meet equally the needs of those who prefer a micro-macro sequence and those with the opposite preference. I have tried to meet this problem by a substantial introductory section, which gives an overview of market organization and an introduction to some central tools of micro analysis. This can lead directly into the fuller examination of micro theory in Part One. But teachers who prefer to go from the introduction to the aggregative analysis of Part Three will find this entirely feasible.

Some areas of micro theory were treated quite summarily in the first edition, and some users of the book found this a deficiency. I believe they are right in the sense that a text should provide a wide variety of teaching options, leaving to each teacher the choice of what to include and what to omit. So Part One has been largely rewritten, with the increase in length which is the price of fuller exposition.

The treatment of international economics has also been substantially enlarged. Heckscher and Ohlin have joined Ricardo in the chapter on trade theory. A chapter has been added on exchange rates, the balance of payments, and the international monetary mechanism. Another significant addition is a chapter on the theory of economic growth, which serves as an introduction to Part Four. The later chapters in this Part have also been heavily rewritten to keep pace with the rapid advance of research on problems of economic growth and development.

In addition to enriching the book in these directions, I have tried to take account of major contributions to the literature since the previous edition; to bring statistics and other factual material fully up to date; to struggle once more with clarity of diagrams, adequacy of summaries, pertinence of discussion questions.

My conception of the ideal elementary course remains unchanged. The course should be regarded as economics for the general reader who will never study economics again, rather than for the small minority of prospective specialists. Its objective is to train students to approach policy issues in the frame of mind with which economists approach these issues, to think like economists. This requires mastery of analytical tools, but these should be necessary tools which are actually used for descriptive and normative purposes. I have tried to be tough about omitting topics which do not clearly pass this test.

Several other judgments have guided the scope and organization of the book:

1. In microeconomics, the whole is more than the sum of its parts. Micro theory often seems unappetizing to students because it is so *very* micro. The spotlight is held too long on the supposed operations of hypothetical business firms. The concept of a national economic mechanism, which transmits and absorbs changes occurring anywhere in the system, becomes lost in the shuffle.

I have tried to emphasize the interrelatedness of the market network, the results that a competitive economy is supposed to produce, and the extent to which the American economy meets these tests of efficient performance. As an accompanying though minor theme, I examine the way in which the same problems of production and distribution are handled in Soviet-type economies, and the problem of appraising the efficiency of these economies.

2. In macroeconomics, long-run economic growth is emerging as the central problem of our time. The rapid growth of output in Soviet-type economies is asserted as proof of their superiority. The fact that U.S. economic growth has since 1950 lagged behind that of Western Europe and Japan gives cause for concern. The determination of the poorer countries of Asia, Africa, and Latin America to accelerate their economic development is a central fact of international relations. Thus the issues examined in Part Four now impress students as especially significant, and this may become increasingly true over the years ahead. In this respect the book can perhaps claim to be forward looking.

3. This claim can be made in another respect as well. In an age when the United States has willy-nilly assumed a position of world leadership, it seems odd that most elementary economics texts focus so heavily on the American economy. The standard allotment of space to the Soviet-bloc countries and the underdeveloped countries combined is about 5 percent. This leaves the student ignorant of many matters on which he should be informed. It also breeds an ethnocentrism which regards our own economic institutions as right and proper, while all other nations are wrong-headed. The 20 percent of space that I have alloted to foreign economies is still not enough, but it is a step in the right direction.

I trust that students will continue to find the book readable and relevant to their world, and that teachers will find it a useful teaching vehicle. I shall continue to be grateful for comments and advice from all quarters. I shall not take all of it, because that way lies the graveyard of encyclopedism. But one may hope that future editions will converge toward that "more perfect book" which is every author's dream.

L. G. R.

West Bend, Wisconsin
September, 1965

Acknowledgments

I am grateful for several kinds of aid, without which this edition could not have been completed. Joanne Clifford, George Grantham, and Gerald Neal helped to assemble and check the basic data. John King made preliminary drawings of the diagrams. Olive Higgins did a careful job of typing draft chapters, compiling and checking the final manuscript, and reading galley and page proofs.

Most especially am I grateful to a number of colleagues who read portions of the revised edition: Robert Clower, Northwestern University; Daniel Fusfeld and Richard Porter, University of Michigan; Ronald R. Olsen, University of Kansas; John Arena, Council of Economic Advisers; and Robert Triffin, Stephen Hymer, Shane Hunt, and William Brainard, Yale University. Their comments were invaluable; but they should not, of course, be implicated in the outcome.

Among members of the Irwin staff, I should like especially to thank Harry Bingham, who did a meticulous editing of the manuscript.

I should not fail to express appreciation to my students in elementary economics at Yale, whose skepticism and zeal for controversy has taught me more than they realized.

L. G. R.

Table of Contents

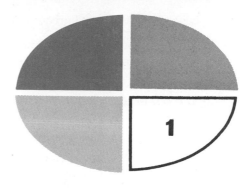

What Economics Is About

> Political economy or economics is a study of mankind in the ordinary business of life; it examines that part of individual and social action which is most closely connected with the attainment and with the use of the material requisites of well-being. Thus it is on the one side a study of wealth; and on the other, and more important side, a part of the study of man.
> ALFRED MARSHALL

> The theory of economics does not furnish a body of settled conclusions immediately applicable to policy. It is a method rather than a doctrine, an apparatus of the mind, a technique of thinking, which helps its possessor to draw correct conclusions.
> JOHN MAYNARD KEYNES

IN A GENERAL WAY, we all know what economics is about. It is concerned with the production, distribution, and use of material goods and services. It deals with the activities of the 5 million business concerns, 4 million farms, 80 million workers, and 50 million households that produced and consumed about $700 billion worth of output in the United States in 1966. As Adam Smith said, economics is "an inquiry into the nature and causes of the wealth of nations."

But just how is economics concerned with these things? What is its approach and method of analysis? What is the "apparatus of the mind" to which Keynes referred? This chapter is an informal chat about these things before we plunge into the subject in Chapter 2.

ECONOMICS AND BUSINESS

Students enroll in economics courses for many reasons—an interest in political issues, a desire to get ahead in business, a curriculum requirement that they would gladly escape. Someone may have told them that economics is practical, that it has something to do with business, that it might lead to success and fortune in the stock market. It is only fair to set this straight at the beginning. The study of economics is not a direct path to riches. The gibe often leveled at economists, "If you're so smart, why aren't you rich?" rests on a misunderstanding. Economists are not especially qualified for stock speculation, and several famous scholars have lost their shirts by ignoring this truth. Still less are they necessarily qualified to manage a business or teach anyone else how to do so.

Economics and business are related, but distinct, studies. Business administration looks at a business concern from the inside, as it were, while economics views it mainly from the outside. The student of business administration sets himself the problems faced by the business manager: How can this company be organized to perform most efficiently and profitably? What personnel, production, marketing, and financial policies will enable the company to survive, grow, and yield an adequate return on the stockholders' investment? The modern manager also wants his company to be considered a good citizen and to take its share of community responsibility. But efficiency and profitability lie at the heart of business management.

It is important that business units should be managed efficiently and that enterprisers should be enterprising. The national economy cannot operate efficiently unless this basic job is being done well. Even Russia has business schools, which have 5-year programs of study, and which each year turn out thousands of accountants, bank personnel, statisticians, pricing and production experts, personnel managers, and economic planners. In addition, a high proportion of the top management of Russian industry is drawn from schools of engineering, as is true to a lesser extent in the United States.

The economist is concerned with the behavior of business units somewhat as a physicist looks at his neutrons and protons. Business concerns are the basic particles of the economic world. The economist views them from the outside, tries to understand their reactions, but does not try to change or improve them. He generally takes it for granted that business managers know their job and are doing it well. His interest is not in what goes on inside a particular company but in its interaction with other companies in the larger economy. The economist does not try to find out how a particular textile mill can be managed most profitably. He does try to analyze what will happen to prices and production in the textile industry if the national demand for cotton cloth falls off.

This is not to say that economics is entirely impractical from a business standpoint. Many ideas first developed by economists have been applied in business management. Analysis of consumer demand, for example, has long been a standard subject in economics. Work in this area has obvious practical applications. If one can predict that a 3 percent increase in consumers' incomes will mean a 5 percent increase in sales of new automobiles, this is an important thing for automobile companies to know. It would also be important to know that a 5 percent rise in new-car prices will produce a 2 percent drop in the number of cars sold. Economists and statisticians have developed ways of making such predictions.

Management people also try to outguess the swings of the business cycle. Will national production and employment continue to rise during the next 12 or 18 months? At what rate? Is there a danger that the economy may instead turn downward into a recession? Correct estimates can make the difference between large profits and serious losses. Economists have developed ways of analyzing fluctuations in national economic activity and have even had some success in prediction. Most large companies now find it profitable to hire a few economists for this sort of weathervane work.

Basic training in economics is normally a required part of a business curriculum. Economists do not object to this—we need the customers. But it is wrong to regard business education simply as applied economics. Business administration is a multidisciplinary study, resting on economics as one pillar, but resting also on psychology, engineering, statistics, and a variety of other disciplines. Above all, it involves the adaptation and fusion of these tools in the solution of management problems.

Perhaps the best way to put the matter is to regard economics and business administration as intersecting circles with some area of overlap. Business education is partly applied economics, but it is not *mainly* that. Economics has certain applications to management, but its *main* applications lie in another direction.

ECONOMICS AND GOVERNMENT

Economics is political economy. Its main applications are to the great issues of economic policy that have been debated for generations.

Who should pay the taxes? Should the rich have to pay a larger percentage of their incomes than the poor?

Should the government aim always to take in exactly as much as it spends? Is there sometimes a case for a budget surplus or deficit? If a country runs a deficit and increases its national debt, will it eventually become bankrupt?

Should manufacturers in the United States be protected against foreign competition by tariffs on imported products? Will goods produced by cheap foreign labor flood the country and cause widespread unemployment if this is not done?

Should the growth of giant corporations be viewed with approval as a step toward greater efficiency or with alarm as leading to monopoly control of industry? If monopoly is a danger, what can be done about it?

Are farmers right in arguing that they have special problems calling for government aid? Is it sensible to guarantee farmers a certain price for corn, wheat, cotton, and other basic products?

What can government do to reduce the likelihood of business depressions? If a depression somehow gets started, what can be done to get out of it?

Why has the national output of the U.S.A. been rising more slowly since 1950 than the national output of the U.S.S.R.? What might be done to increase the growth rate of our economy?

Note that these issues have one thing in common. They all involve *action by government to influence the economy*. The key question in each case is what kind of government action is feasible and wise.

The main purpose of a course in economics is to train you to think systematically about economic issues, correct solution of which may determine the prosperity and even the survival of the nation in the decades ahead. The object is to produce citizens able to pull their weight in a democratic society. Reasonable literacy in economic affairs is also a hallmark of the educated modern man. A prominent economist was once asked by an alumnus why anybody should bother to study economics. He replied, "So as not to be embarrassed in conversation in your club!"

Economics is part of liberal education, of education for citizenship. "Ah," you say, "then economics is really the same thing as politics. The test of a good economist is whether he has correct opinions on political questions." Heavens no! Nothing could be farther from the truth. A left-wing Democrat may be a very good economist or a very poor one. So may a right-wing Republican. There are good and bad economists in every political camp.

The relation of economics to politics can be explained by a simple example. What should the federal budget look like for the fiscal year 1966–67? Should there be a surplus, a deficit, or an even balance? How can the economist contribute to a decision on this issue? Primarily, by raising three kinds of factual question:

a. **What is the present situation?** If present tax rates and expenditure levels were continued without change, what would the budget

picture look like? What would be the size of the deficit or surplus at the
end of the fiscal year? The answer depends on estimates of the level of
business activity in the year ahead, since this has a large influence on tax
receipts and some influence on government expenditures. Estimates of
business conditions can never be completely accurate, and so economists
can give only rough answers to the above questions. Many economists,
however, are engaged in exactly this kind of calculation in the U.S.
Treasury Department, the U.S. Bureau of the Budget, and private
organizations.

b. What are the policy alternatives? Suppose a large budget surplus is in prospect, and the administration of the day decides it would be
better to have a small surplus or an even balance. There are many
different ways by which this might be accomplished. Tax collections may
be reduced, or expenditures may be increased, or both. If it is decided to
reduce tax collections, this can be done by raising personal income tax
exemptions, reducing the basic tax rate, lowering the rates on higher
bracket incomes, reducing the corporation income tax, cutting federal
excise taxes, or doing several of these things together. Economists can
estimate how much each of these steps would reduce tax collections and
can make up various "package" proposals, each of which would have the
same result of reducing the budget surplus by $3 billion or whatever the
desired amount may be.

c. What are the consequences of choosing a particular alternative?
The economist tries to determine, not merely what courses of action are
open, but how the choice of a particular course will affect the operation
of the economy. How would various ways of changing the personal
income tax structure affect the equality of incomes in the country? What
repercussions might be expected on spending, saving, effort, and initiative? How would a change in the corporate income tax affect corporate
saving and investment? How would lowering the excise tax on particular
products—tires, automobiles, cigarettes, transportation—affect the price
and sales of these products? One mark of a professional economist is that
he knows how to take hold of such questions.

On questions of fact, well-trained economists of any political shade
should be in general agreement. Where they disagree, the differences can
be pinpointed, spelled out in statistical terms, and perhaps reconciled.

Basic disagreement begins when one faces the question: *What
should the government do?* Having looked at all the figures and all the
alternatives, what is the wise course of action? Any answer to this
question goes beyond economics in two directions. First, it involves value
judgments. What is a just distribution of personal income? How active a
part should government take in economic affairs? What kind of economic
and political system do we want over the long run? The economist has no
special competence to lay down the law on such matters.

Second, a statement that government *should* do a certain thing

involves a judgment of what is feasible from a political and administrative standpoint. There is no point in drawing up a beautiful piece of
legislation that is certain to be voted down by Congress; nor is there
much point in passing a law that cannot be administered effectively.
Judgments about what can and cannot be done politically are not within
the province of the economist.

To reach decisions on economic policy, then, one needs:

1. A knowledge of economic facts, alternatives, and consequences.
2. Judgments of value.
3. A knowledge of how to get things done through government.

Steps 2 and 3 are *not* economics, and an economist has no special
qualifications in these areas. But economists are also people and have the
same right as other citizens to hold personal values and make political
judgments. Equally good economists may thus come out with different
practical conclusions. There is nothing odd about this. When economists
differ on what should be done, they are differing in their human capacity
as citizens.

THE METHODS OF ECONOMICS

So much for what economists claim to do. How do they do it? What
are the basic methods and techniques? What constitutes proof in
economics?

The Necessity of Measurement

Economics has an advantage in dealing mainly with *quantities.* It is
concerned with prices, hourly wage rates, numbers of people employed,
amounts of goods produced and exchanged, quantity of money and
credit in existence, government receipts and expenditures. These things
are measurable in principle, though actual measurements fall short of
perfection.

Precise measurement, then, is the basis for serious study of
economics. Before trying to explain what goes on in the economy, we try
to discover what actually *is* going on. If one man maintains that national
output is higher this year than last, while another maintains firmly that it
is lower, they cannot get any farther. Agreement on facts is an essential
starting point. So we set out to measure total national output, production
of specific goods and services, exports and imports, the money incomes of
households, price levels and wage levels, and dozens of other things. One
cannot approach economics without such measurements any more than
natural scientists can operate without measures of mass or tempera-
ture.

Preparation and criticism of these measures is the task of *economic
statistics.* There has been enormous progress on this front over the past

two or three generations. In 1900 we had little more than the decennial census data plus a few skimpy price statistics. Today we have a great volume of measurements for almost every conceivable economic quantity, a volume that threatens at times to become overwhelming.

Explanation and Prediction

Measurement of what is happening is only the beginning. Our ultimate hope is to *explain* why things happen as they do. If we can explain past events, we have some chance of being able to *predict* future events. Science always aims at prediction; and practical men are especially intrigued by the possibilities of prediction in economics, since profits and votes may hang on the outcome.

Horseback predictions can sometimes be obtained directly from economic statistics. For example, if you look at statistics of personal income in the United States over the last 30 years, you will find that on the average about 92 percent of personal income after taxes has been spent on consumption while 8 percent has been saved. Except for the war years 1942–45, when goods were hard to get and savings were abnormally large, the savings ratio has not varied far from the 8 percent average. Thus if you have to make a quick estimate of what personal savings will be next year, your safest course will be to take 8 percent of expected personal income.

Such rules of thumb are all right as far as they go. Their limitation is that they give no explanation of *why* the figures behave as they do. It is as though an engineer looked at a machine and observed that a particular wheel always went around so many times a minute but knew nothing about the principles governing the machine's operation. No engineer or physicist would be content to stop at this point. He wants to know *why* the machine behaves as it does. Until he knows this, he cannot be sure that another machine will behave in the same way, nor can he design a machine that would behave differently. Similarly, the economist wants to understand why the American people behave as they do about saving, food buying, working, and other things. He wants to discover the principles behind the statistics.

How can he go about getting this understanding? First, he can ask people why they made certain decisions. There are obvious drawbacks to this method. You can quiz only a small percentage of the population, and you can never be completely sure that you have a representative group. People do not always know why they did what they did, and if they do they may not be willing to tell. Interview questions have to be direct and simple, but the circumstances surrounding a decision are often complex. People can give more reliable answers about recent events than about events in the more distant past. Despite these difficulties, "survey research" has increased greatly in recent years and has added much to our economic understanding.

The standard method of physical science is the controlled experiment, but economists cannot use this method. We cannot shut people up in an isolated camp to observe their reactions. In any case, people's reactions under such artificial conditions would be different from their reactions in everyday life.

So what are we to do? Deprived of the possibility of actual experiments, the economist resorts to *intellectual experiments*. The process of intellectual experiment begins with *observations of behavior*. The important thing is observation of large numbers of families, or business concerns, or what not, rather than of isolated individuals. It isn't very interesting to know that, when Mr. Jones got a $1,000 raise last year, he put $200 of this into extra saving. Mr. Jones may turn out to be an unusual specimen. But if we find out that all families in the United States received $20 billion more income last year and that $3 billion of this went into savings, this is significant. If we can break the total population down into groups, say by income level, and observe the different behavior in these groups, this is even more interesting.

The next stage is to sit down quietly in an armchair and try to reason out why people might have behaved as they did. One can think of many things that might influence family decisions about saving, including the family's present income, its expected future income, its accumulated wealth, fixed commitments for mortgages and time payments, and plans for children's education or other large future expenditures. From what we know of our own reactions, and from what we observe in statistical measurements, we try to estimate the probable strength of these various influences. This is the stage of *hypothesis building* or *theorizing*. At the end, we come out with a set of propositions that may be capable of explaining the facts. We can call this a *theory of household savings*.

Finally, we must go back to the facts and test our hypotheses against observed behavior. Our theory says, for example, that people will react in a specified way to a certain increase in their current income. Well, do they or don't they? The measures of what actually happens are the payoff. If they agree closely with our hypothesis, we can have some confidence that we are on the right track. If not, we must ask what went wrong and start over again. This step is termed *verification, hypothesis testing*, or *statistical inference*. Statistical inference is the economist's substitute for the laboratory he can never have.

It may be necessary to work back and forth several times between hypotheses and verification. We develop certain hypotheses in the first instance. We look at the facts. The facts don't quite fit. So we go back and change our hypotheses, perhaps making them more complicated to take account of things we had overlooked at first. Then we apply another test of statistics against our hypotheses. If we are lucky, the fit will be better, but the hypotheses may need still further revision; and so on and on. In the end, if we are clever as well as lucky, we may come out with a set of hypotheses that agree closely with observed behavior.

Building Hypotheses (Theorizing)

This may seem a bit abstract and difficult. So let's look at another illustration from one of the oldest branches of economics, the theory of consumer demand.

Our problem is to explain what determines the amount of butter bought by the U.S. population in a particular year. Since population is growing all the time, we had better correct this at once by changing the question to read: What determines the amount of butter bought per head of population? One's first thought is that purchases have something to do with price. It seems reasonable that people will buy more of an article when its price is lower than when it is higher. So our first hypothesis is: Purchases of butter vary inversely with the price of butter.

We now look at the statistics and find that the price of butter in 1965 was higher than in 1964; but purchases of butter were *also higher* in 1965, instead of lower as they should have been according to our hypothesis. Something obviously has been left out. A little more thought suggests that how much butter people buy depends partly on their income. If consumer incomes go up, they may buy more butter even though its price has risen.

Another look at the facts (and we should of course look at 20 or 30 years rather than just 2 or 3) shows us that we still don't know everything about butter purchases. The figures jump about in a way which we can't explain satisfactorily by looking only at the price of butter and at consumer incomes. So we scratch our heads again and add hypotheses to take account of such things as:

1. People like butter but they can eat margarine. The lower the price of margarine compared with that of butter, the more people will shift to it to save money. So the price of margarine becomes another factor in our calculations.

2. Butter goes with bread. People usually don't eat spoonfuls of pure butter. So the amount of bread sold per year will affect the use of butter, and this must also go into our equation.

3. You can spread the butter thicker or thinner. As the slim figure and the calorie cookbook have become fashionable, most people spread it thinner. Some actresses even eat dry toast. So we add to our equation another item which the statisticians call a time trend. This shows that, apart from all other factors, butter purchases go down a certain amount each year for reasons which we don't entirely understand but which we lump together as "changes in public taste."

We come out, then, with a more complicated theory including five factors influencing butter purchases instead of only one. If we have good measures of these five factors and of butter sales over a long period of time, we can get some idea of *how much* influence each factor has on the result. This is no place to explain the mysteries of statistical inference, but you can take them on faith. The job can be done. The end result is a formula which might look something like this:

Butter purchases per capita $=0.004$ (consumer income per capita)
$$-0.327 \text{ (price of butter)}$$
$$+0.673 \text{ (price of margarine)}$$
$$+0.018 \text{ (sales of bread)}$$
$$-0.007 \text{ per year (time trend)}$$

Prediction and Proof in Economics

How do we test this complicated hypothesis about butter sales? By seeing how close it comes to explaining actual butter sales year by year. Suppose we take the year 1965. We fill in all the figures for 1965 on the right hand side of the equation—consumer income per capita in that year, butter prices, and so on—and carry out the calculations. The result tells us what butter sales per capita would have been in 1965 if the hypothesis were completely correct. We then look at actual butter sales in 1965 and see how far off we were.

The same process can be carried out for any year in the past. If the hypothesis predicts actual butter sales in most years within 1 or 2 percent, we can regard it as satisfactory. But if it is off by 10 percent on the average, it must be discarded and a new attempt made. Economists have developed demand equations of this type for wheat, sugar, meat, butter, milk, and other staple products; and these typically agree quite closely with actual sales.

Before concluding that economics is an exact science, let's look a little farther. Economic hypotheses are always tested by reference to the past. They have to be, since we have no figures for the future. Yet it is the future in which we are really interested. Are we safe in saying that a formula which fits the facts pretty well for the years 1940–60 will work just as well in 1965 or 1970? It will *if people continue to behave in the future as they have in the past.* This is an important qualification. Hypotheses about consumer purchases and savings are reasonably reliable, because consumers' tastes and habits seem to change rather slowly. But suppose instead we were trying to predict how much companies will spend in 1965 on new plants and machinery. This is a quite variable and unstable figure. Our hypotheses about it are less complete than for consumer behavior, and predictions are likely to be farther from the mark.

Even at best, economic predictions have an "iffy" character. No economist in his right mind would say flatly, "Butter sales next year *will* be 1,700 million pounds." Rather, he will say, "*If* the price of butter is 63 cents, *if* consumer income is 380 billion dollars (and so on through several other ifs), *then* butter sales will be 1,700 million pounds." Even this statement is not sufficiently cautious. Statistical inference yields probabilities rather than certainties. So we must say something like, "If butter prices, consumer incomes, and other relevant factors are as stated, then the chances are 95 out of 100 that butter sales will be between 1,675 and 1,725 million pounds."

Note also that economic predictions relate to a *group* of consumers, companies, workers, or what not; and the larger the group, the more reliable the prediction. It is sometimes argued that economics can't possibly be a precise subject, because it deals with human beings and human beings are unpredictable. If this means that we cannot predict the economic behavior of the Brown family very reliably, the argument is correct. But the economist is not interested in the Brown family. He tries rather to say what 5 million or 50 million families will do under specified conditions, which is a much more feasible undertaking.

MYTHS AND MISUNDERSTANDINGS

The Bogey of "Economic Man"

Economists are sometimes accused of supposing that man is perfectly rational and self-interested, that he responds only to money and is impervious to other motives. A best-seller entitled *The End of Economic Man* was devoted to destroying this economic bogey. The labor was fruitless, because the target was mythical. Economists are not congenitally stupid. They realize that human actions may be motivated by altruism, desire for power or prestige, the urgings of the subconscious, and many other things. It is obvious also that people don't always know what they are doing. Information may be incomplete and inaccurate, actions may be impulsive and mistaken.

But to develop economic hypotheses one need not suppose that people are *perfectly* informed and rational, or that they respond *only* to material advantage. We need suppose only that material advantage is an *important* motive, which operates along with others to shape personal behavior; and that there is *some* rationality and consistency in people's behavior patterns. If this is true, we can predict that most people will respond in a certain direction to certain stimuli.

In a community made up completely of ascetics or psychotics, economic reasoning would break down. But this is not the kind of world in which we live. Most workers prefer to get more pay rather than less, most consumers prefer to pay a lower rather than a higher price for the same product, most corporation officials prefer larger profits to smaller ones. To the extent that people are motivated in this way—whether this constitutes 25 percent, 50 percent, or 90 percent of their total motivation —economic reasoning can predict the general direction of their action. Remember that economists are interested in reactions of people in the mass rather than in predicting the behavior of individuals. If the Widget Company raises wages from $1.75 an hour to $2.00 an hour, I can't predict that Joe Doakes will quit his $1.50 job at the Ajax Company and rush over to Widget. But I am safe in predicting that more workers will apply to the Widget Company for work at the new wage than were applying before. This is all that matters to the Widget Company and to the economist.

Why Bother with Theory?

Another common complaint is that economists spend their time making simple things difficult. Why bother with this difficult work of logical deduction, building up hypotheses, revising and testing them, and developing an elaborate body of theory? Why not simply go out and "look at the facts"? Surely the main currents in economic life are so obvious that one can draw conclusions from simple observation.

The difficulty with this approach is that the facts don't speak for themselves. And there are too many of them. How can one tell which facts are relevant to a particular problem? The facts need to be sorted out, arranged, focused. As soon as you begin to do this you are engaged willy-nilly in selecting hypotheses. You do not avoid theorizing but, since your theorizing is unconscious, it is likely to be bad.

A man who maintains that he is simply looking at the facts means really that he hasn't bothered to make his theory clear to his audience or to himself. He sees, for example, that prices have doubled since 1940. Wages have gone up even more; and unions have been quite active, frequently going on strike for wage increases. From this he concludes, "It is obvious that unions are responsible for inflation." This is not a factual conclusion. It rests on a hidden structure of theory. What set of hypotheses does this man have in the back of his mind? The main hypotheses are:

1. Unions have the power to make wages go up faster than they would go up otherwise.
2. Unions exercise this power.
3. An increase in wages means an increase in production costs.
4. When the cost of producing an article is increased, its price must go up more or less proportionately.
5. Cost increases are the *main* reason why prices rise. Other reasons do not exist or are of minor importance compared with this one.

These hypotheses may or may not be correct. That is not the point at issue. The point is that our observer has leaped to his conclusion without testing his hypotheses or even listing them clearly in his mind. If he had done so, he would have been forced to go through the careful procedure described in the last section. His "obvious" conclusion thus turns out not to be obvious at all. The assertion that a proposition is obvious usually means that the speaker is unwilling to undertake the hard work of finding out whether it is true.

Explanation requires theorizing. There is no escape from this. The only difference is between sloppy, naïve, unconscious theorizing and theorizing in which hypotheses are spelled out thoroughly and subjected to quantitative tests.

Never, never say to your economics instructor, "That may be all right in theory but it doesn't work in practice." His blood pressure will rise sharply, and the reason should be clear to you by now. The purpose of a theory is to describe and explain a certain body of facts. A theory which "doesn't work in practice" in the sense of not corresponding to the facts is simply a bad theory and should be rejected. A carefully constructed and tested theory *will* work, and one must keep improving it until it does.

A WORD ABOUT STUDYING ECONOMICS

Economics is different from any subject you have studied before. It is not like history, or literature, or physics. A few hints on how to approach the subject may save you time and worry.

1. Economics is not memory work. You will not become even an amateur economist by memorizing facts and figures. Economics is a method of thought, a way of taking hold of a problem, breaking it down for analysis, and working systematically toward a solution. It is also a special language, which uses words rather differently from ordinary usage. You become an economist by learning to use this language habitually and correctly, by learning where to find economic statistics and how to interpret them, and by practice in careful reasoning.

2. Economics is an additive subject. It unfolds in a systematic way, what comes later resting on an understanding of what went before. It may be possible in a history text to make sense out of the period 1850–75 even though you missed the chapter on 1780–1800. In economics you cannot skip steps in this way. So do not rush ahead without getting a firm grasp on what you have already read. If you stumble over a sentence or a paragraph, stop and clear it up then and there. If you do this, things will grow clearer as you proceed; otherwise, they are likely to grow foggier.

3. Forget what you think you know about economic issues, because much of what you "know" is wrong. The greatest difficulty in discussing economics is that people already know the answers. They see no need for examining evidence or for careful reasoning and commit the simplest logical errors with unashamed cheerfulness. The purpose of this course is mainly to unteach you what passes for "common-sense economics" among the general public. Any positive knowledge you may acquire beyond this is a sheer bonus.

4. Care in reasoning, and a skepticism of facile arguments, goes without saying. You will learn as you go along that the commonest errors in economics stem from two sources. The first, known as the *fallacy of composition,* lies in supposing that what is true of the parts is necessarily true of the whole. A man who saves 90 percent of his income will grow rich. It does not follow that, if all families in a country save 90 percent of their incomes, the country will grow rich. This would, in fact, be an impossible situation. A company which cuts wages may raise its profits by so doing. But if all companies try to cut wages at once, it is not at all clear that they will raise their profits.

The other common fallacy consists in ignoring the *two-sidedness of economic events.* Consider the argument that a drop in farm prices will "reduce national purchasing power." The farmers who get the lower prices have certainly lost purchasing power. The city housewife, however, will find her food budget lower than before and will have more left over to spend on other things. Her purchasing power has been increased. So it is not at all clear that there has been a drop in national purchasing power. If by the end of the course you have developed the habit of looking automatically at both sides of any economic event, you will have made real progress.

SOME QUESTIONS OF LANGUAGE

One difficulty with using plain English is that the words we use have an everyday meaning. The economist needs to use words precisely and often in a way which differs from ordinary usage. It will be well at this stage to define some of the key words which will be used in later chapters.

We have already spoken of goods and services. An *economic good* is anything which yields satisfaction to someone and which is scarce. It is *scarce* if there is less available than people would like to consume if they could have it free. In this case one will have to pay a *price* for the good. If there is enough to satisfy everyone's wants at a zero price, the article is a *free good.* The same article may be a free good in some circumstances but not in others. Drinking water from a mountain stream is a free good. But water flowing from a city tap is an economic good, since it costs something and users are charged for it in one way or another. Air is normally a free good, but cold air from an air-conditioner in summer is an economic good.

A *service* is an immaterial or intangible good. We speak of the services of the doctor, the entertainer, the teacher. These people do something which we want and for which we are willing to pay, though their product usually does not have a material form. The store clerk and the filling station attendant do not *make* anything, as a factory worker or a carpenter does. But they help us get something we want at the place where we want it, and for this service we are willing to pay.

Production is the making of an economic good or the performance of an economic service. Some early economists, including Adam Smith and Karl Marx, defined the term more narrowly to include only material production. The work of a farmer or shoemaker was considered productive, but the activities of a teacher or musician were labeled "unproductive labor." Modern economics draws no such distinction. Service production stands on the same footing as goods production.

The things which are necessary for production to be carried on are termed *factors of production* or *productive resources*. The most important of these is *labor*. In everyday usage, this term connotes factory work or some other manual activity. But in economics, labor means any form of human effort exerted in production. The bricklayer, the accountant, the doctor, the business executive are all engaged in labor.

A second requisite for production is *capital*. This is a particularly tricky term in economics, because there is a major difference from everyday usage. When an individual speaks of his "capital" he usually means money or securities. Thus it is essential to remember that in economics *capital is not money*. It is machinery, buildings, railroad track and rolling stock, inventories of raw materials, and other *physical* necessities for production. One classic definition runs, "Capital is produced means of production." *Capital goods* are goods which are produced, not for direct use by consumers, but as aids in the production of things which eventually will be used by consumers. *Consumer goods* are finished products for direct sale to consumers.

There is also a major difference from popular usage as regards *investment*. I think of buying a stock or bond as an "investment." A bank which makes a loan and receives a promissory note in return considers this an "investment." Here we are involved with money once more. In economics, however, *investment is the construction of a capital good*. Economics is concerned basically with physical processes rather than with the money which lubricates the wheels of industry. The amount of investment in the American economy in 1964 was *the quantity of capital goods produced during the year*, which had a money value of about $130 billion.

A third important element in production is *natural resources*. Strictly speaking, a natural resource is something given by nature and untouched by human hands, such as rivers, mineral deposits, virgin farm land, or virgin timber stands. As soon as human effort is applied, the resource becomes partly a capital good, a *produced* means of production. An Iowa farm today is partly a natural resource, because certain qualities of levelness, soil texture and composition, natural rainfall, and climate have been there for all time. But it is also partly a capital good, because generations of farmers have added fencing, drainage, tree and stone removal, artificial fertilizers, and other aids to production.

Labor, capital, and natural resources are coordinated in *production units,* such as farms, factories, stores, and transport networks. The work of coordination is done by *management.* Economists sometimes treat management as a separate factor of production, making four factors in all. But it may also be regarded as a specialized high-level kind of labor.

The total output of all production units in the economy, usually calculated on a yearly basis, bears the impressive title *Gross National Product,* usually shortened to GNP. The meaning of this total and the way in which it is calculated will be fully explained in Chapter 19.

For every dollar's worth of *output* produced there must be a dollar's worth of *income* created. Mysterious? Not at all. If a factory produces and sells $100,000 worth of output during a year, it receives $100,000 in return. All of this has to go somewhere. Any of it which is not paid out as wages and salaries, cost of materials purchased, taxes, or dividends must remain in the business at the end of the year (in which case it is still income belonging to the common stockholders who own the business). Thus income created must equal output produced; and instead of speaking of national product we can speak of *national income,* a term which will occur frequently in the chapters ahead.

A final matter of terminology: the difference between *money* quantities and *real* or *physical* quantities. National income and product are measured in dollars. They have to be, since this is the only way we can add up production of pig iron, soy beans, orchestra performances, and shoeshines. But is a dollar this year the same as a dollar last year? As a matter of fact, we know very well that how much a dollar will buy changes considerably over the course of time. Are we not, then, measuring with a rubber yardstick?

Suppose we observe that GNP in 1940 is $100 billion, and that GNP in 1950 is $200 billion. It looks as though production has doubled. But this would be a safe conclusion only if we knew that prices had remained unchanged. What may have happened instead is that the price of every article is double what it used to be, while production has remained unchanged. Thus we cannot draw any conclusion about physical production without making a correction for price changes.

The first step is to construct a *price index* showing what has happened to prices, on the average, year by year. Governmental statistical agencies prepare several such indexes, the most important being the Wholesale Price Index for goods at the manufacturing level, and the Consumer Price Index based on retail prices of goods and services bought by consumers. Armed with such figures, one can proceed to adjust the money totals.

For example, the money value of GNP rose from $100.6 billion in

1940 to $503.2 billion in 1960, or five-fold. But over these years the level of prices rose by 235 percent. Dividing the percentage increase in GNP by the percentage increase in prices (500/235), we find that physical output rose by 213 percent. The result is termed *real GNP*, or *GNP in constant dollars.*

DISCUSSION QUESTIONS

1. What do you think economics is about? What do you hope to learn from this course?
2. Would a business executive be better off for having taken a course in economics? Why?
3. A committee of Congress is considering whether to raise the federal minimum wage from $1.25 to $1.75 per hour. It calls in a group of economists. What can the economists contribute, and what can they not contribute, to the decision?
4. It has been said that if you put any policy question to five economists you will get five different answers. Why might this be true? Would it indicate that economics is purely a matter of opinion?
5. Some people enjoy arguing over whether economics should be considered a science. What are the characteristics of a science? How far does economics possess (or fall short of) these characteristics?
6. Do economic measurements of the past provide a safe basis for predicting what will happen in the future?
7. What do economists assume about human motivation? Is this a reliable basis for predicting how people will react in the real world?
8. What is meant by an economic hypothesis or theory? What function does theory serve? Couldn't we get adequate generalizations about economic behavior simply by "looking at the facts"?
9. Select some problem of prediction similar to the butter sales problem described in the text. Then go ahead and make up your own hypothesis about it. What kinds of statistical information would you need to test your hypothesis?

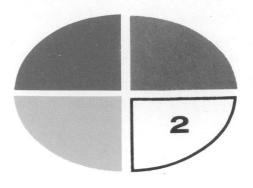

Some Dimensions of the

American Economy

> Young man, there is America—which at
> this day serves for little more than to amuse you
> with stories of savage men and uncouth manners;
> yet shall, before you taste of death, show itself
> equal to the whole of that commerce which now
> attracts the envy of the world.
>
> EDMUND BURKE (1775)

THROUGHOUT PART ONE we shall be dealing with the idea of an economic system, the way in which different parts of the system interlock, and the problem of how one can judge whether the system is operating efficiently. Before discussing these things in general, it will help to have a description of an actual economic system. This could be the economy of Egypt, Australia, or Japan. But why not begin with things closest to home, with the economy of the United States?

An economy is marked off by the political boundaries of a national state. The physical area included may be a whole continent, as in the case of Australia, or the tiny territory of Belgium or Austria. National boundaries matter, because the thing which knits an economic system together is free movement of labor, money, and commodities. These movements are typically easy *within* a country but are subject to check at the national border. One cannot walk into an American grocery store and buy food with Austrian schillings. Movements of people from one country to another for permanent settlement are restricted by immigration laws. Movements of goods among countries are hampered by unfamiliarity of the products, transportation costs, tariff duties, and other restrictions.

In spite of these barriers, there is a large international movement of goods and some international movement of people. There are also ways of converting the money of one country into that of another. Thus, in a loose and figurative way, one can speak of "the world economy." But the great bulk of economic transactions occur within particular countries, and this is why we use the term economic system to mean a *national* economic unit.

A second reason for emphasizing the national state is its importance in economic policy making. International organizations have little control over American economic activity. Our state and municipal governments exercise certain types of control, but the influence of the federal government is predominant. Washington is the focus for decisions on monetary policy, international economic relations, national defense, government spending, agricultural policy, and a host of other matters. Since economics aims to provide a better basis for decisions on these matters, the nation naturally bulks large in economic discussion.

The most striking characteristic of the American economy is its great size. This is not just a matter of geography. There are countries larger than the United States which have only a fraction of its productive capacity. Size for present purposes means *economic* size, as measured by total value of production. U.S. national output is now approaching the phenomenal level of $700 billion a year.

The great size of the American market permits us to use mass production methods. The enormous auto plants in Detroit make sense only in a country which buys six or seven million cars a year. They would not make sense in Chile or Ceylon. The size of our market also permits an unusually diversified pattern of production. In addition to the finished cars, we produce almost all the machine tools, aluminum, electrical apparatus, and other things necessary for automobile production. Almost every conceivable type of capital good and consumer good is produced somewhere in the United States.

The position of a small country is obviously different. It would not be feasible for Jamaica to produce a full range of industrial and agricultural products. It is more efficient to concentrate on items for which Jamaica's resources are particularly well fitted, to export a large part of this production, and to import much of what is needed for domestic consumption.

ACTORS ON THE ECONOMIC STAGE

A national economy includes *consumers* and *producers* of the national product. The basic unit on the consuming side is the family or *household.* There are about 50 million household units in the United States, plus some 10 million individuals living by themselves.

Households play a dual role in the economy. On one hand, they buy the goods and services turned out by producing units. They provide the market toward which productive activity is oriented. On the other hand, households are the ultimate owners of productive resources. These resources are of several sorts. The most important is the labor of the family members. In most households, this is the major source of family income. Households also own the capital used in business, either directly as in the case of small family businesses or indirectly through ownership of stocks or bonds in a corporation. Finally, households own the bulk of the nation's agricultural land in the form of family farms.

The basic producing unit in the American economy is the *business concern.* The great majority of these are small family businesses conforming to the traditional picture of private enterprise. The same person owns and manages the business, takes all the risks, gets all the profit (if any), and can take cash from the till as he needs it. A large proportion of retailing, service activity, and building construction, and a good deal of light manufacturing is organized in this way. There are upwards of three million individual businesses in the United States, to which one might reasonably add some four million farms which are also managed on a family basis. "Little business" is obviously far from dead.

These millions of small businesses, however, produce only about one third of total private output. The remainder is produced by business *corporations.* The corporation is a very interesting institution, which began to be important about a century ago and which has now assumed predominant importance in the economy. Its main features will be described in a moment.

It is not always recognized that *government agencies* are important producers, primarily of services rather than material products. Local governments produce police protection, fire protection, and educational services as well as streets and sewers. The state and federal governments produce highways, educational and research services, national defense, and the administration of justice. These services are important to the citizen, as would be apparent if they were suddenly eliminated. Unlike the product of business concerns, however, government services are usually not sold to individuals for a price. Their cost is assessed against the whole community through taxation. Decisions about how much of a particular service it is worthwhile to provide are made through the process of voting and political representation. How many television sets shall be produced, on the other hand, is decided by individuals going to the store and "voting with their dollars" for this particular product. The former process is usually called *political or collective choice,* while the latter is termed *market choice.*

Households and producing units are linked in a dual fashion: (1)

Households furnish resources for use in production. In return they receive wages, salaries, dividends, and other types of money income. This linkage is shown in the upper half of the diagram below. (2) The producing units take land, labor, and capital and combine them to turn out goods and services. These are then sold back to households, which pay for them with the money received in wages, salaries, and so on. This exchange is shown in the lower half of the diagram.

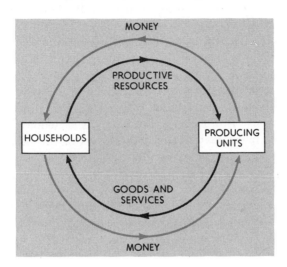

This is often termed *the wheel of wealth,* or *the circular flow of economic activity.* Money moves around the circuit in a counterclockwise direction. Physical quantities—factors of production and finished products—move in a clockwise direction. If we do our arithmetic correctly, the two flows must exactly balance each other. This sketch is highly simplified and ignores many real-life complications, but it is a useful starting point in considering what one means by an economic system.

THE BUSINESS CORPORATION

In the American economy, and in other economies which rely heavily on private enterprise, the most important economic institution is the *business concern.* The purpose of a business concern, no matter how huge or how tiny, is essentially simple. The concern *owns* a certain amount of capital—land, buildings, machinery, inventories of finished and semifinished products. It *buys* additional productive resources, often also called *inputs.* Labor is typically the most important input; but the concern also buys raw materials, electric light and power, transport and communications services, and a variety of other inputs.

The concern combines these purchased inputs with its own capital to produce one or more outputs. These outputs are sold for what they will bring on the market and thus bring in *revenue* to the company. The central business problem is to make sure that revenue is greater than costs, so that there is something left over for the owners of the business. This something left over is commonly called *profit*, and we may accept this usage for the time being, though we shall have to be more precise later on.

The actual bookkeeping for a large business is quite complicated. But the heart of the matter is simple: try to sell whatever you are selling for more than it cost you; try to make a profit.

Profit plays several roles in the economy. An *expectation* of profit is necessary to induce a business to start up or expand. People will not put money into plant and equipment unless they expect some return. The expectation may or may not be realized. Even in prosperous years, many thousands of businesses lose money because of managerial incompetence and other reasons. But for the economy as a whole, the profits of profitable concerns normally exceed the losses of the others. Profits are realized as well as expected. And these realized profits provide a good part of the money needed for industrial expansion, for construction of new plants, machinery, stores, and offices. So profit functions simultaneously as *incentive, reward*, and source of *capital formation.*

This description of business operations applies to the corner grocery and to General Motors, to the concern owned and operated by an individual and to the concern owned by a *corporation*. But there are important differences between these cases. The modern business corporation is only about a century old. Yet in this relatively short time it has become the predominant form of business organization. There are still many businesses operated by individuals or partnerships; but most of these businesses are very small, so that corporations predominate in terms of resource ownership.

What explains this rapid development? What exactly is a corporation? What advantages does it have over other forms of organization?

To start a corporation, you must apply to the government of one of the states, giving details of the proposed organization. If the application is approved, the state issues a *charter* for the corporation. The corporation then becomes a separate legal entity, distinct from any of the people who started it. It can sue and be sued, sign contracts in its own name, and so on. It has the advantage over individuals that it need not die with advancing age. In the words of a great jurist, it is "a being immortal, intangible, existing only in the contemplation of the law."

A corporation has the right to issue certificates of ownership, known as common stock. When the corporation is first formed, individuals acquire stock by subscribing a certain amount of money, say $100 per share, to get the company started. After that the shares are transferable on the open market, and anyone can become part owner of a company by placing a buying order with his broker.

The common stock device has two major advantages. First, when many people can share in the ownership of the business, it becomes possible to raise large amounts of money quickly. If a business has to be large to operate efficiently, as in the case of a railroad or an electric power system, the corporate form is very convenient. Second, the stockholders of a company have *limited liability*. If I operate a grocery store as an individual, and because of poor management the store runs heavily into debt, I am liable for every cent of the debt and may be stripped of everything I own. If I own common stock in a corporation, however, the worst that can happen is that the value of my stock may fall to zero. I cannot lose more than I paid for the stock. Indeed, if I set up my grocery store as a corporation, *its* debts are no longer *my* debts, even though I may own all the stock. Many family businesses are incorporated for precisely this reason.

In addition to the money obtained from common stockholders, a company can raise money by issuing other types of security. The most important are bonds and preferred stock. A *bond* is a certificate of indebtedness. The buyer of the bond lends the corporation a certain amount of money. The corporation promises to pay a certain amount of interest each year and to pay off the face value of the bond at the end of a set period. As backing for this, the bondholders have a claim against the physical assets of the company. If the company fails to pay the interest or principal, they can take control of the company's property and collect the amount due them.

Preferred stock carries a promise to pay a fixed dividend each year, and these payments must be met before any dividends are paid to the common stockholders. It may be provided also that the preferred stockholders' claim carries over from one year to the next, so that if the company falls behind on its payments it must make up the whole amount due the preferred stockholders before the common stockholders get anything. In this case the stock is called a *cumulative preferred* stock. Preferred stockholders do not, however, have a voice in company management.

After deducting that part of the company's property which has been contributed by bondholders or preferred stockholders, the remainder belongs to the common stockholders. This is called the company's *equity capital* or *stockholders' equity*. If there are no bonds or preferred stock outstanding, then the common stockholders own all of the company's buildings, machinery, inventories, and other property.

Each share of common stock participates equally—that is why it is called a "share." If a company has issued 100,000 shares of common stock, of which I own 1,000, then I own one hundredth of everything the company owns. When the company distributes dividends, one hundredth of the total must come to me. I also have 1,000 votes when it comes to electing the company's board of directors or making major policy decisions, such as whether to merge with another company or to issue additional stock. These decisions are normally made at an annual stockholders' meeting.

A Word on Security Prices

A corporate security is a ticket of ownership to physical assets—a stand-in for these assets. This makes it possible for ownership to be traded easily and in small amounts. Paper stock certificates can be passed easily from hand to hand. Pieces of a factory cannot.

Stocks and bonds have value, not just because they are backed by physical assets, but because these assets (usually) yield revenue which provides income for the security owners. If a company earns no profit, and is not expected to earn any in future, its plant has no value and neither will its common stock.

Fixed-income securities, such as bonds and preferred stocks, promise to pay the holder a certain number of dollars per year. Their value depends partly, but not entirely, on the size of this annual payment. A bond paying $10 a year will be worth twice as much as one paying $5 a year, *if both are of the same quality.* What is quality? Essentially, it means *riskiness.* There is always a possibility that the company will do so poorly that it cannot meet the promised payments. The greater this risk, the lower the price of the security.

This is why on the same day you will find one bond promising $5 a year which is priced at $110 on the market, while another $5 bond is selling for only $70. The second bond looks like a bargain; but this is deceptive. The low price means that investors judge that there is substantial risk of the payments not being met. If you are willing to take this risk in the hope of earning more on your money, this bond may be a good buy. But if you are interested mainly in certainty of income, the first bond will be better.

Common stocks are basically different in that they carry no promise of a fixed return. Their return varies from time to time, depending on how much the company earns. Since each owner of a share of common stock is entitled to share proportionately in these earnings, the company's *earnings per share* is a key ratio in financial analysis.

Example: a company has 1,000,000 shares of common stock outstanding. This year, after meeting interest payments on any bonds or preferred stock it may have issued and after paying corporate income tax to the federal government, it has a net profit of $3,500,000. So its earnings per share are $3.50. If this stock is currently selling on the market at $70, then its *yield* is 3.50 divided by 70 or 5 percent. Conversely, the *price-earnings ratio* is 70 divided by 3.50 or 20. This second ratio is the one normally used by financial analysts in trying to judge whether the price of a stock, relative to its earnings, is currently too high or too low.

The common stockholders, though they own all the company's earnings, do not necessarily receive them all in cash. The board of directors may decide to pay out only part of the earnings as dividends on the common stock and put the rest back into capital goods for expanding the business. The stockholders are not being deprived by this arrangement. The new capital goods bought with their money belong to them and will presumably increase the company's earnings in future years, which in turn will increase the value of the common stock. Increase in the value of a stock over time is termed a *capital gain.* Reinvesting part of the company's profits, then, means that stockholders are being asked to sacrifice some current income in the expectation of higher income plus capital gains in the future.

Earnings per share, then, are a more basic consideration than dividends per share. Suppose two companies are each earning profits of $4 per share. Company A decides to pay out $3 per share in dividends, company B only $1 per share. B's stock will not necessarily sell for less than A's. But investors who are interested in maximum current income— say, retired people—will be more likely to buy A's stock; and investors interested mainly in capital gains—say, young people building up an estate—may prefer B's stock.

Suppose a company is in an industry which is expanding very rapidly, the company is well managed, and it is putting a large share of its profits back into plant expansion. It is reasonable to expect that its earnings per share will rise rapidly in future, and people who are looking 10 or 20 years ahead will be eager to buy it on this account. Such a stock may sell at a price which seems much too high in relation to current earnings but which is warranted by the prospect of future growth. It is a *growth stock.* International Business Machines is a well-known example, but there are many others.

There is no royal road to success in buying securities. The nearest thing to a general "tip" is to ignore the behavior of stock market averages and to look carefully into the record of the *specific companies* in which one is interested. These will presumably be companies which correspond with one's own *investment objectives:* for example, moderate but secure returns, or the chance of a larger but less certain return, or low current returns with the prospect of larger capital gains. Regardless of the *general* movement of stock prices, there are always many stocks which are rising and many which are falling, some which are bargains at their current price and others which are not.

Ownership and Control in the Large Corporation

While all corporations are similar in legal structure, they are by no means similar in size. Most of the half-million business corporations in the United States are quite small. Indeed, 60 percent of them have assets of less than $100,000. Most of these are family businesses which have adopted the corporate form to achieve limited liability and other legal advantages.

At the other extreme are such corporate giants as American

Telephone and Telegraph, Du Pont, General Motors, and Standard Oil of New Jersey, each with assets running into the billions. The 250 largest corporations (excluding banks and other financial institutions) control almost half of all nonfinancial corporate assets. These giants are found mainly in transportation, public utilities, and those branches of manufacturing which lend themselves to large-scale production.

Who controls the large corporation? Control is exercised through an annual meeting, which elects the board of directors and votes on major policy issues. Each common stockholder is entitled to come to the meeting and to cast as many votes as he has shares of stock. If he doesn't care to come himself, he can authorize someone else to vote for him. The notice of the annual meeting contains a "proxy" form for this purpose. This is usually made out in the names of one or more of the existing management. Most stockholders sign and return it, thereby handing over their votes to the present management, or else toss it in the wastebasket. But they can legally assign it to anyone, and there are occasional "proxy fights" between rival groups struggling for control of a company.

The difficulty with town-meeting control of a large company is that far too many people are involved. There are many thousands or even hundreds of thousands of stockholders. A.T.&T., the world's largest corporation, has 250 million shares of stock, scattered among more than 2 million stockholders. The largest ball park would not begin to hold these people for an annual stockholders' meeting. In any event, most of them take only a passive interest in the company. They may glance idly through the handsomely printed annual report. If they don't like the way things are going in the company, they sell their stock and that is that.

So who controls the annual meeting and elects the directors of the company? Sometimes one family or group owns a substantial block of stock. If the smaller stockholders are passive and unorganized, the large owners may achieve a dominant position. They may take an active hand in management, or they may leave this to salaried professional managers. In the latter case, the managers have wide discretion in managing the company's affairs, so long as they do not displease the dominant stockholding group.

In other cases, no individual or group owns enough of the common stock to have any appreciable influence on the corporation. Here the management in charge, however it got there in the first place, is the dominant group, and no one can effectively challenge its control. Each year management collects proxies from the scattered and powerless stockholders, and reelects itself to office. As the top officers of the company near retirement age, they select their successors. Management becomes a self-perpetuating body, rather like a university faculty or the leadership of a political party.

It is worth pausing to emphasize the gap between small individual business and large corporate business. The small businessman is owner *and* manager as well. He has a direct, tangible relation to his property. Any profits which are made are *his* profits. He is likely to react violently to encroachment on his property rights, by government or anyone else. He is a traditional, nineteenth-century capitalist.

Who is "the capitalist" in the large corporation? The common stockholder? But he has probably never seen the property which he theoretically owns, and takes only a passive interest in its management. His ownership is a pale shadow compared with that of the farmer or small manufacturer. Is it then the president of the company? But he is a salaried career man. He is expected to turn in a profit, but it is not *his* profit; and his own wealth does not necessarily increase with that of the company.

The managers of American big business are, in fact, a new kind of social group: largely college-trained, starting out as junior executives and working their way up the organizational ladder, looking toward permanent salaried careers rather than owning their own businesses, somewhat footloose and willing to change companies for personal advantage, eventually controlling large amounts of property which they do not own, subject to pressure from stockholders and others but with wide scope for independent decision. The motivation of these men is more complex than that of the small owner-manager. The top business executive is not very different from a political leader, army general, or college president. He is interested in income but also in influence, public reputation, and professional excellence. Being president of A.T.&T. yields craftsmanlike satisfaction as well as a large salary.

This twentieth-century trend has stimulated a wide variety of reactions. Business school deans speak approvingly of "the professionalization of management." Others who feel that the power of business leaders is not adequately controlled speak fearfully of "the managerial revolution." The late Professor Joseph Schumpeter of Harvard feared that the divorce of ownership from management was devitalizing the essence of capitalism. The small owner will take out his rifle to defend his property. But who will mount the barricades for General Motors? The salaried executive class, Schumpeter thought, has neither the will nor the weapons to resist the gradual take-over of economic power by government. Essentially technical and unpolitical in outlook, they will work for whoever is in control—the stockholders, the House of Morgan, or the Department of Defense. Accustomed to large-scale bureaucracy in business, they will settle comfortably into governmental bureaucracy.

GOVERNMENT IN THE ECONOMY

Government is always an important actor in economic affairs. In many times and places, government has dominated economic activity. Even where most production is in private hands, as in the contemporary

United States, government plays a prominent supporting and regulating role. We may distinguish the functions of government as *policeman,* as *producer of public goods,* as *regulator of private economic activity,* and as *distributor of income.*

An ancient function of government is to *maintain law and order.* There can be no effective personal or property rights without a legal system to adjudicate disputes and enforce private contracts, without police protection against theft and violence. If we take these things for granted, it is only because of long custom. In many of the newer countries of the world, absence of firm protection for property rights is a serious barrier to private initiative.

Government functions also as a *producer of public goods.* A public good is something which, if produced at all, becomes available automatically to everyone. The classic example is national defense. It is not feasible to defend part of the citizens and not the remainder. Since use of the service cannot be limited, it is not possible to charge a price for it. There is a collective decision on how much of the service it is worthwhile to produce; and the costs are assessed against the public in the form of taxes.

There are other cases in which, while it would be technically feasible to charge users a price, there seem to be good reasons for not doing so. Everyone sending a child to school could be charged a tuition fee to cover the educational costs; but instead, towns and cities assess the costs against local property owners through a tax on land and buildings. There are two main consequences. First, free education encourages parents to keep children in school longer than otherwise, which presumably benefits the community as well as the child. Second, the costs are distributed differently among families. Families with fewer than average children, or larger than average property holdings, pay more under a tax system than they would under a tuition fee system. Families with little property or many children pay less.

The generally accepted area of public production shades off into a more controversial area in which public or private production are feasible alternatives. Notable examples are rail and air transportation, telephone and telegraph communication, and production of electric light and power. In most countries, these so-called "natural monopolies" are owned and operated by government. In the United States, they are for the most part privately operated but subject to government regulation of prices and service. Television broadcasting is a public monopoly in some countries, a private industry in others, while still others have both private and public systems. In some countries, such as France, government operates all the armament-producing industries. The Swedish government has extensive holdings of mines and forests. Most modern governments are heavily involved in the insurance business. Under our social security system, workers and employers pay payroll taxes so that workers can be insured against loss of income through unemployment, premature disability or death, and eventual retirement. The federal government is also heavily engaged in the banking business through agencies which make loans to farmers, small businessmen, house builders, and others.

The proper boundary between public and private production is always a hotly disputed political issue. Conservatives believe that the public sector has already been overexpanded in the United States and needs to be cut back, while liberals would extend it further in such areas as housing, medical care, and urban redevelopment.

The great bulk of production in the United States remains in private hands. The justification for this is that free competition among rival producers will ensure good service to the consumer at the lowest price. In such cases as electric power and telephone service, however, competition is not feasible; so we establish public agencies to prescribe what services the private monopoly must provide and the maximum prices it may charge. In other cases, there are a few large producers who could clearly do better for themselves by getting together to fix prices instead of continuing to compete; so we have antitrust laws which are supposed to prevent this. Private producers might sometimes be tempted to save money by cutting corners on safety, product quality, or other dimensions of service; so we have federal agencies to control safety practices in aviation and railroading, a Food and Drug Administration to check dangers to public health in those areas, a Federal Trade Commission to detect false or misleading advertising claims, and so on.

This area of *public regulation* has grown greatly in size and complexity since 1900. It is a fascinating blend of law, politics, and economics, in which reality may differ widely from surface appearances. Private economic interests never want to be controlled, and work overtime through political channels to gain control of the personnel and policies of the regulatory agencies. Quite often they succeed, and it becomes hard to figure out who is controlling whom.

Finally, government influences the *distribution of personal income*. As a minimum, it is accepted that no one in the United States should starve; and the private charity on which we used to rely has now been largely supplanted by public charity. The sociological reasons for this include growth in the size of communities, loosening of neighborhood relations, disintegration of family ties, and a relative decline in the financing of churches and private charitable organizations. At any rate, large amounts of public funds now go into payments to the aged, the blind, the dependent children abandoned by one or both parents, the mentally deficient, the physically handicapped, the marginal farmers, the long-term unemployed in declining economic areas. How many of these people might be reclaimed for useful employment, how generously the remainder should be supported, and how the costs should be divided are all live political issues.

The most important way in which government becomes involved in income distribution is through the tax system. There are many ways in which the tax burden might be divided among the citizens. They might be charged on the basis of services received, wherever these can be identified—tuition fees for education, tolls for highway users, and so on. Each citizen might be asked to pay the *same dollar amount* (scarcely feasible in practice, because the poorer citizens would run out of money!). Each might be asked to pay the *same percentage of his income.* Or the higher-income groups might be asked to pay *a larger percentage of income,* as is done under our graduated personal income tax.

We shall explore this issue in depth later in the book. Our concern here is simply to note that government cannot be neutral about income distribution, in the sense of abstaining from decisions about it. Any decision on tax structure *is* also a decision on income distribution; and some decision is unavoidable.

TRADE UNIONISM AND COLLECTIVE BARGAINING

The trade union is a *regulatory agency,* whose main function is to negotiate with employers over terms and conditions of employment. It has important effects on wages, hours, and working conditions, which we shall explore in later chapters.

Trade unionism is one of our oldest economic institutions. The first local unions developed in several eastern cities in the 1790's. National unions with survival power began to appear in the 1850's, and a considerable number have now been in existence for about a century. The American Federation of Labor, a central federation of national unions of which the present AFL-CIO is the lineal descendant, was founded in 1886.

Despite this long history, union membership grew only slowly up to 1930 and was confined largely to the skilled trades. The shock of the Great Depression, the prounion policies of the Roosevelt administration, the economic recovery after 1933, and the severe labor shortages of World War II combined to produce a dramatic rise in union membership from about 3 million in 1933 to almost 15 million in 1945. Union membership leveled off in the mid-fifties at about 17 million and has changed little since that time.

About 30 percent of all wage and salary earners outside agriculture are union members; but this average figure is not very revealing. Transportation, mining, construction, and heavy manufacturing are strongly unionized, with membership in some industries approaching 100 percent. Trade, services, government, and other white-collared occupations are much less unionized. The fact that it is these occupations which have been growing most rapidly since 1945, plus the apparent inability of unionism to penetrate them on a large scale, probably means that total union membership will not increase appreciably in the foreseeable future.

Structurally, there are three main levels of union organization: the *local union* of workers in a particular plant or locality; the *national union,* such as the United Automobile Workers or the International Brotherhood of Electrical Workers, which is a federation of local unions in the same trade or industry; and the *national federation,* such as the American Federation of Labor and Congress of Industrial Organizations, whose membership includes most national unions in the country.

The AFL-CIO is an educational, organizing, and political body. It represents labor on issues pending before Congress and takes an active interest in elections. But negotiation with employers over economic issues, usually termed *collective bargaining,* is the responsibility of the national and local unions in each industry, with the national union gradually assuming a predominant role.

Negotiation with employers goes on at various levels. A small company may bargain with local union officials. Giant corporations such as General Motors or U.S. Steel, on the other hand, bargain with top leaders of the national union. In some cases a group of employers is involved. All the building contractors, printing firms, or garment manufacturers in a particular city may stand together for bargaining purposes.

The result of the bargain is a written contract, usually for 1 year, though some important contracts, such as the steel and automobile agreements, run for 3 years or more. Failure to reach agreement results in a strike, a test of economic staying power, which eventually becomes so costly to the parties that they decide to settle after all. Serious strikes are rare, however, and more than 99 percent of union agreements are renewed each year without a strike.

The union contract normally provides for its own enforcement through a private judicial system, the *grievance procedure.* Any worker who thinks his rights under the contract have been violated can ask the union to discuss the case with management officials. If the case cannot be settled at the shop level, it moves up eventually to top management and union officials; and if they cannot settle it, it goes usually to a neutral arbitrator for decision.

This system of industrial jurisprudence is doubtless the most important single effect of unionism. Without a union, the worker has to accept supervisors' decisions on matters of vital concern, including staying in his job. There is no appeal. With the union, there are clear rules. The fact that management decisions are subject to query and appeal also forces management to be more systematic and consistent in personnel matters and checks arbitrary use of power by foremen and other minor officials.

In addition to this important but intangible effect, unionism has a variety of direct economic consequences: (1) on *wage rates,* at every level from general wage increases in a whole industry down to the hourly wage of a worker on a specific job; (2) on *supplementary income payments,* such as paid vacations and holidays, retirement pensions, insurance, and medical and hospital benefits; (3) on *hours of work,* which are usually specified in detail, with higher pay for overtime beyond the prescribed hours; (4) on *promotion, layoff, and recall* to work, where the union usually tries to emphasize length of service or *seniority;* (5) on *work rules and production methods,* where the union tries to secure as much employment as possible for its members and to shield them against displacement by machinery. The economic effect of these contract provisions will be analyzed in Chapter 15.

THE ORGANIZATION OF PRODUCTION

What is the relative importance of big business and little business in different sectors of the economy? It is easiest to get information on the size of *producing establishments*—farms, retail stores, manufacturing plants, and so on. This is obviously not the same thing as size of *companies.* One manufacturing company, such as U.S. Steel, may own many plants in different locations. Sears, Roebuck or A & P own hundreds of retail outlets. But the individual store or plant remains the basic unit of production, and the size of these units is of considerable interest.

When one looks at the statistics, a striking conclusion emerges. The great majority of producing units are quite small. They seem barely large enough to yield a precarious living to their owner. This is true whether one looks at manufacturing, farming, retailing, or the service industries. The only type of industry in which large units are consistently the rule is public utilities, including railroads.

But while the small establishments predominate in numbers, they are much less important in production. The minority of large establishments in each industry typically produce the bulk of the industry's output.

Look first at the situation in manufacturing (Table 1). There are almost 300,000 manufacturing establishments. But half of these are "holes-in-the-wall" with less than 10 employees. There are only about 27,000 plants in the country with 100 or more workers, or less than 10 percent of the total. Yet this small minority of plants employs about 75 percent of manufacturing workers in the country and accounts for 77 percent of factory payrolls.

In the case of retail stores (Table 2), the best measure of size is not number of employees but amount of business done per year. A highly automated supermarket may employ few workers but have a large sales volume. There are about one and three-quarter million stores in the United States. The dividing line between "small stores" and others may

TABLE 1

Size of Manufacturing Establishments, 1958

SIZE CLASS (Number of Employees)	ESTABLISHMENTS		EMPLOYEES		PAYROLLS	
	NUMBER	PERCENT	NUMBER (000)	PERCENT	MILLIONS OF DOLLARS	PERCENT
1– 4	105,641	35.4	218	1.4	738	1.0
5– 9	50,660	17.0	340	2.2	1,297	1.8
10– 19	46,820	15.7	644	4.2	2,615	3.5
20– 49	46,307	15.5	1,443	9.4	6,058	8.2
50– 99	21,764	7.3	1,513	9.8	6,416	8.7
100– 249	16,132	5.4	2,497	16.2	10,939	14.8
250– 499	6,240	2.1	2,150	14.0	9,709	13.2
500– 999	2,757	0.9	1,893	12.3	9,176	12.4
1,000–2,499	1,363	0.5	2,047	13.3	10,852	14.7
2,500 and over	498	0.2	2,649	17.2	15,950	21.6
Total	298,182	100.0	15,394	100.0	73,750	100.0

Source: U.S. Department of Commerce, Bureau of the Census, *Census of Manufactures*, 1958, pp. 2–2, 2–3. In this and subsequent tables columns might not total precisely because of rounding.

reasonably be set at sales of $100,000 per year, which would amount to about $300 per business day. On this basis, almost three quarters of the stores operating in 1958 were small. Another 20 percent were medium-sized stores with annual sales volume between $100,000 and $1,000,000. Only 1.5 percent of the stores had a sales volume in excess of a million a year.

If one looks at business done, however, the picture is very different. The 1.5 percent of big stores did 31 percent of the retail business of the country, while the 20 percent of medium-sized stores did another 46 percent. This left less than one quarter of the business for the multitude of small retail outlets.

The importance of large-scale retailing is even greater than these figures suggest. Many of the units which appear as small or medium-sized in Table 2 belong to large companies operating chains of retail outlets. Thus the true "independent retailer" is now confined to a small percentage of the market.

The situation in farming is shown in Table 3. The number of farms in the United States has been falling for a long time. From six and a quarter million in 1930, it has now fallen to less than four million. It is striking that almost half of these units contain less than 100 acres. This is scarcely a farm at all for grain growing or livestock production; but for poultry, fruits and vegetables, and certain specialty crops, 100 acres may be quite adequate.

There are about two million farms of more than 100 acres. Only 136,000 farms, or about 4 percent of the total, contain a thousand acres or

TABLE 2

Size of Retail Establishments, 1958

ANNUAL SALES (Thousands of Dollars)	ESTABLISHMENTS		SALES	
	NUMBER	PERCENT	MILLIONS OF DOLLARS	PERCENT
Less than 5	75,064	4.6	254	0.1
5– 9	146,805	8.9	1,014	0.5
10– 19	242,589	14.7	3,468	1.8
20– 29	201,886	12.3	4,884	2.6
30– 49	288,178	17.5	11,131	5.9
50– 99	316,998	19.2	22,288	11.8
100– 299	265,346	16.1	43,482	23.1
300– 499	49,125	3.0	18,766	10.0
500– 999	35,740	2.2	24,602	13.1
1,000–1,999	16,929	1.0	23,357	12.4
2,000–4,999	6,954	0.4	19,714	10.5
5,000 and over	1,295	0.1	15,520	8.2
Total	1,646,909	100.0	188,480	100.0

Source: U.S. Department of Commerce, *Statistical Abstract of the United States*, 1961, p. 836. Includes only stores which operated throughout the year.

more. But note that these large units include almost half of total farm acreage. Once more, a small minority of producing units is responsible for the bulk of economic activity in the industry.

One other feature of American farming may be noted in passing. About 80 percent of all farms are owned by the people who operate them. Only 20 percent of farm operators are tenants. This is a striking change from 1930, when 43 percent of farm operators were tenants and

TABLE 3

Size of Farm Units, 1959

SIZE OF FARM (Acres)	FARMS		ACREAGE	
	NUMBER	PERCENT	ACRES (000)	PERCENT
Under 10	240,699	6.5	1,041	0.1
10– 49	811,118	21.9	21,807	1.9
50– 99	657,656	17.8	47,932	4.3
100–179	772,220	20.9	105,691	9.4
180–259	414,365	11.1	89,477	8.0
260–499	471,385	12.7	165,383	14.8
500–999	199,962	5.4	137,319	12.3
1,000 and over	136,278	3.7	551,713	49.2
Total	3,703,683	100.0	1,120,363	100.0

Source: Preliminary. U.S. Department of Commerce, *Statistical Abstract of the United States* ,1961, p. 619.

only 57 percent were owners. The change reflects the decline of cotton farming in the "old South," which was mainly on a tenancy basis. It also reflects the high prosperity during and after World War II, which enabled many tenants to leave the land for city jobs and many others to buy the land they occupy. Farm ownership, of course, is not always complete. About 40 percent of the farm owners have mortgages, averaging about $9,000 per farm, so that the local banker is often a silent partner in the enterprise.

The coexistence of large and small units in most American industries presents an interesting puzzle. It is not a new phenomenon. The picture shown here for recent years would not be basically different if one looked at 1930 or 1900. One would still find a minority of large units producing the bulk of the output in each industry, and a multitude of smaller units dividing the remainder.

How can "big fellows" and "little fellows" continue to exist side by side in a competitive economy? If large-scale operation is as efficient as we are brought up to believe, why don't the bigger concerns outproduce and undersell the small ones and eventually force them out of existence?

The answer consists of several parts.

First, the industry classification used in Tables 1 to 3 is very broad. Manufacturing is not a single industry but a bundle of industries, which differ greatly as regards the most efficient size of plant. A steel mill or an auto assembly plant must be large to be efficient; but an efficient-sized cotton mill is considerably smaller, and a garment shop can be smaller still. The same is true in agriculture. Cattle ranching takes many acres, but thousands of chickens can be raised on a few acres. Thus if we made up tables for specific types of farming, or manufacturing, or retailing, the variation in size of units would be considerably reduced.

Second, even though a particular size of cotton mill may be most efficient, it may not make a great deal of difference whether the plant is somewhat larger or smaller. A plant half as large as the "right-sized" one may be able to produce a yard of cloth at only 5 percent greater cost. Thus small plants can survive, though they will have lower profits than their more efficient rivals.

Third, the small operator may be able to offset his relative inefficiency in various ways. He can sometimes get a higher price for his product. Studies of retailing usually show that the small independent grocer or druggist charges more than the large chain stores. Yet many people continue to patronize the independent.

The small producer may get by partly by paying lower wages. Wage surveys typically show a direct relation between wage level and size of establishment in an industry. The bigger units pay out part of the gain from their higher productivity in the form of larger paychecks and fringe benefits to employees. This is good public relations and also good union relations.

Finally, the small businessman may survive by accepting a lower income for his effort. In farming, storekeeping, service and repair industries, and other one-man operations, the main cost is the owner's time; and he is free to value this at whatever he pleases. The less efficient he is in comparison with larger units, the less he will earn. Many thousands of small businessmen doubtless end up with less per year than they could earn by taking a salaried job. One can interpret this in various ways: as sheer ignorance and lack of foresight; as chronic overoptimism, an unwarranted expectation that "next year will be better"; or as a deliberate choice of independence even at a lower income.

Whatever the interpretation, the facts are clear. The small business-man survives partly by accepting a low income. Every year many thousands go bankrupt and pass from the scene, but there seems always to be an equal number of new recruits eager to step into their shoes.

FACTORS OF PRODUCTION: LABOR

Before examining what comes out of the production process, let us look at what goes in. The basic *inputs* or *factors of production* are labor, capital, and natural resources; and a few words on each of these is in order.

In the main lobby of the U.S. Department of Commerce building there is a "population clock," whose revolving hands show the population of the United States as of any hour and minute. The hands whiz around quite rapidly. Every 7 seconds a new arrival is registered on the clock, while every 19 seconds there is a subtraction through death. In early 1966, the clock was nearing the 200 million mark.

But this alone does not tell us how much labor the country can count on for production. Very young people, very old people, and a good many in between do not work for pay. Whether to work or not is partly a matter of preference and custom, and the percentage of the population which is at work varies considerably from country to country.

The situation in the United States in 1965 is shown in Figure 1.[1] About 78 million people, or 58 percent of the population aged 14 and over were counted as members of the labor force at that time. More interesting than the total, however, is the distribution of the labor force. Note that more than 90 percent of men in the age range 20–65, and almost 40 percent of all women in this range, were available for work. There is a marked tapering off, however, under the age of 20 and above the age of 65.

This already tells us several things about the American economy and society:

---

[1] Data from U.S. Department of Labor, *Employment and Earnings*, May, 1965, p. 7.

Percentage of Population in the Labor Force, United States, 1965

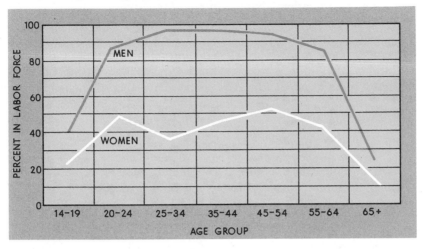

FIGURE 1.

1. For the able-bodied male in the prime of life, work is virtually obligatory.

2. The percentage of women at work, which has risen rapidly since 1900 and is still rising, indicates a society in which women have high independence and status. There are many countries in which this would not be true. In Moslem countries, the percentage of women employed outside the home would be much lower.

3. The low percentage of young people in the labor force indicates the high value placed on education in the United States. The proportion of those aged 16–25 who are enrolled in educational institutions has risen greatly since 1900 and is still rising. It must be a wealthy economy which can afford to keep young people out of the labor force for so long.

4. The American economy is also prosperous enough so that most people over 65 can and do choose to retire from work. Indeed, the retirement age has been creeping down, and now a good many people from 60 onwards retire.

A nation's labor supply is not just a matter of numbers. *Quality* is also important. Labor quality includes physical strength, health, trade skills, regularity of work performance, and responsiveness to material incentives. Some of these things are not susceptible to measurement. One tangible indicator of quality, however, is the *educational level* of the labor force. Education is partly a consumer good, which contributes to a fuller and more satisfying life whatever one's occupation. But it is also a capital good in the sense of inculcating attitudes favorable to high productivity and developing specific vocational skills. A more highly educated labor force can be presumed to be more skilled, more mobile, more aware of occupational possibilities and rewards.

Judged by this yardstick, the quality of the American labor force has risen sharply over the past century. Young people now complete, on the average, many more years of schooling than did their fathers and grandfathers. Present-day workers in the prime ages 20–45 have had about three times as much education as people in the same age groups in 1900.

TABLE 4

Additional Lifetime Income of U.S. Males, Ages 18 to 64, by Years of School Completed and Costs of Education, 1939 and 1958.

YEARS OF SCHOOL COMPLETED	1939	1958
College		
A. Added earnings (Dollars)	39,000	151,000
B. Added costs of education		
(Dollars)	4,348	13,780
C. Ratio A/B	8.97	10.96
High school		
A. Added earnings (Dollars)	25,000	70,000
B. Added costs of education		
(Dollars)	1,636	5,930
C. Ratio A/B	15.3	11.80
Elementary		
A. Added earnings (Dollars)	12,000	47,000
B. Added costs of education		
(Dollars)	344	1,169
C. Ratio A/B	34.9	40.2

Source: Theodore W. Schultz, "Education and Economic Growth," in *Social Forces Influencing American Education,* Sixtieth Yearbook of the National Society for the Study of Education, Part II (Chicago: University of Chicago Press, 1961), p. 79.

Some might still argue that this has no direct connection with productive efficiency, but they would be wrong. There is plenty of evidence that how much people earn is correlated with the length of their education. Thus if people get paid roughly what they are worth, their productive capacity must rise as their education rises.

Schultz's calculations on this are shown in Table 4. By looking at the top right-hand corner of the table you can see that graduation from college will be worth about $150,000 to you over your lifetime. You will get back the cost of your college education 10 times over. Note also that the financial return on a college education has not decreased over the past generation but on the contrary has increased considerably. The

increased earnings resulting from a high-school diploma, however, have
fallen (relatively) since 1939. Now that almost everyone goes through
high school, the added value of a diploma is no longer what it used to be.

What do the people in the labor force do for a living? The kinds of
job at which people were working in 1965 are shown in Table 5. In broad
terms, about one quarter are professional people, technical workers,
executives, and business proprietors. Another quarter work in sales,
clerical, and other white-collar jobs. About one third are manual workers
at every level from laborers to highly skilled craftsmen. More than one

TABLE 5

Occupational Composition of the Employed Labor Force,
United States, 1965

OCCUPATIONAL GROUP	PERCENTAGE OF LABOR FORCE	
Professional, technical and kindred workers	12.5	
Managers, proprietors, and officials (except farm)	10.5	
Total		23.0
Clerical and kindred workers	15.6	
Sales workers	6.5	
Total		22.1
Service workers		12.8
Craftsmen, foremen, and kindred workers	12.5	
Operatives and kindred workers	18.6	
Laborers, except farm and mine	5.2	
Total		36.3
Farmers and farm managers	3.3	
Farm laborers	2.5	
Total		5.8
Total employed		100.0

Source: U.S. Department of Labor, *Employment and Earnings*, May, 1965.

tenth are in service occupations, and only about 5 percent are in
agriculture.

As industries rise and fall in relative importance, and as production
techniques and organization change, the pattern of employment also
changes. The occupational distribution of the labor force in 1900 looked
quite different from the 1965 distribution. One striking tendency over the
long run has been the rapid increase of professional, clerical, and other
white-collar jobs. White-collar workers now form a majority of the urban
labor force, and their preponderance is increasing. Another striking trend
has been the relative decline of agriculture from more than half of the
labor force in 1870 to one twentieth today.

FACTORS OF PRODUCTION: NATURAL RESOURCES

Most countries are not in the comfortable position of the United States. They have difficulty raising enough food to support their populations, even at a low level of living. Agriculture is their basic industry, and land their basic resource. It is an important resource in any country, at any stage of development.

The land *area* of a country does not reveal the amount of economically usable land. Most of the country may be desert or frozen tundra. Even in the United States, with its temperate climate, cropland is a minor part of the total area. The land area of the United States is 2,271 million acres. More than half of this is desert, mountains, forests, public grazing land, and other land not in farms. Another 30 percent is pasture and woodland. Cropland normally used for crops is only about 400 million acres, or 17 percent of the total.[2] In some countries (Belgium, Holland), the percentage of cultivated land would be much higher than this, but in others (Egypt, Saudi Arabia) it would be much lower.

We ordinarily think of the supply of usable land as fixed by climate and geography. It is something which is "just there." But this is not entirely true. The supply of land can often be increased by human effort. The most dramatic examples are large irrigation projects, which may reclaim millions of acres previously idle because of insufficient rainfall. Much can be done also through agricultural research. Development of dry-farming methods, and of drought-resistant crops such as sorghum, enables cultivation to be pushed out into areas of scanty rainfall. Development of strains of wheat with a short growing season has enabled wheat growing to be pushed quite far north in Canada and the U.S.S.R.

The fact that a certain amount of land is available for agriculture does not mean that all this land will be used. The amount of land actually used, and the intensity with which it is used, depends on population pressure in relation to the level of agricultural technology. If population pressure is severe and agricultural methods primitive, as in India, every possible acre will be pressed into service and a great deal of labor will be devoted to each one. But if population is sparser or agriculture more productive, it may not be necessary to put all of the usable land under cultivation. The United States is presently in a position to concentrate its agriculture on a limited acreage of the best land, while retiring less desirable land from active use.

When one turns to natural resources other than land, it is difficult to say much in general terms. The United States obviously has great

---

[2] U.S. Department of Commerce, *Statistical Absract of the United States,* Washington, D.C., 1961, p. 614. Data for earlier years may be found in U.S. Department of Agriculture, *Agricultural Statistics 1960,* Washington, D.C., 1961.

supplies of water power, timber, coal, oil, minerals, and other products of nature. A listing of quantities of each of these things would be tedious and not very instructive. But it may be useful to comment on two aspects of resources which are often misunderstood in popular discussion.

First, when is a resource really a resource? This may seem like a silly question. Surely a resource is a physical quantity of something provided by nature. It is just there, for all time, unless or until it is used up in production. But this common-sense view turns out to be wrong. Resources are relative. Whether a physical object is or is not a resource to the economy depends on *discovery, demand,* and *technology.*

The importance of discovery is obvious. A pool of oil has no economic significance until someone knows it is there. In most countries of the world, geological exploration has been so scanty that no one knows what lies under the ground. Even in the better-mapped United States, there are undoubtedly many "strikes" still to be made.

Demand is also necessary. Someone must want the item in question or want something which can be made from it. The Africans of Kenya and Uganda do not like rhinoceros meat, and so the rhinoceros is a nuisance rather than a resource.

Technical knowledge is a further ingredient. Crude oil was not a resource to the American Indian, but today we know how to extract from it a wide variety of useful products. Technical change can destroy resources as well as create them. Today we count our reserves of anthracite and bituminous coal as a basic resource. But suppose that a century from now developments in solar and atomic energy have provided cheaper sources of heat and power. Then coal may be just a strange black substance in the ground, with no economic value.

Thus natural resources turn out not to be so natural after all. To a significant extent, they are man-made.

Second, what about the scarcity and exhaustibility of natural resources? There is a popular impression that, since these resources are provided in fixed amounts by nature, and since we use up large quantities of them every year, we are bound in time to run out of many types of resources. What then? Will a shortage of basic resources eventually reduce our economic productivity, our military capacity, and our standard of living? Many conferences have been organized, many books written, many millions of dollars spent on research into this problem.

But is it really much of a problem? What happens as one continues year after year to use up the supply of a fixed resource? First, technical change may shift demand away from the item long before the supply has been exhausted. This seems likely to be the case with coal. With the present rapid pace of technical change, it is not much use to predict resource shortages 30 or 40 years ahead, since no one can really say what will be a resource at that time.

Second, as visible supplies of a resource dwindle, exploration for new supplies is intensified. In the case of oil, this search has been spectacularly successful, to the point where many known fields are being held out of production to avoid flooding the market and breaking the world price.

Third, there are few natural products for which there are no substitutes. If the supply of a particular resource decreases, and if exploration does not provide a satisfactory offset, its price will rise. This will stimulate research to discover ways of doing without it and substituting other materials. Aluminum may be used in place of copper, stainless steel in place of aluminum, plastics in place of rubber.

The resource problem is eased also by the availability of international trade. Countries rich in resources are usually eager to sell them, and the United States has been drawing more and more raw materials from foreign sources. This involves the risk of wartime shipping dislocations and the consequent need for strategic reserves. But this is not a problem of resource scarcity.

FACTORS OF PRODUCTION: CAPITAL

Capital consists of *physical goods* used in the production of other goods and services. Capital goods are not directly consumed, but they help to produce things which are desired and consumed by the public. A shoe factory constitutes capital, because it turns out shoes for which consumers are willing to pay a price. A railroad's track and rolling stock are capital, because they produce transportation services for which people are willing to pay. Fences, barns, and farm machinery are part of the capital used in agricultural production.

Most capital in the United States is privately owned, but ownership is not the essence of the matter. Publicly owned assets also yield services and may properly be considered part of the nation's capital. School and college buildings contribute to the production of educational services. Streets and highways provide transportation service. When the British railroads were bought out by the government in 1947 (partly because they were going slowly bankrupt!), they did not cease to be capital because of the transfer of ownership.

We sometimes say that capital goods are *durable*, while consumer goods are used up quickly. But this distinction is also slippery. What about an automobile, which may have a useful life of 15 or 20 years, longer than the life of most factory machinery? Should we not regard the automobile as a capital good, which "produces" the consumer good of transportation service year after year until it is worn out? And what about a home or an apartment house? Is this not a capital good, since it will yield housing service over a long period of time?

Government statisticians count all residential buildings as capital, on the ground that they resemble factories and commercial buildings in being very long-lived. Automobiles, stoves, refrigerators, and other household items are termed "durable consumer goods" and are not counted as capital. But this is a matter of definition, with no firm logical foundation.

Capital goods wear out over the course of time. This is termed *depreciation* and is usually regarded as happening gradually and continuously. The fact of depreciation has important consequences. Suppose there are $1,000 billion worth of capital goods in existence in the United States at the beginning of the year. If no new capital goods are produced during the year, the capital in existence at the end of the year will be less than at the beginning. The same buildings and machines might be standing around, but they will be more nearly worn out. The amount of service left in them will be less by the amount of the depreciation which has occurred during the year.

Production of new capital goods is termed *gross capital formation*. To see how much has actually been added to the capital stock over a certain period, however, we must deduct depreciation on the preexisting capital goods. The result, gross capital formation minus depreciation, is termed *net capital formation*. This is the real addition to capital supply.

The United States has been adding to its capital stock for many years, and this stock has now reached a fantastic total. Goldsmith estimates that the net value of capital goods in the United States in 1958 was $1,367 billion.[3] Our national wealth at this time was thus almost three times the value of our annual output. We had about 3 years' production "stored up" in the form of capital assets. From another standpoint, our capital stock amounted to about $7,500 per head of population, or $20,000 for each member of the labor force.

Who owns all this wealth? About 40 percent of it belongs to business concerns (Figure 2). About the same amount consists of housing owned by families. The decision to count residences as capital is thus a major decision. Without this, national capital would be much smaller, and the ownership proportions would be quite different. Of the publicly owned capital, more than two thirds belongs to state and local governments. But remember that military facilities are excluded, which would have added almost a hundred billion to the total.

The United States is clearly a capital-rich country. We may note also that the supply of capital in the American economy has been rising a good deal faster than the supply of labor. The number of man-hours of labor employed in private production in the United States doubled between 1890 and 1960; but the amount of capital in use increased more

---

[3] Raymond T. Goldsmith, *The National Wealth of the United States in the Postwar Period* (Princeton, N.J.: Princeton University Press, 1962). This total includes only *reproducible* tangible wealth. Land and other natural resources are excluded. Military installations are also excluded.

Net Reproducible Tangible Wealth by Sector, United States, 1958

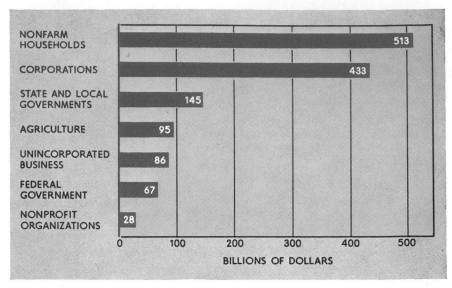

FIGURE 2.

than five times.[4] *Thus capital per man-hour of labor* increased more than
2½ times over this period. This is a major reason why labor has become
more productive over the years. Each man now works with much more
machinery, power, and other physical aids to production. "Automation" is
simply the latest expression of a trend which can be traced far back in
our economic history.

Capital is not spread evenly over all industries in the economy.
Some industries (oil refining, chemicals, air transportation) use a large
amount of capital per worker employed. Other industries (clothing
manufacture, retailing, cleaning and dyeing) use less equipment per
man. The result is wide differences in output per worker. High-capital
industries typically turn out more per man than low-capital industries,
and they also pay higher wages to their employees. The benefits of
capitalism to the worker have often been disputed. The benefits of *capital*
appear to be beyond dispute.

THE PATTERN OF OUTPUT

What does all this labor and capital produce? How large is the
national output? What does it look like, in concrete terms?

The total output of the American economy, worth more than $650

---

[4] John W. Kendrick, *Productivity Trends in the United States* (Princeton,
N.J.: Princeton University Press, 1961).

billion in 1965, staggers the imagination. The number of separate products runs to hundreds of thousands. A list of even the major items would take many pages. Thus one cannot give any detailed description of the outflow of products. But by grouping products into certain broad "families," we can say something about the relative importance of these groups.

The importance of an industry may be gauged either by the number of people it employs or by how much it produces. Both measures are shown in Table 6. Value of output is perhaps the more significant measure, and we shall rely mainly on it.

TABLE 6

Industrial Distribution of National Output
and Employed Labor Force, United States, 1963

TYPE OF INDUSTRY	NATIONAL OUTPUT (Percent)	EMPLOYED LABOR FORCE (Percent)
Agriculture	4.0	6.8
Manufacturing and mining	29.8	25.1
Construction	5.2	6.2
Trade	16.2	20.1
Finance, insurance, and real estate	10.2	4.6
Transportation, communications and public utilities	8.0	5.8
Services	12.4	15.1
Government	13.5	16.3
Rest of world	0.7	
	100.0	100.0

Source: U.S. Department of Commerce, *Survey of Current Business*, July, 1964.

Manufacturing is the most important branch of economic activity, a position which it attained about 1890 and has retained ever since. The proportion of national output coming from manufacturing plants has continued to creep up decade by decade, and now stands at about 30 percent of total production. Within this total are hundreds of different lines of manufacturing. These are usually grouped into two broad categories: "hard goods" or durable goods, which includes steel and other metal products, machinery, automobiles and transportation equipment, household appliances, and the like; and "soft goods" or nondurables, which includes food products, textiles, clothing, and so on. The durable goods group is now the larger of the two, and its preponderance is increasing.

Second most important is the trade sector, which makes up about one sixth of national output. The wholesalers and retailers in this category produce the service of getting goods from the producer to the ultimate user, of providing convenient locations in which families can have access to goods produced all over the world. With the growing size and complexity of the American economy, the task of distributing goods has become steadily larger relative to the task of physical production.

Third in order come the services produced by government. They now constitute one eighth of national output, a considerably larger percentage than a generation ago, due mainly to heavier military expenditures. Private service industries produce a bit more than 12 percent of national output. This group includes medical, legal, and other professional services; the entertainment industries; personal services such as barbering and beauty care; laundering and dry cleaning; and the work of servants in private households.

Two impressions stand out from Table 6. One is the small size of the historic agricultural sector. Agriculture, forestry, and fisheries together now turn out less than 5 percent of national output. The political turmoil over agricultural policy relates to a shrinking part of the economy. A second striking fact is that industries concerned with physical production now constitute only half of national output. This is true even if we stretch a point and count transportation and utilities as part of the "goods" group along with manufacturing, mining, construction, and agriculture. The remaining "service" sectors—trade, finance, services, and government—make up half of national output, and their share is growing year by year. When we speak of the output of goods *and services*, therefore, the second term is not an afterthought. More and more of our productive activity takes an intangible rather than a physical form.

A different basis for classifying productive activity is according to the purchaser of the product, the ultimate customer. The customer may be a private household, a business concern, a government agency, or a foreign buyer. The relative importance of these groups in 1964 is shown in Table 7. This table is based on principles of national income accounting, which we shall not examine in detail until Chapter 19. All that need be said here is that the table includes only *finished products,* at the stage of passing into use by an ultimate purchaser.

Consumers, as one might expect, are much the largest customers for the national output. They regularly buy around 70 percent of each year's production. Note the large proportion of this which consists of expenditure on services rather than on physical products. Purchases of services make up about 40 percent of all household expenditure.

Government agencies are the second largest group of customers, taking about one fifth of all goods and services produced. State and local governments are the main buyers of ordinary or nonmilitary products, but heavy purchases of military items by the federal government make its total somewhat larger. This reverses the historic relationship which

TABLE 7

Gross National Product in 1964 by Type of Purchaser

	BILLIONS OF DOLLARS		PERCENT OF TOTAL
Consumer purchases		426.3	67.8
Durable goods	58.7		9.3
Nondurable goods	177.5		28.2
Services	162.6		25.9
Residential construction	27.5		4.4
Business purchases		65.3	10.4
Buildings	21.1		3.4
Machinery and equipment	39.4		6.3
Change in inventories	4.8		0.7
Government purchases of goods and services		128.4	20.4
Federal	65.3		10.4
State and local	63.1		10.0
Net exports of goods and services		8.6	1.4
Exports	37.0		5.9
Imports	28.4		(−4.5)
Total		628.7	100.0

Source: *Survey of Current Business*, September, 1965, p. 25.

prevailed before 1940, when federal purchases were considerably smaller than state and local purchases.

Third in line come business organizations. Remember that the total here does not include purchases of materials which are to be worked over some more and then resold to someone else, such as purchases of leather by a shoe factory or cotton yarn by a weaving mill. Table 7 includes only business purchases *for final use.* This means basically purchases of buildings and machinery—in short, *capital formation.* This is not a big item, forming only about 10 percent of GNP. But it is a strategic item in the economy for two reasons. First, it is the source of new productive capacity and thus a major source of economic growth. National production is higher this year than last, mainly because part of last year's output went into office buildings, factories, machine tools, commercial aircraft, and other things that will contribute to greater production over the years ahead.

Second, business purchases of plant and equipment are irregular from year to year, depending on sales and profits in the immediate past and businessmen's guesses about the future. Business purchases fluctuate considerably more than consumer purchases. These fluctuations are a major element in the "business cycle."

WHO GETS THE PRODUCT?

The gross national product of the United States in 1965 was more than $650 billion. Now for every dollar of goods produced and sold there must be a dollar of income created. We can speak interchangeably of national *product* or national *income*. They come to the same thing.

Who gets all this money? And why do they get it? People receive income mainly because of their command over factors of production. They supply the services of these factors to producing units, and receive a cash payment in return. Factors of production can be divided broadly into animate (labor power) and inanimate (capital and natural resources). The return to the former is usually termed *labor income,* and that to the latter, *property income.*

Property income goes by various names—interest, dividends, profits, rents. These are all returns to ownership. Farmers, storekeepers, and other independent proprietors also receive income partly as a return on the land and capital which they own. Labor income appears mainly in the form of wage and salary payments, which alone make up about *two thirds* of national income in the United States. Farmers, small businessmen, and independent professional men do not pay themselves a salary; but most of what they receive is also a payment for personal effort.

Labor income and property income are hard to untangle statistically, mainly because it is hard to split the incomes of farmers and independent business and professional men into a "labor share" and a "property share." Making the best guess one can about this, however, it appears that more than three quarters of all income in the United States today is labor income, and less than one quarter is property income.[5]

Property owners do less well than these figures suggest, because they get considerably less than the income which theoretically "belongs" to them. About half of corporation profits are taken by the federal government in income taxes. Of the remainder, companies usually put about half back into the business and pay out the other half in dividends. Thus dividend payments come down to roughly a quarter of the original profit total. If one looks at income *actually received,* then, property income amounts to only about 15 percent of all personal income.

A different kind of question is how much income is received by each household in the economy, regardless of the source from which it comes. How many households fall in each "income bracket"? This bears directly on the degree of income equality or inequality in the country. The situation in 1962 is shown in Table 8, which covers all families of two

---

[5] The basis for this estimate, and the way in which labor and capital shares have changed since 1900, is explained in detail in Chapter 16.

TABLE 8

Distribution of Families by Annual Income, 1962

ANNUAL INCOME (Before Income Taxes)	NUMBER OF FAMILIES (000)	PERCENT OF FAMILIES	AGGREGATE INCOME RECEIVED	
			(Millions)	(Percent)
Under $2,000	3,217	6.9	3,905	1.0
2,000– 2,999	2,902	6.2	7,313	1.9
3,000– 3,999	3,835	8.2	13,491	3.5
4,000– 4,999	4,592	9.8	20,715	5.4
5,000– 5,999	5,075	10.8	27,918	7.3
6,000– 7,499	7,487	16.0	50,436	13.2
7,500– 9,999	8,730	18.6	75,057	19.7
10,000–14,999	6,941	14.8	82,956	21.7
15,000 +	4,111	8.7	100,424	26.3

Source: U.S. Department of Commerce, *Survey of Current Business*, April, 1964, p. 6.

or more people living together but does not include individuals living alone.[6]

Despite the growth of equalitarian beliefs and policies in recent decades, income distribution is still quite unequal. At the bottom, many households still have annual incomes at the incredibly low level of $2,000 or less. At the other extreme, the 8 percent of families with incomes above $15,000 receive about one quarter of all personal income. These high incomes come partly from concentration of property ownership in a minority of the population but also from high business salaries and professional earnings. Most of the inequality of household incomes *must* be due to inequality of wages and salaries, since these provide the great bulk of all income received.

Remember, however, that the incomes in Table 8 are *before* payment of federal income taxes. The personal income tax rate rises steeply with rising income. People in the range of $20,000–$50,000 a year pay about a quarter of their incomes in income tax, and people above $100,000 pay about half.[7] Thus the distribution of income after taxes is somewhat more equal than the distribution of pretax incomes. Whether we have gone too far, or not far enough, in leveling incomes through taxation is a hotly disputed political issue which will be discussed in Chapter 16.

---

[6] There were about 10 million individuals living by themselves in 1962. These were mostly young people just breaking into the labor market, or older retired people. On this account they fall heavily into the lower-income brackets. To include them would give a biased view of "normal" family incomes.

[7] Tax rates are even higher than this. But because the rates are so high, tax lawyers and accountants have become very ingenious at discovering loopholes, deductions, and adjustments which bring down the tax actually paid.

SUMMARY

1. An economic system consists of *households* and *producing units* —mainly private business concerns in the United States, though government agencies are also important producers.

2. There is a circular flow of money and services between the two groups. Households sell services to producing units for money and spend this money on the output of the producing units.

3. Almost all large business concerns, and many smaller businesses, are organized as corporations. The corporation can mobilize large amounts of money by issuing securities, and its owners have the advantage of limited liability.

4. Most large corporations are controlled, not by the mass of small stockholders, but by the executives who manage the company's affairs. This separation of ownership from control has produced important changes in the nature of modern capitalism.

5. Government functions in the economy as policeman, producer of public goods, regulator of private economic activity, and distributor of personal income.

6. The trade union is an important regulatory agency. It enables workers to appeal from management decisions which affect their job tenure or working conditions. Union contract rules also affect wage rates, supplementary benefits, hours, job security, work speeds, and production methods.

7. Most producing units in the American economy are quite small. The minority of large units, however, produces the bulk of output in most fields.

8. The growth of the nation's labor supply depends on population growth, changes in the proportion choosing to work, changes in the working week, and improvements in the quality of labor through education and other means.

9. Natural resources are partly given by nature; but they depend also on discovery, demand, and technology.

10. Capital consists of buildings, machinery, and other durable goods used in the production of goods and services. Over the last century in the United States, the supply of capital has risen much faster than the supply of labor.

11. About 70 percent of our national output is bought by households for consumer use. About 20 percent is bought by government, and 10 percent consists of capital goods bought by business concerns.

12. More than three quarters of the income *earned* in the United States, and about 85 percent of the income actually *received*, is payment for work. The balance is income from property ownership.

13. Income distribution among households is still quite unequal. The top 15 percent of families receive almost 40 percent of all income (*before* payment of federal income taxes). The bottom 15 percent of families receive about 4 percent of total income.

DISCUSSION QUESTIONS

1. Why is a nation a logical unit for economic study? What other geographic units might be interesting for various purposes?

2. Why do we attach special importance to *households* and *producing units* in analyzing an economy? Are the two always clearly separated? (Contrast, for example, Nigeria and the United States on this point.)

3. What monetary transactions go on between households and
   a) Private producing units?
   b) Governmental producing units?

4. Would you expect the economic decisions (on prices, wages, expansion of the business, etc.) reached by the professional managers of a large corporation to differ from those which would be reached by an individual owner-manager? Why?

5. "The dominance of professional management in large companies has reduced ownership to secondary importance. Whether nominal ownership is vested in private stockholders or in government may make little difference to the operation of the enterprise." Discuss.

6. Which goods and services should be produced by government and which by private producers is a hot political issue in most countries. How would you try to draw a proper boundary line?

7. The text says that government cannot be neutral in the matter of income distribution. But maybe this is wrong. Can you construct a tax-and-expenditure system which would be strictly neutral?

8. Is it true that "big business" now dominates most branches of the American economy, and that our professed policy of encouraging small business is simply a sentimental survival from the past? If big business is so efficient, how does small business survive?

9. Should one expect a country's labor supply to grow at the same rate as its population? From your general knowledge (the chapter doesn't tell you), can you estimate what has happened in the United States since 1900?

10. How would you expect the labor supply of the United States (relative to population) to compare with that of West Germany? Of India?

11. The Ford Foundation once gave a research organization quite a few million dollars to study the urgent problem of our dwindling natural resources. After years of research the organization published a large volume which concluded that the problem was not serious after all. Why do you suppose they reached this conclusion?

12. Can one draw a clear line between *capital goods* and other goods? On what basis?

13. What is the approximate division of our gross national product among private consumer purchases, government purchases, and business purchases of capital goods? What things influence this division? Would you expect the percentages to look similar or different in other countries of the world— say, in Japan, the U.S.S.R., the Republic of the Congo, and Switzerland?

14. Considering that most income in the United States is now labor income rather than property income, wouldn't one expect the distribution of income among households to be reasonably equal? How do you explain the degree of inequality which still exists?

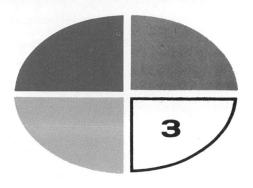

The Subsistence Economy;

The Planned Economy

> Q. What is the difference between capitalism and socialism?
>
> A. Under capitalism, man exploits man. Under socialism, it's just the opposite.
>
> OVERHEARD IN WARSAW

THE ECONOMIES of India, the U.S.A., and the U.S.S.R. seem on the surface to be very different from each other. Yet all economies perform the function of producing and distributing goods. To do this any economy must answer several questions:

1. Which members of the population shall engage in productive labor, how much work shall they do, and what shall they work at? This is the problem of *labor supply*.

2. How much effort shall be devoted to producing goods for immediate consumption, and how much to producing tools and equipment that will make possible greater production in the future? This is the problem of *capital supply*.

3. How much of each good and service shall be produced? What amount of resources shall be devoted to producing cotton cloth, television sets, superhighways, and the thousands of other things included in national output? This is the problem of *resource allocation*.

53

4. What methods of production shall be used? Shall one grow corn with a great deal of hand labor and little machinery or with much machinery and little labor? This is the problem of *production methods.*

5. How shall the national output be divided among the population? How much is each individual and household entitled to receive, and on what basis? This is the problem of *income distribution.*

The answers to these questions are interrelated. A man's income is related to how much work and what kind of work he does. Methods of production depend on available supplies of labor and capital. But the five questions are logically distinct, and each provides a vantage point for analyzing how an economy operates.

Every national economy answers these questions; but the institutional arrangements for reaching the answers differ considerably. Very broadly, one can distinguish *subsistence economies, planned economies,* and *market economies.* None of these ever exists in pure form. But it is helpful to think about them in pure form, just as it is useful to reason about pure chemical substances, frictionless space, and other things no one will ever see.

In a *subsistence economy* the basic unit is the family, clan, or tribe. Each unit produces all its requirements and consumes everything it produces. The nation is simply a conglomeration of these self-sufficient units, each living in economic isolation. Economic decisions are made in patriarchal fashion by the family head or tribal chief, within the bounds of established tradition. Many rural areas of Africa, Asia, and Latin America come quite close to this pattern of subsistence organization.

In a *planned economy* the means of production and the authority to make economic decisions belong to the state. Control is concentrated in a central planning board, which decides what is to be done in every corner of the economy. The nation is organized, in effect, as a single giant corporation. In this pure form, a planned economy would be quite cumbersome and inefficient, and so complete central planning is never found in actuality. But the economies of the U.S.S.R. and other communist countries go a long way in this direction.

A *market economy* is the polar opposite of a planned economy in the sense that economic decisions are highly decentralized. Each member of the labor force chooses his job independently. Each household decides what to buy with its money income. Each business concern decides what to produce, what production methods to use, and where to sell the product. Anyone is free to go into any line of production and to make or lose money by so doing.

The central mystery of a market economy is this: If economic decisions are made by millions of individuals, each doing precisely what he wants, what keeps the system from flying apart? May not the decisions of different people be so inconsistent that everything breaks down in confusion? How do conflicting interests and choices get reconciled with each other? This was long considered *the* central problem of economics, and it is still one of the most intriguing branches of economic study.

The market economy, like other pure types, is something no one will ever actually see. But the economies of the United States, Britain, the West European countries, and the British dominions come closer to this pattern than to any other.

Since each of these forms of organization is important in large areas of the world, each requires discussion in a general introduction to economics. There is no preordained sequence for this discussion. I choose to begin with subsistence economies and planned economies because they seem inherently simpler. The basic economic decisions are made by identifiable people, in one case a patriarch or tribal leader, in the other a central planning board. Thus the nature of the decisions stands out quite clearly. In a market economy, on the other hand, no one *makes* decisions for the economy as a whole. Overall decisions *get made* through an interlocking network of markets, in which the personal decisions of millions of individuals are registered and reconciled. To explain how this happens is a bit complicated, so it seems best to leave it until after the simpler cases have been considered.

THE SUBSISTENCE ECONOMY

It is instructive to picture the economic choices faced by Robinson Crusoe on his island. This is not as farfetched as it may seem. Crusoe is a shorthand symbol for any isolated household which meets its needs from its own production, rather than through trade with other households. Most of the world still lives in this way. Crusoe, the hillbilly in the Appalachians, and the poor peasant in South India are brothers under the skin.

If Crusoe is lucky, he will have been cast away on a fertile island. It may perhaps have breadfruit trees, the fruit of which has all the vitamins and minerals needed to sustain life. So, waking up his first morning on shore, Crusoe sets out to gather his daily breadfruit.

He will soon discover two things. First, the amount he can eat in a day is limited. The first breadfruit will seem delicious, because he is very hungry. But the second will not yield as much satisfaction as the first, the third will add still less satisfaction, and so on. He has discovered the principle of *diminishing marginal utility* from consumption.

It will turn out also that, as he gathers more fruit, each one will become more expensive in terms of time. The first few he may be able to knock down with a stick from the tree under which he is lying. But to get more he will have to climb the tree, and to get still more he will have to travel to other trees farther from home. So each additional hour he spends gathering breadfruit will yield less fruit than the one before. He has now discovered the principle of *diminishing marginal productivity* of labor.

At some point it will strike him that the game is no longer worth the candle. He will get increasingly hot and tired, and leisure to sit on the sand or swim in the ocean will look more and more attractive. At the same time, the reward for additional effort is declining, because the number of fruit he can collect per hour is falling, and the satisfaction from consuming each additional fruit is also falling. When he reaches the point at which the prospective reward from working an extra hour is less

FIGURE 1. Each point on AD shows a combination of fish and breadfruit which Crusoe could collect in 6 hours' time. This is called a production possibilities curve or production frontier. Points outside the frontier, such as E, are not feasible, because they would require more labor time than Crusoe has decided to exert.

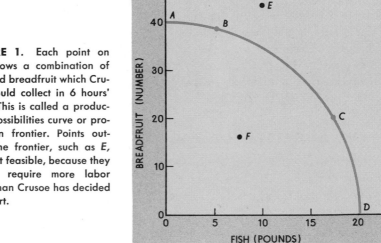

Crusoe's Production Possibilities Curve

than the prospective pleasure of ocean swimming, he will quit for the day. He has solved the problem of *income versus leisure*. Or, if you like, he has determined his own *labor supply*.

Now let's make Crusoe's life a bit more complicated. He wants to add some protein to his diet, and he really likes fish. There are plenty of fish in the nearby waters, so he decides to spend some of his time catching them. The problem now is how to allocate his one productive resource, labor time, between catching fish and collecting breadfruit.

One pertinent consideration is his productivity in these two directions. Let's make a little chart of this (Figure 1). If he spends his whole working day—say, 6 hours—on breadfruit, he can collect a total of 40 (point A). If he spends his whole day on fish, he can catch 20 pounds (point D). By dividing the day between the two, he can produce various *combinations* of the two products. Thus he might produce 5 pounds of fish and 36 breadfruit (point *B*), or 18 pounds of fish and 20 breadfruit (point *C*), or any number of other possibilities. The line *AD*, connecting all the combinations which Crusoe could produce in 6 hours, is termed his *production possibilities curve* or *production frontier.*

Why "frontier"? Because points outside the frontier (looking *away* from the origin to the northeast) are not feasible with the resources available. A point such as *E*, which indicates more of both products than point *B*, could be reached only by working more than the 6 hours to which Crusoe has decided to limit himself. Points within the frontier are all feasible but not preferable. Production at point *F*, for example, would mean working only 3 or 4 hours a day—having too much leisure and too little consumption. So Crusoe will want to produce at some point on *AD*.

The production frontier is a basic concept applicable to any economy, from the simplest to the most complex. Every economy has such a frontier, defining what it can produce with the resources available and the known methods of production. Over the course of time, the frontier moves outward as resources grow and production methods improve. The economy can never operate outside the frontier existing at the moment; and it will not want to operate inside the frontier, for this would mean that some resources are left unemployed. Operating exactly on the frontier is essentially what we mean by "full employment." But there are many points on the frontier, many bundles of goods which can be produced with the same resources. This is why there is always a problem of *choice*—the guns-versus-butter choice which a nation faces in wartime, the more-steel-mills *versus* better-housing choice faced by planners in the U.S.S.R., and so on.

How does Crusoe face this problem of choice? At what point on the production frontier will he produce? This depends on his *consumption preferences,* on how well he likes fish relative to breadfruit. If he is very fond of fish, he may end up in the neighborhood of point *C*. But if a little fish goes a long way with him, he may prefer a point near *B*. The common sense of this is obvious; we shall be more precise about it in Chapter 6.

So far we have had Crusoe working with his hands; but on the fishing front, at least, he could do better with a net. Perhaps he can weave one from reeds along the shore. But how is he to find time to *both* gather food (produce consumer goods) and weave nets (produce capital goods), while still working only 6 hours a day? Here is one way: suppose this Monday he eats only three quarters of the food he collects and stores up the other quarter. He does the same on Tuesday and Wednesday. Then, on Thursday, he can eat this stored food and spend the whole day working on his fish net. Repeat this prescription every four days, and eventually the net will be finished.

Here Crusoe has been saving, by consuming less food each day than he might have consumed. In fact, he has been saving a quarter of his income. The incentive to do this is that it enables him to *build capital goods,* which will increase his productive capacity and his potential income in the future. With the fish net he can catch perhaps twice as many fish per hour. Then he can eat more, or loaf more, or put in still more time on capital building—most likely he will choose some combination of these three things.

How much will Crusoe decide to save? This depends, first on the additional productivity of the capital goods. If the fish net triples his fish output per hour, he has a stronger incentive to build it than if it raises his output only 20 percent. The other consideration is his weighing of the present versus the future. This is partly an objective matter: if the island is on a main shipping lane and there is a good chance of his being picked up in a week, it would be foolish to spend much time building anything but bonfires. If he is likely to be stuck on the island indefinitely, it will pay to take a longer view. But there is also a subjective element. There are ants and grasshoppers in the human population and, depending on which Crusoe is, he may save much or little.

We have now extracted all we can from Crusoe, short of raising an income distribution problem by bringing in the man Friday. So let's turn to a more complex economy which is still essentially the same. Consider a tribal village in western Uganda. There is one graveled road leading from the village to the capital city 250 miles away. Young men sometimes go to work in the city for a while and bring back radios, bicycles, and other things which they have bought with their savings. Apart from this, everything used in the village is produced and consumed on the spot.

The question of who shall work, and at what tasks, is settled by immemorial custom. Women till the fields and gather the crops. Children herd the cattle. Men do the heavier work of clearing new land, building irrigation ditches, house building, and so on. They also hunt and fish and, in the happy days before the white man, used to engage in tribal warfare. In the time left over, they sit under the banana trees and discuss village politics. The men show a strong preference for leisure as against productive effort, though they do not allow the same degree of choice to their women.

Even this small village with its simple agriculture produces a considerable range of products: grain, plantains, and bananas from the ground; milk and meat from the cattle; fish and wild game; alcoholic drinks brewed from the bananas; clothing woven and tailored by the women in the evenings; and simple articles of furniture fashioned from wood by the men. This raises a typical economic problem of distributing the available labor time among various lines of production in such a way as to achieve greatest satisfaction. Note that decisions will be based both on the villagers' liking for different articles of consumption and on the difficulty of producing them. The men may catch few wild antelope *either* because they do not find them very tasty or because the time required is much greater than for other foods.

There is also a problem of capital supply. The villagers might devote their full time to producing goods for immediate consumptions. Alternatively, they may spend some time fashioning crude fish nets, spears, bows and arrows, shovels, hoes, and the like. These things will increase the productivity of their work and enable them to live better in future. They may also spend time on land clearing, terracing, drainage and irrigation ditches, road building, and other agricultural improvements. They may build larger and more comfortable houses, perhaps substituting tin roofs for the traditional thatched roofs. And by eating less meat for the time being, they can gradually build up the size of their livestock herds, which are a major capital asset.

These are all primitive forms of saving and capital formation. By consuming less than they might during the current year, the villagers can enjoy a larger income in later years. The basic condition for capital formation is also apparent: natural resources and the people's productive capacity must be large enough so that it does not take their full time every day just to win a bare livelihood. If it did, they could never get ahead of the game, never set aside enough of their basic resource—labor time—to improve the tools of production.

The income distribution problem is simple. Each family consumes what it produces. The family, however, is an "extended family," a group of perhaps 30 or 40 people linked by blood and marriage, instead of the smaller individualistic family which is customary in the West. Each member is entitled to his share of the family food supplies. Thus how much a particular villager gets depends on the output of a large group rather than on his personal productive effort.

The Uganda village, in short, contains most elements of the economic problem. There are worker-consumers with certain attitudes toward work, leisure, savings, and consumption; with a stock of technical knowledge and personal skills; and with preferences among different consumption goods. There is a more or less plentiful supply of natural resources. There is a supply of capital goods which can be added to, simply maintained, or allowed to wear out without replacement. These are the same elements which underlie economic choice in complex economies. And whether in a complex economy or a self-sufficient village, economic decisions are shaped by *natural resources, technical possibilities,* and *personal preferences.*

THE PLANNED ECONOMY

There is no fully planned economy in the world, nor is there ever likely to be. Central planning implies that in the center of the economy sits a group of controllers who issue detailed orders on the quantity of each product to be produced in the coming year; how much labor and materials each factory shall have to produce its output quota; how many people in the country shall be employed, where they shall work, and what they shall be paid; and all other details of economic life.

Even with high-speed computers and a large statistical staff, it would be difficult to draft and enforce a consistent plan embracing all these matters. Nor is there any need for such comprehensive control. One can control the essentials without controlling everything; and there is an obvious advantage in allowing plant managers, workers, and consumers to exercise some initiative within the framework of the overall program.

The economies of the communist countries, then, are partially planned economies. One could also call them *priority* economies. Industries to which the government attaches high priority for military or development reasons are closely planned and supervised. Others are left to ride along with looser controls. Moreover, alongside the element of central direction, these countries provide opportunities for individual choice similar to that exercised in capitalist countries. The blending of direction and choice, and the way in which the blend has changed over the course of time, is in fact the most interesting feature of these economies.

The U.S.S.R., as the oldest and most productive of the communist countries, is the natural one to select for illustrative purposes. One should bear in mind that many things about the Soviet economy are still not known to Western scholars, and also that economic institutions are still evolving, so that what one says today may be outmoded tomorrow. What we have to say can be organized under four heads: (1) planning organization; (2) decisions on what shall be produced; (3) decisions on production methods; and (4) income distribution, including the question of who works and at what jobs.

Planning Organization

Production targets for key raw materials and finished goods are set in Moscow. Planning is not all-inclusive, and targets are not always achieved, but the development of the economy in its broad outlines is guided from a central point.

Who does the planning? The main groups involved in economic planning at present are these:

1. *The Council of Ministers (Cabinet) of the U.S.S.R.*, headed by the Premier, which is the supreme policy-making body. It might be argued that the Presidium of the Communist Party, which dominates political life under the Soviet one-party system, is really the supreme governing authority. But the leadership of the Party and the government is so closely intertwined that one cannot draw any significant distinction between them. Major questions of economic policy are usually discussed

first at Party Congresses, and decisions of the Council of Ministers are then made within the framework of Party directives.

The Council of Ministers makes strategic decisions on such matters as: the feasible growth rate of the economy over the next several years; the division of national output between consumer goods and capital goods; the allocation of capital goods among public utilities, manufacturing, agriculture, housing, and so on; the pace of development in different regions of the country; and the distribution of new plants among these regions.

2. *The State Planning Commission* (*Gosplan*) takes these general directives and turns them into a detailed draft economic plan, containing production targets for each controlled commodity and a division of the proposed output among the various republics. It discusses this draft plan with officials of the republics and eventually brings back an agreed-upon plan for final ratification by the Council of Ministers. It also collects a great deal of statistical information on the operation of the economy.

3. The U.S.S.R. is divided into 15 republics, which correspond somewhat to American states, except that 2 republics—the Russian Federated Republic and the Ukraine—contain two thirds of the country's population and more than two thirds of its economic activity. The *Republic Council of Ministers* is responsible for production carried on within its borders. For products produced and consumed entirely within the republic, it is the sole authority. For "all union commodities," where production and allocation must be coordinated for the country as a whole, each republic negotiates with Moscow concerning its share in the total program. Once a final plan is agreed on, officials of the republic are responsible for meeting the specified targets.

4. The *Republic Gosplan* carries on the detailed work of planning and supervising production within the republic, under general direction of the Council of Ministers. The relation is the same as that between the U.S.S.R. Council of Ministers and the U.S.S.R. Gosplan.

5. *The Regional Economic Council* (*Sovnarkhoz*). The larger republics are divided into a number of regional economic units, though a small republic may have only one such unit. There are presently upwards of a hundred regional economic councils in the U.S.S.R. Each sovnarkhoz has planning and supervisory responsibility for plants in its region. The sovnarkhoz usually has a staff of several hundred people. It is divided into industry divisions covering the main types of production in the region and also has functional or staff divisions concerned with manpower, finance, transportation, and the like.

6. The lowest operating unit is the plant or *enterprise*. The enterprise director is appointed by the sovnarkhoz of his region and is responsible to it. Management is based on "one-man responsibility." While lower officials of the enterprise may criticize and discuss matters of policy, decision rests with the director, and he alone is responsible for

success or failure. Most enterprise directors are engineers, and the Russians find it difficult to understand how we can allow men to rise to top management positions in the United States without engineering training.

This does not indicate the full complexity of Soviet economic organization. For example, certain products of major military importance are managed directly from Moscow, and regional officials have no authority over them. At the other extreme, industries of purely local importance operate under the city council and higher planning bodies take no account of them. This includes service and repair establishments, baking and other local food processing, and even plants below a certain size engaged in producing bricks and other building materials.

Planning procedures.   Having brought the actors onto the stage, let us examine what they do. There are three types of plan: the long-range plan, the annual plan, and the quarterly plan. Long-range targets are necessary as a guide to current planning, and particularly as a guide to development projects, which will take several years to complete. If steel production is to rise by 30 percent 5 years from now, development of new ore mines may be necessary at once. A major hydroelectric project may take 5 to 10 years to complete. While 5 years is the commonest planning period, there was a 7-year plan from 1959 through 1965.

The annual plan, however, is the yardstick for current industrial operations. Preparation of this plan begins about a year in advance of the period which it is to cover. Early in 1966, Gosplan U.S.S.R. began drafting the plan for production of all-union commodities during 1967. By April this may be far enough along to be broken down by republics and passed on to the republic governments. Each republic Gosplan must then break down its quota of each product among the sovnarkhoz units. It must also add plans for articles produced and controlled within the republic, for which Moscow prepares no figures. Republic Gosplan then sends down to each sovnarkhoz tentative output quotas for each item to be produced in its region. The sovnarkhoz, finally, breaks these figures down into quotas for individual enterprises. As the plan moves downward, it takes on more and more bulk and detail, and more of a concrete operating character. As one official put it, "The plan rolls up like a snowball."

Even before this downward process is completed, there has been set in motion a reverse current of plans and proposals, often termed "planning from below." This begins at the grass roots with the individual enterprise, the personnel of which has the advantage of knowing better than anyone else what it is capable of producing. Each enterprise passes up to its sovnarkhoz its own proposed plan for 1967—how much it can produce, and how much labor, materials, and supplies it will need to produce this amount. There is a good deal of gamesmanship in drafting these enterprise plans. A Soviet manager is judged, promoted, and to some extent paid according to his success in achieving the plant's output quota for the year. Failure is regarded at best as inefficiency, at worst as sabotage. It pays, therefore, to get as low a quota as possible by concealing the true productive capacity of the plant. If things go poorly during the year, there is a safety factor. If things go well, the manager may be able to exceed his plan targets and earn a good bonus.

Sovnarkhoz officials, of course, are supposed to discover any such minimizing of capacity. It is quite common for enterprise plans to be adjusted upward by 5 to 10 percent at the sovnarkhoz level. The sovnarkhoz then puts all its enterprise plans together and transmits them to the republic Gosplan, which after further scrutiny and adjustment passes them on to Moscow. Gosplan in Moscow thus finally gets in its hand a picture of what everyone at lower levels believes the economy is capable of producing.

These "feasible figures" often fall short of the "desirable figures" which were passed down originally from Moscow. Moreover, the discrepancies will vary from one product to another, so that the original program is thrown out of balance. This leads to much additional adjusting and reconciling of targets in Moscow and to much bargaining between Moscow and the republics, the republics and the sovnarkhozy, and so on down. Finally, the revised plan is brought back to a full-dress conclave in Moscow attended by the Council of Ministers, key Gosplan officials, and representatives of the republics. When approved by this meeting the figures arc final and binding. If the process is completed by November of the year before which the plan is to take effect, everyone is well satisfied. It is not uncommon, however, for the new year to begin before final targets have been approved.

The final plan has three main components: (1) A list of the outputs expected from each industry of all-union importance. This means capital goods industries, industries of military importance, key foodstuffs, and a few other key consumer goods industries. (2) Balance sheets for the materials necessary to produce these outputs, showing how much of each material will be available during 1967 from current production, reserves, or imports, and where the available supply will go. Control sheets of this sort currently are prepared for upwards of a thousand materials. There is also prepared a balance sheet of available and required manpower, broken down by industries and regions. (3) A production and cost plan for each enterprise, showing the list of products which it is expected to produce, and the quantities of labor, fuel, materials, and other supplies which it is allowed to purchase during the year. These three elements of the plan are interrelated and should ideally be fully consistent.

Little need be said of the quarterly plans which are prepared for each enterprise. They make the production targets more concrete by reducing them to months and calendar quarters, provide a basis for reporting current operations, and introduce some flexibility into the annual plan. A plant which turns out to have unexpectedly great productive capacity may find its quota increased during the year, while a plant which runs into legitimate difficulties may argue for a reduction in its original schedule.

Enforcing the plan. The fact that production goals are announced with much fanfare does not mean that these goals will be met. What controls are available to ensure that production during the year will go roughly according to plan? Four main devices are used for this purpose:

1. *Control through the State Bank (Gosbank)*. Each enterprise has an account at Gosbank, and all payments between enterprises are made by bookkeeping transfers. Cash is drawn out for the weekly payroll, and this also is charged against the enterprise's account. The manager of the Gosbank branch with which an enterprise deals thus has his finger on the pulse of the enterprise. The enterprise's output plan for the year is accompanied by a financial plan, showing how much it will receive from sale of its products, how much it is allowed to spend for labor and materials, and how much short-term credit it may have to cover inventories and goods in transit. The enterprise may overdraw its account for good cause, but this requires the consent of Gosbank. If the enterprise seems to be departing seriously from plan, this consent presumably will not be given.

2. *Supervision by the Sovnarkhoz*. Each industry division of the sovnarkhoz is expected to keep in close touch with plants in its industry, to obtain and analyze their operating reports, to help them out with production problems, and to call them to account for serious failures. As a last resort, the enterprise director may be removed and replaced. In American terms, the Soviet enterprise corresponds somewhat to a branch plant of a parent corporation (the sovnarkhoz), which has ultimate responsibility for its performance.

3. *Multiple Channels of Information*. In an effort to prevent enterprise directors from concealing a record of poor performance, the system provides numerous channels through which independent reports can be passed up to higher authorities. The chief accountant of the enterprise has a direct line to the accounting department of the sovnarkhoz, and has considerable independence in his dealings with the director. He is expected to act as the "financial conscience" of the enterprise and to report discrepancies between plan and performance. There is a Communist Party cell in every enterprise, and from this group reports can travel up to Moscow via Party channels. Large enterprises and enterprises of military significance usually have members of the security police attached to them, who report directly to their superiors. The chairman of the trade union organization in the plant can make reports to higher union bodies.

All these precautions are not necessarily sufficient. Everyone connected with an enterprise has some interest in forming a common front

against higher officialdom. It is not uncommon for the director, accountant, and other local officials to form a coalition to present misleading
reports of performance or even falsify records and accounts. Having done
this, they are all involved and must stick together to make their story
hold up.

4. *Financial Incentives.* The system makes it worthwhile for
management officials and workers to produce effectively. Most workers
are paid on a piece-rate basis under which earnings rise proportionately,
or even more than proportionately, with the quantity produced. Management officials, in addition to a basic salary, receive a bonus geared to
fulfillment of the plant's output plan. The director of a successful
enterprise draws a large part of his income from this source. Part of any
profit earned by exceeding the output target also goes into an Enterprise
Fund, which may be used in part for building worker apartments (still
scarce and highly valued by Russian workers), for health and recreational facilities, and other employee benefits. To the extent that these
direct incentives are effective, the need for outside supervision and
control is reduced.

Decisions on What to Produce

No general rationale for planning decisions has ever been set forth
in Soviet writings. One leading Western student of the Soviet system says
simply: "They do it the way they do it." But one can say a little more
than this. First, Soviet plans have always had a strong bias toward capital
goods production. Resources have been poured unstintingly into steel,
machinery, electrical equipment, power production, and other lines of
heavy industry. Close to 30 percent of gross Soviet output each year goes
into capital goods, compared with about 20 percent in the United States.
This is a high rate of investment. It has meant holding back on
production of consumer goods and keeping living standards below what
would have been possible otherwise—certainly below what people would
have chosen of their own accord.

If pressed for a justification of this austere policy, Soviet leaders
would say that it was essential to build a powerful industrial base to
protect the country against military attack. There is historical warrant for
this view. Without the rapid industrialization of the country from 1928 to
1940, there is little doubt that it would have been conquered by Germany
in 1942–43 and world history would have taken a decidedly different
turn. Soviet leaders would also argue that higher saving today will mean
greater consumption tomorrow. The rapid buildup of basic industrial
capacity will eventually make possible a great outpouring of consumer
goods and a much higher standard of living. Soviet leaders surpass even
Americans in their confident belief in material progress.

The basic planning decision, then, is what proportion of resources
shall be devoted to capital goods. Next one faces the question: What
types of capital goods? This is in effect a decision about which lines of

industry are to be expanded most rapidly. A decision to build a major hydroelectric project on the Volga implies a need for certain quantities of earth-moving equipment, trucks, cranes, turbines, steel, cement, and labor. A staff of engineers can translate the finished project into the components necessary to produce it, and these can then be fitted into current production schedules. Since capital goods form such a large part of national output, much of the production plan follows automatically from decisions about industrial expansion.

But how is it decided which lines of production are to be expanded in the near future, and at what rate? This is a major policy decision and is arbitrary in the sense that it rests on no single rule. During a particular 5-year plan, two or three sectors of the economy are singled out as the main obstacles to further development and productive resources are channeled heavily into these sectors. After a time this means that these sectors become overdeveloped relative to other parts of the economy, and new bottlenecks emerge, which are attacked in the next plan period. At various stages of Russian economic development the leading role has been played by steel and machinery, electric power, transportation, military equipment, light metals, and chemicals. At the present time, chemicals, power, and machinery are receiving primary emphasis, but there is also considerable emphasis on housing and farm equipment.

It is difficult to find any guiding principle for the planning of consumer goods output. Certainly production is not guided, as it is in a capitalist system, by consumers' preferences expressed through purchases in the market. How, then, can the authorities discover "what people really want"?

This problem is not yet as serious in the Soviet Union as it would be in the United States. The reason is that most consumer goods production in the Soviet Union still consists of basic necessities. Luxury goods, where consumer fancy has widest sway, play a minor role in the economy. For basic items of food, clothing, and housing one can set up rough standards of physical need. Nutritionists can say how many calories per day, how much fat and protein, how much minerals and vitamins, are necessary to sustain health and working efficiency. These requirements can be converted into pounds of bread, potatoes, vegetables, meat, and other foods. Housing standards are more arbitrary; but once one decides on so many square feet of floor space per person, one can calculate how many new houses and apartment buildings will be necessary to attain this standard. The housing deficit in the Soviet Union is still so staggering that one cannot make any mistake in building as much as resources permit. Clothing requirements are also flexible, but one can set minimum targets for coats, suits, shirts, shoes, and other items; and these can be converted into yards of cloth, quantities of leather, and so on.

Minimum consumer requirements seem to be scheduled into the annual plan in the same way as capital goods. Consumer goods production above the minimum is largely an unplanned residual, both in the sense that output targets are not even set for many products and in the sense that fulfillment of targets is not viewed with the same urgency as would be true of steel, power, or machine tools. If there is steel left over after priority needs have been met, some of this may go into passenger cars, refrigerators, and other consumer goods; but it is not considered urgent that any particular output of these items be attained in a particular year. There is a general intent to raise the output of most consumer goods year by year, and gradually to approach the consumption levels of Western Europe and the United States. But there is not the feeling of driving urgency about this that one encounters in the realm of investment goods.

Agricultural production is not as thoroughly planned as industrial production. The basic unit of Soviet agriculture is the collective farm. These farms are large by American standards—there are less than 100,000 of them, compared with our 4 million farms. Even a small collective has several thousand acres of land and several hundred people. The workers on the farm are divided into work teams, each under a foreman, somewhat in factory fashion. They are paid partly through an allowance of grain, potatoes, and other farm produce and partly through a cash wage per hour. How much one gets depends on his work assignment and the skill involved in the work. A tractor driver gets more than a milkmaid. Families on the farm may also rent small plots of land, usually half an acre to two acres, for private cultivation. What a farmer raises on his private plot can be sold in the nearest town market and the money is his.

Total agricultural production really is not planned at all. What is planned is the amount of grain, potatoes, meat, and other staples which the government expects to buy from the farms and ship to the city to feed the urban population. State purchasing agencies contract with each farm to buy specified amounts of produce at specified prices, and the farm must treat these deliveries as a first obligation. What is left over is theirs. If they work hard and the weather is good, they will eat well. If not, they will eat poorly.

Production from the private plots is, of course, unplanned, and this is an important part of total farm output. The private plots produce almost all the poultry and eggs, and more than half the meat, milk, potatoes, fruits, and vegetables. Collective cultivation, on the other hand, accounts for the great bulk of the grain, feed and forage, cotton, sugar beets, and industrial raw materials. Soviet officials do not like the private plot system, which they regard as old-fashioned and capitalistic; but it is so productive that they have not yet been able to get rid of it.

Production Methods and Operating Efficiency

The problem of production methods divides into two subproblems: (a) the basic design of plant and equipment; (b) utilizing each plant so as to obtain greatest output from a certain amount of labor and materials.

Basic production design.   The central fact here is the severe short-age of capital goods. Despite strenuous efforts to build up steel and machinery capacity, there has never been anything like enough capacity to meet all military and industrial needs. Labor is not abundant either, but it is relatively more plentiful than capital. Logically, this should lead to production methods which use a good deal of labor and which economize on capital—*labor-intensive methods*, in economic parlance.

The Soviet economy has, in fact, been bent in this direction, and in two main ways. First, whole sectors of the economy have been starved of capital and have had to make out with simple production methods. Agriculture is the outstanding example. The number of tractors, cultiva-tors, combine harvesters, milking machines, and other machines on Soviet farms is tiny compared with the technical possibilities and with the amounts used in more advanced countries. Soviet agriculture depends mainly on human and animal power. In 1960 there were still more than 10 million horses on Russian farms. (How many would one see in a day's drive through Illinois or Iowa?) It takes 40 percent of the Soviet labor force to feed the Soviet population, while less than 10 percent of the labor force suffices for this purpose in the United States. This means that each Soviet farm worker is turning out much less than each American farmer. This is due partly to difficulties of supervision and management, less use of fertilizers, poorer seed and livestock strains, and other factors. But it is due above all to the low level of farm mechanization.

The transportation system has also been kept on short rations. Road mileage and numbers of trucks and buses are low by American standards, so that the work of moving goods and people piles up on the railroads. In 1957 railroads still were carrying 90 percent of all freight traffic in the U.S.S.R., compared with 39 percent in the U.S.A. The Soviet rail system even carried three fourths of all passenger traffic, which has almost disappeared from American rail lines. An American railroad official would be happy if he could have the volume of business handled by his Soviet counterpart. But he would be unhappy with the equipment given him to do the job. The supply of freight cars, passenger cars, and locomotives is deficient in both quantity and quality. The steam locomo-tive is almost a museum piece in the United States. The U.S.S.R. in 1958, however, was still using 11,000 steam locomotives and only 2,000 electric and diesel-electric engines.

Second, even in the preferred industrial sector, capital has been economized by using methods which are more labor-intensive than those used in the United States. The central production operations are quite well mechanized. The carding, spinning, and weaving departments of textile mills, the main assembly lines in auto and truck plants, look much like their counterparts in the United States. But supplementary opera-tions—getting materials to the machines, finishing and packing, getting finished products to the shipping room, and so on—make more use of hand labor than is true here. One sees few automatic conveyor systems or mechanical lift trucks in Soviet factories.

Current operating efficiency.   In addition to the grand strategy of plant design, there are a multitude of detailed, tactical problems of production method. Given the same machinery, materials, and labor, some managers will get more output than others. The job of the enterprise director is to produce the maximum from the supplies allotted him by higher authorities. How much output he gets will depend on his skill in arranging the plant layout, subdividing production processes, scheduling production, hiring the right quantity and quality of labor, and motivating workers and supervisors to a high rate of effort.

The Soviet manager is stimulated to efficiency by a carrot and stick technique. On the negative side, he must operate within the framework of the plan. He may spend only certain amounts on labor, materials, and other supplies, and he must produce a certain volume of output. His success is judged by conformity to the cost side of the plan as well as the output side. Moreover, he is expected to do better year by year. Rising productivity is built into the system in the sense that each year the planning authorities specify that the plant must increase output and reduce costs.

A manager who falls seriously short of the planned targets can expect demotion. In the Stalin era he would have been accused of "wrecking" or "sabotage," and might have been shot or sent to Siberia. In the more relaxed atmosphere of today, he will suffer only a loss of status and salary. The successful manager, on the other hand, can expect promotion to a larger enterprise or may become an official of the sovnarkhoz or the republic. Most Soviet managers seem to feel that directing a large enterprise is the best job available in the system. This is partly because the director of a successful enterprise earns substantial bonuses, while a salaried official of the republic or national government does not. (American businessmen resist taking jobs in Washington for the same reason!) If the enterprise succeeds in increasing output above or reducing costs below the planned level, part of the resulting profit comes back to management officials as bonus. This may run to 50 percent or more of the manager's basic salary.

The incentive system of Soviet managers, in short, bears considerable resemblance to that of American business executives. The intrinsic satisfaction of doing a good administrative job, desire for the esteem of one's superiors and inferiors, hope of promotion to larger responsibilities, and financial incentives combine to induce managers to put forth their best efforts.

Even with these incentives the efficiency of Soviet industry leaves much to be desired. There are several reasons for this. First, the cost and output norms are matters of bargaining rather than scientific determination. The enterprise director may agree to ambitious targets and then struggle to fulfill them. Or he may, by hard bargaining and concealing his true productive capacity, secure low targets which can be met with little effort. It is not surprising that managers prefer the second course, which gives them a safety margin in case of trouble and a chance of earning large bonuses by overfulfilling a plan which was too low in the first place.

Another difficulty is that the output norms are not entirely clear. Greatest importance usually is attached to total value of output in rubles. The plant also is given physical targets for its various products and is expected to produce the right assortment of products as well as the proper total value. But if some of the products are overpriced relative to the cost of producing them while others are underpriced, the enterprise has a strong incentive to fulfill its value plan by concentrating on production of the high-priced items. Enterprises often depart from their assortment for this reason, and these departures are not effectively policed.

Difficulties may arise even if the production targets are specified solely in physical terms. Textile plants have sometimes been given targets of so many million yards of cloth, without specifying how wide the cloth is to be. Since it is cheaper to produce a yard of 30-inch cloth than one of 50-inch, there is a tendency to concentrate heavily on the narrower widths, even though this may not meet the preferences of buyers. Moreover, a plant may produce goods which are adequate in quantity but not in quality. In a sellers' market where goods of every sort are scarce, the customer has little alternative but to accept the faulty goods and make the best of it. Quality control has been a major problem in Soviet industry from the beginning.

Finally, greater importance is usually attached to the output plan than to the cost plan. Controls over expenditure on labor and materials are not very firm. If a director meets his output quota, there is a tendency to wink at how he did it. Success thus may be achieved by using more inputs than were really necessary. The combined effect of these things is to produce a lower level of operating performance than exists in comparable plants in the United States.

The Distribution of Income

Farm incomes versus city incomes.   About 40 percent of the Soviet labor force still works the land. How much they get for what they grow thus has a great effect on the distribution of income. This is a major political issue in almost every country. In the Western countries, government typically intervenes on the side of the farmer. By supporting prices above the level which they would reach in a free market, government transfers income from city consumers to farm producers.

In the Soviet Union, government policy for many years worked in the opposite direction. The collective farms were obliged to deliver specified quantities of farm produce to the government at artificially depressed prices, prices which yielded very low incomes and living standards. These foodstuffs were resold to the city population at much higher prices, and the government pocketed the difference. This policy served a dual purpose. The fact that farm incomes were held much below city incomes provided a strong incentive for people to move to the city, and this was necessary to provide labor power for the rapid expansion of urban industry. The food extracted from the remaining farm population served to feed the urban labor force as it worked on the enormous program of construction and heavy industrial development.

There is no doubt, however, that this policy was pushed too far and that farmers were squeezed too hard during the Stalin era. The prices which the government paid for food hardly rose at all between 1937 and 1950. Meanwhile, the prices which farmers had to pay for manufactured goods doubled and redoubled. Even considering the fact that farmers were able to sell part of their production outside government channels at higher prices, they suffered severely during these years. One expert has estimated that the real income of the farm population was cut in two.

Small wonder that the farmers did not produce enthusiastically. The peasant has an infinite capacity for quiet sabotage, and the government paid dearly for its niggardliness. Farm workers spent as much time as possible on their private garden plots and as little as possible on the main farm operations. Farm production consistently fell short of the planned targets and in many lines was not much higher in 1950 than in 1910.

After the death of Stalin, there was a drastic shift to a profarmer policy. There was a thorough reorganization of controls over agriculture and a substantial increase in farm prices. Government prices for food purchased from collective farms were about seven times as high in 1958 as in 1950. Farm income from all sources is estimated to have tripled during this period. Incomes on the more efficient farms seem now to have risen close to parity with the incomes of factory workers.

Wage and salary incomes. Urban wages and salaries are set in a labor market which does not differ strikingly from our own. Workers in practice have the right to move freely from one job to another. Labor is so scarce that a good worker knows he can find a job wherever he goes.

This means that each enterprise has to work out a "package" of wages and other conditions which is attractive enough to recruit and hold the labor it needs. Wage schedules have to be tailored to hiring requirements. Steel, machinery, and other heavy industries offer considerably higher wages than light manufacturing, partly because of the nature of the work, but also to make sure that these high-priority industries can get all the labor they need. Wages are also considerably higher in the colder eastern regions of the Soviet Union. The government can appeal to people's Soviet patriotism to go out and colonize these unattractive areas, but a good lacing of money is a wonderful help to patriotic spirit.

Other important characteristics of the wage-salary structure are:

1. A substantial spread between rates for skilled and unskilled labor. It is common in manufacturing plants to find skilled mechanics earning two to three times as much as common laborers—a wider spread than one would find in most industries in the United States. This is meant to induce workers to better their skills, and thus meet the needs of an expanding industrial economy which has a chronic shortage of skilled labor.

2. Extensive use of piece-rate systems, under which a worker's earnings are based on how much he produces. Piece-rate payment is used even more widely in Russia than in the United States, and for the same reason—to stimulate each worker to produce up to the limit of his individual capacity. Under piece-rate payment, a worker's official wage rate may give little clue to his earnings. His job may call for a basic rate of 100 rubles a month; but if he is proficient and hard working, he may turn out enough product to earn 150 rubles or more.

3. High rates for manual work compared with those for white-collar jobs. It is startling at first glance to find that the girl on a spinning machine in a Tashkent cotton mill earns 100 rubles a month, while a typist in the office of the same plant earns 50 rubles. Plant officials explain, "We pay for what is important—for production." The decisive point, however, is that they can *get* enough typists at the 50-ruble wage.

4. Good salaries and perquisites for industrial managers. The Russians have, from an early stage, recognized the key importance of skilled management and have been willing to pay for it. The director of a medium-sized industrial plant earns, in salary and bonuses, five or six times the earnings of a common laborer in his plant. In addition, he usually is provided with a car, a house, vacation allowances, and other perquisites. When one considers that the top income tax rate in Russia is only 13 percent, the income difference after taxes between laborer and chief executive is probably about the same in Russian industry as in American industry.

Income distribution among households.   Information on family incomes, comparable to that given for the United States in Chapter 2, is not available for the U.S.S.R. But it seems likely that household income distribution is more equal there than here. Property income, which in the United States flows mainly to the upper-income brackets, is almost absent in the U.S.S.R. Moreover, a number of services are provided free by government. All medical and hospital services are free. Not only is college education free, but students receive living allowances from the government. Housing is heavily subsidized, and rents are low by Western standards. Since these free and subsidized services count as part of family income, and since they are open to all comers, the result is a considerable equalization of living standards.

The Soviet System: A Mixed Economy

This completes our tour of the Soviet economy. We have seen how the Soviet system works out, on a much larger scale, the same basic decisions which must be made in a subsistence economy. These decisions are made partly through administrative orders but also partly through individual choice and initiative similar to that which operates in a market economy.

Administrative decisions determine (1) the broad division of national output between consumer goods and capital goods; (2) the distribution of capital goods among different lines of industry, which determines their relative rates of expansion; (3) specific production targets for a long list of industrial raw materials, metals, machinery, building materials, housing, foodstuffs, and other basic consumer products. This planned sector accounts for most of national output and shapes the broad contours of economic development.

What does this leave for individual choice and initiative? Mainly the following:

1. Workers can choose where to work, what kind of work to do, and how hard to work. These choices are made in much the same way in the U.S.S.R. as in the U.S.A. and other industrial countries. The main inducement which steers workers in one direction or another is the money earnings and fringe benefits offered by various jobs.

2. Consumers can decide how to spend their money incomes. Until recently, choice has been limited by the fact that incomes were too low to cover more than basic necessities. As income levels rise, however, and as the variety of consumer goods increases, consumer choice will take on greater meaning; and it seems likely that there will be pressure on government to give greater weight to consumer preferences in planning production.

3. A considerable part of production is subject to local decision rather than central control. This is notably true of farm output and particularly of production on farmers' private plots. It is true also of local manufacture for local use, and of local service industries, which comprise a sizable percentage of Soviet output.

4. Even where output targets are centrally determined, how much is actually produced and how efficiently it is produced depends on the effort and initiative of management officials. These people are motivated by a mixture of prestige and power considerations, material rewards, promotion possibilities, and other incentives, which does not seem to differ greatly from that of their counterparts in capitalist countries.

It has become fashionable to refer to the United States as a "mixed economy," meaning that government carries on a considerable part of national production and also intervenes in many ways in the private economy. What is not so widely recognized is that the U.S.S.R. is also a "mixed economy." The mixture is quite different from our own, but the difference is one of degree rather than of black-and-white contrast. Moreover, the Soviet mixture has been changing rapidly since the early fifties, and will undoubtedly continue to change in the future.

Western economists, to the extent that they have any missionary urge to save souls abroad, can hope that Soviet officials will gradually discover the advantages which (we believe) are inherent in individual initiative, price "cues" as against administrative orders, and wide use of market mechanisms. There is no doubt that some Soviet administrators do realize these things. The main obstacles to acting on this knowledge are doubtless the *political* centralism of the Soviet system and the difficulty of reconciling free choice in economic matters with the tight discipline of a one-party state. There is also the ideological need to avoid any obvious imitation of capitalist methods and to sanctify any new departures by copious quotations from Marx. Fortunately, Marx wrote several thousand pages, many of them reasonably obscure, and this simplifies the task.

SUMMARY

1. Any economy must reach decisions concerning (1) how much work the population shall do; (2) how much effort shall be devoted to providing for the future by producing capital goods; (3) how much of each consumer good and service shall be produced; (4) what production methods shall be used; (5) how much of the national output each household shall receive.

2. An isolated Crusoe works out decisions on these points for himself. His decisions will depend on: the natural resources of his island; the production methods which he knows or can invent; his preference for income *versus* leisure; his preferences among available types of consumer goods; and his weighing of present consumption *versus* future consumption.

3. In a more complex subsistence economy, decisions will be influenced also by custom, family structure, and the authority of family heads and village officials.

4. In the planned economy of the U.S.S.R., the division of national output between consumer goods and capital goods is a strategic decision made at the highest level of government.

5. Production of basic foodstuffs, standard clothing, and other key consumer goods is planned to meet minimum standards of physical need. Nonessentials receive lower priority and output typically falls short of official targets. Agricultural production by its nature cannot be planned as tightly as industrial production.

6. Industrial managers are stimulated to operate their plants efficiently by a combination of plan controls, promotion and prestige rewards, and money incentives.

7. Decisions about how much to work and where to work are left largely to the individual worker. The system of wage rates is so constructed as to enable high-priority industries to recruit the labor they need.

8. Wage differences between laborers, skilled workers, managers, and professional people are probably about as wide in the U.S.S.R. as they are in the U.S.A. Differences in household income are smaller, however, because property income is absent and because many services are provided free by government.

9. The Soviet system is a mixed economy. Many things are planned, some more tightly and effectively than others. But a good many other things are left to individual choice and initiative.

DISCUSSION QUESTIONS

1. The economic choices listed at the beginning of the chapter sound quite difficult. Yet the text says that they actually get made in the American economy. What is the evidence for this statement?
2. How will Crusoe's pattern of work and consumption be affected by
   a) whether his island is very fertile or very barren?
   b) his previous education and work experience?
   c) whether he has a strong preference for certain consumer goods which are unusually difficult to produce?
   d) whether he is (economically) shortsighted or farsighted?
3. "People in an African village or a Pacific island may be poor, but at least they are happy. They have no economic problems." Is this correct?
4. What would an economy planned completely from the center look like? Is such a system feasible in practice? Why, or why not?
5. Is the annual economic plan of the U.S.S.R. actually "made in Moscow"? How do groups at lower levels influence both the construction of the plan figures and the course of events after the plan has been announced?
6. Compare the responsibilities and rewards of a Soviet enterprise director with those of a U.S. corporation president.
7. What are the main resemblances and points of difference between the Soviet economy and the American economy?

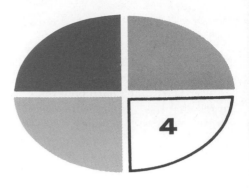

The Market Economy

> " 'Tis so," said the Duchess; "and the moral of it is 'Oh! 'tis love, 'tis love that makes the world go round!' "
>
> "Somebody said," whispered Alice, "that it's done by everybody minding their own business!"
>
> "Ah, well! It means much the same thing," said the Duchess.
>
> *Alice's Adventures in Wonderland*

> Once you have gone to market you have told the whole world.
>
> RUSSIAN PROVERB

MARKETS AND PRICES

FEW PEOPLE IN THE UNITED STATES live as isolated Crusoes. Nor does anyone sit in Washington deciding how much of each good shall be produced. How, then, are the key economic decisions made? Russian leaders refer to capitalist economies as "unplanned," "chaotic." Yet these economies actually show a great deal of order and stability. What is it that produces order rather than chaos?

I go down to the supermarket on Saturday afternoon and lay hands on a market basket. No one has any notice of my coming. Yet the goods I want are usually there, and at about the prices I had expected to pay. The people who produced the goods may be thousands of miles away. They know nothing about me and care less. Yet their activities are somehow coordinated with my desires. Writers with a poetic bent have sometimes compared a market economy to an astronomical system, with self-interest playing the role of gravity and millions of consumers and producers whizzing harmoniously about in their respective orbits.

What holds the economy together? A brief answer, which will take several chapters to develop, is that the system is coordinated through an interlocking network of *markets*. The key feature of each market is the *price* prevailing in the market. These two terms have a special meaning in economics and require a word of explanation.

Markets

The term "market" does not refer just to fishmarkets or fresh vegetable stalls, or even to retail trade in general. Every good and service is regarded as having a market, in which supplies of the good are bought and sold. There is a market for basic steel, electric power, textile machinery, cotton cloth, dry cleaning, barber services, and every other item produced in the economy. Moreover, a product may pass through a series of markets before reaching the ultimate user. A farmer sells wheat to a miller, who sells bran to a food manufacturer, who sells bran flakes to wholesale distributors, who resell to retail grocers, who supply consumers in the retail market.

There are also markets for the basic services used in production—for land, labor, and capital. Thus we speak of the "money market," in which lenders provide funds to borrowers at a specified rate of interest. In the "labor market," employees deal with employers, exchanging so many hours or weeks of labor for a certain wage.

A market is not necessarily, or even usually, a single place. The distinguished British economist, Alfred Marshall, stated that: "A market is an area within which buyers and sellers are in such close communication with each other that price tends to be the same throughout the area." Some markets are virtually worldwide. This is true of many basic raw materials, and also of securities of the U.S. government and of leading U.S. business concerns. The requirements for a wide market are that the product be sufficiently standardized that it can safely be bought and sold without being seen, and that its value be high relative to the cost of transporting it. Gold, precious stones, and gilt-edged securities, whose value is high and transport cost low, are the international commodities par excellence. But other staples such as copper, aluminum, rubber, coffee, cocoa, wool, and cotton also enjoy a world market.

Other markets are national in scope. Men's and women's clothing can be shipped anywhere in the United States at a cost which is small relative to the value of the merchandise. A clothing manufacturer in any part of the country, then, is in direct competition with makers of the same item in other regions and must watch their prices. This is true also of other light manufactured goods. As one gets into heavier products with a low value per pound, shipment to distant points becomes less feasible, and the market shrinks to regional or local proportions. Each city has its own sand and gravel quarries, which do not compete with suppliers in other cities. Brick factories have a narrow market area because of the great weight and low value of their product.

Retail markets, particularly markets for groceries and other staple necessities, are centered in a single town or city. But the rise of the automobile has made retail markets larger than they used to be. An enterprising housewife will drive to a suburban market or even to the next town if she detects a substantial advantage in quality or price. The market area of each town thus interlocks with that of neighboring towns in an endless chain.

The size of the labor market depends on the level of labor in question. An outstanding business executive, scientist, actor, or surgeon enjoys a national market. He is known throughout the country, is well informed about opportunities in other areas, and will move to another location if it offers sufficient advantage. For most manual, clerical, and subprofessional jobs, however, one can take the locality as the relevant market area. A worker who is settled in a community and perhaps owns a home there is unlikely to know about, or to be much interested in, jobs in other cities. These local labor markets are linked, however, by the possibility that people *might* move if the wage level of City A rose much above that of City B. This possibility is sufficient to keep wage levels of nearby cities reasonably well in line with each other.

Prices

A "price" is the amount paid for a specified quantity and quality of any good or service, the amount for which it exchanges in the relevant market. Bricklayers are paid, say, $4 an hour in Minneapolis. This is the price at which this kind of labor is sold by workers in the Minneapolis labor market. Thus a wage rate is a price. An interest rate is also a price —the price paid for use of a certain quantity of money for a stated period of time. Most frequently, price is used in its everyday meaning of the amount paid for a pair of shoes or a pound of butter. But when the term is used in a general way, when one speaks of "competitive pricing" or "the price mechanism," it should be taken to include wage rates, interest rates, rents, and other payments for productive services.

SCARCITY AND CHOICE

The Fact of Scarcity

Even with the great productive resources of the United States, we are not able to produce nearly as much as we should like to consume. The "economy of abundance" is not yet a fact. Perhaps we have as much as we *need* in the eyes of some austere outside observer, but we do not have as much as we *want*.

Any group which doubts this statement can convince itself by a simple experiment. Let each member of the group take a piece of paper. Write down the annual income which you would like to have when you are 35 years old, married, and have three children. Then average the figures for the group. It usually turns out that the group average is two or three times the *actual* average income of all families in the United States. It is not possible for everyone in the country to live at anything like the level which each of us considers desirable for himself.

The same result appears from household surveys in which families are asked how much additional income they need to live adequately and without worry. The figure mentioned is typically 10 to 20 percent higher than the family's current income, and this is as true of families with $10,000 a year as of families with $5,000 a year. Almost everyone wants just a little more. The doubling of real income per capita since 1935 has not made Americans noticeably more content with their lot. Wants continue to grow faster than the means of satisfying them, and the higher incomes in prospect for the year 2000 will still be inadequate to the needs which we shall feel *at that time*.

It may seem that this reduces economics to a dead end of complete futility. A Burmese student at Yale once wrote a doctoral thesis to prove that the main hope for the future lies in reducing man's wants instead of increasing his productive capacity. Leaving this issue to the philosopher, let us see how mankind adjusts to its urge toward consumption. Even in the wealthy United States, there are still three million families with incomes below $2,000 a year. For these people, scarcity of resources is no psychological fancy but a bitter fact of daily experience. In many other countries the average family reaches depths of poverty which have to be seen to be believed. In most countries the increase of economic resources, wise use of these resources in production, and careful distribution of the national output are matters of vital importance.

The Necessity of Choice

Scarcity lies at the root of economics. If all goods were free as air, there would be no need to economize resources and no economic problem. The central fact of scarcity forces hard choices. More of this means less of that. The main choices which must be made were listed at the beginning of Chapter 3. They are:

How much work shall people do?
What proportion of national resources shall be devoted to capital formation?
What goods shall be produced, and in what quantities?
What production methods shall be used?
Who shall get what is produced?

A common thread runs through these choices. They are all of the "more or less" variety. Shall we have a little higher consumption standard at the cost of a little less leisure? Shall we have a little greater future productive capacity at the cost of a little less current consumption? Shall some families have a little more income at the cost of some others having less? And so on. In economic terminology, they are *marginal* choices, involving small plus and minus adjustments at the margin of decision.

If one were designing a new economy from the ground up, it would be necessary to consider an enormous variety of possible permutations and combinations. But no country is ever actually in this position. The economy is a going concern, adjusted to grinding out a certain bill of goods and distributing them in a certain way. The relevant and feasible decisions are to push out a bit in one direction and to cut back a bit in another.

Nor can these decisions be made independently of each other. Each of the five types of decision can be treated as logically independent and singled out for separate analysis. But in practice all are interdependent, and a change in one area involves adjustment in the others as well. A change in the supply of labor in the economy, or in the supply of capital goods, or in the distribution of money income sets up repercussions which will spread to every part of the economy before the effects are exhausted.

Solution of the resource allocation problem thus involves simultaneous decision on a large number of questions, and decision on each point involves the decisions which are being made at the same time on all the others.

At this point the reader will surely throw up his hands and exclaim, "Why, that's impossible! Nobody in the United States supervises the economy in that fashion. And even if anyone wanted to, the human mind couldn't possibly cope with the problem." Yet all the decisions we have outlined do get made, in the United States and in every other country; and they were being made long before discovery of the electronic computer.

How can this be? The task of this chapter is to explore how the key economic decisions get made in a largely private economy such as that of the United States. Most decisions are left to the millions of workers, households, and business managers, and their choices feed back through markets in a way which regulates the course of economic activity. It will take some time, however, to develop this cryptic statement.

A SIMPLIFIED MARKET SYSTEM

It will be helpful first to look at a simple picture of a market economy, designed to highlight the key markets and prices and to show their interrelations. The excuse for this is that the real world bears some resemblance to this simple model. An understanding of this simplified system will help us in exploring the complexities of the actual American economy at a later stage.

Our model rests on several foundation stones, or *assumptions,* which should be kept clearly in mind for the rest of this chapter. These are suppositions about the setup of markets and the behavior of people in the system, without which we should be unable to reach definite conclusions. The main assumptions are:

1. Government is left on the sidelines for the time being in order to explore the operation of a *purely private economy.* All production in the system is carried on by private business units.

2. All markets in the system are characterized by *pure competition.* This implies that:

   a) Any person in the economy can enter any market if he sees a chance of gain by so doing and can operate on either the buying or selling side. There are no legal or other barriers to entrance into any market.

   b) There must be large numbers of buyers and sellers so that the dealings of any individual are a small part of total transactions in the market, hence will have little influence on the prices established.

   c) Buyers may not get together to beat down the market price, nor may sellers conspire to raise it. "Rigging" of the market is forbidden.

Few actual markets meet these requirements. The New York Stock Exchange comes very close, however, and so do the commodity exchanges for wheat, corn, cotton, sugar, cocoa, and other staples. Most other markets fall short of these specifications to a greater or lesser degree.

3. Everyone willing to work at existing wage scales can find work. The model is one of a *full-employment economy.* This does not mean that we ignore the importance of depression and unemployment in actual economies, but this problem is reserved for later treatment in Part Three. Meanwhile, the full-employment assumption means that increased output of any product in the system must be accompanied by reduced output of one or more other products. Since everyone is at work, increased employment at one point in the system means reduced employment somewhere else.

4. The workers, housewives, business executives, farmers, and others in the system are reasonably well informed about prices in the markets in which they operate. But they do not need to be perfectly informed for the system to operate effectively.

5. People in the system are interested in material well-being, in monetary gain. We suppose that a worker will normally prefer a higher wage to a lower wage for the same kind of work, that a housewife will prefer a lower price to a higher price for the same article, and that a businessman will prefer larger profits to smaller ones.

So much for the underpinnings of the model. Now what does it look like? The system is sketched in Figure 1. It includes three types of organization: households, producers of goods and services, and retailers. These groups are linked by four types of market: labor markets, money markets, producers' markets, and retail markets. The curlicues in each market are steel springs, intended to suggest that tension is being exerted on the market from both sides—the buying or demand side and the selling or supply side.

Goods move from left to right across the chart, while money flows in the opposite direction. Since the households at the extreme left are the same households which appear at the extreme right, the chart could be

The Chain of Markets

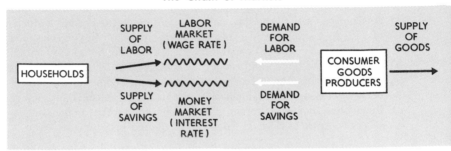

FIGURE 1.   Each market in the system is linked to many other markets.

curled over to form a continuous circle, the "wheel of wealth" shown in Chapter 2.

The drastic simplification of reality involved in this diagram is apparent. The American economy includes millions of households, producing units, and retail outlets. Listing each of these separately would extend the chart downward for several miles. Moreoever, rarely is all the work of producing a finished good done in a single enterprise, as suggested by our one box for producers. There are usually numerous stages of processing on the way from raw materials to final sale, and inserting these stages would stretch out the diagram in the horizontal direction. What we have done is to collapse or condense the "real-world diagram," both horizontally and vertically, to make it printable and comprehensible.

SOME CHARACTERISTICS OF THE MARKET ECONOMY

Figure 1 was constructed to explain the key economic decisions made in a market economy. Before turning to that problem, however, let us look at some general characteristics of this kind of economy.

One Market, One Price

Under pure competition, there can be only one price for a specified product. If one seller tries to charge more than the prevailing price, buyers will abandon him and buy elsewhere. If he offers goods below the prevailing price, buyers will flock to him so fast that he will conclude that he can safely raise prices. The large number of buyers and sellers in the market, and the possibility of shifting from one to another, forces all dealings in the direction of a single price. This price gives a "thermometer reading" of the situation prevailing in the market in question. The economic mechanism may be thought of either as a network of interconnected *markets* or as a network of interconnected *prices*, each indicating the situation in the market to which it relates.

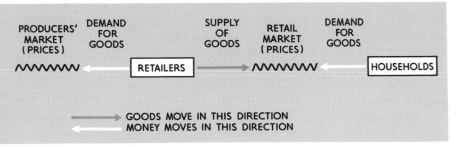

Price Determined by Supply and Demand

A nineteenth-century wit remarked, "Teach a parrot to say 'supply and demand' and you have an economist." The fact that the term has become a cliché should not blind us to its remarkable usefulness. Price obviously *is* influenced by pressure from both sides of the market—from sellers supplying the good or service, who will cease supplying it if the price falls too low, and from buyers, who want the product but will feel obliged to stop buying it if prices rise too high. The markets in Figure 1 have been represented as steel springs to indicate that tension is exerted on the market from both the supply and demand sides. A tug on the spring from either side will be felt at the other side, and will lead to a different quantity of the product being exchanged in the market at a different price.

The Interrelation of Prices and Markets

Each market is related to every other market in the system. This means that the prices which measure the state of the market also are interrelated. What will happen if consumers decide to buy more television sets and fewer radios? Retailers of television sets will find merchandise moving off their shelves at a brisker pace (right-hand side of Figure 1). They no longer will feel obliged to offer special discounts and clearance sales, which amounts to an increase in their selling price. Next they will order more sets from the manufacturers. Faced with this rush of business, manufacturers may raise their prices. Certainly they will try to increase production, and the prosperity of the industry may cause new companies to set up in television production. This will increase the demand for metals, glass, and other materials going into the sets, for certain kinds of machinery, for bank loans, and for labor to produce the increased output. Thus the impact is felt finally in the markets for productive services (left-hand side of Figure 1). Higher wages may be offered voluntarily to attract the necessary number of workers, or if there is a union, it may take advantage of the situation to demand a wage increase.

Even this is not the end of the story. Increased demand for television parts will cause expansion of all the industries supplying those parts, and the impact will stretch back to iron and copper mines, lumber mills, and silica sand for glass production. Movement of labor to the expanding television industry will force other companies to recruit more actively and probably to raise their wages. The effects will be felt eventually in thousands of markets, many of them remote from the initial point of impact.

Meanwhile, the hapless radio producers will be faced with an opposite sequence of events. Some of them may manage to convert their plants and become television manufacturers. Unless they do this, they will be faced with declining sales and profits, and their material suppliers and workers will suffer along with them. The reader can trace out for himself the sorry sequence of events resulting from a permanent *drop* in demand for a product.

It is now clearer why we are justified in speaking of an economic *system*. Using the dimensions of Figure 1, markets are linked in a horizontal direction by technological processes, by the flow of materials through successive stages of processing and distribution until the finished good reaches the ultimate user. They are cross-linked in a vertical direction by the existence of alternatives and the consequent possibility of choice. Consumers may decide to use more of commodity A and less of B. Producing units may decide that one sort of machine or material does the job better than another. Workers may decide that they prefer to work at company X rather than company Y.

A shift in one market is transmitted through these vertical and horizontal linkages into markets which on the surface seem quite remote from the first. A market economy may be visualized as a kind of giant computer, constantly receiving information from all parts of the system and working out appropriate adjustments. A shift in one market starts lights flashing all through the machine, and many prices and outputs may have to change before the computer settles down once more with a sigh of contentment. A major function of economics is to analyze and predict these indirect effects, which the man on the street typically overlooks.

The Basic Data: Individual Preferences and Production Possibilities

A market economy is individualistic in the sense that its operation depends on the preferences and choices of the millions of individuals in the system. This obviously cannot mean that each person's preferences are independent of those of others. Any social psychologist could demonstrate that this is not so. But however preferences are determined, whether people are herd-minded or as independent as Crusoe, their choices are *registered* by individual acts of buying and selling in various markets. These are the ultimate pressures to which the market economy responds.

The term *preference* may suggest something whimsical or intangible, simply a vague attitude of mind. But economists use the term in a more precise sense. *Consumer preference* implies that a man knows how much a particular product is worth to him relative to each other product he buys. He knows how much of product A he would give up to get a certain amount of product B; and since he has only so much income, he has to make this kind of decision every day. Similarly, one can speak of *worker preferences*. If a man can choose his working hours, as many people can to some extent, he must balance the attractiveness of extra income and extra leisure. In choosing among jobs, he may decide that a strenuous and uncomfortable job should pay him 50 cents an hour more than a light, pleasant job; and so on.

The other thing which we take as given in analyzing a market economy is *methods of production*. Even for a single product, we speak usually of *methods* rather than of a single method. There are many different ways of using land to grow wheat. The farmer may use a great deal of machinery and little labor or simpler tools and more labor. He may spend more or less on drainage, fertilizers, improved seed, and other supplies. We assume that the producer knows all these alternative possibilities and makes an informed choice among them. But we do not at this stage ask where new production methods come from, any more than we ask where consumer and worker preferences come from.

Equilibrium and Disturbances of Equilibrium

The term *equilibrium* will occur frequently in later chapters, so it is best to get the general sense of it at the outset. Equilibrium is a state of balance, a condition which will continue unchanged until disturbed by some outside event. If the market price of a product is $3, and if at that price the quantity which suppliers wish to sell exactly equals the amount which users are willing to buy, the market is in equilibrium. The same quantity will continue to be exchanged at the same price, week after week and month after month, until there is some change in behavior on either the buying or selling side.

One can even imagine a situation in which all markets in the economy would be in equilibrium at the same time. Suppose each individual has preferences as regards working and consuming, and that these preferences continue unchanged over time. Suppose also that no one upsets the applecart by inventing new products or new production methods. We might then expect that the economy would settle down gradually into a steady state—producing the same quantities of each good month after month, hiring the same amounts of labor for each job, and so on.

Now we know that no actual economy operates in this fashion. Why is this?

1. One important disturbing factor, general waves of prosperity and depression, has deliberately been left out of the picture and will continue to be ignored until Part Three.

2. A major source of disturbance is the invention of new products and new methods of production. When a major new product appears and catches on, other products have to move over, as it were, to make room for it. Some existing products suffer a loss in sales and some disappear entirely.

3. There are spontaneous shifts in consumer preference. Even without the appearance of new products, taste and fashion may shift away from certain goods and toward others. As slimness becomes fashionable, people will eat less potatoes and more lettuce.

4. There are spontaneous shifts of preference at the other side of the diagram. An increased preference for leisure, or increased preference for white-collar jobs compared with blue-collar jobs, will clearly have important repercussions. So will a decision to save more and consume less or vice versa.

5. War obviously produces severe dislocations in the economy. Less important short-term disturbances can result from unusually good or bad harvests, shifts in economic conditions in other countries, long strikes in key industries, and a variety of other factors.

A market economy can be regarded as a basically stable and self-adjusting mechanism which is constantly being jolted and modified by these various disturbances. The water level of the ocean is essentially stable; but on top of this one finds tidal movements, the long "rollers" of mid-ocean, smaller waves, and tiny ripples whipped up by surface winds. Any actual economy displays a similar "choppiness." Basic, slow-moving changes are in process, and on top of these are a multitude of transient disturbances. Economics helps one to sort out these various layers of disturbance and assess their relative importance.

ECONOMIC DECISIONS IN A MARKET ECONOMY

It may seem that we have made a long detour from the problem with which this chapter began: how the key economic decisions are made in a market economy. Having gone this long way round, however, we can now take a shorter route home.

Work and Leisure

Decisions in this area are made by many millions of workers and potential workers. They have to decide three things: whether to work at all, how much work to do, and what to work at.

1. The decision whether to work at all is heavily influenced by economic necessity and social pressure. Except for the wealthy, a decision not to work means a decision not to live very well; and in the United States it is unfashionable for an able-bodied male to remain idle even if he can afford to do so. Single women are also expected to work from school-leaving to marriage. Married women, on the other hand, usually have a real alternative between taking jobs and not taking them. This group shows a growing preference for work outside the home. The reasons include smaller families, mechanical aids to housekeeping, and a steady widening of the range of occupations considered normal and proper for women. The percentage of women aged 25–44 who are in the labor force increased from 18 percent in 1890 to about 40 percent at present.

2. Having decided to enter the labor force, one must next decide how much work to do. This depends on the shape of individual preference systems. A man who values income highly because he has a large family or expensive tastes may prefer to work long hours for a large paycheck. A man with fewer responsibilities or of a more idle temperament may prefer to work fewer hours.

This kind of decision is also influenced by social custom and industrial practice. In modern industry, it is not feasible for each worker in an enterprise to choose his own working hours. All must abide by a standard schedule. Throughout a large part of American industry, the standard is now 8 hours a day, 5 days a week, with 2 to 4 weeks of vacation during the year. Standard hours have fallen greatly since 1900 and undoubtedly will continue to fall in the future.

The existence of a standard schedule in each establishment does not mean that the individual is entirely without choice. Different industries have different practices, ranging from 30 hours a week in some to 50 hours or more in others. A man can choose to enter a long-hour or a short-hour industry. Many plants also work overtime during busy periods, and workers have the option of putting in for overtime or avoiding it. A worker with a high preference for income may even hold two jobs at the same time. These people are often called "moonlighters," and there are now several million of them. On the other hand, people with a low income preference can often find part-time employment. Married women who need time for household duties often adjust in this way. Of the seven million part-time workers in the United States, more than four million are women.

3. Each person also must decide *where* to work—at what kind of job, for what company, and in what part of the country. True, the middle-aged machinist cannot suddenly decide to become a doctor. A long-time resident of Oakland isn't really concerned with jobs in Youngstown. In the formative high-school and college years, however, the range of choice is potentially as wide as the economy itself. This means that, *given sufficient time*, the number of people choosing to work in certain occupations or areas may rise substantially while preference for other types of work may decline. Even the factory operative usually has a modest range of choice among specific jobs and employers.

Each worker presumably chooses the job which yields maximum advantage in view of his own preference system. This does not mean that he necessarily chooses the highest-paying job he can find. He may be influenced by whether the job is close to home, whether he has friends in the plant, whether the work is hard or easy, and any number of other things. Adding all these things together, he chooses the job which offers him the most attractive "package" of conditions. If it should happen that two jobs are alike in every respect except wages, most people will doubtless choose the higher wage.

Each employer competing in the labor market, then, must work out a package of conditions good enough to attract and hold the number of workers he needs. If he wants 750 employees, then there must be 750 people in the community who value his terms of employment more highly than the terms offered by rival employers. Some workers may be firmly wedded to the plant by long habit, or because they find the work inherently congenial and attractive. But there will be others who are closer to the margin of decision, who are wavering between a job in plant A and plant B. It is these "marginal" people who must be persuaded. Wages are typically a key device for persuading them, partly because money is after all important, and partly because wage levels can be adjusted more rapidly than most other conditions of employment.

Thus workers' preferences encounter the terms offered by employers in the labor market. Through the market there is worked out a pattern of wages and other terms of employment such that each worker is reasonably content with his job choice and each employer is able to hire the number of workers he needs.

Capital Goods and Consumer Goods

Business units need more than labor to set up in production. They need buildings and machinery, which may be elaborate and expensive. How can they get the money to buy these things? In our simplified economy, they would have to borrow from households. This would be done in the "money market." In this market the individual hands over a certain amount of money (say $100) and gets in return either a definite promise (in the case of a bond or preferred stock) or a reasonable expectation (in the case of a common stock) of receiving a certain money payment each year (say $5). In this case the rate of interest is $5/100 = 5$ percent. The rate of interest is the "price" of money in the capital market, just as the rate of wages is the governing price in the labor market.

Where do households get the money which they hand over to business? Presumably from saving, i.e., from spending on current consumption something less than their current income. The inducement to save is that, by reducing current consumption, one can earn interest payments and thus enjoy higher consumption in future years. This kind of choice, indeed, is often termed a "choice between present goods and future goods."

Whether a person is more or less savings-minded will depend on such things as: whether his earnings may be expected to rise or decline in future years; whether family responsibilities are increasing or decreasing; whether savings are needed for some major expenditure such as a house or college education of children; plans for retirement; and whether the person is temperamentally farsighted or shortsighted, reckless or conservative. The amount saved will also be influenced strongly by the size of the family income. People with large incomes save on the average a much higher percentage of their incomes than people in the low-income brackets.

The supply of savings, shaped by these personal preferences, encounters the demand for savings by business units on the capital market. Through the working of the market, a rate of interest is established and a certain volume of savings is exchanged. How does this affect the operation of the economy? Suppose that in a particular year the net output of our model economy is worth $500 billion. Under the simple conditions assumed here, all of this will be distributed to individuals in income payments. Personal income = net national product = $500 billion. Now suppose that 20 percent or $100 billion of this is put into savings while the remaining $400 billion is spent on current consumption. If the economy is to be in balance, the output of consumer goods cannot exceed $400 billion, since this is the amount that households have allocated to purchase of consumer goods. But we supposed originally that total output of the economy was $500 billion. What has become of the other $100 billion? This consists of capital goods production. The $100 billion which savers hand over to business concerns is used to buy this quantity of capital equipment.

This situation may be sketched as follows:

	Spent 400	=	Consumer goods output 400	
Total Income 500				Total Output 500
	Saved 100	=	Capital goods output 100	

For our simple economy to be in balance, the distribution of national output between capital goods and consumer goods must precisely correspond with the distribution of personal income between savings and consumption. Money flows and goods flows must match. If people decide permanently to increase the proportion of income saved, the structure of production will gradually respond to this decision. The percentage of output going into capital goods will rise and the percentage going to consumer goods will fall.

Whether an economy is a low-savings economy or a high-savings economy is clearly very important. Where households are unwilling to postpone consumption and insist on spending almost all their incomes, the supply of loanable funds will be small and the rate of interest high. Only business ventures which promise high returns can be undertaken. Additions to the country's stock of plant and equipment will be slow. Production methods will be simple, output per worker small, and living standards low. These conditions characterize many of the underdeveloped countries, where the level of savings is close to zero.

A high propensity to save, on the other hand, makes for moderate interest rates, a rapid buildup of the country's capital stock, use of increasingly elaborate techniques and equipment, and a steady rise of living standards. Rising incomes, of course, make it still easier to save in the future, and the buildup of capital goods becomes cumulative.

What Kinds of Consumer Goods?

The choices examined thus far determined the amount of labor available in the economy, which sets a ceiling on total output, and the broad division of output between consumer goods and capital goods. This leaves unsettled the question of what kinds of consumer good shall be produced and in what quantities. Why do we turn out seven million cars this year rather than five million or nine million? Why 600 million pairs of shoes rather than a larger or smaller quantity? We have already seen that this is a difficult problem under central planning and is not solved very satisfactorily. How is the same problem solved in a market economy?

A rough answer, which will be spelled out more fully in the next several chapters, is that the amount of each good produced is determined by weighing costs of production against the price which consumers are willing to pay. Under pure competition, business concerns will grind out more and more of a product as long as consumers will buy it at a price sufficient to cover the cost of making it. Production is thus guided by consumers' preference systems as expressed by their purchases in retail markets.

Suppose that at a particular time men's shoes could be produced and retailed at $15 per pair, including a reasonable profit to all concerned. Consumers are so avid for shoes, however, that they are willing to pay $25, and the market price settles for the time being at this level. This price obviously yields handsome returns to all the sellers in this particular chain of markets—retailers, wholesalers, shoe manufacturers, leather makers, and the rest. The result will be a strenuous effort to turn out more of this profitable item. Existing shoe companies will expand their production, and new companies may be set up.

As the production of shoes rises, however, two things will happen. The price offered for shoes in the market will fall, following the general principle that increased quantities of any product can be sold only by lowering its price. The cost of producing additional shoes may also rise, but it may not. In any event, the fall in price will gradually reduce the gap between price and cost, and eventually a point will be reached at which there is no incentive to expand shoe production further.

Under pure competition, in short, a positive price-cost gap signals an expansion of production, while a negative gap (a loss) signals curtailment of production.

The concept of "cost" deserves additional comment. Cost of production is, on the surface, a certain quantity of money. The shoe producer must pay certain amounts for labor, for leather, for other supplies and materials, and for interest on the capital invested in the enterprise. But these money costs have a deeper economic significance. Consider labor, which is the most important cost item for the economy as a whole. Our shoe producer has to pay, say, $2 an hour to hire an additional worker. Why must he pay this? Because the worker is worth this much to some other employer—say, a furniture manufacturer. If the labor market is competitive, as we have supposed it to be, the shoe producer must pay at least as much as the man would be worth elsewhere in order to bid him away into shoe production. If the man goes to work on shoes, however, he cannot work on furniture, and the output he might have produced there is lost to the economy. The real cost of his shoe output is thus the value of the furniture output which he does not produce. Economists term this *opportunity cost*—the value of foregone opportunities.

The significance of equality between price and cost now becomes more apparent. Price measures the valuation which consumers place on an additional pair of shoes, the benefit which they expect to derive from this item. Cost, traced back to its root meaning of *opportunity* cost, measures the valuation placed on the articles which must be sacrificed to make possible production of the extra pair of shoes. When these two valuations are precisely equal, consumers cannot be benefited by any further shifting of resources into or out of shoe production. If all product markets are in this sort of equilibrium, one can argue that the economy is doing the best possible job of satisfying consumer preferences.

The Choice of Production Methods

When one speaks of "cost of production," one means cost of production *by a certain method*. Different methods will yield different levels of cost. How, then, does a business concern decide what method to use for a particular product? This is an especially important question in designing a completely new plant. Once the plant has been built, the range of choice is narrower; but one can still make modifications so as to save labor by using more machinery or vice versa.

Decision on this point requires two kinds of information. First, one must know what alternative combinations of labor, capital, and other factors are *technically possible* for the level of output desired. But this alone cannot determine which alternative is *economically preferable*. To determine this we must know the prices of the various factors. Then we can calculate production costs by each method and choose the method which yields lowest cost.

The way in which this will work itself out is almost self-evident. In an economy where labor is scarce and expensive, as it is in the United States, the scales will be tilted in favor of mechanization and automation. Countries with abundant labor and little capital, on the other hand, will lean toward simpler methods. The relative scarcity of labor and capital is reflected in their relative prices; and these prices lead producers to choose methods which economize on the scarcer factor and make more use of the abundant one. This is efficient from the standpoint of the individual producer and also makes best use of national resources.

But haven't we assumed too readily that businessmen are invariably well informed and rational? How do we know that they will select and use the lowest-cost methods of production? The answer is that under pure competition efficiency is the price of survival. If some companies can produce shoes for $15 per pair, others must learn to do the same if they are to continue in the industry.

Competitive pressure forces each producer to make correct decisions about production methods and to run his plant efficiently. If anyone in an industry develops improved methods leading to lower costs, other producers must eventually fall in line. The penalty for being inefficient is elimination from the economy. This is a major argument for competition as a method of economic organization.

The Distribution of Income

The final question which our market economy must answer is what share each individual or family shall receive of the national output. Why do some people receive 10 or 20 times as much as others? To what extent are these differences inherent in a market economy and to what extent can they be altered by community action?

In a market economy, people receive income as *owners of labor and capital* which they contribute to the production process. Each person's income depends on the *quantity* of resources which he contributes multiplied by the *price* which these resources fetch on the market. The problem of resource prices has already been examined. The rate of interest is determined in the capital market, the wage rates for various types of labor in the labor market. But what determines the quantity of resources which each person owns?

How much capital a man owns depends on how much he has inherited and how much he has added to or subtracted from this amount. He can add to his inheritance by saving or subtract from it by spending beyond his current income. If it were not for the inheritance factor, one could say simply, "How much you own depends on how much you save." Inheritance is quite important in practice, however, and this weakens the argument that property income is justified by personal merit or sacrifice. The feasibility of passing on property intact depends a good deal on the inheritance laws of the country and on whether the government levies estate taxes at death.

Capacity for productive labor is partly inborn. Some occupations require natural talents which occur only rarely in the population. One cannot mass produce concert violinists, ballerinas, or big-league pitchers capable of winning 20 games a year. People with these talents are bound to command a premium price. Capacity to perform most jobs, however, is largely a matter of training. There are many young people in the country who are capable of being average machinists, accountants, professors, salesclerks, or lawyers. But how many people, and *which* people, actually get into these occupations depends on opportunity to acquire the necessary education and experience. This is particularly important for law, medicine, science, and other professional occupations. Even in the United States, and to a greater extent in most other countries, cost of education and limitations of university capacity restrict the number of people who can get into the higher occupations. Thus these occupations, in addition to the earnings which they could command in a free market, receive an additional premium resulting from artificial restriction of supply.

It follows that the distribution of income in a country depends partly on its institutional structure and is in no sense immutable. One can always alter income distribution by changing the pattern of resource ownership. If one would like to see a more equal distribution, one can try to enlarge the educational bottlenecks which restrict access to the higher occupations; and one can try to bring about a more equal distribution of property ownership. Such measures tackle the income distribution problem in a fundamental way, and in a way which does not interfere with the operation of the market mechanism.

In addition, of course, government can alter income distribution through taxation, and most governments do a good deal of this. How far this tendency should be carried is a subject of intense political controversy, to which we shall return in Chapter 16.

CONCLUDING COMMENTS

The Market Provides Answers

We have tried to demonstrate that a market economy is capable of answering the key economic questions posed at the outset. Given the distribution of resource ownership, personal preference systems, and the production possibilities set by technology, one can deduce how much of each product will be produced and what it will sell for, where each person will work and how much he will be paid. One may think of the appropriate price-production pattern as being worked out in a flash by solving a large number of equations in a computer or, more realistically, as being approximated through the trial-and-error process which goes on in any actual economy.

An attractive feature of the market economy is that the answers are worked out on a *decentralized* basis, through millions of individuals making their own decisions in thousands of different markets. There is no need for a central planning board to supervise the process from on high. The decentralized system has advantages in terms of flexibility, speed, and opportunity for personal initiative.

The Interdependence of Markets

This point has already been made but deserves to be emphasized. A shift in preferences or technology, while its initial impact may be mainly on one market, sets up repercussions which will be transmitted to many other markets before the system settles down into a new equilibrium. The self-adjusting character of the system depends on this linkage and interdependence of markets.

Space does not permit detailed illustration of this point; but the reader will find it instructive to do a few "finger exercises" on his own account, starting with a change somewhere in the system and trying to trace out the repercussions of the change. Consider, for example, the following:

1. A shift of workers' preferences *away* from bituminous coal mining.
2. A shift of consumers' preferences *away* from potatoes and *toward* lettuce.
3. Introduction of a completely new product—choose your own—into the economy.
4. A shift of workers' preferences toward leisure, leading to a general shortening of the work week.

If you can work out cases of this sort successfully, you will have absorbed the essence of this chapter.

A Guiding Thread: The Marginal Principle

This chapter has tried to explore the full range of decisions which have to be made in any economy. These may seem on the surface to be quite different from each other, yet there is a unifying principle which runs through them all. This is commonly termed the *marginal principle*. It means that economic choices are typically between small or *marginal* quantities. The consumer does not choose between buying a great quantity of beef and giving up beef altogether. He asks rather: "Seeing how prices are this week, will it be worthwhile for me to buy *a little more* beef and perhaps *a little less* pork?" He is comparing, not *total* quantities, but *marginal* quantities. He is weighing the possible advantage of making small adjustments at the boundaries of his present consumption pattern.

Similarly, our shoe manufacturer is not in the position of deciding between building six new shoe factories and going out of business completely. His typical problem is this: "I'm turning out 500 pairs a day. If I went up to 550 pairs a day, could I sell the extra 50 pairs for enough to cover the cost of making them"? Would the extra income or revenue cover the extra costs? The manufacturer is not reasoning about his total output but about a small or marginal change in his rate of output.

The worker considering whether the money he would get for working overtime on Saturday morning is attractive enough to outweigh not being able to take his son fishing is engaged in a marginal calculation. So is the householder wondering whether the interest he will get on a $100 U.S. savings bond outweighs the pleasure of spending the money right away. So is the plant manager trying to calculate whether the savings from an improved machine will repay the cost of the machine.

Individuals throughout the economy are constantly engaged in millions of calculations of this sort. Each tries to work out a pattern of behavior which will yield greatest satisfaction in terms of his preference system. If these calculations are being made correctly, then the system is performing as efficiently as it can within the limits of people's preferences and the basic resources available.

The Market as Reconciler of Conflicting Interests

A competitive economy performs another important function, so obvious that it is in danger of being overlooked. It produces a working compromise among the conflicting interests of individuals and groups in the economy. Indeed, it is the only way of achieving such a compromise without central economic control.

Consider the inevitable difference of interest over income distribution. Everyone wants more, and there just isn't enough to go round. This could lead, and in some societies has led, to armed conflict. Competitive pricing of labor and capital on free markets at least provides a clear principle for income distribution, a principle which can readily be explained and which has managed to win a considerable measure of public agreement.

Consider also the fact that the things consumers want to have produced may not correspond at all closely to the kinds of work people would like to do. Some of the products in greatest demand may require work which is heavy, hot, and generally uncongenial. Men might prefer to spend their days in work which is light, leisurely, and creative, but which yields products of little market value. This conflict is resolved by pressures from the two sides meeting in the market and reaching a working adjustment. The product in great demand commands a relatively high price. This means that the industry can afford a relatively high wage rate. High wages are sufficient, at least for some workers, to offset the natural unpleasantness of the work, and the industry is able to recruit a labor force. Coal mining is a good example.

In the opposite case of work which is naturally congenial, one can hire people at low wage rates, the low wages being offset by the pleasantness of life on the job. These wages permit the product to be offered at low prices; and low prices induce the public to take more of the product, even though their preference for it is not high. Thus some people are able to work in these pleasant occupations. There are people who say they would paint, act, or play the violin "for nothing"—and they must mean it, because most artists earn very little. By performing for next to nothing, they create a market for their services and are able to follow their career preference.

Consider, finally, the conflict of interest between each group of producers in the economy and the consuming public. Each producer group—the farmers, the steel producers, the retail druggists, and the rest —would really like to mulct consumers by charging a high price for their wares. Talk about "public service" is a thin veil for mercenary motives.

Where pure competition prevails, however, producers are obliged to work for minimum returns. Each producer is compelled to work at full efficiency and to provide the community with goods at minimum cost. This is not done out of altruism. Producers continue to be as selfish as ever, but competition channels their selfishness in a direction useful to the community. As Adam Smith concluded, ". . . thus each is led, as though by an invisible hand, to promote a good which was no part of his intention."

Some Limitations of the Competitive Model

Finally, we must consider a basic objection to everything we have been saying. Some people argue that the present-day American economy differs so greatly from our simplified competitive model that analysis of the latter has little bearing on the former. A purely competitive economy might work excellently, but the actual economy is full of defects and blemishes.

There is a good deal to this. If you look back at the assumptions we made in setting up the simplified model, you will see that all of them are open to question. This is true especially of the full-employment, no-government, and competitive-market assumptions.

It is not true that market economies always operate at full employment. There is nothing about a market system which will prevent occasional recessions or which will bring the economy rapidly back to full employment. Indeed, it is possible for an economy to go along year after year with part of its resources idle. The American economy had heavy unemployment (of labor *and* capital) from 1930 through 1941 and moderate unemployment from 1958 through 1964. This does not prove that a market economy is *undesirable*, but simply that it is *incomplete*. It must be supplemented by government actions designed to maintain full employment. These actions lie mainly in the areas of taxation, government spending, and control of money supply.

Next we must recognize the existence of public goods produced by government. Here we cannot apply the price = cost rule to determine the proper rate of output, since there is no price. The decision on how much to produce is made through political, rather than market, processes. Again, this demonstrates *incompleteness* of the market economy. The 20 percent or so of national output produced by government remains outside its scope.

The most damaging criticism is that in the actual economy pure competition is a rarity, and serious restrictions on competition are the general rule. We have with us the railroads, electric power companies, and other "natural monopolies"; the many lines of industry dominated by a few giant firms—steel, petroleum, automobiles, and the rest; the farm organizations demanding government price fixing and subsidies; the unions doing their best to abolish competition in labor markets. So it can be argued that a model of the economy which assumes the prevalence of competition is not very relevant to practical affairs.

This is a major issue, which cannot be dismissed in a paragraph or two. We shall come back to it several times, particularly in Chapters 9, 12 and 13. Briefly and dogmatically, one can say that many (not all) economists would subscribe to the following view:

The monopoly elements in the American economy are serious. Most of them are probably irremovable. Because of them the decisions made in the economy are both less predictable and less desirable than they would be if all markets were fully competitive. In appraising the efficiency of the American economy, and in comparing it with other national economies, we must take it as it actually is and not pretend that it corresponds to the simple competitive model.

While *pure* competition is rare in the actual economy, *effective* competition is quite pervasive. Most product prices, most wage rates and interest rates, are subject to competitive pressures. It is also possible that some sectors of the economy could be made more competitive than they now are through antitrust action and other government policies. Such policies are not foredoomed by any inevitable trend toward increasing monopoly.

The theory of purely competitive markets remains useful in several respects. First, it provides a definition of what we mean by an efficiently functioning market economy, a useful yardstick or point of departure. Second, while few markets behave *exactly* like purely competitive markets, many behave *somewhat* in this way. And interestingly enough, the ideas about demand, supply, and costs which were developed originally to analyze competitive markets turn out to be necessary also for understanding what goes on under monopoly. Finally, many of the general ideas advanced in this chapter—that markets are interrelated, that events in one market may have wide repercussions on others, that both supply and demand pressures influence price—are not much affected by the precise blend of monopoly and competition in the economy.

SUMMARY

1. This chapter analyzes the operation of a private economy in which all markets are characterized by pure competition. Review the concepts of *market, price,* and *pure competition.*

2. Important characteristics of this economy are: there can be only one price in a particular market; each price is influenced by supply and demand; all prices and markets in the system form an interlocking network.

3. The results which the economy produces depend on individual preferences and production possibilities. Specifically, there are (*a*) *consumer preferences among products;* (*b*) *worker preferences between income and leisure;* (*c*) *preferences between present consumption and future consumption,* which determine the amount of saving; (*d*) known *alternative methods of producing* a particular good.

4. Decisions about working are made by individual workers in response to the terms offered in the labor market.

5. The division of national output between consumer goods and capital goods depends on decisions about saving.

6. The amount of each consumer good which will be produced depends on a balancing of its cost of production against the price which consumers are willing to pay. Price is significant because it measures benefit to consumers. Money cost is significant because it measures real or opportunity cost. (Review the definition of this term.)

7. Each product will be produced by the method which, given the price of labor and capital, yields lowest total cost per unit of output.

8. Each person's income depends on the quantity of resources which he contributes to production and on the price which these resources command in the market.

9. Through all these decisions runs the guiding thread of the *marginal principle*. Economic choice typically involves small adjustments at the margin of decision.

10. One can make a strong argument that a purely competitive economy leads to a pattern of production which is the best one can do with the resources available. But this argument is subject to important qualifications, which will be spelled out more fully in later chapters.

DISCUSSION QUESTIONS

1. What are the main assumptions underlying the model of a competitive market economy?

2. It is sometimes said that these assumptions are so far from reality that reasoning based on them can have no practical application. What do you think about this?

3. The text says that each market is linked to every other market in the system. What are the reasons for this linkage? Can you imagine a market which would be completely insulated against events in other markets?

4. What is the meaning of *equilibrium* in a market? Would you expect ever to find a market in equilibrium in the real world? If not, what is the use of the concept?

5. In a complex industrial economy, how much opportunity is there for expression of personal preferences concerning work and leisure?

6. Why and how will household saving decisions influence the kinds of goods produced in the economy? (Take an extreme case: Suppose no one saved any of his money income. What would the structure of production look like?)

7. How does the market determine when production of a consumer good has reached just the right level?

8. Is *cost of production* merely a quantity of money or does it have a deeper significance? Explain.

9. In a market economy, why does each person receive the amount of income he does? To what extent can this distribution of income be considered *natural*? Even if natural, is it necessarily just?

10. Why is *the marginal principle* important in reasoning about a market economy? See how many illustrations of this principle you can think of.

11. If "everybody minding their own business" works out so well, shouldn't government refrain from intervening in the economy? Where and why may government action be justifiable?

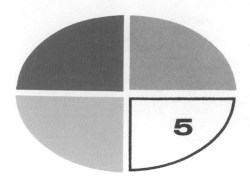

5

Demand-Supply Analysis

John Stuart Mill
By a mighty effort of will
Overcame his natural bonhomie
And wrote "Principles of Political Economy"
EDMUND CLERIHEW BENTLEY

WHAT DETERMINES how much of a particular good will be produced in the economy? What determines the price at which it will sell? These questions are really the same, for at a specific price only so much of a good can be sold.

Our task here is to explain the *system of prices* which exists in a market economy. But we could equally well say that we are explaining the *system of quantities produced.* We could also say that we are studying the *allocation of productive resources:* for a certain pattern of output requires a corresponding allocation of land, labor, capital, and management.

Economists explore this problem by means of *demand-supply analysis.* There are two kinds of pressure at work in a market. On one side is the willingness of purchasers to buy larger or smaller quantities of the product, depending on its price. On the other side is the willingness of sellers to produce and bring to market various amounts of the product, depending on the price which they expect to receive. Demand-supply analysis is a way of separating these forces, analyzing each in turn, and then bringing them together to explain price and output.

In this chapter we describe the main outlines of demand-supply analysis and show how it can be applied to practical problems. In

Chapter 6 we shall go deeper into the personal wants and spending decisions which lie behind demand, and in Chapter 7 we shall consider the cost calculations which underlie supply.

INDIVIDUAL DEMAND

Demand stems from people's desire to consume. This is obvious in the case of shoes, automobiles, breakfast cereals. But raw materials and semifinished goods are also demanded because they will turn into consumable products. Labor and capital goods are demanded because of what they can produce. The demand for labor, capital, and materials is usually termed a *derived demand,* since it is derived from the demand for finished consumer goods. For the moment, we concentrate on final demand, leaving derived demand to a later point.

In our type of economy, consumer demand is usually expressed through markets. But this is not always true. The public has decided that certain things—highways, national defense, primary and high-school education—can be provided most efficiently on a community basis. Instead of paying for these things in the market, we pay a price through taxation. Preferences are expressed through political channels rather than market channels. But it remains true that unless a good or service is desired, it will not be produced. For the present, we concentrate on private goods, leaving discussion of public goods to Chapter 16.

Let's look, then, at Mr. A's demand for a finished, private consumer good—say coffee. First of all, what *is* demand? How do we describe it?

Demand is a List (or Schedule) of the Quantities Which Will Be Bought at Various Prices

You will avoid much confusion by remembering that, in economics, the term demand *always refers to a schedule.* It is *not a single quantity.* If we want to focus on the quantity which will be bought at some particular price, we call it the *quantity demanded.*

To describe Mr. A's demand for coffee, we must specify the quantity demanded at each of the various possible prices for coffee. For example, Mr. A's demand schedule might look as in Table 1. If the price is $2.50, he will get along with only 1 pound. At lower prices he will buy more until, if the price fell to 25 cents, he would buy 10 pounds a month.

The same information is shown graphically in Figure 1. Since coffee is usually bought in pound packages, its graph would consist of a series of disconnected points. For products where the quantity purchased can be increased by very small amounts, the demand schedule becomes a continuous line like the solid line in Figure 1. Such a line is called a *demand curve.* We shall be using demand curves very freely as we go

TABLE 1

PRICE OF COFFEE (Dollars per Pound)	QUANTITY BOUGHT (Pounds per Month)
2.50	1
2.25	2
2.00	3
1.75	4
1.50	5
1.25	6
1.00	7
0.75	8
0.50	9
0.25	10

along; so it is well to remember that a demand curve is simply a graphic picture of the demand schedule, the list of prices and quantities purchased.

Why is it reasonable to expect that demand curves slope downward from left to right, i.e., that people will normally buy more of a good at a

At a Lower Price, Larger Quantities Will Be Purchased

FIGURE 1. This is a graph of Mr. A's demand schedule for coffee. Each point means that, if the price were as shown on the vertical axis, Mr. A would buy the number of pounds shown on the horizontal axis. If the price and quantity intervals were made very small, the graph would become a continuous line, termed a *demand curve*.

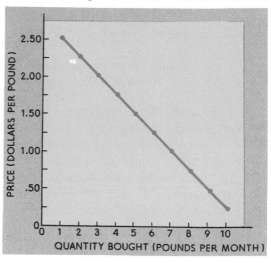

lower price? The traditional line of proof, explained more fully in Chapter 6, rests on the notion of satisfaction or *utility*. Why do I buy a product at all? Obviously, because it yields me some sort of satisfaction. But a second unit of the product will usually not yield as much satisfaction as the first, and a third will yield still less. As I go from being a one-car householder to a two-car or three-car householder, the utility yielded by additional cars will decline. Nineteenth-century economists called this the *law of diminishing marginal (or additional) utility*. If this law holds, then I will not be willing to pay as much for a second car as I would for the first; and to get me to buy a third car, the price would have to be still lower. My demand curve for cars slopes downward to the right.

We seem, then, to be on safe ground in concluding that consumers will buy less of a product if its price rises, and more if its price falls. But the ground is more treacherous than it appears. We can be sure of this result only if we specify a number of conditions. The most important are:

1. Buyers' preferences must remain unchanged. If we allow Mr. A's preferences to jump about at the same time that the price of coffee is shifting, we can no longer be sure of the outcome.

2. The desirability of the good to consumers must be *independent* of the market price. Without this stipulation, a price cut might sometimes *reduce* the quantity sold. If the price of diamonds fell drastically, they might cease to be prestige symbols and engagement rings might contain emeralds instead.

3. Buyers' incomes must remain unchanged. If Mr. A's money income rises at the same time that coffee prices rise, he may end up buying more coffee rather than less.[1]

4. Prices of other products must remain unchanged. This is especially important for closely related products, such as tea, cocoa, soft drinks, sugar, and cream. We must hold these prices constant if we wish to observe the pure effect of a change in coffee prices on coffee sales.

5. Prices must be expected to continue at about their present level. If coffee rises 10 cents a pound and consumers fear it will rise another 10 cents next month, they may rush out and buy heavily to beat the price rise. *Speculation on price changes* may mean that a price increase, at least for a while, will *raise* sales of the product instead of reducing them.

The principle of demand may now be restated in stricter form: A consumer will purchase less of a product the price of which has risen, and more of a product the price of which has fallen, *provided* that his

---

[1] Strictly speaking, if the price of one item in the consumers' budget falls and other prices remain the same, his real income *cannot* remain unchanged. He can now buy more than before, hence his real income must have risen. If the good in question is a small item in peoples' budgets, it is safe to ignore this complication, as is normally done in demand analysis. But if the item takes a large part of the budget, one may encounter the "Giffen paradox." Sir Francis Giffen, a nineteenth-century British economist, noted that, when Irish potato prices rose in bad years, many Irish families consumed *more* potatoes rather than less. Why? Because with high potato prices and no increase in their money incomes they were now too poor to afford meat and other foodstuffs. How did they keep alive? By eating more potatoes.

income and his preference system remain unchanged, that the prices of all other products remain unchanged, and that present prices are expected to continue indefinitely in the future.

MARKET DEMAND

Will *total* purchases of a product obey the same principle as purchases by an individual consumer? Will a decline in shoe prices, everything else in the economy remaining unchanged, lead to an increase in shoe purchases? Yes, it will. The reason is that total national demand is simply the sum of the demands of individual households. A drop in shoe prices will cause at least some families to buy more shoes, and thus there will be more shoes bought in the country as a whole.

A hypothetical list of how many pairs of shoes might be bought at various price levels is shown in Table 2. This is termed a *market demand*

TABLE 2

Market Demand Schedule
for Men's Shoes

PRICE OF SHOES (Dollars per Pair)	QUANTITY BOUGHT (Millions of Pairs per Year)
30	85
27	110
24	130
21	160
18	190
15	240
12	300
9	375
6	500

schedule. As we go down the price column to lower and lower prices, we find larger and larger quantities appearing in the purchases column. The same information is shown graphically in Figure 2. *DD* shows the amount which purchasers would be willing to buy at various alternative prices. This *demand curve* is drawn as a continuous line, indicating that price can be varied by very small amounts and that sales will always respond.

Figure 2 looks deceptively simple. Since we shall be using demand curves frequently in later chapters, we had better pause to consider exactly what they do and do not mean. Three main points should be kept in mind:

1. A demand curve is *not* a historical chart showing the course of events over a period of time. The demand curve does *not* say that if price

Market Demand Obeys the Same Principle as Individual Demand

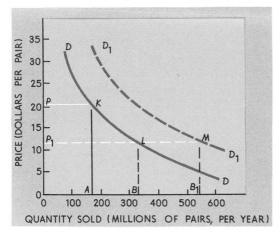

FIGURE 2. *DD* is a demand curve. Each point on the curve shows how many pairs of shoes consumers would be prepared to buy at a specified price. D_1D_1 indicates a change in demand to a higher level.

falls from *OP* in 1965 to OP_1 in 1970, then the quantity sold will increase from *OA* to *OB*. Over this period, preferences, incomes, and other prices will certainly have changed, and thus the basis we laid down for constructing a demand schedule will have been swept away.

The demand curve is an analytical, not a historical, concept. All the points on the curve hold true *simultaneously* and at the same moment of time. They represent alternative possibilities, only one of which can actually be realized. *If* price were to be *OP*, then quantity sold would be *OA*. If instead the price were to be OP_1, then quantity sold would be *OB*. But only one of these possibilities can be realized in a particular market at a particular time.

2. The term *change in demand* is often used incorrectly. If price in Figure 2 rises from OP_1 to *OP*, and sales consequently fall from *OB* to *OA*, many people would say that "demand has fallen." *This is wrong.* Consumer preferences have not changed, and the demand curve is exactly where it was. There has simply been a *change in the quantity demanded* in response to a change in price.

Movement from one point to another *on the same demand curve—* in this case, from *L* to *K*—is *not* a change in demand. A change in demand occurs only when *the whole demand curve shifts to a new position.* Suppose *DD* moves upward to the position D_1D_1. This is truly an increase in demand, because whatever the price, it will now be possible to sell more than with the previous demand curve. At price OP_1, for example, one can now sell OB_1 units of product instead of *OB*. The movement from *L* to *M* does represent a change in demand, while that from *L* to *K* does not.

Why might demand rise from DD to D_1D_1? Basically, because of a change in one or more of the things which we specified earlier as constant: people's preferences, their incomes, and the prices of other goods.

3. The figures for the table and for Figure 5–2 were pulled out of the air to illustrate the principle that demand curves slope downward to the right. But if we were dealing with a real product in the real world, we could not make up figures in this way. Any actual demand curve has a specific shape. Some products have a very steep demand curve, indicating that consumers will buy almost as much at a high price as a low price. In other cases, purchases may fall off sharply as the price rises, which would mean a flat demand curve. The shape of a particular demand curve depends, for example, on whether the product is basic to the consumption pattern of most households, or an optional item which can readily be sacrificed. The demand curve for bread obviously is different from that for silk scarves. It depends also on whether there are close substitutes for the product. If close substitutes are available, people will shift to these as the price rises, and sales will fall off rapidly. Salt has a steep demand curve precisely because there is no good substitute for it.

Elasticity of Demand

The shape of demand curves may strike the reader as an abstract and unreal subject. To businessmen, however, it is a matter of intense practical concern. If a company cuts its price by 10 percent, will sales increase by 5 percent, or 15 percent, or 25 percent? If costs are rising and the company is considering a price increase, will sales fall off only slightly or a good deal? The answer can make the difference between good profits and large losses. Companies and management consulting firms spend large amounts of money trying to find out what the demand curves for various products look like.

It is unsatisfactory to refer to demand curves simply as "steep" or "flat," particularly since this depends on the scale used on the axes of the supply-demand diagram. Look again at the shoe demand curve in Figure 2. Suppose you made the horizontal distance corresponding to 100 million pairs of shoes twice as large as before. The demand curve would *look* much flatter, wouldn't it? Yet demand would be just the same as before. Similarly, you could make this demand curve look much steeper by enlarging the *vertical* scale on the diagram.

We need a more precise measure of just how quantity sold responds to a change in price. The measure which economists use for this purpose is termed *elasticity of demand*. This measures the relative effect on quantity sold (Q) of a change in price (P). More precisely

$$\text{Elasticity } e = -\frac{\% \text{ change in } Q}{\% \text{ change in } P}.$$

Consider the effect of a 1 percent reduction in price. If quantity sold increases by more than 1 percent, so that $e > 1$, we say that demand is *elastic*. If quantity sold rises less than 1 percent, so that $e < 1$, demand is said to be *inelastic*. The borderline case, where $e = 1$, is referred to as one of *unit elasticity*. Since we are dividing a positive Q change by a negative P change, or vice versa, the result would be negative. Hence we add a negative sign to the elasticity formula to convert this back to a positive number.[2]

It is sometimes said that demand for "necessities" is inelastic, while demand for "luxuries" is elastic. But on this basis cigarettes would have to be classified as a necessity, since demand for them is quite inelastic.[3] It is better to say that elasticity depends on the fixity of consumption habits *and especially on the availability of substitutes for the product*. The larger the number of substitutes available, and the closer substitutes they are in consumers' eyes, the more elastic the demand schedule. This is why demand for one brand of a product with many competing brands is usually quite elastic.

The concept of elasticity can be illustrated by a hypothetical demand schedule for men's shirts (Table 3). Opposite each price in column 1 we enter in column 2 the quantity which could be sold at that price. In column 3 we multiply P by Q to get total sales revenue at that price. Thus at a price of $12, sellers of shirts would receive a total revenue of $300 millon; at $11, they would receive $385 million; and so on.

Once we have completed column 3, we can calculate how much *additional* revenue sellers will get by moving from one price and sales level to another. Thus the change from $12 to $11 raises revenues by $85 million; the next reduction from $11 to $10 yields additional revenue of $115 million; and so on. These figures are entered in column 4.

For many purposes, we are interested in knowing additional revenue *per unit sold*. Thus when price is cut from $12 to $11, 10 million additional shirts are sold, yielding additional revenue of $85 million. Additional revenue *per shirt*, then, is $8.50. This is termed marginal revenue,

---

[2] The percentage price change used in measuring elasticity should be small, since what we want to know is elasticity in the neighborhood of a specific price, perhaps the price existing at the moment. Ideally, we would like to measure elasticity at a single *point* on the demand curve. We can do this by making the assumed change in P smaller and smaller, so that the change in Q also becomes extremely small. This yields a measure of *point elasticity*.

The formula given above is, strictly speaking, a measure of *arc elasticity*. It measures the average elasticity of the section (or arc) of the demand curve lying between the beginning price and the ending price. The larger the percentage price change we use, the less will the measure of arc elasticity tell us about elasticity at any one point.

[3] The price elasticity of demand for cigarettes has been estimated at between 0.3 and 0.4. See S. M. Sackrin, "Factors Affecting the Demand for Cigarettes," *Agricultural Economics Research*, July, 1962, pp. 81–88.

TABLE 3

Market Demand Schedule for Men's Shirts

PRICE (Dollars) (1)	QUANTITY SOLD (Millions per Year) (2)	TOTAL REVENUE (Millions of Dollars per Year) (3)	ADDITIONAL REVENUE (Millions of Dollars) (4)	MARGINAL REVENUE PER UNIT SOLD (Dollars) (5)	ELASTICITY OF DEMAND (6)
12	25	300			
			85	8.50	3.83
11	35	385			
			115	7.70	3.71
10	50	500			
			85	5.70	2.48
9	65	585			
			95	4.75	2.27
8	85	680			
			90	3.60	1.92
7	110	770			
			70	2.30	1.56
6	140	840			
			20	0.60	1.13
5	172	860			
			0	0.00	1.00
4	215	860			
			−35	−0.60	0.86
3	275	825			
			−75	−0.75	0.77
2	375	750			
			−200	−1.10	0.57
1	550	550			

the revenue per unit of sales resulting from a small change in the selling price. The marginal revenue resulting from successively lower prices is entered in column 5.

Note an important relation between columns 3 and 5. So long as total revenue is increasing, which is true down to a price level of $5, marginal revenue is positive. The change from a $5 to a $4 price, however, brings no change in total revenue. Marginal revenue is zero. Below $4, further price reductions *reduce* total revenue, so marginal revenue is negative. This yields a simple rule:

MR *is positive, zero, or negative as*
TR *is increasing, constant, or decreasing.*[4]

---

[4] Suppose we made the price intervals in the table smaller and smaller, finally reaching a continuous function as charted in Figure 3. Then marginal revenue is

But wait a minute. Hasn't something gone wrong here? How can shirts which are sold for $11 yield a marginal revenue of only $8.50? Well, figure it out. By cutting the price from $12 to $11 we sell 10 million more shirts per year. So it looks as though total revenue is increased by $11 × 10 million = $110 million. But this is wrong. For in order to sell this amount, we have to lower the price for all shirts sold during the year. The 25 million shirts which could have been sold anyway at $12 are now being sold at $11, which reduces sales revenues by $25 million. So the addition to total revenue is only $110 million − $25 million = $85 million; and marginal revenue per additional shirt sold figures out to $8.50.

This yields another important rule: if price must be cut to sell a greater number of units, the *marginal revenue per unit sold will be lower than the price*. The reason is the price cut on earlier units which is necessary to sell the additional units. (Go down the table and verify that *MR* per unit in column 5 is always lower than *P* in column 1.)

Finally, by comparing each *percentage* change in *P* with the corresponding *percentage* change in *Q* and applying the elasticity formula, we can calculate elasticity of demand. These calculations are shown in column 6.[5] Note that elasticity varies widely from the top of the column to the bottom. So if someone asks, "What is the elasticity of demand for shirts?" the answer cannot be given as a single figure. One can give a figure for elasticity of demand *at a specific price;* or one can reproduce column 6 and say, "elasticity will vary in this way for various price ranges."

Note also that as long as elasticity is greater than 1, total revenue rises as price is reduced. When *e* = 1, total revenue is unaffected by a price change. When elasticity falls below 1, a price cut will reduce total revenue.

The information in Table 3 is shown graphically in Figure 3. The demand curve *DD* is charted from the price and quantity information in

---

simply the rate of change of total revenue with respect to quantity sold,

$$MR = \frac{dTR}{dQ}.$$

Thus *MR* must be positive for rising *TR*, zero for constant *TR*, and negative for decreasing *TR*.

[5] Strictly, each figure in this column measures *arc elasticity*, or average elasticity over the $1 price interval involved. There is a small problem in the calculation, which some readers may already have spotted. When price falls from $12 to $11, how do we calculate the percentage change in price? Is it $\frac{1}{12}$ or $\frac{1}{11}$? Similarly for the quantity change. The convention is to take neither the higher nor the lower figure, but rather the midpoint of the range. Thus the first figure in column 6 works out to:

$$-\frac{10/30}{-1/11.5} = 3.83 \ .$$

columns 1 and 2. *TR* comes from column 3. *MR*, marginal revenue per unit sold, comes from column 5. But note an important difference. In the table, we showed price declining a dollar at a time. (To show it declining a cent at a time would make the table a mile long!) In Figure 3, however, we have "smoothed out" the curves to show what would happen if price were varied by extremely small intervals.

Note that the chart obeys the rules laid down earlier. As long as $e > 1$, *TR* is rising and *MR* is positive. Where $e = 1$, *TR* is constant and *MR* is zero. When $e < 1$, *TR* is falling and *MR* is negative.

Figure 3 demonstrates that visual impressions of the shape of a de-

Demand and Revenue Curves for Men's Shirts

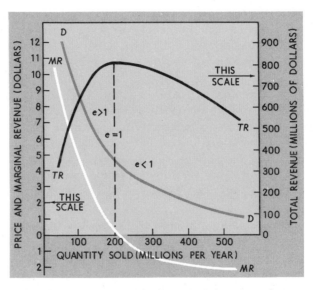

FIGURE 3. The demand curve *DD* and the marginal revenue curve *MR* are drawn with reference to the left-hand vertical axis. The total revenue curve *TR* refers to the right-hand axis. Note that when $e > 1$, *TR* is rising and *MR* is positive. When $e = 1$, *TR* is constant and *MR* is zero. When $e < 1$, *TR* is falling and *MR* is negative.

mand curve can be very misleading. The upper part of the curve appears quite steep, yet it turns out to be elastic. The lower portion looks flatter, yet it is inelastic. How can this be? The explanation is that elasticity is based, not on *absolute* changes in prices and quantities, but on *percentage* changes. In the upper range of Figure 3, a dollar cut in price is only a small percentage change, because we are starting from a high base. A sales increase of 1,000 shirts, however, is a *big* percentage increase, because we are starting from a low sales volume. Hence our elasticity measure, $-\dfrac{.\%\ \text{change in } Q}{\%\ \text{change in } P}$ turns out to be large and demand is elastic. In the lower range of the curve, the percentage price changes are getting steadily larger and the percentage quantity changes steadily smaller. The shrinking numerator and the growing denominator causes the elasticity measure to fall.

The marginal revenue concept is useful in calculating how a producer can make the most money. Suppose you own a spring of mineral water, from which you can draw off as much or as little as you like each day. The water costs nothing to produce. There are no rival producers. The demand curve for mineral water slopes downward in the usual way. Your problem is to set a price and rate of output which will yield greatest revenue. Total revenue will be largest where MR is zero, that is, where the MR curve intersects the X-axis. So this is the rate of output you should choose. For goods which cost something to produce, the problem becomes more complicated, but the central principle remains the same: it will pay to expand output so long as the marginal revenue from an additional unit exceeds the additional cost of producing it.

Additional Elasticity Measures

Income elasticity of demand.   What we have been discussing is, strictly speaking, *price elasticity of demand*, that is, the relation between price and quantity sold. Suppose, instead, that we wanted to measure the effect of a change in buyers' *incomes*. As their incomes rise, consumers buy more of most goods and services; but purchases of some things rise a good deal faster than of others. Purchases of bread and vegetables rise slowly, purchases of vacation trips and college education rise rapidly. To a businessman or an investor wondering how a particular industry will fare over the years ahead, *income elasticity of demand* is very important.

The definition of income elasticity of demand is parallel to that of price elasticity:

$$\text{Income elasticity} = \frac{\%\text{ change in quantity sold}}{\%\text{ change in income}},$$

price and all other conditions being held constant.[6] If a 5 percent increase in consumers' incomes means a 5 percent increase in sales of a product, its income elasticity is 1. If people were completely satiated with a good and would buy no more of it whatever their incomes, its income elasticity would be zero.

There have been many statistical studies of income elasticity, which show a consistent pattern. Basic foodstuffs have the lowest income elasticities, typically between 0.4 and 0.7. Housing normally falls in the

---

[6] There is no need for a minus sign in this elasticity formula. A positive change in income is normally accompanied by a positive change in quantity sold, so income elasticity is positive. There are some goods, usually termed "inferior goods," of which people buy *less* as their incomes rise; but these are exceptional cases.

range 0.6 to 0.9, and clothing in the range 1.0 to 1.5. The highest income elasticities, in the range 1.5 to 2.0, are for things like cosmetics and beauty care, travel, recreation and entertainment, health care, education, and other personal services; and so production of these things shoots up fastest as national income rises.

We saw that price elasticity can be measured precisely only at a specific price and will differ in different price ranges. Similarly, income elasticity depends on the income level one is considering. In very poor countries, where people spend almost all their incomes on food, income elasticity of demand for food is close to 1. In richer countries it is considerably lower, and in the United States has been estimated as low as 0.25.

Cross-elasticity of demand.   We noted earlier that purchases of one product depend not only on its own price but on the prices of other products which are consumed along with it or which are substitutes for it. If the demands for products A and B are related, then a change in B's price will affect the sales of A. The strength of the relation is measured by the *cross-elasticity of demand.*

The cross-elasticity of demand for product A in terms of B is $\dfrac{\% \text{ change in quantity of A}}{\% \text{ change in price of B}}$. This resembles the ordinary elasticity formula except that we now use the price of B in the denominator. The other difference is that ordinary price elasticity is normally positive, while cross-elasticity may be either positive or negative. A cut in B's price may increase or decrease the sales of A, depending on the relation between them.

If a cut in B's price raises A's sales, then A and B are *complementary products*—like cars and gasoline. If a cut in B's price reduces A's sales, then A and B are *substitute products*—like butter and margarine. If cross-elasticity is zero, the two goods are *independent* in consumption.

Interpreting the Demand Curve: Consumers' Surplus

Look closely at the demand curve in Figure 4. Starting at the top, we see that some people would be willing to pay a price close to OA in order to have a little of the product. Other people, or perhaps the same people, would be willing to pay a bit less than this for additional amounts. As we travel down the demand curve, and people's desire for the product is more thoroughly satisfied, the price they will pay for additional amounts of the good declines.

But what do they actually pay? Suppose the quantity of the good available is OQ. Running up to the demand curve, we see that all of this can be sold at a price OP. In a competitive market, then, price will be OP, and consumers will spend an amount $OPBQ$ on the product.

Do Consumers Get More than They Pay For?

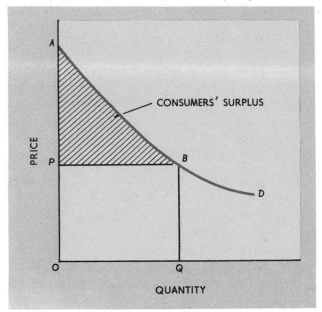

FIGURE 4. *AD is the demand curve for a consumer product. Its price is OP, and the quantity purchased is OQ. The total amount consumers pay is OP × OQ = OPBQ. But if necessary they would be willing to pay the larger amount OABQ. The difference between what they do pay and what they would pay, the shaded area PAB, is termed a "consumers' surplus."*

But does this measure the satisfaction they get from this good? Not at all. Consumers located near A would have been willing to pay a much higher price rather than go without the good. Almost all other consumers would have been willing to pay *something* more. Only for the people located near B is the satisfaction they are getting approximately equal to what they have to pay.

A monopolist with complete control of this product could sell a little of it at a price near OA. People whose demand for the good is high would pay this rather than go without. Then he could dole out a little more at a slightly lower price, to satisfy the next bit of demand. By moving down the demand curve in this way, arriving at B when his supply was used up, he could collect from consumers the whole area OABQ. So this area, the maximum they would hand over in return for OQ of the good, must indicate the satisfaction they get from consuming this amount.

But because they are not "held up" in this way, they pay only the amount OPBQ. The difference between what they actually pay and what they would be willing to pay is the shaded area PAB. Marshall labeled this "consumers' surplus," a bonus of satisfaction which consumers get from the product.

Consumers' surplus is not precisely measurable. The areas in Figure 4, including the "surplus" *PAB*, are dollar totals. But these dollars belong to thousands or millions of consumers, who differ in tastes and income level. We cannot say that a dollar to one man is the same as a dollar to another. So when we add them together, the result cannot be taken literally as measuring a certain amount of consumer satisfaction or enjoyment.

But the idea of consumers' surplus is still suggestive. Suppose a good that people are used to consuming were suddenly banned from the market. Someone might argue that consumers have suffered no loss. They are no longer getting any of the product; but they aren't spending any money on it either, so the two things cancel out. But this is not correct. When they were free to buy the good, they were getting some consumers' surplus from it, and this they have now lost.

Moreover, people would suffer a greater loss of satisfaction from the disappearance of some goods than from others. These goods, because of the location of their demand curves relative to their price, yield an unusually large amount of consumers' surplus. This accounts for our feeling that goods are not created free and equal, that some are more important than others. This intuitive feeling has a genuine basis in fact.

Special Cases of Demand

A few special demand situations are shown in Figure 5. D_1 shows completely inelastic demand, with the same quantity being sold regard-

Special Cases of Demand

FIGURE 5. D_3D_3 is a demand curve with unit elasticity throughout its length. Total revenue, which is $P \times Q$, is the same for all points on the curve. The other two curves illustrate extreme cases of zero elasticity and infinite elasticity.

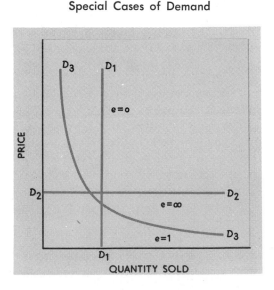

less of price. This obviously couldn't go on forever—price couldn't climb up into the sky without having some effect on sales. But one might find something close to zero elasticity over a certain range. Whether a small part for a Chevrolet costs $1.00, $1.50, or $2.00 is not going to have much effect on the number of parts sold.

D_2D_2 shows the opposite case of a demand curve which is infinitely elastic. The amount sold has no effect on price. The classic illustration is the demand for wheat from a particular farm. The farmer can sell 1,000 bushels, 5,000 bushels, or 10,000 bushels. The market price will be the same. But if this farmer expanded to the point of owning half the wheatland in the country, he could no longer sell as much as he chose without affecting the market price. Only a small seller in a large industry can safely assume that his demand curve is horizontal.

D_3D_3 shows a demand curve which has unit elasticity throughout. Whether the price is high or low, sales revenue will be the same, a change in price being just offset by an opposite change in quantity.

Derived Demand

Our illustrations to this point have involved articles bought by consumers. What about the multitude of products—raw materials, semifinished goods, machinery, building materials—which are bought by one business concern from another and never enter the retail market? Do such goods have demand curves? Of course they do. Since the demand for these things rests on, or is derived from, the demand for some final product to which they contribute, it is termed a *derived demand*. The demand for bricks is derived from the demand for buildings. The demand for steel is derived from the demand for finished goods using steel. The demand for a particular kind of labor is derived from the demand for the finished product of that labor.

The shape of a derived demand curve has the usual meaning. It's elasticity shows whether sales are very responsive to price changes or only slightly responsive. This depends mainly on three things:

1. *Elasticity of demand for the final product.* An increase in the price of materials or labor going into a finished good will raise its cost of production, and this will normally raise its price. If, as the price of the final product is raised its sales fall off rapidly, then sales of the materials used in making it will also fall off rapidly. Thus the more elastic the demand for the product, the more elastic will be the demands derived from it.

2. *The importance of the item in total cost.* Suppose a certain item constitutes $10 of the cost of a $100 product. The price of the material now rises 10 percent, so that the same quantity costs $11 instead of $10. To "cover" this cost increase, the price of the final product would have to be raised from $100 to $101, or by 1 percent. Suppose elasticity of demand for the final product is unity. Then its sales will fall 1 percent,

and sales of the material will also fall 1 percent. Note that, although demand for the final product has unit elasticity, demand for the material in question is very inelastic—a 10 percent price increase causes a drop of only 1 percent in sales. The reason is that the material is such a small part of total cost that an increase in its price has only a small impact on price and output of the final product. This is sometimes termed "the importance of being unimportant."

Suppose the material had cost $60 out of the $100 price of the product. Then, if we suppose the product demand curve has unit elasticity as before, a 10 percent increase in the price of the material may produce a 6 percent increase in the price of the product, and sales of both product and material will fall 6 percent. Demand for the materials is considerably more elastic than before. This leads to a second principle of derived demand: demand for an intermediate good or a factor of production will be more elastic the larger its share in the cost of the final product.

3. *The availability of substitutes.* We have been supposing that, when the price of a material or component is increased, producers of the final product will have to go on using it anyway. This may or may not be true. There will often be some possibility of substitution. As cotton becomes more expensive, rayon and other synthetics will be used instead. As the price of steel rises, it may be feasible for some purposes to substitute aluminum, copper, or other metals. As wage rates rise, employers will make greater use of automatic process which use less labor. The greater the possibilities of substitution, the more elastic will be the demand for the intermediate good in question.

Elasticity of a derived demand curve, in short, varies directly with elasticity of demand for the final product, with the percentage which the item forms of total production costs, and with the availability of substitutes in the production process.

SUPPLY AND EQUILIBRIUM PRICE

Demand is only one of two sets of forces influencing price. Buyers are only one side of the market. What about the sellers on the other side of the market? How is the price which exists in the market going to affect the amount they will be willing to produce and sell?

The Supply Schedule

This is a complicated question. The answer depends on the nature of the industry. It depends also on the period of time which we take into account. The amount which will be supplied at a particular price next year may be larger or smaller than the amount which will be supplied today. These and other factors influencing the shape of the *supply schedule* will be examined in Chapter 7.

The purpose here is simply to show how supply conditions interact with demand conditions to determine the market price and quantity sold. So for illustration let us select a situation, quite common in practice, in which larger quantities will be offered on the market at higher prices. This possibility is shown pictorially in Figure 6. SS is a *supply schedule* or *supply curve.* Each point on it shows the amount per year which sellers of the product will be willing to bring to market at the price in question. The fact that the curve slopes upward to the right says that producers will offer more goods at higher prices.

We must observe the same cautions about the supply curve which we noted earlier in the case of demand. Specifically:

1. The supply curve is *not* a historical curve linking prices and quantities sold in different time periods. It shows alternative possibilities

The Market Supply Schedule

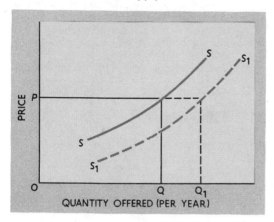

FIGURE 6. SS is a supply curve. Each point on the curve shows how much of the product sellers will offer at a specified price. S_1S_1 shows an increase in supply—more offered at each price than was true previously.

available *at a moment of time.* If price *were* at a certain level, *then* a certain quantity would be offered on the market. But only one of these possibilities will actually be realized at a particular time.

2. The supply curve for each good has a specific shape, depending on how easy or hard it is to expand production. The shape of the supply curve is of great importance to buyers. If the supply curve slopes up steeply, this means that an increased demand can be gratified only at substantially higher prices. Conversely, a gently sloped supply curve indicates that production can be expanded readily and that higher demand will not cause much increase in price.

3. The supply curve, like the demand curve, can be given a definite shape only if we suppose that certain other things remain constant. In the case of demand, we assumed that buyers' preferences, their incomes, and the prices of substitute products were known and constant. In the case of supply, the most important things which we hold constant are the methods of production and the supply conditions of the materials, labor,

and other things needed for production. If any of these things should change, the old supply curve vanishes and a new one appears.

4. A movement from one point to another on SS is *not* a change in supply. It is simply a change in the quantity offered in response to a change in price. A change in supply means *a shift of the entire curve to a new position,* such as S_1S_1 in Figure 6. Note that at any price sellers will now offer more goods than before. At the price OP they will now supply OQ_1 units instead of OQ. Thus a rightward shift of the supply curve indicates an *increase in supply.* This might happen because improved production methods have been developed, which make it possible to turn out the product at a lower cost and offer it at a lower price. In the converse case of a decrease in supply, SS would move upward to the left.

Demand, Supply, and Equilibrium Price

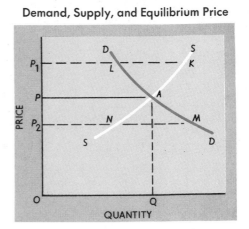

FIGURE 7. If demand and supply are in this position, the market price will be OP and the quantity exchanged will be OQ. Other prices, such as OP₁ and OP₂, will not be feasible. Explain why.

Market Equilibrium

We are now in a position to bring the demand and supply curves together on the same diagram, as is done in Figure 7. What is the point of this diagram and what does it tell us? The intersection of DD and SS defines a price (OP) and a quantity sold (OQ) which have a special significance. We call these the *equilibrium price and quantity* in the market. This means two things:

1. If the price OP somehow gets established, it will persist. It is in fact the only price which precisely "clears the market," the only price at which the amount consumers are willing to buy exactly equals the amount producers want to sell. This being so, there is no reason for the price to change until there is a shift in DD or SS.

2. If the market price starts out either above or below OP, forces will operate to move it toward OP. Suppose, for example, the market

"opens" on a particular morning at price OP_1. What will happen? At this price the amount sellers stand ready to offer (P_1K) is much larger than the amount buyers are willing to take (P_1L). As soon as this becomes apparent, some sellers will begin to offer the product at lower prices. Thus the market will begin to slide down the demand curve, with no logical stopping point until it reaches point A.

Suppose, on the other hand, that the market starts off at OP_2. At this low price, the amount buyers want (P_2M) is much larger than the amount producers are willing to supply (P_2N). Some of the eager buyers will now begin to bid up the price, preferring to pay a bit more rather than go unsatisfied. As this process goes on, the market travels up the demand curve, and there is no reason for it to stop short of A.

OP, in short, is the only price which is stable and will maintain itself so long as the underlying demand and supply conditions continue unchanged.

Does the demand-supply diagram *explain* price and output? Not in any ultimate sense. A full explanation requires that one know everything which lies behind the SS and DD curves. Behind the demand curve lies the whole array of consumer preferences. Behind the supply curve lie many things which we still have to examine—notably, costs of production. But these things affect price *through* their effect on the position of the demand and supply curves. Anything which affects the price of a product must do so either by altering the willingness of consumers to buy (*DD*) or the willingness of producers to bring various quantities to market (*SS*). The demand-supply apparatus thus gives us a basis for *classifying* the ultimate determinants of price and for reasoning about them in an orderly manner.

The reader will encounter the demand-supply diagram repeatedly in later chapters, in a wide variety of practical applications. It is important at this stage, therefore, to master the logic of the diagram so thoroughly that it becomes a habitual method of thought.

APPLICATIONS OF DEMAND AND SUPPLY: THE ECONOMICS OF PRICE FIXING

The reader may already have asked himself: Suppose the government just steps in and *fixes* a price? "The price of bananas will be so-and-so, on penalty of fine or imprisonment." What happens then to all our reasoning about supply and demand?

It is certainly possible for government to pull a price out of the air and enforce it by legal decree. This is the general rule in planned economies and happens quite often in other countries. This does not mean, however, that demand-supply analysis becomes irrelevant. On the contrary, it is essential to an understanding of *what will happen as a result of the fixed price*.

Price Supports and Farm Surpluses

Suppose the government guarantees farmers a minimum price for wheat, and that this is above the equilibrium price which would exist in a free market. This situation is illustrated by Figure 8. The equilibrium

A Price Support System for Wheat

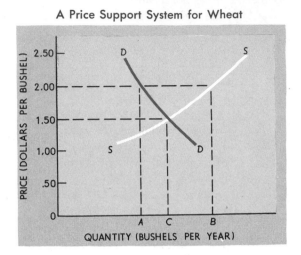

FIGURE 8. At a guaranteed price of $2 per bushel, the supply of wheat exceeds the quantity demanded. What might be done to equalize supply and demand?

price with this supply-demand situation would be $1.50 per bushel. At this price, OC bushels of wheat would be produced and sold, and the market would be cleared. Farmers maintain, however, that $1.50 per bushel is not a fair return for their efforts and persuade Congress to intervene. Congress decrees that the price shall be $2 per bushel, and enforces this by binding the government to buy wheat at this price.

What will happen? Farmers respond to the higher price by increasing wheat plantings and now turn out OB bushels per year. Consumer purchases, however, are reduced by the higher price and fall to OA. The difference between production and sales is AB. This "surplus wheat" piles up in the hands of government which, unless it can ship the excess abroad at bargain prices, must simply hold and store it. But this is only a short-range solution. Next year's crop will bring in more surplus wheat, and the government's stockpiles will eventually become unmanageable.

One possible avenue of escape is to take away from farmers the right to grow and sell as much wheat as they choose. Each wheat farmer might be required, for example, to reduce the number of acres sown to wheat by one third. But reduction of acreage may not be very effective. Farmers take their poorest land out of cultivation, and then pile more fertilizer, labor, and equipment onto the remaining acres. Thus they may end up growing about as much as before on the reduced acreage.

A more drastic approach is to set a marketing quota for each farmer, which permits him to sell only so many bushels per year at the controlled price. By careful calculation, it might be possible to make these quotas add up to just the amount *OA*. There would then be a *managed equilibrium* in the sense that consumers would be willing to buy at $2 all the wheat that farmers were legally permitted to sell. But the price to the consumer is still an inflated price.

The complexities of actual farm price support legislation are examined in Chapter 14. The point here is simply to demonstrate that one cannot decree a price and leave it at that. Certain consequences follow, which necessitate further controls. *Price* regulation usually leads quite quickly to *quantity* regulation as well.

Price Ceilings and Black Markets

The same conclusion is reached by examining a situation in which government sets a *price ceiling*, a maximum price which is *below* the market equilibrium. This was done on a large scale during World War II. The resulting situation is shown in Figure 9. The market equilibrium is

Price Ceilings and Black Markets

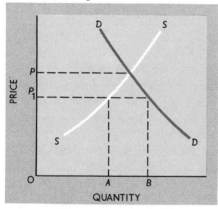

FIGURE 9. At a ceiling price of OP_1 the quantity demanded exceeds the available supply. What is likely to happen next?

OP, the legal ceiling OP_1. Instead of a "surplus" as in the wheat case, we now have a "shortage." At the ceiling price consumers would like to buy *OB* units of the product, but only *OA* units are available. The difference, *AB*, represents unsatisfied demand for the product.

Which lucky customers will get the limited quantity available? Unless some control system is installed, people may simply line up in front of the store. The early-comers at the head of the line will be served, while those at the end get nothing. Favoritism and bribery spring up. The storekeeper keeps a stock of the product "under the counter" for favored customers, or he insists on "tie-in sales." This means forcing the customer to take some slow-moving item which he doesn't want in order to get the scarce item he does want.

If the good is a necessity, and if one wants to achieve a fair distribution of the available supply, this can be done through *rationing*. Ration coupons can be issued to each family, entitling it to buy a specified quantity of the product. Storekeepers are forbidden to sell the product except to people holding ration coupons. If the system is well managed, the number of coupons issued should just add up to the supplies available (*OA*). Once more we have a managed equilibrium, in which price control is supported by quantity control.

Rationing was used on a large scale during World War II for gasoline, tires, fuel oil, meat, canned goods, dairy products, coffee, sugar, and other foods. Supplies of these things were well below what people would have liked to buy with their high wartime incomes. Rationing helped to distribute the scarce supplies in an equitable way. The system led, however, to difficult problems of evasion and enforcement. A buyer whose ration coupons had run out could often get supplies by offering more than the official ceiling price. This was illegal, but some sellers were willing to break the law for enough money. A new class of middlemen grew up who specialized in getting scarce goods from producer to consumer outside the rationing system and at premium prices. These deals were called *black market* transactions.

Pricing Consumer Goods in the U.S.S.R.

We saw in Chapter 3 that production of consumer goods in the U.S.S.R. is not geared very closely to consumer preferences. Yet consumer goods are distributed through retail outlets at a market price, and consumers have free choice of goods within the limits of their incomes. This seems contradictory. What is the explanation?

The matter may be cleared up by a diagram. Figure 10 shows the demand and supply curves for washing machines in the U.S.S.R. If this were a market economy, production would be carried to the intersection point of *DD* and *SS*. Output of washing machines would be *OG* and price would be *OF*.

But the Soviet authorities do not use this type of reasoning. Washing machines use metal and other scarce resources which might better, they conclude, be going into tractors and machine tools. So Gosplan decides to limit washing machine production for 1963 to *OA*. The authorities want to distribute this output through stores in the usual way and without the necessity of rationing. How to do it? Simple enough. Just add on to the production cost *AB* an excise tax (called in Russia a turnover tax) of *BC* and set the retail price at *AC* = *OP*. At this high price, consumers are willing to buy just the number of washing machines (*OA*) which the planners have decided to produce. A managed equilibrium once more!

But Soviet planners have to guess where *DD* is, just as capitalist

The Washing Machine Industry in the U.S.S.R.

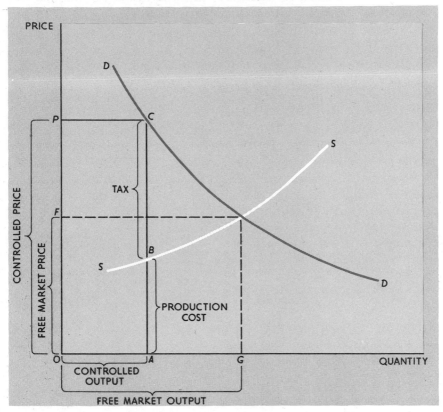

FIGURE 10. In a market economy, output would be OG and price OF. But central planners may decide to produce a smaller quantity, such as OA, and sell it at OP. The price includes a tax of BC in addition to production cost AB.

producers do, and they don't always succeed in setting prices which will exactly "clear the market." One hears of shortages of certain items and of people bribing storekeepers to let them know when a consignment of some scarce article is due to arrive. This means that the articles in question have been underpriced. Note that any price below OP in Figure 10 would create a "shortage" of washing machines.

Other articles, however, are sometimes overpriced. Around 1960 the authorities found that some expensive items—cameras, wristwatches, radio and television sets—were not moving off retail shelves as rapidly as they were being produced. One could conclude that the turnover tax on these articles was too high, leading to a price above the level corresponding to OP in Figure 10. A simple remedy would have been to cut the turnover tax and the retail price. The government did not want to do this, however, and gave as a reason that it would reduce the Treasury's tax collections. Instead, an effort was made to raise demand curves by introducing the capitalist device of installment credit.

The Union Scale for Coal Miners

Demand-supply analysis is applicable not only to product markets but also to markets for the factors of production. Consider the occupation of coal mining. Many things will influence a man's attitude toward this kind of work—the physical exertion required, danger, underground conditions, seasonal irregularity of employment. But included in these things is the rate of pay. The higher the wage, the more people will consider it worthwhile to work as coal miners.

As usual in analyzing one market, we suppose conditions in all other markets—in this case, wage rates for all other occupations—to remain unchanged. Then our conclusion is that the higher the wage for coal miners *relative to wages in other occupations,* the greater the supply of coal miners. So we can construct a supply schedule for coal miners, which will slope upward to the right in the usual way (Figure 11).

Demand-Supply Analysis Works Also in Studying Wages

FIGURE 11. *DD* and *SS* are demand and supply curves for coal miners. The equilibrium wage is *OW* and equilibrium employment *OE.* Suppose, instead, that employers and the union negotiate a wage of OW_1. This reduces the number of jobs from *OE* to OE_1, and also increases the number of people seeking work in the industry from *OE* to OE_2. We end up with "surplus labor" $E_1E_2 = AB$.

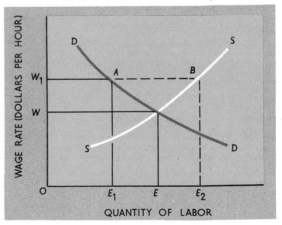

There is also a demand curve for coal miners. If the wage rate is increased, everything else remaining unchanged, what will happen? First, employers will have a stronger incentive to use machinery instead of labor wherever possible. They will use more mechanical coal-cutters, more loaders and conveyors, larger excavating machines for open strip mining—and fewer men. The price of coal will also tend to rise and, if the prices of oil, gas, and other competing fuels have remained unchanged, sales of coal will fall. This also means reduced employment. So for a single occupation we can say that the higher its relative wage rate, the smaller will be employment in the occupation.[7] The demand curve slopes downward to the right.

If the demand and supply curves at a particular time are as shown in Figure 11, the equilibrium wage for coal miners is OW. At this wage, employers will want to hire OE men. Exactly the same number will prefer working as miners to working at something else, and all will be employed.

But there is no reason why the actual wage need be OW. Suppose the United Mine Workers demands a higher wage, say OW_1, and employers agree rather than face a strike. At this wage, only OE_1 workers will be demanded; but supply is considerably larger, since OE_2 workers will now prefer to work as miners. The market is no longer in equilibrium. There is a "labor surplus" equal to the distance $E_1 E_2 = AB$.

What will happen to these surplus workers? Some of them may become discouraged and depart to seek work in other industries. But many are likely to hang around the mines hoping for occasional work or an eventual full-time job. This will mean continuing unemployment, often termed "wage distortion unemployment." Some workers, too, may undercut the union by offering to work for less than the union scale. This is one reason why, particularly in small-scale industries with many employers, a union may have difficulty in keeping the industry organized and may be unable to raise wages much above the market level.

This example may seem almost too close to reality, so a word of caution is in order. We are not asserting that the heavy unemployment in the Appalachian coalfields is due to the wage policies of the United Mine Workers. Some of it may be; but there are also other reasons for the decline in coal production and employment. How much wage policy has contributed is a difficult question requiring careful investigation.

On Repealing the Law of Supply and Demand

The remarkable success of demand-supply analysis has led to some misunderstandings. For example, it is often asserted that "You can't repeal the law of supply and demand." The element of truth in this is that *demand and supply schedules* are definite, objective things. They depend on personal preferences and production possibilities. They change only slowly, and can certainly not be changed by waving a wand.

Moreover, while it is often possible to decree a price higher or lower than the market equilibrium, this price may be hard to enforce. It

---

[7] Remember that this conclusion can definitely *not* be extended to the labor force as a whole. If *all* wages are raised simultaneously, it does not follow that total employment will be reduced. What will happen is a problem in macroeconomics, to be considered in Part Three.

usually injures some actual or potential buyers and sellers in the market, who will consequently try to evade it. And even if enforced, it may create difficulties which compel still more regulation. Controlling a market is a little like squeezing a balloon—it puffs out in one direction just when you think you have it under control in another.

Where competitive markets are feasible, then, there is a presumption that it is best to let them regulate prices and quantities exchanged, and that intervention to alter market results will have mischievous consequences.

SUMMARY

1. As one consumes additional units of any product (per period of time), the satisfaction yielded by the last unit decreases. This is known as the *principle of diminishing marginal utility*. It explains why a consumer will normally buy more of any product only at a lower price.

2. Since total demand is the sum of individual demands, it behaves in the same way. A reduction in price leads to an increase in quantity sold. The *demand curve* slopes downward to the right.

3. Movement from one point to another on the same demand curve is *not* a change in demand. A change in demand means that the whole curve has shifted to a new position.

4. *Elasticity of demand* is $-\dfrac{\% \text{ change in } Q}{\% \text{ change in } P}$. It is measured at a point or over a small distance on the demand curve. The same demand curve will have different elasticities at different points.

5. Where $e > 1$, demand is elastic; where $e = 1$, demand has *unit elasticity*; where $e < 1$, demand is *inelastic*.

6. *Total revenue* (TR) is price $\times$ quantity sold. *Marginal revenue* (MR) is the additional revenue per unit of sales resulting from a small change in price.

7. If demand is inelastic, total revenue moves in the same direction as price. As price falls, TR falls and MR is negative. If demand is elastic, total revenue moves in the opposite direction from price. As price falls, TR rises and MR is positive. In the borderline case of $e = 1$, TR is constant and MR is zero.

8. *Income elasticity of demand* is defined as $\dfrac{\% \text{ change in quantity sold}}{\% \text{ change in income}}$.

9. *Cross-elasticity of demand* is defined as $\dfrac{\% \text{ change in quantity of A}}{\% \text{ change in price of B}}$. The sign of this coefficient indicates whether products A and B are *complementary* in consumption, *substitutes* in consumption, or *independent* in consumption.

10. Demand for raw materials, semifinished products, and factors

of production is *derived* from the demand for the finished product. The elasticity of a derived demand curve increases with the elasticity of demand for the final product, with the percentage which the item forms of production costs, and with the availability of substitutes in the production process.

11. The *supply curve* shows the quantities which sellers of a product will offer at various market prices. It will normally slope upward to the right.

12. The intersection of the supply and demand curves defines an *equilibrium price and quantity exchanged.* If a different price is established initially in the market, it will tend to move toward the equilibrium price; and once there, the price will be stable so long as the underlying demand and supply conditions continue unchanged.

13. It is possible to fix prices by law above or below the market equilibrium. But awkward consequences may follow. If farmers are guaranteed a support price *above the equilibrium level,* there will be excess supply, and government will have to buy the surplus output. If it does not want to accumulate these surpluses, it must regulate farm production. If government sets a price ceiling *below the equilibrium level,* the result will be excess demand leading to rationing of the product.

14. Soviet planners try to price each consumer good at a level such that consumers will buy just the quantity which the planners have decided to produce. They try to hit the demand curve; but they do not take the demand curve as a guide in deciding how much to produce.

DISCUSSION QUESTIONS

1. Is the principle of diminishing marginal utility always valid? Can you think of exceptions to it?

2. "The principle of demand states that if the price of a product falls, more of it can be sold. But if diamonds fell substantially in price, people would buy less rather than more. So there must be something wrong with the principle." Comment.

3. Suppose we find that the price of new cars is higher this year than last year, but sales are also higher. Does this disprove the principle of demand? What has probably happened?

4. One sometimes sees statements such as "the demand for men's shirts is elastic." What is wrong with such a statement?

5. You are a producer with complete control of the supply of some product. You are trying to decide whether a 10 percent reduction in price will raise or lower your profits. What information would you need to reach a decision?

6. You are an investor trying to estimate which industries in the American economy are likely to show the largest increases in output over the next 20 years. Are there any concepts in this chapter which would help you?

7. Labor has a demand, like everything else, and this is a *derived* demand. Using the principles of derived demand explained in the text, list (*a*) several types of labor which you would expect to have a highly inelastic demand; (*b*) several types of labor for which you would expect demand to be more elastic.

8. You are a union president, and you have a good estimate of the elasticity of demand for labor in your trade or industry. Would you be able to make practical use of this information? How, and why?

9. Is it reasonable to draw the supply schedule as sloping upward to the right
   a) In the case of goods?
   b) In the case of labor?
   Explain why in each case.

10. In what sense does the demand-supply diagram explain (or fail to explain) why the price and quantity exchanged are what they are?

11. Is it always true that if the price in a market starts out above or below the equilibrium level, it will move toward that level? Can you construct a situation in which this will not be true?

12. "Apparent surpluses or shortages are always fictitious. They indicate simply that price has been set above or below the equilibrium level for the market in question." Discuss.

13. Would it help a Soviet planner to know the demand schedules for each consumer good in the economy? Why?

APPENDIX: TIME, SPECULATION, AND MARKET STABILITY

We defined the equilibrium price in a market as the price which, if established, would remain unchanged so long as DD and SS remained unchanged. But then we made a second statement which looks similar but is quite different: that if a price other than the equilibrium price gets established in the first instance, the market will operate to move the actual price toward the equilibrium price. This is not always true in actuality, and we must explain why.

The Cobweb Theorem

One complicating factor is that supply adjustments often require considerable *time*. Producers look at the prevailing price, revise their production plans, and 6 months or a year later, the new supply becomes effective. Consider a market in which DD and SS remain unchanged, but supply adjustments always take 6 months. Buyers' adjustments to a new price, on the other hand, are assumed to be instantaneous.

Look first at Figure 12 (*a*). When our story opens, the market is at position 1, with a price of OP_1 which is above the equilibrium level OP. Producers, therefore, plan for the level of output corresponding to a price of OP_1, which is shown by point 2 on SS. Six months later, this larger supply appears on the market. But this supply can be sold only at a lower price, and the market moves to position 3. This low price discourages production, and producers now plan for the lower output at point 4. Six months later, output is cut to this level. But this drop in supply drives price up again to point 5, and so on.

But note that with each move around the "cobweb," the market is coming closer to the equilibrium price and output. After two complete circuits, it is very close indeed. The movement of the price level itself is shown in Figure 12 (b). Price is fluctuating, but the size of the

A Converging Cobweb

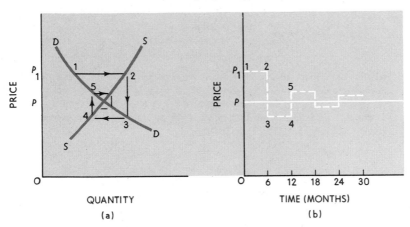

QUANTITY

(a)

TIME (MONTHS)

(b)

FIGURE 12.   OP is the equilibrium price in this market. But the market starts off at a higher price (point 1). When producers have adjusted supply to this price, which we suppose takes 6 months, we move to point 2; price falls immediately to 3; and so on. The arrows trace the course of the market as it moves closer and closer to the equilibrium position. In (b) we show the movement of price alone, with time on the horizontal axis. Fluctuations become smaller over time, and price comes closer and closer to OP.

fluctuations is diminishing, and we come ever closer to the equilibrium level OP.

Look now at Figure 13 (a). Here our cobweb seems to have run away. On each round we get farther and farther away from equilibrium. The price fluctuations in Figure 13 (b) get larger and larger. (It is obviously possible to set up a borderline case between Figures 12 and 13, in which we orbit around the diagram in exactly the same path, never getting any closer to equilibrium or any farther away.)

If you look closely at Figures 12 and 13, you will see that the difference between them comes down to the *relative slopes of DD and SS*. In the stable case, Figure 12, we drew SS *steeper* than DD in the neighborhood of equilibrium. In the unstable case, Figure 13, SS is *flatter*

An Explosive Cobweb

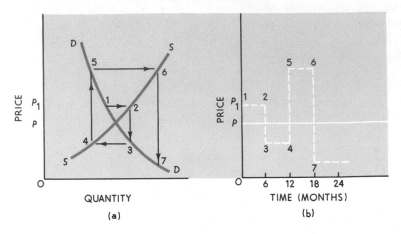

QUANTITY

(a)

TIME (MONTHS)

(b)

FIGURE 13. This is the same kind of diagram as Figure 12. But here the cobweb explodes outward instead of converging inward. Price moves farther and farther away from equilibrium. What is there in the shapes of the DD and SS curves in Figures 12 and 13 which produces this difference in the result?

than DD. If we drew them with exactly the same slope, we should get the borderline case of a "constant orbit" cobweb.

Now in practice we hardly ever get the explosive fluctuations shown in Figure 13. This must mean that DD and SS usually have the "right" relative slopes. But why should this be? The main reason is probably that producers are not too badly taken in by price fluctuations. They have a good idea of what the equilibrium or "normal" price should be. If the actual price is much above that level, they will expect it to fall. So they will not expand output as much as if they innocently expected the high price to persist forever. Similarly, they will expect a low price to be temporary and will not contract output very much. But this amounts to saying that over short periods SS *is usually quite steep,* so that the stability condition is satisfied. *Stability of expectations* contributes to *stability of markets.*

The Function of Speculation

"Speculator" is traditionally a term of ill repute. It suggests a greedy fellow "cornering the market" in a commodity, then reselling it at a large profit. But speculation can actually serve a useful purpose.

The best illustrations come from staple farm products. Suppose a normal year's output of a certain crop is OQ, which with demand at DD would mean a price of OP (Figure 14). But this year the weather is unusually good, and there is a bumper crop of OQ_1. If the whole crop

How Speculation Can Stabilize Price and Consumption

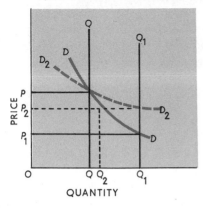

FIGURE 14. OQ is the "normal" annual crop of this farm product. *DD* is the demand of users of the product. So OP is the normal equilibrium price. But this year there is a bumper crop OQ_1 which, if sold to users, would drive price down to OP_1. Speculators, however, are willing to buy at anything below the normal price. By adding their demand to users' demand, we obtain the *total* demand curve D_2D_2. So price will be OP_2, sales to users OQ_2, and additions to speculators holdings Q_2Q_1.

had to be sold immediately, this could only be done at a price of OP_1, about half the normal level.

The product is storable, however, and it is traded on an organized commodity exchange. The traders on the exchange include some people who are neither suppliers nor users but pure traders or speculators. These people reason that if price is unusually low this year, it will be higher next year; so it will pay to buy the commodity now and hold it for resale later. Remember that *DD* shows only the demand by *users* of the product. When we add the demand of speculators, we get a new *total* demand curve D_2D_2. Note that speculators' demand—the horizontal distance between *DD* and D_2D_2—becomes ever larger *the farther actual price falls below the normal or expected future price.* Similarly, at any price *above OP,* speculators expect the future price to be lower, and they will be *selling* in the market rather than buying. So above *OP,* total demand is *less* than users demand, and D_2D_2 lies to the left of *DD.*

With a crop of OQ_1, then, price will be determined by the intersection of Q_1Q_1 and D_2D_2, and so will settle at OP_2 instead of OP_1. This is considerably closer to the normal level. Moreover, instead of the whole crop being sold to users at once, only OQ_2 is sold to users and the remainder, Q_2Q_1, is stored by the speculators for later sale.

The reader can work out for himself the opposite case of an unusually poor crop, with a consequent threat of skyrocketing prices. With present price above the expected future price, speculators will be *selling* rather than buying. This will hold down the rise of prices and also increase the supplies available for immediate use.

In this case, then, speculation serves two useful purposes: *it reduces the fluctuation of price around its normal level;* and *it evens out the rate of consumption* by diverting supplies from bumper years to poor years. If the speculators have guessed the future correctly, they will be rewarded by a profit. But if there are many speculators on the market, all equally expert, the profit will be small—just enough to keep them interested in continuing the game. What makes the game really interesting is that they are not all equally expert, nor do they all view the future the same way at the same time. So the unusually shrewd and experienced can make a substantial profit, not so much at the expense of the public as at the expense of their fellow speculators who guessed wrong.

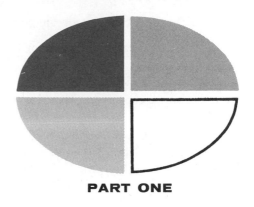

PART ONE

THE ECONOMICS OF

PRICES AND MARKETS

If you're going to write, don't pretend to write down. It's going to be the best you can do, and it's the fact that it's the best you can do that kills you.

DOROTHY PARKER

Not that the story need be long, but it will take a long time to make it short.

HENRY THOREAU

THE PROBLEM of what determines the value of a good—that is, its price relative to other goods—was already puzzling economists in the seventeenth and eighteenth centuries. One common idea was that value had something to do with cost of production. In the 1820's, the British economist David Ricardo developed the theory that goods will exchange in proportion to the labor used in their production, taking account of skill or quality of labor (1 hour of carpenters' labor, say, equaling 3 hours of ditchdiggers' labor), and taking account of the indirect labor embodied in the capital goods required to make the product. Crusoe's net-weaving labor, as well as his fish-catching labor, is part of the cost of producing fish. Ricardo's theory is sometimes called a *labor theory* of value; but it is more correctly termed a *cost-of-production* theory.

Ricardo's theory held sway for a half century. But it did not take account of the fact that, to have value, a good must be useful as well as costly. Spending a great deal of labor on an article cannot make it valuable unless consumers are willing to buy it. And an emerald picked up from a stream bed is very valuable, even though little labor is needed to bring it to market. In the 1870's and 1880's, several economists developed the proposition that value depends heavily on the *utility* of an article to prospective buyers.

But utility alone is also a one-sided explanation. Cost cannot be ignored. In the 1890's, Alfred Marshall developed a synthesis of the two ideas. Value, he said, depends equally on utility, which is the basis of consumer demand, and on cost of production, which underlies supply. It is as useless to ask whether supply or demand predominates as to ask which blade of a scissors does the cutting.

This approach proved so useful in analyzing product markets that it was quickly extended to markets for the factors of production. Marshall, John Bates Clark of Columbia, Irving Fisher of Yale, and others developed demand-supply theories of wage rates and interest rates. Demand and supply became the central tools of what we now call microeconomics—the analysis of prices and quantities exchanged in specific markets. ("Micro" because we are looking at small areas of the economy in detail, under a microscope, as it were.)

The main outlines of demand-supply analysis have already been presented in Chapter 5; but now we want to explore the subject more thoroughly. Following John Gunther, we might call the next two chapters "Inside Demand and Supply." Demand comes basically from consumers, so in Chapter 6 we ask how households go about making the standard Crusoe decisions: how much of each good to buy in the market, how much and what kind of work to do, how much to save for the future. In Chapter 7 we go behind supply to look at the operations of producing units. We examine the main kinds of production cost and the way in which costs behave as the amount of production is increased or decreased. In the course of this, we get a precise definition of what it means to produce at lowest possible cost, which is an important aspect of economic efficiency.

Having examined the foundations of demand and supply, we put the two parts of the picture together to explain price and output determination in product markets. We draw a major distinction between markets in which there are many sellers (Chapter 8) and markets in which there are one or a few sellers (Chapter 9). Where there are many producers of a product, they will not be able to get together to control price and output; and, since each producer is relatively small, it will not be hard for additional producers to enter the industry. Price cannot long remain above costs of production, including a "normal" profit; for this will lead new producers to set up, and the increased output will drive down the price until it just covers costs.

Where there are only a few producers, on the other hand, they may get together on prices; and where there is a single monopolist, he need consult no one but himself. In both cases, price may be held above cost, and profits may be abnormally large. The high price means that less of the output is produced and sold than consumers would prefer.

What about markets for the factors of production? Demand for these factors comes from producing units. The amount which a producer will pay for one more unit of a factor, say a man-hour of labor, depends on how much that unit adds to his output. This is called the *marginal productivity* of the factor; and our first job in Chapter 10 is to define and explain this idea. We then go on to discuss the most important kind of factor market, the labor market. The demand for a particular kind of labor, which depends on its marginal productivity, combines with the supply of that kind of labor, which depends on workers' choices among occupations, to establish a market wage for the job. If people are completely free to choose among jobs, the wage rates for all jobs in the economy must form a consistent system such that no one has any incentive to shift from what he is doing. We also consider the possibility that the wage may be set above the competitive level because of union pressure or government regulation and explore the possible consequences.

Chapter 11 discusses the returns to other productive resources, particularly interest and profit. There is considerable difference of opinion among economists as to the nature and necessity of profit, and the main explanations will be examined.

After completing this grand tour of the market economy, one is bound to ask oneself: what does it matter? How efficiently does a market economy perform? What does it matter whether an economy is coordinated through markets, through central planning, or some mixture of the two? This forces us to set up a yardstick of efficiency. Crudely, an economy is efficient if it produces the maximum output of goods and services from a given quantity of resources and if the assortment of goods produced corresponds to the wishes of the population. In Chapter 12 we first spell out this statement more precisely. We then apply the efficiency yardstick to the American economy, on one hand, and to the Soviet economy, on the other. This is an interesting exercise in itself; and it also provides an excellent general review of microeconomics.

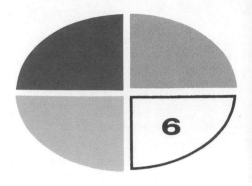

Household Economics

and Demand

> Economy is going without something you
> do want in case you should, someday, want some-
> thing you probably won't want.
>
> ANTHONY HOPE

THE HOUSEHOLD is a basic unit in the economy. Its spending decisions determine the demand for consumer goods, and indirectly, for raw materials and factors of production. Its decisions about saving influence the rate of capital formation. Its decisions about who in the family shall work, and how much work each shall do, determine the supply of labor.

These decisions are interrelated. Decisions about how much work to do, which means how much income to earn, are related to the satisfaction derived from spending this income on consumption. Saving decisions involve balancing the satisfaction from consuming right now against that of having higher consumption later on.

From an economic standpoint, the household is a satisfaction-producing organization, just as a business unit is a goods-producing organization. Its problem is to get greatest satisfaction with least effort or discomfort. More precisely, the problem is to maximize *net* satisfaction after deducting the effort required to earn it. This implies that satisfaction from consumption is commensurable with the disutility of effort and that the two can be balanced against each other. This is what we assumed about Crusoe in Chapter 3. It is what we mean by treating the household as an economic *unit* rather than as a bundle of unrelated activities.

This chapter will explain briefly how a rational householder would go about solving the problem of maximizing net satisfaction. The discussion also has an important bearing on the issue of overall economic efficiency. A market economy is usually said to be "consumer-guided," that is, responsive to household preferences and decisions. For this to be an advantage, we must suppose that household decisions make sense, that people are actually able to do the best for themselves. What does it mean to do the best for yourself? We must pin down this notion more precisely.

DECISIONS ABOUT SPENDING

How would a rational consumer go about getting the most for his money? What *is* a rational consumer? In analyzing consumer behavior, economists usually assume that:

i. Consumers "know what they want." They have definite goals—freedom from hunger, shelter against the elements, security for the future, protection against domestic thieves and foreign foes, prestige in the community, rest and recreation. They also know how much they value one goal as against another.

ii. They know the effectiveness of various goods and services in attaining these goals—how much a new dress will contribute to prestige or how much a sirloin steak will reduce hunger.

iii. They know the price at which each good can be obtained in the market.

iv. Each consumer uses this information in such a way as to maximize his total satisfaction. This "does not imply (as almost all of its critics state) that the individual seeks to maximize money or wealth, that the human soul is a complex cash register. It does not affect the formal theory of demand in the least whether the individual maximizes wealth, religious piety, the annihilation of crooners or his waistline."[1]

These assumptions have been subjected to heavy criticism. It has been argued that people do not have definite goals, that they are interested mainly in developing new wants rather than in gratifying old ones; that consumers are poorly informed, led around by the nose by advertisers, and don't know what they are buying; and that we are creatures of custom and routine, buying usually on the basis of habit rather than rational choice.

The truth doubtless lies somewhere between the economist's picture

---

[1] George J. Stigler, *The Theory of Price* (New York: Macmillan Co., 1947), p. 64.

of rational man and the critics' picture of ignorant, habit-ridden man. Much purchasing is done on the basis of habit, and up to a point this is efficient. Conscious decisions take effort. It would be a nuisance to recalculate our whole life scheme every time we go to the store, to display what Professor J. M. Clark of Columbia has termed an "irrational passion for dispassionate rationality." It is also true, however, that habits respond to *marked* changes in the prices and availability of goods, provided one allows time for the word to get round. Consumers are better buyers of some things than of others. On items which are bought very frequently, people are bound in time to acquire some expertise. Ignorance is greater as regards unique purchases, where one cannot learn from repeated experience.

There is a further practical justification for our three assumptions: they enable us to say something definite about consumer behavior. Without them we could only say "people may do anything," which would not be much help. Moreover, hypotheses based on these assumptions bear a distinct resemblance to what we see people doing in the real world. They provide insight into, though not a full explanation of, actual consumer behavior.

Diminishing Marginal Utility

What shall we call the satisfaction which people get from consumption? Nineteenth-century economists labeled it *utility* and laid down an important principle about it. They reasoned that the more of a good I am already consuming, the less will an additional unit of it add to my satisfaction. They considered this a self-evident principle, which anyone can confirm by looking inside himself, and called it the law of *diminishing marginal* (= additional) *utility.*

Suppose Mr. A, a confirmed coffee drinker, could have only one pound of coffee a month. This would yield a large amount of utility. It would give him that first morning cup which makes it possible to face the day's work.

But perhaps instead of one pound a month he can have two. Now he can have a second cup of coffee at breakfast or perhaps a cup in mid-morning. This will yield additional utility, though not as much as that yielded by the first pound. A third pound per month will mean that he can drink coffee at lunch or in the evening. This will add to his satisfaction, but by less than the second pound did. And so on. Eventually, when he has enough coffee to drink all he can hold, an additional pound will yield no utility at all.

This can be made more concrete by setting up a *utility schedule* for Mr. A (Table 1). Column 3 of the table shows how much additional satisfaction (marginal utility) Mr. A gets from each additional pound of coffee per month. The qualification *per month* is important. Consumption must always be shown as a *quantity per unit of time.* Otherwise we get

TABLE 1

Mr. A's Utility Schedule for Coffee

POUNDS PER MONTH (1)	TOTAL UTILITY (2)	MARGINAL UTILITY (3)
0	0	
		7
1	7	
		6
2	13	
		5
3	18	
		4
4	22	
		3
5	25	
		2
6	27	
		1
7	28	
		0
8	28	

into the absurdity of saying that 52 pounds of coffee (per year) can have as high a marginal utility as 1 pound of coffee (per week). Note that the entries in column 3 decline as we go down the column, in accordance with the principle of diminishing marginal utility. In this example, Mr. A would never wish to drink more than 7 pounds a month, since the eighth pound has a marginal utility of zero.

The second column shows Mr. A's *total utility* from consuming various amounts of coffee. Note that each entry in this column is obtained by adding up the entries in column 3 down to the level in question. Thus if Mr. A is consuming 4 pounds per month, his total utility is the sum of the marginal utilities of the first, second, third, and fourth pounds, i.e., $7 + 6 + 5 + 4 = 22$. As consumption increases, total utility rises as long as marginal utility remains positive. But when marginal utility falls to zero with the eighth pound, total utility ceases to rise.

Could marginal utility ever become negative? Yes, it could if one had so much of a product that part had to be thrown away and if this took trouble or expense. Tomatoes normally have a positive marginal utility; but a surplus of overripe tomatoes in my garden could be a nuisance.

The information in the table is shown graphically in Figure 1. The height of each rectangle shows the marginal utility yielded by an additional pound of coffee. The rectangles decline steadily in height,

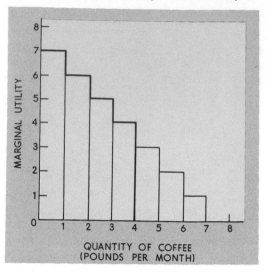

Diminishing Marginal Utility from Consumption

FIGURE 1. Each rectangle shows the amount of marginal (= additional) utility yielded by an additional pound of coffee per month. Note that each additional pound has lower marginal utility than the one before.

eventually reaching zero. The sum of the rectangular areas out to any point on the horizontal axis shows the total utility derived from consumption at that level. For example, if 4 pounds a month are being consumed, total utility is the area within the heavy black lines in the figure.

The staircase appearance of Figure 1 comes from the fact that we are dealing with whole pounds of coffee. Suppose we could buy coffee in very small amounts—ounces or half ounces—so that consumption could be varied by tiny steps. Then the rectangles in Figure 1 would become very thin. If they became thin enough, we should end up with a continuous line such as MU_c (marginal utility of coffee) in Figure 2. We shall normally use such lines from here on. They need not be straight lines, of course, but may show varying degrees of curvature. The only requirement is that they must slope downward from left to right.

The *height* of MU_c at any point shows the *marginal utility* of the last small unit of the product which has been added to consumption. The *area under* MU_c out to any point on the horizontal axis shows the *total utility* yielded by that rate of consumption. For example, at a consumption level of 4 pounds per month, total utility is the shaded area $OABC$.

Even with these simple ideas about utility, we can begin to draw some interesting conclusions. It is often said that the "economy of abundance" is either here or just around the corner. Professor Kenneth Galbraith of Harvard has argued that Americans now live in an "affluent society." What do such statements mean? Taken literally, "abundance" would mean that for every consumer and for all products, marginal utility has fallen to zero. This is clearly untrue. So being a bit more

Marginal and Total Utility

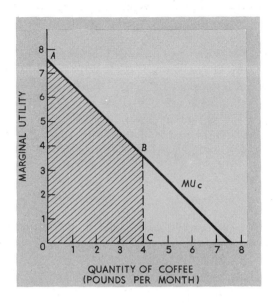

QUANTITY OF COFFEE
(POUNDS PER MONTH)

FIGURE 2. If consumption can be varied by very small amounts, the rectangles of Figure 1 become very thin and can conveniently be smoothed to a continuous line such as MU_c (marginal utility of coffee). The height of this line at any point shows the marginal utility of the last small unit of the product which has been added to consumption. The area under MU_c out to any point shows the total utility yielded by that rate of consumption. For example, at a consumption level of 4 pounds per month, marginal utility is BC and total utility is equal to the shaded area OABC.

charitable, what these writers must mean is that, for most people and products, marginal utility has reached a *low* level—low enough that total utility is high and people's wants are well satisfied. Is this actually true? Let each reader give his own answer.

Consider next the famous diamonds-water paradox, which puzzled the classical economists. Water is obviously more useful and necessary to life than diamonds. Yet diamonds command a much higher price. How can this be? Ingenious and even tortured reasoning was developed to explain the paradox. Today, we can give a simple explanation based on the distinction between marginal utility and total utility.

The total utility yielded by water is very great—indeed, the utility of the water needed to sustain life might be regarded as infinite. Since water is relatively abundant, however, the marginal utility of the last gallons used is low. Diamonds, on the other hand, are rare relative to the desire for them, so their marginal utility is high. The satisfaction yielded by the last unit of a good, and hence the price people can be induced to pay for it, is measured by marginal rather than total utility. This is why diamonds cost more than water.

Allocating the Consumer's Budget

It is all very well to set up a marginal utility schedule for one good. But the typical household has to distribute its spending over hundreds of different goods and services. How can it do this in a way which will yield greatest satisfaction? This is not an academic question. Every household faces it every day and answers it more or less effectively.

Once we begin talking in terms of money, we need a different version of the marginal utility curve. From now on, the horizontal axis of our diagrams will show, not *physical units* of a good, but *amounts of money* spent on the good. For clarity, it will be best to call this a *marginal utility of expenditure* (*MUE*) curve. In order to draw it we need to know both my liking for coffee, as expressed in the *MU* schedule, and the price of coffee. For example, suppose that my third pound of coffee per month yields 10 "utils" of satisfaction. The price of coffee is 50 cents per pound. Then the *MUE* at this point is $10/50 = 0.2$ utils per penny. By a similar calculation we might find that the *MUE* of money spent on a sixth pound is only 0.1 utils per penny. If we designate the price of coffee as P, then

$$MUE = MU \cdot \frac{1}{P}.$$

If P is constant, then *MUE* must fall continuously from left to right, because *MU* falls steadily as larger quantities are purchased.

Look now at a simple case in which a family buys only two goods, product A and product B, distributing its total budget of $5,000 a year between them. The "money" *MUE* curves for these goods are shown in Figure 3. Lay a string horizontally across the diagram, which we may call *II* (for income). Move the string up or down until you get a combination of expenditures, $OA + OB$, which just uses up the family's income. Note that $OA + OB = \$3,000 + \$2,000 = \$5,000$. (This can be done by experiment. If expenditure is below income on the first try, so that there is

How to Get the Most for Your Money

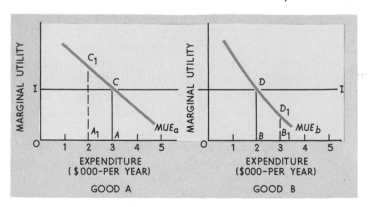

FIGURE 3. The problem is how to distribute my annual budget of $5,000 a year between goods A and B. Rule: the marginal utility of expenditure on A must equal the marginal utility of expenditure on B. So I should spend AO = $3,000 on A, and OB = $2,000 on B, because AC = BD. Why would OA_1 and OB_1 not be a correct combination of purchases?

money left over, lower II so that the family buys more of both goods; conversely if expenditure is too high. After all, this is what an actual family would do!)

Why is the combination $OA + OB$ the best that the family can do? First, it is using its total income, so it cannot get more of one good without giving up some of the other. Second, *the last dollar spent on product A yields precisely the same utility as the last dollar spent on product B.* When the family is spending $3,000 on good A, the utility of the last dollar is AC. Similarly, the utility of the last dollar spent on B is BD. But AC and BD are equal, because II was drawn horizontally across both diagrams.

Suppose, instead, that the family had chosen to spend only $OA_1 = $2,000$ on A, and $OB_1 = $3,000$ on B. Then the last dollar spent on A would have a utility of A_1C_1, while the last dollar spent on B yields utility of B_1D_1. A_1C_1 is obviously larger. It follows that if the family shifted a little money from B to A, it would be gaining more than it would lose. Total satisfaction would be increased. If it shifted, say, $100 in the first instance, it would move a short distance down MUE_a and a short distance up MUE_b. But the marginal utility of expenditure on A would still be higher, so it would pay to shift another $100; and so on, until one reached the points C and D, where marginal utility is equal and no further gain is possible.

Now imagine hundreds of additional MUE curves for other products, extending out to the right of Figure 3, with II running across all of them. Then if the family spends on each good the amount indicated by the intersection of II with the MUE curve, it will be getting the same utility from the last dollar spent on each product. Since it cannot gain by shifting money from one good to another, this spending pattern yields maximum satisfaction.

The rule for rational budget allocation, then, is that *the marginal utility of expenditure on each good purchased must be equal.* If there are n commodities in the consumer's budget, the condition for maximum satisfation is that:

$$MUE_1 = MUE_2 = MUE_3 = \cdots = MUE_n.$$

We saw earlier that, for any good,

$$MUE = MU \cdot \frac{1}{P} = \frac{MU}{P}.$$

So the rule for maximum satisfaction can be written also as:

$$\frac{MU_1}{P_1} = \frac{MU_2}{P_2} = \frac{MU_3}{P_3} = \cdots = \frac{MU_n}{P_n}.$$

The marginal utility yielded by a unit of each good must be proportionate to its price.

We noted in Chapter 5 that a family's purchases of a good will be influenced by its tastes, by the price of the good, and by the prices of related goods. It is now clear that purchases also depend heavily on income. The effect of income is illustrated in Figure 4. For simplicity

My Spending Pattern Will Vary with My Income

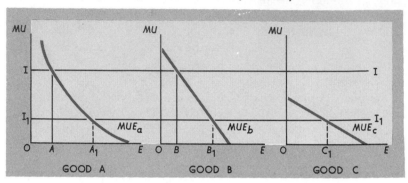

FIGURE 4. If I have a small income, corresponding to the income line *II*, I can buy only OA + OB and cannot afford good C at all. With a larger income corresponding to I_1I_1, I can buy $OA_1 + OB_1 + OC_1$.

show only 3 goods instead of 300. We ignore saving for the time being, and suppose that all income is spent on consumption. If the family's income is small, its consumption pattern might be defined by *II*. It buys small amounts of A and B, but "cannot afford" any of C, i.e., the MUE_c schedule falls entirely below the income line. (When you say you cannot afford something, you mean really that its marginal utility per dollar to you is not as high as that of the things you do buy. You can always afford the things that matter *enough*.) As usual, $OA + OB$ equals the family's income.

Suppose now the family's income were much larger. Then its consumption pattern might be defined by I_1I_1. It buys a good deal more of A and B, and also buys some C which it did not buy before.

While the effect of an increase in income is to add new goods to the family's budget and to increase its purchases of most things it was already consuming, this may not be true of *every* good. Family budget studies show that a higher income usually means *smaller* purchases of such things as margarine, potatoes, beans, and cheap lines of mass-produced clothing. These things are called *inferior goods*—not a term of reproach but simply an indication that use of these goods is negatively related to income.

DECISIONS ABOUT SAVING

So far we have assumed that this year's income is all spent on this year's consumption. This is true of many families with low incomes. But at higher income levels many families decide to save part of this year's income for use in later years. What considerations influence this kind of decision?

Only a few misers put their savings under the mattress. Income saved is usually put into forms which are expected to return a larger income in the future. If you put money in a savings account, you receive interest each year and can get back the amount you put in whenever you choose. If you buy an 8-year government savings bond for $18.75, you will get back, say, $25 when the bond matures. If you buy a common stock, you will usually get cash dividends and can turn the stock back into cash whenever you wish.

In all these cases the saver is really *buying future income*. He is trading $1 of spending today for the possibility of spending something more than $1 sometime in the future. This future income can be regarded as a good with its own utility schedule. We can chart it and add it to all the other *MUE* curves which the consumer uses in reaching his budget decisions.

Look at the household illustrated in Figure 5. The left-hand chart

Balancing Consumption and Saving

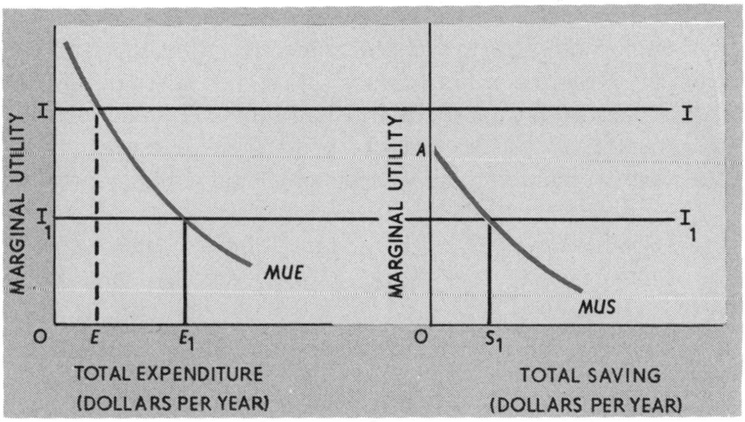

FIGURE 5.   On the left-hand side, *MUE* shows the marginal utility of dollars spent on current consumption. On the right-hand side, *MUS* shows the marginal utility of dollars saved for use in the future. The usual rule for rational choice applies: the consumer should divide his budget so that *MUE* and *MUS* are equal. If his income is very low, corresponding to *II*, he "cannot afford" to save anything. But with a higher income, indicated by I_1I_1, he can spend more, OE_1, and save OS_1 as well.

shows its marginal utility curve for spending on current consumption. Where does this curve come from? It is based on the utility schedules for individual goods, which were illustrated in Figure 4. We saw there that if the consumer is allocating his budget correctly, the marginal utility of the last dollar spent on each good will be identical. Any level of total spending, then, corresponds to a certain level of marginal utility; and this relation is shown by *MUE* in Figure 5. The curve must fall from left to right in the usual way: the greater the amount spent, the lower the marginal utility yielded by the last dollar.

The *MUS* (marginal utility of saving) schedule is shown on the right side of the chart. The dollars along the horizontal axis are *current* dollars—dollars saved today out of today's income. On the vertical axis, the distance *OA* shows how much utility the individual gets *today* from the first $1 of income saved *today*; and so on for lower points on *MUS*. Why does *MUS* slope down to the right? Because it represents expected satisfaction from *future consumption*.[1] Since consumption in any time period yields diminishing marginal utility, this should be true of future consumption as well as present consumption. Saving is also done partly for security reasons; but here the same rule applies. The more security I already have, the less an additional bit of security adds to my satisfaction.

Given the *MUE* and *MUS* schedules, we can apply the standard rule for rational choice: the consumer should save an amount such that his utility from the last dollar spent equals that from the last dollar saved. At the low income indicated by *II* in Figure 5, his income line lies entirely above the *MUS* curve. He "cannot afford" any saving, and will spend an amount *OE* equal to his total income. With the larger income corresponding to I_1I_1, he will maximize satisfaction by spending OE_1 and saving OS_1. As usual, OE_1 and OS_1 must add up to his total income. If his income were still larger, he would spend more *and* save more than before. A rise in family income normally raises both spending and saving.

The *MUS* schedules of different families must differ considerably, because at any income level—say, $10,000 a year—one finds some families that save a good deal and others that save nothing at all. Why is this so? What determines the height and shape of a family's *MUS* schedule?

One important consideration is how much property the family has already accumulated. Other things equal, a man who has already accumulated $100,000 will not be as eager to save as a man who is starting from zero.

A second consideration is whether this year's income is expected to continue in future. If a family has been used to getting $10,000 a year, its scale of living will be adjusted to that income level. This year, through an unexpected windfall, it has an income of $12,500, but this is not expected to continue. It would not be sensible, then, for the family to raise its consumption level substantially. Much of the extra $2,500 will probably go into saving.

---

[1] True, a wealthy man often builds up an estate which is expected to outlast his own lifetime. So *he* will not be spending the future income. Presumably, the prospect of his children or grandchildren being able to spend their legacies at some future time yields him utility at present, and this influences his savings decision.

There are important differences in families' future needs relative to expected future income. A young man who expects that his salary will be rising for many years will react differently from an older man looking forward to a low retirement income. A family faced with college expenses for children will behave differently from a family without such expenses. Research studies have shown that there are systematic differences in savings behavior at different stages of a family's life cycle.

It is sometimes argued that the rate of interest, which determines how much today's dollar will grow by next year, has an important effect on saving. If a dollar is expected to grow to $1.10 by next year, saving it will yield more utility than if it is expected to grow only to $1.05. So a rise in the interest rate will raise the *MUS* schedule and cause a higher proportion of household income to be saved; and conversely for a drop in interest. Many economists, however, doubt that this is very important compared with other influences on saving decisions. We shall go further into this in Chapter 11.

Apart from objective circumstances, people differ in their foresight or anticipation of the future. It is reasonable that a dollar of income next year should not be valued as highly as a dollar right now—next year I may not be here to enjoy it. Moreover, expected future satisfactions do not register as sharply on the mind as current satisfactions. So a future dollar shrinks in importance, and the farther away it is the more it shrinks, like railroad tracks disappearing in the distance. But some people discount the future at a much higher rate than others. People who *have a high time preference* for present over future income may appear shortsighted or spendthrift. Similarly, a man who values next year almost as much as this year *has low time preference*, and may appear thrifty, or farsighted. No praise or reproach is intended. These are preferences like any others, among which the economist must be neutral.

Given a family's *MUS* and *MUE* schedules, saving depends upon income. Taking the community as a whole, income is of dominant importance. Statistical studies show that, as we go up the income scale, the average amount saved per family rises steadily. Saving also rises as a percentage of family income.

DECISIONS ABOUT WORK

So far we have not asked where income comes from. Most of it comes from working; so decisions about work are a basic part of household economics. There is no law which says how many hours a man must work. He can get by with 30 hours a week in some occupations, or he may put in 40 hours in another, or he may get 50 hours by working overtime or holding a second job—"moonlighting." Several million people in the United States do hold two jobs at present.

How many hours a week does it pay to work? Each extra hour yields extra income, which can be spent or saved and hence yields extra utility, though at a diminishing rate. But time off for rest and recreation also yields utility. It takes time to spend and enjoy one's income. We must assume that these different kinds of satisfaction are commensurable and can be weighed against each other. People obviously do weigh them in reaching decisions about how much to work.

On this basis we can construct Figure 6. Along the horizontal axis

How Much Work to Do: Balancing Income and Leisure

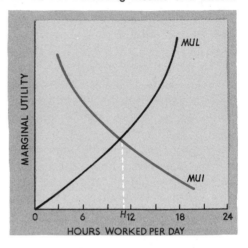

FIGURE 6. *MUI* shows the declining marginal utility of income as this man works more hours per day. *MUL* shows the rising marginal utility of leisure as work hours are lengthened, *i.e.*, leisure hours are decreased. The best workday for this man would be *OH*, where *MUI* and *MUL* are equal. Why would he get less satisfaction by working fewer or more hours than this?

we show the 24 hours a day which are available to be divided between work and leisure. Each point on the axis shows a possible combination of the two. As we move from left to right, work increases and leisure decreases. *MUI* shows the marginal utility of the income derived from additional work. It slopes downward to the right in the usual way. Since an hour of leisure is an hour of *not working*, we can show the marginal utility of leisure (*MUL*) on the same diagram. As we move to the right on the diagram, the amount of leisure is decreasing, and so its marginal utility is rising. Hence *MUL* slopes upward from left to right.

The reasoning behind this shape of *MUL* is simple. If work hours were zero, the worker would have so much leisure that the last hour would yield him little satisfaction. Leisure might even have negative utility, if he is ashamed of sitting at home idle. But as working hours are lengthened, each hour chopped off his leisure is more precious than the last. So as we move to the right on the diagram in the direction of more work and less leisure, the marginal utility of leisure rises steadily.

The man in Figure 6 would do best for himself by working *OH* hours per day. Why? Because if he worked less than this, the marginal utility of income would be higher than that of leisure. He could gain by trading a little more leisure for income, thus moving to the right toward *OH*. Any hours beyond *OH*, however, would involve a loss of satisfaction, since in this range *MUI* is below *MUL*.

People differ widely in their attitude toward leisure; and so some choose to work a great deal and others very little. If we want to be polite, we can say that Joe Doaks has a high preference for leisure, a high MUL curve. If we want to be rude, we can say he is lazy. Some people seem to be naturally work-shy, while others work with compulsive zeal. A person with a wide range of athletic, cultural, or other interests, a person who is skillful in getting satisfaction from leisure, will have a higher MUL schedule than a person of limited interests. (One of the objects of a liberal education is supposedly to raise your MUL curve!) The kind of work a person is doing also has a bearing. If the work is exhausting, monotonous, or otherwise unpleasant, leisure will seem more attractive than if the work is intrinsically pleasant and interesting.

This last point amounts to saying that work usually involves *disutility* or negative satisfaction. The extent of this disutility, however, varies widely from job to job. The more unpleasant the job, the more the balance of choice will be tilted in favor of leisure and the shorter will be the preferred work week.

A man may choose to work long hours, not because his valuation of leisure is low, but because his desire for income is great—he has a high MUI curve. This depends partly on the size of his family responsibilities. In boom periods, many factories work overtime, and their workers have a chance to bid for overtime hours at premium pay. Research studies show that married men with families put in substantially more overtime than young, single workers whose income needs are lower. Even with the same family size, however, some men will aspire to a high standard of living and work hard to attain it, while others will choose to work less and live less well.

People sometimes have income which is independent of work. Suppose the man in Figure 6 has a great-aunt, who leaves him some securities which bring in $2,000 a year. How will this affect the amount of work he does? If he earns $3,000 a year from work, his total income is now $5,000. The last dollar he gets from work is now the 5,000th dollar in his income instead of the 3,000th dollar; so it must have lower marginal utility than before. The marginal utility of income *from working* is reduced, and, everything else remaining the same, he will prefer to work less.

In all this we have taken the worker's *hourly wage rate* as given. To determine any point on MUI, say the point directly above 8 hours of work, we perform two operations. First, we multiply this number of hours by the wage rate to get the number of dollars earned per day. Then we must determine the marginal utility of the dollars earned in the last hour. If the wage rate changes, this changes our calculations. And we cannot be sure whether a wage increase, say, will lead a man to work more hours or fewer hours. The fact that an extra hour of work now yields more income is by itself an inducement to work the extra hour. But the fact that his labors earn him greater income for *all* hours, not just the extra hour, means that his income is higher, and so the marginal utility of extra income is less than before. These two effects pull in opposite directions, and on balance the man may work either more hours or less.

Some economists have speculated that, on the average for the entire labor force, the income effect is predominant; and that higher wage rates will cause a reduction in average hours per worker. Over the past century, there has been both a great increase in real wage rates and a marked reduction in weekly and yearly hours of work. If the reduction of hours represents a deliberate choice based on workers' preferences, this seems to support the hypothesis of an inverse relation between wage levels and labor supply.

This question is of practical importance also in the realm of tax policy. A 20 percent income tax imposed on a man whose income comes entirely from work amounts to cutting his wage rate by 20 percent. Will the fact that an hour's work now yields less income cause him to work less than before? Or, on the contrary, will he work longer hours to restore his take-home pay to its previous level and maintain his standard of living? Either result is quite possible. Research studies on actual reactions to income taxation have so far been inconclusive.

THE EQUILIBRIUM OF THE HOUSEHOLD

To sum up: a supposed virtue of a market economy is that it is responsive to individual choices—choices about spending, about saving, about working. Each household has an opportunity to work out a pattern of life which, given its particular goals and preferences, will yield maximum satisfaction.

This chapter has attempted to define "maximum satisfaction." It appears that maximizing satisfaction involves the household in a set of interlocking calculations. The amount of work to be done (and this may include work by the wife or other household members as well as the husband) must be chosen so that the marginal utility of the income gained just equals the marginal utility of the leisure sacrificed. Saving must be carried to the point where the utility of the last dollar saved just equals the utility of the last dollar spent. Spending must be spread over the goods and services available so that the last dollar spent on each yields the same utility. If all these choices are being made correctly, the household is *in equilibrium*, that is, it cannot increase its satisfaction by a move in any direction.

This definition of overall equilibrium would be interesting even if no one behaved in precisely this way. But the question how far households actually do behave in this way is, of course, important. This divides into two subquestions: first, how far do existing economic institutions allow people to make the kinds of marginal calculation outlined above? Could households exercise rational choice even if they were fully capable of it? Second, how rationally do households use the opportunities for choice which are open to them? A word on these points will provide a fitting conclusion for the chapter.

As to opportunity, households are perhaps best off in the distribution of *current purchases*. Rarely does any one dictate what you shall buy. Almost every conceivable good and service is available in some nearby retail outlet. The main problem is limited information. The quality and performance of some complex products is hard for the consumer to appraise; and a good deal of misinformation is spread deliberately by producers. Ignorance and misinformation is concentrated in certain kinds of product, however, and these do not form the bulk of consumer purchases.

As to *saving*, there is now a large volume of compulsory saving over which individuals have little control. The federal Old-Age, Survivors, and Disability Insurance system (OASDI) obliges most workers and employers to set aside certain amounts of money while a man is employed to provide him with a retirement pension, or a disability allowance should he become disabled before retirement, or death benefits for his family in the event of premature death. There are also many private pension systems, set up by companies or by union-employer negotiation, which are binding on the individual employee.

Establishment of compulsory savings systems does not affect our earlier argument so long as *the amount of compulsory saving is less than the person would have saved voluntarily.* His voluntary saving will now be lower than it would have been, but total saving may be the same. But OASDI and other compulsory savings systems have doubtless forced many low-income families to save *more* than they would have done voluntarily. In defense of this interference with free choice, it can be argued that most families are quite shortsighted, as witness the high proportion of old people who ended up living on their children or on relief in pre-social security days. Compulsory saving for old age or disability is probably a desirable corrective for this shortsightedness; but it does involve interference with individual choice.

The choice of *how much work* to do is somewhat constrained by law and custom, but perhaps not as seriously as appears at first glance. The federal Fair Labor Standards Act and union contracts have established a basic 40-hour week in many industries, and that is that. But why does the standard week hover around 40 hours? This must be within a reasonable distance of the hours which the average worker would choose voluntarily. If not, there would probably be agitation in the unions and in Congress to change the standard. Moreover, there are still local or intrastate industries which work 48 hours or more a week; and some industries work as little as 30 hours. There are opportunities to volunteer for overtime work or to hold a second job. There are a growing number of part-time jobs. Several million workers, mainly women, voluntarily work less than a full week. Businessmen, professional men, and farmers have wide scope to vary their hours. In farm areas located near cities, many farmers hold full-time jobs in town and run a farm on the side. Long hours, but high income.

It seems, then, that there is wide scope for economic choice for households. But how fully do households exploit the opportunities which are open to them? How closely do they conform to the canons of rational choice? We do not have nearly as much evidence as one would like. If full evidence were available, the picture would doubtless come out quite mixed. Certainly not *every* household makes *precise* economic calculations *every day* of the year. Household heads differ in intelligence and temperament, and the accuracy of their economic calculations will differ accordingly. Calculations are often rough, and leave some difference in marginal utilities instead of reaching precise equality. People may not respond to small changes in income, prices, or wages, but may wait until the changes have become large enough to be worth thinking about. In between these spasms of decision, they follow habitual routines, which may be a sensible way of conserving mental effort.

With all these qualifications, there seems to be a *strong element* of rational choice in household behavior. Within the limits of their imperfect information, people do try to do the best for themselves. They do find their way gradually toward cheaper and better goods, toward better jobs, toward preferable hours of work, and so on.

SUMMARY

1. The marginal utility of a good is the satisfaction derived from the last unit consumed (per period of time). Marginal utility decreases as the number of units consumed increases. This is called the principle of *diminishing marginal utility.*

2. The individual's demand schedule for a good is derived from the marginal utility schedule. It slopes downward to the right because of the principle of diminishing marginal utility.

3. The marginal utility of *expenditure* on a good depends on the marginal utility of the good *and* on its price. $MUE = \dfrac{MU}{P}$.

4. A household maximizes its satisfaction from consumption by allocating its budget so that the last dollar spent on each good yields the same marginal utility. The rule can be stated as:

$$MUE_1 = MUE_2 = MUE_3 = \cdots = MUE_n$$

or

$$\frac{MU_1}{P_1} = \frac{MU_2}{P_2} = \frac{MU_3}{P_3} = \cdots = \frac{MU_n}{P_n}.$$

5. Decisions about saving can be analyzed in the same way. The rational householder will divide his annual budget so that his utility from the last dollar spent on current consumption equals the utility he expects to derive from the last dollar saved.

6. Families with the same income this year may save different amounts, depending on how much property they have already accumulated, their prospective expenditure needs in the future, whether this year's income is expected to continue, and their valuation of the future compared with the present. On the average, however, saving rises as family income rises, both in absolute terms and as a *percentage of income*.

7. A worker will select his preferred hours of work by balancing the marginal utility of income against the marginal utility of additional hours of leisure. Individual preferences on this point differ substantially, both because of differences in the valuation of leisure and differences in desire for income.

8. An increase in a man's hourly wage rate may lead him to work either more hours or fewer hours. In the United States, taking the labor force as a whole over the past hundred years, rising wage levels have been associated with a marked reduction of hours per worker.

9. If a household reaches correct decisions on allocation of consumption expenditures, rate of saving, and amount of work to be offered in the market, it will have attained a position of maximum satisfaction. If all households in the economy do this, total consumer (and worker) satisfaction will be at a maximum.

DISCUSSION QUESTIONS

1. "Economists assume that consumer wants emerge spontaneously, and that producers respond by providing what consumers desire. It would be more accurate to say that producers create wants by developing new products, which consumers are then persuaded to purchase. The producer-dominated consumer is a reality, while the consumer-guided producer is largely a fiction." Discuss.

2. Review the main kinds of good you purchase. Can you think of any which do *not* obey the principle of diminishing marginal utility?

3. Does the "equal *MUE*" rule provide a sensible basis for consumer budget decisions? How close do you come to observing this rule in your own purchases?

4. Is saving always a Good Thing? Under what circumstances might zero saving or negative saving (borrowing) be quite rational?

5. "While the interest rate plays a large role in economic theory, it actually has a minor effect on savings decisions compared with other circumstances." Do you agree? What are some of the "other circumstances"?

6. High-income households save much more, both absolutely and as a percentage of income, than do low-income households. So it would seem that

the rich should get steadily richer. Actually, however, the proportion of all property owned by the richest 5 percent of the population has not increased in recent decades. Can you think of any explanations for this apparent paradox?

7. "The idea that workers can make a free choice between income and leisure is far from reality. When you take a job, you take the hours that go with it, and that is that." Discuss.

8. It is sometimes argued that union contracts and labor legislation have reduced working hours so much that most workers are getting less income and more leisure than they really prefer. What is your own hypothesis on this point? What kinds of facts might be gathered to test your hypothesis?

APPENDIX: THE INDIFFERENCE-CURVE APPROACH TO HOUSEHOLD DECISIONS

Many economists view the utility approach used in this chapter with considerable suspicion. It is not hard to see why. After all, what *are* the units on the vertical axis of our utility diagrams? Imaginative textbook writers sometimes label them "utils." Mr. A's first pound of coffee yields him 7 utils of satisfaction, the next pound 6 units, and so on. Nineteenth-century economists were inclined to regard a unit of satisfaction as a measurable quantity, like a pound or a foot. You could add and subtract them, show them as areas on a diagram, and so on.

But many modern economists regard this as dubious psychology. You can *feel* satisfaction, but you cannot *measure* it. You can also *compare* satisfactions. A man can say that one unit of a good, or one bundle of goods, yields more satisfaction than another; but he cannot say precisely how much more. All he can do is *rank* satisfactions as greater or less.

Moreover, it is argued, all the conclusions we have reached about household behavior can be reached equally well by another route, a route which carries no implication that utility is measurable. The key concept in this alternative approach is the *indifference curve*. This is a curve linking positions of *equal satisfaction*, among which the individual will consequently be indifferent. This may look complicated at first glance. But it is a quite simple and useful tool. We shall apply it first to decisions about current spending on consumer goods, and then see how it can be applied also to decisions about saving and working.

The Choice of Consumption Goods

Consider the case of Mr. Bibber (Figure 7). He has a fixed income each month to spend on food, and he eats only two foods, meat and potatoes. He is entitled to choose various combinations of these; but since his income is limited, he can get more of one item only by giving up some of the other. His food preferences are indicated by a curve, I_1, showing

Mr. Bibber's Food Preference System

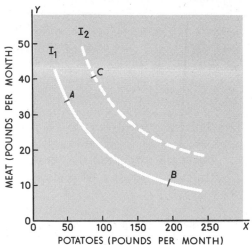

FIGURE 7. I_1 is an indifference curve. It shows combinations of meat and potatoes which would be equally acceptable to Mr. Bibber. So does I_2. The higher curve shows a higher level of satisfaction, since on it he can have more of both goods.

different combinations of the two articles which would be equally acceptable to him. He would be equally content with much meat and very little potatoes (point A), or far more potatoes and a small meat allowance (point B). As we move down the curve from A, its shape tells us how much additional potatoes it would take to compensate Mr. Bibber for the loss of a certain amount of meat. It shows the terms on which he is willing to substitute one product for the other. As we move closer to B and the amount of meat diminishes, it will take more and more potatoes to get Mr. Bibber to give up a pound of meat. This seems like a reasonable supposition. Finally, we may reach a rock-bottom level at which Mr. Bibber is unwilling to give up any more meat no matter how many potatoes he is offered. At this point I_1 becomes a horizontal line.

This construction, an indifference curve, is a very flexible and useful device. Different attitudes toward the two commodities can be shown simply by differences in the shape of the curve. If the consumer regards the two products as close substitutes, almost interchangeable with each other, I_1 will be a shallow curve, close to a straight line. If he does not regard them as very good substitutes for each other, the curve will bend down more toward the origin. In the extreme case, where Mr. Bibber insists on a specific "package" of so many pounds of meat and so many pounds of potatoes and is unwilling to substitute at all, the indifference curve would become a right angle with the point of the angle showing the one preferred combination.

"But," you may ask, "what about a point like C? Here he has *both* more meat and more potatoes than at A. So why won't he simply move up to C and stay there?" Of course, Mr. Bibber would prefer C to A if he had enough money to buy greater quantities of both products. C lies on a higher indifference curve representing a higher level of living. This second curve is shown by I_2. There are in fact a large number of indifference curves for Mr. Bibber, lying one above the other, and filling the whole space in the diagram. Each corresponds to a different satisfaction level, and Mr. Bibber naturally will climb to the highest one that his actual income level permits. The totality of his indifference curves for all levels of satisfaction is termed his *preference system.*

The notion of a preference system seems abstract and unreal on first acquaintance. One reason is that our illustration involves choice between two commodities only, whereas real-world choices are obviously more complex. But there is no logical difficulty in extending the idea of a preference system to embrace 10, 50, or any number of commodities which may be available for consumer choice.

So far we have not asked how much of any product—say meat— Mr. Bibber will actually buy. This depends, not just on Mr. Bibber's preferences, but also on his income and on product prices. We can demonstrate this by setting up the indifference diagram in a slightly different form (Figure 8). On the vertical axis we show pounds of meat bought per month. But on the horizontal axis we now show the dollar amount he spends per month. If prices are constant, this money income represents his command over *goods in general.* So the indifference curves, such as I_1 and I_2, show the rate at which he is willing to trade a reduction in meat for an increase in everything else he buys.

Suppose Mr. Bibber's monthly income is $OP = \$40$; and suppose the price of meat is \$1 per pound. Then if he spent all his money on meat, he could buy $OM = 40$ pounds of meat per month. Alternatively, if he bought no meat, he would have $OP = \$40$ per month to spend on other things. Or he can choose some intermediate combination. All the

Purchases Depend on Price and Income

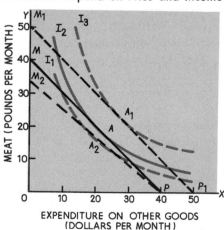

FIGURE 8. The budget line *MP* shows all combinations of meat and other things which Mr. Bibber can buy with his income. He will select the combination shown by *A*, where *MP* touches the highest indifference curve he can reach. If his income rises to P_1, his budget line becomes M_1P_1 and his purchases rise to A_1. If the price of meat rises, his budget line shifts to M_2P and his purchases fall to A_2.

combinations open to him lie along the straight line *MP*. (Why is *MP* a straight line? Because its slope depends on the price of meat, which we have taken as constant.)

We may call *MP* his *consumption possibilities line* or his *budget line*, since it shows all the combinations of meat and other goods which he can buy with his income. He cannot move to any position above *MP* because he hasn't enough income. He will not choose any position below *MP* because that would mean leaving some of his income unspent— "throwing money away."

How much meat will Mr. Bibber actually buy? He must settle for some point on *MP*. Given this limitation, he will naturally try to reach the highest possible indifference curve (or satisfaction level). The highest indifference curve which is touched by *MP*, therefore, will be the best he can do. This is I_2 in Figure 8, and his preferred combination is shown by *A*, the point at which *MP* is tangent to I_2. Here he is buying about 22 pounds of meat and has about $18 per month left to spend on other things.

A little thought reveals why Mr. Bibber cannot profitably move in any direction from *A*. If he tries to move right or left along I_2, he cannot do so because all points on I_2 except *A* lie *above MP*, i.e., they represent combinations which cost more than his income. If he tries to move up or down along *MP*, he can do so but will find himself on a *lower indifference curve* representing a lower level of satisfaction.

The tangency of *MP* and I_2 has an important economic meaning. At the point of tangency, *A*, the slope of *MP* is just equal to the slope of I_2. But what is the slope of I_2? It shows the rate at which Mr. Bibber *is willing* to substitute meat for other goods in his consumption pattern. The slope of *MP*, on the other hand, shows the rate at which he *can* substitute in view of existing prices. He is in equilibrium when his *subjective* rate of substitution just equals the *objective* rate permitted by the market.[2]

How will Mr. Bibber's meat purchases be affected by changes in his income or in the price of meat? Suppose first that his income rises to $OP = \$50$ per month, while the price of meat remains unchanged. The maximum amount of meat he can buy is now $OM_1 = 50$ pounds a month. His new budget line is M_1P_1, parallel to *MP* at a higher level. (Why is it parallel? Because the slope of the budget line depends on the price of meat. Since this has remained unchanged, M_1P_1 will have the same slope as *MP*.) The highest indifference curve he can reach is now I_3, and he

---

[2] This is the same thing as the $\dfrac{MU_a}{P_a} = \dfrac{MU_b}{P_b}$ rule reached in the body of the chapter. This can be converted to the form $\dfrac{MU_a}{MU_b} = \dfrac{P_a}{P_b}$. The first term is the subjective rate of substitution, while the second is the objective or market rate.

will settle at A_1, where M_1P_1 is tangent to I_3. He buys more meat than before and also more of other things.[3]

Now let's keep Mr. Bibber's income constant at $40 per month and raise the price of meat to $1.25 a pound. The most meat he can buy is now $OM_2 = 32$ pounds a month. The budget line becomes M_2P. (Note that the slope of the budget line has changed because of the change in price.) The best position which Mr. Bibber can now reach is A_2, the point at which M_2P is tangent to the lower indifference curve I_1. The price increase without any increase in income has lowered his satisfaction level, which is what common sense would suggest.

Mr. Bibber now buys less meat than he did before. His meat purchases have fallen for two reasons: (1) the fact that meat prices have risen while his money income remains unchanged means that his purchasing power is reduced. He is less "well off" than before. Note that he also buys less of other goods than he did before, even though their prices are unchanged. This is termed the *income effect*. (2) Since meat is now *relatively* more expensive than before, he buys *relatively* less meat and more of other things. He substitutes other goods for meat in his consumption pattern. This is termed the *substitution* effect.

The income and substitution effects normally work in the same direction. The income effect can run in the opposite direction, however, and in rare cases might be big enough to outweigh the substitution effect. Then one encounters the "Giffen paradox" mentioned in Chapter 5.

To sum up: Mr. Bibber's meat purchases depend on (1) his income; (2) the price of meat; (3) the prices of all other goods he buys; and of course (4) his basic tastes and preferences, reflected in the shape of the indifference curves. This is fully consistent with our earlier results using the utility approach.

The Choice of Spending or Saving

We saw earlier in the chapter that a saver is really *buying future income*. Consider a man wondering whether to save part of this year's income in order to earn interest which will add to his income next year.

On the horizontal axis of Figure 9 we show this year's consumption. On the vertical axis we show interest earnings which would form additions to next year's income. The indifference curves show combinations of present expenditure and future interest income which would be equally satisfactory to Mr. Goldbilt. As he cuts down his present spending, it will take larger and larger interest payments to compensate him; so the indifference curves, as usual, become steeper as we move up to the left. If there is a minimum level of living below which he will not go, his indifference curves will become vertical at that level.

---

[3] While this is the general rule, it is not an invariable rule. The indifference map could be shaped so that, as Mr. Bibber's income rises, he buys *less* of the product in question. This would be the case of an *inferior good*, already noted.

Saving Varies with Income and the Rate of Interest

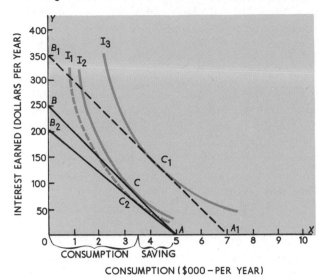

CONSUMPTION ($000 – PER YEAR)

FIGURE 9. If the market rate of interest is 5 percent, Mr. Goldbilt can earn $50 interest for each $1,000 saved. If his income this year is OA = $5,000, his possibilities curve is AB. He will choose position C, where AB is tangent to the highest indifference curve he can reach. If his income rises to $7,000, his possibilities curve becomes A_1B_1, and he will move to C_1, where he saves more and spends more than before. If with the $5,000 income the rate of interest falls to 4 percent, his possibilities curve becomes AB_2 and he will be forced down to C_2.

What possibilities are actually open to him? This depends on his income and on the rate of interest. Suppose his income is $OA = \$5,000$ and the market rate of interest is 5 percent. Then if he saved all his income, he could earn $OB = \$250$ of interest next year. If he spends all his income for consumption, he will, of course, earn zero interest; and he can do anything in between. His budget line is AB, showing all combinations of current spending and future interest earnings which are possible within the limits of his income. Its slope depends on the rate of interest, and will be steeper as the interest rate rises.

Mr. Goldbilt's best position in these circumstances will be at C, where AB is tangent to I_2, the highest indifference curve he can reach. So he cannot gain by a change in any direction. Here the rate at which he *is willing* to substitute present for future income (shown by the slope of I_2) just equals the rate at which he *can* substitute them through the money market (shown by the slope of AB).

Suppose now that his income rises to $OA_1 = \$7,000$. By saving all of this he could earn interest of $7,000 \times 5$ percent $= \$350$. His budget line becomes A_1B_1, parallel to AB (since the rate of interest is unchanged) but at a higher level. He can now reach the higher indifference curve I_3, and his preferred position will be at C_1. Note that he is now saving more *and* spending more than before, which is the general rule as income rises.

The other thing that may happen is that the rate of interest may change. Go back to the first position in which his income is OA. Suppose now that the interest rate falls to 4 percent. The maximum he could earn even by saving all his income is now only $5,000 × 4 percent = $200. His budget line is AB_2 instead of AB.

This forces him down to a lower indifference curve, I_1, and he will settle at O_2, where AB_2 is tangent to I_1. Here he is spending more of his current income and saving less than he was before. It seems reasonable that if the reward for saving falls, the amount of saving done will decline.

It is possible, however, that some savers may not react in this way. Suppose you are determined to have a fixed amount of interest income in the future—say, $1,000 per year—for retirement or some other purpose. You are what has been termed a "target saver." Then if the interest rate is 5 percent, you can attain your objective by saving $20,000. But if the interest rate falls to 4 percent, you will have to save $25,000. Thus your saving will *increase* as the interest rate *decreases*. We could illustrate this kind of reaction by giving a different shape to the indifference curves in Figure 9.

The Choice of Work versus Leisure

Let's look finally at how this same approach can be applied to decisions about hours of work. Mr. Restwell's work preference system is shown in Figure 10. Mr. Restwell is, say, a commission salesman who can work as few or as many hours per week as he wishes. He can get more income by working longer hours, but this means a sacrifice of leisure. On the vertical axis we show weekly income in dollars. On the horizontal axis we show various ways in which Mr. Restwell might divide, say, 100 waking hours per week between work and leisure. Hours worked appear above the line, leisure hours below the line, and the two, of course, move in opposite directions. As we move to the right, leisure increases and hours worked decline.

The indifference curves I_1 and I_2 show different combinations of income and leisure which Mr. Restwell would consider equally attractive. At a point far to the right on I_1, indicating short hours and low income, he will be willing to work longer for only a little more income. As we move up I_1 to the left, however, and his work week becomes steadily longer, it takes more and more money to persuade him to work an extra hour. This behavior seems reasonable on a common-sense basis.

The Choice of Work versus Leisure

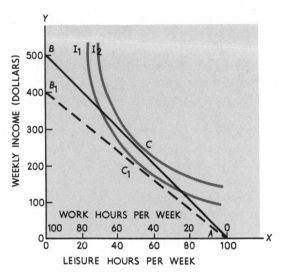

FIGURE 10. The horizontal axis shows different ways in which Mr. Restwell can divide his 100 waking hours between work and leisure. As we move to the right, leisure increases and work decreases. The indifference curves I_1 and I_2 show combinations of income and leisure which would be equally acceptable to Mr. Restwell. If the wage on his job is $5 an hour, his possibilities curve is AB, and his preferred position is C, where AB is tangent to the highest possible indifference curve. A drop in the wage rate to $4 would shift the possibilities curve to AB_1, and force him down to a less satisfactory position at C_1.

Where Mr. Restwell will come out depends on the wage rate for his job. Suppose this is $5 an hour. Then if he worked the absolute maximum of 100 hours per week, he could earn $OB = \$500$. If he doesn't work at all, shown by OA on the horizontal axis, he will, of course, earn zero; and he can do anything in between. His budget line is AB, the slope of which depends on the hourly wage rate. His preferred work week is shown by point C, where AB is tangent to the highest possible indifference curve. At this point he is working about 50 hours and earning $250 per week.

As always, this result depends on the shape which we give to the indifference curves. With a stroke of the pencil we can make Mr. Restwell greedy or abstemious, idle or diligent, and bring him out with a long work week or a very short one. And while for illustrative purposes we can do anything we choose, it must never be forgotten that each individual's work preference system is a real and unique thing.

The outcome depends also on the slope of AB, i.e., on the hourly wage rate. Suppose that, instead of $5, the wage rate were only $4. Mr. Restwell's possibilities curve is now AB_1, and the best adjustment he can make is at C_1, where AB_1 just touches the indifference curve I_1. Since I_1 is below I_2, this is a less satisfactory position than before—it is impossible to be as well off at a lower wage rate as at a higher one.

Will the lower wage cause Mr. Restwell to work longer hours or shorter hours than before? In Figure 10, he ends up working longer hours. But this will not necessarily be true in all cases. The best way to see this is to regard the hourly wage rate as *the price of leisure*. How can

I get an additional hour of leisure? By working one hour less than before. But this means giving up the wage that I might have earned in that hour. So the higher the wage, the higher is the price of leisure; and conversely.

A lower wage, then, means a cut in the price of leisure. Just like the meat price change noted earlier, this sets up two conflicting reactions: (1) Since leisure is now cheaper than before, there is an incentive to buy more of it, that is, to work shorter hours. This is the *substitution effect*. (2) But at the lower wage level Mr. Restwell is also poorer than before. So he will feel less able to afford all the good things of life, *including leisure*. This *income effect* will stimulate him to work longer hours, in order to bring his weekly income back closer to its previous level.

The outcome depends on which effect is stronger in a particular case. If the income effect predominates, as we have shown it doing in Figure 10, a lower wage rate will mean longer hours, and a higher wage rate shorter hours. The opposite result is quite possible, however, and could be illustrated by altering the shape of the indifference curves.

Production Economics, Costs,

and Supply

Business is really more agreeable than
pleasure; it interests the whole mind, the aggregate nature of man more continuously and more
deeply. But it does not look as if it did.

WALTER BAGEHOT

PRODUCING UNITS are the counterpart of the household units studied in
Chapter 6. Households buy goods and supply factors of production. Producing units buy factors of production and supply goods and services.

Instead of "producing unit" we usually say "business firm." But we
should remember that government agencies such as the U.S. Post Office
or the New York State Department of Education are also producing
units. So are farms, lawyers' offices, hospitals, and many other units
which we do not commonly regard as businesses.

Producing units come in all shapes and sizes. They range from the
one-man farm or grocery store to the giant corporation employing
hundreds of thousands of workers. But there is a basic similarity in their
production operations. All use labor, capital, raw materials, and other
inputs. Use of these inputs involves *costs of production*. The inputs are
used to produce outputs which are sold on the market for a *price*. Over

163

the long run, this price must cover the necessary costs, else production will not continue.

Because costs are so important, we must look carefully into where they come from. What does it cost to produce a ton of steel? Why this amount rather than something else? The answer involves the following considerations: (1) The steel company has to buy buildings and machinery, labor, coal, limestone, iron ore, power, and other *factors of production*. So its production costs depend partly on the price of these factors. (2) Steel can be produced by various methods—for example, by methods which use very little labor or by methods which use a good deal more labor. So cost depends partly on the method of production. (3) The size of the plant and of the company will make a difference. It is usually said that there are "economies of large-scale production." On the other hand, one hears that "a business can get too big." (4) Cost depends not only on the size of the plant but on how much it is turning out. In some years steel mills operate at 90 percent of capacity, in other years at 50 percent. This makes a substantial difference to cost per ton of steel.

Altogether, then, we must examine *factor prices, production methods, size of enterprise,* and *rate of output.*

THE PRICE OF THE FACTORS

Like other prices, factor prices are determined in markets and are subject to the twin pulls of supply and demand. We illustrated this in the coal miner case in Chapter 5, and will go into it more thoroughly in Chapters 10–11. So there is no need to say much at this point. We shall simply assume that there is a competitive market for each factor, that this market establishes a price, and that any producer can get as much of a factor as he wants by paying the market price. This will not always be true in actuality. A company may be so big, or the supply of a particular factor so limited, that an increase in the company's purchases will raise the market price. But we shall ignore this complication for the time being.

We should comment, however, on one point which is quite important in small businesses. What happens if a producer does not have to buy factors in the market because he already owns them? The small storekeeper owns his own labor, and he has $50,000 which he uses to build and equip his store. Does use of these factors still involve a cost? Yes, it clearly does. The cost of a producer-owned factor is usually termed an *imputed cost* and is equal to what the factor could otherwise have earned in the open market.

To calculate accurately how well his business is doing, our storekeeper should pay himself the same salary which he could have earned by working, say, as a salaried manager of a chain store. If he would have cost the chain store $7,500, he should cost himself the same amount. He may, of course, value independence for its own sake. While he would have demanded a $7,500 salary from the chain store, he may be equally content to earn $6,000 a year in his own store. In this event, one cannot say that it is uneconomic for him to follow his own preferences. Many farmers, storekeepers, and other small proprietors do earn less than they could by working for hire. But it is hard to say how far this results from a deliberate preference for independence, and how far it is due simply to limited foresight and bad bookkeeping.

The imputed cost rule applies also to the storekeeper's capital. If he could put his $50,000 into securities and earn a 5 percent return, then he should pay himself $50,000 × 5 percent = $2,500 per year in his capacity as capitalist. This is a genuine cost of operating his business.

Without these calculations we cannot tell whether the storekeeper is covering his costs or not. Suppose that at the end of the year, after paying for goods bought and other purchased inputs, he has $10,000 left over. He might be inclined to call this "profit." But actually he is just breaking even. If we deduct the imputed cost of his labor and capital, we have $10,000 − $7,500 − $2,500 = 0. *Profit is a surplus in excess of all costs, including imputed costs.* If he had $11,000 left at the end of the year, then he would indeed have made a profit of $1,000. But if he came out at the end of the year with $9,000, he would have lost $1,000.

A large business is managed by salaried executives, and imputed labor cost is of little account. Imputed capital cost, however, usually is important. A company should expect to earn a competitive rate of return on its investment in plant and equipment. *Imputed interest is a cost.* Only if there is a surplus left after deducting imputed interest has the company made a true profit.

How large is this competitive or "normal" rate of return? Five percent? Six percent? Seven percent? It is impossible to give a general answer, since the competitive rate of return varies with circumstances— the country, the time period, the kind of industry. For stable industries such as electric light and power, public utility commissions have often set it in the neighborhood of 6 percent. For riskier industries, it might be higher. Marshall devised a famous, though circular, definition: the rate of return is normal when there is no incentive to change the amount of capital employed in the industry. Some companies may still be coming into the industry, and others may be dropping out. But if the inflow and outflow just balance, then earnings are normal. This is still a good operational definition.

Economic definitions differ on this point from accounting definitions and from everyday usage. In economics, *imputed interest is not profit.* It is a necessary return on the owners' capital, required to induce them to use capital in this line of production rather than in something else. *This level of return is always included in the cost schedule.* To say that price equals cost, then, is the same as saying that industry is earning a normal rate of return.

Profit, on the other hand, is the *difference between the actual rate of return and the normal rate.* Profit can be either positive or negative—positive if price is above cost, negative if price is below cost. *Example:* a company is earning 3 percent on the owners' capital. We somehow determine that the normal return in this industry is 6 percent. The accountant would say that the company is earning a 3 percent profit. The economist would say that profits are $3 - 6 = -3$ percent. In the following chapters we shall try to use profit consistently in its economic meaning.

THE METHOD OF PRODUCTION

The cost of producing a good depends not only on factor prices but on what quantity of each factor is used in production; and this depends on the method of production. There is no such thing as *the* cost of producing a good; there is only the cost of producing a good *by a certain method.*

We assume that each producer will seek out and use the method which yields least cost per unit of output. In a competitive industry, this is a reasonable assumption, for if one producer does not use the best method others will. The product price will tend toward the cost of production by the least-cost method. A producer who is not using the best method will have higher costs and subnormal earnings and will in time be forced out of the industry.

Where a producer has a monopoly or is otherwise sheltered from competition, he is not *forced* to adopt the least-cost method. But it is still worth his while to do so, since he can thereby increase his·profit. At any rate, we give him the benefit of the doubt.

What is involved in discovering and using the least-cost method of production? At least three things. First, a producer must possess all the technical knowledge available at the time. He must be able to sort over and choose from the existing stock of technical know-how.

Second, whatever method he chooses must be operated efficiently in an engineering sense. *Engineering efficiency* means getting the largest feasible output from any set of inputs or, conversely, using the smallest quantity of inputs to produce a given output. It means not wasting inputs, not using two men to do one man's work.

But *engineering* efficiency is not synonymous with *economic* efficiency. There are a half-dozen ways of weaving cotton cloth, ranging from a hand loom operated in the household to fully automated power looms requiring little labor. All of these are in use in various parts of the world. Each can be operated efficiently in the engineering sense of not wasting inputs. But this does not tell us which yields least cost per yard of cloth, which is *economically* efficient. To discover this we must know the price of each factor of production. The economically efficient method will be one which economizes on factors which are relatively expensive by using more of factors which are relatively cheap.

Suppose it takes *only* labor and capital to produce cotton cloth. Forget about other factors for the time being. On the vertical axis of Figure 1 we show quantities of plant and machinery, on the horizontal axis quantities of labor. Each point on the diagram represents a certain combination of labor and capital, capable of producing a certain amount of product. Let's examine different possible ways of producing 1,000 yards of cloth a day. This might be done by a combination such as P_1, using a lot of automatic equipment and not much labor. Or it might be done by a combination such as P_6, using much more labor and simpler machinery. The other points represent other intermediate techniques. By joining

How to Compare Methods of Production

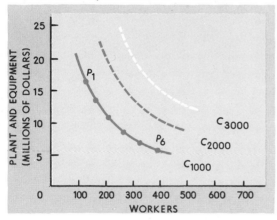

FIGURE 1. The curve C_{1000} shows different combinations of labor and capital, any of which would produce 1,000 yards of cloth per day. It is called an *isoquant* for *equal quantities* (of output). The higher curves show combinations needed for 2,000 and 3,000 yards per day.

these points we get the curve C_{1000}. This is called an *isoquant*, for *equal quantities* of output produced by alternative methods.

To draw C_{1000} as a continuous curve implies that labor can be substituted for capital by very small degrees, so that there are innumerable ways of making cotton cloth. This might or might not be true in a particular case. In agricultural production, something close to continuous substitution usually is possible, which is one reason why economists like to draw illustrations from agriculture! In other cases there may be only a few standard techniques among which a producer must choose. In the extreme case where there is only one known method, requiring a fixed combination of labor and capital, the isoquant reduces to a right-angle curve on the diagram. But this degree of rigidity in production methods is rare.

Suppose that instead of 1,000 yards a day we wanted to produce 2,000 yards a day. This would take more labor, or more capital, or both. By plotting all feasible combinations for this rate of output, we derive the isoquant C_{2000}, lying above and to the right of C_{1000}. Similarly, C_{3000} is the isoquant for 3,000 yards of cloth a day. The whole area of Figure 1 is, in fact, filled with isoquants, lying one above the other, and each indicating a slightly higher rate of output. The diagram as a whole is often called a *production surface*.[1]

When we say that a producer has full knowledge of existing technology, this means that he knows the production surface for his product. But how will he choose among the available possibilities? What production method will he actually use?

Least-Cost Method Depends on Factor Prices

FIGURE 2.   AB shows different combinations of labor and capital which could be bought for the same amount of money. The combination chosen will be that which yields greatest output. This is where AB touches the highest possible isoquant at point C. If labor were cheaper and capital more expensive, the cost line might look like A_1B_1, leading to a more labor-using production method at C_1.

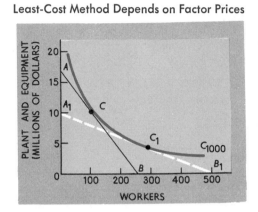

A producer has greatest freedom of choice before he has set up in business. So consider a man thinking about going into cloth production. His resources will allow him a production budget of $1 million a year, to be divided among wages for labor and interest on investment in plant and equipment. The market rate of wages for textile operatives is $2.00 an hour, and the interest rate is 6 percent. The production map of Figure 2 is the same as in Figure 1.

If he puts all his money into hiring labor, he can hire $OB = 250$ workers. If he does nothing but buy plant and equipment, he can afford a

---

[1] *Surface* because, if we showed output in a third dimension, we would be moving up a mountain slope to the northeast on the diagram. The isoquants are equivalent to geographical contour lines on this surface. They show how one can move around the "production mountain" while staying at the same "height" (rate of output).

Several characteristics of isoquants are worth mentioning: (1) They are convex to the origin. What does this mean? It means that as you substitute more of one factor for another—say, machinery for labor—it takes increasing amounts of the abundant factor to offset the loss of another unit of the scarce factor. In common-sense terms, the possibilities of saving labor (without sacrificing output) taper off. (2) The curvature of the isoquants reflects the *ease* with which factors can be substituted for each other. If two factors were fully substitutable, the isoquant would be a straight line—they would in fact be the *same* factor. As substitution becomes more difficult, the isoquants bend in more toward the origin. (3) Isoquants cannot intersect. Why? Because this would mean that it takes *less* of one or both factors to produce a *larger* amount of the product, which contradicts our assumption that producers never waste inputs.

plant worth $OA = \$16\%$ million.[2] Neither A nor B is a feasible position—he can't operate with only one factor. But by connecting A and B we can show all the other possibilities which are open to him within the limits of his production budget. Any point on AB shows a combination of labor and capital which will cost $1 million a year. (Verify this by picking a couple of points and making the calculation.) AB is an *equal cost* or *isocost* line. Since the distances OA and OB depend on the prices of labor and capital, the *slope* of AB also depends on these prices.

Our producer will want to operate somewhere on AB. He cannot go above it, since he does not have enough money, and to operate below it would mean leaving part of his resources idle. He will also want to get the greatest output he can for his production budget. He will want *to reach the highest possible isoquant.* This is C_{1000}, which is just touched by AB; and his least cost production method is indicated by C, where AB is tangent to C_{1000}.

Why is C the best position he can attain? He cannot move away from C along C_{1000} in either direction, because he would then be exceeding his budget. He could move from C upward or downward along AB, but he would then be on a lower isoquant with a lower rate of output. Only at C can he attain *maximum output per dollar of cost* or, the same thing in reverse, *minimum cost per unit of output.*

Suppose now that the relative factor prices were drastically different. Suppose labor cost only $1 per hour while the rate of interest was 10 percent. Then he could buy more labor (OB_1) if he wanted to, but the maximum amount of capital he could get (OA_1) is lower. His budget line would be A_1B_1, the shallower slope of which represents the marked change in factor prices. The best production combination is now C_1, using considerably more labor and less capital than before.

So we conclude that the *economically* best method of production depends on *relative factor prices.* If one factor becomes more expensive, it pays to use less of it and more of other factors. Each automobile produced in the United States today embodies much less labor and much more capital than was true 50 years ago. This is not just because inventors have become more ingenious. It is partly because labor has become much more expensive. The highly automated machines used in automobile plants today would not have paid off in 1910 even if producers had known about them, because labor was still quite cheap. They do pay today. The AB line has become steadily steeper, and producers have responded by shifting to "laborsaving" methods (which we could equally well call "capital-using" methods).

This explains also why one finds different production techniques in

---

[2] With a 2,000-hour year, and a wage rate of $2 per hour, each worker will earn $4,000 a year. Multiplied by 250, this yields an annual wage cost of $1 million. Similarly, an interest charge of 6 percent on a plant worth $16⅔ million yields an annual interest cost of $1 million.

different countries. American textile mills are highly mechanized, with one worker tending a large number of machines. In India, much of the cloth comes from "cottage industries," using simple equipment and much more labor. This does not necessarily mean that Indian production is "backward." The basic fact is that labor is abundant and cheap in India, while capital is scarce and expensive. So it makes sense for Indian producers to use more labor and less capital per unit of output than is true in the United States. To imitate our methods would be quite uneconomical for them.

It is hard to overcome the "common-sense" feeling that the most highly mechanized production methods *must* be economically preferable. Both engineers and ordinary citizens are inclined to be "machine happy." It is true that additional mechanization will usually save *some* labor; but beyond some point the savings are made at inordinate cost. Blind mechanization could easily lead a producer to a point above C on C_{1000} in Figure 2, where production costs would be higher for the same level of output. How far it pays to go at a particular time depends on relative factor prices. Simpler methods are preferable until rising wage levels make fancier methods economical. Engineering possibilities must be subjected to economic analysis.

COST AND SCALE OF ENTERPRISE

Let's review where we have gotten so far: given the prices of the factors, and given the production possibilities map, a producer can choose the production method which yields lowest cost per unit of output. From here on, *we assume that producers have actually made this kind of analysis and acted accordingly*. The cost schedules discussed in the remainder of this chapter are not just any old costs. They are the *lowest feasible costs* which producers can achieve by correct choice of methods plus efficient management.

Size of Plants

We proceed now to the relation between costs and scale of enterprise. The phrase "economies of large-scale production" suggests that a larger plant can attain lower costs than a small one. Is this always true? Is it true indefinitely or only up to a certain point? Can a plant or a company become "too large"?

There obviously are economies of large-scale production. A larger plant can usually achieve greater subdivision and specialization of production processes. In a small custom workshop, a shoemaker may perform all the operations needed to turn out a shoe. In a large factory, these operations are finely subdivided. It may be boring for the worker to make the same few motions all day long, but he learns to do them faster, he wastes no time in changing from one task to another, and he can use tools which are specialized to a particular job. Subdivision of production operations is an essential basis for mechanization.

In some industries, the basic production equipment is very large. The huge machines which stamp out auto bodies, the automatic equipment which drills all the holes in the cylinder block in one operation, the miles of assembly line, and the large ovens which spray and bake paint on the car would be very expensive for a small producer. But when thousands of cars a day are fed through the plant, the cost per car can be cut to a low level. Large plants can also afford to mechanize many supplementary operations, such as bringing materials to the production floor and packaging and shipping the finished product.

Eventually, however, one reaches a point at which the plant is large enough to take full advantage of existing technology. A still larger plant would bring no additional savings, and costs would actually begin to rise because of the problems of supervising and servicing a very large establishment. The more acres over which a plant is spread, the greater the cost of getting materials and people from one part of the plant to another. To this must be added growing difficulties of supervision and coordination. The plant which is neither too large nor too small, which can attain least cost per unit of output, is said to be of *optimum scale.*

The size of the optimum plant differs greatly from one industry to another, depending mainly on whether the industry uses *large and indivisible capital goods.* The extreme case is a railroad, where you have to lay a track over the whole route before starting operations; or a hydroelectric power installation, where the dam comes in one piece. Auto assembly plants have large optimum scale, partly because the body-stamping machines, automatic engine-boring machines, and other basic equipment items are large and indivisible. Steel mills and oil refineries are large for the same reason.

At the other extreme, take a shop producing men's shirts. The basic tool is a power sewing machine. Each operative has his own machine and does all the stitching on the shirt. So the choice is between a shop with, say, 20 workers and 20 machines and one with 100 workers and 100 machines. Over a considerable range the choice will not make much difference, because the savings from putting more man-machine units side by side are not large.

A recent study estimated that the optimum scale of plant, measured by annual output, was only about half a million dollars in the women's dress industry. But it was 27 million for steel works and rolling mills, 26 million for glassware, and 70 million for inorganic chemicals.[3]

A more interesting figure is the optimum scale of plant *relative to*

---

[3] T. R. Saving, "Estimation of Optimum Size of Plant by the Survivor Technique," *Quarterly Journal of Economics,* November, 1961, pp. 569–607. The estimates are, of course, subject to numerous limitations, which are fully described in the original source.

total output of the industry. This has a bearing on the feasibility of competition. If a plant has to produce 25 percent of the industry output to achieve minimum costs, then there is room for only four optimum-sized plants in the industry. The result is a semimonopolistic situation. Nor can this be cured by antitrust action, since it is not feasible to disintegrate a single plant. If, on the other hand, a plant can be efficient with 0.5 percent of the industry output, there will be room for a couple of hundred producers. It will also be easier for new producers to enter the industry, and the situation will be generally more competitive.

Professor Saving's findings on this point are encouraging to believers in competition. In more than half of the 132 manufacturing industries he investigated, the optimum scale of plant was estimated at less than 1 percent of industry output, and in more than 90 percent of the industries it was less than 5 percent. It seems also that over a considerable range, plant size does not make a large difference in costs. This is probably why one often finds medium-sized plants and larger plants coexisting in the same industry, without much difference in their profit showing.

Size of Companies

In many industries there are only a few *companies,* and each of these is very large. Where companies are large, this is usually not because the individual plants must be large, but rather because the company has combined many plants under one management. If these plants perform the same kind of operation—a chain of grocery stores or a number of auto assembly plants—this is called *horizontal integration.* If the plants perform successive stages in the same production process—say iron ore mining, ore shipping, pig iron production, steel smelting and rolling, and production of finished steel products—this is termed *vertical integration.* If the company controls plants in a number of different industries, it is often called a *conglomerate enterprise.* Such industrial giants as Du Pont, General Motors, or Standard Oil of New Jersey exhibit all of these characteristics simultaneously. Some of their production is vertically integrated, they operate many parallel plants doing the same kind of operation, and they also operate in a variety of different industries.

It is important, then, to distinguish clearly between optimum scale of *plant* and optimum scale of *company.* Even after plants have reached the most efficient size, there may be additional economies in putting a number of plants under common management. Every company must have a president, treasurer, personnel director, sales manager, legal counsel, and so on. If these costs of top management can be spread over 10 million units of output a year instead of 1 million, unit cost will be lower. Managements also differ widely in their managerial capacity. An unusually able management can be regarded as a large and indivisible machine which needs a large enterprise to make full use of its services. For products where advertising is important, there is a substantial minimum cost of making a national appeal to consumers through magazines, radio, and television. There is a saving in spreading this cost over as large a volume as possible. A company which buys materials and supplies on a large scale can get quantity discounts which reflect genuine economies in sales, transport, and handling costs. A large company can afford expert staffs for research, development, and production engineering. It is in a better position to introduce new or improved products and to keep up with the march of technology.

If a large company can gain these various economies, why do companies ever stop growing? Why doesn't one company gobble up a whole industry, or perhaps several industries? The usual answer is that, as a company gets larger, it also becomes harder to manage. Even the ablest company president has only a limited amount of time and energy. He can hire more and more other executives to help him as the enterprise grows; but this also has its limitations. The wastes of bureaucracy are not confined to government. A very large corporation may have so many layers of executives, so much delay and error in transmission of instructions and information, so wide a gap between top management and people on the plant floor, that it becomes muscle-bound and ends up with higher costs than a smaller concern. This is alleged to have been true of some of the famous early "trusts," including International Harvester and United States Steel. These companies have survived and grown over the years; but their share of total output in their industries has fallen considerably, while the share of smaller, lower-cost competitors has risen.

Evidence on optimum scale of enterprise is hard to get. None of the methods which have been tried is very reliable. One approach is to ask executives in an industry how large a saving in unit costs results from having several plants rather than one under the same management. The consensus of executives in a group of industries studied by Professor Joe Bain was that the savings were small—typically, not more than 2 or 3 percent.[4] Another approach, with different limitations, is to compare profit rates for different sizes of company in the same industry.[5] In manufacturing, at least, it appears that really small companies have high costs and low profits. Costs fall considerably as one moves from small companies to those of moderate size. Beyond that, however, size does not make a great difference. The largest companies in an industry typically do not earn larger profits, and often earn lower profits, than their medium-sized competitors. The evidence suggests that a company can

[4] Joe Bain, *Industrial Organization* (New York: John Wiley & Sons, Inc., 1959), p. 351.

[5] The difficulties in this sort of comparison include: products may not be precisely comparable; different companies may have been operating at different percentages of capacity during the period of the study; and profits for a particular year may have been affected by special circumstances unconnected with production costs.

become too big, and that there are natural checks which prevent one company from swallowing up the economy.

The preceding discussion can be summarized in a parable: suppose I am planning to start a new company for widget production. I hire a firm of management consultants and put the following question to them: If I set up an organization to produce 50,000 widgets a year, what is the lowest cost I can obtain per widget? What will be the cost if I plan for a capacity of 100,000 or 150,000?

The consultants' report, expressed in a graph, might look something like Figure 3. The vertical axis shows cost per widget, usually called

The Effect of Size on Cost

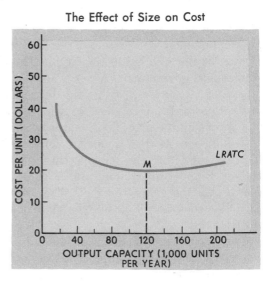

FIGURE 3. *LRATC* is a planning curve or long-run average total cost curve. It shows the lowest unit cost which could be attained by companies of various sizes. Its shape shows that up to a point, large-scale production reduces unit cost, but eventually cost turns upward again. Point *M*, the minimum point on *LRATC*, indicates the optimum scale of company.

unit cost or *average total cost*. The horizontal axis shows various amounts of potential production. Note that this is production of the *company*, not of a single plant. If the optimum scale of plant is 10,000 widgets, then to produce 100,000 widgets I would need to build 10 plants. I can see what my unit cost would then be and plot this as a point on Figure 3. Similarly, I can see what unit cost would be with five plants and a company capacity of 50,000 widgets, and plot this as a second point. By joining up a large number of such points, we get the curve *LRATC*.

LRATC is a *long-run average total cost curve*. It is also often termed a *planning curve*, since it is used in reaching decisions on setting up or expanding plant capacity. The minimum point of the curve, which here is *M*, corresponding to an output capacity of 120,000 widgets, is called the *optimum scale of company*. A company of this size would have lower unit costs than either a larger or smaller company—or so my consultants tell me. The shape which we have given to *LRATC* is that suggested by research findings. As company size increases, unit costs fall rapidly for a while, but the decline tapers off. Beyond *M*, unit costs begin to rise again but not very steeply. Over a wide middle range, size of company does not make a *large* difference in unit cost of production.

COSTS AND THE RATE OF OPERATION

Now suppose I have actually set up in production. I have burned my bridges. And to simplify the story without changing its essence, let's suppose I am operating only one plant rather than several. My potential output is now limited to what I can squeeze out of this one plant. But I can always produce less than this, down to and including zero. And how much I produce will affect my unit cost of production. Let's examine why this is so.

We must first distinguish two kinds of cost:

1. *Fixed (or Overhead) Costs.* These are *costs the amount of which is not influenced by the plant's production level.* They continue even if the plant stands idle, and they do not increase when it is run at full capacity. Property taxes, fire insurance, interest on borrowed money, and salaries of top-management officials are examples of overhead costs. Machinery will deteriorate and become obsolete whether or not it is used in production, so part of the depreciation cost of equipment is overhead.

What things are counted as overhead depends on the *length of time* considered. If you consider only a day or two, almost all costs are fixed. You cannot lay off even plant employees, let alone your office staff, on a day's notice. Over a period of several months, fewer things are fixed and more are variable. Plant workers can be laid off, office staff reduced, raw material orders curtailed, and other expenses trimmed. If you look 20 years ahead, almost everything becomes variable. Old plants can be worn out, old equipment discarded, the company itself liquidated.

The customary distinction between fixed and variable costs assumes a rather short period—say, 6 months or so—during which a company cannot do much about plant, equipment, or basic executive staff. The company is stuck with these expenses, which for this reason are often called "sunk costs." It cannot reduce them by producing less or even by shutting down.

How do fixed costs behave? Since their total amount is constant, fixed cost per unit produced or *average fixed cost* falls steadily as the rate of production increases. Suppose the fixed costs of my widget plant are $100 per day, as shown in Table 1. Then if I produce only five widgets a day, average fixed cost will be $100/5 = $20. But by producing 10 units a day, I could cut this to $10, and the more I produce, the lower the figure will be. Average fixed cost for various rates of output is calculated in

TABLE 1

Costs and Rate of Operation, ABC Manufacturing Company

OUTPUT (Units)	FIXED COST (Dollars)		VARIABLE COST (Dollars)			TOTAL COST (Dollars)	
(1)	TOTAL (2)	AVERAGE (3) = (2)/(1)	MARGINAL (4)	TOTAL (5)	AVERAGE (6) = (5)/(1)	TOTAL (7) = (2) + (5)	AVERAGE (8) = (3) + (6)
0	100	∞		0	0	100	∞
			12				
1	100	100		12	12	112	112
			12				
2	100	50		24	12	124	62
			12				
3	100	33.3		36	12	136	45.3
			12				
4	100	25		48	12	148	37
			12				
5	100	20		60	12	160	32
			12				
6	100	16.7		72	12	172	28.7
			12				
7	100	14.3		84	12	184	26.3
			12				
8	100	12.5		96	12	196	24.5
			12				
9	100	11.1		108	12	208	23.1
			12				
10	100	10		120	12	220	22
			12				
11	100	9.1		132	12	232	21.1
			14				
12	100	8.3		146	12.2	246	20.5
			16				
13	100	7.7		162	12.5	262	20.2
			18				
14	100	7.1		180	12.9	280	20.0
			21				
15	100	6.7		201	13.4	301	20.1
			24				
16	100	6.3		225	14.1	325	20.4
			27				
17	100	5.9		252	14.9	352	20.8
			31				
18	100	5.6		283	15.7	383	21.3
			35				
19	100	5.3		318	16.7	418	22.0
			39				
20	100	5		357	17.9	457	22.9

column 3 of Table 1, and charted in Figure 4.[6] Note that the average fixed cost curve, AFC, falls continuously from left to right.[7]

This reduction of unit cost by producing more units is commonly called "spreading the overhead." It explains why producers are usually eager to produce more and why their eagerness increases in proportion as fixed costs bulk large in their total cost picture. Railroads, whose fixed costs are a high proportion of the total, search strenuously for more freight volume to help "absorb" these costs. Steel mills, automobile producers, and other "heavy" manufacturing industries also benefit greatly from increases in sales volume.

Fixed Cost per Unit Falls Continuously

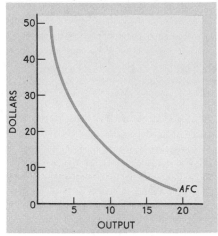

FIGURE 4. AFC shows average fixed (or overhead) costs per units of output. AFC declines continuously as output increases.

The second category of costs is:

2. *Variable (or Direct) Costs.* As the name implies, these are costs which vary with the rate of production. The main direct costs are labor and raw materials. But power, wear and tear on equipment arising from use, and various other costs enter in.

But *how rapidly* do direct costs increase as output increases? Will costs go up less than proportionately, or just in proportion, or perhaps

---

[6] There is the same problem here which we noted earlier in charting utility and demand. Arithmetical illustrations have to proceed by "jumps" of one or more units in output, which when charted yield a series of unconnected points. For graphic analysis, however, it is more convenient and elegant to work with continuous curves. When we draw a continuous curve such as AFC, we are implying that output can be varied by extremely small amounts.

[7] AFC is a rectangular hyperbola, which approaches the two axes asymptotically. If we take any point on AFC, drop lines to the two axes, and calculate the area of the rectangle, this area will be the same regardless of the point chosen. Why? Because this area measures units of output × fixed cost per unit = total fixed cost = a constant.

more than proportionately? This is important from a profit standpoint and has a bearing on how much it pays to produce.

To frame this question more precisely, we must define a new term: the cost of producing one additional unit of product is known as the *marginal cost* of that unit. (Marginal means *additional*, just as it did when we were discussing marginal utility or marginal revenue.) What we want to know, then, is how marginal cost behaves as output is increased. There is no universal answer. It depends on the production setup of the industry. A common situation is that in which equipment is highly divisible and, while the whole plant is always there, the part of it actually used can be increased gradually as production is stepped up. In a weaving mill you can activate 1 man to tend 20 looms, or 2 men and 40 looms, or 10 men and 200 looms. The same is true for a garment shop or any other operation where there is a standard man-machine ratio.[8]

In this case, marginal cost could remain constant over a wide range. Each additional unit of production will require the same amount of material, the same number of man-hours of labor, the same amount of machine time for processing, and so on. Thus output can be stepped up again and again without causing marginal cost to rise.

But this cannot go on forever. The very notion of plant capacity implies that there are limits beyond which it will be difficult or impossible to increase production. As a company tries to squeeze more and more production out of the same plant, marginal cost must eventually begin to rise. Why is this? The normal plant work force will have to be increased, and the new workers may be less efficient than the old. Overtime work becomes necessary and has to be paid for at premium rates. If second or third shifts are used, output per man will be lower on these than on the day shift. When equipment is in constant use, it cannot be maintained so effectively, and machine breakdowns will increase. The plant may become so crowded that men and materials get in each others' way, with a loss of time and output.

In column 4 of Table 1, we suppose that our widget factory behaves in this fashion. Marginal cost remains constant at $12 per unit up to an output of 11 units a day. Then it begins to rise—slowly at first, then more steeply. This behavior of marginal cost is shown by *MC* in Figure 5.

The other curve in Figure 5, the *AVC* curve, shows the *average variable cost* per unit for various rates of output. Why does this diverge

---

[8] Granted, this illustration would not work well for steel, automobiles, or other industries using large and indivisible machinery. Granted also that, even in the textile mill case, a *very* low rate of output might involve high direct costs, because in addition to the weavers, you have to hire supervisors, repair mechanics, janitors, and others in order to operate at all. So for a while marginal cost might fall as the services of these people are more fully utilized. But since plants rarely operate at 20 percent of capacity, this qualification is not very important.

Variable Cost per Unit Eventually Rises

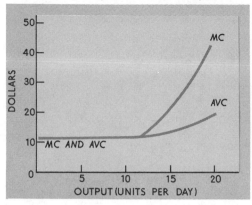

FIGURE 5. MC shows the marginal (= additional) cost of each extra unit of output. AVC for any output shows the average variable cost per unit for that amount of output. MC and AVC may remain constant for a time, but must rise eventually.

from the *MC* curve? Because the two stand for different things. Marginal cost is the additional cost for *one unit* only. Average variable cost is the average for *all the units* produced up to that point. As long as *MC* is constant, *AVC* will also be constant and equal to it. When *MC* begins to rise, *AVC* must also rise, but more slowly, because it is being "pulled down" by the lower costs of earlier units included in the average. The calculation of *AVC* is shown in columns 5 and 6 of Table 1. Total variable cost in column 5 is found by summing up the cost of each unit from column 4. Then in column 6 we get average variable cost by dividing the total by the number of units produced.

The company manager, of course, is interested in how he comes out overall, when fixed and variable costs have been added together. This addition is performed in column 8. Adding average fixed cost (column 3) to average variable cost (column 6) yields average total cost (column 8). The *ATC* curve in Figure 6 is thus the (vertical) sum of the *AFC* and *AVC* curves.

Note that average total cost falls for a long time, because average fixed cost is falling fast enough to more than offset the rise in direct costs. Eventually, however, the rise in direct costs begins to predominate and *ATC* turns upward. Lowest cost per unit is achieved at point *Q*, with an output of 14 units. This is the most efficient rate of operation and is defined as the *capacity* of the plant. The plant can produce more or less than this, but at any other rate of production, unit cost will be higher.

Capacity in the economic sense of least-cost rate of output differs from capacity in the everyday sense of maximum possible output. Every year the McGraw-Hill Publishing Company surveys a large number of manufacturing enterprises and asks them, among other things, what percentage of their capacity they are currently using and what percentage they would prefer to use. The preferred rates of operation are usually

Average Total Cost First Falls and Then Rises as Output Is Increased

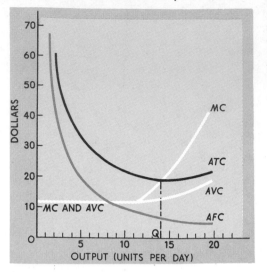

FIGURE 6. Average total cost, ATC, is the sum of AFC and AVC for any rate of output. It falls for a time, because AFC is falling faster than AVC is rising; but eventually the opposite becomes true and ATC turns upward. Production OQ, for which ATC is a minimum, is defined as the *capacity* of the plant.

in the neighborhood of 90 percent. Here the companies are using "capacity" in the ordinary sense. They are saying, in effect, that the minimum point of their *ATC* curves is at about 90 percent of the maximum they could produce. The last 10 percent would involve high marginal costs and rising average total cost.[9]

The fact that *MC* intersects *ATC* at the minimum point of *ATC* is not an accident, and we can show that this must always be true. Take a group of boys averaging 6 feet in height and add another boy 5 feet 8 inches tall. The average of the group will now be lower than before. But if we added a boy taller than the previous average, say 6 feet 2 inches, the average height of the group would rise. The same principle holds here. So long as the cost of an additional unit of output is *below* the average cost of previous units, i.e., so long as *MC* is below *ATC*, then *ATC* must decline. But when we begin adding units the cost of which is *above* the previous average, i.e., when *MC* rises above *ATC*, then *ATC* must begin to rise. Hence *MC* must intersect *ATC* at its minimum point.

It should be emphasized that *ATC* includes *all* necessary costs of production, including a normal rate of return on invested capital. Thus, any time the producer is getting a price above *ATC*, he is making a profit and has an incentive to expand. If he is getting less than *ATC*, his profit is negative, and if the situation continues, he will consider dropping out of the industry.

---

[9] See *Measures of Productive Capacity* (Hearings before the Joint Economic Committee, 87th Cong., 2d sess. [Washington, D.C.: U.S. Government Printing Office, 1962]), especially testimony of Mr. Douglas Greenwald, Economics Department, McGraw-Hill Publishing Co.

OUTPUT UNDER PURE COMPETITION

Now that we know the cost of producing widgets, we can go on to a related question: how do I decide how many widgets to produce per day? How do I select the best rate of plant operation, the rate which will maximize my profit?

Costs alone are not a sufficient basis for this decision. I must know also how much I can get for each widget; and this depends partly on the kind of market in which I am operating. Let's begin with the simplest case of pure competition. My output is such a small part of total industry output that I can vary my rate of sales without affecting the market price. The price is given to me from the outside and is unaffected by my own actions.

To put the same point in another way: *The demand curve for my product is horizontal at the prevailing price.* This is illustrated by the horizontal lines in Figure 7. If, for example, the market price is *OP*, my demand curve is *PP*. I can sell any amount I wish at that price. If, on the other hand, the market price were *OP₁*, my demand curve would be *P₁P₁*; and so on.

Note another important feature of this case: under pure competition, price and marginal revenue are the same thing. If I can sell an additional unit with no reduction in price, then my revenue is increased by the full price of that unit. So *marginal revenue equals price and is constant.* If the market price is *OP*, then *PP* is *both* my demand curve and my marginal revenue curve.

Determining the Best Rate of Output

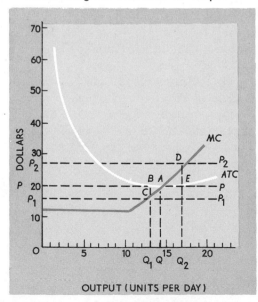

FIGURE 7. To determine the proper rate of output, look at the price line and the MC curve. The firm will make most profit (or least loss) by producing the output for which price = MC. To determine the profit level, look at the price line and the ATC curve. If price is above ATC, there is positive profit; if it is below, there is negative profit.

To determine the most profitable rate of output, we must bring cost and revenue together in a single picture, such as Figure 7. Actually, we need only two of the cost curves from our previous diagrams, the MC and ATC curves. On the demand side, we show several possible prices, in order to see what will happen in each case.

Suppose, first, the market price of widgets were $10. At this price, and in fact at any price below $11, the plant cannot afford to operate. The marginal cost of producing each widget would be higher than its price, and the company would be out of pocket on every unit sold. So it is best to shut down the plant completely. The company will be losing money to the extent of its overhead costs, but it will lose less by shutting down than by operating.

What if the market price rises to $16, indicated by P_1P_1? Now the plant can afford to operate, since the price of a widget is sufficient to cover the direct cost of producing it. How much will it pay to produce? The answer is OQ_1, or 13 units per day. Why is this? Because up to this point the price is more than sufficient to cover the marginal cost of producing additional units. The marginal cost of the thirteenth unit, however, is just equal to its price, since P_1P_1 intersects MC at this point. And if production were pushed beyond OQ_1, marginal cost would rise above the price line. Units to the right of Q_1 would cost more to produce than could be gotten for them on the market, and so their production is unprofitable.

Note that at output OQ_1, profits are negative, since price is below average total cost by the amount BC. This is too bad, but the company cannot do anything about the market price, and it will lose less by producing at OQ_1 than at any other rate. At this output, it is covering its variable costs and earning enough in addition to cover part of its overhead. If it shut down, it would still have to pay overhead costs and would have no income at all. (Check back to Table 1 and verify that, with a $16 price, the company will lose more at zero output than at an output of 13.)

A happier situation is shown by the price OP. It will now pay to increase production to the intersection of PP and MC, which occurs at $OQ = 14$ units. At this point, price just equals average total cost, and the firm is earning a normal return. If price should rise to OP_2, it will pay to increase production further to $OQ_2 = 17$ units. And now the company will be making positive profits, since the price of each unit exceeds average total cost by the amount DE.

This leads to a rule for production decisions under pure competition: *A producer will make maximum profit (or suffer minimum loss) by producing the output for which marginal cost is equal to price.* Since price and marginal revenue are the same thing, marginal cost must also equal marginal revenue. Thus the rule can be stated as:

$$MC = P = MR .$$

The supply curve of the individual producer under pure competition, then, slopes upward to the right. As the price of the product rises, the price line intersects *MC* at higher and higher points, and it becomes profitable to produce more and more output. The shape of the firm's supply curve rests on the shape of its marginal cost curve.

OUTPUT UNDER MONOPOLY

Consider a case at the opposite pole from pure competition. I am the only widget producer in the country. The demand curve for widgets is *my* demand curve. Since the demand curve for any product slopes downward, my demand curve will slope downward, and I must lower the price if I want to sell more.

The competitive producer adjusts his output to a price given by the market. But the monopolist can set his own price and adjust output accordingly.

In Figure 8 we draw in the *MC* and *ATC* curves as before. The demand curve is *D*, and the associated marginal revenue curve is *MR*. Note that *MR* falls faster than *D*. Why? Because to sell an additional unit of product, I must lower the price on *all* units sold. So the additional revenue which that unit yields is less than its price.

Suppose I know the facts and am interested in making the largest possible profit from my operation. How much should I produce, and what price should I charge? On one side, I must consider the cost of producing an additional unit of output. On the other hand, I must consider how much it will add to my revenue. I will do best by observing the rule: *produce that quantity for which marginal cost equals marginal revenue.*

Maximum Profit for a Monopolist

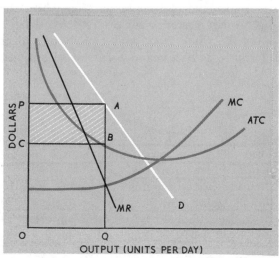

FIGURE 8. I have a monopoly of the widget industry. *D* is the demand curve for widgets, and *MR* is the marginal revenue curve. My *MC* and *ATC* curves are just as before. I will make maximum profit by producing OQ units, where MC = MR. I can sell this amount at a price OP = AQ. My profit is AB per unit, and my total profit is the shaded area PABC.

In Figure 8 this quantity is OQ, corresponding to the intersection of MC and MR.

The logic of the $MC = MR$ rule is clear. At rates of output to the left of Q, MR is greater than MC. Selling one more unit will add more to revenue than it does to cost. So it pays to produce this unit, and another, and another, until Q is reached. But then one should stop. Any unit beyond Q would add more to cost than to revenue, hence would reduce profit.

So much for my output. Now what price should I charge? Looking at the demand curve, we see that the output OQ can be sold for a price OP. So I will operate at point A on the demand curve, with a healthy gap between price and ATC. For output OQ, average total cost is QB. Remember that this includes the normal return on capital which would be earned under pure competition. With a price of QA, then, I make a profit of AB on each unit. My total profit—profit per unit times the units sold—is the shaded rectangle $PABC$. This is a larger profit than I could make at any other point on the demand curve.

Note that there is no difference between the monopolist and the pure competitor in degree of selfishness or in general principles of behavior. Both try to maximize profit. Both observe the $MC = MR$ rule. But because of the difference in their market situations, the consequences of following this rule will be different. Price will typically come out higher and output lower under monopoly than it would have under pure competition.

The idea that business concerns aim at maximum profit has been subjected to much criticism and debate. The modern executive of a large corporation, it is argued, is not much interested in maximizing profit. Even if he were, demand and cost curves shift so rapidly that he couldn't possibly succeed in hitting the maximum-profit point. We shall come back to this interesting issue at the end of Chapter 9. Meanwhile, the profit maximization principle is worth mastering for two reasons: there is *something* to it, even if it is not the whole story; and it provides a clear take-off point for what might otherwise be a vague discussion of business motivation.

SUMMARY

1. The cost of producing one unit of a product depends on the prices of the factors used, the method of production, the size of the producing enterprise, and the rate of plant operation.

2. Cost includes the market price of purchased factors and the *imputed cost* of producer-owned factors, calculated at what the factor could have earned in alternative uses. Imputed labor cost is important in small businesses, and imputed capital cost is important in large enterprises.

3. Profit is a surplus over all costs, including imputed costs. It can be either positive or negative.

4. A product can usually be produced by several different methods, using different amounts of the factors of production. A curve linking different combinations of two factors (say, labor and capital) which will produce the same amount of output is called an *isoquant*.

5. Given the known methods of production—that is, given the isoquant map—and given the price of each factor, one can determine which method will yield lowest production costs. The lower the relative price of a factor, the more of that factor it will pay to employ. The least-cost method of cotton weaving will use much more labor in India than in the United States.

6. A curve showing the lowest unit production cost which can be attained by various sizes of enterprise is called a *long-run average total cost curve* (*LRATC*), or a *planning curve*. Unit costs fall for some time because of the production and distribution economies open to large enterprises; but eventually they begin to rise because of difficulties of supervision and coordination. The size of enterprise which has lower unit costs than any other is termed the *optimum scale* of enterprise.

7. Costs can be divided into *fixed costs*, which are independent of the rate of plant operation, and *variable costs*, which do vary with output. The addition to variable costs resulting from an additional unit of output is called *marginal cost*.

8. As output is increased, marginal cost may remain constant for a considerable time; but it must eventually rise as output nears the physical maximum of the plant. When MC begins to rise, average variable cost (AVC) must also rise; and when the rise in AVC begins to exceed the decline in average fixed cost (which is always falling), then average total cost (ATC) begins to rise.

9. The least-cost rate of plant operation is that for which ATC is a minimum. This is termed the *capacity* of the plant and is normally below the physical maximum rate of output.

10. Under pure competition, a producer can sell as much as he wishes at the market price. He faces a horizontal demand curve for his product. Since price is constant, it follows that *marginal revenue is constant and equal to price*.

11. The producer under pure competition will make maximum profit (or incur minimum loss) by producing that output for which marginal cost is equal to price. At this rate of output:

$$MC = P = MR.$$

12. A monopoly producer faces a sloped demand curve for his product, and so marginal revenue is less than price. He will also do best by choosing the rate of output for which

$$MC = MR,$$

but note that P has dropped out of the equation. Since P is now higher than MR, it will also be higher than MC.

DISCUSSION QUESTIONS

1. Review your understanding of the following concepts: imputed cost; profit; engineering efficiency; economic efficiency; isoquant; production surface; least-cost method of production; long-run average total cost curve; optimum scale; fixed costs; variable costs; marginal cost; short-run average total cost curve; plant capacity; maximum-profit output under pure competition; maximum-profit output under monopoly.

2. Is the problem of producing at least cost important only to business concerns or is it important to all of us? Explain.

3. What is meant by a "normal rate of return"? Return to *whom,* and on *what?*

4. Suppose the statistics for all U.S. business corporations in 1966 showed an average return of 7 percent on owners' investment. Does this indicate that 7 percent is the normal rate of return defined above?

5. "While there may be many possible ways of producing a good, there is always one best way. The engineer's job is to discover this method and apply it." Discuss.

6. Can you think of situations in which there is literally only one known method of production? How do such situations change the conclusions reached in our discussion of production methods?

7. What are the main economies and diseconomies associated with different sizes of *plant?* With different sizes of *company?*

8. What practical difference does it make whether the long-run average total cost curve in a particular industry is saucer-shaped or cup-shaped? Which is more common in practice?

9. Why does the short-run average total cost curve first decline and then rise? Why must MC intersect ATC at the point where ATC is a minimum?

10. Why is capacity in the economic sense typically below capacity in the everyday sense?

11. How will a producer under pure competition decide his best rate of output?

12. Will a company sometimes produce even at a loss? Why? When will it pay to shut down completely?

13. Suppose a company's fixed costs suddenly double—say, because of a sharp increase in property taxes. Will this affect its output decisions in the short run? In the long run?

14. "The monopoly producer acts on precisely the same principles as the purely competitive producer. The fact that his decisions have different economic consequences arises solely from his different market situation." Do you agree? Explain.

APPENDIX: THE RELATION OF SHORT-RUN AND LONG-RUN COST CURVES

In this chapter we analyzed two different kinds of cost curve. The long-run *ATC* curve, or planning curve, shows the effect on unit costs of a *larger or smaller scale of enterprise*. It is called "long run" because building new productive capacity, and more especially wearing out and abandoning old plant capacity, takes a considerable time.

The short-run *ATC* curve, on the other hand, shows the effect on unit costs of a *higher or lower rate of production from an enterprise of fixed scale*. You have made your basic decision on how much production capacity to build. Now all you can do is produce more or less from this fixed plant (or plants); and your costs vary accordingly.

How are these two kinds of curve related? Suppose you build a plant designed for a certain level of output, corresponding to a certain point on *LRATC*. You can still vary the output of the plant within limits. But then you will be operating on the short-run *ATC* for a plant of that size. In Figure 9, a plant designed for output OQ_1 will have a short-run *ATC* curve like $SRATC_1$. But if you had built a larger plant designed to produce OQ_2, you would be operating on $SRATC_2$; and so on. The long-run curve *LRATC* contains a very large number of *SRATC* curves, each

There Is a Short-Run ATC Curve for Each Point
on the Long-Run ATC Curve

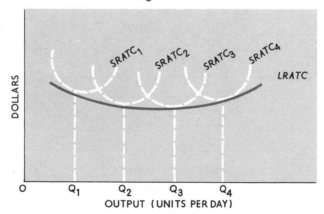

FIGURE 9. Any point on *LRATC* indicates minimum unit cost for a certain scale of enterprise. Once the scale has been chosen, the enterprise is operating on the *SRATC* curve corresponding to that scale. Four short-run curves are shown for illustration. $SRATC_3$ is the short-run curve for an enterprise of *optimum* scale, i.e., one which yields lowest possible unit costs.

corresponding to a slightly different scale of enterprise, and all "sitting on top" of the *LRATC*.

Why must they sit on top? Think for a minute about the economic meaning of Figure 9. Suppose you had built plant 1 in the first instance, intending to produce in the neighborhood of OQ_1. But now demand for the product turns out to be very high, and you would like to produce OQ_2 instead. You may be able to get this much output from plant 1, but it will be quite expensive, since you will be traveling up $SRATC_1$ to the right at higher and higher cost. But if you allow enough time to build additional capacity—a "long" period—you can move onto $SRATC_2$, and you can get output OQ_2 at much lower cost. *Moral:* For any rate of output, you can get a lower unit cost if you have time to adapt your production capacity to just that rate of output. This is why the *LRATC* must always be below the *SRATC*'s which it embraces.

Note also that one of these scales of enterprise is better, in the sense of permitting a lower *ATC*, than any other. This is $SRATC_3$, which was designed for output OQ_3, corresponding to the minimum point of *LRATC*—the *optimum scale* of enterprise.

This kind of diagram also helps to explain where cost and price will settle down in a purely competitive industry over the long run. Look at Figure 10, showing the cost levels attainable by producers in a certain

Long-Run Equilibrium of a Firm in Pure Competition

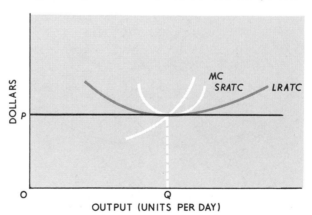

FIGURE 10. Under pure competition, each producer is forced toward the optimum scale OQ, where unit cost is at the lowest possible level OP. The price cannot remain permanently higher than OP, since positive profit would cause an influx of new producers. Nor can it remain permanently lower for the opposite reason. If costs and demand remained stable long enough for things to settle down, each producer would reach an equilibrium position in which $P = MC = SRATC = LRATC$. With some qualifications to be added later, this gives a definition of ideal economic efficiency.

industry. Each producer will tend to move toward the optimum scale OQ. Since he can sell as much as he chooses at the prevailing price, there is no marketing problem to check his expansion. Since he can get a lower unit cost by moving toward OQ, there is a positive inducement to do so. There is also a negative inducement in that if he fails to move toward OQ while other producers are doing so, he will find himself in trouble with high costs and probable losses.

Suppose now that all producers have established enterprises of optimum scale and are operating on the short-run curve $SRATC$. We can now show that OP is the only feasible price level over the long run. As usual, we prove this by asking what would happen if it were *not* so. Suppose price were above OP. Then each producer would operate where $P = MC$, and hence where $P > ATC$. Producers would have positive profits. But if entrance to the industry were unrestricted, which is one of the conditions for pure competition, new producers would come in to take advantage of this profit opportunity. Their additional production, however, would drive price down toward OP. When price reached OP, profits would be zero (that is, earnings would be normal), there would be no incentive for more producers to enter, and the industry would be in equilibrium.

By a similar chain of reasoning it can be shown that a price below OP would involve losses, which would drive producers out of the industry until reduced production raised the price to OP once more.

OP, then, is the *long-run equilibrium price for the industry*. In long-run equilibrium,

$$P = MC = SRATC = LRATC .$$

This is an optimum position, because unit production costs are at the lowest point permitted by existing factor prices and technical knowledge. Each enterprise is of optimum scale and is being run at the optimum rate. If all industries in the economy were simultaneously in this position, there would be no way to increase total output with the resources available. This is why the idea of full competitive equilibrium remains useful as a definition of economic efficiency, even though no actual economy may approach it very closely.

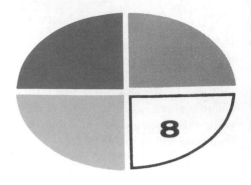

Competition among the Many

Now THAT WE have seen where demand and supply come from, we can return to our main theme: what determines the price and output of each good in the economy? What determines the allocation of productive resources among various products?

Types of Market Structure

The answer depends not only on demand and cost conditions but on the *structure of the market* for the product—how many sellers there are, how many buyers there are, whether sellers get together on price, and so on. We shall usually look at markets from the *seller's side*, on the assumption that sellers are fewer and bigger than buyers and that their policies are of dominant importance. But we shall also note cases in which buyers are few and important—for example, the large chain store buying from many small manufacturers.

A key market characteristic is whether there are *many or few sellers* of the product. What do we mean by "few"? This is not a matter of numbers but a matter of behavior. We say that there are "few" sellers if a price change by one seller will be noticed and reacted to by other sellers. "Few" means few enough so that they can keep track of each other. By the same token, there are "many" sellers when no one of them is important enough for others to pay attention to his actions. The market with many sellers is an anonymous market, where each seller is free to make his own decisions without worrying about the reactions of his rivals.

Fewness of sellers means that each is large *relative to the size of the market*. Often they are large in absolute size as well, as in the case of automobile or basic steel production. But fewness need not mean bigness. A small town usually has only a few banks, movie theaters, doctors, lawyers. Here is fewness without bigness.

Competition among the few has a different tone from competition among the many. It is mainly where sellers are few that one encounters the activities which constitute "competition" in everyday parlance: rivalry for sales, accusations about price cutting, emphasis on advertising and marketing, efforts to develop a distinctive product, close watch on the actions of one's competitors. Where there are many sellers, on the other hand, people pay no attention to each other. It is one of the paradoxes of language that in this situation—the essence of free competition from the economist's standpoint—sellers do not behave "competitively" in the ordinary sense. A purely competitive market is completely impersonal.

A second dimension of market structure turns on the *homogeneous* or *differentiated* character of the product. A certain grade of wheat, beef, steel sheets, bituminous coal, or fuel oil is a homogeneous product. Because the essential qualities of the product are few and measurable, they can be identified by a grade which tells the buyer all he needs to know. There is no basis for advertising such a product, since this could add nothing to the buyer's information. Nor is there any reason for buyers to prefer one seller over another. The products of various sellers are completely substitutable for each other. If, in addition, there are many sellers, we have a situation of *pure competition*.

If the product is differentiated, on the other hand, *the product of one seller is not a perfect substitute for that of another*. Different brands of soap, cigarettes, or automobiles are examples. Note that the test of differentiation is in the mind of the buyer. It does not matter whether different brands of toothpaste are physically different so long as buyers are convinced that they are different. To strengthen such convictions is a major purpose of advertising.

The services provided by retail stores and service establishments are also differentiated products. A box of Wheaties sold in two different groceries is not the same product to me as a buyer. One grocery may be nearer to my home than the other. One grocer may be more accommodating as regards credit, delivery, and other services. I may prefer the personality of the checkout girl in one store to that of her opposite number. For these or other reasons, I may prefer to buy at one store rather than the other. This preference, which ties me in some measure to one seller, means that the market is no longer purely competitive.

When a situation like this exists, we have what has been termed *imperfect competition* or *monopolistic competition*. The latter term underlines the fact that each seller has a distinct product and a group of regular customers who prefer that product. As regards this group, he has a limited degree of monopoly power. He has his own demand curve and is not tied to a uniform market price. If he raises his price above that of other sellers, he will lose some but not all of his customers. It he cuts his price below that of others, he will gain some customers, but everybody will not rush to him. Some will remain loyal to their customary seller. The strength of dealer loyalties or brand loyalties can be judged from the elasticity of the demand curves of the various sellers.

Three other dimensions of market structure may be given briefer notice. The *number of buyers* in the market is important. The number of consumer buyers in retail markets is typically large. But there are other markets in which buyers are few: the canner or meat packer buying from many farmers, the large auto company buying parts from many suppliers, or the large mail-order house buying from many manufacturers. There is no reason why the two sides of the market need be symmetrical. The market may include many sellers and many buyers, few sellers and many buyers, few buyers and many sellers, or few people on each side. Economists have spent much time analyzing situations where a single buyer confronts a single seller, a case known as bilateral monopoly: for example, the United Mine Workers bargaining with all coal companies over the wage rate for miners.

Freedom of entrance to the market is important. There are industries in which the costs and risks of setting up in business are so great that new producers are effectively barred. Entrance to some businesses and occupations is restricted by licensing regulations. In such cases, price and output will differ from what they would have been with complete freedom of entrance.

The *market behavior* of sellers and buyers—in particular, whether they reach independent decisions or whether they cooperate in various ways—can make a substantial difference. Even where sellers are few, they may conceivably operate at arm's length. On the other hand, they may try to regulate prices, allocate shares of the market, and freeze out new producers. If they can do this without falling foul of the antitrust laws, they should be able to make more money.

We have emphasized five things: number of sellers in the market, number of buyers in the market, homogeneous or differentiated character of the product, conditions of entrance to the market, and market behavior of buyers and sellers. And there are still other market characteristics which we might have examined. By taking all possible combinations of these characteristics, one can construct a large number of market situations. To analyze all of these would take a book in itself. We propose instead to select a few cases of special interest and importance.

In this chapter, we explore what happens under *pure competition* and *monopolistic competition*. Both situations involve many sellers, many buyers, free entrance to the market, and absence of price fixing or other collusive action. In both cases, we can say that competition is *free* or *atomistic*, since each seller is a small atom in the market universe. The difference is that *under pure competition the product is homogeneous, while under monopolistic competition it is differentiated.*

In the next chapter we shall examine cases in which there is one seller (*monopoly*) or only a few sellers (*oligopoly*).

PRICE AND OUTPUT UNDER PURE COMPETITION

We have already noted the importance of *time* in market adjustments. If the price of a consumer good is changed, consumers will not change their buying habits very much this week or next week. The demand curve will be highly inelastic. But if we allow time for word of the change to get around and for consumers to rethink their buying patterns, there will be a larger sales response. The longer the period allowed for adjustment, the more elastic the demand curve.

Time is important also on the side of supply. If we consider only a day or two, supply may be completely fixed. But if we allow a few weeks or months, the supply of most goods can be increased by operating plants at a higher rate. If we allow still more time, new plants can be built and supply increased in this way. Which kind of supply increase we are talking about will make a decided difference to costs, as we saw in Chapter 7. In fact, one cannot really draw a supply curve without specifying the adjustment period to which it relates.

It is useful to distinguish three different periods:

1. The *market period,* in which all goods available for sale have already been produced.
2. The *short period* or *short run,* which is long enough to allow changes in the rate of production from existing plants, but not long enough to allow construction of new plants.
3. The *long period* or *long run,* which is long enough for new plants to be built and new producers to enter the industry.

Note that these are *functional* definitions rather than *clock-time* definitions. They run in terms of *what happens* over the course of time rather than in terms of so many weeks or months. Thus the market period, during which available supplies remain fixed, may be a day for fresh strawberries, a month for cotton textiles, a year for corn production or labor supply.

Little need be said about price determination in the market period, which is illustrated in Figure 1. The supply curve is a vertical line, indicating that supply is fixed for the time being. This being so, price is determined solely by the level of demand. The higher the demand, the higher the price, and vice versa.

This diagram is useful in explaining the gyrations of prices for perishable products. Fresh fish is the classic example. The catch on a particular day determines market supply, and this supply has to be sold

With Supply Fixed, Price Depends Solely on Demand

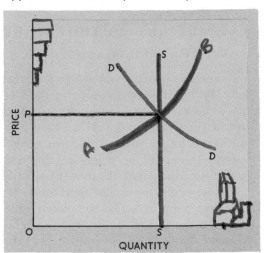

FIGURE 1. With supply fixed at *OS*, price depends solely on the level of demand. If demand is *DD*, price will be *OP*.

for whatever it will bring. (This illustration, however, dates from before the invention of the deep-freeze. What effect would you expect the possibility of freezing fish to have on the shape of the supply curve?)

Price and Output in the Short Run

The distinguishing feature of this period is that plant is fixed but output can be varied. So each producer is operating on the short-run cost curves described in Chapter 7. Under pure competition, a producer will produce at the point where price equals marginal cost. As price rises, it will be worth his while to produce more, because the higher price compensates him for a rising marginal cost.

By the definition of pure competition, we have many producers in the industry. So how do we get a total supply curve for the product? Quite simply: by adding together the supply curves for all producers. This is illustrated in Figure 2. At the left of the diagram are cost curves for three producers, companies A, B, and C. At the right is a demand-supply diagram for the industry as a whole. Note that the output scale on the industry diagram is laid out in millions, while that for each producer is in thousands.

Suppose the price of this product were OP. Then, by looking across to company A's marginal cost curve, we see that it will produce an output of Oq_a. Similarly, B will produce Oq_b, C will produce Oq_c, and so on for each of the other producers. If OQ is total output at price OP, then

$$OQ = Oq_a + Oq_b + Oq_c + \cdots + Oq_n.$$

This gives us one point on the industry supply curve S.

Next, suppose the price were OR. Then the total industry output at this price will be

$$OT = Ot_a + Ot_b + Ot_c + \cdots Ot_n.$$

This gives us a second point on the supply curve for the industry. By repeating this for many alternative prices, we can trace out the whole supply curve.

This leads to an important conclusion: *the short-run supply curve of an industry always slopes upward.* It does so because it is based on the marginal cost curves of individual producers. Its slope reflects the higher cost of forcing more and more product out of a fixed number of plants.

Which of the various prices we assumed in tracing out the supply curve will be the actual price? This depends on demand as well as supply. If the demand curve were D in Figure 2, the short-run equilibrium price would be OU, and the quantity produced would be OV. If the demand curve shifted upward, say to D_1, both price and output would be higher. This leads to a second principle: *in the short run, under pure competition, a rise in demand raises both price and output;* and conversely for a fall in demand.

By calling OU a short-run equilibrium price, we are implying that it may not prevail indefinitely; and in this case, it clearly would not. Note that each producer in the industry is producing Ov, and that price is above average total cost. Profits are positive, and this provides incentive for new producers to enter the industry. Given sufficient time, new plant capacity will be built and put into operation. The amount of product forthcoming at each price will be greater than before. The supply curve S, therefore, will shift to the right and intersect D at a lower point, forcing down the price and raising industry output.

We can show also that a short-run equilibrium price such as OP could not persist. All companies are now making negative profit and have an incentive to get out of the industry. As companies are squeezed out of the industry, less output is forthcoming at each price. S shifts to the left, intersects D at a higher point, and the price rises.

Over the long run, then, the industry can be in equilibrium only at the price *OR*. Why is this? Because with this price each producer is operating at the minimum of his *ATC* curve and just earning a normal rate of return. There is no incentive for producers to leave the industry or for new producers to enter. Any short-period price higher or lower than *OR* will cause the industry supply curve to shift in such a way that price moves back toward *OR*.

This neat thermostatic control of price and output seems almost too good to be true. Is it anywhere near the facts of life? One way in which we have deliberately simplified reality is by supposing that all companies have identical cost curves. Only so can we maintain that *OR*, which is a

Total Supply Is Obtained by Adding the Output of All Producers

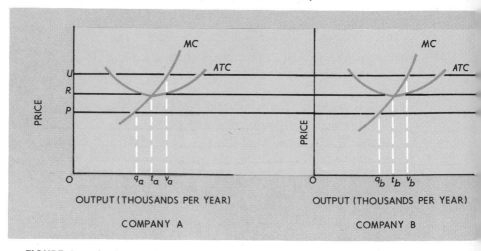

FIGURE 2.   The left-hand diagrams show short-run cost curves for three of the many producers in a competitive industry. The demand-supply diagram at the right shows the total industry situation. For any price such as *OP*, we can draw a horizontal line

zero-profit price for company A, will also be a zero-profit price for companies B, C, and so on. In reality, there may be considerable cost differences among companies in the same industry. We have also talked rather glibly about producers being tempted into, or forced out of, an industry. Tempting new producers in is not difficult; but to reduce capacity in an overexpanded industry is a slow and painful process. We shall say more about these real-life complications in a moment; but first we must complete our sketch of pure competition by examining long-period adjustments.

Price and Output in the Long Run

The distinctive feature of the long run is that productive capacity can be expanded or contracted. New plants can be built or old ones abandoned. In a growing economy, most industries are increasing their productive capacity over the years. What does this do to cost and price? Will addition of more plants raise the level of costs in the industry, or lower it, or leave it unchanged?

Let us frame this question more precisely. Consider a purely competitive industry in full equilibrium. *Each company is operating at capacity, and each is of optimum size.* Price just equals average total cost and all is well. Now demand increases, so price rises and positive profits appear. This causes new companies, presumably also of optimum size, to enter the industry. What will this do to the cost level of existing

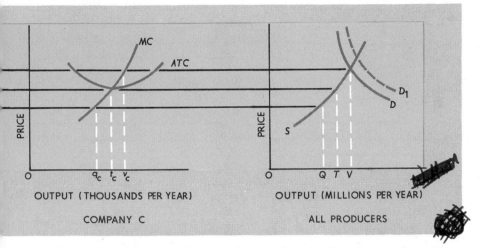

OUTPUT (THOUSANDS PER YEAR)

COMPANY C

OUTPUT (MILLIONS PER YEAR)

ALL PRODUCERS

across the company diagrams to determine how much each will produce at that price. Adding these up gives total industry output at that price, i.e., a point on the industry's S curve.

producers? Will costs be increased, or decreased, or remain unchanged? Where will cost and price settle down after the industry has adjusted fully to the new level of demand?

There are three possibilities. These possibilities are usually termed *constant costs, increasing costs,* and *decreasing costs.* Let us look at these in turn.

Constant costs. One possibility is that new companies entering the industry will have the same cost level as the old ones and that the cost level of existing producers will remain unchanged. This requires that this industry's demand for labor, materials, and other factors of production form a small part of total demand for these factors, so that expansion of the industry will not affect factor prices. If it is true that expansion of capacity leaves everyone's costs unchanged, then the industry's long-run supply curve will be horizontal. Production can be expanded to any desired extent with no increase in unit cost and no need for a permanently higher level of prices.

Constant cost is probably a common situation in manufacturing, trade, services, and other industries. The argument for assuming constant cost can be put simply as: why not? If the labor, land, capital, and other factors used in an industry are doubled, why shouldn't the product also double? If the product does double, and if factor prices remain unchanged, unit production cost will be unchanged. It is departures from constant cost, rather than constant cost itself, which require special explanation.

Increasing costs. There are industries in which productive capacity can be added only at higher cost, and where the long-run supply curve consequently slopes upward. Why might this be? One possibility is that the industry uses such a large part of some factor of production that expansion of the industry's demand for that factor raises its price. An industry localized in one area, and which needs to expand its labor force, may have to offer higher wages to induce workers to migrate to the area from other communities.

Another possibility is that, while more units of the factor can be bought for the same price, additional units are less and less productive in the industry in question. Capacity for scientific work, for example, differs widely among individuals. To increase the number of scientists substantially, as we have been trying to do recently, means drawing on people who are less and less well suited for the purpose. Thus cost per unit of scientific output goes up.

A classic illustration of this possibility is wine growing. Good wine land requires an unusual combination of soil composition, rainfall, slope, exposure to sun, and shelter from storms. The amount of first-class land available is limited. If wine growers know their business, as they should after several hundred years, the best land will be put into cultivation first. As demand continues to increase, land which is less and less well adapted to vineyards will have to be used. This land will produce smaller yields for the labor and materials used, which means higher marginal costs for added units of output. The more demand increases, the more marginal costs will rise. The top-quality land will also be worked more intensively by using more labor, fertilizers, and equipment per acre. But this also leads to rising marginal costs, as extra gallons of wine are won with greater and greater effort.

This is a common situation in all the extractive industries. It is easy to take out the largest and most accessible trees from a stand of virgin timber. As one goes farther away from transportation and into smaller trees, marginal costs will rise. Copper mines differ greatly in depth of the ore body below the surface, thickness of the veins, and copper content of the ore. The cheapest known sources of ore will be exploited first. As demand increases, it becomes necessary to use thinner veins and lower-grade ores at higher cost per pound of copper.

Decreasing costs. Are there cases of the opposite sort, in which expanding an industry will lower production costs? There are several reasons why this may happen. One possibility is that the industry consists of a single large installation, which for the time being cannot be operated at the optimum rate because demand is insufficient. A small and poor country may have one good hydroelectric power source. To tap this source means building a large dam, generating plant, and transmission system. Since the country is underdeveloped, the immediate demand amounts to only a fraction of plant capacity. Overhead is not spread effectively, and average total cost is high. As the economy grows and power demand rises, the industry can operate at lower and lower points on its ATC curve.

Where the optimum scale of production is very large relative to demand, the industry cannot be organized on a competitive basis. This is why electric power, railroading, telephone service, and the like are often called "natural monopolies."

Can we find any reasons for decreasing cost while remaining within the bounds of pure competition? One possibility is that larger output for the industry may make possible a finer subdivision and specialization of work among individual companies. One set of plants may do nothing but spin cotton yarn, another group nothing but weaving, another group may do cloth dyeing and finishing, and so on. In this way, each plant may get larger production volume and lower unit costs *on a specific operation* than could be had if each plant performed all the operations from raw material to finished products.

Another possibility is that, by operating on a larger scale, an industry may be able to get some of the factors at lower cost or, what amounts to the same thing, get more efficient factors at the same price. Where there are many retailers, as in New York City, one finds schools of retailing. If going through such a school makes managers more efficient, the industry's costs should be reduced. Where a manufacturing industry has become localized in a certain area, it gradually creates a pool of skilled and experienced labor which did not exist in the first instance and which raises labor efficiency throughout the industry. Production of key materials and supplies can be delegated to supplementary producers, who can achieve larger output and lower costs as the industry expands. The Akron tire plants can get vulcanizing chemicals more cheaply by buying them from a nearby chemical plant than by producing them themselves; but this chemical plant could not be built until the tire industry became large enough to make the venture profitable.

An expanding industry may be able, for that matter, to buy electric power and transportation more cheaply by enabling *those* industries to operate closer to capacity and hence at lower unit cost. But this is a "lifting by one's own bootstraps" kind of explanation: to explain decreasing cost under pure competition in this way, you have to start with one or more industries which are *not* purely competitive!

To sum up: the long-run supply curve of an industry, like any supply curve, is a schedule of the prices required to call forth various amounts of output. Its shape depends on which of the cost conditions just described prevails in the industry. If the industry is subject to increasing costs, it will have a rising supply curve such as S_1 in Figure 3. Higher prices will be necessary to call forth increased production. A constant cost industry will have a horizontal supply curve such as S_2. If the

The Long-Run Effect of a Change in Demand Depends on the Supply Situation

FIGURE 3. When the curtain rises, this industry is operating at A on the demand curve D. S_1, S_2, and S_3 are possible long-run supply curves, corresponding to the cases of increasing, constant, and decreasing costs. Demand now rises to D_1. The long-run effect may be to raise price, leave it unchanged, or lower it, depending on which supply situation prevails. Output will rise in all three cases, but by differing amounts.

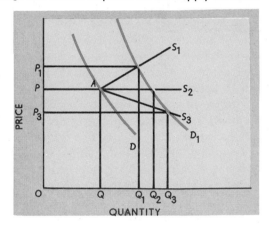

industry is subject to decreasing costs, the supply curve will slope downward as in S_3.

The long-run effects of a shift in demand will differ in these three cases. Suppose an industry is operating at point A, with price OP and output OQ. Demand now rises to D_1. In the increasing cost case, the long-run effect will be a rise in the price to P_1. In the constant cost case, price will remain unchanged, while in the decreasing cost case it will fall to P_3. The new quantity produced will be smallest under increasing costs, largest under decreasing costs.

Can one conclude from this that increasing cost industries are "bad industries," while decreasing cost industries are "good industries"? Some nineteenth-century economists did reason in this way. They liked manufacturing, which they thought was often subject to decreasing costs, and disliked agriculture as an increasing cost industry. They believed government could usefully tax increasing cost industries to restrain their expansion, while bestowing subsidies on decreasing cost industries to stimulate their growth.

But what is wrong with an increasing cost industry? If output expands and costs are forced up, this must be in response to rising consumer demand. The industry continues to obey the principle that the cost of the last unit produced just equals the price which consumers are willing to pay for it. The fact that price rises is *itself* a restraining factor on expansion. What other restraint can be justified?

One possible source of complaint is this: if increasing cost is due to the fact that the units of some productive factor differ in quality, then as demand rises, the owners of the superior units will receive larger incomes. When demand for food is high enough so that even poor farm-land is being used, the owners of the best land will be able to demand a high rent for its use. (It was partly the sight of rich landlords living on their "unearned increment" which turned nineteenth-century British economists against the agricultural industry.) When an average scientist is getting $10,000 a year, the really good scientist may be getting $50,000.

This reduces to a complaint that certain factor suppliers are getting bonuses which they have done nothing to deserve, since they arise from inherited talents, natural fertility or favorable location of land, and other things which cannot be ascribed to personal merit. The legitimacy of this complaint will be considered when we examine factor pricing in Chapter 10. Meanwhile, one thing should be said: the remedy in these cases, if remedy is needed, would lie in a direct attack on the incomes of factor owners—presumably through income taxation. This is an entirely differ-ent thing from *taxing the output of a product* in which these factors happen to be used. There is no case for special penalties on the *output* of an increasing cost industry.

WORKING THE MARKET MECHANISM: ADJUSTMENTS THROUGH TIME

We live in a dynamic, ever changing economy. Few markets are ever in equilibrium, and if so they would not stay there long. Demand and supply curves for various products are constantly changing. The practical purpose of demand-supply analysis, then, is mainly to explain *change* rather than stability. We use it to explore the train of events which will be set off by a shift in demand or supply conditions.

Shifts in Demand

Consider first the repercussions set off by a rise in demand for a product. Why may demand increase? Presumably because one or more of the things which we held constant in constructing the demand curve have changed. People's incomes may have risen. There may have been a shift in preferences. Or the price of some related product may have changed.

So, for whatever reason, DD in Figure 4 shifts upward to D_1D_1. What will happen? Immediate consequences are one thing, eventual consequences another. To trace out the chain of events, we show in Figure 4 three supply curves, corresponding to our three time periods. S_m is the market supply curve, its vertical shape indicating that supply cannot be increased immediately. S_s is the short-run supply curve, indicating the possibility of increasing production from existing plants. S_l, the long-run supply curve, reflects the costs involved in adding fresh plant capacity. S_l has been drawn horizontally on the assumption that we

Immediate Effect of a Demand Increase Differs from the Ultimate Effect

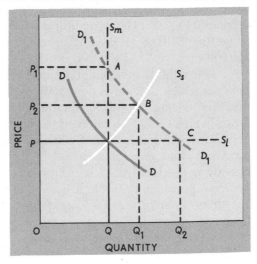

FIGURE 4. S_m, S_s, and S_l are the market, short-run, and long-run supply curves for this industry. If demand rises from DD to D_1D_1, the industry will move immediately to the market equilibrium at point A, then to the short-run equilibrium at B and finally back to long-run equilibrium at C. The permanent effect is a rise in productive capacity from OQ to OQ_2.

are dealing with a constant cost industry; but it could also be drawn to show increasing or decreasing long-run costs.

The first effect of the demand increase will be a rise in price. Price will rise from P toward P_1, corresponding to the intersection of S_m with the new demand curve D_1. At this attractive price, the industry will rush to get out more product. Additional labor will be hired, more materials bought, and plants worked longer hours.

The industry will expand along S_s which rises because of the rising marginal cost of working plants closer to capacity. Output will move from Q toward Q_1, and as this happens, price will decline from P_1 toward P_2. At B, where S_s intersects D_1, the industry will be in short-run equilibrium.

But price P_2 still yields positive profits. So, if the higher demand is expected to be permanent, companies will begin planning to expand, and new producers will move into the industry. As new plants come into production, the industry's output expands beyond Q_1 toward Q_2. The industry travels down the demand curve toward C, price declines from

P_2 toward the old level P, and returns in the industry recede toward normal.

The end result is as follows: the industry's productive capacity has been enlarged; output has expanded from Q to Q_2; profit is zero, as it was at the beginning; and price is also just what it was originally. (This last conclusion, of course, depends on the assumption of constant costs. If S_l sloped upward, the new permanent price would be higher than before.)

The consequences of a permanent decline in demand can be traced out in the same way. The short-run effect is a drop in price, output, and rate of return. Negative profits, if continued long enough, will force some companies to liquidate or shift to other products. New producers will be discouraged from entering the industry. Thus the industry's productive capacity will shrink. As this happens, price and rate of return gradually rise toward the original level. When earnings have returned to normal, the thermostat clicks, and contraction of the industry ceases. The long-run results are: smaller capacity; smaller output; zero profit, as before; and (under constant cost) no change in price.

Note the nicety of this mechanism. Upward or downward shifts of demand trigger off upward or downward price-profit movements. These induce an appropriate expansion or contraction of productive capacity. As adjustments in capacity are completed, prices and profits return to normal levels. The end result is a reallocation of resources corresponding to the new pattern of demand.

At one time, economists puzzled over this question: is demand or supply more important in determining price? Marshall's comment on this was that one might as well ask which blade of a scissors does the cutting. Both blades are necessary. The relative importance of the demand and supply blades does depend, however, on the length of time considered. In the market period, with supply fixed, demand does all the work. In the short run, both demand and supply have an influence. In the long run, supply becomes of dominant importance.

Shifts in Supply

The supply curve may shift as well as the demand curve. An *upward* shift of SS would mean that it is more difficult than before to produce any given amount of the product. Such a shift is unusual in practice. Much more typical are *downward* shifts of SS. These result mainly from a factor which has been ruled out of consideration up to this point, progress in science and technology. Technical progress can take the form of turning out a better product at the same cost, or the same product at lower cost, or most commonly, both together. In the early years of a new industry, costs often fall dramatically, though progress may slow down as the industry matures.

The effect of downward supply shifts is shown in Figure 5. Each of

the small supply-demand sketches relates to a different period of time—
say 1960, 1970, and 1980. We assume that demand for the product is
growing over time, and that at any given time the industry is subject to
constant costs. In the absence of technical progress, the growth of
demand would lead simply to greater production at the same cost and
price level. The industry would travel to the right along SS. But instead,

A Shift in Supply over Time

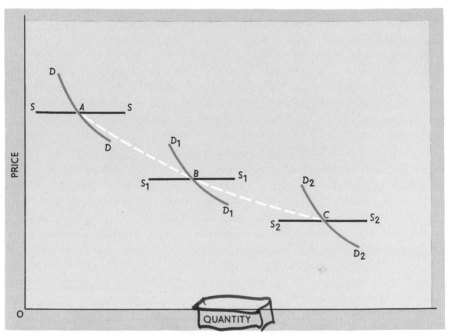

FIGURE 5.   *DD* and *SS* refer to 1960. D_1D_1 nd S_1S_1, show the same industry in 1970, and
D_2D_2 and S_2S_2 in 1980. Demand is rising, while at the same time the long-run supply
curve is being lowered by technical progress. The industry expands along the dotted
line *ABC*, usually termed a *historical cost curve.*

technical progress drops the level of costs, first to S_1S_1, then to S_2S_2. So
the industry travels along the path shown by the dotted line linking the
equilibrium points *A*, *B*, and *C*. This line is sometimes called a *historical
cost curve.*

The rate of technical progress differs widely from one industry to
another, and this has important consequences for the production pattern
of the economy. All industries are in competition with each other for the
consumer's dollar. Those which are most successful in reducing costs and
prices will be able to travel out fastest along their demand curves. If one
takes two cross sections of the economy 10 or 20 years apart and observes
which products have shown greatest increase in output, one finds a

strong association between increases in output and *relative* decreases in price.

MONOPOLISTIC COMPETITION

It is logical to consider this case next because of its strong resemblance to pure competition: there are many sellers, free entrance to the industry, no collusion among sellers or buyers. The only difference is that the product is differentiated. The product of one seller is not identical with that of another in buyers' eyes. Thus each seller has a kind of limited monopoly, a monopoly of his own product. Hence the label "monopolistic competition," devised by Professor Edward Chamberlin. This combination of many sellers and a differentiated product is common- est in the retail trade and service industries; but it is approximated also in some branches of manufacturing, where there are many producers each selling under its own brand name.

What is the advantage of having your own brand? Basically, it enables you to develop your own clientele, a following of regular customers whom you hope will come back to you again and again. Statistical studies have estimated that the probability of repeat purchases of a branded product is quite high, sometimes as high as 0.8. This means that out of 100 customers buying a certain brand, 80 will come back to the same brand next time.[1] One object of advertising is to raise this percentage by strengthening the brand loyalty of existing customers. The other objective is to win new customers by tempting people away from other brands which they previously purchased.

To the extent that a seller can develop brand loyalty, he gains some independence in price setting. If he raises his price above that of other sellers, he will lose some, but not all, of his customers. If he cuts his price below that of other sellers, he will gain some customers, but others will stay with their usual brands.

Under pure competition, each producer must sell strictly at the market price. He faces a horizontal demand curve, such as D_1 in Figure 6, which is determined by the market and is identical for all sellers. But the seller of a differentiated product has an individual demand curve, such as D_2 or D_3. The demand curve of a seller under monopolistic competition shows the effect on his sales of a variation in his price, *the prices of all other sellers remaining unchanged.* It shows, that is, the effect of a *relative* change in his price up or down. The size of the effect is indicated by the elasticity of demand. If the demand curve is D_2, a small

---

[1] Estimates for a number of consumer products will be found in two articles by Lester G. Telser: "The Demand for Branded Goods as Estimated from Consumer Panel Data," *Review of Economics and Statistics*, August 1962, pp. 300–324; and "Advertising and Cigarettes," *Journal of Political Economy*, October, 1962, pp. 471–99.

price change will produce a large increase or decrease in sales. If the demand curve is D_3, the sales effects will be much smaller.

What determines the elasticity of demand for one seller under monopolistic competition? Basically, the strength of customer attachment —"brand loyalties," or "store loyalties." A demand curve such as D_2 indicates that customer loyalties are weak and easily overcome by a variation in price. D_3 shows a situation in which brand loyalties are strong and in which it is hard to shake people loose from their customary brand, even by a substantial price change.

Product Differentiation Tilts the Firm's Demand Curve

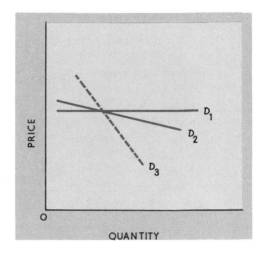

FIGURE 6. The seller of a homogeneous product faces a horizontal demand curve like D_1. Product differentiation and brand preferences, however, tilt the firm's demand curve to an extent which depends on the strength of consumer attachment. D_2 illustrates a case of weak consumer attachment to the firm's brand, D_3 a case of strong consumer attachment.

What do companies' demand curves look like in practice? Probably more like D_2 than D_3. Professor Telser's estimates show an elasticity of 5.7 for different brands of frozen orange juice, 5.5 for instant coffee, 4.4 for regular coffee, and 3.0 for margarine. There is also indirect evidence from the fact that rival sellers under monopolistic competition usually sell at very nearly the same price. They hesitate to test consumer loyalty by going much above the prices charged by other sellers. They *act as though they believed* that their demand curves are highly elastic.

How does the monopolistic competitor decide how much to produce and what price to charge? For this we must know his cost curves as well as his demand curve; and we shall assume as usual that he is interested in maximum profit. Suppose, then, his situation is as shown in Figure 7. The rule for maximum profit is that production should be carried to the point where $MC = MR$. Up to this point, each additional unit adds something to profit; beyond this point, additional units would subtract from profit. The producer in Figure 7, then, should produce OQ, which he can sell for a price of OP. This is a profitable position, since price is above ATC.

We must next ask whether this profitable situation can continue. This leads us to look beyond the individual seller to his rivals in the industry. To simplify matters, let's suppose that *each producer in the industry has the same demand and cost schedules,* and that these are as shown in Figure 7. Thus when we look at one producer we are really looking at them all.

Can all producers in an industry, then, continue in the position shown in Figure 7 and continue to make positive profit? Only if they can bar new competitors from the industry. But in defining monopolistic competition we assumed that entrance to the industry was free. So new

A Monopolistic Competitor Follows the MC = MR Rule for Maximum Profit

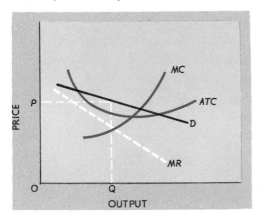

FIGURE 7. This shows a possible cost-demand situation for one company under monopolistic competition. The company will make greatest profit by producing OQ, for which marginal revenue equals marginal cost. The output can be sold at a price OP, which yields positive profit. (Can this situation continue indefinitely?)

producers will come in to share in the positive profits. But this will take away some of the sales of existing producers. The demand curves of existing companies shift to the left.

How far can this go? It will continue so long as people in the industry are making positive profit. So demand curves will continue to decline until they reach the position shown in Figure 8, where D_1 just touches the ATC curve. The marginal revenue curve moves downward to MR_1. So each company, following the $MR = MC$ rule, will produce OQ units, sell them for OP, and earn only normal returns. When this point is reached, there is no inducement for new producers to enter, and the industry is in equilibrium.

Note that the adjustment mechanism is identical with that for pure competition. Positive profit triggers off entrance of new producers, which drives price down to the zero-profit level. Conversely, if we start with producers making negative profit (i.e., with D lying *below* ATC throughout), the opposite sequence of events will follow. Some producers will be forced out of the industry, which leaves more business for the remainder, so that demand curves rise until they are just tangent to ATC.

If entrance to the industry is free, the final equilibrium must be in a zero-profit position.

We have not yet said whether *ATC* should be considered a *short-run* or a *long-run* cost curve. Since we are concerned here with long-run industry equilibrium, it seems that *ATC* should be interpreted in a long-run sense. In Figure 8, then, *OC* represents the *optimum scale of com-*

Monopolistic Competition, like Pure Competition, Leads to a Zero-Profit Equilibrium

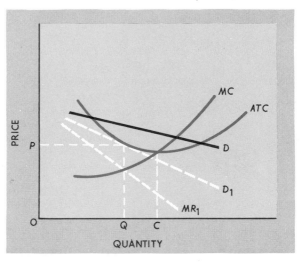

FIGURE 8. When the curtain rises, each producer in this industry has *D* and *ATC* curves which permit a positive profit. As new producers enter the industry to share in these profits, company demand curves fall gradually to the position D_1. In this position, each company will produce OQ, charge a price OP, and have zero profit. Note that each company's size, OQ, is below the optimum scale OC which would permit lowest unit cost.

pany, while *OQ* is the actual scale of the typical company. Since *OQ* is less than *OC*, each company is too small to achieve lowest unit cost. Average total cost is higher than it need be, and the price to buyers is higher in consequence. From another standpoint, there are too many producers in the industry. The amount being produced could be turned out by a smaller number of companies, each operating at capacity.[2]

It is debatable how far this constitutes a criticism of monopolistic competition. The apparently excessive number of sellers is, at least partly, a *result* of consumer preferences, as expressed in the tilted demand curve. Where the preference is based on *location,* as in retailing, consumers get a *quid pro quo* through not having to travel so far to shop. Even in the case of brand preference, consumers evidently *think* that they gain by being able to choose one brand over another. If not, brand loyalty would vanish, and company demand curves would become horizontal.

So far we have concentrated on price and output. But this makes the problems of the monopolistic competitor look simpler than they actually are. Under monopolistic competition, the firm must decide not only what price to charge but *what kind of product* to produce. And in addition to the usual *production* costs, it must reach decisions about *selling costs.*

The essence of monopolistic competition is that buyers *think* there are differences in the products of different companies. The differences are sometimes slight or even fictitious. But producers also have the option of making genuine changes in the product if it seems this would pay. There is often a choice of producing a higher-quality product at one level of costs and prices, or a lower-quality product in a lower price range. This is standard practice throughout the clothing industries and is common for other consumer goods. The availability of different price-quality packages enlarges the range of choice open to consumers. The lower price lines, while sometimes stigmatized as "shoddy goods," may bring a product within the reach of low-income groups who could not otherwise afford it. In the case of food and drug products, however, product deterioration can be injurious to health. The U.S. Food and Drug Administration accordingly sets minimum standards which limit producers' discretion at the lower end of the quality range.

How does a producer decide what quality of product to offer? Presumably by the kind of marginal calculation with which we are already familiar. In the short run, of course, he is limited by the reputation and price level of his existing products. But over a longer period he can try to move down or up in the quality range. He can calculate the extra cost of making a slightly better product and then estimate how much higher a price he could get for it. If the shift would produce marginal revenue in excess of marginal cost, it is worthwhile. He can make a similar calculation for a still better quality; and so on. Eventually he will reach a point where further improvement of the product does not pay.

When we drew Figure 7 to discover the company's best-profit position, we were assuming that the decision about product had already been made. The product must be specified before cost or demand curves can be drawn. What we are now saying is that a producer may have a large number of cost-demand diagrams to consider, one for each variety or quality of product he might make. He should look these over to find the one which will allow the *largest profit rectangle.*

The possibility of product variation adds a new dimension to competition. It opens up new possibilities for business ingenuity, for success and error, for profit or loss.

The seller of a differentiated product has selling costs as well as production costs. Through his sales staff, through advertising, and in other ways he seeks to reach the buying public and to push his product. The purpose of this activity is to *influence the position of his demand curve.* From a defensive standpoint, a company must make a sufficient sales effort to offset the sales efforts of rival producers, to prevent them from winning away its customers and shifting its demand curve to the left. If it wants to go on the offensive and take customers away from others—shift *their* demand curves to the left and its own to the right—it will have to spend more than this. Each additional dollar spent on selling will have some impact on the demand schedule and bring some increase in sales. But sales effort, like other kinds of effort, runs eventually into diminishing returns. The returns to additional "doses" of selling effort taper off and will eventually fall to zero.

At what point should a company stop? You should already be ahead of this question. Still another marginal calculation must be made. Suppose you put an additional thousand dollars into selling, using the sales *methods* which will yield maximum results for the money. How many more units could you sell? And how much would these units, after deducting the cost of producing them, add to your net revenue? If the answer is more than a thousand dollars, the extra sales effort is worthwhile. Make a similar experiment with another thousand dollars of selling expense; and so on. Eventually you will reach a point at which an additional unit of selling expense would barely repay itself. On the usual principle of equating marginal revenue and marginal cost, you should stop at this point.

While these competitive sales efforts appear necessary to the firm, are they also useful to the economy? Or do they use up resources with no corresponding benefit to consumers? We defer this issue until the next chapter. Advertising reaches major proportions mainly where sellers are few, as in automobiles, gasoline, or cigarettes. The reasons why this is so, and the economic consequences, will be examined when we discuss this kind of industry.

COMPETITIVE INDUSTRY IN PRACTICE

Some industries in the economy are purely competitive, and many others are monopolistically competitive. So to some extent we can check our theoretical conclusions by observation. How does the actual operation of competitive industries compare with the picture presented above?

Many of the things one can observe and measure come out about as they should. Rates of return on capital are only moderately above the long-term interest rate, so the zero-profit rule is well observed. Returns do not differ drastically from one competitive industry to another. They tend to be higher in rapidly expanding industries and lower in declining industries, as one would expect.

Output is responsive to demand, rising most rapidly where demand is shifting rapidly to the right. Output and price are also responsive to cost. Industries in which cost curves are falling rapidly because of technical improvement show a relative decline in prices and a relatively large expansion of output.[2] Demand and cost trends are interrelated. Where demand and output are rising rapidly, technical progress is encouraged, and companies are able to "grow up" quickly to optimum scale. These cost reductions bring lower prices, which stimulates sales and output, reinforcing the expansion process. This is a familiar cycle during the first few decades of a new industry.

In several respects, however, the operation of competitive industries is more complicated than simple theorizing may suggest. First, we often draw the long run ATC curve quite U-shaped, which implies that there is a sharply defined optimum scale of enterprise and that producers must move toward this point to minimize costs and survive in competition. So one might expect in each industry to find producers about the same size. Actually, one finds substantial size differences. Small producers exist alongside others 10 or 20 times as large. Why is this? The most plausible explanation is that the long-run ATC curve is usually quite shallow, more like a saucer than a soup bowl. Rather than a sharply defined optimum scale, one has a wide range of feasible sizes, which may differ by no more than a few percent in total unit cost. So one finds producers distributed over this range rather than bunched in the middle.

It is not necessarily true either that small companies always want to get bigger, even where they could reduce unit costs by so doing. Small business is very much a personal and family matter. Where getting money for expansion would mean sharing control of the business with bankers or outside investors, the family may prefer to sit tight and maintain its control. The managers of the business may feel that they already have enough to do and that expansion would get them in over their heads. Businessmen have to make a choice of work *versus* leisure, like anyone else, and this may set limits to the scale of enterprise.

Second, we often assume for simplicity that the ATC curves of competing producers are at about the same level. Price will adjust itself to this level; and anyone who has higher costs will suffer losses and will eventually be forced out of operation. Statistical studies, however, usually show considerable variation between the highest-cost and lowest-

---

[2] For evidence of this during the 1950's, see Harold Solozin, "Inflation and the Price Mechanism," *Journal of Political Economy*, October, 1959, pp. 463–75.

cost producers in an industry. What are the reasons[3] for this? One reason is the *differences in scale* already mentioned. The smallest producers in an industry are apt to have markedly higher costs. Differences in *geographical location* are sometimes important. Wage rates, a large cost element in most industries, vary considerably by region of the country and by size of city. Location may also yield lower shipping costs or other advantages. There are substantial differences in *managerial efficiency*. In principle, this should be canceled out by equivalent differences in managerial salaries. Custom sets an upper limit, however, to how much a company can decently pay its top executives. It is likely that the productivity gap between the best managers and an average manager is wider than the salary gap, so that the companies lucky enough to have the best managers get some cost advantage.

It is not hard, then, to think of reasons why cost differences may develop. But why are the high-cost producers not forced out of operation? Well, perhaps most of them are. The argument that costs should be equalized is an argument about long-run equilibrium. But any snapshot of an industry at a particular moment catches it in a state of *disequilibrium*. Some of the high-cost producers may be newly established companies, which have not had time to learn the tricks of the trade or to grow up to efficient size. Either they will grow up and achieve lower costs, or they will vanish from the industry as failures. Some may be older concerns with antiquated machinery or management, which are also on their way to oblivion. But some high-cost concerns may continue in operation because the owner deliberately accepts a subnormal return rather than fold up a business which has become his way of life.

Recognition of cost differences helps to solve at least one theoretical problem. When we assumed equal costs and showed all producers making losses, we said this would be corrected by "producers leaving the industry." The thought may have occurred to you: *which* producers will leave? If they are all equally efficient, how can one choose? Do they have to play eeney, meeny, miney, mo? We can now answer this question: the least efficient, who are making largest losses, will be the first to go. Conversely, when the industry is profitable and expansion is in order, the lowest-cost producers will expand first and farthest.

This leads us, however, to a third difference between theory and reality. The profit thermostat regulating the capacity of competitive industry works much better for expansion than for contraction. Positive profit plus free entrance can be counted on to produce expansion after

---

[3] We mean genuine reasons rather than accidental or statistical reasons. Differences in accounting practices, for example, may produce an apparent difference in unit costs where no real difference exists. Again, one plant may have been operating at 60 percent of capacity, another at 80 percent of capacity, in the month the survey was made. If the ATC curves of the two are identical, the former will show higher unit costs, because it was operating farther to the left on its cost curve. Products of the various enterprises may not be strictly comparable; and so on.

the short time required for plant construction. But to squeeze producers out of an overexpanded industry which is suffering losses can be a slow and painful process, a matter of decades rather than years. It takes time for producers to recognize the probable bleak future, time for plants to wear out, time to bring oneself to face community criticism for throwing men out of work. Witness the prolonged death throes of the New England cotton mills and many of the Appalachian coal fields. In these cases, one often hears criticism of competition as a harsh taskmaster and demands that government step in with price guarantees or other forms of aid.

Fortunately, these cases are not too common. In a growing economy, demand for most goods and services is increasing. So what mainly happens is that *some industries expand faster than others*. The market operates to channel new resources into industries whose demand curves are rising most rapidly. Other industries can shrink *relatively* without suffering an absolute decline which would force them to release labor and capital.[4]

SUMMARY

1. The number of sellers and the standardized or differentiated nature of the product are important aspects of *market structure*. This chapter considers the cases of many sellers of a standardized product (*pure competition*), and many sellers of a differentiated product (*monopolistic competition*).

2. In the *market* period, supply is fixed and price depends solely on the level of demand.

3. In the *short period*, plant capacity is fixed, but rate of plant operation can be varied. The producer's supply curve, which is identical with his marginal cost curve, slopes upward to the right. Since total output is the sum of the outputs of individual companies, the supply curve of the industry also slopes upward to the right.

4. While a company is in short-period equilibrium where price equals marginal cost, it will be in long-run equilibrium only if price also equals average total cost; that is, if the price line touches the *ATC* curve at its minimum point. If price is above *ATC*, there is positive profit, and the company has an incentive to expand capacity; and conversely if the price is below *ATC*.

5. The *long-run supply curve* depends on what happens to an industry's cost level as production capacity is increased. Extractive

---

[4] Professor Stigler reports that out of 98 manufacturing industries examined over the years 1947–56, only a half dozen actually lost capital. At the other extreme, the seven most rapidly growing industries increased their capital at more than 11 per cent per year. The average rate of increase for all industries was about 6 percent a year. George J. Stigler, *Capital and Rates of Return in Manufacturing Industries* (Princeton, N.J.: Princeton University Press, 1963).

industries may be subject to *increasing costs* due to their use of a scarce natural resource. In most other industries, it seems reasonable to expect *constant costs*. But in some cases, one may find *decreasing costs* arising from *external economies*.

6. Demand-supply analysis is useful mainly in tracing the results of a shift in demand or supply conditions. The *immediate effect* of a permanent increase in demand is a higher price and positive profits. The *short-run effect* is an increase in the rate of operation of existing plants. The *long-run* effect is construction of new productive capacity. In a constant cost industry, after all adjustments have been completed, unit cost, price, and earnings will have returned to their original level.

7. If we admit technical change to the picture, an industry's supply curve may shift downward over time as a result of technical progress. The industries which are most successful in reducing unit cost and price tend to show largest increases in output over the years.

8. Under monopolistic competition, each seller has a downward-sloping demand curve because of the existence of brand preference or dealer preference. The strength of customer attachment to a particular seller is indicated by the elasticity of his demand curve.

9. Under monopolistic competition, as under pure competition, positive profit will attract new producers and negative profit will lead to withdrawal of producers. The industry is in long-run equilibrium only when profit is zero.

10. Industry equilibrium under monopolistic competition involves more sellers, each producing less, and at a higher unit cost, than would be the case under pure competition. But since this occurs in response to customer preferences it is questionable whether it should be considered inefficient.

11. The monopolistic competitor, in addition to deciding on price and output, has to reach decisions on *type of product* and level of *selling expenditures*. These decisions are made on the usual basis of equating marginal revenue and marginal cost. Instead of considering only one cost-demand diagram, the producer has to consider a large number of alternative diagrams, from which he chooses the one which permits greatest profit.

12. Competitive industries in practice operate somewhat differently from the textbook picture. The most important differences are: the existence of a wide range of company sizes in the same industry; the existence at any moment of sizable differences in the cost levels and profit levels of competing producers; and the slowness with which productive capacity is withdrawn from declining industries.

DISCUSSION QUESTIONS

1. Suppose you were asked to classify industries in the United States into a few general categories, based on their *market structure*. What would you

need to know about each industry, and how would you construct your classification?

2. What will determine the actual calendar length of
   a) The Marshallian *market* period?
   b) The Marshallian *short* period?

3. Why does the short-run supply curve for an industry slope upward? Will the price determined by intersection of the demand curve and the short-run supply curve continue to prevail in the future? Why, or why not?

4. Classical writers believed that manufacturing industries were usually subject to *decreasing costs*. Explain clearly what this means. What reasons can you find for agreeing or disagreeing with the classical view?

5. A purely competitive industry in long-run equilibrium experiences a rise in demand. What will happen:
   i) Immediately?
   ii) In the short run?
   iii) In the long run?

6. Suppose one observes that the price of a product has fallen substantially (relative to prices in general) over a period of 20 years. What has probably happened?

7. You undoubtedly buy many products which are sold under conditions of monopolistic competition. Review the strength of your attachment to these brands, dealers, etc. What does this mental experiment suggest to you about the probable elasticity of the sellers' demand curves?

8. "While theorists have made much of the distinction between pure and monopolistic competition, the practical outcome is very nearly the same." Do you agree? Explain.

9. You are put in charge of a research project, designed to test how closely the results of "real-world competition" resemble the textbook results.
   i) What figures would you try to collect for each competitive industry?
   ii) What general conclusions might you expect to reach?

Competition among the Few

> Here's the rule for bargains. "Do other men for they would do you." That's the true business precept.
>
> CHARLES DICKENS

THERE ARE MANY dimensions of market structure, and so there are many ways of classifying product markets. We have chosen to emphasize the dividing line between markets in which there are *many sellers*, and where competition is consequently atomistic, anonymous, impersonal; and those in which there are *few sellers*, and where competition is overt, visible, direct. The tactics popularly regarded as "competitive" are more characteristic of the second situation than the first.

"Few," as noted earlier, means few enough so that each can keep watch on the actions of his rivals and must also consider their reactions to whatever he may do. Independent action is not possible. Any action is like a move in a chess game where one must look several moves ahead. Concretely, few may mean as many as 20 or 30. It may also mean only three or four. A common situation is one in which there are a half-dozen substantial producers, plus a fringe of smaller companies who are regarded as harmless by the big producers so long as their sales are only a small part of the industry total.

REASONS FOR FEWNESS OF SELLERS

Fewness of sellers arises where the capacity of each firm is large *relative to the size of the market*. This may be because the market itself is small. The small city with its half-dozen banks, three or four building

216

contractors, a few movie theater operators, and so on, illustrates this possibility. But this situation is common also in manufacturing. The complex and mechanized industry of the United States requires thousands of small parts and components, tools, gadgets, chemical materials, and other specialty products, which are sold to other companies rather than to the general public. A certain gadget may be quite essential, yet a few plants may be able to handle the total national demand. There are also many highly specialized consumer goods whose market is so limited that there is room for only a few producers.

For this reason, the line between many sellers and few sellers does not correspond closely with the line between small business and big business. There are many small businesses which, because they cater to a limited market, are in an oligopoly or even a monopoly position.

In other cases, the total market is large, but the individual sellers are also very large. The list of industries in which a few large companies provide most of the national output reads like a *Who's Who* of American manufacturing. It includes aircraft, aluminum, automobiles, basic steel, cigarettes, copper rolling, distilling, heavy electrical equipment, railroad cars and locomotives, soap, sugar refining, synthetic fibers, telephone equipment, and tires.

These situations arise partly because of economies of scale. In industries using complex processes and large machine units, the optimum scale of plant will be large. There may be further economies in merging a number of plants under common management, though these are more debatable.

There are other advantages of size which provide a standing incentive to the merger of competing concerns. Size may make it easier to *control the price* of the product and bar potential competitors from the industry. Size may confer *bargaining advantages* vis-à-vis customers or suppliers. Moreover, the process of merging two or more companies into a new company can bring substantial profits to the "insiders" in charge of the merger. These things should be kept separate from true economies of scale. The latter increase the efficiency of the economy, while the former do not.

The most dramatic case, the single seller, is best exemplified by electric power, telephone service, and other public utilities. These are extreme examples of economies of scale. Once you have set up a telephone network, you get lower unit costs by exploiting it as fully as possible. While it would be technically possible to set up a second network, this would clearly be uneconomic. Industries of this sort are commonly termed *natural monopolies*.

PRICE SETTING UNDER OLIGOPOLY

The case of few sellers is trickier than the cases analyzed in Chapter 8. Where there are many sellers, each can try to maximize his own profit without considering anyone else. From conclusions about what each seller will do, we can deduce what will happen in the industry as a whole. But where sellers are few, each must ask himself not only, "What should I do?" but also, "What will the others do?" The answer to the second question may determine the answer to the first. This *interdependence* of action makes it hard to predict the outcome.

The few sellers may be selling either a homogeneous product or a differentiated product. In the former case, they must sell at the same price. In the latter case, this is not strictly necessary; but there is still a strong tendency to sell at about the same price. Analysis of the two cases follows similar lines. We shall assume that we are dealing with a

The Kinked Oligopoly Demand Curve

FIGURE 1. D_1D_1 shows what happens to company A's sales if it can change its price while all other sellers leave theirs unchanged. D_2D_2 shows what happens if A's price changes are fully matched by other sellers. If A reasons that other companies *will* match a price cut but will *not* match a price increase, its effective demand curve is the heavy line D_1ED_2. The "kink" at E produces a sharp break in MR; and MC can move up or down considerably without changing the company's best price and output.

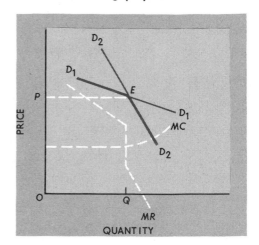

differentiated product, since this raises interesting questions about advertising and selling costs.

The position of an oligopolist selling a differentiated product is illustrated in Figure 1. He is currently operating at E, producing OQ units and selling them at price OP. What will happen if he departs from this price? There are various possibilities. One is that everyone else in the industry will do just what he does, raising prices when he raises them and vice versa. In this case, his demand curve might look like D_2D_2. If all sellers raise and lower prices together, each can expect to keep his established share of the market. So D_2D_2 will be a small replica of the demand curve for the product as a whole, its elasticity depending on the characteristics of the product.

Suppose, on the other hand, that when company A changes its price, all other sellers leave theirs unchanged. In this case, A's demand curve will be much more elastic. In a situation where brand preferences are not strong, it might look like D_1D_1. If the company cuts its price while others do not, it will gain heavily in sales, while if it raises prices on its own, it will lose heavily.

Company A may expect different reactions depending on the *direction* of its price change. It may expect that a price increase will *not* be followed by others in the group. What would this mean? It would mean that the group considers the existing price level high enough. So they will veto any move to increase it. We can see from D_1D_1 that company A would then lose heavily in sales, so in fact it will not try to raise prices on its own. Company A may also expect that, if it cuts prices, other sellers *will* also cut them. If A were allowed to reduce prices single-handed, we see again from D_1D_1 that it would make a large gain in sales and cut heavily into the markets of other sellers. So they will not let A get away with it. They will cut too. Instead of moving to the right along D_1, then, A finds itself moving down along D_2, which shows the effect of all sellers changing prices together.

In this case, A's effective demand curve consists of the heavy line, which follows D_1 upward but D_2 downward. The demand curve has a "kink" at the existing price level. The kink in the demand curve means that there is also a break in the marginal revenue curve, MR. If A cuts its price and others follow, MR drops to a much lower level.

To complete the picture, we draw A's marginal cost curve, MC. Let's suppose that this intersects MR somewhere in the vertical break. Two conclusions follow. First, by the $MR = MC$ rule, company A is producing the most profitable amount and charging the right price. Second, MC can move upward or downward over a considerable range without upsetting this result. So long as MC continues to intersect MR within the vertical break, there is no incentive to change price or output.

This may help to explain the observed rigidity of prices under oligopoly. In markets with many sellers, prices change frequently in response to slight demand and supply changes. Where sellers are few, there is usually a set price for a considerable period, and this is changed only in response to substantial changes in cost or demand. The kinked demand curve is one plausible explanation of why this might happen.

Setting the "Right" Price

The kinked demand curve helps to explain why, once an industry is settled at a certain price, it will show considerable resistance to any price change. But it doesn't explain why the price is where it is. In drawing Figure 1, we simply supposed that the price was OP. But why OP rather than something else?

The trouble is that we cannot determine price from a diagram *for one seller only*. Under oligopoly, any member of the group can veto a proposed price by selling for less. So any viable price must reflect a group consensus. The problem is to explain how a price is reached *which everyone finds it in his own interest to observe*.

As a starting point, let's make the usual assumption that each seller has the same cost and demand curves. Let's assume also that all sellers always charge the same price. The pertinent demand curve for each seller, then, is a curve showing what happens when everyone raises or lowers prices together. The demand curve in Figure 2 is drawn on this basis. The cost curves have their usual shapes. We have drawn the curves so that the firm has a chance to make positive profit.

If the company in Figure 2 were the only one in the industry, and if it wanted to maximize profit, its course would be clear. It should produce OQ, the level of output for which $MR = MC$, and charge a price OP.

Now if instead of one company there are six, each with the cost-demand situation in Figure 2, isn't it also clear what they should do? Why don't they put their heads together and *agree* to charge the price

Oligopolists Can Maximize Profit by Agreeing to Charge the Monopoly Price

FIGURE 2. We noted earlier that a company will make maximum profit by producing where $MC = MR$. The oligopolist shown here will do best, therefore, by producing OQ and charging OP. (The demand curve D assumes that all companies raise and lower prices together.) If the other members of the oligopoly group have the same cost and demand curves, all will maximize their profits by agreeing to fix price at OP.

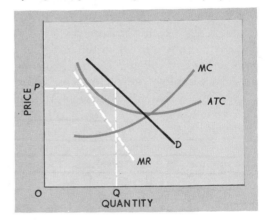

OP? This will yield maximum profit to each company and hence to the group. So one might expect that complete cooperation among oligopolists would lead to the same result as monopoly.

Prices doubtless are fixed at or near the maximum-profit level in some cases. Open price fixing is, of course, illegal in the United States. If rival producers get together and agree to observe a set price for a product sold in interstate commerce, they are violating the antitrust laws. This prevents open, formal arrangements to control prices and production. In some countries, members of an industry can legally form a trade association or cartel which sets prices, allots production quotas to each company, and regulates admission of new companies to the industry. Such associations are illegal in the United States.

So price fixing is illegal. But most businessmen do not feel that it is *wrong*. Indeed, when demand is falling and profits are low, they are apt to argue that it is essential. When the law prohibits something which many people still want to do, the effect is to drive the prohibited practices underground. There is much informal evasion of the antitrust laws, which is hard to discover and eliminate. The telephone still works, and the quiet talk in a corner of the golf club can be quite effective.

A common control device is *price leadership*. Price changes are announced first by some bellwether company, perhaps U.S. Steel for steel prices, one of the Standard Oil companies for oil products, and so on. The "leader" in an industry need not always be the same company, but may change from time to time. Once the leader has spoken, everyone else in the industry announces an identical price change.

How does the leader decide where to set prices? In some cases, price leadership is a cloak for a secret agreement. The industry confers on a change, and one company is selected to announce it. But this is not necessarily the case. The leader may have some independence of judgment and action. Other members of the industry, in effect, delegate to one company the responsibility of working out price strategy for the group. This company may be selected because it is big, because it is the traditional pacesetter, or because of a strong figure in the company's management. But the leader is not free to do anything he may feel like. Unless he takes account of the interests and views of other companies, he will not remain leader indefinitely.

This is one way of getting controlled pricing without the necessity of a conference before every price move. Some court decisions have termed this method "conscious parallelism of action." The U.S. Department of Justice has attacked it under the antitrust laws, but its legal status is still unclear. It is difficult to see what could be done about it, even if it were held illegal. One can scarcely forbid rival companies to match each others' price changes, since the same product must be sold at about the same price by all producers.

Some Obstacles to Agreement

The antitrust laws are not the only obstacle to price fixing. There are other reasons why "gentlemen's agreements" about prices may break down or may lead to prices below what a monopolist would charge:

1. It makes considerable difference whether there are 3 companies in an industry or 30 companies. If there are only two or three producers, prices can be controlled by telephone or mental telepathy. If there are several dozen companies, it takes a good deal of discussion and paper work. This leaves a trail which antitrust investigators can pick up.

2. If there are enough producers, there are likely to be a few "uncooperative" ones. One reason may be the existence of substantial cost differences in the industry. The assumption that all producers have the same cost level is usually not justified in practice. Consider an industry in which production costs for most companies fall in the range $1.00 to $1.10 per unit. Several companies, however, are able to produce for $0.80 per unit. These low-cost producers have the whip hand. They may decide to follow a policy of "live and let live," and go along with the industry on

a price of, say, $1.10. This will cover the costs of all companies and yield the low-cost concerns a handsome profit. On the other hand, they may prefer a strategy of "cut and expand." They may cut prices to, say, $0.90 per unit. This will gradually force higher-cost companies out of the industry and allow the low-cost companies to take over more of the market. To the extent that there are low-cost companies with expansionist aspirations, it will be hard for the industry to follow a high-price policy.

3. In some cases an industry is divided between producers of advertised national brands sold at a relatively high price, and producers of unbranded merchandise who must undersell the national brands in order to win a market. It is difficult to line this second group up behind a price agreement, since their very existence depends on lower and more flexible prices. Producers of unbranded nylon hosiery, for example, have never been willing to cooperate with the big-name manufacturers on price strategy.

4. There may be other differences of economic interest among members of an industry. There may be honest differences of opinion about the location of the industry demand curve. Or there may be old-fashioned individualists in the industry, who object to price fixing as a matter of principle. Harvey Firestone, Sr., was such a person, and his insistence on independent action was one reason for severe price competition in the tire industry during his lifetime. Henry Ford played a similar role in the early days of automobile manufacturing.

5. The pressure of large buyers such as Sears, Roebuck; Macy's; or A & P helps to break down price agreements among manufacturers. By dangling a large order under a manufacturer's nose, and by threatening to shift the order to another manufacturer, they can sometimes induce a company to cut prices. Some large retailers have also set up their own manufacturing units.

Where the mass distributor buys from a multitude of small pea canneries, shoe factories, or pants producers, it may exert pressure which is severe and even unfair. But the situation is different for the large manufacturers of electric appliances, tires, paint, or window glass in their dealings with Sears, Roebuck or Montgomery Ward. These manufacturers are big enough to hold their own, and without some counterweight would probably take advantage of the consumer. The mass distributor, by exercising what Professor Galbraith has termed "countervailing power," produces a more equal balance of forces in the market and a lower level of prices.

6. Even though a few companies produce 60 or 70 percent of an industry's output, there may be numerous small producers who share the remainder of the market. Their existence depends on being able to sell at lower prices than their larger rivals. If the big fellows raise prices too much, the advantage of the small companies increases, their sales expand

and begin to cut seriously into the sales of the big companies, and the latter may be forced to beat a retreat. The existence of a fringe of small competitors thus exerts a restraining influence on the price policies of the industry leaders.

Where entrance to an industry is easy, *potential* competition also has a restraining influence. If prices are high and profits attractive, new companies will come in. Unless the leading companies are astute enough to follow a moderate price policy, they will gradually lose ground. There are cases in which a "trust" once controlled 70 percent of an industry but now has only 20 or 30 percent.

For these reasons, all one can really say about pricing under oligopoly is, "it depends." Price will usually settle at a level somewhere *between* that which would be charged by a single monopolist and that which would exist under atomistic competition. It is probable that the larger the number of companies in the industry, the more closely will price approach the competitive level. But this is simply a hypothesis, and it would be difficult to prove that it *must* be so.

SALES RIVALRY AMONG OLIGOPOLISTS

Let's return to the case in which the oligopolists are able to set price at the monopoly level and earn substantial profits (see Figure 3). This is not necessarily the end of the matter. Unless it is possible to bar people from the industry, this high profit level will attract a flow of new producers. The available business will be split up finer and finer, and the market share of the old companies will decline, i.e., their demand curves will shift to the left. This can go on until each company is earning no more than a normal return. This would happen if demand fell to the position D_1D_1 where it just touches the ATC curve. Each company is now able to sell only OQ_1, considerably less than before.

Things cannot get worse than this—at least, they cannot *remain* worse. If still more newcomers enter the industry and demand falls completely below ATC, some companies will decide to go out of the business, and D_1D_1 will begin to rise again. The position in which D_1D_1 is just tangent to ATC is thus an equilibrium position for an oligopoly group with no limits on entrance.

What is wrong with this equilibrium from a public standpoint? Companies in the industry are earning only normal returns. Each company, however, is operating much below the minimum point on its ATC curve. Plants are partially idle because too many companies have come in to take advantage of the fixed price. The resources employed in the industry are greater than needed for the volume of output, and this is economically wasteful. Price to consumers remains too high and output too low, compared with what would happen under atomistic competition.

Suppose companies in the industry are able to maintain the fixed price *OP and* to bar new producers. Will they then be secure and happy? Not necessarily. Note that even with output *OQ*, the typical company in Figure 3 is operating well below capacity. If it could somehow get a larger share of the market, it could spread its overhead more widely, secure lower unit costs, and earn larger profits.

This pressure of excess capacity provides a standing temptation to secret price cutting. This is especially likely during a business cycle downswing, when sales fall off and excess capacity increases. Even though *quoted* prices are maintained unchanged, prices actually *paid* by customers may be reduced by secret discounts and concessions. In the steel industry, for example, there has sometimes been a considerable gap

New Producers May Eliminate Oligopoly Profit

FIGURE 3. *D* and *ATC* are the same as in Figure 2. As before, the company will maximize profit by producing OQ. If entrance to the industry is open, however, the positive profit will attract new producers. As they take away more and more business, the company's demand curve will fall eventually to D_1D_1, where it just touches ATC and profit is zero. (Why will it not fall even farther?) Note that output has fallen to OQ_1, leaving the company with much excess capacity.

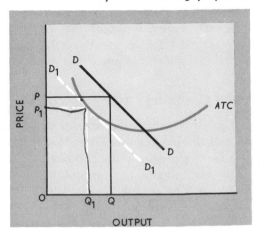

between official prices and actual prices. Price cutting constitutes reprehensible conduct in the eyes of one's competitors, and it can be profitable only so long as it remains undetected. Once your competitors catch on and begin to cut *their* prices, the game is up. Professor Stigler has devised some ingenious formulas for estimating the chances of "getting away with it" in a particular case.[1]

One way to ward off the danger of price cutting would be to regulate each company's share of the market, to fix *OQ* as well as *OP*. If company A has been allotted 15 percent of total industry sales and is not allowed to sell any more, there is no point in price cutting. But since such action is illegal under the antitrust laws and is readily detectable, it has never gained a wide foothold.

Price competition is not, of course, the only way of getting more business. Other possible ways are through product variation and intensified sales efforts. With price cutting frowned on as "unethical," the

---

[1] George J. Stigler, "A Theory of Oligopoly," *Journal of Political Economy,* February, 1964, pp. 44–61.

struggle for sales is diverted mainly into these other channels. Indeed, the term "competition" in ordinary parlance connotes sales and product rivalry. The intensity of competition in this sense results partly from absence of competition in the sense of free and independent pricing.

Product competition sometimes involves slight or even imaginary changes in the product; but the changes can also be real and substantial. A notable recent case is the "horsepower race" among automobile producers. Throughout the 1950's, cars grew longer, wider, and heavier; horsepower rose steadily; gasoline mileage fell; and more and more new features—automatic transmissions, power brakes, power steering, and so on—were added. The cost of these changes to the companies was reflected in higher prices to car buyers, who also bore higher costs for gasoline consumption, car repairs, insurance, and so on. A group of economists has estimated that in 1959 the annual cost of producing and operating the 1959 models was over $5 billion, or almost $1,000 per car, *more* than it would have cost to produce and operate the same number of 1949-model cars.[2] The cumulative cost from 1950 through 1960 was of the order of $30 billion.

Were the product improvements which consumers got as a result of this competitive struggle worth the added costs? One can argue that they must have been, since consumers chose to pay the higher prices. But did they have much choice? Their main alternative in the late 1950's was to buy smaller and more economical cars imported from Europe. Imports did rise rapidly, and, when they reached half a million a year, the American manufacturers took alarm, backtracked, and launched their own "compact" models. The continued increase of product size and price was limited in the end by foreign rather than domestic competition.

The other main avenue of sales rivalry is advertising. One should distinguish two types of advertising: (1) *informational* advertising communicates the fact that certain goods are available at a specified place and price. The department store advertisement and the classified ad are examples. Newspapers, and to a lesser extent radio, are the principal media. (2) The kind of advertising with which we are concerned here is of a different sort. We are all familiar with it, though it is hard to find a good one-word label. It conveys little positive information. Indeed, it often conveys misinformation—"little white lies" about the product, supposedly harmless because hardly anyone takes them seriously. The aim is to associate the product with beautiful women, handsome men, gay occasions, gracious and affluent living—to

---

[2] This estimate takes account of the fact that the 1949 cars could have been produced more cheaply in 1959 because of improvements in production methods. It takes account of higher gasoline consumption by the 1959 models, but not of higher repair bills, insurance, and other operating costs. For a full description of methods, see Franklin M. Fisher, Zvi Griliches, and Carl Kaysen, "The Costs of Automobile Model Changes since 1949," *Journal of Political Economy,* October, 1962, pp. 433–51.

impress the magic name on one's subconscious so that it pops out automatically as one goes down the store aisle. The television commercial is the prototype, though radio and magazines are also important media. The total cost runs to many billions a year.

What does this kind of advertising accomplish? It is often said that advertising *creates demand.* It would be more correct to say that advertising tries to *shift demand.* Chevrolet's advertising is intended to raise the demand for Chevrolets and to lower the demand for Fords and Plymouths. It is possible, of course, that the intense barrage of automobile advertising to which the public is subjected may raise the *total* demand for automobiles. But where does this demand come from? Since consumers' incomes remain the same, it must come from *reduced* consumption of some other product. Once more, the effect is a *shift* in demand rather than an an addition to demand. Advertising can *create* demand only if, by making the public more eager for goods in general, it raises the percentage of total consumer income spent and reduces the proportion saved. But savings banks try to prevent this by engaging in heavy advertising themselves.

An oligopolist engaging in competitive advertising, then, is trying to shift his demand curve to the right. But he may or may not succeed; for his rivals are also engaged in the same effort. If one company's advertising agency comes up this year with an especially clever slogan, it may win sales for the time being. Over a period of years, however, rival advertising campaigns may about cancel out, leaving everyone's demand curve in the same position as before. But everyone's costs are higher by the amount of the advertising bill.

It seems quite possible for competitive advertising to be carried to irrational lengths, in the sense that the last dollar spent on advertising yields less than a dollar of additional revenue. In this event, the sensible thing would be for the oligopolists to call each other up and agree to save money by reducing their advertising budgets. But competitors who are cooperative on prices may well be uncooperative on sales efforts. Most executives are convinced that advertising is a Good Thing, and to question this is a serious heresy in the business community. There is also a certain "armament race" aspect to advertising. Each company watches the others, and, if Ford appropriates more money for advertising, Chrysler and General Motors feel obliged to do the same. There may be some parallel between the rivalry of national states and the empire-building proclivities of big-business executives. The fact that general disarmament would pay doesn't mean that it will happen.

Who pays for advertising? Sales costs are part of the costs considered in determining the company's price and output. Like other costs, they are paid eventually by the consumer. So the "program which is being brought to you by the courtesy of . . ." is really coming by courtesy of yourself (unless you carefully avoid buying any of the company's products). In return for paying the advertising bill, consumers get free radio and television programs. Whether this is a necessary or preferable way of financing radio and television is an interesting issue, but one which lies outside the scope of our present discussion.

An important incidental effect of advertising should be noted. It now constitutes a major barrier to entrance into some industries. In the case of a heavily advertised product, it may be impossible for a new competitor to start out small in hopes of growing up gradually. You have to start with a barrage of national advertising at the outset. This can cost many millions of dollars; and the results are quite uncertain. (The ill-fated Edsel car, which even the great Ford resources did not succeed in promoting, is a classic case.) If you make the effort and fail, you have nothing to show for your money. This risk deters most people from even trying to enter the more heavily advertised industries; and small companies in these industries find themselves squeezed inexorably by the sales pressure of their larger rivals. The losing battle of the small automobile manufacturers, the small-town brewers, and other similar groups could be cited.

MONOPOLY

A seller is said to have monopoly power *if he is able to influence the price of his product*. The seller under monopolistic competition has some degree of monopoly power. So does the oligopolist. Only under pure competition is monopoly power entirely absent.

But the word comes from a Greek word meaning "one seller"; and in ordinary parlance a monopolist is someone who controls the entire supply of a product. What is a "product"? We think of it as being something distinctive, something for which there is no ready substitute. But there are few things for which there is no substitute. The producer of Dairy Maid butter has a monopoly of his own brand; but since other brands are close substitutes, his market power is small. Does butter as a whole, then, constitute a product? In various times and places oleomargarine, lard, peanut butter, and other things have been used on bread instead of butter. So perhaps it is bread spreads of every type which should be considered "a product." The contribution of these spreads to the diet is primarily fat. But fat may also be obtained from meat, vegetable oils, and other sources. So should not the whole category of fats and oils be treated as a product? The chain of substitutes goes on and on, in ever widening circles. A monopolist in the strict sense would have to control everything produced in the economy.

We get around this difficulty by defining a product on the basis of *a major gap in the chain of substitutes*. Goodyear and Firestone tires are close substitutes for each other, and it would not make much sense to treat them as separate products. But there is no good substitute for automobile tires as a whole. When we come to such a gap, we consider everything inside it as a single product. A company which produces all of such a thing has a monopoly.

In this case, the demand curve for the product belongs to one company. The company *is* the industry. The power of the monopoly depends on the elasticity of demand. No monopoly is ever perfect. The Aluminum Company of America had a monopoly of aluminum production for 50 years; but there are considerable possibilities of substitution among aluminum, copper, steel, and other metals. The New Haven Railroad has a monopoly of rail transportation between Boston and New York, but people can make this trip by airplane, bus, or automobile. These things are all reflected in the demand curve.

Monopoly, like oligopoly, often has its roots in economies of scale. The outstanding examples are of the transportation and public utility industries, where a large installation must be built at the outset and fixed costs are high relative to variable costs, so that *ATC* slopes downward over a wide range. Once the plant is built, it pays to use it as fully as demand permits. These industries are "natural monopolies," not because it would be *technically unfeasible* to have two, three, or more producers, but because it would be *economically inefficient* to do so.

At the other end of the scale, monopoly may arise because the market is very limited. Demand may be small enough so that one moderate-sized plant can provide all the necessary output. If one company gets an early start, and if it expands output as rapidly as demand rises, there may never be room for anyone else to break into the industry. Most monopolies in manufacturing are monopolies of little things, not of big things. And everyone has seen towns with one bank, one hotel, one electric repair shop, one dry cleaner.

In still other cases, monopoly exists where it doesn't have to. The market may be large enough to support several producers of optimum scale. But if one company gets a head start and determines to keep out would-be competitors, it may be able to do so. One way of doing this is through *patent control*. If the product involves a new production process, the company can secure from the U.S. Patent Office an exclusive right to this process for a period of 17 years. Anyone who tries to duplicate it is liable to suit for infringement of patent. Threat of an expensive patent trial can be a powerful weapon in the hands of an established concern, even when its legal case is not strong. And if enough new features can be added to the process to warrant new patents, exclusive rights can be extended over a longer period.

Another possibility is *control of an essential material.* The Aluminum Company of America for many years bought up newly discovered deposits of bauxite ore, either using them itself or preventing any rival producer from using them. In this way it managed to keep control of the industry for a long time after its original patent protection had run out.

Control of labor supply is another possible device, found mainly in local rather than national industries. Local associations of building contractors, trucking concerns, laundry and dry-cleaning establishments, and the like have sometimes signed union agreements under which the union promises that its members will not work for anyone who is not in the association. This does not make it impossible for new companies to get established, since they can try to recruit nonunion labor; but it certainly makes it more difficult.

Cost, Price, and Output under Monopoly

How will a monopolist set about doing the best for himself? And how does the result differ from that which would be reached under competitive conditions?

Maximum Profit for a Monopolist

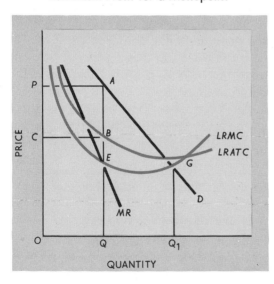

FIGURE 4. These are demand and long-run cost curves for a one-company monopoly. The monopolist should follow the MR = MC rule and build a plant just large enough to produce OQ. His profit is shown by the rectangle PABC. The strength of the monopoly is indicated by the ratio AE/AQ, often called the *degree of monopoly*.

It is best to consider these questions in terms of the long run rather than the short run. The long-run problem is how much plant capacity will be constructed in a particular industry. Will the amount of capacity built be larger or smaller under monopoly than under atomistic competition? And what will this do to price and output?

In Figure 4 we show a long-run *ATC* curve for a particular product, with the corresponding marginal cost curve. Remember that each point on these curves represents a different scale of enterprise. The cost curves show what happens to cost as scale is increased. Optimum scale is at *G*, the minimum point of *LRATC*.

We next draw in the demand and marginal revenue curves for the product. Applying the usual $MR = MC$ rule, we see that the monopolist will make most money by building just enough capacity for output OQ, and by selling this amount at price OP. This yields the profit rectangle $PABC$, which is larger than any other he could secure.

Unlike the result in pure competition, there is a substantial gap between price and marginal cost. This gap can be taken as a measure of the strength of the monopoly. Indeed, the ratio of the gap to the price itself, *i.e.*, AE/AQ, has been termed the *degree of monopoly*. This measure is obviously related to the elasticity of demand. The more inelastic the demand curve, the higher the degree of monopoly.[3] So the intelligent monopolist will try to get hold of a product for which there are only poor substitutes and which most people consider a necessity.

What is wrong with monopoly price and output from a public standpoint? One can single out at least three disadvantages:

1. It is clear from Figure 4 that too little of the product is being produced. Why can we say this? Because at the monopoly output OQ, there is a large gap between the price $OP = QA$, which indicates how badly buyers want the product, and the marginal cost of producing it, QE. Under pure competition, on the other hand, output of each product is carried to the point where cost and benefit exactly balance, where the price people are willing to pay for the last unit produced just covers the cost of producing it.

Restriction of output to OQ means that too small a quantity of economic resources is being used in the industry. Some labor, capital, and other resources which consumers would prefer to see devoted to this product are not being devoted to it. Instead, they are forced to seek employment elsewhere in the economy, which means that one or more other products are being *over*produced. This misallocation of resources is the basic disadvantage of monopoly.

2. A second consequence is that the monopolistic company makes profits for which it performs no economic function. This is sheer tribute levied on the hapless buyer. Consumers are likely, on the average, to have smaller incomes than the owners of stock in the monopoly business, and the effect is thus a transfer of income from lower brackets to higher brackets. But even if the buyers were richer than the monopolistic seller, exaction of monopoly profits constitutes an arbitrary redistribution of income.

3. Price isn't everything. Service, quality, and other aspects of the bargain are important. One disadvantage of dealing with a monopolist is that he can push you around on these things as well as on price. A competitive seller cannot do this. If he falls down on service or quality, the customer simply says good-bye and goes across the street. But when

---

[3] It can be shown that $\dfrac{AE}{AQ} = \dfrac{P - MR}{P} = \dfrac{1}{E}$
where E is the elasticity of demand. The smaller is E, the higher the degree of monopoly.

you cannot go anywhere else, and the seller knows this, he may take advantage of it by being slow on deliveries or service calls and unreliable in performance.

The urge toward maximum profit, of course, does not operate without restraint. The federal government regulates transportation rates, and most of the states regulate rates for electric power, intrastate telephone calls, and other public utilities. This does not remove all the disadvantages of monopoly; but it probably makes price lower and output larger than would be the case otherwise. Even without regulation, fear of public criticism may cause a monopolist to charge less than the maximum-profit price. Moreover, unless the monopolistic company's position is very secure, it may fear that large profits will tempt other companies to enter the industry or to develop substitute products, and may take this into account in its price policies. This can still be regarded as maximizing its profit, but taking a long view of the future rather than a shortsighted view.

Price Discrimination

So far we have considered only the simplest case, in which a product is sold in one market at a uniform price. There are cases, however, in which a product is sold to distinct groups of buyers; and if the markets can be kept distinct, it may be possible and profitable to charge a different price in each. This is termed *price discrimination.*

It seems plausible that it will pay to charge higher prices in markets where demand is less elastic, lower prices where demand is more elastic. This is demonstrated for a two-market case in Figure 5. D_1 and D_2 are the demand curves in the two markets, MR_1 and MR_2 the marginal revenue curves. Demand is clearly more elastic in market 2. By adding D_1 and D_2 *horizontally* for each possible price, we obtain total demand for the product, D_T; and similarly, we can add MR_1 and MR_2 horizontally to obtain MR_T. The marginal cost of production is shown by MC.

Now how should the monopolist proceed? As usual, he should produce to the point where marginal revenue equals marginal cost *for output as a whole,* i.e., where $MC = MR_T$. This indicates an output of OC. Next, he will want to divide this output between the two markets so that his *marginal revenue in each market is the same.* Why? Because if there were a discrepancy, he could raise his profits by shifting output from the market where MR is lower to that where it is higher. The point A on MR_T, corresponding to the proper *total* output, was obtained by horizontal addition of MR_1 and MR_2. So to "dis-add" them we draw a horizontal line from A across to the Y-axis. By noting where this intersects the two marginal revenue curves, we see that OA units of output should be sold in market 1 and OB units in market 2, where $OA + OB = OC$. This satisfies the equal-marginal-revenue requirement. Finally, knowing the quantity sold in each market, we can run up to the demand curves to get the prices, which will be AP_1 in market 1 and BP_2 in market 2. So we get the expected result: price is higher where demand is less elastic.

This will work only if the seller can keep the markets sealed off and prevent any seepage between them. If customers can buy in the low-price market and resell in the high-price one, a price differential becomes impossible. But it is often possible to achieve a clear separation of markets. For example, the inelastic market may be the market within the

A Monopolist Selling in Distinct Markets Should Charge Different Prices to Maximize Profit

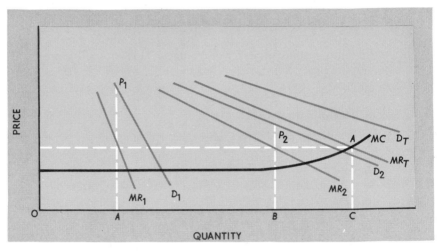

FIGURE 5. D_1 and D_2 show the demands of two distinct groups of customers served by the same monopolistic seller. Total demand D_T is obtained by adding D_1 and D_2 horizontally; MR_T is obtained by adding MR_1 and MR_2. The monopolist should produce OC, where MC = MR_T. He should sell OA of this in market 1 and OB in market 2, since this equalizes his marginal revenue in the two markets. The result is a lower price, BP_2, in market 2, which has the more elastic demand curve; and a higher price, AP_1, in market 1.

country, while the elastic market is the foreign market, where the product must be sold in competition with goods from other countries. If the seller can make sure that the goods he exports at lower prices are not reimported to the home market, discrimination can work. Doctors usually charge rich patients higher fees than poor ones. This works because the rich man can't change his name and his bank account in order to have an operation. Railroads charge one rate for shipping cattle, another for shipping iron ore. The cattle can't change their skins to travel at a lower rate.

A familiar case of discrimination is in the pricing of electric power. The highest rate is for current used in lighting, since substitutes are poor and demand inelastic. Customers get a lower rate for current used in water heating or house heating, since here electricity is in competition with gas, oil, and coal. A still lower rate is charged to factories and other industrial users, partly because they buy in large quantity, but partly because of competition with other energy sources.

Price discrimination can sometimes increase total output, as compared with what would happen under a uniform price policy. Discriminatory pricing of railroad transportation and electric power is usually justified on the ground that it enables these enterprises to work closer to full capacity. A further effect is a redistribution of incomes among various classes of buyers. Some pay more, others less than they would pay under a one-price policy. About the merit of this effect, economics has little to say. It is often considered fair that doctors should levy an unofficial income tax on their more prosperous patients, while providing cheaper service to low-income people. But this is an ethical judgment, not an economic judgment.

DO BUSINESSMEN MAXIMIZE PROFIT?

We must now face an issue which so far we have detoured around. The $MR = MC$ rule assumes that businessmen seek maximum profit. This is plausible for atomistic competition, on a "survival-of-the-fittest" basis. We need suppose only that *some* of the competitors are single-minded about minimizing costs and reaching correct price-output decisions. Then the others will be forced into line or they will vanish. The survivors will be "economic men" of necessity.

But what about oligopoly and monopoly? If the company's demand curve lies above the ATC curve over some range (and one object of business strategy is to maneuver the company into this favorable position), its management has a range of discretion. It is not *forced* to adopt any one price-output policy. In this situation, will company executives necessarily pursue maximum profit? May they perhaps do something quite different?

It is desirable first to separate problems of *information* from problems of *motivation*. One line of argument is that businessmen would like to maximize profit but that they can't possibly know enough. So they fall back on simplified rules of thumb which are quite different from the rules explained above. A second line of argument is that business executives have multiple objectives, of which profit is only one. Profits belong to the stockholders, not to the corporate executive. What *he* wants is salary, fringe benefits, power, prestige, and other things which may be only loosely related to profit. Let's examine each of these arguments briefly.

Shortcuts and Rules of Thumb

The executives of a large business live in a much more complex world than we have recognized so far. A large company may have hundreds or thousands of products. When these come from the same plant, the exact cost of each is hard to determine. The position of the demand curves for each product can never be known precisely. Worse still, it is expected *future* demand and costs which really matter, and the future is far from predictable.

Moreover, it is not feasible to decide everything afresh each day. An executive's time and energy are limited. Very frequent changes of price and output would also be upsetting to customers, competitors, and workers. So once a decision is made, it usually stands until circumstances have changed enough to warrant a reconsideration.

Even if business executives could carry through the elaborate calculations needed to maximize profit at every moment, it would doubtless not be worthwhile to do so. Gathering information and reaching decisions involves costs, and these have to be set against any possible benefits. It is more sensible to aim at coming somewhere *near* the maximum-profit position *on the average* over the months and years. And it is sensible to use simplified rules of thumb as an aid to quicker decisions. Two common devices for this purpose are *average-cost pricing* and the *break-even chart*.

Average-cost or "full-cost" pricing starts by calculating the total unit cost of a product on the basis of current or estimated production volume. A percentage markup is then added, and the result is the product price. Research studies have shown that this technique is widely used by manufacturing companies. The percentage markup is traditional also in wholesale and retail trade.

On the surface, this method seems to be based entirely on cost and to ignore demand and marginal revenue. But how is the size of the markup decided? Here we find demand lurking in the background. The percentage used varies among industries and even among companies in the same industry. (Companies usually have different cost levels. So if they all sell at the same price, they *cannot* be getting the same markup over cost.) The markup may also vary with the swings of the business cycle. Consistent application of a standard markup would have odd results. During a recession, output falls, which tends to raise total unit cost because of the overhead factor—the company moves to the left on its *ATC* curve. So consistent use of the same markup would mean *raising prices* as sales decline in recession and *lowering prices* as sales rise during prosperity. This is not the way producers actually behave. They find it expedient to accept a smaller markup in bad years than in good. Demand is taken into account.

Nor is there any logical inconsistency between (1) *deciding on price and output* by applying the $MR = MC$ rule, and (2) *stating the price* as a percentage over total unit cost. We could take any of the cost-demand diagrams used in this chapter, measure the gap between price and the ATC curve, then express this as a markup over ATC. The *manner of expression* does not tell us how the price was actually determined.

One must admit, however, that while average-cost pricing *could* be quite consistent with maximum profit, it is unlikely to be so in practice. Since demand and cost conditions are constantly changing, the correct markup would change every day. It is impractical, however, to change prices this often. So a company is likely at some times to be overpricing its product (compared with the price which would yield maximum profit), and at other times underpricing it. If it comes out about right on average, this may reflect shrewd management—or it may be a lucky accident.

Another common technique for analyzing price-output problems is the *break-even chart*. One way of setting up such a chart is shown in Figure 6. The reason why this chart looks so different from the ones

A Break-Even Chart

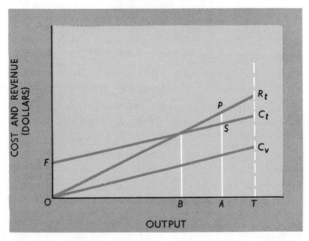

FIGURE 6. C_v is variable cost and C_t total cost for various levels of output. R_t shows the revenue which this output would bring at a specified price. The company would "break even" ($R_t = C_t$) at output OB. If the company is able to sell OA units at this price, it will make a profit of PS.

presented earlier is that it uses *total cost* and *total revenue* curves rather than average or marginal curves.

In Figure 6, C_v is total variable cost, C_t is total cost including overhead, R_t is total revenue. To draw C_v as a straight line assumes that variable costs increase at a constant rate as output rises; that is, that marginal cost and average variable cost are constant. This is obviously a simplification of reality. But marginal cost may be approximately constant over an output range from, say, 30 percent to 90 percent of plant capacity. If the company actually operates within this range most of the time, the simplification may be warranted.

C_t is obtained from C_v by adding overhead costs. Overhead is, by definition, a fixed amount, shown by the distance OF. So C_t runs parallel to C_v at this fixed distance above it. The slope of the revenue curve R_t assumes a certain price for the product. It shows how revenue would behave if more and more output were sold at this same price. A higher assumed price yields a steeper R_t line, a lower price a flatter one. The company is not naïve enough to think that it actually could sell any quantity it wished at the same price. Prospective sales are one of the key items to be determined. But one has to start somewhere. So the company selects a price, perhaps the one prevailing at the moment, or a new price proposed by the sales department, and asks itself, "How would various levels of sales at this price affect our profits? How much would we have to sell to at least break even?"

The *break-even point* is the output for which total revenue equals total cost, *i.e.*, the point at which R_t crosses C_t and begins to rise above it. The break-even point in Figure 6 is OB. At outputs below this, the company would be covering variable costs but would not be covering all its overhead, so it would be making a loss. Any output above OB will bring a profit. The break-even output is usually expressed as a percentage of plant capacity.[4] If capacity output is OT, the break-even percentage is OB/OT. This is the meaning of such statements as, "Steel prices are now so high that the industry can break even at 50 percent." Given the level of costs, a *higher* price (steeper slope of R_t) means a *lower* break-even point, and vice versa.

Now comes the critical question: how much will the company actually be able to sell at the price assumed in drawing R_t? Suppose the best guess about prospective sales is OA. If these sales actually materialize, the company will have revenues of AP minus costs of AS, leaving a profit of PS. It also has a *safety margin* in the estimates, since sales could fall short of OA by the distance AB without involving the company in losses. Executives are likely to look at the safety margin as well as the prospective profit in judging whether the situation shown by the chart is satisfactory.

A single break-even chart, such as Figure 6, shows the results of a specific course of action: a certain product, certain production and selling costs, a certain price, and an estimate of sales volume. Choice among alternative courses of action, then, involves *comparing different charts* to find the one with the most favorable outcome. For example,

---

[4] In this section we are almost bound to slip into using business terminology rather than economic terminology. By "capacity" executives usually mean rated capacity in an engineering sense, or a production rate which would be exceeded only in unusual circumstances. This will normally be above the minimum of the short-run ATC curve.

separate charts can be drawn for different possible prices. A simple comparison involving only two prices is shown in Figure 7. The revenue

Using the Break-Even Chart to Compare Alternatives

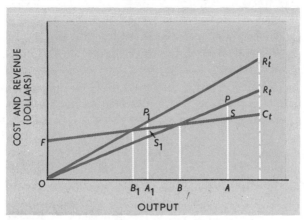

FIGURE 7. This is the same as Figure 6 with the addition of a new revenue curve R'_t based on a higher assumed price. Estimated sales at this price are OA_1 and profit P_1S_1. Since this is smaller than PS, the company will do better at the lower price corresponding to R_t.

line R_t is the same as in Figure 6. But suppose the company is considering also a higher price, shown by the revenue line R'_t. The break-even point with this price would be B_1, and the estimate of probable sales is A_1. Why is OA_1 smaller than OA? Because the company (except in the case of pure competition) is confronted by a sloped demand curve. A higher price normally means lower sales.

In this case, the lower price indicated by R_t yields both a larger profit margin ($PS > P_1S_1$) and a larger safety margin ($AB/OA > A_1B_1/OA_1$). But the result will not always be so clear-cut. One price may yield a higher profit but a smaller safety margin than another, in which case the choice will depend on the weight which executives give to each of these objectives.

In the same way, one could construct a series of charts for different products or different variations on the same product. One could set up a series of charts, all assuming the same price, but showing different levels of selling expense and corresponding differences in estimated sales. The usefulness of the procedure depends on the accuracy of the underlying figures, and particularly of the sales estimates. The break-even chart is simply a tool for organizing information so as to allow executives to survey rapidly a variety of possibilities. The decisions which result may or may not come close to maximizing profits, depending on the judgment and intuition of the executives. There is certainly no *logical* inconsistency between an effort to maximize profits and the use of this particular tool.

The Motivation of Executives

The great majority of businesses are still owner-operated. The small businessman who maximizes profit is at the same time maximizing his own income. The case for assuming that he will try to do so is similar to that for assuming people normally prefer higher wages to lower wages or more consumption to less.

But what about the large corporation? Here management is in the hands of salaried executives, nominally responsible to the stockholders, but often a virtually self-perpetuating body. This cleavage between ownership and control in the large corporation raises basic questions about executive motivation. How much do salaried executives care about profit? What other things do they care about? How far does their behavior deviate from the simple picture drawn in the last two chapters?

There are many reasons why salaried executives should continue to be interested in profit. First, the company's profit rate is the clearest indicator of managerial success. A management which regularly turns in substantial profits, or which does better this year than last year, or which does better than competitors in the same industry, earns esteem in business circles and gets written up in popular magazines and business school case books. Second, profits are necessary if the business is to grow and expand. Management generally regards expansion as normal and desirable. Third, executives often share directly in profits through stock ownership in the company, or through bonus schemes related to profits. Fourth, consistent failure to make money can land a management in serious trouble. It may mean a cold shoulder from the bankers, loss of competitive position in the industry, even the horrid spectre of a stockholders' revolt.

But to say that executives have an interest in profit does not mean that they are interested *only* in profit or that they are interested in *maximum* profit. Professor Herbert Simon and others have suggested that we should replace the concept of the "maximizing" executive with that of the "satisficing" executive, who aims merely at a *satisfactory* profit rate. Provided this target is achieved, he will not worry much about whether still larger profits might have been earned by a different route.

What other objectives enter into executive motivation? Executives are certainly interested in the *growth* of the enterprises they manage. Growth is considered normal and meritorious. There is something wrong with a company which fails to grow. Moreover, growth correlates well with the personal interests of the executive. Power, prestige and influence are important sources of executive satisfaction. The larger the business, the greater the executives' prestige and influence. Studies of executive salaries have shown that they are also highly correlated with size of company. So there is a direct incentive for the executives to try to make the company bigger and thus increase their own rewards.[5]

This kind of motivation may partially offset the tendency toward monopolistic restriction described earlier in this chapter. A monopolist, or a member of a "cooperative" oligopoly group, should logically hold down his size and output to the maximum-profit level. But growth-minded executives may push beyond this to an output which still yields satisfactory profits, but where output is larger and price lower than in the simple monopoly solution. The growth drive may also lead to heavy emphasis on research and development, product improvement, introduction of new products, and diversification of company activities into other branches of industry. A company can expand only so far in one line; but it can expand almost indefinitely by adding new lines of activity.

The commonest way for a company to grow is to retain and reinvest part of its learnings instead of passing them all out in dividends to stockholders. But to go too far in this direction may interfere with another important objective—*management security.* If stockholders receive too small a return, they may begin to wonder whether they shouldn't have a different management.

Management's control and security may be threatened also if the profit rate itself becomes low or negative. A key fact here is the *uncertainty* about the results of any business decision, which arises from uncertainty of future costs and demand. An executive has not merely to make a best guess about the probable outcome, but also to estimate the chances that the result will be better or worse than expected. If the worst should happen, he may be in trouble with his superiors and the stockholders. So he may well aim for a smaller but more secure profit as compared with a larger potential profit which is also subject to large risks. The problem of rational *decision making under uncertainty* has received much attention from economists in recent years.

All things considered, it still seems useful to learn the rules for maximizing profit under conditions of complete certainty. For one thing, this brings out clearly the influence of different market structures. One can say that the behavior of a monopolist is likely to be biased in a low-output, high-price direction; and that a "cooperative" oligopoly will show more of this bias than a situation where cooperation is looser. But one should beware of thinking that the intersection of curves on a cost-demand diagram can reveal precisely what will happen in a particular case.

---

[5] If there were a good market for business executives, and no psychological or institutional barriers to movement, a man could achieve the same end by moving up from smaller to larger companies; and this does happen to some extent. But there is a marked tendency to stay within, and grow up with, a particular company. Inter-company shifts are fairly rare at the highest executive levels.

MONOPOLY, OLIGOPOLY, AND COMPETITION

In the past two chapters, we have developed propositions about business behavior under various market structures. The purpose was partly descriptive but also partly normative. We would like to be able to decide whether some market structures are preferable to others. What can we actually say on this point?

One problem is that these different market forms are not practical alternatives to one another throughout the economy. Transportation and public utilities are the special province of monopoly. The question of how these industries would perform under atomistic competition is meaningless. At the other pole, agriculture is the traditional domain of pure competition. One cannot imagine wheat growing organized as a monopoly any more than the New York Central Railroad run "competitively."

There are situations, however, in which alternative market structures are possible and a direct comparison makes sense. Consider an industry in which optimum plant size is small relative to total demand, so that there is room for a hundred or more producers. Many branches of manufacturing are in this situation, as are the retail and service industries in large cities. Then each plant might be owned by a separate company, leading to atomistic competition; or one might have a few oligopolists each owning numerous plants; or, if the law permitted, all the plants might be operated by a single monopolist.

How will these differing forms of organization affect price and output in the industry? We can get a clear result *if* we assume that the form of organization makes no difference to each plant's *ATC* curve. Then monopoly or fully cooperative oligopoly will yield highest price and lowest output. If the oligopolists do not cooperate fully, price will be below the monopoly level; and if the infighting is severe, it may be as low as under atomistic competition. In general, atomistic competition is the safest route to minimum price and maximum output.

If this were the whole story, trust busters could lay about them with good conscience. Keep the industry organized in many small companies, and you will get best results. But the assumption that costs will be the same under any form of organization begs the question, and argument rages mainly around this point. Two separate issues are involved: (1) Which form of organization leads to lowest cost *at a particular time?* (2) Which form of organization is most conducive to technical progress and lowering of costs *over the course of time?* Economists are still far from agreement on the answers.

The level of *ATC* curves at a particular time is obviously not a fact of nature. It depends on the scale of enterprise and on the effectiveness of management. The argument for large companies leans heavily on economies of scale, that is, *scale of enterprise*, since we have assumed that *plants* are already of optimum size. A larger company, it is argued, can achieve economies in selling, purchasing, financing, and other types of expense which will reduce costs per unit of output. It can give full scope to the talents of top-quality management; and it can make greater use of outside management consultants in the search for maximum efficiency.

Against this it is argued that, while scale of plant has an important effect on costs, scale of enterprise does not. Having 10 plants under the same management rather than 1 will reduce costs only slightly. Moreover, there are diseconomies of scale as well as economies; and a large monopolist or oligopolist may readily expand beyond the optimum size. Where producers can control the price, there is no automatic check on excessive size, as there is under atomistic competition.

It is argued also that managers will work hardest under atomistic competition because they must do so or suffer elimination from the industry. Fear of failure is a stronger spur than hope of gain. The monopolist or cooperative oligopolist is usually assured of positive profit. True, he could earn a still larger profit by an energetic effort to reduce costs. But why should he? Why not relax a little? The best monopoly profit is a quiet life. So if one wants a guarantee of efficient management, the best guarantee lies in atomistic competition.

In addition to these arguments, we have noted special possibilities of inefficiency under oligopoly. Oligopolists who refrain from competing with each other in price, but who still want more sales, are forced to turn to advertising and other forms of nonprice competition. These can involve costs which outweigh any benefit to consumers. Moreover, if the oligopolists are unable to exclude new companies, they may end up operating much below capacity, with needlessly high unit costs and prices. One is tempted to conclude that oligopoly yields the worst of both worlds, and that outright monopoly would be preferable. But this may be too hasty. So long as there are several producers in an industry, there is always the possibility that they may cut prices, improve products, and do other things which benefit the consumer. Monopoly is apt to be lethargic and also hard to get rid of.

The second issue is which form of organization is likely to be more progressive in lowering costs and improving products over the course of time. Here it is argued that inventions and improvements now come mainly from systematic research, that this is best organized on a large scale, and that only a large company can bear the necessary costs. Further, the possibility of monopoly profit makes the risks of innovation bearable. Large companies do typically devote a higher percentage of their revenues to research and development than small companies. And one can point to laboratories such as those of General Electric, Bell Telephone, and Du Pont, which have an impressive research record.

The most striking fact about industrial research is its heavy concentration in a few industries. Two thirds of the total goes to aircraft and space vehicles, electrical equipment and communications, and chemicals. These are industries which draw on one or more of the natural sciences, which include many large companies, and which are closely related to military and space programs. Since the federal government now provides most of the money for industrial research, it is naturally allocated heavily in these directions.

Small companies, it is said, are handicapped in organizing research; and industries organized on a small scale are apt, for this reason, to be technically unprogressive. Looking only at one point in time, it may be true that the oligopolist is exacting higher prices and profits than would prevail under atomistic competition. But if one looks a few years ahead, this is more than offset by a faster rate of decline in costs and prices due to industrial research.[6]

But this line of argument has not gone unchallenged. Inventions may come from many sources. The most basic scientific discoveries are apt to come from university laboratories, while industrial laboratories concentrate more on improvements and practical applications.[7] The lone-wolf inventor is still important. Government laboratories are important sources of innovation in agriculture and public health and could be so in other fields. Small-scale producers don't necessarily have to do their own inventing. The manufacturers of coal-mining machinery, textile machinery, and printing machinery have been a major source of technical progress in those industries. So the fact that coal mines, textile mills, and printing shops are small and competitive has been no bar to technical progress. An even more striking case is agriculture, which has benefited from commercial research on farm machinery, fertilizers, hybrid corn, and other things as well as from government-sponsored research. So although this is one of our smallest-scale industries, it has had one of the highest rates of productivity increase over the past generation.

From this welter of conflicting opinion, everyone must draw his own conclusions. We return to this issue in examining antitrust legislation in Chapter 13.

SUMMARY

1. Fewness of sellers (*oligopoly*) arises where the capacity of each firm is large relative to total demand for the product. This may occur either because the firms are large or because total demand is small.

---

[6] For a strong statement of this view, see Henry H. Villard, "Competition, Oligopoly, and Research," *Journal of Political Economy,* December, 1958, pp. 483–97.

[7] Interesting evidence on this point is contained in D. Hamberg, "Invention in the Industrial Research Laboratory," *Journal of Political Economy,* April, 1963, pp. 95–115.

2. Under oligopoly, price may settle anywhere between the level which would be charged by a single monopolist and the level which would exist under pure competition; and quantity produced will vary correspondingly. While it might be logical for oligopolists to agree on the monopoly price, there are several reasons why this may not actually happen: price fixing is illegal; there may be differences of economic interest among the oligopolists; pressure by large buyers may break down the united front of sellers; and numerous small producers may exert a restraining influence on the large producers.

3. Even if oligopolists can agree on a profitable price, profits may be eroded by the entrance of new producers or by the growth of selling expenses. Below-capacity operation and excessive selling expenses are common sources of waste in oligopoly industries.

4. *Monopoly* exists where there is only one seller of a product, "product" being defined by a major gap in the chain of substitutes. A monopolist will determine price and output according to the $MR = MC$ rule. Price will be higher and output lower than would be the case under pure competition. Monopoly distorts the allocation of resources by admitting too little labor and capital to the monopolized area, thereby forcing more resources to seek employment in other (competitive) sectors of the economy.

5. Where a monopolist sells the same product in two or more distinct markets with differing elasticities of demand, he will maximize profit by *price discrimination*, setting lower prices in the markets where demand is most elastic. This is a common practice in pricing railroad transportation and electric power.

6. The complexity of actual pricing decisions leads executives to adopt shortcut procedures. One of these is *average-cost pricing*, which means adding a percentage markup to average total cost. This is not necessarily inconsistent with maximizing profit in accordance with the $MR = MC$ rule.

7. The *break-even chart* uses total cost and total revenue curves to determine the consequences of a particular price and sales volume. The sales volume at which $TR = TC$, and above which profit begins, is termed the *break-even point*.

8. There is reason to think that profit, the dominant incentive of the manager of a small business, is also a major incentive to the corporate executive. Theories which assume an effort to maximize profit are a good starting point for analysis of business behavior.

9. Comparisons of the results of monopoly, oligopoly, and competition tend to assume that plant cost curves will be the same in all three cases. But this is actually unlikely. One issue is which situation will produce most efficient management, and hence lowest ATC curves, at a particular time. A second issue is which situation will produce most rapid technical progress, and hence fastest decline in ATC curves, over the course of time.

DISCUSSION QUESTIONS

1. What is meant by *monopoly power* in a market? When we say that a single seller has *a monopoly,* what does this mean? How can one measure the strength of a monopoly position?

2. What are some of the reasons why a monopolist might charge less than the price which would maximize his immediate profit?

3. Under what conditions can a monopolist charge different prices to different groups of customers (or to the same customers for different purposes)? Isn't it unfair for him to do this? Should government regulatory agencies permit this practice?

4. When we say that oligopoly means "few sellers," *how* few do we mean? Does it make any practical difference whether the oligopoly group numbers 5 or 25?

5. What are the main reasons why an oligopoly group may fail to establish a firm price agreement?

6. It is often argued that advertising increases demand, which makes possible production at lower unit cost, which permits lower prices to consumers. Under what conditions would this argument be valid?

7. Suppose that for the next 10 years the automobile manufacturers, instead of making annual model changes, continued to turn out an unchanged 1967 model. What would be the effects
   i. On the companies?
   ii. On consumers?

8. "The businessmen who make pricing decisions never heard of marginal cost or marginal revenue. They use an entirely different set of concepts. The price theory expounded in economics textbooks is of little use in explaining actual business behavior." Discuss.

9. "The usual analysis of monopoly power is highly misleading. True, a monopolist or oligopolist may charge higher prices at a moment of time. But over the course of time he is likely to reduce costs and prices faster than would a horde of small competitive producers." Do you agree? Why, or why not?

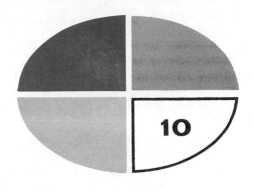

Labor Markets and Wage

Determination

A man's value is that which he sets upon himself.   RABELAIS

As in other things, so in men; not the seller but the buyer determines the price. For let a man (as most men do) rate themselves at the highest value they can; yet their true value is no more than it is esteemed by others.

THOMAS HOBBES, *Leviathan*

IN CHAPTERS 8 and 9 we examined price and output determination in *product* markets. In Chapters 10 and 11 we round out our survey of the market economy by analyzing the pricing of *productive services.*

Why do we say "productive services" instead of "factors of production"? These are closely related but distinct ideas. A *factor* is a human or material agent able to contribute something to production: a man, a machine, a building, an acre of land. A factor is a *stock* of stored-up productive power, capable of being exerted over a longer or shorter period in the future. The *service* is the actual use of the factor over a certain period. It is a *flow per unit of time.* The price of a productive service cannot be expressed without a time dimension. Examples are the cost of a man-hour of a certain grade of labor, a machine-hour of a certain type of machine, the use of a building for a month, or an acre of farmland for a year.

If we know the price of a service, we can derive the value of the factor which yields it. From the annual rental of an acre of farmland, we can calculate what the land is worth. From the expected future yield of a piece of machinery, we can calculate its present value. The method of doing this, known as *capitalization,* will be explained in Chapter 11. The same method is applicable in principle to labor services. A man who will be able to earn certain amounts year after year in the future has a certain value today. In a slave society, this would be his price in the market. In our society, people cannot be bought and sold. But this does not affect the economics of the matter. A worker has value just as a machine or building has value, and for the same reason: the stream of services which he can render in the future. This is why a baseball club can collect a large amount from another club by selling it the right to employ a star player.

Factors of production are owned by households and are the main source of household income. Each household's income depends on the quantity of factor services it supplies and on the market price of these services. A household which supplies high-priced kinds of labor, or which owns much land or capital, will have a higher income than one which does not. For this reason, the pricing of productive services is often called *the theory of distribution.* If we know the market price of each service, and if we know how the ownership of factors is distributed among households, we can explain the distribution of money income among them.

How Many Factors?

How many factors of production are there? The classification can be as fine as we wish. In a large enterprise, using hundreds of kinds of labor and a great variety of machines, we could define each of these as a separate factor. But to get an overview of the economy, it is convenient to group similar factors of production into broad categories. The question is how these broad dividing lines should be drawn.

The English classical economists had a clear answer, which dominated the teaching of economics for a century. The basic types of factor were *land, labor,* and *capital.* Each factor received a different type of income: *rent, wages,* and *interest* (which they called "profit"). And each factor belonged to a distinct social class: the landed gentry, the working class, and the industrial bourgeoisie.

Land was considered unique because it was provided in fixed amounts by nature. Supply being fixed, the rent of land depended solely on demand. As demand rose because of the food requirements of a growing population, rents would rise continuously, and the landlords would get an ever growing share of national income.

Labor was unique because the factor itself is not for sale, and because its supply depended mainly on population growth. Most of the classical school, following Malthus, were population pessimists. They believed population would increase so rapidly that wages would be held down to a bare subsistence. If wages should rise temporarily above this level, fewer people would die of malnutrition and disease. Population would increase faster, and wages would be pressed down again. Some economists, to be sure, conceded that the "subsistence level" is a matter of custom rather than of physical requirements alone. If wages could stay high long enough for workers to raise their customary standard of living, and if they were willing to defend this standard by limiting the size of their families, then the increase might be permanent. But on the whole, the pessimists held the field.

Capital was unique in being material (unlike labor) but reproducible (unlike land). Its increase depended on the profits earned by capitalists and on their willingness to save and reinvest these profits. (Landlords were considered a profligate class who spent their incomes on high living and *would* not save, while workers *could* not save because of their low incomes.) Looking about them, English economists saw that the industrial bourgeoisie was thrifty and was piling up capital at an impressive rate. But as this went on, they believed that the rate of profit must fall, and eventually reach such a low level that further saving would be discouraged. The economy would then enter the famous *stationary state:* wages at a subsistence level, interest rate low and constant, landlords sleek and happy, and no further change until the millenium.

The classical three-factor classification grew out of a certain social milieu and served a definite purpose. It was part of a theoretical scheme which professed to explain how the main social classes were faring at the moment and how they might be expected to fare in the future. It was a cornerstone of what has been called "the magnificent dynamics" of the classical school.

But after 150 years of institutional and theoretical development, the old scheme no longer looks so useful. The division among factor owners in late twentieth-century United States is not nearly so sharp as in early nineteenth-century Britain. The American farmer is worker and capitalist as well as landowner. Many professional and managerial workers own substantial amounts of capital and derive an important part of their income from this source; and ownership of securities is spreading gradually down the income scale. The small businessman is also usually both worker and capitalist.

The supposedly unique characteristics of each factor have also been blurred by closer analysis. Land was supposedly different because it was fixed in supply. But is this true only of land? By no means. What about inherited personal talents, so important in the creative arts and professions? These are also "given by nature," are in fixed supply, and depend on demand for their earnings. A building or machine, once built, is also in fixed supply for its lifetime, which is often quite long.

Nor is it really true that land is "given by nature" and cannot be increased by human effort. *Creation* of new land is rare, though it has been done in Holland; but *improvement* of land is very common. A large part of the value of most American farms derives, not from the original properties of the soil, but from expenditures on clearing, draining, fencing, construction of farm buildings, and so on. These improvements are capital; and the distinction between land and capital has broken down rather completely. We shall follow the modern practice of treating land as not differing importantly from other material agents of production.

In the same way one might argue that the labor and capital categories overlap. How much of the income of an electrician, an accountant, or a chemist is a return to innate ability and effort? How much is a return on the money spent in training for these occupations? If we include in training costs, as we should, the money the person could otherwise have earned during his additional years of education, training is a substantial item for skilled manual and clerical jobs and a very substantial item for executive and professional occupations. So human productive capacity *can* be increased through investment, just like plant and equipment capacity. The result of investment in training is, in fact, often termed *human capital.*

There are, nevertheless, important differences between investment in human and nonhuman capital. Human investment occurs mainly in the first 25 years of life; and for the most part, people do not invest in themselves. The decisions are made by parents and others who provide the necessary finance. (Another important difference: there is no well-developed market for loans to be used in human investment, as there is for loans to be used in material investment.) The *return* on the investment, however, does not come back to the people who made it. They doubtless get satisfaction from seeing their children well launched in life. But the cash return accrues to the person in whom the investment has been incorporated. He is also limited in certain ways: he cannot issue a mortgage on himself, or sell himself to another, as the owner of physical capital can do. He can cash in on his "human capital" only by working, by drawing the higher wage which his enhanced productive capacity commands in the market.

Another important difference: the seller of labor is more intimately involved in the bargain than is the man who risks only his capital. The satisfactions and dissatisfactions arising from work are part of the total experience of the worker-consumer. So we conclude that "people are different from things" and treat labor as a different kind of factor.

Labor and capital do not organize and manage themselves. So in classifying productive services, economists often set up a category which is variously termed "management," "coordination," "entrepreneurship," "risk bearing." Those in this category hire labor and physical equipment, pay the market rate for these services, sell their product at the market price, and keep any profit (or loss) which may remain. The difficulty of pinning down this category, however, shows up in its varied treatment in the professional literature. What is this "extra" factor? What exactly does it do? Why should it receive a return, and what determines the size of the return it does receive? Does the return exist at all—do profits exceed losses for the economy as a whole? We had best leave these questions until next chapter.

DEMAND FOR A PRODUCTIVE SERVICE: MARGINAL PRODUCTIVITY

The price of a productive service is determined by demand and supply. The forces explaining labor supply differ from those explaining the supply of capital goods, so on the supply side each must be analyzed separately. On the demand side, however, there is a general principle which applies to any productive service. This is the principle of *marginal productivity*.

Marginal here has its usual meaning of *additional*. The *marginal product* (*MP*) of a service is the additional output obtained by using an additional unit of the service. What the producer is interested in, however, is the revenue he obtains by selling this additional output. The money return from the physical output secured by using an additional unit of a service is called its *marginal revenue product* (*MRP*).

If the product is sold under conditions of pure competition, so that additional amounts can be sold at a constant price, then marginal revenue product is simply the physical marginal product multiplied by the product price:

$$MRP = MP \times P.$$

In our subsequent reasoning we shall usually be dealing with *MRP* rather than with *MP* itself. A money measure is needed when we want to compare the marginal product of a factor in different companies or industries or to compare the marginal product of a factor with its cost.

In deciding how much of a service to use, a producer is concerned with both its productivity and its cost. The cost of an additional unit of a service may be called the *marginal factor cost*. If the service is sold in a purely competitive market, and the producer can buy as much of it as he wishes at the market price, then marginal factor cost is equal to this price. We shall assume that this is typically true. Situations in which it may not be true will be considered in the Appendix.

We can now state the general principle: a producer will employ any service up to the point at which *marginal revenue product equals marginal factor cost* (which on our assumptions *equals factor price*.) For any factor, *x*, the producer will use the amount at which:

$$MRP_x = MFC_x = P_x .$$

The rationale of this principle is the usual one of maximum profit. If the *MRP* of a service is greater than its cost, then the last unit employed yields a net gain. A rational producer will presumably go on to use additional units. Conversely, if marginal revenue product is less than cost, the last unit used involves a loss, and its use will be discontinued. The producer can earn maximum profit only where marginal revenue product and marginal factor cost are equal.

We shall apply this principle first to labor, which is not only the most important factor but also the most tangible and familiar. For labor our principle says that the *marginal revenue product of labor must equal its wage rate.* Crudely, "labor is paid what it is worth."

This is often wrongly called the *marginal productivity theory of wages.* It cannot by itself be a theory of wage *determination,* since it says nothing about labor supply. Nor does it say anything about the institutional circumstances under which wages are determined. The wage may be set by government decree, or through union-management negotiation, or determined in a competitive market. Marginal productivity analysis says only that *if* the wage is at a certain level, producers will regulate their hiring of labor so as to make its marginal productivity equal to the wage. Marginal productivity is a *theory of demand for labor.*

THE GENERAL LEVEL OF REAL WAGES

It will be convenient to work downward from the general to the specific. We begin by asking what determines the average level of wages in an economy at a particular time, proceed to examine wage determination for broad occupational groups, and get down finally to the detail of wage differences in particular cities and companies.

In examining the general wage level, it is best to work in real or physical terms. One reason is that to use the money wage level would land us in difficulties which we cannot clear up until Part Three. For the time being, we detour around these monetary difficulties by talking in terms of labor's *physical* productivity and labor's *real* (or commodity) wage. Note that the vertical axis of Figure 1 is defined in units of physical output produced and received by workers.

MP in Figure 1 shows the *marginal physical product of labor.* The quantity of land, buildings, machinery, and other productive resources is assumed to be given and constant.[1] The downward slope of *MP* tells us that as more and more labor is applied to the fixed supply of other factors, the marginal physical product of labor declines. The classical

---

[1] We usually also assume, however, that the *form* of capital equipment can be varied so as to cooperate most effectively with whatever quantity of labor happens to be available. If there are only a few workers available in an agricultural country, each can ride a combine; but if population is very dense, each may have to get along with a scythe. This may seem at first an odd and unrealistic assumption. Yet given enough time, there is no doubt that the form taken by capital in a country *is* adapted to the amount of labor available.

The General Level of Real Wages

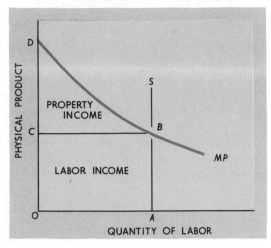

FIGURE 1. MP is labor's marginal physical productivity schedule. It is also the demand schedule for labor. If labor supply is OA and all workers are employed, labor's marginal physical product and the real wage rate will be OC = AB. Total output is OABD, of which labor receives OABC (employment × the wage rate = OA × OC). The remainder goes to the owners of land and capital.

economists called this the *law of diminishing returns.* Today we usually call it the *law of variable proportions.* This principle, which is described more fully in the Appendix, states that: *if the quantity of one productive service is increased, the quantities of all other services remaining constant, the resulting additions to output will decrease after a certain point.* This seems reasonable on intuitive grounds, and has been verified by evidence from a wide variety of production processes.

The slope of *MP* reflects the substitutability of labor for capital, that is, the ease with which a given stock of capital can be rearranged to cooperate with increasing quantities of labor. If known techniques of production are so rigid that it is difficult to use additional labor, even with adequate time to readjust the form of capital goods, then *MP* will fall steeply. If production methods are flexible and substitution easy, it will fall more gradually.

The *height* of *MP* above the X-axis is very important, since it shows whether a given number of workers will have a low or high physical productivity. The height of *MP* depends mainly on three things:

1. The *quantity of other factors* used along with labor. This includes natural resources, capital goods, and economic organization. The last factor includes both the efficiency of management in particular companies and the effectiveness with which the whole production apparatus of a country is coordinated, through markets or in other ways.

2. The *state of technical knowledge.* A single invention, such as hybrid corn or synthetic fibers, may enable the same quantities of labor and capital to turn out much more product.

3. The *quality of the labor force.* The same number of people may turn out more or less product, depending on their health, education, technical training, and motivation.

The horizontal axis of Figure 1 shows units of labor supply. Since a worker may work longer or shorter hours, it is best to total the *man-hours of labor available,* rather than the number of people in the labor force. We assume also for the moment that all workers are equal in skill and personal efficiency, so that they are fully interchangeable in production.

Total labor supply depends on the size of the population; the proportion of each age and sex group which is in the labor force; the standard hours of work in each industry; and personal preferences, expressed in finding ways of working more or less than the standard hours. Total labor supply is inflexible over short periods. There are indications that it may be somewhat responsive to opportunities for employment. More people may enter the labor force, or they may be willing to work more hours, when the demand for labor is high. But it is not far wrong to draw the supply curve of labor at a particular time as a vertical line, such as *AS* in Figure 1, indicating that just *OA* man-hours of labor are available.

If *OA* man-hours of labor are available, and if all this labor is employed, the marginal productivity of labor will be *AB*. If the labor market is fully competitive, the real hourly wage rate will also be *AB = OC.* Why is this? Because each employer adjusts his employment so that the marginal product of the last unit of labor used just equals the rate of wages. If the wage were above *OC*, employers would reduce their use of labor, and the whole labor force could not be employed. Conversely, the wage rate cannot remain below *OC*, because then employers would be trying to hire more labor than there is available. Competition among employers will raise wages to the level *OC.*

There is a dangerous simplicity and power about Figure 1 that can lead to wrong conclusions. So some cautions are necessary. First, we should not say that the wage level *will* be *OC*. This is the equilibrium toward which the labor market would tend under pure competition. But government or unions may be able to maintain a real wage above *OC*. And during World War II, most governments tried to hold real wages below *OC*, which led naturally enough to a severe "labor shortage."

Second, even if the wage *OC* is established, it does not follow that the available labor will always be fully employed. Over short periods, the demand for labor fluctuates with the swings of the business cycle, for reasons to be explained in Part Three. So employment may be close to *OA* at cycle peaks, but will fall below this during recessions. Figure 1 is a long-run construction which ignores short-term fluctuations.

With this caution, what can we learn from Figure 1? First, it shows us the *physical output* of the economy at a certain time. Suppose only a few workers were employed. Their output would constitute a thin sliver along *OD*, at the left-hand side of Figure 1. Adding more workers adds more slivers of output, filling up the area under *MP* as we move from left to right. Finally, if *OA* workers are employed, total output is the area under *MP* up to this point, i.e., *OABD.*

Moreover, Figure 1 shows us how this output is divided between workers and others. With OA workers employed, each receiving a wage OC, total labor income is $OA \times OC = OABC$. The remainder, the triangle BCD, must go to the owners of other factors. If we overlook entrepreneurship for the moment, and treat land as part of capital, we can call BCD simple *property income*. The analysis thus yields a division of national output between suppliers of labor and suppliers of capital. This is usually called the *functional distribution of income* or the distribution of income into *factor shares*.

The kind of analysis we have been applying to labor can equally well be applied to capital. In next chapter we shall construct a diagram similar to Figure 1, but with units of capital along the X-axis instead of units of labor. The MP curve will then show the marginal productivity of capital and, if we know the amount of capital available, we can determine the rate of return of capital. On this kind of diagram, the bottom rectangle constitutes property income, and the triangle at the top is labor income.

Will the results of the two diagrams be consistent? If labor is paid its marginal product and if capital is paid its marginal product, will the labor and capital shares together just equal the total product? This is not necessarily true; but there is one simple case in which it will be true. Suppose an increase in labor and capital inputs always leads to proportionate increase in output. A 1 percent increase in labor and a 1 percent increase in capital results in a 1 percent increase in total product. This amounts to assuming that the economy as a whole shows *constant returns to scale*.[2] If total output behaves in this way and if labor and capital are paid at rates equal to their marginal product, it can be shown that the labor and capital shares will just use up the total product available.

These ideas about functional income distribution can be applied to a wide range of practical problems. Let's look briefly at two applications: the question of how returns to labor and capital will behave over the course of time in a growing industrial economy such as the United States; and the question whether unions can raise the real wage level above what it would be without unions.

Look again at Figure 1, and think now in terms of *change* rather than equilibrium at a point of time. What kinds of change will alter the real wage level OC? We can separate the possible changes into two groups: those affecting the supply of labor and those affecting the height of the MP schedule.

The supply of labor depends, as we have seen, on size of

---

[2] An example of this kind of production relation is $Y = VK^a \, L^{1-a}$, where Y is output, K and L are capital and labor, and V is a constant. This production function is usually termed a Cobb-Douglas function after its discoverers, one of whom was a mathematician and the other the economist Professor Paul Douglas of the University of Chicago (later Senator Douglas of Illinois).

population, the proportion of the population which enters the labor force, and hours worked per person. Each of these behaves differently over time. Population normally increases, and this has certainly been true of the United States throughout its history. The proportion of the population in the labor force, as we saw in Chapter 2, has changed very little since 1890 or so. Hours of work per week and per year have been falling for a century or more. This is a normal consequence of rising real incomes. Leisure is also one of the good things of life, and as incomes rise, people buy more leisure as well as more commodities. On balance, labor supply rises over the course of time, but less rapidly than population. The decline of hours offsets part of the population increase.

If this were all that were happening, employment would be moving out to the right along the *MP* curve, and real wages would be falling. Increased labor supply by itself makes for lower real wages. But here we encounter the second element in the situation—the height of the *MP* schedule. Any increase in the supply of capital and other factors raises the marginal productivity of labor. So does invention of improved products and production methods. In the United States over the past century there has been a high rate of technical progress and a rapid accumulation of capital goods. So labor's *MP* schedule has been shifting upward rapidly over the years.

The course of wages, then, depends on a race between rising labor supply and rising productivity. If labor supply is rising rapidly while productivity is sluggish, real wages may stagnate or decline. Some of the less developed countries are in this situation. But if increases in productivity keep ahead of the growth of labor supply, real wages will rise. This has been the normal situation in the United States, Canada, Britain, Japan, Australia, and the countries of northwestern Europe over the past century. It is illustrated in Figure 2, where the solid lines represent the situation at one point of time, the dotted lines the situation 50 years later. The effect of rising labor supply is swamped by the productivity increase from MP_{1920} to MP_{1970}.

For the United States, Figure 3 shows the increase in real hourly earnings in manufacturing since 1889. The size and steadiness of the increase is impressive. An hour of work today yields more than five times as much real income as did an hour of work in 1889. Note also the close parallel between the rise of real wages and the increase in physical output per man-hour.[3]

An increase in the real wage rate does not necessarily mean an

---

[3] The productivity index covers the entire private economy, while the wage index relates to manufacturing only. The two are thus not strictly comparable. Note also that the productivity index shows *average productivity* per man-hour, while the wage rate is related to *marginal productivity*. In a way, this makes the close coincidence of the two series even more surprising.

Real Wages Normally Rise in a Progressive Economy

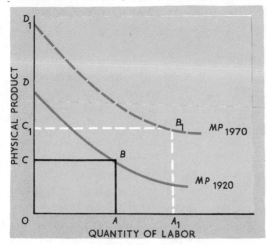

FIGURE 2. The solid lines show the situation in 1920. The broken lines show the situation in 1970. The increase in labor supply from OA to OA_1 tends to depress the real wage rate; but this is more than offset by the rise of labor's physical productivity schedule. Note that, while the *real hourly wage rate* is much higher in 1970, *labor's share of total output* may or may not be higher.

Man-hour Output and Real Hourly Earnings in Manufacturing,
United States, 1889–1965 (Indexes, 1929 = 100)

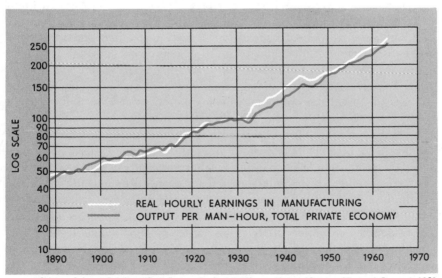

Sources: Solomon Fabricant, *Basic Facts on Productivity Change*, National Bureau of Economic Research, 1958; U.S. Council of Economic Advisors, *Economic Report of the President*, 1965.

FIGURE 3.

increase in labor's share of total output. The ratio $OA_1B_1C_1/OA_1B_1D_1$ in Figure 2 may or may not be greater than the ratio $OABC/OABD$. This depends on the slope of the marginal productivity schedule, which in turn depends on the ease or difficulty of substituting labor for capital in production. In Chapter 11 we shall present some statistics indicating that there has been a moderate increase in labor's share of national income over the past 50 years. But this is the result of historical circumstances rather than of logical necessity.

A word now on the possible impact of unionism. There is no question that unions can sometimes raise wages for a particular occupation, plant, or industry. But can they raise real wages for the labor force as a whole? If so, they would have to do it by affecting the height of the *MP* schedule or by changing the supply of labor.

Unions do some things which raise the *MP* schedule and other things which lower it; but it is hard to say which effect predominates. In some companies and industries, unions probably succeed in getting a larger share of revenue as wages and leave a smaller share for profits. This may reduce the rate of increase in capital supply, both by reducing these companies' incentive to expand and leaving them with less money to spend on expansion. In some industries, too, union regulations concerning work speeds, production methods, and use of unnecessary labor have reduced output per worker. On the other hand, union pressure for higher wages has doubtless stimulated technical progress and improvements in production and personnel management. One can point to many cases in which a union has demanded wage increases which the company honestly believed it could not pay. But when faced with the necessity of doing so, management has buckled down and found ways of improving production methods so as to pay the higher wage.

There is no consensus among economists as to whether unionism on balance has raised the productivity schedule or lowered it; and it would be hard to support either opinion with solid evidence.

A much clearer effect of unionism is via the supply of labor. Unions have worked actively to restrict immigration to the United States; to lower the proportion of people in the labor force by raising the minimum age for beginning work and lowering the age of retirement; to reduce the standard work week; and to reduce hours worked per year by demanding more paid holidays and longer vacation periods. These policies add up to a considerable reduction in the man-hours of labor available, and this must have raised the real wage per man-hour. One can conclude with fair assurance that unionism has raised the average level of real wages in the United states; and that this has been done mainly, or perhaps entirely, by restricting total labor supply.

WAGE RATES FOR A SPECIFIC KIND OF LABOR

The average wage for all labor is a statistical fiction. The reality is a wide variety of wage rates for particular kinds of work. A farm laborer may earn $1 for an hour of work, a stenographer $2, a bricklayer $5, a doctor $10. What explains these differences? Why may one kind of work pay 10 or 20 times as much as another?

Each kind of labor can be regarded as having a separate market; and its price is determined by the interaction of demand and supply in this market. We can safely return now to using money rather than physical units in our demand-supply diagrams. One kind of labor is a sufficiently small part of the economy that we can take its demand curve as independent of its price. A wage increase for shoe workers will not affect total purchasing power enough to alter the demand curve for shoe workers.

Marginal Productivity and Demand

Employers demand labor because it is productive. So we must ask what happens to labor's marginal productivity as more and more labor is used in a particular industry.

Look first at a single company. The company has fixed amounts of various nonlabor factors: buildings, equipment, management. Suppose we were able experimentally to vary the amount of labor used with these fixed factors, starting with just a little labor, then using more and more. We can be certain that beyond some point the marginal physical product of labor will begin to fall. This follows from the law of variable proportions. We were really drawing on this principle when we asserted in Chapter 7 that marginal cost curves eventually begin to rise. Why does marginal cost turn up? Because marginal product turns down.

If marginal physical product (MP) is falling, then marginal revenue product (MRP) must also be falling; and it will, in fact, usually fall at a faster rate. The reason is that additional units of output can be sold only at a lower price. This is usually true even for a single company: except in the case of pure competition, the company is faced with a downward-sloping demand curve. If one considers an entire industry, the product demand curve *must* slope downward to the right. The marginal revenue from each additional unit sold is less than its price. So as more labor is hired, its MRP falls for a double reason: each additional man contributes less physical product; and each additional unit of product contributes less to revenue.

A diagram may be helpful at this point. The vertical axis in Figure 4 is laid off in dollars, so that it can be used to measure both revenue productivity and the wage rate. The horizontal axis shows employment in the industry, measured in man-hours. MRP shows the behavior of marginal revenue productivity as more and more labor is used in the industry.

If the wage rate at a particular time is OW, employers will wish to employ OE man-hours of labor. Why? Because at this point the marginal revenue product of labor just equals the price of labor. If employers stopped short of OE, they would be in a range where $MRP > OW$, i.e., labor is contributing *more* than it costs. So it would pay to expand

Labor Demand in One Industry

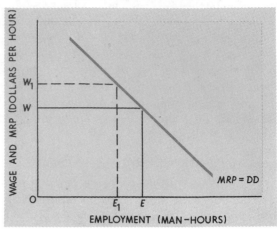

FIGURE 4. *MRP is labor's marginal revenue productivity schedule. Since employers will hire up to the point where MRP = the wage rate, we can read off from MRP the employment corresponding to any wage rate. MRP is the industry's demand schedule for labor.*

employment. But to go beyond *OE* would mean moving into a range where labor contributes *less* than it costs. Thus *OE* is the most profitable level of operation. Similarly, if the wage rate were OW_1, employment would be OE_1; and so on. The *MRP* curve, in fact, *is* the industry's demand curve for labor, and can equally well be labeled *DD,* as we shall do in later diagrams. It tells us that, as the wage for one kind of labor rises (all other wages and prices remaining constant), less of that kind of labor will be demanded; and conversely, a lower relative wage will mean more employment.

What determines the elasticity of an industry's demand curve for labor? The answer can be important—for example, to a union considering the possible impact of a wage demand. Would a (relative) increase of 10 percent in an industry's wage level reduce employment by 10 percent? Or only by 1 percent? In the latter event, the effect may be considered small enough to be ignored.

Four factors influence the elasticity of demand for labor. These apply, indeed, to demand for any productive service and go back to the principles of derived demand explained in Chapter 5. They are:

(1) *Elasticity of Demand for the Product.* Suppose a 10 percent wage increase raises total unit cost 5 percent and that product prices also rise 5 percent. If elasticity of demand for the product is low, say 0.5, sales will fall by only 2½ percent. But if elasticity were higher, say 2.0, sales and employment would fall 10 percent because of the same wage increase. The more elastic the demand for the product, the more elastic the demand for the labor used in making it.

(2) *The Proportion Which Labor Costs Form of Total Production Costs.* If labor is only 10 percent of the total, then a 10 percent wage increase will raise total unit costs only 1 percent. The effect on product

prices, sales, and employment will be small. But if labor forms 80 percent of production costs, the impact will be greater. On this account, a skilled craft union covering only a small part of an employer's labor force is in a stronger bargaining position than a plant-wide union. The cost of buying off the craft group is small, and this lessens the employer's resistance; and the employment effect is too small to deter the union from an aggressive wage policy.

(3) *The Difficulty of Substituting Other Factors for Labor in Production.* In some cases the existing technique of production may be the only known method, and the possibility of modifying it to save labor may be small. But in other cases, there may be alternative methods involving greater mechanization. At a higher wage, one or more of these methods will become profitable and will be brought into use. The greater the number of known alternative methods, and the more laborsaving they are, the greater the elasticity of demand for labor.

(4) *The Supply Curves of Productive Services Other than Labor.* (This is harder to grasp than the three previous points.) Look at it this way: the reason for lower employment at a higher wage is that production costs rise, product prices rise, sales and output are reduced, and purchases of productive services are reduced. Suppose, however, that the industry uses some factor—say a specialized raw material with no other uses—the supply curve of which is highly inelastic. As the industry's demand for this material falls, this will drive down its price. This reduction in the industry's costs serves as an offset to the higher costs resulting from the wage increase. So the increase in total cost and price will be smaller, and the drop in sales and employment smaller, than they would be without this cushioning factor. In this case, labor's gains are partly at the expense of the owners of this other factor.

To sum up: an industry's demand for labor will be more inelastic— that is, a wage increase will produce a *smaller* drop in employment—in proportion as: (1) demand for the product is inelastic; (2) labor costs form a small proportion of total costs; (3) the known possibilities of substituting capital and other factors for labor are small; and (4) supply of one or more nonlabor factors is inelastic.

Worker Preferences and Supply

It seems plausible that the supply curve of a particular kind of labor will slope upward to the right. This means that, as the wage rate in one occupation increases *relative to that in other occupations,* more people will prefer to work at this occupation rather than at something else. The hourly wage rate is, of course, only one element affecting the attractiveness of a job. The worker must consider also the time and cost of learning the occupation, the degree of physical or mental effort required, the standard work week, regularity of employment, prospects for promotion, physical conditions of work, the social esteem in which the job is held, and other things. Since people's preference systems differ, workers will evaluate these conditions differently. Some may find a particular kind of work so congenial that they would do it even for a low wage. Others who find it only moderately attractive will require a higher wage before choosing it instead of something else. But we can be sure that, as the relative wage level rises, the number seeking employment in the occupation will also rise.

There is the further consideration that labor markets for most kinds of work are local markets. There is a market for secretaries in Boston, in Washington, in Atlanta. Movements from one area to another involve

Wage Determination in an Industry

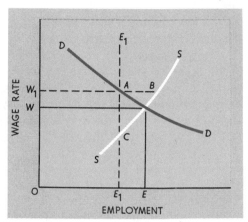

FIGURE 5. DD and SS are the industry's labor demand and supply curves. Under pure competition, OE workers would be employed at a wage of OW. A strong union might insist on the wage OW_1, but in this event only OE_1 workers would be hired.

financial and psychological costs, and will be undertaken only for an offsetting gain in wages. As the relative wage in one area rises, however, more and more people will consider it worth their while to migrate from other areas. This provides a second reason for upward-sloping labor supply curves. Detroit wages rose so high partly because the auto companies had to attract many workers from the South.

Competitive and Regulated Wages

If the labor market is competitive, and if we know the position of the demand and supply curves for an occupation, we can say how many will be employed in the occupation and what they will be paid. The intersection of DD and SS in Figure 5 defines a wage rate, OW, and an employment level, OE. This is an equilibrium position in the sense that, if it were to be established, no one would have any reason to alter it. At the wage OW, employers want to hire OE workers, and just this number of workers will seek employment in the occupation. The quantities offered and demanded balance, and the market is cleared.

We see from the demand curve that the wage OW equals the marginal revenue product of the last worker employed. The supply curve tells us that this is also the wage necessary to induce the last worker employed to shift over from some other occupation. A competitive labor market equalizes the attractiveness of various occupations *to the workers at the margin of choice.*

Note another interesting thing: the worker located right at the intersection of *DD* and *SS* feels that it is barely worth his while to work in this occupation at the wage *OW*. But workers lower down on *SS* are getting a kind of bonus. They would be willing to work at this job for less than *OW*; but they can get *OW* anyway, because that is the wage needed to tempt the marginal man. This difference between what people get and the minimum they would take may be called a *producers' surplus,* similar to the *consumers' surplus* discussed in Chapter 6. The growth of a diversified economy with hundreds of occupations, by permitting fuller development and gratification of individual work preferences, adds to producers' satisfaction, just as a vast array of alternative consumer goods adds to consumer satisfaction.

The fact that *OW* is the equilibrium wage for this occupation under pure competition does not mean, of course, that this wage will actually be established. Suppose that for some reason people are not free to enter the occupation at will and that the number admitted is held down to OE_1. Then, from the demand curve, we see that the wage will be OW_1; and this wage will be perfectly stable so long as the controls on entrance continue. Or government may set a legal minimum wage higher than *OW*; and this will also be stable provided it can be policed. Or a trade union may enter the picture.

Suppose the members of this occupation belong to a union, and the union concludes that the "market wage" *OW* is too low. What can be done about it? There are at least three ways in which the union might try to raise the wage level above *OW*.

First, the union might try to raise the demand for its labor. One way of doing this would be to raise demand for the product. The Ladies' Garment Workers' Union has helped New York dress manufacturers to finance advertising campaigns designed to establish New York as a world fashion center and to raise the demand for clothes made there. The Hatters' Union has conducted energetic, though largely unsuccessful, propaganda against bareheadedness in men. A union will normally join with employers in its industry to lobby for tariff protection which, by reducing the flow of competing imports, raises the demand for domestically produced goods. If the labor demand curve can be raised, it may be possible to raise both wages *and* employment.

Second, the union might try to restrict labor supply. If it can hold the number admitted to the occupation below *OE*, then a wage above *OW* will automatically result. Union apprenticeship rules are often pointed to in this connection. Even in skilled trades where apprenticeship programs exist, however, most workers still manage to learn the trade without passing through these programs. There is little evidence that apprenticeship rules have any effect on numbers. Where a union has succeeded in restricting numbers, it has usually relied on a state or municipal licensing system—witness the efforts of the barbers, the building trades, the taxi drivers, and others.

Efforts to restrict numbers are usually not necessary, for there is a more direct and effective route to the same end. The union may simply insist that employers pay a certain wage, say OW_1, under threat of a strike. Then employers will be willing to hire only OE_1 workers, and the number who can find employment in the occupation is automatically limited.

This wage and employment level clearly involves a misallocation of labor resources. Looking up E_1E_1, we see that the marginal product of the last worker employed (E_1A) is much higher than the supply price of this last worker (E_1C). This gap indicates that employment in the occupation is too low. The economy would gain by raising employment to OE, where marginal product and supply price are equal. Moreover, the workers who would be employed in this industry under competitive conditions but are now excluded from employment, shown by E_1E, must find employment somewhere else. Their efforts to do so will drive down the marginal productivity of labor and the wage level in other occupations, further widening the gap between these other occupations and the privileged group shown in Figure 5.

To the extent that unions hold their wages above the competitive level, then, they are driving down wages in the occupations which the excluded workers are obliged to enter. The higher wages of the unionized groups are secured partly at the expense of workers in nonunion occupations.

From the possibility that unionism *might* have this effect, one should not leap to the conclusion that it actually does so. Holding wages above the competitive level is not always easy. Employers have an incentive to resist the union pressure; and if the companies involved are large and farsighted, their resistance may be quite effective. Where employers are small and mobile, on the other hand, the union may have trouble keeping the industry organized. From the supply curve in Figure 5, we see that the numbers of workers who would prefer to work in this industry at the wage OW_1 is W_1B. But employers are willing to hire only W_1A. There is a "labor surplus" of AB. These workers may vanish quietly into other occupations. But they may also hang around this industry in the hope of getting employment. They may try to get jobs by offering to work for less than the union wage; and new nonunion shops may spring up to employ them. In textiles, clothing, and other small-scale manufacturing industries, actual and potential non-union competition has set narrow limits to what the union could do.

WAGE DIFFERENCES AMONG OCCUPATIONS

Having examined wage determination for a specific kind of labor, let us now shift our focus to the fact of wage *differences* among the hundreds of occupations in the economy. How are the earnings of these groups related to each other? How are the markets for different types of labor linked in a general market system?

The linkage comes through the fact that people have a choice among a variety of occupations. In a purely competitive economy, anybody could enter any occupation which seemed attractive to him. It is worth exploring this idea a bit to see what pattern of relative wages will result. Labor will flow into a particular occupation so long as people see a net advantage in choosing that occupation rather than something else. The higher the wage for occupation A, the more people will prefer it to other types of work. This upward-sloping supply curve, together with the demand curve for occupation A, will determine a market wage. The same is true for occupations B, C, D, and so on. If the whole system is to be in equilibrium, the last man engaged in occupation A, the *marginal* man,[4] must consider it just worth his while to remain there rather than shift to something else. So, too, for the marginal men in each of the other occupations. This has been termed *the principle of equal net advantage* —equal, that is, from the viewpoint of the people at the margin of decision. When the economy reaches a position in which no one feels that he can gain by switching occupations, then all labor markets are in balance and the relative wages for various occupations are in equilibrium.

Does this mean that wage rates for various occupations must be equal? Obviously not. *Equal advantage* does not mean *equal hourly wages*. Occupations differ in natural attractiveness, the ease or difficulty of learning them, and many other respects. If a particular occupation has poor working conditions, high training costs, or other disadvantages, a higher wage will be necessary to offset these things and tempt enough people into the occupation. Concretely, a higher wage might be necessary to compensate for:

1. Unpleasant or hazardous working conditions. One reason why coal mining carries a high wage rate is that the chances of accidental death are higher than in most other jobs.

2. A high degree of physical or mental effort. Heavy manual labor ordinarily pays more than light jobs such as floor sweeper, elevator operator, or night watchman.

---

[4] Note that here we are using *marginal man* in a somewhat different sense from a few pages back, where we were considering the economy as a whole and assuming all labor to be homogeneous.

3. Irregularity of employment. One reason for high hourly wage rates in the building trades is that construction drops off during the winter months and most workers get considerably less than a full year's work. High hourly earnings are necessary to yield reasonable annual earnings.

4. Risk of failure. A man can be less certain of succeeding as a lawyer, storekeeper, or corporation executive than he can as a bricklayer or gardener. If people are deterred by risk, a higher level of earnings in business and the professions will be necessary on this account. On the other hand, if you do succeed in these fields, there is a chance of great success. Adam Smith argued that the existence of a few big prizes, plus the "over-weening confidence" which most men have in their own ability and good fortune, would lead *more* people to enter these risky fields than would be true if returns were perfectly certain. Many people participate eagerly in lotteries, in which ticket holders as a group are sure to lose, but a few will win large amounts.

5. Time and expense of training. To set up in medical practice may take 10 years of higher education at a cost of $25,000 or more. There is a further cost in that during these years the student could have been earning a salary in some other occupation. The doctor's earnings over his working life must be enough to repay these initial costs with interest. The same is true of other occupations requiring higher education such as law, engineering, and teaching.

In a purely competitive economy, wage differences among ccupations would be *equalizing* differences. They would equalize the net advantage of various occupations to people on the margin of decision. Most people would be within the margin and would regard their occupations as clearly preferable to anything else. Those least attached to their present occupation, the marginal men, would be indifferent as between their present job and the next best thing. No one could make a net gain by changing jobs. This would be a "correct" system of wage differences in the sense of corresponding to peoples' occupational preferences.

What would a system of purely competitive wage differences look like? Looking at actual wage relations does not give a reliable answer, because of the numerous restrictions on competition in actual labor markets. Competitive wage differences would probably be somewhat smaller than the differences presently existing in the United States. Business and professional earnings would be less far above manual workers' earning than they actually are, and the earnings of skilled labor would not be so far above those of common labor. But this is only a surmise, which would be hard to test statistically.

Labor markets, in practice, are far from fully competitive. Various restrictions impede the free flow of labor and affect relative wage rates. One such interference has already been described. A particular group may organize itself and insist on a rate of payment above the competitive level. Trade unions and professional associations have this as one of their major purposes. If they succeed, the result is that fewer people can be employed in the occupation than would be able to work there at the competitive wage.

Another restriction on free choice of occupation is the cost of higher education, which is essential for the professions and important for a business career. Millions of families in the United States cannot afford to finance a long period of college training, and some who could afford it do not encourage their children to go to college because of limited knowledge and foresight. Government and private scholarship systems help somewhat but are far from adequate to the need. For some occupations, there is a physical bottleneck in training capacity. There is considerable agreement, for example, that too few places are available in medical schools and that too few doctors are being graduated. It is expensive to build medical schools, however, and the federal government, which could provide the necessary resources, has not moved vigorously in this direction. These barriers reduce the flow of people into the higher occupations below what it would be if there were complete freedom of choice. The result is to raise earnings in these occupations above the competitive level.

OCCUPATIONAL WAGE DIFFERENCES IN THE UNITED STATES

We have approached the problem of wage differences by starting with the concept of purely competitive labor markets and then bringing in restrictions which may cause actual wages to differ from the competitive pattern. Let us now look at actual wage differences in the United States and see whether they are understandable in these terms. We do not have wage rates for each type of work in the economy, but we do have information about yearly earnings, and this can serve as a rough substitute. Table 1 shows the median annual earnings of men employed full-time in various types of work in 1965.

Several things stand out from this table. Earnings of *self-employed business proprietors* are lower than one might have expected. Grocers, filling station operators, and other small independent businessmen earn less in a year than the skilled manual worker. Why is this? Some people may prize independence so highly that they deliberately choose self-employment knowing that it will mean lower earnings. But the more important reason is that small businessmen *expect* to make more than they do. The man who puts his life's savings into a corner grocery visualizes himself as the founder of a new A & P. Most of these people turn out not to have much business ability and end up in bankruptcy. But

TABLE 1

Median Income of Male Full-time Workers, by
Occupation Group, United States, 1965

OCCUPATION GROUP	MEDIAN ANNUAL EARNINGS, 1965
Professional, technical, and kindred workers	
Self-employed	$14,167
Salaried	8,311
Managers, proprietors, and officials (except farm)	
Self-employed	6,195
Salaried	8,828
Clerical and kindred workers	6,225
Sales workers	6,948
Craftsmen, foremen, and kindred workers	6,613
Operatives and kindred workers	5,738
Laborers, except farm and mine	4,487
Private household workers	. . .
Service workers, except private household	4,861
Farmers and farm managers	2,598
Farm laborers and foremen	2,243
All civilian workers	6,302

Source: *Current Population Reports,* Series P–60, No. 44, May, 1965, p. 4.

Adam Smith's principle of large prizes and overoptimism keeps a fresh supply of would-be businessmen springing up every year.

Salaried executives do considerably better than independent proprietors. Yet note that the average for this group is only $2,200 a year above that for skilled craftsmen. The president of a large corporation may receive several hundred thousand dollars a year in salary and fringe benefits. Looking at these peak salaries, one is apt to forget that for every president of General Motors there are hundreds of department heads within General Motors earning modest salaries. And for every General Motors there are hundreds of small corporations with lower salary levels. The chance of a large income induces many people to go into business careers in the hope of hitting one of the big prizes, but few actually do.

What about the small group of top-management people who in effect set their own salaries? There is not a perfect market for corporation presidents, and their salaries are influenced more by personal leverage than by demand and supply. Research studies suggest that a major factor is the size of the organization: the larger the company, the higher the president's salary. This may be partly because increasing size of company means more layers of administrative organization. Companies often reason that salaries at each level should be a certain percentage above those at the next lower level. Thus if one goes up through six layers of superstructure instead of three, one comes out whith higher salaries at the top.

The highest-paid group in the economy are the *independent professional practitioners,* such as doctors, lawyers, dentists, and engineers. Medicine yields highest average earnings of any occupation; and the independent professional group as a whole earns 60 percent more than the average salaried man in business. Part of these higher earnings can be traced to the cost of extra years of education, but only part can be explained in this way. The remainder is a monopoly gain arising from the fact that many people who would like to train for the professions cannot afford to do so. If scholarship or loan funds were adequate to support all qualified candidates through the training period, the increased supply of professional people would gradually lower the price of their services, and this monopoly gain would disappear.

The man with a *white collar* has traditionally enjoyed more prestige than his blue-collared neighbor, and for most of our history he has enjoyed higher earnings as well. As recently as 1940, the annual earnings of clerical workers were above those of manual workers. More recently, however, the manual workers have pulled ahead. The average skilled craftsman is now well ahead of the average clerical worker, and the semiskilled factory operative is almost abreast of him. An important reason is the great increase in the percentage of young people finishing high school. High-school graduates often regard manual labor as beneath them and white-collar jobs as their natural right. The rise in educational levels has thus increased the supply of white-collar workers, which tends to lower their price, and at the same time depleted the supply of manual workers, tending to raise their price.

The reversal of the traditional relation between white-collar and blue-collar earnings is thus explained partly by shifts of labor supply curves. But two other factors are probably important. The high level of business activity since 1940 has meant that most manual workers now get closer to a full year's work than they did during the thirties. This would raise annual earnings even without any change in relative wage rates. Moreover, the growing strength of unionism among manual workers, while white-collar workers remain largely unorganized, may have something to do with the shift in relative earnings.

Semiskilled workers earn about 30 percent more than *laborers,* and *skilled workers* about 50 percent more. The advantage of the upper manual groups has decreased considerably over the course of time. Fifty years ago, hourly wage rates for craftsmen were typically double those of laborers in the same industry. Today, they usually receive one third to one half more than laborers. This shrinkage of the gap between skilled and unskilled workers can be explained on a supply-demand basis. Fifty years ago, the supply of unskilled labor was inflated by mass immigration of untrained workers from Europe, large-scale movement of American farm boys from country to city, and much dropping out of school at an early age. This ample supply depressed laborers' wages and gave the craftsman a large wage advantage. Today the supply of unskilled labor is much diminished. Mass immigration ended in 1923, the farm population is now too small to make its former contribution to the urban labor supply, and far fewer students drop out before the end of high school. So, it is not surprising that the price of unskilled labor has risen faster than the price of higher grades of labor, narrowing the gap between them.

At the bottom of the income pyramid stands the *farm population*. At no time during the past 50 years has the average farm laborer earned half as much as the unskilled factory worker, even including the value of board and room which the farm laborer often receives. Farm operators do better, but not a great deal better. How can this be? Why don't all the farm workers rush off immediately to the city?

There are probably several reasons for the depressed level of farm wages. The demand for farm labor has been falling off for a long time. Agricultural production has not been expanding as fast as other sectors of the economy. A country can eat only so much, no matter how rich it may become. In addition, the rapid mechanization of agriculture—tractors, combines, cotton pickers, milking machines, and the rest—has enabled more to be produced with less labor. On the supply side, rural birth rates are relatively high, and this holds up the supply of farm labor. Growing supply combined with shrinking demand is the basic explanation of the low level of farm incomes.

This still does not explain why the farmers do not rush off to the city. If enough of them did this, the supply of farm labor would shrink, that of factory labor would rise, and the income gap would gradually close. But there are serious obstacles to this movement. Country people do not have a clear picture of job opportunities in the city, they are attached to their home areas, and they hesitate to face the costs and risks of movement. Many people do move from country to city despite these obstacles. But the *movement is not fast enough* to drain off the chronic excess of rural population and to close the income gap.

It does seem that supply-demand reasoning, modified by a recognition of imperfections in actual labor markets, is helpful in analyzing wage differences among major occupational groups. The finer details of the wage structure will always defy precise analysis. No demand-supply diagram will tell us why one job in a factory pays precisely 4 cents an hour more than another. But such questions, while they may be important to the personnel manager, are not of much interest to the student of the national economy. The economist is interested in explaining the broad contours of the national wage structure and how these change over long periods of time. For this purpose, one can get a good deal further with supply-demand analysis than without it.

WAGE DIFFERENCES WITHIN AN OCCUPATION

We must now take a further step toward reality by exploring why workers earn different amounts even within the same occupation. Take any occupation you wish—machinists, carpenters, laborers, domestic servants—and go around the country inquiring how much people earn. You will usually find sizable differences, even within the same city, and still larger differences among geographical regions.

Regional Wage Differences

The highest wages in the United States are found on the Pacific coast, particularly in Seattle, Portland, and San Francisco. Another high-wage belt runs from New York through Pittsburgh to Detroit and Chicago. Wages then taper off as one goes west into the farm states, north into New England, or south toward the gulf coast. The lowest wages in the country are found in rural areas of the deep South.

These differences are partially offset by differences in living costs. It costs less to live in a small town in Minnesota than it does in Chicago or Detroit, and it costs still less in a small town in Mississippi. The difference in *real* wages is thus less than the difference in *money* wages. But the offset is not complete. There are still sizable differences in real wages, and these require explanation.

Broad regional differences can be explained largely on a supply-demand basis. The southeastern states have a relatively high rate of population increase. Until recently the main outlet for this labor was in agriculture, where labor productivity and wage rates are low. A factory could come into a southern town with a wage level high enough to recruit labor out of agriculture, yet considerably below the level of competing factories in other regions. Suppose farm workers in South Carolina are getting $0.50 an hour, while the wage level in northern textile mills is $1.50 an hour. A textile mill setting up in South Carolina with a wage level of $1 an hour will be able to draw as much labor as it needs out of agriculture and also to undersell its northern competitors. (There is no evidence, incidentally, that a worker in Birmingham or Atlanta produces less than a worker in Boston or Chicago, given identical equipment, training, and supervision.)

This situation should set off a chain reaction: many new plants should spring up in the South to take advantage of lower labor costs. Their lower costs will enable them to undersell and take business away from northern plants. Northern production will decline, or at least fail to expand as fast as southern production. The demand for labor in the South will rise rapidly, while labor demand in the North will stagnate. This means that wage rates in the South will rise relative to those in the

North, and the gap between the two regions will gradually shrink. The original situation, in short, was not an equilibrium situation. Through the normal working of economic forces, through movement of industry from North to South and movement of labor from South to North in search of higher wages, the system should gradually approach an equilibrium. Wages would not necessarily become equal in the two regions, but they would come a good deal closer together.

Something like this has actually been going on over the past 50 years. The rate of industrial expansion in the South has been considerably faster than anywhere else except the west coast, and a number of manufacturing industries are now largely southern industries. As this has happened, wage levels in the South have risen and there has been a gradual shrinkage of the North-South differential in many industries, though not in all.

Differences by Size of City

There is usually a considerable difference in wage levels between large cities and small towns in the same region—between Chicago and West Bend, Wisconsin, or between Atlanta and Newton, Georgia. Even after adjusting for the lower living costs in small towns, there remains a difference in real wage levels.

One reason for the lower wage level of small towns is that they can attract labor readily from the farm population. High rural birth rates produce a surplus of labor which has to seek urban employment. A small-town personnel manager can usually pull in all the labor he needs by spreading the word through the surrounding countryside. The large city has to attract labor mainly from smaller towns and cities, and it must offer enough of a wage premium to induce people to move.

There is a natural corrective to unduly large city-town differences, just as there is to interregional wage differences. The lower wage level of the small town offers employers a standing inducement to move there from the city. This is particularly true of "footloose" types of manufacturing with little fixed equipment and a high labor cost ratio, such as garments, shoe manufacture, textiles, furniture, canning, and meat packing. There has been considerable movement of these industries into smaller communities in recent decades.

Wage Differences in the Same City

One of the most puzzling things about labor markets is the fact that companies in the same city often pay considerably different rates for what seems to be the same kind of labor. Studies of many occupations in many cities by the U.S. Bureau of Labor Statistics show that the highest plant in the city often pays 50 percent above the lowest plant for the same job. This conflicts sharply with the principle that there can be only one price in a competitive market. What is the answer?

The apparent differences may be partly spurious. The different wage rates may not apply to the same *quality of labor* applied to the same *job duties*. Even "common labor" is not identical from one plant to another. The work may be heavy and exhausting in one plant, lighter and easier in another. Working conditions, fringe benefits, and other job characteristics may differ. The workers involved may also differ in personal efficiency. A high-wage company may set strict hiring specifications designed to fill the plant with people of superior efficiency; and because its jobs are attractive and people want to hang on to them, it may be able to demand a better level of performance. The fact that the wage level of company A is 25 percent above that of company B does not mean that company A's *labor cost per unit produced,* which is what really matters to management, will be 25 percent higher. Labor cost may not be higher at all, if the high-wage policy is accompanied by careful hiring and effective supervision.

Suppose that after correcting for these things one still finds "genuine" differences in wages for precisely the same quality of labor and type of work. How are these differences to be explained? One possible explanation is union pressure. A union sometimes pushes a particular company out of line with the rates paid by other employers. There are other cases, however, in which a company apparently just chooses to pay wages above the general level in the area.

These cases are rather puzzling. Why should any company choose to pay more than the prevailing market rate for labor? Does this not run counter to the natural urge to maximize profits? The companies following a high-wage policy are usually large, well managed, and often sheltered from price competition by a monopoly or oligopoly position. They usually enjoy profits which are large and secure enough so that management can allow itself the luxury of paying superior wages. As executives walk through the plant, it is nicer to be greeted with genuine friendliness than veiled hostility, and paying "the best wages in town" certainly contributes to this. A high wage level makes it easier to recruit high-quality workers and to demand good job performance, and may help the company to stave off the union or live with the union. It is understandable, therefore, that some managements should choose a high-wage policy in preference to squeezing out the last drop of profit.

At the other end of the scale, one finds plants which are paying below-average wages and even so are making little or no profit. This may happen in an atomistic industry where demand is falling; or it may be because the plant has antiquated methods or machinery, poor location, or some other handicap; or it may be due to poor management. Low wages are more apt to reflect managerial incapacity than managerial greed.

Differences in Personal Efficiency

There are wide differences in personal capacity among people in professional, administrative, scientific, and artistic work, which go far toward explaining differences in earnings in these occupations. Even in the simplest manual operations, some people have greater physical stamina, faster reflexes, better concentration, and other advantages which enable them to turn out a good deal more in an hour's time.

This reflects itself partly in the job area to which people gain admission. Proficient and eager workers stand the best chance of getting into the high-wage plants which have first pick of the area labor force. They also have best chance of promotion to higher occupational levels. Both things mean higher earnings for able people.

Even within the same plant and work group, one may find substantial differences in personal capacity. This is sometimes recognized by establishing a "rate range" rather than a single rate for each job. Machinists may be placed in a rate range of $2.50 to $2.90 per hour, and may be given "merit increases" within this range based on the foreman's judgment of their work.

Differences in ability may also be recognized through *piece-rate* or *incentive* payment, under which how much the worker receives depends on how much he produces. This is widely used in manufacturing processes where each worker's output can be identified, and where quantity of output rather than quality is the main consideration. The hope is that payment by results will stimulate each worker to produce up to the limit of his ability. This objective is never entirely accomplished. There is typically pressure on the faster members of a work group to hold back so as not to show up their slower colleagues. Workers also have a well-grounded suspicion that if they produce so much that their earnings become "unreasonably high" in the eyes of management, the piece-rate is likely to be cut. Incentive payment doubtless produces a higher level of effort than one would get under time payment. It also produces a quiet but determined battle of wits between workers on the one hand and foremen and time-study men on the other.

SUMMARY

1. A *factor of production* is a human or material agent the *services* of which are useful in production. While the number of factors is large, they can be grouped conveniently into the categories of *labor* and *capital*. Management or *enterprise* is sometimes treated as a separate factor.

2. The *marginal product* (*MP*) of a factor is the additional output obtained by using an additional unit of the factor. *Marginal revenue product* (*MRP*) is the amount which sale of this output adds to the producer's revenue.

3. The demand for a factor rests on its productivity. A producer will employ any factor up to the point at which marginal revenue product equals marginal factor cost. If the factor is sold in a purely competitive market, where a producer can buy any amount at an

unchanged price, this price is the marginal cost of the factor. The producer, then, will use that amount of the factor for which

$$MRP_x = MFC_x = P_x \,.$$

4. If the quantity of one factor is increased, the quantities of all other factors remaining unchanged, the marginal product of that factor will decrease after a certain point. This is called the *law of variable proportions*. Applied to the economy as a whole, it enables us to construct a schedule of the marginal physical product of labor, which will slope downward from left to right.

5. The *MP* schedule for labor is also a demand curve for labor. Given this schedule, and given the available labor supply in man-hours, we can determine the real wage rate at which all available labor will be employed.

6. The height of labor's *MP* schedule depends on existing supplies of natural resources and capital equipment, the state of technology, the quality of the labor force, and the effectiveness of economic organization. The real wage level varies *directly* with changes in any of these things; and it varies *inversely* with the quantity of labor. In the United States and other industrial countries, upward shifts of the *MP* schedule have more than offset the increasing quantity of labor, and real wages have risen consistently.

7. Unionism could raise the general level of real wages by raising labor's *MP* schedule, by reducing the supply of labor, or by raising wages where employers have been strong enough to depress them below the competitive level. It seems likely that the most important effect has been via reduced labor supply.

8. The demand for labor in a particular industry depends on labor's marginal revenue product in that industry. The *MRP* schedule always slopes downward from left to right. The supply curve of labor to an industry slopes upward from left to right, because at higher wages more people will prefer to work in this industry rather than elsewhere.

9. The demand and supply curves for a particular kind of labor establish an equilibrium wage rate for that labor. It is possible, however, to set a wage rate above the market equilibrium by law or union contract. This reduces the number employed in the industry and increases the number who prefer to work there, creating a "labor surplus" which may in time undermine the fixed wage.

10. Some variation of wages is necessary to equalize the net advantage of different occupations. These may be termed *natural, equalizing,* or *competitive* wage differences. But part of the variation which one observes in actuality arises from barriers to free movement of labor among occupations. This is particularly important for the professional and managerial occupations, where costs of higher education are a significant barrier.

11. Interesting characteristics of the earnings structure in the United States include: relatively high earnings of independent professional people; relatively low earnings of small independent businessmen; earnings for routine sales and clerical work which are little above the level of manual labor; and a depressed earnings level for both farm laborers and farm operators.

12. Wages for the same kind of labor vary considerably according to region of the country, size of city, size of company, type of industry, and efficiency of the individual worker. These differences are largely, though not completely, explainable in terms of supply-demand reasoning.

DISCUSSION QUESTIONS

1. Throughout this chapter we have generally assumed that factor services are sold in purely competitive markets. What would be the necessary conditions for a purely competitive labor market? To what extent do you think that actual labor markets in the United States meet these conditions?

2. It is often said that, in the absence of a union, the bargaining power of the individual worker is usually less than that of the employer. Can you give a precise definition of "bargaining power"? Why might the employer's bargaining power (however you have defined it) be superior? What would you expect to be the economic consequences?

3. What determines how rapidly a country's real wage level will rise over the course of time? From what you know of the following countries, how would you expect their rate of wage increase to compare over, say, the years 1945–65: Canada, U.S.A., Japan, U.S.S.R., Brazil, India?

4. Do you think that trade unionism has had a significant effect on the *general* level of real wages in the United States? Why, or why not? What kinds of evidence might you collect to test your opinion?

5. Why is it reasonable to draw the labor supply curve to a particular industry as sloping upward to the right? When we do this, are we assuming that everyone is employed? What if there is unemployment?

6. Why do labor demand curves slope downward to the right? What determines the elasticity of the demand curve?

7. There are indications that some unions have been able to raise the wages of their members significantly (compared with what those wages would have been in the absence of unionism), while other unions have not. What makes the difference? What conditions are most favorable to union success?

8. Where does the higher income received by members of a "successful" union come from? Does somebody else lose what the union members gain? Who might this be?

9. Why would different occupations pay different wage rates even if all labor markets were purely competitive? How do you think this (hypothetical) pattern of wage differences would compare with the pattern which actually exists in the United States?

10. Is it desirable to equalize the money wage for a particular kind of labor

in all regions of the United States? Does it make any difference to the answer whether we are talking about steel-workers or filling station attendants?

11. Aren't piece rates the fairest basis for wage payment, since each worker earns what he produces? How would you go about setting a correct piece rate for a particular job, and what problems might you encounter?

APPENDIX: THE LAW OF VARIABLE PROPORTIONS

This principle, which we passed over briefly above, deserves further explanation. The problem is, what will happen to output as one factor of production is varied, the quantities of all other factors being held constant. We call these others the *fixed* factors, and the one in which we are interested the *variable* factor. We then change the amount of the variable factor only, and observe what difference this makes to output. The added product resulting from the use of one more unit of the variable factor is its *marginal product*.

Take a simple illustration from agriculture. The fixed factors are a 1,500-acre farm and a certain quantity of tools and equipment. Labor is the variable factor. We suppose that, while the quantity of tools and equipment remains constant, its *form* can be varied so as to cooperate most effectively with whatever quantity of labor happens to be available. This assumption means that we are thinking in long-run rather than short-run terms.[5]

Now let us add men to this land and equipment and see what happens to the output of wheat. The first man might not produce much, because he has too much ground to cover. The marginal product of a second man might well be higher, because the work can be subdivided and each acre worked more intensively. The third and fourth men may also add increasing amounts to the product. As more and more men are added, however, the marginal productivity of labor must eventually begin to decline, since each man is cultivating less acreage with less equipment. Finally, an additional man would add nothing to output. One might even reach the situation, alleged to exist in some Asian countries, where the rural population is so dense that people get in each other's way and marginal productivity is negative.

The principle can now be stated more precisely: *if the quantity of one productive service is increased, the quantities of all other productive services remaining fixed, the resulting additions to output will decrease after a certain point.* The classical economists called this the *law of*

---

[5] Without this assumption one runs into some nice problems: 10 men are working on a farm with 10 spades. Now an eleventh man appears. He has no spade. How can he produce anything at all? One answer is that, given time, the farmer can reshape his capital into 11 spades with shorter handles. It has been suggested also that the eleventh man could be set to work carrying beer for the rest!

diminishing returns and derived it as we have done by applying more and more labor to land. But the principle applies equally to any factor. We could hold labor and capital constant and vary the amount of land, with the same result. The principle is now usually called *the law of variable proportions.* It could also be called the principle of *diminishing marginal productivity.* It rests not only on logical deduction but on evidence from a wide variety of production processes.

The results of our farm experiment are shown arithmetically in Table 2, and are charted in Figure 6. The marginal productivity curve *MP* rises to a peak, then declines toward zero, and finally becomes negative. The average productivity curve, *AP,* which shows *average* output per worker at each level of employment, has a gentler upward and downward slope. Note that *MP* intersects *AP* at the point where *AP* is a maximum. This is the same principle we observed earlier in drawing marginal and average cost curves. So long as *MP* is above *AP,* i.e., so long as each new worker adds more than the average output of the workers previously employed, this keeps pulling the average *up.* But when *MP* falls *below AP,* it begins pulling the average *down,* and so AP begins to fall.

We cannot tell directly from Figure 6 how many men it will pay to use on this farm. To determine this, we must know the price of wheat and the cost of labor. Suppose farm labor costs $2 an hour, or $4,000 per year, and any number of workers can be hired at that wage. Suppose the price of wheat is $2 a bushel and, the market being perfectly competitive, any amount can be sold at this price. Then we can set up our problem as shown in Figure 7. The average and marginal productivity curves are drawn as before, but now the vertical axis is laid out in *dollars* instead of *bushels.* (Since 1 bushel = $2 throughout, the shapes of the curves are not affected). The marginal curve *MRP* now shows how much an additional worker adds to the value of output, i.e., his *marginal revenue product.* Similarly *ARP* is a curve of *average revenue product* per worker.

The yearly cost of each worker is $4,000 a year or *OW.* So we draw a horizontal *wage line* at this height and observe where it intersects *MRP.* The employment level *OE,* corresponding to this intersection, is the most profitable one for the enterprise. The reasoning behind this should by now be familiar. Up to *OE,* each worker is adding more dollars in output than he costs in wages, so it will pay to employ him. The next man beyond *OE,* however, would add less than the amount of his wage. His *MRP* is below the wage line, so it would not pay to hire him. Labor should be hired up to the point at which its wage equals its marginal revenue product.

This holds equally for the purchase of any other productive service. A producer, as we saw in Chapter 7, usually has a problem of combining two or more factors so as to achieve lowest production costs. Suppose he is using two factors, *L* and *C.* Then he will employ factor *L* up to the point at which

TABLE 2

Wheat Output per Year
(Hundreds of Bushels)

NUMBER OF WORKERS	TOTAL PRODUCT	MARGINAL PRODUCT	AVERAGE PRODUCT
0	0		0
		10	
1	10		10
		20	
2	30		15
		30	
3	60		20
		40	
4	100		25
		37	
5	137		27.5
		34	
6	171		28.5
		31	
7	202		28.9
		28	
8	230		28.7
		24	
9	254		28.2
		21	
10	275		27.5
		18	
11	293		26.7
		15	
12	308		25.7
		12	
13	320		24.6
		9	
14	329		23.5
		6	
15	335		22.3
		3	
16	338		21.1
		0	
17	338		19.9
		−3	
18	335		18.6
		−6	
19	329		17.3
		−9	
20	320		16.0

The Law of Variable Proportions

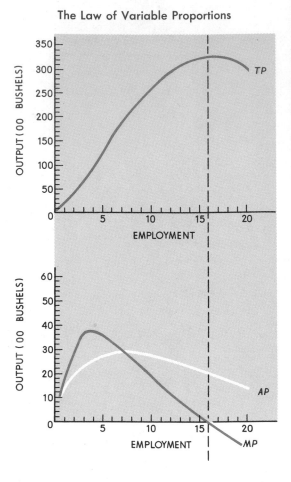

FIGURE 6. This shows the result of applying increasing amounts of labor to a fixed amount of farm land and equipment. *TP, AP,* and *MP* show respectively *total product, average product per worker,* and *marginal product.* Note that *MP* intersects *AP* at the maximum of *AP;* and that *MP* eventually becomes negative.

Determining the Level of Employment

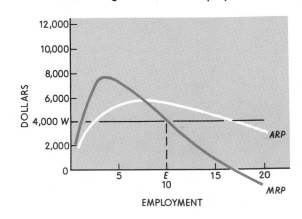

FIGURE 7. *ARP* and *MRP* have the same shape as in the previous diagram, but now show the *revenue* product of labor. If the wage is *OW,* it will pay to employ labor up to *OE,* where *OW* = *MRP.*

$$MRP_L = P_L$$

And he will use C to the point at which

$$MRP_C = P_C$$

It follows that

$$\frac{MRP_L}{MRP_c} = \frac{P_L}{P_c}$$

A producer will achieve lowest unit cost by combining the factors in such proportion that the ratio of their marginal productivities equals the ratio of their prices.[6]

Buying Power in Factor Markets

We saw in Chapter 9 that a company may have monopoly power in the product markets in which it sells. By the same token, it may have buying power in one or more of the markets in which it buys productive services. This is called *monopsony* power. It means that the company, by altering the amount of a service it buys, can influence the price of the service.

Take a company in a small community in a remote area, where it is the only employer of labor—a paper mill in northern Maine, or a textile mill in a small North Carolina town. The whole supply curve of labor in the area is *its* supply curve. Suppose this curve is S in Figure 8. The company can always get more labor, but only by paying a higher wage. Or, to put it in reverse, it can depress the wage rate by hiring less labor. It is a *monopsonist* in the labor market.

Note another significant thing: *the cost of hiring additional labor is greater than the wage rate.* If the company hires an extra man it must raise the wage rate, not just for him, but for everybody it employs. Let us call the cost of this extra man the *marginal factor cost of labor,* shown in Figure 8 by *MFC.* Since an extra man costs more than his wage (because the higher wage must be generalized to all employees), *MFC* must lie above S. The reasoning is exactly the same as when we demonstrated that the marginal revenue curve slopes downward more steeply than the demand curve.

---

[6] This result is identical with the geometrical solution reached in Figure 2 of Chapter 7. The slope of an isoquant at any point shows how much of one factor must be added to make up for the loss of a small amount of the other factor and leave production unchanged. It shows, that is to say, the *relative* marginal productivities of the two factors or, in this case $\frac{MRP_L}{MRP_c}$. The slope of the producer's budget line, on the other hand, depends on the relative prices of the two factors, that is, on $\frac{P_L}{P_c}$. At the point where the budget line is tangent to the highest possible isoquant, the slopes of the two must be equal, i.e., $\frac{MRP_L}{MRP_c} = \frac{P_L}{P_c}$.

The Rules Change When an Employer Can Set His Own Wage

FIGURE 8. *S* is the labor supply curve to a company which has *monopsony* power in the labor market. *MFC,* the marginal cost of an additional worker, rises more steeply than *S*. (Why? For the same reason that *MR* falls more rapidly than *DD*.) The company will hire *OE* workers, the number for which *MFC = MRP*, and it can get these workers for a wage *OW*. But if the wage is forcibly raised to *OW₁*, it will pay the company to expand employment to *OE₁*.

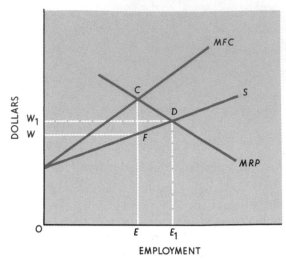

How many men should the company hire? To decide this we must know the marginal revenue product of labor, *MRP*. Knowing this, we can say that the most profitable employment for the company is OE, where *MRP* intersects *MFC*. If the company went beyond this, the next man would cost more than he would add to company revenues; so he will not be hired.

From the labor supply curve *S*, we see that *OE* workers can be hired at a wage rate *OW*. So since the company is able to set the wage, it should set it at this level. Unlike the situation in the perfectly competitive factor markets discussed in Chapter 10, there is now a *gap between the wage rate and labor's marginal product,* shown by the distance *CF*. (Note the parallel with the gap between price and marginal cost which results from monopoly in product markets.) Joan Robinson of Cambridge University has labeled this gap *exploitation* of labor. Exploitation in this technical sense does not necessarily mean a low wage; it means simply that the wage is below the marginal revenue product.

Suppose now that a minimum wage board or a union succeeds in establishing a higher wage, *OW₁*. The company must pay this wage regardless of how few or how many workers it hires. This amounts to making the supply curve of labor to the firm horizontal along the line *W₁D*—in a sense, restoring the equivalent of a perfect labor market. The company now has no incentive to restrict employment as a way of depressing wages. Its best course will be to hire up to the point *D*, at which *MRP* equals the prescribed wage. So employment will rise to *OE₁*.

Thus one reaches the paradoxical result that *raising* wages from *OW* to *OW₁* has *increased* employment, contrary to the normal result.

Note, however, that this is true only *up to* OW_1. If the prescribed wage is pushed above this level, we move up the *MRP* curve to the left and employment drops again.

While this is an interesting theoretical curiosity, its practical importance is probably not very great. The supply curve of labor to the firm is usually very elastic, so that any gap between S and *MFC* is small. Why is S elastic? Partly because the labor force is usually underemployed, and more people can be recruited at about the same wage by dipping into the unemployed pool.

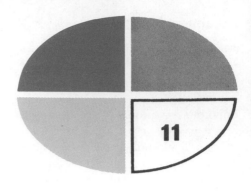

Capital, Interest, and Profit

Get money, by fair means if you can; if not, get money.

HORACE, *Epistles*

There are few ways in which a man can be more innocently employed than in getting money.

SAMUEL JOHNSON

MORE THAN three quarters of the income received by factor owners in the United States is labor income. The remainder goes to those who own material instruments and supply their services in production. Most of this return is interest, and our main task in this chapter is to explain what determines the size of these interest payments.

Discussions of capital and interest involve three related ideas: (1) *real capital*—land, buildings, machinery, inventories, and other physical agents of production (this is the basic meaning of the term); (2) *money capital* or investable funds—streams of money which are available for buying physical capital; (3) the *saving* or *waiting* which is necessary for capital creation. If the economy's resources are fully employed, more capital goods can be produced only if fewer consumer goods are produced.

These differing concepts make capital theory probably the most confused and least satisfactory branch of economics. Is interest basically a physical return, arising from the fact that capital goods yield a marginal product? Or is it a monetary phenomenon, determined by demand and

supply for loanable funds in the money market? Both viewpoints have
something important to contribute. In this chapter, however, we shall
adhere generally to the physical interpretation and leave monetary
analysis to Part Three. In particular, we shall take no account here of the
existence of the commercial banking system, with its mysterious power to
"create money."

Again, is interest paid because of the *productivity* of capital goods,
or because of the *impatience* of consumers, who will postpone present
consumption only in the expectation of higher consumption in the future?
After our exposure to demand-supply analysis, it should be clear that
these are not *alternative* explanations but two sides of a single explanation. Productivity is dominant on the demand side of the capital market,
while household savings preferences are an important factor on the
supply side.

We must be careful also in our treatment of capital to distinguish
between the *stock* of capital goods in existence at a particular time and
the *flow* of new capital goods coming into existence per unit of time. It is
one thing to ask: What was the marginal productivity of the amount of
capital in existence on July 1, 1966? This is the kind of question we shall
be examining in this chapter. It is obviously similar to the questions we
raised in Chapter 10 about the marginal productivity of a certain
quantity of labor. It is another thing to ask: Supposing that $100 billion
of new capital goods are constructed during the year July 1, 1966–July 1,
1967, what will be the marginal productivity of this new capital? This
question, relating to what is usually called the *marginal efficiency of
investment,* will be examined in Chapter 20, where we analyze how
business concerns set their level of current investment.

We saw in Chapter 10 that, in a progressive industrial economy, the
real wage rate rises consistently and quite rapidly over time. The interest
rate, however, can go down as well as up and sometimes has gone down
for quite long periods. Figure 1 shows the yield of long-term U.S.
government bonds, which is a good indicator of interest rates in general,
from 1919 to the present.[1] Note that the figure reached about 5½ percent
in 1920, at the peak of the boom following World War I. It then sagged
to a low of little more than 2 percent at the end of the depressed thirties.
During World War II, when the federal government was the major borrower, the interest rate was fixed by government policy along with most
other prices and wages. About 1950, yields began to rise once more, and
have been around 4 percent in recent years.

An index of yields on top-quality corporate bonds (Moody's Aaa
rating) is included for comparison. Note that this fluctuates closely with
government bond yields, but is normally ½ percent to 1 percent higher.
The reason is that even the best corporate bonds are not quite as secure

---

[1] Data are from U.S. Department of Commerce, *Survey of Current Business.*

Yield on Long-Term U.S. Bonds and High-Quality
Corporate Bonds, 1919–65

FIGURE 1.

Yields on Selected Types of Security, United States, 1857–1965

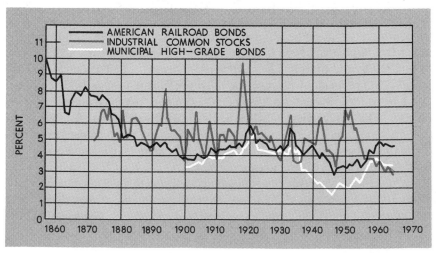

FIGURE 2.

as a government bond. This illustrates a general principle: the riskier a security, the more it must yield to induce investors to buy and hold it. The difference between the government bond yield and the corporate Aaa bond yield is a *risk premium*.

A still longer perspective is provided by Figure 2, which runs back to the nineteenth century. The figures show ups and downs in interest rates, with a declining tendency over the long run.

Why do Figures 1 and 2 have the shape that they do? Why do bond yields in the United States show a sagging tendency over the past century? Why were yields particularly depressed during the thirties, and why did they revive markedly during the fifties?

Looking at the matter on a world scale, why do interest rates differ substantially in different countries? In 1964, for example, the yield of long-term government bonds was as follows:[2]

Pakistan	3.90%	Canada	5.19%
Switzerland	3.97	U.K.	6.03
U.S.A.	4.15	Italy	6.26
Australia	4.72	Egypt	6.40
India	4.74	Peru	7.23

The purpose of this chapter, then, is to provide tools for explaining the difference between interest rates in the United States in 1965 and Japan in 1965 or between the United States in 1965 and 1900. We are interested in broad tendencies over substantial periods of time. Short-period changes between one year and the next, which are considerably influenced by monetary institutions and monetary policy, will be analyzed at the proper point in Part Three.

THE RATE OF INTEREST

The Productivity of Capital

Our discussion subdivides as usual into demand and supply considerations. Business concerns demand capital goods because they make a positive contribution to production. But the physical basis of productivity is not as obvious in the case of capital as in the case of labor. So we must first ask *why* capital goods have a marginal product and how the size of this product can be estimated.

As early as Chapter 3, we noted that building capital goods means using more *roundabout* or *time-consuming* methods of production.

---

[2] Data from *International Financial Statistics*, July, 1965. The reader should be warned that these are *money* rates of return rather than *real* rates, i.e., they are not adjusted for price level changes. One reason for high money interest rates in some of the less developed countries is that the price level is expected to continue rising rapidly in the future.

Crusoe had to cut his consumption while building his fish nets; but he got a larger supply of consumption goods in the end. Roundabout methods of production are more productive, sufficiently so to warrant the waiting involved.

The importance of sheer time can be dramatized by some familiar illustrations. A vineyard owner sets aside a cask of wine worth $100, lets it age for 10 years, then sells it for $200. By waiting for 10 years he has realized a gain of 100 percent. Whipping out our compound interest tables, we see that this amounts to a return of 7.2 percent per year. Or suppose a man buys an acre of land, clears it, and plants young trees. This costs him $1,000. He then waits 20 years for the trees to reach a size at which they can be sold to a paper mill as pulpwood. He cuts the trees, hauls them to the mill, sells them, and has $2,500 left over. His return is 150 percent over 20 years, or 4.5 percent per year. This measures the productivity of the resources originally devoted to tree growing.

An apartment house, a factory building, or a machine also represent time-using methods of production. A machine can be regarded as a certain amount of stored-up labor, the labor used in its construction. This labor is gradually released and converted into product over the lifetime of the machine. Once more, *waiting* is involved. And once more, the reward of waiting is an enlarged product.[3]

Calculating the productivity of a machine, however, is more complicated than in our earlier wine and tree cases. Consider a wheat farmer who has been harvesting his 300 acres in the old-fashioned way, using a binder to tie the sheaves, hiring labor to set up the sheaves in the field, and then carrying them in hayracks to the threshing machine. This costs him 60 man-days of labor at $10 per day, or $600, plus $300 for upkeep of the binder and other expenses, or a total of $900. He now has an opportunity to buy for $4,000 a combine which does the whole operation at once and eliminates the need for the hired labor. It will last for 10 years, so he should set aside $400 each year to replace it when it is worn out. This is usually called a *depreciation allowance*. Repairs, gasoline, and other operating expenses are estimated at $100. His total harvesting cost, then, is $500, and he can save $400 per year compared with the old method.

The combine each year saves $400/4,000 = 10$ percent of its cost. It

---

[3] To be fully correct, we should say that the machine represents a certain amount of stored-up *labor and capital;* for, of course, other machines were used along with labor in making this machine. But, a Marxist would object, these other machines were also basically stored-up labor; and so were the still earlier machines used to make them. So, if we trace back to the time of Adam, there *is* nothing but stored-up labor power. There is no separate productivity of capital, and capital is not entitled to any interest payment.

This seems patently incorrect. If no one since the time of Adam had done any waiting, no capital goods would have been built. And since waiting is distasteful, capital goods are always scarce relative to the possibilities of using them. The rate of interest is a measure of this scarcity and a device for allocating scarce capital among alternative uses.

may thus be said to have a *productivity* of 10 percent. If the farmer can borrow money to buy the machine for anything less than 10 percent, he will profit by doing so. Suppose he can borrow $4,000 at 6 percent interest. His interest charges will then be $240 per year. But since he saves $400 a year in operating expenses, he is $160 better off than before.

Large corporations are constantly engaged in calculations which, while much more complicated than this, have the same general character. A.T.&T. has been gradually replacing long-distance telephone operators by automatic equipment for direct dialing. This involves estimating the cost of the new equipment, the consequent saving in operating expenses, and converting this to a yield on cost. If expenditure of $100 million on equipment will save $8 million annually in operating costs, the yield is 8 percent. These calculations are not revealed to the general public. We know, however, that A.T.&T. has been raising large amounts of money for new equipment by selling bonds or debentures at interest rates running up to 5 percent. The prospective yield of the new equipment, therefore, must be above 5 percent.

These examples involve changes in production methods. But the same sort of calculation is required in starting a new company, increasing its production capacity, launching a new product line, or doing anything else which means spending money on plant and equipment. The basic question always is how the prospective return from the investment, after deducting all the attendant expenses, compares with the initial cost. The percentage rate of return measures the productivity of the particular capital goods in question.

Capitalization: The Value of Assets

A machine or other capital good is bought because it is productive. After deducting the cost of the other factors used along with it and depreciation on the machine itself, there is something left over which is the net product of the machine. And this net product continues year after year until the machine is worn out. A capital good, then, yields its owner *a stream of future income.*

If we know the cost of the capital good and the size of the future income, we can convert the income into a *percentage yield* on the initial cost. This is what we did in the combine example. Then, by comparing the yield with the rate of interest, we can tell whether purchase of the machine is worthwhile.

Alternatively, if we know the size of the future income stream, and if we know the rate of interest, we can calculate *how much the machine itself is worth* to its user. This process of deriving the value of an asset from its future yield is known as *capitalization.* It applies to any physical asset—a machine, a farm, an apartment house. It can be applied also to stocks, bonds, and other securities.

Take a piece of equipment which will yield a net income of $1,000 next year, another $1,000 the year following, and so on. How do I work back from this future income stream to the present value of the machine? Concentrate first on the $1,000 I expect to receive next year. This is not worth the same to me as $1,000 today. The psychological reason for this was noted in Chapter 6: future income shrinks in peoples' minds, and the farther away it is, the smaller it appears. There is also an objective reason. If the market rate of interest is 5 percent, and if I put out about $950 at interest today, this will grow into $1,000 a year from now. Thus next year's $1,000 yield from my machine is equivalent to only about $950 today. To be precise, it is worth $1,000/1.05 = 952.38. The present value of an income item due 1 year hence is obtained by *discounting that income by the rate of interest.*

The $1,000 which the machine will yield 2 years from now must be discounted more heavily, since it is farther away. And we apply the same principle. If the interest rate is 5 percent, $1 put out at interest today will in 2 years be worth $1 \times (1.05)^2$. To get the present value of income 2 years hence, we throw this into reverse. The $1,000 two years away is worth today $1,000/(1.05)^2 = \$907.03$.

If the machine will last 20 years, and will fall apart at the end of that time, then the present value of *all* the future income it will yield is:

$$\frac{1,000}{(1.05)} + \frac{1,000}{(1.05)^2} + \frac{1,000}{(1.05)^3} + \cdots \frac{1,000}{(1.05)^{20}} .$$

This works out at $12,462.21. To the prospective buyer, *the present value of the machine equals the present value of the future income stream which it yields.* So this machine is worth $12,462.21. Why? Because if I buy the machine at that price, and if the future yields work out as expected, I will have earned the market rate of interest on my investment.

Suppose now that the market price of the machine is only $10,000. Then it is highly profitable to buy it, and there will be a strong demand from companies in the industry concerned. But as more and more of these machines are built and installed, two things will happen: the expected future product of each machine will fall because of the principle of diminishing marginal productivity, and so its present value will fall. Moreover, its price may rise if the machine-producing industry is subject to increasing cost. Where will equilibrium be reached? At the point where the *present value of the machine just equals its market price.* It will not pay investors to go beyond this point, and new purchases of the machine will cease. A little reflection shows that this is the same as saying that investment will be carried to the point of which the expected rate of return (on equipment cost) equals the rate of interest. When this is true, it must be true also that the price of the machine equals its present value.

In one special case, the capitalization formula becomes very simple. Suppose the asset is expected to last forever, and will yield an income of $R per year for all time to come. Then if the rate of interest is i, the present value V of this machine is:

$$\frac{R}{(1+i)} + \frac{R}{(1+i)^2} + \cdots + \frac{R}{(1+i)^n} + \cdots$$

By the formula for an infinite series, we see that:

$$V = \frac{R}{i}.$$

The value of an asset varies inversely with the rate of interest. If the rate of interest rises, the present value of capital goods falls. If the price of capital goods has not changed, investment will be discouraged.

Determining the Rate of Interest

We saw in Chapter 10 how to construct a marginal productivity schedule for labor. By the same procedure we can construct a marginal productivity schedule for capital. To do this, the quantity of all other productive resources, and especially the quantity of labor, must be held constant. The technology of production is also given and constant. And

Determining the Rate of Interest

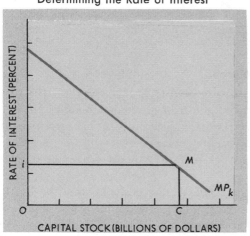

FIGURE 3. MP_K is the marginal productivity schedule of capital for the economy. If the amount of capital in existence at a particular time is OC, the rate of interest will be Oi.

we assume that whatever quantity of capital may be available can be put into the *physical forms* which will maximize its productivity. For long-period problems, this assumption of the malleability of capital is not unreasonable.

We now ask how variations in the quantity of capital will affect its marginal product. If only a little capital were available, it would be spread thinly over the entire labor force. The small amount of capital possessed by each worker would have a high yield. But the law of variable proportions tells us that, as more and more capital is applied to the same number of workers, its marginal yield will fall. The national marginal productivity schedule for capital slopes downward, like MP_k in Figure 3.

The *height* of this schedule depends on the supplies of other productive factors and on the state of technology. Its *slope* depends on the ease with which capital can be substituted for other factors. The greater the substitutability of capital, the less rapidly will its marginal productivity fall as its quantity is increased.

Turning to the supply side, there is at any moment a certain *stock* of capital in existence, the accumulated result of investment decisions over a long period in the past. The only way to sum up the diverse types of capital in the economy is by adding their dollar values, as is done in Figure 3. But essentially, we are concerned with *physical amounts* of capital. If, because of a general price increase, capital which was valued at $1,000 billion this year is valued at $1,100 billion next year, this is *not* an increase in the stock of capital for present purposes. So the dollars on the horizontal axis of Figure 3 must be understood as dollars of constant purchasing power.

If today's stock of capital is OC, the last bit of capital will have a marginal product of MC. Concretely, this might be 6 percent per year. Just as in the case of labor, the rate of return to capital will tend to equal the marginal product of the last unit employed. The market rate of interest will tend toward $Oi = MC$.

Changes in the Rate of Interest

One important application of Figure 3 is in analyzing how the rate of interest is likely to behave over time in a growing economy. On one hand, the capital stock normally increases year by year. The amount of new capital built exceeds the amount which wears out or becomes obsolete. Increase in the capital stock is in fact almost synonymous with economic growth.

If only this were happening, however, the outlook would be bleak. The marginal productivity of capital, and with it the rate of interest, would fall year after year as the economy traveled to the right down the MP_k schedule. The falling interest rate would discourage saving, and both new saving and new capital creation would eventually cease.

But fortunately, as C is moving out to the right, MP_k is shifting upward year by year. What accounts for the upward movement of MP_k? Basically, two things. The first is the growth of population and labor force. New workers need new tools, even if there is no change in production methods. They also need new houses, schools, urban facilities, highways, and so on. Population growth presents opportunities for *capital widening*—an increase in capital stock which simply parallels the increase in labor force and does not, therefore, depress the marginal productivity of capital.

The second factor is research and invention. By creating new products which displace older ones, research speeds the obsolescence of existing capital and creates opportunity for investment in new kinds of industry. The great waves of investment set off by the discovery of electric power and of the internal combustion engine are still fresh in memory. Today we see heavy investment in television, aircraft, electronic products, and chemicals. This is associated with a rising and rapidly changing pattern of consumption.

Research also contributes to *capital deepening*—a rising ratio of capital to labor in production. Use of more capital per worker with unchanged production methods would lower the marginal productivity of capital. But with technical change in the picture, it need not do so. Invention can keep the MP_k schedule moving upward at a rate which more than offsets the growing quantity of capital.

So both C and MP_k are shifting over the course of time; and the question is which will move fastest. The long-term course of interest rates depends on a race between thriftiness on one side and population and technology on the other. In the United States, over the past century, it appears that population and technology have not quite kept up in the race. During the booming sixties, interest rates have remained somewhat below the level of the booming twenties, and even farther below the levels of 1860–1880. But we are still some distance from the 1 or 2 percent which the classical economists believed would usher in the stationary state, and which Lord Keynes thought would produce the "euthanasia of the rentier." Indeed, if technical progress continues to accelerate and if we do not become too exorbitantly thrifty, we may never reach it.

We can use this analysis also to explain interest rate differences among countries; for example, why interest rates in less developed countries are typically above those in the United States and Western Europe. Almost by definition, the less developed countries are capital-poor countries. The accumulated stock of capital is small, and it is increasing very slowly because of the low rate of saving in these countries. At the same time, labor supply, and with it the need for capital, is rising rapidly because of a high rate of population growth. Using a diagram similar to Figure 3, one can easily show why this will produce an interest rate which is high and perhaps rising over the course of time.

The Function of Interest

Over the course of history, interest has often been viewed with suspicion. Medieval theologians denounced it as "usury." Marx denied the productivity of capital and with it the legitimacy of interest. In the U.S.S.R. and most other communist countries, interest on the capital used in producing a good is not counted as part of cost. So it is important to ask what function the rate of interest serves and what difficulties arise when one tries to dispense with it.

We could say that interest is necessary to call forth saving; but this would not be a strong line of argument. We are not sure that the rate of interest has a marked influence on household savings decisions. Moreover, there are institutional devices for bringing about saving which do not depend on personal decisions at all. Corporate saving is one such device. Another possibility, more important in other countries than in the United States, is for government to save part of its tax revenue and use this for capital construction.

But suppose the amount of saving is decided, no matter how. What does saving accomplish? The fact that all income is not spent on consumer goods means that not all the resources of the economy need be used in producing consumer goods. Saving *liberates resources,* which would otherwise have been producing for direct sale to consumers, and makes them available for production of capital goods. What seems to be just a supply of money is really a supply of resources, of capital goods in embryo.

If these resources could be gotten free of charge, the demand for them would be limitless. Who could not use an extra story on his office building, a plant addition, or more powerful and productive machinery? But the potential supply of capital goods is not unlimited. So one major function of interest is to *restrain the demand for capital goods within the limits of feasibility.* Without this restraint, the quantity of capital goods demanded would greatly exceed the resources available and would overstrain the economy.

In addition to limiting the total amount of capital constructed, an economy must decide the specific kinds of capital to be built: how much resources shall go into new plants in each industry, how much into improved machinery, how much into offices, stores, and apartments? Here the rate of interest serves a *rationing or allocating function.* Any project with a yield equal to or higher than the rate of interest, so that its sponsor can afford to borrow money at that rate, will be undertaken. Any project with a lower prospective yield will be abandoned. Thus the market settles the vital question of *who* shall participate in the limited capital pool. This amounts to deciding the directions in which the productive capacity of the economy shall be enlarged.

The job which interest does on this front is best visualized by supposing that interest does not exist. Suppose you are a member of the central planning board in Hungary or Poland. One of your jobs is to decide how much new capital shall be added to each industry in the economy during the coming year. Any capital which you allocate to an industry is, from the industry's standpoint, a free gift. You are not entitled to charge interest on it because, in Marxist theory, capital produces no return. So how do you decide that industry A shall receive a certain amount, and industry B another? How do you decide whether it will pay to adopt a production method using more capital and less labor? You would certainly have difficulties.

These difficulties are, in fact, so serious that central planners eventually learn to behave in an un-Marxian way and bring in interest calculations through the back door, as we shall see in the next chapter.

Interest calculations, then, play a necessary role in a capital-using economy. Why do we say "capital using" rather than "capitalistic"? Because the functional justification of interest has nothing to do with who owns the capital, who receives the interest, or even whether interest payments are made at all. Interest serves the same economic functions even if all capital is publicly owned.

RENT AND QUASI RENT

If factor markets are competitive, each factor gets paid what it is worth. This in two senses. The return to a factor equals its marginal productivity in the industry where it is used; and this return also equals the potential productivity of the factor in other industries where it might have been used. A certain price is necessary to induce the factor to transfer to this use from some other use. This *transfer cost* or *opportunity cost* is a necessary cost of production. If the product market is competitive, then over the long run the product price must equal the total opportunity costs of the factors used in producing it. In this sense we can say that *factor prices govern product price.*

But is this always true? What about a factor which has only one use, and the supply of which is fixed? It is going to be used in this industry or not at all. There is no transfer problem. How is the return to such a factor determined?

Consider this case: there is just a certain amount of land in eastern France suited to producing Burgundy wine. There is no way to increase the supply of such land, and it has no other possible uses. Suppose further that the actual winegrowers are tenants, who must rent their land from the landowners for so much per acre. Their demand curve for land, based on its marginal revenue productivity in winegrowing, is shown by DD in Figure 4. The fixed supply of land is shown by the vertical line SS. Under these conditions, land has a marginal productivity, and so will command a return, of OP per acre. The total return to the landowners is OPRS.

Note that the size of this return depends solely on the level of DD, which in turn depends on demand for the product. If the French population continues to grow and drinking habits remain unchanged, then the demand for wine will rise. DD for vineyards will also rise, and landowners will receive ever higher returns per acre. But suppose someone launches a milk-drinking campaign, as one French premier tried (unsuccessfully) to do, and demand for wine falls off. Then the return

The Return to a Fixed Factor Depends Solely on Demand

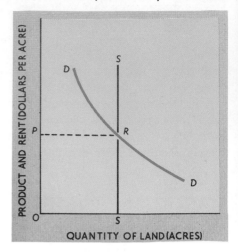

FIGURE 4. *DD* is the demand curve (= the marginal revenue productivity curve) for wine-producing land in Burgundy. Only *OS* acres of such land are available. Since *DD* and *SS* intersect at *R*, the rent of an acre of land will be *RS* = *OP*. The rent depends solely on the height of *DD*, and will rise or fall with it. The same amount of land will be used whatever the rent.

per acre will also decline, and there will be nothing the landowners can do about it. Here, then, the rule seems to be reversed: *the price of the product governs the price of the factor.*

Note also that, whether the return is higher or lower, the total acreage *OS* will continue to be used in wine production. The price of the factor has no effect on its supply. It is not, therefore, a necessary cost of production. It is usually called a *noncost outlay* or *rent.*

But suppose we approached a particular farmer in the region. He would certainly accuse us of being impractical theorists and would consider our conclusions quite wrong. He would say, "Of course rent is a necessary cost. Unless I pay the standard rent of *OP* per acre to the landlord, he won't let me use the land and I'll be out of business." This is true from the standpoint of a single producer. If land is rented on a competitive basis, then anyone who wants an acre must bid it away from other would-be farmers by offering the market price *OP*.[4] From the

---

[4] The argument is not altered materially if the farmer owns the land instead of renting it. For proper bookkeeping he should still, in his capacity as farm operator, pay a rent of *OP* to himself as landowner, because he could get this amount by leasing the land to someone else. For the same reason, he should pay himself competitive wages for his labor and the market rate of interest on his buildings and other equipment. (Perhaps one reason why such calculations are rarely made in practice is that on this basis most farms would turn out to be losing ventures!)

Nor does it matter whether we talk in terms of *rent* per acre or *price* of an acre of land. Like any other income-yielding asset, the value of land is derived from the future stream of rents which it is expected to yield. *Price is derived from rent,* by applying the principle of capitalization explained earlier. An increase in the revenue product, and therefore in the rent, of a piece of land will bring a corresponding increase in its price; and conversely. Here again the true situation is opposite to what it appears on the surface. The owner of a highly productive property will say that he must charge a high rent because he had to pay a high price for the property. The true relation is the reverse. The price was high *because* the property was very productive and yielded a high rent.

standpoint of the whole winegrowing industry, however, the land is still costless. The reason is that it can produce nothing in any alternative use, and so its transfer cost is zero.

We chose vineyards for our example in order to make the assumption of "no alternative use" plausible. If instead we had chosen an acre of Illinois farmland, we would have been in trouble. For this acre might be used to produce wheat, corn, oats, hay, milk, or pork. Any one of these industries which wants the land will have to pay what it would have yielded in some other use. So here there is an opportunity cost to the industry as well as to each farmer; and it seems that land is not basically different from labor or capital.

We can get around this, if we wish, by treating all agricultural production as a single industry. Then, since the amount of land available for farming is virtually fixed, we can regard the total return to farmland as a rent, the size of which depends on the total demand for farm products. This was the path taken by Ricardo and the British classical economists. Crowded into a small island with a rapidly growing population, they visualized the demand for foodstuffs rising without limit while the supply of land remained fixed. Land rent would rise higher and higher, and landowners would grow richer and richer.

While the rent principle is usually illustrated from agriculture, the concept itself is wider. It is *fixity* and *specialization* of factor supply which matters, not the physical characteristics of the factor. Urban land yields rent as much as farmland. The amount of land available for office buildings in lower Manhattan is strictly limited. As demand rises, the rent per acre of this land also rises; and so does its price, which is derived from the rent through capitalization. Land covering a rich oil pool, or a mountain containing a rich copper deposit, yields a rent determined by demand for these products.

The rent concept is not even limited to property income but includes also part of the income from labor. If the supply of first-rate violinists is fixed, and if they have no alternative use,[5] then their income is a rent, comparable in every way to that of our vineyard owners. If the demand for concert performances is high, violinists' incomes will be high. If it is low, they will earn little. In any case the rate of return will make no difference to the supply of the service. It is hard to judge how common such situations are, and how much of labor income is really a rent rather than a wage. But the rent element is probably important throughout the creative arts, the professions, and business administration.

---

[5] In actuality, almost any factor has some alternative use. Vineyards could be used for wheatgrowing. Violin virtuosos could be drugstore clerks. Strictly, it is only the *difference* in return between the actual use and the second-best use which constitute rent to the factor owner. But if the second-best use is *much* less productive, we can ignore it and treat the whole income as rent without being far off.

Economic rent, then, performs no economic function. It accrues to those who own the fixed productive services; but the size of the payment does not affect the supply of the services. This "unearned increment" has seemed to some to be an ideal object of taxation. Henry George, who almost became mayor of New York in 1886 on the Single Tax ticket, believed that taxation of land rent was fair, because landowners had done nothing to earn it; feasible, because they wouldn't be able to do anything about it; and desirable, because this one tax would yield enough to relieve the public of paying any other taxes.

George's proposal was limited, sensibly, to land itself, and did not extend to buildings and improvements. Apartment houses and office buildings are reproducible; and they will be built up to the point at which they yield no more than a normal return on cost. Their return is interest, not rent. If government tries to take away part of this return, the owners *can* do something about it. They can decline to put up any more buildings. The French government maintained low, fixed rent ceilings on houses and apartments from World War I through World War II. It is not surprising that residential construction virtually ceased during this period.

If the tax is limited to income from land, the landowners cannot do anything about it. If half of the rent OP in Figure 4 is taxed away, owners have only half as much income. But they will not withdraw their land from use, because then they would have no income at all. Whether this would be fair is another matter. If the people who originally bought Manhattan island from the Indians had held onto it, and their descendants were now drawing many millions of rent per year, one might question whether they should be so highly rewarded for sitting still for three centuries. The mayor of New York might perhaps reclaim part of what the Indians gave away. But the fact is that this land has changed hands many times since the original purchase. The man who last year paid a million dollars for a piece of Manhattan real estate, expecting it to yield him $50,000 a year, is no different from other men who bought corporate stocks or government bonds. He would have a legitimate complaint if the rules of the game were suddenly changed and a special tax imposed on income from one type of property. This would amount to a partial expropriation of those who had been unlucky enough to buy land rather than some other type of asset.

Land and certain kinds of labor provide the clearest cases of fixed supply. But *in the short run*, capital goods are also in fixed supply. A new plant will not be built unless it is *expected* to yield normal returns. But *after* the plant is built, it is simply there and must take its chances. If demand prospects improve, the plant may yield more than expected. But if demand falls off unexpectedly, returns may be subnormal. There is nothing the owner can do about it in the short run. His return is determined by the state of demand, just like the landowner's return. For this reason, Marshall termed the short-run return to a capital good a "quasi rent."

The difference from true rent is that old capital goods do wear out and new capital goods can be built. The level of returns influences producers' decisions about whether to enlarge capacity, maintain capacity, or allow capacity to shrink through wearing-out of capital. So, over a period of years, the level of returns in a competitive industry must approach that in other industries, as we saw in Chapter 8. The industry must yield "normal quasi rents," or what we have called simply normal returns.

PROFIT

Income distribution does not consist simply of workers receiving wages and owners of capital goods receiving normal rates of return. There is such a thing as profit. The profit share of income is important, not because it is large, but because of the conditions under which it arises and the functions it performs. There are several possible reasons for profit. Unlike the other income shares, for which we were able to give a unified explanation, profit requires a multiple explanation.

1. **Monopoly profit.** Under monopoly or cooperative oligopoly, it is possible to fix price above average total cost and so earn a profit over the long run. This kind of profit, however, may not show up in the profit statistics.

Take a simple example. A company builds a plant costing a million dollars, to make a product of which it is the only producer. Suppose the normal rate of return in competitive manufacturing industries is 5 percent, so that under competition this plant would yield an income of $50,000 a year. Because of its monopoly position, however, the plant actually earns $100,000 a year. This earning power will soon be reflected in the valuation of the company's assets. The $100,000 a year return, capitalized at 5 percent, means that the assets are worth $2 million, even though they cost only $1 million to build. ($2,000,000 \times 5$ percent = $100,000.)

This may be reflected in the company's balance sheet. Under assets, the balance sheet may show $1 million as the value of plant and equipment and another $1 million as the value of "patent rights," "goodwill," or "intangible assets." If we divide this $2 million of assets into the $100,000 annual return, it appears that the company is earning only the normal 5 percent. But the economic profit is still there, even though the calculations of accounting profit do not reveal it.

The earning power of the monopoly will be reflected also in the market value of its stock. It will rise to a price which, when divided into annual earnings per share, gives a yield which is the same as that on other stocks of comparable quality. If you look over the stock market pages and calculate price/earnings ratios for a large number of companies you will find that stocks of semimonopolistic concerns do not yield more than stocks of companies in competitive industries. Since people are always free to shift funds from one stock to another, the market operates to level out differences in yield. But this does not mean that there are no monopolies and no monopoly profit.

2. Competitive profit. Under atomistic competition the members of an industry, on the average and in the long run, earn only normal returns. But this does not mean that every company earns normal returns every year. There may be an upward shift of demand for this industry's products. Eventually productive capacity will be expanded to meet the increased demand; but this takes time. During the period before the new plants come into production, existing producers earn positive profits. This kind of profit serves an important thermostatic function; but it is by nature a fleeting thing. It shrinks and disappears as soon as it has done its job of drawing more resources into lines of production where demand has risen or cost has fallen.

We saw also in Chapter 8 that some producers may have lower costs than others, and so be able to earn profits even in the long run. If a company has lower costs, this must mean that one or more of the factors it uses can be purchased for less than the general market price. If all factor markets were perfect, this could not happen. But factor markets, particularly the markets for labor and for executive services, are by no means perfect. So there is a possibility of continuing profit based, not on monopoly position in *product* markets, but on an advantageous position in one or more *factor* markets. Such profits, like monopoly profit, will be reflected in the valuation of the company's assets and the price of its stock; so they may not show up in the statistics on rates of return.

3. Profit and innovation. This concept is associated particularly with Joseph Schumpeter, a noted Viennese economist who came to the United States and taught at Harvard. Schumpeter distinguished between *invention* of a new product or production method and the actual application of an invention in production. The latter he termed *innovation,* which he regarded as the specific function of the *entrepreneur.* Innovation requires imagination, energy, ability to mobilize capital, willingness to take risks. Schumpeter thought that few people have these qualities. So any major innovation will be pioneered by one or a few men. If it succeeds, it may bring large profits to the first producers.

After the few have shown the way, the many will follow. If there are no restrictions on entrance, more and more resources will flow into the industry, product prices will be reduced, and eventually the industry will settle down to earning only a normal return. The profit from innovation is a vanishing profit. But it may take quite a long time to vanish; and meanwhile the original entrepreneur has been well repaid for his efforts.

Schumpeterian profit can be regarded as the rent of a productive resource—entrepreneurship—which is fixed in supply. The larger the supply of this kind of ability in a particular country, the more rapid will be the exploitation of new production opportunities, the more dynamic the economy, and the lower the level of entrepreneurial profits. While the supply of entrepreneurs may be fixed in the short run, it can be enlarged over the course of time by education, by cultural changes which increase the prestige of the businessman, and by a lightening of government restrictions on innovation. The alleged shortage of entrepreneurship in many of the less developed countries is probably due, not so much to any difference in the inherent capacities of the population, as to cultural and institutional factors.

4. **Profit and uncertainty.** This view of profit stems mainly from the work of Professor Frank H. Knight of the University of Chicago. Knight argued that profit would not arise if the future could be forseen with certainty. If future shifts in demand, technology, and factor prices could be visualized today, then the appropriate actions would be taken today. Upward and downward adjustments of capacity would be smooth, and the profit thermostat would not be needed.

The same would be true if there were uncertainties about the future, but if these uncertainties were of a kind which could be insured against. Many personal risks—that my house will catch fire this year, that I will have various kinds of illness, that I will die, that I will be involved in an auto accident—are quite predictable for a whole population, though they are uncertain for any member of the population. So an insurance company can calculate how large a premium it must charge in order to compensate the people who suffer loss in a particular year. It knows about *how many* they will be, though not *who* they will be.

If a company could buy insurance against the possibility that consumers may turn against its product, that it may lose a large government contract, that new machinery may make its present plant obsolete—then (for it) these uncertainties would no longer exist. It would have shifted them to the insurance company. The insurance premium would be put down as a production cost, and from there on it could calculate as though the future were certain. Producers actually do this to some extent. Companies often carry death and disability insurance on their top executives, as an offset to the loss from being deprived suddenly of their services. Lloyd's of London will insure an opera singer against loss of his voice or a pianist against damage to his fingers.

But the major uncertainties of business cannot be disposed of in this way. Knight believed that willingness to face noninsurable uncertainties is limited and must be paid for. *Profit is the reward for bearing uncertainty.*

Uncertainty means that you may end up with negative rather than positive profit. If the chances of negative and positive profit seem exactly equal, then it is foolish to take a chance rather than get a guaranteed return on a government bond. The businessman must *expect* that he has a better than even chance. Suppose the best estimate he can make of his probable return is 8 percent,[6] and that the rate of interest at the time is 5 percent. Then the difference, 3 percent, is his *expected profit;* and if he considers this sufficient to compensate for the uncertainty involved, he will go ahead.

In uncertain situations, then, it is necessary for profits to be *expected.* Is it necessary also for profit to be *received?* Not in any one case. But over the economy as a whole, positive profits must exceed negative ones. Otherwise the expectation of profit will become implausible, willingness to bear uncertainty will decline, and the system will lose vitality. The expectation of profit, backed up in some measure by actual earning of profit, is central to the operation of a private enterprise economy.

How Important Is Profit?

It is difficult to estimate the size of *economic* profit in the United States. Even figures on *accounting* profit are available only for incorporated businesses, which leaves out most of retailing, service, and agriculture. Table 1, derived from business income tax returns, gives accounting profits for all business corporations since 1949. Losses of companies making losses have been deducted from the profits of the remainder, and corporate income taxes have also been deducted. The remainder is calculated first as a rate of return on the owners' capital, and second as a percentage of net national product. There seems to have been a slight decline in profit levels over the period, and there are sizable year-to-year changes associated with the business cycle.

It is clear from Table 2 that rates of return vary widely in different types of industry. Finance and manufacturing stand relatively high, mining and agriculture relatively low. Within manufacturing, we have selected a few industries at the top of the earnings range and a few others near the bottom. Note that in the high-profit branches of manufacturing, oligopoly is the general rule, while the low-profit industries are typically closer to atomistic competition.

The difficulty comes when we try to convert these accounting figures into economic terms. On one hand, the accounting figures are too low because, as we saw in our monopoly example, a sustained high rate of return will be reflected in the value of the company's assets. So the rate

---

[6] In practice, he would usually have in mind more than one possible outcome. He might estimate, for example, that there are 3 chances in 10 that he will earn 4 percent, 4 chances in 10 that he will earn 8 percent, and 3 chances in 10 that he will earn 12 percent. Then by taking an average, in which each of these possible rates is weighted by its probability, we see that the *most probable expected return* is 8 percent. $\dfrac{(3 \times 4) + (4 \times 8) + (3 \times 12)}{10} = \dfrac{80}{10} = 8.$

TABLE 1

Net Accounting Profit, All Business Corporations, after Corporate Income Taxes, 1949–64

YEAR	PROFIT AS PERCENT OF STOCKHOLDERS' EQUITY	PROFIT AS PERCENT OF NET NATIONAL PRODUCT†
1949	8.9	6.6
1950	11.3	8.6
1951	9.0	6.4
1952	7.7	5.3
1953	7.5	5.3
1954	7.0	5.0
1955	8.5	6.3
1956	7.9	6.1
1957	7.1	5.5
1958	5.5	4.6
1959	6.5	5.5
1960	5.5	4.8
1961	5.7	4.6
1962	*	4.9
1963	*	5.0
1964	*	5.2

* Not yet available.
† As calculated by the Office of Business Economics, Department of Commerce. These figures differ slightly from those prepared by the Internal Revenue Service. For a detailed explanation
of differences in method, see the cited source.
　　Source: U.S. Department of Commerce, *Survey of Current
Business*, July, 1964.

of return on *present value* of assets may be only moderate, while the
return on *original cost* of assets may be quite high. On the other hand,
the accounting figures are too high, because they include *imputed
interest* on the owners' capital, and this must be deducted in order to see
whether any economic profit is present. How much should we deduct for
this purpose? Government bond yields averaged about 3 percent during
the fifties. The yield of top-quality corporate bonds averaged about 4
percent. The rate of return in public utilities, a very low-risk industry
subject to government price controls, was near 5 percent.

However we decide this question, it seems likely that there *is*
positive profit in the American economy as a whole. But the average rate
of profit is not high. At a rough guess, one might put it in the range of 2
to 3 percent on the value of owners' capital. As a proportion of national
income, profit is no more than 2 percent of the total.

How do we explain the amount of profit which does exist?
Monopoly? Dynamic change in competitive industries? Innovation and
entrepreneurship? Risk bearing? Take your pick, and you can scarcely be
wrong, because each of these contributes in some measure.

TABLE 2

Net Accounting Profit after Corporate Income Tax, as
Percent of Stockholders' Equity, 1961,
Selected Branches of Industry

MAJOR SECTORS	
Finance, insurance, and real estate	6.4
Manufacturing	6.3
Wholesale and retail trade	4.9
Transportation, communication, and public utilities	4.8
Services	4.3
Construction	3.1
Mining and quarrying	3.0
Agriculture	1.7
SUBSECTORS OF MANUFACTURING	
Tobacco manufactures	13.2
Motor vehicles and equipment	10.4
Chemicals	9.9
Instruments and related products	8.5
Apparel	6.0
Furniture and fixtures	4.7
Textiles	4.3
Leather and leather products	4.3
Lumber and wood products, except furniture	3.0

Source: U.S. Treasury Department, *Statistics of Income*, 1961–62, pp.
197–204.

Finally, a word on the justifiability of profit. In many parts of the
world, "the profit system" is a term of reproach; and in the United States
it is a favorite theme for student political clubs and debating societies.
Without getting into the argument, one may suggest that it is a good idea
to define targets carefully before opening fire. People who think they are
attacking profit are often at bottom attacking one or more of the
following:

1. Property income in general.   One can argue on ethical grounds
that income should be earned by working, and that some stigma attaches
to property income. There is no reason, however, to distinguish profit
from any other form of property income. Most of what is called profit
should, in fact, be regarded as imputed interest.

2. Inequality of income.   Property ownership is highly concentrated. Most property income is received by a small minority of the population, and this aggravates the overall inequality of income distribution. If
inequality is the real target, the line of attack lies through the tax system.
The personal income, corporate income, and inheritance taxes already
have a strong leveling effect. Whether more or less should be done in this
direction is naturally a matter of political controversy.

3. Monopoly power.   Most of the profit in the American economy

arises in semimonopolistic industries. An attack on profit, then, is largely synonymous with an attack on business monopoly. This has been a traditional subject of political debate in the United States for a century or more.

The logic of these three lines of attack is quite different, and the practical remedies available are also different. Lumping them together in an omnibus attack on profit arouses a suspicion that the critic has not thought through his position.

The positive justification of profit is that it is necessary to induce businessmen to take risks, start new ventures, improve products and production methods. The total price paid for this service in the American economy is not great; and if at any time it seems to be getting too large, the tax collector is always available to rake more of it back into the U.S. Treasury. A country which is not willing to pay for entrepreneurship in this way must elicit it in some other way. In some routinized sectors of the economy, such as rail and air transport, electric power, communications, the government entrepreneur may turn out to be a satisfactory substitute. But it remains to be demonstrated that this can work well in manufacturing, trade, and other sectors where the opportunity and the need for innovation are greater.

SUMMARY

1. Capital goods, like other factors of production, yield a marginal revenue product. This is usually measured as a percentage return per year on the cost of the capital good. Purchase of a capital good is profitable if its percentage return is equal to or greater than the market rate of interest.

2. If we know the expected future returns from a capital good, and if we know the rate of interest, we can calculate the *present value* of the capital good. This procedure is called *capitalization.*

3. Given the supply of labor and other productive resources, and given the state of technology, the larger is the nation's capital stock, the lower will be the marginal productivity of capital. The national MP_k schedule slopes downward to the right.

4. At any time, there is a definite amount of capital in existence. The marginal productivity of this amount of capital determines the rate of interest.

5. In the advanced industrial countries, the capital stock is normally growing. At the same time, the MP_k schedule is being raised by increases in the supply of labor and other productive resources and by technical progress. Depending on the relative strength of these forces, the interest rate may either rise or fall over time.

6. The interest rate serves to *restrain the demand for capital goods*

within the limit of available resources and also to *allocate resources* among specific types of capital good. These are necessary functions in any capital-using economy.

7. If a factor is in fixed supply and can be used for only one purpose, its return depends entirely on demand for its product. Such a return is called a *rent*. While land provides the commonest illustration, certain scarce human abilities also command a rent.

8. The existence of *profit* even in competitive industries has been variously explained as: arising from *lags in adjustment* of an industry to demand increases or cost decreases; a return to the *entrepreneurs* who pioneer an *innovation* in products or production methods; a necessary reward to businessmen for bearing noninsurable risks or *uncertainties*.

9. Actual or realized profit is not large, probably not more than 2 percent of national income. Potential or anticipated profit is nevertheless an important incentive to economic activity.

DISCUSSION QUESTIONS

1. If you look at financial magazines you will find a large number of different rates of interest. Which of these correspond most closely to "the rate of interest" discussed in this chapter?

2. Cannot the productivity of a capital good be attributed entirely to the labor used in making it? Is there any such thing as a separate productivity of capital?

3. Why does an increase in the supply of labor raise the marginal productivity schedule of capital?

4. Would you expect the rate of interest to have risen or fallen over the past 50 years in Japan? In Britain? In India? Why? (See whether you can check on what actually happened.)

5. Can one make a case for taxing the rents of fixed and specialized factors more heavily than other types of income? If you had been a New York voter in 1886, how would you have reacted to Henry George's single-tax proposal?

6. The difference between *accounting* profit and *economic* profit was explained in Chapter 7. Can you restate the distinction?

7. What do you consider the most reasonable explanation for the existence of economic profit?

8. Political views of profit have ranged all the way from regarding it as a sacrosanct personal right to treating it as an antisocial form of income which should be eliminated. What is your own view?

Markets, Planning, and Economic Efficiency

> Society is composed of two great classes:
> those who have more dinners than appetite, and
> those who have more appetite than dinners.
>
> SÉBASTIEN R. N. CHAMFORT

IN CHAPTERS 3 and 4 we outlined two patterns of economic organization: a centrally planned economy on the Soviet model and an economy coordinated through a network of competitive markets. The analysis of a market economy was then elaborated by looking more closely at particular kinds of market, beginning with product markets and going on to markets for productive resources. We want now to stand back and look again at the market economy as a whole, this time from the standpoint of judging its performance. How good a system is it? What are its main strengths and weaknesses?

The same questions may be asked about the planned economy. We are apt to assume that central planning must be inefficient, just as the Russians assume that capitalism is inefficient. Yet the national output of the U.S.S.R. has risen rapidly since 1950. Perhaps planning works better than we think. At any rate, we should make a systematic effort to find out.

THE IDEA OF GENERAL EQUILIBRIUM

The first thing to be said about the market economy is that it is a system. It is not, as its critics have sometimes claimed, a state of anarchy.

305

It is not a mere patchwork collection of markets. The price-quantity decisions reached in one market are related to those in other markets. The system as a whole can be counted on to make the billions of decisions required for the economy to function. Let's review the main kinds of decision and see how they tie in with each other.

1. There is a market for each kind of consumer good and service. On the demand side of the market stand consumers, spending their incomes so as to achieve greatest satisfaction. On the supply side stand producers, deciding how much it pays them to bring to market. The equilibrium price which emerges in the market has the *incentive* function of inducing a certain level of production; and it has the *rationing* function of ensuring that consumers will buy just the amount being produced.

2. The producing unit, in addition to deciding how much to produce, must also decide how to produce it. It has at its disposal the known methods of production, devised by scientists and engineers. It also knows the price of each productive service and will choose the method which minimizes unit cost. So the cost curves which underlie the market supply curves are curves of *minimum feasible cost*.

3. But the prices of the productive services, while a single producer can usually take them as given, are not given for the economy as a whole. They are one of the things to be decided in the system. The demand for a productive service is derived from the value of its product. We have seen how the marginal revenue product curves of individual producers can be added to yield total demand for a factor. Households now stand on the supply side of the market, deciding how much to save, how much work to do, and where to work. The market price for each service, just like a product price, serves the dual function of calling forth a certain supply and at the same time rationing this supply among alternate uses.

4. The market prices of productive services, which are *costs* to the producer, constitute *income* to the households who own the factors of production. Each household's income depends on the amount of land, labor, and capital services it supplies, and on the price which these command in the market. With this income, households come into the market for consumer goods. We are back where we started.

We often speak of these decisions as following each other chronologically. Consumers decide to buy certain quantities of goods, producers respond by turning out these quantities, this generates a certain demand for productive services, factor owners receive income for supplying these services, then they respend this money on the next round. But in practice all these things are going on *simultaneously*. And the flows of productive services and commodities through the economy must be *consistent*, so that surpluses do not accumulate in one part of the system and shortages in another. Prices of products and factors, moving upward and downward as needed, are the *regulators* by which this consistency is assured.

Behind the market mechanism are the guiding forces of household preferences and production possibilities. These are usually taken as lying outside of economic analysis, as "given conditions" into which we do not inquire. Let's suppose, by a heroic effort of imagination, that these basic conditions stay unchanged long enough for the system to adjust fully to them. Then a price and a quantity would be determined in each market, the results in all markets would be consistent, and they would remain unchanged so long as the given conditions remained unchanged. The economy would settle down into a steady state—producing the same goods by the same methods, distributing them to the same people, hiring the same workers for the same jobs, year after year. This view of the economy as a network of interacting and mutually consistent markets is usually termed *general equilibrium*. It is associated with the name of Léon Walras, a French mathematical economist who demonstrated that such a system would be capable of deciding all prices and quantities simultaneously.

The given conditions do not in fact stay unchanged. People's preferences are constantly shifting, and engineers are upsetting the applecart by developing new products and production methods. There are also waves of prosperity and depression, which we deliberately leave out of the picture until Part Three. But we can still regard the market economy as a basically stable and self-adjusting mechanism, which is constantly being jolted and modified by outside disturbances. The economy is straining toward equilibrium at any moment, even though it never arrives there.

ECONOMIC EFFICIENCY UN●ER PURE COMPETITION

So we can show that a market economy works. But how *well* does it work? Are the results which it produces desirable, correct, efficient?

"Efficiency" has a variety of meanings. We use it here in the sense of extracting maximum satisfaction from a given amount of productive resources. This is usually called *static efficiency*, or *efficiency of resource allocation*. It is one desirable feature, though not the only desirable feature, of an economy, and it is worth defining with some care.

How do we test for the presence of static efficiency? By looking at the economy to see whether we can rearrange inputs or outputs so as to increase anyone's satisfaction. So long as it is possible to make someone better off without making anyone else worse off, the economy is not efficient. We have reached an optimum position *only when it is impossible to make any individual better off without making someone else worse off.* This is usually called a *Pareto optimum,* after the Italian economist who first defined it.

Why is the definition framed in this cautious way? Could we not sometimes increase community welfare by benefiting one individual at the expense of another—say, by taking money from Mr. A and giving it to Mr. B? Maybe. But we cannot be sure. Most economists now take the view that one cannot compare or add up the satisfactions of different individuals in any scientifically rigorous way. This means that we cannot, as economists, decide that one distribution of income is preferable to another, even though as citizens we may make value judgments on the matter. Only if we can benefit Mr. A *without* hurting Mr. B can we demonstrate that total welfare has increased.

This section has two aims: to define the necessary conditions for a Pareto optimum and to show that if all markets are purely competitive these conditions will be realized. This will reveal the basis for the common-sense belief that "competition is a good idea." It will also help us to distinguish clearly between the abstract model of a purely competitive economy and the actual American economy of the present day.

The conditions for a Pareto optimum have all been laid down in earlier chapters and need only to be summarized here. Let us start from product markets and work through to factor markets.

1. **The consumer choice condition.** Each consumer distributes his budget in such a way that the marginal utility of each good purchased, relative to its price, is identical. If we designate goods by A, B, C . . . , then for each consumer:

$$\frac{MU_A}{P_A} = \frac{MU_B}{P_B} = \frac{MU_C}{P_C} = \ldots = \frac{MU_N}{P_N}.$$

If a consumer's budget is not meeting this condition, he can gain satisfaction by shifting money from one good to another.

Under pure competition consumers have adequate *opportunity* to satisfy this condition, since they can buy any good in any quantity at the market price. The assumption that consumers actually succeed in equating marginal utilities is an act of faith; but so would it be in any other type of economy.

2. **The product distribution condition.** The relative marginal utilities of any two goods must be the same for each consumer in the system: If we designate consumers by 1, 2, 3, . . . , then:

$$\frac{MU_A}{MU_B}_1 = \frac{MU_A}{MU_B}_2 = \frac{MU_A}{MU_B}_3 = \ldots = \frac{MU_A}{MU_B}_N.$$

If this condition is not met, we could increase satisfaction by re-shuffling commodities among consumers. Suppose that for consumer 1 the ratio MU_A/MU_B is higher than for consumer 2. This indicates that consumer 1 has *relatively* too little of product A, while consumer 2 is in the opposite position. There can be mutual gain by consumer 1 obtaining more of A from consumer 2 in exchange for some of B; and they will continue to gain until the marginal utility ratio is the same for both households.

Under pure competition, *the market price of each good is the same to all buyers;* and we can show that where this is true, the present condition is satisfied. Each consumer, if he is allocating his budget correctly, will reach a position in which $\dfrac{MU_A}{P_A} = \dfrac{MU_B}{P_B}$ which is the same as saying that $\dfrac{MU_A}{MU_B} = \dfrac{P_A}{P_B}$. But since P_A and P_B are market prices which are the same for all buyers, P_A/P_B is identical for all households. Hence MU_A/MU_B must also be identical.

3. The correct output condition. Production of each good and service in the system must be carried to the point at which price equals marginal cost. The reasoning behind this rule was explained in Chapter 7. Suppose that, for product A, $P_A > MC_A$. This shows that the valuation consumers would attach to an additional unit of A is greater than the cost of the resources needed to produce this unit. But this cost, being an *opportunity cost,* measures the valuation which consumers place on the other goods these resources are presently producing. Since product A is valued more highly, consumer satisfaction would be increased by shifting resources to produce more of A and less of other things.

We demonstrated also in Chapter 7 that this rule will be satisfied under pure competition. Since a producer can sell any amount he wishes at a constant price, he will always do best by producing at the point where $P = MC$.

4. The least-cost condition. Unit cost of production for each good must be at the lowest level permitted by existing technology. This requires, first, that plants be of optimum scale and that they be operated at (economic) capacity. Second, it requires that factors of production be combined in the right proportions. Specifically, the quantity of each factor used in producing a particular good must be such that the ratio of a factor's marginal product to its price is the same for all factors. If we designate factors as $a, b, c, \ldots$, then:

$$\frac{MP_a}{P_a} = \frac{MP_b}{P_b} = \frac{MP_c}{P_c} = \cdots = \frac{MP_n}{P_n}.$$

Suppose this condition is not being met—for example, MP_a/P_a is higher than for the other factors. The high marginal productivity of factor a, relative to its cost, indicates that the producer is using too little of this factor. He can get more output per dollar by buying more of factor a and less of other factors.

To paraphrase Adam Smith, we might say that under pure competition producers are kicked by an invisible boot into satisfying the least-cost condition. This is the price of remaining in business. Anyone is free to come into a competitive industry, set up a plant of optimum scale, run it at the optimum rate, and achieve the least-cost combination of factors. Over the long run, product price will settle at a level which just covers this minimum cost. Any producer who fails to achieve minimum cost will experience losses and will eventually be forced out of operation.

5. The factor allocation condition. The marginal revenue product of each factor must be the *same in all uses*. The need for this condition is obvious. If factor *a* has a higher marginal revenue product in industry 1 than in industry 2, then national output can be increased by shifting more of the factor to industry 1. As this happens, its marginal productivity will fall in 1 and rise in 2. When MRP_a becomes equal in the two industries, nothing can be gained by further shifting.

The proof that this condition will be satisfied under pure competition is straightforward. The market price of any factor will be the same to all producers. But each producer, in order to satisfy conditions 3 and 4, must hire each factor up to the point at which its marginal revenue product equals the factor price. Hence the marginal revenue of the factor must also be the same in all uses.

6. The factor supply condition. For each household in the system, the marginal valuation of leisure lost from the last hour of work supplied should be just compensated by the wage rate; and the consumption satisfaction lost from the last dollar of saving should be just compensated by the rate of interest. Suppose this condition is not met—for example the satisfaction yielded by Mr. A's hourly wage is greater than the satisfaction provided by the marginal hour of leisure. His satisfaction could be increased by lengthening his working hours to the point at which the marginal valuation of leisure is just offset by the wage.

Under pure competition, each household is free to offer as much labor and saving as it chooses, guided by its preferences and by market rates of return. The assumption that households will try to behave economically as factor suppliers is as firm (or shaky!) as the assumption that they will behave economically as consumers.

7. The occupational choice condition. The tasks performed by members of the community should be so allocated among them as to involve a minimum of sacrifice, because everybody is doing the work he likes best (or dislikes least) and for which he is best fitted. This condition is required because of the great diversity of jobs in the economy and the wide variation of people's work preferences and abilities. If it is met, we can be sure that no switching of two people between jobs could lighten one person's burden without either raising the other person's burden or causing a drop in output.

This condition will be met if people are able to choose freely among alternative occupations. The rational individual will choose the job which, on the basis of wage rate and all other conditions, strikes him as most attractive. This will lead to an optimum distribution of workers among jobs.

Consider Mr. A, whose income is below Mr. B's. Then A must have chosen his job in preference to B's either because, lacking aptitude for B's occupation, he could not have earned B's income in it; or because he sees other disadvantages in B's job which more than offset the higher wage. In neither case would there be a gain from moving A to B's job. In the first case output would fall, and in the second case A would feel worse off than before.

We conclude that, if all markets in the economy are purely competitive, all of the efficiency conditions will be satisfied. But note that we have reached this result mainly by *defining* pure competition in such a way—absence of restrictions on individual decision, full knowledge of alternatives, rational pursuit of economic satisfaction—that fulfillment of the efficiency conditions follows as a logical consequence.

The Ideal and the Actual

The purely competitive economy is a nice kind of utopia—logically elegant, politically attractive. So attractive is it that one must guard against identifying the competitive model with the real world and against concluding that if government would only leave the economy alone, all would work out for the best. The sophisticated case for laissez faire should not be vulgarized into blanket approval of all private economic activity.

The extent to which product and factor markets in the United States differ from the competitive ideal should be evident from the preceding few chapters. In some areas of the economy competition is absent; in other areas markets are seriously defective. The economy doubtless could be made more competitive than it is; but this in itself implies an active role for government. Competitive markets do not necessarily spring up and persist of their own accord. Government action is often needed to establish markets or improve their operation.

Equally important, there are many economic problems with which the market mechanism does not deal. The market mechanism does handle the problem of static efficiency—getting the most from a given bundle of resources. But static efficiency isn't everything. What about the rate at which resources *grow* over the course of time? How do we know that resources will always be *fully employed*? Is the *distribution of income* yielded by the market necessarily desirable? What about basic *public services* which must be provided through government or not at all? Decisions on these matters have to be made outside, or at least alongside, the market mechanism.

Let's review briefly, first the main *gaps* in the market mechanism, and then its major *imperfections.*

GOVERNMENT ACTION OUTSIDE THE MARKET MECHANISM

Economic Growth

The market mechanism answers the question of how to distribute a *given* amount of productive resources among various lines of production. It is less clear that it provides a satisfactory answer to the question of how fast these resources should *grow* over the course of time.

The growth of the nation's stock of capital equipment is heavily influenced by household decisions about saving and consumption. But on what ground can one say that these decisions are *correct* from an overall standpoint? Why should the preferences of the present generation be taken as decisive for the level of investment, which will affect the welfare of many generations to come? If this generation is shortsighted in some measure, why should the national economy be similarly short-sighted?

These questions are important even in prosperous industrial countries. They are even more important in the less developed countries, where voluntary household savings are typically small. Suppose the government of one of these countries decides that development should be accelerated and that more of the country's resources should be diverted to capital goods at the expense of current consumption. Can one say that this interference with private decisions is necessarily wrong?

Economic growth depends also on *the rate of technological progress.* In reasoning about static efficiency, the state of technology is always taken as given. But where does technology come from? Can a private market economy be counted on to produce a rapid flow of new inventions? Or are there things which government can usefully do in this connection?

Economic Stability

However good the market system may be for allocating economic resources *at full employment,* it does not solve the problem of how to achieve and maintain full employment. One can construct on paper an ideal market economy which could not deviate far from full employment and in which deviations would be quickly corrected. But this is not the world in which we live. There is nothing in actual market economies which insures them against waves of depression, or for that matter against chronic underemployment. Maintenance of near-capacity operation requires deliberate stabilizing actions which only government is in a position to take.

Public Services

It has always been recognized that there are community needs which cannot be met through individual choice in the market place. National defense cannot be sold to the citizens in small pieces. It must be produced by government and financed through a system of taxation.

This raises several questions: (1) *What types* of production fall properly within the public sector? Police protection and national defense are clear cases. Public education and public highways are generally accepted. As one gets into such things as health, housing, and social insurance the degree of controversy increases. Where should the boundary be drawn?

2. *How much* of each public service should government produce? What is a proper level of expenditure on defense, education, highways, and the rest? It is difficult to apply the test of marginal cost = price because these services are usually not sold at a price. What principles can we find as a substitute?

3. How should the *tax burden* be distributed? This is closely related to the issue of personal income distribution. By tilting the tax scales in one direction or another, government can make the distribution of income after taxes more equal or less equal than before.

The theory of prices and markets does not answer these questions, and we are forced to reach beyond it for other bases of decision.

Income Distribution

In a competitive economy, individuals are paid according to their contribution to production. One can argue that this is a fair and proper basis for income distribution, but then one is talking philosophy as well as economics. If someone else argues on ethical grounds that the talented and efficient should be taxed to support their weaker brethren, one cannot prove him wrong by appealing to economic theory. Income distribution is bound to be a subject of political struggle, in which the results of the market will be modified to some extent.

The struggle is partly over the pattern of *resource ownership*, on which the market distribution of income basically depends. In reasoning about static efficiency, resource ownership is always taken as given. But this does not render it immune to criticism at a more fundamental level. Property ownership in the United States is still concentrated in a minority of families. Should these families be allowed to pass on their holdings intact to their descendants? Or should property be taxed away at death and each generation obliged to start afresh in the economic race?

Similar questions arise with respect to the distribution of personal skills and capacities. These are partly inherited, but they depend also on training and education. The setup of higher education is especially strategic in determining how many people, and which people, can qualify to become accountants, dentists, architects, or electrical engineers. Government can affect the outcome by its expenditures on educational facilities, teaching salaries, and scholarship or loan funds. This amounts to changing the institutional structure within which people compete for a livelihood. It is a change in one of the givens of the competitive problem.

GOVERNMENT ACTION TO IMPROVE THE MARKET MECHANISM

The argument that a system of private competitive enterprise leads to maximum efficiency rests on an idealized picture of the system, in which everyone is perfectly informed and all markets are purely competitive. But these conditions are not feasible in all sectors of the economy, and even where they are feasible, competitive markets will not spring up and persist of their own accord.

There are numerous industries in which atomistic competition is not feasible. In the area of public utilities, it would be inconvenient and expensive to have more than one producer in the same territory. In many other industries, there is room for only a few producers, because the optimum scale of plant is large relative to total demand. The consequence is oligopoly, and it is difficult to make members of an oligopoly group behave competitively in the sense of following independent price and production policies.

In these cases the regulatory force of competition is not operative. What can be put in its place? The possibilities include informal supervision and pressure on the industry, regulation of prices and service by a government board, and government operation. In any event, there would be widespread agreement that unchecked exercise of monopoly power cannot be permitted.

Even where competitive markets are feasible, they will not necessarily arise, persist, and operate effectively. Government action may be needed to make effective competition possible. Such action, while sometimes criticized as meddlesome intervention, is fundamentally pro-private enterprise.

Government can sometimes *create markets* where they would not otherwise exist. A good example is the local offices of the state employment services. These are not used by workers and employers as fully as they might be. But to the extent that they are used, they enable each employer to find out what labor is available and each worker to find out what job vacancies exist in the area. This permits a more effective matching of unemployed workers and available jobs.

The effectiveness of competition can often be improved by *provi-*

sion of information. It is often argued with some reason that consumers are so ignorant and misinformed that their preferences provide only a dubious guide to production decisions. But one need not conclude that consumer choice should be supplanted or that a wise and benevolent government should give people what is *really* good for them. The moral is rather that government should provide information on the basis of which consumers can pursue their interests more effectively. Information activity includes setting objective grades and standards, as is done for many food and drug products, so that buyers can determine more accurately what they are getting. It includes the efforts of the Federal Trade Commission and other agencies to prevent false advertising statements. It includes the testing of products and distribution of facts about performance by such private groups as Consumers Union and Consumers Research.

A special case of this sort is provision of technical and market information to *small business* concerns. There are numerous industries in which production can be carried on efficiently by small independent units. But small producers cannot afford to set up large research and development laboratories or to make elaborate market surveys and economic forecasts. These activities need to be organized on a larger scale, and their results made generally available. The classic case in American experience is agriculture, where small private producers have been aided effectively by an elaborate network of government research, education, marketing, credit, and advisory services. Many lines of industry and trade could benefit from this same sort of cooperative effort.

Even though competition may be more efficient, collusion to set prices and regulate production is usually more profitable. So government is called on to *prevent collusive action* and to protect competitive markets. The work of the Department of Justice and other federal agencies on this front will be examined in the next chapter.

The argument for competitive industry usually assumes that *money costs of production are an accurate measure of social costs.* While this is broadly true, one can find instances in which it will not be true. If a factory pollutes a stream in which people would like to fish or swim, or if it sends out dense clouds of smoke which deposit soot for miles around, there are costs to the community which will not be counted as costs by the company concerned. If a company works its employees hard to the age of 50 and then lays them off to be supported on relief, it is imposing a cost on the community which should be (but will not be) covered by the price of its products. Such discrepancies between private and social cost can often be corrected by government action.

This is one example of a broader economic phenomenon which has been termed *neighborhood or external effects.* Competitive economic theory is ultraindividualistic in assuming that the satisfactions of each individual in the system are independent of the behavior and satisfactions of other people. This is clearly not true. If my neighbor keeps a barking dog, or gives noisy parties, or drives his car very badly, this has an effect on me. On a broader plane, if other citizens are free not to educate their children beyond the fourth grade or to go about in public with communicable diseases, this affects me and my family. These neighborhood effects justify police protection, compulsory education, health regulation, and other things which restrict freedom of individual choice.

An important case of interdependence among economic units involves the *external economies* discussed in Chapter 8. The costs of one company or industry may depend on those of related companies or industries. Simultaneous expansion of several related industries may lower costs for all of them. It will be worthwhile from an overall standpoint to stimulate such expansion, even though it would not pay any one company to go ahead on its own. This is an especially important consideration for countries in the early stages of industrialization.

What Remains of the Competitive Case?

We argued initially that a system of purely competitive markets could be ideally efficient. How far do the gaps and deficiencies in actual markets reduce efficiency below the theoretical ideal? No quantitative answer can be given to this question. We cannot say that total satisfaction is 70 percent, or 80 percent, or 90 percent of what it would be if our economic resources were ideally deployed and used. But listing the possible sources of inefficiency is helpful in forming a rough impression.

The writer would judge that the American economy rates quite *high* in terms of static efficiency. This judgment is prompted partly by observing the difficulties which the planned economies have encountered in trying to reach the same decisions by other methods. The market settles many complex issues skillfully but unobtrusively, so that its advantages are not always appreciated. The main sources of welfare loss in our economy, in order of decreasing importance, strike me as follows: (1) underemployment of resources, which may have averaged as much as 10 percent in recent years; (2) financial, informational, and other obstacles to effective choice among occupations; (3) external effects, particularly in medical care, urban housing, and community development, which are inadequately cared for by private markets; (4) informational obstacles to effective consumer choice; (5) monopoly power over prices and wages. Some economists would give item 5 a higher rank. My low ranking is based partly on a judgment that neither business monopolies nor trade unions take full advantage of the power which in theory they might exert.[1]

The "anatomy of market failure," in Francis Bator's trenchant phrase, provides us also with an anatomy of public policy. Political writers and practitioners often portray government as the natural opponent of private enterprise. They imply that acceptance of a market economy reduces, or should reduce, government to the role of policeman. This is a major misunderstanding. Even the most pro-private enterprise government one could find in the world (West Germany? Japan?) finds itself faced with unavoidable tasks: creating and improving private markets, controlling monopoly, producing collective goods, correcting biases in private production due to external effects, regulating the level of economic activity, reflecting popular judgment on income distribution. These activities are complementary to, rather than opposed to, private economic activity. Government may overregulate and stifle private initiative; but it *need* not do so. We should not stigmatize the instruments of government because they are potentially capable of misuse.

VARIETIES OF ECONOMIC PLANNING

It is only fair that the efficiency standards we have applied to the market economy should now be applied to the planned economies of the socialist countries. An initial difficulty here is that we are not dealing with a homogeneous species. Economic planning operates somewhat differently in Poland and in the U.S.S.R. Yugoslavia is still more of a maverick. If we had information about China, it would probably also show important differences. So it is best to begin by exploring some alternative varieties of planned economy.

The Command Economy

First, every quantity in the system might be decided at the center. Gosplan sitting in Moscow might decide where each individual in the U.S.S.R. is to work, the quantities of inputs to be used and the outputs to be produced by each producing unit, and how much of each consumer good shall be delivered to each household. This planning could be done entirely in physical terms. If money was used for accounting convenience, it would play a purely passive role.

Such a system would require a vast amount of information at the center, and a great deal of calculation to ensure that inputs and outputs were consistent—that the right quantities of each resource were available

---

[1] Other economists have also concluded that the welfare loss from monopolistic misallocation of resources is quite small. See, for example, Arnold C. Harberger, "Monopoly and Resource Allocation," *American Economic Review*, May, 1954, pp. 77–87; and David Schwartzman, "The Burden of Monopoly," *Journal of Political Economy*, December, 1960, pp. 627–30.

at the points needed, and that the exact quantities of goods produced were taken off the market. But in this day of high-speed computers, the problem might conceivably be solved. Perfect computation might serve in place of perfect competition.[2]

It is harder to visualize the vast *administrative* effort which would be needed to control the economy by directives from a central point. Each household would have to receive ration coupons for each good, each worker would have to receive his marching orders, each production manager would be given detailed instructions for the conduct of his enterprise. There would also have to be checks on how far these orders were obeyed and penalties for noncompliance.

In such a system, *prices* would perform no function. A worker would work at a particular job because he was told to, not because he was induced to do so by a certain wage. The prices set on consumer goods would have no bearing on the quantities consumed.

The central controllers might try to discover and take account of consumer preferences and worker preferences; but it would be hard to do this without markets and prices. Alternatively, the controllers might follow their own preferences and hunches about production and distribution. Given sufficient political control, they could impose any pattern they might choose.

Decentralization: Market Socialism

Suppose that, as premier of a socialist country, you decide that centralized physical planning cannot work well. You have read some Western textbooks on economics and learned about the advantages of competitive markets. Could you run the economy by setting up a simulated market system, even though land and capital continue to be publicly owned? How would such a system work?

First, you would leave workers free to choose jobs on the basis of relative wage rates and other advantages. The wage for each kind of labor would be set by supply and demand, just as under capitalism. Second, you would leave households free to spend their money incomes according to their preferences, and prices of consumer goods would vary with changing consumer demand. Third, you would set up free markets for raw materials, semifinished products, and capital goods; and these would be traded back and forth among producing units. Finally, you would establish government banks, from which any producing enterprise could borrow funds for expansion by paying the market rate of interest.

---

[2] See the interesting discussion in P. J. D. Wiles, *The Political Economy of Communism* (Cambridge, Mass.: Harvard University Press, 1962).

What instructions would you give the managers of the government-owned enterprises? Would you need to tell them anything at all? By looking at the prices of the factors of production, they can figure out how to minimize costs. By looking at prices for the various goods they might produce, they can choose those which are most profitable. They can set output rates according to the $P = MC$ rule. By comparing the return on their capital with the rate of interest, they can tell whether it will pay to borrow money for expansion of the enterprise. So all you really need to tell them is "Go ahead and make money." It will probably help to give the managers a share in the profit as an extra incentive. Capitalistic? Possibly. But quite sensible as a route toward static efficiency. And if you succeed in maximizing the satisfactions of the population, aren't you still being a good socialist? *Use of free markets as a device for resource allocation is not tied to any one system of property ownership.* It is quite compatible with public ownership of productive resources, and the reasons why this combination is rare are political rather than economic.

Such a system, usually termed *market socialism*, stands at the opposite pole from the command economy. It can be regarded as a form of planning, but it involves *planning through markets*, with maximum use of price indicators and incentives. By leaving decisions to individual enterprise managers, workers, and consumers, it minimizes the need for central directives and administrative staff. Its economic advantages are similar to those of pure competition under capitalism.

These ideas have been discussed a good deal in the U.S.S.R., and have been experimented with in Czechoslovakia and some of the other East European countries. The economy which comes closest to market socialism at present is Yugoslavia. Here wages in each enterprise are set by collective bargaining and market pressures. Product markets are generally free, with prices set by competition or negotiation among the enterprises concerned. Consumers express their preferences through their purchases, which guide production much as under capitalism.

Agriculture is still largely in private hands. Enterprises outside agriculture are publicly owned and are governed in principle by a Workers' Council representing employees and management. In practice, management seems to have the dominant voice, with workers exerting an influence on wages and other matters which concern them directly. Each enterprise is free to produce what it chooses and sell it to any available buyer. So enterprises in the same industry compete—indeed, Yugoslavia has an antitrust system to prevent their getting together and fixing prices! Part of an enterprise's profit may be paid in bonuses to workers and management, and part is available for reinvestment. A large part of profit, however, is paid in taxes to the local municipality and the central government.

The central government has a dominant voice in deciding how the national product shall be divided between consumption and investment, and executes its decisions through the state banking system. From the profits tax and other sources, it accumulates each year a substantial investment fund. Any enterprise wanting to expand faster than its own funds permit can apply to the state bank for a loan at the going rate of interest. The interest rate is set at a level which will equate the expected demand for funds with the available supply. So while government controls the *amount* of investment, the *allocation* of investment is determined by competition among enterprises rather than by central planning decisions. Capital flows to points in the economy at which demand is rising or new products and processes are being introduced.

State Monopoly

Centralized physical planning is such a cumbersome system that it has never been tried for long. Something like it existed in Russia during the Civil War years, 1917–21, and in China during the commune experiment of the late fifties; but in both cases the result was serious disorganization of production. The opposite pole of market socialism, while economically feasible, is suspect on political grounds. It looks too much like the "anarchy of markets" which Marxists denounce as a basic defect of capitalism. It also involves a relaxation of central political control. If enterprise managers are left free to reach their own economic decisions, what will they do next? May they not become powerful enough to stage a "managerial revolution" and threaten the control of the ruling Communist Party? So the Yugoslav system is still regarded as somewhat heretical and dangerous.

What compromises are possible between these extremes? One possibility is to leave the two ends of the market chain free and control everything in between. Let workers choose jobs freely, and let consumers spend their incomes freely. But control the production apparatus by direct administrative orders. This amounts to treating the economy as a giant enterprise, of which each producing unit is merely a branch plant controlled from above. The state becomes an all-embracing monopoly.

The control system of the U.S.S.R. is not too far from this pattern. But as we noted in Chapter 3, the production apparatus is too vast to be controllable in detail from a single point. This has led to creation of intermediate control bodies on industrial and regional lines, between the top authorities in Moscow and the individual producing units. Even these intermediate bodies can't control everything, and a certain amount of authority is left to the enterprise manager. Some of this is given to him legally, some he just takes informally to get his job done. If all the regulations to which he is subject were strictly observed, he probably could not act at all. So in the end he decides which rules to break. The interesting economic question is whether he uses his limited authority in ways which increase efficiency or reduce efficiency.

THE EFFICIENCY OF SOVIET PLANNING

At this point we narrow the discussion from central planning in general to the planning system currently used in the U.S.S.R. The institutions and practices were described in Chapter 3. We now ask how the results measure up to the tests of static efficiency. This time let us start at the factor supply end.

1. The occupational choice condition. This is well fulfilled. Workers are free to choose and change jobs at will. The most serious restriction on labor mobility is the housing shortage, which leads people to remain in jobs where they have assured housing. Financial barriers to higher education, and hence to entry into the upper occupational levels, have been largely removed. Women have unusual freedom to enter the full range of occupations. Wages and salaries are set essentially on a supply-demand basis, to call forth the amount of labor needed in each area and occupation. True, wage setting is overcentralized, and the centrally determined wage scales get out of date. But when a Soviet manager finds that he cannot get the labor he needs at the official wage, he gets around this in the same ways as a U.S. personnel manager. The worker can be put in a higher job classification than the one to which he is really entitled. Or, for pieceworkers, time standards can be set generously, so that actual earnings rise above the official hourly rate.

2. The factor supply condition. As regards labor supply, this condition is also well met. There is a chronic shortage of labor, and anyone wanting to work can readily find a job. There is the problem that existence of a standard work week makes it difficult for the individual to tailor his working hours precisely to his income-leisure preferences. It is perhaps harder in the U.S.S.R. than in the U.S.A. to get around this by "moonlighting," working overtime, or running a sideline business (this last being illegal, though not unknown).

There is a major difference between the two systems, however, in the matter of capital supply. While personal saving is encouraged in the U.S.S.R., and interest is paid on savings accounts, these savings are relatively small. Most saving is done by government, either from tax revenues or from the profits of state enterprises. The planning authorities decide how much new capital equipment shall be produced each year. A higher proportion of productive resources has been devoted to capital goods, and a smaller proportion to consumer goods, than is true in most Western countries. Soviet leaders have deliberately sacrificed the present to the future. They have restricted living standards today to make possible higher living standards, plus greater industrial and military might, tomorrow.

If one holds that the division of national output between capital goods and consumer goods should be based on individual preferences, the Soviet system is open to criticism. Soviet citizens would almost certainly have preferred to consume more in the present and make less provision for the future. Their preferences on this point have been violated.

One can also argue, however, that the present generation is naturally shortsighted, that people give too much weight to their desire for immediate consumption and too little to the welfare of their grandchildren. Is it not a legitimate function of government to offset this shortsightedness and to take a long view of the community's interest? Soviet leaders may have gone too far in this respect. But who is to say that they have, and how would one go about proving it?

3. The factor allocation condition.   It is here that we begin to have serious doubts about Soviet efficiency. In a competitive market economy, this condition is met by setting a standard price for each factor of production and letting each producer buy as much as he wants at that price. Then if each producer buys up to the point where the price of the factor equals its marginal revenue product, the marginal revenue product of the factor is equal in all uses and factors are properly allocated.

There are two main reasons why this result is not achieved in the Soviet system. The first is that land and capital have no price. In Marxian economics, labor alone is productive. There is no place for land or capital productivity and no place for interest or rental charges. How, then, are land and capital allocated? They are rationed according to planners' decisions about which lines of production should be expanded; and this may lead to sizable variations in marginal product from one use to another.

One might think there is no difficulty in the case of labor, since each grade of labor has a standard price which the enterprise must pay. But there is still the problem of equating labor's price with its marginal revenue product. Labor's marginal revenue product in a particular use depends on the product price. In a competitive market economy, one can take this price as reflecting the importance which (marginal) buyers attach to the product. It is a *scarcity price*. But in Soviet practice this is not so. *Product prices are cost-plus prices*. They are obtained by taking average unit production cost and adding the "planned profit" rate for the industry. They are supply-determined, and demand has little to do with them.

Moreover, the cost calculation itself is incomplete because of the absence of any charge for use of capital. To this extent production costs are understated, and the degree of understatement varies from industry to industry. The cost of goods requiring much capital equipment comes out relatively too low, while the cost of goods with a high labor content is relatively too high. This bias in the costing system produces a bias in the price system which interferes with correct calculation of marginal product and proper allocation of resources.

4. The least-cost condition.   For this condition to be met, the factors must be combined in such proportions that their marginal products are proportionate to their prices. Here again we encounter the difficulty that there is no interest charge on capital. But labor does have a price, and the amount an enterprise can spend on wages is controlled. This produces a tendency to substitute capital for labor wherever possible, to give preference always to the most capital-using method of production. Capital is still relatively scarcer in the U.S.S.R. than in Western capitalist countries; but because this is not reflected in the price system, it does not have its proper influence on the choice of production methods.

A notable example was the controversy over hydroelectric versus thermal plants for electric power. Hydro plants require more initial capital but have lower operating costs, and engineers in the industry were pushing them on this account. Premier Khrushchev finally intervened in favor of thermal plants on the common-sense ground that capital is scarce and has to be economized.

Actually, many of the Soviet engineers in charge of designing new plants have rediscovered the interest rate idea, and use it as a guide to decisions. Suppose one design involves spending $100,000 more on plant, but yields a saving of $10,000 a year in operating expenses. Then the extra expenditure will have been recovered in 10 years. This is usually called the *payout period* in the United States and the *period of recoupment* in the U.S.S.R.

Whether a capital good will pay for itself in 6, 8, or 10 years is often used as a test of its worthwhileness by Soviet engineers. The calculations are quite similar to those made in a capitalist business. Interest, having been chased out the front door, has come in at the rear. Use of these methods is somewhat furtive, however, and is frequently criticized by orthodox Marxists. The standard payout period used varies considerably from industry to industry, with the consequence that use of capital is pushed more intensively in some fields than in others. Greater standardization of this period throughout the economy, i.e., movement toward an equal marginal yield of capital in all uses, would improve the efficiency of production.

A second difficulty lies in the area of managerial incentives and performance. In reasoning about a capitalist producer we assume that he will always get maximum output from a given bundle of inputs. We justify this, first, by saying that he has an *incentive* to behave in this way, because a reduction in unit cost means an increase in profit. Moreover, under pure competition he will be *forced* to behave in this way in order to remain in production.

The manager of a Soviet enterprise has no single criterion of success. He is subject to a multiplicity of targets and directives, which are partially contradictory, and some of which are taken more seriously than others. The most important target is typically *total value of output.* But there may also be *physical output targets* for major products. On the input side, the plant is limited to a certain budget for wages and to certain quantities of equipment and raw materials. After covering these costs, the enterprise is expected to end the year with a certain "planned profit." The financial plan, however, is not taken as seriously as the output plan. The manager's bonus and promotion chances depend mainly on meeting the output targets. If he does well on the production side, but incurs excessive costs, his superiors are apt to wink at this. The heavy emphasis on sheer physical output makes for neglect of costs. Another problem, noted in Chapter 3, is that the Soviet manager has a strong incentive to conceal from his superiors how much his plant could really produce, in order to get a "soft" set of targets and earn a good bonus. Higher officials are supposed to detect such underestimates of capacity, but they can scarcely succeed completely.

The emphasis on production volume, and the cost-plus basis of pricing, work against efficiency in other ways. The economy is always overscheduled, everything is scarce, producers are always operating in a sellers' market. Where the price of an article creates no difficulty in selling it, producers don't worry much about prices, and consequently do not worry about costs. High costs can always be "covered" by adding on the planned markup. Especially in natural resource industries such as farming and mining, there is no clear basis for closing down submarginal units. Government encourages farming in poor regions by paying higher prices to farmers there, even though output might be increased by using the same labor and capital to work good land more intensively. Inefficient coal mines are kept in operation by adjusting the prices they receive to their level of unit costs, even though the same fuel equivalent could be obtained more cheaply from good mines or from other sources such as oil.

Soviet economists and planners seem to believe that long-run cost curves slope downward indefinitely, that larger production units are always more efficient. This belief in "giantism" has doubtless led to production units which are beyond optimum size, particularly in agriculture, where the difficulties of managing a large unit are especially great. Nor does it seem that the problem of efficient location of industry has been well solved. Wiles asserts that "the most important . . . criterion by far is local political pull. Plants go to areas where local officials, especially Party officials, are important or unscrupulous."[4]

So one reaches the paradoxical result that, in a country where supreme importance is attached to material production, the control structure leads to considerably less output than could be obtained from the same resources.

5. The correct output condition. Decisions on how much of each good to produce clearly are *not* guided by the $P = MC$ rule, or indeed by any sort of price-cost comparison. This would mean, in Soviet eyes, that planners were yielding to "the anarchy of the market." They assert their independence of the market by *first* deciding what is to be produced. After this is done, costs can be calculated. Then price setting follows as a rather minor operation. For everything except consumer goods, prices are set by adding a moderate markup to average unit costs. For consumer goods there is a high markup, which varies from product to product, and is designed mainly to adjust the amount bought by consumers to the amount which the authorities have decided to produce.

Consumer prices are apparently intended to be market-clearing prices. But actual prices often miss the target, occasionally on the high side (leading to unsold goods which have to be moved by installment credit, advertising, and other devices) but more often on the low side (leading to bare shelves, lines of unsatisfied customers, and under-the-counter dealing). Some prices are set deliberately below the market-clearing level. The leading case is apartment rents, which are very low, even though modern housing is still extremely scarce. Prices of private automobiles are also "too low," because output is very small and the market-clearing price would be very high. This leads to a wait of several years between deciding to buy a car and actually getting one.

Consumer preferences, then, are *not* binding on production decisions. The size of the markup needed to clear the market, or the length of the line of unsatisfied customers indicates how much consumer demand for each product is going unmet. It would be possible to use this as the main guide for production planning, and to increase production fastest in those lines where unsatisfied demand was greatest. But there is no indication that Soviet planners do this in any systematic way.

6. The consumer choice condition. Consumers have free choice of goods at the prevailing prices; and goods are distributed through retail outlets in the usual way. We have already noted, however, that prices bear no close relation to costs of production. Some products carry a high excise tax, called a "turnover tax"; others have a much lower tax. No one knows how these decisions are made. But one can surmise that they reflect partly planners' judgments of essentiality, the more essential goods carrying lower tax rates. They also reflect capacity to produce a particular item. The tax is set to produce a price at which consumers will just purchase the planned output, as explained in Chapter 5.

The result is similar to the result of monopolistic restriction, and may be illustrated by Figure 1. Take two products, A and B, which we assume to have similar demand curves and the same unit production cost OC. In a market economy, these products would be priced at OC and the same quantity of each (OQ) would be produced. In the Soviet production plan for 1967, however, the quantity of product A is set at

Production Decisions Can Distort Resource Use

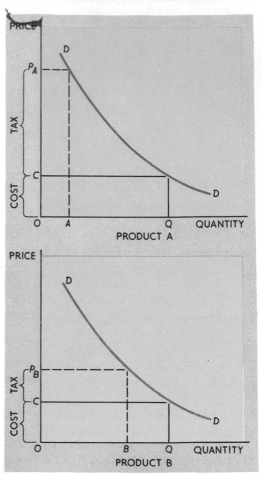

FIGURE 1. Both products have the same unit cost of production and the same demand schedule. The planners, however, decide to produce only OA of the first and OB of the second. Turnover taxes are set so that just these quantities can be sold.

OA, the quantity of B at OB. In order to clear the market, A must be priced at OP_A, which means adding a large turnover tax CP_A to production costs. Product B must be priced at OP_B, which will mean adding the lower tax rate CP_B.

This involves misallocation of resources in terms of satisfying consumer preferences. Product A is being (relatively) underproduced while Product B is (relatively) overproduced. The value which consumers place on an additional unit of A is shown by OP_A, while the value placed on the last unit of B is shown by the much lower figure OP_B. Consumer satisfaction could be increased by shifting resources from B to A, since consumers would value the extra output of A more than the amount of B which they would have to give up. How serious this misallocation is in practice we do not know, since we have no list of turnover tax rates; but it is probably a serious defect of the system.

Statistical Measures of Efficiency

Two main sources of inefficiency have been considered in this section. First, the pattern of output is not geared closely to consumer preferences. Second, the economy does not produce this pattern of output at minimum cost. The first kind of inefficiency will not show up in production statistics, where one ruble's worth of output is as good as another. But the second should show up in *productivity* statistics, in output per unit of labor and capital.

Interpreting productivity figures is a tricky business. Suppose resources were being used just as efficiently in the U.S.S.R. as in the U.S.A. Factor supplies, however, differ in the two economies. The U.S.S.R. has *relatively* more labor and less capital than the U.S.A. So one might expect that, in producing a given product, Soviet producers would use more labor and less capital per unit of output than we do. In this event, output per unit of labor would be *lower* in the U.S.S.R. than in the U.S.A., while output per unit of capital would be *higher* in the U.S.S.R.[5]

The productivity measurements do tend in this direction.[6] Output per man-hour in Soviet industry appears to average half or less of the American level. There are wide differences among industries in this respect. In some, labor productivity is about at the American level, while in others, it is less than one tenth as great. Output per unit of capital, on the other hand, is often higher in the U.S.S.R. In rail transportation and pig iron production, for example, the U.S.S.R. utilizes its capital more intensively and gets higher returns per unit of equipment. But this is not true in all industries.

The productivity gap between the two economies is widest in agriculture. Yields per acre for most major crops are less than half those in the United States; and labor requirements are much higher. It takes three times as many farm workers in the U.S.S.R. to produce the same amount of milk, five times as many to produce a given quantity of potatoes, and seven times as many to produce the same amount of grain.

---

[5] Example: Suppose the United States uses 75 men and 2 automatic coal cutters to produce 150 tons of coal a day, and suppose that the U.S.S.R. attains the same output with 150 men and 1 automatic cutter. Then labor and capital productivities would compare as follows:

	Labor Productivity (*Tons per Man*)	*Capital Productivity* (*Tons per Machine*)
U.S.A.	2	75
U.S.S.R.	1	150

[6] For a review of available evidence, see Robert W. Campbell, *Soviet Economic Power* (Boston: Houghton Mifflin Co., 1960). See also some interesting estimates in Joseph S. Berliner, "The Static Efficiency of the Soviet Economy," *American Economic Review, Proceedings,* May, 1964, pp. 480–89.

The result is to tie down in agriculture about 40 percent of the Soviet labor force, compared with our 7 or 8 percent. One reason is the lower level of mechanization in Soviet agriculture—only one fifth as many trucks and tractors, only one quarter as much electric power as on American farms. There has also been less use of fertilizers and other inputs. These differences can gradually be overcome. But one wonders whether giant farm units using wage labor can ever achieve the efficiency level of the (largely) owner-operated, family-size forms in the United States.

When one adds labor and capital together to get an overall productivity measure—output per unit of total resource input—the Soviet economy seems clearly less efficient than the American economy. But how *much* less cannot be said with certainty. There are difficult statistical problems in totaling inputs and in comparing output in rubles with output in dollars. Bergson estimates that in 1960, per unit of labor and reproducible capital, the net national product of the U.S.S.R. was only 54.9 percent of that in the U.S.A.[7] But he also discusses at length the hazards of any such comparison. One must remember, too, that differences in economic organization are only one of numerous factors affecting relative productivity. The resource base of the two economies is substantially different. The labor force also is considerably different— for example, 49 percent of employed workers in the U.S.S.R. in 1960 were women, compared with only 33 percent in the United States.

A Concluding Comment

This critical account of Soviet efficiency is apt to induce a complacent "look how much better we do things" frame of mind. To put matters in perspective, let us repeat that static efficiency isn't everything. Overall appraisal of an economy must give some points for full employment of resources, on which the U.S.S.R. would rate high; and for economic security and personal income distribution, on which it would also get a good score. One must also consider the growth of output over time. Since 1950 the Soviet economy has had one of the highest growth rates in the world. Why this contrast between static and dynamic efficiency? How can an economy with so many structural defects continue to expand so rapidly? We shall return to this tantalizing puzzle in Part Four.

Part of the answer is that planning is not static. Planners can learn from past errors, and methods can be improved. There has been a definite lift in Soviet productivity since the end of the Stalin era, with its highly centralized administration, very arbitrary output targets, and reliance on terror for enforcement. One should expect further improvement of planning methods in the future.

---

[7] Abram Bergson, *The Economics of Soviet Planning* (New Haven, Conn.: Yale University Press, 1964), p. 341.

It is tempting to speculate on some of the possible lines of future improvement. They may include:

1. Greater use of electronic computers and of refined conceptual schemes to yield *consistent* physical output plans. Preparation of balances for thousands of items by hand is a slow process. It is impossible to explore a wide variety of alternatives, and to carry the calculations through enough successive approximations to reach a high degree of consistency. The speed of electronic equipment permits a more thorough searching of alternatives. A *consistent* plan will still not necessarily be an *efficient* plan, i.e., it will not necessarily meet the tests of static efficiency. But it is at least a beginning.

2. There is no reason why planners could not give increasing weight to consumer preferences in planning consumer goods output. The machinery is there, in the form of retail markets through which consumer choices can establish demand curves for each product. The main structural reform needed would be to work toward an equal tax on all consumer products. If gloves are taxed 75 percent, the same rate should be levied on shirts, stockings, tables, washing machines, and motor scooters. (Food might be exempted, as it often is under state sales taxes in the United States.) Then prices, while not *equal* to cost, would be *proportionate* to cost, which can be defended as a "second-best" basis for pricing. Consumers would still be getting less of everything than they would like, but they would feel the pinch equally across the board. Quantities produced would be guided by consumer preferences as shown in demand curves, rather than by planners' ideas about what consumers want or should be given.

Changes might also be made in retailing practices. There is chronic complaint from Soviet consumers about the monotony, poor styling, and poor quality of consumer products. Since all goods are scarce, manufacturers have the whip hand. They unload what they choose to produce on the state retail outlets, which must then unload the goods on consumers. The retailing organizations might be given more authority to bargain with manufacturers over design and quantity, and even to stop buying from factories which fail to meet reasonable standards. This would involve some idle capacity and apparent waste in the short run. But if it succeeded in breaking the mentality of a sellers' market, it could bring great advantages to consumers over a longer period.

3. The Soviet government has already gone some distance in raising farm prices and putting them on a regular commercial basis. But why not go the whole way? Why shouldn't the state trading organizations which buy food for city consumers have to depend entirely on offering sufficiently attractive prices to get the deliveries they want? And why shouldn't each collective farm be left free to plan its output so as to make most money in view of prevailing prices for various products? This would offer greater incentive for agricultural efficiency. It would also induce

each farm to specialize in products for which it has greatest natural advantage, something which has not been true of Soviet agriculture in the past. Each farm should also have more latitude than it now has to reach independent decisions on quantity and type of machinery to be purchased, use of fertilizers, crop rotation, and other problems of farm management.

4. Industrial enterprises are subject to a multiplicity of targets and controls. The manager is told in detail what to produce, and how much labor, materials, and other inputs he may use. Targets are set for unit costs, man-hour output, machine utilization, and many other things. Different targets may conflict, diverting effort into wasteful directions.

Couldn't the control system be streamlined to advantage by substituting a single criterion of success, the yearly profit of the enterprise? Tell the manager to go ahead and make money but don't try to tell him how. Leave it to him to juggle inputs so as to achieve lowest production costs and to arrange his output pattern to get greatest sales revenue. Then, assuming that product and factor prices have been set correctly, he will be making best use of the resources committed to his care. A good profit showing could be rewarded through both profit sharing and promotion.

A more drastic departure would be to allow enterprises to reach their own decisions about expansion, and to bid for the necessary funds on a competitive basis. This would be a move toward the Yugoslav pattern of market socialism, and is doubtless too unorthodox to be considered in the U.S.S.R. in the near future; but it would not be surprising to see such experiments in some of the other East European countries.

5. Greater use could be made of the interest rate concept, both in choosing production methods and in allocating investment funds among sectors of the economy. This is a major power of the central planners at present. One can scarcely expect them to sacrifice it and to substitute slavish obedience to interest yields. But they might usefully estimate the yield of capital in various fields before reaching final decisions. Then if they decide to go contrary to the interest criterion, they are at least making a deliberate rather than an ignorant choice. Over the past 20 years, the marginal yield of investment in agriculture, transportation, and housing has probably been *much* higher than in other fields. And it is interesting that housing and agriculture, at least, have recently been getting heavier emphasis.

It has been said that nature imitates art. Similarly, events have a way of catching up with ideas. The reforms suggested above were discussed in the first edition of this book and have been widely discussed by other economists, Eastern and Western. As this edition goes to press, the following things have happened: several hundred enterprises producing consumer goods in the Moscow and Leningrad regions have been given permission to produce on the basis of orders from retail outlets.

They can determine their own production pattern, and deal directly with retailers on matters of design, quality, and price. Overall profit showing, rather than physical output targets, has been accepted as the key criterion of enterprise success. Assuming that the new system operates well, it seems likely to be extended to other branches of industry and other parts of the country. It is significant also that authority over pricing throughout the U.S.S.R. has been transferred to a new high-level agency, and the whole system of product pricing is apparently going to be reconsidered at a fundamental level.[8]

To balance the picture, one should add that the market economy of the United States is also susceptible of improvement and is in fact being improved over the course of time. Some product and factor markets are becoming more effectively competitive, barriers to free occupational choice are being lowered, progress is being made in economic analysis of public services, business cycle fluctuations are being reduced, income distribution is being reshaped, and the poverty problem is diminishing. These lines of improvement will be explored at length in Parts Two and Three. The market economies of the United States and other Western countries are certainly engaged in a quiet, long-run competition with the planned economies which will go on for decades or generations. Which type of economy will improve its performance most rapidly, whether the gap in performance (thus far favorable to the West) will widen or diminish, is perhaps the leading politico-economic issue of our time.

SUMMARY

1. An economy has reached a position of *static efficiency* when, with the available resources and technology, it is impossible to make any individual better off without making someone else worse off. Such a position is often called a *Pareto optimum*.

---

[8] A New York *Times* news report of August 29, 1965, reads in part as follows:

"The Soviet government Saturday announced the establishment of a high level agency for the administration of prices in the national economy. The move was regarded as a key element in the steady drive toward economic reform based on the profit motive. . . .

"The creation of the price agency follows publication of articles in the Soviet press in which leading economists pointed out that radical changes in the Soviet price structure would be essential if the profit motive, as a basis for Soviet planning and production, was to be a success.

"Now that a decision evidently has been made to introduce self-regulating levers like supply and demand into the once rigidly planned Soviet economy, economists contended, a thorough overhauling of the price system is essential to make the proposed reforms meaningful.

"In contrast to the western type of market economy, where prices are an independent force determining production, resource allocation and consumption, prices in the Soviet economy have been manipulated by central authorities as one of the instruments intended to accomplish planned goals.

"The problem for Soviet planners now is to devise a system that will enable them to retain enough control to insure fulfillment of national goals, and yet allow enough flexibility to promote more efficient workings of a market mechanism."

2. There are several basic conditions for static efficiency. Review these and make sure that you understand them.

3. If all markets in an economy are purely competitive, it can be shown that the efficiency conditions will be realized.

4. This does not mean, however, that actual market economies such as that of the United States are ideally efficient. Actual product and factor markets contain numerous imperfections. And there are important economic problems which the market mechanism may not solve satisfactorily. These include *full employment of resources,* the *desirable rate of economic growth,* the *proper level of public services,* and the *desirable distribution of income.*

5. Government action to create and improve markets, and to resolve issues which the market mechanism does not resolve, is quite consistent with a general commitment to a market economy.

6. There are several logical variants of economic planning: the *command economy,* involving centralized physical controls over all aspects of economic life; *market socialism,* a decentralized system making maximum use of prices and markets; and *state monopoly,* an intermediate system which has been dominant in the U.S.S.R. and most of the other socialist countries.

7. The Soviet economy meets some of the static efficiency conditions quite well but does less well on others. The pattern of output is not geared closely to consumer preferences; factors are not efficiently combined because of failure to count interest and rent as costs and because of other oddities of the pricing system; and the system of control over individual enterprises does not provide a strong incentive to minimize costs.

8. Productivity statistics suggest that the static efficiency of the Soviet economy is substantially below that of the American economy. An overall evaluation, however, would have to take account of growth rate, employment of resources, income distribution, and other relevant considerations.

9. The efficiency of the Soviet economy could be improved by taking more systematic account of consumer preferences, giving greater freedom of decision to enterprise and collective farm managers, substituting overall profit incentives for detailed physical controls, using the interest-rate concept effectively, and revising the pricing system to help accomplish these objectives. There are already indications of considerable progress along these lines.

DISCUSSION QUESTIONS

1. "The idea of a purely competitive, perfectly efficient economy is really utopian. Actual market economies depart so widely from this model that it has little value as a yardstick." Discuss.

2. What are the most serious shortcomings of the American economy from the standpoint of static efficiency?

3. Some proponents of the market economy argue that it can provide solutions for all economic problems of any consequence; and that government, apart from providing a few essential public services, should rely on private initiative. Criticize or defend this point of view, as you prefer.

4. Try to sort out the economic activities of our federal government into two groups:
   a) Those which are a necessary supplement to the market economy.
   b) Those which can be regarded as in conflict with the market economy, and which may reduce economic efficiency.

5. "Centralized planning of a complex economy has proved unworkable again and again. Faced with this fact, planners always try to limit their task by leaving some decisions to individuals throughout the economy." Discuss.

6. What are the main deficiencies of Soviet economic planning, from the standpoint of static efficiency?

7. "One may grant that, in terms of static efficiency, the Soviet economy is outclassed by the best of the market economies. But the Soviet economy has advantages on other fronts—continuous full employment, a high growth rate, an equitable distribution of income, real equality of economic opportunity. Overall, one can argue that it performs at least as well as the leading capitalist economies." Discuss.

8. You are a Russian economist, and have been appointed chairman of a top-level committee to recommend improvements in the Soviet planning system. What are the main issues to which you would draw attention in your report?

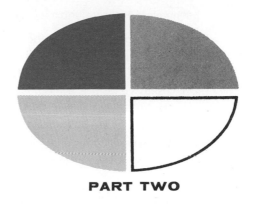

GOVERNMENT AND THE

MARKET ECONOMY

Every boy and every gel
That's born into this world alive
Is either a little Liberal
Or else a little Conservative.

W. S. GILBERT

When we reflect how difficult it is to move
or deflect the great machine of society, how impossible to advance the notions of a whole people
suddenly to ideal right, we see the wisdom of
Solon's remark, that no more good must be attempted than the nation can bear.

THOMAS JEFFERSON

ONE CAN construct on paper a purely private economy, watched over
by a caretaker state; but no one has ever actually seen such an
economy. In all capitalist countries, government performs important
economic functions, and these functions have been gradually increasing. This has led to acrimonious political debate. To some, government
is a beneficent instrument for promoting the general welfare. To others,
government action spells creeping socialism and suppression of private
initiative.

While most economic activities of modern governments seem legitimate in principle, this leaves wide room for debate. Is the scale of a particular program too large or too small? Is it well designed to achieve the objectives at which it is aimed? Are there new lines of activity that government might usefully pursue? These economic issues are the core of modern politics. In Part Two we run the gamut of the issues and ask what we can learn by applying economic analysis to them. The sequence of discussion is as follows:

1. We can all agree that competition is a fine thing. But how competitive is the American economy in practice? Is the trend toward freer competition or toward greater concentration of market power? What is government now doing, and what more can it do, to enforce competitive behavior? (Chapter 13.)

2. In some sectors of the economy, competition has deliberately been limited or abandoned. Public utilities are unavoidably monopolistic, and their prices are regulated by government commissions. About half of agricultural production is covered by guaranteed minimum prices, accompanied in some cases by production controls. Retail competition in some products has been significantly restricted by resale price maintenance laws. What is the effect of these policies, and to what extent should they be continued? (Chapter 14.)

3. Turning to factor markets, we consider first the supply and pricing of labor. What do trade unions try to get from employers and how do they go about it? How does collective bargaining affect wage rates, labor supply, hours of work, and labor productivity? Does an overall evaluation of unionism indicate benefit or harm to the economy? What can be done to reduce the likelihood of crippling strikes, particularly in industries whose continuous operation is important to public safety and convenience? (Chapter 15.)

4. Inequality in personal income distribution is sometimes considered a shortcoming of a competitive economy. How unequal is income distribution in the United States, and is inequality increasing or decreasing over the course of time? How far should leveling of personal incomes be a deliberate object of government policy? What is the effect of taxes and transfer payments on income distribution at present? (Chapter 16.)

5. After examining the organization of private production, we turn to the public economy. How much is presently spent on providing public services? Do we have too much of these services or too little? We

usually cannot apply the test of price = marginal cost. Is there anything which can be put in its place? What kinds of tax are levied to cover the cost of public services? Who pays each type of tax, and how does this add up for the revenue system as a whole? It turns out that the overall tax burden is unevenly distributed, by income level and by region of the country. Is the present distribution of the burden desirable and, if not, what changes can be suggested? (Chapter 17.)

6. Thus far the discussion has been confined to a single country. What about competition across national boundaries? What determines the products a country exports and imports? If free competition within a country has desirable effects, can the same be said of free international trade? Is there any justification for protective tariffs and other types of trade restriction? (Chapter 18.)

Part Two, in sum, covers the *microeconomic* issues of government policy, applying to them the analytical tools developed in Part One. *Macroeconomic* problems of monetary control, fiscal policy, and other policies to promote economic stability and growth are left to a later stage, since they require concepts that will not be developed until Part Three.

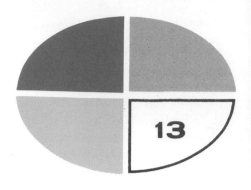

Promoting Competition

Monopolies are odious, contrary to the
spirit of free government and the principles of
commerce, and ought not to be suffered.
MARYLAND DECLARATION OF 1776

THE MAIN TRADITION of economic thought in the United States favors
competitive private enterprise. But is competitive enterprise a feasible
objective? It is often argued that there is so little competition left in the
American economy that we cannot rely on it as an organizing principle.
So we must begin by inquiring whether this is true. How competitive is
the American economy? Is the trend toward freer competition or the
reverse? Will efforts to preserve competition be frustrated by the march of
history?

THE IMPORTANCE OF MARKET POWER

It would be nice if one could toss industries into boxes labeled
"monopoly," "oligopoly," and "atomistic competition." One difficulty with
this is that oligopoly is a matter of degree. Oligopoly can mean that three
companies produce all the industry's output. But it can also mean that
there are 20 important producers plus a fringe of smaller competitors.
The price-output results will probably be closer to those of atomistic
competition in the 20-company case than in the 3-company case. Where
does "strong oligopoly" leave off and "weak oligopoly" begin?

One can learn something, however, by looking at the proportion of
a market which is occupied by a few producers. The situation in

manufacturing is suggested by Table 1. In one third of all manufacturing industries, producing one quarter of manufacturing output, the four leading companies turned out half or more of the industry output. These are situations of strong oligopoly. At the opposite extreme, another third of the industries, producing 40 percent of manufacturing output, had less than 25 percent of their output controlled by the four leading companies. These are situations of weak oligopoly or atomistic competition. A middle third of industries had between 25 and 50 percent of their output controlled by the top four companies. It must be emphasized, however, that the operation of an industry depends on relations among the leading companies, on the number of smaller companies, and on the ease with which new companies can enter the industry. Two industries with the same percentage of output controlled by the top four companies may show quite different economic behavior.

TABLE 1

Industrial Concentration in Manufacturing, 1954

PERCENT OF INDUSTRY SHIPMENTS SUPPLIED BY THE LARGEST FOUR FIRMS	NUMBER OF INDUSTRIES	PERCENT OF INDUSTRIES	PERCENT OF ALL MANUFACTURING SHIPMENTS
75–100	40	9.2	8
50– 75	101	23.3	17
25– 50	157	36.2	35
0– 25	136	31.3	40
	434	100.0	100.0

Source: Joe Bain, *Industrial Organization* (New York: John Wiley & Sons, Inc., 1959), p. 120.

Turning to other sectors of the economy, *public utilities* are typically monopolies subject to public regulation of prices and service. This sector includes electric power, gas and water supply, local street transportation, and telephone and telegraph service. Freight and passenger *transportation* typically shows a high degree of seller concentration. The number of railroads, truck or bus companies, and airlines serving the same route is usually small. Radio and television broadcasting, motion picture production, and magazine and newspaper publishing are also highly concentrated industries.

The situation in *mining* is variable. Metallic mining, including iron, copper, aluminum, lead, and zinc, usually shows high concentration. Stone, sand, clay, and gravel have numerous small producers. Bituminous coal is marked by atomistic competition, and so is crude petroleum production except for output controls imposed by legislatures.

Agriculture is atomistically competitive in the sense that there are millions of producers, none of whom supplies a significant part of total output. Within the last generation, the working of competition has been modified by government control legislation. But about half of farm output continues uncontrolled, and even where controls exist, farmers react to them in atomistic fashion. The *forestry* and *fishery* industries show a low degree of concentration.

The situation in *retail distribution* varies with the size of the city, large cities having more sellers of a particular product than small towns. It varies also with the type of retailing. There are more groceries and clothing stores than there are building material dealers, new-car dealers, or fluid milk distributors. On the whole, retailing is less concentrated than manufacturing, and something approaching atomistic competition is quite frequent.

Local *service* industries present a similarly diversified picture. They range from moderately high concentration in some lines (hotels, motion pictures) to something close to atomistic competition in laundry and dry cleaning, household service, and other areas. In general, this group of industries lies toward the atomistic pole.

The construction industry is really a group of related industries. For commercial and industrial buildings, apartment houses, highways, and other large projects, there are usually only a few companies in each area. The number of house builders is much larger, and they compete in essentially atomistic fashion. The same is true of the subcontractors who do painting, plumbing, electrical, and other types of building work.

How does this add up for the economy as a whole? The highest degree of seller concentration is found in public utilities, transportation, communications, metal mining, large contract construction, and heavy manufacturing. At the other pole, conditions approaching atomistic competition are found in agriculture, forestry, and fisheries; house building and subcontracting; coal mining and nonmetallic mining; most of the service industries; and a large proportion of retail markets. In between one finds every possible shading of weak, moderate, and strong oligopoly. At a rough estimate, one might say that two thirds of private output in the United States is produced under conditions of reasonably effective competition, while one third is produced under severe restrictions on competition.

TRENDS IN INDUSTRIAL CONCENTRATION

In addition to looking at the current situation, one must consider long-run tendencies. Has industrial concentration been increasing or decreasing? Does this provide any clue to what may be expected in the decades ahead?

In any economy one finds forces working in both directions, some making for a decrease in industrial concentration, others for an increase. The outcome is not preordained, but depends on the balance of forces at a particular time; and it will be different in different lines of production. The forces making for *greater* industrial concentration include:

1. Technical developments usually increase the economies of large-scale production and hence the optimum size of producing units. The feasible number of competitors in a particular market depends partly on the optimum size of plant relative to total demand. If technical progress raises the optimum size of plant faster than demand rises, industrial concentration will tend to increase.

In manufacturing, at least, the average size of plants has been rising quite rapidly. Between 1904 and 1947, total manufacturing output rose at almost 4 percent a year. The number of manufacturing establishments, however, rose less than 1 percent a year. Thus output per establishment rose about 3 percent a year. The greater part of the rising manufacturing output came from *larger* plants rather than *more* plants. The rate of increase in plant size differs widely from industry to industry—highest in cigarettes and chemicals, lowest in meat packing and gloves. But out of 46 industries, only 1 (cordage and twine) showed a decrease in plant size over the period.[1]

2. In addition to factors increasing the most efficient size of *plant,* there may be factors increasing the most efficient size of *company.* The difficulty of managing a very large enterprise is supposed to set natural limits to the growth of companies. But modern communications systems, the growing use of computers, developments in organizational theory, and improved business education may be relaxing these limits quite rapidly. It may be as easy to manage an enterprise with 100,000 workers today as it was to manage one with 5,000 workers 50 years ago.

3. Even though efficiency is not increased, monopoly profit can be gained by merging competing companies to achieve control of prices and production. Businessmen may be expected to take advantage of such opportunities where the legal situation permits.

4. Financiers who promote the merger of competing concerns can also make substantial profits. How? Simple enough. Buy up the old companies for $300 million and sell $400 million worth of stock in the new merged company to the general public. This then leaves $100 million for company officials, investment bankers, lawyers, and other insiders. This was a big factor in the growth of the early railroad empires, the many manufacturing mergers in the period 1880–1910, and the mushrooming of public utility holding companies in the 1920's. Controls over stock flotation are tighter now than they were before 1929, but there is still plenty of money to be made from arranging mergers.

5. The increasingly expensive advertising of branded products makes it harder than it used to be for a new company to break into an

---

[1] Saul S. Sands, "Changes in Scale of Production in United States Manufacturing Industry, 1904–1947," *Review of Economics and Statistics,* November, 1961, pp. 365–68.

industry. The new venture must be backed by a large advertising budget; and if the effort to penetrate the market fails, this money will be lost. A well-established concern is in a better position to take such a gamble than a new enterprise, and even so it may not succeed. The Ford Motor Company is reported to have spent $350 million in developing and promoting the Edsel car, which failed to win market acceptance and was discontinued after a short time.

What forces are working in the opposite direction to reduce industrial concentration?

1. The markets for most products have grown through general economic expansion. If the total output of an industry is growing, industrial concentration will decline unless the leading companies grow at least as rapidly. One might expect that established companies, having an inside track, would at least keep pace with the growth of total demand. But there are some cases in which they have not. In a number of the famous early "trusts"—steel, tobacco, oil refining, aluminum, farm machinery—the proportion of output controlled by the leading companies today is considerably smaller than it was 50 years ago.

2. Transportation has improved and become cheaper. Where transportation is expensive, local producers are sheltered from the competition of those in other localities. In the early nineteenth century, the local grist mill, sawmill, cobbler, and so on had a monopoly in their immediate area. The railroad brought products of one area into competition with those of another, and gradually created regional or national markets for most consumer goods. The automobile has had a similar effect as regards retailing and service industries. When one can jump into one's car and shop anywhere in a 20-mile radius, the number of dealers who are in competition with each other is much greater than if one had to go about on foot or by streetcar.

3. While we think of technical change as making for larger production units, this is not always true. Improvements in electric transmission and the development of portable generating units, for example, have made it possible to set up groups of power-driven machines almost anywhere. No longer must the textile mill be built near a waterfall and built large enough to take full advantage of the power installation. The mill may now be built almost anywhere and may be larger or smaller without much difference in operating efficiency.

4. The rapid pace of technical progress in recent decades has also increased competition *across industry lines.* An established product may find itself undercut and eliminated by a development in another area of the economy. With the discovery of synthetic yarns, chemical companies found themselves in the textile business. Television sets undercut motion pictures. There is a growing tendency for companies well established in one industry to spread out in other directions, increasing the severity of competition in the areas which they enter.

5. The growth of large *buyers* in many markets, while it does not reduce the concentration of sellers, does offset and reduce their market power. The outstanding example is the rise of the large retail chains and their price struggles with the manufacturers.

6. Government policy can cut in either direction. A lowering of tariff barriers exposes domestic producers to more severe competition from producers abroad, and this has been the tendency in the United States since the mid-thirties. But tariffs can also be raised, with restrictive effects on competition. Vigorous antitrust enforcement can reduce industrial concentration, while lax enforcement will work in the opposite direction. Government can restrict competition by regulating farm prices, crude oil production, or other matters; or it can decline to intervene in these ways.

These conflicting tendencies will balance out differently in different industries. One will find sellers' market power increasing in some sectors of the economy while at the same time it is decreasing in others. In adding things up for the economy as a whole, there is a further complication, the changing importance or *weight* of various sectors. Agriculture is a much smaller part of the American economy than it was a hundred years ago. Transportation, communications, and public utilities are relatively larger. Such changes alter the mix of monopoly and competition in the economy, apart from what is happening *within* each sector.

How have things worked out in the United States over the past century? It is a safe guess that the American economy in 1870 was more atomistic than it has been at any time since. Agriculture was still the dominant industry. Manufacturing produced only 16 percent of total output, and most production was on a small scale. Big business meant the railroads and not much else.

Between this time and 1905, there was a significant increase in industrial concentration. The main development was a massive merger movement in manufacturing, which at the same time became a more prominent part of the total economy. Between 1880 and 1904, there were over 300 major industrial combinations. These absorbed about 5,200 separate plants, and by the close of the period controlled about 40 percent of the manufacturing capital of the country. Among these combinations, 78 controlled 50 percent or more of the output of their industries. Market domination by a single large company reached an all-time high in manufacturing around 1905, from which it has since receded somewhat.

Between 1905 and 1935, the most important development was the growing importance of the public utility sector and the combination of utilities into giant holding companies. There was also increased concentration in retail distribution. In 1905, there were only two major grocery chains controlling about 2 percent of national sales. By 1935 the five largest chains controlled one quarter of grocery sales. Similar trends were evident in other retail fields. But the growth of large retailers may well have intensified competition in retail markets. It serves also to offset manufacturers' market power and can produce a lower level of manufacturers' prices and profits.

Within the manufacturing sector, there was little change in concentration between 1905 and 1935. In some new industries, such as automobiles and tires, concentration increased as producers were weeded out through bankruptcy. In older industries, on the other hand, concentration tended to decline from the peak reached at the end of the merger movement. Increased vigor of antitrust enforcement after 1910 may have been partly responsible.

It is noteworthy that there has been no tendency toward further increase of industrial concentration since about 1935. Concentration in the utility sector has declined through the growth of smaller companies and the breaking up of the largest holding companies under federal legislation passed in the New Deal period. There has been no significant trend one way or the other in manufacturing and other sectors. In manufacturing, the growth of large companies plus occasional mergers has been offset by the enormous expansion of the total national market over the past 30 years. The atomistic agricultural sector has continued to decline in relative importance. But the retailing and service industries, which also tend in an atomistic direction, have increased in importance. Thus the economy seems for the time being to have settled down on a plateau, with little movement in either a competitive or monopolistic direction. The 200 largest nonfinancial corporations, which owned more than half of all corporate assets in 1935, held a somewhat smaller percentage in 1955.

We can conclude that there is no convincing evidence of an inevitable decline of competition. Any tendency in this direction over the past century has been gradual and intermittent, and there have been strong forces working in the opposite direction. There is no firm basis for asserting that efforts to strengthen the forces of competition in the economy are foredoomed to failure.

The general desirability of competition, and the unlawfulness of efforts to restrict it, were laid down in the Sherman Act of 1890 and the Clayton Act and the Federal Trade Commission Act of 1914. These statutes, usually termed "the antitrust laws," remain the cornerstone of our policy concerning competitive markets. To explain their meaning and practical effect is the main purpose of this chapter.

THE LAW AGAINST COLLUSIVE AGREEMENTS

Section 1 of the Sherman Act provides that "every contract, combination . . . or conspiracy, in restraint of trade or commerce among the several States, or with foreign nations, is hereby declared to be illegal."

How has the Supreme Court interpreted and applied this provision over the years since 1890? Some things are clear. A direct agreement on prices among rival sellers (or buyers) is illegal. So is any agreement which would have the effect of raising prices or reducing output. An agreement that each company in an industry will produce only so much per month, or that no one will build new productive capacity, or that existing capacity will be shut down or destroyed, would be illegal. The law also bans any agreement to share the total market by allocating customers or territories or by each company accepting a fixed percentage of total industry output.

It is important to note that *existence* of a collusive agreement is illegal, regardless of the economic consequences. The courts have assumed that the effects will be harmful. The Justice Department does not have to prove that prices have actually been raised or that profits are exorbitant. Nor will it do the industry any good to argue that the market power secured by the agreement has been used in a responsible manner. The existence of such market power is itself unlawful.

As one goes beyond simple price or output agreements, one gets into more doubtful territory. Industry-wide trade associations, perfectly legal in themselves, often carry on activities which verge on restriction of competition. These activities include:

1. Promotion of uniform accounting methods for calculating production costs. From this it is a short step to try to ensure that the costs of different companies will come out at about the same level, and from this to adding on a "reasonable" profit margin. This could lead to a standard price schedule which all companies would be urged to observe under penalty of being considered "uncooperative" or "unethical." To go this far would doubtless be illegal, but one can stop a step or two short and leave people to draw their own conclusions.

2. Price-filing or bid-filing systems, under which members send the association full information on new prices. Building contractors in an area may agree to file with the secretary of the association their proposed bids on a particular contract. This makes it possible to put pressure on low bidders to come up to the general level. The group may even agree that a certain contract shall go to a particular company, in which case other contractors will be instructed to file higher bids. In a manufacturers' association, each company may agree to give 30 days' advance notice of a price change. If a company proposes a price cut which would be unwelcome to its colleagues, the association secretary has 30 days in which to talk the company out of it.

3. Preparation of statistics on production, inventories, sales, and future demand. One association, for example, sent its members each month an estimate of prospective demand for the industry's product in

the following month. Each company president had in his desk drawer a figure showing his company's "normal" percentage of the industry's output. Multiplying this percentage by the association total gave him his production schedule for the month. This simple device succeeded in controlling total industry output, sharing it among the member companies on an agreed basis, and protecting prices at a profitable level. There was never any *direct* price agreement, but the arrangement was nevertheless attacked by the Justice Department and was discontinued.

Strong oligopoly poses difficult problems. Suppose three or four companies control three quarters of an industry's output. Once these companies get used to each other's way of doing business, they need scarcely talk to each other to maintain effective control of prices. If they do talk to each other, no one is going to know about it. Discussions will be on the telephone or over the luncheon table, with no records kept and no evidence of agreement. Price leadership can be used to announce price changes, other companies simply following any move by the leader. The antitrust sleuth finds it hard to pick up the trail of such arrangements. Even if he does, what kind of court order can he secure? Can members of an industry be forbidden to speak to each other socially? Can companies be forbidden to sell at the same price?

The crime defined by the Sherman Act is one of "conspiracy," and the courts have been reluctant to act unless collusion can be proved. At the same time, they have been worried by oligopoly situations and the ease with which prices can be manipulated under them. There has been some tendency to move in the direction of holding that "conscious parallelism of action" is an offense under the law, even when agreement cannot be proved. Simple price leadership will normally not be held unlawful. But if the companies also maintain an elaborate similarity of policy on other terms of sale such as quantity discounts, price differentials between various qualities and types of produce, and freight charges or delivered price arrangements, the courts may find a breach of the law. It is unlikely that "all that much parallelism" could occur without intimate cooperation among the companies.

What can be done about a proven case of illegal price fixing? The Antitrust Division of the Department of Justice, which has main responsibility for prosecuting these cases, can use either or both of two procedures. First, it can file a criminal action under which the companies and the executives responsible, if convicted, are liable to fines of not more than $50,000 and imprisonment for not more than one year. This is not as forbidding as it may sound. The respectable business executives who appear in these cases do not look like criminals, and juries have been reluctant to convict them on criminal charges. But the potential effectiveness of criminal procedures should not be written off. In 1961 several high officials of the major electrical manufacturing companies were fined and sent to jail for agreeing to fix prices of heavy electrical equipment.

The companies, in addition to fines, had to pay large damages to the government agencies and private utilities to whom they had sold this equipment. They suffered damaging publicity, and were ordered to desist from price agreement in the future.

The other possibility is a civil suit, which may be filed alone or along with a criminal action. If the defendants are found guilty in a civil suit, the judge normally issues an *injunction,* a "don't do it again" kind of order, forbidding continuation of the unlawful practices. If the companies violate the injunction, they can be fined for contempt of court. This achieves much the same result as a criminal suit but without the stigma of a criminal conviction.

How much effect has the prohibition of collusive agreements had on the American economy? The law has certainly checked the development of the industrial cartels which flourish in many other countries. In view of the acknowledged deadening effect of cartels on competition and efficiency, this is an important accomplishment. In addition, the law has doubtless reduced the number of price-fixing agreements and understandings. It has not entirely eliminated them; but the possibility of prosecution has a restraining effect, just as every speeder does not have to be picked up to discourage speeding. The most serious loophole in the law is the difficulty of detecting friendly cooperation among large oligopolists.

An incidental and unintended effect of the law has been to stimulate outright merger of competing companies. Competition among rival concerns can be restricted either through agreement or by absorbing the rival concerns into a larger company. While the Sherman Act made agreement illegal, mergers were more loosely controlled, and the urge to suppress competition was thus diverted in the latter direction. The campaign against collusion intensified the problem of monopoly. This leads us to the second main facet of the antitrust laws.

THE LAW AGAINST MONOPOLIZING

Section 2 of the Sherman Act states that "every person who shall monopolize, or attempt to monopolize, or combine or conspire . . . to monopolize any part of the trade or commerce among the several states, or with foreign nations, shall be deemed guilty of a misdemeanor. . . ." The primary thrust of this section is against *exclusion* of competitors from an industry. The Clayton Act goes further in listing specific exclusionary practices:

1. A common device of the early "trusts" was predatory price cutting. A new competitor would be greeted by severe price cuts in his area of operation, the trust's losses on these sales being made up by its profits in other areas. The competing concern could thus be driven into bankruptcy and forced to sell out or come to terms with the trust. Section

2 of the Clayton Act, which prohibits price discrimination where the effect may be to lessen competition, was intended to strike at this practice.

2. Another early device was the "tying contract," under which the buyer of company A's product agreed not to buy from any competing company. If company A was the dominant producer, and buyers had to be sure of getting its products, they might be forced into tying contracts which effectively prevented any new producer from gaining a foothold. Such contracts are forbidden by Section 3 of the Clayton Act.

3. Section 7 of the Clayton Act, as amended and strengthened in 1950, prohibits mergers where the effect "may be substantially to lessen competition, or to tend to create a monopoly."

What does the law mean? The offense under the Sherman Act is *monopolizing*, rather than a *monopoly*—a kind of activity, rather than a state of being. One element of the offense is clear. There must be either a single company or a small group of companies occupying a predominant position in a particular market, a position such that one can make a case that competitors have been eliminated or potential competitors prevented from entering. How large a share of the market must the monopolist or the oligopoly group occupy in order to become suspect? The courts have never been willing to say, but some clues can be drawn from past decisions. A company occupying 90 percent of a market, as Alcoa did in the aluminum ingot market at the time of the antitrust suit against it in 1945, is certainly vulnerable. A few companies occupying two thirds or more of a market would probably be subject to attack. If the share held by the top four or five companies fell below 50 percent, antitrust prosecution would probably not be successful. There can be a good deal of market power in the economic sense without monopolization in the judicial sense.

Given concentration of an industry in a few hands, there are at least three standards which might be used to determine whether there has been an offense against the Sherman Act:

1. On the most lenient interpretation, the monopolist or oligopoly group would have to be found guilty of deliberately and effectively excluding competitors from the industry. Further, the methods used would have to go beyond the bounds of ethical business practice, to the point where they might be regarded as predatory and unfair.

2. On a stricter interpretation, exclusion of competitors even by normal and legitimate business methods might be considered unlawful. Thus a company or group of companies which always expanded ahead of demand, leaving no possible loophole for new rivals, or which bought up all available sources of raw material for a product, or cornered all available patents, or put other obstacles in the way of potential producers, might be found guilty.

3. The above interpretations rest on the *conduct* of the parties. A more severe interpretation would rest on the *structure* of the market, and would make mere possession of undue market power unlawful, regardless of how it had been acquired or maintained. This would go in the direction of forbidding *monopoly* in the economic sense—a state of affairs, without reference to specific actions which might be construed as monopolization.

For many years the courts held mainly to the first interpretation. The oil and tobacco trusts were dissolved by the courts, not just because they were big, but because they had used unfair tactics against competitors. A group which could keep out competition by gentlemanly methods was safe. The dictum that "mere size is no offense" was frequently reiterated. The government failed to win a conviction in the steel case of 1920, even though U.S. Steel alone produced half of the nation's basic steel at this time and the top eight companies produced about 70 percent.

Since the New Deal period, however, antitrust enforcement has been more vigorous and the tone of judicial opinion has shifted. Court decisions have veered toward the second interpretation above: exclusion of competitors by a group which has "too much" of the market is unlawful, even if it is accomplished by fair and normal business methods. The Supreme Court has not yet been willing, however, to go all the way to the third interpretation that mere possession of undue market power is unlawful. It came almost to this point in the Aluminum Company decision of 1945, which involved a long-standing case of market power; but since then the Court seems to have drawn back from this advanced position.

STRONG OLIGOPOLY: THE "TOUGH NUT" FOR ANTITRUST

It remains doubtful, therefore, whether one can get at gentlemanly and well-behaved oligopoly under the present antitrust laws. What to do about steel, copper, aluminum, oil refining, automobiles, heavy machinery, electrical equipment, cigarettes, and the rest? Parallel action is achieved without overt agreement, so that it is difficult to invoke the ban on collusion. Exclusion of competitors is so discreet—indeed, usually requires no positive action because of the heavy costs of entry in these industries—that the courts hesitate to support a finding of monopolization. There is considerable agreement that uncontrolled market power in these industries can have harmful effects. There is little agreement as to what, if anything, might be done about it.

Some students of the problem have suggested a legal limit on the size of companies. This could be either an absolute limit on size of assets or number of employees, or a provision that no company may supply more than a specified percentage of output in a particular market. The feasibility of such proposals is doubtful. A uniform limit on absolute size would be meaninglessly high for small-scale industries but might be unduly restrictive where large-scale plants are essential. A 25 percent share of a particular market might be innocuous under some circumstances, quite dangerous in others. Most companies, too, make a variety of products. Which one would be used in testing whether a company's market share is too large? Exercise of judgment on such points would be necessary no matter how the law might be written.

Most experts, therefore, favor continuation of a case-by-case approach under the Sherman Act, involving examination of each industry on its merits. The most powerful remedy available under the Sherman Act is dissolution, the breaking up of a company into several smaller companies. The remedy has been employed sparingly, the courts being almost as reluctant to impose capital punishment on a corporation as on an individual. The old Standard Oil and American Tobacco trusts were divided in 1911 into a number of successor companies, and a few other dissolutions decrees have been issued since that time. If it were desired to use this device for a real drive on oligopoly, it might be necessary to amend and clarify this portion of the Sherman Act. Two leading authorities have suggested[2] that Section 2 of the Act be amended so that (a) "unreasonable market power" would itself be made unlawful, with no need to prove nefarious conduct by the companies concerned; (b) the courts would be instructed to dissolve the companies, provided no lesser remedy appeared adequate and provided that dissolution would not unduly reduce efficiency.

There are two main types of dissolution procedure: (1) *horizontal* dissolution, under which a company owning several plants producing the same kind of product is ordered to dissolve and set up several smaller companies; and (2) *vertical* dissolution, in which a company controlling successive stages of a production cycle—say, everything from mining bauxite ore to producing aluminum pots and pans—is required to get out of some of these stages.

Horizontal Dissolution

Horizontal dissolution was applied in the early oil and tobacco cases. It clearly could be applied to many of the present highly concentrated industries if this seemed expedient. The 3 major cigarette producers could be divided into 10 or more companies, since each has several plants. The basic steel producing operations of U.S. Steel could

---

[2] Carl Kaysen and Donald F. Turner, *Antitrust Policy, A Legal and Economic Analysis* (Cambridge, Mass.: Harvard University Press, 1959). Professor Joe Bain has added the weight of his authority to this suggestion in *Industrial Organization* (New York: John Wiley & Sons, Inc., 1959), pp. 608–9.

be divided into at least three clusters, centered on Pittsburgh, Gary, and Birmingham. Altogether, one could probably make 20 or more efficient-sized steel companies out of the present half-dozen leading producers. In the window glass industry, there are only 4 companies but about 20 plants, which could form the basis of separate companies. American Can, which produces more than half of all tin cans in the country, has about 60 plants, which could be reorganized into a number of new companies. These illustrations are not intended as advocacy, but simply to suggest technical possibilities.

Wouldn't breaking up large corporations in this way reduce industrial efficiency? This involves our earlier distinction between the efficiency of large *plants* and the efficiency of adding similar plants together into a large *company*. The first question is not involved here, since no one proposes to dismember individual plants; but it is worth noting that the efficiency of mammoth plant units is often exaggerated. In most manufacturing industries, the optimum scale of plant is small enough relative to the size of the market so that the industry could accommodate at least 10 to 20 efficient-sized plants, and often many more than this. In a study of 20 manufacturing industries, Bain found only 2 (automobiles and typewriters) which had what he termed "very important" economies of plant size, i.e., the optimum plant size exceeded 10 percent of market capacity, and unit costs would be raised by 5 percent or more at half this size.[3] On the basis of one plant per company, then, one could usually get enough companies to produce reasonably effective competition.

But are there not important gains in efficiency from having a number of plants organized under common management? One must distinguish between bargaining advantages and genuine economies. A giant corporation may be able to drive a harder bargain with material suppliers, bankers, and others from whom it buys; and it can often manipulate product prices to advantage. But these are not gains from the standpoint of the economy as a whole. Genuine economies would have to come mainly from the following sources:

1. A large company may be able to hire unusually capable managers, who then have a chance to use their talents over a wide range of production. Against this must be set the possibility that large-scale organization may lead to excessive paper work and red tape, delayed decisions, internal intrigue, and other types of bureaucratic inefficiency.

2. Selling costs per unit may be reduced by being spread over a large volume of output, even though production costs are no lower.

3. In industries which rest on complicated scientific techniques large-scale organization of research and development may produce better results than could be obtained from a number of smaller laboratories.

---

[3] *Op. cit.*, p. 348.

This is not certain, however, and there is no reason why a large research organization must be supported and accompanied by a giant production organization. Government agencies, universities, trade associations, private consulting laboratories, and other groups are active in the research field and provide possible alternatives to the one-company research center.

The extent to which there are genuine economies from multiplant organization is unclear. Bain obtained estimates from management people on this point in 12 of the 20 manufacturing industries which he studied, with the following results:

For six of the twelve . . . the existence of any significant multi-plant economies was denied, even though in three of these six industries the larger firms had attained substantial multi-plant development. For the remaining six of the twelve cases, some multi-plant economies were claimed to exist to the extent that a firm with three to ten plants would be more efficient than a one-plant firm. But the extent of cost reduction . . . was generally estimated as 'small,' 'slight,' or not exceeding 2 or 3 percent.[4]

In some cases, then, horizontal dissolution might involve loss of efficiency. On the other hand, the public would benefit from the more competitive behavior which would result from having 20 companies in the industry instead of 3 or 4.

Vertical Dissolution

Many of our economic giants derive their strength in part from vertical integration, from controlling an entire production cycle. The leading steel companies produce everything from iron ore to tacks and nails. The major oil companies own oil wells, pipelines and tanker fleets, oil refineries, and chains of retail gas stations. There may be some gain in efficiency from this adding together of successive production processes, though the gains are harder to visualize than in the case of horizontal integration. What is clear is that vertical integration confers great bargaining advantages, and may enable the integrated company to put an economic squeeze on its smaller competitors.

The Aluminum Company of America, for example, was for 50 years the sole producer of aluminum metal in the United States. In addition, the company produced a wide variety of finished aluminum products. A number of smaller companies bought aluminum from Alcoa and fabricated it into various end products. Alcoa, because of its dominant position at each level of the industry, could determine the prices of both aluminum metal and finished aluminum products and thus determine the "spread" available to cover manufacturing costs. This spread could be varied to make things easier or harder for the little fellows in the industry. Suppose Alcoa raised the price of primary aluminum without

---

[4] *Op. cit.*, p. 351.

raising the price of finished products. This made no difference to its own profits, since the price it charged itself for aluminum was purely a matter of internal bookkeeping. It made a great difference to the profits of the small producers, however, and could obviously be used to drive them out of existence.

To prevent this sort of economic pressure, the Antitrust Division has sometimes sought a dissolution decree restricting the major companies to a specified level of operation. The major motion picture producers, for example, were ordered to get out of theater operations, because the court judged that this gave them an unfair competitive advantage over picture producers who did not own theaters. New companies were set up to take over theater operation, and these companies bought the theaters from the producing companies at a negotiated price. A leading student of the oil industry has proposed that the major refining companies be ordered to get out of both the pipeline business and the filling-station business.[5] This would give the small independent refiners a freer hand in buying and transporting crude oil and in disposing of their products through retail outlets.

Other Approaches to the Oligopoly Problem

While dissolution is the most direct and effective approach to the problem of strong market power, several other techniques deserve mention:

1. Something can be accomplished through investigation and publicity. Government agencies can spell out clearer standards of good economic performance for an industry, analyze the operation of our closely controlled industries in the light of these standards, and publicize the results. The industries concerned typically resist even this mild form of public surveillance as "snooping" into private business affairs. But these industries, by virtue of their importance in the economy and the fact that they are not subject to the usual discipline of competitive markets, become "vested with a public interest." Adequate knowledge of their operations is necessary as a basis for wise public policy.

Some would go further. Those who fear that the ease with which prices can be raised under strong oligopoly may contribute to chronic price inflation have suggested that wage and price increases in these industries be made subject to approval by a government board. The missing check of market competition would be replaced by government regulation. The wisdom of such proposals is doubtful. Government price control has not worked very well in the public utility industries, for reasons which will be explained in the next chapter. It seems unlikely

---

[5] Eugene V. Rostow, *A National Policy for the Oil Industry* (New Haven, Conn.: Yale University Press, 1948). This proposal was violently attacked in the press as, among other things, "socialistic." Actually, the proposal was aimed at stronger competition and freer private enterprise.

that it would work any better in steel, oil, or copper. If one dislikes the prospect of direct controls, however, the logical alternative is to make the structure of these industries as competitive as possible through the dissolution technique. Some sort of control over private market power there must be. If we are unwilling to institute competitive controls, it seems likely that events will move toward the opposite pole of government regulation.

2. The prospects for competition are improved by the fact that the market for most products is growing. If one could ensure that most of the growth would come either through new companies or the expansion of smaller existing companies, the market domination of our present industrial giants would gradually diminish. Over a period of 40 or 50 years, one could achieve considerable decentralization without actually dissolving existing companies. There seems in any event to be some tendency for older companies to expand less rapidly than smaller or newer companies. United States Steel had about two thirds of the basic steel producing capacity of the country when it was formed in 1901. Today its proportion has fallen to about 30 percent. Another classic case is the International Harvester Company, whose share of the farm machinery market fell from three quarters in 1911 to less than one quarter today.

Government can aid this tendency in a variety of ways. The sale of aluminum plants built with government funds during World War II to two new producers, Kaiser and Reynolds, provided Alcoa with its first serious competition. Wherever there is a choice in disposing of government-owned facilities or in placing government contracts, this could be used to build up efficient small producers. As a minimum, there should be a clear policy of not favoring the largest producers and not increasing industrial concentration through government sales and purchases. The federal Small Business Administration is active in this area and is helping in particular to meet the capital needs of small business. A company with assets below $5 million and annual net income below $2.5 million, and which has been unable to secure a regular bank loan, can apply to the SBA. Approved loans are typically repayable over a period of 5 to 10 years, and carry interest rates ranging from 4 to 6 percent. The SBA also helps to finance intermediary organizations, termed small-business investment companies, which then advance funds to small concerns.

3. It is important also to prevent the formation of new industrial giants through merger of competing firms. A vigilant procompetitive policy could have prevented the formation of U.S. Steel and other companies whose market power constitutes a continuing problem. Certainly such agglomerations should be prevented in the future.

Until 1950 the check on mergers was weak. But Section 7 of the Clayton Act was amended in 1950 to forbid one company to acquire either stock or the physical assets of another company in the same type of industry where the effect "may be substantially to lessen competition" or where the merger would "tend to create a monopoly." The indications are that the Supreme Court intends to apply this prohibition quite strictly. Several merger cases have been decided in favor of the government. Mergers have been prohibited even where the merging companies had only a small (by past Sherman Act standards) share of the product market. And the judgments have been forward-looking rather than backward-looking. The Court has addressed itself to the question: "What will more mergers of this same sort do to the structure of the industry? Is this the point at which a line should be drawn?" This goes beyond the traditional Sherman Act interpretation that substantial injury to competition must already have occurred before relief will be granted.[6] If the Court continues to follow this line of reasoning, further restriction of competition by the merger route may be effectively prevented.

4. Where a monopoly or oligopoly has been aided by tariff protection, the tariff can be lowered to give consumers the benefit of competition from other countries. We shall argue in Chapter 18 that the tariff is a dubious device, which can be justified only in exceptional cases. It is especially dubious where it serves to protect, not competitive private enterprise, but private monopoly power.

To sum up: it is sometimes argued that we can do *nothing* about concentrated market power. This is surely incorrect. It would be fair to say that we cannot do anything very spectacular very quickly or by relying entirely on one approach. We must try a variety of approaches—checking further concentration through merger, dissolving large concerns here and there, strengthening the competitive power of small enterprise, analyzing and publicizing the economic performance of concentrated industries—with a view to making gradual progress over the course of decades. General intent, sense of direction, and vigor of action are the main things.

EXCEPTIONS TO ANTITRUST

While the antitrust laws remain our basic charter in the matter of monopoly and competition, a variety of exceptions have grown up over the years. Two of the most important, agricultural price controls and retail price fixing, are examined in Chapter 14; but several others will be reviewed briefly here.

Patent Protection

Anyone who believes he has developed an original product or production method can take it to the Patent Office in Washington and

---

[6] For an analysis of the first decision under the new antimerger provisions, see D. D. Martin, "The Brown Shoe Case and Antimerger Policy," *American Economic Review*, June, 1963, pp. 340–58.

apply for a patent. Something like 50,000 applications are filed every year. An overworked staff of patent clerks spends a few hours searching the files to see whether any similar device has been patented in the past. If they can find none, and if the new device doesn't seem too ridiculous, a patent will be issued. This gives the patent owner exclusive right to the product or process for 17 years. Anyone else who makes anything too similar to it can be sued for patent infringement and, if found guilty, will have to pay damages.

A patent is a legal grant of monopoly, immune from question or prosecution under the antitrust laws. The original purpose of the patent system was to reward the lone-wolf inventor by protecting the use of his discovery for a long enough period to yield him some financial return. Large returns for successful inventions would supposedly spur more people to tinker and experiment and would increase the amount of inventive activity. In modern times, however, an inventor is more likely to sell his patent to a corporation than to exploit it himself; and an increasing proportion of inventions are made in corporation laboratories by salaried reserach workers. The main present-day argument for patents, then, is that the system is necessary to induce companies to spend large amounts on research and development. Why should a company maintain an elaborate research organization if discoveries are immediately thrown open to all its competitors? Protected use of the discovery for 17 years enables the company to recover the money which has been sunk in developing it.

There is doubtless good reason for some degree of patent protection, but many students of the patent system feel that its original intent has been distorted over the course of time and that it now offers unreasonable protection to monopolistic activities. Common criticisms include:

1. Patent law is complicated, patent lawyers are high priced, and patent suits are long and expensive. The threat of patent litigation has thus become an important weapon of intercorporate warfare. A large company has sometimes gone to a smaller competitor and said in effect: "Your product encroaches on certain patents which we own. We propose to sue you. Stop it, or else." The charge of patent infringement may or may not be warranted. What matters in such a situation is not the merit of your patent but the size of your purse. The small company, faced with ruinous legal expenses, must usually accept the terms laid down by the larger one. It may be forced to pay royalties to the big company under a patent license, or to accept a merger, or to go out of business.

2. A patent can be used to hold a new product or process off the market instead of putting it on the market. There are cases in which application of a new technique has been long delayed because it would have upset existing production methods and reduced the value of present plant and equipment.

3. A company which wants to produce under a patent belonging to another company can do so by getting a license from the patent holder, which usually involves paying a royalty of so much per unit produced. Large companies which own overlapping patents in the same area will often issue licenses to each other to avoid any threat of patent suits, an arrangement known as *cross-licensing*. Or all patents in an industry may be turned over to a trade association or a special company set up for the purpose, which then issues licenses to each of the participating companies. This is known as a *patent pool*.

Licensing arrangements can operate in a way which liberates and strengthens competition. The automobile industry has long had a patent pool under which patents owned by one company are available to all other companies without restriction and without charge. But licensing systems can also be used to restrict and suppress competition. The companies in a cross-licensing agreement or a patent pool may refuse to license any newcomer, thus barring new companies from the industry. Or the licensing arrangements may be used to divide up the market, with each company retaining a monopoly in a specified field.

Patent licenses have also been used to limit the amount of a product which can be manufactured and the price at which it can be sold. One of the most elaborate arrangements of this sort was developed by the Hartford-Empire Glass Company, which held the key patents on machinery used in glass bottle manufacturing. A bottle manufacturer was given a license to produce under these patents only on condition that he produce a certain kind of bottle, in specified quantities, sell only within a certain geographic area, and at a specified price. The entire national market for many types of bottle was thus subdivided and controlled. Anyone who questioned or violated the prescribed arrangements was simply put out of business by withdrawing his license. This arrangement was eventually broken up by court order after the Justice Department brought suit under the antitrust laws.

These criticisms have been accompanied by proposals for reform of the patent system, with a view to retaining essential protective features while minimizing harmful effects on competition. Some of the main suggestions which have been made are:

1. The validity of disputed patents might be submitted to a special patent court, with all expenses being borne by the government to remove any disadvantage of weaker companies.

2. It could be spelled out clearly in law that patent licensing may not be used to fix product prices, set output quotas, divide up markets, and impose other restraints on competition. Such restraints have already been held illegal in the Hartford-Empire case and other cases, but the law might be made more explicit on this point.

3. It might be provided that a patent owner must issue a license to any other producer on payment of reasonable royalties.

4. Since World War II, most of the money spent on scientific research has come from the federal government, either through its own laboratories, or through grants to universities and research institutes, or through paying the research expenses of business concerns. Yet the inventions resulting from this research are often patented by companies or individuals. Where invention has been financed by government, it would seem that the resulting patents should belong to government and should be made available to all comers.

Union Activity in Product Markets

In considering the economic consequences of unionism one must distinguish between (*a*) bargaining with employers over wages and other terms of employment in the *labor market,* which we leave for analysis in Chapter 15; and (*b*) intervention to fix prices or restrain competition in the *product market,* which falls logically within the scope of this chapter.

Unions have a direct interest in product prices, since it is price which gives the employer the wherewithal to meet his wage bill. An employer in a small-scale, competitive industry may sometimes find his selling price reduced to the point where he feels compelled to cut wages or go out of business. A union in such an industry has a practical interest in "stabilizing" prices (which always means raising them!) in order to remove pressure on the wage level, and the union can sometimes control prices more effectively than the employers.

Suppose the dry-cleaning industry in a city is "menaced" by price competition. Companies undercut each other on prices, profits are low and uncertain, efforts to reach a price agreement are unavailing. To the rescue rides the International Brotherhood of Teamsters. It organizes the delivery truck drivers, and perhaps the plant employees as well, and signs a wage agreement with each company. But it does more than this. It organizes a price-fixing agreement among the employers and undertakes to police the agreement. A company which cuts prices now finds its labor supply cut off and is quickly forced back into line. Dave Beck, originally west coast head of the Teamsters and later International President, perfected and applied this technique to numerous retailing and service industries in Seattle, and was awarded every sort of civic honor by grateful businessmen. It has since been extended to many other areas of the country.

This sort of union-employer combine flourishes also in building construction. The building contractors in a city form an association, one purpose of which is to present agreed bids on public contracts and to divide the available business on a controlled basis. They agree with the local building trades unions that they will employ only union members, and the unions agree that their men will work only for members of the contractors' association. This forces all contractors to join the association and observe the price-fixing agreement, on penalty of getting no labor. Part of the arrangement may be a cash payoff by the companies to key union officials, but this is petty larceny compared with the grand larceny which the contractors perpetrate on the public.

In other cases a union has acted on its own to shut off competition. Local 3 of the International Brotherhood of Electrical Workers in New York City has long had a rule that switchboards and other electrical apparatus shipped into New York from outside must be disassembled and rewired by members of the Local. This effectively excludes outside manufacturers from the New York market.

There is a curious anomaly in the antitrust laws at this point. If *employers alone* conspire to fix prices or restrict competition, they are breaking the law. If *employers and unions* together do the same thing, the scheme is still illegal. But *if the union acts alone,* without visibly conspiring with employers, it can impose any restraints on pricing and competition which it may choose. The Clayton Act provides that "labor is not an article of commerce," and this has been interpreted by the courts as meaning that independent actions of a labor organization cannot be prosecuted under the antitrust laws. A union can strike against a price-cutting employer, refuse to work for a new company, impose a ban on products from outside the area—all quite legally so long as no one can prove that employers are involved in the scheme.

This situation is illogical. It seems desirable to amend the law so as to distinguish between matters of *labor relations* and matters of *commercial competition* in product markets. As regards the latter, anything which would be unlawful for business concerns to do in the product market should be equally unlawful for trade unions. To hold otherwise is to open a large gap in the antitrust system, through which price agreements can ride intact so long as employer participation cannot be proved.

Transactions within a State

The antitrust laws cover only activities affecting interstate commerce. A good deal of local retailing, service, and construction activity does not cross state lines and is immune to federal regulation. Many states have their own antitrust laws, but there is usually no provision for enforcement, and the statute remains a dead letter.

The general tenor of state and municipal regulation is in fact highly anticompetitive. State and local governments are more vulnerable than the federal government to concentrated pressure by business groups, demanding legislation to restrict competition in their particular bailiwick; and the inert majority of consumers which is hurt by such legislation puts up no effective defense.

Most states have laws which discriminate against out-of-state producers. There is an almost incredible variety of such restrictions.

Many states maintain their own plant quarantine systems, which are designed partly to protect local nurserymen. "Fresh eggs" are sometimes defined as eggs laid within the state, "fresh fruits and vegetables" as state-grown produce. Some states discriminate against trucks which come in loaded as against those which come in empty. Most states have laws requiring preference for residents in making state purchases or awarding contracts, and many cities do the same. Dairy farmers cannot ship milk to a particular city unless their farms have been inspected and approved by state or local health authorities; simple refusal to inspect farms outside the state is sufficient to bar them from the market. Most states prohibit transportation of alcoholic beverages into the state except by authorized dealers. This does not promote temperance, but it does protect dealers' margins.

There is point in Wilcox' comment: "These measures have the same defects as do barriers to international trade. In fact, they may be more harmful, since the area they leave open to competition is a smaller one. As we move from 'Buy American' through 'Buy Indianan' and 'Buy Middletown' to 'Buy Main Street,' the consequences differ, not in kind, but in degree."[7] Carried to their logical conclusion they would carve up the vast free trade area of the United States, a major source of our economic efficiency, into hundreds of Balkan principalities surrounded by high trade barriers.

Similar observations may be made on state licensing requirements for various occupations. These are doubtless legitimate for professions which require long training and which involve public health and safety, such as medicine, dentistry, and law. But state licensing systems have been extended far beyond these proper boundaries. Wilcox points out that "there are as many as 75 trades where entry is restricted by law . . . most states license barbers, beauticians, chiropractors, funeral directors, surveyors, and salesmen of insurance and real estate. A number of states also license such tradesmen as plumbers, dry cleaners, horseshoers, tree surgeons, automobile salesmen, and photographers. Altogether, there are more than 1,200 occupational license laws, averaging 25 per state."[8]

Administration of these laws is usually entrusted to a board composed entirely of members of the occupation. A group of plumbers decides what is a proper examination for a plumbers' license, administers the examination, and decides who has passed and who hasn't. Since the members of any occupation have a direct interest in holding down the number admitted to it, it would be surprising if these laws were not administered with restrictive intent. Supervision by state government officials is usually nominal and often entirely lacking.

---

[7] Clair Wilcox, *Public Policies toward Business* (rev. ed.; Homewood, Ill.: Richard D. Irwin, Inc., 1960), p. 348.

[8] *Ibid.*, p. 348.

These two types of law are restrictive and antisocial. Many of them are thinly disguised "grabs" by small groups in the economy. They persist because the public doesn't know about them, and because each one seems to take only a small bite out of the consumer. One can hope that citizens of each state and community will gradually become better informed about what goes on in their own backyards and take greater interest in preserving free occupational choice and free competition.

A WORD ON ENFORCEMENT

The achievements of the antitrust laws to date are certainly substantial. Direct price-fixing agreements have been driven underground, and their scope and effectiveness severely limited. Business concerns have been warned off any close approach to single-firm monopoly. Unfair and predatory tactics against smaller competitors have been ruled out of bounds. Companies have been given reason to worry about standing out on the landscape as "too big" in their respective industries. One reason why some oligopolists have cheerfully watched their market share shrink is the consolation of greater immunity to antitrust prosecution.

How much can we expect to make of the antitrust approach in the future? This depends on what we want to make of it, and particularly on how much money and manpower we devote to enforcing the law. The effectiveness of any piece of economic legislation can be predicted by looking at the budget of the enforcing agency. The statute books are cluttered with impressive-looking laws which mean nothing because no one is doing anything about them. Lobbyists and legislators know well that the best way to fight legislation is not to oppose its passage but simply to cut off funds for enforcement.

This was essentially the fate of the antitrust laws from 1890 to 1935. The annual budget of the Antitrust Division of the Department of Justice never rose above $200,000, and the number of lawyers employed was never more than 25. This small group was supposed to preserve competition through the whole of American industry! Considering the discrepancy between the enormous resources of business corporations and the tiny resources of government, it is amazing that the antitrust laws had any effect whatever. The number of prosecutions started by the Antitrust Division was less than 10 per year until 1906, and typically between 10 and 20 per year from 1906 to 1939.

The antitrust laws began to be enforced more seriously during the late New Deal period. Between 1934 and 1942 the budget of the Antitrust Division rose from $154,000 to $2,325,000; the number of lawyers employed rose above 200, and the number of cases started per year began to exceed 50. After some slackening during the war years, antitrust activity revived after the war and has continued on a higher plateau under both Republican and Democratic administrations, with an average of close to 50 cases being started each year.

If the policy of promoting competition is to be taken seriously in the future, there is need for further enlargement of the staff and budget of the Antitrust Division. The Division is still much smaller than the police force of the District of Columbia, and tiny compared with the number of companies and the volume of activity which it is responsible for monitoring.

There should also be a shift in the emphasis of enforcement activities. About half of the antitrust actions initiated since 1890 have involved three groups of industries: food processing and distribution, building materials production and distribution, and the service trades. By contrast, there has been little activity in steel, nonferrous metals, chemicals, machinery, electrical equipment, and other branches of manufacturing.

The main thrust of the law has clearly been against collusive agreement in small-scale industry rather than against monopoly and oligopoly in large-scale industry. There are practical reasons for this. In terms of winning public support for antitrust, it is expedient to concentrate enforcement on industries which are widely distributed throughout the country and which come into direct contact with consumers. The food processing, service, and building construction industries meet this requirement; basic steel, chemicals, and electric turbines do not. Moreover, the state of the law and the outlook of the courts must be considered. The Antitrust Division knows it can win a case against outright collusion by little business, but it is not sure how far the courts will support it in moving against tacit collusion by big business. Since the enforcement budget is so small, it seems sensible to concentrate it on cases where the chances of success are highest.

One would not want to suggest that the Antitrust Division should act less vigorously against outright collusion than it has in the past. But it might well act more vigorously against concentrated oligopoly, and shift the emphasis of enforcement toward heavy manufacturing. The difficulties in doing this are obvious. The Sherman Act might have to be amended in certain respects. Larger enforcement funds would be needed. Political opposition would be intense. This brings us back to the basic question of how far we mean what we say about the desirability of competitive markets. If we do mean it, positive movement in a competitive direction is not going to be achieved painlessly.

SUMMARY

1. At a rough estimate, two thirds of private output in the United States is produced under conditions of reasonably effective competition, one third under monopoly or strong oligopoly.

2. Certain forces in the economy are always making for greater industrial concentration, while others are working in the opposite direction. Over the last 30 years the two sets of forces seem to have just about offset each other.

3. The Sherman Act of 1890, and the Clayton Act and Federal Trade Commission Act of 1914, are usually known collectively as "the antitrust laws." They prohibit open agreement among competitors to fix prices or control production, and such agreements have been largely prevented; but tacit collusion among a few large companies has not been checked.

4. The antitrust laws also forbid *monopolizing*, that is, action by one or more dominant companies to exclude competitors from an industry. But the courts have not yet gone so far as to hold that mere *existence* of market power is itself unlawful.

5. The most difficult problem under antitrust is strong oligopoly, where a few large companies are able to regulate prices by tacit agreement. One approach is through dissolution of large companies into smaller ones, which could sometimes be done with little or no loss in efficiency. But this is a drastic remedy which the courts have hesitated to apply.

6. Other lines of approach include investigation and publicity, support for new enterprises and small enterprises, prevention of further concentration through mergers, and tariff reductions to permit foreign competition.

7. The antitrust system could be strengthened by changes in patent legislation, by preventing unions as well as business concerns from restricting competition in product markets, and by eliminating state laws which restrict competition.

8. The Antitrust Division of the Department of Justice needs a substantially larger staff and budget. This would permit more vigorous activity in oligopolistic industries which thus far have been largely neglected.

DISCUSSION QUESTIONS

1. Has the average *size of company* been increasing in the United States over the past century? What are the main reasons? Does this necessarily mean an increase in *industrial concentration* or a lessening of competition? Explain.

2. Some economists have advocated that situations of concentrated oligopoly be attacked by dissolving each of the leading companies into a number of smaller companies. Would this be economically desirable? Do you know enough about a particular industry to discuss the issue with respect to that industry?

3. Suppose next week the major steel producers announce a general increase

in steel prices. As head of the Antitrust Division, you suspect that the law has been violated. How would you go about proving it? If you could prove it, what remedies would you ask the court to apply?

4. President Kennedy in 1962 made a strong public statement against a proposed increase in steel prices. Was this an unjustified interference with private industry?

5. How have the courts interpreted the Sherman Act prohibition against *monopolizing?* What does a company have to do to fall foul of this provision?

6. Contrast the meaning of monopoly in law and in economics.

7. The antitrust system has been variously evaluated as:

   a) An ineffective effort to maintain a competitive system which is inevitably on the decline.

   b) An activity which may not do much good but certainly does no harm, and is worth continuing as a minor arm of our national economic policy.

   c) A useful device which has done a good deal to slow down the growth of monopoly power and collusive agreement.

   d) A potentially powerful weapon which, with adequate staffing and enforcement, could maintain effective competition in most sectors of the economy.

   State and defend your own evaluation (which need not correspond with any of the above).

8. To what extent is union activity to restrict competition in *product markets* now limited by the antitrust laws? What changes in the law might be desirable?

9. Do you know how many laws restricting competition in intrastate industries are on the statute books in your state? See whether you can find out. Which of these laws seems justifiable to you, and which should be repealed?

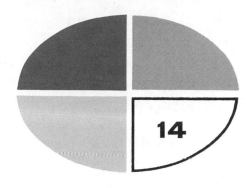

Restricting Competition

> "It seems to me that th' on'y thing to do is to keep pollyticians an' businessmen apart. They seem to have a bad inflooence on each other. Whiniver I see an aldherman an' a banker walkin' down th' street together I know th' Recordin' Angel will have to ordher another bottle iv ink."
>
> FINLEY PETER DUNNE

THE POLICY OF CONTROLLING industry through competitive markets has never been applied to every sector of the economy. Public utilities have been accepted as inevitably monopolistic and have been made subject to government regulation. In other industries, atomistic in structure and competitive by tradition, it has been charged that competition works unfairly and that government should intervene to ensure fair prices for producers. The outstanding case is agriculture, which has been subject to extensive regulation of prices and production since the early thirties.

NATURAL MONOPOLY: REGULATION OF PUBLIC UTILITIES

This group of industries includes electric power, gas, telephone and telegraph communication, railroading, local street transportation, and a number of others. The characteristic feature of a public utility is that optimum scale is very large, so that long-run marginal cost continues to fall with increasing size. This makes it efficient to have only one company operating in a particular area. So consumers must depend for an essential service on a monopoly which, left to itself, might fail to provide adequate service or might charge unreasonable prices. The public can be protected only by giving a public body power to control prices and service.

Regulatory agencies have been set up both at state and federal levels. Electricity and gas service, telephone service, and other services within a single state are usually regulated by a state agency, usually termed the public utility commission or public service commission. Interstate distribution of electricity, rail transportation, and other activities reaching across state lines are regulated by a galaxy of federal commissions, including the Interstate Commerce Commission, the Civil Aeronautics Board, the Federal Power Commission, and the Federal Communications Commission.

The existence of these agencies is certainly essential, but their record of performance is unimpressive. There are several reasons for this:

1. Although some outstanding people have served on these commissions, the average caliber of commission members is not high. No special qualifications or experience are required. Many appointments are frankly political. Low salary levels make it difficult to attract or keep capable people.

2. Staffs are too small to do an adequate job. The budgets of the state utility commissions average less than a half-million dollars per year. A single utility company may spend much more than that on legal and accounting talent. Regulation is essentially a battle between public and private experts, but the scales are heavily weighted in favor of the latter.

3. The powers of the regulatory commissions are mainly negative rather than positive. They can forbid a utility to raise prices, but they are not equally well equipped to bring about price reductions.

4. Because regulation of profits affects property values, utility companies can appeal commission decisions to the courts under the Fourteenth Amendment. This makes utility regulation somewhat cumbersome, expensive, and uncertain.

5. The economic issues involved in utility regulation are complex and difficult. An understanding of the unsatisfactory results of utility regulation to date requires a brief review of these underlying issues and problems.

SOME ECONOMIC ISSUES IN REGULATION

It seems simple enough to say to a private monopoly, "You must sell your product at a fair price," and to set up a board charged with enforcing this edict. This approach is often advocated, not only for public utilities, but for highly concentrated manufacturing industries such as basic steel. If an industry is raising prices too fast or making too much money, why not set up a board to regulate its prices? A century of experience in utility regulation reveals the host of difficulties involved in such an attempt. Only the most important of these can be outlined here.

"Fair Return on Fair Value"

The courts have ruled that the owners of utilities are entitled to a fair rate of return on a fair valuation of the property. But they have not been willing to lay down definite principles for determining either fair value or fair return. The meaning of these terms is argued out afresh in each case.

One major issue involves the difference between the original cost of a plant and the cost of building the same plant today. Consider a steam generating plant built by an electric power company for $10 million at the depressed price levels of 1935. To build the same plant today might cost $25 million. Which is the "fair value" of the property? Should the company be allowed to earn 6 percent on original cost, which would mean $600,000, or 6 percent on reproduction cost, which would be $1,500,000? During a long upswing of prices, the companies will be strongly in favor of reproduction cost, while the commissions will usually favor original cost. During a downswing of prices, the positions are reversed. The courts have usually given the not very helpful advice that "both principles must be given due consideration."

Another difficulty is that the 1935 plant will be partly worn out by 1965. How much should be deducted from its value on this account? There are various possible ways of calculating depreciation, and much room for argument concerning them.

After the value of the company's property has been decided, the next question is how high a return the company should be allowed to earn on this value. The yield of an investment, as we saw in Chapter 11, normally includes the pure rate of interest plus a risk premium which varies with the riskiness of the enterprise. There is not much risk involved in operating a public utility, since it usually controls an essential service with a stable or expanding market. The rate of return on public utility property, therefore, should presumably be not very far above the rate on a long-term, riskless government bond. But precisely what rate should be allowed depends on the judgment of a particular commission. The permitted rate has usually been between 5½ and 8 percent, toward the low end of this range during the thirties and forties when all interest rates were low, higher during the fifties when money rates generally were higher.

Control of Operating Costs

If price to the public is to be fair, not only must profits be reasonable but operating costs should be held to a minimum. Production costs, however, result from decisions of private management. The utility commissions, while they usually have legal authority to investigate operating costs and disallow specific items, actually do so only in cases of flagrant abuse. A lax management can allow costs to creep up higher than necessary, and then apply to the commission for higher rates which will enable it to earn the customary return on these inflated costs.

The argument is not that executives of public utilities are less efficient than executives in other lines of industry. This may or may not be true, and a factual test would be difficult. The point is simply that they *can* be inefficient and still survive. There is no automatic check on inefficiency such as exists in a competitive industry. Nor is there a strong financial incentive to improve efficiency over the course of time.

Government price regulation falls short of being a satisfactory substitute for competition partly because it does not exert strong pressure for maximum efficiency.

Negative Control versus Positive Initiative

Proper economic performance by an industry is a positive concept. It requires that plants in the industry be of optimum scale and be managed with maximum efficiency. It requires that output be increased

Different Output Policies for a Utility

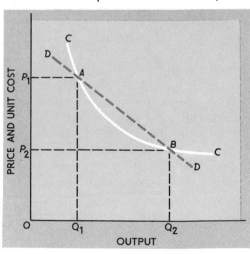

FIGURE 1. CC is the long-run average total cost curve. The company can earn a normal profit at *either* A or B. A cautious management operating at A may decide to stay there, even though expansion would be in the public interest.

so long as it can be sold at a price which will cover marginal cost. It requires aggressive expansion of plant capacity where necessary to meet this production objective.

If these things are to be done, however, they must be done through management initiative. The commission can scarcely compel them. Its powers are essentially negative, to prevent exorbitant prices and profits.

The inability of a utility commission to take positive steps toward desirable economic performance may be illustrated by Figure 1. *CC* is the long-run average total cost curve for a particular utility. It shows the unit cost of producing various quantities of output after allowing time for construction of new plant capacity. It includes whatever return on capital is allowed by the controlling commission. *DD* is the product demand curve. Suppose the utility is presently operating at *A*, with price OP_1 and output OQ_1, and earning just the rate of return which the commission allows. On the surface everything seems all right, but it really isn't. If demand is as shown, the company could afford to build new plant capacity and expand to *B*, where it would be selling output OQ_2 at price OP_2. Here it would still be covering costs and earning the allowable rate of return, while consumers would be getting more of the product at a lower price.

To move from *A* toward *B* requires positive action. Management must gamble that the demand curve is as elastic as shown and that larger outputs can be sold at a profitable price. But since the company is already earning satisfactory profits at *A*, it may decide to sit tight and not take the risks of expansion. Managers of monopolies seem often to underestimate the elasticity of their demand curves and to follow a conservative policy of low output and high prices. If they can be forced to cut prices, this turns out to be profitable. But they have to be forced, and the typical public utility commission is reluctant to do this.

The Possibility of Net Losses

A utility commission is supposed to set a price which covers average total cost including a fair profit. But this will not necessarily yield the best price and output from a community standpoint. We concluded in Part One that output of each product in the economy should be expanded to the point at which price equals *marginal cost*. But this will not always yield a reasonable profit to the company, and may involve losses.

Consider the situation sketched in Figure 2. Here we have an enterprise with a large plant and heavy overhead costs. As output is expanded, average total cost falls steadily, and for a long time marginal cost lies below average cost. The standard illustration is a main-line railroad. Buying and building the right of way, laying the rails, and maintaining the roadbed involves heavy fixed costs. But once the road is there, the more tons of freight are run over it, the lower will be the average cost per ton. Eventually marginal cost and finally average cost will turn upward, presumably because the railroad gets overcrowded with trains. But capacity may be considerably above the actual rate of operation, as in the case shown.

What price policy should be followed in this case? Ordinary principles of utility regulation might lead to operation at *A*, where the enterprise can earn just a normal profit with price OP_1 and output OQ_1. Our standard of economic efficiency, however, requires that output be expanded so long as price is above marginal cost. This would lead to operation at B, with price OP_2 and output OQ_2. At this point, however, the company cannot break even. Price is below average total cost by the distance BC. Since the commission cannot order a company to accept an unprofitable price, it cannot enforce such a policy. The price OP_2 would be feasible only with public subsidy or public operation of the industry.[1]

Correct Output May Involve Losses

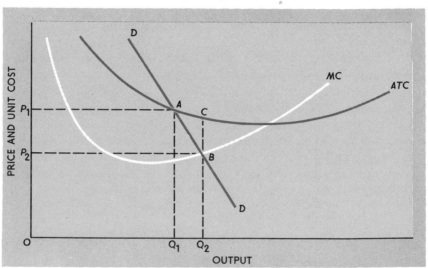

FIGURE 2. In this situation a public utility commission might order a price of OP_1, since with this price and output OQ_1 the company will just cover average total costs. It is economically desirable that output be increased to OQ_2, that is, to the point at which price equals marginal cost. But this would mean a loss to the company, so will not be done.

Declining Demand and Vanishing Industries

There are other cases in which losses are inevitable and price regulation may provide no workable solution. Consider a utility whose demand curve is shifting downward over the years. Railroad passenger service, the New York subway system, and city bus systems are good illustrations. The rapid growth of private auto travel has meant a downward shift in demand curves for these types of public transportation.

---

[1] There has been considerable discussion among economic theorists over whether a government enterprise *should* necessarily equate price and marginal costs, and over what form of taxation should be used to make up the losses resulting from such a policy. The discussion is mainly academic rather than practical. Boards of publicly owned monopolies are about as conservative as those of private monopolies. They are usually ordered by law to cover all costs of their operation, and thus tend in the direction of point A rather than point B.

Suppose such an industry in its heyday enjoys the demand *DD* in Figure 3. It operates at *A*, gets full use of its facilities at a low price, earns reasonable profits, and all is well. *DD* now begins to shift downward. Volume declines and unit cost rises. The company and the public utility commission will see only one answer: raise prices to cover the higher costs. The industry travels up *ATC* to the left. This can go on until

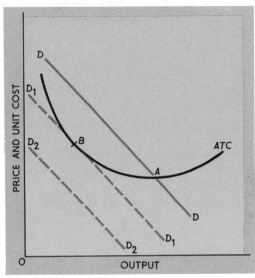

The Vanishing Industry Case

FIGURE 3. If this utility's demand curve falls below *D₁D₁*, there is no longer any price which will cover average total cost. Either service must be abandoned or losses must be subsidized by government.

demand has fallen to D_1D_1. Here the utility can still break even by operating at *B*, with considerably higher prices and lower volume than at the outset.

But suppose demand falls farther to D_2D_2. Now the remedy of raising prices breaks down. There is no longer *any* price which will cover average total cost. Either service must be abandoned, or a government subsidy provided, or government must take over the enterprise and run it at a loss. One can find examples of all three developments. The public bus systems have been abandoned in some American cities and replaced by jitney taxi service or by nothing at all. State and city governments have granted subsidies to support railroad commuter service into New York City and other East Coast communities. In other cases, declining industries have been unloaded on the government and turned into public corporations.

Transportation: Competition among Monopolists

Although we have been regulating transportation for several generations, public policy remains ill-defined and ill-coordinated. The railroads were regulated originally to prevent their charging exorbitant rates for passenger and freight transportation, of which they had a monopoly except for limited competition from the waterways. As road and air transport have increased in importance, however, the problem has become one of equalizing competitive opportunities among the various transport media, so that each can perform the functions in which its relative efficiency is greatest.

We are not within sight of this objective at present. Most types of transportation are subsidized by the public, but the subsidies vary erratically from one type to another. The railroads, while they received large land subsidies in the nineteenth century, have received little since that time. Trucks and buses contribute to highway costs through taxes on motor vehicles, tires, and gasoline; but they are still subsidized to some extent. Air and water carriers receive free use of the air and waterways and large public contributions to the cost of shipbuilding, harbors, and airport construction. There is some reason for the railroads' complaint that the scales of competition are tilted against them, and that this is one reason for the steady decline in their percentage of the transportation business.

The orientation of regulatory policy is restrictive and anticompetitive. There is no positive drive to promote cheap, efficient transportation by whatever medium proves best suited to a particular task. The tendency is rather to protect vested interests, to restrict competition among the various media, to keep everyone in business somehow, and to prevent newcomers from getting a foothold if this will inconvenience established companies. New airlines cannot be established, and existing airlines cannot fly new routes, without CAB approval. New trucking concerns must apply for a license, and this is generally refused if it appears that the new concern would cut into the business of existing truckers or of the railroads. Instead of setting only maximum rates on freight transport, the ICC now sets minimum rates for both railroads and truckers, to control competition and regulate the amount of business going to each carrier. The railroads maintain that this prevents them from moving promptly to meet trucking competition.

These policies may keep everyone alive, but they certainly don't keep everyone efficient. Part of the difficulty is that no one agency is responsible for taking an overall view of transportation policy. The Bureau of Public Roads goes merrily ahead sponsoring roads and highways, the ICC regulates railroading and trucking, the Civil Aeronautics Board handles air transport, and the Maritime Commission subsidizes shipping. No one has the job of thinking about rational policy for transportation as a whole. There are probably few sectors of the economy which stand to gain more from thorough review and a fresh approach.

PUBLIC OWNERSHIP AS AN ALTERNATIVE

Private management combined with public regulation is only one answer to the utility problem. The main alternative is public ownership and operation of natural monopolies. This alternative has been widely employed in Britain, the British Commonwealth countries, Western Europe, and many of the less developed countries—in fact, almost everywhere outside the United States.

The relative advantages of private and public operation have been argued for decades. Some of the points most commonly made in favor of public ownership are:

1. It simplifies the structure and responsibilities of management. The American pattern of public utility regulation involves two-decker management. There is a full-fledged private management responsible for decisions on business policy. But on top of this is placed a public board responsible for supervising what private management is doing. If the public utility commission is to do its job effectively, it must have a large staff of experts and technicians paralleling the staffs of the companies it regulates. This is expensive, time-consuming, and apt to be mutually frustrating. Under government operation these two layers are merged into a unified management, responsible for operating the enterprise in the public interest.

2. It establishes public service as the criterion of successful performance and allows this criterion to be applied in a positive way. Management can devote its full attention to defining economic policies which will serve the public interest and to putting them into operation. A management responsible to private stockholders is bound to be biased toward policies which yield maximum profit.

3. It reduces the financial restrictions on management decisions. Government does not go bankrupt, while business concerns do. A private corporation cannot afford losses over any extended period. Yet there may be circumstances, as noted in the previous section, in which it is desirable to provide a public service at a price below full cost. This can be done by handing over government money to a private company to cover its losses, as we now do for passenger airlines and merchant shipping; but this procedure is obviously subject to abuse. If an enterprise is unlikely to be profitable in the foreseeable future, there is much to be said for nationalizing it and bearing the costs directly rather than indirectly.

The main considerations against public ownership are suggested by the battle cry of "politics and bureaucracy." Specifically, it is charged that:

1. A government enterprise is under irresistible public pressure to make uneconomic decisions. The unions will expect a government agency to be a model employer and to give in with good grace to wage demands. At the same time, consumers and politicians will object to raising product prices enough to cover the higher costs. Particular areas of the country will work through political channels to get plants and facilities located there, whether or not the location makes sense from a cost standpoint. This political pulling and hauling may lead to losses which will have to be met from general tax revenues.

2. Political intervention in appointments may make it difficult to recruit management officials on a merit basis. Salary restrictions on public officials also make it hard to compete with private business for top talent. The result may be mediocre and unimaginative leadership of public enterprises.

3. The management of a government monopoly may be characterized by rigid procedural rules, elaborate paper work, and skilled buckpassing. This can cause serious delay in decisions, poor service, and arbitrary treatment of customers. The seriousness of this risk depends a good deal on how the public industry is organized. Bureaucratic tendencies are more likely to develop in a regular government department than in an independent public corporation such as the British Railways or the Tennessee Valley Authority. One must remember also that bureaucracy is not unknown in private business. The management procedures of our railroads have a charmingly antiquated character which would do credit to any government bureau.

There is no magic in public ownership which will automatically solve the economic problems of an industry. Naïve socialists have sometimes imagined that nationalizing a private industry would usher in the new Jerusalem. Production would now be "for use, not for profit," whatever that may mean. Wages could be raised and prices lowered, managers would immediately become efficient and public spirited, the union lion would lie down with the management lamb. They have been quite surprised to find that on the morning after nationalization everything remains much as before. It is still hard to figure out how fast capacity should be expanded, what prices should be charged, whether operating losses are justifiable, and so on. It is hard to mediate the conflicting pressures from workers, consumers, legislators, and others. Good day-to-day management continues to be a hard, unremitting task, never perfectly performed.

EXCESSIVE COMPETITION: THE CASE OF AGRICULTURE

To this point we have been considering industries in which competitive organization is impossible and in which the regulatory force of competition must be replaced by public control. We now turn completely around to consider cases in which competition not merely exists but it is claimed that competition is excessive and harmful. The most important industry in this category is agriculture.

An initial difficulty is that there is no single agricultural problem for which one might be able to find a single solution. There are several distinct problems, of which the most important are chronic overexpansion of productive capacity, high sensitivity of farm prices to shifts in demand or supply, and poverty among the marginal fringe of the farm population.

These problems must be explained before considering possible remedies.

BASIC ECONOMIC PROBLEMS OF AGRICULTURE

Chronic Overcapacity

Many countries of the world have difficulty feeding their population from their own production. The American problem is precisely the reverse—a problem of plenty rather than want. American agriculture is geared to turn out more produce than the market will take at acceptable prices.

What is the evidence for this assertion? How can one tell whether an industry is overexpanded relative to others in a market economy? If the market mechanism is working effectively, the marginal productivity of labor and capital employed in each line of industry will be approximately equal. The money return to a factor of production is a rough. measure of its marginal productivity. Thus one should find that labor of the same skill and quality earns roughly the same wage at different points in the economy. If labor in a particular industry earns substantially less than comparable labor in other industries, this indicates some blockage in the market mechanism. There is too much labor, and probably too much of other resources, engaged in the low-wage industry.

There is abundant evidence of low earnings in agriculture relative to urban industries. Hired farm labor has never in modern times earned even half as much as unskilled factory labor, and the ratio has usually been closer to one third. The incomes of farm operators, including the value of farm produce consumed at home, are typically less than half those of semiskilled factory operatives. Considering that farming involves considerable skill, versatility, and independent judgment, that the farmer works a longer week and year than the factory worker, and that his income includes some return on his capital, this is an odd situation. The farmer is apparently right in claiming that competition has been working to his disadvantage.

How did American agriculture get into this situation? Through a chronic tendency over the past 50 years for the supply of farm products to rise more rapidly than the demand for them. These demand and supply trends are deep-seated and require a word of explanation.

The *demand* for foodstuffs depends basically on the number of mouths to be fed. The rate of population growth in the United States fell off considerably from 1914 to 1940 because of the cessation of mass immigration and a considerable drop in birth rates. This had a depressing effect on agricultural demand. Since 1940, birth rates have risen once more, and the U.S. population has been increasing at about 1½ percent per year. This bulge in the population curve will be quite helpful to agriculture, as the babies of the fifties grow up into adolescents with voracious appetites during the sixties. It is uncertain, however, whether population growth will continue at the same rate or will taper off again.

Most products can depend, not only on growth of population, but on the rise of people's incomes and living standards. Even if population were stationary, producers of household appliances, restaurant meals, and vacation trips could count on a rising sales volume. Agriculture, however, benefits less from rising incomes than do other industries. Food is a basic necessity and, while people eat somewhat better as they become better off, their spending on food rises much less rapidly than their incomes. Professor Theodore Schultz has estimated that, at present U.S. income levels, an increase of 10 percent in people's incomes produces an increase of something like 2½ percent in demand for food. (The *income elasticity of demand* for food, in other words, is about 0.25.) The main thing which happens as people's incomes rise is not that they buy more food, but that they shift to more expensive foods—less beans and more sirloin steak. They also demand more service with their food—more processing, fancier packaging, freezing, and so on. But this means increased demand in manufacturing and retailing rather than in agriculture.

Suppose population continues to increase at around 1.5 percent per year. Suppose also that personal income per capita rises at the long-term average of about 3 percent. With an income elasticity of 0.25, per capita food consumption will rise about 0.75 percent per year, and total demand for farm products will rise 2.25 percent per year. If supply rises faster than this, there will be downward pressure on farm prices. Since agriculture is already overexpanded, farm output should rise *less* than 2.25 percent a year over the next decade or two to redress the supply-demand balance.

The actual tendency of agricultural output has been to increase faster than this appropriate rate. Output has risen sharply since 1940, even though acreage planted has declined slightly and the farm population has fallen by one third, from 30.5 million in 1940 to 21 million in 1960. How could output rise so much when the number of farms and farm workers was falling? The answer lies in a sensational rise of agricultural productivity. Output per worker in agriculture in 1960 was more than double that in 1940, a much higher rate of productivity increase than in the economy as a whole. Farmers now use much more mechanical equipment than they did a generation ago. Capital per farm worker, measured in constant dollars, almost doubled between 1940 and 1960. Chemical fertilizers are used more intensively and effectively. Hybrid corn and other improvements in seed, improved control of plant diseases, improved breeds of livestock, and many other developments have contributed to higher productivity. There has been an increase in average size of farms in some regions, as the more successful farmers have bought out people retiring or moving to the city; and this has enabled machinery to be used more effectively. There is no indication that the possibilities in these directions are being exhausted or that the rise of farm productivity is slackening.

This rapid increase in productive capacity, combined with a slower rate of increase in demand, accounts for the present overexpansion of agriculture. Overexpansion is particularly serious in cotton, which has suffered from the competition of synthetic fibers and from loss of export markets; and in wheat, where domestic demand is sluggish and a world wheat surplus available at low prices hampers our export position. There is less overcapacity in dairy products, fruit and vegetables, and cattle raising, where demand trends are more favorable and export markets are not important. There is thus a dual problem of cutting back total agricultural capacity and of redistributing the remaining capacity among products, getting more of it into lines for which demand is expanding and leaving less in products such as wheat and cotton where demand is especially weak.

The problem of overcapacity is aggravated by the low price elasticity of demand. For many manufactured goods, a 10 percent increase in output might mean only a 10 percent drop in price. But in the case of agriculture, a 10 percent increase in output may mean a 30 to 40 percent drop in price. This means that a *small* excess production of a particular crop has a *large* depressing effect on the growers' incomes. The amount of overcapacity in agriculture is not large—probably of the order of 5 to 10 percent of total agricultural production. Yet this small output surplus would, if prices were left completely free, drive them down to a level which farmers would regard as intolerable.

Short-Term Instability of Farm Prices

Inelasticity of demand, combined with fluctuating and uncontrolled production, tends to produce large year-to-year swings in farm prices and incomes. Farm prices are much more vulnerable than most other prices to the ups and downs of the business cycle. Suppose that in a year of normal prosperity wheat production is OQ, demand is DD, and price is OP (Figure 4). Now a depression sets in. Demand falls to D_1D_1. Oligopolists in a manufacturing industry would probably react to this by cutting output in order to hold up prices. But farmers cannot control production in this way. There are too many of them, and it is not to the interest of one farmer to reduce his wheat acreage unless others do the same. They are likely, then, to keep right on producing OQ, and this (unless the government intervenes through price supports) will mean a drastic drop in wheat prices to OP_1.

The accident of an unusually good crop is also likely to cut farmers' incomes. This follows directly from inelasticity of demand, which means that larger quantities produce less revenue. Suppose that because of unusually favorable weather the wheat crop is OQ_2 instead of the normal OQ. With demand unchanged at DD, price will drop from OP to OP_2. The "good year" turns out not to be so good after all, for wheat growers' total income (OQ_2BP_2) is a good deal smaller than the income in a normal year $(OQAP)$.

These wide swings in prices not only involve personal hardship but also make it harder for farmers to make a rational choice among alternative lines of production. There is widespread agreement that government should try to smooth out these price fluctuations.

Fluctuations in Wheat Prices

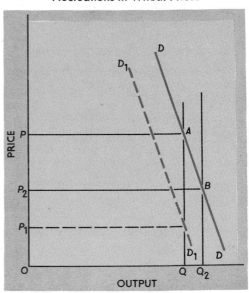

FIGURE 4. Starting from demand *DD* and price *OP, either a* decline in demand to D_1D_1 or a bumper crop which raises output to OQ_2 will cause a sharp drop in wheat prices.

The Marginal Farmer and Rural Poverty

The *average* income of farm families is a misleading figure, because it conceals great variation among them. The wheat farmer with 5,000 acres of good cropland, or the rancher with 10,000 head of beef cattle, is at one end of the scale. At the other is the family with 50 acres of wornout land, barely able to feed itself and to buy a few necessities in town. These are all farm families, but they are worlds apart.

There are about four and a half million so-called "farm units" in the United States. But only two million of these have market sales of $2,500 or more per year.[2] These are the core of our farming industry, and produce more than 90 percent of marketed farm output. They are clearly capable of producing as much as the national market can absorb at

---

[2] The top 3 percent of our farms, each with annual sales of $25,000 or more, produce about one third of total commercial output.

reasonable prices. The remaining farm units may thus be regarded as surplus.

Where and what are the remaining farm units? Many of them should not be called farms at all. One and a half million are classified by the census as "part-time and residential farms." The people who live on them usually get most of their income from nonfarm sources and are not really part of the farm problem.

This leaves upwards of a million full-time commercial farms with annual sales of less than $2,500. Almost half a million have cash sales of less than $1,200. After deducting costs of farm operation, this leaves too little for decent family living. The low earnings of these families reflect low productivity, due to a number of causes: too little acreage to employ the full time of the farmer and his family; land which is eroded, depleted of fertility, or unproductive for other reasons; inadequate equipment and poor farming methods; and tenancy arrangements which sometimes give the tenant little incentive for productivity. The greatest concentration of such families is found in the old cotton areas of the Southeast, but they are found also in the cut-over areas of the Lake States, on the fringes of forest regions, and on dry land near the western edge of the Great Plains.

These families constitute a special problem. Raising farm prices doesn't help them much, because they have little to sell. The general answer to their problem is clear: they shouldn't be where they are. They should be on better land or larger farms in other locations, or they should be out of agriculture altogether. But it is not easy to accomplish this in a society which believes in free choice of occupation and residence, and where people can use their freedom to make mistakes.

THE POLICY OF FARM PRICE SUPPORTS

With this background, let us look briefly at the poultices which we have been applying to our agricultural ailments over the past 30 years. Many things have been done about agriculture, but the policy which has gradually assumed central importance is that of price supports. Not all agricultural products are covered by the system. The products which must be supported by law are: cotton, wheat, corn, dairy products, tobacco, rice, peanuts, wool, mohair, tung nuts, and honey. Certain others may be supported if the Secretary of Agriculture so decides. Under this optional provision, support prices have been established for soybeans, cottonseed, oats, barley, rye, flaxseed, beans, and sorghum grain. The products under price support make up about half of total agricultural output, while the remaining half is still sold at free market prices.

A price support is a guaranteed minimum price. If the market establishes a still higher price, well and good. Price is free to fluctuate upward, but it may not fall below the support level. How is the support price calculated? A central concept here is *parity,* which means essentially that the price a farmer receives for his product should bear the same relation to the price he pays for industrial products as it did in some base period. Crudely, "If a bushel of wheat bought a cotton shirt in 1950, it should buy the same shirt today." *Example:* Suppose that in 1950 the price of wheat was $2 per bushel. Instead of shirts we should use some average of all goods purchased, and the government does calculate each month an index of "prices paid by farmers." Suppose that in 1950 this index stood at 100. By 1960 it has risen to 120, an increase of 20 percent. The parity price of wheat in 1960, then, is 20 percent higher than in 1950, or $2.40 per bushel.[3]

The parity price is an arbitrary figure. Take the question of what year or years should be chosen as the base period for parity calculations. There is no scientific answer to this question. The tendency has been to select a base period during which farm prices were unusually high relative to nonfarm prices, in order to get the highest possible parity price. Moreover, there is no reason why the price of wheat should rise at the same rate as prices of other products for all time to come. Divergent price movements in the economy are normal, reflecting mainly the differing rates of productivity increase in different industries. Carried to its logical conclusion, the parity concept would mean that all prices in the economy must march along forever in lockstep. The parity price, despite its pseudoscientific appearance, is actually a piece of "political arithmetic."

But there is more political arithmetic to come. How close should the government come to full parity? Should the minimum guaranteed price be 50 percent of parity, or 75 percent, or 100 percent? This is a central issue in political battles over farm legislation. While the decision is partly arbitrary, the state of demand for farm products can be found lurking in the background. During World War II, demand was very strong and farm prices were allowed to rise to 110 percent of parity before ceilings could be imposed. Postwar needs abroad plus the Korean War kept demand strong through the early fifties, and support prices were typically set at 90 percent of parity. As demand receded toward more normal levels, the administration fought for and secured from Congress a flexible system under which the Secretary of Agriculture could set prices for basic products anywhere between 75 and 90 percent of parity, depending on the supply-demand situation for a particular product.

---

[3] The actual calculation of parity prices is considerably more complicated than this example suggests. Different base periods have been used for different products, usually with a view to getting the highest possible support price for each! Recently, an effort has been made to shift over to a moving base, which would be an average of prices received and paid in the most recent 10-year period. Thus parity prices for 1963 would rest on a base of 1953–62. This has advantages over a fixed base, which tends to get more and more obsolete as it recedes into the past.

Support prices for corn, wheat, cotton, and other basic products in recent years have been close to the 75 percent minimum, while dairy products and others defined by law as nonbasic have been supported at rates down to 60 percent of parity. The price support system thus makes some concession to economic realities.

How does the government make good on its commitment to support the price of cotton at, say, 32 cents per pound? By standing ready to buy any quantity which may be offered on the market at this price. If demand is good or the crop small so that the market equilibrium is above 32 cents, all is well and the government need do nothing. But if the market weakens and the price threatens to fall below 32 cents, the government is bound to start buying and to buy as much as necessary to maintain the price. The lower private demand falls, the more government must buy. In recent years government has held something like a full year's crop of wheat, corn, and cotton, stored in warehouses all over the country at considerable expense.

The fact that the system rests on government purchase and storage explains why it has been confined to nonperishable products. Livestock producers have occasionally descended on Washington to demand support prices for meat, but have invariably been turned down. The deep-freeze lockers of the country are not adequate to hold the meat surplus which would accumulate under a support system. Where supports have been used for products which do not store very well, the result has been a fiasco. Some years ago the large holdings of potatoes in government warehouses began to sprout at an embarrassing rate. Part of the supply was dyed black and disposed of as cattle feed, part was simply destroyed. Potatoes have been out from under supports since that time.

Who gains and who loses under a price support arrangement? The main effects can be explained by a demand-supply diagram (Figure 5). DD and SS are the demand and supply curves for cotton or wheat, or whatever. OP and OQ are the equilibrium price and output which would result in a free market. In the absence of government intervention, buyers would pay and producers would receive $OPBQ$. Instead of this, government undertakes to support prices at OP_1. Immediately a gap opens up between the amount which buyers are willing to take off the market (OQ_2) and the amount which farmers want to produce at the support price (OQ_1). The "surplus," $OQ_1 - OQ_2$, must be purchased and stored by government. The consequences are:

1. Farmers' incomes are increased to $OP_1B_1Q_1$. Only part of this income comes from private buyers (OP_1AQ_2). The remainder comes from the government in return for government purchases ($Q_2AB_1Q_1$).

2. Consumers get less of the product than before, but pay more money for this reduced amount.

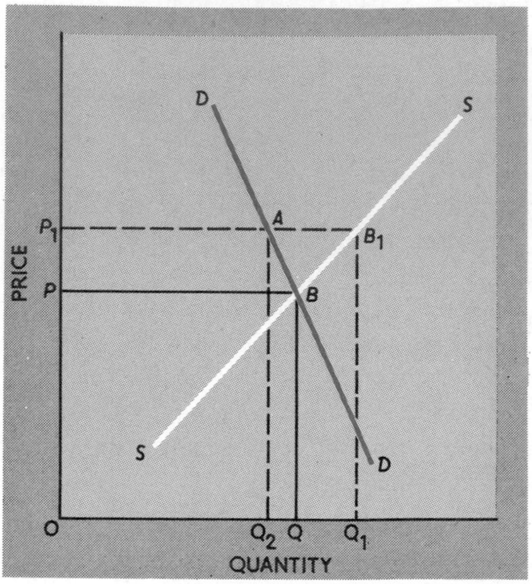

FIGURE 5. Supporting price at OP_1 instead of the equilibrium OP reduces consumption and leads to a surplus of $AB_1 = Q_2Q_1$. Consumers pay more both as food buyers and taxpayers, and this money is transferred to farmers.

3. In their capacity as citizens, consumers are taxed an amount $Q_2AB_1Q_1$, which the government turns over to the farmers in return for the "surplus" produce.

The most embarrassing feature of the system is the tendency for ever-larger quantities of unsold produce to accumulate in government warehouses. Is there any way to avoid this? What about restriction of production? If farmers could be limited to producing OQ_2 instead of OQ_1, then the system would be in balance after a fashion. Present farm legislation provides for production controls on the six basic commodities. After a referendum of growers, in which the control proposal must get a two-thirds majority, the Secretary of Agriculture is empowered to impose production controls. He can say, for example, that only so many million acres may be planted to winter wheat in 1966, and can allocate this total by states, by counties, and by individual farms. The acreage planted to wheat, corn, and cotton has been restricted since the early fifties.

This has still not prevented the accumulation of large surpluses. What happens when a farmer is told that he must cut his wheat acreage by one third? First, the acres which he takes out of production are the least productive acres. The best land continues to be used for wheat. Second, the farmer concentrates fertilizer, labor, and equipment on these remaining acres, works them more intensively than before, and raises the yield per acre. A cut of 20 or 30 percent in acreage, then, may yield little or no reduction in output. The logical response would be for the government to cut acreage still further; but this could lead eventually to a situation in which each farm was only one third utilized, and the foolishness of the system would become transparent.

Thus the accumulation of surpluses continues. Government holdings of commodities acquired through price support operations now total more than $5 billion. In addition to the money tied up in these products, much of which will eventually be lost through spoilage or cut-rate sales, there are heavy warehousing expenses. The only outlet for any considerable part of this surplus lies in foreign countries.

There may have been a case for price supports as a temporary measure under the depressed conditions of the thirties. But as so often happens, what began as a palliative has hardened into a permanent policy. This policy does not get at the basic agricultural problems and has in fact retarded the search for fundamental remedies. The most important defects of the price support program are:

1. It has laid a heavy tax on the nonfarm population, both directly to provide money for government purchase and storage and indirectly through higher food prices. Nor is this clearly a transfer from higher-income urban groups to lower-income rural groups in the population. There are many millions of low-income families in the cities, and food is a large item in their budgets. On the receiving end, the benefits of price supports go mainly to the larger farmers who market most of the farm produce.

2. The program has made little contribution to the problem of rural poverty. The poorest million farms in the country bring little produce to market, so higher market prices cannot add much to their incomes. The larger and more productive a commercial farm, and the less it really needs price supports, the more it benefits from the present program.

3. The program has aggravated the overcapacity which constitutes the basic problem of American agriculture. Guaranteed high prices have kept farms in production which might otherwise have been withdrawn from production and have stimulated expansion of output when contraction was in order. High prices have also choked off demand and made it harder to find market outlets for our productive capacity. This is particularly serious as regards wheat and cotton. U.S. cotton prices are so far above the world level that we are almost out of the export market, which has been taken over increasingly by Brazil, Mexico, Egypt, and other producers. In the domestic market, high cotton prices make it easy for producers of synthetic fibers to undersell cotton and take over more and more of the clothing business. U.S. wheat prices are out of line with those of Canada, Argentina, and other major producers, and our export position has suffered accordingly. A policy of pricing farm products out of the market is not in the long-run interest of the farm population.

4. The logical outcome of guaranteed prices is production control through quotas reaching down to the individual farm. Such a system is clearly undesirable. It keeps all existing farms in operation, but allows each to be operated at only a fraction of its full capacity. Land, equipment, and the farmer's time are all underutilized. Moreover, the

pattern of production becomes frozen. Production of each crop must continue on the same farms, in the same states, in perpetuity. New producers cannot break in, and established producers will not shift to other crops because they would lose their valuable quota privileges. Shifts of production which may be desirable because of changing markets and technology are effectively prevented.

SOME POSSIBLE DIRECTIONS FOR FARM POLICY

This is not the place to develop a comprehensive policy for American agriculture. The issues are complicated and even lifetime students of agriculture are not in full agreement. But one could probably get widespread agreement on the following propositions:

1. The key to a solution of agriculture's problem lies partly outside agriculture, in a rapid and sustained growth of nonagricultural industries. A rapid rise in consumers' incomes raises the demand for farm products. An abundance of urban job opportunities pulls labor off the land and helps hold farm production within bounds. Thus general economic growth is helpful on both the demand and supply sides. Schultz has estimated that (in the United States) urban industries must expand three to four times as rapidly as agricultural production for agriculture to remain in a healthy condition.[4]

2. Elimination of overcapacity requires that a substantial acreage be permanently retired from agriculture. The percentage reduction in acreage must be larger than the desired reduction in output, because of the tendency for the remaining acres to be worked more intensively. During the late fifties, the federal government moved in this direction through the "soil bank" program, but the deposits in the bank were neither large enough nor permanent enough to meet the need. An effective program should incorporate the following characteristics:

   a) The retirement of land from agriculture should be permanent rather than temporary. This amounts to government buying the land rather than renting it, as under the soil bank program.
   b) Emphasis should be on retirement of whole farms rather than parts of farms. In this case the farm operator would probably retire or move to town. If only part of a farm is taken out of production, the farmer will stay on the land and be underemployed.
   c) Priority should be given to retirement of marginal, low-income farms. This would reduce rural poverty as well as farm production.
   d) The program should probably be several times the size of the original soil bank program. This would mean a large initial cost to the government. But

---

[4] Theodore W. Schultz, *Agriculture in an Unstable Economy* (New York: McGraw-Hill Book Co., Inc., 1945).

it would be a once-for-all cost and would remove the need to buy up large surpluses in future years.

3. If land and labor are to be taken out of agriculture and without hardship to the people involved, ways should be found to ease the transition of ex-farmers to urban employment. The first essential is to have enough jobs available through a vigorous full-employment program. The state employment services could help to advise people in rural areas as to where the job outlook is most promising. It might also be desirable to advance moving costs to farm families leaving for the city, to be repaid over a reasonable period in the future.

4. Pricing of farm products should be returned as rapidly as possible to the free market, keeping only the safeguards against depression to be described in a moment. With the scaling down of farm capacity already suggested, market prices should yield adequate incomes to the efficient family-sized farm. Reliance on market pricing would eliminate the problem of burdensome surpluses and the need for production controls. Market prices would also perform their traditional function of shifting land and other resources toward farm products the demand for which is rising away from products where demand is declining.

5. There remains the problem of sharp drops in farm income in depression years. A depression which produces little decline in industrial prices can produce a drop of 20 or 30 percent in farm prices. This degree of instability is more than farmers can reasonably be asked to bear, and there is a good case for some form of protection against it.

A possible approach to the problem has been suggested by Professor Schultz. During prosperity there would be no effort to raise farm prices or incomes above market levels. At the onset of depression, however, a support program would go into action. Government could announce that a depression exists when full-time unemployment rises above some specified percentage of the labor force or when total national output falls by a specified amount. This announcement would set in motion remedial measures designed, not to support farm *prices*, but to support farm *incomes* through direct cash payments.

Suppose that the price of wheat just before the depression began was $2 per bushel. There would be no effort to hold the price of wheat at this level. On the contrary, it would be allowed to fall to whatever extent might be necessary to clear the market. But at the same time government would guarantee the farmer cash payments based on a specified percentage of the predepression price. This percentage could be generous or niggardly. If it were established at 85 percent, wheat farmers would be guaranteed an income of $1.70 per bushel sold. As soon as the market price fell below $1.70, the government would begin cash payments to make up the difference. If at the bottom of the depression the price of wheat had fallen to $1.20, government would be paying farmers a direct subsidy of 50 cents a bushel. Subsidy payments would continue until *either* the market price climbed back above $1.70 *or* the depression was officially declared over.

This would provide depression protection for farmers, similar to the unemployment compensation system for wage earners. It can be justified both as disaster protection for farmers and as a way of sustaining purchasing power during depression. Its merit, indeed, is that it *is* strictly a depression measure. It would not require subsidies to farmers in good years, nor would it involve perpetuating obsolete price levels. There would be a new "parity level" at the peak of each prosperity period.

EXCESSIVE COMPETITION: THE RETAILING REVOLUTION

Until well into the twentieth century the small, owner-operated retail shop was the order of the day. The corner grocer, the druggist, the hardwareman, and the lumberyard operator were key figures in the community. They sold on credit as well as for cash, waited on the customer, ran the packages around to his home if required, and provided a highly personalized retailing service.

Beginning about 1920, the position of the small merchant was challenged by a rapid increase of large retail units, usually linked in chains covering a region or even the entire country. This tendency was particularly strong in grocery, drug, auto accessory, and general or department stores. These mass distributors often bought directly from the manufacturer, eliminating the wholesaler on whom the small merchant had traditionally relied. By large orders, hard bargaining, and eliminating the wholesalers' margin they were able to buy cheaper than the small retailer. In terms of store operations, it turned out that the optimum-sized retail unit was much larger than had previously been realized. The mass distributors were able to handle merchandise at substantially lower unit costs than their smaller competitors. Finally, the chains operated on a cash-and-carry basis. Self-service instead of the hovering sales clerk, elimination of expensive delivery systems, and abolition of credit with its accompaniment of collection costs and bad debts, reduced retailing costs and made possible lower prices.

For these reasons drug and grocery chains could undersell the small retailer by 10 percent or more and still make handsome profits. To most people this price advantage more than offset the loss of credit and delivery services. Customers flocked to the large retailers, and their share of the national market rose rapidly. This was essentially a technological revolution, involving displacement of high-cost retailing methods by lower-cost methods.

But while consumers rejoiced, the small merchant was panicked.

The mortality rate of retail shops has always been high. But the rise of mass distributors accelerated the demise of small merchants, and the survivors found their profits severely squeezed. Cries of outrage soon reached Congress and the state legislatures, accompanied by demands that something be done.

Three main things were done. Many of the states passed laws levying a license fee on retail stores, the size of the fee rising steeply with the number of stores operating under common ownership. This gambit was not very effective. The states did not dare levy high enough taxes to offset the cost advantages of chains and put them out of business. Moreover, the taxes were obviously discriminatory and were held unconstitutional by many state supreme courts. These laws have now generally been repealed.

At the federal level, the Robinson-Patman Act of 1936 provided that price discrimination by a seller which might injure competition among his buyers was illegal unless the seller could prove that the price difference was justified by a difference in costs. This was intended to hamper the mass distributor in bargaining with manufacturers and to prevent him from getting goods at much lower prices than his small competitors. This objective was only partially attained. Chains were able to get around the act by contracting for a manufacturer's total output or by setting up their own manufacturing facilities.

A third device was the state "fair trade" or "resale price maintenance" laws. These laws permit a manufacturer of a branded article to specify a fixed retail price below which no retailer may sell his product. The technique is for the manufacturer to sign a contract with one or more dealers under which they promise, as a condition of receiving his product, that they will not sell it for less than a specified price. Thus far the restriction is not serious, for some retailers might refuse to sign, and it would take the manufacturer a long time to line up all dealers in a state. But resale price maintenance laws commonly provide that, when a price-fixing contract has been signed with one dealer, it becomes binding on *every* retailer in the state, whether or not he has signed it or even heard of it. Any retailer who violates the fixed price is punishable under state law. The result is a monopolist's dream—legalized *private* price fixing, with no public control or standards of reasonableness, but with public enforcement of the fixed price.

The purpose of these laws is to provide a generous guaranteed margin between the retailer's buying price from the manufacturer and his selling price to the consumer. They are promoted mainly by associations of independent retailers in various fields, particularly drugs and cosmetics, liquor, books, photographic equipment, and electrical appliances. The prescribed margins are based on the costs of the small retailer and are intended to prevent the more efficient mass distributors from selling at lower prices and expanding their share of the market. Consider, for example, a drug item on which the manufacturers' price is $1. A small pharmacist might retail this at $2.50 to cover his costs and earn what he considers a reasonable profit. A large drug chain with lower costs and markups could retail the item profitably at $1.75. In a free market, the retail price would tend toward $1.75. The small man's profits would be squeezed, and he might be forced to the wall. Under resale price maintenance, the small dealers see to it that the minimum price of the article is set at $2.50 or better, and the large chain must observe this price. The chain is thus prevented from passing on its lower costs to the public and winning more customers through lower prices.

It is sometimes argued that retail price fixing benefits the manufacturer as well as the merchant. The manufacturer, it is said, has a valuable asset in his brand name. This value is likely to be impaired by price cutting, since the public tends to reason that low price indicates low quality. There may be a little to this but not very much. On the whole, manufacturers have little to gain from retail price fixing. Political pressure for this type of legislation comes mainly from retailers' associations. Once a resale price maintenance law has been passed, the association sets to work to "persuade" manufacturers to set high fixed prices on their products. If a manufacturer is reluctant, he is brought into line by a threat to boycott his products unless he signs up. Most manufacturers find it prudent to go along with the system, but this does not prove that they are convinced of its merit or that they would try to control retail prices if given free choice.

The immediate effect of a resale price maintenance law is to raise prices of the products covered by it. A number of research studies have found that the effect on prices is substantial. But the matter does not stop there. Guaranteed retail margins encourage various kinds of economic waste. Merchants who are forbidden to compete with each other in price will try to compete through lavish store layouts, delivery facilities, credit terms, advertising, premiums, and the like. Selling costs are needlessly inflated. Moreover, attractive profits combined with inability to control entrance leads to multiplication of retail units. The available business is split up finer and finer, each store operates below capacity, and retailing costs per unit of goods sold are higher than they need be. Retailers can then argue that, since their costs are so high, they must have the protection of resale price maintenance in order to survive. Thus the wheel comes full circle.

There is little doubt that resale price maintenance laws are undesirable. Fortunately, the consequences have been less harmful than might have been expected. The products which lend themselves well to price maintenance comprise only about 10 percent of all retail sales. Food and clothing, where prices fluctuate considerably and brand names are of minor importance, have been little affected. Chain and department stores have gotten around the legislation by introducing their own brand names, which they are free to price as they choose and which are typically priced below the national brands. Finally, there is widespread violation of the fixed resale prices by discount houses and other retail outlets. This is difficult to police, partly because of the number of outlets involved, partly because of doubts about the constitutionality of the price maintenance laws, and partly because manufacturers are lukewarm toward the system. But the fact that price maintenance laws are only partially effective does not justify them. Outright repeal of these laws would be preferable.

SUMMARY

1. Public utility industries are inherently monopolistic, and this has led to regulation of price and service by state and federal agencies.

2. Public regulation, while it protects against exorbitant profits, does not ensure maximum operating efficiency, adequate expansion of plant capacity, or an equating of price with marginal cost. The control boards are hampered by the negative nature of their powers as well as by inadequate staffing.

3. Most countries outside the United States prefer public owner-ship and operation of utility industries. The question of private versus public operation is a technical one, to be decided in each case on grounds of economic efficiency.

4. The basic problems of American agriculture are chronic overex-pansion of productive capacity, short-term instability of farm prices, and low productivity and incomes for the bottom quarter or so of the farm population.

5. Government agricultural policies, which involve guaranteed minimum prices for about half of farm output, have not attacked these problems successfully. The price support system has laid a substantial tax on consumers, benefited mainly the larger farmers who need it least, aggravated the problem of overcapacity, and led toward detailed government control of farm operations.

6. Policy should now be oriented toward reducing farm acreage substantially and permanently, restoring free pricing and free choice by farmers of what to produce, and maintaining farm incomes during depression.

7. Over the past 50 years there has been a gradual displacement of small independent retailers by large chain stores. One way in which the independents have tried to fight back is by sponsoring "fair trade laws" which permit retail price fixing. These laws maintain a needlessly high level of prices, lead to wasteful selling expenditures, and encourage an inefficiently large number of retail units.

DISCUSSION QUESTIONS

1. "The natural monopolies present a simple regulatory problem. It is necessary only to empower a government agency to set reasonable prices and profits." Discuss.

2. Compare the merit of private *versus* public ownership of electric utilities, railroads, and other natural monopolies.

3. When would it be economically desirable for a utility to charge a price below average total cost? How could such a policy be carried out in practice?

4. Local public transportation appears to be a vanishing industry in most cities. What, if anything, can be done about this? (This same question might be raised concerning railroad passenger transport in the northeastern states.)

5. How did American agriculture get into its present situation of chronic overcapacity?

6. What kind of production control system would be necessary to support the present price controls while preventing accumulation of surpluses? What can one say about the economic consequences of such a price-production control system?

7. A favorite proposal (at least among nonfarmers!) is to dismantle price and production controls by stages and to move toward reliance on market pricing. Is this a feasible line of policy? How would you do it?

8. What are the economic consequences of a resale price maintenance law? Why have these laws been less effective in practice than they appear on paper?

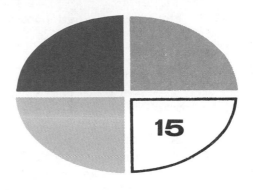

Competition and Monopoly

in Labor Markets

"Well, it's too bad that th' golden days has passed, Hinnissy. Capital still pats Labor on th' back, but on'y with an axe. Labor rayfuses to be threated as a frind. It wants to be threated as an inimy. It thinks it gets more that way. What do I think iv it all? Ah, sure, I don't know. I belong to th' onfarchnit middle class. I wurruk hard, an' I have no money. . . . No man iver sthrikes in sympathy with me."

"They ought to get together," said Mr. Hennessy.

"How cud they get anny closer together thin their prisint clinch?" asked Mr. Dooley, "They're so close together now that those that are between them are crushed to death."

FINLEY PETER DUNNE

IT IS USUALLY SAID, with reason, that labor markets are quite imperfect. Moreover, the imperfections are of a sort which bear especially hard on the sellers of labor. The market is not a neutral instrument.

THE STRUCTURE OF LABOR MARKETS

There are at least three reasons for this. First, there is typically excess labor available in the market. The economy reaches full employment only occasionally, at the peak of an unusually strong business upswing. It may be said that this is not an inherent characteristic of labor markets, that government could hold the economy closer to full employment by correct monetary and fiscal policies. This may well be; but until we have had greater success in doing this, underemployment must be taken as a characteristic of most labor markets in most years.

Ready availability of labor undermines the worker's bargaining position, since the employer can replace him from among the unemployed. It also creates an atmosphere of "job scarcity," and makes the worker less willing to quit one job in hope of a better one. But willingness to quit is the worker's main bargaining weapon; and anything which reduces this works to his disadvantage.

Second, the seller of labor is a necessitous seller. He needs the job to maintain the flow of money income to his family. Few working families have more than a few hundred dollars' of savings. The situation has been improved somewhat by the state unemployment compensation systems; but these make up only a minor part of the wages lost through unemployment.[1]

The employer also needs the worker; but his need is less immediate. If he does not hire one worker, he can usually find another. Even if he finds no one, he will not go hungry himself. Anyone who has hunted for a job knows the psychological situation which this creates. The employer can safely adopt a "take-it-or-leave-it" attitude. The worker, who needs immediate income and who is convinced that jobs are always scarce, is likely to take the first job offer he gets; and for the same reasons, he may cling to an unsatisfactory job rather than try his luck in the market. Resort to the market, which may spell opportunity for the businessman, strikes the worker as hazardous and unpleasant.

Third, the level of information in the labor market is deplorably low. This is true on both sides. An employer has difficulty in locating the best workers available for a particular vacancy and in judging their abilities in advance of employment. The worker's ignorance is even more profound. He normally knows little about wages and conditions in plants other than the one in which he is currently employed. He is dependent on gossip and rumor, and much of what he "knows" turns out to be wrong. So the flow of labor toward more advantageous jobs, which we took for granted in theorizing about wages in Chapter 10, is seriously impeded.

There are additional difficulties in the way of an employed worker who wishes to better himself by changing jobs. Most companies are

---

[1] On this point see Richard A. Lester, "The Economic Significance of Unemployment Compensation, 1948–1959," *Review of Economics and Statistics,* November, 1960. Over this period, total unemployment compensation payments amounted to only about 20 percent of total wage losses from unemployment.

reluctant to "pirate" labor from other companies, and in many areas there are gentlemen's agreements on this point. A worker employed in one company who applies to another will usually not be hired unless his present employer agrees to release him. This reduces the competitiveness of the labor market.

Finally, labor markets are highly segmented. Two lines of segmentation—geographic and occupational—are especially important. Geographically, each town or city constitutes a distinct labor market. Even in the age of the automobile, most people will not seek work far from their homes; and they are reluctant to move to another area where work may be available. So if employment opportunities in an area decline sharply, the result is a "stranded population," much of which will remain unemployed year after year. The most dramatic recent examples are the New England textile workers who were stranded by the shift of this industry to the South, and the coal miners in the Appalachian region who have suffered from a sharp decline in mining employment since World War II.

On the occupational side, there is no market for labor in general. There are markets for chemical engineers, college teachers of French, accountants, carpenters, retail clerks, domestic servants. Just as movement among geographical markets is retarded by cost and uncertainty, so movement among occupational markets is impeded by educational and training requirements. It is quite academic for a plumber aged 30 to decide that he should have been a doctor instead. He or his family would have had to make this decision when he was 18 or earlier.

In recent decades there has been a marked shift of demand toward professional, technical, and managerial occupations, and away from unskilled and semiskilled labor. This has left unemployed hundreds of thousands of people with little skill and often little education, who do not have the qualifications needed for the occupations in which demand is expanding. This problem will not be met merely by creating better labor market machinery or by raising the total demand for labor. It will require reeducation and retraining on a larger scale than has been attempted up to this point.

These structural features of labor markets have ramifications on the *level of unemployment, the allocation of workers among jobs,* and the *determination of wage rates.* There is bound always to be some *frictional unemployment,* because workers displaced from one job do not find their way instantaneously to another. But if the time needed to find work is increased by poor information, lack of central labor marketing machinery, and occupational or geographical maladjustment of labor supply, frictional unemployment will be higher than it need be. The same things interfere with an optimum allocation of workers among jobs, i.e., an allocation which correctly reflects workers' job preferences on one side and their productive capacities on the other. To the extent that square pegs end up in round holes, the people concerned are frustrated and the economy's productive capacity is reduced.

As regards wage determination, the labor market tips the balance of advantage in favor of the employer. It becomes possible for one company's wage level to be lower than that of other companies employing comparable kinds of labor. Why do the employees of this company not rush off immediately to higher-wage companies, as would happen in a purely competitive market? Partly because they are fearful and security-minded, partly because there may or may not be vacancies in the higher-wage companies. In product markets, unsold goods usually can be sold by cutting the price. But it is not feasible for unemployed workers to displace existing employees by lining up outside the plant and offering to work for less.

Supporters of unionism argue that unions are needed to redress the balance of power in wage setting. Critics of unionism maintain that it often does more than this. A strong union may push wages in one company or industry above the level which would prevail under pure competition and exact a monopoly advantage for its members.

Whatever one's view on this point, it is important to realize that the unionized labor market continues to have most of the structural defects of the nonunion market: the possibility of chronic underemployment; a low level of information among workers and employers; lack of a good central labor exchange; geographical immobility of labor; and maladjustment between workers' skills and the skills which are in active demand. The machinery of union-management negotiation is not adapted to cope with these problems. Some of them have to be tackled on a community-wide basis, others on a regional or national basis.

The problems of improved labor marketing are hard to dramatize and so are in danger of being overlooked. But few objectives of public policy are more important, and recent legislative actions (the Area Redevelopment Act of 1961, the Manpower Development and Training Act of 1962, the Economic Opportunity Act of 1964) indicate growing recognition of this fact. The possibilities of constructive labor market action include:

1. **Strengthening of the U.S. Employment Service.** This consists of 50 state employment services, with about 1,900 local offices and a total staff of some 15,000 people. Every city of any size has an Employment Service office, which registers unemployed workers, and refers them to vacancies listed by employees in the area. Most of the labor market traffic, however, continues to bypass the Employment Service. It has been estimated that only about one sixth of all new hirings are made through this channel.

One reason is that the Service deals almost entirely with the unemployed, who must register there to be eligible for unemployment compensation. This lends a certain relief flavor to the activity, leads employers to suspect that Employment Service registrants are the least desirable segment of the labor force, and makes them reluctant to list job vacancies there. It would be helpful to have a clear separation of unemployment compensations and job placement activities and clear recognition of the Employment Service as an *economic* agency rather than a *welfare* agency. It would be useful also to make a more determined effort to register employed workers who are interested in changing jobs. This smacks of "labor pirating" and would no doubt be resisted by many employers; but it seems essential if the local Employment Service office is to become a real clearinghouse for labor.

2. Vocational information, counseling, and training for young people. The critical decisions, which largely determine a person's future occupational level, are made during the high-school years. At this stage, therefore, there should be a maximum effort to mobilize all available information on probable job opportunities and on the individual student's abilities and preferences. A comprehensive program on this front would include such things as: projection of future demand for labor in various occupations, reduced wherever possible to a regional or local level; vocational training programs, oriented toward expanding occupations, for students who intend to go to work immediately after high school; aptitude testing and vocational counseling services in the school; and special effort by the local Employment Service office to register and place each year's graduating group. Much is already being done in these directions, but much more could be done.

There is, of course, a continuing need for vocational information and advice at the college level. There is also a problem of financing the costs of higher education for students from low-income families. This is especially important for professions with a long training period, such as law, medicine, or college teaching. Since this is closely related to income distribution, we shall leave the economics of scholarship and loan funds until next chapter.

3. Adult education and retraining programs. It is certainly desirable to do a good job of training and advising school graduates from here on out. But what about those who have left school over the past 40 years, who are still in the labor market, but whose skills and education do not qualify them for today's jobs? Hundreds of thousands of these people, many entirely unskilled and even illiterate, were left on the shelf despite the vigorous economic expansion of 1961–65. Many have been unemployed for years on end. There is a clear need for large-scale retraining programs to fit these people for employment in expanding occupations.

The first serious attack on this problem was through the Manpower Development and Training Act of 1962, which was amended and enlarged in 1963. This provides programs of vocational training, including basic education for those with very little schooling, running from 52 to 72 weeks. Trainees receive a weekly living allowance, which may not be more than $10 above the average state unemployment compensation payment. Upwards of 100,000 trainees were enrolled during the first year of the program, the most popular occupations being typing and stenography, nursing, machine operating, automobile repairing, and welding. Training is offered only in occupations for which the Employment Service certifies that there is an expanding demand, and the Employment Service is also responsible for placing trainees at the end of their course.

Additional training funds, aimed particularly at young men aged 16 to 21, were provided in 1964 and 1965 as part of President Johnson's antipoverty program. While this program is still in the experimental and development stage, we seem to be nearing the point at which anyone seriously interested in "second-chance" education and training will be able to get it.

4. Aids to geographical movement. Unemployed workers in depressed areas, who must leave their home localities to find employment, present a special problem. In addition to retraining these people, it may prove desirable to contribute to their moving expenses. Britain, Sweden, and a number of other countries are already doing this at moderate cost and to good effect. Moving allowances should not be regarded as welfare payments but as an economic investment designed to raise the employability of the labor force.

THE ECONOMICS OF COLLECTIVE BARGAINING

The potential economic impact of labor market programs is probably as important as the economic impact of collective bargaining. But unionism and collective bargaining are colorful as well as important, so we proceed now to consider them. Space considerations force us to limit the discussion severely. Using the ideas developed in Chapter 10 about labor demand and supply, productivity, and wage determination, what are the main effects which collective bargaining might have on the size and distribution of national output? What evidence is there on the actual importance of these possible effects? Looking at these effects, does collective bargaining seem on balance to be economically useful or harmful institution?

Institutional Arrangements for Collective Bargaining

A word first on how bargaining is carried on. The commonest sort of bargaining is between officials of a single company and officials of the local union which has bargaining rights in that company. But the scope of bargaining tends to expand to cover all companies which compete closely in the same product market. There is a simple reason for this. If the carpenters' union in Milwaukee charges contractor A $4 an hour for carpenters' labor but allows contractor B to hire labor for $3, B can consistently underbid A for construction contracts. So unions typically try to enforce the principle of *the standard rate*. The simplest way to enforce it is for the union to drive a single bargain with the whole group of competing employers.

In some industries competition is confined to a single city. This is typically the case in house building, newspaper printing, local trucking, cleaning and dyeing, and other service industries. Here one usually finds a local union bargaining with an association representing employers throughout the area. The teamsters bargain with the local trucking association, the typographical union with all the newspaper publishers, the carpenters or plumbers with the local building contractors' association, and so on. When an agreement is reached, it becomes binding on all unionized employers in the area.

In manufacturing, competition among employers is usually on a regional or national basis. The logical outcome would be a single bargain between the national union and a national employers' association for the industry. But in a country as large as the United States this is not always easy to arrange, and many employers object to it on principle or because they think they can drive a better bargain through independent action. Thus one finds a wide variety of arrangements, of which the commonest are:

1. *Industry-wide bargaining,* in which a union bargains with a national employers' association or with several regional associations. This is found in railroading, coal mining, hosiery, pottery, men's and women's clothing, merchant shipping, over-the-road trucking, and a number of other industries.

2. *Pattern bargaining,* in which the union singles out one or a few leading companies in the industry as its point of attack. The terms secured from these companies set the pattern for the year, and an effort is made to bring other companies into line under threat of strike. This comes close to industry-wide bargaining, but is not quite the same thing, since there is scope for different terms if a particular company can make a case for exceptional treatment. This approach is used in automobiles, where the union usually selects either Ford or General Motors as its prime target; in basic steel, where U.S. Steel has been the traditional point of attack; and in electrical equipment, where the union tries to set an initial pattern in either General Electric or Westinghouse.

3. *Company-by-company bargaining.* Here local union officials play a more prominent role, while in the first two cases national officials bear the brunt of negotiations. Even where local bargaining prevails, the national union tries to ensure some consistency in wage and other terms of employment. The national convention or the executive board may specify standard demands which each local is expected to put forward in a particular year. National field representatives usually sit in as advisers

on local negotiations and can object to serious deviations from national policy. In many unions, too, local agreements are not effective until they have been approved by national headquarters. The object is to bring an industry-wide perspective to bear on local negotiations and to see that no employer gains a competitive advantage over his rivals.

The outcome of collective bargaining is a written agreement, often termed a *union contract*. But this kind of contract is not enforced by going to court. It is observed voluntarily, because both sides find it to their interest to observe it. It is perhaps better termed a *collective agreement*—collective because it covers a number of workers and frequently a number of employers as well. The agreement usually runs for a year, though some unions negotiate 2-year or 3-year agreements. Some time before the agreement expires the two sides choose representatives, formulate demands, and begin negotiations over terms of the next agreement. If they are unable to settle their differences before the old agreement expires, a strike usually follows. But more than 99 percent of the agreements which expire each year are renewed successfully without a strike.

The signing of an agreement does not end all differences of opinion between union and management. The wording of the document is never perfectly clear. The union may contend that clause 12 of the agreement should be interpreted in a certain way, while management views it as meaning something quite different. There may also be disputes over facts. The agreement says that a worker may be fired for drinking on duty. A foreman fires John Jones for drinking, but Jones says the foreman is wrong and appeals the case. Should Jones stay fired or shouldn't he? If peace is to be maintained in the shop from day to day, there is need for judicial machinery to decide issues of fact and interpretation arising during the life of the agreement. Without this, the union would either have to accept all management decisions during the year or would have to strike frequently over small grievances.

This need is normally met by a *grievance procedure,* which is a standard feature of collective agreements. It provides that an aggrieved worker may take his case to his union representative, who will discuss the matter with the foreman. If the matter is not adjusted at this level, it is passed up to successively higher levels of union and management, perhaps culminating in discussions between a national union official and the company's vice president in charge of industrial relations. If agreement cannot be reached even at the top, the case is usually referred to a neutral arbitrator from the outside, and both sides agree to accept his decision.

Economic Consequences of Collective Bargaining

What difference does it make whether wages and other terms of employment are set by union-management negotiation or set unilaterally by the employer in the context of labor market forces? What are the economic consequences of collective bargaining? This is a hard question, since it involves comparing what is with what might have been. Would automobile workers earn less than they actually do if they had remained unorganized? How much less? How would one find out? One is bound to speculate about such questions even if one cannot answer them conclusively.

Wages and Income

A union is a monopoly in the sense that it substitutes a regulated wage rate for a market-determined rate. But the theory of business monopoly is not helpful in analyzing unionism. It is plausible to assume as a first approximation that the business monopolist maximizes profit. But the union is not selling labor at a profit, and it is not clear that it has an incentive to maximize anything. We are forced to devise some other basis for analyzing union policy.

One approach is to regard the union as a political body whose leaders are concerned mainly with survival of the organization and with keeping themselves in office. They must win enough in wages and other benefits so that the members do not become dissatisfied to the point of revolt. This suggests some common-sense rules: never take a wage cut; make sure that wage increases at least keep up with cost of living increases; try in addition to win as much as other unions which might be considered comparable to your own.

The union cannot, of course, write its own ticket. Employer resistance must also be considered. This will vary with economic circumstances—the poorer the profit prospects, the harder a fight management will put up. In a depressed industry or a depressed year, union leaders may have to settle for no gain and explain this to the members as best they can.

This kind of analysis is not very precise and does not answer the question whether unionism tends to push wages in some industries out of line with those in other industries. Nor does one get an easy answer by looking at wage statistics. For comparative purposes, one should know what the relative wage levels of different industries would be if all were unorganized. Or more strictly, what relative wages would prevail if all industries were unorganized *and if all labor markets were perfectly competitive?* Obviously we cannot know, and so we are forced back on estimates subject to considerable error.

Economists who have worked on this problem[2] conclude that some unions at some times have raised the relative wage level of their

---

[2] See, for example, Albert Rees, *The Economics of Trade Unions* (Chicago: University of Chicago Press, 1962), chap. iv; and H. Gregg Lewis, "The Effects of Unions on Industrial Wage Differentials," in the N. B. E. R. conference volume *Aspects of Labor Economics* (Princeton, N.J.: Princeton University Press, 1962).

industries, while other unions at other times have not. A union is in the best position to enforce out-of-line wage rates where: (1) entrance to the industry is difficult, so that it is hard for new nonunion firms to get established; (2) the workers involved are in a strategic position and can stop production by walking out, as is true of truck drivers or building tradesmen; (3) the group does not cost much to buy off, because its wages form a small percentage of production costs; (4) industry profits are high because of rapid technical progress or a rapid rate of increase in demand. In short, an inelastic and rapidly rising demand curve for labor is favorable to abnormally large wage increases.

Even successful unions have rarely won a large wage advantage for their members. Estimates run usually in the range of 10 to 20 percent, i.e., wages of the unionized group are this much higher, relative to other wages, than would be true under nonunion conditions. The moderate size of the impact is surprising. Why have unions in the most strategic positions not secured larger relative gains? One element in the answer has already been suggested: the union official is not a maximizing monopolist but a political leader. Why should he try to extract the last cent from employers if he can satisfy his members by just "keeping up with the Joneses" in the matter of wages? He may be conscious also that very large wage increases will reduce employment in the industry and hence the size of his dues-paying membership. In some industries a union which pushes wages too high may be undercut by the growth of nonunion companies operating at lower wage levels. The union must reckon also with employer resistance to wage rates which are clearly out of line with those for comparable labor. These and other checks have apparently been sufficient to prevent major distortion of interindustry wage relations.

A second major effect of collective bargaining is on the relative wage levels of companies within the same industry. Under nonunion conditions, it is not uncommon to find a range of 30 or 40 percent between the highest-wage and lowest-wage firms in an industry. As an industry becomes unionized, the union typically tries to move toward a uniform wage level for competing companies—a standard local scale where competition is on a local basis, a national wage scale where competition is national in scope. This means, of course, leveling up intercompany differences rather than leveling down. Suppose that before unionization companies in the industry were paying common labor at rates varying from $1.25 to $2.00 per hour. The union may try in the first instance for a minimum rate of $1.75 throughout the industry. But the union scale is not applied inflexibly. If a company can convince the union that paying the standard rate would put it out of business, it may be allowed to pay less. Unless a company is hopelessly inefficient, the union hesitates to push it over the cliff and throw people out of work. At the upper end of the scale, companies already paying above the standard rate will not be allowed to level down; but they may be allowed to mark time while the rest of the industry catches up with them. The union's strategy is gradually to herd companies in the direction of a common wage level, with full equalization as an ultimate ideal.

Efficient, high-wage companies will not be hurt by this policy. But the less efficient companies are put under pressure to raise their efficiency or perish. Some sources of inefficiency, such as obsolete equipment or poor location, may turn out to be irremovable. But if the main difficulty is poor administration, management may be able to offset the higher wage level by working harder. Union wage pressure can be a powerful stimulus to management effort and efficiency.

Unions argue that the principle of the standard rate is fair and natural. If a loomfixer is worth so much per hour to one textile mill, he should be worth the same amount to another. In a purely competitive labor market, workers of the same skill and efficiency would receive the same wage. The union is simply trying to offset the deficiencies of actual labor markets and to duplicate the results of pure competition. A further argument is that the standard rate "puts a floor under competition," and prevents any company from gaining an unfair competitive advantage by underpaying its workers.

These arguments are persuasive for companies in the same geographical area. Some question may be raised, however, about the wisdom of leveling up plants in different areas. Suppose a shirt factory in Chicago is competing with a shirt factory in a small Wisconsin town where living costs are 10 percent lower. It can be argued that the Wisconsin plant, instead of being forced to the Chicago level, should be allowed to pay 10 percent less, which would still give its workers the same living standard as the Chicago workers. One consideration is whether it is desirable, as a matter of social policy, to encourage decentralization of industry from metropolitan areas to smaller centers. Leaving a gap between small-town and big-city wage rates will encourage decentralization, while complete leveling will discourage it. A similar problem arises as regards the southern states, which have traditionally had somewhat lower living costs and considerably lower wage rates than the northern states. The wage gap has encouraged industrialization of the South, and closing this gap would probably retard the rate of industrialization. Which course is desirable is not just a question of equity to wage earners but also a question of national policy on industrial location.

A third important effect of collective bargaining is on the *form* in which workers receive their incomes. The weekly paycheck is by no means the whole story. Workers also receive paid vacations, paid holidays, year-end and other special bonuses, company retirement pensions, free medical and health care under employer-financed schemes, supplementary unemployment benefits, severance pay, and a variety of other benefits. In the nation's larger corporations, these indirect payments now form 25 percent or more of total labor costs, and the percentage is rising each year. Union pressure is largely responsible for the rapid spread of such payments. The wage bargain has become quite complicated, and a "package" of (say) 10 cents an hour may consist of a 5-cent-an-hour increase in wage rates plus increases in supplementary benefits which cost the company another 5 cents per payroll hour.

The first question is whether the union, by scattering its demands over wages and supplementary benefits, is able to get more than it could otherwise. Probably not, or at least not much more. In the illustration just given, if the company was willing to concede a total package costing 10 cents an hour, it would probably have been willing to give about the same amount as a straight wage increase. So the main effect of union pressure for fringe benefits is not to increase workers' total income but to alter the distribution of this income—less in direct wage payments, more in supplementary benefits. It is an interesting question whether unions have gone further in this direction than their members would prefer. Cases have been reported in which the members, when given a choice of alternatives, voted to take the total increase in wage rates and to skip the supplementary benefits. But it is true also that members benefit from and appreciate health care, pensions, and the like when they actually receive them, even though they might not have been farsighted enough to "buy" these things by foregoing immediate wage increases. One can argue that union leaders' emphasis on supplementary benefits is a desirable corrective to workers' shortsightedness.

Hours of Work

One of the most striking trends in American industry is the great reduction in the work week over the past century. The early New England textile mills worked an incredible 72-hour week. Today the 5- or 5½-day week, with 35 to 40 hours of working time, is the general practice. In addition to this reduction of weekly hours, there has been a considerable reduction in *annual* hours of work through the spread of paid holidays and vacations. Long-service employees now generally receive from 2 to 4 weeks vacation, and most companies provide from 6 to 10 paid holidays during the year.

Unions have taken the lead in pushing for reduction of working hours. The rise of productivity and real wages over the past century would doubtless have brought some reduction in any event. With rising hourly wages, a rational worker would use part of his larger income to "buy" more leisure. It is not easy, however, for the worker to make his preferences effective. He cannot bargain with the employer for an individual hours reduction as he can for an individual wage increase. Everyone in the plant must work the same schedule, and so reduction of hours requires an institutional decision. Employers have been slow to make such decisions, and unions have had to nudge the employer again and again.

Until recently, reduction of the work week probably added to national output. Experimental studies have shown that reducing hours from, say, 60 to 54 typically increases weekly output per worker. Reducing hours again from 54 to 48 will probably still bring output gains. The shorter week means that workers are more thoroughly rested, less subject to illness and accidents, able to work harder and to turn out more per hour. But as hours are shortened, this effect tapers off. Eventually the increase in output per hour will no longer outweigh the reduction in hours, so that weekly output must fall. Just where this point is depends on the kind of work, and particularly on how much muscular effort and fatigue is involved. For most kinds of work it seems likely that a reduction of hours from 40 to 30 would mean a drop, though not a proportionate drop, in weekly output.

We have thus reached the point at which hours reduction is beginning to cost something in terms of output and real income. Unions in the future will be increasingly in the position where to cut hours will mean giving up some income which their members might have enjoyed. This does not mean that hours should not be cut, for workers may consider the increased leisure worth what it costs. But the choice needs to be put clearly before union members so that they can reach an informed decision.

Union leaders probably tend to overshoot the mark and to press for shorter hours than the members would choose if they were in possession of all the facts. Straight thinking is beclouded particularly by the fallacious notion that shorter hours are a remedy for unemployment. Whenever there is serious unemployment in an industry or in the economy at large, unions argue that unemployment could be eliminated by reducing the work week. Suppose there are a million workers attached to the automobile industry. With current demand for cars and modern production methods, only 750,000 workers are needed, while the remaining 250,000 are unemployed. Could this situation not be corrected by reducing the work week from 40 hours to 30? A million workers employed 30 hours a week would provide the same number of man-hours to the industry as 750,000 working 40 hours a week; and if we overlook the possibility that output per man-hour might change in the process, the whole million could now be hired.

But employment in the proper sense of man-hours worked has not been increased by this change. What has happened is that unemployment, instead of being concentrated on certain workers, has been spread evenly over the whole labor force. *Full-time* unemployment has disappeared, but this is paid for by the fact that everyone now gets less work and income than before. This sort of work-sharing may be appropriate to tide over a temporary slump. It is not an appropriate way of meeting a permanent decline in an industry's demand for labor. The only genuine remedy for the situation is to create enough job opportunities elsewhere in the economy so that the 250,000 surplus automobile workers can move out of that industry into others.

In the same way one can show that cutting hours is not an appropriate remedy for general depression. It does nothing to create additional employment, but simply spreads a low volume of employment more evenly over the available labor force. The proper approach is to raise total demand for labor.

Working hours, then, is an area in which union pressure has had a healthy effect in the past but may have undesirable effects in the future.

Job Tenure and Job Security

Union contracts usually regulate the conditions under which workers may be hired, transferred, promoted, laid off, or discharged.

As regards hiring, the union office sometimes serves as an employment exchange. This is traditional in industries such as building construction where the workers are skilled craftsmen, the demand for them fluctuates irregularly, and many employers are too small to maintain their own recruitment systems. When a man is needed, the employer calls the union office, and the business agent looks about for a suitable candidate. It is understood that union members will be given preference in employment, and that only if the union office is unable to refer anyone will the employer look elsewhere. This kind of arrangement, known as a *closed shop*, was outlawed by the Taft-Hartley Act of 1947 and may no longer be written into union contracts. It continues on an informal basis, however, in printing, building construction, and certain other industries where it has been customary for generations.

A much commoner kind of provision is the *union shop* which is found in about two thirds of all collective agreements. This does not limit the employer's freedom of hiring or the right of any worker to seek a job. But once a man has been hired, and if he survives the probationary period, he must join and remain in the union as a condition of continued employment. This means basically that he must pay dues, which in most unions run between 1 and 2 percent of workers' monthly earnings. Beyond this he is free to take as much or as little part as he chooses in union affairs. The union shop is usually accompanied by a *checkoff* clause, under which union dues are deducted from the worker's paycheck along with social security and other deductions and are turned over directly to the union by the employer.

The union shop is legal under federal law, but has been banned by state law in a number of southern and western states. The basic argument for the union shop is that, since the union bargains for all workers in the plant, all workers should contribute to its support. We do not allow residents of a town to decide whether or not to pay taxes in return for the educational, police, and other services which the town provides. Why should any worker be allowed to get a "free ride," receiving all the benefits of the union contract and the grievance machinery, but contributing nothing to the cost of these services? A supplementary argument is that a union whose security is guaranteed can afford to be more reasonable and constructive in collective bargaining. If people can drop out at will, the union must engage constantly in selling itself to the workers. The simplest way to do this is to denounce the employer and keep stirring up grievances against him. Only a secure union can admit that the employer is sometimes right and settle issues in ways which all members may not approve.

Against the union shop, it is often argued that it interferes with the right to work. The state antiunion shop laws are usually termed "right-to-work laws." This rests on a misunderstanding. Except for a few unions which exclude Negroes, women, or other categories of worker from membership, the union shop does not prevent anyone from getting a job or the employer from hiring anyone he chooses. (These discriminatory membership provisions are, of course, undesirable and should be eliminated.) The effect of a union shop is to bar *the right to work at a particular company without paying union dues*. The burden imposed on workers is mainly financial. A few workers may have conscientious objections to unionism and may feel compulsory membership as a violation of personal freedom; but these cases are rare. It is usually the worker's pocketbook which is hurting, not his conscience.

The central issue is whether workers gain enough from a strong union to warrant taxing all employees for its support. One's opinion on this is bound to depend on one's assessment of how much workers gain through collective bargaining. Those who feel that workers would do about as well for themselves without a union should logically oppose the union shop. Those who believe that workers benefit materially from unionism will be inclined to support it. There is thus no demonstrably right answer to the union shop debate even at an objective level, and certainly not in the hurly-burly of bargaining, where the divergent interests of union and management typically lead them to take opposite sides.

A less controversial but very important group of rules are those governing transfer, promotion, and layoff. A vacancy opens up for a desirable job in the plant. Who shall get first chance of promotion to it? A decline in business means that some workers must be demoted or laid off. Who shall be the first to go?

Standard union policy is to require, first, that insiders be given preference over outsiders. Present employees must be given a chance to bid for promotion before the employer looks elsewhere. Workers who have been laid off during a slump must be given the option of returning to work before new people are hired. Second, in choosing among insiders, main emphasis is placed on length of service or seniority. If two workers bidding for promotion have approximately equal ability, the senior man will normally be given preference. In case of layoff, those with least seniority will be laid off first and recalled last.

Definite rules on these matters enable each worker to know where he stands, and reduce the possibility of arbitrary action by foremen and supervisors. A worker's security in his job increases with length of service, which seems a fair arrangement. The seniority system has, nevertheless been criticized on the ground that, if people are thoroughly secure in their jobs, they will work less effectively. The psychological basis for this argument seems doubtful. Are fear and insecurity really the best stimuli to effort? A more cogent argument is that undue emphasis on seniority in promotions may block talented young people from working up quickly to positions worthy of their ability. This is a problem, and management usually tries to retain enough flexibility to recognize outstanding merit.

Finally, the union contract normally provides that workers may be discharged only for specified reasons, and that the union may appeal any discharge which it considers unjustified. For older workers and long-service workers, in particular, discharge is a drastic penalty which should be exercised with restraint. A high proportion of discharges are appealed by the union through the grievance procedure, and many end up in arbitration. Protection against unjustified discharge is perhaps the greatest single benefit which a union brings to its members. An outside check on management's actions also makes for clearer disciplinary policies and more careful execution of those policies. Indeed, the growth of unionism has produced a major tightening and improvement of personnel administration throughout American industry.

Work Speeds and Production Methods

It has often been remarked that the employment bargain is open-ended. It specifies how much the employer must pay, but not how much effort he is entitled to get in return. How much should the worker deliver for his hour's pay? Under piece-rate or incentive payment, this comes down to time-study decisions on how many seconds or minutes should be allowed for each production operation. Under hourly payment, it may come down to decisions on the speed of assembly lines or the number of machines which one worker must tend. On unmechanized hand operations, it comes down to a daily battle of wits between worker and foreman.

Unions insist that decisions on work speeds and work assignments be brought under joint control. The result is sometimes a slower pace of work and hence higher labor costs per unit of output. Automobile assembly lines do not run as fast as they did in preunion days. But to say that this is economically harmful would amount to saying that employers' judgments are always right and that the worker is not entitled to an opinion. The worker clearly is entitled to an opinion on anything which so intimately affects his daily life on the job. There may be cases in which work speeds have been reduced to an unreasonable extent. In general, however, it seems likely that union pressure has resulted in a better balance between workers' interest in moderate work speeds and consumers' interest in high output at low cost.

Workers are convinced that full employment is a rarity and that there are typically not enough jobs to go round. So some unions have tried to create additional employment for their members by requiring the hiring of unnecessary men, or severely limiting the tasks which each worker may do, or requiring the use of antiquated tools and time-consuming methods. Other unions have resisted displacement of labor by improved machinery and production methods. Such policies are particularly likely in industries where employment is declining because of technical progress or declining demand for the product.

Railroading is a good example of a declining industry in which the unions have struggled to maintain employment by enforcing traditional work rules. The effort to force continued employment of firemen in diesel locomotives has caused several threatened rail strikes and is still not fully resolved. The building trades, while by no means declining, have opposed prefabrication of housing, insisted that building materials be cut and prepared at the building site rather than the factory, set needlessly high quality requirements in some cases, and taken negative attitudes toward such modern developments as spray painting. Professors Haber and Levinson of the University of Michigan estimate that restrictive practices in the building trades have raised on-site labor costs by 8 to 24 percent, depending on the area, and have raised the selling price of a house by 2 to 7 percent.[3]

Unions in manufacturing have usually not resisted technical progress; and where they have resisted, they have not succeeded for very long. Employment in automobiles, basic steel, and some other heavy manufacturing industries has been shrinking gradually as a result of mechanization and automation. Unions in these industries, instead of opposing the new developments outright, have concentrated on cushioning the shock to their members in various ways: adequate notice of impending layoffs; provision for transfer of displaced workers to jobs in other plants of the same company; early retirement of older workers with adequate pensions; and substantial severance pay for workers laid off permanently. In return for cooperation in these matters, employers have been given a free hand on mechanization decisions.

---

[3] William Haber and Harold M. Levinson, *Labor Relations and Productivity in the Building Trades* (Ann Arbor: University of Michigan Bureau of Industrial Relations, 1956), especially chaps. vii–ix.

In Summary

Even this brief account reveals the wide-ranging impact of union policies. Some of the consequences described can be set down as broadly favorable: for example, the equalizing of wage scales for competing companies in the same industry, the control of work speeds and work assignments, the recognition of earned rights in a job through length of service, the protection of employees against arbitrary discipline and discharge. But other unfavorable effects can be cited: for example, some distortion of wage relations between industries, some tendency to minimize the importance of merit as against seniority in making promotions, inflation of costs in some industries by employment of unnecessary labor or antiquated methods. Since the size of most of these effects is hard to measure, it is almost impossible to say whether the desirable consequences outweigh the undesirable ones or vice versa. The reader must make up his own balance sheet.

One word of caution: a trade union is more than an economic institution. It is also a club, a forum, a political body. A final judgment on the social utility of unionism should not be based on economic grounds alone but should take these other roles into account.

PUBLIC POLICY TOWARD COLLECTIVE BARGAINING

Whatever we may think of unions, they exist and are likely to exist in something like their present form for a long time to come. We turn now to examine the legal controls on unionism and collective bargaining and some of the proposals for reform in the control system.

Until recently, unions were controlled entirely through the courts of law. Anyone injured by, or fearing injury from, a union could sue for damages or seek an injunction ordering the union to desist from striking or other actions. Pickets could be arrested for disrupting traffic or other offenses. Public policy was represented by a legal tradition which was critical of, and even somewhat hostile to, trade unionism.

The first important statute on labor relations was the Norris-LaGuardia Act of 1932. This Act, which forbade injunctions against peaceable strikes and other normal union activities, struck down the strongest legal weapon in the hands of employers. Freed from this legal disability, it was believed that unions could hold their own with employers and that there was no need for government to intervene further.

This laissez-faire policy was superseded almost immediately, however, by a policy of positive government support for union organization, embodied in the National Labor Relations Act (Wagner Act) of 1935. A union claiming to represent a majority of workers in a plant or other unit could appeal to the National Labor Relations Board for a secret ballot to test its claim, and if successful would be certified as bargaining agent. The employer was then obliged to bargain with the union and to sign a written agreement. He could not discharge men for union membership or discriminate against the union in other ways. Complaints of "unfair labor practices" by the employer could be taken to the National Labor Relations Board.

Aided by this legal protection and by favorable economic conditions, unionism flourished mightily between 1935 and 1945, to the point where many felt that the balance of power had swung too far in labor's direction. A wave of postwar strikes in 1946 contributed to a critical public attitude and to election of a Republican congressional majority in the fall of that year. In 1947 Congress passed the Labor Management Relations Act (Taft-Hartley Act). This Act continued the NLRB and its election machinery and continued the prohibition of unfair labor practices by employers. But it added a list of unfair labor practices by unions—refusal to bargain, intimidation or coercion of workers, strikes to upset an NLRB election, secondary boycotts—which could be appealed to the NLRB by aggrieved employers or workers. It also prohibited the closed shop, encouraged state legislation to limit the union shop, set up a special procedure for national emergency disputes, provided that union officials must file non-Communist affidavits, and a number of other things.

The objective of the Wagner Act was to encourage unionism by prohibiting certain antiunion tactics of employers. The stated purpose of Taft-Hartley was to equalize the legal position of the parties by prohibiting certain tactics of both sides. Taft-Hartley also implied that the individual worker might need protection against the union as well as against the employer, and that the general public needed protection against crippling strikes.

Public opinion continued critical of unionism during the fifties. Congressional investigations revealed numerous instances of financial and other malpractices in union government. The Landrum-Griffin Act of 1959 undertook to regulate internal union affairs in considerable detail.

Since 1930, then, the federal government (and to a lesser extent the state governments), has gotten deeper and deeper into regulation of union organization and union-management relations. Labor relations has become a lawyer's paradise, into which it is unwise for a nonlawyer to venture. But we may enumerate briefly the main kinds of thing which are now subject to specific regulation.

1. Union recognition. A union which claims to represent a majority in an "appropriate bargaining unit" may apply to the NLRB for certification. (The NLRB, incidentally, decides what is an "appropriate unit" in each case—a single craft, all workers in the plant, several plants of the same company, or what not—this issue often being hotly contested by the parties.) If the union's claim is upheld by a name check or a secret

ballot, it is certified as bargaining agent. The employer is then bound to bargain in good faith with the union. He is not obliged to make concessions, but on any point where agreement is reached, he must be willing to sign a written contract. A certified union may not be challenged by another union for at least a year, but after that time a new election may be held if demanded. Workers may also petition the NLRB for an election to "decertify" an established union which is believed to have lost its majority status.

2. Union and employer tactics. The employer may not discharge or otherwise discriminate against workers for union membership. Nor may he threaten or coerce them—for example, by saying that "if you join the union, this plant will close down." He is free, however, to make speeches and express his disapproval of the union in a nonthreatening manner. On its side, the union must bargain in good faith with the employer. (There have been cases in which the union simply laid a completed contract in front of the employer with a "take-it-or-leave-it" attitude.) The union may not threaten or coerce workers into joining the union. It may not pressure an employer to deal with it where another union has been certified by the NLRB. It may not pressure an employer with whom it has no direct dispute to induce him to stop doing business with another employer who is the real object of the union's attack (a "secondary boycott").

3. Content of the agreement. It is doubtful whether anyone intended the federal government to get into the business of deciding what may or may not be written into a union contract. The law, however, requires both union and employer to bargain in good faith over "terms and conditions of employment." What is a term or condition of employment? Can the union demand a voice in management decisions on price policy or plant location? Can the employer demand changes in internal union procedures? By deciding such issues in hundreds of cases, the NLRB has defined what the parties are not obliged to bargain about, and by implication, what things are not part of a normal union contract. In addition, no contract may contain a closed shop clause binding the employer to hire only union members, though some contain provisions amounting almost to the same thing.

4. Strikes. Peaceable strikes for normal union objectives are clearly lawful. But if the object of a strike is unlawful—for example, to upset the results of an NLRB election—all activities in support of it become unlawful. And even in a lawful strike, physical violence against nonunion workers or others is not permissible. There is considerable scope for local law enforcement officials and local courts to decide what constitutes peaceful picketing.

The volume of strike activity is not high. With rare exceptions, such as 1946, time lost per year through strikes averages less than 1 percent of the man-days worked in unionized industries, or considerably less than the time lost through illness, accidents, and absenteeism. While these strikes may cause loss to the parties, they usually involve little inconvenience to the public; and they are part of the cost of operating a collective bargaining system. It is mainly the threat of a strike which causes the parties to compromise their divergent demands and reach an agreement. If a strike occurs, the mounting losses on both sides continue to exert pressure, and when the losses become heavy enough, the strike will be settled. Viewed from this standpoint, a strike is one route toward eventual agreement.

There are certain industries, however, in which continuous operation is essential. A railroad strike has a disruptive effect on the national economy. So does a long strike in basic steel. Strikes in local transportation, police or fire protection, electric power, food and fuel deliveries, or hospital service can endanger public health and safety. There is no satisfactory federal procedure for handling such disputes. The Taft-Hartley procedure, which provides for an 80-day waiting period while a public board investigates and reports on the dispute, has not worked very well. The disputants typically sit out the waiting period and then proceed with their strike plans. If the dispute is important, it usually ends in mediation by the Secretary of Labor or even the President. Several of the states have laws covering strikes in local utilities and public services, of which the Massachusetts and New Jersey laws are perhaps the most effective. But none of the existing procedures is fully satisfactory, and handling of these emergency disputes continues to be one of the most difficult and challenging areas of industrial relations.

5. Union government.   A union has traditionally been regarded as a voluntary private association, comparable to a lodge or club, whose internal affairs were of no public concern. With the growing economic power of unions, this view has become less and less appropriate. During the forties and fifties the courts became more receptive to suits over internal union matters. In 1959 the Landrum-Griffin Act set up legislative standards for union conduct and vested broad enforcement powers in the Department of Labor.

Briefly, the law requires that regular financial reports be made available to the members and filed with the Department of Labor. Financial transactions by a union officer which might involve him in a conflict of interest with the union must be reported. Direct embezzlement of union funds is, of course, forbidden; and employers may not bribe a union official to influence his conduct in collective bargaining. All members must be given an equal right to participate in union meetings and elections. Local union elections, and election of delegates to the national convention, must be by secret ballot. Local officers must be elected at least every 3 years, and national officials at least every 5 years. No union member may be fined, expelled, or otherwise disciplined without a full and fair trial. Former convicts and former members of the Communist Party are forbidden to hold union office for a specified period of years.

Most unions are honestly and efficiently governed. Financial malpractices have existed in a minority of unions, however, such as the Teamsters, some of the building trades unions, and the New York longshoremen's union. The Landrum-Griffin Act should help in detecting and prosecuting such malpractices. Apart from this, it is doubtful that the Act will bring major changes in union government. Control of union affairs, at both local and national levels, is normally concentrated in a small minority of workhorses. Only during crises will more than 5 or 10 percent of the members appear at the local union meetings. So long as the union is delivering satisfactory gains, most members prefer to have others do the work and make the decisions. It is certainly desirable, however, that members be protected in their right to criticize or oppose the existing leadership without threat of economic reprisal.

Hardly anyone is satisfied with our present national labor policy, which is the result of a long series of political compromises. Union leaders would like to see many Taft-Hartley and Landrum-Griffin provisions repealed. Many employers believe that the law should be even tougher on unions than it is at present. But there is no agreement on what kind of new labor legislation should be written if we could wipe the slate clean and start fresh. This is because there is little consensus in the American community on the economic merit of collective bargaining. Without an agreed framework of general objectives, there can be little agreement on specifics.

One common but drastic proposal is abolition of national unionism, sometimes euphemistically described as "prohibiting labor monopoly" or "applying the antitrust laws to labor." A union would be forbidden to bargain with more than one employer in the same industry. Each local union would be confined to one company and would be on its own, without the support of a national organization. The result would be a marked power shift in favor of the employer and a sharp drop in union influence on wages and other terms of employment. What one thinks of this proposal depends essentially on how one answers the questions posed at the end of last section: Are the economic effects of collective bargaining on balance beneficial or harmful? Does unionism have other social and political consequences which should be weighed in the balance?

One of the most experienced scholars and practitioners of labor relations, President Clark Kerr of the University of California, has advanced a drastic proposal of a different sort.[4] He believes that

---

[4] Clark Kerr, "Industrial Relations and the Liberal Pluralist," *Proceedings of the Seventh Convention of the Industrial Relations Research Association* (1954), pp. 14–15.

government has gotten much too involved, and needlessly involved, in the details of union-management relations. He thinks it might be well to sweep the slate clean and go back to a much simpler system with only the following provisions:

1. A government mediation service for industrial disputes, but without arbitration or other compulsory powers.
2. Conduct of representation elections, as is now done by the NLRB.
3. A law limiting union pressure on third parties to get at an employer.
4. A law guaranteeing certain elementary rights—admission to union membership without discrimination, free and equal participation in union affairs, and outside review of expulsion from membership or other penalties imposed by the union.

This would be in a sense a return to the laissez-faire position of the Norris-LaGuardia Act. It would also bring us closer to the position of most other Western industrial nations, in which unions and employers work out their own bargains apart from government, without the maze of regulations which we have created over the years.

LEGAL REGULATION OF WAGES

Only a minority of workers in the economy are organized into trade unions. Some of the lowest-paid groups—farm laborers, domestic servants, store clerks, hotel and restaurant employers, manufacturing workers in rural areas of the country—are largely nonunion. There has consequently been a demand for federal and state laws to set minimum wage rates for all employees. These laws can be regarded either as an alternative to collective bargaining or as a backstop for collectively bargained wage rates. Unions such as the Textile Workers, which have had poor success in organizing their industry and have been threatened continuously by nonunion competition, have been interested in minimum wages for the latter reason.

We have already noted that it is common to find some employers in an area paying considerably less than others for the same kind of labor. These employers are not necessarily greedy nor are their operations necessarily profitable. They are apt to be companies which, because of poor location, inefficient management, or other reasons, are able to earn little profit even when paying substandard wages.

What will happen if a minimum wage is imposed at a level such that the bottom 10 or 20 percent of employers are forced to raise their wages? The most obvious effect is that workers in these companies will get more money. It is also probable, however, that fewer workers will be employed in these companies than before. If labor's marginal productivity schedule remains unchanged in each enterprise, the amount of labor hired will decline as the wage rises.

This decline of employment in the formerly low-wage firms is a positive effect of wage regulation. It is not desirable that some employers be allowed to pay less than competitive wage rates and so be encouraged to absorb additional labor. This will mean overallocation of labor to these enterprises, underallocation to others. It is desirable that each enterprise pay a competitive wage, and that it equate labor's marginal productivity with the wage. Workers displaced in the process should be transferred to other industries. Assuming a full-employment policy which makes enough jobs available, the new allocation of labor will be more productive than the old.

A minimum wage system may affect the supply of labor as well as the demand. The quality of individuals in the labor force varies considerably. There is a fringe of workers whose productive potential is low because of inadequate education and training, low intelligence, physical handicaps, or other disabilities. Employers may be willing to hire such people provided they can pay them enough below the standard rate to offset their lower output. But if a minimum wage is imposed which requires everyone to be paid as much as a worker of standard efficiency, employment of these substandard workers becomes unprofitable and they will be laid off, at some cost in personal hardship and national output.

The basic federal law in this area is the Fair Labor Standards Act of 1937. This Act sets a minimum hourly wage for manufacturing and other industries in interstate commerce. It also requires overtime payment for hours in excess of 40 per week, with some flexibility for seasonal adjustment of hours in agricultural processing and other seasonal industries. Most of the industrial states also have minimum wage laws applying to stores, hotels, restaurants, laundries, and other intrastate industries. Separate minima are often set for each industry, usually after hearings before a public board. The minima are typically well below the federal level.

The minimum wage under the FLSA has been raised by Congress from 25 cents an hour in 1940 to 40 cents in 1945, 75 cents in 1950, $1.00 in 1955, and $1.25 in 1963. These revisions follow an interesting pattern. When a new minimum is set, it is usually about 50 percent of the average hourly earnings in interstate industries. After the minimum is set, the actual wage level continues to rise and the percentage which the minimum forms of the actual gradually falls. When it has fallen to 35 percent or so, Congress gets busy and raises it once more. The minimum wage, in short, lags behind the movement of market rates rather than forcing the pace.

The effect of each revision is to force up a limited number of "stragglers" at the bottom of the wage structure, whose rates are seriously out of line with those prevailing elsewhere. The number of workers affected is typically less than 5 percent of all covered workers, and these are almost entirely in the southern states. The main effect of the FLSA has probably been to bring southern workers in interstate industries somewhat closer to the wage level of comparable industries in the North, and by the same token raised them farther above the wage level of intrastate workers in the South than they would be otherwise. But because the wage impact has been moderate, the employment impact has also been limited. Case studies made after each increase in the minimum fail to reveal any substantial displacement of labor from southern industries.

The FLSA does not seem, either, to have ruled many people out of employment because of its limited coverage of the labor force. Low-quality workers who cannot get hired in interstate industries at the federal minimum can seek employment in intrastate industries. If there is a state minimum wage which rules them out even there, areas such as agriculture and domestic service remain uncovered by any minimum. Thus one effect of the minimum wage system is to sort workers out among several levels of employment on a quality basis.

SUMMARY

1. Certain characteristics of the labor market tend to give the employer a bargaining advantage over the individual worker: there is typically a surplus of labor in the market; the worker needs a job more than the employer needs a particular worker; the worker's knowledge of alternative opportunities is very limited; and competition for labor is often restricted by employer agreements. In addition to biasing the determination of wage rates, imperfect labor markets produce a needlessly high level of frictional unemployment and a failure to match workers' qualifications and preferences with job requirements.

2. Improvement of labor markets would benefit both workers and employers, and increase economic efficiency. Possible lines of action include strengthening of the U.S. Employment Service; improved vocational training, counseling, and placement of high-school students; similar facilities at the college level, plus adequate scholarship and loan funds where required; "second-chance" retraining programs for adults who lack basic literacy or work skills; and financial aids to movement out of declining areas.

3. The *wage effects* of collective bargaining include: some distortion of the relative wage levels of different industries; greater equality of wages among competing companies in the same industry; some decrease in wage differences between larger and smaller communities, and between the northern and southern states; and a growing percentage of workers' income taking the form of supplementary or "fringe" benefits rather than direct wage payments.

4. The *nonwage effects* of collective bargaining include: a marked reduction in weekly and annual hours of work; greater security of job tenure, and greater emphasis on length of service as a factor in promotion or layoff; some reduction of work speeds in certain industries; and some resistance to displacement of labor by improved work methods.

5. Any judgment on the desirability of unionism involves a complex balancing of all these consequences. It should also include consideration of political and social consequences as well as economic effects.

6. Our national policy toward collective bargaining has varied from a negative attitude embodied in court decisions before 1930, to a laissez-faire policy in the Norris-LaGuardia Act of 1932, to positive encouragement of union organization in the Wagner Act of 1935, to a neutral or slightly antiunion position in the Taft-Hartley Act of 1947, to further regulation of internal union affairs in the Landrum-Griffin Act of 1959. One reason for this vacillation of policy is wide disagreement on the merits of unionism within the American community.

7. A serious unsolved problem of industrial relations is orderly adjustment of disputes and prevention of production stoppages in "essential industries."

8. A minimum wage law which brings low-wage companies closer to the level which would prevail in a purely competitive labor market is likely to reduce employment in those companies; but this improves the overall allocation of labor and is not a disadvantage. A more serious problem is that a minimum wage tends to rule some workers out of employment by making it unprofitable to employ people of low productive capacity.

9. Our federal minimum wage under the Fair Labor Standards Act has exerted little pressure on wages and so has had little impact on employment.

DISCUSSION QUESTIONS

1. Is it correct to say that, under nonunion conditions, the employer's bargaining power is usually greater than that of the individual worker? How would you define "bargaining power" in this connection?

2. What do we mean concretely by "a more perfect labor market"? What benefits—to workers, to employers, and to the community—would result from improvement of labor markets?

3. What did you learn in high school about the requirements and rewards of various occupations? What additional information might have been useful to you at that stage?

4. You are now preparing to enter the labor market in a few years' time. In what capacity? Why? Do you have adequate information on training requirements, nature of the work, prospective salaries, methods of locating jobs?

5. What is collective bargaining? What is the function of the collective agreement? Of the grievance procedure? Is it desirable that all unresolved grievances be submitted to arbitration?

6. What are the economic considerations behind union pressure for the standard rate? Over what geographical area is the standard rate policy applied? What are the economic effects of the policy?

7. It is often alleged that unionism distorts the relative wage levels of different industries, as compared with what would happen in a competitive labor market. How would you get evidence to test this proposition?

8. Is reduction of hours an appropriate remedy for unemployment in a particular industry? In the national economy?

9. On what principles could one determine the proper length of work week? Do you think there is any bias in collective bargaining toward setting hours which are either too long or too short?

10. Federal law permits the union shop, but some states have banned it. Who is right?

11. It is sometimes argued that a union which bargains with all employers in an industry has undue monopoly power, and that each union should be restricted by law to bargaining with one employer. What do you think of this proposal?

12. Draft a model law for settlement of disputes in essential industries, indicating what industries you include in this category.

13. Congress has recently been debating proposals to raise the federal minimum wage from $1.25 an hour to some higher level. What evidence would you look at in trying to decide whether an increase, and how large an increase, is warranted?

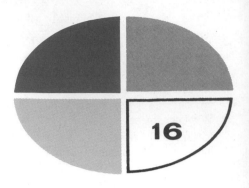

16

Income Distribution, Inequality,

and Poverty

Some people's money is merited,/And other
people's is inherited,
But wherever it comes from,/They talk about it
as if it were something you got pink gums
from.
This may well be,/But if so, why do they not
relieve themselves of the burden by transferring it to the deserving poor or to me?
. . . .
The only incurable troubles of the rich are the
troubles that money can't cure,
Which is a kind of trouble that is even more
troublesome if you are poor.
Certainly there are a lot of things in life that
money won't buy, but it's very funny—
Have you ever tried to buy them without money?
OGDEN NASH

A STANDARD CRITICISM of capitalist economies is that, while the average
level of income may be high, this income is unequally distributed. There
are extremes of wealth and poverty. So we must look further into who
gets how much in the United States, whether income distribution has
been growing more equal or less equal over the course of time, what

418

government has been doing about it, and what we may need to do in the future.

THE DETERMINANTS OF INCOME DISTRIBUTION

The bare facts of income distribution were set out in Chapter 2. But now we must try to explain why the distribution looks as it does.

There are close to 50 million families in the United States, plus more than 10 million individuals living by themselves. The median income of unattached individuals is surprisingly low—only about

TABLE 1

Distribution of Families by Annual Income, before Federal Income Tax, 1962

ANNUAL INCOME (Before Income Taxes)	NUMBER OF FAMILIES (000)	PERCENT OF FAMILIES	AGGREGATE INCOME RECEIVED	
			(Millions)	(Percent)
Under $2,000	3,217	6.9	3,905	1.0
2,000– 2,999	2,902	6.2	7,313	1.9
3,000– 3,999	3,835	8.2	13,491	3.5
4,000– 4,999	4,592	9.8	20,715	5.4
5,000– 5,999	5,075	10.8	27,918	7.3
6,000– 7,499	7,487	16.0	50,436	13.2
7,500– 9,999	8,730	18.6	75,057	19.7
10,000–14,999	6,941	14.8	82,956	21.7
15,000 +	4,111	8.7	100,424	26.3
Total	46,890	100.0	382,215	100.0

Source: U.S. Department of Commerce, *Survey of Current Business*, April, 1964, p. 6.

$2,700 in 1960. The reason is that these are mainly young people who have not yet developed substantial earning power, or handicapped people unable to hold a regular job, or older people dependent on modest pensions. Older people, in particular, have serious income problems. For most purposes, however, it is best to concentrate on the family units which include 95 percent of the population.

The distribution of family incomes in 1962, before federal income taxes, is shown in Table 1. We start with the pretax distribution because we wish to examine how much people receive in the first instance through the operation of the market economy. At a later stage we shall examine how much of this income is taken by taxation.

The median income for all families at this time was about $6,750, that is, half the families in the country had less than this while the other half had more. At the bottom of the scale, about 13 percent of the families were living on incomes of less than $3,000 per year. At the upper end, 23 percent of the families had incomes above $10,000. This top group received 48 percent of all money income.

Why just this degree of inequality, no more and no less? We saw in Chapter 10 that people receive income by providing productive services to the economy. How much an individual receives depends on how much capital or labor power he owns and on the price which these services command in the market. This clue enables us to sort out the determinants of income distribution into four boxes: the distribution of income from labor; the distribution of income from property; the relative size of the labor and capital shares; and a group of other considerations, of which the most important are the relative size of the farm and nonfarm populations, the relative earnings of Negro and white workers, the number of wage earners per family, and the number of people in the population who are unable to work for one reason or another.

Income from Labor

More than three quarters of income produced in the United States goes to those who provide labor services. So the distribution of labor income is the most important single determinant of overall income distribution. We saw in Chapter 10 that the labor market establishes widely differing wage rates for different occupations, from floor sweepers and farm laborers at the bottom to surgeons and corporation presidents at the top.

In a dynamic economy, these occupational wage differences may either widen or narrow over the course of time. If demand for the higher skills is rising rapidly, while supply is restricted by educational or other bottlenecks, occupational wage differences may widen. But as educational and training facilities are expanded, the supply of technical and professional manpower may rise faster than demand, and wage differences narrow again.

In addition to variation in wage rates per hour, there is considerable variation in hours worked during the year. A skilled man worth $4 an hour, if he works a 2,000-hour year, will come out at the end of the year with $8,000. But suppose that, for health or other reasons, he prefers to work only part time. Or suppose there is a recession and he is laid off for part of the year. In this event, he may work only 1,000 hours and earn only $4,000.

This produces shifts in income distribution over the business cycle. During a depression many people are partly or wholly unemployed and drop into the lower-income brackets. Inequality of incomes increases. During prosperity these people are reemployed, their annual incomes rise, and inequality is reduced.

Income from Property

Between 20 and 25 percent of income produced in the United States is allocated to property owners. The amount actually paid out to these property owners is smaller, since businesses save and reinvest part of their earnings. But reinvested profits belong to the owners of the business, just as much as the cash dividends they receive.

Most income-yielding property is held by a small minority of the population. The top 5 percent of income recipients in the United States receive more than two thirds of the dividend payments and about half of all property income. The concentration of property incomes is much greater than that of incomes from work. The top 5 percent of income recipients get only about 10 percent of total wage and salary payments.

The upper-income groups do not consist mainly of idle coupon clippers. It is unfashionable in America to live without working. A recent survey showed that only 2 percent of families with incomes above $15,000 were living solely on property income. About two thirds of these household heads held salaried jobs, while almost all the remainder were self-employed. The high-income family usually combines property income with substantial income from work. The property element, however, makes the overall income distribution more unequal than it would be otherwise.

The Labor and Property Shares

Since labor income is distributed more equally than property income, the relative size of the labor and capital shares becomes important. If labor's share of total income is rising, this will make for a more equal distribution of household incomes, while a rising capital share will have the opposite effect.

The division of income between labor and capital was examined in Chapter 10. The amount each factor receives depends mainly on the quantity of the factor employed in production and on its marginal productivity. These determinants will obviously be changing over the course of time. In the United States, the amount of capital in use has been rising about twice as fast as total labor supply. So, *if relative factor prices remained unchanged,* the capital share would be rising. But this proviso begs the question. The rapid increase of capital means that its relative marginal productivity is falling, so the interest rate is falling relative to the wage rate. The faster increase in quantity of capital, and the relative decline in its rate of return, work in opposite directions. So, on balance, capital's share of income produced may either rise or fall.

There is considerable (though not unanimous) agreement among scholars that the share of labor has increased moderately since 1900, while the capital share has fallen. Three recent studies may be cited.

Irving Kravis estimates that the property share of national income fell from 30.6 percent in 1900–1909 to 23.8 percent in 1949–57.[1] Kendrick's calculations for the private economy, excluding government production, show the property share declining from 30.1 percent in 1899 to 18.6 percent in 1957.[2] Finally, Denison finds the property share falling from 30.5 percent in 1909–13 to 22.7 percent in 1954–58.[3] While these studies use somewhat different methods, they all show property income shrinking from something like 30 percent at the beginning of the century to not much more than 20 percent today.

The increase in labor's share arises partly from the decreased importance of land, which is lumped with capital in these studies. Denison estimates that returns to land were about 9 percent of national income in 1909–13 but only 3 percent in 1954–58. The main explanation, however, is that the real wage level has risen much faster than the rate of return to capital. Kendrick estimates that the real wage per man-hour of labor was almost four times as high in 1957 as in 1899. Real income per unit of capital, however, rose only about 15 percent over this period. This checks closely with Denison's conclusion that real earnings of reproducible capital rose only about 20 percent between 1909 and 1957.[4]

Additional Considerations

Several other considerations deserve brief mention. First is the fact that income levels in agriculture are substantially below those in urban occupations. So some people should leave agriculture, and people have been leaving in large numbers. People who move from agriculture typically raise their income level. Thus the relative decline of the agricultural sector reduces the proportion of low-income families. If by a flight of fancy one can imagine the agricultural sector completely eliminated, income inequality would be considerably reduced.

Second, employers tend to prefer white workers over Negro workers. Partly because of this demand bias, Negro workers typically receive lower wages than white workers for comparable work.[5] They are also usually consigned to the lower occupational levels, and suffer disproportionately from unemployment. To the extent that these disabilities are removed through improved educational and training facilities for Negroes, reduction of discriminatory hiring practices, and maintenance

---

[1] Irving B. Kravis, "Relative Income Shares in Fact and Theory," *American Economic Review,* December, 1959, pp. 917–49.

[2] John W. Kendrick, *Productivity Trends in the United States* (Princeton, N.J.: Princeton University Press, 1961), p. 121.

[3] E. F. Denison, *The Sources of Economic Growth in the United States* (New York: Committee on Economic Development, 1962), p. 30.

[4] Denison, *op. cit.*

[5] For a recent analysis of the evidence on this point, see Alan B. Batchelder, "Decline in the Relative Income of Negro Men," *Quarterly Journal of Economics,* November, 1964, pp. 525–48.

of high overall demand for labor, income inequality in the nation will be reduced.

A third factor influencing household income is that the household may include more than one wage earner. Particularly striking is the growing tendency for married women to work after they are past the peak of child-care responsibilities. Half of all women aged 45–54 are presently in the labor force, and the proportion is expected to increase to 56 percent by 1975.

If married women's propensity to work were randomly distributed over all income brackets, it would not alter the national income distribution. But this is not the case. There is a clear inverse relation with the husband's income level, i.e., the lower the husband's income the greater the likelihood of the wife working.[6] The fact that double incomes are more common at the lower occupational levels tends to pull up the bottom of the income distribution.

Finally, there are several million households in the country which have no member in the labor force. Many of these people may have worked at one time, but have been disabled by accident or disease. Many are older people past working age. There are many broken homes, in which the wife cannot look after the children and hold a job at the same time. This group will be analyzed in our later discussion of poverty, since it constitutes the hard core of the poverty problem.

People who lack productive capacity may receive income payments outside the production process. These are usually called *transfer payments*. They include private pension payments, public pensions under the social security system, government payments to farmers, unemployment compensation, aid to special groups such as the blind or dependent children in broken homes, and general public relief. The more generous are these transfers, the fewer people will fall into the lowest-income brackets.

In sum, the following developments will make for a *more equal distribution* of household incomes: a reduction of wage differentials between the higher and lower occupations; a high level of demand for labor, which will permit everyone to work as many hours per year as he prefers; a reduction in the inequality of property ownership; a reduction in the property share of national income; a decline of agricultural employment as a percentage of total employment; a reduction of Negro-white differentials in wage rates and employment opportunities; increased opportunity for women to seek and find jobs; a reduction in the proportion of the population unable to work; and larger transfer

---

[6] For evidence on this point see Clarence D. Long, *The Labor Force Under Changing Income and Employment* (Princeton, N.J.: Princeton University Press, 1958), chap. vi; and Jacob Mincer, "Labor Force Participation of Married Women," in *Aspects of Labor Economics* (Princeton, N.J.: Princeton University Press, 1962), pp. 63–106.

payments to those who lack work capacity. (You can compile a list of developments making for a *less equal distribution* by throwing each of these points into reverse.)

RECENT TRENDS IN INCOME DISTRIBUTION

So much for possibilities. What has actually been happening in the United States over the past several decades? Has the distribution of household incomes become more or less equal, and why?

In order to talk about trends in income distribution, we need a more precise measure of this concept. One common measure is illustrated in Figure 1. On the horizontal axis we measure percentages of household

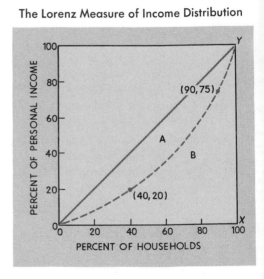

The Lorenz Measure of Income Distribution

FIGURE 1. Each point on the dotted line shows the percentage of income received by a certain percentage of household units. The shallower the line, the more equal the distribution of income. A numerical measure of income inequality can be obtained by calculating A/A + B.

units, while the vertical axis shows percentages of total personal income. If income distribution were perfectly equal, then the first 20 percent of households would receive 20 percent of total income, the first 40 percent of households would receive 40 percent of income, and so on. Income distribution would be represented by points along the straight line *OY*.

We may imagine also the opposite extreme of perfect inequality. Suppose one household received all income in the economy, while the other 99.999 percent received nothing at all. Income distribution would then follow the path *OXY*.

Any actual income distribution will fall between these extremes. Suppose a particular country in a particular year has the distribution shown by the dotted line in Figure 1. This is called a Lorenz curve, after its originator. The curve shown represents a moderately unequal distribution. The lowest 40 percent of families receive only 20 percent of total income, while the top 10 percent receive 25 percent of income. If we call the area above the dotted line A, and the area below the line B, we can get a numerical measure of inequality by calculating $A/A + B$. This is sometimes termed the *Gini coefficient*. It can have any value between 0 (complete equality) and 1 (complete inequality).

A movement toward greater income equality is shown by a shallower Lorenz curve and a drop in the Gini coefficient. A move toward inequality means a bending outward of the Lorenz curve and a rise in the Gini coefficient.

The course of events in the United States since the mid-thirties is shown in Table 2 and Figure 2. The years 1935, 1950, and 1960 have been

TABLE 2

Distribution of Family Personal Income, before Federal Income
Taxes 1935–36, 1950, 1960

QUINTILES (20 Percent Groups)	INCOME BEFORE TAXES					
	MEAN ANNUAL INCOME (1960 Dollars)			SHARE OF ALL PERSONAL INCOME (Percent)		
	1935–36	1950	1960	1935–36	1950	1960
Lowest	827	1,299	1,576	4.2	4.8	4.6
Second	1,840	2,976	3,758	9.3	10.9	11.0
Third	2,803	4,405	5,581	14.2	16.1	16.3
Fourth	4,206	6,045	7,721	20.8	22.1	22.6
Highest	10,161	12,622	15,585	51.5	46.1	45.5
Total	3,951	5,469	6,845	100.0	100.0	100.0

Sources:
1935–36: L. G. Reynolds, *Labor Economics and Labor Relations*, 4th ed., p. 514.
1950. *U.S. Income and Output*, 1958, p. 161.
1960: *Survey of Current Business*, April, 1962, p. 14.
Figures are adjusted to 1960 dollars using Consumer Price Index (1947–49 = 100) revalued to 1960 = 100.

selected for comparison. Table 2 shows the mean income of the lowest 20 percent of families, the next 20 percent, and so on in each year, adjusted to dollars of comparable purchasing power. It shows also the percentage of all personal income received by the lowest 20 percent, the next 20 percent, and so. The corresponding Lorenz curves for 1935 and 1960 are charted in Figure 2.

There has clearly been a shift toward greater income equality. The shift occurred mainly between 1935 and 1950—actually, between 1935 and 1945. From 1945 to the present, there has been little change in the pattern of distribution.

To understand the reduction of inequality between 1935 and 1945 we must look back to the basic factors already described. We shall find that most of them were working in an equalizing direction over this period.

There was a marked reduction in occupational wage differentials from 1935 to 1945. Wages of manual workers rose relative to white-collar salaries, and laborers' wages rose relative to those of skilled workers. The reasons for this were explained in Chapter 10.

Employment opportunities were much more plentiful during the

Distribution of Household Income before
Federal Income Tax, United States, 1935–36
and 1960

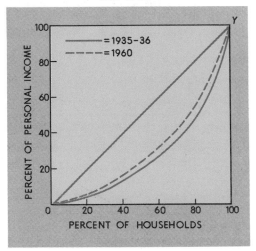

FIGURE 2.

forties than during the thirties. The many low incomes in 1935 reflected partly the heavy unemployment at that time. After 1940 these people were reabsorbed into employment, with a consequent increase in their annual incomes.

Another particularly depressed group during the 1930's was the farm population. During and after World War II, the high demand for food raised farm prices and brought a relative improvement of the farmer's position. This narrowed the income distribution for the nation as a whole.

Property income has been a declining proportion of total personal income. Business profit rates have not fallen appreciably. But the proportion of profits *paid out as dividends* has dropped, mainly because of increases in the corporate income tax. Rent, interest, and dividends, which formed 22 percent of personal income in 1929, had fallen to 13 percent by 1961. Since these types of income are received mainly by the wealthier groups, the result has been to pull their incomes down closer to the national average.

In addition to the reduced importance of property income, there are indications that it became more equally distributed between the 1920's and the 1940's. Kuznets has calculated that during the 1920's the top 5 percent of income recipients got more than 80 percent of dividend payments and more than 55 percent of all property income. By the late forties, however, they were getting only 70 percent of the dividends and about 40 percent of all property income.[7]

Finally, the New Deal era brought a marked increase in transfer payments to low-income groups, including old-age pensions and assistance, unemployment compensation, veterans benefits, aid to dependent children, and general relief. These payments helped to raise the bottom of the income distribution.

Since the late forties, these tendencies have slowed down and in some cases been reversed. There has been little further shrinkage of occupational wage differences, and in some industries differentials have widened. Rising interest rates have checked the drop in the relative importance of property income. Studies by Professor Lampman for the National Bureau of Economic Research suggest that the distribution of property ownership has become less equal in recent years. Increases in pension rates, unemployment compensation rates, and other transfer payments have done little more than keep pace with price inflation. On balance, income distribution since 1950 has shown no marked trend toward either greater or less inequality.

If one were to speculate about the future, it seems safe to predict that income distribution a generation from now will be more nearly equal than it is today. Some of the forces working toward equality are strong and apparently irreversible: the decline of white-collar earnings relative to manual workers' earnings, the shrinkage of the low-income farm population, the reduction of Negro-white income differentials, greater opportunity for working women, more adequate social provision for those unable to work. There does not seem to be an equally strong array of forces working in the other direction.

INCOME REDISTRIBUTION: THE MARKET APPROACH

The present distribution of income is not necessarily ideal. And there are things which can be done about it. We can and do alter income distribution through the tax structure, through transfer payments, and in other ways. What government should do in this respect is a classic political issue.

We must distinguish first between measures which affect income distribution *through* the market mechanism and measures which operate

---

[7] Simon Kuznets, *Share of Upper-Income Groups in Income and Savings* (New York: National Bureau of Economic Research, 1953).

outside the market. On the former there is little disagreement in principle, while the second is more controversial.

We noted in earlier chapters that one source of inequality is limited access to the higher occupations. Doctors, lawyers, engineers, and business executives have substantial incomes partly because there are few of them, relative to the market demand. Earnings of laborers and farmers are depressed because there are too many of them. There are barriers to movement up the occupational ladder.

This suggests that important gains can be made by enabling people to shift from low-productivity occupations to others where their productivity and earnings would be higher. If a factory laborer worth $4,000 a year can be converted into a doctor worth $15,000 a year, this is a step forward both for him and for the community. The man has more interesting work and larger income, and he is contributing more to national output.

It is hard for people of mature age to make large occupational shifts. Most of the shifting has to be accomplished by enabling young people to enter the managerial and professional occupations. The main obstacle is the cost of higher education for these occupations. The average cost of a B.A. degree in the United States is now close to $10,000. An M.D. may represent a cash outlay of $25,000 or more. (Moreover, the income which a person gives up by going to college for several years when he might have been working must be counted as a cost of his training.) Many families in the United States cannot consider an investment of this size. Despite the tradition of "working your way through college," many able young people are barred from higher education on financial grounds. This is injustice to the individual and economic waste to the community.

There are at least two ways of breaking this financial bottleneck: through *loans* and through *scholarships.* One can argue that, since the individual benefits from professional training through higher income, he should be required to pay the training costs. This would mean setting up a loan fund from which students could borrow up to some maximum amount, with repayment spread over a period of years after graduation. The student himself would have to estimate whether the prospective gain in income from added training would be sufficient to repay the loan and leave some margin of advantage.[8] College vocational advisers could give

---

[8] This is essentially the calculation which a business manager must make in deciding whether to buy an item of capital equipment (Chapter 11). The student should count as a cost not only his educational expenses but the income which he might have earned by going to work after high school instead of entering college. These costs would be accumulated forward to graduation day at an appropriate rate of interest. On the income side, one would have to estimate future income over the student's lifetime *in excess* of what he could have earned without the advanced training; and this gain in income would be discounted back to graduation. An excess of gain over cost would indicate that the training is worthwhile.

the student information on prospective earnings in various occupations and also give tests which would help him to gauge his own abilities. Since ability is not subject to precise measurement, and since earnings in the higher occupations vary widely with ability, each student would still be gambling somewhat. But it would be *his* gamble. Lack of initial capital would be removed as a barrier to free choice. The question of how many people should be educated for each occupation, and who they should be, would be left to individual decision.

Many colleges and universities have modest loan funds, and the record of repayments has been good. New York and a few other states have established state loan funds; and private lending agencies are moving increasingly into this area.

A second possibility is scholarship grants from public funds. This is common practice in many countries. In Britain the great majority of university students hold government scholarships. The number of students, however, is much smaller relative to population than in the United States. In Russia students admitted to universities and training institutes automatically receive a living allowance as well as free tuition. The allowance is meager and parents still have to contribute something if the student is to live well, but the bulk of the cost is borne by government.

We have gone some distance in this direction in the United States. Private colleges often have substantial scholarship funds. State colleges and universities provide free or low-cost tuition. We have had one experience with federal grants covering both living costs and tuition—the "GI program" for veterans of World War II and the Korean War. This seems to have operated well from the standpoint of both the students and the universities. More recently, federal money has been allocated for graduate fellowships in engineering, science, and mathematics under the National Defense Education Act of 1958. Science and engineering were selected on the politically appealing ground that "the Russians are doing it" and that these occupations have special significance for national defense.

Important additional steps have been taken during the sixties. The Health Professions Educational Assistance Act of 1963 provided federal assistance to university loan funds for prospective physicians, dentists, and optometrists. In 1965, as part of a broad program of support for higher education, Congress approved the first federal scholarships for undergraduates. It was estimated that some 140,000 undergraduates would receive scholarships during the first year of the program. In addition, the 1965 act enlarged the loan facilities available to needy students. In states which have not acted to establish their own student loan funds, students can apply to banks or other private lending agencies. If the applicant and the loan terms meet prescribed standards, the loan will be guaranteed by the federal government.

The economic difference between loan and scholarship systems is illustrated in Figure 3. DD and SS are the demand and supply curves for, say, medical service. We suppose, however, that the supply of doctors is restricted artifically to OE because only this number can finance the cost of medical training from their own resources. Employment in the profession is thus limited to OE, and doctors' incomes settle at OW.

Suppose we set up a loan system which allows anyone to enter medical school if he believes that future income will cover the cost of the loan. The true supply curve SS now becomes operative and A emerges as the equilibrium position. The number of doctors increases to OE_1 and their annual incomes fall to OW_1. This is a loss to the doctors who were

Economics of Loans and Scholarships

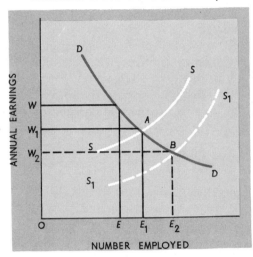

FIGURE 3. SS and DD are supply and demand curves for medical service. We suppose that the number of doctors is limited to OE by restricted access to training. With a loan system, SS becomes operative, the number in the profession rises to OE_1 and incomes fall to OW_1. With a scholarship system, supply increases to S_1S_1, numbers increase to OE_2 and incomes fall to OW_2.

previously earning OW. But it benefits the new doctors who are now able to get into the profession; and it enables the public to buy more medical service at a competitive price.

Suppose we go further and give each medical student a scholarship which covers all costs of his training. This operates like a reduction in production costs of a commodity and shifts the supply curve of doctors rightward to S_1S_1. For a given level of expected income, more people will be willing to undertake medical training than before. The long-run equilibrium is now at B, with OE_2 doctors earning an annual income of OW_2.

Compared with the previous equilibrium at A, there are the following effects: (1) Doctors trained before the scholarship system went in lose by the change, for they have already paid the cost of their education but will now receive incomes lower than they had expected. (This could conceivably be met by a lump-sum payment to these doctors.) (2) Doctors trained after the new system begins neither gain nor lose. Their prospective income is lower, but this is offset by the reduction in educational costs. (3) Consumers of medical services benefit from a lower price. OW_2 is in fact a subsidized price, since it does not cover the full cost (including training expenses) of providing the service. (4) This subsidy, the annual scholarship budget, comes from the taxpaying public. If the people paying the taxes are a different group from those who receive the medical services, there is an income transfer from the former to the latter. If the two groups coincide, there is no transfer; but consumers of medical services are then paying a hidden tax cost in addition to the visible price which they pay in the market.

The scholarship system is open to objection on the ground that consumers are getting more medical service than they would choose at a price covering full cost, and that they are paying more for this service than they think they are paying. On the other side, it can be argued that medical service has neighborhood effects extending beyond the individual, that people *should* get more of it than they would pay for voluntarily, and that interference with market pricing is justifiable. This is essentially the argument for free elementary and high-school education. The public would certainly take less of these services if given the option of paying a full-cost price or going without. How far this line of reasoning should be extended to health and other services is a problem of political choice for the community.

This case has been developed at length because education probably offers widest scope for altering income distribution through the market mechanism. But there are other possibilities as well. Government can help marginal farmers to transfer to other occupations. To the extent that this reduces excess agricultural capacity and enables the remaining farmers to earn equilibrium incomes, the effects are favorable. Government can also help to accelerate movement from depressed areas to expanding regions of the country. Such programs have favorable income effects while involving minimum interference with market allocation and voluntary choice.

INCOME REDISTRIBUTION OUTSIDE THE MARKET: GENERAL CONSIDERATIONS

Government can also alter income distribution by superseding the market. Public services which benefit everyone may be financed by taxes which weigh most heavily on the well-to-do. Government can make cash payments to certain groups in the population out of tax revenues. Such transfers are typically in an equalizing direction, from higher brackets to lower brackets.

How far government should go in equalizing incomes is a classic political issue. At one time economists believed that they could give a scientific answer to this question. The answer was that a transfer of income from richer to poorer people would increase total satisfaction.

The reasoning can be explained with the aid of Figure 4. Consider a simple community consisting of two men, Mr. A and Mr. B. We suppose that their capacity for deriving satisfaction from income is identical, and that for each man the satisfaction derived from an additional dollar of income decreases continuously as his income rises. Money is used to buy goods, and consuming additional goods yields decreasing marginal utility as explained in Chapter 6.

A Simple Argument for Income Equalization

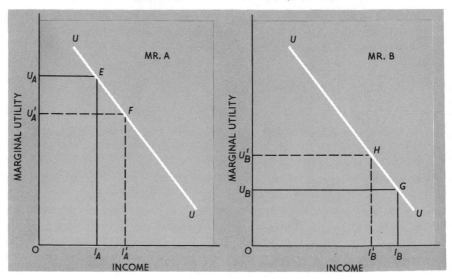

FIGURE 4. Mr. A and Mr. B have the same capacity to derive satisfaction from income, shown by *UU*. But B's income of *OI_B* is much larger than A's income of *OI_A*. Hence the marginal utility of income to B (*OU_B*) is much smaller than A(*OU_A*). Transferring income to A will add to his satisfaction more than it reduces B's satisfaction, so total satisfaction will be increased.

These assumptions are sketched in Figure 4. Mr. A and Mr. B have identical marginal utility curves, *UU*, which fall steadily from left to right. But they have different incomes. *B* is a well-to-do fellow with an income of *OI_B* while A's income of *OI_A* is only about one quarter as large. So the marginal utility of income to B (*OU_B*) is much less than to A (*OU_A*). It thus seems that the *combined* satisfaction of the two men could be increased by shifting some income from B to A. Suppose we levy a tax on B which reduces his income to *OI'_B*, and give this money to A, raising his income to *OI'_A*. The satisfaction lost by B as we move up his utility curve from G to H is clearly less than that gained by A in moving from E to F. Thus total satisfaction has been increased. Indeed, since *OU'_A* is still greater than *U'_B*, it would pay to transfer some more income from B to A, and to continue this process until the incomes of the two men are equal.

People who advocate greater equality have this reasoning in the back of their minds. They feel that an extra dollar means a lot to the poor, while to the rich man it means very little. But the argument has been undermined by economic theorists, who point out that its assumptions are dubious and cannot be verified by observation. How do we know that marginal utility curves slope steadily downward? Perhaps appetite grows with eating, and utility curves may slope upward for a while. And how do we know that different people have the same capacity to derive satisfaction from income? Perhaps the well-to-do man, whose income has allowed him to cultivate expensive tastes, has a much higher utility curve than the poor man. Perhaps he derives just as much satisfaction from his last dollar as the poor man does from his. This aristocratic line of argument may seem unconvincing, but can one prove that it is wrong? There is no way to get inside the skins of Mr. A and Mr. B, or to compare their subjective satisfactions. And this weakens the classical argument for income equality.

But even if one concludes that utility is unmeasurable, there are other arguments favoring greater equality of income:

1. Inequality reduces satisfaction because of the necessity of "keeping up with the Joneses." Whatever my income may be, there is always someone around with twice as much, and I feel under pressure to emulate his standards. (There is also someone around with only half as much as I have, but the satisfaction I get from looking down on this fellow is less than the discontent I feel from looking at the man above me.) Without changing my income, my satisfaction could be increased by reducing the gap between me and those higher up. Since everyone except the top man in the income distribution presumably feels this way, general satisfaction could be increased by a reduction of inequality.

2. In a democracy where people are legally and politically equal, how can one justify large differences in income and consumption levels? Doesn't inequality undermine democracy by giving the wealthy a disproportionate influence in political affairs?

3. The case for greater equality can be argued also on religious and ethical grounds. If people will not voluntarily follow the Biblical injunction to "sell what thou hast and give to the poor," perhaps their consciences should be aided by the tax collector.

4. Property income is sometimes regarded as particularly open to ethical criticism. "Unearned income" from property is considered inferior to wage and salary income. Since property income goes mainly to the higher brackets, one can argue that it is right to redistribute some of it through taxation.

5. An important economic argument relates to maintenance of full employment. There is chronic danger, it is argued, that money savings will exceed the amount which businessmen and others are willing to borrow. When this happens there is a deficiency of spending in the

economy and production and employment fall. Thus anything which reduces the level of savings in the economy will reduce the likelihood of unemployment. Since wealthy people save a large proportion of their incomes while poor people save very little, transfer of income from rich to poor will reduce saving and increase consumer spending.

The difficulty is that these arguments can be countered by an equal number on the other side. Those who believe government should not set out to redistribute income contend that:

1. Wage and salary income, which makes up four fifths of personal income, is received for services performed. It is unjustifiable to take away from people what they have earned through their own efforts.

2. There is also an ethical basis for property income. Property is simply congealed labor, the result of *past* effort plus saving. The state is no more entitled to take away the fruits of past labor than of present labor.

3. To the argument that inequality arouses envy and discontent, one can retort that envy may stimulate productive effort. One can try to keep up with the Joneses by working harder or climbing to a higher occupational level. Conversely, if income differences become too small, no one may consider it worthwhile to undertake skilled and difficult work. The wage and salary differences which emerge in a competitive labor market ensure an adequate supply of labor to costly, strenuous, or unpleasant jobs.

4. Taxation may have other harmful consequences. A heavy income tax may make people decide to work fewer hours and spend more time on the beach. Taxation of business profits, by reducing the return on investment, may cause less investment to occur. This will mean slower growth in productive capacity and national output. One can argue that what the country needs is more saving rather than less saving, and that heavy taxation of large incomes and business profits reduces saving to an undesirably low level.

It is clear, even from this brief listing, that economic analysis can never determine what is a correct income distribution. This remains at bottom a matter of ethical conviction and political preference. A man of one opinion cannot hope to convince a man of different mind by sheer weight of evidence. Like many problems in political economy, this issue is essentially one of *degree.* Scarcely anyone would advocate *complete* equality of incomes. At the other extreme, few people today would defend the degree of inequality which existed in Britain around 1800, or which exists today in some of the less developed countries of the world. The practical question is always *how much* equality is feasible and desirable at a particular time.

The trend of economic policy in Western industrial countries during this century has been toward greater income equality. But this does not prove that the policy is right in any absolute sense. It may merely prove, as embittered aristocrats contend, that there are more voters in the lower brackets!

REDISTRIBUTION OUTSIDE THE MARKET: U.S. EXPERIENCE

How far have we already carried the tendency toward equalization of incomes through the government budget? In a general way, we know that the fiscal system operates in an equalizing direction. Most of the transfer payments go to people in the brackets below $5,000 a year, while the federal personal income tax falls heavily on the brackets above $5,000.

But any effort to be more precise than this runs into two kinds of difficulty. First, who actually pays various types of tax? Does the corporation income tax fall entirely on the stockholders or is some of it added on to product prices? What about sales and excise taxes, social security taxes, and the rest?

Second, who benefits from the provision of government services? In some cases the benefits can be traced to a particular group. School expenditures benefit people who have children, agricultural research and extension benefits farmers, and so on. But it is difficult to allocate military expenditures, foreign aid, and general government overhead. The simplest assumption is that each citizen benefits equally from these expenditures, but they could also be allocated on the basis of income or property ownership.

For these reasons an analysis of how government operations change the distribution of real income involves many assumptions and much hard statistical labor. One effort of this sort is shown in Table 3.[9] Though the results are necessarily rough, they suggest a substantial redistribution of income. Comparing the final distribution after taking account of government operations with the initial distribution, one finds that the percentage share of the lowest bracket has more than tripled, rising from 1.4 to 5.0 percent. The top bracket, on the other hand, has fallen from 26

---

[9] Data for this Table and for Figure 5 are adapted from Alfred H. Conrad, "Redistribution Through Government Budgets in the United States, 1950," in Alan T. Peacock (ed.), *Income Redistribution and Social Policy* (London: Jonathan Cape, 1954), pp. 178–268.

The initial income in the first two columns includes only income from work or property, exclusive of transfer payments. It may be regarded as the "pure" or "original" distribution which is later modified by government action.

The main steps in going from this distribution to the final distribution at the right-hand side of the table were: (1) transfer payments were added in; (2) federal, state, and local taxes were deducted, using specific assumptions about who pays various types of tax; (3) the value of free government services, taken as equal to their cost, was allocated among the various income brackets. For defense and other general services of government, it was assumed that each citizen shares equally in the benefits. The assumptions and procedures used are spelled out in detail in the original source.

percent to 18 percent. The amount of income which has been redistributed downwards works out at almost $17 billion, or about 9 percent of total personal income.

TABLE 3

Government Impact on Income Distribution,
United States, 1950

MONEY INCOME CLASS (Based on Initial Income)	DISTRIBUTION OF SPENDING UNITS (Percent)	INITIAL INCOME		FINAL INCOME ADJUSTED FOR TAXES, TRANSFERS, AND GOVERNMENT SERVICES	
		Billions	Percent	Billions	Percent
Less than $1,000	14	2.804	1.43	9.736	5.0
1,000–1,999	19	16.188	8.23	21.860	11.3
2,000–2,999	21	28.466	14.47	31.734	16.4
3,000–3,999	19	33.750	17.16	34.790	18.0
4,000–4,999	11	27.438	13.95	26.211	13.6
5,000–7,499	11	36.370	18.49	33.968	17.6
7,500 and over	5	51.687	26.28	34.747	18.0
Total	100	196.703	100.00	193.046	100.0

While the fiscal system has a marked equalizing effect, it falls far short of full equalization. Even in the final distribution, average income per spending unit is $13,364 in the highest bracket compared with $1,337 in the lowest bracket. It would have been necessary to redistribute an

The Government Impact on Income Distribution, 1950

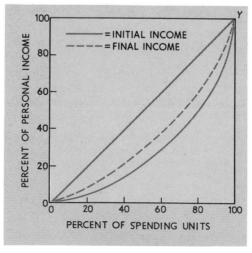

FIGURE 5.

additional $43 billion to bring about equal income per spending unit. The fiscal system of 1950, therefore, resulted in moving the initial income distribution about 28 percent of the way toward full equality (which is taken as simply a measuring rod, not necessarily a desirable objective).

The leveling effect of fiscal operations is shown graphically in Figure 5. Note the substantial difference between the Lorenz curves representing initial and final distributions.

ELIMINATING POVERTY

We cannot expect agreement on the wisdom of transferring income from people with $25,000 a year to those with $5,000 a year. But one might get agreement on the desirability of eliminating really substandard conditions. For the first time in human history, it is now technically feasible to eliminate poverty over a vast area such as the United States. It would be gratifying if the United States could be the first large nation to accomplish this task. If we do not, we can be fairly certain that several other countries will have accomplished it within the next generation. Competition in abolishing poverty should not be less challenging than competition in armaments or space rockets.

How many people in the United States can be regarded as living in poverty? There is no precise answer, because standards of living are conventional and change over time. What was acceptable in 1850 is considered substandard today. If we take as our standard the "American way of life" depicted in the slick-paper magazines, most Americans are impoverished. But this is unrealistic. The definition of poverty must be constructed with an eye to how most people are actually living. If the target is set too high, it becomes useless as an objective.

The standard commonly used at present is an annual income of $3,000 for a city family, often taken as a family of four. This can be refined by allowing for differences in family size, rural *versus* urban living costs, and other relevant considerations. But these refinements do not greatly change the estimated number of people living below the poverty line.

Estimates for selected years since 1947 are shown in Table 4. There has been an encouraging decline in the percentage of families below the poverty line, from 31.7 percent in 1947 to 18.5 percent in 1963; and the decline is presumably continuing. But 18 percent is still more than 9 million families, not counting the millions of single individuals who are also below the poverty line.

The main reason why the percentage of families living in poverty has fallen is the steady rise in average family incomes. As the general level of income rises, one can expect that the proportion *below* any benchmark figure will decline. So why not wait for the problem to solve itself? If family incomes continue to rise at the present rate for another generation, won't poverty disappear automatically and without special effort?

This argument is valid *for people who are able to participate fully in the market economy.* The trouble is that most of the poverty group are not in this category. About half of them are people who cannot work at all because of age, disabling accidents, mental or physical deficiencies, or the need to care for dependent children. For these people the continuing rise in the national wage level is irrelevant, since they cannot earn wages. Most of the remainder are people who are seriously disadvantaged in the labor market because of limited education and training, racial discrimi-

TABLE 4

Percent of Families with Less than $3,000 Annual Income, United States, Selected Years

YEAR	PERCENT OF FAMILIES WITH LESS THAN $3,000 ANNUAL INCOME (1963 Prices)	MEDIAN INCOME OF ALL FAMILIES (1963 Prices)
1947	31.7	$3,896
1950	31.2	3,961
1953	25.8	4,542
1956	22.2	5,051
1959	21.4	5,337
1963	18.5	5,873

Source: L. E. Galloway, "The Foundations of the War on Poverty,'" *American Economic Review*, March, 1965, pp. 122–31.

nation, geographical remoteness from centers of expanding employment, and other reasons. Potentially employable they may be; but in actuality they have no jobs or only irregular and precarious jobs. Because of their tenuous connection with the labor market, they are left behind in the rising tide of affluence which benefits their fellows.

The continued rise in average income levels will certainly continue to reduce the percentage of impoverished families; but it will not eliminate poverty within the forseeable future. There is a hard core, amounting to perhaps 10 percent of our population, who can be lifted above the poverty line only by programs directed specifically to that end.

Who are today's poor, and why are they poor? An interesting analysis has been made by a group of scholars at the University of Michigan's Survey Research Center.[10] From a national sample of

---

[10] James N. Morgan, Martin H. David, Wilbur J. Cohen, and Harvey E. Brazer, *Income and Welfare in the United States* (New York: McGraw-Hill Book Co., Inc., 1962).

families they secured information on family income and on a variety of other family characteristics. The results were then expanded to provide estimates for all families in the United States.

Using a poverty yardstick adjusted to take account of differences in family size, they concluded that about 20 percent of American families were living in poverty. But when one asks why, there is the difficulty that poverty may arise from a half-dozen sources. A particular family may have several of these characteristics. So which is really the "cause" of its poverty? To meet this difficulty the authors devised a sequential analysis, starting with factors which by themselves would be sufficient to explain poverty. If the household head is aged, this would be a sufficient explanation. Again, if he has serious physical or mental disabilities, one need look no further.

The results of this analysis are shown in Table 5. The number of families for whom a certain characteristic can be considered the prime source of poverty appears along the *diagonal* of the table. For example, the total of disabled family heads is 1.7 million; but of these 0.9 million are also aged, which by itself would explain their poverty. So we say that only the remaining 0.8 million are poor *because* of disability. Again, there are an estimated 2.9 million poor nonwhite families. But about half of these are aged, disabled, or have other clear sources of poverty. The number who have no visible handicap except being nonwhite is only 1.4 million.

The results suggest that close to half the families (4.7 million out of 10.4 million) were poor because of inability to work. This includes the aged, the disabled, and the female heads of broken homes. The remainder presumably had some work ability but were nevertheless unable to earn an adequate income. This group includes 1.4 million Negro families, presumably those at the bottom of the Negro population in terms of education, job training, and employability. Of the 1.0 million self-employed, the majority were probably marginal farmers. There remain 0.9 million who reported that they were usually employed but got only part-time work during the sample year; and a residual group of 2.4 million families for whose poverty there is no obvious explanation.

This analysis of the sources of poverty has a direct bearing on the question of remedies. For people who are actually or potentially employable, the answer is to find jobs at which they can work productively at market wage levels. For people without work ability, direct cash support is the only alternative.

Work Opportunities for the Employable

The fact that a person is able-bodied and willing to work does not by itself make him employable. He must possess job skills which make him valuable to an employer. The need for training is intensified by the evolution of our complex, highly mechanized economy. Demand for labor is shifting rapidly toward white-collar, technical, and skilled

TABLE 5

Proportions and Aggregate Estimates of Heads of Poor Families Having Characteristics Related to Poverty within Likely Causes of Poverty

LIKELY CAUSES OF POVERTY	AGED	DISABLED	SINGLE AND HAS CHILDREN	USUALLY EMPLOYED, UNEMPLOYED IN 1959	NONWHITE	SELF-EMPLOYED BUSINESSMAN OR FARMER	NONE OF THESE
1. Aged	100% 2.8 mil.	32% .9 mil.	1% .04 mil.	2% .04 mil.	22% .6 mil.	8% .2 mil.	0%
2. Disabled (not 1)		100% .8 mil.	15% .1 mil.	4% .03 mil.	26% .2 mil.	17% .1 mil.	0%
3. Single and has children (not 1–2)			100% 1.1 mil.	14% .1 mil.	43% .5 mil.	3% .01 mil.	0%
4. Usually employed, worked less than 49 weeks in 1959 (not 1–3)				100% .9 mil	29% .2 mil.	0%	0%
5. Nonwhite (not 1–4)					100% 1.4 mil.	14% 0.4 mil.	0%
6. Self-employed businessman or farmer (not 1–5)						100% 1.0 mil.	0%
7. Not 1–6							100% 2.4 mil.
All	2.8 mil.	1.7 mil.	1.2 mil.	1.1 mil.	2.9 mil.	1.7 mil.	2.4 mil.

Source: James N. Morgan, Martin H. David, Wilbur J. Cohen, and Harvey E. Brazer, *Income and Welfare in the United States*, p. 195.

manual workers. Opportunities for unskilled work are shrinking. The worker who is illiterate or completely unskilled is likely to find himself unemployable.

The problem of Negro unemployment, while it arises partly from employer and union discrimination, is due also to low levels of education and job training. The millions of Negroes who migrated from southern farms to northern industrial centers during the forties and fifties had been seriously deprived of educational opportunities in their home communities. In 1960 almost one quarter of the total Negro population aged 24 and over had less than 5 years of schooling, and could be classified as functionally illiterate.

The federal antipoverty program, initiated by the Economic Opportunity Act of 1964, thus focuses heavily on education and training, with particular attention to young people. Title I of the Act provides funds to enroll up to 100,000 people aged 16 to 21 in a Job Corps, which includes two kinds of residential training center: conservation camps in rural areas, which combine work on conservation and recreational projects with repairing basic educational deficiencies; and residential centers in urban areas, which combine basic education with job training. This part of the program aims to give a second chance to young people who have left school before acquiring the general literacy or the vocational skills which would make them good employment prospects. These early dropouts have a high unemployment rate and, having become used to idleness, drift easily into delinquency and crime. To reclaim them by a year or two of training for perhaps 40 years of productive employment is a sound economic investment.

Other provisions of the Act are intended to assist students from needy families to resume or continue regular high-school or college education. Under the work-training program, the federal government will enter into agreements with state and local governments or nonprofit organizations to pay part or all of the cost of full- or part-time employment to enable young people aged 16 to 21 to stay in high school, or to return to high school if they have dropped out. It is expected that some 200,000 young people will participate in this program. At the college level, the Act provides a work-study program under which the federal government will enter into agreements with colleges and universities to provide part of the cost of part-time employment for undergraduate or graduate students from low-income families. This program is expected to involve some 150,000 students.

While training the young is particularly important, older workers also often need retraining and relocation. The activities in this area under the Manpower Development and Training Act of 1962 were described in Chapter 15. They focus on unemployed workers who, because they live in depressed areas or because they lack job skills currently in demand, stand little chance of reemployment. As this program attains full proportions, it should do much to remold the labor force in the direction of expanding labor demands.

The Role of Social Insurance

People who normally work and earn adequate incomes may fall into the poverty group through temporary or permanent loss of earning power. Most workers suffer unemployment at one time or another. Everyone who lives long enough eventually becomes unable to work through old age. Even before this, a worker may be disabled by accident or disease. His earnings may be interrupted by illness, which also involves extra costs for medical care. If he dies prematurely, his family may be left with no means of support.

The chances of these things happening can be estimated, just as one can estimate the probability of a house burning down or a car being involved in an accident. This makes it possible to apply the principle of insurance and to make advance provision through reserve funds. Most countries now have social insurance funds to which the worker and his employer contribute while he is working, and from which he is entitled to draw specified amounts when unable to work. This may not involve much transfer of income to wage earners from other groups in the population. The worker contributes part of the cost himself. The remainder comes mainly from payroll taxes on the employer which, according to best guesses about tax incidence, are either shifted back to the worker in lower wages or shifted forward in higher prices to consumers, of whom workers form a large proportion. The main transfer of income, then, occurs *within* the wage-earning population and is a transfer between periods of working and not working. The result is to level out the worker's lifetime income and to prevent his falling into poverty because of the normal hazards of industrial life.

The risks of unemployment, disability, and old age are covered by insurance funds established under the Social Security Act of 1935; but the cash benefits provided are quite low. The maximum old-age pension is still only $204 a month after the 1965 Amendments; workers in the lower wage brackets receive even less. Unemployed workers covered by unemployment compensation receive, on the average, only 30 to 35 percent of their normal weekly wages. Since wage levels and living standards are constantly rising, a scale of payments which may have been adequate in 1960 will be obsolete in 1970. Frequent revision of benefit scales is necessary to ensure that the Social Security system meets its original purpose of preventing hardship for regular workers who have contributed to the system from their earnings.

A sizable amount of poverty results from large families. A man and wife with $3,000 a year are perhaps not "poor." A man, wife, and six children with the same income certainly are poor.

Many of the advanced industrial countries meet this problem

through a system of family allowances. These involve monthly government payments of so much per child, independent of the father's wage or other family income. They are *social* payments, not *relief* payments. The bank president receives the same monthly allowance for his child as the street sweeper.

The idea of family allowances has not made much headway in the United States and seems unlikely to do so. The income tax system, of course, provides a $600 allowance for each dependent. But this brings greatest benefit to those in the highest tax brackets. Consider the man with a wife, six children, and a $3,000 income. He is entitled to a dependency allowance of 8 × $600 = $4,800. Perhaps he has other allowable deductions of $300. So he has deductions of $5,100 to set against $3,000 of income. He will obviously pay no income tax. But neither does he benefit from his $2,100 of "unused" deductions. The total of such unused deductions at present is estimated at $20 billion dollars, mostly in families with children.[11]

This has led to the proposal of a *negative* income tax for people in this situation. If the negative tax rate were set at, say, 30 percent, the man in our illustration would receive a government payment of .30 × $2,100 = $630. This would raise his annual income and help to lift his outsize family above the poverty line. It would cost considerably less than a general system of family allowances and would bring greatest benefit to those with lowest incomes. (It would, in fact, not show up in the federal budget as a cost but simply as a reduction in personal income tax collections.)

Income for the Nonemployable

These lines of action would make a deep bite into the poverty group. Ideally, no family whose head is able and willing to work would be poor.

But this would not take care of the whole problem. There remain "the halt, the lame, and the blind," the people of low physical or mental capacity, the unemployable or barely employable, the people who never work regularly enough to come within the orbit of the wage system. There remain also the broken homes with dependent children, in which the mother cannot work without depriving her children of essential care.

For these people, direct cash relief remains the only resort. Why not say that all people in these categories shall be brought up to some minimum income level, which could be adjusted for variations in family size and regional living costs. The objection that relief will discourage willingness to work does not apply in these cases, since work capacity is

---

[11] Robert J. Lampman, "Approaches to the Reduction of Poverty," *American Economic Review*, May, 1965, pp. 521–29.

absent by definition. (In borderline cases, where it is suspected that work capacity is present but motivation is lacking, this could be tested by requiring the person to enter a training program as a condition of continued relief. The "willingness-to-work" test requires, however, that there be *enough vacant jobs available in the economy*. To apply this test in a slack labor market is pointless and unfair.)

We do have relief systems at present—probably too many of them. The brunt of the burden falls on local governments, but relief scales vary from area to area and are typically inadequate. There is a variety of federal programs for specific groups—the aged, the blind, mothers with dependent children—administered through the states but supported by federal grants. A single national program, based on a standard definition of need and eligibility, might be more equitable and efficient and might not cost much more than existing programs.

It was estimated in 1964 that the "poor" group in the population had a total income of $25 billion, of which about $10 billion came from social security benefits, local relief, and other transfer payments. To bring everyone in this group up to a level of $3,000 per family or $1,500 per unrelated individual would have required an additional $12 billion.[12] Remember, however, that we have proposed to take care of all the employable poor through the measures outlined in the previous section. The cost of lifting the "hard core" of unemployables above the poverty line would probably be in the range of $6–8 billion per year, or about 1 percent of our GNP. Would it not be worthwhile to spend as much in eliminating poverty on earth as we are presently spending to land on the moon?

SUMMARY

1. The distribution of household incomes is determined by: relative wages and salaries for different occupations; the distribution of property ownership; the division of total income between labor and capital; and a variety of other factors, including the relative size of the farm population, differences in earnings between Negro and white workers, and women's participation in the labor force.

2. The degree of income inequality at a particular place and time can be measured by the *Lorenz curve* and the *Gini coefficient*.

3. In the Western industrial countries there seems to be a long-run trend toward greater equality of pretax incomes. In the United States, income distribution became considerably more equal between 1935 and 1945, but there has been little change from 1945 to the present.

4. Government can act to change the distribution of income either *through* the market mechanism or *outside* the market mechanism. The

---

[12] Lampman, *op. cit.*, p. 523.

most important example of the first type is steps to reduce the financial barrier to higher education through loan or scholarship systems.

5. Government also shifts income outside the market system through taxes and transfer payments. There is at present a substantial downward transfer from richer to poorer groups. Whether we are doing too much or not enough in this direction is a highly controversial question. There are economic arguments on both sides, but economics alone cannot provide a definite answer.

6. The proportion of families with incomes below $3,000 a year, which can be taken as a working definition of poverty, has fallen from about 31 percent in 1947 to 18 percent in 1963. About half of the poverty group cannot work because of age, disability, or household responsibilities. The remainder are employable but are presently unemployed or have low productivity for a variety of reasons.

7. The employable group can be raised to an adequate income level by educational and training programs, by maintaining adequate overall demand for labor, and by social insurance against old age, disability, and unemployment. For those who cannot work, cash relief seems the only alternative.

DISCUSSION QUESTIONS

1. What are the main reasons for inequality of personal incomes in the United States? To what extent are these inherent in a private market economy?

2. Why was there an appreciable reduction of income inequality between 1935 and 1950? Would you expect further reductions in the future? Why, or why not?

3. The text says that reducing the barriers to free occupational choice would lead to a gain in economic welfare. How can one measure this gain? Who gets it?

4. It is often said that there is a *shortage* of doctors (also of engineers, physicists, college teachers, etc.) in the United States. What would constitute evidence of such a shortage?

5. Is there an economic case for free (= full scholarship) education for technical and professional occupations? Or only for a system of repayable loans? In the scholarship case, how would one decide *how many* people should be admitted (and financed) for training in each field?

6. Income inequality can be further reduced by transfers through the government budget. How far should a country go in this respect? What are the main considerations pro and con?

7. What might be done to reduce concentration of property ownership and hence of property income? For example, would heavier inheritance taxes be desirable?

8. Explain clearly the difference between a policy of equalizing incomes and a policy of eliminating poverty. Would you support the latter policy unqualifiedly? or with qualifications?

9. Do you know what educational and job-training activities are going on in your home community under the federal antipoverty program? Do all young people interested in further training have a chance to get it?

10. What do you know about relief scales and relief administration in your community? What changes in the present system would you recommend?

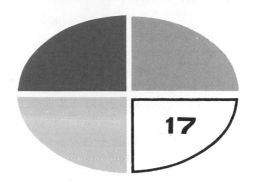

The Public Economy

"It was as true," said Mr. Barkis, "as taxes
is. And nothing's truer than them."

CHARLES DICKENS

To tax and to please, no more than to love
and to be wise, is not given to men.

EDMUND BURKE

MOST OF THE THINGS I consume are bought from private sellers at a market price. How much of each article I get depends on my ability and willingness to pay the price. For the nation, the amount of each article produced depends on the balancing of consumer preferences and production possibilities explained in Part One.

Alongside this private economy there exists a public economy operated on quite different lines. I cannot go to the store and buy a certain quantity of national defense. I do not pay a price for sending my child to the local public school or driving my car over the state highway. Public services have two distinguishing characteristics: they are usually provided without charge to the individual recipient, and they are available equally to all comers. I cannot choose to go without national defense and consume a great deal of public education, while my neighbor makes the opposite choice. The principles of choice, market pricing, and resource allocation which apply in the private economy no longer apply in the public sphere.

But the government has no magic power to commandeer resources or make something out of nothing. The resources needed to build highways, operate schools, and maintain the defense establishment must be bought and paid for. The money comes from taxes levied on the citizens. Here is where trouble starts. We all enjoy using government services, particularly when we can view them as falling from the sky without cost. But we hate to pay the taxes which lurk in the background.

What kinds of good and service are typically provided through public channels? Why not others as well? Where should we draw the line between the private economy and the public economy? How can we judge whether the government is producing too little or too much of a particular service? Is there anything in the public economy which corresponds to the rule of price = marginal cost in the private economy?

Who should pay the taxes required to finance public services? What types of tax do we use at present, and who pays them? What problems arise from the fact that services are provided and taxes levied by several layers of government? These issues are the focus of this chapter.

THREE FUNCTIONS OF GOVERNMENT BUDGETS

Government budgets perform three main functions:[1] (1) The *allocation* function. A tax reduces the amount of money which people have available for spending on privately produced goods and services, and this frees resources in the private economy. As government spends the tax money, however, government use of resources increases in a way which offsets the drop in private use. An increase in the level of taxes and expenditures *reallocates* resources from the private to the public economy. This reallocation is accompanied by changes in the structure of production and employment, since the things on which government spends money will differ from the things on which consumers would spend the same money.

2. The *distribution* function. Government may levy just enough taxes to cover the cost of public services. But it may also levy taxes on some people in the economy in order to transfer the proceeds to other people, who then have this money available for private spending. This does not alter the level of government services or affect the allocation of resources between the private and public sectors. It is a transfer of private purchasing power, and these payments are accordingly called *transfer payments.* The question of how far government should go in this direction was examined in Chapter 16.

3. The *stabilization* function. During the past generation it has been realized increasingly that the government budget can be used to

---

[1] The terminology used here follows the analysis of Richard A. Musgrave, *The Theory of Public Finance* (New York: McGraw-Hill Book Co., Inc., 1959), especially Part I.

correct extremes of inflation or deflation. The prescription for a counter-cyclical budget policy is easily stated, though it is not easy to apply. If the economy is fully employed and prices are rising, total spending is excessive and should be reduced. One way of doing this is to have the government take in more money than it spends, that is, run a budget surplus. Conversely, during an unemployment period when more spending is needed, one possible policy is for the government to spend more than it takes in, or run a deficit. The practical difficulties of designing and applying such a policy will be examined in Part Three.

In this chapter we assume that functions (2) and (3) are being performed satisfactorily. The economy is in a state of full employment with stable prices. Some community consensus has been reached on what constitutes a proper distribution of income, and the appropriate transfers are being made through the government budget. Leaving these matters aside, we focus here on function (1), on the *management of the public household*. What services should be provided by government? In what quantity should they be provided? How should the costs be divided among the taxpaying public?

PUBLIC EXPENDITURE: QUESTIONS OF PRINCIPLE

Scope of the Public Sector

In Part One we argued that a system of competitive markets is an efficient mechanism for meeting consumer wants. The fully competitive economy is admittedly a utopia. But even our imperfect market mechanism seems reasonably efficient in guiding production and reaching decisions about resource allocation. Why, then, do we depart from it for certain types of production? Why can't all the services we need be privately produced and sold at a market price? Why is there any need for government production?

The case for government production rests on one or another of three considerations: the *public character* of the good, the existence of major *economies of scale*, or the existence of significant *external effects*. A word about each of these.

The hallmark of a *public good* is that Mr. A's consumption of the good does not interfere with, or reduce the possibility of, Mr. B's consuming the same good. For goods produced and sold in private markets, there is always a distributive problem. More for me means less for you. But in the case of a public good, more for me *does not* mean less for you. If a city sets up a smog control system, Mr. A benefits from breathing the purer air. But this does not interfere with the same benefit being enjoyed by Mr. B and all other residents of the community.

Further, it is impossible to exclude individuals from consuming a public good. In private markets, those who will not pay the price do not get the product. But for public goods this *principle of exclusion* is unworkable. The national defense establishment protects us all willy-nilly. It is not feasible to let some people use the city streets and not others. So if one tried to finance these services on a price basis, the attempt would surely fail. No one would pay the price, because he could continue to enjoy the service without paying. The service must be financed in a different way, through taxation.

Where *economies of scale* are important, increased output of the good brings a steady reduction in unit costs. The *LRATC* curve falls continuously to the right. This normally means that the production unit is large and indivisible (you cannot build a small piece of the Golden Gate bridge or of a national telephone network), and that fixed costs are large relative to variable costs.

To take an extreme case, suppose that a certain bridge, once it is built, has no repair or maintenance costs. Since all costs are fixed, the *ATC* curve is identical with the *AFC* curve, and slopes downward continuously to the right. Marginal cost is zero.

Here, unlike the public-good case, it would be feasible to charge a toll and to exclude anyone who will not pay the toll. But would this be desirable? We learned in Chapter 7 that output of a good is at the correct level when its price equals marginal cost. Since marginal cost here is zero, price should also be zero. People should be allowed to use the bridge free of charge.

The common sense of this is evident. Since it costs nothing for one more person to pass over the bridge, excluding anyone from crossing would reduce his satisfaction with no saving in cost, so is inefficient.

If a private monopolist were allowed to build and operate the bridge, he could perhaps set a high enough toll so that the bridge would "pay for itself." But this violates the $P = MC$ rule and is economically undesirable. It is preferable that the bridge be publicly constructed and operated free of charge.

While this is a polar case, it is not far from the actual situation for highways, ports, airfields, power installations, or railroads. Variable cost is not zero, but it is low compared to fixed costs. Average total cost typically slopes downward over the whole range of feasible operations, and the *MC* curve lies continuously below the *ATC* curve. In such cases, following the economically desirable $P = MC$ rule will involve a loss and require a subsidy. This does not per se prevent private operation of such enterprises. Government might require a private company to set the correct price, and make up the loss through a subsidy payment. Or a government regulatory board might permit the company to cover costs by using price discrimination, a kind of "second-best" arrangement. But either procedure is somewhat cumbersome and unsatisfactory. So in most countries these industries are considered to fall naturally within the public sector.

The third situation is that of strong *external effects*. These arise when a producing unit imposes costs or confers benefits on the community which are not reflected in its own costs and revenues. A factory may impose additional costs, for example, by air pollution, water pollution, or unhealthy work conditions. Such things are usually taken care of by government regulations requiring the enterprise to avoid certain practices or to pay for eliminating the nuisances it has created.

What about the case where a producing unit confers benefits on the community which it cannot recapture through its selling price? These benefits may be either to other producing units or to consumers. As an example of the former, Eckstein notes the case of the storage reservoir created by Hungry Horse Dam on the Columbia River,

which carries over water from wet seasons to dry and also from wet years to dry. When the water is released, it passes through 12 downstream dams, generating power at each one—in fact, three-fourths of the resultant power is generated at the downstream dams. A private company would not develop Hungry Horse; most of the benefit would accrue to other private power companies, some local public companies, and the U.S. government. The result: Hungry Horse is a public-power dam.[2]

On the consumption side, market theory normally assumes that each person's consumption is independent. My consumption of good A benefits me and nobody else. But there are cases in which this is not true. The outstanding example is probably education. If my neighbors send their children through high school and college, this benefits me and my children. Moreover, there is a public interest in a literate, enlightened citizenry capable of responsible self-government. So it has long been accepted that government should both require education up to some minimum level and provide funds to make this possible. Similar considerations apply to public health programs. It is in my interest that other families should not contract diseases which might spread to my family.

There are additional reasons for government production in certain cases. Some enterprises which may eventually "pay off" involve heavy initial costs and unusually large risks. We may some day see space cargo ships carrying rare minerals from moon to earth. But no private company could afford the vast cost of space exploration. Similarly, the economic feasibility of producing atomic power is still uncertain. So the cost of building and operating experimental nuclear reactors has been borne largely by government. Indeed, most of the money for scientific research —the results of which are hard to forecast, and which benefit mainly the

---

[2] Otto Eckstein, *Public Finance* (Englewood Cliffs, N.J.: Prentice-Hall, Inc., 1964), p. 12.

community rather than the original inventor—now comes from the federal government.

There are cases in which defects of consumer knowledge and foresight may cause people to buy less of a good than they would buy if they were perfectly informed. The U.S. government operates something akin to an insurance system under the Social Security Act. Why is government in the insurance business? Because experience before 1935 indicated that most people, left to themselves, will not voluntarily save enough during their working lives to provide decently for their retirement, and so become dependent on the community or their children. It is often argued that similar considerations apply to the costs of medical and hospital care and that these should be covered by a comprehensive public insurance system. The Social Security Act was amended in 1965 to provide this protection for older people, whose medical costs are apt to be unusually heavy.

A decision that government should intervene to ensure adequate production of a particular service leaves many questions open. The service may be provided by the federal, state, or local governments, or by some multicommunity organization such as the New York Port Authority. Production may be organized through a regular government department such as the Post Office, through a semiautonomous public corporation such as the TVA, or through a mixed private-public corporation such as the Communications Satellite Company. Instead of government producing the service, it may contract with private organizations to produce it, as is done for most federal research expenditures. Or government may simply provide consumers with funds and let them purchase the service where they wish. Returning veterans of World War II and the Korean War were given cash awards to cover the cost of college attendance or vocational training, and could use these awards at any approved training institution.

Efficiency in Government: Economics in the Small

In the sphere of private production there are definite rules about how much of each good to produce, how to produce that amount most economically, and what price to charge. As we enter the realm of government production, do we leave these guidelines behind us? Or is some of the reasoning in Part One still useful in the public sphere?

The answer is both yes and no. On some of the larger questions— how much does it pay to spend on national defense?—there is nothing comparable to the solutions provided by the market mechanism. But on more limited questions, economic analysis often can be applied to advantage. We consider three examples: cost-benefit analysis, the problem of least-cost production, and the pricing of public services.

We concluded in Part One that production of each good should be carried to the point at which the benefit yielded by the last unit just equals the cost of producing it. There are cases in which the benefits from a public project can be estimated, and by comparing these benefits with estimated costs, one can judge whether the project is worthwhile. Consider a multiple-purpose river development project, which produces a combination of electric power, flood prevention, irrigation, and improved navigation. For power output, one can estimate the price at which the power can be sold on a commercial basis. The value of flood prevention can be judged by the property damage resulting from past floods. As regards irrigation, one can compare the cash value of crop production on irrigated land with production on the same land before irrigation. For navigation benefits, one can estimate the probable increase in tonnage carried by water, and how much it would have cost to move this tonnage by rail or other methods. Adding these things, one gets an estimate of total benefits from the project which can be compared with the probable cost. This type of calculation is used by the Army Corps of Engineers, the Bureau of Reclamation, and other agencies concerned with river development.[3]

In the area of education, too, one can make rough cost-benefit calculations. Consider the cost to the community of having a high-school graduate complete a college course in engineering. The cost consists of the income which he could have earned during the years he is enrolled in college, plus the cost to the college of providing his training (which will usually be greater than the actual tuition charge). These costs are an investment designed to raise his productive capacity, and the extra capacity he acquires is in fact often called "human capital." The return on this capital can be measured roughly by the difference between the man's future earnings as an engineer and what he could have earned as a high-school graduate. If the rate of return is higher than that on alternative kinds of physical or human investment, this indicates that more engineers should be trained.

Suppose now it has been decided to produce a certain amount of some public service. There is still the problem of how to produce this amount at minimum cost. Here we can use the same principles as in private production. How can the post office handle a specified volume of mail at lowest unit cost? What size and location of school buildings, what combination of teachers and physical plant, will minimize the cost of producing a certain quality of education? Just as in private production, we know that operating units should be of optimum scale; that the factors of production, given their prices, should be combined in the least-cost way; that where several techniques of production are available, the most economical should be chosen. These are familiar problems to efficiency engi-

---

[3] For an analysis of the theoretical and practical difficulties in such calculations, see Otto Eckstein, *Water Resource Development* (Cambridge, Mass.: Harvard University Press, 1958).

neers and management consultants. There is no reason why these expert analysts should not be used as heavily in public production as in the private economy.

Secretary Robert McNamara, Charles Hitch, and others have pioneered in applying economic analysis within the Department of Defense, to the dismay of some military officers and congressmen, but with a substantial saving of resources. Instead of the traditional allocation of the defense budget among Army, Navy, and Air Force, the budget is now classified by functions to be performed: strategic retaliatory forces, continental air and missile defense forces, general-purpose forces, and so on. This makes it possible to pose the question of how a particular function can best be performed, not as a problem of jurisdictional rivalry among the services, but as a problem of cost and efficiency.

Suppose, for example, that the strategic retaliatory forces must be prepared on command to deliver a certain weight of bombs on specified targets. This could conceivably be done by conventional bombers, by missiles stationed in the United States, or by mobile missiles fired from submarines. The costs of each technique can be calculated, and a combination developed which will achieve the objective at minimum cost.

A third area for economic analysis involves pricing of public services. It is never *necessary* to charge a price for a public service, since government can use the taxing power to cover costs. But it may be quite *appropriate* to charge a price where those who benefit from the service are a clearly identifiable group. Transportation, communications, and electric power services are normally sold at a price. We charge prices to those who send mail through the Post Office system. Farmers who receive irrigation water normally pay something for it; and so on.

In such cases the public authority, by experimenting with various price levels, can learn something about the shape of demand and marginal revenue curves. Average and marginal cost curves can be calculated, and the $P = MC$ rule applied. To say that this can be done in principle, however, does not mean that it is easy to do in practice. The customer groups naturally mobilize political pressure to secure prices below marginal cost; and very often they succeed. A notable example is our low second- and third-class postal rates, which cause the public to be deluged with large amounts of "junk mail." Higher rates based on delivery costs would reduce both the Post Office deficit and the cost of emptying waste baskets all over the country.

Price devices could probably be used to good effect in areas where they are not now used. Highways and city streets, though built at taxpayers' expense, are treated thereafter as though their use was free. So commuters abandon the mass transit facilities, causing them financial distress, and come pouring into town by the thousands in their automobiles. The resulting congestion sets up an outcry for larger and faster access routes to the city. But better highways attract still more traffic, and one is involved in an endless cycle of road building—congestion—more road building—still more congestion. Some economists think it would be appropriate to charge the commuter motorist a price equivalent to the marginal cost he imposes on the community. This could be done by charging a substantial toll for access to the central city or by making downtown parking really expensive. This would also divert part of the commuter traffic to more efficient mass transit facilities, which presently have unused capacity and low marginal costs.

The Level of Public Services: Economics in the Large

We have argued that economic analysis can often be applied effectively to public production. But the yardstick melts when we come to the larger issues. Consider a public good, or a good with large external effects, which either cannot be priced or for which it does not seem expedient to charge a price. We can still say that production of the service should be carried to the point where marginal social benefit equals marginal cost. More broadly, production of all public services should be carried to the point at which the last dollar spent on them yields consumers the same utility they could have obtained from spending this dollar on privately produced goods. Only then are resources being properly allocated between the private and public sectors.

Unfortunately, however, this test is not operational. What *is* the marginal social benefit of the last dollar we are now spending on national defense, or on elementary education, or on the national highway network? In the absence of prices and of any market test of consumer demand, we just do not know. So we cannot be sure whether these goods are being overproduced or underproduced, relative to each other and relative to private good and services.

This is a frustrating situation. Could we perhaps get around it in the following way: people get satisfaction from public services, just as they do from privately sold goods and services. They must therefore be presumed to want public services, to have a demand for them. It should be possible then, to construct Mr. Jones's demand curve for highway services just as we construct his demand for food or clothing. He would probably pay a good deal for a two-lane highway to drive to work from his home in the suburbs. If the highway were made wider and better, it would yield some additional benefit, and so would additional highways linking him with other communities. These benefits taper off, however, and Mr. Jones's demand curve would fall from left to right in the usual way.

Suppose we got demand curves for highway service from every-body in the country and added them together to get a total demand curve. The cost of building increasingly fancy highway systems can be estimated, giving a supply curve for highway services. By noting the intersection of the demand and supply curves, could we not read off the proper level of highway expenditure?

This would be a nice solution. But there are two major difficulties. First, there is no objective way of discovering the demand curves of the citizens. For privately marketed goods, buyers reveal their preferences by their behavior in the market. In the case of public services, however, people have an incentive to conceal and understate their preferences. Expressing a high preference could lead to paying higher taxes. Expressing a low preference costs you nothing, since you know that you will have equal access to whatever level of service the government decides to provide. Second, there are problems in adding up preferences. The people who benefit from a particular service are not exactly the same people who pay the corresponding taxes. Provision of the service thus involves a transfer of income from one group to the other. A decision to provide a certain level of service is also a decision that a certain income distribution is desirable, and there is no scientific basis for reaching decisions about income distribution.

This leaves us with no clear guide to the proper level of expenditure on public services. There seems no alternative but to accept the results which emerge from the political process. Political decision making is admittedly imperfect. It is not feasible to submit every expenditure decision to a popular referendum. And when legislative representatives take action on spending bills, it is not clear just whom or what they are representing. A voter choosing among alternative candidates is probably not much influenced by the candidate's views on particular spending programs. He may be influenced by whether the candidate or his party is identified with "high spending" or "low spending." But he is apt to be vulnerable to the candidate who promises simultaneously to raise expenditures, reduce taxes, and balance the budget.

How does the political process work out? Does it contain any inherent bias toward "overspending" or "underspending"? Does it lead to a higher or lower level of public services than the citizens would prefer on the basis of full information and rational reflection? There are wide differences of opinion on this point. One school of thought maintains that government is biased toward overspending. The voters, it is argued, have an optical illusion on this matter. They regard public services as free goods and fail to realize that they must be covered by taxes. Thus they press for more service than they would if the costs were clearly visualized. In the legislative lobby, groups urging new spending are likely to be better organized than those urging tax reductions. Spending programs usually benefit a specific group, which will therefore press hard for them. Tax reductions benefit the citizens at large, whose interest in them is consequently diffuse and ill organized. This school of thought relies also on the spectre of the power-hungry bureaucrat, eager to expand his empire in accordance with Parkinson's Law.

An opposing school maintains that we have been seriously under-spending on public services. The media of mass communication, it is argued, assiduously promote the idea that private production is "good," while government functions are "bad" or at least suspect. Taxes are of course "bad," since they are extracted by force from a groaning citizenry. But spending by these same citizens on the products of private business is "good." The public is urged constantly by high-pressure advertising to buy more and fancier consumer goods. No similar advertising campaign is conducted on behalf of better schools and hospitals, urban redevelop-ment, natural resource conservation, and other public goods. As a result, too much effort goes into producing private consumption goods, while too little goes into providing public services. We pack our plastic dishes into our nylon picnic bag and climb into our chrome-ornamented car. We then drive our undereducated children through smog-filled air on an overcrowded highway to lunch in a weed-ridden park beside a polluted stream.

Which school of thought is more nearly correct? There is no objective way of deciding. Both schools may be right with respect to different types of public expenditure. A public program which benefits a small, well-organized group may readily be overexpanded as a result of political pressure. Consider the irrigation and land reclamation programs, designed to "make the desert blossom like the rose." These certainly benefit the landowners, who often get irrigation water well below cost. But in view of our already large agricultural surpluses, the national benefit from these programs is probably negative. Another example is the costly program of subsidies to American shipbuilders and the U.S. merchant marine. There is admittedly a defense consideration here, but defense needs could probably be met adequately at a fraction of the present cost.

A belief that government budgets could be reduced in such areas is not at all inconsistent with a belief that they could usefully be expanded in others. Public services which benefit the amorphous, inarticulate mass of the community may often be underdeveloped. In public production, just as in private production, people often have to be shown new consumption possibilities through imaginative entrepreneurship. There was little public demand for slum clearance and urban renewal until the possibilities had been demonstrated by some enterprising public officials.

PUBLIC EXPENDITURE: TYPES AND TRENDS

There is a cliché to the effect that the American economy is characterized by "big business," "big labor," and "big government." Government expenditures, it is said, have been rising disproportionately fast in recent decades and have now reached alarming proportions. This suggests several quantitative questions: How does one measure the economic importance of government relative to the private economy? How rapidly has the relative importance of government been rising, and why? What are the major purposes of public expenditure? What is the distribution of functions among different levels of government?

There are several possible measures of the significance of government operations: (1) *total government expenditure* indicates roughly how much is being collected each year in taxes. But this total includes a large volume of transfer payments which go right back to the citizens. Thus it is a good deal larger than: (2) *the cost of providing public services*. This indicates the proportion of our productive resources which is being devoted to satisfying community wants, or the proportion of national output organized on a tax-supported rather than a private market basis. Most of the materials required for public services, however, are purchased from private business concerns. In 1964, business sales to government amounted to about $64 billion. If we deduct this amount we get a still smaller total, (3) *the cost of direct government production*. This includes only goods and services produced by government agencies, not those which are simply *purchased and distributed* by government. Basically, it is the public payroll.

These three totals compared as follows in the calendar year 1964: total government expenditure, including transfer payments, was $175 billion. The cost of providing public services was $128 billion. Output produced directly by government came to $64 billion. One can pick and choose among these figures, depending on the purpose in mind. In terms of resource use, the second and third totals are most significant and we shall concentrate on them here.

Direct Government Production

One approach to the importance of government is to ask what proportion of national output is produced by government agencies or, thinking in terms of inputs, what proportion of our resources is used in direct government production? The most important input is labor, and we have reliable figures of public and private employment. Table 1 and Figure 1 show government employment as a percentage of total employment at intervals from 1900 to 1965, and also the division of employment among the federal, state, and local governments.

Judged by the employment yardstick, government has tripled in relative importance since 1900. Civilian employees of the government were 4.5 percent of all workers in 1900, 12.1 percent in 1965. If members of the armed forces were added, about one sixth of all employed workers were working for various levels of government in 1965.

Contrary to popular impression, the federal government is not the largest producer of ordinary or nondefense services. The state and local governments have more than twice as many civilian employees as the federal government. Local government alone provides more than half of all civilian public employment, mainly because of the great size of the school system. The federal government's share of civilian public employment has risen only slightly since 1900. It is mainly the military establishment which makes the federal government loom so large on the budget scene.

TABLE 1

Government Employment as a Percentage of
Total Employment, United States, 1900–1965*

	1900	1910	1920	1930	1940	1950	1960	1965
Federal								
Military	0.5	0.4	0.8	0.5	1.1	2.8	3.6	4.9
Nonmilitary	1.1	1.2	1.7	1.4	2.2	3.5	3.3	1.9
State	0.3	0.3	0.5	0.7	1.1	1.8	2.3	2.6
Local	3.1	3.4	4.0	5.4	5.9	5.4	6.7	7.6
Total	5.0	5.3	7.0	8.0	10.3	13.5	15.9	17.0

* Figures through 1940 are adapted from S. Fabricant, *Trend of Government Activity since 1900* (New York: National Bureau of Economic Research, 1952). The 1965 data are from U.S. Department of Labor, *Employment and Earnings,* June, 1965. All school employees are classified as local through 1940. For later years they are distributed between local and state governments in proper proportion. The federal figure for 1940 excludes emergency relief workers.

The share of the nation's capital resources used by government has also risen. Fabricant estimates that in 1900 the government owned about one sixteenth of the nonmilitary capital assets of the country. By the late forties, government owned about one fifth of all nonmilitary assets, with

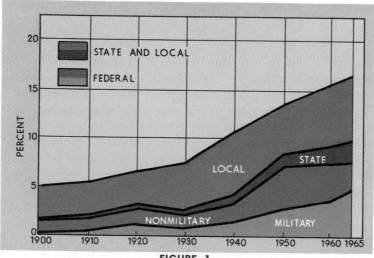

Government Employment as a Percentage of
Total Employment, United States, 1900–1965

FIGURE 1.

an estimated value of more than $50 billion. If military items were also included, government's share would be even higher. Most of this increase occurred during the years 1929–46.

Cost of Public Services

In addition to the public payroll, government buys large amounts of goods and services from private industry. This includes the work of contractors in building new schools, highways, airports, and other facilities; the cost of military aircraft, missiles, and other defense products; and a great variety of supplies for the daily operation of government agencies. By adding government purchases to government payrolls we get the *cost of providing public services* or, what amounts to the same thing, *government expenditures exclusive of transfer payments.* By calculating this total as a percentage of GNP we can see how much of our national output is being channeled through government rather than through private markets.

TABLE 2

Government Payrolls and Purchases as Percentage
of Gross National Product, 1903–64*

	1903	1913	1929	1939	1949	1954	1961	1964
Federal								
Military	0.8	0.6⎫	1.3	1.4	5.3	11.3	9.4	8.9
Nonmilitary	1.1	1.3⎭		4.3	3.4	1.8	1.6	1.6
State and local	4.5	5.2	6.9	8.7	6.9	7.6	9.7	10.1
Total	6.4	7.1	8.2	14.4	15.6	20.7	20.7	20.6

* Data on government payrolls and purchases were derived as follows:
  1903–13: S. Fabricant, *Trend of Government Activity since 1900*, Tables D-4, pp. 225–234.
  1929–64: *Survey of Current Business,* July, 1964, and May, 1965

Table 2 shows the situation in selected years since 1900. Expenditure trends have been broadly similar to the employment trends shown in Table 1. The proportion of national output absorbed by government has more than tripled, from a bit over 6 percent near the beginning of the century to about 21 percent at present. Local and state governments are the main providers of civilian services, being about six times as important in this respect as the federal government. At the federal level, the most dramatic development has been the sharp increase in military expenditures. Before 1940 these typically formed only one tenth of all government spending and around 1 percent of GNP. Today military spending is about half of the total cost of public services and about 9 percent of GNP.

Where Does the Money Go?

One fifth of our national product is a lot of output. What concrete form does this take? What are the main types of service provided by each level of government? Figures 2a, 2b, and 2c show the situation as of 1961.

The federal government provides basically national defense. This may be news to businessmen who find themselves regulated by the ICC,

Cost Distribution by Level of Government and Type of
Service, United States, 1963–64
(Percent)

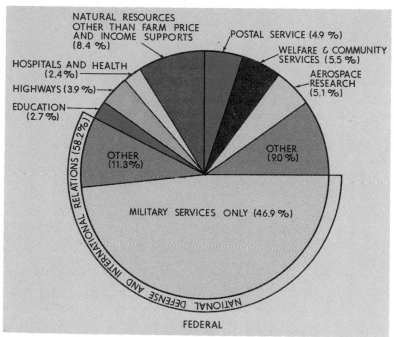

FIGURE 2a.

FTC, SEC, FPC, FCC, CAB, and other alphabetical agencies. These activities are important, but they cost little in money and manpower. If we include the foreign aid and atomic energy programs as part of the defense effort, national defense absorbs about three quarters of the cost of federal services. Everything else has to fit into the remaining quarter.

At the state level, education and highways form more than half of all costs. Educational expenditures include grants to localities for the public school system plus the cost of the state universities and other institutions of higher education. The states have traditionally borne the main burden of highway construction, though increasing support is now being received from the federal government. Other important state services include health and hospital care, natural resource conservation, and law enforcement. Relief expenditures are also important, but these are transfer payments and consequently do not appear in Figure 2b.

The main local service has always been the public school system. Since 1945, school expenditures have risen unusually fast because of the

Cost Distribution by Level of Government and Type of
Service, United States, 1963–64
(Percent)

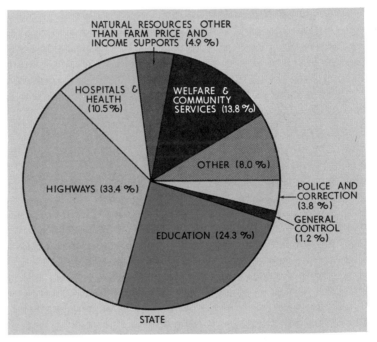

FIGURE 2b.

population upsurge, which has greatly increased the number of children to be trained. Today, local governments devote about half their resources to education. The next largest item is streets and roads, which includes country roads in rural areas as well as streets and sidewalks in the cities. Other sizable items are police protection, fire protection, water supply, trash and garbage collection, hospitals, and libraries. There are also important transfer payments in the form of cash relief.

Altogether, then, three quarters of the cost of public services in the United States goes for four items: national defense; education; roads, streets, and highways; and police, fire, and health services. General government administration, the "swollen bureaucracy," takes only a small percentage. It is an illusion to think that large amounts of money can be cut from government budgets without also cutting the level of service provided.

Behind the Uptrend

This analysis of the content of public services makes it easier to visualize what lies behind the long-term rise in government expenditures. Particularly important have been:

1. **The changed international situation.** The United States in 1900 still stood on the fringes of world politics. The game was being

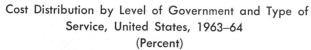

Cost Distribution by Level of Government and Type of Service, United States, 1963–64

(Percent)

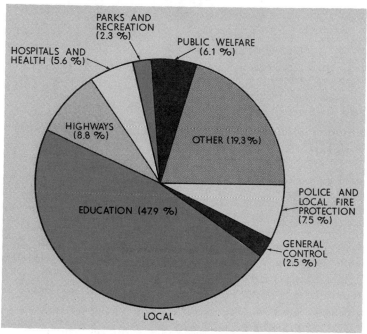

FIGURE 2c.

played out in Europe among the traditional great powers—Britain, France, Germany, Russia, and the Austro-Hungarian Empire. Fascinating as the game was, no one expected it to erupt in major wars, the last of which had ended almost a century before with the downfall of Napoleon. In these circumstances, our military establishment of 100,000 men was an inexpensive sideshow.

No one need be reminded of the very different circumstances of the

1960's. After two destructive world wars, which have left their residue of expense, the United States and the U.S.S.R. have emerged as superpowers in a world torn by dissension. Tension between these powers and their adherents seems likely to continue for many years. This necessitates a larger military establishment than existed before 1940, while at the same time the cost of modern weapons has greatly increased. It is a far cry from the machine guns and field artillery of 1918 to the long-range missiles and atomic submarines of today.

2. Urbanization of the population. In 1900 only 40 percent of the American people lived in towns and cities. Today the proportion of town-dwellers is two thirds and still rising. City people consume more public services per head than country people. The farmer draws water from his own well, disposes of his own trash and garbage, protects his property as best he can from fire and theft, needs no streets, sewers, or public parks. In the city these functions are provided at public expense. The resulting network of municipal services, while counted as part of national output, should perhaps be considered an unavoidable cost of complex, congested urban living.

3. Rising real incomes. Real income per capita in the United States almost tripled between 1900 and 1960. Higher incomes increase the demand for almost everything, but for some things more than others. Food and other necessities show a low income elasticity of demand. Most services, on the contrary, show a high income elasticity. Thus as real incomes rise, production of services rises a good deal faster than production of commodities. This is true of such privately produced services as travel, entertainment, vacation resorts, medical care, and beauty care. It is true also of public services. As living standards rise, people demand longer and better schooling, fancier highways, faster postal service, more adequate police and fire protection.

Not only does the volume of public services rise for these reasons, but these services become relatively more expensive to provide. They are essentially labor services, and in our economy the price of labor rises steeply over the long run. Nor is there the same opportunity to substitute capital for labor which one finds in commodity production. A doubling of auto workers' wages over 20 years will not double the price of an automobile, because of the possibility of substituting machinery for labor and making improvements in production methods. But a doubling of policemen's salaries will come close to doubling the cost of police protection. The radio patrol car, to be sure, covers more ground than the foot patrolman, and the eye of the television tube is now peering over the shoulder of the schoolteacher. But the possibilities of capital substitution are still limited, and both public and private services seem bound to become more expensive over the course of time.

4. Rising educational standards. Education deserves special mention because it absorbs such a large part of state and local budgets

and because demand for education has risen so spectacularly. For every thousand pupils enrolled in Grade 5 in 1910, only 139 graduated from high school and only 23 succeeded in finishing college. High-school graduates were a small aristocracy. Today high-school graduation proves mainly that one has lived to the age of 18, and even college graduation is so common that it gives no assurance of a high-income job. Out of a thousand fifth grade pupils in 1952, 581 graduated from high school and 301 went on for at least some college training. The ratios in the sixties will doubtless be higher still.

This educational revolution is due partly to the higher income level of the country. Rising incomes make it less necessary for youngsters to begin contributing to the family budget at an early age. Rising incomes also provide taxable capacity to cover the cost of educating people for longer periods. Added to these economic factors is the traditional American belief that "education is good for you." It will help you adjust to adult life, find a wife or husband, get a better job, and derive greater enjoyment from your leisure time.

At any event, enrollment has risen substantially since 1900. Enrollment in colleges and universities has increased more than tenfold, from 237,000 in 1900 to over 4½ million in 1963, a number which is expected to double by 1970. When one considers also the increased variety and complexity of the subjects taught, improvements in the style of classrooms and dormitories, and the great increase in teachers' salary levels, it is clear why educational expenditures have increased not only absolutely but as a percentage of national income.

5. The car and the highway. The inventor of the internal combustion engine unwittingly launched a huge increase in future public expenditures. The passenger car has now largely replaced rail travel as well as local subway and bus systems. The truck has cut deeply into railroad freight traffic. The auto and truck manufacturers, however, do not provide roads on which their vehicles can run. This remains a public responsibility. As the number and speed of vehicles has increased, standards and costs of highway construction have risen steadily. The costs have gotten beyond the fiscal capacity of the states, and increasing federal subsidies have become necessary. The 41,000-mile interstate network of superhighways, started in 1958 and expected at that time to cost about $25 billion, is being financed to the extent of 90 percent from federal funds. The federal government also contributes to support of the older national and state highway systems.

Cars and highways are complementary goods, but one falls in the private and the other in the public sector. Private decisions to buy cars and trucks compel public decisions to allocate more resources to road building. Thus an item which bulked small before 1900 has become a major object of public expenditure.

The growth of public expenditure, then, reflects a long-term in-

TABLE 3
Sources of Tax Revenue, Fiscal Year 1963–64

TYPE OF TAX	FEDERAL		STATE		LOCAL		TOTAL	
	$ Million	Percent	$ Million	Percent	$ Million	Percent	$ Million	Percent
Personal income	48,697	53.8	3,415	14.1	376	1.6	52,488	38.0
Corporate income	23,493	26.0	1,695	7.0	...	...	25,188	18.2
Property	...	...	722	3.0	20,519	87.2	21,241	15.4
Sales taxes, excises, and customs	(14,776)	(16.3)	(13,957)	(57.6)	(1,806)	(7.7)	(30,538)	(22.1)
Customs duties	1,252	1.4	...	...	...	...	1,252	0.9
General sales taxes	...	...	6,084	25.1	1,170	5.0	7,254	5.2
Motor fuel	2,696	1.4	4,059	16.9	33	0.1	6,788	4.9
Alcohol and tobacco	5,526	6.1	2,060	8.5	113	0.4	7,699	5.6
Other sales & excises	5,301	5.8	1,754	7.2	489	2.1	7,544	5.5
All other	3,542	3.9	4,454	18.4	841	3.6	8,837	6.4

Source: U.S. Bureau of the Census, Governmental Finances in 1963/64, p. 22.

crease in demand for public services, based on rising incomes, urbanization, and other growth trends in the economy. One should expect that public expenditures will continue to absorb at least the present proportion of our productive resources and probably a gradually rising proportion. The only possibility of sizable reductions lies in the military sphere, but this would require favorable developments in the international situation which are not now in sight.

PUBLIC REVENUE: TYPES OF TAX

While government raises some money through borrowing, most of what is spent comes from taxation. Table 3 shows the main sources of *general* tax revenue at each level of government in a recent fiscal year. The table does not include every type of government income. For example, it does not include revenues from commercial sales by government enterprises, such as sale of electric power by TVA or sale of subway services by the New York City system. Nor does it include the payroll taxes levied to support the old-age pension and unemployment compensation systems. This money goes into separate trust funds earmarked for pensions and unemployment benefits. The government runs a large insurance business as it were, alongside its other operations. But there is no need to mix this into our picture of how general government services are financed.

The amount of tax revenue *collected* at each level of government does not correspond with the amount *spent* at that level. The federal government makes cash grants to the states for various purposes, and the states in turn make grants to local governments. The emphasis of Table 3 is on tax *collections* rather than on where the money is eventually spent.

The tax sources used by different levels of government overlap considerably. While the federal government is the main recipient of income taxes, some states also tax personal and corporate income. The states join the federal government in taxing alcohol, tobacco, and motor fuels. Both state and local governments use sales taxes, and a few localities even levy income taxes. A half century ago, the revenue sources of each level of government were quite distinct. As expenditure needs have grown, however, each level has tried to tap more and more sources. This has produced a complicated overlapping network of taxation. Whether the present structure could be simplified to advantage by federal-state agreement is an important practical problem.

While tax structures overlap, the "center of gravity" differs for each level of government. Four fifths of federal revenue comes from income taxes on individuals and corporations, and excise taxes provide almost all the remainder. The main sources of state revenue are gasoline and motor vehicle taxes, general sales taxes, and personal and corporate income taxes. These provide about 70 percent of state tax collections. At the local level, the general property tax is still of overwhelming importance, providing more than 85 percent of tax revenues.

These differences in center of gravity are important for discussion of whether certain services should be provided by the federal government or at lower levels. This is often debated as a matter of high principle, of political centralism versus "states rights." But it is also a matter of hard cash. To say that something should be done by the federal government amounts to saying that it should be financed from income taxes. To push it down to the state level means that the funds will come largely from sales and excise taxes. Local responsibility means reliance on the general property tax. Since different people pay these various types of tax, this is a pocketbook issue which can generate heated argument.

The Personal Income Tax

This tax has been the outstanding fiscal development of the twentieth century. Along with its twin, the corporate income tax, it gives the federal revenue system great elasticity and enables Washington to collect enough to both cover federal expenditures and part of state and local expenditures.

The 1965 level of personal income tax rates is shown in Table 4. The tax rises by steps or "brackets," only a few of which are shown here, with

TABLE 4

Tax Rates on Personal Income, United States, 1965*
(Married Couple Filing Joint Return, Two Dependents,
Standard Deductions Only)

GROSS INCOME (1)	DEDUCTIONS (2)	TAXABLE INCOME (3)	MARGINAL TAX RATE (Percent) (4)	AMOUNT OF TAX (5)	AVERAGE TAX RATE (Percent) (6)	INCOME AFTER TAX (7)
$ 1,000	$2,600	$ 00	14	$ 0	0	$ 1,000
2,000	2,600	00	14	0	0	2,000
5,000	2,900	2,100	15	306	14	4,694
10,000	3,400	6,600	19	1,114	18	8,886
15,000	3,400	11,600	22	2,172	19	12,828
20,000	3,400	16,600	28	3,428	21	16,572
25,000	3,400	21,600	32	4,892	23	20,108
50,000	3,400	46,600	50	15,360	33	34,640
100,000	3,400	96,600	60	43,140	45	56,860
200,000	3,400	196,600	69	108,634	55	91,366
300,000	3,400	296,600	70	178,600	60	121,400
400,000	3,400	396,600	70	248,600	63	151,400
500,000	3,400	496,600	70	318,600	64	181,400

* The actual tax schedule contains many more steps in column (1), with the marginal tax rate rising gradually from step to step. This simplified version is intended merely to indicate the general nature of the system. It assumes that only the standard deductions are taken. Larger deductions would, of course, reduce the tax paid.

each increment of income subject to a higher rate than the one before. The *marginal* tax rate, the rate on the last increment in an income of given size, is shown in column (4). Beginning at 14 percent, it rises to a ceiling of 70 percent on all income over $200,000.

The *average* rate, the percentage of the whole income which must be paid in taxes, is shown in column (6). For an income of $20,000, for example, the marginal tax rate is 28 percent, but the average rate is only about 21 percent. At the $100,000 level, the marginal rate is 60 percent, the average rate about 45 percent. The average tax rate is always less than the marginal rate. It is "dragged down," as it were, by the lower marginal rates on earlier increments of income.

If, as one goes from lower to higher income brackets, a tax takes an *increasing* proportion of people's incomes, the tax is said to be *progressive*. A tax which takes the *same percentage* at each level of income is a *proportional* tax. A tax which takes a decreasing percentage from the higher incomes is termed *regressive*—it bears most heavily on the lowest income groups in the population. By this test the U.S. personal income tax is steeply progressive.

In practice, the progression is less steep than Table 4 would suggest. Few people actually pay more than half their income in taxes. Figures published by the Treasury Department show that in 1961 (when the tax schedule was higher than today, with marginal rates ranging from 20 to 91 percent), taxpayers reporting gross income of between $50,000 and $100,000 paid on the average only 34 percent of their income in taxes instead of the 45 percent indicated by the tax table. People with incomes of $200,000 to $500,000 paid 44 percent of their income in taxes instead of the 75 percent suggested by tax schedules at that time (Table 5).

Why do actual tax rates work out lower than the rates in the official schedule? The reason is partly that there are numerous deductions from gross income before the income tax is computed. These include charitable contributions, taxes paid to state and local governments, and medical expenses above a certain level. Interest on certain types of security, notably state and municipal bonds, is exempt from federal taxation. People in the top income brackets have a strong incentive to invest in tax-exempt securities.

There are also ways of reducing one's income for tax purposes a good deal below one's true income. These methods are termed tax *avoidance*, to distinguish them from illegal *evasion* of taxes by simply not reporting income received. One method, widely used in business, is to take part of one's compensation in the form of an expense account rather than in salary payments. Or part of an executive's compensation may be put into a prepaid retirement annuity which is not counted as income until he begins drawing pension payments. Or he may be given the right to purchase company stock at a reduced price (a stock option). The higher the marginal rate of tax, the greater the incentive to tax avoidance.

This has become a highly developed art, to the great benefit of the legal and accounting professions.

Although large incomes are charged the highest rates, they do not provide the bulk of tax collections. More than half of personal income tax receipts come from incomes below $10,000, because that is where most of the personal income of the country is concentrated (Table 5). People with incomes of $100,000 and over provide only 6 percent of tax

TABLE 5

Individual Income Tax Returns with Income
by Adjusted Gross Income Classes, 1961
(Number of Returns in Thousands,
Income in Millions of Dollars)

ADJUSTED GROSS INCOME CLASS	NO. OF RETURNS	ADJUSTED GROSS INCOME	INCOME TAX AFTER CREDITS	PER CENT OF ALL TAX COLLECTION
Under $1,000	6,988	3,692	41	0.1
$ 1,000–$ 1,999	7,265	10,693	482	1.1
2,000– 2,999	6,745	16,864	1,057	2.5
3,000– 3,999	6,695	23,410	1,840	4.4
4,000– 4,999	6,583	29,620	2,639	6.2
5,000– 9,999	20,784	144,984	15,936	37.7
10,000– 14,999	4,125	48,553	6,951	16.5
15,000– 19,999	890	15,151	2,577	6.1
20,000– 49,999	854	24,532	5,612	13.3
50,000– 100,000	110	7,268	2,484	5.9
100,000– 199,999	22	2,951	1,206	2.9
200,000– 499,999	6	1,750	764	1.8
500,000– 999,999	1	663	297	0.7
1,000,000 and over	*	806	342	0.8

* Less than 500
Source: *Statistical Abstract of the United States,* 1964, p. 399

payments. Large incomes are conspicuous, but there aren't many of them; and the amount of taxes which they provide is reduced by the possibilities of avoidance just described. The main reason for levying high marginal rates on large incomes is not that they yield much revenue but rather that they gratify a widespread sentiment against income inequality.

There has been much controversy over the indirect effects of the personal income tax on the supply of labor and capital. On a common-sense basis, one might argue that if the government takes away a sizable percentage of each hour's earnings, people will not work as many hours as they would otherwise. But the income tax cuts in two directions, which tend to offset each other. On one side, it amounts to lowering the real wage rate per hour of effort. An individual dividing his time between work and leisure finds work less rewarding than before. To put the same point in reverse, he finds that leisure has become less expensive. So, according to the normal principles of substitution, he will choose less work and more leisure.

But the tax also reduces the individual's weekly income. Unless income is of no account to him, he will feel some inclination to work *more* hours to regain his former income and scale of living. This *income* effect works in the opposite direction from the *substitution* effect, and there is no firm basis for predicting which will predominate. The outcome will depend on the shape of individual preferences for income and leisure, the distribution of personal incomes, and the steepness of the tax progression.

It is difficult to investigate this matter statistically. There have been a few studies of independent professional men who can work a longer or shorter week and can retire at an earlier or later stage of their careers. The results are inconclusive. It typically appears that some members of the group have adjusted to the tax structure by working more, others have decided to work less, and the net effect on labor supply has been small.[4]

More significant may be the effects on the supply of capital. One cannot be sure how far the upper-income groups react to heavy taxation by cutting consumption and how far by reducing saving, but the effect on saving must be substantial. Nor is this reduction of private saving offset by an increase in government saving, since the tax revenue is used mainly for current government expenses. There is thus a reduction in saving for the economy as a whole. Whether this should be viewed as good or bad depends on whether one thinks that "undersaving" or "oversaving" is a more serious danger in our type of economy, a problem which will be explored in Part Three.

In addition to an overall reduction in capital supply, there may be an especially sharp reduction in the supply of equity capital for new or risky enterprises. Venture capital on a large scale used to come mainly from wealthy individuals, while the low- and medium-income groups have always tended toward savings accounts, annuities, and fixed-income investments.

The Corporate Income Tax

This is on the surface a remarkably simple tax. The first $25,000 of profits is taxed at a rate of 22 percent, and everything over that at a rate of 48 percent. The object of this gradation is to aid small enterprises

---

[4] See in particular George Break, "Income Taxes and Incentives to Work: An Empirical Study," *American Economic Review*, September, 1957, pp. 529–49

which, because they cannot tap the general capital market, must grow mainly through reinvestment of earnings. This degree of aid, however, is probably too small to have much practical effect.

While this tax is simple in principle, it is complicated in practice by the fact that "profit" is such a slippery concept. Determining a company's profit for the year requires the determination of its costs. One thorny problem is the size of depreciation charges on plant and equipment. Suppose a company buys a $100,000 piece of equipment which is expected to have a service life of 20 years. A simple straight-line formula yields annual depreciation of $5,000, which is entered as a cost item. But if the company were allowed to write off the item over a 5-year period, as has sometimes been done as a special incentive to companies in defense production, the annual depreciation charge would be $20,000. Cost would be higher, profit lower, and the company would pay less income tax. After the end of the 5-year period, the situation is reversed. The company will be paying *more* income tax than if it had spread out the depreciation over a longer period. But meanwhile it has staved off the evil day. And a rapidly expanding company can stay ahead of the game for a long time.

Who pays the corporate income tax? The traditional answer has been the corporation, which means the common stockholders. The reasoning behind this conclusion is simple: under either monopoly or competition, the intelligent business manager will adjust his production and selling price to make maximum profit. It will not pay him to alter this adjustment, even though the government decides to take away half his profit in taxes. Even with a tax, it can never pay to make *less* profit than you were making before.

But this view has not gone unchallenged. Another school of thought argues that the corporate income tax is at least partially shifted forward to consumers. The argument is that, where producers have some power over price, they will interpret the corporate income tax as an added cost and will raise prices to cover this cost. They will aim to make their profit rate *after* taxes as high as their previous profit rate without the tax. The national income statistics provide some support for this argument. Interest and profit rates are somewhat lower today than they were in the 1920's, when corporate income taxes were negligible. But they are not 50 percent lower. So it does seem that part of the tax impact on the corporation has been recaptured from consumers.

The issue is of considerable practical importance. If the corporate income tax fell fully on stockholders, it would be a *progressive* tax, since stockholding is concentrated in the higher income brackets. But to the extent that it falls on consumers, this is not true. Again, if the tax falls on the corporation, it will reduce both the incentive to new investment and the funds available for new investment. But to the extent that the tax is shifted, this argument no longer applies.

The Excise Tax

The venerable history of this tax is attested by the Scotch ballad, "The de'il's awa' wi' th' exciseman," a sentiment warmly echoed by later generations. It is a tax on the production or sale of a commodity, usually a necessity with inelastic demand which can be counted on to produce a dependable revenue. Salt and matches have been favorite objects of taxation in many countries. Today alcohol and tobacco are usually mainstays of the excise tax system. This is sometimes justified on the moral ground that heavy taxes, which means high prices, will discourage the use of these harmful articles. But people cling to tobacco and alcohol with remarkable tenacity. There is not much discouragement of consumption, but for precisely this reason, there is a tax yield which delights the treasury authorities.

During World War II in the United States, the need to increase federal revenue and discourage private consumption led to a great multiplication of excise taxes. Excises were imposed or raised on automobiles, trucks, tires, gasoline, passenger travel, telephone and telegraph bills, theater admissions, night club entertainment, and a wide variety of allegedly "luxury" products, including jewelry, furs, luggage, radio sets, cameras, sporting goods, and musical instruments. This was justified as a temporary way of meeting the war emergency. But temporary taxes have a way of becoming permanent, and most of these excises lingered on until the mid-sixties. By that time federal excise taxes were yielding about $15 billion a year. More than four fifths of this, however, came from five items: alcohol, tobacco, cars and accessories, gasoline, and telephone bills. Many of the other items were little more than nuisance taxes with a small revenue yield.

In 1965 the Johnson administration recommended, and Congress enacted, a bill designed to cut annual excise tax collections by about $5 billion through staged reductions over several years ahead. Many of the minor excises were abolished immediately, and even the major 10 percent tax on new automobiles will have disappeared by 1969. The only major excises remaining at that time will be those on alcohol, tobacco, and motor fuel. Taxes on motor fuels are usually justified as a way of forcing highway users to contribute to highway costs; and most of the revenue from these taxes is set aside in special funds for highway construction.

An excise tax is levied on the supplier of a good or service, but part or all of the tax is typically shifted forward to the buyer. Consider a product produced at constant long-run cost and sold under competitive conditions (Figure 3). DD is the demand curve and PS the long-run supply curve. Equilibrium price will be OP and output OQ. Now an excise tax of PP_1 is placed on each unit produced. This addition to costs raises the supply curve to P_1S_1, and leads to a new equilibrium with price OP_1 and output OQ_1.

In a Competitive, Constant Cost Industry,
the Consumer Pays the Full Excise Tax

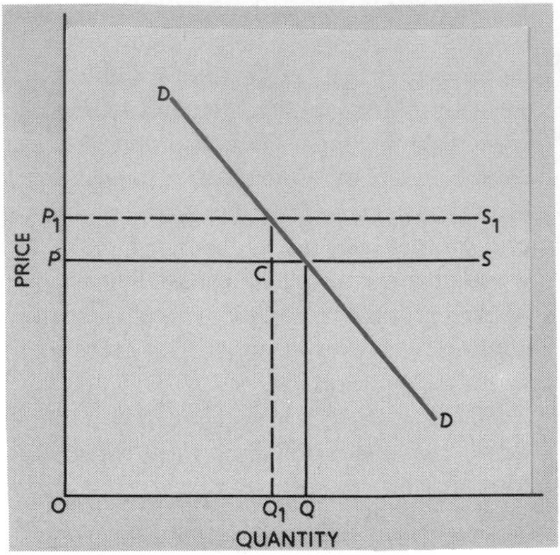

FIGURE 3. *DD* is the demand curve and *PS* the long-run supply curve. Imposing an excise tax of PP_1 raises the price of the product from OP to OP_1 and reduces the quantity produced from OQ to OQ_1.

These are long-run results and take time to work themselves out. After the dust has settled, however, it turns out that:

1. Output of the product is permanently reduced. The extent of the reduction depends on the elasticity of demand.

2. The price of the product to consumers is raised by the full amount of the tax. The entire tax has been shifted forward. Note that this result depends on the assumption of constant costs. If the supply curve were forward sloping, indicating an increasing cost industry, the price rise would be less than the amount of the tax.

3. The result depends also on the assumption of a competitive industry. If the product were sold by a monopolist, and if he were maximizing profit before the excise was imposed, he could not avoid bearing part of the tax through reduced profits.

In Figure 4 the solid lines are the cost and revenue curves of a monopoly producer. The monopolist maximizes profit by producing the output for which $MR = MC$. This is OQ, and the price at which this output can be sold is OP. Now the government imposes an excise tax of CC_1 dollars per unit. This raises both the marginal cost and average cost curves, which shift upward to MC_1 and ATC_1. The best the monopolist can now do is to produce where $MR = MC_1$. So he will produce OQ_1 and sell it for OP_1. His profit is now lower than before. This follows from the fact that he was already maximizing profit *before* the tax was imposed. But if you are skeptical, draw in the two profit rectangles and compare them.

This reasoning applies to any situation in which the producer faces a sloped demand curve, that is, to monopoly, oligopoly, and monopolistic

Under Monopoly the Producer Bears
Part of the Tax

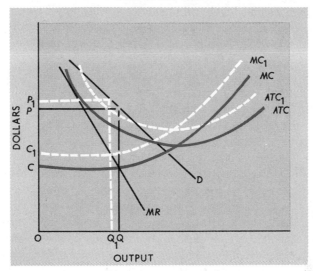

FIGURE 4. The solid lines show the company's position before the excise tax is imposed. Output of the product is OQ
and price OP. Now an excise tax of CC_1 per unit shifts the
cost curves upward to MC_1 and ATC_1. The new output, where
MC_1 intersects MR, is OQ_1 and the new price is OP_1. At this
price the monopolist's profit must be less than before.

competition. In these cases the producer's profit is reduced by the excise.
Consumers also bear part of the burden through higher prices and
reduced consumption of the good.

The items which provide most of the excise tax revenue are articles
of mass consumption. A family with $5,000 a year spends a larger *per-
centage of its income* on cars and accessories, gasoline, tobacco, alcohol,
and telephone service than does a family with $20,000 a year. The low-
income family consequently pays a higher percentage of its income in
excise taxes than does the high-income family. Excise taxes are *regressive*.
They take about 5 percent of the income of the poorest group in the community. This drops to less than 2 percent for those with incomes above
$10,000 a year.

The Sales Tax

This is basically a state tax. State expenditures on highways,
education, and other items have risen rapidly since 1945 and are still
shooting upward. On the revenue side, the states are squeezed between
the general property tax, where they must defer to the localities, and the
income tax, where they cannot compete too heavily with the federal
government. So they have turned to the general sales tax, which promises

a large yield with low collection costs. About two thirds of the states now have sales taxes, at rates ranging mostly between 2 and 4 percent. The tax is assessed at the retail level and normally applies to all commodities but not to services. A number of states exempt food, which reduces the tax burden on the poorest families, and a few exempt medical and health supplies.

Retailers are usually required to compute the tax separately from the price of goods sold, and to show it as a separate item on the customer's bill. The intent is that the buyer shall pay the tax, and we can take it that this result is largely achieved. It follows that a general sales tax is regressive. As one goes up the income scale, the percentage of income spent declines and the percentage saved rises. The percentage of family spending which goes for services rather than goods also rises with increasing incomes. Thus the *percentage of income spent on goods only,* which is the basis of the sales tax, must go down with rising income. Calculations made some years ago for the state of Illinois indicated that in the $1,000–2,000 range, 80 percent of family income was spent on items subject to tax. But families with incomes above $10,000 spent only 45 percent of their income on taxable items, hence were taxed only about half as heavily as the poorest groups.

The Property Tax

This is the mainstay of town and city finance and is well known to every householder. Each May, I receive a bill stating the assessed value of my house and lot, the tax rate for the year, and, by simple multiplication, the amount which I owe the city. It is quite clear who pays this tax. I do. So do my neighbors. So do farmers and landowners in general. The only possibility of significant shifting is in the case of office and commercial buildings, residential apartments, and other buildings constructed for rent. Over the long run, people will not put money into building projects unless they yield as much as other types of investment. Property taxes will have to be counted as a cost, along with maintenance and other operating costs, and will be passed on to the tenants in rent charges.

The property tax is moderately regressive, though not so strongly as sales and excise taxes. It takes close to 5 percent of incomes below $2,000, but only 3½ percent of incomes above $10,000 a year.

THE IMPACT OF TAXATION

How do these taxes add up in terms of the total impact of the tax structure? Musgrave's exstimates, shown in Table 6, rest on detailed assumptions about shifting which are described in the original source. The 1954 data are now some distance in the past, but recent changes in the tax structure would not change the general drift of the conclusions.

The total impact of the U.S. tax structure in this year was mildly progressive as regards the brackets below $10,000 a year, in which the great bulk of the population was concentrated. Familes with incomes of less than $2,000 a year paid about 23 percent of their incomes in taxes, while families between $7,500 and $10,000 paid about 30 percent. The progressive effect of the personal and corporate income taxes slightly outweighed the regressive effect of sales, excise, and property taxes.

Above $10,000 a year, income taxes dominate the scene increasingly and give a sharper progressive tilt to tax payments. The average of 40

TABLE 6

Distribution of Tax Revenue by Income Class, United States, 1954
(Percent of Adjusted Money Income Paid in Tax)

INCOME CLASS	PERSONAL INCOME TAX	CORPORATE INCOME TAX	EXCISE AND SALES TAX	PROPERTY TAX	ALL TAXES
Under 2,000	3.1	3.9	10.7	4.8	22.8
2,000– 3,000	5.4	4.0	9.6	4.3	23.5
3,000– 4,000	7.3	3.4	8.7	4.1	23.8
4,000– 5,000	8.6	3.3	8.3	4.1	24.7
5,000– 7,500	11.9	3.8	7.8	3.8	27.4
7,500–10,000	14.7	4.3	7.1	3.6	29.9
Over 10,000	15.4	14.7	4.1	3.4	39.5
All incomes	11.1	6.5	7.3	3.8	29.4

Source: Derived from Tables A–2, A–4, and 2 of Richard A. Musgrave, "The Incidence of the Tax Structure and its Effects on Consumption," in Joint Committee on the Economic Report, *Federal Tax Policy for Economic Growth and Stability*; papers submitted by panelists appearing before the subcommittee on tax policy, November 9, 1955.

percent tax payments for all families above $10,000 is not very revealing because it covers such a wide range of incomes. A more detailed breakdown would show progression all the way up the scale.

THE TAX SYSTEM: SOME UNSETTLED ISSUES

Who Should Pay the Taxes?

The previous section provides a factual background for discussion of tax policy. But it is only a background. We cannot conclude that "whatever is, is right." Many people believe that the present tax system has grave defects. Scholars have been seeking correct principles of taxation for centuries, so far without much success. The themes which recur most frequently in the literature are the "benefit principle" and the "principle of ability to pay."

The benefit principle.   Taxes are levied to provide public services which benefit the recipients. Is it not reasonable, then, that each person should pay taxes proportionate to the benefits which he receives? On this view, the taxpayer is "buying" public services with his tax payments, much as he buys goods and services in private markets.

This principle is useful where a public service benefits a clearly defined segment of the population and where there is some basis for assessing the amount of the benefit. People who use the highways benefit from highway construction, and their consumption of gasoline is a rough measure of how much they drive. Hence it makes sense to tax gasoline and earmark the proceeds for highway construction.

But what about general government services, of which national defense is the classic example? Who benefits from defense expenditure, and in what measure? One approach starts from the proposition that all citizens are free and equal. Protecting Mr. A against foreign invasion is worth precisely as much as protecting Messrs. B, C, D, and the rest. On this reasoning, each individual should contribute the same absolute amount. Another approach, however, stresses the fact that it is mainly the *property* of Messrs. A, B, C, and D which is being protected. Or perhaps it is their accustomed way of life, which is linked with income level. On this basis, it would be legitimate to charge each household according to its property holdings or current income. There is no objective basis for choosing among these or other possible alternatives. Thus the benefit principle trails off into a maze of philosophical uncertainties.

The principle of ability to pay.   Another ancient maxim is that people should contribute to the public treasury "according as they are able." This referred originally to inherent personal faculties. The mighty warrior or the clever merchant should contribute more than the village idiot. In modern times, it has generally been interpreted in terms of wealth or income. The nineteenth-century British economists used the doctrine of decreasing marginal utility to justify progressive taxation, on the ground that a dollar taken in taxation means less loss of satisfaction to the rich than to the poor. More recently, however, this application of marginal utility has become suspect for the reasons outlined in Chapter 16.

The search for indisputable principles of taxation thus leads into a dead end. Decisions about tax levies, like those about public expenditure, emerge from a political process which is our only guide to the preferences of the electorate. Differing schools of thought may try to sway citizens and legislators. But in a democratic community all elements must accept the results of the political process—at least until the next election.

Neutrality in Taxation

It is generally accepted as desirable that a tax system should interfere as little as possible with individual choice in the private sector of the economy. Public expenditure necessarily means a diversion of resources from private consumption and investment. The private economy must "move over" to make room for the public economy. In doing this, however, there should be minimum distortion of the choices which people are still free to make between private goods and services, between saving and consumption, between work and leisure, and so on. The ideal tax system should be *neutral* as regards these choices.

The concept of tax neutrality has been used particularly as an argument against excise taxation. Consider a simple community in which consumers have a choice between product A and product B, at market prices determined in the usual way. The government now finds that it needs to raise a million dollars more in taxes. One way to do this is to put an excise tax on A. This raises the price of A and tilts the balance of consumer choice against it. People find themselves consuming less of A and more of B than they preferred in the first instance. It is usually argued that consumer satisfaction would be increased if the government, instead of taxing A, simply deducted a million dollars from people's incomes and left them free to choose between A and B at the old prices. Precise demonstration of this point requires an indifference diagram and the usual simplifying assumptions. But even on a common-sense basis, it seems reasonable that consumers will be worse off if government goes around the economy attaching arbitrary penalties to consumption of particular products. Unless there is some social reason why people *should* be discouraged from using a particular product, one cannot justify the discrimination involved in excise taxes.

The difficulty is that income taxes, sales taxes, and most other general taxes involve their own type of distortion. An income tax influences the choice between work and leisure, and may cause people to do either less or more work than they "really prefer." It also influences choice among occupations by reducing the relative income (after taxes) of the higher-paid jobs. A general sales tax amounts to a tax on spending and tilts the balance in favor of saving as against consumption. Most actual sales taxes apply to goods only, and thus tilt the balance of consumer choice against goods in favor of services. The only truly neutral tax is a poll tax—so much per head, regardless of income or anything else. But this is a very regressive tax which has little to commend it on other grounds.

Even if full neutrality is unfeasible, one can perhaps think in terms of degrees of neutrality. An income tax is more nearly neutral than excises on specific commodities. A general tax on spending is more neutral than a sales tax limited to certain types of good, and so on. The broader the base of the tax, and the fewer the possibilities of substitution which it leaves uncovered, the more nearly does it meet the criterion of neutrality.

Relations among Levels of Government

The size of the United States, and the provision of public services by several layers of government, raises complicated fiscal problems. There is the obvious problem of achieving a reasonable division between the tax sources tapped, and the functions performed, by different levels of government. There is also a more subtle problem of maintaining a balance between resources and responsibilities at each level over the long run.

We have seen that the state and local governments are the main providers of peacetime public services. The states and localities have borne the brunt of the tremendous increase in demand for education, highways, and municipal facilities over the past 20 years; and these demands show no sign of slackening in the years ahead.

But the main sources of state and local revenue are inelastic. (We define as *inelastic* a tax whose yield, based on a fixed structure of rates, rises less than proportionately to increases in national income. Conversely, a tax whose yield rises more than proportionately to growth of national income may be termed *elastic*.) The sales tax, bulwark of state finances, is inelastic. Why? Because as national income rises, the percentage devoted to purchase of goods declines, while the percentage spent on services rises. The property tax, on which town and city government so largely depend, is in danger of being seriously inelastic because assessments tend to lag behind rising property values. (Over the past 20 years, however, local governments have done a remarkable job of raising assessments, and the yield of property taxes has risen about as fast as that of sales taxes.) The personal income tax, on the other hand, is elastic, because as incomes rise, more and more people are pushed up into higher brackets where they are taxed at higher rates. Lucky federal government! How can it lose over the long run?

The lower levels of government are trapped between rapidly rising needs and restricted tax sources. Eckstein has estimated that, on the basis of tax levels and expenditure trends in the late fifties, the state and local governments will by 1968 have a combined deficit of about $3.5 billion.[5] But the federal government, on the basis of "medium" assumptions about federal expenditure, will have a budget surplus by 1968 of $7.5 billion. The federal government thus seems in danger of having too much money, while other levels of government have too little.

What might be done to correct this imbalance? There are several possibilities: (1) The federal government might take over functions now being performed by the states and localities, thus lightening their expenditures and increasing its own. (2) Without any change in the

[5] Otto Eckstein, *Trends in Public Expenditures in the Next Decade* (New York: Committee on Economic Development, 1959), p. 9.

present division of functions, the federal government might share more heavily in the *cost* of certain functions through larger grants to the states. The federal government has already assumed a larger share of highway expenditures, and many are urging larger federal contributions to school construction costs and other educational expenditures. (3) Federal tax rates might be lowered, and the space left in family budgets might be filled, at least partially, by increases in state and local taxation. This could keep both groups of budgets in balance without any change in the present division of expenditures.

Which of these courses should be chosen raises questions of political philosophy. Advocates of local autonomy are not going to agree with advocates of centralized federal responsibility. The *economic* stakes involved in the choice are of two kinds. First, what degree of progression do we want in the total tax structure of the country? If one favors a high degree of progression, this leads to a preference for the personal income tax, which in turn leads to a preference for federal spending. People of this mind should logically favor alternatives 1 or 2. If one wants less progression than at present, this indicates heavier reliance on sales, excise, and other regressive taxes, which means a preference for state and local taxation. This leads logically to a preference for alternative 3.

Second, how far should the federal budget be used to equalize the level of public services in different parts of the country? Equalization of service is an accepted principle within each state. State highways do not suddenly deteriorate when they pass through a low-income area, then pick up again when they come to a prosperous district. State grants to the localities for education help to reduce disparities of educational opportunity.

But what about differences among the states? There are wide differences in per capita income and taxable capacity. In 1963, personal income per capita in Delaware ($3,250) was two and a half times that in Mississippi ($1,379). The poorer states tax their citizens just as heavily *relative to their incomes* as do the richer states. Indeed, the percentage of personal income collected in state and local taxes is somewhat higher in the three groups of southern states than in the industrial Northeast. But because these high rates are applied to a small income base, the tax yield is disappointing.

Left to their own devices, the poorer states would have to get along with lower levels of roads, education, health, and other public services. The most direct way of reducing these disparities is through cash grants to the poorer states from the federal budget. Federal revenues come in disproportionate measure from the wealthier states. The Middle Atlantic and East North Central regions had 45 percent of U.S. personal income in 1957, but contributed almost 58 percent of federal tax revenues. The reason is the predominance of income taxation in the federal system. The use of cash grants-in-aid thus means that federal revenues drawn in good measure from the wealthier states are being used to support public services in the poorer states. There is a *geographical* transfer of income as well as a transfer from higher to lower income brackets.

Those who approve this transfer will exclaim, "Why of course! This is a basic advantage of our federal union. We are Americans first and citizens of Alabama second. Any American, wherever he lives, is entitled to a decent basic level of public service. If New York and Connecticut have to be milked to make this possible, so be it." But colorful rhetoric could also be employed on the other side. Having raised the issue, we leave it to the reader's own reflection.

SUMMARY

1. Government budgets perform an *allocation* function, a *distribution* function, and a *stabilization* function. This chapter is concerned only with the allocation function.

2. Certain goods and services are produced by government because of their *public* character. The hallmark of a public good is that it is impossible to exclude individuals from consuming it, and so it cannot be sold at a price.

3. In other cases, public production is justified by the existence of major *economies of scale*, so that *MC* lies continuously below *ATC*, and production of the economically correct amount will involve loss to the producer. A third possible reason for public production is existence of significant *external effects*, as in the case of education.

4. There is wide scope for application of economic analysis to public production. For example, cost-benefit analysis can be used to determine whether a particular project is worthwhile; the least-cost method of production can be analyzed just as in the private economy; and economics can be applied to the pricing of public services where prices are appropriate.

5. There is usually no objective basis for determining how *much* of a particular public service should be produced. This decision is made through the political process. There is disagreement over whether this process is biased toward overproduction or underproduction of public services.

6. Production of government services has tripled in relative importance since 1900 and now forms about one fifth of national output. Federal expenditures are primarily for defense. State and local expenditures are mainly for education, streets and highways, and police, fire, and other protective services.

7. The main reasons for the relative increase in government services are the deterioration of international relations, urbanization of the population, rising real incomes, rising educational standards, and the highway demands created by the automobile.

8. A *progressive* tax is one which takes an increasing proportion of income as one goes up the income scale. A *regressive* tax is one which takes a decreasing proportion of the higher incomes.

9. The federal government relies mainly on the personal and corporate income taxes, which are progressive. States rely mainly on sales taxes and local governments on property taxes, which are regressive. The overall impact of the U.S. tax system is mildly progressive in the brackets below $10,000, more steeply progressive above that level.

10. Some tax authorities have argued that taxes should be assessed on the basis of benefits received, while others have emphasized ability to pay. Economics provides no clear basis for choice between these principles.

11. It is generally accepted that a good tax should be *neutral,* that is, should not interfere with individual choice in the private sector of the economy. But since none of the leading types of tax is neutral, one is faced in practice with a choice of evils.

12. Federal revenues tend to rise more rapidly than national income over the course of time, while state and local revenues tend to rise less rapidly. This squeeze on state and local finances might be met by (1) the federal government taking over more functions, or (2) the federal government making larger cash grants to the states, or (3) reducing federal tax rates and raising state and local tax rates.

13. The choice among these approaches is a political choice, depending partly on how one feels about income redistribution between income brackets and between geographical regions.

DISCUSSION QUESTIONS

1. Explain clearly the *allocation function* of government budgets. What additional functions does the U.S. federal budget perform?

2. List as many examples of a *public good* as you can. Why can such goods be produced only by government?

3. "The fact that production of a good has marked external effects or strong economies of scale may justify government intervention to raise the level of output; but it in no way justifies government operation of the productive facilities. It will usually work better to offer adequate subsidies or other incentives to private producers." Discuss.

4. Professor Milton Friedman of the University of Chicago has suggested (in his *Capitalism and Freedom,* University of Chicago Press, 1962) that the quality of education would be improved if education at all levels were organized as a competitive industry. Let each parent be given a certain amount per child for educational expenses, and let him buy education wherever he prefers, adding to the government grant from his own resources if he wishes. How well do you think such a system would work?

5. Suppose you were appointed Postmaster General of the United States. Would you try to reduce the annual deficit of the postal system? If so, what measures would you suggest?

6. Do you think our governmental system contains any inherent bias toward underproduction or overproduction of public services? Explain.

7. What are some alternative measures of the size of government operations? Which best indicates the importance of government in terms of *production* or *resource use?*

8. Excluding military services, how much has government production increased as a percentage of total production since 1900? What are the main reasons?

9. Why might the personal income tax either *increase* or *decrease* the amount of work done? How would you get evidence concerning the actual effect?

10. It is often supposed that an excise tax is paid entirely by buyers of the product. Under what conditions will this actually be true?

11. How far are the tax sources used by our several levels of government separate from each other, and how far do they overlap? Should this overlapping be reduced?

12. Why is there a tendency for the federal government to be overfinanced and for lower levels of government to be underfinanced? What are some alternative ways of meeting this problem, and which would you prefer?

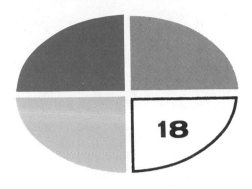

The International Economy

> Our interest will be to throw open the doors of commerce, and to knock off its shackles, giving perfect freedom to all persons for the vent of whatever they may choose to bring into our ports, and asking the same in theirs.
>
> THOMAS JEFFERSON

> Free trade, one of the greatest blessings which a government can confer on a people, is in almost every country unpopular.
>
> THOMAS BABINGTON MACAULAY

EVEN THOSE WHO BELIEVE in free competition within a country often question the extension of this principle to international trade. Competition among American business concerns may be all right, but let's not admit foreigners to the game. Let's "buy American" and "keep American dollars at home." There is something about foreign trade which seems mysterious and different.

One obvious difference is that factors of production move more freely within countries than between countries. If the marginal productivity of labor is higher in California than in Oklahoma, and if California workers consequently earn more, labor will flow from Oklahoma to California. If capital yields more in southern textiles than in northern textiles, investment will grow in the South and shrink in the North. Factor mobility can be expected to reduce differences in rates of return within a country. But movement of labor from country to country is severely restricted by immigration laws; and capital movements are also restricted in various ways. As a consequence, there is no reason to expect equalization of wage levels and interest rates among different countries.

How freely commodities move among countries depends partly on transportation costs, partly on national policies. The great reduction of transportation costs over the past century and a half has been a powerful force swelling the volume of world trade. National policies have varied, tending at times in the direction of free trade, at other times placing severe restrictions on trade.

A country's participation in world trade is influenced by the size of its economy. A country with a limited resource base and a small internal market cannot possibly produce all the goods it may wish to consume. It usually exports a few products for which it has natural advantages and imports a wide array of other goods from the rest of the world. Countries which normally export 30 to 50 percent of their GNP include Belgium, the Netherlands, Eire, Iceland, Cuba, Panama, Jamaica, British Guinea, Peru, Venezuela, Ceylon, and Ghana. At the other pole are very large countries with diversified resources and a vast trading area within their own borders. These countries can be largely self-sufficient. The list of countries whose exports are normally less than 10 percent of GNP includes the United States, the U.S.S.R., China, India, Pakistan, and Brazil. International trade is important even to these countries. For the smaller countries, it is vital.

A slightly confusing aspect of international trade is that it usually involves two or more *currency units.* In the Galeries Lafayette in Paris, I see a bottle of perfume priced at 50 francs. What will this cost me in dollars? I cannot tell until I know the *rate of exchange* between francs and dollars. An exchange rate is a special kind of price, the price of one national currency in terms of another. We shall not ask at this point how these prices are determined. We simply take it for granted that national currencies are exchangeable at standard rates.

This chapter aims to do three things. First, we must ask *why* countries trade with one another, and what determines *which* goods a country will export and import. Can we show that there is normally a gain from trade and explain how this gain is divided among the participants? Second, it will be interesting to look briefly at the size and direction of world trade. Who trades with whom, and in what products? The figures for the United States will be of special interest here. Third, we shall examine the effect of trade restrictions. Are there valid arguments for tariff protection, and if so, what are they? What has been the course of U.S. tariff policy over the years, and where do we stand at this moment?

THE BASIS OF TRADE: COMPARATIVE CHEAPNESS

Why do nations export certain goods and import others? In some cases the reason is clear. Bananas and coffee cannot be grown in the United States, so we buy them abroad. In other cases our raw material supplies are insufficient for our needs, so we buy copper from Chile, iron ore from Canada and Venezuela, and oil from the Middle East. But why do we buy large amounts of manufactured goods from Britain, Western Europe, and Japan? We are ourselves a great manufacturing nation. In fact, we export large amounts of manufactures *to* these same countries. What are the reasons for this kind of trade?

One's first thought might be that a country will export goods which it can produce cheaply and, since wages are a large part of production costs, a country with a low wage level will have an advantage. Imagine, for example, that trade is opened up for the first time between the United States and Japan. Will Japan, with its lower wage level, be able to undersell us in everything? Suppose for a moment that this were to happen. Japan is exporting large amounts of merchandise and importing nothing. What would be the consequences? First, the boom in Japanese industry would cause wages and prices to rise in Japan. Second, to pay for our imports from Japan we would have to buy large amounts of Japanese yen. Because of this increased demand, the price of the yen would rise in the foreign exchange markets. For both reasons, Japanese goods would become more and more expensive in the United States.

At the same time, American goods would become cheaper in Japan. Suppose that at the beginning the exchange rate is $1 = 100 yen. Now because of the great demand for yen the rate changes to $1 = 50 yen. (This is an *increase* in the value of the yen, which is now worth 2 cents instead of 1 cent; and it is a *decrease* in the value of the dollar.) So a product selling for $100 in the United States, which originally cost 10,000 yen in Japan, will now cost only 5,000. American goods are becoming cheaper and hence more attractive to the Japanese. On the other hand, a Japanese product selling at 1,000 yen, which used to cost Americans $10, will now cost $20 at the new exchange rate.

As the value of the yen continues to rise, more and more Japanese goods will be "priced out" of the American market. Conversely, more and more American goods will move into the Japanese market as their price (in yen) declines. So Japan's exports will shrink and her imports will rise until the flow of trade is balanced. At this point the exchange rate will become stabilized.

What goods will Japan still be exporting to us when equilibrium has been reached? Isn't it clear that these will be the goods which it can produce most cheaply *relative to other Japanese goods?* Similarly, we will ship to Japan goods in the production of which we are unusually efficient. The basis for trade is that a country's labor, capital, and other resources are not equally effective in every line of endeavor. The goods for which a country's production resources are especially effective, and which consequently have relatively low unit cost and price, are the ones which will be exported, while goods which are relatively expensive to produce at home will be imported.

An Illustration of Comparative Cheapness

The principle of comparative cheapness can be illustrated by the hypothetical figures in Table 1. The table shows for each product the

TABLE 1

Comparative Prices, United States and United Kingdom

COMMODITY	U.S. PRICE (Dollars)	U.K. PRICE (Pounds)	PRICE RATIO (Dollars/Pounds)
Radio tubes (dozen)	1	1	1
Wheat (bushel)	2	1	2
Coal (ton)	30	10	3
Wool cloth (100 yards)	150	30	5
Shoes (dozen pairs)	280	40	7
Bicycles (each)	90	10	9

U.S. price in dollars, the British price in pounds, and the ratio of the dollar price to the pound price. Note that we cannot say whether any product is actually cheaper in the United States or in Britain. This depends on the rate of exchange, which we do not yet know. But even without this we can say something about *comparative* cheapness. Looking at the right-hand column, we see that the ratio of the dollar price to the pound price varies greatly. Items toward the top of the table are comparatively cheap in the United States. Items toward the bottom are comparatively expensive in the United States, and comparatively cheap in Britain. We get the same result by looking down each of the first two columns. In the United States a bicycle is worth 90 times as much as a dozen radio tubes, while in Britain it is worth only 10 times as much. Again, we reach the conclusion that bicycles must be comparatively cheaper in Britain.

Given these relative prices, which we suppose are based on production costs, the movement of trade depends on the rate of exchange. Suppose the rate were £1 = $10. Then everything would be absolutely cheaper in the United States, and all six items would be exported to Britain. But this could not continue. There would be a great supply of pounds and no demand, and the price of pounds would fall. Conversely, suppose the rate were £1 = $0.50. This would make everything cheaper in Britain, trade would move solely from Britain to the United States, and so this also turns out to be an unfeasible exchange rate.

Some intermediate exchange rate, however, will be feasible in the sense of balancing the flow of trade. At a rate of £1 = $4, for example, it would pay to ship the top three items in the table from the United States to Britain, and to ship the bottom three items from Britain to the United States. (A little arithmetic on each product will show why this is true.) The rate of exchange slices through the middle of the list of price ratios in Table 1. Products above the line move in one direction, those below the line in the opposite direction.

THE PRINCIPLE OF COMPARATIVE ADVANTAGE

We have argued that trade depends on the comparative cheapness of products in different countries. But on what does cheapness depend? If goods are produced under competitive conditions in each country, prices will reflect money costs; and these costs reflect quantities of land, labor, capital, and other resources used in production. If radio tubes are relatively cheap in the United States, this means basically that they are cheap *in terms of the physical resources required to produce them.* To put the matter in reverse, American productive resources are particularly well adapted to production of radio tubes, more so (still following Table 1) than they are to production of bicycles. The United States has a *comparative advantage* in radio tube production, while Britain has a *comparative advantage* in bicycle production.

This does not tell us, and we need not know, anything about *absolute* levels of productive efficiency in the two countries. U.S. productive resources may have higher productivity in each and every line of production. Now if the United States were exactly twice as productive as Britain in every line of activity, there would be no basis for trade and no trade would occur. (The ratios in the right-hand column of Table 1 would all be the same.) But in actuality our productivity advantage is *uneven*—much greater in some lines than in others. So it pays us to concentrate on products in which our productivity advantage is greatest, in which we have a *comparative advantage,* and to import those in which our advantage is least.

The notion of comparative advantage is sufficiently important that it will be worthwhile to illustrate it from various points of view. The principle applies within countries as well as between countries, and so we can begin with a domestic illustration. Consider five farms, each of which

TABLE 2

Comparative Advantage in Farming

FARM	POTENTIAL BEEF PRODUCTION (Tons per Acre)	POTENTIAL PORK PRODUCTION (Tons per Acre)	BEEF/PORK RATIO
A	5	50	0.1
B	40	200	0.2
C	50	150	0.33
D	30	75	0.4
E	30	60	0.5

has the option of feeding beef cattle for market or of growing corn and fattening hogs. The amount of beef each farm could produce if it concentrated entirely on beef is shown in the first column of Table 2, the amount of pork which could be produced by concentrating on pork production appears in the second column and the ratio of potential beef output to pork output appears in the right-hand column.

What will each farm produce? We cannot tell without knowing the prices of beef and pork. A farm will specialize in beef if its prospective receipts are greater in that line, that is, if potential beef production $\times$ price of beef $>$ potential pork production $\times$ price of pork. This is the same as saying

$$\frac{\text{potential beef production}}{\text{potential pork production}} > \frac{\text{price of pork}}{\text{price of beef}}$$

Suppose beef is selling at $1 a pound and pork at 30 cents, so that the second ratio is 0.3. Then farms C, D, and E, whose beef/pork production ratio is greater than this, will produce beef. Farms A and B will find themselves better off producing pork. The price ratio slices through the middle of the table, just as the exchange rate did in our earlier case, and determines the most profitable line of production for each farm.

Note that the farms specializing in each product need not be those which are *absolutely* best in that line. Farm A is the poorest pork producer in the group. Yet it will cling to pork production longer than anyone else, even if pork prices are only a little more than one tenth of beef prices. The reason is that, while farm A is a poor pork producer, it is an even worse beef producer. Comparative advantage can mean *either* that one is particularly good at the product in question or particularly bad at other things. The fact that certain desert areas in Nevada concentrate on sheep grazing doesn't mean that these areas are absolutely best for this purpose, but since their productivity in other lines would be close to zero, they have a *comparative advantage* in sheep production.[1]

This suggests a second illustration, involving trade between regions of the United States. Why doesn't each region produce everything it needs? Why not "keep New England money at home"? Why are some kinds of production located mainly in one region, others mainly in another?

Regional specialization arises because a product can usually be produced more efficiently in some parts of the country than in others. For primary products this may be due to climate, soil fertility, or natural resources. In manufacturing, it may be due to a highly skilled labor force,

TABLE 3

A Case of Interregional Trade

	BEEF PRODUCTION (Lbs. per Day of Labor)	SHOE PRODUCTION (Pairs per Day of Labor)	PRICE RATIO BEEF/SHOES
Texas	200	40	5
New England	40	20	2

development of subsidiary industries supporting the main industry, long managerial experience, closeness to materials, or closeness to markets.

Suppose Texas and New England were separate countries, with no trade between them; and suppose that the productivity situation was as shown in Table 3. We use labor input as a shorthand device for input of resources in general, and suppose that within each region products will exchange according to the ratio of labor input. Then, in New England, a pair of shoes will exchange for 2 pounds of beef. In Texas, however, the "beef price" of a pair of shoes will be much higher—5 pounds of beef instead of 2.

Suppose now that trade is opened up between these "countries." Surely it will occur to some New Englander to ship shoes to Texas, where their "beef price" is higher than at home, and to ship beef in the opposite direction. Ship 200 pairs of shoes to Texas, where they can be exchanged for 1,000 pounds of beef, bring this back to New England and trade it for

---

[1] This illustration serves also to amplify a point made during the discussion of agricultural policy in Chapter 13: agricultural resources will be allocated most effectively if prices are left free to indicate the state of demand and if farmers are left free to switch from one product to another on the basis of comparative advantage. Government price and production controls interfere with the operation of comparative advantage and thus with location of production in the best areas for each product. This reduces the efficiency of the agricultural sector.

500 pairs of shoes, export these to Texas and get 2,500 pounds of beef, and so onward to riches. But as our trader and his friends get to work, the price of shoes will begin to rise in New England and fall in Texas. Overlooking transportation costs, the price ratio will eventually become the same in both regions.

Table 3 does not tell us where the price ratio will settle down. To discover this, we would have to know the demand and supply curves for each product in each region. Suppose the price settles at 4:1, four pounds of beef exchanging for a pair of shoes. Then each region has gained from the opening up of trade. By concentrating on shoe production and importing beef, the New Englanders now get for a day's labor 80 pounds of beef (= 20 pairs of shoes). Without trade they could have gotten only 40 pounds. The Texans also gain by concentrating on beef production and importing shoes. For a day's labor they can now obtain 50 pairs of shoes (= 200 pounds of beef), whereas formerly they could have gotten only 40 pairs. It appears that Texas has gained less than New England, but this is because we chose 4:1 as the new price ratio. If the ratio settled at a level more favorable to Texas, say 3:1, the Texans would gain more and the New Englanders less. *The division of the gains depends on the terms of trade.* But at anything between the original price ratios of 2:1 and 5:1, each region will gain something.

Note one curious thing about this case. Texas has greater productive capacity than New England in both products. One's first thought, then, might be that Texas will do best by producing everything for itself. Yet Texas actually gains by importing shoes and shipping beef in return. Texas has an *absolute* advantage in everything; but it has a *comparative* advantage in beef, where its absolute advantage is greatest. New England has a *comparative* advantage in shoes, where its absolute disadvantage is least.

This is not quite the end of the story. If economic resources are more productive in Texas in every line of endeavor, people in Texas will enjoy a higher standard of living. *Real* wage rates, which are based on absolute productivity, will be higher in Texas than in New England. If people respond to economic advantage, and if movement between the two regions is easy, one should see a migration of New Englanders to Texas to take advantage of the higher wage levels there; and there should also be an outward movement of capital from New England to take advantage of higher profit rates. The movement of labor and capital should continue until productivity levels and income levels have been brought close to equality in the two regions.

The results of this case may be summarized as follows:

1. Where two regions are linked by trade, each will export the products in which it has *comparative* advantage. This is true regardless of absolute productivity levels in the two regions.

2. The gain from trade is the increase in total output which results from each region specializing in the products in which it has comparative advantage.

3. The division of this gain between the regions depends on the price ratio which is established for the products exchanged. (In international dealings this is called *the terms of trade,* defined most simply as the ratio of the prices a country receives for its exports to the prices it must pay for its imports. If a country's export prices rise relative to import prices, we say that its terms of trade have improved, and conversely.)

4. Over long periods, differences in *absolute* productivity levels among regions tend to be eliminated by movement of labor and other resources toward the high-productivity regions.

Comparative Advantage: The International Case

Suppose we revised the side headings in Table 3 to read "France, Norway," and the column headings to read "herring, perfume." Would the conclusions be changed? In most respects, no. In international trade as in interregional trade, each country tends to export products in which it has a comparative advantage.

But what lies back of comparative advantage? What determines comparative cheapness in the last analysis? The approach used in the last section, and which we shall continue to use a bit longer, is the Ricardian or labor cost approach. Ricardo's theory of international trade was consistent with his theory of domestic trade. The value of a product, he argued, must in the long run depend on its cost of production; and the *amount of labor required to produce it* can be taken as a good yardstick of production costs.[2] So goods would exchange in proportion to the amount of labor embodied in them.

If this worked for domestic trade, why not for foreign trade as well? Take two countries, each producing the same goods. (The classical writers usually chose England and Portugal, with cotton cloth and port wine as the products. But let us take the United States and Switzerland, with wheat and watches as the products.) The cost of producing each good in each country can be reduced to labor units; and within each country, the relative price of the products will equal their relative labor costs. Suppose also that each good is produced under constant cost conditions, so that relative costs and prices are independent of how the country's resources are divided between its two outputs.

---

[2] Ricardo recognized, of course, that there are different qualities of labor, but thought that they could be converted to some common unit, say a man-hour of completely unskilled work. Thus an hour of carpenter's work might be counted as two of these standard man-hours; and so on. The labor embodied in the capital goods used in producing a product must also be counted as part of cost. Ricardo also recognized interest as a legitimate cost, but thought it would not be far wrong to take interest charges as a uniform percentage of labor cost for each good.

The United States has 200 man-days of labor available (we could equally well say 200 million, but small numbers are more convenient). It takes 1 man-day of labor to produce a bushel of wheat, but 4 man-days to produce a watch. So, on the labor cost principle, one watch will be worth 4 bushels of wheat.

The U.S. production possibilities curve is shown in Figure 1. By

Production Possibilities in the United States

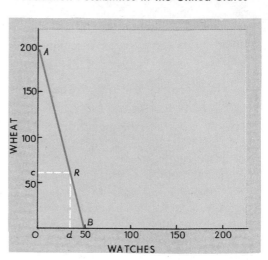

FIGURE 1. The line *AB* shows all combinations of wheat and watches which the United States can produce with the 200 man-days of labor available. For example, if it grows Oc bushels of wheat it can also produce Od watches. The *slope* of the line *AB* measures the price of watches in terms of wheat, which is 1:4.

putting all our labor into wheat production, we could grow $OA = 200$ bushels of wheat. If we produced nothing but watches, we could produce $OB = 50$ watches. Or we can produce various combinations of the two, shown by different points on *AB*. The steepness of *AB* indicates the relative price (= the relative labor cost) of the two products, which is 4:1. The fact that this ratio is constant, i.e., that *AB* is a straight line, depends on our assumption that each good is produced under constant costs.

How much of each good will actually be produced cannot be determined from the cost ratios. We would have to know also the demand curve for each product. But we would undoubtedly produce and consume some combination, such as $Oc + Od$.

Now look at Switzerland, which also has 200 man-days of labor available. In Switzerland, as in the United States, 1 man-day of labor will produce a bushel of wheat. But Switzerland also has an unusually productive watch industry, in which 1 man-day of labor is enough to produce a watch. So in Switzerland the price ratio is 1 bushel = 1 watch.

The production possibilities curve for Switzerland is A_1B_1 in Figure

Production Possibilities in Switzerland

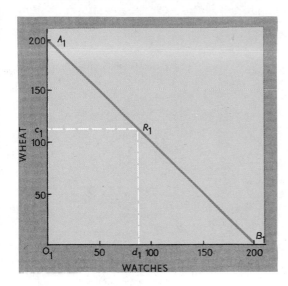

FIGURE 2. Here A_1B_1 shows all combinations of wheat and watches which Switzerland can produce—for example, Oc_1 of wheat plus Od_1 of watches. As before, the slope of A_1B_1 measures the price of watches in terms of wheat, which is 1:1.

2. It is a straight line because of the constant cost condition; and its slope, which is 1:1, measures the price ratio of the two products. Once more, we cannot say where production will actually settle without having demand information; but it might be at P_1, with Oc_1 of wheat and Od_1 of watches.

Now these two economies, which have previously been operating independently, are allowed to trade with each other; and it is clear that trade will be profitable. The Swiss watch producers, who can get only 1 bushel per watch at home, will see that they can get 4 bushels per watch in America, and will start exporting. The American wheat producers, who can get a higher (watch) price in Switzerland than at home, will also start exporting.

As trade continues, the price ratios will begin to shift. The relative price of watches will fall in the United States as Swiss watches come flooding in, while the relative price of wheat will fall in Switzerland. If we overlook transportation costs, and if there are no tariffs, the price ratio must eventually be *identical* in both countries. Why? Because they have become in effect a single market, and under competition there cannot be different prices in the same market.

The new price ratio will depend on the demand for each product in each country. But it will probably be at some point between the two previous ratios.

What will happen to production and consumption in each country? Look at Figure 3, which combines the information in Figures 1 and 2.

There is a little trick about the construction of Figure 3: to get both countries on the same diagram, we locate their origins at opposite corners of the chart. The origin for the United States is at O, and its production possibilities curve looks just as before. But the origin for Switzerland is

The Gain from Trade

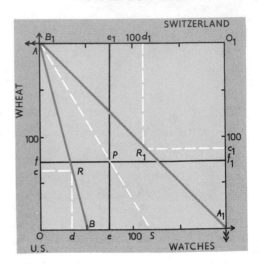

FIGURE 3. AB and A_1B_1 are the production possibilities curves shown in Figures 1 and 2, but the origin of the Swiss diagram is now located in the upper right-hand corner at O_1. Before trade begins, the United States is producing at point R and Switzerland at R_1. With trade, it is possible to move to a point such as P, where each country has more of both products than before.

now located in the upper right-hand corner at O_1. (Study this a bit to make sure that you understand how it works.)

The new price ratio is shown by the dotted line AS. Note that its slope is intermediate between that of the two old price lines, AB and A_1B_1. At this price ratio, it will pay the United States to produce only wheat and import all its watches. Out of a wheat production of OA we can consume, say, Of bushels. By trading the remainder, fA, at the new price ratio we can buy $Oe = fP$ watches. By comparing points P and R, one can see that we now have *more of both wheat and watches than before*. We are now operating outside our old production possibilities frontier.

The Swiss on their side will specialize completely in watches. By selling us B_1e_1 ($= oe$) of watches, they can buy O_1f_1 ($= fA$) of wheat. So they also end up at P, above their old production possibilities frontier and with more of both products than before.

Each country has gained by concentrating on the product in which it has comparative advantage. The division of the gain between them depends on the new price ratio, that is, on the *terms of trade*. The further AS swings down toward AB, i.e., the higher the relative price of watches, the more of the gain will go to Switzerland. In the unlikely event that AS coincides with AB, all the gain would go to Switzerland and none to the United States. (The price of watches cannot go *higher* than the old U.S. price ratio. Why? Because then the United States would produce watches at home instead of importing, and trade would cease. Neither side can *lose* by trade, since it always has the option of not trading.)

From the fact that both countries are now able to consume more than before, it follows that total production must have increased. You can verify this from Figure 3 by adding up wheat and watch production before trade began and comparing it with the new levels after trade. Free international trade, by permitting each country to specialize according to its comparative advantage, tends to *maximize world production*.

The classical writers tended to treat a day's labor in one country as equivalent to a day's labor in another. This is obviously not true in actuality. But the assumption of equal labor quality is not essential to the argument. Just as Ricardo could convert skilled labor into equivalent units of "standard" or unskilled labor to get a neat theory of prices, we can adjust for international differences in labor productivity in reasoning about international trade.

Suppose that, over the economy as a whole, a man-hour of labor in the United States produces twice as much as in Britain. Since real wages depend on productivity, the general wage level in Britain will be about half that in the United States. Since the lower wage level is just offset by lower productivity, this does not per se give Britain a competitive advantage in world trade. So what will happen to trade? We come back to the principle that trade depends, not on differences in productivity levels between countries, but on productivity differences among different industries in the same country, i.e., on *comparative advantage*.

U.S. workers are paid twice as much as British workers because *on the average* they are that much more productive. Relative American and British productivity, however, will differ a good deal from one industry to another. In producing electric light bulbs, say, American productivity may be four times as high as in Britain; so with American wages only twice as high, the unit cost and price of light bulbs will be lower in this country. We can successfully export light bulbs to Britain and undersell her in the markets of third countries. But suppose that in cement production our output per worker is just the same as in Britain. Here the shoe is on the other foot. With wages only half as high, they can undersell us and have a flourishing export trade.

This reasoning stands up well to statistical tests. Sir Donald Mac-Dougall of Oxford made a classic analysis of British and American productivity and exports as of the late thirties. More recently, Professor Stern of Michigan has analyzed American and British exports of manufactured goods in 1950, at which time American wages were about three times the British level. His results are shown in Table 4. In most of the 15 industries where American output per worker was more than three times that in Britain, our exports were also larger than British exports. But in the 24 industries where our output per worker was less than three times the British level, they typically had an export advantage.

TABLE 4

	TOTAL NUMBER OF INDUSTRIES	U.S. EXPORTS LARGER THAN BRITISH	U.S. EXPORTS SMALLER THAN BRITISH
U.S. output per worker more than three times British	15	11	4
U.S. output per worker less than three times British	24	3	21

Source: Robert M. Stern, "British and American Productivity and Comparative Costs in International Trade," Oxford Economic Papers, October, 1962, p. 288. The earlier MacDougall results appeared in the Economic Journal, 1951, pp. 697–724, and 1952, pp. 487–521.

The Basis for Trade: A Modern Approach

A substantial revision of trade theory stems from the work of two Swedish economists, Eli Heckscher and Bertil Ohlin. Nineteenth-century writers struggled valiantly to reduce all factors of production to labor equivalents. The Heckscher-Ohlin analysis emphasizes the existence of multiple factors and is directed mainly at the question of how differing factor supplies in different countries will affect the pattern of trade.

Their reasoning is developed under quite simple assumptions. Each country in the system is characterized by pure competition, full employment, and constant costs in all industries. Each factor is of the same quality in all countries. The same production techniques are known and available to all countries. There are no transportation costs and no barriers to trade. Since these conditions never hold in full measure, the Heckscher-Ohlin conclusions are only possible tendencies rather than unavoidable results.

Countries are allowed to differ, however, in their endowment of the factors of production. Suppose one country has a large stock of capital relative to its labor force. Let us call this Industria. Another country is densely populated but has little capital. Call this Agraria. These differing factor proportions will be reflected in factor prices. In Industria, the wage level will be high and the interest rate low, while Agraria will have high interest and low wages.

How will this affect the structure of production in each country? A basic consideration is that production of different goods requires different factor proportions. Suppose for each industry we calculate the amount of capital equipment used per man-hour of labor. We shall find some industries in which this ratio approaches zero: custom tailoring, fine jewelry and goldworking, other handmade quality products. These industries are very *labor-intensive*. At the other pole are industries, such as oil refining, in which the use of labor approaches zero, and so the capital-labor ratio approaches infinity. This is the *capital-intensive* pole. Every industry in the economy can be ranked along a scale running from one pole to the other.

In Agraria, labor costs little and capital costs much; so products lying toward the labor-intensive pole will be *relatively cheap*. (Any tourist can verify this observation. In the Orient one gets low prices for haircuts, rickshaw rides, or hand-tailored suits; but durable consumer goods requiring much capital may be as expensive as in the United States.) In Industria, on the other hand, capital-intensive goods, are *relatively cheap* and labor-intensive goods are expensive.

Agraria and Industria now discover each other, and trade develops between them. It is clear where comparative advantage will lie. Agraria has an advantage in labor-intensive products. These products will be exported to Industria, and their production within Agraria will expand. Agraria's production of capital-intensive goods will diminish, since it will import more of these from Industria where they are relatively cheap.

These changes in production in Agraria will react on factor prices. The capital-intensive industries which are contracting in Agraria will release a good deal of capital but little labor. The expanding export industries, on the other hand, will demand much labor and only a little capital. So total demand for labor will rise, and the wage level will move upward. Capital, however, is now less scarce than before, so interest rates will fall.

In a similar way we can work out the sequence of events in Industria. Because of import and export trends in Industria, and the consequent changes in its structure of production, wage rates will fall and interest rates rise. Industria's ability to import labor-intensive goods from Agraria compensates for the scarcity of labor at home, reducing the essentiality of labor and depressing its rate of return.

This means that, for each factor, the rates of return in the two countries *move toward each other*. Wage levels in the two countries become more nearly equal than they were before trade began; and so do interest rates. If this went on long enough, the price of each factor could conceivably become equal in the two countries. This is the result which would be attained by free international movement of the factors themselves. Since factor movements are restricted, *free movement of commodities serves as a substitute for movement of factors* and affects factor prices in the same direction.

This result has usually been called *the factor-price equalization theorem*. But remember the thin ice of assumptions on which it rests. In this imperfect world, "It ain't necessarily so."

One major effort to test this reasoning has produced apparently paradoxical results. Professor Leontief of Harvard calculated the machinery-labor ratio in American export industries and in import-competing industries, i.e., industries where we have some home production but also import from abroad. In the first group of industries we presumably have a comparative advantage, and in the second group, a comparative disadvantage. The accepted view is that capital is the abundant factor in the United States, while labor is scarce and expensive. So on Heckscher-Ohlin grounds we should have a comparative advantage in the more capital-intensive industries. One would expect a *higher* machine-labor ratio in our export industries than in import-competing lines.

Much to everyone's surprise, the results come out wrong; and the experts are still trying to figure out why. Leontief found that the machine-labor ratio in the export group was slightly lower than in the other group.[3] In an effort to resolve the paradox, he questioned the basic Heckscher-Ohlin assumption that factors are of equal quality in all countries. Because of long industrial experience, superior education, and other factors, American workers produce much more than workers abroad. Perhaps we should recognize this by counting each American worker as the equivalent of, say, three foreign workers. If we multiply the American labor force by three, labor turns out to be truly our abundant factor, and the statistical results are "right" after all!

The Dynamics of Comparative Advantage

A serious limitation of most trade theory is that it gives only a snapshot at a moment of time. It says that, given the factor endowment of each country, the technology of production, and the state of demand, one can deduce comparative advantage and the pattern of trade; and these deductions will hold good for as long as conditions remain unchanged.

But, of course, they do not remain unchanged. Technology is essentially dynamic and is being altered continuously by new inventions. Factor proportions change as natural resources are developed or discovered and as labor and capital supplies grow at different rates. Trade itself alters factor supplies—for example, by enabling an underdeveloped country to import capital goods. So a country's comparative advantage 10 years from now will differ from what it is today; and it may be very different 50 years hence.

At any time, there are recently developed industries whose technology is still evolving rapidly. The country which pioneered in developing a new industry will have comparative advantage in that field for some time. But not indefinitely. Technical ideas spread, and what one country has done, others can learn to do. So the original leader must be prepared to bow out eventually and move on to newer fields.

The classic case is the British textile industry, whose dominance in

---

[3] The results, in dollars of capital equipment per man-year of labor, were $11,622 for the export industries and $13,658 for the import-competing industries as of 1947. For 1951, the results were $12,977 for the first group, $13,726 for the second. See W. W. Leontief, "Domestic Production and Foreign Trade: The American Capital Position Re-examined," *Proceedings of the American Philosophical Society,* 1953, pp. 332–49 (reprinted in *Economia Internazionale,* 1954, pp. 9–38); and W. W. Leontief, "Factor Proportions and the Structure of Foreign Trade: Further Theoretical and Empirical Results," *Review of Economics and Statistics,* November, 1956, pp. 386–407.

the world market originally earned Britain the title of "workshop of the world." But during the nineteenth century, factory production of textiles spread to the United States, Western Europe, and Japan. Britain is now almost out of the textile business. Japan will be displaced in its turn by other countries of Asia and Africa, where labor is even cheaper and more abundant; but Japan is shifting nimbly to electronics, machinery, and shipbuilding.

The United States has initially gained, and eventually lost, world predominance in one area of technology after another. But there has always been something new, and our total exports have kept on growing. For several decades we had almost a monopoly of automobile exports; but that day is no longer. We used to ship large amounts of heavy electrical generating equipment to Europe, based on the technical leadership of the American companies. After a time, innovation in the United States slowed down, competitors abroad caught up, and European companies can now compete effectively in the American market. We pioneered the development of the radio industry and built up a substantial export volume. But this is a light, labor-intensive industry, in which low-skilled women assemblers are particularly effective. Now that the technology has spread throughout the world, good transistor sets are flowing back into the United States in large volume from Japan.

Kindleberger relates the story of "a General Electric salesman who visited Japan on two occasions ten years apart. On the second he sold no item which had been included in the first order, and many of these—light bulbs, household switches, etc.—were being made in Japan and exported to the United States. But since technology had not stood still in the United States, and since trade is based on differences in technology and new goods, his order the second time was larger than the first."[4]

THE PATTERN OF WORLD TRADE

How important is trade in the world economy? Who are the big trading nations? What do they sell, and to whom do they sell it?

A Long View of Trade

World trade has had its ups and downs. The period 1870–1914 is often regarded as the "golden age." The free-trade movement, spurred by Britain's repeal of import duties on wheat in 1846, reached its height about 1870. Tariffs in most countries rose somewhat after that time; but trade restrictions remained moderate, and the volume of trade was spurred by a steady reduction of transport costs. Between 1870 and 1913, world trade rose at an average annual rate of 3.4 percent. This was

---

[4] Charles Kindleberger, *International Economics* (3d ed.; Homewood, Ill.: Richard D. Irwin, Inc., 1963), p. 127.

appreciably above the annual increase in world production, so that a growing proportion of total output was entering international trade.

The years 1914–45 provide a bleak contrast. World War I caused great loss of life and capital, broke down national boundaries and customary trade relations, and disrupted the relation of the various European currencies. Before this damage had been repaired, the Great Depression struck a massive blow at most countries of the world. Many countries tried to save themselves by a "beggar-my-neighbor" policy of restricting imports while pushing exports, a policy which could not possibly succeed when everyone tried it at once. The effect on world trade was disastrous. Between 1913 and 1938, trade grew only 1 percent a year, and relative to world production it *fell* substantially. World production of manufactures in 1936–38 was 85 percent above the 1913 level; but world trade in manufactures was 8 percent below 1913. World War II once more cut the volume of trade and distorted its pattern.

But just when many had written off world trade as of declining importance, history once more confounded the prophets. Since World War II there has been a remarkable rebound, and international trade has grown faster than ever before. Since 1950 the volume of world trade has risen at better than 6 percent a year, considerably higher than the increase in world production. Once more a rising proportion of world output is being traded with other countries. True, the 1965 trade volume of around $150 billion is still less than 10 percent of world production. But for many countries trade relations are of crucial importance.

The experience of several important trading countries over the years 1870–1960 is shown in Table 5. For most countries, the percentage of output exported was lower in 1938 than in 1913. But 1950 shows a recovery, and the 1960 figures are even higher.

There has been much discussion among economists over the existence of a "law of declining trade." It has been argued that, as a country's internal market grows, it can support more and more kinds of industry within its own borders. This diversification of production means that it need draw fewer goods from abroad, and its import and export ratios will tend to decline. It is argued also that services, which are usually nonexportable, become a larger share of national output as a country gets richer. Again, the effect is to diminish the ratio of trade to GNP.

The figures for the United States and United Kingdom provide some support for this hypothesis. Their 1960 trade ratios are clearly below those of a century ago. For most other countries, however, there seems to be no clear trend over the long run.

The Pattern of Trade in the Sixties

Europe has always been the hub of world trade; and this continues to be true today. About 40 percent of the world's exports originate in

Western Europe alone. Moreover, the bulk of European trade is with other European countries. This tendency has been accentuated by the development of regional trade groupings: the European Economic Community or "Common Market" (Belgium, Netherlands, Luxembourg, West Germany, France, Italy); and the European Free Trade Association (Britain, Norway, Sweden, Denmark, Austria, Spain, Portugal). Reduc-

TABLE 5

Ratio of Merchandise Exports to GNP at Current Prices (Percent)

	1870	1913	1938	1950	1960
Belgium	...	...	26.5	22.1	29.8
Denmark	21.2	29.1	20.1	21.5	24.9
France	...	...	6.9	10.4	11.8
Germany	13.1	17.0	5.4	8.6*	16.6†
Italy	10.8	11.3	6.3	8.6	11.4
Netherlands	...	...	17.4	28.3	35.9
Norway	...	23.0	14.5	18.6	19.9
Sweden	17.7	22.1	16.4	19.8	21.0
Switzerland	...	...	14.2	19.7	22.4
United Kingdom	18.8	19.8	8.2	16.3	14.1
United States	6.3	6.1	3.6	3.5	4.0
Canada	...	...	15.7	17.5	14.7

* Federal Republic, excluding Saar, and West Berlin.
† Federal Republic, including Saar, and West Berlin.

Source: This table is derived from Angus Maddison, "Growth and Fluctuation in the World Economy, 1870–1960," *Banca Nazionale del Lavoro Quarterly Review*, June, 1962, p. 14.

tion of tariff barriers within each of these groups has stimulated the intercountry flow of trade.

Although U.S. trade is small relative to our own GNP, it forms about one sixth of total world trade. Our exports are double those of our nearest competitors, West Germany and the United Kingdom. The detailed makeup of our foreign trade will be examined in a moment.

The communist countries as a group have exports roughly equal to those of the United States. The U.S.S.R. and the East European countries have tried to plan a systematic exchange of products through the Committee on Economic Cooperation (COMECON), intended as a rival to the Common Market organization. Nationalist sentiment has hampered this effort, however, and each country still maintains a rather high degree of self-sufficiency. About two thirds of the trade by communist countries is with other communist countries; but trade with noncommunist countries has been increasing rapidly in recent years. The East European countries have long-standing trade ties with Western Europe.

The less developed countries furnish close to a quarter of world

TABLE 6

A World Trade Matrix, 1962
(Millions of U.S. Dollars, f.o.b.)

DESTINATION SOURCES	U.S.	CANADA	EEC	EFTA	JAPAN	OTHER DEVELOPED COUNTRIES*	LATIN AMERICA	OTHER LESS DEVELOPED COUNTRIES†	COMMUNIST COUNTRIES	WORLD
United States	$ ...	3,744	3,588	1,937	1,408	1,458	3,096	3,874	116	21,362‡
Canada	3,516	...	432	983	202	202	274	146	184	5,939
EEC	2,452	308	...	7,500	310	2,390	1,640	4,760	1,280	20,640§
EFTA	1,636	614	5,350	...	205	2,960	860	3,510	865	16,000§
Japan	1,410	125	270	320	...	325	315	1,940	215	4,920
Other developed countries*	958	77	1,820	2,380	525	410	155	1,005	720	8,050
Latin America	3,250	300	1,810	1,030	335	262	620	928	665	9,200
Other less developed countries†	2,253	662	5,035	3,395	1,300	1,183	410	4,652	950	19,840
Communist countries	80	25	1,255	1,085	185	560	700	1,615	11,565	17,070
World	15,555	5,855	19,560§	18,630§	4,470	9,750	8,070	22,430	16,560	123,021

* Australia, New Zealand, South Africa and West European countries not in EEC or EFTA: Finland, Greece, Iceland, Ireland, Spain, Turkey and Yugoslavia.
† Countries not included elsewhere.
‡ Includes $2,141 million of U.S. exports not distributed by destination, for security reasons.
§ Excludes intra-EEC and intra-EFTA trade.

Source: GATT—International Trade, 1962.

exports. Considering that this group includes the bulk of the world's population, one might wonder that the ratio is not higher. The obvious answer lies in low productivity and low purchasing power. The trade of the less developed countries still consists largely of shipping primary products to the industrial countries and buying manufactures in return. There is still relatively little trade of the underdeveloped countries *with each other*. It may be true that there is a large potential in this direction, but it has scarcely begun to be tapped.

Source \ Destination	I	NI
I	25 M 25 P	20 M
NI	20 P	5 P + M

In terms of *types of commodity*, world trade is about evenly divided between manufactures and primary products. Manufactured exports come about 95 percent from the industrial countries. Even as regards primary products, the industrial countries' exports exceed those of the less developed countries. The reason is that the great agricultural exporters of the temperate zone—Canada, United States, Australia, New Zealand, Denmark—all fall in the industrial group.

With slight simplification, then, the pattern of world trade among the noncommunist countries is as shown above. (*I* means industrial countries, *NI* nonindustrial countries, *M* manufactured goods, and *P* primary products. The figures in the boxes are percentages of total trade, and do not add to 100 because of rounding.)

The trade of the industrial countries with each other forms about half of total world trade. Moreover, because of rapid output growth in the industrial countries since 1945, the figures in the upper left-hand box have been tending to rise, and the less developed countries' *share* of world trade (though not the absolute volume) has tended to decline. This has caused great concern in the less developed countries over how they can boost their exports or, alternatively, reduce their dependence on the advanced countries by developing their own manufacturing industries.

Main Features of U.S. Foreign Trade

It will be useful to say a bit more about how our own trade relations have changed over the years. The basic information is provided in Tables 7–10, which speak for themselves, and to which we need add only a brief comment.

TABLE 7

Structure of U.S. Exports, 1850–1964
(Percent of Total)

PERIOD	CRUDE MATERIALS	CRUDE FOODSTUFFS	MANUFACTURED FOODSTUFFS	SEMI-MANUFACTURES	FINISHED MANUFACTURES
1851–60	61.7	6.6	15.4	4.0	12.3
1881–90	35.9	18.0	25.3	5.2	15.6
1901–10	31.0	10.6	20.1	12.8	25.6
1921–30	26.0	8.5	11.8	13.3	40.8
1951–55	13.0	7.1	5.6	11.6	62.7
1961–64	10.9	9.7	6.4	14.8	58.2

Source: *Historical Statistics of the United States; Statistical Abstract, 1965.*

TABLE 8

Structure of U.S. Imports, 1850–1964
(Percent of Total)

PERIOD	CRUDE MATERIALS	CRUDE FOODSTUFFS	MANUFACTURED FOODSTUFFS	SEMI-MANUFACTURES	FINISHED MANUFACTURES
1851–60	9.6	11.7	15.4	12.5	40.5
1881–90	21.3	15.4	17.8	14.8	30.8
1901–10	34.0	11.9	12.1	17.2	24.8
1921–30	37.1	11.8	11.4	18.2	21.4
1951–55	26.3	19.5	10.1	23.7	20.4
1962–64	19.5	10.7	10.8	21.2	37.8

Source: *Historical Statistics of the United States; Statistical Abstract, 1965.*

TABLE 9

U.S. Exports by Destination, 1860–1964
(Percent of Total)

PERIOD	EUROPE	CANADA	SOUTH AMERICA	CENTRAL AMERICA	ASIA	AFRICA AND OCEANIA
1860	74.8	6.9	4.7	8.8	2.4	2.5
1871–75	80.2	6.4	4.0	7.2	1.0	1.2
1891–95	79.5	5.5	3.7	6.8	2.3	2.2
1911–15	64.0	14.2	5.2	7.7	5.6	3.3
1931–35	47.4	14.8	7.0	8.0	17.3	5.5
1951–55	23.4	18.8	15.1	10.9	13.7	5.3
1962–64	33.6	19.4	9.2	8.3	21.7	7.8

TABLE 10

U.S. Imports by Source, 1860–1964
(Percent of Total)

PERIOD	EUROPE	CANADA	SOUTH AMERICA	CENTRAL AMERICA	ASIA	AFRICA AND OCEANIA
1860	61.3	6.7	9.9	12.5	8.3	1.3
1871–75	55.6	5.9	11.0	16.6	9.7	1.3
1891–95	50.6	4.6	14.9	16.3	10.8	2.7
1911–15	46.6	7.7	12.8	14.5	15.8	2.5
1931–35	30.1	13.8	14.3	10.3	28.7	2.8
1951–55	20.2	22.5	21.2	12.0	16.3	7.7
1962–64	28.2	22.4	14.4	8.3	18.9	7.8

The changes in *kinds of good traded* are what one would expect in a country making the transition from an agricultural economy to the world's leading industrial nation. Before 1900, food products, minerals, and other raw materials were dominant in our exports. Around 1900, however, our manufacturing industries reached the stage at which exports of manufactured goods began to exceed food exports; and this trend has continued. Today, three quarters of our exports consist of manufactured products, and we sell more manufactures abroad than any other country. This contradicts the view that our high wage level puts us at a *general* disadvantage in competing with the manufacturers of other nations.

One fifth of our imports consist of tropical food products such as coffee, tea, cocoa, sugar, and bananas. Another quarter of our imports are minerals, oil, rubber, and other raw materials needed to feed our giant industrial machine. Rather surprisingly, more than half of our imports are manufactured goods; and these come mainly from Japan, Canada, Britain, and Western Europe. Yet we also export a large volume of manufactures to these countries. Why do the rich countries of the world take in each other's washing in this way? The answer lies in the principle of comparative advantage. For some manufactured goods, the United States is the lowest-cost location in the world. For other types, Japan or Britain or Italy may be the most efficient location. Thus all can gain by exchanging their particular specialties.

This casts an interesting sidelight on the dilemma: what happens when the whole world becomes industrialized? In the past, much of world trade has consisted in the underdeveloped countries shipping food and raw materials to Europe and North America, taking manufactures in return. But now every country wants to industrialize and produce its own manufactures. So what happens? Won't the basis for world trade dry up and disappear? On the basis of trade relations among the present industrial nations, the answer seems to be no. Development of manufacturing in all countries will not eliminate comparative advantage. West Africa may end up as the world's leading textile producer, Japan as the largest shipbulder, India as one of the lowest-cost steel centers. Each nation can continue to exchange its specialties, and the volume of world trade may rise rather than fall. But this depends on the course of world politics more than on economic considerations. World trade *could* flourish in the peaceable international community which is not yet in sight.

As regards the direction of our foreign trade, the most striking feature is growing *diversification* over the course of time. The other countries of North and South America have grown in importance to the point where they now account for almost half our imports and exports. Asia has also grown in relative importance, mainly because of the remarkable expansion of the Japanese economy. Our trade with Europe, which was of dominant importance before 1914 has now dropped to about one third of the total. But it is still large in absolute terms, and the phenomenal growth of Western Europe since 1950 means that it will continue to be a major trade partner in the future.

BARRIERS TO TRADE: THE TARIFF CONTROVERSY

If our earlier conclusion that trade between two regions or countries is mutually beneficial was correct, it follows that barriers to trade will be harmful. Building a tariff wall between Texas and New England would hurt consumers on both sides of the wall.

Why, then, do most countries have tariff systems and other restrictions on free movement of trade? Are political leaders simply irrational? Did they not study elementary economics? The broad answer is that restriction of imports, while rarely in the interest of the population as a whole, is often in the interest of specific industries which are subject to import competition. These industries work hard to restrict imports, while the general public is apt to remain apathetic. Moreover, the arguments for trade restriction are easily intermingled with patriotic sentiment. It is easier to get the public aroused about protecting American labor and capital against foreign competition than it would be to whip up sentiment for "protecting Illinois labor and capital" against "Alabamian competition," though the logic of the two cases is similar.

There are numerous types of trade restriction,[5] but the import tariff

---

[5] A type which has been particularly important since the 1930's is the *import quota*. Here a country specifies how much of a particular commodity may be imported from abroad, and perhaps even how much may be imported from particular countries. This goes naturally with a system of exchange control, which requires importers to come to the government for their foreign exchange requirements. Exchange controls and import quotas are found particularly in the less developed countries of Asia and Latin America. But the United States also uses quota restrictions on oil, copper, lead, zinc, and certain agricultural products.

is historically the most important, and we shall concentrate on it here. Further, we shall concentrate on the protective aspects of the tariff rather than on the revenue which it yields. During the 1850's, about 90 percent of federal revenue came from customs duties. During the 1950's, however, less than 1 percent of federal revenue came from this source. Arguments over the tariff today thus turn mainly on its price and production effects rather than on its revenue effect.

A tariff is a tax on imports. The importer is required to pay either a

Effect of a Tariff on Imports

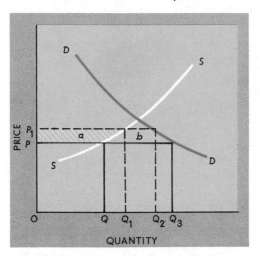

FIGURE 4. With free trade (solid lines) the product sells in the United States at the world price OP. U.S. production is OQ, imports QQ$_3$, and consumption OQ$_3$. A tariff of PP$_1$ per unit (dotted lines) raises the price to OP$_1$. Consumption falls to OQ$_2$, imports fall to Q$_1$Q$_2$, and home production increases to OQ$_1$.

certain percentage of the value of the imported article (an *ad valorem* duty), or so many dollars and cents per physical unit imported (a *specific* duty). The effect of imposing a tariff on a product which is produced both in the United States and abroad may be illustrated by Figure 4. *DD* and *SS* are the demand and supply curves for the product in the United States. *OP* is the "world price," the price at which the article can be imported from other countries. Under free trade, this price will prevail in the United States as well. By seeing where the price line intersects the U.S. supply curve we discover that *OQ* of the product will be produced in the United States. *QQ*$_3$ will be imported and total American consumption will be *OQ*$_3$.

Now suppose the United States imposes a specific duty of *PP*$_1$ per unit. Importers must now pay the world price plus the tariff and will have to sell the product in the United States for *OP*$_1$. Going across the *DD*, we see that U.S. consumption of the product will decline from *OQ*$_3$ to *OQ*$_2$. U.S. production, however, will increase from *OQ* to *OQ*$_1$, which was presumably the point of putting on the tariff. With U.S. production up but consumption down, imports will fall to *Q*$_1$*Q*$_2$.

Who gains and who loses from the tariff? The direct effects are:

1. There is a *revenue* effect, an increase in the customs receipts of the government. This is equal to the rectangle b (Q_1Q_2 units of imports $\times$ PP_1 tax per unit). This is of course not a gain from a national standpoint, since the customs revenues are paid by buyers of the product.

2. There is a *protective* effect, shown by the increase in domestic production from OQ to OQ_1. Some American producers who would not have been able to cover costs and survive at a price of OP are able to keep going at OP_1.

3. There is a *redistribution* effect, a transfer of income from consumers to companies in the industry. The marginal producer, located right at Q_1, has production costs of OP_1 and is just able to survive with the tariff protection. But everyone else in the industry is receiving more than he needs. The increased profit to the industry is shown by the shaded area a.

4. There is likely also to be an *export* effect. Putting a United States tariff on some item coming from Italy will probably lead the Italians to retaliate by higher duties against U.S. exports to that country. Even if there is no direct retaliation, a drop in U.S. payments for imports means that other countries have fewer dollars with which to buy goods from us. Unless we are willing to lend or give away more abroad, our exports will have to fall. Thus, against the increase in employment and profits in the protected industry one must set a drop in employment and profits in other U.S. industries which send part of their product abroad. Nor is this an even exchange from a national point of view. The export industries which are hurt are presumably those in which we have comparative advantage, while the protected industry presumably does not have comparative advantage in the world market. If it did, it would need no protection.

The effects may be summarized as follows: The industry which receives the tariff protection is benefited; other American industries engaged in export trade are hurt; total national output is reduced by a diversion of resources from products in which the United States has comparative advantage to products in which it does not; and consumers of the protected product get less of it at higher prices.

These effects are unfavorable on balance. Why, then, is tariff protection so widely practiced? Surely there must be some arguments in its favor. In reasoning about this, one must distinguish carefully between the interests of a particular industry and the interests of the national economy. A tariff is normally beneficial to producers of the protected product and the higher the tariff the better, up to the point at which imports are excluded entirely. Tariff increases enable the domestic industry to produce more, charge higher prices, earn more money, and employ more people. So it is not surprising that industries subject to import competition should lobby energetically for tariff protection.

Specious reasoning begins when an industry sets out to prove that "what's good for us is good for the country." This is typically done by focusing solely on benefits to the industry while ignoring or denying the injury to consumers and exporters. The argument is often supported by pseudoscientific reasoning. It is argued, for example, that it is fair to impose a tariff sufficient to equalize costs of production at home and abroad. If an item costs 40 cents to produce in the United States and can be bought abroad for 20 cents, then there should be a 20 cent tariff to "maintain fair competition between American and foreign producers."

This so-called "scientific" tariff principle has actually been written into law in some cases. Consider its implications. What is the standard for determining cost of production in the United States? Should one take the costs of the most efficient existing producer or of the least efficient producer? Should one consider the potential costs of new producers who might be able to survive at a higher price? A glance at Figure 4 shows that by going up the supply curve far enough one can justify any tariff one wants to, including a tariff high enough to exclude imports completely. In effect, the "scientific tariff" advocates are saying that whenever foreign producers can undersell *any* American company in *any* product, their advantage should immediately be canceled out by tariff duties. Whatever else this may be, it certainly is not scientific. It denies the principle of comparative advantage and in fact denies the possibility of any profitable trade among nations.

If self-interested arguments are to be discounted, what about the national interest? Are there circumstances in which tariff protection can be justified on national grounds? There are several:

1. **National defense.** Adam Smith, pioneer advocate of freer trade, nevertheless asserted that "defense is of more importance than opulence." The United States would be ill-advised to import long-range missiles or missile components. It can be argued that we need to preserve some watch production because watchmakers' skills are readily transferable to fuses and other military items. But one must not stretch the national defense argument too far. Everything which we might want to use in wartime need not be made within the United States in peacetime. Some stockpiling is feasible, and some foreign sources are reasonably secure. Maintaining an adequate number of watchmakers does not necessarily involve maintaining a large watch industry. We have many millions of trained military reservists, although only a fraction of this number are under arms at any one time. It shouldn't be any harder to organize a "watchmakers' reserve" than a naval air reserve.

2. **Infant industries.** This famous argument for protection, expounded in Alexander Hamilton's *Report on Manufactures*, has always been popular in countries in the early stages of industrialization. The argument is that a new industry may be relatively inefficient in its early years, while plants are being expanded to optimum size, labor and

management skills developed, and market connections established. During this period it is vulnerable to low-cost competition from more experienced foreign producers. If it can be sheltered for a time by tariff barriers, however, efficiency can be raised to the point where it can compete with foreign producers on a free basis. The "infant" will have grown up and the protective walls can be dismantled. This argument was used to justify protecting American manufactures against foreign (primary British) competition during the early nineteenth century. It is widely used today by the countries of Asia, Africa, and Latin America which are trying to push industrialization in the face of competition from more advanced industrial countries.

This is an argument for *temporary* or transitional protection for industries which, when fully developed, will turn out to have comparative advantage in the countries concerned. It is not an argument for *permanent* protection. It is not applicable to industries which will never be able to attain a competitive position in world markets. Its application in a particular case, therefore, requires careful investigation of prospective costs and revenues.

Even in valid cases, there is the practical difficulty that the infants often refuse stubbornly to grow up and be cut loose from the apron strings. They get used to the high prices and profits guaranteed by the tariff wall and fight against its removal, even when fully capable of standing on their own feet. Protection which was supposed to be temporary thus often turns out to be permanent after all. Tariffs with a terminal date, or tariffs shrinking at a specified rate, might provide an answer to this problem.

3. Terms of trade.   A country which is a large buyer of a certain product can sometimes alter the price to its advantage by imposing an import duty. Suppose the United States is the sole importer of coffee and Brazil the sole exporter. Suppose, further, that coffee supply in Brazil is completely inelastic. Coffee growers bring the same amount to market regardless of price. If the United States now imposes an import tax of 10 cents a pound, this will lower the price received by Brazilian producers by 10 cents while leaving the price to U.S. consumers unchanged. The Brazilians bear the full brunt of the duty while the U.S. Treasury gets the revenue. (Verify this if you wish by sketching a supply-demand diagram.)

Even if conditions were not this extreme—the United States simply the major importer, Brazil the major supplier, supply highly inelastic rather than completely inelastic—the United States could gain something from this sort of maneuver. This would not be regarded as a gentlemanly act by the Brazilians, however, and might lead to economic retaliation. It can scarcely be advocated as good national policy, particularly for an economically powerful nation such as the United States.

4. Antidepression measures.   It will be shown in Part Three that,

if the United States were suffering from depression, and if it could cut its imports without anything happening to its exports, the result would be a rise in U.S. production and employment. On a common-sense basis, "money which was being spent abroad will now be spent at home." Demand for domestic products will rise, and employment will rise with them. This works hardship on other countries, of course, since the reduction of imports by the United States will throw people out of work abroad. For this reason it is often termed a "beggar-my-neighbor" policy. It is doubtful also whether the policy is feasible for any length of time. Other countries would certainly retaliate to cut their imports from the United States, so that any advantage we might gain would be of short duration.

5. Making haste slowly. On a different plane stand arguments which relate, not to imposing a tariff in the first instance, but to removing it where it has been long established. Lowering a tariff amounts to forcing down product prices and may have a disruptive effect on the industry concerned. Plants may be closed down, and workers faced with the necessity of moving to other jobs. These resource transfers are painful, and the economists' argument that it is all for the general good is likely to be received with ill grace. This is not a positive argument for tariffs, or an argument for inaction in lowering them. It is simply an argument for gradualism. Tariffs should be lowered gradually and judiciously—preferably during prosperity rather than depression, with due notice to all concerned and with advance planning to help plants and labor to convert to new uses.

What does this boil down to? In the U.S. case, imposing import restrictions to solve temporary depression problems or to lower the prices which we pay to other countries seems shortsighted and inadvisable. The infant industry argument, whatever merit it may have possessed in 1820, is surely no longer applicable to the world's leading industrial nation. This leaves national defense as the only argument for protecting U.S. production of items which are in fact closely related to national security and which cannot survive without such protection.

ISSUES IN AMERICAN TRADE POLICY

The Trend of Trade Policy

The United States was for many years a strongly protectionist country. During the early nineteenth century, protective tariffs were erected as a way of nurturing new manufacturing industries and enabling them to withstand the competition of British manufactures. But these infant industries declined to grow up; and tariff protection, instead of being a transitional device, became a permanent feature of national policy. The center of protectionist sentiment was the industrial Northeast and the Republican party. Support for freer trade came mainly from export industries, which at this time meant principally agriculture. Free trade sentiment was particularly strong in the South, with its interest in cotton exports. The Republican party dominated national politics from the Civil War until 1930, and the protectionist forces usually came out on top. The peak of this movement was reached with the Smoot-Hawley Act of 1930, which raised tariffs to an all-time high and led to retaliatory action by many other countries.

The Democratic victory of 1932 brought a sharp shift toward freer trade accompanied by a transfer of tariff-making authority from Congress to the Executive branch. The Trade Agreements Act of 1934 authorized the President to negotiate with other countries for a reciprocal lowering of tariff barriers, reductions by the United States to be matched by concessions of equal value by the other party. No tariff, however, could be cut below 50 percent of the 1934 level. This grant of authority to the President was subsequently renewed by extending the Trade Agreements Act each time it expired. Particularly significant was the renewal of 1945, which authorized the President to reduce tariffs by 50 percent of the rates in effect *on January 1, 1945*. Thus duties which had already been cut 50 percent under the original act could be reduced by another 50 percent, or to 25 percent of the 1934 level.

Between 1934 and 1948, trade agreements were negotiated with 29 countries, including all our important trading partners. Duties were cut on about 90 percent of all dutiable imports. In over three quarters of these cases, the rate of duty was reduced by 45 percent or more, and a quarter of our imports experienced tariff reductions of 66 to 75 percent.

The amount collected in tariff duties fell from 47 percent of the value of dutiable imports in 1934 to 28 percent in 1945 and 12 percent in 1953.[6] About half of this decline seems to have been due to tariff reductions under the Trade Agreements Act. The remaining half was due to the great rise of prices between 1934 and 1952, which automatically reduces the restrictiveness of a *specific* duty (though not of an ad valorem duty). *Example:* A tariff of $1 each is imposed on a certain grade of cotton shirt. If the import price of the shirt is $2, this is a 50 percent duty. But if the price doubles to $4 and the tariff is not changed, the rate has fallen to 25 percent.

Thus in about 15 years the United States was transformed from a high-tariff country to a moderate-to-low tariff country. Tariff rates today, which are not very different from those in effect in 1950, lie mainly between 10 percent and 20 percent of the value of imported products. These rates are not negligible, but in few cases are they high enough to be prohibitive.

During the fifties the movement toward tariff reduction lost

[6] Howard S. Piquet, *The Trade Agreements Act and the National Interest* (Washington, D.C.: The Brookings Institution, 1958), p. 25.

momentum. Congress continued to renew the Trade Agreements Act, but grudgingly, and with limitations which made it easier for American producers to campaign against proposed tariff reductions by appealing to the U.S. Tariff Commission or the Office of Defense Mobilization.

The drive toward freer trade was resumed by the Kennedy administration in 1962. The immediate occasion was the rapid progress of the European Economic Community or "Common Market," which includes France, West Germany, Italy, Belgium, Holland, and Luxembourg. The treaty establishing the Community provides for gradual reduction of tariff barriers among the member nations, and reduction is actually proceeding ahead of schedule. It provides also for freer movement of labor and capital and a variety of other steps which together come close to full economic union. Many Europeans hope that economic integration will provide a favorable setting for closer political ties.

But while tariffs are being reduced within the Community, they remain up against the outside world. This raised the possibility that the United States might gradually be frozen out of its largest foreign market. The Kennedy administration argued that the best way to avoid this was to give the President power to bargain with the E.E.C. for a lowering of their external tariff in return for reductions in our own. Public support for the proposal was strong, and protectionist sentiment seemed weaker than in previous years. The outcome was the Trade Expansion Act of 1962, passed by substantial majorities in both House and Senate.

The new Act runs for a period of 5 years. It permits the U.S. government to bargain for reductions of up to 50 percent in most existing tariffs, and to negotiate on broad categories of goods rather than on individual items. Tariffs which are already below 5 percent can be eliminated entirely. A novel provision is that, for products in which the United States and the E.E.C. countries together account for 80 percent of world trade, we can bargain with the E.E.C. for complete abolition of tariffs.

The Act also provides transitional assistance to companies and workers hit by foreign competition resulting from tariff reductions. Companies may receive tax relief, government loans, and technical aid in converting facilities to different products. Displaced workers may receive cash payments of up to $61 per week for a maximum period of 78 weeks. These benefits are considerably more generous than those provided by the state unemployment compensation systems. There is provision also for retraining programs to help workers learn new skills which are in active demand.

The U.S. and the E.E.C.

Negotiations among the major trading nations are now carried on within the framework of the General Agreement on Tariffs and Trade, or GATT. This is a multilateral trade agreement dating from 1948, which has been subscribed to by about 70 countries. These include all the Western industrial nations, plus many of the larger underdeveloped countries, plus Poland, Czechoslovakia, and Yugoslavia from Eastern Europe.

The main feature of GATT is the most-favored-nation principle: if a country makes a tariff reduction to any member of GATT, this is extended automatically to all other members. There is also an agreed-upon code of rules governing trade, designed to discourage quantitative import restrictions and export subsidies. GATT headquarters in Geneva, and the conferences held under its auspices provide a forum for international discussion of trade matters.

Every few years, when the time seems propitious, there is a general conference or "round" of trade negotiations. Delegates come from each member country with lists of the tariff concessions they are prepared to make and with ideas of what concessions they would like to get in return. They then settle down for prolonged negotiation between pairs of countries over particular commodities. How much a country will concede to another country in these discussions is influenced by the fact that what it does for one it must do for all. Finally, at the end of the round, GATT compiles and publishes the new tariff schedules.

The most recent round opened in Geneva in 1965 and is still grinding away at this writing. The American negotiators are armed with authority under the 1962 Act to cut U.S. tariffs up to 50 percent across the board. The hope is that the E.E.C. countries will be willing to lower their common external tariff to the same extent and that other trading nations will do the same. Success in these discussions would bring the world as close to general free trade as it has been in the last century. In 1965, about a quarter of U.S. and E.E.C. tariff rates were already at 5 percent or less, and few were above 20 percent.

The thorniest problem in discussions with the E.E.C. countries involves agricultural policy. The E.E.C. countries have substantial tariffs on grain and other key products, designed to maintain a protected price level for their own farmers. We would like to maintain, and if possible increase, our large agricultural exports to these countries, presently running at about $1,250 million a year. So in return for our willingness to cut tariffs on industrial goods, we have been urging the E.E.C. countries to be cooperative on import duties for agriculture. How far we shall succeed in this effort remains in doubt.

East-West Trade

Trade between the communist and noncommunist countries fell to a low ebb during the tensions aroused by the Korean War; but since that time it has increased rapidly. Exports to the communist countries from other countries rose from $1.4 billion in 1953 to about $5 billion in 1963, and arc probably above $6 billion by now.

The United States has participated only slightly in this expansion. Our total exports to the communist countries in 1963 were only $166 million, less than those of Austria. This compares with exports of $668 million by Germany, $411 million by Britain, $284 million by France, $276 million by Canada, and $241 million by Japan.

The main reason for this poor showing is that Washington has discouraged commercial contacts with the communist countries. The official view has been that to sell to these countries or buy from them will strengthen their economies, and that this is harmful to the United States. For products of direct military usefulness this view is doubtless valid; and there is a tacit agreement among the Western countries not to supply these products. But for consumer goods and capital goods in general, there seems no obvious reason why exchange of goods with a communist country should benefit their economy more than it benefits ours. In any event, these goods are normally available from other Western countries, which do not share our view of the harmful effects of trade. So we do not succeed in denying these goods to the communist world, but simply penalize our own exporters and importers.

There is some indication that the U.S. position in this matter is gradually changing. In 1965 both an official study group and an influential private business group[7] issued reports favoring judicious enlargement of East-West trade; and there have been steps toward more active trade discussions with the U.S.S.R. and the East European countries. The U.S.S.R. is so large and diversified that its foreign trade is of only marginal importance. The East European countries, with their smaller and more export-oriented economies, are more actively interested in developing better trade relations.

The Less Developed Countries

The less developed countries earn much more foreign exchange through their exports than they receive in loans and grants. So they are naturally eager to enlarge their trade with us on reasonable terms. The most recent expression of this interest was the creation in 1964 of a United Nations Conference on Trade and Development (UNCTAD), headed by the Argentine economist Raul Prebisch, one of the most eloquent spokesmen of the underdeveloped world.

What adjustments in our trade policies would benefit the less developed countries without undue detriment to our own economy? Several things have been suggested:

1. Abolition of all tariffs on tropical food products. These serve no protective purpose, and the revenue gained by our government comes partly from agricultural producers in the poorer countries.

2. Support for well-designed schemes to stabilize the world price of

---

[7] *East-West Trade* (New York: Committee on Economic Development, 1965).

major primary products, whose price gyrations are a major source of economic disturbance in the less developed countries. We are already participating in a world coffee agreement, not to mention the long-standing world wheat agreement (where we are on the export side of the table along with Canada, Argentina, and others). It seems possible that workable plans could be devised for a number of other products.

3. Another suggestion is that the industrial nations might extend the tariff concessions they make to each other to the underdeveloped countries, but *without requiring the latter to reciprocate*. Nigeria or Peru could ship us cotton textiles at a low tariff rate, but would be allowed to maintain high tariffs to protect their own production. The argument for this is that, if the underdeveloped countries are to raise their exports at all rapidly, they must begin to add exports of manufactures to their traditional exports of primary products. Since their "infant" manufacturing industries are relatively inefficient at this stage, they should be allowed special protection until they have become more firmly established.

4. One could go even further and allow manufactured goods from the less developed countries to enter our market at a lower tariff than that imposed on comparable goods from the developed countries. While ideas of this sort are advanced hopefully in UNCTAD circles and in other gatherings of the "have-not" nations, it seems unlikely that the "haves" can be persuaded to go quite this far.

SUMMARY

1. International trading and financial relations require a *foreign exchange market,* in which the currency of one country can be converted into that of another. The chief operators in this market are large private banks and central (government) banks. An *exchange rate* is the price of one currency in terms of another.

2. A country normally exports products which are comparatively cheap at home compared with prices abroad, and imports goods which are comparatively cheap in other countries. Underlying comparative cheapness of a good *in terms of money* is comparative cheapness *in terms of the physical resources required to produce it*. This is usually termed *comparative advantage*.

3. Trade that is based on comparative advantage leads to larger total output than if each country (or region) produced all its own requirements. This economic gain is usually divided between the trading partners, the exact division depending on the price ratio or *terms of trade* between their products.

4. When we take account of differing factor endowments, a country will tend to specialize in products requiring much of the factor which is relatively abundant (and hence cheap) in that country. For example, a

country with abundant labor will specialize in labor-intensive products.

5. Because this specialization raises the demand for (and hence the price of) the abundant factor, the price of the same factor in different countries will be more nearly equal with trade than without trade. This is usually called the *factor price equalization theorem.*

6. The volume of international trade, after languishing from 1914 to 1945, has experienced a remarkable recovery since 1945. It is still only about 10 percent of total world production, but many of the smaller countries export 20 or 30 percent of their output.

7. The United States has shifted over the past century from being a raw materials exporter to being mainly an exporter of manufactured goods. Changes in factor supplies and technical progress have altered our comparative advantage.

8. A tariff is a tax on imports. It benefits the protected industry by enabling it to sell more goods at a higher price. But consumers are injured, and so are export industries which suffer retaliation by foreign countries.

9. Most arguments for the desirability of tariffs are fallacious. But one can justify temporary protection for promising *infant industries,* and continuing protection for industries which are essential to *national defense.* It is also reasonable that, where a tariff has long existed, it should be withdrawn gradually rather than suddenly.

10. Until 1930 the United States was a high-tariff country. But under the Trade Agreements Act of 1934, as subsequently renewed and extended, tariffs were more than cut in half by 1950. During the fifties, Congress was grudging in approving further tariff reductions. The Trade Expansion Act of 1962, however, portends a new period of tariff cutting and perhaps an approach to free trade within the North Atlantic community.

DISCUSSION QUESTIONS

1. Considering only two countries, and thinking in money terms, what determines which products each country will export to the other?

2. Define the *principle of comparative advantage.* Why might it pay Texas to import from New England goods which could be produced with less labor in Texas?

3. In the early fifties some European economists argued that the United States has such superior productivity that it can undersell the rest of the world in *all* lines of production. Do you see any weaknesses in this argument?

4. One might expect labor-abundant countries such as Ceylon or Nigeria to have comparative advantage in textiles, clothing, and other light consumer goods. Yet they continue to import large amounts of these products.

Why is this? Do you know of any labor-abundant areas which do specialize in and successfully export light manufactures?

5. "The argument that the ratio of trade to GNP will fall as a country's per capita income rises is logically unassailable. If we see a country in which this is not happening, then we simply haven't waited long enough." Discuss.

6. Would you expect that trade among the industrial countries will increase in the future as a percentage of total world trade? Why, or why not? Would such a tendency be to the disadvantage of the less developed countries?

7. Who gains and who loses from a tariff on imports? Can one demonstrate that the losses normally outweigh the gains? How?

8. It is sometimes argued that a tariff which equalizes the cost of producing an article in the United States and abroad simply puts competition on a "fair" basis. What do you think of this reasoning?

9. Are there valid arguments for tariff protection? Which of these are important in the United States at present?

10. There are a growing number of plans for regional economic integration, such as the European Economic Community. How would you expect such a plan to affect:
    a) Countries included in the arrangement?
    b) Countries excluded from the arrangement?

11. Despite all theoretical reasoning, many people retain a conviction that tariffs are necessary "to protect the American workingman against the products of cheap foreign labor." What would you say to a person holding this view?

12. When the United States several years ago sold a large amount of wheat to the U.S.S.R., there was considerable disagreement over the wisdom of the move. What would your own view have been?

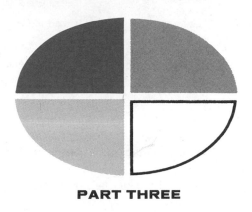

PART THREE

THE ECONOMICS OF

INCOME AND EMPLOYMENT

Bell, book, and candle shall not drive me back,
When gold and silver becks me to come on.
WILLIAM SHAKESPEARE, *King John*

WE HAVE now reached a turning point in the course. Parts One and Two focused on particular industries and markets. They raised questions of this sort: Supposing that national output in 1966 is $700 billion, how much of this output will consist of breakfast cereals, automobiles, potatoes, cement, and so on? What will be the market price of each product? How much cash income will go to each individual in the economy?

Throughout this discussion we took the general level of economic activity for granted. We assumed that the economy runs along quietly at capacity year after year. But everyone knows that this is not true. Sometimes the system operates well below capacity. Plants are partly idle and many workers are unemployed. At other times production shoots up and unemployment shrinks. We know also that the price level fluctuates widely. These price swings can be quite upsetting, and we need to understand why they occur.

In Part Three, therefore, we focus on forces affecting the economy as a whole, on what is usually termed *aggregative economics* or *macro-*

economics. This analysis is related, of course, to the microeconomic analysis of Part One. The whole is the sum of its parts. But macro-economics involves a different emphasis and point of view. We ask, not what determines the demand for television sets, but what determines *total demand* in the economy; not what determines the price of new cars, but what determines the *average level of all prices;* not why a particular industry is expanding, but why *most industries* are ex-

Production and Unemployment, 1918–65

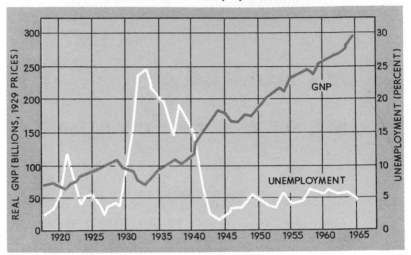

FIGURE 1.

panding at one time and contracting at another. This effort to explore the central heartbeat of the economy requires new concepts, and a more thorough analysis of money supply, spending, and saving.

A good way to introduce these issues is to look at the behavior of the American economy since World War I. The colored line in Figure 1 shows changes in the physical output of the economy. The white line shows the percentage of the labor force that was completely unem-ployed. The unemployment figure, naturally enough, moves in an opposite direction to the production figure.

Note the jittery movement of production and employment, and the frequent reversals, of course. After the postwar depression of 1920–22, production rose quite strongly until 1929. Then occurred the cata-strophic decline of 1929–33. This depression shook the economy to its foundations, and led to the wave of New Deal legislation. Despite gov-ernment efforts to promote recovery, unemployment remained unusually high and production unusually low until the onset of World War II. During the war, production rose to unprecedented heights and unemployment almost vanished.

Most economists, smarting from the Great Depression and still nervous about the future, predicted a serious depression after World War II. It came as a pleasant surprise that the drop of production in

Wholesale Price Index, 1918–65

FIGURE 2.

1946 was brief and mild. The economy then set off on a period of sustained expansion, broken only by mild recessions in 1948–49, 1953–54, 1957–58, and 1960–61. During the late forties, consumers and business concerns were catching up on things they had been unable to buy during World War II; and after 1950, the Korean War gave a new stimulus to demand and production. The rate of expansion slackened from 1957–61, then rose again during the early and middle sixties.

The historical record raises several major questions. Why do we have these ups and downs of production? The downswings since 1945 have been mild, but they are still annoying. Must we put up with these interruptions of progress every 3 or 4 years? What can be done to immunize the economy against declines and to accelerate its upward movement?

Now look at Figure 2, which shows changes in the average level of prices. The depression after World War I brought a sharp break in prices, which then remained almost stable through the prosperous years 1922–29. The 1929–33 depression brought another sharp price decline —the nickel hamburger, the $500 new car, the restaurants advertising "all you can eat for 60 cents." Prices rose again during the partial recovery of the thirties, and advanced more sharply during and immediately after World War II. There was a smaller spurt of prices during the first year of the Korean War.

Since the Korean War ended in 1953, the trend of prices has been mildly upward. Prices have not fallen during recession and have risen a bit during prosperity. Wages have risen substantially in bad years as well as good. This has led to predictions that our economy has entered an era in which prices will move in only one direction—up.

Is this prediction correct? If so, who is responsible? Business groups blame unduly large wage increases. Union leaders retort by blaming business for demanding exorbitant profit margins. Is a continued mild uptrend in prices harmful to the economy, or can it be exhilarating? If it is harmful, can anything be done about it? Can we have *both* a high level of spending, leading to capacity production and full employment, *and* a stable level of prices?

These are very practical questions, and many people feel strongly about them. Economists are by no means agreed on the answers. But if we cannot always provide answers, we can at least explain what the shooting is about and help the reader to formulate his own views intelligently rather than emotionally.

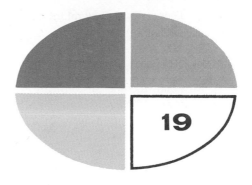

National Income: Meaning

and Measurement

Never ask of money spent
Where the spender thinks it went.
Nobody was ever meant
To remember or invent
What he did with every cent.

ROBERT FROST

IN ORDER TO TALK about the total output of an economy, as we propose to do in Parts Three and Four, we need some way of defining and measuring this output. We shall be speaking frequently of gross national product, national income, and similar quantities. Where do they come from? How are they estimated? What assurance have we that the estimates are reliable? To find out, we must explore a subject usually known as *national income accounting.*

While the effort to measure national output goes back for centuries, national income accounting is a recent development. Detailed and comparable estimates for the United States go back only to 1929. A few other countries were preparing national estimates before World War II. Since 1945 this kind of work has been accelerated by the Statistics Division of the United Nations, which has assisted member countries to set up national income measurements and publishes annual statistics for most countries of the world.

A few years ago the writer encountered in London an economist friend who is a leading authority on national income. He had just gotten off a plane from India and was about to board one for Brazil. On being asked how he managed to get around the world so much, he explained, "After all, old man, *every* country has a national income." He was quite right. There are national income estimates for Kenya and Jamaica, for Burma and Iran. If there aren't figures for Togoland and the Fiji Islands,[1] there soon will be.

National income accounting is now the central framework for describing and analyzing a national economy. If one asks what is going on in a particular economy, whether it is advancing or declining, or how its internal structure is changing over the course of time, the answers run in terms of national income tables. So it is necessary to get this measurement system clearly in mind. Having done this, we can use the system to explore short-term fluctuations of national income in Part Three, and long-term economic growth in Part Four.

A PRODUCTION STATEMENT FOR ONE COMPANY

Our problem is to add up all the productive activity going on in an economy during a certain period. Production is carried on mainly in business units, of which there are several million in the United States. Let us first consider, therefore, how we might picture the activities of a single company over a year's time. If we can do this for each company, we can then add up the activities of all companies to get a picture for the nation as a whole.

TABLE 1

Production Statement for the X Manufacturing Company, 1966
(Thousands of Dollars)

ALLOCATIONS		SOURCES	
Depreciation	80	Sales to Company A	300
Taxes other than corporate profit taxes	30	Sales to Company B	600
Wages and salaries	680	Sales to Company C	450
Social insurance contributions	25	Other sales	200
Net interest	10	Inventory increase	100
Corporate profit tax	55	Total value of production	1,650
Net dividends	35		
Undistributed profits	35	Minus: Goods and services purchased from other producers	700
Total allocations of value added	950	Total value added	950

---

[1] As a matter of fact, there *are* estimates for the Fiji Islands. They were collected by an enterprising British economist who traveled from island to island by sailboat, busily counting piles of copra in every port.

Table 1 shows the X Manufacturing Company's operations during 1966. It is adapted from the ordinary income statement or "profit and loss" statement. It is constructed according to the principles of double entry bookkeeping. In old-fashioned physics, at least, "whatever goes up must come down." In accounting, "whatever comes in must go out." Every dollar which the company receives has to end up somewhere. If it is not paid out for materials, labor, taxes, or other expenses, it must have stayed in the company and will show up as profit. The right-hand side of the table shows the value of what the company produced during the year. The left-hand side shows where the money went, including how much of it stayed behind in the company's hands. And the two sides must always balance.

Sources of Funds: "Value Added"

Table 1 deserves careful study. Look first at the right-hand side. The company has manufactured and sold to its various customers $1,550 thousand worth of goods. It has also produced $100 thousand worth of goods which were not sold during the year but are sitting in the warehouse as increased inventory. Since what we are after is total production during the year, this amount must be added. (The inventory figure might have been negative instead of positive. The company might have sold more than it produced, and thus reduced inventories.) Thus we come out with total production of $1,650 thousand.

But did the X Company itself produce this much? It used up during the year $700 thousand worth of materials and service purchased from other companies—raw materials, electric power, trucking and freight services, office supplies, and so on. This $700 thousand constitutes production by these other companies, not by the X Company. What the X Company has really produced is the *difference* between the value of the ingredients purchased from other companies and the value of its own finished product. This difference of $950 thousand dollars is termed *value added* and is considered the true production of the X Company for the year.

The importance of calculating in this way becomes clear when we try to add different companies' production together into a national total. Consider what would happen otherwise. Wheat worth $100 is sold to a miller who grinds it into flour worth $150, after which it is baked into bread worth $300, and finally retailed to consumers for a total of $450. How much has been produced in the process? Is it $100 + $150 + $300 + $450 = $1,000? No, it is not. Total production is only $450, the amount which consumers pay for the final product. Where is the catch? The catch is that in the $1,000 total the value of the original wheat is counted *four* times, the value added by the miller is counted *three* times, and the value added by the baker is counted *twice*. The only way to eliminate this double counting is to deduct, at each stage of production, the materials purchased from people at earlier stages and to count only value added at that stage as true production. In this example, value added is $100 for the wheat farmer, $50 for the miller, $150 for the baker, and $150 for the grocer: $100 + $50 + $150 + $150 = $450, which is the right answer.

Allocations or Uses of Funds

Where does the money go? Every dollar's worth of production must be accompanied by a dollar's worth of expense or profit. How does this work out on the left-hand side of Table 1?

The first item, *depreciation,* is money set aside to cover wear and tear on buildings and equipment and to replace them when they are worn out. Suppose a machine costs $50,000 and is expected to wear out at the end of 10 years. Then according to the simplest ("straight-line") depreciation formula, the company will put aside $5,000 each year. At the end of the 10 years it will have the $50,000 necessary to buy a new machine. Depreciation charges are a necessary cost of production. Unless they are set aside, the company is "living on its capital." Its equipment will eventually wear out, and there will be no money available to replace it.

The next item is mainly *property taxes* paid to the city or county, plus *excise or sales taxes* which the state and federal governments collect on some products. *Wages and salaries,* a large item in most companies, needs no explanation. Most employers must also contribute a certain percentage of payrolls to finance the state unemployment compensation and federal old-age pension systems—hence *social insurance contributions.* The company may also have to pay *interest* to bondholders or to banks which have lent it money.

These items, plus purchased materials which have already been deducted on the right-hand side of the account, make up all the *costs* of running the enterprise. What's left, if anything, is an accounting *profit.* The X Company did well in 1961 and came up with a profit of $125 thousand. This gets split three ways, shown by the last three items on the left-hand side. A large share goes to the federal government under the corporate profit tax. The remainder may be paid out to the stockholders in dividends or held back to expand the business. The X Company in this year made a 50–50 split.

Thus we have managed to account for $950 thousand, which must and does equal the value of production on the right-hand side. Note that all the items on the left-hand side represent *income* to somebody, while the items on the right-hand side represent value of *product.* The table may thus be regarded *either* as an income statement or a product statement. We shall see that the same is true of production statements for the economy as a whole. This is why one finds the terms *national income* and *national product* used interchangeably.

A PRODUCTION STATEMENT FOR THE ECONOMY

Now let's see what is involved in adding up the activities of all production units in the economy. Most production comes from business corporations, and we have already seen how to handle them. Provided we are careful to eliminate double counting by deducting purchased materials at each stage, we can add the figures for all companies in the country and come out with a statement looking just like Table 1, though the totals now run in billions instead of thousands. On the right-hand side this will show *total value added* by the productive activities of all companies. This can be viewed also as *total production for final use,* since production of materials by one company for sale to other companies has been eliminated in the totaling. On the left-hand side, our consolidated statement shows the *total income* resulting from corporate activities, including corporate tax payments and business profits. Total income must equal total product, just as for a single company.

There is no difficulty either in adding the production of the several million farmers, grocery storekeepers, and other small producers whose businesses are not set up as companies. Their production statements are actually simpler than the one we set up for the X Company. The farmer pays for his purchased materials, pays his property taxes, and perhaps pays a little interest to the local banker. What's left over is his net income for the year. We may say, if we like, that part of this income is really wages for his labor, part is interest on his investment in the farm, and part may be profit. But it's all income, and it's all his. The same is true for grocery store operators, professional practitioners, and other individual proprietors. In the U.S. national income accounts, the incomes of all such people are lumped together as *income of unincorporated enterprises.*

What else remains to be added? The federal, state, and local governments hire a lot of people and spend a lot of money. So they must be producing something. Government production, as we saw in Chapter 17, mainly takes the form of services; and these services are usually not sold in the market for a price. So what value can we attach to them?

National income estimators have adopted a simple rule on this point: government services are worth what they cost. The value of government's product equals the money spent to provide it. This assumes that the citizens know what they are doing. If they don't think a particular public service is worth its cost, they can get after their elected representatives to have it reduced or eliminated. But there is no way to *prove* that government production is worth precisely this much and no more. To anyone who questions the soundness of the present rule, all one can say is "Go find a better one."

With government, as with other producing units, we must avoid double counting. Suppose the cost of all government services in 1966 was $150 billion. Of this amount, $50 billion was paid to government employees while $100 billion was paid to business concerns for goods and services—everything from missiles and space vehicles to carbon paper for Washington offices. Can we say that the value added by government was $150 billion? Obviously not. The $100 billion of government purchases has already been counted as part of the output of private industry and cannot be counted again. We are left with $50 billion, which leads to a simple rule: *value added by government equals the government payroll.* This $50 billion goes into the value of national product on the right-hand side of the sheet, and the same $50 billion goes into the wage and salary item on the left-hand side. The statement continues to balance.

Have we now finished adding up the national income? Not quite. There are a few other things which do not enter the market place and are not sold at a price, but which it seems legitimate to count as part of national income. We call these *imputed income,* to indicate that no cash transaction is involved. The largest items are: (1) The value of farm produce consumed on the farm. This is usually valued at the price which the farmer could get by selling it rather than at the retail price he would have to pay if he were buying it. It can be argued that this value is too low, and that this is one reason why farm incomes always look so low compared with city incomes. (2) The rental value of owner-occupied houses. If a tenant pays rent to a landlord, we say that this measures the services yielded by the house, and should therefore be counted as part of national product. Suppose now the tenant buys the house. There is no longer any monthly rent. Yet the house yields the same service as before, and it would seem odd not to continue counting it as part of national product. We estimate, therefore, what the homeowners of the country would have to pay for the services of their houses if they were renting them, and this is added to both sides of the national production statement.

Imputation could be carried even farther, and there are nice questions about how far it should be carried. Johnny's haircut by the neighborhood barber adds $1.50 to national product. Johnny's haircut at home by the porridge-bowl method adds nothing to national product. What about housewives' labor put into cooking, cleaning, and household management? Valued at the cost of a hired housekeeper, this would add a large amount to national product. But national income statisticians have not been this daring, and production within the household is not counted. This has paradoxical results: the widower who marries his housekeeper is reducing national income!

The result of this adding-up is shown in Table 2. The figures are now billions instead of thousands. They are still hypothetical, though not very different from the actual U.S. figures for 1964. Table 2 bears a strong resemblance to Table 1, but a few changes should be noted. On the

TABLE 2

Production Statement for the Economy, 1964
(Billions of Dollars)

ALLOCATIONS		SOURCES	
Depreciation	55	Value added in the market economy	
Taxes other than corporate		Sales to consumers	350
income taxes	58	Sales to business	90
Wages and salaries	334	Sales to government	64
Social insurance contributions	31	Increase in inventories	4
Income of unincorporated		Net sales to foreign	
enterprises	52	countries	7
Rental income of persons	18	Value added by government	64
Net interest	15	Other nonmarket (imputed)	
Corporate profits taxes	26	production	50
Net dividends	20		
Undistributed profits	20		
Current surplus of government			
enterprises	1		
Gross national income	630	Gross national product	630

sources side, we have added government production and imputed production. And sales by private producers have been broken down by *type of purchaser,* to show how much output went to consumers, how much to business concerns, and how much to government.

One thing looks odd in the table: how can there be any "sales to business" by other businesses? Didn't we wash these out in the totaling process? We did wash out all transfers of materials and services *to be used up in current production.* The "sales to business" shown in Table 2 include only plant construction, machinery, and other capital goods destined to last beyond the current year. They are *final sales,* and as such stand on the same basis as final sales for consumer use or government use. This item, which will turn out to be important in our later discussion, is usually termed *plant and equipment investment* or *private fixed investment.*

There are a few additions also on the allocations or income side of the table. *Income of unincorporated enterprises* has been added to include the earnings of farmers, small unincorporated businesses, independent professional men, and the like. Some government enterprises, such as the TVA, do sell their products for a price. The profits or losses of these enterprises appear under *current surplus of government enterprises. Rental income of persons* includes not only cash rents paid by tenants but the imputed rent of owner-occupied houses. With these additions, the table is just like Table 1, and once more the two sides must balance. Gross national product and gross national income are the same thing looked at from different standpoints.

TABLE 3

U.S. National Income and Product, 1964
(Millions of Dollars)

Compensation of employees:	365,345	Personal consumption	
Wages and salaries	333,539	expenditures	398,907
Supplements	31,806	Gross private domestic	
Income of unincorporated		investment	92,876
enterprises	51,137	Government purchases of	
Rental income of persons	18,210	goods and services	128,356
Net interest	15,153	Net exports of goods and	
Corporate profits:	64,836	services	8,560
Corporate profit tax	27,644		
Dividends	17,249		
Undistributed profits	19,943		
Inventory valuation adjustment	− 292		
National income	514,389		
Indirect business taxes	58,040		
Business transfer payments	2,340		
Statistical discrepancy	− 542		
Less: Subsidies minus current			
surpluses of government			
enterprises	−1,237		
Net national product	572,990		
Capital consumption allowances			
(depreciation)	55,709		
Gross national product	628,699	**Gross national product**	628,699

Source: *Survey of Current Business,* August, 1965.

U.S. GROSS NATIONAL PRODUCT IN 1964

The national income accounts prepared by the U.S. Department of Commerce look a bit different from Table 2. It will be a good idea to examine the official figures for 1964, partly so that you will recognize this kind of table when you meet it, partly to illustrate the varying ways in which such tables may be constructed. Table 3 gives the Department of Commerce data for 1964, with only slight rearrangement.

The right-hand side of the table, as before, shows the value of final production during the year, including government production and imputed production. Output is now subdivided, however, on the basis of *who bought it.* This reflects the strong interest of economists in business cycle analysis during the crucial period when our national income accounts were taking shape. Consumer spending, business spending, and government spending behave differently during the business cycle, and so it was considered important to separate them out. But this kind of breakdown is also significant for other purposes.

It is easy to see how the items in Table 3 are derived from those in Table 2. *Personal consumption expenditures* is the sum of sales to consumers and imputed production. *Gross private domestic investment* is the sum of capital goods sold to business, housing construction (which is also counted as investment), and increase in inventories. *Government purchases of goods and services* is the sum of business sales to government and the government payroll.

On the left-hand side of Table 3, almost all the items are familiar from previous tables, though their order has been slightly reshuffled. The main newcomers are *inventory valuation adjustment,* a technical adjustment which need concern only the specialist,[2] and *statistical discrepancy,* which needs a word of explanation. We must now break down and confess that the national income division of the Department of Commerce does not actually collect income statements for every producer in the economy and add these up as we have supposed. Figures to fill in the different totals in Table 3 are collected from a wide variety of sources, and most of them are estimates of varying degrees of reliability. When all the spadework has been done and the two sides of the table have been added up, they should logically balance. But unhappily they don't, because of gaps and errors in the basic information. "Statistical discrepancy" is simply an item put in to *make* the table balance. It may be positive or negative, and amounts to saying, "We slipped up somewhere."

One final point should be emphasized because it is often misunderstood. *Only income arising from current production enters the national income table.* Suppose I sell 100 shares of A.T.&T. stock on the New York market and the buyer pays me $6,500. Is this $6,500 income? No, it is not. It is simply a change in my assets from one form to another. Instead of holding one asset (stock) I now choose to hold a different one (cash). The transaction has nothing to do with production; and so the money received is not counted as income in my personal accounting or in the national income accounts. You can see why this principle makes sense. Without it, a burst of feverish activity on the stock exchange would show up as an increase in national output.

The principle applies to any other transfer of assets. If I sell a house

---

[2] The reason for this is that part of the increase (or decrease) in value of inventories shown in the right-hand side of the table may have resulted from a change in price levels rather than a change in quantity of inventories held. Since the object of Table 3 is to get at physical quantity of output during the year, we want to take out of the inventory total any change resulting from price movements. The inventory valuation adjustment is an effort to do this, and may be either positive or negative depending on which way prices have moved.

or a used car, the money received is *not* income. If a company goes out of business and sells its plant and equipment to another company for $10 million, this payment is *not* income. If you are ever puzzled about how a particular payment should be treated, apply this simple test: did the recipient get it for participating in production? Only if the answer is yes does the item enter the national income accounts.

The Grand Total and Some Smaller Totals

We have been explaining how a lot of building blocks are piled on top of each other to arrive at gross national product. Now let's see how the blocks can be taken apart to get smaller totals which are interesting for various purposes. We start at the top with the biggest figure and work down to smaller and smaller subtotals.

1. Gross national product.   This is the most global of national income concepts. GNP professes to total up all of the productive activity in a particular country during a certain period of time. It is the best single answer to the question, "What did we turn out in the United States in 1964?"

But this seemingly solid figure is no stronger than the rules by which it is constructed. It depends on what we agree at the beginning shall be considered production. Marxists include only *material* production; and so the GNP totals for Russia, Poland, and other communist countries do not include the services of teachers, doctors, civil servants, entertainers, and the like. They leave out part of what we would consider to be national output. The U.S. figures include some kinds of imputed income but leave out others, notably household production. Thus the total can be increased or decreased by changing the rules of the game.

Two other misunderstandings should be avoided. First, *GNP is not a measure of consumer welfare.* An increase in GNP from one year to the next may mean an increase in output of consumer goods, or it may not. Part of the increase, or conceivably the whole of it, may be in business investment or in government activity. The tremendous increase of GNP during World War II was accompanied by only a modest rise in civilian consumption.

Second, *GNP is not a measure of productive efficiency.* In economics, efficiency is usually measured by the ratio of output to input. If a country's output rises 5 percent in a particular year *with no increase* in the use of labor, capital, land, and other inputs, this is a 5 percent increase in efficiency. But if inputs have also risen 5 percent, there has been no change in efficiency. The economy is simply bigger, not more efficient. The GNP figure tells us nothing about inputs and therefore says nothing about efficiency.

2. Net national product.   Another possible criticism of GNP is that it overstates how much has been produced during the year, since it fails

to take account of the wearing out of factories, machinery, office buildings, houses, and other capital goods. Part of the year's output must be devoted to replacing this depreciation, which is also termed *capital consumption.* Only after providing for replacement can one tell how much of the 1964 product is available for use *without eating into capital.* This remainder, GNP minus capital consumption, is termed *net national product* or NNP. Table 3 shows that in 1964 GNP was $628.7 billion, capital consumption was $55.7 billion, and NNP was consequently $573.0 billion.

The terms *gross* and *net* have this meaning wherever one meets them. Thus *gross business investment* is the amount of new plant and equipment built during the year, plus additions to inventories. But some plant and equipment wore out during the year, indicated by the size of depreciation allowances. By deducting depreciation from gross investment we get *net business investment* or the net increase in the stock of productive equipment.

A serious difficulty with NNP is that the capital consumption allowance on which it rests is one of the more uncertain figures in the national income table. The main ingredient in estimated capital consumption is the amount put aside for depreciation by business concerns. The Department of Commerce is forced to take these business estimates at face value. But how do we know that they precisely measure the wearing out of capital during the year? Some companies may overdepreciate, others may underdepreciate, and the net result is unclear. Since capital consumption is rather a guess, NNP is a guess also. So, having explained what it means, we shall make little use of it in later chapters. In discussing ups and downs in total production, we shall usually fall back on the more solid GNP figure.

3. National income. Suppose we stop looking at Table 3 as a total of *production* and look at it as a total of *incomes.* We ask now how much income workers, investors, and other suppliers of the factors of production have earned in the course of the year's activities. This is useful for various purposes, such as calculating labor and capital shares in national income.

The sales value of the year's output, after providing for depreciation, is NNP. Isn't this the figure we are seeking? Not quite. Everything which producing units receive in return for goods sold is *not* available for the factors of production. Business concerns must pay sales taxes, excise taxes, property taxes, and various other fees and licenses. These are shown in Table 3 as *indirect taxes,* to distinguish them from the direct tax on corporate profits. After deducting indirect taxes and a few smaller items, we see that *national income,* the total earnings of the factors of production, amounted in 1964 to $514.4 billion.

4. Personal income. Not all the income which Table 3 shows as

belonging to the factors of production actually reaches them. This is notably true of profit income. The government takes close to half through the corporate income tax, and boards of directors vote to hold back part of the remainder. Thus the stockholders may end up getting a quarter or less of "their" profits. There are also deductions from labor income. The amount which a worker pays into social security and private pension funds, as well as what the employer contributes on his behalf, is counted as belonging to him, but he never sees it.

On the positive side, people receive some income which has not been earned in the course of current production. Veterans receive various cash benefits, farmers receive government checks for land taken out of production, workers receive unemployment compensation payments and old-age pensions, relief cases receive checks from the city, and so on. All these government *transfer payments* are counted as part of personal income. There is also a small volume of business transfer payments through pensions and other private welfare plans. In 1964, transfer payments of every sort totaled $55.7 billion.

Personal income, then, is income actually received from every source, including transfer payments, before payment of personal income taxes.

5. Disposable income. This is simply personal income *after* pay-

TABLE 4

	MILLIONS OF DOLLARS
Gross national product	628,699
Minus: Capital consumption allowances	55,709
Equals net national product	572,990
Minus: Indirect business taxes	58,040
Plus: Other minor items	561
Equals national income	514,389
Minus: Corporate profits taxes	27,644
Undistributed profits	19,943
Corporate inventory valuation adjustment	−292
Social security contributions	27,796
Plus: Government transfer payments	34,246
Net interest paid by government	19,112
Business transfer payments	2,340
Equals personal income	494,996
Minus: Personal income taxes	59,211
Equals disposable income	435,785
Consumption and interest payments	409,453
Savings	26,332

Source: *Survey of Current Business*, August, 1965.

ment of income taxes. It is how much money people finally have left to spend or to save. It is an interesting figure for retailers and consumer goods manufacturers, since it indicates the size of the consumer market. If disposable income is rising, most businesses can expect to find their sales rising as well.

The relation among these totals can be illustrated in several ways. A

GNP and Some Smaller Totals, 1929–64

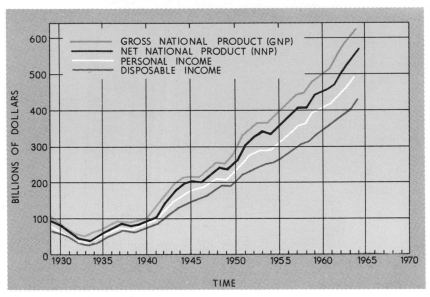

FIGURE 1. The subtotals normally rise with the grand total. But the gaps between them have widened, mainly because of heavier taxation. All values are calculated in 1964 dollars.

simple arithmetical tabulation is shown in Table 4.

The behavior of some of the GNP subtotals over the years 1929–64 is shown in Figure 1. Note that they typically move in the same direction and at about the same pace. The gaps between them, however, have widened over the course of time. The gap between NNP and personal income has widened mainly because of the substantial increase in corporate profit taxes, sales and excise taxes, and social security taxes. The gap between personal income and disposable income has widened because of the heavier bite of the personal income tax. These heavier tax drains, of course, are the counterpart of increased government expenditures. The upshot is that consumers' disposable income, which was 80 percent of GNP in 1929, was a bit under 70 percent in 1964.

Another useful way to present national income information is in the form of an income flow chart (Figure 2). Here we separate the three major types of spending: personal consumption expenditure, business investment, and government purchases of goods and services. These are usually designated as *C, I,* and *G,* and you will meet them frequently in

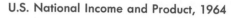

U.S. National Income and Product, 1964

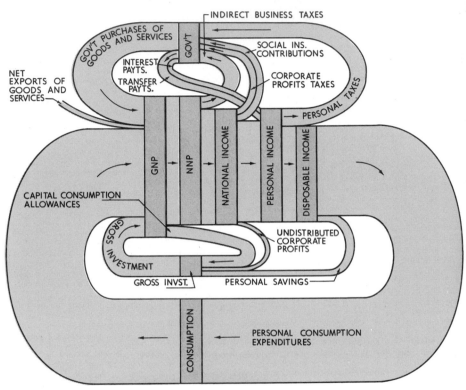

FIGURE 2.

later chapters. Figure 2 also shows the sources from which funds for each type of spending are derived. Households receive income mainly for services in production, but also as transfer payments from government; and this income is divided between consumption and personal saving. Government receives revenue from the various tax streams flowing in at the top of the chart. Money for business investment comes from depreciation allowances, undistributed profits, and personal saving.

The way in which *C, I,* and *G* have behaved over the past 35 years is shown in Figure 3. Note that personal consumption has at all times dominated the GNP total, but that its share of the total is lower today than in 1929 while the share of government has risen substantially.

GNP by Type of Spending, 1929–64

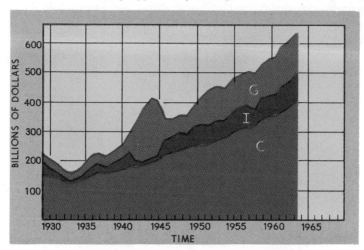

FIGURE 3. All the components have risen, but government has risen fastest. Note the impact of the severe 1929–33 depression and of World War II from 1941–45. All values are calculated in 1964 dollars, i.e., they have been adjusted for price level changes from year to year.

USES OF NATIONAL INCOME: COMPARISONS OVER TIME

Learning these concepts may have seemed tedious, but they greatly increase one's ability to analyze economic events. We shall suggest a few of their main uses and indicate some pitfalls which await the unwary user.

One use of national income figures is for historical analysis of how a country's output has changed over long periods of time. Has U.S. national output risen steadily or intermittently? At what rate, on the average? Are we getting richer by 2 percent a year or 5 percent?

The first difficulty in tackling these questions is that we are working with a rubber yardstick. All our figures of national output are expressed in dollars. But a dollar sometimes measures a larger quantity of physical goods and sometimes a smaller quantity, depending on changes in prices. When prices rise, our yardstick shrinks—a dollar equals less goods than before; and when prices fall, the yardstick expands again.

The technique of adjusting for price changes was described in Chapter 1. Its accuracy depends on the accuracy of the price indexes which are used in the process. Since price indexes are never perfect, the deflated or *constant dollar* figures which result are never completely reliable.

The difference made by adjustment for price changes is illustrated in Figure 4. Part of the apparently rapid increase of GNP since 1940 is due to price increases. When we revalue this output at the lower prices of 1929, the rate of increase is reduced. Real output, or output measured in constant dollars, rises more gradually than output measured in current dollars. It is a sound rule never to use current dollar figures for comparisons over any extended period of time.

U.S. Gross National Product, 1929–64

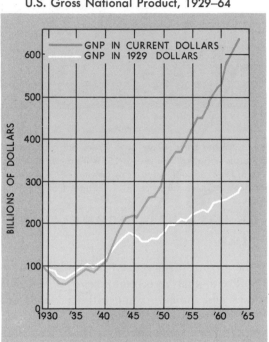

FIGURE 4.

Even after the price experts have done their best, we are far from being out of the woods. Here are a few brain teasers:

1. The deflation procedure assumes that we are dealing with unchanging products. Prices may vary up and down, but the products being priced are supposed to remain constant. But in practice product quality is always changing, usually for the better. The 1965 Ford is not the 1935 Ford. The dacron and cotton shirt of 1965 is not the same as the cotton broadcloth shirt of 1940. Quality can sometimes be measured. One can discover how many thousand miles a four-ply tire will run before the tread is gone. If a tire costs 20 percent more in 1965 than in 1950, but if it will also run 20 percent more miles, there has been no increase in the

price *per thousand miles of use*. But in many cases no such measurement is possible.

One of the writer's colleagues argues persuasively that there was no real increase in consumer prices between 1950 and 1965, although the Consumer Price Index showed a rise of about 30 percent. His argument is as follows: Give a family a 1950 Sears, Roebuck catalog and a 1965 Sears catalog. Give them $1,000 and allow them to make up an order list from *either* the 1950 or 1965 catalog, but not from both. If the family decides to use the 1965 catalog, which he believes most people would do, this must mean that they consider the higher 1965 prices more than offset by improved quality.

Quality improvements, whether measurable or not, are certainly important. To the extent that they are not allowed for in our price indexes, the rise in price levels is overstated and the rise in real GNP is consequently understated.

2. This difficulty becomes even more serious if some goods disappear completely from the shopping list and new articles take their place. How does one compare the price of a horse and carriage in 1890 with the price of a "horseless carriage" in 1940? Or the cost of traveling a thousand miles by Pullman car in 1910 with first-class jet air fare for the same distance in 1965? What about products which don't replace anything, because nothing like them existed before? Television sets, vitamin pills, sulfa drugs, electronic computers, isotopes, and many other things now included in our national "market basket" are recent developments. They had no price in 1930 because they didn't exist.

Price indexes and GNP totals are not well adapted to covering drastic changes in the items going into national output. Over short periods during which people's way of life stays much the same, our measurements work reasonably well. But as we stretch out the period covered, we run into increasing difficulty. How much does it mean to calculate that the average American lives 3.2 times as well in 1965 as he did in 1870? The truth is that he lives very *differently*. By present standards, he seems to be living much better. But it is a bold man who would attach an exact percentage figure to the improvement.

There is a similar difficulty, as we shall see, when we try to make comparisons between countries with very different ways of life. Does an average American family live twice as well as an average Russian family? Three times as well? Certainly the *pattern* of life is very different. How much more one can say is open to question.

3. For judging increases in consumer welfare it is important to look at the *makeup* of GNP as well as its size. Nobody eats GNP. We must focus on that part of GNP which is destined for consumer use. And perhaps not all of that. The New York executive spends a good deal on railroad tickets for commuting from his home in the suburbs. This counts

as part of the national product which he "enjoys." But does it add to his satisfaction? On the contrary, it is a time-consuming nuisance. The more money he spends in this way, the *worse* off he is.

Simon Kuznets, a leading authority on national income, argues that many things which we count as part of national output should be considered *costs* rather than *products*. The costs involved in sustaining enormous metropolitan areas—travel costs to and within the area, subway systems, high rents arising from urban crowding, police protection, and other overhead expenses—should be deducted from national output. Similarly, Kuznets maintains that national defense costs should not be counted as part of national product. Since these types of expense have been increasing with disproportionate speed, we may not be getting better off as rapidly as the GNP totals suggest.

4. GNP measures outputs, not inputs. It says nothing about how much effort was needed to produce a certain output. Here we can strike an optimistic note, for the amount of effort going into the national product has been declining for at least a century. Our grandfathers worked a 60-hour week, our fathers a 48-hour one. Our children will probably work no more than 30 hours a week, and have a couple of months vacation besides. If we include this gain in leisure time, welfare has been rising faster than the output figures indicate.

5. The rules about imputed output affect the behavior of GNP over the course of time. Before 1900, housewives in the United States did most of the baking, clothes making, laundry, and other household services. Since these things were done at home without pay, they didn't count as part of national output. Since 1900, more and more of this work has been shifted outside the home. We have prepackaged and precooked foods, commercial bakeries, garment factories, commercial laundries and dry-cleaning establishments, repair shops of every description. The output of these establishments is bought and sold, hence *is* counted in GNP. Thus even if people consumed no more food or clothing than before, it would *look* as though GNP had increased. For this reason, the actual increase in consumer goods production since 1900 is doubtless somewhat less than the apparent increase.

Despite these doubts and qualifications, we shall go boldly ahead in later chapters to compare GNP figures for a hundred years and more. But the reader has been warned to keep tongue in cheek and not to take the figures more seriously than they deserve.

USES OF NATIONAL INCOME: COMPARISONS OVER SPACE

In this international age, people want to make income comparisons among countries. The United Nations has to do this for the practical reason that member nations are supposed to contribute to the U.N. budget in proportion to their national incomes. No wonder every government has to have a national income estimater! People interested in the comparative strength of capitalist and communist economies want to compare GNP in Britain, the United States, or Japan with GNP in Russia, Poland, or China. People interested in the less developed countries want some measure of how badly off these countries are. Is GNP per head higher in Mexico than in India? Is Indonesia better off than Ghana?

The problems involved in international comparisons are similar to those involved in comparisons over time for the same country. First, there is the problem of currency units. Japanese GNP is in billions of yen, while U.S. GNP is in billions of dollars. How do we get from dollars to yen, or marks, or rupees?

One simple expedient is to use the official exchange rate between the two currencies. A U.S. dollar at present exchanges for about 5 Indian rupees. So we can take the GNP of India, divide by 5, and say that the result represents Indian GNP "converted to U.S. dollars." The trouble with this is that official exchange rates may not correspond closely to the actual buying power of the two currencies in their home countries. Anyone traveling in England in the early fifties could observe that a British pound would buy at least as much as $4 would buy in the United States. The official exchange rate, however, was £1 = $2.80. The pound was undervalued. Similarly, the Japanese yen was undervalued in the late fifties, and visitors to Japan came home laden with radios, cameras, and pearls. South American currencies, on the other hand, are usually overvalued. They will not buy as much as the corresponding amounts of U.S. money would buy at home, and so tourists find few bargains in Latin America.

Suppose we forget official rates and set out to find the proper ratio between the dollar and the yen. We could make up a shopping list of consumer goods, see what the whole list would cost in the United States in dollars, and then what it would cost in Japan in yen. If the U.S. cost is 100 dollars and the Japanese cost 20,000 yen, one might say that 1 dollar = 200 yen is a proper conversion factor. But how do we get our shopping list in the first place? Japanese consumption habits are different from those in the United States. If we start with a "Japanese market basket" and price these items in both countries we shall get one result, while if we start with a "U.S. market basket" we shall get a different result. A common compromise is to try both procedures, get two exchange ratios, and then average them.

Suppose we have handled the currency conversion problem in one way or another. GNP totals for other countries of the world have been converted into dollars. We next divide each country's GNP by its population, to get national output *per capita*. We are then able to make up a comparative listing such as the one shown in Table 5 below.

The *ranking* of countries in this table is doubtless correct. Living standards in North America are above those in Western Europe, most European countries are above the Latin American group, and Latin America is generally above the African and Asian countries with the exception of Japan. Anyone who has traveled widely in the African and Asian countries can testify to their very low consumption levels. The table does tend, however, to exaggerate the absolute *distance* between the richer and poorer countries. To say that the average American lives 30 times as well as the average Nigerian or 20 times as well as the average Filipino is spuriously precise and in some ways misleading.

TABLE 5

Gross National Product per Capita, Selected Countries, 1962

COUNTRY	GNP PER CAPITA* (U.S. Dollars)	COUNTRY	GNP PER CAPITA (U.S. Dollars)
United States	2,691	Greece	394
Canada	1,807	Mexico	356
Sweden	1,703	Turkey	211
Australia	1,416	Brazil†	179
West Germany	1,349	Egypt†	156
France	1,300	Philippines†	125
Great Britain	1,288	Nigeria†	86
Puerto Rico	825	Pakistan	74
Italy	688	India	73
Japan	504	Burma	52
Argentina†	462		

* Gross domestic product, at factor cost, converted to U.S. dollars at official exchange rates. From U.N. *Yearbook of National Accounts Statistics*, 1963, pp. 321–24, 327–30.
† Data for these countries converted at estimated purchasing power parity rather than at official exchange rates. Method explained in original source.

There are several reasons for this. First, we are comparing an overwhelmingly rural population living largely on a subsistence basis, in Burma or Indonesia, with a dominantly urban population living in a cash economy in the United States. It might make some sense to compare farmers living in the mountains of Java with hillbillies in the southern Appalachians. But it makes little sense to compare the Javanese farmer with people in New York City or Chicago.

Second, we are comparing very different patterns of life. The Japanese middle-class house, with its sliding wooden panels, simple furniture, absence of central heating, secluded and beautiful garden, and staff of low-paid servants, involves much less cash outlay than the more elaborate and mechanized middle-class household in the United States.

But if the Japanese family spends one quarter as much, does this mean it is living only one quarter as well? From some philosophical standpoints, it may be living better. The problem is similar to that of comparing Americans in 1960 with Americans in 1860.

A third problem is the great importance of nonmarket production in the poorer countries. The rural household in these countries does almost everything for itself. Food growing, cooking, clothes making, laundering, barbering and other personal services, manufacture of simple household furniture and utensils, gathering of fuel, and many other things are done in the home. The national income statistician is apt to overlook these things except for food production, and even food is typically undervalued by being taken at the farm price rather than the retail price. No wonder the output figures for these countries come out so low. It would be interesting to see how different the results would look if everything done by the Indian housewife were revalued on a cash basis.

Finally, consumption is important only in relation to need, and need is relative to climate and other things. The fact that people in the northern United States have to build solid houses, spend money on heating, and change to warm winter clothing is not a *gain* in their standard of living. It is a *cost* of living in a cold climate.

This is not to say that we shouldn't make intercountry comparisons; but until the bases of comparison have been improved, the figures should not be taken too seriously. Professor Kuznets has tried to make rough adjustments for some of the factors mentioned and concludes that the United States, instead of being 30 times as well off as the poorest countries, is perhaps only 10 to 15 times as well off.[3]

SUMMARY

1. For a single production unit, total *output produced* equals total *income created*.

2. The same principle applies when the output of individual units is added to get totals for the national economy. *National product equals national income.*

3. In making this addition, one must avoid double counting by deducting the cost of materials purchased by a production unit and showing as its output only the *value added* in production.

4. One must include also the value of services produced by government, which is taken as equal to the government payroll; and certain items of imputed income, of which the most important are farm produce consumed on the farm and the imputed rent of owner-occupied dwellings.

---

[3] Simon Kuznets, *Modern Economic Growth: Rate Structure, and Spread* (New Haven, Conn.: Yale University Press, 1966), chap. vii.

5. Review the relations between *gross national product, net national product, national income, personal income,* and *disposable income* by studying the summary listing at the end of that section.

6. In tracing changes in a country's GNP over the course of time, one must first correct for price changes to get *real GNP* or *GNP in constant dollars.* Even after this has been done there remain logical difficulties arising from changes in quality of products; disappearance of some products and appearance of others; the fact that some items consumed in a complex urban society can be regarded as costs rather than additions to income; changes in the input of effort required to produce a certain output; and shifts of production from the household to the market or vice versa.

7. For these reasons GNP comparisons become less meaningful as one extends the period covered.

8. Similar problems arise in GNP comparisons among countries at the same time. Such comparisons are complicated by differences in patterns of life, rural versus urban residence, importance of nonmarket production, and the needs imposed by climate and geography. This prevents any precise measurement of the income gap between the richer and poorer nations.

DISCUSSION QUESTIONS

1. Why can't one add up the value of sales for all producing units to arrive at national product? What must one add up instead?

2. Why must the two sides of the national production statement total to the same amount? Which side of the account do you think is easier to estimate in practice?

3. What is meant by imputed output? Which items of imputed output are counted as part of GNP in the United States and which are not counted?

4. What do you think of Kuznets' argument that some kinds of production are "regrettable necessities" which do not add to consumer satisfaction and should not be counted as part of national income?

5. Explain the relations between GNP, NNP, national income, personal income, and disposable income. For what purposes might one be interested in each of these totals?

6. It has been argued that changes in product quality muddy up the significance of price level changes. Is there any practical way around this difficulty?

7. Suppose one observes a doubling of real GNP per capita in the United States over a certain period. The conventional conclusion might be that "people are twice as well off as they used to be." What qualifications should be made to this conclusion?

8. Granted that GNP figures do not accurately measure changes in welfare over long periods, is there any better technique which might be used?

9. Do national income statistics give a correct impression of the gap in living standards between the richest and poorest countries of the world? Explain.

10. If you think that GNP figures are not a reliable basis for intercountry comparisons of real income, what other comparisons would you suggest?

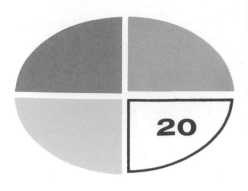

The Level of National Income

THE NATIONAL INCOME concepts of Chapter 19 help us to measure and describe changes in the economy. But they do not *explain* these changes. Why was United States GNP in 1965 about $670 billion? Why wasn't it higher or lower? Production cannot rise above the capacity of the economy, which is limited by available supplies of labor, capital, and other resources. But there is no law which prescribes that the economy must operate at full capacity. Why does the American economy operate close to capacity in some years and a good deal below capacity in others?

A related question is what determines the level of prices. Suppose all prices had been twice as high in 1965. Then the money value of GNP would have been $1,340 billion. Why weren't prices twice as high, or half as high? What determines the price level anyway?

In Part One we learned how to analyze the operation of a particular market. The forces operating in a market can be summarized in supply and demand curves, which determine the quantity and price of the goods exchanged. Can the same sort of reasoning be applied to the economy as a whole? Are there forces working systematically to determine the *total* production of goods and services and the *general* level of prices? And can these forces be summarized in a way similar to the supply-demand diagrams of Part One?

It is a challenging task to explain the great tidal movements of the economy. It is also a task of great practical importance. Every so often the economy turns downward into recession. Unemployment mounts and cries of alarm fill the air. Many remedies are offered to check the decline and set the economy back on the upward path. Which of these proposals are useful, which are ineffectual, and which may be positively harmful? One cannot judge without understanding why production and employment move up or down.

Another practical question: Since 1945, except for war years, the American economy has operated below capacity *even in periods of peak prosperity.* Unemployment has usually been higher than most people would consider desirable. The yearly rate of increase in U.S. GNP has been below that of many other industrial countries. Why this sluggishness in the economy? What steps could be taken to move output up closer to capacity? This has become a matter of public concern and political debate.

Until the 1930's most economists maintained that a capitalist economy tends naturally to operate at full capacity. A depression was only a temporary setback, which did not require corrective action by government. If economic forces were left to work themselves out, they would automatically check the slump and restore prosperity. This view was severely shaken by the Great Depression. In 1940, after 11 years of below-capacity operation, about 15 percent of the American labor force was still unemployed. This does not look like a self-adjusting economy. Eleven years is a long time to wait for economic forces to operate. In the end, capacity operation was restored by World War II rather than by natural recovery.

Alongside the orthodox view, there were always economic heresies, such as those advanced by John Hobson, William T. Foster, Waddill Catchings, and Major Clifford Douglas, founder of the "Social Credit" movement. These men maintained that there is a fatal flaw in the economy which prevents it from operating at a stable level. The economy, they argued, turns out a steadily increasing flow of goods, but does not provide enough purchasing power to take these goods off the market. Every so often a shortage of purchasing power develops. Then goods pile up in the stores, businesses reduce production, and workers are unemployed.

In this bald form the argument is surely incorrect. Think back to the logic of national income accounting. The two sides of the account always balance. For every dollar of goods put on the market, there is a dollar of income created. This is received by somebody and is available for spending. There is no built-in leakage of income from the system which would mean an *unavoidable* shortage of purchasing power. True, income may go to households or businesses which choose not to spend it. But this is a different matter. It depends on human decisions, and human decisions can be changed.

So we must discard both of the older views—the view that the economy tends naturally toward capacity operation, and the view that it must suffer frequent relapses because of a structural defect. In a particular economy at a particular time, there are forces operating to determine an equilibrium level of production and employment. But this equilibrium will not necessarily be at the level of capacity operation. It may by good fortune just be at that level; but it may also be above or below it.

What are the basic economic forces at work? How do they determine an equilibrium level of output, and where will this be? This chapter and the next are aimed at answering these questions.

INCOME AND SPENDING

Everyone would agree that the level of demand affects the level of production and that demand involves spending. Most discussions of prosperity and depression take spending as a point of departure. Consider the following common-sense "explanation" of depression: "Why is business bad? Because there is not enough spending. Why isn't there enough spending? Because people's incomes are low. Why are people's incomes low? Because business is bad." This sort of circular reasoning cannot explain anything. Yet one hears it repeatedly in popular discussion.

Autonomous and Induced Spending

How can we get out of this circle and onto a useful method of analysis? The clue is that, while spending is heavily influenced by income, it does not depend *solely* on income. With the same level of income, people may decide to save more and spend less or vice versa. We have also developed credit and borrowing, which makes it possible to spend more than one has.

With no change in income, then, any economic unit can suddenly decide to spend more or to spend less. This is termed an *autonomous* change in spending. But if income changes first and spending changes simply as a consequence, this is termed an *induced* change.

This difference may be illustrated as follows: Consumer income this month is $100 billion, of which $90 billion is spent and $10 billion is saved. Suppose consumer income next month rises to $101 billion, and that consumers continue to divide their incomes between spending and saving in the same proportion. Then next month consumer spending will be $90.9 billion, and saving will be $10.1 billion. There has been an *induced* increase of $0.9 billion in consumer spending. But this cannot be used to explain anything, because it is simply a result of the $1 billion increase in income. We did not explain where this $1 billion came from. We simply supposed it. This leaves us in the position of the Greek who maintained that Atlas was supporting the earth but could not answer the question, "Who is supporting Atlas?"

Suppose, instead, that consumer income next month remains unchanged at $100 billion, but that consumers reduce their saving ratio. They decide next month to spend $91 billion instead of the previous $90. This *autonomous* increase of $1 billion in spending *can* be regarded as a prime mover. It will lead to an increase in retail sales, which in turn will stimulate output and employment.

Now we seem to be on the right track. An autonomous increase in spending anywhere in the economy will have an expansionary effect. It will certainly cause an increase in sales, probably an increase in production and employment, and possibly an increase in prices. An autonomous decrease in spending will have opposite effects.

Types of Spender

To see how autonomous changes in spending can occur, let's go back to the classification of customers for national output used in Chapter 19. We saw that the whole of national output must be sold to consumers, business concerns, government agencies, or foreign buyers. Let us look briefly at each of these groups.

Consumers are the largest customers for national output. Yet this is the sector in which surprises are least likely to occur. American consumers as a whole behave rather consistently, saving 7 or 8 percent of disposable income and spending the remainder. Changes in consumer spending are mainly induced by income changes. Large autonomous changes occur only in unusual circumstances, such as war or threat of war. In 1941–42 and again in 1950–51 millions of families rushed to the stores to stock up on key items "before the hoarders got all the goods."

The *business* spending which is significant here is what we called in Chapter 19 *business investment*, or final sales to business. Its main components are investment in plant and equipment, investment in inventories, and residential construction. Each of these has an autonomous element and is rather volatile. They rise rapidly at some times and drop at others, with a consequent impact on total spending.

Government agencies now buy about 20 percent of national output. An increase in government purchases raises total spending, while a cut in purchases lowers it. Taxation works in the opposite direction. An *increase* in taxation *reduces* spending, since it leaves consumers with less income than before. A cut in taxation leaves people with more money in their pockets and thus raises spending.

Foreign buyers provide part of the demand for our goods and services. An increase in foreign spending on our products has the same stimulating effect as an increase in domestic spending. Exports of goods and services will rise, and U.S. production and employment will increase.

But we buy abroad as well as sell abroad. An increase in our imports from other countries has a depressing effect. Why is this? Because more goods are available for sale on the American market, but no new domestic purchasing power has been created to absorb these goods. The truism that "for every dollar of goods produced there is a dollar of income created" no longer works if the income has been created *abroad* while the goods are shipped for sale *here*. Put another way, an increase in the amount of U.S. income spent on foreign goods leaves less available for purchase of domestic production.

A Check List of Forces

We can now list the autonomous changes which may raise or lower the level of spending; and we can be sure that this is a *complete* list, because of the completeness of the national income accounts on which it is based. Anything which affects the level of national income must do so through one of these channels.

SECTOR	AUTONOMOUS CHANGES PRODUCING EXPANSION	AUTONOMOUS CHANGES PRODUCING CONTRACTION
Consumer	Increase in consumption expenditure	Decrease in consumption expenditure
Business	Increase in plant and equipment investment	Decrease in plant and equipment investment
	Increase in inventory investment	Decrease in inventory investment
	Increase in residential construction	Decrease in residential construction
Government	Decrease in tax rates	Increase in tax rates
	Increase in expenditure programs	Decrease in expenditure programs
Foreign	Increase in exports	Decrease in exports
	Decrease in imports	Increase in imports

This list is useful in several ways. First, it provides a test of alleged causes of economic expansion or contraction. If someone argues that a certain development will raise national income, one can ask: Which of the expansionist channels is it going to affect? How do we know? Can we be sure that there will not be offsetting (depressing) effects on other items in the table?

Second, it provides a rudimentary basis for economic forecasting.

One can go down the list and ask what will probably happen to each of these quantities over the next year and so build up an estimate of national income. This is a rather primitive technique, but some professional forecasters do little more than this.

Third, it provides a framework for discussion of public policy. Suppose the economy is in depression and the problem is how to get out. One can begin by asking what it might be feasible to do to each item in the expansion column. There may be several levers which can be manipulated with some prospect of success. Having analyzed each of these, one can go on to the problem of choosing which levers to pull.

The problem is not always too little spending. Occasionally in the United States, and more frequently in some other countries, there has been a problem of too much spending, leading to price inflation. The contraction column of the table then becomes pertinent, and one must look down it for ways of reducing spending.

AGGREGATE ECONOMIC EQUILIBRIUM

In Part One we became familiar with the concept of equilibrium in a particular market. In equilibrium, the amount of a product which people are willing to buy at the prevailing price equals the amount which sellers are willing to supply. A similar approach can be used for the economy as a whole. *Aggregate demand* is total spending from all the sources listed above—spending by consumers, businesses, government, and foreign buyers. *Aggregate supply* is the total value of goods and services being produced in the economy. The economy will be in equilibrium, with no tendency to expand or contract, only if aggregate demand and aggregate supply are equal.

If aggregate demand exceeds aggregate supply, an expansion is set in motion. If the economy is operating well below capacity, this will be mainly an increase in production and employment. But as expansion proceeds, some industries approach capacity, and their prices begin to rise. Eventually, one may reach a stage at which the whole economy is operating at capacity and output increases are no longer possible. If aggregate demand still exceeds aggregate supply, the only effect will be a rise in the price level.

If aggregate demand falls short of aggregate supply, a contraction is set in motion. This could take the form of a drop in prices, or a drop in output, or some mixture of the two. In the present American economy, most prices are hard to reduce, partly because it is not feasible to cut wage rates which form the bulk of production costs. Insufficient demand, then, leads mainly to a drop in production and employment.

There is an important difference, however, between reasoning about overall economic equilibrium and reasoning about equilibrium in one market. In dealing with a single market, one can safely assume that *supply and demand are independent.* An increase in production of potatoes will not increase the demand for potatoes. But in analyzing the national economy, the assumption of independence no longer holds. An increase in total output *will* raise incomes, which will lead to an induced rise in spending. Aggregate supply and aggregate demand are interrelated.

A Basic National Income Identity

Let us explore this interrelation by looking at an economy in which business concerns must finance any new investment by borrowing from households. There is no business saving. Government is included, and can run either a budget surplus or a deficit. We ignore foreign trade for the time being, since this would complicate the story without adding anything essential.

Gross national product can be viewed either as total *output* or as total *income.* Thinking first in terms of output, all output must go either into consumption (C), business investment (I), or government purchases (G). Hence we see that

$$GNP \equiv C + I + G.$$

The identity sign $\equiv$ is used to indicate a statement which must be true by definition.

Turn now to the income side and consider all the places where income can go. All the income generated in the course of production is paid over to government in taxes (T), or is saved by households (S), or is spent on consumption (C). So from this standpoint

$$GNP \equiv C + S + T.$$

But since things which are equal to the same thing are equal to one another

$$C + S + T \equiv C + I + G.$$

Canceling out C and shifting T to the right side, we arrive at

$$S \equiv I + (G - T).$$

Saving equals investment plus the government deficit. This is often termed the *basic national income identity.*

If we simplify the economy still further by leaving government out of the picture, this identity reduces to

$$S \equiv I.$$

Saving must equal investment. They are in fact the same thing: the unconsumed part of current output.

The Condition of Aggregate Equilibrium

But if the economy always balances out in this way, how can it ever be out of equilibrium? How can there ever be an expansion or contraction in national income?

The answer lies in a simple but vital distinction between *past transactions* and *future plans*. Our national accounting measurements always refer to a completed period in the past. We close the books at the end of the year and total up consumption, saving, and other key items. We then find that the identities just listed hold good. They *must* be true by the nature of the accounting system, as was explained in Chapter 19.

But suppose that instead of the past we are looking forward to the future. Here we stand on January 1, 1967, considering the movement of the economy over the year ahead. Now instead of *completed investment* we are interested in *planned or intended investment*. Similarly, it is *planned saving, consumption, and government budgets* which are pertinent.

For the rest of this chapter, whenever we use one of the standard national income concepts, we shall use it in its *future or intended* sense. S means *intended saving*, I means *intended investment*, and so on. It is important to grasp and remember this point, since the whole analysis depends upon it.

Can we now continue to maintain that (planned)

$$S = I + (G - T)?$$

By no means. Consider that savings and consumption decisions are made by some 50 million households, with no central coordination. Investment plans are made separately by many thousands of large businesses and millions of smaller ones. Budget plans are made by thousands of state and local units as well as the federal government. These decisions could conceivably add up in such a way that the amount households are planning to save just equals the amount which business concerns and governments are planning to borrow. But this would be no more than an accident, and is in fact very unlikely.

But suppose this accident does occur, and that (planned)

$$S = I + (G - T).$$

What does this mean? The left-hand side shows the amount which households are planning to pull out of the income stream through saving. The right-hand side shows the amount which business and government units are planning to add to the stream by spending beyond their current incomes. Consider the present level of national income as the water level in a tank. Then if the outflow of water through the "savings pipe" is just balanced by the amount pumped in through the "investment pump," the level of the tank will remain unchanged. The system is in equilibrium.

This basic condition for aggregate equilibrium can be met in a variety of ways. Suppose that at the present level of national income households wish to save $100 billion. Thus the equilibrium condition becomes

$$100 = I + (G - T).$$

A little figuring reveals that the economy could be in balance with investment of $100 billion and a balanced government budget; or with investment of $120 billion and a budget surplus of $20 billion; or with investment of $80 billion and a budget deficit of $20 billion; or with any other combination which adds up correctly. Some of these combinations may be considered preferable to others, but they are similar in that any of them would maintain the current level of income unchanged.

Now what happens if the multitude of spending plans do not add up in this way? Suppose that (planned)

$$S > I + (G - T).$$

This means that the amount leaking out through the savings pipe is greater than the amount being added by the investment pump. There is a deficiency of total spending, and the level of income must fall. This means, incidentally, that households will not actually be able to save as much as they had intended, because their incomes will be lower than they expected. This brings out an important principle: If there is a divergence of plans on the two sides of the equation, *the gap is closed by a change in the level of income.*

Suppose the gap is in the other direction. Suppose that (planned)

$$S < I + (G - T).$$

The amount pumped in by business investment and government deficits exceeds the amount drawn off in savings. In this case the level of national income will move upward. As incomes rise, people will save more than they had intended originally. Once more the gap in plans sets up a movement of national income in a direction which tends to close the gap.

In sum,

If $S = I + (G - T)$, the level of income will remain **unchanged.**
If $S > I + (G - T)$, the level of income will **fall.**
If $S < I + (G - T)$, the level of income will **rise.**

THE LEVEL OF NATIONAL INCOME

So far so good. We have seen how a divergence in spending plans can raise or lower the level of national income. But we still have no way of defining what the equilibrium level of income will be at a particular time.

A clarification is necessary here to avoid misunderstanding. In Chapter 19 we drew a careful distinction between gross national product, net national product, and national income. Precise definition of this last term is important if one is really interested in income, and in the division of income into labor and property shares.

But when the man in the street, or even the man in Washington, speaks of "national income," he usually *means* gross national product. This is the significant total if one is interested in changes in national output and employment. At any rate, it is the total with which we are concerned here. What we want is a way of defining the equilibrium level of GNP. But we shall use the term national income as interchangeable with GNP, bowing on this point to popular usage.

The usual approach to the problem is illustrated in Figure 1. On the horizontal axis we lay out GNP, or national output. On the vertical axis we lay out total spending on national output by consumers, businesses, and government.

Now what is the meaning of aggregate equilibrium? It means that producers are able to sell just what they are producing, so that they have no incentive to produce either more or less. The requirement for equilibrium is that *expenditure on national output must equal the cost of national output* (including the "normal" profit with which we became familiar in Part One.) So let's lay out a line, *OO*, running up from the origin at an angle of 45 degrees. At any point on this line, total output and total expenditure are equal. Thus *any position of aggregate equilibrium must lie on OO*. One can regard *OO* as a kind of supply curve, since it shows the conditions under which various levels of production would be forthcoming. If expenditure were $400 billion, then $400 billion of output would be forthcoming on a sustained basis. If, instead of this, expenditure were $500 billion, then $500 billion would be produced; and so on up to the output capacity of the economy. (What happens if demand rises above capacity we leave until the next chapter.)

We set against this on the demand side the expenditure schedule, *EE*. This shows the amount which all spending units will desire to spend at various levels of national income. It refers to *planned* or *intended* spending. *EE* shows planned spending rising as income rises, which seems logical. But note that *spending rises less rapidly than income*, because saving is also increasing. The reasons for drawing *EE* in this way will be explained in a moment.

The logic of *EE* is broadly the same as that of the demand curve for a single product. It is an "iffy" or hypothetical construction, a snapshot of spenders' intentions at a moment of time. It says that *if* at this moment national income were $500 billion, then households, businesses, and governments would want to spend $550 billion. *If*, on the other hand, income were to be $700 billion, spenders would want to spend $650 billion. Since only one such possibility can be realized, only one point on *EE* is pertinent at a particular time.

Aggregate Economic Equilibrium

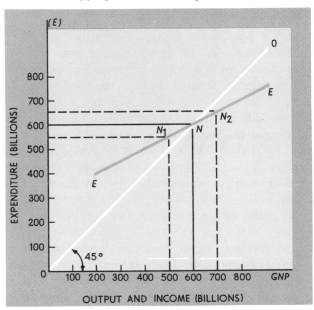

FIGURE 1. At any point on OO expenditure and output are equal. So any equilibrium position must lie on OO. The expenditure schedule *EE* shows planned spending at each level of income. Note that spending rises with income, but less rapidly. The intersection of *EE* and OO at N defines the equilibrium level of income, which is $600 billion.

In constructing *EE*, just as in constructing a demand curve, we assume that certain things are known and constant. For each level of income, we must assume some distribution of personal income among households. (Rich families typically save more than poor ones.) Each household is supposed to know definitely how much it would spend and save at various income levels. Similarly, each business concern and government unit is supposed to have definite spending plans for the period ahead. Monetary conditions and interest rates must be taken as given, since they will affect spending plans. The price level must also be taken as given, so that we can work with "constant dollars." What happens when some of these given conditions change will be explored in later chapters.

Once we know the location of *EE,* we can determine the equilibrium level of national income. The equilibrium is defined by the intersection of *OO* and *EE* at *N.* At this point total spending is $600 billion, and the volume of goods being produced is also $600 billion. So producers can find a market for their current output. Everything will go along smoothly so long as the underlying conditions remain unchanged.

The fact that *N* is an equilibrium position can be shown also by supposing that output is at some other level and asking what will happen. Suppose output were running at only $500 billion per year ($N_1$). Looking across to the expenditure axis, we see that planned expenditure at this income level would be $550 billion, well above the level of current production. This excess demand would give businesses an incentive to expand production, and the system would move to the right toward *N.*

Suppose, on the other hand, that production somehow reached a level of $700 billion ($N_2$). Could this level be sustained? No, it could not, because total expenditure would be only $650 billion. There would be a shortage of demand, unsold goods would pile up, and production would be cut back.

The white arrows on the horizontal axis of Figure 1 indicate that, if actual output is anywhere below the equilibrium level of $600 billion, output will tend to rise. Conversely, if output is above the equilibrium level, it will tend to fall.

Three cautions should be added:

1. There is nothing particularly *good* about equilibrium. It is a position of rest, but not necessarily a desirable position. Point *N* in Figure 1 might turn out to be a long way below the capacity of an economy. Only by a stroke of luck would it coincide with the point of full employment.

2. The fact that the economy at any moment may be regarded as *moving toward* an equilibrium position such as *N* does not mean that it will actually get there. Long before this has happened, *EE* will have changed its location, which means that *N* has also shifted, and the economy then sets off after this new will-of-the-wisp.

3. In a sense, we are not interested in equilibrium positions at all. The main usefulness of Figure 1 is to help in analyzing conditions of *change.* Take the "business cycle." What happens during a recession is that *EE* starts to drop, pulling production down after it. After a while it hits bottom and begins moving upward again. *Question:* How can this wavy up-and-down dance of *EE* be made less violent than it has been in the past?

Those who complain of the sluggishness of the American economy over the past decade are saying that even in the best years, *N* has been below full capacity. *Question:* What could be done to raise *EE* so that it would intersect OO at a higher level, a level corresponding to full employment? These are problems of change, but we need an equilibrium diagram to get at them effectively.

COMPONENTS OF SPENDING: CONSUMPTION

We have now gotten ahead of the game by drawing a schedule for total spending without saying anything about the behavior of different types of spenders. So we must backtrack and look at what determines spending decisions. Let's start for simplicity with an economy consisting only of households and business concerns. All saving is done by households and all investment by business concerns. We leave government on the sidelines, to be brought back into the picture in the next chapter.

The central fact about consumer spending is this: *as GNP rises, consumer spending also rises, but by a smaller amount.* Conversely, a decline in GNP produces a smaller decline in consumer spending.

This result stems from the behavior of individual households. Both logic and observation suggest that when a household receives additional income, *it will spend part but not all of that income.* Some of the added income will go into saving. This tendency was first emphasized by Lord Keynes, who made it a key feature of his theoretical system and coined a new term, *the marginal propensity to consume (MPC).* If a family, on receiving an additional $100, increases its spending by $75, its marginal propensity to consume is 75/100 or 0.75. There is a twin concept, *the marginal propensity to save (MPS),* which in this case would be 25/100 or 0.25. Since all family income must be either saved or spent, the two propensities must add up to 1.

Each household has its own spending schedule, indicating how it would behave at various levels of family income. These schedules have a characteristic shape. Even if income is very low, a family will spend some minimum amount on basic necessities. If necessary, it can spend beyond its income for a while by not paying bills and by borrowing. This is called *dissaving* or *negative saving.*

The consumption schedule of the Jewkes family is shown in Table 1 and Figure 2. Note that to the left of B the family is dissaving. At B, where its income has risen to $6,000 a year, it is just breaking even. Above this level, it begins to make positive savings, shown by the widening gap between CC and the 45 degree line.

The consumption schedule for this family was drawn with a marginal propensity to consume of 2/3. Each increase of $1,000 in income brings increased spending of $667 and increased saving (or reduced dissaving) of $333. Geometrically, the MPC is the *slope* of CC. We have assumed that MPC is constant for all levels of income, so that CC is a straight line. This would not necessarily be true in practice, but it is a useful first approximation.

TABLE 1

Consumption Schedule of the Jewkes Family

(Dollars per Year)

DISPOSABLE INCOME (1)	CONSUMPTION EXPENDITURE (2)	MARGINAL PROPENSITY TO CONSUME (MPC) (3)	AVERAGE PROPENSITY TO CONSUME (APC) (4)	NET SAVING (5)	MARGINAL PROPENSITY TO SAVE (MPS) (6)	AVERAGE PROPENSITY TO SAVE (APS) (7)
0	2,000		.00	−2,000		− 00
		0.667			0.333	
1,000	2,667		2.67	−1,667		−1.67
		0.667			0.333	
2,000	3,333		1.67	−1,333		−0.67
		0.667			0.333	
3,000	4,000		1.33	−1,000		−0.33
		0.667			0.333	
4,000	4,667		1.17	− 667		−0.17
		0.667			0.333	
5,000	5,333		1.07	− 333		−0.07
		0.667			0.333	
6,000	6,000		1.00	0		0.00
		0.667			0.333	
7,000	6,667		0.95	333		0.05
		0.667			0.333	
8,000	7,333		0.92	667		0.08
		0.667			0.333	
9,000	8,000		0.89	1,000		0.11
		0.667			0.333	
10,000	8,667		0.87	1,333		0.13

We can now define an additional term, the *average propensity to consume* (*APC*). This is consumption expenditure as a percentage of income, and is shown in column (4) of Table 1. Similarly, the *average propensity to save* (*APS*) is the percentage of income saved, and appears in column (7). Note that, as we move to the right along *CC*, even though the *marginal* propensity to consume remains constant, the *average* propensity to consume is falling steadily. At the break-even point *B*, the *APC* is 1.0. But at the $10,000 income level, the *APC* is 8,667/10,000 = 0.87. If we went up to an income level of $50,000, and the *MPC* continued unchanged, we should find that the *APC* had fallen to about 0.7.[1]

---

[1] This follows from the equation for the consumption schedule *CC*, which is
$$C = a + bY$$
where *C* is consumption, *Y* is income, *a* is the intercept *OC* on the vertical axis, and *b* is the slope of *CC*. The average propensity to consume is
$$\frac{C}{Y} = \frac{a + bY}{Y} = \frac{a}{Y} + b.$$
Since *a* and *b* are constants, the value of this expression declines as *Y* increases.

This suggests that families in higher-income brackets will typically consume a smaller percentage of their income than families in lower brackets. This will be so even if the high-income families have consumption schedules of the same slope as the poor families, i.e., if *MPC* is the same at all income levels. In actuality, there is considerable evidence that high-income families have not only a lower *APC* but also a lower *MPC* than poor families. Instead of being a straight line throughout, *CC* bends

Consumption Schedule for the Jewkes Family

FIGURE 2. The Jewkes' consumption schedule, CC, shows how much the family would spend at various levels of annual income. To the left of B, that is, below $6,000 a year they spend more than they receive. To the right of B, spending is below income and there is positive saving.

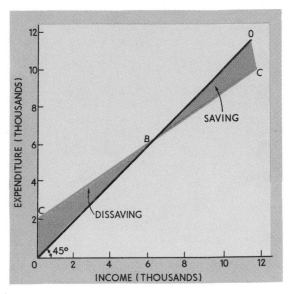

and flattens out as we move to higher incomes.[2] This causes the *APC* to fall even faster than it otherwise would.

The upshot is that, as one goes up the income ladder, one finds families saving not only larger absolute amounts but also a larger proportion of their income. The results of one budget study on this subject are shown in Table 2. Note that families with incomes below $2,000 per year were dissaving. But families with $5,000–$7,500 per year had an *APS* of 12.7 percent, and those with incomes of $10,000 and over had an *APS* of 33.1 percent.

A shift of income from one bracket to another may thus affect total spending and saving in the economy. But here we must be cautious. The fact that high-income families have a lower *APC* is not conclusive. The crucial question is whether they also have a lower *MPC*. We need to

---

[2] See on this point M. Bronfenbrenner, T. Yamane, and C. H. Lee, "A Study in Redistribution and Consumption," *Review of Economics and Statistics*, May, 1955, p. 153 ff. This study shows the *MPC* falling from 0.98 for families with incomes of $2,000–$3,000 to 0.60 for families with incomes about $7,500. It should be emphasized, however, that the issue is still not resolved to everyone's satisfaction.

know what happens to the marginal dollar when it is transferred from one household to another.

Suppose we transfer a dollar from well-to-do Mr. A, who has an *MPC* of 0.6, to Mr. B, a relief client with an *MPC* of 1.0. Mr. A will reduce his saving by 40 cents and his consumption by 60 cents. Mr. B's consumption will rise by the full dollar. So overall, there will be a rise of 40 cents in consumption expenditure and a drop of 40 cents in saving. Such transfers could reduce national savings considerably. Depending on whether one considers oversaving or undersaving a greater threat to the

TABLE 2

Savings-Income Ratios by Income Class, 1950

INCOME AFTER TAXES	AVERAGE INCOME	AVERAGE SAVING	SAVING/INCOME RATIO (Percent)
Under $1,000	574	−316	−55.2
$ 1,000–$1,999	1,510	− 3	− 0.2
$ 2,000–$2,999	2,497	2	0.1
$ 3,000–$3,999	3,486	195	5.6
$ 4,000–$4,999	4,438	404	9.1
$ 5,000–$7,499	5,862	744	12.7
$ 7,500–$9,999	8,837	2,509	28.4
$10,000 and over	16,290	5,392	33.1

Source: Irwin Friend and Stanley Schor, "Who Saves," *Review of Economics and Statistics*, May, 1959, Part 2, p. 217.

economy, one might or might not regard the shift as desirable. In any event, the shape of the *national consumption schedule* depends not only on the schedules for individual households but also on how income is distributed among them.

A possible national consumption schedule is shown in Figure 3. It resembles the household consumption schedule of Figure 2, except that we are now dealing with billions of dollars instead of thousands. Total saving is negative to the left of *B*, zero at *B*, and positive to the right of *B*.

The region to the left of *B* is of little economic importance. It doesn't mean much to say that consumer spending would still be $100 billion even if GNP were zero, because the system would presumably have collapsed before then. The only modern instance of negative total saving occurred at the bottom of the Great Depression in 1932–33.

The main use of both the consumption schedule and the total expenditure schedule is in analyzing short-term fluctuations in GNP. We are usually looking ahead for at most a few years. So we are actually interested in a small section of *CC*, running from moderately below to moderately above the point at which the economy is currently operating.

Before proceeding to business investment, we must pause to explain an apparent paradox. We saw in the Jewkes family case that a *constant MPC* means a *falling APC* as income rises. The shape of *CC* in Figure 3 implies that this is true also for the national economy. As the economy grows and we move to the right on the GNP axis, it seems that the percentage which consumption forms of GNP will fall steadily, while the savings percentage will rise.

The National Consumption Schedule

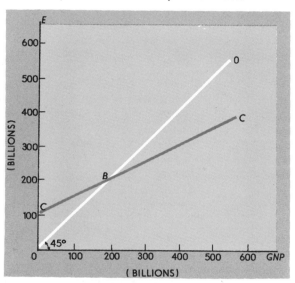

FIGURE 3. The national consumption schedule, CC, shows how much all households in the country would plan to spend at each level of GNP. As in the case of the Jewkes family schedule, there is negative saving to the left of *B*, positive saving to the right of *B*.

When one looks at the statistics, however, one gets a surprise. In the United States since World War II, consumer spending has been consistently close to 0.8 of private available income. So *APC*, the proportion of income consumed, does *not* seem to fall as GNP rises. Indeed, Kuznets' studies indicate that this has been true over a much longer period. He finds that the proportion of national income saved has not changed materially since 1870, though real income has risen several fold since then.

How can we explain this result? The explanation is partly that *CC* in Figure 3 is a very short-run schedule. It is designed to show consumption reactions over a few calendar quarters. Over such short periods, households are quite "set in their ways," and their consumption habits may not respond much to a change in income. A sudden increase in income may go largely into saving, and a drop in income may be offset largely by reduced saving. This amounts to saying that the (short-run) *MPC* may be quite low.

Given a longer period for adjustment, however, people are quite capable of finding ways to use additional income. Former luxuries come to be regarded as necessities, and new products appear to stimulate consumer demand. This gradual increase of living standards in response to rising incomes may be viewed as an *upward shift* of the short-run consumption schedule (Figure 4). The schedule rises from CC to C_1C_1,

The Consumption Schedule Drifts Upward over Time

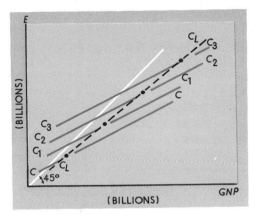

FIGURE 4. CC shows short-run consumption reactions at a particular time. C_1C_1 shows the same reactions ten years later, when people are habituated to higher living standards; and so on. Because of continued upward shifting of the short-run schedule, consumption over the long run follows the path shown by C_LC_L.

then to C_2C_2, and so on into the future. The small circles may be regarded as representing the normal level of income at periods 10 years apart, so that C_3C_3 carries a date 30 years later than CC. When these are linked up, they form the *historical expenditure schedule* C_LC_L.

Why should CC shift upward over the course of time? One hypothesis is that a family's spending depends, not on its *absolute* income, but on its income *relative* to that of other families within its horizon. If the income of every family rises by 20 percent, but they keep the same standing relative to each other, there is no reason why any family should change the distribution of its income between saving and consumption. This competitive aspect of consumption was stressed long ago by Veblen, and has been given more precise form by Duesenberry and others.

The appearance of new products which open up different patterns of consumption is perhaps an important factor. If Americans had their present incomes but could spend these only on 1890 products (an impossible and self-contradictory hypothesis), they would probably spend a smaller percentage of their incomes than they actually do.

Adding more and more horse carriages, kerosene lamps, overstuffed furniture, and ice cream sodas to the family budget would eventually seem unsatisfying. But the ranch-style suburban home, the automobile, aviation, electric applicances, radio and television, and other things have completely transformed consumption standards. The new way of life may or may not be more satisfying than the old. It certainly requires more money and helps sustain the propensity to consume.

The advertising fraternity may be partly responsible for American devotion to consumption. Without the constant whipping up of consumers' appetites by television commercials and other methods, people might spend less than they actually do. (Banks and other savings institutions try to redress the balance by counteradvertising against consumption!) But the inventors and engineers who keep the stream of new products flowing must carry the main responsibility.

COMPONENTS OF SPENDING: INVESTMENT

Gross private investment is now more than $100 billion a year, a substantial part of the GNP total. This item is particularly interesting because, unlike consumer spending, it varies considerably from year to year and is a prominent feature of the "business cycle."

What determines the level of *planned or intended investment* at a particular time? This amounts to asking why businessmen are interested in acquiring new capital goods. The answer is that they expect a monetary return from one or other of two sources: (1) They may acquire capital goods to *increase production capacity*. In this case they must expect that, after selling the additional output and deducting all labor and material costs, there will remain an adequate return on the capital used. (2) They may acquire capital goods to *reduce production costs*, perhaps by substituting machinery for labor or more productive machines for less productive ones. If unit cost is lowered, selling prices remaining unchanged, unit profit and total profit will rise.

These categories of *capacity-oriented investment* and *cost-oriented investment* are not mutually exclusive. The same new piece of equipment will often increase capacity and also lower unit production costs.

We saw in Chapter 11 that, if we know the cost of a capital good, and if we know how much income the good is expected to yield in the future, we can calculate the *percentage rate of return*. For example, building a particular plant might yield an expected return of 20 percent.

There are millions of business concerns in the economy; and at any time they will be considering millions of possible investment projects. Suppose we had in front of us engineering estimates on every last one of these, giving the cost of the new capital and the expected rate of return; and suppose we then ranked the projects from those with highest returns to those with lowest. There would undoubtedly be some investment opportunities with yields of, say, 50 percent or better; and these would absorb a few billions of investment expenditure. If we lower the yardstick to a 40 percent return, some more projects would "pay off," and feasible investment expenditures would be larger. The amount of investment with an expected yield of 30 percent would be still larger; and so on down—if we wish—all the way to zero.

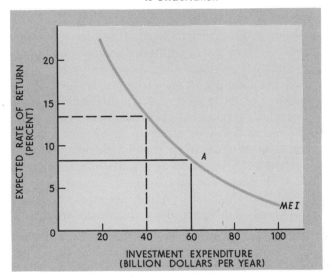

Expected Returns Fall as More Investment Is Undertaken

FIGURE 5. This is the marginal efficiency of investment (*MEI*) schedule for the nation. Point A shows that, if $60 billion of new investment projects were undertaken next year, the least profitable of these projects would yield an expected return of 8 percent. Any other point on *MEI* has the same significance.

In this way we can trace out the marginal efficiency of investment (*MEI*) schedule in Figure 5. This shows, for any level of investment expenditure we select, the expected yield on the last dollar—hence *marginal* efficiency. For example, if $40 billion were spent on new capital goods this year, the marginal efficiency of investment would be 13 percent. As the amount of expenditure increases, marginal efficiency falls, because we are adding projects with lower and lower rates of return.

Given this roster of investment opportunities, how much investment will actually be undertaken this year? It can be argued that this will depend on the market rate of interest. A businessman will carry out an investment project only if the expected return is at least equal to the interest rate. If he borrows money at 8 percent to finance a project yielding only 5 percent, he has made a bad bargain. Even if he is using money saved from the company's profits, he should charge himself the market rate of interest, since he has the alternative of lending the money to someone else. The market rate should be counted as an imputed cost.

If we know the rate of interest, then, we can read off the level of investment from the *MEI* schedule. Suppose the interest rate is 8 percent. Then all projects down to point *A* on the *MEI* schedule will be undertaken, and those below that point will not. The level of planned investment will be about $60 billion.

The proposition that investment depends on the rate of interest, however, has been frequently challenged. It has been argued that many other things will influence the executive's decision: how much money he has available from depreciation allowances and retained profits, how close to capacity his plant is operating, the business outlook for the near future, the riskiness of the projects he is contemplating, and so on. In research studies where businessmen are asked what factors they consider in making investment decisions, the rate of interest is mentioned less frequently than some of these other things. On this ground the skeptics argue (*a*) that the *MEI* schedule at a particular moment is probably quite *inelastic* with respect to the interest rate—it may be almost a vertical line, indicating that just so much investment is in prospect; and (*b*) that the *MEI* schedule shifts about quite violently in the short run because of changes in the business outlook and other factors. The changes in investment we actually observe may be due mainly to *shifts* of the schedule rather than to movements along the same schedule because of interest rate changes.

There is something to both lines of argument. The interest rate is of some importance, particularly at certain times and for certain kinds of investment, and a higher interest rate does cause some reduction of investment plans. But it is also true that the *MEI* schedule undergoes sharp rightward and leftward shifts from time to time, and that numerous factors other than interest affect investment plans. The more important of these deserve brief description.

Risk

It is no accident that the word "expected" recurred frequently in our discussion of investment plans. The return from a prospective investment is always an estimate, not a certainty. It depends on a whole series of subestimates about sales prospects, product prices, factor prices, and production efficiency. So a 20 percent expected return calculated in this way will not be valued as highly as a 20 percent *guaranteed* return on a "sure thing." Depending on the confidence which the executive feels in his estimates,[3] and depending on whether he is temperamentally inclined toward taking risks or prefers to avoid them, he may rate this return as equivalent to only 10 percent on a sure thing, or even 8 percent, or 5 percent. A change in his estimates or attitudes will have more effect on the investment decision than a small variation in the rate of interest.

The risk element explains why businessmen often seem to be demanding exorbitant returns on proposed investments. Businessmen usually talk in terms of the "payout period," that is, the number of years required for the net income from an investment to equal its original cost. A company may have a rule of thumb that new machines must pay for themselves in 3 years, or that a new plant must pay out in 5 years. At first glance these rates of return seem very high. But when we adjust them for the risk that the expected return may not materialize, they are a good deal lower.

Internal Funds

Most of the funds for business investment are accumulated within the company instead of being borrowed through the market. In 1964, for example, new machinery purchases plus new construction (excluding houses) totaled $60.5 billion. In the same year, corporations' depreciation allowances and undistributed profits totaled $53.9 billion. Companies normally prefer internal to external funds. To secure external funds the company must either borrow, in which case it is faced with fixed interest charges, or it must sell new common stock, which "dilutes" the ownership of the existing stockholders and could conceivably risk loss of control of the company.

This aversion to external financing has two consequences. First, most companies rely solely on internal funds. The size of these funds determines, or at least limits, the amount of investment undertaken. It is considered normal that whatever money is at hand should be reinvested in the most promising projects available. Decisions about business saving and business investment are strongly interrelated.

Second, while companies perhaps should take the market rate of interest into account in deciding how to use their internal funds, there is little indication that they actually do so. The interest rate, therefore,

---

[3] The estimation of risk is a highly technical subject, the complexities of which can only be hinted at here. It normally involves, not a single expected rate of return, but a range of possibilities. Suppose there is a 50–50 chance that project A will yield either a 60 percent return or a zero return. Then by a kind of averaging we can say that the estimated return is 30 percent. Suppose project B promises a 1 in 4 chance of a 20 percent return, a 2 in 4 chance of 30 percent, and a 1 in 4 chance of 40 percent. Here, too, the simple average of expected returns is 30 percent. But the two situations are obviously not equivalent. An investor with an aversion to risk will probably choose project B, since the *worst* he can do here is 20 percent, while in the A case his return may fall to zero.

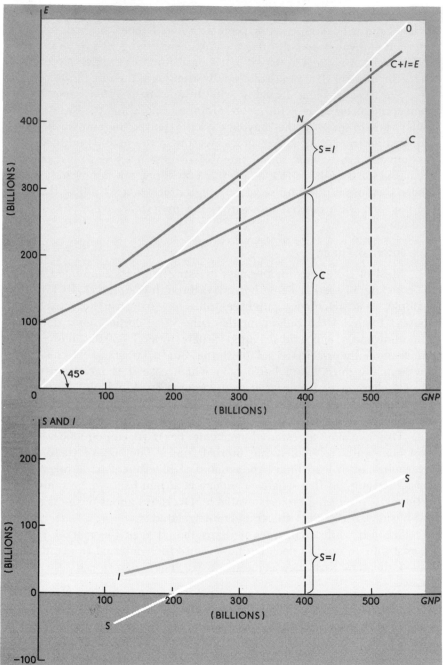

Consumption, Investment, and Equilibrium Income

FIGURE 6. The *lower* panel shows the level of planned investment and intended saving at various levels of income. The economy can be in equilibrium only when these two quantities are equal, that is, at $400 billion. In the *upper* panel we add planned investment to consumption to get the total expenditure schedule, *E*. The intersection of *E* with *OO* at *N* defines the equilibrium level of income, which must of course be the same as that derived by the other method.

affects mainly investors who lack internal funds and must resort to the market. The most important of these groups are: (a) families building houses, who normally make only a small down payment and borrow the remainder; (b) state and local governments, which float bond issues to cover large projects such as highways, water and sewerage systems, schools, and other public buildings; and (c) businesses which, for one reason or another, want to invest more than their internal resources allow. This includes small businesses just getting started, companies in rapidly expanding industries which have unusually large investment needs, and public utilities whose earnings are regulated by government. Whenever would-be investors must resort to the market, the interest rate is likely to have some effect on their plans.

The Level of National Income

The level of national income, and its rate of increase in the recent past, also affects the volume of planned investment. There are several reasons for this. First, at a higher level of income more industries will be producing close to capacity; and this raises the question whether it would not be wise to increase capacity. If a company fails to expand at the right time, or at the same rate as competitors in the industry, it may lose in competitive position over the long run. Second, a rising level of sales tends to be projected into the future. High demand generates an atmosphere of optimism and a willingness to take major investment decisions. Conversely, during recession businessmen turn pessimistic and postpone investment projects. Third, as national income rises, business profits and retained earnings also rise; and we have just seen that these internal funds are the main source of finance for new investment. As businesses find themselves with more money in hand, they become more willing to increase their investment plans.

This has a bearing on how we should draw the investment schedule in our national income diagrams. If the interest rate were really all that mattered, and if the interest rate were at a certain level, then the level of planned investment would be fixed. The investment schedule would be a horizontal straight line. But if investment plans depend partly on the level of GNP itself, then the investment schedule will be tilted upward as we have drawn it in Figure 6, indicating that a higher level of GNP corresponds to a higher level of planned investment.

EQUILIBRIUM IN THE NO-GOVERNMENT ECONOMY

In our simplified economy, the consumption schedule and the investment schedule provide all the information we need to determine the equilibrium level of national income. This can be explained in either of two ways, which come to the same thing, and are sketched in the upper and lower panels of Figure 6.

The upper panel is laid out in the same way as Figure 1. The horizontal axis shows total output. The vertical axis shows total expenditure, which consists of consumer spending and investment spending. First we draw in the national consumption schedule from Figure 3. Now add on top of this the amount which business concerns will plan to invest at each level of income. This gives us the $C + I$ line, which shows how much will be spent on consumption and investment together.

By the reasoning used for Figure 1, equilibrium income is defined by point N. Only at this point will total spending just cover the cost of the goods and services being produced. If output were either higher or lower, one can show that the system is not in balance and will move back toward N.

The same information is shown from a different viewpoint in the lower panel of Figure 6. Instead of the consumption schedule, we draw here its twin, the saving schedule SS. Note that the point of zero saving in the lower panel lies directly below the break-even point of the consumption schedule in the upper panel. To the left of this point, saving is negative, and to the right it is positive.

Now draw in the investment schedule II, showing planned investment at each level of national income. Note that the height of this schedule above the horizontal axis in the lower panel is equal to the distance between C and $C + I$ in the upper panel.

In this simple economy without government, the requirement for aggregate equilibrium is that (planned)

$$I = S.$$

Thus the equilibrium income level is defined by the intersection of SS and II, which occurs at $400 billion. This is the same result reached in the upper panel, and this must be so, since the two diagrams rest on the same basic data.

In equilibrium, then, output $= $400 billion, consumption $= $300 billion, and saving $=$ investment $= $100 billion. The savings drain is exactly matched by the volume of planned investment, and all is in order.

Thrift: Private Virtue A Public Vice?

In the American tradition, saving is a Good Thing. This despite the constant effort of advertisers and finance companies to separate the consumer from his dollars and to encourage indebtedness.

Can what is good for the individual be bad for society? Two centuries ago Bernard de Mandeville, in his *Fable of the Bees*, asserted that the lavish spending of the French courtiers was socially valuable because it provided employment for great numbers of jewelers, perfumers, dressmakers, and wine producers. If the nobles ever learned to save their money, this employment would be lost and the French economy would fall into stagnation. More recently, many economists have been concerned about the possibility of "oversaving." If people save too much, it is said, there may be insufficient demand leading to general depression.

Who is right? Should saving be encouraged or discouraged? The problem can be analyzed by using the ideas we have just developed. In Figure 7 we have drawn the saving schedule, SS, just as it looks in the

The Economic Consequences of Thrift

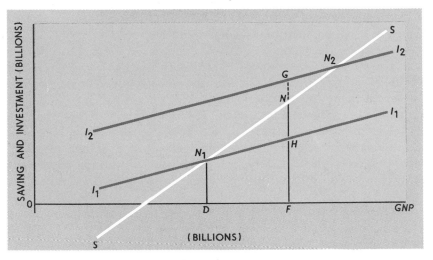

FIGURE 7. Suppose the saving schedule has the position SS, and that OF constitutes full employment. Then if the investment schedule is I_1I_1, the propensity to save is excessive. The level of income will be only OD, and people will actually be able to save only N_1D instead of the NF which they would like to save at full employment. Conversely, if the investment schedule is I_2I_2, the propensity to save is insufficient, and inflation will follow.

lower panel of Figure 6. We need also to define the output capacity of the economy, the output corresponding to "full employment." Suppose this is OF. Then if income were at this level, the amount people would plan to save is NF.

Now, depending on the level of planned investment, this propensity to save may be either excessive or insufficient. Suppose the investment schedule is located at I_1I_1. If under these conditions people try to save NF, this is too much in the light of the planned investment of HF. As a matter of fact, they will not be able to save NF. If they try, planned saving will exceed planned investment. Output and income will fall, until the system reaches equilibrium at N_1. Because income is lower, actual savings will be only N_1D.

This underlines an important principle: How much people actually save does not depend just on how much they would like to save. If they try to save too much (relative to planned investment), national income will fall and they will end up saving less than they desired. This is sometimes called *the paradox of thrift*.

An opposite situation exists if the investment schedule is I_2I_2. Here there is undersaving in the sense that, at full employment, the amount saved (NF) falls short of what businessmen wish to invest (GF). This will mean an inflationary expansion of the economy, with rising prices but little increase in output. This can be prevented only by forcing down the investment schedule so that it intersects the savings schedule at N, or by raising the savings schedule so that it cuts the investment schedule at G. In this situation, increased saving would help to combat inflation and would benefit the economy as well as the individual.

The United States, Britain, and Western Europe seem to have been in this position frequently during the nineteenth century. Business investment plans often ran ahead of available savings, leading to complaints of a "shortage of capital." This doubtless helped to strengthen the belief that thrift is a civic as well as a personal virtue. Nor is this belief, and the circumstances which justified it, a matter of ancient history. Since World War II, many of the Western industrial nations have been chronically short of savings, not to mention the more acute shortages in the less developed countries.

Thus to the question "Would an increase in thrift help or hurt the economy?" one can only answer, "It all depends." It depends heavily on the level of planned investment at the time and place in question.

Saving and Investment: Equal or Unequal?

We have emphasized that there is no need for *planned* saving to equal *planned* investment. Yet we have also said that, looking back at any past period, saving and investment are necessarily equal. How can these statements both be true?

Suppose the economy last year produced $400 billion of output, with saving and investment balanced at $100 billion and consumption at $300 billion. For next year, households, expecting the same income, plan to spend and save as before. But business concerns reduce their planned investment for next year to $80 billion. Aggregate demand falls from $400 billion to $380 billion. Producers, not realizing this, go ahead and produce $400 billion of output, and are unpleasantly surprised to find that they can sell only $380 billion. What happens to the remaining $20 billion? It sits in the warehouse, forming an (unintended) addition to business inventories.

When we compile the national accounts at the end of the year, what shall we find? GNP is $400 billion. Realized saving is $100 billion. *But realized investment is also $100 billion*—$80 billion of intended investment plus $20 billion of unintended investment in inventories. So, looking backward, S and I balance out. This is not a satisfactory balance, however, for producers will not like to see unsold goods piling up in inventories. As they become aware that aggregate demand has fallen, they will reduce their production plans for next period, and GNP will move downward.

Suppose the opposite happens. Planned investment for next year is raised from $100 billion to $120 billion. Aggregate demand rises from $400 billion to $420 billion. Then producers will be pleasantly surprised to find that they can sell more than the $400 billion of goods they are currently producing. Where will they get the extra $20 billion of goods? By taking them out of inventories. This $20 billion reduction in inventories is a negative investment, or *disinvestment*. Once more, looking backward, realized S = realized I = planned I − unintended inventory disinvestment:

$$100 = 100 = 120 - 20 \, .$$

For the next period, producers will increase their output plans, and GNP will move upward.

For any past period, then, realized S and I must be equal. Any gap in plans at the beginning of the period is closed by an unplanned increase or decrease in inventories, which serve as a buffer. This *ex post* equality of S and I does *not* mean that the economy is in equilibrium. It is in equilibrium only when planned S and I are equal, when plans are fully realized, and when unintended inventory changes are zero. Any surprises, pleasant or unpleasant, lead to an upward or downward movement of GNP.

SUMMARY

1. An *induced* change in spending is one which occurs in response to a prior change in income. An *autonomous* change is independent of any change in income. Autonomous changes are of primary importance in explaining a rise or fall in national income.

2. Autonomous changes are particularly likely to occur in business spending on plant and equipment, inventions, and construction. But they can occur also in the consumer, government, or foreign trade sectors.

3. The economy is in equilibrium only if total spending from all sources equals the cost of the goods and services being produced. Canceling out consumption from both sides, we can show that equilibrium requires that

$$S = I + (G - T) \, .$$

The amount being drained out of the income stream through saving must be offset by an equal amount pumped in through investment and/or a deficit in the government budget.

4. This condition is always satisfied for any *past* period, since the rules of national income accounting ensure that income and product will be equal. But it is not necessarily satisfied if the terms are re-defined to mean *plans* for a future period.

5. If *planned*

$$S > I + (G - T)$$

there will be a deficiency of spending in the next period and national income will fall. Similarly, if *planned*

$$S < I + (G - T)$$

spending will exceed the value of current output, so output and/or prices will rise. There is an expansion of national income.

6. To define the equilibrium point precisely, we construct a diagram on which the vertical axis shows total (planned or intended) expenditure, and the horizontal axis shows gross national product. We lay out a line *OO* running up from the origin at an angle of 45 degrees, at any point on which total spending and total output are equal. Thus *any equilibrium position for the economy must lie on OO.* We also lay out an expenditure schedule *EE*, which shows the amount of planned expenditure at each level of national income. Since spending rises less rapidly than income, *EE* slopes upward less steeply than *OO*, hence must intersect it. *The intersection of EE and OO defines the equilibrium level of national income.*

7. The expenditure schedule is made up of several components: a *consumption schedule,* an *investment schedule,* a *government expenditure schedule,* and a *net foreign trade schedule.*

8. The *national consumption schedule* depends on the consumption schedules of individual households and on the distribution of income among them. There has been considerable debate, but no final agreement, on whether greater equality of incomes raises or lowers the consumption schedule.

9. The fraction of any increase in income which goes into increased consumption is termed the *marginal propensity to consume.* The fraction going to increased saving is the *marginal propensity to save.* Since all income must be spent or saved, *MPC* and *MPS* add up to 1. The *MPC* is the same thing as the slope of the consumption schedule.

10. The proportion of total income spent is the *average propensity to consume;* and the proportion saved is the *average propensity to save.* The *APC* and the *APS* must also add up to 1. Be sure you understand why a *constant MPC* means a *declining APC* as income rises.

11. The (short-run) consumption schedule, as usually drawn, shows *APC* decreasing and *APS* increasing as income rises. Yet when we look at statistics over long periods we find that the percentage of income saved has remained roughly constant. Given time, people find ways of spending their larger incomes, and the national consumption schedule keeps shifting upward.

12. The *marginal efficiency of investment* (*MEI*) schedule shows, for any level of investment expenditure which might be undertaken in the next period, the expected rate of return on the last dollar of investment. How much investment will actually be undertaken depends partly on the rate of interest; but it is influenced also by availability of internal funds and by the level of national income.

13. In a simplified, no-government economy, the equilibrium level of national income can be defined either by the intersection of *EE* with the 45-degree line, or by the intersection of the *S* and *I* schedules. Given the position of the *I* schedule, there is only one position of the *S* schedule which will result in full employment for the economy. The actual *S* schedule at any time may be higher than this ("oversaving") or lower than this ("undersaving").

DISCUSSION QUESTIONS

1. What is the difference between *autonomous* changes and *induced* changes in spending? Why can only the former be used to explain changes in the level of national income?

2. List the possible types of autonomous change in spending. Which of these are most important in the American economy at present?

3. In what sense is it always true that

$$S = I + (G - T)?$$

4. What happens if planned *S* does not equal planned $I + (G - T)$?

5. What is the meaning of the *EE* and *OO* lines in the national income diagram? Why will the economy be in equilibrium only at the intersection of these lines?

6. What is the meaning of the *consumption schedule* for an individual family? What is the *marginal propensity to consume*? The *average propensity to consume*?

7. Assume we know the consumption schedule for each family in the economy. What else must we know in order to construct the national consumption schedule?

8. The consumption schedule suggests that, as national income rises, the percentage of income saved will also rise. The national income of the United States has risen greatly over the past century, yet the percentage of income saved has remained about the same. Can you explain this apparent contradiction?

9. Distinguish clearly between the meaning of the *MEI* schedule in Figure 5 and the *I* schedule in Figure 6. How will the shape and location of the former affect the latter?

10. Sketch two different ways of showing aggregate equilibrium in a simplified economy without government. Why do these come to the same thing?

11. During the Great Depression of the thirties, it was argued that the American economy suffers from a chronic tendency toward oversaving, and that the saving schedule should be lowered by heavier taxes on large incomes and other devices. How would you evaluate this argument in the light of experience since 1940?

12. Explain how inventory changes operate to produce equality of *realized* saving and investment despite discrepancies in planned *S* and *I*. Using this reasoning, can you predict how business inventories might be expected to behave
   a) In the first few months of a business recession?
   b) In the first few months of a business upswing?

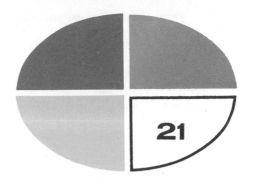

The Level of National

Income (Continued)

Money, the life blood of the nation,
Corrupts and stagnates in the veins
Unless a proper circulation
Its motion and its beat maintains.
JONATHAN SWIFT (*1720*)

THE SIMPLIFIED ECONOMY of Chapter 20 is not a close approximation to the actual American economy for several reasons. First, saving decisions are made by businesses as well as households, and much of the money needed for investment comes from business saving. Second, government expenditures are a substantial part of total demand; and tax payments to government determine how much income businesses and households have left to spend. So we must consider how government can be fitted into the picture. Third, we have not yet taken account of the existence of international trade.

The first new element, business saving, is large and important. In 1964, household saving was $26.3 billion. Corporate depreciation allowances in this year were $34.0 billion and undistributed profits were $19.9, yielding *gross business saving* of $53.9 billion.

It is quite easy, however, to fit business saving into the framework of our previous analysis. We simply redefine saving to mean household saving *plus business saving;* and we draw the national consumption and saving schedules on this basis. How will this affect the position of the schedules? Suppose that the funds which businesses now save and reinvest were all paid out as dividends to stockholders, and the stockholders could decide how to use this income. Would total saving be as high as it is now? It seems unlikely that it would. If this surmise is correct, the existence of business saving increases total saving and reduces consumption, i.e., lowers the level of the consumption schedule.

COMPLETING THE PICTURE: THE IMPACT OF GOVERNMENT

Taxation affects the consumption schedule in the same way as business saving but even more heavily because of the size of the tax "take." Government tax collections rise as GNP rises, because most taxes are related directly or indirectly to income. This is true most obviously of the personal and corporate income taxes. But revenues from excise and sales taxes will also increase, since production and sales are rising.

Let's assume as a first approximation that taxes take the same percentage of any increase in GNP, and let's define this as the *marginal rate of taxation* (*MRT*). If the *MRT* in a particular instance were 0.3, the effect of a billion dollar increase in GNP might be as follows:

GNP increases	$1,000 million
Of which taxes take	300
Leaving an increase in private disposable income of	700
Out of this businesses save	100
Leaving an addition to consumer income of	600
Of which consumers save	100
And increase consumption expenditures by	500

While these figures are simply illustrative, they are perhaps not far from the mark for the American economy at present. They explain why it is plausible to draw a national consumption schedule with a slope of only 1:2. At first glance this seems odd. Surely if consumers get their hands on an extra billion of income, they will want to spend more than half of it. But remember that we are here relating the level of consumption to *the level of GNP*. A large part of any increase in GNP is drained off by taxation and business saving without reaching the consumer.

While government drains off income through taxation, it adds to the flow of income through its expenditure programs. Next to consumers, government is the largest buyer of goods and services. Government spending is typically planned well in advance—in the case of the federal government, 12 to 18 months in advance. Most state legislatures meet bienially and approve expenditures for 2 years ahead. Government expenditure (G) can thus be taken as independent of short-run fluctuations in national income. When we add it on top of consumer spending and investment spending, as in Figure 1, we get a new total expenditure line $(C + I + G)$. This runs parallel to the $(C + I)$ line, the vertical

Equilibrium Income with Government Included

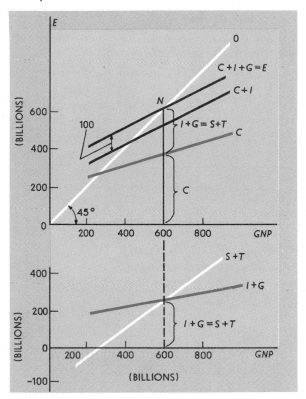

FIGURE 1. The upper panel shows how we build up the expenditure schedule, E, by adding C, I, and G. The equilibrium level of national income is determined by the intersection of E with the 45-degree line at N. Only at this point is the amount drained from the income stream by S and T just offset by the amount pumped in from I and G. When we chart $S + T$ and $I + G$ in the lower panel, their intersection must lie directly under the equilibrium point derived in the upper panel, at a GNP level of $600 billion.

distance of $100 billion between them representing the constant volume of government expenditure.

We can now draw a picture of national income determination with government included (Figure 1). The logic of this is just the same as that of Figure 6 in Chapter 20, so little explanation is required.

First we draw in the consumption schedule, C, remembering now that its slope depends on taxation and business saving as well as household saving. The "gap" between C and the 45-degree line at any GNP level is

$$S_h + S_b + T, \text{ or } S + T \text{ for short}.$$

Note that the gap widens rapidly as GNP rises.

Next we add the investment schedule, I, and finally the government expenditure schedule, to arrive at the total expenditure schedule $E = C + I + G$. By the reasoning used earlier, we can show that the system will be in balance only at N, that is, at a GNP of $600 billion. Only at this point will the total amount which spenders plan to spend equal the value of output which producers plan to produce.

A second view of equilibrium is shown in the lower panel of Figure 1. Here the $S + T$ line shows the gap between consumer spending and GNP at each level of GNP. It shows, in other words, how much spending must come *from some other source* if a certain level of GNP is to be maintained. The $I + G$ line shows how much additional spending will actually be forthcoming.

But we saw in Chapter 20 that the economy will be in equilibrium only if the amount of income which vanishes down the $S + T$ drain is offset by the amount coming in through the $I + G$ pump. The basic condition of equilibrium is that (planned)

$$S + T = I + G.$$

This will be true only where the $S + T$ and $I + G$ lines intersect, and this must accordingly be the equilibrium level of GNP. The equilibrium level in the two panels of Figure 1 is necessarily the same, since they are based on the same information.

This conclusion is both more realistic and less discouraging than the $S = I$ condition stated at the end of Chapter 20. There it looked as though, if the amount which people choose to save at full employment exceeds the amount which businesses are willing to invest, the economy is in trouble. Full employment cannot be maintained. But with government in the picture there are additional possibilities. If aggregate demand is too low to permit full employment, taxes can be cut, which will raise C and probably I as well. Another possibility is that government may borrow and use some of the savings which business is unable to use. This happens on a substantial scale in the United States. State and local governments typically borrow upward of $5 billion a year, and the federal government is also a net borrower in most years.

In short, if the relation of S and I is not satisfactory, government can try to raise GNP by manipulating G and T. The art of doing this is called *fiscal policy,* and will be examined in next chapter.

COMPLETING THE PICTURE: THE IMPACT
OF FOREIGN TRADE

In the United States, exports and imports form only a small percentage of GNP. We are a largely self-contained or "closed" economy. Most other economies, partly because they are smaller and less diversified, depend more heavily on foreign trade. So we must indicate briefly the effect of trade in an "open" economy.

When a country engages in trade, the supply of goods available to it includes imports (M) as well as domestic production; and aggregate demand includes foreign demand for the country's exports (X). The GNP identity thus becomes

$$Y + M \equiv C + I + G + X, \text{ or}$$
$$Y \equiv C + I + G + (X - M), \text{ or}$$
$$C + S + T \equiv C + I + G + (X - M).$$

And the condition for aggregate equilibrium is that (planned)

$$S = I + (G - T) + (X - M).$$

If $(X - M)$ is positive, that is, if we are shipping abroad more goods than we are getting in return, we must be extending credit to other countries. We are engaging in *foreign investment,* and the size of $(X - M)$ measures the amount of this investment. The offsets to domestic savings now include *domestic investment plus the government deficit plus foreign investment.*

How will exports and imports vary with changes in GNP? What is the shape of the *export and import schedules?* Exports are usually taken as determined solely by the level of demand in foreign countries and as independent of the country's own output. So the export schedule is drawn as a horizontal straight line, like X in Figure 2.

Imports, on the other hand, clearly are not independent of GNP. A higher level of national income will raise demand not only for goods produced at home but for imported goods. As GNP rises, imports will also rise. The import schedule, M in Figure 2, slopes upward to the right. The relation between a small increase in GNP and the resulting increase in imports is called the *marginal propensity to import* (MPM). If a billion-dollar increase in GNP raises M by $50 million, the MPM is $50/1000 = 0.05$. The MPM is the slope of the import schedule just as the MPC is the slope of the consumption schedule.

The MPM for the United States at present is estimated at about 0.04. A dollar rise in income means an extra 4 cents spent on foreign goods. For small countries which are more heavily engaged in foreign trade, however, the MPM is considerably higher.

Imports, like taxation and savings, constitute a *leakage* from the domestic income stream. If national output and income rise by a billion dollars, some is drained off into extra purchases of foreign goods, hence is not available to purchase domestic output. The import drain, like the tax and savings drains, acts as a brake on any expansion of GNP; and the higher the *MPM*, the harder the brake takes hold.

The *X* and *M* schedules are subject to shifts over the course of time; and it is easy to see how these shifts will affect the equilibrium level of GNP. A rise in *X* adds to aggregate demand and raises the equilibrium level of GNP, while a fall in *X* reduces it. When we come to imports, the relation is reversed. A *drop* in *M raises* demand for domestic output. A drop in *M* indicates decreased willingness to spend money on foreign goods, which amounts to a shift of demand toward domestic products.

Changes in GNP Alter a Nation's Trade Balance

FIGURE 2. The export schedule, *X*, depends on foreign demand and can be regarded as independent of the country's own GNP. Imports rise as GNP rises, however, so M slopes upward. The slope of M indicates the country's marginal propensity to import *(MPM)*. At higher GNP levels the country may have a trade deficit rather than a surplus.

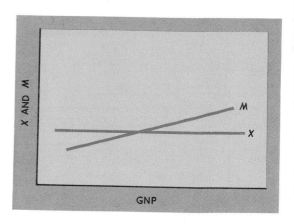

This creates a serious temptation for a country during depression periods. *M* can always be forced down by tariffs, import quotas, and other devices to shut out foreign goods. So if country A has heavy unemployment, shutting out imports may seem a promising way of raising demand for local goods and stimulating recovery. Such a policy will, of course, reduce output and employment in the other countries which formerly sold to country A. So it amounts to a policy of "exporting unemployment" or "beggar my neighbor." Moreover, it may not work for long, because other countries can play the same game if they want to. They can offset the drop in their exports to country A by restricting their imports from A. As everyone gets into the import-restriction game, there will be a general decline in world trade, with no one's export surplus improved and no one's unemployment problem solved. This is what happened during the Great Depression of the thirties, when import restrictions multiplied and world trade shrank catastrophically.

CHANGES IN SPENDING: THE MULTIPLIER

To construct an aggregate expenditure schedule, we assume that the underlying C, I, G, X, and M schedules are known and constant. But actually they are jumping about all the time, and so the expenditure schedule is continually shifting. What happens when the expenditure schedule moves up or down? How much, and how quickly, will this alter the equilibrium level of GNP?

Effect of a Shift in the Expenditure Schedule

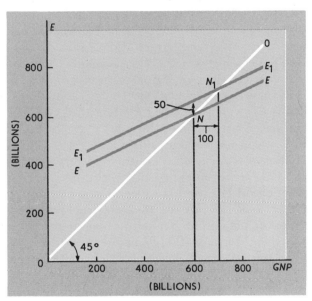

FIGURE 3. Here a rise of $50 billion in planned spending, from *EE* to *E₁E₁*, raises the equilibrium level of income by $100 billion. This is termed *the multiplier effect*. The size of the multiplier depends on the slope of *EE*, which is termed the *marginal propensity to spend*. The steeper the slope of *EE*, the larger the multiplier.

To see why the expenditure schedule may shift, one need only refer to the list of spending decisions given early in Chapter 20. Any autonomous change in spending plans—in the consumer, business, government, or foreign sectors—will change the expenditure schedule. Such changes are occurring all the time, and so the expenditure schedule is constantly changing position.

What does this do to the equilibrium level of national income? Clearly, a rise in the expenditure schedule will tend to *raise* the level of income, while a drop in the schedule will *lower* it.

The effect is illustrated in Figure 3. We start from an expenditure schedule EE. Suppose for one reason or another the schedule shifts upward by \$50 billion to E_1E_1. It now intersects OO at a higher level, N_1. National income will begin to rise, and expansion will continue until a new equilibrium has been reached at \$700 billion.

Now note a curious thing: the increase in spending which set off the process was only \$50 billion. But the result is to raise the level of income by \$100 billion. The original impact has been *multiplied* by 2 in the course of transmission. How did this happen? And why did the *multiplier* turn out to be 2 rather than some other figure?

In terms of geometry, the answer lies in the slope of EE. Both EE and E_1E_1 were drawn with a slope of 1:2. So a vertical distance of 50 units corresponds to a horizontal distance of 100. Experimenting with a pencil will convince you that if the slope of EE were steeper than this, the multiplier effect would be larger. Conversely, if the slope were smaller, the multiplier effect would also be smaller.

But what does the slope of EE mean in economic terms? It shows *the increase in spending which will accompany a specified increase in income*. Drawing EE with a slope of 1:2 means that a dollar (horizontal) increase in income is accompanied by a 50 cent (vertical) increase in spending. This ratio of increased spending to increased income is termed *the marginal propensity to spend;* and its size determines the size of the multiplier effect. A higher marginal propensity to spend, which would mean a steeper slope of EE, would produce a larger multiplier.

What determines the size of the marginal propensity to spend? Suppose an expansion of output generates an additional dollar of income. Will this whole dollar be respent on domestic production? No, it will not, because parts of the dollar will "leak away" in various directions. Part of it will be drained off by taxation, some will go into savings, and some will be spent on imported goods.

Suppose the marginal rate of taxation (MRT) is 0.25. Then out of an additional dollar of income only $1 - MRT = \$0.75$ will become available as private income; and only part of this will be spent on consumption. Suppose the marginal propensity to consume (MPC) is 0.7. Part of this increased spending will be on imported goods. Suppose the marginal propensity to import (MPM) is 0.033.

Then out of an additional dollar of income there will be respent on domestic goods only

$$(1 - MRT)\,(MPC - MPM) = (1 - 0.25)\,(0.70 - 0.033)$$
$$= 0.75 \times 0.667$$
$$= 0.50 \,.$$

The marginal propensity to spend is one half.

There is a simple relation between the size of the marginal propensity to spend and the size of the multiplier. If we indicate the multiplier by M, we find that

$$M = \frac{1}{1 - \text{marginal propensity to spend}}$$

$$= \frac{1}{1 - (1 - MRT)(MPC - MPM)}.$$

This says that the *larger* the marginal propensity to spend, the *larger* will be the multiplier effects of an autonomous increase in spending. Put differently, the *smaller* are the leakages into savings, tax collections, and imports, the *larger* the multiplier will be.

ANOTHER VIEW OF THE MULTIPLIER

The logic of this may become clearer if we consider the multiplier as operating (as it actually does operate) *over the course of time.* Start with an equilibrium situation in which the economy is running along at an even level. Now suppose there is an autonomous rise in spending of $1 billion per calendar quarter because of, say, an increase in planned investment. If investment was previously running at $10 billion per quarter, it now becomes $11 billion. And suppose that the new level of $11 billion is maintained quarter after quarter into the future.

What happens next? The $1 billion is received by companies producing new plant and equipment, who pay out most of it to their workers, suppliers, and stockholders. But they may save some of it, and they pay something to the government in corporate income taxes. The workers and stockholders also spend part of what they get, save part, and pay part in taxes. Altogether, then, how much of the original $1 billion will come back into the market on the next round? If we continue with the illustrative figures used above, in which the marginal propensity to spend was one half, the answer is that there will be $0.5 billion of new spending.

This $0.5 billion goes from retailer to wholesaler to manufacturer, leads to production of additional goods, and finally gets passed out again as income. If the marginal propensity to spend has remained unchanged, on the next round there will be additional spending of half the $0.5 billion, or $.25 billion. This money then goes whizzing around the system and reappears as $0.25 billion of income in the next round. People proceed to spend half of this $0.25 billion, and so on and on.

How much income will finally result from the original $1 billion of new investment? The amount, in billions, is

$$1 + 0.5 + 0.5^2 + 0.5^3 + \ldots .$$

By the formula for an infinite geometric progression, this sums up to

$$\frac{1}{1 - 0.5} = \frac{1}{0.5} = 2 .$$

Thus an autonomous increase of one dollar in spending eventually adds two dollars to national income. And a *permanent* rise of $1 billion in the level of planned spending raises the equilibrium level of national income by $2 billion.[1]

How long does the multiplier process take to work itself out? By adding $1 + 0.5 + 0.25 + 0.125 = 1.875$, we find that more than 90 percent of the impact will be felt during the first four rounds. But how long is a "round," in actual calendar time? This depends on how long it takes for money to travel the circuit from consumers through the business system and back to consumers again. In the United States, this period seems to be something like three months, so that it is roughly correct to

Operation of the Multiplier over Time

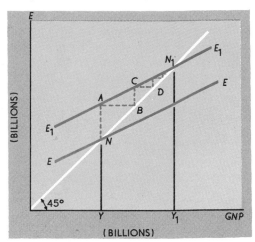

FIGURE 4. In practice the multiplier takes time to work out its effects. An increase in planned spending of NA this quarter generates increased income of AB next quarter, which leads to additional spending of BC in the following quarter; and so on. Thus the economy gradually approaches the new equilibrium at N_1.

take each round as equal to a calendar quarter. Most of the impact of an autonomous increase in spending will be felt within the first year after it occurs.

This version of the multiplier is illustrated in Figure 4, where the dotted lines trace the process of adjustment. The initial increase in spending, NA, goes chasing through the economy and reappears as an equal amount of income, AB. Half of this amount is respent, so there is a new wave of spending, $BC = \frac{1}{2}AB$. This goes through the circuit and comes out as a second round of new income, $CD = BC$. Half of this income is respent, and so on and on, bringing the economy closer on each round to the new equilibrium at N_1.

---

[1] Suppose that planned investment rose by $1 billion for only one quarter and then returned to its previous level. What would happen? The income effect of this one-shot increase would gradually dwindle, and after a few rounds would have become insignificant. For the level of national income to be raised *permanently*, the increase in planned spending must also be permanent.

This analysis supposes that *EE*, after having shifted upward, sits quietly for a year or two while the economy adjusts to the new equilibrium. This is unlikely to happen in practice. Long before N_1 has been reached, the expenditure schedule will have shifted once more, and the economy will be off chasing its tail toward some new equilibrium. This method of reasoning is nevertheless useful. It tells us the *direction of movement* which will be induced by a shift in *EE*, and something about the size and speed of the movement.

The multiplier operates downward as well as upward. A drop in planned spending by consumers, business, or government will set off a more than proportionate decline in income. In the present illustration, income would fall by twice the initial drop in spending. This is part of the story of what happens in a business recession.

EMPLOYMENT: FULL, LESS THAN FULL, AND OVERFULL

So far we have not tried to appraise the equilibrium positions described in our diagrams. Equilibrium has been treated simply as a fact, as showing what is "in the cards" for the economy. But the outcome is not a matter of indifference. Some levels of national income are more desirable than others.

It is generally agreed that the economy should operate close to capacity. It should make full use of available supplies of labor, capital, and other resources. Since plant and equipment is diversified, it is hard to sum up this element in productive capacity. It is easier to add up the national labor supply, and so we tend to judge the use of our capacity by the percentage of the labor force employed. There is also a humanitarian reason for concentrating on utilization of human capacity. An idle machine may reduce national output, but the machine is not annoyed. An unemployed worker does suffer feelings of worthlessness, failure, and insecurity. Thus a high level of employment is a natural objective for any society.

How much employment do we want? "Full employment" is the standard phrase. But how full is "full"? It is not feasible for everyone in the country to be at work every day. We must allow for normal labor turnover—people laid off who must find new jobs elsewhere, people changing jobs of their own accord, and young people seeking work for the first time. Hunting jobs takes time, and so a certain proportion of the labor force is always "unemployed between jobs." This unavoidable minimum is usually termed *frictional unemployment.*

Frictional unemployment in the United States is often estimated at about 4 percent of the labor force. Thus "full employment" will be reached when 96 percent of the labor force is at work. *NF* in Figure 5 indicates the output level corresponding to this volume of employment, which is assumed to be $600 billion.

Defining full employment, however, is a far cry from *attaining* it. Where the economy will actually operate depends on the position of the expenditure schedule. *EE* might intersect *OO* precisely at *N*, so that equilibrium would be reached at full employment. This would be a happy coincidence. But it is more likely that *EE* will lie above or below this ideal location.

Full Employment and Alternative Levels

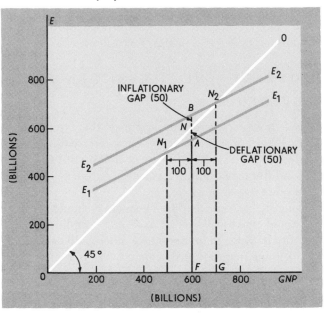

FIGURE 5. At *OF*, with GNP of $600 billion, there would be full employment. But if the expenditure schedule is in the position E_1E_1 there will be a spending deficiency or *deflationary gap* of $50 billion; and because of the multiplier effect the equilibrium level of income at N_1 will be $100 billion below full employment. Conversely, if the expenditure schedule is in the position E_2E_2, there will be excess demand or an *inflationary gap* of $50 billion and the price level will have to rise.

Suppose the expenditure schedule is in the position E_1E_1. Then the economy cannot reach full employment. For at an output of $600 billion there would be spending of only $FA = \$550$ billion. There is a deficiency of $50 billion, shown by the distance *AN*. This is termed a *deflationary gap*, because it has a depressing or deflating effect on the economy. Note that although the deflationary gap is only $50 billion, the equilibrium level of income at N_1 is $100 billion below full employment. The multiplier effect is working against us here.

Does this mean that we must find $100 billion of additional spending to pull the system up to full employment? No, it does not. We need find only $50 billion, the amount of the deflationary gap. If E_1E_1 can be raised vertically by $50 billion, it will intersect OO at N. The multiplier effect will convert the initial impulse of $50 billion into a rise of $100 billion in national income.

Suppose, instead, that the spending schedule is located at E_2E_2. Now if producers turn out $600 billion of output, they will find that total spending adds up to $650 billion. There is excess demand of $NB = \$50$ billion. This is termed an *inflationary gap*. It makes life pleasant for anyone who has goods to sell, raises profits, and produces energetic efforts to expand output.

But how can this be? How can national income rise above the full-employment "ceiling"? The answer is that *physical* production cannot rise above the full-employment level or at least not much above it.[2] What can happen, however, is a rise in prices for the same quantity of output. And if people demand more goods than business concerns are able to produce, prices will be marked up. Such a general increase in prices is usually termed inflation.

PRICE MOVEMENTS: CAUSES AND CONSEQUENCES

In earlier sections we assumed a constant price level. A rise in the expenditure schedule produced a rise in physical output, while a drop in spending brought a drop in output. But through all this, the price level remained unchanged.

Is there any justification for such an assumption? If the level of spending rises, why don't prices rise instead of, or along with, physical output? If spending drops, why don't prices drop also?

Price Behavior in the United States

Price movements in the United States since the end of the Korean War are shown in Figure 6. The wholesale price level has risen only slightly, and the prices consumers pay for *commodities* have also risen only moderately. The sharpest increase has been in consumer prices for *services*. This is worth a word of explanation, since it will probably continue in future.

Wages and salaries rise every year; but the effect of this on

---

[2] In reality, capacity output is a zone rather than a single point. One can squeeze out more production by working men and machinery overtime and by hiring people who would not ordinarily be considered employable. This "overfull employment" may add a few percentage points to national output. For simplicity, however, we often assume that there is a precise limit to employment and output, and that expansion of total spending beyond this will lead *only* to an increase in prices.

commodity prices and service prices is different. If an auto worker in the Ford assembly plant in Detroit earns 15 percent more than he earned 5 years ago, this doesn't necessarily mean that car production costs and car prices are increased. There has probably been enough improvement in production methods over these years to raise the worker's productivity 15 percent and leave unit costs unchanged. The opportunities for raising a

Service Prices Have Been Rising Faster than Goods Prices

FIGURE 6. This chart shows a price index for all commodities at the wholesale level, a price index (the Consumer Price Index or C.P.I.) for everything bought by consumers, and a subdivision of the C.P.I. into commodity prices and service prices. Note the more rapid rise in the price of services.

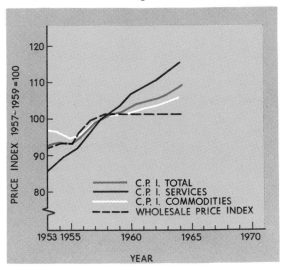

barber's productivity are more limited. If he is going to get his 15 percent and keep up with the auto worker, he will have to do it by raising the price of haircuts. Similarly for doctors' fees and prices for every sort of personal and professional service. So the Consumer Price Index seems subject to built-in increases in the service component. To keep the overall index unchanged, it would be necessary for retail prices of commodities to fall steadily year after year.

Looking again at the Wholesale Price Index, perhaps the best single indicator of price movements, we note a significant fact. During periods of business recession—1953–54, 1957–58, 1960–61—the price level has not declined. Drops in aggregate demand have produced drops in output but not in prices. Now if aggregate demand falls, this means that demand for certain products must have fallen. Some product demand curves must have shifted downward. If demand and supply curves have the shapes shown in Chapter 5, this should normally mean a drop in output *and* in price. Why does output in fact bear the main weight?

One reason is that recessions are mainly recessions in business investment. The drop in demand falls most heavily on building materials, machinery, steel and other metals, and to some extent on automobiles and durable consumer goods. But these industries are characterized generally by oligopoly and controlled pricing. Even in slack periods, producers rarely try to win business away from each other by the ungentlemanly method of cutting prices. Nor do they think it sensible to all reduce prices together, since they regard demand for their products as quite inelastic. So they hold prices unchanged and ride out the recession.

This still does not explain the firmness of prices in industries with many competitors. Here we must rely on a general business sentiment against price cutting, plus the tradition of fixed markups, which means that a product price cannot fall unless some element of cost falls. Somebody has to make the first move, and nobody does. The fact that many wages are now fixed by union agreement, and that wage cutting has gone completely out of fashion even in nonunion labor markets, sets a firm floor under costs and prices. Recessions since 1945 have, of course, been very mild, involving drops of only a few percent in total demand. A recession which lasted longer and went deeper might be sufficient to break through the price floor; but this is not an idea we want to test out by experiment.

Turning to business upswings, we note that prices tend to creep upward, particularly in years of strong expansion such as 1955–57 and 1964–65. Why is this so? To put the question in reverse: under what conditions might we expect to experience expansion *without* price increases?

Suppose supplies of all raw materials can be expanded smoothly at constant cost. Suppose wage rates behave "sensibly," i.e., rise no faster than man-hour output, so that unit labor costs do not increase. Suppose each producing unit has a definite production capacity, that its labor and material costs per unit of output remain constant up to the capacity point, and that beyond that point no output can be obtained at any price. Suppose, finally, that the economy is so perfectly synchronized that all producing units hit their capacity point at the same moment.

Then we might expect business upswings to follow a path such as *ACD* in Figure 7. We start with production at point *A*, where all industries are operating at, say, 80 percent of capacity. Now for one reason or another aggregate demand starts rising. As this happens, we move rightward along *AC*, with physical output expanding *and prices constant*. Oligopoly and markup pricing are in a sense helpful because, since unit costs are not rising, there is no reason for prices to rise.

All of a sudden, however, every industry hits full capacity at *C*. We can move no farther to the right on the output scale. If aggregate demand keeps on rising, there is only one direction in which we can go—*up* the price scale in the direction *CD*.

In this kind of economy a rise in aggregate demand would first affect *only* output and later, beyond the capacity point, would affect *only* prices. The prescription for price stability would be simple: try to hold aggregate demand at such a level that the economy just reaches C without going beyond it. Easier said than done, no doubt; but at any rate a clear guideline.

But the American economy is not that simple. As we move rightward from A, prices will remain stable for a while. But when we get to B, where the economy is operating at, say, 90 percent of capacity, some

Prices May Begin to Rise before Output Reaches Capacity

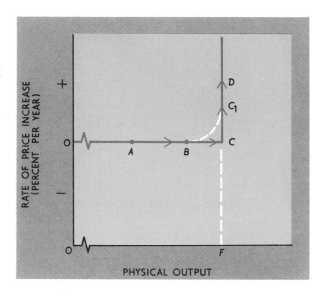

FIGURE 7. The economy is currently producing at point A, and prices are stable. Capacity output is OF. Aggregate demand now begins to rise. We can define conditions under which prices will remain stable until output reaches OF, after which only the price level will rise. In the actual economy, however, prices typically begin to rise before capacity is reached, so that we move along ABC_1D instead of $ABCD$.

prices begin to edge upward. As we push farther to the right, the rate of price increase accelerates. Finally, if we are really determined to hit full capacity, we shall find prices rising quite fast. The economy moves along the curved path BC_1 rather than the right-angle path BCC_1. If we want completely stable prices, we must stop expansion at B, well short of capacity. If we push the economy to capacity, we may find prices rising 10 percent a year.

Why does the economy behave in this awkward way? It must be because some of the things we assumed in constructing an economy which would follow the right-angle path are not true in actuality. Start at the beginning with raw material supplies. Agricultural crops come in only once a year. Mineral supplies are hard to expand at short notice, and expanding them may involve higher unit costs. A rapid economic expansion raises raw material prices because of inelastic supply curves; and the rise may be intensified by speculative buying based on expectations of price increases.

Wages are not always well-behaved. Unions sometimes can and do win wage increases large enough to force up unit labor costs; and they are more likely to do this as the level of production and profits rises while the level of unemployment declines. Moreover, even if wages were well-behaved *on the average,* there could still be trouble. The reason is that, while the wage level moves up rather evenly for all industries, labor productivity behaves quite differently from one industry to another.

Suppose labor productivity rises this year by 3 percent on average for the economy as a whole, and that each and every worker in the economy receives the appropriate 3 percent increase. In industry A, however, labor productivity has risen only 1 percent. Result: its unit labor cost is higher than before, and sooner or later its price level will rise. Industry B, on the other hand, has had a productivity increase of 5 percent. Its unit labor cost is now lower than before, and it could afford a price reduction which would offset the increase in industry A. But will industry B make the reduction? Maybe—and maybe not, particularly if it is an oligopolistic industry where prices are subject to control. It appears, then, that our wage-price mechanism contains a built-in bias. Where price increases are in order, you can be sure they will be made. Where price reductions are in order, the reductions may be slow and incomplete.

The assumption of a fixed production capacity for each company and industry is also unjustified. Even when a plant has reached the output for which it was designed, one can usually get more out of it by overtime work, double-shifting, delaying maintenance and repairs, and so on. But this means higher unit costs, for which producers may reasonably demand higher prices.

Finally, and very importantly, the degree of underuse of capacity at any time varies considerably from industry to industry. While some industries are still underemployed and crying out for more demand, others will already have reached the capacity point. This is one reason why price increases at high employment start off gradually, then accelerate as more and more industries hit capacity operation.

In actuality, then, there is no single *full-employment point,* such as we assumed earlier in this chapter. There is rather a *high-employment zone,* such as *BC,* which may be fairly wide. When we say we are aiming at full employment, we mean really that we want a desirable level of employment. And this is related to how much inflation we are willing to tolerate. The unfortunate fact is that the further up in the high-employment zone we decide to operate, the stronger will be the upward pressure on prices. Conversely, insistence on price stability will require a higher unemployment rate than we might like to see.

The choice problem is illustrated by the possibility curve in Figure 8, often called a "Phillips curve" after one of its earliest exponents.[3] Each point on this curve represents a feasible combination of unemployment rate and rate of price increase. At some level of unemployment, here

The Trade-off between Inflation and Unemployment

FIGURE 8. The possibility curve traces out all feasible combinations of unemployment level and rate of price increase. Thus one can have 5 percent un-employment with stable prices (A), or 3 percent unemployment with prices rising 1½ percent a year (B), or any other combina-tion falling on the curve. Point C, on the other hand, while it is a preferable position, is not a feasible one.

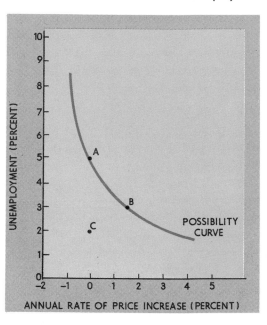

estimated at 5 percent, prices would remain stable. If unemployment were forced down to 1 percent, prices would be rising at more than 5 percent a year. The curve has been drawn convex upward to indicate that, as the rate of price increase is accelerated, this will produce smaller and smaller declines in unemployment. This seems a realistic supposition for our type of economy.

The shape of the possibility curve at a particular time is institution-ally determined. For example, one reason why the U.S. economy now runs into rising prices during an upswing, even when output is well

[3] A. W. Phillips, "The Relation Between Unemployment and the Rate of Change of Money Wage Rates in the United Kingdom, 1862–1957,"*Economica*, November, 1958, pp. 283–99. See also the thorough discussion of this and other ap-proaches to analysis of inflation in Martin Bronfenbrenner and Franklyn D. Holzman, "Survey of Inflation Theory," *American Economic Review*, September, 1963, pp. 593–661.

below capacity, is the aggressive policies of strong trade unions and quasi-monopolistic business concerns. With greater restraint by private monopolists, it might be possible to get unemployment down to 3 percent instead of 5 percent before encountering rising prices. The possibility curve would bend in more toward the origin. Anything that can be done in this direction obviously should be done.

Given the situation at a particular time, policy makers confront the problem of *selecting a point on the possibility curve*. Preferences on this are certain to differ. People who are particularly vulnerable to unemployment may prefer a point far to the right on the curve. People on fixed salaries who are in no danger of unemployment will prefer a point further to the left. Political liberals may want point *B*, while conservatives may prefer *A*. Everyone might agree that *C*, with low unemployment and stable prices, is best of all. But this is shadowboxing, since *C* is not a realistic possibility. In the end, there must be a choice of some point which does lie on the possibility curve and can be accepted as the least bad of feasible alternatives.

Without such a decision on objectives, one cannot decide what to do in a particular situation, nor can one appraise past policy actions. For example, the Federal Reserve System is frequently criticized as too tough in controlling business upswings. It is argued that interest rates are usually pushed up too fast and far so that borrowing and investment are unduly restricted. The underlying fact is that the System attaches greater weight to price stability and less weight to maximum employment than do many of its critics. Reflecting the conservative outlook of the banking community, it prefers a position rather high on the possibility curve. The critics are really saying that they would have chosen a lower position. This is the kind of issue on which no one can be "right" in any absolute sense.

Having posed the problem, we leave it for the time being. We shall return to it later in our general review of macroeconomic policy in Chapter 26.

Serious Inflation: Mechanics and Remedies

Let us look now at cases of aggravated inflation, in which the price level is rising at, say, 10 to 50 percent a year. The United States has experienced such increases only during and after major wars; but other countries have experienced them more frequently. The Brazilian price level has been rising quite fast for a hundred years. (A leading Brazilian economist is quoted as saying: "When our price level rises less than 15 percent a year, everyone denies that there is any inflation. Between 15 and 30 percent, the Finance Minister makes speeches against it. If it goes above 30 percent, we try to do something.")

Rapid price increases originate in excessive aggregate demand, a situation usually called "demand inflation" or "classical inflation." Look again at E_2E_2 in Figure 5. What does this really mean? The quantity of goods that the various spending groups are trying to buy (BF) is greater than the quantity which can be produced ($NF = OF$). There is $50 billion of *excess demand,* and the system is not in equilibrium. If production could be increased to OG, equilibrium could be reestablished. But by saying that OF represents full capacity we have also said that production of OG is impossible.

Where total demand is excessive, it may be hard to say just *whose* demand is unduly high. It can be any or all of the major groups. In one famous economic model,[4] inflation is set off by the fact that, with the economy already operating at full employment, business concerns insist on investing more than consumers are willing to save.

Planned I > Planned S.

The business concerns get the extra money to carry out their investment plans by borrowing from banks (take this on faith for the moment). They use this money to hire away labor and other resources from consumer goods production to capital goods production. Output of consumer goods falls, their prices rise, and consumers end up with less goods than they had expected. This is called *forced saving,* and seems rather a dirty trick. The economists who developed this theory, however, viewed it tolerantly because the end result was more productive capacity for the economy, usually considered a Good Thing.

While inflation arising from overinvestment is quite possible, it is probably less common than excess demand from government sources. The inflation experienced by the belligerent countries in World War I and World War II stemmed from very large increases in government purchases. Chronic inflation in some of the less developed countries today arises partly from rising expenditure on public services and development projects, combined with inability to raise tax revenues at a corresponding rate.

At any rate, for whatever reason, the economy finds itself with excess demand. The only way to keep prices stable in this situation is to force E_2E_2 back down to a level where it intersects OO at N, so that demand and output are in balance. Somebody's demand for goods has to be reduced. Business investment can perhaps be reduced by higher interest rates. Government can cut its own spending plans. If this is undesirable, as it would be in war emergencies, consumer spending can be cut by heavier taxation. Another possibility is to ration goods, giving people just enough ration tickets to buy the quantities of goods which are available. This is obviously another species of forced saving. Rationing is

---

[4] The classical statement is found in Joseph Schumpeter, *The Theory of Economic Development,* published in German in 1911 and in English in 1934. (Cambridge, Mass.: Harvard University Press, 1934 and 1949).

an awkward and expensive device, and is used mainly in war periods when excess demand is great and the inflation threat is severe.

If neither of these things is done, prices will begin to rise. But how much? Why not by exactly 8⅓ percent? Then the $600 billion worth of goods at the old price level, which is all the system can produce, will be *called* $650 billion worth of goods at the new price level. Thus people will be able to spend the $650 billion which they are apparently determined to spend, and all will be well.

But won't people soon realize that they have been tricked in this process? They are spending $650 billion all right, but because of the price increase they are *not getting as many goods as they originally intended to get*. What they wanted was $650 billion worth of goods *at the old prices*, and they are not getting this much because their dollars now buy less than before.

They may possibly just sit back and take it.[5] But they don't have to, and the chances are they won't. They are likely to react by trying to increase their spending, in the hope of still getting the things they originally desired. If the price of machinery has risen, businesses will raise their investment budgets. As cement, asphalt, and other elements in highway construction go up, government budgets will have to be raised. As prices of consumer goods rise, and housewives look reproachfully at their husbands, there will be a drive for wage increases.

Now the fat is in the fire. Business concerns, whose labor costs are higher than before, feel they have a legitimate case for further price increases; and, since spending is so high, they feel confident that their customers will pay the higher prices. But now workers come back and say, "Ah, living costs have risen some more, so we must have still higher wages." So it goes, round after round up the wage-price spiral, each group blaming the other and asserting its own innocence. And in a sense both are innocent, since the original cause was an unduly high level of aggregate demand, for which no one is particularly to blame.

Where will it all end? It might never end. If each group can offset any increase in the price level by raising its own money income, and if all continue stubbornly to insist on getting more goods than the economy can produce, prices could go on rising year after year. If people become panicky enough, the rate of inflation can accelerate to the point where money becomes worthless. Alternatively, the movement may slow down and reverse itself.

A conclusion that anything can happen is not very useful. If we try to push beyond this and ask, "On what does the outcome depend?" one can think of at least three considerations: the size of the "squeezable"

---

[5] This would amount to saying that they are now satisfied with less goods than they thought they wanted, i.e., that E_2E_2 has fallen. This is one way by which equilibrium might be reestablished, but not a very likely one.

groups in the economy; the extent of built-in lags in the spending mechanism; and the nature of consumers' and businessmen's price expectations.

1. While each group in the economy may struggle to increase its money income to keep pace with the inflation, not everyone succeeds. Pensioners, bondholders, and others with fixed money incomes can do nothing for the time being. Salaries of civil servants and many other white-collar groups may be virtually fixed in the short run. These people, then, are forced to reduce their consumption, to engage in forced saving. But their private misfortune is a public benefit. It slows down the rate of increase in money demand and thus has a braking effect.

2. Wage earners may also have to engage in forced saving if there is a long lag between price increases and wage increases. Suppose all workers are covered by union contracts which can be reopened only once a year; and that during the year the price level rises 25 percent. Even if at the end of the year workers are fully compensated by a 25 percent wage increase, their consumption has been cut meanwhile. Unfair? Maybe so, but also a brake on inflation.

The other important lag is between an increase in wages or other production costs and the consequent increase in product prices. Again, the longer the lag in price adjustments the slower the rate of inflation. An economy in which prices and wages can be adjusted once a week will be subject to more violent inflationary spirals than one in which adjustments can be made only once a year.

3. An important consideration is people's expectations about how prices will move in future. Rising prices may stimulate either of two reactions. If the rise is expected to continue and accelerate, and if people speed up their purchases in order to "beat the price rise," then the rise will be intensified. On the other hand, a marked rise in prices may lead people to feel that "prices are too high," that the trend will be reversed, and that it will be wise to wait and buy later. If this belief becomes strong enough, spending schedules will begin to drop; and when this happens, the inflation is over. An expectation of price stability is thus a powerful force *making* for price stability. This is probably one of the main reasons why inflations in the Western industrial countries typically slow down after a while instead of running away.

The Outlook in the United States

Barring major wars, there seems no reason to expect that the American economy will experience enough excess demand to produce "serious inflation." The prospect is rather that our price level will rise a bit during each prosperity period, level off during recession, and rise once more during the next boom. This is often termed a *ratchet movement* of the price level. Its result is a gradual upward drift of prices over the long run. It would not be at all surprising if the Wholesale Price

Index rose at an average rate of 1 percent a year over the next generation.

How strong the updrift of prices will be depends partly on how hard we try to push the economy toward capacity operation. The price rise from 1953 to 1965 was so mild partly because the economy was well below capacity most of the time. If our political leaders in the future select a different point on the Phillips curve, we may have lower unemployment and larger price increases. Whether this would be desirable we leave for later discussion.

SUMMARY

1. Government expenditure (G) adds to aggregate demand, while tax withdrawals (T) reduce demand. When we include government in our picture of the economy, the condition of aggregate equilibrium is that (planned) $S = I + (G - T)$.

2. Similarly, exports are an addition to aggregate demand, while imports reduce demand for domestic products. The full condition for aggregate equilibrium in an open economy, then, is that (planned)

$$S = I + (G - T) + (X - M)$$

3. An upward or downward shift of the expenditure schedule typically produces a larger change in the equilibrium level of national income. This is termed *the multiplier effect*. If a rise of $1 billion in planned expenditure raises the equilibrium level of income by $2 billion, the *multiplier* has a value of 2.

4. The size of the multiplier depends on the *marginal propensity to spend*, that is, on the *slope of the expenditure schedule*. The greater the marginal propensity to spend, the larger the multiplier; and conversely.

5. The marginal propensity to spend depends on what fraction of any increase in income leaks away into *increased saving, increased tax payments*, and *increased spending on foreign goods*. The larger these leakages, the smaller the marginal propensity to spend, and the smaller the value of the multiplier.

6. The multiplier can be understood most readily by viewing it as operating *over the course of time*, through successive rounds of spending, enlarged incomes, and respending.

7. The *equilibrium level* of national income at a particular time is not necessarily the *desirable or full employment level*. The expenditure schedule may be so low that there is serious unemployment; or so high that demand exceeds the output capacity of the system, leading to rising prices. In the former case there is a *deflationary gap*, in the latter case an *inflationary gap*.

8. The American economy since 1945 has been characterized by price stability during recessions and a mild upcreep of prices during expansion periods. The fact that many wages and prices are controlled rather than atomistically competitive, the differing rates of productivity increase in different industries, the fact that unit costs of production usually rise as capacity is approached, and the fact that different industries reach capacity at different times during an expansion, all contribute to this behavior of prices.

9. Full employment in practice is a zone rather than a single point. Moving higher within this zone involves stronger upward pressure on prices. Setting a national income goal means choosing one of many possible combinations of unemployment rate and rate of price increase.

10. Rapid inflation typically originates in excessive aggregate demand, which may stem from an excess of planned business investment over planned saving, or from excessively large government budget deficits, or both together. The only real corrective is to reduce the level of aggregate demand.

11. Once an inflation is underway, it may speed up or it may slow down and taper off. The outcome is influenced by the size of the "squeezable" or fixed-income groups in the economy, the frequency of wage and price adjustments, and the nature of consumers' and businessmen's price expectations.

DISCUSSION QUESTIONS

1. In Chapter 20 we defined the equilibrium level of national income as the level at which planned saving equals planned investment. How is this definition changed when we bring government into the picture?

2. "A surplus of exports over imports constitutes a net addition to aggregate demand. A nation should always try, therefore, to maintain as large an export surplus as possible." Do you agree? Why, or why not?

3. Why will an autonomous increase in spending raise the equilibrium level of GNP by *more* than the amount of the increase? What determines the size of this "multiplier" effect?

4. Explain the difference between the "serial" version of the multiplier and the "instantaneous" version. Do the two lead to the same conclusion?

5. Why do we usually define full employment in terms of manpower rather than plant capacity? Would the two definitions necessarily coincide?

6. What is the meaning of an "inflationary gap," or a "deflationary gap"?

7. If there is a deflationary gap of $30 billion, will the economy then produce just $30 billion less than full-employment output? Explain. How large an autonomous increase in spending will be required to attain full employment?

8. Why, during an economic upswing, does the price level typically begin

to rise before the economy is operating at full capacity? What does this do to the definition of "full employment"?

9. Is the possibilities curve shown in Figure 8 completely unchangeable? Can you think of any concrete steps which might alter its position?

10. Rapid inflation typically results from excessively high aggregate demand. What are the possible sources of excess demand? What are the main things that can be done to eliminate the excess?

11. What determines whether an inflationary movement will slow down or accelerate? Does the fact that inflations usually slow down and taper off after a while mean that government need not be concerned about them?

Taxes, Public Spending, and

Fiscal Policy

> Let us have the courage to stop borrowing
> to meet continuing deficits. Stop the deficits.
> FRANKLIN D. ROOSEVELT (*Speech, July 30, 1932*)

> Let us all be happy and live within our
> means, even if we have to borrow the money to
> do it with.
>
> ARTEMUS WARD

ISN'T THERE a simple and straightforward way of holding total demand at the right level through the federal budget? If total spending threatens to be too high, can't it be reduced as much as necessary by levying heavier taxes? If, on the other hand, demand is too low and the economy is operating below capacity, can't this be corrected by increasing government spending or by lowering taxes to permit more private spending? The use of government budgets to regulate total spending is usually called *fiscal policy*.

TAXES, PUBLIC SPENDING, AND NATIONAL INCOME

The way in which the government budget affects the level of spending was suggested in Chapter 21, but we must now go into this question more thoroughly.

A Few Preliminaries

When we speak of "the federal budget," just what do we mean? The *administrative budget*, which is submitted to Congress by the President each January, is a legal document which follows conventional rules of government accounting. It includes all expenditures which require appropriations by Congress and all revenues which go into the general funds of the Treasury. The surpluses and deficits which you see reported in the newspapers usually refer to the administrative budget. But the administrative budget does not fully reflect government's impact on the economy:

1. It excludes some important operations of government, notably the social security system. Each year government collects billions of dollars in payroll taxes under this system. The money goes into a trust fund, which is used to meet old-age pension, disability, and unemployment compensation payments. In most years since the system began, more money has been going into the trust fund than has been coming out. Thus government cash receipts from the public are understated by the administrative budget, and any budget deficit (in cash terms) is correspondingly overstated. Another large trust fund not included in the administrative budget is the highway fund set up as part of the federal-state superhighway program, which receives certain earmarked taxes on gasoline and motor vehicles.

2. It makes no distinction between government purchases of goods and services, transfer payments, and government lending operations. These are all treated equally as part of government expenditure. The economic effects of these transactions, however, are quite different.

In what follows, therefore, we shall use a different budget concept —*government transactions on income and product account,* or the government sector of the national income table. This includes only *transactions which give rise to current income,* thus omitting lending and similar operations. But it does include *all* current transactions, bringing in the social security system and the highway trust fund. It separates transfer payments from government purchases of goods and services. And it counts taxes as a deduction from income at the time they are incurred rather than when they are actually paid, which may be as much as a year later. This is a realistic procedure, since businesses and wealthy individuals do put aside money currently to meet later tax payments.

The "income and product budget" is calculated and published quarterly by the national income staff of the Department of Commerce. It typically shows a larger surplus (or smaller deficit) than the administrative budget.

We shall follow the terminology used in previous chapters. *Government expenditure means government purchases of goods and services.* Remember that only government purchases of goods and services enter into the value of GNP. So when we want to add government spending to private spending, as we did in Chapter 20, we must use the term in this sense.

Transfer payments we shall regard as negative taxes. They increase the disposable income available for private spending, just as taxes reduce disposable income. When we speak of taxes, therefore, we shall mean *net taxes* or *tax receipts minus transfer payments.*

EXPANSIONIST EFFECT OF THE BUDGET

Government spending, as we saw in Chapter 21, counts as an addition to private spending. A dollar spent by government is as good as any other dollar in its direct effect on the flow of income. Taxes, on the other hand, reduce the disposable incomes of households and businesses and thus lower the level of private spending.

Suppose expenditures and tax receipts are equal, so that the budget is precisely balanced. One might then think that government is a neutral factor in the economy and that the budget has no effect on the level of national income. But this turns out not to be true. *Even a balanced budget has an expansionist effect.* We shall try first to explain this proposition in words, and then give a graphical illustration.

Look at it this way: When government spends an additional dollar on goods and services, the full amount of this dollar enters the income stream. But when government collects an extra dollar in taxes, private spending is not reduced by a full dollar. It is reduced only by the amount which would have been spent out of this dollar. The remainder of the tax comes from money which would have gone into private saving. The expansionist effect of the dollar spent thus exceeds the depressing effect of the dollar taxed, leaving a net addition to total spending and hence to the equilibrium level of national income.

Suppose the economy is operating below full employment. The President decides to give things a boost by spending an additional $50 billion on highways (or anything else you prefer). But he has a conservative Secretary of the Treasury, who insists that this expenditure must be covered by taxes. What will happen? The government takes away $50 billion of private income through the taxes. But at the same time it creates $50 billion of income which it pays out for the highway projects. Hence *private income remains unchanged.* Consumer spending and business investment can remain as high as before. But GNP has increased by the value of the highways built, or by $50 billion.

This is usually termed the *balanced budget theorem.* It asserts that an increase of x dollars in government spending, even if fully covered by an increase of x dollars in tax receipts, will raise the equilibrium level of national income by x dollars. Thus an economy with a government sector will have a higher equilibrium income than one without government.

To see whether there is any catch in this, let's do it over again with geometry (Figure 1). We start with the expenditure schedule in the position EE. The slope of this schedule, which is the marginal propensity to spend, is ½. The equilibrium level of income is $600 billion.

Now government enters the scene with its $50 billion highway program. This by itself would raise total spending $50 billion to E_1E_1, and the multiplier effect would raise national income to $700 billion.

But the Secretary of the Treasury insists on his $50 billion of taxes. People now have $50 billion less in their pockets than they had before the taxes were imposed. So they will spend less than before. How much less? The answer depends on the marginal propensity to spend, which we have assumed to be ½. If income drops by $50 billion, spending will drop $25 billion.

The Balanced Budget Theorem

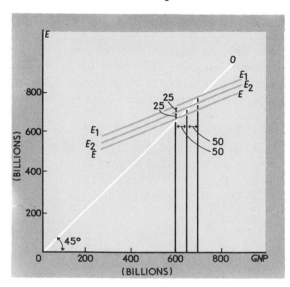

FIGURE 1. A $50 billion increase in government spending would by itself raise the expenditure schedule from *EE* to *E₁E₁* and, through the multiplier effect, raise the equilibrium level of income by $100 billion. But if $50 of new taxes are imposed to balance the increased spending, this lowers the expenditure schedule to *E₂E₂*. The end result is that the equilibrium level of income rises by $50 billion, or just the amount of the (balanced) increase in the government budget.

Thus the expenditure schedule drops by $25 billion, from E_1E_1 to E_2E_2. Why doesn't it drop all the way back to EE? Because part of the tax revenue comes out of saving rather than spending. So the new equilibrium level of national income, $650 billion, is higher than the level of $600 billion from which we started and it is higher by just the amount of the budget increase.

This argument is not watertight. It assumes that the basic propensities to consume and invest remain unaffected by an increase in the government budget, which would probably not be true in practice. Some kinds of government spending might frighten businessmen enough to cause a drop in private investment. But other kinds of spending, of which highways are a good example, will raise the profitability of many businesses and thus stimulate private investment. We have also assumed a rather odd kind of tax, which would yield the same $50 billion *regardless of the level of income.* Most actual taxes are not of this character.

Because of these and other considerations, one cannot assert that in practice a balanced increase of *x* dollars in the government budget will raise national income by precisely *x* dollars. The effect may be either larger or smaller, but there is little doubt that it will be in an expansionist direction.

THE IMPACT OF TAXATION

The federal tax structure in the United States has one outstanding characteristic: tax revenues rise sharply with an increase in national income and drop sharply when national income falls. The reasons lie in the nature of the personal and corporate income taxes, and in the importance of transfer payments.

1. **The personal income tax.** As national income rises, the incomes of most families in the country also rise. They move up into higher "tax brackets." As this happens, the *percentage* of their income taken in tax increases. So tax receipts rise, not just proportionately to income, but more than proportionately.

This can be explained by an illustration. Year 1 in Table 1 is a recession year in which incomes are at a low ebb. The economy now embarks on a boom, culminating in the prosperous Year 2. Between these two years each family's income rises by $1,000. We assume that the larger the income, the higher the percentage of income taken by taxation, as is true in our system.

Note what happens to tax receipts as income rises. The increase in personal income between Year 1 and Year 2 is 33.3 percent. But tax receipts rise by a whopping 57.5 percent. Of the $30,000 increase in income, $13,500 or 45 percent is drained off by an increase in tax payments. This will have a strong braking effect on any expansion of income.

It is instructive also to work the table in reverse. Suppose income falls from the level of Year 2 to the level of Year 1 as a result of recession. Income *received* drops by $30,000. But personal income taxes also drop by $13,500. Thus the drop in *disposable* income is only $16,500, or 55 percent of the original decline in GNP. The braking effect works on the downswing of the cycle as well as the upswing.

2. **The corporate income tax.** The wide swings of business profits in our economy have already been mentioned. Profits rise faster than national income during a boom and fall faster during a recession. About half of corporate profits go to the federal government in taxes. Because profits fluctuate so widely, the yield of the corporate income tax rises

sharply in prosperity and drops sharply in recession. The braking effect on the economy is similar to that of the personal income tax.

3. Transfer payments. These payments rise substantially during recession and fall during prosperity. A recession means that more people are out of work, so unemployment compensation payments rise. Farm prices are likely to be falling, so government has to pay out more under price support schemes. Since jobs are hard to find, older people may decide to drop out of the labor market and begin drawing their pensions. During an upswing, these tendencies go into reverse and transfer payments shrink.

TABLE 1

Effect of Progressive Income Taxation

YEAR 1					YEAR 2				
ANNUAL INCOME	NO. OF FAMILIES	TOTAL INCOME	AVERAGE TAX RATE (%)	TAX RECEIPTS	ANNUAL INCOME	NO. OF FAMILIES	TOTAL INCOME	AVERAGE TAX RATE (%)	TAX RECEIPTS
2,000	10	20,000	20	4,000	2,000			20	
3,000	10	30,000	25	7,500	3,000	10	30,000	25	7,500
4,000	10	40,000	30	12,000	4,000	10	40,000	30	12,000
5,000			35		5,000	10	50,000	35	17,500
Total	30	90,000		23,500		30	120,000		37,000

These changes in transfer payments work in the same direction as the swings in tax receipts. During recession, disposable income falls less than one might expect *both* because the tax "take" is reduced and because transfer payments are increased. During prosperity, the increase in the tax take *and* the decline in transfer payments slows down the rate of increase in disposable income.

The Built-in Stabilizer

On a common-sense basis one can see that this must have a stabilizing effect on the economy, tending to brake both expansions and contractions of national income. Moreover, the gyroscopic effect works automatically, with no need for diagnosis or deliberate action. This effect of the tax structure is usually referred to as the *built-in stabilizer*.

This common-sense impression can be pinned down by noting that taxation *reduces the slope of the consumption schedule*. In the no-government economy, this slope depends solely on the marginal propensity to consume. But when taxation enters, an addition to personal income means less spending than before. Not only does some income go into saving but some is taken by taxation.

The shape of the revised consumption schedule depends on the tax structure. Two possibilities are illustrated in Figure 2. Let C be the original consumption schedule, with no taxation. Suppose a tax is introduced which is collected on all income received and is strictly proportional to income. This changes the consumption schedule to C_1. It remains a straight line, but with a reduced slope. The difference in slope between C and C_1 is equal to the marginal rate of taxation, which we have assumed to be constant.

Effect of Taxation on the Consumption Schedule

FIGURE 2. C is the untaxed consumption schedule. A proportionate tax on all income will rotate it downward to C_1. A progressive tax structure, under which rates rise as income increases, will give it a shape like C_2.

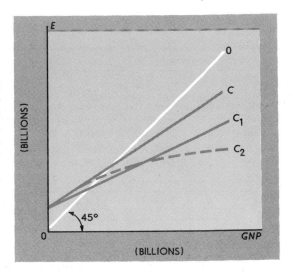

Consider now a tax which exempts income below some minimum amount, say $2,000 per year. As a person's income rises above this minimum, the marginal rate of taxation also rises. This is a progressive income tax of the type used in the United States. It results in a consumption schedule such as C_2. This schedule is curved rather than straight, flattening out at higher income levels.

Since consumption is much the largest item in total expenditure, a reduced slope for the C schedule means a reduced slope for the expenditure schedule as well. The practical consequences of this fact are illustrated in Figure 3. Start with the expenditure schedule E, which includes a "primitive" or "untaxed" consumption schedule. The slope of E is steep and the multiplier is large. Suppose there is an autonomous drop of m dollars in planned spending, which lowers E to the position E_1. Then national income will fall all the way from Y to Y_1.

Suppose now that because of income taxation the consumption schedule, and therefore the expenditure schedule, has the reduced slope shown by E'. Then an autonomous drop of m dollars in spending will lower it to E'_1. Note that now the equilibrium level of income falls only to Y'_1. The tax system has cushioned the fall in income.

By working the diagram in the opposite direction one can show that the stabilizing effect works on the upswing as well. The tax structure reduces both the upper and lower limits within which the economy can fluctuate, and holds cyclical swings within a narrower range.

The strength of the built-in stabilizer depends mainly on two things:

1. The income level at which taxation begins. Almost all tax systems exempt incomes below a certain level, on the ground that it is unjust to tax the very poor. The higher the exemption, the smaller the stabilizing

Effect of Taxation on Income Stability

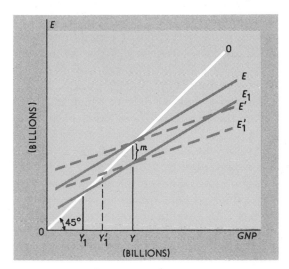

FIGURE 3. Suppose income taxation reduces the slope of the expenditure schedule from E to E'. Then the same drop of m dollars in planned expenditure will produce a smaller decline in GNP than would have occurred without taxation. Income falls only from Y to Y'₁ instead of from Y to Y₁.

effect of the system. An exemption of $5,000 would produce less stabilization than an exemption of $2,000, since the proportion of personal income subject to tax would be much lower.

2. The progressiveness of the rate structure. If one wants to take away 30 percent of taxable income, this can be done in various ways. It can mean a proportionate 30 percent tax on all income above the exemption level. Or it can mean a schedule under which the marginal rate starts at 10 percent but rises to 90 percent on the largest incomes. The latter system will cause tax receipts to shoot up considerably faster than national income and will consequently have a stronger stabilizing effect.

THE MEANING OF FISCAL POLICY

So far we have considered taxation and expenditure in isolation. We have seen that an *increase* in government expenditure *raises* the equilibrium level of national income, while a *cut* in expenditure *lowers* it. For taxation, the effects run in the reverse direction. An *increase* in tax rates *lowers* private spending and the equilibrium level of income, while a *cut* in tax rates *raises* the income level.

But in the real world, taxes and spending go together. Actual budget making involves, or at least should involve, a careful adjustment of tax and expenditure levels relative to each other. The combination chosen for a particular year constitutes a *fiscal program. Fiscal policy is the choice of a fiscal program.*

Choosing a particular fiscal program involves choosing a certain size of budget surplus or deficit. It involves also an assumption about national income for the year ahead. The reason is that tax receipts depend heavily on the level of income. So without an assumption on this point, one can have no idea of how the budget will come out.

Suppose government, on the basis of its best guess about next year's national income, chooses a program which just balances expenditures and tax receipts *at that income level.* This does not mean that the budget will actually come out balanced at the end of the year. If national income is higher than expected, there will be an automatic budget surplus. If it is lower, there will be a deficit. The large federal deficits which occur in recession years arise mainly from the abnormally low level of income rather than from deliberate decisions.

The meaning of fiscal policy may be clarified by looking at Figure 4.[1] A particular fiscal program is represented by a *budget line,* such as *A* in the diagram. At any point on this line, the level of federal spending and of tax rates is exactly the same. As one moves up to the right, however, the budget deficit decreases and eventually turns into a surplus. The main reason is that higher levels of national income yield larger revenues even at the same tax rates. The steepness of the budget line depends mainly on the marginal rate of taxation.

A different fiscal program is shown by line *B.* The difference between the programs is shown by the *vertical* distance between the two lines. Note that *at the same level of income,* program B involves a considerably larger deficit (or smaller surplus). This must mean that tax rates are lower or expenditures higher. Since either action will tend to raise national income, program B is more *expansionist* than program A.

The actual deficit or surplus in a particular year depends on two things: on the fiscal program, shown by the location of the budget line; *and* on the level of national income.

One paradoxical result is that a tax cut or an expenditure increase can *reduce* the federal deficit instead of increasing it. Either of these steps shifts the budget line downward. But it also, through the multiplier

---

[1] This is adapted from a similar diagram in the *Economic Report of the President,* January, 1962, p. 79.

effect, raises the level of national income; and this tends to raise tax revenues and reduce transfer payments. If the multiplier is large and the budget line quite steep, the secondary effects might outweigh the original shift and produce a smaller deficit or even a surplus. This possibility is

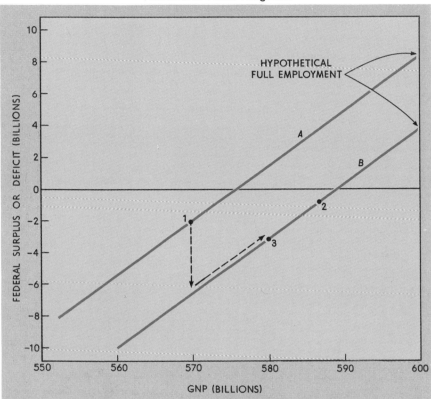

Alternative Fiscal Programs

FIGURE 4. An unchanged fiscal program, such as line A, can produce either a surplus or deficit, depending on the level of GNP. Program B is more expansionist than A because, at the same GNP level, it involves a larger deficit or smaller surplus. Shifting from program A to program B involves an immediate increase of $5 billion in the deficit. But if the multiplier is 2 and the marginal rate of taxation is 30 percent, GNP will rise by $10 billion, leading to a $3 billion increase in tax collections. So one ends up at point 3, with a deficit only $2 billion larger than in the original position 1.

shown by a movement from position 1 on line *A* to position 2 on line *B*. Under these conditions we could quite literally "spend ourselves rich."

While this is a hypothetical possibility, it is not a realistic one for the American economy. Given the present structure of the economy, a more expansionist fiscal program will in fact produce a larger deficit— but not as much larger as one might think. Suppose the economy is operating below capacity and needs an expansionary push. Government decides to spend $5 billion more next year, leaving tax schedules unchanged. If the multiplier is 2, national income will rise by $10 billion. With present tax structures, about 30 percent of any increase in national income is drained off into federal revenues. Tax collections rise by $3 billion. So despite the original increase of $5 billion in spending, the deficit increases by only $2 billion. The economy moves from 1 on line *A* to 3 on line *B*. The drop in the budget line is partially offset by the fact that one is operating farther to the right in terms of national income.

A simple way of comparing the impact of different fiscal programs is through the concept of the *full-employment surplus*. This is the budget surplus (or deficit) which would result from a given program *if* GNP

The Federal Budget Impact, 1960–64

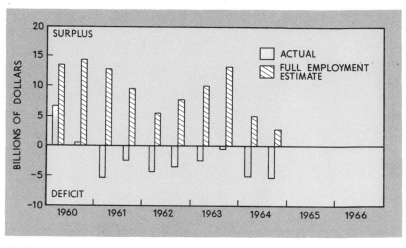

FIGURE 5. Estimated full-employment surplus in the federal budget, by calendar half years, 1960–64.

were at the full-employment level. In terms of Figure 4, it is the height at which a particular budget line hits the full-employment boundary at the right of the diagram.

The estimated full-employment surplus for several recent years is shown in Figure 5.[2] Note that in 1960, budget policy was quite restrictive, with a full-employment surplus of about $13 billion. This was reduced during 1961 and 1962 by a considerable increase in expenditures and by tax concessions to corporations in the form of more liberal depreciation allowances. By late 1962, however, the surplus was creeping up again, while the economy, with almost 6 percent unemployed, was operating

[2] *Annual Report of the Council of Economic Advisers,* January, 1965, pp. 62–64. Full employment is defined as that level of output which would reduce full-time unemployment to 4 percent of the labor force.

well below capacity. President Kennedy accordingly recommended to Congress a sizable cut in income taxes to raise private spending and stimulate the economy. Congress did not act on the proposal in 1963, and the full-employment surplus rose some more.

Early in 1964, however, Congress, at the urging of President Johnson, cut personal and corporate income tax rates by amounts which, at 1964 income levels, yielded tax savings of $8.4 billion. Additional cuts estimated at $4.6 billion were scheduled to take effect in 1965. In mid-1965, with the economy vigorous but still below full employment, the President recommended, and Congress enacted, a new round of cuts, this time in federal excise taxes, totaling about $2 billion immediately and several billion more in later years. The result was to hold the full-employment surplus to a low level during 1964 and 1965.

The 1964–65 program of income tax reductions seems to have worked much as its supporters predicted. By mid-1965, consumer disposable income was about $10 billion a year higher as a direct result of the tax cuts. If one takes a multiplier of 2 as roughly correct, this would by itself raise GNP by about $20 billion. Moreover, the program had a favorable effect on business investment. The drop in the corporate income tax rate from 52 to 48 percent left corporations with about $3 billion of additional profits available for investment; and the upsurge of consumer spending provided a strong incentive to expand plant capacity. A good part of the $8 billion rise in plant and equipment investment between early 1964 and mid-1965 should probably be credited to the tax program.

Between the second quarter of 1964, when the cuts become effective, and the third quarter of 1965, by which time most of the impact had been felt, GNP (at annual rates) rose by about $50 billion or 8 percent. Federal cash receipts were $4 billion *higher* in the fiscal year 1965 than in fiscal 1964, despite the cut in rates, and the federal deficit was reduced by $2 billion. One cannot say precisely how much of this performance should be credited to the tax program.[3] The economy would perhaps have continued to expand in any event, though at a slower rate. But it cannot be doubted that the tax reductions had a marked stimulating effect, and that the program must be rated as a successful venture in fiscal policy. Much of the credit should go to Professor Walter Heller of the University of Minnesota, chairman of the Council of Economic Advisers from 1961 to 1964, who persuaded two Presidents, the Secretary of the Treasury, and influential leaders of Congress that it could be constructive to cut taxes in the face of a federal deficit.

---

[3] For a good analysis of the complexities involved, and for some carefully qualified estimates, see Arthur M. Okun, "Measuring the Impact of the 1964 Tax Reduction," Paper delivered to the American Statistical Association, Philadelphia, September 10, 1965.

TAX CHANGES VERSUS EXPENDITURE CHANGES

The fiscal program can be altered by changing *either* tax rates or government expenditure. Is there anything to choose between these two types of change? The expenditure lever, as we have seen, is somewhat more powerful. If expenditures are raised by $1 billion, the whole amount goes directly into the income stream. But if government releases $1 billion of private income through tax cuts, only part of this will be spent and the rest will be saved. So it will take a larger tax cut to achieve the same effect on national income.

A more important consideration, however, is that taxation and government expenditure play different roles in the economy. *The function of government expenditure is to allocate resources to production of public services.* Expenditure should be set at a level which, *assuming full employment,* will divide national output between private and public production according to the preferences of the citizens. Under full employment, any increase in public services involves a diversion of resources from private production. If the public, acting through Congress, decides that it prefers to have an extra billion dollars worth of labor and materials devoted to national defense rather than to consumer goods, that is that. The task of Congress and the administration is to appraise and reflect these public preferences.

The implication is that government expenditures should not be varied to offset short-term fluctuations in national income. This is partly because it is difficult to vary public construction programs quickly. But more basically it is because the level of government services should be decided by long-term priorities. A new school or highway needed next year is presumably needed just as much whether the year happens to be a good one or a poor one. It is unnecessary to rethink the proper level of government activity every year because of business cycle swings.

If this is accepted, the burden of fiscal policy falls mainly on taxation (remembering always that transfer payments count as negative taxes). The *function of taxation is to regulate total spending so as to achieve a desired level of output and employment.* It is customary to state this objective as *full employment without inflation.* But this rather dodges the issue, as we saw in Chapter 21. High employment and price stability are to some extent competitive, and one is forced to choose some combination of the two.

Once the objective is decided, and after there has been a forecast of total spending for the period ahead, one can say in which direction taxes need to be adjusted. If the level of spending threatens to be too high, leading to undue inflation, then tax rates should be raised to drain off this excess demand. But if the problem is insufficient demand, taxes should be lowered to raise private spending.

The latter course will involve a budget deficit, possibly a substantial deficit. People who dislike deficits will object that such a program is "inflationary." This depends on what one means by inflation. If one means simply a rise in the level of spending, then a budget deficit will have this effect. But if the level of total spending is too low, this is precisely what the economy needs. If one uses inflation in the proper sense of a rise in the price level, the effect of a budget deficit depends on the economic circumstances. If the economy is operating well below capacity, a deficit will mainly increase output and will have little effect on prices. Under these conditions the inflation objection is unwarranted.

If we treat expenditures and taxation as having quite different functions, what becomes of the historic connection between them? What becomes of the balanced budget? The answer is that under this approach *the budget surplus or deficit is not a direct object of public policy.* Expenditure levels and tax levels are determined independently on the basis of the function which each is expected to perform. Then we let the deficit or surplus fall where it may. Taxes and expenditures are planned, but the balance between them is not planned.

This approach to fiscal policy has been accepted by most economists for a generation. High officials of the federal administration, expert bodies such as the Commission on Money and Credit, and numerous business groups have endorsed it. But there continues to be strong opposition from some groups in Congress and in the business community; and since tax powers are vested in Congress, it remains uncertain how rapidly the newer views will be incorporated in public policy. The bold and sensible actions of 1964–65 are encouraging but not yet conclusive.

Suppose Congress were persuaded to adapt this approach to the federal budget. How would it work out over the long run? Would budget surpluses in some years roughly balance deficits in other years? Or would deficits preponderate, leading to a gradual rise in the national debt? The answer depends on the strength of private spending, and particularly the level of business investment. In a period of active investment, such as 1945 to 1955, a correct use of fiscal policy would add little to national debt and might even reduce it. But during the 1930's, when private investment virtually collapsed, fiscal policy necessarily involved a preponderance of deficits. It is ironic that the quite small federal deficits of the New Deal era were widely assailed as leading to the downfall of the American economic system. With the benefit of hindsight, it seems clear that considerably larger deficits were called for.

OTHER IDEAS ABOUT THE BUDGET

1. The annually balanced budget. A traditional view in public finance has been that the budget should balance in each fiscal year.

Whatever one can say for this principle at the state and local levels, as applied to the federal budget it has little merit. In fact, if taken seriously, it would have pernicious effects. It would mean *raising* tax rates during recession, to offset the natural decline in tax revenues, and *cutting* taxes during inflation to avoid a budget surplus. This is just the opposite of what should be done. Even exponents of "sound finance" rarely go this far. Deficits are accepted so long as they are unplanned and can be treated as nobody's fault, but proposals for deliberate deficits to stimulate the economy are strongly resisted.

The argument for annual balance in the federal budget is essentially a political argument. It rests on the view that there is a built-in tendency toward overspending. Self-interested groups of citizens are always eager to batten on the public purse. Power-hungry bureaucrats work constantly to expand their empires. Congressmen are too weak to resist these pressures. So the only remedy is to tie a ball and chain around government's ankle by saying, "If you want to spend, you've got to tax." How much there is to this line of reasoning you can judge as well as the next person.

2. The balanced budget at full employment.   This idea comes closer to modern ideas about fiscal policy. It has been espoused by, among others, the Committee for Economic Development, a responsible and respected business group. Under this proposal, government expenditures would be determined independently on the basis of economic priorities. Next, one would estimate how much the economy could produce at full employment. Finally, one would set tax rates so that, *if the full employment income were actually achieved,* tax receipts would just equal expenditures.[4] So long as the economy was below full employment, there would be an automatic deficit and the budget would be working in the right direction.

This is not really a laissez-faire program, though it may look like one. In a growing economy, and with progressive tax schedules, the full-employment surplus will tend to rise over time. To hold it at zero will require tax reductions from time to time.

It is an optimistic approach, however, since it implies that private consumption and investment will normally be high enough to maintain full employment without the stimulus of a government deficit. This may or may not be true in practice. Or it may be true at some times and not at others. Business investment is buoyant in some years, depressed in others. It is doubtful, therefore, that one can prescribe a zero level, or any other level, of full-employment surplus as equally appropriate to all occasions.

---

[4] The C.E.D. formulation is actually a bit more conservative than this. "It should be the policy of the government to set its expenditure programs and tax rates so that they would yield a constant, moderate surplus under conditions of high employment and price stability." (Committee for Economic Development, *Fiscal and Monetary Policy for High Employment* [New York, 1962], p. 26.)

Troublesome as it may be, fiscal-policy makers have no alternative but to "play it by ear."

3. Capital and current budgets.　An interesting type of budget system, developed in Sweden during the 1930's and since adopted by a number of other countries, distinguishes between the *current* expenditures of government and its *capital* expenditures. Most government expenditure falls in the current category—the civil service payroll, the pay and subsistence of the armed forces, purchase of materials for current use, interest on the public debt, and other transfer payments.

But there is also a large volume of expenditure on such things as schools, hospitals, post offices and other public buildings, superhighway systems, military installations, flood control, navigation, and reforestation projects. These are capital investments which will yield benefits to the public over a long period to come. There is no inherent reason why their full cost should be assessed against taxpayers in the particular year during which they are constructed. Why not finance them by issuing long-term bonds, and then assess interest charges against taxpayers who use the facilities in future years? If a private corporation builds a turnpike, it raises the money by selling bonds. If government builds the same turnpike, why shouldn't it finance it in the same way?

The state and local governments do operate to some extent on this basis. Part of the cost of capital projects is raised through borrowing rather than through current taxation. Between 1900 and 1958, for example, state and local government debt increased by $55 billion. But there was something to show for it. Over this same period the estimated value of assets owned by state and local governments rose by $195 billion.[5]

At the federal level, one should distinguish the issue of *proper economic accounting* from that of *proper fiscal policy*. From an accounting standpoint, it would be desirable to include government capital formation as part of total capital formation. The fact that we do not do this at present gives an inaccurate view of what is happening in the economy, and makes our national accounts noncomparable with those of countries which do measure government capital formation.

From a fiscal policy standpoint, however, it would be wrong to tie how much the federal government should borrow in a particular year to how much it is spending on capital formation in that year. This would be just as undesirable as any other rigid budget formula. The size of the federal surplus or deficit should be adjusted to the prospective level of aggregate demand in the economy. If one wants to argue that the federal deficit isn't really a deficit because the government has a lot of physical

---

[5] From $5 billion in 1900 to $203 billion in 1958. See Raymond W. Goldsmith and Robert E. Lipsey, *Studies in the National Balance Sheet* (Princeton, N.J.: Princeton University Press, 1963), p. 43.

assets to show for it, well and good. But this is public relations rather than economics.

THE QUESTION OF THE DEBT

There is still a widespread public feeling that increases in public debt are unsound and dangerous, and that reducing the debt should be a major objective of fiscal policy. So we must look into this question before concluding.

TABLE 2

Public Debt in the United States, 1930–64
(Billions of Dollars)

YEAR	FEDERAL GOVERNMENT (End of Fiscal Year)	STATE AND LOCAL GOVERNMENTS	YEAR	FEDERAL GOVERNMENT (End of Fiscal Year)	STATE AND LOCAL GOVERNMENTS
1930	16.2	18.5	1950	257.4	24.2
1931	16.8		1951	255.2	27.0
1932	19.5	19.2	1952	259.1	29.6
1933	22.5		1953	266.1	32.7
1934	27.1	18.9	1954	271.3	37.9
1935	28.7		1955	274.4	43.2
1936	33.8	19.5	1956	272.8	48.0
1937	36.4		1957	270.6	52.5
1938	37.2	19.4	1958	276.4	57.2
1939	40.4		1959	284.8	62.4
1940	43.0	20.2	1960	286.5	67.2
1941	49.0	20.2	1961	289.2	75.0
1942	72.4	19.7	1962	298.6	80.9
1943	136.7	18.7	1963	306.5	86.7
1944	201.0	17.5	1964	317.9	92.2
1945	258.7	16.6			
1946	269.4	15.9			
1947	258.3	16.8			
1948	252.3	18.7			
1949	252.8	20.9			

Sources: *Historical Statistics of the United States*, pp. 728–30. *Statistical Abstract of the United States*, 1961, pp. 388–89. U.S. Department of Commerce, *Governmental Finances*, 1961; *Survey of Current Business*, May, 1965.

The growth of public debt in the United States since 1930 is shown in Table 2. Most of the increase in federal debt occurred between 1941 and 1945. The rise of state and local debt, on the other hand, has occurred largely since 1945. It represents mainly school construction to educate the offspring of the "baby boom," and to a lesser extent the cost of highways and other public improvements.

But however acquired, doesn't this debt represent a burden on the population? How much of a burden, and for whom?

An important clue lies in the distinction between *real burdens* and *financial burdens*. The *real cost* of a public expenditure consists of resources which might otherwise have been put to some other use. It is an *opportunity cost*. This cost depends on the level of economic activity. In a period of heavy unemployment, one can argue that resources diverted to public use would otherwise be doing nothing. Their opportunity cost is zero. But if resources are fully employed, an increase in public production means an equivalent drop in production for private use. It is this drop which constitutes the real burden of the public expenditure.

At the height of World War II, the American economy was operating beyond the point of normal full employment. Manpower, plant capacity, transportation, and other resources were stretched tight. Something like half of all resources was devoted to war production. If this had not been necessary, most of these resources would have been available for private consumption and investment. To the extent that resources were withdrawn from consumption, the population of the country "paid for the war" directly through a lowering of living standards. This cost could not be "passed on to future generations," since the future generations weren't around at the time!

There probably was some shifting of the war burden to future years, since resources were withdrawn from investment as well as consumption. Except for war plants and facilities, investment virtually ceased. Thus future periods were deprived of the flow of goods which might have resulted from investments which were in fact not made. But this argument is largely conjectural. It is possible that the low investment during the war contributed to an abnormally high rate of "catching-up" investment after the war, so that by 1960 our capital stock was as great as if the war had never occurred.[6]

Turning to the financial side, what is the significance of the fact that the national debt increased fivefold during the war years? The most obvious result is that more taxes must be raised each year to pay interest on the debt. The federal budget for 1964–65 included about $11 billion for interest charges. The corresponding figure for 1939–40 was about $1 billion.

Is this an added burden on the people of the United States? It clearly would be if the U.S. government bonds were owned by residents of Peru. In this case, our taxpayers would have to hand over each year $11 billion to the Peruvians for interest payments. This could not be done for long from our gold reserves, and the Peruvians might not even want

---

[6] This seems to have been true in Germany, Japan, and the U.S.S.R., where great wartime devastation was followed by very heavy postwar investment. There may be some underlying principle that "the farther you fall, the higher you bounce."

that much gold. So eventually we would have to make payment by shipping goods of that value to Peru. This would reduce consumption levels in the United States and constitute a real burden on the population.

But the national debt is not held by Peruvians. It is held almost entirely by people and corporations within the United States. "We owe it to ourselves." So the taxes raised to pay interest on the debt come back into the pockets of people in this country. If the impact of the federal tax system were exactly the same as the ownership of the debt, this would amount merely to each person shifting money from one pocket to the other. To the extent that this is not true, the transfer affects the distribution of personal income. But it remains true that, for the population as a whole, the rights to receive interest balance off the obligations to pay interest. There is no burden of the debt in the sense that my house mortgage imposes a burden on me.

This does *not* mean that the size of the debt is unimportant. Paying interest on the debt requires tax levies, and levying taxes always harms the private economy to some extent. "There are no good taxes." Personal income taxes affect incentives to work; business taxes affect the ability and incentive to invest; excise taxes penalize consumption of certain products and distort the pattern of production. Even if the $100 which I pay the government in taxes comes right back to me as interest on government bonds which I own, I am worse off as a result of the transfer.

The inconvenience resulting from additional taxation is often termed *tax friction*. The tax friction resulting from the national debt can be measured by the percentage of national income which must be raised in taxes to pay interest on the debt. This depends on three things:

1. The size of the debt.
2. The rate of interest on the debt.
3. The size of the national income.

An increase in the size of the debt or the rate of interest increases the weight of the debt, while an increase in national income reduces it. If interest rates remain stable, the inconvenience of the debt increases only if it is growing faster than national income. If national income is rising 5 percent a year, the debt can also rise 5 percent a year without the economy being any worse off than before.

Table 3 shows interest payments on the federal debt, calculated as a percentage of GNP, at two-year intervals since 1929.

While the debt has risen from $17 billion in 1929 to over $300 billion at present, its economic significance has risen much less than this. In 1929, interest payments on the debt were 0.65 percent of GNP. Today they are higher, but not startlingly so, at about 1.75 percent of GNP. Note also that the interest burden is somewhat *lower* today than it was at the end of World War II. The debt has continued to rise gradually, and interest rates have also risen, but this has been more than offset by the rate of increase in GNP.

The tax friction due to national debt typically falls during peacetime and rises sharply after major wars. It has been estimated that interest on the national debt of Great Britain amounted to 7.7 percent of

TABLE 3

Interest Payments on the Federal Debt, 1929–64

CALENDAR YEAR	GNP ($ Billions)	INTEREST PAYMENTS ($ Billions)	INTEREST PAYMENTS (Percent of GNP)
1929	104.4	0.678	0.65
1930	91.1	0.695	0.72
1932	58.5	0.599	1.02
1934	65.0	0.757	1.16
1936	82.7	0.749	0.91
1938	85.2	0.926	1.07
1940	100.6	1.041	1.03
1942	159.1	1.260	0.79
1944	211.4	2.609	1.23
1946	210.7	4.722	2.24
1948	259.4	5.211	2.01
1950	284.6	5.750	2.02
1952	347.0	5.859	1.69
1954	363.1	6.382	1.76
1956	419.2	6.787	1.62
1958	444.2	7.607	1.71
1960	503.2	9.179	1.82
1962	560.3	9.120	1.63
1964	628.7	10.900	1.73

Source: *Historical Statistics of the United States,* p. 139; *Statistical Abstract of the United States,* 1961, pp. 301, 389; and *U.S. Treasury Bulletin,* April, 1964, and April, 1965.

GNP in 1818, soon after the end of the Napoleonic wars. During the peaceful nineteenth century, it fell substantially. But by the end of World War II, it was back up to 6.2 percent of GNP or about three times the U.S. level.

But are we not getting out of the problem too easily? What about the principal of the debt? Must we not repay this at some time in the future? The answer is emphatically NO. Personal debts have to be repaid because people are mortal. My creditors want to make sure that I pay off my debts before I am gathered to my fathers. (Hence the length of time for which a bank will give a house mortgage decreases as the borrower's age increases!) But nations do not suffer from this human frailty. So there is no reason why national debt must be paid off, and in fact it rarely is. It may be reduced a bit in years of budget surplus. But for the most part, as old debts mature, the government simply "refunds" the debt by issuing new securities in place of the old.

All this is an accepted part of our financial system. Banks, insurance companies, colleges, and wealthy individuals hold large amounts of government securities in their portfolios. To them, these certificates of national debt appear as *assets*. And they are preferred assets because of the ease with which they can be converted into cash and the negligible risk of default. If the supply of such assets ever shrank materially through retirement of national debt, large investors would be embarrassed because they could not find such riskless assets elsewhere.

SUMMARY

1. In this chapter the *government budget* means government transactions on income and product account. *Expenditure* means government purchases of goods and services. *Taxation* means net taxes or tax receipts minus transfer payments.

2. Government expenditure by itself raises the equilibrium level of national income. Even if tax receipts are equal to expenditure, the budget has an expansionist effect. This is usually termed the *balanced budget theorem*.

3. Taxation by iteslf reduces private spending and lowers the equilibrium level of income.

4. The present U.S. tax structure is so constructed that tax receipts rise a good deal faster than national income on the upswing, and fall faster on the downswing. This has an automatic braking effect on fluctuations in national income, usually termed the *built-in stabilizer*.

5. *Fiscal policy* is the deliberate adjustment of tax rates and government expenditure to achieve a desired level of national income. A specific combination of tax and expenditure levels constitutes a *fiscal program*.

6. The federal surplus or deficit in a particular year depends on two things: the fiscal program, and the level of national income. Because the latter is somewhat unpredictable, the budget result is often substantially different from what was intended.

7. The main consideration in choosing a fiscal program is the current and prospective level of national income relative to the output capacity of the economy. If the economy is operating below capacity, a more expansionist program is needed; and conversely if spending threatens to be excessive.

8. Short-run changes in the fiscal program should be brought about mainly by varying tax rates. Government expenditure should be set at a level which, *assuming full employment,* will allocate the nation's resources between private and public production according to the preferences of the citizens. These preferences presumably change rather slowly, and so it is not appropriate to vary expenditure to offset short-term fluctuations in national income.

9. A national debt owned within the country is not a burden in the sense that private debt constitutes a burden. It does, however, involve the inconvenience of raising more taxes to meet interest payments to bondholders. This *tax friction* can be measured by the size of interest payments as a percentage of GNP.

10. There is no reason why national debt need be reduced over the long run. It is quite feasible for the Treasury to pay off old bonds and certificates as they mature by selling new securities of equivalent value.

DISCUSSION QUESTIONS

1. In discussing the effect of taxation and government expenditure on national income, how should one define expenditure? Taxation? The budget?

2. Why will a balanced increase in the government budget raise the equilibrium level of income? What qualifications must one attach to this conclusion?

3. Does the balanced budget multiplier theorem tell one anything about the desirable level of government expenditure?

4. How does the U.S. federal tax structure affect the shape of the consumption schedule?

5. What is meant by saying that our tax structure operates as a "built-in stabilizer"? Does the stabilizer work on the upswing as well as the downswing?

6. What is meant by a *budget line?* Why does this line slope upward to the right? What determines the slope?

7. Suppose federal tax rates are cut by an amount which, at present GNP levels, would reduce tax collections by $10 billion. Expenditures remain unchanged. Will the federal deficit rise by $10 billion? Explain.

8. Is it possible for a tax cut to *reduce* the budget deficit? What conditions would be necessary for this to occur?

9. Suppose the economy is operating below capacity, and one wants a more expansionist fiscal program. Should one raise expenditures, or lower taxes, or both? Why?

10. Some fiscal theorists argue that the size of the budget deficit or surplus should not be a direct object of policy. What is the rationale of this position? Do you agree with it?

11. "Budget balancing" can mean several different things. What are some of the possible meanings?

12. In what sense does an internally held public debt constitute a "burden"? How can one measure the size of the burden?

13. Is there any need to "pay off the national debt"?

14. What does retirement of public debt mean in concrete terms? Under what economic conditions would such action be appropriate?

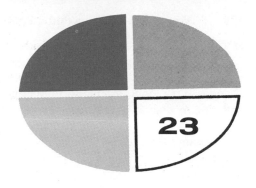

The Supply of Money

> Money is indeed the most important thing in the world; and all sound and successful personal and national morality should have this fact for its basis.
>
> GEORGE BERNARD SHAW

THERE IS a close relation between money and spending. The relation was put graphically by Sir Dennis Robertson, who called the amount of money in existence "money sitting," while spending was "money on the wing."

The fact that money exists doesn't tell us that it will be spent, or how rapidly it will be spent. This is why it seemed wise to start out in Chapters 20–22 by analyzing the basis for spending decisions, and what happens when these decisions change. But, on the other hand, money cannot be spent *unless* it exists, and an increase in the level of spending is apt to be accompanied by an increase in the quantity of money. So we need to understand where money comes from, the ways in which the quantity of money can be controlled, and the extent to which monetary controls can help in avoiding extremes of depression or inflation. These questions form the substance of Chapters 23 and 24.

THE NATURE OF MONEY

Money is as money does. Anything which members of a community are willing to accept in payment for goods or debts is money. Large round stones serve the purpose on the island of Yap. They can't be carried around in one's pocket. Indeed, the happy inhabitants of this island don't have pockets. The stones remain immovable on hillsides throughout the island; but each stone has an owner, and ownership changes as payments are made. One large stone fell out of a boat years ago and lies in deep water some distance offshore. It is still wealth to its owner and counts as part of the island's money supply.

Among the Bantu tribes of East Africa, animals serve as a means of payment. A prospective bridegroom must pay the father of the bride so many cattle, sheep, or goats as a "bride price." Monetary systems have been based on cowrie shells, wampum, cloth, and beads. A prisoner-of-war camp during World War II developed an elaborate system of exchange in which cigarettes were accepted as currency.

Gold and other metals have always exercised a special fascination. They are durable, they can be fashioned into personal ornaments and art objects, and this commercial value reinforces their value as money. From Greek times until quite recently, money in the Western world meant metal coins which circulated partly by order of the sovereign but also by virtue of their metallic content.

The next stage in the development of modern monetary systems came with the rise of banking institutions in Europe during the fifteenth and sixteenth centuries. Banks gradually learned that they could issue paper notes which would be generally accepted as a means of payment. A bank note meant originally that the banker had an equivalent amount of gold in his vaults, which he promised to pay to the holder of the note on demand. But so long as people had faith in the bank's soundness, there was no reason for them to demand payment. The notes passed freely from hand to hand because of the general belief that they were "as good as gold." After a time, most payments came to be made in this way, and coins were reduced to serving as small change.

Still more recent is the practice of making payments by check. Most businesses and individuals now hold ready cash in the form of a checking account. One occasionally reads of an old lady with a passion for keeping bundles of bank notes in brown paper bags, but these stories make the headlines only because they are so rare. Most people regard a checking account as perfectly safe, and so it is. In the unlikely event that your bank should fail, deposits up to $10,000 are guaranteed through the Federal Deposit Insurance Corporation. Bankers refer to checking accounts as *demand deposits,* because the owner is entitled to withdraw them at any time on demand, without advance notice.

It may seem odd to regard checking accounts as money; but they meet the test of general acceptability. Checks written by a business concern, government agency, or other institution are normally accepted without question. So are personal checks with at most a quick glance at your driver's license. In addition, purchases are made increasingly on credit. When the bills roll in at the end of the month, how are they paid? By check, of course. This is much more convenient than going to the bank for paper money, and it also provides a ready record of what you have spent.

In mid-1965, there was about $35 billion of coins and paper currency in circulation. Demand deposits in the hands of the public totaled about $125 billion. Thus demand deposits now form about four fifths of total money supply in the United States. Moreover, check money circulates faster than other kinds of money. More than 90 percent of all payments in the United States are made by check. So when we ask what determines the amount of money in existence, the main problem is what determines the amount of demand deposits.

We count checking accounts as money. Why do we not also count savings accounts? These are called *time deposits,* because the holder can be required to give a certain period of notice before withdrawing them. In normal times, most banks overlook this requirement, and savings accounts can be withdrawn as freely as checking accounts. The total amount of time deposits in mid-1965 was $185 billion.

For that matter, why do we not count holdings of short-term government securities, which can be turned into cash without notice and with little risk? These resemble money in certain respects. They provide a safe way of holding reserve funds, and are counted as part of the liquid assets of businesses and individuals. Savings accounts and short-term government securities are often lumped together as *near money.*

But they are still not *quite* money. They are not directly and universally transferable. You can't go to the store and spend a savings account or a U.S. Treasury bill. They must first be converted into real money, which is then used as a means of payment. In the case of securities, the terms on which conversion can be effected are typically uncertain. A company knows that it can always sell its holdings of U.S. Treasury bills for cash; but the price of Treasury bills varies from day to day, and the outcome is uncertain until the bills are sold. Thus if I put a thousand dollars into securities, I cannot know how many dollars I will be able to realize in a year's time. The same thousand dollars put into a checking account will always be worth a thousand dollars. The difference is important. This is what one means by saying that money possesses *complete liquidity.*

The fact that we do not count near money as identical with true money does not mean that the amount of near money in existence is unimportant. Quite the contrary. If households and businesses have large holdings of savings accounts and government securities, this may make them more venturesome in spending their current incomes. For a couple of years after World War II, consumer spending almost equaled consumer income, and personal savings dropped almost to zero. This was partly because consumers had accumulated many billions of savings during the war, which gave them a feeling of safety and increased their readiness to spend.

THE BUSINESS OF BANKING

There are banks and banks. Certain types of banks, important in their own right, lack the power to create demand deposits and hence are of no concern to us here. Examples are: (1) *Investment banks* or *underwriters.* These are securities merchants, who float new bond and stock issues on the general market. (2) *Savings banks,* whose business is to accept savings or time deposits. Money put into a savings account is usually left with the bank for a considerable period. This justifies the bank in putting the money into house mortgages, bonds, and other long-term securities. These securities earn interest, which constitutes the income of the bank. The bank pays interest at a lower rate to the depositors, covering its costs and hopefully making a profit from the spread.

The banks whose operations influence the money supply are called *commercial banks.* They are dealers in money or, if you prefer, dealers in loans. They also perform certain service functions. My bank receives my paycheck from my employer every month, allows me to draw checks on the account, sends me a statement at the end of the month, and deducts a service charge for its trouble. But this is an unexciting and not very profitable operation. The lifeblood of commercial banking is sizing up would-be borrowers and advancing them money for a price.

Why is this sort of banking called *commercial?* Because in the early days most bank borrowers were engaged in commerce. Their need for loans is readily explained. A wholesaler buys a shipment of shoes from a manufacturer and must pay for it within 30 days. He will eventually resell the merchandise to retailers and collect for it, but this may take 90 days. How does he get the money to pay off the shoe manufacturer? If his business reputation and credit standing are satisfactory, he can go to a bank and borrow the necessary money. The bank adds the amount of the loan to his checking account. He gives the bank a promissory note backed by the merchandise itself as *collateral.* (Collateral is something which the bank can lay hands on if the borrower fails to repay the loan. If I borrow money to buy a car, the bank can take over the car if I default on the payments. The car is collateral.)

Commercial bank lending is typically of this "tiding over" sort. A farmer needs money in the spring for seed, fertilizer, other farm costs, and living expenses. He must survive until the crop ripens in the fall, or until his cattle or hogs have been fattened and sold. The answer? A 6-month bank loan, secured by animals or farm machinery as collateral. A manufacturer must buy raw materials and hire labor to work on products which may not be sold for months to come. He may need a bank loan to carry him through the intervening period.

A commercial bank provides *circulating capital* or *working capital*, which tides over the period between the beginning of a production process and the sale of the final product. This period is usually short. Hence commercial bank loans typically run between 1 and 6 months, with 3 months perhaps the commonest period. Commercial banks do not usually provide long-term money for plant construction. These *fixed capital* needs must be met by reinvesting profits or by selling new securities in the capital market.

The line between short-term and long-term lending is often unclear in practice. A company may never borrow for more than 3 months; but as one loan is repaid, and if the company continues to need money, the bank may immediately extend a new loan of the same amount. This can go on for years, provided the company continues to meet the bank's standards of financial soundness. In such cases the bank becomes a continuing partner in the enterprise, fortifying it with ready cash as needed, while on the other hand looking over management's shoulder and keeping an eye on the books. The company, so long as it continues to operate successfully, has a permanent source of working capital. But the fact that loans must be renewed every 3 months or 6 months enables the banker to bail out quickly if the business seems to be going downhill.

We can now see why the level of business borrowing moves up and down with the level of production. Suppose manufacturers believe an economic upswing is underway and decide to step up production schedules. They must immediately begin to lay out more money for payrolls, raw materials, and other operating expenses. Where will the money come from? Some companies may be able to draw on accumulated cash reserves, but others will go to the banks seeking larger loans.

Suppose the banks are willing to make additional loans. They can do so simply by adding the amount of the loans to the borrowers' checking accounts. Thus demand deposits rise. But demand deposits are money, the most important kind of money in the modern economy. So we reach an important conclusion: An increase in the level of economic activity is normally accompanied by an increase in the quantity of money.

The converse is also true: A drop in economic activity is normally accompanied by a decline in demand deposits. If production is dropping, businesses need less working capital than before and find themselves paying off old loans faster than they are requesting new ones. But how does a business (or an individual) pay off a loan? By allowing the bank to *deduct* the amount of the loan from its checking account. Repayment of loans thus means a drop in demand deposits.

This parallel movement of money supply and productive activity says nothing about causation. We are not asserting that changes in the quantity of money *cause* changes in the level of production, or vice versa. The interrelation is more complicated than this, as will appear in the next chapter.

BANK ASSETS: INCOME AND SECURITY

A good way to dig deeper into the nature of commercial banking is to look at the assets which banks hold and the liabilities which they owe. Instead of selecting a particular bank, let us look at the totals for all commercial banks in the United States at the beginning of 1965. (Table 1).

TABLE 1

Consolidated Balance Sheet; All Commercial Banks
January 1, 1965

ASSETS (Millions)		LIABILITIES (Millions)	
Cash and interbank		Owners' capital	27,795
deposits	37,581	Time deposits	126,720
Balances with Federal		Demand deposits,	
Reserve Banks	17,581	including interbank	
U.S. government securities	62,991	deposits	180,451*
Other securities	38,796	Other	11,955
Loans	175,589		
Other	14,383		
Total	346,921	Total	346,921

* This figure is considerably larger than the $125 billion mentioned earlier as part of the money supply. The main reason is that it includes deposits held by one bank in another, and also government deposits, which are not considered part of money supply.
Source: *Federal Reserve Bulletin,* June, 1965.

A central concern of any commercial bank is security and liquidity. The liability side of Table 1 shows that the banks of the country are obligated in theory to pay out fantastic amounts to depositors. Demand deposits can be withdrawn at once, and time deposits can be withdrawn on 30 days' notice. Thus it seems that households and businesses could descend on the banks and demand upwards of $200 billion in cash. They would not get very far, since there is only about $30 billion of cash in existence. This would amount to a general collapse of the banking system, which could happen only in extreme emergency. Something close to this did happen in early 1933 at the bottom of the Great Depression. Widespread public demand for cash led to the failure of many banks and finally to a "bank holiday," during which all banks were closed by government order until public confidence could be restored.

While a general "run" on the banks is unlikely, a particular bank may be faced with substantial and unexpected withdrawals. So it must stand ready to meet any demands for cash payment. The first three items on the asset side of Table 1—cash, balances with the Federal Reserve, and U.S. securities—constitute successive lines of defense on which a bank can fall back to meet its obligations.

Cash

Banks normally hold some money in the till to meet depositors' requests for cash. Bills and coins are now a minor part of the monetary system, and the demand for cash is reasonably predictable. Moreover, while some customers are demanding cash from the bank, others will be returning cash for deposit. Thus a bank can get along with a remarkably small amount of currency, usually only a few percent of its total liabilities.

Reserves

Should there be unusually heavy withdrawals of cash from a bank, it can fall back on its next line of defense—its checking account with the Federal Reserve Bank of its district. The Federal Reserve Banks, of which there are 12 in the United States, are *central banks* or *banker's banks*. They deal almost entirely with the commercial banks rather than with the general public. Their operations will be explained in the next chapter. Meanwhile, we may note that commercial banks which are members of the system maintain substantial checking accounts, usually called *reserves*, with the Reserve Bank of their district. If a bank suddenly needs $50,000 of additional currency, the Federal Reserve ships it this amount of Federal Reserve notes, at the same time deducting $50,000 from the bank's checking account.

The minimum reserves which a commercial bank must carry are specified by law. A bank normally prefers to have reserves somewhat above the legal minimum, since it is only these "excess" or "free reserves" which can be drawn on for day-to-day operations. The drawback is that a checking account at the Federal Reserve earns no interest. It is an unproductive investment for the bank compared, say, with putting the same amount into government securities.

Government Securities

An important type of bank asset is short-term securities of the federal government. These earn interest and are readily salable should the bank run short of reserves. They are in fact often termed *secondary reserves*.

At the end of 1965, there was about $267 billion of U.S. securities in the hands of banks, business concerns, and individuals. (In addition, there was some $47 billion of special issues not available to the public, such as the securities held by the Old-Age, Survivors, and Disability Insurance system.) Commercial banks owned $57 billion, or about one fifth of the total. Their holdings were largely in the form of Treasury bills and certificates. These short-term securities are particularly attractive to the commercial banks, which dislike committing money for long periods.

The disadvantage of short-term federal securities is the low rate of interest which they carry. They typically pay something between 1 and 3 percent, whereas money put into business loans will yield 4 to 6 percent. On the other hand, government securities are safe and can readily be converted into cash.

Bank holdings of government securities fluctuate in response to the demand for business loans. If the demand for loans is rising, the banks try to meet it, both to keep the goodwill of their customers and to earn higher rates of interest. If necessary, they will sell some government securities and shift the money to loans. Conversely, in slack times when loans are being repaid faster than new loans are being demanded, the banks find themselves with idle resources which they can put back into securities. Earning 2 percent is better than earning nothing at all.

Loans

Commercial banks are basically lending institutions. Thus the largest category of bank assets is loans to businesses and households. We have already seen what happens when a loan is made. The borrower gives the bank a promise to pay, a piece of paper which counts as an asset. The bank gives the borrower an addition to his checking account, which increases the demand deposit item on the liability side of Table 1. The *loans* item on the asset side of Table 1 is the sum total of pieces of paper certifying that people owe the banks money. These are certificates of private indebtedness, just as a government bond is a certificate of public indebtedness. Commercial banks are in the business of buying certificates of indebtedness, public and private.

Bank loans include such things as: "commercial loans" in the old sense of loans to wholesalers, retailers, exporters, importers, and other merchants; working capital loans to manufacturers; agricultural loans to farmers (though a good deal of this is now handled by federal lending agencies); loans to consumers, where the commercial banks now offer vigorous competition to the personal finance companies; and mortgage loans for residential and commercial construction.

The volume of loans is only partly within the control of the commercial banks. It takes two to make a loan, and the borrower normally takes the initiative. The bank's influence is limited to being more or less receptive to loan applications and to varying the interest rate which it charges. No matter how receptive the banker may be, no matter how reasonable his terms, businessmen will not request loans unless they expect to earn a profit on the money. If the economy is in recession, loan applications will decline, and they will be revived only by an upturn in business activity.

BANK LIABILITIES: DEMAND DEPOSITS AND CREDIT CREATION

When I write a check for $100, this is an order to my bank to deduct $100 from my account and transfer it to the recipient of the check. He then deposits it in his bank and gets the amount added to his balance. If we both have checking accounts in the same bank, the transaction is simple. The bank deducts $100 from my account and adds $100 to his. The bank's total deposits remain unchanged.

But suppose a check drawn on bank A is deposited in bank B. Bank A then owes bank B that much money, and a transfer between the two banks is necessary. It is likely, however, that at the same time some checks drawn on bank B will have been deposited in bank A, so that the two debts will partially cancel each other. These cancellations are carried out through a central clearinghouse in each city. Each morning every bank sends to the clearinghouse all the checks which it has received drawn on other banks in the city. The totals are added up. A bank which has sent in more dollars worth of checks on other banks than others have sent in against it receives a payment of that amount. A bank which has an adverse balance must pay in that amount to the clearinghouse. How does a bank "pay up" in such a case? By writing a check on its account with the Federal Reserve Bank of its district. Thus a bank which has more checks drawn against it than are being deposited with it suffers a reduction in its balance at the Federal Reserve.

If a check drawn in one city is deposited in another, the clearance procedure is more elaborate but not basically different. Again, the important thing to the individual bank is whether the total checks drawn against it are greater or less than the checks it is receiving drawn on other banks.

The term *demand deposits* is confusing. It suggests that to get a checking account I must *deposit* something in the bank. This idea seems so reasonable that it is hard to dislodge from one's mind. There is even an element of truth in the idea, for this is certainly one way to acquire a checking account. I can come into the First National Bank of Illyria and open a checking account by depositing either a check which I have received or a bundle of paper money. But note that *this does not alter the amount of money in the economy*. If I deposit a check, the increase in my checking account is exactly offset by a reduction in someone else's checking account. Total demand deposits remain unchanged. If I deposit cash, this increases the amount of demand deposits in existence, but it reduces cash in circulation by an equal amount. Total money supply remains unchanged.

How, then, can there ever be an increase or decrease in the supply of money? The answer is that there is a second way in which demand deposits can originate. Suppose I am a manufacturer with a growing business which requires more working capital. I ask my banker for a loan of $100,000 and, after looking into the soundness of the business, he approves the loan. What does he give me? Not a bale of $100 bills. He simply adds $100,000 to my checking account. In return, I give him a piece of paper promising to repay the money by a specified date. The transaction affects the bank's balance sheet as follows:

ASSETS		LIABILITIES	
Loans	+100,000	Demand deposits	+100,000

Here is an increase in demand deposits coming right out of the blue. My need for a loan has increased the money supply of the economy.

This apparent ability to create something out of nothing has subjected bankers to much criticism and complaint. There is a limitless supply of would-be borrowers, each very creditworthy in his own eyes. The banker, they feel, has only to agree. For can he not create new money at the stroke of a pen? If he declines to do so, is he not being mean and niggardly? "The monied interests," with their stubborn refusal to turn the money tap wide open, have been a favorite target of politicians.

A banker hearing this kind of talk comes as close to foaming at the mouth as a banker ever could. He will maintain stoutly that his power to make new loans is strictly limited. He is likely to say, "Create money? Why, I can't do that. I can only lend out money which other people have first deposited with me."

What is the truth of the matter? Can the banks create money or can't they?

CREDIT CREATION: A MONOPOLY BANK

Suppose there is a single bank, with branches all over the country, which has a monopoly of the commercial banking business. This bank is required by law to maintain a balance with the Federal Reserve System equal to 20 percent of its demand deposits. And suppose that at the moment the bank is just meeting this requirement. Its Federal Reserve balance is exactly 20 percent of its demand deposits. It also has exactly the amount of till money which it considers necessary. In this situation the bank is indeed tied hand and foot. It is loaned up, as bankers say. If I approached it for a loan, it could only say "So sorry."

But help is on the way. Out of the hills comes a prospector who has found $1 million worth of gold nuggets in a canyon. Instead of gambling them away he turns them over to the bank, which credits his checking account. The bank then passes the gold on to the Federal Reserve, thereby increasing its balance at the Fed by $1 million. The effect on the bank's position is:

ASSETS		LIABILITIES	
Balance at Federal Reserve	+1,000,000	Demand deposits	+1,000,000

The bank's reserves have now been increased, so it can presumably increase its loans as well. By how much? The answer depends on the legal reserve ratio. If the ratio is 20 percent, the bank can make new loans of $4 million. Its balance sheet will then have changed as follows:

ASSETS		LIABILITIES	
Balance at Federal Reserve	+1,000,000	Prospector's demand deposits	+1,000,000
Loans	+4,000,000	Borrowers' demand deposits	+4,000,000

At this stage the bank has once more reached the limit of its lending capacity. Its extra $1 million of reserves will support the extra $5 million of demand deposits but no more than this. It must now mark time until there is some further addition to its reserves.

In this simplified case one can conclude that:

1. There is a definite ceiling to the bank's lending capacity. This is determined by the size of its reserves and by the legal reserve requirement. If the legal ratio is 20 percent, it can lend only up to the point at which demand deposits are five times the reserves on hand. When the bank has reached this ceiling, it cannot increase loans without an addition to its reserves.

2. An addition to reserve enables the bank to increase its deposits by several times the amount of the addition. The degree of deposit expansion depends on the required reserve ratio. A reserve ratio of 20 percent will permit a fivefold expansion, as in our illustrative case. With a

10 percent ratio, deposits could be increased by 10 times the increase in reserves; and so on.

3. This principle operates equally in the opposite direction. A reduction in reserves will force a deposit reduction of several times that amount. Starting from a loaned-up position, and with a 20 percent reserve ratio, a drop of $1 million in reserves would compel a reduction of $5 million in demand deposits.

The size of bank reserves is thus the central lever of the monetary system. An upward or downward movement in reserves has a multiple effect on the feasible level of demand deposits. This flexibility of the system permits the money supply to change rapidly in response to business requirements, but it is sometimes criticized as a source of instability and an aggravating factor in business cycles.

CREDIT CREATION: A MULTIPLE BANKING SYSTEM

How far do these principles apply to the U.S. banking system, which contains thousands of banks operating independently of each other? Let us consider this case, assuming again that all banks must keep legal reserves of 20 percent.

If all banks in the system are loaned up, the answer is the same as before. There can be no increase in loans without an addition to reserves. But here comes our helpful prospector once more. He must now choose a particular bank for his deposit, which we shall call bank A. As before, the bank sends the gold to the Federal Reserve and receives a $1 million addition to its reserve balance.

How much can the bank lend on the basis of this increase in reserves? An inexperienced banker might reason as we did in the previous case: the $1 million of new reserves will support an additional $5 million of demand deposits. Demand deposits have already increased by the $1 million which was credited to the prospector's account. This leaves $4 million which the bank can lend.

In the present case, however, this answer would be wrong. The reason is that people do not borrow money to let it sit in the bank. They borrow it to spend. If a bank adds $4 million to checking accounts through new loans, the borrowers will immediately start writing checks against this amount. They are entitled to spend it all, and the only safe assumption is that they will spend it all in the near future.

In the previous case, where all checks drawn against the monopoly bank come back to branches of the same bank, this presents no problem. Money never leaves the bank, and the $5 million of new demand deposits will always remain covered by the $1 million addition to reserves.

In a multiple banking system, however, each bank must assume that the checks drawn on it will be deposited in *other* banks. If bank A goes blithely ahead and lends $4 million dollars, it will soon find other banks descending on it *via* the clearinghouse demanding payment of this $4 million. The bank has only $1 million of new reserves available to meet this obligation. So bank A is in trouble, and the official who authorized the new loans is in disgrace.

How much *can* bank A safely lend on the basis of its increased reserves? The answer in this case is $800,000. Why is this? Because even if this amount is checked out of bank A at once, and the bank has to pay over $800,000 of its new reserves to other banks, it still has $200,000 left to set against the prospector's demand deposit of $1 million. The 20 percent reserve requirement is satisfied, and the bank is in balance.

This can be explained most clearly in balance sheet terms. The first effect of the prospector's gold deposit on bank A's balance sheet is as follows:

ASSETS		LIABILITIES	
Balance at Federal Reserve	+1,000,000	Demand deposits	+1,000,000

Bank A now lends $800,000 to customers. After the loans have been made, but before any of the money has been checked out, the bank's books will look as follows:

ASSETS		LIABILITIES	
Balance at Federal Reserve	+1,000,000	Prospector's demand deposits	+1,000,000
Loans	+ 800,000	Borrowers' demand deposits	+ 800,000

Now the borrowers proceed to spend the full amount of their loans, and all the checks they write are deposited in other banks, which bank A must repay by drawing on its account at the Federal Reserve. After this has happened, bank A is left in the following position:

ASSETS		LIABILITIES	
Balance at Federal Reserve	+200,000	Prospector's demand deposits	+1,000,000
Loans	+800,000		

Since the increase in reserves is 20 percent of the increase in demand deposits, the bank is all right. But if it had tried to lend more than $800,000, its reserves would have been depleted to the point where it could no longer meet the legal reserve requirement.

This is the end of the story as far as bank A is concerned, but it is not the end for the banking system as a whole. Other banks in the system have now gained $800,000 of reserves through the withdrawals from bank A. Thus they are in a position to increase *their* loans, creating demand deposits in the process. How much can they lend? By the same reasoning used for bank A, they will be able to lend $\frac{4}{5}$ of the increase in reserves, or $640,000.

This $640,000 is now checked out by the borrowers and deposited in still other banks, which gain reserves to this extent. These larger reserves will justify increased loans and demand deposits amounting to $\frac{4}{5}$ of $640,000; and so on and on.

When the process has worked itself out, demand deposits will have increased by

$$1,000,000 + 1,000,000(\tfrac{4}{5}) + 1,000,000(\tfrac{4}{5})^2 + \ldots + 1,000,000(\tfrac{4}{5})^n .$$

The sum of this series is:

$$1,000,000 \left(\frac{1}{1 - \tfrac{4}{5}} \right) = 1,000,000 \left(\frac{1}{\tfrac{1}{5}} \right) = 5,000,000 .$$

The original increase in reserves has thus permitted a multiple expansion of demand deposits. The size of the expansion depends on the required reserve ratio. Since the reserve ratio was assumed to be one fifth, the increase in deposits is five times the increase in reserves.

What has happened here? The $1 million increase in reserves, which started out as a single lump in bank A, has been spread around among a large number of banks through the drawing and deposit of checks. But none of it is extinguished. Wherever it ends up, it serves to support demand deposits of five times its own size. Thus *for the banking system as a whole* it is now possible to have $5 million more in demand deposits than it was possible to have previously. The conclusion reached in the discussion of a single monopoly bank holds in this case as well. The banking system *can* create money. It can lend several times the amount of any increase in reserves, the size of this leverage depending on the required reserve ratio.

If we look only at one bank, the "banker's reasoning" is quite correct. A bank which is already loaned up cannot lend anything more until it has had an increase in reserves, and it can lend no more than the amount of this increase. Indeed, it must lend somewhat less than this to remain in a safe position.

The banking system as a whole, however, can do something which no bank within it can do individually. It can pyramid an increase in reserves into a multiple expansion of deposits. At the end of the process, a consolidated balance sheet for all banks in the system will show the following changes:

ASSETS		LIABILITIES	
Balances with Federal		Prospector's demand	
Reserve	+1,000,000	deposits	+1,000,000
Loans	+4,000,000	Borrowers' demand	
		deposits	+4,000,000

This is exactly the result which we reached in the monopoly bank case.

CREDIT CREATION: SIMULTANEOUS EXPANSION IN A MULTIPLE SYSTEM

The case just examined is remote from real life. It is unlikely that an increase in reserves would go entirely to one bank, and that other banks would have to sit idly by while the reserves were gradually redistributed among them through successive rounds of depositing and relending.

The forces which increase or decrease bank reserves are examined in the next chapter. They include deposit and withdrawal of cash by the public, movements of gold into and out of the United States, actions of the U.S. Treasury, and actions of the Federal Reserve System. These forces are likely to hit many banks at about the same time and in the same direction.

Suppose, for simplicity, that all banks are receiving additions to their reserves at the same time and at the same rate. Then each bank is safe in lending more than it has received, *provided it keeps in step with other banks in the system.* Why? Because if each bank increases its demand deposits at the same rate as other banks, it can assume that the extra checks which are going to be drawn against it will be offset by extra checks drawn against other banks and deposited with it. It need no longer fear the loss of reserves which would follow if it were the only bank in the system making new loans. If all banks are expanding simultaneously, each can move directly and rapidly toward a 5 to 1 expansion of demand deposits on the basis of its new reserves. We are back, in effect, to the monopoly bank case.

Reality is never this simple. Changes in bank reserves do not hit all banks with equal force. During an expansion some banks will gain reserves faster than others, and part of their gains will be spread around to other banks as described in the previous section. On the whole, however, a model of simultaneous proportionate expansion of reserves and deposits is more realistic than any other.

It is worth noting that a *reduction* in the required reserve ratio has the same effect as an *increase* in reserves. Suppose that at a particular time there are $100 billion of demand deposits, which are just covered by $20 billion of reserves. The Federal Reserve decides to lower the reserve ratio from 20 percent to 15 percent, so that the banks need only $15 billion of legal reserves. This leaves them with $5 billion of *free or excess reserves,* which will permit an increase in demand deposits of $5 \times \dfrac{100}{15} = \$33.3$ billion.

All our illustrations have involved *increases* in bank reserves and deposits. The system is expanding most of the time, and positive arithmetic is easier to grasp than negative arithmetic. Everything which has been said about expansion, however, applies equally to contraction. If the banking system is loaned up, and if it then *loses* reserves (or the Federal Reserve *raises* reserve requirements), the banks will be obliged to reduce demand deposits by several times as much. How is this done as a practical matter? Mainly by making new loans at a slower rate than old loans are being repaid.

Does this sound confusing? What happens when a loan is repaid? A wholesaler has borrowed $50,000 from a bank on a 3-month promissory note. At the end of the 3 months, unless the loan is extended or renewed, the bank automatically *deducts* $50,000 from the wholesaler's checking account. *Repayment of loans extinguishes demand deposits.* If the banks stopped making new loans completely, and simply waited for old loans to be paid off, demand deposits would fall quite fast. Actually, they need never go this far. By merely holding back, so that repayments run ahead of new loans, they can gradually reduce demand deposits to any desired level. This process is termed *credit contraction.*

SUMMARY

1. In the United States today, money consists largely of *checking accounts* or *demand deposits* at commercial banks.

2. The main business of a commercial bank is to make short-term loans to business concerns and households. *Making a loan creates a demand deposit.* Conversely, repaying a loan extinguishes a demand deposit. Thus the amount of "checking account money" in existence moves up and down with the volume of bank lending.

3. Partly because of business prudence, but mainly because of legal requirements, a commercial bank must hold a *reserve* equal to a specified percentage of its deposits. This takes the form of a checking account with the Federal Reserve Bank of its district.

4. If a bank's actual reserve percentage is just equal to the

percentage required by law, it is said to be *loaned up*. It cannot increase its volume of loans unless it receives an addition to its reserves.

5. Under the U.S. system of many independent banks, a bank which receives an addition to its reserves cannot lend more than the amount of the addition—in fact, somewhat less. This is because it must assume that the loans will be spent rapidly, leading to deposit of checks in other banks and a consequent transfer of reserves from the first bank to these others.

6. But this transfer of reserves enables other banks to increase *their* loans; and so on through successive cycles. *For the banking system as a whole,* loans can rise eventually by several times the amount of the original increase in reserves. Review the last few pages of the chapter to make sure you understand just how this works.

7. Everything which is true of expansion is true also of contraction. If bank reserves fall, loans will have to fall by several times as much.

DISCUSSION QUESTIONS

1. What are *demand deposits?* Why do we count them as part of the supply of money?

2. Why do we *not* count savings deposits and holdings of short-term government securities? Should these be included in money supply?

3. What are the main functions of a commercial bank? What other kinds of banks are there, and what do they do?

4. Why do businesses need short-term loans? Why do commercial banks limit themselves largely to this kind of lending?

5. A commercial bank is supposed to make money, but it is also supposed to avoid insolvency. How does a bank go about balancing these two objectives?

6. In what ways may a demand deposit originate? When does a new demand deposit increase the supply of money?

7. Explain the following: *bank reserves; legal reserve requirement; loaned up.*

8. Suppose one bank in a multiple banking system receives an addition of $1 million to its reserves. (Start from a loaned-up position, and assume a specified reserve requirement.) How much can *this bank* lend on the basis of the increased reserves? How much can *the banking system as a whole* increase its loans?

9. A banker will often say: "I can't create money. I can't make additional loans unless someone comes in and deposits some money with me." When is this statement true? When is it not true?

10. One sometimes hears complaints of a "shortage of credit." What might this mean concretely? Why should there ever be a shortage of credit when creation of new demand deposits is apparently so easy?

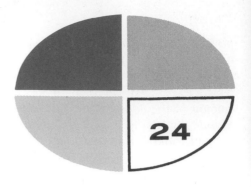

24

The Impact of Monetary Policy

Money knows nobody; money has no ears;
money has no heart.

HONORÉ DE BALZAC

PROSPECTORS FROM THE HILLS are not the main reason for changes in bank reserves, despite our example for Chapter 23. What are the actual reasons why reserves may increase or decrease? What control powers does the Federal Reserve System have, and how are these powers used to influence the supply of money? And how does the supply of money influence interest rates, spending, and production?

We now think of the Fed mainly as a vehicle for controlling the availability and cost of money on a national scale and for moderating the swings of the business cycle. But in the laissez-faire atmosphere of 50 years ago, such a program would have seemed radical and impractical. The Federal Reserve System was created in 1913 to serve limited and practical needs: to provide a rapid and effective system of check clearance; to provide a single fiscal agent for the federal government; to enforce rules of sound lending procedure on individual banks through periodic reports and visits by bank examiners; to provide a readily expansible supply of hand-to-hand currency; and to ward off "financial panics" (which had occurred with disastrous effect in 1873, 1884, 1893, and 1907) by creating a "lender of last resort" to which the commercial banks could turn in an emergency.

In the course of providing for these needs, however, the authors of the Act in 1913 gave the Federal Reserve power to influence the level of bank reserves. Its powers were enlarged by a major revision of the Act in

644

1935, following the banking collapse of 1933. As the Fed has gained experience in using its powers, and as belief has grown that business cycles can be moderated by deliberate action, the emphasis of the System's operation has shifted toward overall monetary control. The original service functions remain important but are now generally taken for granted.

STRUCTURE OF THE FEDERAL RESERVE SYSTEM

Most countries have a single central bank located in the national capital. Some of the European central banks are much older than our own. The Bank of Sweden dates from 1656, the Bank of England from 1694, and the Bank of France from 1800.

Because of the geographical diversity of the United States and the influence of sectional interests in Congress, it was decided to create 12 Federal Reserve Banks with headquarters in commercial centers throughout the country. These banks are located in Boston, New York, Philadelphia, Richmond, Atlanta, Cleveland, Chicago, Minneapolis, St. Louis, Kansas City, Dallas, and San Francisco. Each bank has jurisdiction over a "Federal Reserve District," comprising states in its normal trading area.

All commercial banks with national charters must be members of the Federal Reserve System, and state banks may become members by meeting certain qualifications. Some 7,000 state banks either have not been able to qualify or have been unwilling to accept the controls and obligations of Federal Reserve membership. The 6,000 or so banks which are members, however, have about 85 percent of the demand deposits in the country; and many of the nonmember banks carry their reserves in member banks. The great bulk of banking activity thus falls within the orbit of the System.

The 12 Federal Reserve Banks are *central banks* or *bankers' banks*. This is true in a double sense. First, each of them is owned by the member banks in its district. Second, Federal Reserve dealings are almost entirely with the commercial banks and the U.S. Treasury.

Despite their private ownership, they are in a real sense *public banks*. Their main function is to influence the volume and cost of money in a way which will promote stable prosperity. They are not primarily profit-making institutions. After the member banks have received a guaranteed annual 6 percent return on their capital subscriptions, almost all remaining Federal Reserve profits are turned over voluntarily to the Treasury.

The System is directed by a seven-man Board of Governors, located in Washington and appointed by the President with the advice and consent of the Senate. (When we speak loosely of "the Board" or "the Fed," it is usually this group that we have in mind.) Members of the Board are appointed for 14-year terms, one term expiring every 2 years.

This protects the Board against domination by a particular administration and to some extent immunizes it against pressure from Congress. This vaunted independence of the Fed presents difficulties as well as advantages and has given rise to considerable controversy.

The Board of Governors appoints three of the nine Directors of each Federal Reserve Bank. (Of the remaining members, three are expected to be commercial bankers, and three are chosen to represent industry, agriculture, and commerce. All six are elected by member banks in the district.) The chief officers of each bank, the president and first vice-president, must be approved by the Board of Governors. In addition, the Board of Governors dominates the strategic *Federal Open Market Committee,* which decides on Federal Reserve purchases and sales of government securities. Thus despite the separation into 12 regional banks, the System approaches the centralization of authority found in the central banks of other countries.

The most important feature of the Federal Reserve System is its power to influence the size of bank reserves and the legal reserve requirement. The principal control powers are:

1. The System can lend to member banks at a specified rate of interest, which is called the *discount rate.* This rate is altered from time to time, reflecting Federal Reserve objectives and changing conditions in the money market.

2. The System can buy and sell federal securities in the open market, an activity known as *open market operations.* These transactions have a direct impact on member bank reserves and are the main instrument of day-to-day monetary policy.

3. The System can alter within specified limits the percentage reserve which member banks must carry against their deposits. The outside limits within which the Board must operate, and the actual requirements in force in 1965, are shown in the following schedule:

	MINIMUM RESERVE PERCENTAGE	MAXIMUM RESERVE PERCENTAGE	ACTUAL RESERVE REQUIREMENT, JUNE 1, 1965
Demand deposits			
Reserve cities (large and medium cities)	10	22	16½
Other member banks (smaller cities and towns)	7	14	12
Time deposits	3	6	4

Federal Reserve activities may be made more concrete by looking at a combined balance sheet for the 12 banks as of mid-1965 (Table 1). Let us examine some of the major items, starting on the asset side.

TABLE 1

Consolidated Balance Sheet, Federal Reserve Banks
June 30, 1965
(Millions of Dollars)

ASSETS		LIABILITIES	
Gold certificates	13,670	Federal Reserve notes	34,907
U.S. government		Member bank reserves	18,229
securities	39,100	Other deposits	1,049
Loans, discounts, and		Deferred availability	
advances	710	cash items	4,692
Cash items in process of		Capital and surplus	1,188
collection	6,041	Other liabilities	443
Other assets	987		
Total	60,508	Total	60,508

Source: *Federal Reserve Bulletin*, July, 1965, p. 974.

Gold Certificates

Gold has not circulated as money in the United States since 1933. Newly mined gold within the country, and gold coming into the United States from abroad, must be delivered to the Treasury at a price of about $35 per ounce. It is then interred in a vault at Fort Knox, thus completing its journey from underground to underground. The Treasury sells gold at the fixed price for jewelry, dental, and other requirements; and it stands ready to provide gold for shipment abroad in settlement of international transactions. For this purpose, a ready reserve of gold bullion is kept in the vaults of the Federal Reserve Bank of New York, well guarded against enterprising members of the underworld.

When the Treasury buys a million dollars worth of gold, it hands over to the Federal Reserve a gold certificate for a million dollars. The certificate is a kind of warehouse receipt, indicating that there is that much actual gold around—in New York, in Fort Knox, or somewhere. The total of gold certificates in existence, then, roughly equals the amount of gold owned by the Treasury. This amount is influenced by international financial developments which are in some measure outside our control. During the late 1930's, gold flowed in tremendous volume from strife-torn Europe to presumably safer havens in the United States. Treasury holdings rose from $4 billion in 1934 to $22 billion in 1941. From 1941 to 1958, the U.S. gold stock remained relatively constant in the range of $20–22 billion. Since 1959, however, there has been a considerable drain of gold out of the United States because of sizable deficits in our balance of payments.

Gold certificates are the basic assets of the Federal Reserve System and the main reserve against its various liabilities. The Fed is required by law to hold gold certificates equal to 25 percent of the total of Federal

Reserve notes plus member bank reserves. In this limited sense, gold is still the basis of our monetary system, and the gold stock sets the ultimate limit to expansion of currency and credit.

But this limit is flexible, and may even be regarded as fictitious, since it can be altered at any time by congressional action. Until 1945 the requirement was a 40 percent gold reserve against Federal Reserve notes and 35 percent against member bank deposits. The circulation of currency rose so rapidly during World War II, however, that the gold reserves began to wear thin, and it appeared that the Fed would soon be right up against the limit. At this point, Congress obligingly lowered the reserve requirement to 25 percent. It would doubtless do so again if the present requirement threatened to become restrictive.

U.S. Government Securities

The Fed is a large holder of Federal securities, mostly of short duration, though it also holds several billion dollars' worth of issues running 5 years or longer. The System is in the market literally from day to day, buying or selling securities to raise or lower member bank reserves. These dealings are carried on between the Federal Reserve Bank of New York and a specialized group of 15 to 20 dealers in government securities. The effect of these open market operations will be examined in a moment.

Federal Reserve Notes

Turning to the liability side of Table 1, we find that the largest item consists of paper currency issued by the Federal Reserve System.

In the early days of American banking, much of our paper money consisted of notes issued by individual commercial banks, backed only by the bank's promise to redeem them in coins or U.S. currency on demand. These notes passed freely from hand to hand so long as everyone had faith in the bank's promise. Quite often, however, this faith was misplaced. A bank issued notes too liberally, or made unsound loans, ending up in bankruptcy, which left its notes worthless. The Federal Reserve Act provided, therefore, that notes could no longer be issued by individual banks but only by the Federal Reserve System.

If you take a bill from your wallet, you will probably find that it is a Federal Reserve note. The only other important kind of paper money now circulating is the U.S. Silver Certificate, issued in denominations of $1 to $10.

Issuance of Federal Reserve notes is a passive activity of the System. The amount in circulation depends on how much cash people want to carry in their pockets at a particular time. The amount goes up with rising incomes and has increased rapidly since 1940. Anyone with a checking account can go into his bank and say, "I want some cash." The bank will give him cash and reduce his account by that amount. If the bank runs short of till money, it can order some notes from the Federal Reserve bank of its district, which will send the notes and reduce the bank's reserve balance correspondingly. Where does the Federal Reserve bank get the notes? It gets them from a Treasury official in Washington, who gets them from the Government Printing Office, where they are printed. In return the Fed must put up a deposit of the same amount, at least 25 percent of which must be in gold certificates and the remainder either in gold certificates or government securities.

If people find that they need less cash, an opposite series of events occurs. Currency flows back to the banks for deposit, and the banks pass the excess currency on to the Federal Reserve and receive credit in their balances. The Federal Reserve can either stockpile the currency for the time being or pass it back to the Treasury. An inflow of currency from the public builds up checking accounts at each stage. An outflow of currency to the public reduces checking accounts all along the line.

Member Bank Reserves

These are the checking accounts which each member bank is required to maintain with the Federal Reserve Bank of its district. They are assets to the member banks and liabilities of the Federal Reserve System, which owes this amount to its members. The importance of member bank reserves has already been emphasized. They determine the amount of demand deposits which a particular bank may carry, and thus limit its lending power. The total of member bank reserves limits the lending power of the banks as a whole. Reserves are thus the focal point for control of the banking system. *Monetary policy* is essentially policy designed to affect the banks' ability to lend by altering the level of bank reserves.

THE TECHNIQUES OF MONETARY POLICY

Before describing how the Federal Reserve influences the supply and cost of money, we must note that there is another large operator in the money market. This is the United States Treasury, which is constantly issuing and retiring government securities in large volume, and which has a practical concern with the level of interest rates.

Treasury Financing Activities

The federal budget might be exactly in balance, with tax income just equaling expenditures on goods and services. In most years, however, the Treasury has either a deficit which must be covered by selling securities or a surplus which can be used to retire securities.

Suppose there is a deficit of $5 billion in a particular year. The fact that government is putting $5 billion more into the income stream than it is withdrawing from the stream through taxation affects the level of spending in the economy. This *fiscal effect* of the deficit was analyzed in Chapter 22. In addition, depending on who buys the securities which are sold to finance the deficit, there may be an effect on the quantity of money. It is this *monetary effect* which interests us here.

Federal securities may be sold to individuals and corporations outside the banking system, or to commercial banks, or to the Federal Reserve Banks. These transactions have different monetary consequences.

1. If the Treasury sells $5 billion of bonds to investors outside the banking system, the quantity of money is not affected. The buyers pay by check, so their demand deposits are reduced by $5 billion. But as the Treasury spends the money, demand deposits are increased by the same amount.

2. Suppose the securities are sold to commercial banks, which pay by crediting the Treasury on their books. Then as the Treasury spends the money, demand deposits in the hands of the public rise by $5 billion without an offsetting decrease elsewhere in the system. Money supply has risen by $5 billion. The balance sheet effect is as follows:

MEMBER BANKS			
ASSETS		LIABILITIES	
U.S. securities	+5 billion	Demand deposits	+5 billion

This assumes that the banks were not loaned up to begin with, and so had room for this increase in demand deposits.

3. The expansionary effect is even stronger if the securities are sold directly to the Federal Reserve System. In this case the Treasury's balance at the Federal Reserve is increased. As the Treasury spends the money, it issues checks on the Federal Reserve to private parties, who deposit them in their banks, which then present them to the Federal Reserve for credit. When the money has all been spent, the result is as follows:

MEMBER BANKS			
ASSETS		LIABILITIES	
Reserves	+5 billion	Demand deposits	+5 billion
FEDERAL RESERVE BANKS			
ASSETS		LIABILITIES	
U.S. securities	+5 billion	Member bank reserves	+5 billion

Not only has money supply risen by $5 billion, but member bank reserves have risen by $5 billion, which permits a further multiple expansion of the money supply.

Financing a Treasury deficit by selling securities to the banking system is not very different from financing the deficit by printing new money. The former procedure seems more respectable, possibly because it is harder to understand. It is also more expensive, since the Treasury pays interest on the securities which it would not have to pay on new currency issues. During World War II, the Treasury covered its enormous deficits by selling $90 billion of securities to commercial banks and the Federal Reserve, in addition to the $105 billion which it was able to sell to private investors. The result was a great increase in the nation's money supply, which contributed to price inflation during and after the war.

The Treasury is heavily involved in the money market even when it is not running a surplus or deficit. The reason is that much of the public debt consists of short-term securities. In mid-1965 there was about $92 billion of outstanding issues with maturities of 1 year or less. Thus many billions of issues fall due each year and are normally *refunded* by issuing new securities. If the new issues are bought by precisely the same people who held the old securities, there is no monetary effect. But the Treasury may take advantage of the occasion to issue a different type of security aimed at a different group of investors. It may try, for example, to sell long-term bonds to nonbank investors and use the proceeds to pay off short-term issues held by the banking system. This would constitute a *lengthening of the debt.* By tracing through the balance-sheet effects in the usual way, we see that there will be a drop in demand deposits in the hands of the public and thus in the money supply.

Decisions about the length of new federal security issues, the market at which they should be aimed, and the rate of interest which must be offered to attract investors are made by a group of Treasury officials responsible for *debt management.* There is no need here to delve into this specialized and esoteric art. It is enough to say that debt management often involves switching of funds among different types of investors and that this has monetary consequences.

The Problem of Monetary Control

If Federal Reserve policy were the only force acting on member bank reserves, the control problem would be considerably simplified. But this is not the case. Reserves are changing all the time because of currency movements into and out of the banks, gold movements into and out of the country, changes in Treasury cash balances, and other factors. Thus even if the Federal Reserve does nothing at all, member bank reserves will still fluctuate from day to day. A sizable research staff, mainly in the Federal Reserve Bank of New York, is engaged in keeping track of these movements and trying to predict them for the near future. These estimates are checked by higher officials in New York and Washington in the light of their experience and "feel" of the money market.

Suppose Federal Reserve officials conclude that, as things are going, member bank reserves will shrink over the next week by $200 million. This will reduce the banks' lending ability and make for a tightening of credit. What should the Federal Reserve do? This depends on the objectives which the System is pursuing at the time. If Federal Reserve officials feel that credit restriction is in order, they may simply abstain and allow the prospective shrinkage of reserves to occur. Inaction does not necessarily indicate neutrality or indifference to monetary developments. It can be a matter of deliberate policy.

Suppose, however, that the Fed considers that member bank reserves are now at about the right level. In this event, it will act to raise member bank reserves by $200 million to offset the decline which would otherwise occur. Such action to offset an undesired movement of reserves is usually termed *defensive policy*. If the policy is successful, the statistical charts will show bank reserves moving along on an even level week after week. This does not mean that the Federal Reserve has been inactive, as might appear at first glance. On the contrary, it means that its action has been deft enough to offset fluctuations which would otherwise have occurred.

Finally, Federal Reserve officials may feel that monetary expansion is in order and that member bank reserves should be increased by, say, $300 million. In this case they will have to raise reserves by $500 million to offset the prospective decline of $200 million and still come out with the desired increase. These are the main permutations of Federal Reserve policy: abstaining and letting nature take its course; a defensive policy of "leaning against the wind" to offset undesirable changes; and an active policy aimed at reversing the prospective course of events.

Open Market Operations

Once the Federal Reserve had decided what to do, how does it go about doing it? The main instrument of day-to-day policy is purchase and sale of federal securities. Decisions on this front are made by the Federal Open Market Committee, consisting of the seven members of the Board of Governors, the president of the Federal Reserve Bank of New York, and four other presidents of Reserve banks. The Committee meets every three weeks. In addition, its members and key staff officials normally confer every morning over a telephone hook-up and arrive at decisions for the day. Actual trading is carried out through a trading desk in the Federal Reserve Bank of New York, since New York is the center for dealers specializing in government securities.

The impact of these operations is rapid and direct. When the

System buys $100 million of securities, it pays by check on the Federal Reserve Bank of New York. If the seller is a commercial bank, this check gives it an immediate addition to its reserve balance. If the seller is an individual or a nonbank corporation, it deposits the check in a commercial bank, which presents it to the Federal Reserve and receives credit. The balance sheet effect in this case is as follows:

MEMBER BANKS			
ASSETS		LIABILITIES	
Reserve balances	+100	Demand deposits	+100
FEDERAL RESERVE BANKS			
ASSETS		LIABILITIES	
U.S. securities	+100	Member bank reserves	+100

When the System sells securities, opposite effects occur. The buyer gives the Federal Reserve a check drawn on his commercial bank. The Fed deducts this amount from the bank's reserve balance. Thus member bank reserves shrink.

The principle involved is simple: Federal Reserve purchase of securities *raises* member bank reserves, while Federal Reserve sale of securities *lowers* reserves. The effect on bank reserves is almost instantaneous, and its size is certain. This plus the fact that the size of security operations can be adjusted precisely to the supposed need makes them a natural choice for day-to-day use.

While the first impact of open market operations is on bank reserves, there are also important secondary effects. Suppose the Federal Reserve wants to tighten credit and consequently begins selling federal securities. This immediately lowers member bank reserves, which is a step in the desired direction. In addition, the increased supply of U.S. securities coming onto the market will lower their price. Now if the *price* of a fixed-interest security falls, its *yield* necessarily rises. Moreover, since the network of interest rates is interconnected, an increase in yield on one kind of security will tend to be transmitted to other securities. Thus there will be general upward pressure on interest rates, including rates charged on bank loans, and this will discourage borrowing. This is in line with the Federal Reserve's objective of restricting credit.

Member Bank Borrowing and the Discount Rate

A major complaint against the pre-1913 banking system was its inelasticity under pressure. There was no central reservoir of funds to which banks could resort in time of need. The authors of the Federal Reserve Act were at pains, therefore, to provide ways by which any solvent bank could draw on the virtually unlimited resources of the System to meet temporary emergencies.

A member bank can secure Federal Reserve funds and increase its reserve balance in either of two ways:

1. It may sell commercial paper to the Federal Reserve Bank of its district. This is known as *discounting*. EXAMPLE: A bank brings to the Federal Reserve a promissory note from one of its customers for $100,000, due in 3 months' time. The discount rate at the time is 4 percent. The Federal Reserve discounts the note by deducting from its face value interest at 4 percent for 3 months, or $1,000. The remaining $99,000 is added to the member bank's reserve balance.

2. A simpler technique, and the one mainly used in practice, is a direct loan from the Federal Reserve to the member bank. The bank puts up either commercial paper or (more commonly) U.S. securities as collateral for the loan. The Federal Reserve charges interest on the loan at the existing discount rate.

The volume of member bank borrowing is not large. The banks dislike being in debt to the Federal Reserve, and try to work their way out of debt as quickly as possible. The Federal Reserve also looks with suspicion on any bank which draws too heavily on its borrowing privilege and can if necessary cut off further credit. The possibility of borrowing, however, provides a breathing space for any bank which finds itself suddenly short of reserves. It gives a few weeks of grace during which the bank can make an orderly readjustment of its position.

The existence of this escape valve permits the other Federal Reserve powers to be used with greater assurance. Open market operations and changes in reserve requirements are general instruments, whose impact cannot be tailored to the situation of particular banks. Federal Reserve sale of securities reduces bank reserves in general, but it is impossible to say in advance which banks will be hit and how hard. Banks with sizable excess reserves may be little affected, while banks which are already loaned up may suddenly find themselves in a deficit position. The Federal Reserve is nevertheless free to push open market operations as vigorously as it wishes, for if the policy leaves a particular bank short of reserves it can always cover itself temporarily by borrowing. Over the longer run, of course, the bank will have to work its way back to a safe reserve position by going slow on loans and holding down its demand deposits. This is precisely the result at which the open market operations were aimed.

Each of the 12 Federal Reserve banks sets its own discount rate. The rates are usually the same, however, and policy for the whole System is coordinated through the Board of Governors. The discount rate is normally raised gradually during a business upswing, keeping more or less in step with the rise of other short-term interest rates. In a recession, the discount rate is usually cut substantially.

An increase in the discount rate has two effects. Since it increases the cost of borrowing from the Federal Reserve, it strengthens the member banks' unwillingness to remain in debt. More important, it serves as a signal to the banking community of the direction in which Federal Reserve policy is moving. A discount rate increase indicates that the Federal Reserve feels that expansion of loans should be slowed down and that it intends to exert pressure toward that end. This usually encourages member banks to raise their own lending rates—a step which is bound to be unpopular with borrowers, but which can now be defended on the ground that "this is what the Fed wants us to do." Similarly, a lowering of the discount rate is a signal for more liberal lending policies and lower interest rates.

Member Bank Reserve Requirements

The ability to change reserve requirements is a powerful instrument. Profit considerations lead a commercial bank to keep its resources as fully invested as possible and to operate near the legal reserve minimum. Thus an increase in reserve requirements immediately throws many banks into a deficit position and forces them to restrict their lending. The weapon is in fact so powerful that it is not used for delicate adjustment of monetary conditions from week to week. For short-term purposes, the Fed relies on frequent open market operations, supported by occasional adjustments of the discount rate. Reserve requirements are changed less frequently, and mainly to offset substantial long-term movements in bank reserves.

During the 1930's, an enormous inflow of gold from abroad raised bank reserves sharply, while at the same time depressed business conditions prevented the banks from increasing their loans materially. The result was large excess reserves, which for the time being put the commercial banks virtually beyond Federal Reserve control. In an effort to "mop up" these excess reserves, the Fed doubled reserve requirements between 1936 and 1938.

Since World War II, however, the banks' reserve position has been quite tight. Loans to businesses and consumers have grown steadily, reflecting rising production and price levels in the economy. But bank reserves have grown little, and were actually cut by the heavy gold outflows since 1959. The Federal Reserve has had to lower the legal requirements several times to keep the banks in a viable position. By 1965 the legal reserve ratios had been cut to 16½ and 12 percent, or about the middle of the range permitted by present legislation.

The Coordination of Policy Instruments

While the three control powers of the Federal Reserve System are legally separate, in practice they are used together to achieve the System's objectives of monetary restriction or monetary ease. The Fed will usually lead off with open market operations. This is particularly appropriate for defensive policy or where only small positive effects are desired. For larger adjustments, open market policy may be supported by changes in the discount rate. Changes in reserve requirements are made least frequently, and usually only when the Fed wants to produce a substantial easing of monetary conditions. Note that the lowering of reserve requirements since 1953 was concentrated in the recession years of 1954 and 1958.

The way in which these policy instruments are coordinated may be illustrated by the course of events during a business upswing. Suppose business loans and demand deposits have been rising for a couple of years. Production is nearing the physical capacity of the system. Price indexes are edging upward, arousing fears of inflation. The Fed decides that the time has come to put on the monetary brakes. It begins by selling off, say, $500 million of short-term government securities. This lowers member bank reserves, and some banks find themselves below the legal minimum. These banks will probably tighten their lending policies. They may borrow from the Federal Reserve as a temporary expedient. They may also decide to sell some of their own holdings of government securities. These offerings, plus those of the Federal Reserve System, lower the market price of short-term government securities. This amounts to an increase in yield on governments, which makes for a general rise in short-term interest rates.

As interest rates rise, the Federal Reserve typically "follows the market upward" by raising its own discount rate. It does not like to get much ahead of the market, but neither does it lag materially behind it. The increase in the discount rate usually leads the member banks to raise the interest rate which they charge on business loans. This makes borrowing less attractive and helps to achieve the Federal Reserve objective of credit restriction.

These lines of policy will be pursued as long as the threat of overexpansion continues. Open market sales and discount rate increases will go on, hand over hand, for as long as necessary to achieve the desired braking effect.

ADVANTAGES AND LIMITATIONS OF MONETARY POLICY

The usefulness of monetary policy depends on whether the problem is to combat inflation or unemployment. Monetary policy is more effective on the former front than on the latter. "You can't push on a string," as the saying goes. During a recession the Federal Reserve can strengthen bank reserves, reduce interest rates, and establish an attractive atmosphere for borrowing. But it cannot directly affect the will to borrow. So long as business prospects seem poor, borrowers will hold off and the desired increase in loans and spending will not materialize.

It is toward the top of a boom which is threatening to pass over into inflation that monetary policy really comes into its own. As a technique for inflation control, monetary policy is alleged to have several advantages:

1. Decisions on monetary policy can be reached and applied rapidly, since power is concentrated in the Board of Governors. Fiscal policy, on the other hand, depends on the slower processes of congressional approval and administrative action.

2. The effectiveness of monetary action is reasonably certain. By sufficiently vigorous action, interest rates can always be raised to a level at which the brakes take hold.

3. Monetary policy is an impersonal, thermostatic device, which produces its effects through the market mechanism. It is neutral as among individuals and groups in the economy. If the Federal Reserve succeeds in restricting credit, some would-be borrowers will be left unsatisfied. But the Federal Reserve does not presume to say which borrowers or which projects shall be dropped from the list. This is left to negotiation between private borrowers and lenders.

But the effectiveness of monetary control should not be overstated. Monetary policy in practice is more complicated and less effective than appears from textbook examples. These difficulties and limitations deserve brief attention.

Conflicting Signals

What are the targets of monetary policy? How does the Federal Reserve decide whether tightening or loosening of credit is in order?

It is usually said that monetary policy should promote high employment and a stable price level. But these indicators sometimes point in different directions. Suppose the economy is coming out of a recession. Production and employment are rising but are still well below full capacity. Between 5 and 6 percent of the labor force remain unemployed. The price level, however, is rising at 2 percent a year. What should the Federal Reserve do? Should it follow a low-interest policy to stimulate further increases in production? Or should it tighten credit to hold down the price level?

Decisions about monetary policy are *not* automatic. They require judgment and the weighing of various objectives. Some critics of monetary policy feel that Federal Reserve officials, reflecting the outlook of the banking community, give too great weight to preventing inflation and too little weight to promoting production and employment. They err, it is argued, in the direction of chronic tightness of credit and an unduly high level of interest rates. Federal Reserve officials reply that they are doing no more than is necessary to check inflation and that without a stable price level we cannot have sustained prosperity and rapid economic growth.

Prediction and Timing

Monetary action may be faster than most other policies, but it is far from instantaneous. It usually takes several months after an economic downturn or upturn before one can be sure of the direction of movement. There are cases in which appropriate Federal Reserve action was seriously delayed because the System misjudged the turning point.

Even after the Federal Reserve has decided to move, it takes considerable time for the effects to work themselves out. When credit is being restricted, it takes time for bank lending policies to be adjusted to a tighter reserve position, time for borrowers to react to higher interest rates, and time for financial decisions to be translated into production plans. Even after borrowers have decided to borrow less, it may be 6 to 12 months before this shows up in the level of spending.

"Slippage" in the Controls

If businesses and individuals could get funds only by borrowing from commercial banks, and if the banks could get increased reserves only at the option of the Federal Reserve System, the monetary authorities would have close control over the level of demand deposits. But this is not the case. Over the past half century there has been a great increase in the importance of nonbank lenders, such as savings and loan associations, insurance companies, personal finance companies, and other *financial intermediaries*. Large corporations also have liquid funds which can be used to provide their customers with *trade credit* (an understanding that bills need not be paid for a specified period, such as 60 or 90 days). True, these intermediaries are dependent to some extent on bank loans, and a restriction of bank credit may force them to tighten their own credit terms. But monetary policy impinges on nonbank lenders only indirectly, and its impact is therefore less predictable.

Another important development since 1940 is that commercial banks and other business corporations have large holdings of government securities which can be sold off as needed. A company which cannot obtain more bank credit can still get money by selling securities. A bank which finds itself short of reserves can follow the same course, selling securities and using the proceeds to build up its reserves.

During the boom of 1954–57, when the Federal Reserve was trying to tighten credit, the commercial banks sold $10.9 billion of government securities, other financial institutions sold $3.7 billion, and nonfinancial corporations sold $3.6 billion. During the recession of 1957–58, when monetary controls were relaxed, the banks bought back $9.7 billion of securities and nonfinancial corporations bought $2.3 billion. This pattern of selling securities when money is tight and buying them back when money is easy has been rather consistent during the fifties and sixties.

It takes two to make a trade. Who was buying governments when banks and business concerns were selling? First, purchases by individual investors have moved in a reverse direction from those by business concerns. Individuals have bought when businesses were selling, and vice versa. Part of the answer, too, lies in the changing budget position of the federal government. During boom periods, when banks and other businesses want to sell securities, the Treasury may be running a surplus which enables it to buy up and retire its issues. During recession there is always a budget deficit. The Treasury finances the deficit by issuing additional securities, which are absorbed mainly by business concerns and the banking system.

Changes in the Velocity of Money

Monetary policy operates on the *quantity* of money in existence. Credit restriction during an upswing can slow down or prevent an increase in the money supply. But monetary policy cannot control the *uses* to which money is put. With enough ingenuity, people can find ways of making the same amount of money do more work than before. Warren Smith has commented that:

when credit conditions are tightened and the creation of new money through the banking system is restricted, pressures are automatically set up which cause the financial system to "hunt" for methods of mobilizing the existing money supply more effectively, thus permitting it to do part, or perhaps even most, of the work that would have been done by newly created money had credit conditions been easier.[1]

How much work money is doing can be measured by dividing the value of GNP by the money supply. The result is termed the *income velocity of money*. It shows how many dollars of production were financed by each dollar of money in existence. Income velocity has shown an upward tendency since World War II, rising from about 2 in 1945 to around 4 in 1965. Moreover, it tends to rise during boom periods and to fall during recession. These swings have often been considerably larger than the changes in the quantity of money. During the expansion of 1954–57, the quantity of money rose only 6 percent, but velocity rose 17 percent. During the recession of 1957–58, the quantity of money remained unchanged, but velocity fell 3 percent. During the long upswing of 1961–65, both the quantity of money and its velocity rose about 11 percent.

---

[1] *Staff Report on Employment, Growth, and Price Levels,* prepared for the Joint Economic Committee, 86th Cong., 1st sess. (Washington, D.C.: Government Printing Office, 1960), p. 344.

Federal Reserve efforts at credit restriction on the upswing, then, are partially offset by increases in the effectiveness with which money is used. Households and business concerns adapt themselves to holding less money, relative to their incomes, than they did before. This permits national income to go on rising faster than the increase in money supply.

One can make a virtue of necessity by arguing that this provides a desirable degree of elasticity. Without this flexibility, the monetary brakes might take hold too hard and bring the economy grinding to a halt. But one cannot have it both ways. One cannot argue *both* that our financial system is quite flexible, which seems to be true, *and* that monetary controls are precise and predictable, which seems not to be true.

Possible Conflict with Treasury Objectives

All borrowers prefer low interest rates, but most of them can't do anything about it. There is one borrower, however, which can try to do something about it. This is the U.S. Treasury.

Interest on the national debt is now a large item in the federal budget, amounting to some $11 billion in fiscal year 1965. A difference of 1 percent in the interest rate on federal securities makes a difference of about $3 billion in cost to the government. Thus the Treasury Department has a natural interest in low rates, and its influence is apt to be exerted in this direction. It is particularly unhappy if the Federal Reserve is forcing down the price of federal securities and forcing up interest rates just when the Treasury needs to float a large new issue. At such times there is likely to be discussion of the need for Federal Reserve "cooperation" with the Treasury. The implication is that the Federal Reserve should abandon its effort at monetary control for the time being, and help out the Treasury by keeping interest rates low.

Conflict of Internal and External Considerations

Measures which would be desirable for internal reasons may conflict with the country's international economic position. An excellent example of this occurred during the winter of 1960–61. The American economy was in recession, and the Federal Reserve had taken the usual steps to reduce interest rates. Meanwhile, the European economies were booming, and interest rates in most of them were well above the American level. This caused a large shift of funds from New York to England, West Germany, Switzerland, and other countries in search of higher yields. (National governments, central banks, and international business concerns have many billions of liquid funds, which they can invest temporarily in one country or another as they see fit. A substantial difference in short-term yields in different countries produces a movement of funds toward the high-interest locations.) This contributed to a heavy outflow of gold from the United States in 1960–61 and aroused fears of a "run on the dollar."

What should be done in such a situation? Some urged that American interest rates should be raised toward European levels to check the shifting of funds and the consequent outflow of gold. But to do this would discourage investment and interfere with recovery from recession. Should priority be given to internal recovery or to adjustment of the balance of payments? This sort of conflict adds one more complication to the life of Federal Reserve officials.

Uneven Impact of Monetary Policy

The assertion that monetary policy is neutral as among groups in the economy is questioned by some observers. True, the Federal Reserve does not set out deliberately to discriminate against certain types of business. But is not a restriction of bank credit inherently discriminatory? It is argued that this may be true in at least three respects:

a) Some companies have larger internal resources than others, and hence are less dependent on bank borrowing. Federal Reserve policy hits companies which depend heavily on the commercial banking system.

b) Some types of investment are more sensitive than others to changes in the rate of interest. A rise in interest rates may have little effect on manufacturing investment but may cut heavily into house building and local government projects.

c) Some would-be borrowers have a higher credit rating and better banking connections than others. When the banks are forced to restrict loans, they will still try to accommodate the companies with top credit rating. Thus the impact of restriction may fall largely on smaller and newer businesses which are regarded as less creditworthy.

Statistical studies suggest that small concerns do suffer more than big ones during periods of tight money, both because of lower credit standing and smaller internal resources. But the evidence is not as clear-cut or striking as some of the complaints from small business might lead one to expect.

Defenders of monetary policy argue that these effects are not discriminatory in any meaningful sense. An increase in any price "discriminates" against people who can no longer pay the price and in favor of those who can. But one cannot conclude from this that no price should ever be raised. The rate of interest, it is argued, is no different from any other price in this respect.

WHAT DOES MONETARY POLICY ACCOMPLISH?

In earlier chapters we argued that the level of national income depends on the spending plans of consumers, business concerns, and government, which together make up the total expenditure schedule. If monetary policy affects the level of national income, it must do so by changing the plans of one or more of these groups. Is there reason to believe that it does have this effect, and how is the result produced? An approximate answer to this question can be given quite briefly. A more thorough analysis will be found in the Appendix to this chapter.

Interest and the Level of Spending

1. Monetary policy alters the supply of money. The strength of this effect cannot be gauged simply by looking at monetary statistics. During a business upswing, the expansion of production and bank borrowings makes for a marked increase in demand deposits. A policy of monetary restraint shows up in the fact that demand deposits rise *less* than they would have risen in the absence of such a policy. But since one can never say "what would have happened if," the quantitative effect of monetary control is hard to estimate. On the downswing, demand deposits tend to fall as business declines. But the Federal Reserve can pump new money into the stream through security purchases, and may thus prevent the money supply from falling or even increase it.

2. The supply of money affects the rate of interest. We saw in Chapter 11 that the interest rate can be regarded as *the price of money*. From the lender's standpoint, it is the reward for giving up money, for "parting with liquidity." From the borrower's standpoint, it is the price which must be paid for increased cash in hand.

We can thus fall back on the familiar principle that an increase in the supply of anything will lower its price, and vice versa. An increase in the quantity of money leads, other things equal, to a fall in the rate of interest, while a reduction in the quantity of money will raise interest rates. One exception to this principle is explained in the Appendix, but it can be taken as a safe guide in most circumstances.

3. The rate of interest affects the level of spending. Looking first at consumers, a rise in interest rates may lower the consumption schedule by raising saving, or reducing borrowing, or both. It is usually said that saving is painful and that people have to be paid for doing it. The more they are paid, i.e., the higher the rate of interest, the more they will set aside out of current income. While this proposition has sometimes been questioned, it is probably dependable as a general rule.

Will a rise in interest rates cause families to borrow less for cars, furniture, electric appliances, and the like? Many consumers, of course, do not realize what rate of interest they are paying. They look only at the monthly payment, which depends on the purchase price of the article and the length of the loan as well as the rate of interest. If a rise in interest rates can be offset by a price reduction or a spreading out of payments, it may pass unnoticed. But usually a higher interest rate will mean larger monthly payments, and this should cause some reduction in consumer borrowing. It seems safe to conclude that a rise in interest rates will typically lower the consumption schedule.

Turning to business concerns, it is usually argued that a higher interest rate means less investment. As the cost of borrowing rises, more and more potential investment projects will appear unprofitable and will be abandoned or postponed. The logic of this is almost self-evident, and was explained in Chapter 20. But investment decisions are also influenced by the business outlook, risk considerations, profit levels, and other things. The cost of borrowing is only one factor, and may often be a minor factor, in investment decisions.

Factual studies suggest that the situation differs for different types of investment. Investment in inventories is probably not much affected by interest rate changes. Nor is plant and equipment investment by larger business concerns, where availability of internal financing is a dominant consideration. Even in public utility industries, where plant life is long and interest charges are important, there is little evidence of any appreciable effect of interest rate changes.

Interest rate changes do seem to have an impact on residential and commercial construction, on state and local government construction expenditures, and on investment by small businesses which cannot float securities on the national market and are heavily dependent on bank borrowing.[2]

As regards both the consumption and investment schedules, then, one can predict the *direction* of the effects induced by monetary policy. An increase in the rate of interest will lower the C and I schedules, and hence the equilibrium level of national income. A decline in the interest rate tends to raise the C and I schedules, and thus to raise the level of income. But there is considerable difference of opinion about the *size* of these effects. Some believe that raising the interest rate 1 or 2 percent will reduce spending very little, while others think the effect will be substantial. These differences of opinion lead to differing judgments about the practical usefulness of monetary policy.

Credit Rationing and the Level of Spending

There is a second route by which monetary policy may alter the level of spending. Banks do not lend automatically to any company which is willing to pay the going rate of interest. They look into details of the borrower's business, including its ratio of current assets to current liabilities, its past earnings record and future prospects, the purposes for which the loan will be used, and the assurance that the loan can be repaid. After this appraisal, the bank may decide to grant the loan in full, scale it down to a smaller amount, or reject it entirely. The volume of loans made always falls short of loan applications. The money market thus operates differently from a vegetable market, in which anyone with the price can get the goods.

The severity of the bank's appraisal is influenced by the state of its

---

[2] On this range of problems see Warren Smith, *op. cit.*, pp. 362–94.

reserves. Toward the peak of a boom, would-be borrowers are pressing in from every side. Suppose the Federal Reserve now moves to cut bank reserves. The banks will respond, not only by raising the interest rate, but by imposing tougher requirements on prospective borrowers. They may decide to consider only applications of straight A quality, and A— or B+ propositions may go by the board. Conversely, if reserves are ample and the banks are eager for business, they can get more business by lowering their standards for loan applications. There is evidence that bank lending standards do vary in this way over the course of the business cycle.

Thus monetary policy produces effects through *lenders'* reactions as well as through *borrowers'* reactions, through changes in the *availability* of credit as well as the *cost* of credit. Even if borrowers are quite insensitive to interest rates, changes in the toughness of bank lending policies may raise or lower the expenditure schedule. Some economists would say that this effect is more important than the interest rate effect.

Would Automatic Rules Work Better?

The Federal Reserve Board will never win a popularity contest. It has the peculiar misfortune to come under attack from precisely opposite standpoints. One school of thought holds that the Board, because of its close working relations with the financial community, takes an unduly conservative view of the economy. It worries too little about unemployment and too much about possible price increases. It tends to put on the monetary brakes too early and to stop every expansion short of full employment.[3] Moreover, monetary restriction operates mainly by cutting back investment, which hampers long-run economic growth.

This line of criticism has led to proposals for reducing the independence of the Board and subjecting it more clearly to the federal administration. Monetary policy, it is argued, needs to be coordinated closely with other aspects of national economic policy. There can be no room for a semiautonomous agency, particularly one which is suspected of having a strong policy bias.

An opposite kind of proposal is to take the Fed further out of the political arena and, in a sense, to abolish monetary policy by subjecting the money supply to a fixed formula. No Board of Governors, it is argued, can be clever enough to anticipate and make correct adjustments to the short swings of the economy. They are likely to make about as many errors as correct decisions. Their proper task is to provide a stable monetary environment over the long run by expanding the money supply

---

[3] Nor is this tendency necessarily confined to the United States. For an interesting effort to analyze the motivation of Canadian monetary authorities, see G. L. Reuber, "The Objectives of Canadian Monetary Policy, 1949–61: Empirical 'Trade-Offs' and the Reaction Function of the Authorities," *Journal of Political Economy*, April, 1964, pp. 109–32.

at a rate which will finance a growing GNP at stable prices. A steady annual increase of 4 percent in bank reserves (and hence in potential money supply) is often mentioned as an appropriate rule, this being about the rate at which real output may be expected to grow over the years ahead.

This proposal comes sometimes from hard-line anti-inflationists who suspect the Fed of being too soft rather than too tough in curbing aggregate demand; sometimes from neoliberals who distrust government authority in general; sometimes from monetary economists who are impressed with the technical difficulty of reaching correct policy decisions. It has the attractiveness of any automatic device. No longer need the Board of Governors lie awake nights worrying about the next step in monetary policy. They need only follow the rule. But how effective would such a rule be? Whatever may be true in the long run, the velocity of money is certainly not stable in the short run. It shows a marked tendency to rise during business upswings and to fall during downswings. This amounts to saying that individuals and businesses have some latitude in their spending plans. Spending does *not* depend only on the amount of money in one's possession.

A smooth expansion of the money supply, then, would not necessarily produce a steady increase in spending. Nor would it prevent spending from dropping occasionally for the same reasons for which it drops at present. True, if spending dropped and the Federal Reserve continued doggedly to increase bank reserves according to the rule, there would be a rise in the lending capacity of the banking system. But this situation, while favorable to economic recovery, will not by itself initiate recovery. It takes borrowers as well as lenders to bring about an expansion of bank loans, and the presence of excess reserves does not directly affect the incentive to borrow.

These are limitations of *any* sort of monetary policy, whether discretionary or automatic. But it is not clear that an automatic formula gets around them more successfully than the present exercise of discretion by the Board of Governors. It is doubtful that there is any foolproof gyroscope which will relieve us of the necessity of using judgment and making occasional mistakes in monetary management.[4]

---

[4] For an interesting effort to compare Federal Reserve performance with what would have happened under various types of automatic rule, see Franco Modigliani, "Some Empirical Tests of Monetary Management and of Rules versus Discretion," *Journal of Political Economy,* June, 1964, pp. 211–45. He concludes that from 1952–60, when the Federal Reserve was most nearly free to consider only output and price objectives, "one finds that monetary management was rather effective. . . . It led to relatively small errors, except possibly through parts of the 1957–58 recession; and it outperformed, usually by healthy margins, all of the conventional rules. . . ." (p. 243). But before 1952, when the Fed was obliged by Treasury agreement to support the government bond market, and from 1960 on when it was heavily concerned with balance-of-payments objectives, its performance in terms of domestic price-output objectives was less satisfactory.

SUMMARY

1. Although the Federal Reserve System consists of 12 regional banks, important policy decisions are coordinated through the Board of Governors in Washington. And while in theory the Board is not subject to Presidential control, in practice it works closely with the Treasury and other agencies of government.

2. Monetary policy is directed at *member bank reserves*. The Fed operates by buying and selling securities in the *open market,* by varying the *discount rate* at which it will lend to member banks, and (less frequently) by altering the *reserve ratio* which member banks must carry against their deposits. By coordinated use of these powers, the Fed can increase or decrease the amount of *free or excess reserves* in possession of the banks and thus influence their ability and willingness to lend.

3. During a business upswing, the Fed typically restricts bank reserves by selling securities and gradually raises the discount rate. This forces up private interest rates and also leads banks to ration credit more carefully. This lowers the consumption and investment schedules, which has a braking effect on the expansion.

4. During recession, the Fed bolsters bank reserves by buying securities, lowers the discount rate, and may lower reserve requirements. This brings lower bank interest rates and more liberal lending policies. But since the volume of loans depends also on the attitude of borrowers, and since borrowers are usually pessimistic during recession, monetary measures may not be sufficient to check the decline. Fiscal action is more dependable during a downswing.

5. While monetary control seems simple in principle, there are a number of practical complications, including: judgment in deciding when and how hard to apply the brakes on an expansion; the time lag between policy decisions and the time at which these decisions begin to affect spending; slippage in the controls arising from the existence of financial intermediaries, and from large bank and business holdings of federal securities which can be sold as needed; the possibility that restrictions on the *quantity* of money may be offset by increases in the *velocity* of money; possible conflict between Treasury and Federal Reserve objectives; and possible conflict between internal stability considerations and external balance of payments considerations.

6. The linkage between our monetary discussion of Chapters 23–24 and the theory of income determination in Chapters 20–21 is as follows: Monetary policy alters the supply of money; the supply of money affects the rate of interest; the rate of interest (and variations in the liberality of credit rationing at this rate) affects the consumption and investment schedules; and this affects the equilibrium level of national income. The

Appendix to this chapter provides a more complete synthesis of monetary analysis and income analysis.

DISCUSSION QUESTIONS

1. How do Federal Reserve open market operations affect member bank reserves?

2. What is the discount rate? How does a change in the discount rate affect the behavior of the commercial banks?

3. What is the point of the legal reserve requirement? Why is the legal requirement changed only infrequently?

4. Explain how the Federal Reserve moves to "put on the brakes" during a business upswing. What are some of the practical difficulties in deciding what to do and when to do it?

5. Why is monetary policy less effective in checking a downswing than in braking an upswing?

6. How does a tightening of monetary controls affect the behavior of the member banks? Is the effect solely on the rate of interest or are there other effects as well?

7. How does monetary policy influence the total expenditure schedule and the level of national income?

8. Would you favor legislation instructing the Federal Reserve System to increase member bank reserves at a certain percentage rate each year?

If the Appendix is assigned, these additional questions are relevant:

9. Explain the logic of the *quantity equation.* What is the difference between the quantity equation and the quantity *theory* of money and prices?

10. What are some of the difficulties involved in explaining price movements solely, or mainly, by changes in the quantity of money?

11. Explain the nature of the *transactions, precautionary,* and *speculative* demands for money. Which of these is related mainly to the level of income? Which is related to the rate of interest?

12. Given the level of income, how will the interest rate be affected by a change in the quantity of money? Given the supply of money, how will interest react to a change in the level of income? Illustrate diagrammatically.

13. Explain the derivation of the *IS* and *LM* curves. How can one use these curves to determine simultaneously the rate of interest and the level of income?

14. Why can we label certain sections of the *LM* curve as "Keynesian" and "classical"?

15. Using the *IS-LM* apparatus, explain the reactions set off by
    a) A rise in the expenditure schedule.
    b) An increase in money supply.

APPENDIX: A SYNTHESIS OF MONETARY ANALYSIS AND INCOME ANALYSIS

The modern theory of income determination is a lineal descendant of earlier theoretical systems. Money played a large role in these systems, which usually went under the name of *monetary theory*. It will be useful to glance at some earlier ideas about money before considering its role in modern income analysis.

The Fisher Equation

Until quite recently, economists thought of full employment as the normal condition of the economy and of any deviation from full employment as temporary and self-correcting. Monetary forces, it was believed, reflected themselves mainly in movements of the *price level;* and attention was consequently focused on the relation between money and prices.

One line of reasoning was as follows: for every sale made in the economy, the number of dollars changing hands must equal the value of the goods sold. Thus the total amount of money spent in the country during a year must equal the total value of goods and services exchanged during that period.

Total spending may be thought of as the amount of money in existence, M, multiplied by the average number of times each dollar changes hands during the year. This second quantity, usually designated as V, is termed the *transactions velocity of money*. Total spending during the year, then, is MV.

The value of the goods and services exchanged may be thought of as the quantity of each good, T, multiplied by its price, P. Thus the total value of transactions during a year is PT, where P is an index of average prices of and T represents the physical quantity of goods exchanged.

Now total spending must equal the value of goods sold. They are simply different ways of looking at the same transactions, one from the standpoint of the buyers and the other from that of the sellers. It follows that

$$MV \equiv PT.$$

This is the famous *quantity equation* or *equation of exchange,* often identified with Professor Irving Fisher of Yale.

On its face the equation is simply a truism. It resembles the $S \equiv I$ formula in that it is true by definition for any past period. It does not necessarily say anything about causal relations in the economy.

With a few embellishments, however, the quantity *equation* can be turned into a quantity *theory* of money and prices. The velocity of money, it can be argued, depends on banking institutions and people's money-holding habits. These are reasonably stable over short periods, and so V can be taken as roughly constant. Moreover, if one regards full employment as the normal state of affairs, production cannot change much over short periods, and T can also be taken as constant.

With V and T constant, and only M and P left to vary, the outcome is clear. An increase in M will produce a proportionate change in P. Double the quantity of money, and the price level will also double. Cut the quantity of money and prices will fall.

The simplicity of this theory, and the sweeping conclusions which could apparently be drawn from it, attracted a wide following. Most economists have gradually become convinced, however, that the theory is too good to be true. V turns out not to be very stable in the short run, tending to rise during business upswings and fall during downswings. More serious, T moves up and down over the course of the cycle. Indeed, it is these fluctuations in output in which we are mainly interested; but the quantity theory is not oriented toward fluctuations in T and does little to explain them.

The flexibility of V means that it is possible for spending to rise or fall with no change in the quantity of money. Moveover, under sellers' inflation the impetus to price increases comes from the cost side rather than the demand side. So one cannot regard money as the only prime mover in the economy. The quantity theory fails to highlight the forces behind the spending decisions on which total demand depends.

The Cambridge Equation

A different form of the quantity equation stems from the work of Professor Alfred Marshall of Cambridge, and is hence usually termed the *Cambridge equation.* It starts from the proposition that the quantity of money people wish to hold in cash or checking accounts is related to the size of their incomes. The fraction of their incomes which people choose to hold in money was designated by Marshall as k. Then the money holdings of any individual or business will be $m = ky$. EXAMPLE: I have an income of $500 a month, and keep on the average $250 in my pocket and my checking account. Thus my k is 0.5, and my money holdings satisfy the condition

$$250 = 0.5 \,(500) \,.$$

Since all the money in existence at a particular time must be held by somebody, we can sum up for the economy as a whole and conclude that

$$M = kY$$

where M is the average money stock over a certain period, Y is total money income during the period, and k is the ratio of money holdings to income.

Marshall's k is the same kind of creature as Fisher's V. Marshall thought that k could be regarded as roughly constant over short periods. He also supposed the economy to be fully employed, so that output does not change. Suppose now that the quantity of money increases. What will happen? People find that their money holdings are above the level, k, to which they are accustomed. They will try to get rid of the excess by spending it. Since output cannot rise, increased spending serves only to raise the price level. As prices rise, people's money incomes also rise. This expansion of income will continue until the ratio of money holdings to income has fallen to the normal level k. At this point, people are once more willing to hold the enlarged money supply, and the system is in equilibrium.

A little calculation shows that this occurs when the price level has risen by the same percentage as the original increase in money supply. Thus we reach Fisher's conclusion by a different route: a change in the quantity of money leads to an equal proportionate change in the price level.

Marshall's system is subject to some of the same criticisms as Fisher's system. K does not remain constant over time, any more than V does. Nor does output remain constant over time. The Cambridge equation was, nevertheless, a substantial improvement. It focused attention on people's reasons for holding money balances and on the relation of this to spending plans. It was a step toward the thoroughgoing analysis of spending which characterizes the modern approach.

Money and Interest in Modern Dress

Modern monetary theory starts from the observation that there are several reasons for holding money rather than just one reason, and that the amount of money held is related to the rate of interest as well as the level of income.

The demand for money may be divided into three parts:

1. Transactions demand.   It is convenient to keep something in one's pocket and one's checking account to pay for current purchases. Given a certain income, the amount carried depends on personal habits and business practices. One could get by with a very small balance by buying entirely on credit and paying all bills by check on the first of the month. But most people pay bills intermittently over the month and also make cash purchases, which requires a sizable average balance. Business concerns also carry substantial cash balances to pay for current purchases.

These practices can be assumed to remain stable over short periods. Thus the transactions demand for money depends mainly on the number of transactions to be carried out, i.e., on the value of national output and income.[5] A larger national income means a proportionate increase in the transactions demand for money.

Transactions demand is probably little influenced by interest over the normal range of interest rates. If the interest rate becomes very high, however, people may try to economize on their cash balances so that they can put more into securities or savings accounts.

Transactions Demand for Money Depends on Interest and Income

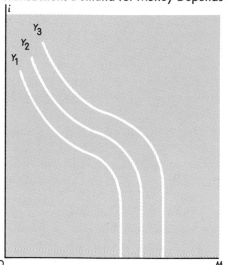

FIGURE 1a. A separate demand curve must be drawn for each level of income. Y_1, Y_2, and Y_3 show demand at successively higher income levels. A diagram of the *precautionary* demand for money would look similar to this one.

These suppositions are shown graphically in Figure 1a. The rate of interest is shown on the vertical axis, the quantity of money on the horizontal axis. Each Y line shows the transactions demand for money at a certain level of national income. It is completely unresponsive to the rate of interest over most of its length. If the interest rate becomes very high, however, people become willing to get along with less money for transactions purposes, so the demand curve bends to the left.

The demand curve Y_1 assumes a specified level of national income. Suppose instead that there is a higher income level. Then the transactions demand for money will be higher, say at Y_2, which lies to the right of Y_1. A still larger income will move the money demand rightward to Y_3 and so on.

2. **Precautionary demand.** If future receipts and expenditures were completely certain, the money carried for transactions purposes would cover all one's needs. But the future is never completely certain. A check which is supposed to arrive at a certain time may not arrive. I may have to make a business trip out of town on short notice. Before the

---

[5] In this Appendix, as in earlier chapters, we shall continue to use the term national income as equivalent to gross national product. And for convenience of notation, we shall use the letter Y instead of the more cumbersome GNP.

invention of the credit card, this might have meant paying for the trip first and collecting from the boss later. A car accident or a sudden illness in the family may lead to unforeseen needs for cash.

Most people, therefore, will not be content to hold the bare minimum of cash needed to cover normal transactions. They will want a "rainy day" reserve in addition. This precautionary demand, like transactions demand, probably depends mainly on the size of incomes. As a man's income rises, he buys more safety as well as more of everything else.

The precautionary demand for money thus resembles the transactions demand curves shown in Figure 1a. There will be a different demand curve for each level of national income, and these curves will be unresponsive to interest except at very high rates. Because of this similarity, it has not seemed necessary to draw a separate diagram for precautionary demand.

3. Speculative demand.   This type of demand affects investors, including business concerns as well as better-off individuals. While these people are a minority of the population, they hold large money balances; and the size of their holdings is related to the state of the securities markets.

Since speculative demand for money is a phenomenon of the securities markets, it has no direct connection with the level of production. Thus we have only one demand curve instead of a separate curve for each level of national income. What does this demand curve look like? In particular, how is the speculative demand for money related to the rate of interest?

It is helpful to recall that the rate of interest moves in the *opposite* direction from the price of bonds and other fixed-interest securities. To say that the interest rate is *rising* is the same as saying that security prices are *falling;* and vice versa. Now as security prices fall, more and more people will conclude that prices are "too low," i.e., below their normal or long-run level, and that they will rise back toward this level at some later point. In an effort to "buy at the bottom," they will shift out of cash and into securities. Speculative holdings of money decline. Conversely, as security prices rise (= the interest rate falls), more and more people will conclude that prices are now "too high," and will shift out of securities into cash. The speculative demand for cash increases.

This produces the kind of demand curve shown in Figure 1b. *The speculative demand for money varies inversely with the rate of interest.* This amounts to saying that people will be more willing to hold securities the lower their prices.

Note one important feature of Figure 1b. At the interest rate i_0, the speculative demand curve for money becomes infinitely elastic. What does this mean? It means that at this level the yield on securities is so unattractive that investors will not increase their securities holdings at all. If additional money is pumped into the system, they will simply hold it in idle balances. This is usually termed the *liquidity trap*. The practical consequence is that *the monetary authorities cannot force the interest rate below* i_0. This limits the power of the central bank to take useful corrective action during a depression.

4. Total demand. The total demand for money, obtained by adding these three types of demand, will look as shown in Figure 1c. There is an infinite number of demand curves, each corresponding to a different level of national income, of which only three are shown here. Each curve slopes downward in response to lower interest rates until it reaches the critical minimum i_0, at which point it becomes infinitely elastic.

Speculative Demand for Money

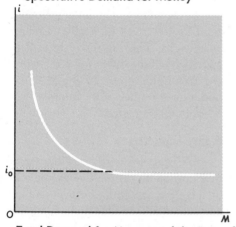

FIGURE 1b. As the rate of interest falls (= securities prices rise), people will hold less securities and more money. At some minimum rate, i_0, any additional money will be held idle.

Total Demand for Money and the Rate of Interest

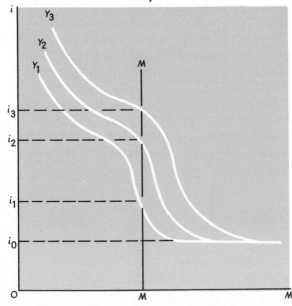

FIGURE 1c. The total demand curves Y_1, Y_2, and Y_3 are a composite of the underlying demand curves in Figures 1a and 1b. Given such a demand curve, and given the supply of money, one can determine the rate of interest. Thus if demand is Y_1, and money supply is OM, the interest rate will be i_1.

If we know the supply of money as well as the demand, we can determine the rate of interest. Suppose OM is the quantity of money in existence, so that MM is the money supply curve. And suppose that at the present level of income the demand curve for money is Y_1. Supply and demand must be equal, since all the money in existence at a particular time must be held by somebody. Thus the rate of interest must be i_1, determined by the intersection of Y_1 and MM.

A higher national income Y_2, with the same quantity of money, will produce a higher interest rate i_2, defined by the intersection of Y_2 and MM. A still higher income Y_3 will result in the interest rate i_3, and so on. Thus we conclude that, given the money supply, *the interest rate varies directly with the level of national income.*

Suppose now that we take national income as fixed, say at Y_1, and make money supply the variable factor. Move MM to the left, indicating a smaller supply. The equilibrium rate of interest will be higher. Enlarge the money supply by moving MM to the right. The interest rate will be lower. This leads to a second proposition: *The interest rate varies inversely with the quantity of money.* (This holds good *until* one strikes the horizontal section of the demand curve, when the interest rate becomes unresponsive to further increases in money supply.)

Income Determination in a Monetary Economy

We seem to have made a considerable step forward. In Chapter 20 we said that, in order to draw a consumption or investment schedule, one must assume some rate of interest. But this rate was pulled out of the air. Now we have shown how the interest rate itself is determined by the operation of the system.

But wait a moment. Are we as far ahead as we thought? All we have shown is that we can determine the rate of interest provided we know the supply of money *and the level of national income.* But in practice, of course, the level of national income is the great unknown. This is what we really want to determine in the end. So we seem to be going around in a circle.

The difficulty is that, having brought money into the picture, we have two equilibrium conditions to satisfy instead of one. These are:

1. **Equilibrium in product markets.** Total spending on goods and services must equal the cost of goods and services produced. We saw in Chapter 20 that this condition is satisfied when

$$S = I + (G - T)$$

or in the simplified no-government case,

$$S = I .$$

2. **Equilibrium in the money market.** This requires that the amount of money people want to hold must equal the amount of money

in existence. If we designate the former as L, and the latter as M, the condition is

$$L = M .$$

Suppose we know the quantity of money in existence. (We have to take *something* as fixed in order to get anywhere at all!) But both national income (Y) and the rate of interest (i) are left free to vary. *Problem:* To find a combination of Y and i which will satisfy *both* of the equilibrium conditions simultaneously. If we can do this, we shall have a stable equilibrium for the economy, in which money supply, interest rate, and the total expenditure schedule will be mutually consistent.

Is this a soluble problem? Yes, it is. The solution can be shown in several different ways. The one chosen here requires effort to grasp; but it ties up a lot of things in a neat way.

Since we are now trying to determine Y and i simultaneously, our diagrams from here on will show Y on the horizontal axis and i on the vertical axis. The eventual solution, then, will be a *point* on this sort of diagram, a satisfactory pair of values for the two variables.

Start with the first condition of equilibrium, $S = I$, and look at

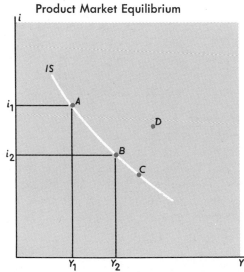

Product Market Equilibrium

FIGURE 2. *IS* contains all combinations of national income (Y) and interest rate (i) which satisfy the conditions $S = I$. Thus A, B, and C are possible equilibrium positions for the economy, while D is not.

Figure 2. Choose any rate of interest, i_1. Now, for this rate of interest there must be some level of national income which will make S equal to I. The rate of interest determines a certain amount of investment, so we must find a level of income at which people will choose to save just this amount. Suppose this turns out to be Y_1. Then point A on the diagram, with coordinates i_1, Y_I, is one point at which the $S = I$ condition is fulfilled.

But there are obviously many more such points. Choose a lower rate of interest, i_2. With lower interest, there will be a larger volume of investment. If the saving-investment equality is to hold, there must be more saving, and this will happen only at a higher level of income. The required level of income turns out to be Y_2. This gives us another point, B, which meets the $S = I$ condition. By repeating the same process we discover a third point, C; and so on.

By linking together all such points, we derive the curve IS. This is the *locus of all combinations of* i *and* Y *which satisfy the* $S = I$ *condition*. Wherever the economy may settle, then, it must be at some point along this line. Point D, for example, cannot be an equilibrium point because it does not satisfy one of the basic conditions.

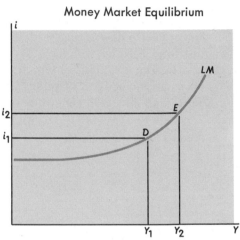

Money Market Equilibrium

FIGURE 3. *LM* contains all combinations of Y and *i* which satisfy the condition $L = M$. Only points on this line, such as D and E, are possible equilibrium positions for the economy.

Turn now to the second condition, $L = M$, and look at Figure 3. We proceed as before. Choose any rate of interest, i_1. Given this rate, the amount of money people wish to hold depends solely on the level of income (refer back, if you need to, to Figure 1c). But the quantity of money in existence is fixed. Thus we can find some income level at which people are just willing to hold this fixed amount of money. Suppose this turns out to be Y_1. Then point D gives us one combination of i and Y which satisfies the $L = M$ condition.

Choose another rate of interest, i_2. At this rate, it will take a different income level, Y_2, to equate L and M. This gives us a second point E. By discovering more and more such points and joining them up, we obtain the LM curve in Figure 3. This is *the locus of all combinations of* i *and* Y *which satisfy the* L = M *condition*.

Why does LM slope upward to the right? As we move to the right, we are moving toward higher levels of income. People will thus want to hold larger money balances for transactions and precautionary purposes. But the amount of money in existence is fixed. So the larger transactions-precautionary demand can be satisfied only by persuading people to hold *smaller* balances for speculative purposes. This requires a rise in the rate of interest, since speculative balances vary inversely with interest. The rate of interest must rise enough to reduce the speculative demand for money by the same amount that the higher level of income has raised the transactions-precautionary demand. Only in this way can the $L = M$ condition continue to be satisfied with a fixed amount of money.

Note, however, that the early section of LM has been drawn as a horizontal line. This corresponds to the horizontal section of the money demand curve in Figure 1c. This portion of Figure 1c, it will be remembered, indicates that at some (low) level of interest rates people will accumulate idle balances indefinitely instead of buying securities.

General Equilibrium: Simultaneous Determination of Interest Rate and National Income

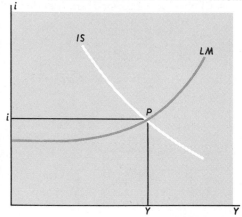

FIGURE 4. Any equilibrium position for the economy must lie on both *IS* and *LM*. The only point of which this is true is the intersection point *P*. Hence the level of income will be *Y* and the interest rate *i*.

This is the region of the liquidity trap. Starting from such a situation, as income rises the increased transactions-precautionary demand for money can be met for awhile by drawing off idle balances with no need for a rise in the interest rate. Eventually, however, the economy reaches a point at which further balances will be released only at a higher rate of interest. At this point *LM* turns upward.

Once the construction of the *IS* and *LM* curves has been grasped, the solution of our problem becomes simple. Look at Figure 4, where the two are brought together. Each curve shows a basic condition of equilibrium. For the economy to be in equilibrium, *both* conditions must be satisfied at once. The equilibrium combination of interest rate and national income *must* lie on *both IS* and *LM*. But this can happen only where the two curves intersect. The intersection at *P*, then, defines the general equilibrium of the system. The interest rate will settle at *i* and the level of national income at *Y*. And this will be a stable position so long as the underlying conditions—the expenditure schedule, the money demand curves, and the quantity of money—remain unchanged.

Changes in the Level of National Income

In practice, the underlying conditions never do stay unchanged for long. The chief usefulness of the $IS - LM$ diagram is as a tool for exploring the reactions which will be set up by any change in the basic conditions. Two examples will make the point.

An Increase in the Expenditure Schedule

Suppose first that the IS curve shifts rightward to $(IS)_1$ (Figure 5). This means that, at each rate of interest, people are now willing to spend more than before. We need not ask why. An increase in planned spending by consumers, business concerns, or government might be responsible.

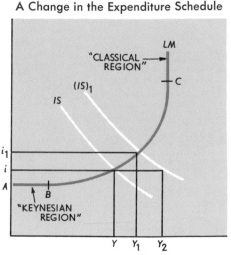

A Change in the Expenditure Schedule

FIGURE 5.   Over the upward-sloping region BC, a shift of IS will change both the interest rate and the level of income. Below B, the effect will be entirely on income; above C, it will be entirely on the rate of interest.

What reactions will be set up by this shift? The answer depends on the shape of LM. Three cases may be distinguished:

1. Suppose that $(IS)_1$ intersects LM somewhere in the range BC, over which LM slopes upward to the right. (This is probably the commonest case, and is the one illustrated in Figure 5.) Then equilibrium will be reestablished at the intersection of $(IS)_1$ and LM. The rate of interest will rise from i to i_1, and national income will rise from Y to Y_1. The increase in spending will raise *both* national income and the rate of interest.

Note, however, that national income rises less than it did in the simple multiplier analysis of Chapter 21. The reason is that in Chapter 21 we assumed the interest rate to be unaffected by any shift in total demand. If this were so, and if the rise from IS to $(IS)_1$ left the interest rate unchanged at i, then the multiplier effect would push national income all the way out to Y_2. But in the present case the interest rate does rise. This acts as a brake on expansion and limits the rise in national income to Y_1.

2. There is a case, however, in which the simple multiplier analysis yields correct results. Suppose that both IS and $(IS)_1$ intersect LM in the range AB, i.e., the region of excess speculative balances. Then the rise in spending will not raise the rate of interest. Without the interest brake, the multiplier will be left to work out its full effect in terms of higher income.

This has been labeled the "Keynesian region" in Figure 5, because Lord Keynes called attention to this possibility and thought it was important in practice. In the abnormally depressed conditions of the 1930's, interest rates may have reached the irreducible minimum which Keynes visualized, but this possibility has been of little practical importance since 1940.

3. A third possibility is indicated by the vertical section from C upward in Figure 5. At C the rate of interest is so high (security prices are so low) as to produce a general conviction that the movement will be reversed. Everyone has shifted into securities, and speculative holdings of money have fallen to zero. All the money in existence is being held for transactions and precautionary purposes. But we have assumed that these holdings are a constant proportion of income. Thus if the money supply is fixed, national income is fixed, and we can move no farther to the right on the diagram. The LM curve becomes vertical.

Suppose that the IS curve intersects LM at or above C. If IS rises still higher, the new intersection point will be immediately above the previous one. The only effect will be a rise in the interest rate, and there will be no effect on national income. This has been labeled the "classical region" in Figure 5, because these results correspond to those often assumed in economic theory before 1930.

"Real-life economies" are probably moving most of the time within the range BC, and the results which hold within that range are most likely to be of practical importance.

An Increase in Money Supply

Consider now the effects of a change in the money market (Figure 6). The banks, influenced by Federal Reserve policy, have become willing to lend more than before at the same rate of interest. Thus LM moves rightward to the position $(LM)_1$. What will happen? The IS curve now intersects the monetary curve farther to the right, so that there is a new equilibrium level of interest and national income. But note that these variables change in opposite directions. National income *rises* from Y to Y_1. The rate of interest *falls* from i to i_1. Moreover, a quick pencil test reveals that these results hold even if IS intersects LM in its vertical or "classical" region.

The relative size of the two effects depends on the slope of IS.

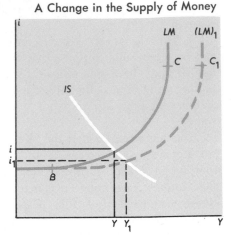

A Change in the Supply of Money

FIGURE 6. An increase in the supply of money shifts *LM* rightward, say to $(LM)_1$. The normal result will be a *rise* in national income and a *fall* in the rate of interest. But if *IS* intersects *LM* in the Keynesian region to the left of *B*, the increase in money supply will be ineffective.

Suppose *IS* is very steep, i.e., savings and investment decisions are little affected by changes in the rate of interest. Then an increase in money supply will mean a marked drop in the rate of interest, but only a small increase in national income. A very flat *IS* curve will lead to opposite results. The flatter the shape of *IS*, the greater the impact of an increase in money supply on national income.

This analysis helps to illustrate why equally good economists may reach different conclusions about the effects of monetary change, and thus come out with different policy recommendations. Such disagreements can often be put in the form of differences of opinion about the shape and location of the *IS* and *LM* functions. These are questions of fact. As continuing research throws more light upon them, the range for legitimate difference of opinion should gradually narrow.

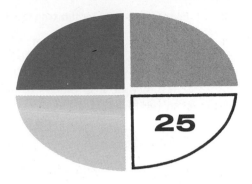

Fluctuations in National Income

All Mathematics would suggest / A steady straight line as the best,
But left and right alternately / Is consonant with History.

W. H. Auden

The ebb will take off what the tide brings in.

Thomas Fuller

THE NATIONAL INCOME DIAGRAMS in earlier chapters are still photographs of the economy at a moment of time. They say that, if the expenditure schedule is in a certain position, the economy will be tending toward a certain level of national income. If the expenditure schedule shifts, the equilibrium level of income will change.

We must now examine how the expenditure schedule actually does shift over the course of time. It could conceivably go on rising steadily year after year. But in practice it does not do this. Every few years there is a setback, and expenditure and national income drop for a year or so before the upward climb is resumed. The task of this chapter is to follow these movements as if with a movie camera and to explore what determines their timing and shape.

We shall concentrate on *description, explanation,* and *prediction* of these swings in economic activity. What do they look like? What things go up most rapidly during an expansion, and what things fall most in recession? How can one explain the turning points in economic activity? Why does an expansion always reverse itself after a while instead of going on upward forever? What progress has been made toward predicting future economic movements?

These questions are important. Elections are won or lost, businesses prosper or fail, people lose their jobs or find new jobs—all according to the swings of the business cycle.

DESCRIPTION

The nature of economic fluctuations can be judged from Figure 1, which is the chart shown in the introduction to Part Three. Note that every few years national output drops and unemployment rises. Then after a short time the movement is reversed. Output rises and unemployment falls.

Production and Unemployment, 1918–65

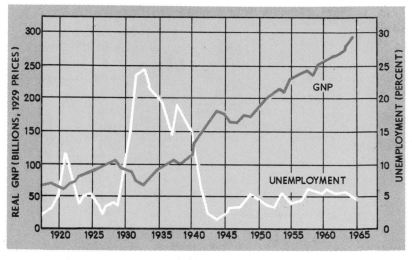

FIGURE 1.

These sawtooth movements are often called business cycles, but this can be misleading. "Cycle" suggests greater regularity than actually exists. If expansions and contractions followed each other at regular intervals, there would be no forecasting problem. The thing which keeps everyone sitting on the edge of his chair is uncertainty about when the next turn will come. Some economic expansions (1924–26, 1927–29, 1958–60) peter out after a couple of years. But one, the 1938–45 expansion associated with World War II, lasted almost 7 years; and the strong upswing which began in 1961 lasted more than 5 years. The average duration of an upswing is something like 3 years. But an average is not an insurance policy.

The term "cycle" also connotes a strong similarity among different expansions and contractions. It suggests that we can find a single "business cycle theory" which will account for all of them. Few economists today would accept this view. There is a certain family resemblance among successive cycles. But each has individual characteristics, involving a combination of circumstances which will never recur in just the same form. Cycles differ in length, in size, in the combination of forces responsible for the upswing, in the reasons for ending of prosperity, and in the severity of the relapse.

It may be better, therefore, to speak of *economic fluctuations* or *fluctuations in national income*, which carries no implication of regularity or uniform causation.

One other problem of terminology: In popular usage, periods of economic expansion go by such varied names as "recovery," "prosperity," "boom." Periods of declining activity may be called "slumps," "recessions," "depressions." All this is rather confusing. Let us agree, therefore, to call a period of rising activity an *upswing*, and a period of declining activity a *downswing*. The point at which an upswing ceases and reverses itself we shall call the *upper turning point*. The end of a downswing is the *lower turning point*. A complete fluctuation, then, consists of a lower turning point, an upswing, an upper turning point, and a downswing. If this sounds less exciting than boom and slump, it has the advantage of saying exactly what we mean.

What goes on during one of these fluctuations? The most striking thing about them is the divergent movement of different elements in the economy. During a downswing some things fall a lot, others fall a little, while some go right on rising. In general, the things which fall most on the downswing also rise most on the upswing. It is necessary to say a bit about these differences in movement, since they provide some clues to why the fluctuations occur.

Some Things Fluctuate Widely

Among the items which show sizable fluctuations are:

1. *Business inventories* of raw materials, goods in process, and finished products. Businesses typically add substantially to inventories on the upswing and reduce them on the downswing.

2. *Machinery and equipment* expenditures also rise sharply on the upgrade and fall off during contraction. Note the wide fluctuations of this item in Figure 2.

3. *Consumer spending on durable goods,* notably automobiles, furniture, and household appliances. These purchases are postponable and are financed partly by borrowing. During a period of economic uncertainty some families will be unwilling or unable to borrow and will postpone their purchases to a more favorable time. Consumer spending on food, clothing, and services, on the other hand, has not declined in any of the downswings since 1945.

Economic Fluctuations Are Mainly Investment Fluctuations

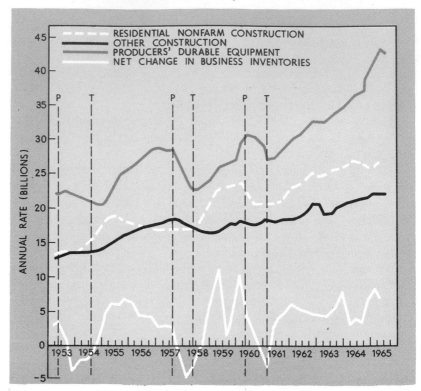

FIGURE 2. *P* indicates a cycle peak or upper turning point. *T* indicates a cycle trough or lower turning point. The dating is that used by the National Bureau of Economic Research.

4. *Production of durable goods.* With business spending on machinery and consumer spending on durable goods both falling, it stands to reason that output of durable goods must fall on the downswing. A downswing *is* mainly a decline in steel, metals, machinery, automobiles, and other durable goods industries. In recent downswings the total output of nondurable goods has dropped scarcely at all.

5. *Employment* rises and falls with production. On the downswing, several million people may be laid off completely and several million more reduced to working part time.

6. *Business profits* may fall by 25 percent or so in even a mild downswing, then shoot up the same distance or more during the next upswing.

7. *Tax receipts* of the federal government fluctuate for the reasons noted in Chapter 22. Even the mild downswings of the fifties brought drops of $5 to $8 billion in federal revenues, mainly because of smaller receipts from the corporate income tax. The upswings of 1954–57,

1958–60, and 1961–66 brought increased revenues of close to $20 billion
—in the last case despite the large 1964–65 cuts in tax *rates.*

8. *Interest rates,* particularly short-term rates, move up and down
substantially over the cycle. This is partly a natural result of fluctuations
in the demand for money, partly a reflection of monetary policy.

Some Things Always Go Up

Among items which fluctuate little with general economic activity, we
may note:

1. *Government purchases of goods and services.* State and local
government expenditures have risen quite steeply since 1945, and the rise
has continued right through the downswing periods. Federal expenditures have had a milder uptrend, and also show little relation to general
economic activity.

2. *Consumer spending on nondurable goods and services.* This has
risen sharply during upswings, leveled off a bit during downswings, but
shows no period of actual decline.

3. *Wage rates.* Wages have risen in bad years and good. The rise has
been slightly less rapid during downswings than during upswings, but
the difference is not marked.

4. *The price level.* Both the Wholesale Price Index and the Consumer
Price Index have edged up gradually over the past 20 years. The advance
slows down and sometimes stops for a while during downswings; but
except for a mild drop in prices during the downswing of 1948–49, there
has been no general price decline in the United States since 1938.

Much more could be said about the behavior of the economy during
periods of expansion and contraction.[1] But perhaps we have said enough
to set the stage for an analysis of why these fluctuations occur.

EXPLANATION

It would be satisfying to discover a general cause of economic
fluctuations, a single source of the uneven heartbeat of the economy. But it
has gradually become apparent that there is no one prime mover. Each
upturn and downturn is complex and to some extent unique. One needs an
eclectic rather than a monocausal approach.

There are two main things to be explained. First, after the economy
has started moving up or down, why does it build up momentum and
keep going in the same direction for a considerable time? Second and
more difficult, why does the movement reverse itself after a while? After

---

[1] The great center of research on this subject is the National Bureau of Economic Research in New York. Anyone who wants to delve into detail will find a
wealth of publications by Wesley C. Mitchell, Arthur F. Burns, Geoffrey H. Moore,
Solomon Fabricant, and other past and present members of the Bureau staff.

production has been rising for several years, the production index levels off and then starts to decline. Why doesn't expansion continue indefinitely?

Investment: Autonomous and Induced

Since economic fluctuations are centered in the investment industries, we must look further into the short-run behavior of business investment. A basic distinction here is between *autonomous* and *induced* investment. The latter is capacity-oriented investment, occurring in response to changes in consumer demand. Demand for shoes rises 10 percent. If the shoe industry is presently operating at capacity, it will have to increase its capacity 10 percent to keep up with the expanding market.

Autonomous investment, on the other hand, is independent of current consumer demand. An example is investment in the early automobile factories. There was no prior demand for the product, since the product didn't exist. But some businessmen believed that, by starting to turn out this new product, they could tap a potential desire for it and develop an effective demand. New-product investment, then, is autonomous; and so is a good deal of the investment in cost-reducing improvements. Scientists and engineers are every day turning up improvements in production methods which are so profitable that they will be adopted even if consumer demand is not rising.

Autonomous investment could conceivably go on at a steady pace year after year, but this is unlikely to happen in practice. True, invention and innovation are going on all the time. But there are major and minor innovations. At one end of the scale is the small adjustment on a machine which increases its efficiency by 5 percent and which earns someone a $100 prize from the company suggestion system. At the other extreme are the inventions which led to the railroad, electric power production, telephone communication, and the automobile.

A major innovation gives rise to a wave of capital investment. First, a few pioneers demonstrate that the new technique is feasible and that the public will take the product at profitable prices. After this, imitators swarm into the new industry. Investment is heavy, plant capacity and output grow rapidly. But eventually the potentialities of the new industry are fully exploited, output tapers off to a plateau, and investment falls.

To sustain the upward momentum of the economy one needs a series of major innovations, following each other at regular intervals, so that as the force of one new development tapers off, there is something else to take its place. But this cannot be counted on. No matter how many well-financed research laboratories there may be, one cannot be sure of producing the equivalent of a new automobile industry every decade. Putting more money into scientific training and research should raise the *average rate* of invention, but it cannot make it completely regular. Significant discoveries cannot be turned out on the assembly line.

The late Professor Joseph Schumpeter regarded the irregularity of autonomous investment as the main explanation of the business cycle. A cycle upswing is a period during which businessmen are swarming into one or more new fields of activity. As capacity catches up with demand for these products, prices and profits fall, new investment declines, and we enter the cycle downswing.

Swings in Induced Investment: The Acceleration Principle

If autonomous investment is likely to fluctuate, induced investment is certain to fluctuate. This can be explained by a simplified illustration. Table 1 shows a company operating in an industry in which technology is such that it takes $2 of plant and equipment to produce $1 of product per year. When the scene opens in 1961, the company is operating at capacity, producing $100 million of goods per year from a plant costing $200 million. We suppose that $10 million of the company's equipment wears out each year and has to be replaced just to keep capacity unchanged. This appears as *replacement investment* in column (4). To increase capacity requires additional *net investment,* shown in column (5). *Gross investment* is the sum of the two and appears in the final column.

We do not try to explain the sales figures in column (1). We simply assume that sales behave irregularly, first rising for a while and then falling. What we intend to show is that, because of the fluctuation in sales, there will be even larger fluctuations in investment. This is usually called *the acceleration principle,* because sales variations are magnified or "accelerated" into wider swings of investment.

TABLE 1

Hypothetical Illustration of the Acceleration Principle
(Millions of Dollars)

YEAR	SALES (1)	REQUIRED STOCK OF CAPITAL (2)	ACTUAL STOCK OF CAPITAL (3)	REPLACEMENT INVESTMENT (4)	NET INVESTMENT (5)	GROSS INVESTMENT (6)
1961	100	200	200	10	..	10
1962	110	220	220	10	20	30
1963	125	250	250	10	30	40
1964	135	270	270	10	20	30
1965	140	280	280	10	10	20
1966	140	280	280	10	..	10
1967	135	270	270	..	..	..
1968	125	250	260	..	..	..
1969	125	250	250	..	..	..
1970	135	270	270	10	20	30
1971	150	300	300	10	30	40

In 1961, sales and capacity are in balance, so the company invests only the $10 million needed to replace worn-out equipment. In 1962, however, sales rise by $10 million, requiring new plant capacity of $20 million. Adding this to the $10 million of replacement gives gross investment of $30 million for that year. The course of events in subsequent years can be traced by working down the table. Note that net investment occurs only in years when sales are rising. Note also that in some years even replacement investment vanishes. Why is this? Because in these years sales are falling. The company can afford to let its plant wear out and its capacity shrink, since it still has enough (in 1968, more than enough) capacity to produce all it can sell.

Two points deserve special emphasis. First, the fluctuations in demand for the product produce magnified or accentuated fluctuations in gross investment. An increase of 25 percent in sales between 1961 and 1963 produces a *fourfold* rise in gross investment. A decline of less than 5 percent in sales from 1965 to 1967 causes gross investment to plummet to zero.

Second, the *level* of gross investment depends on the *rate of increase* in sales. In 1964, a slowing down of the rate of increase of sales as compared with the previous year causes an actual *drop* in investment. So the downturn of investment in column (6) *precedes* the downturn of sales in column (1), even though sales are the causal factor. This is the most interesting feature of the accelerator, and helps to explain why a business upswing may slow down and eventually topple over.

On the downswing, investment stays at zero while the capacity built during the boom gradually wears out. Note that wearing out of capacity will eventually require some replacement investment even if sales do not rise. Even if sales in 1970 remained at their depression level of $125 million, this would require plant capacity of $250 million. Since 1969 capacity is only $250 million and would wear down to $240 million by 1970, there will have to be replacement investment of $10 million in 1970 to meet production requirements.

The acceleration principle is applicable to other important categories of investment—for example, investment in housing. We could set up an example similar to Table 1 to show that a *decline in the rate of increase* of demand for housing will produce an absolute decline in house building. One can also generate fluctuations in business inventories by the acceleration principle. Since inventory fluctuations play an important role in business cycles, we give a simplified example in Table 2.

A common principle of inventory management is to keep inventories at a constant ratio to current sales. The department store in Table 2 tries always to maintain a 2:1 ratio. As its sales fluctuate, and it has unintended additions to or withdrawals from inventory, it will try to bring inventories back to the desired level. In period 1, the store is running along smoothly, with sales at 100 and inventory at 200. It will

TABLE 2

The Acceleration Principle Applied to Inventories

PERIOD	SALES DURING PERIOD	DESIRED INVENTORY AT END OF PERIOD	ORDERS TO ADJUST INVENTORY	ORDERS TO REPLACE GOODS SOLD	TOTAL ORDERS
1	100	200	0	100	100
2	115	230	30	115	145
3	130	260	30	130	160
4	145	290	30	145	175
5	150	300	10	150	160
6	140	280	−20	140	120
7	130	260	−20	130	110
8	130	260	0	130	130
9	140	280	20	140	160
10	150	300	20	150	170

order from manufacturers just enough to replace the goods it has sold, i.e. 100 units, as shown in the final column. In period 2, however, sales rise to 115 units, requiring an inventory of 230 units. To reach this level at the end of the period, it will have to order 115 units to replace the goods sold plus 30 units to build up inventory, or a total of 145 units. So an increase of 15 percent in the store's sales raises its orders to manufacturers by 45 percent—the accelerator once more.

The buildup of inventories continues through period 5. In period 6, however, sales drop and the accelerator goes into reverse. The store now wants to reduce inventories, to engage in *inventory disinvestment*. How does it do this? Simply by ordering fewer goods than it is currently selling. In period 6, it sells 140 units but buys only 120, so inventories drop from 300 to 280. Investments drop again in period 7. Just as on the upswing, a small change in sales produces a large change in orders to manufacturers.

Note that the turning points in new orders *precede* the turning points in sales. In period 5 sales are still rising, but the *rate of increase* has diminished. This brings a decline in new orders, because of the slackening of inventory investment. Again, in period 8, sales are at the same level as in the previous period. Orders begin to rise, however, because the store has stopped disinvesting in inventories.

By working the accelerator and the multiplier together, we can generate a "built-in" business cycle. True, there must be a push to set the machine going, an autonomous increase in spending from one source or another. Given this, the multiplier generates increased income and additional spending by consumers. As sales begin to increase, the inventory accelerator takes hold, and manufacturing activity rises even faster. This generates additional income, sales rise some more, and the rush to invest in inventories gains momentum. As manufacturing plants begin to near capacity, the plant and equipment accelerator takes hold, and investment rises some more. Through the multiplier this generates still more income, sales rise again, and so on and on.

To keep the upswing going, sales of finished goods must continue to rise. Moreover—and this is what really matters—they must *rise at a constant or increasing rate.* Any slackening of the rate of increase in sales, as we have seen, is sufficient to cause a decline in both inventory investment and plant and equipment investment. If this happens, the multiplier goes into reverse and income begins to fall.[2] Maintaining an economic upswing is rather like racing a motorcycle up a steep slope. As soon as the machine loses momentum, it is in danger of toppling over.

The Mechanism of Expansion

With these principles as background, let us look more concretely at what goes on during a typical cycle. Let us ask first how an upswing feeds on itself and develops enough momentum to continue for several years at a time. We break into the cycle just after the lower turning point. An upswing has begun and has continued long enough to convince the business community that recovery is underway. What happens from this point on?

1. The early stages of recovery are a good time to carry out investment plans. The banking system has excess reserves. Interest rates have tumbled during the downswing. Capital goods manufacturers have idle capacity so that one can get prompt delivery of machinery and materials. Prices and wages are as low as they are likely to be in the foreseeable future. Labor is plentiful. Thus for anyone considering an investment project, the economic environment is unusually favorable.

2. Who is in a position to invest on the upswing? Young industries whose markets are growing at a rapid rate are particularly important. Such industries know that they must build new capacity, and the only question is when. They may hold back on the downswing until they can gauge its seriousness, and also in the hope of benefiting from lower costs at the bottom. But once the upswing is clearly underway, there is no longer any reason to delay. These industries will come strongly into the market for capital goods, and expansion projects initiated at this time

---

[2] This impressionistic account can be made more precise by using some simple algebra. Well worth reading is the classic article on the subject by Paul A. Samuelson, "Interactions between the Multiplier Analysis and the Acceleration Principle," *Review of Economics and Statistics* (1939), pp. 78–88 (reprinted in the A.E.A. *Readings in Business Cycle Theory,* ed. Gottfried Haberler [Homewood; Ill.: Richard D. Irwin, Inc., 1944]). By selecting different values for the multiplier and the accelerator, one can generate a violent cycle which becomes progressively wider, or one which repeats itself indefinitely, or one which becomes progressively milder.

may take 2 or 3 years to complete. The length of the physical *gestation period* on large construction jobs is one reason why activity keeps moving upward for a considerable time.

Even industries which are not increasing capacity must do considerable investment. Old equipment wears out or becomes obsolete as superior machinery is developed. New products may require different types of equipment. This replacement and modernization investment is timed with some reference to economic conditions. When profits are falling and the future is unclear, many companies follow a "wait and see" policy. They let old equipment wear out and do nothing about it, which for the time being intensifies the downswing. The longer the downswing continues, the more of this postponed replacement demand is built up for the future. Once the upswing is underway, this potential demand becomes effective and helps raise the level of investment.

3. Some industries have cycles of their own. Building construction seems to follow a cycle of 15 to 20 years in length. If an economic upswing occurs at a time when the building cycle is also on the upgrade, the vigor of construction activity adds momentum to the upswing. But if the building cycle is in a contraction phase, this acts as a drag on the economy. It makes the general upswing shorter and weaker than it would be if building were also expanding.

4. Another feature of the early upswing is a rise in inventory investment, explainable by the accelerator principle. As sales of finished goods begin to rise, there will be an inventory buildup all along the line from retailers back through manufacturers to raw material suppliers. This can add several billions a year to total business investment.

There is a further reason for a rise in inventory investment. In industries where raw materials are important and where material prices fluctuate widely, a manufacturer is unavoidably involved in price speculation. A tire company is partly a producer of tires, partly a speculator in rubber prices. So as soon as an upswing is underway many companies, reasoning that material prices are bound to rise, will order unusually large amounts in order to "beat the price rise."

5. With additional investment going on for these reasons, the upswing is clearly on solid ground. Part of the increased income generated in the capital goods industries is spent on consumer goods, thus raising demand and output in those industries. Increased employment in consumer goods production generates still more income, most of which is respent on the next round; and so on through the familiar multiplier process. Because of the large size of the consumer goods sector, the *absolute* increase in consumption during an upswing is typically larger than the increase in investment, even though it may have been investment which provided the initial push.

6. As the level of income rises, more and more industries find themselves operating close to capacity and begin to consider whether

they shouldn't build new capacity. The rising cost of investment during a boom operates as a deterrent. But this is typically outweighed by the facts that the sales outlook is good and that companies are making substantial profits which can be plowed back. There is also a competitive element at work. A company usually aims to keep at least its present share of sales in its industry, and preferably to gain a larger share. This means that its expansion plans must keep pace with those of rival companies. If demand for the industry's products is expected to be 20 percent higher 5 years from now than it is today, there will be a competitive scramble to see who can "get there fastest."

Thus we get *induced* investment, operating in the manner of our accelerator example. Because of the high mechanization of many industries, the effect is substantial. During the strong upswing of 1961–65, for example, sales of new machinery rose from about $29 billion in 1961 to $45 billion in 1965, or more than 50 percent. Construction of plants, stores, office buildings, and the like also rose by about $5 billion.

These cumulative, mutually reinforcing increases in consumption and investment readily explain why the pendulum keeps swinging in the same direction for several years at a time. It is harder to explain why the upswing eventually slows down and reverses itself. Just when people have become confident about continued economic expansion, the rug is pulled from under them, and the economy heads downward into recession.

Why is this? Must the boom come to an end? Couldn't a downturn be prevented, if only we were sufficiently clever? In the present state of knowledge the answer seems to be no. To explain why is the next stage in our story.

The End of Prosperity

We saw earlier that, to the extent that the upswing depends on the accelerator, aggregate demand must keep rising *at a constant or rising rate*. This may well happen, at least for a while. But it may also not happen. Some of the components of total spending may stop rising, or may rise more slowly than before. Consumers may decide that they don't like this year's automobile models and may reduce their spending on durable goods. A drop in federal spending, unaccompanied by a drop in tax rates, can break the back of a boom. This was a factor in the downturn of 1953. As the Korean War came to a close, federal purchases of goods and services were cut by about $15 billion between the first quarter of 1953 and the first quarter of 1954. This was an unusual event. But even a failure of government expenditure to rise at the same rate as tax revenues are increasing will have a depressing effect on total spending.

Most likely of all, however, is that business investment will eventually lose momentum and rise more slowly than before. Autonomous investment is naturally erratic and unpredictable; and induced investment has vagaries of its own, as we have seen. The reasons for an eventual slackening of investment are to some extent built into the pattern of the previous expansion. Several points deserve mention:

1. In the early stages of an upswing, there is usually heavy inventory investment to restore the normal ratio of inventories to sales. But once this has been accomplished, the rate of inventory investment slackens. Now if businessmen increased inventories this year by $10 billion, and if next year they increase them only $5 billion, this amounts to a *cut* of $5 billion a year in investment. A careful look at Figure 1 suggests that this typically happens during the last half of an upswing.

The same analysis applies to replacement and modernization of equipment. There is a tendency to delay this kind of investment on the downswing because of the uncertain business outlook. Thus the economy enters the upswing with a backlog of deferred demand. Once the upswing is underway, there is no longer any reason for delay. Businesses rush to make up for lost time. Orders for new equipment are placed at a rapid rate. The backlog of demand begins to shrink, and after a couple of years may be largely exhausted. This means a drop in demand for machinery and related items.

2. Another prominent feature of the upswing is a rush to increase plant capacity in industries with a strong uptrend of demand. But future movements of demand are always conjectural, and plant expansion may undershoot or overshoot the mark. Overshooting is especially likely in competitive industries where numerous firms are trying to estimate both the increase in total industry demand and the share of the market which they can hope to capture. If many firms are overoptimistic, total plant capacity can easily outrun the increase in demand. Since plant construction takes time, it may be several years before this becomes apparent. But as more and more plants come into operation and it becomes apparent that the industry is overexpanded, further plant construction will cease. This is an additional reason why investment, after rising for a few years, may weaken abruptly and unexpectedly.

3. Investment is a physical as well as a financial process. The feasible rate of investment is limited in the short run by the capacity of the capital goods industries, by the supply of metals, machinery, building materials, skilled construction labor, and so on. These industries enter the upswing with much idle capacity, and so for a while their production can expand rapidly. If the upswing carries to the point at which the capital goods industries are working to capacity, however, the rate of increase in investment must decline.

Capacity limitations do not compel an actual downturn of investment. But they can compel a drop in the rate of increase. This leveling off of investment must fairly quickly, after the multiplier has done its work, mean a leveling off of GNP. And this has awkward implications.

4. The upswing may or may not carry to the point at which there is

upward pressure on the price level. If it does, another unstable and reversible element enters the scene. Part of consumer and business spending now becomes an effort to beat the next price increase. It depends on an expectation of further price increases in the future. If anything happens to shake this expectation, this "scare buying" will diminish or disappear; and the overbuying which was induced by fear of price increases will be offset by underbuying for some time.

5. How far have we gotten in demonstrating that the boom contains the seeds of its own destruction? We have shown that part of the investment on the upswing is of a sort which naturally goes into reverse after a while. Inventory investment, deferred replacement demand, and buying based on expectation of price increases are all of this character. Competitive overexpansion of particular industries during the upswing may lead, when it is eventually discovered, to a drop of investment in those industries. If the monetary authorities become concerned about rising prices and apply the credit brakes, this can also check the rise of investment.

Thus investment *may* level off or decline even before the capital goods industries are working at capacity. If the upswing carries these industries to capacity, investment *must* taper off for physical reasons. And this implies that the increase in GNP will also taper off.

But what is wrong with this? Why can't the economy taper off at a high level and move along a gently rising plateau? There are at least two reasons. First, a reduced rate of increase in consumer demand cuts induced investment via the acceleration principle. Second, most businessmen do not believe that the economy can hold indefinitely to a stable level of activity. They do not believe in "prosperity plateaus." They believe in cycles, having been conditioned to this by a century of economic history. As soon as an expansion begins to level off, many businessmen say "Ah! We are nearing the end of this upswing. The sensible thing now is to go slow on our investment plans and see what happens." As this impression spreads, it helps to bring on the downturn. And then everyone can say, "How clever we were. We knew it all the time."

Big Downswings and Little Ones

The growth of production and employment is interrupted every few years by a downturn. Since 1850 there has been only one peacetime upswing which continued longer than about 4 years,[3] and many were cut short after 2 to 3 years. But some downswings are long and severe, while others are brief and mild. In the Great Depression of the thirties, GNP dropped by about 30 percent between 1929 and 1933, and full recovery

---

[3] Geoffrey H. Moore (ed.), *Business Cycle Indicators* (Princeton, N.J.: Princeton University Press, 1960), Vol. I, p. 670.

was not achieved until the war boom of 1941–45. In the four downswings between 1946 and 1965, on the other hand, GNP never dropped more than 5 percent. This is sometimes taken as indicating that major downswings are no longer possible in the American economy.

What makes the difference between a small downswing and a large one? One important factor is the stage of the building cycle, which has its own slow-moving pattern cutting through the fluctuations of general business. If building construction is moving upward, one can count on a sizable volume of investment in good years and bad. Suppose all other investment dropped to zero. Then national income could drop only to the point at which saving equaled building investment (or, more realistically, building investment plus the federal deficit). This sets a floor to the downswing, and the higher the level of building activity the higher this floor will be.

But suppose the economy is in a downward phase of the building cycle. Then building activity provides less support, and downswings can go farther before hitting bottom. This was the situation in the 1930's. The building cycle reached a peak in 1925 and then turned down. By the time of the general downswing in 1929, building had fallen too low to provide much support. Throughout the fifties, on the other hand, building construction was high and rising. Each time a downturn occurred, the continued strength of building activity helped to arrest the downswing.

Another important factor is the uneven occurrence of major investment opportunities. A major downswing could occur because of a temporary lack of major inventions and innovations. It has been suggested that this may have happened after 1929. Heavy investment in electric power and automobiles helped to sustain prosperity during the twenties. But as these industries moved toward maturity, no new industries of equal importance appeared to maintain the momentum of investment. The downturn of the building cycle in 1925 served as an additional drag. Hence the severity of the 1929–33 downswing.

Contrast with this the situation during the fifties. By this time many important discoveries dating back to the thirties and forties were ripe for commercial application. The list includes automation in factory and office, computers and other electronic devices, applications of atomic energy, jet aviation and rocketry, major developments in chemicals and petrochemicals. These areas have generated a large volume of autonomous investment, oriented toward long-term development and largely independent of current demand. This flow of assured investment, plus the high level of construction activity, has sustained national income during the postwar period. Downswings have not been able to develop momentum. In each case the economy has hit bottom and rebounded after 9 to 12 months.

This can be illustrated by some arithmetic. The figures are pulled

out of the air but are not far from the mark for recent years. Suppose the
pattern of investment at the upper turning point is as follows:

Residential construction	$20 billion (annual rate)
Autonomous business investment	25
Induced business investment*	25
Inventory change	5
Total investment	$75 billion (annual rate)

* This is a gross investment, and includes all items which may be subject to short-term cyclical influences. It includes replacement and modernization of equipment as well as plant expansion based on expectations of rising demand. Our assumption that half of business investment is sensitive to short downturns and half is not is arbitrary. But it may be a reasonable estimate for this period.

Suppose that on the downswing the inventory figure drops to −5 billion, and that induced investment drops to 20 billion. House building and autonomous business investment remain unchanged. Thus total investment declines by 15 billion. If the marginal propensity to spend is 0.5, then the multiplier is 2 and GNP will fall by 30 billion. At present GNP levels, this would be a fall of about 5 percent.

Suppose, on the other hand, that house building and autonomous business investment were declining year by year. This would lower the automatic "floor" under the economy, and permit deeper and longer declines in GNP. It is these two components of investment which really make the difference.

Concerning the probable behavior of the American economy during the next decade or two, one can only speculate. There is little evidence that private investment is inherently more stable than it used to be. The chief difference from earlier decades is the reduced value of the multiplier, due mainly to the greater importance of federal taxes and transfer payments. Recent estimates put the value of the multiplier in the neighborhood of 2, whereas pre-1940 estimates were usually between 3 and 4. Thus a $10 billion drop in investment now generates only a $20 billion decline in GNP instead of a $30 or $40 billion decline. This fact, plus the likelihood that any federal administration would move vigorously to combat a major downswing, warrants a belief that depressions on the 1929–33 scale are now impossible. But medium-sized downswings, larger than anything we have seen since 1940, are still within the bounds of possibility.

PREDICTION

What's going to happen next on the economic front? Everyone would like to know. Economic forecasting has become a favorite indoor sport of journalists, commentators, sales managers, and public officials. The quality of these forecasts varies greatly. Many are so vague or loaded with weasel words that the forecaster can hardly lose, but by the same token the user of the forecast can hardly benefit.

A good way to separate the men from the boys is to see whether a forecast uses numbers. Economics is a quantitative subject, and masses of current statistical information are now available. Unless an economic writer indicates a grasp of this material and is willing to spell out his predictions in figures, he cannot be taken seriously.

The more reputable methods of prediction may be classified as: (1) barometric forecasting; (2) analytical forecasting using the GNP framework; (3) econometric forecasting, which is also analytical but somewhat more complicated.

Barometric Forecasting

This method does not require any theorizing about the causes of economic fluctuations. It is purely inductive. It rests on the observation that things have happened in a certain way in the past and a surmise that they may happen similarly in the future.

The best-known example is the work of the National Bureau of Economic Research. Research workers at the Bureau have analyzed the movement of several hundred economic variables over a long period in the past, beginning in some cases as early as 1870. Particular attention has been paid to upper and lower turning points in each series, which presumably reflect the rhythm of overall economic fluctuations. From an examination of this material, the Bureau has established a precise year and month for each upturn and downturn in general economic activity. By comparing the turning points of a particular series with that for business in general, one can discover whether the series typically reverses itself earlier than general business, or at about the same time, or later.

On this basis, the series have been classified into three groups: (1) *Leading series*, which typically turn up and down in advance of general business. Included in this group are business failures, stock prices, new orders for durable goods, building contracts, average work week in manufacturing, new incorporations, and sensitive wholesale prices. (2) *Roughly coincident series*, which turn at about the same time as general business. This group includes employment, unemployment, industrial production, GNP, freight carloadings, corporate profits, and wholesale prices (except farm and food products). This amounts to saying that these are the series to which the Bureau attaches greatest weight in *defining* the turning points in general business, and also that these major indicators move quite closely together. (3) *Lagging series*, which move somewhat behind the swings of general business. Among this group are personal income, retail sales, consumer installment debt, manufacturers' inventories, and bank rates on business loans.

How can this kind of information be used by the economic fore-caster? It is no use to look at the lagging series, because by the time they move, the horse is already out of the barn. Even the coincident series do not help on prediction, though they can *confirm* a turning point 2 or 3 months after it has occurred. The only way to obtain an advance tip-off is to look at the leading series, which normally move ahead of general business. If five or six of these have already turned up or down, one can conclude that a turning point in economic activity is near.

TABLE 3

Average Timing of Selected Leading Series before 1957, and Their Timing in the 1960–61 Recession

SERIES	FIRST YEAR COVERED	MEDIAN LEAD (−) OR LAG (+) IN MONTHS		LEAD OR LAG AT 1960–61	
		Peak	Trough	Peak	Trough
Liabilities of business failures*	1875	− 6.5	−7	−12	−8
Industrial stock prices	1871	− 3.5	−6	−10	−4
New order, durable goods	1920	− 5.5	−2	−11	−1
Residential building contracts	1915	−14	−6	−17	−2
Commercial and industrial building contracts	1919	− 8	−2	no contraction	
Average work week, manufacturing	1920	− 6.5	−4	−12	−2
New incorporations	1860	− 2	−6	0	−3
Sensitive wholesale prices	1892	− 2	−1	− 6	−2

Sources: Data to 1957 are from R. A. Gordon, *Business Fluctuations* (2nd ed.; New York: Harper & Bros., 1961). They were compiled originally by Geoffrey H. Moore of the National Bureau. Leads for 1960–61 were calculated by the writer, using the Bureau's standard dates of May, 1960, for the upper turning point and February, 1961, for the lower turning point.
* This series is used in *inverted* form. Failures *rise* as business activity *falls*, and vice versa. Hence leads and lags refer to the inverted series.

Since particular interest attaches to leading series, their past per-formance is shown in Table 3. The figures in the first two columns show the *average* number of months by which each series has been ahead of general business at downturns and at upturns. These averages, unfortu-nately, conceal a good deal of variation from one cycle to the next. A series which shows an *average* lead of 4 months at the downturn may vary all the way from a lead of 12 months to a lag of 4 months in different cycles. Blind reliance on any one indicator can be quite misleading. A particular series will sometimes "flash the signal" a good deal too early, while in other cases there may be no signal at all until after the fact.

There are two main reasons why a series may be a leading series: (1) It may measure something which foreshadows a change in productive activity. An increase in building contracts normally means a rise in construction work a few months later. A rise in new orders for durable goods leads directly to increased activity in the metals and machinery industries. An increase in incorporations means that the new businesses will shortly be spending money on plant and office facilities.

2. A series may express the combined opinion of experienced observers about what lies immediately ahead. When large investors become convinced that a downswing is "bottoming out" and will soon end, they will buy securities immediately to get in at the bottom. Thus the stock market will turn up before the upturn in physical production. The same is true of raw material prices and other items included in the "sensitive wholesale price" index.

The barometric approach rests on economic logic. There are good reasons why the leading series *are* leading series on the average. But the method also involves certain weaknesses:

a) The variability in the behavior of individual series has already been noted. A series which is "well-behaved" most of the time may deceive you in a particular case by reversing itself too early or too late.

b) Most economic series show small, irregular fluctuations from month to month. If an index declines in a particular month, one cannot tell immediately whether this is a real turning point or a minor variation which will be reversed next month. It may take two or three months to be reasonably sure, and this cuts into the forecaster's precious margin of time.

c) In addition, most series are not available to the public until 2 or 3 months after the period which they cover. This is one reason why business organizations often collect their own indexes, which may have limited coverage but can be gotten out faster than the official government figures.

Thus even if a leading series does genuinely lead in a particular case, the forecaster is bound to be several months behind in reaching a firm conclusion.

Note also that this method predicts only the turning points. With good luck it may predict a future downturn, or at least confirm the downturn soon after it has occurred. But it says nothing about the probable depth and duration of the downswing. Similarly for an upswing. Barometric methods are thus useful mainly for short periods of time in the vicinity of a turning point. At other times, which means most of the time, analytical methods will be found more useful.

The last two columns of Table 3 show how one would have fared by using this method to predict the business peak of May, 1960, and the trough of February, 1961. The indicators would not have been very helpful in anticipating the 1960 downturn. One of them never turned down at all. Most of the remaining series turned down about a year in advance of the general business decline. They gave the right signal but a good deal too early. The indicators performed better on the upturn, most of them turning up 1 to 3 months ahead of the general business recovery.

Analytical Forecasting

This approach rests on the theory of income determination developed in Chapter 20. It starts from the components of total demand and the relations among them. It consists of estimating the components of demand, combining them into an estimate of GNP, and then crosschecking the results for consistency. The outcome is a detailed forecast of GNP and its main components, usually by calendar quarters, for a year or so ahead.

While the essence of the approach is easily stated, its application is more difficult. One difficulty is that "everything depends on everything else." Business investment in the next quarter will have some relation to consumer spending. But consumer spending depends on income, which depends partly on business investment. It seems that we cannot estimate any one component of GNP without already knowing the others.

There are two ways of breaking out of this circle. One way, quite important in econometric forecasting, is to use *lagged relationships*. If consumer spending in the *next quarter* depends on disposable income in *this quarter* (which we already know), we can make an independent estimate of this item. Similarly, if business investment next quarter can be related to business profits over the past four quarters (which we already know), we are on firm ground.

Another thing we can do is to take some components of GNP as independent of everything else, at least as a starting point. Obvious candidates include government spending, business investment, and exports. Let's see how far we can get by first estimating these items, then working back to consumer income and expenditure, and then crosschecking the results.

Look first at *government purchases of goods and services*. Each January the President sends Congress his proposed budget for the fiscal year running from July 1 of that year to July 1 of the following year. By midsummer, Congress has finished working over the items in the budget and has determined the final figures. We are then on reasonably firm ground for four quarters ahead.

There is no central source of information on state and local government expenditures. But this item can safely be projected on the basis of past trends. Over the past decade it has risen consistently at about 10 percent per year.

The most important *investment* item is business expenditures on *plant and equipment*. This includes industrial construction, commercial construction, and machinery purchases. There are several indicators of future investment plans. Early each year the Department of Commerce and the Securities and Exchange Commission send a questionnaire to a large number of business concerns asking how much they expect to spend on plant and equipment during the year. The results are published in the March issue of the *Survey of Current Business*. The results of this survey typically come close to the amount actually spent during the year. The margin of error averages about 3 percent, and in some years has even been less than 1 percent. Information on recent business profits, on construction contracts awarded, and on new machinery orders serve as useful supplements to the Commerce-SEC results.

Residential construction moves more erratically. Efforts to predict its movement on the basis of consumers' incomes, surveys of consumers' intentions, and surveys of builders' plans have not been very successful. Availability of mortgage money, and the prevailing interest rate on mortgages, seem to be important factors. Construction contracts awarded provide some indications for the near future. Something can also be learned by analyzing basic factors affecting the demand and supply for new housing, such as the marriage rate, migration rates from country to city and city to suburbs, the existing supply of unsold new houses, the vacancy rate in apartment buildings, and the price of old houses.

Inventory change is an important component of investment but is also difficult to predict. *Fortune* magazine and Dun and Bradstreet make quarterly surveys of companies' inventory plans. One can also look at sales by manufacturers and retailers, the ratios of present inventories to sales, and how the current ratios compare with those which have been normal over the past. If the current inventory/sales ratio is considerably above normal, for example, there may be an effort to reduce it in the quarters ahead.

The Department of Commerce prepares forecasts of U.S. *exports and imports,* which are reported frequently in the *Survey of Current Business*. The International Monetary Fund and other international agencies also take an active interest in this field. Exports are inherently difficult to predict, since they depend on income levels throughout the world as well as on our competitiveness in foreign markets. But this is a small item in our GNP accounts and moderate errors are not important.

After estimating each of these items, we add them up and find that the total comes to, say, $200 billion. The next step then is to incorporate this into a projection of total GNP, including consumer expenditures. We know that consumption is closely related to disposable income. Something like 92 percent of income is normally spent and the remainder is saved. We also know that disposable income is a good deal smaller than GNP. Government takes a large amount in taxes, though part of this comes back in transfer payments. Business savings are another substantial item. So we must examine probable tax receipts and transfer payments, corporate profits, and business savings. On the basis of this we conclude that disposable income will be, say, 70 percent of whatever GNP turns out to be.

From here on we proceed as follows:

$$\text{GNP} = \text{consumption} + \text{investment} + \text{government}$$
$$\text{expenditure} + (\text{exports} - \text{imports})$$
$$Y = C + I + G + (E - M)$$
$$\text{but } I + G + (E - M) = 200$$
$$\text{hence } Y = C + 200$$
$$\text{or } C = Y - 200 \tag{1}$$

We also know that $C = 0.92Y_d$, where Y_d is disposable income. And we know that disposable income is 0.70 of Y. Thus

$$C = 0.92Y_d$$
$$= 0.92(0.70Y)$$
$$= 0.644\ Y \tag{2}$$

Solving equations (1) and (2), we find that $Y = 561.8$ billion and $C = 361.8$ billion. This becomes our prelimininary estimate for the period we are considering.

This estimate still needs cross-checking and revision. It rests on economic relationships which, on the average, have held true in the past but which may need to be modified for the immediate future. In particular, it is wise to make an independent projection of consumer expenditure based on past trends and to see how this compares with the total of 361.8 billions obtained above. Separate estimates are usually made for consumer expenditure on nondurable goods and services, which is a very stable item, and expenditure on durable goods, which is more volatile. Within the durable goods category, automobile purchases are so variable and important that they deserve a separate estimate.

An annual survey of consumers' buying plans conducted by the Survey Research Center of the University of Michigan, and a more recently developed survey by the Census Bureau, provide help on this front. Results of these surveys are published in the *Federal Reserve Bulletin* and have considerable predictive value. What consumers say they are planning to do about buying new cars, for example, yields a more accurate forecast of car sales than one would get by looking at consumer income alone.

There are also cross-checks of the "where is the money coming from" variety. Estimated business investment can be set against the funds available from depreciation allowances, retained earnings, and possible reduction of cash reserves. Any uncovered balance will have to be met by security sales to the public and bank borrowing. If the results indicate a substantial rise in business borrowing, this may push up interest rates, which may cause some lowering of investment plans.

It is useful to compare estimated government receipts and expenditures. Suppose the preliminary estimates indicate a large federal deficit. This suggests several possibilities: there may be something wrong with the estimates; or the estimates may be correct, but the size of the prospective deficit may lead to efforts to reduce it; or the deficit may actually materialize, in which case Treasury sale of securities to cover it will affect interest rates, bank reserves, and availability of credit to private borrowers.

After making these checks, one may want to revise some of the items in the preliminary estimate. The GNP equation must then be solved again to produce a new forecast, which can be checked by the same methods as the original estimate.

The results to this point are all in dollar terms. To judge the probable movement of physical output and employment, we must make a further estimate of changes in the price level.

It is helpful to examine the estimated level of GNP relative to the physical capacity of the economy. The closer the projected level of GNP is to full capacity, the more reason to expect that part of the rise will take the form of price increases rather than output increases. One can also see whether there have been recent price increases in metals, raw materials, and other basic products which will gradually work their way through to the finished goods level. It may make a difference whether important labor contracts are expiring and whether sizable wage increases are in prospect. Agricultural prices require a separate estimate, since they move differently from industrial prices.

Out of all this comes an estimate that the general price level will be, say, 2 percent higher a year from now than it is today. If the dollar value of GNP has been estimated at 5 percent higher, this means physical output will rise 3 percent over the year. Finally, the output estimate can be converted into an employment estimate on the basis of past relationships between volume of output and man-hours of labor required to produce this output.

Econometric Forecasting

This is an attempt to make analytical forecasting more precise by applying statistical techniques to quantitative information about the economy. It focuses on the major GNP categories, especially the components of consumption and private investment. The problem is to estimate each of these so as to get a close approximation to total GNP. The analysis uses quarterly rather than annual data, since the purpose is to predict short-term movements in the economy; and the forecasts usually run no more than two to four quarters ahead of the present.

Suppose we wish to estimate household consumption for the next quarter. Theory suggests that the change in consumption will be related to the change in GNP. So, using C for consumption, Y for GNP, and Δ to indicate the change from one period to the next, we write a relation of the form

$$\Delta C = a + b \, \Delta Y.$$

Here ΔC is the dependent variable and ΔY is the independent variable on which we are relying to "explain" ΔC. The constants a and b are termed *parameters*.

Now we come to the crux of the matter: what values for a and b will give us the most accurate prediction of ΔC? At this stage we resort to past experience. Suppose we have quarterly figures for the years 1950–65, giving us 64 observations of ΔC and ΔY. We proceed to "fit" our consumption equation to these figures, using regression techniques which you may have encountered in statistics courses. This yields values for a and b which, if we had used them over the years 1950–65, would have given a more accurate prediction of ΔC than we could have gotten with any other values. The regression analysis also gives us measures of the variance between our predicted ΔC's and the true values, measures of "goodness of fit."

If the fitted equation yields close predictions of ΔC, we may stop at this point. But this would be unusually good luck. More probably, there will be a degree of variance which makes us uneasy about using the equation to forecast the future. We will then try to reduce the variance by altering the form of the consumption equation—for example, by adding other independent variables which might logically have some bearing on consumption. Finally, after a good deal of such tinkering, we get an equation with a fit which we consider good enough for operating purposes.

We repeat this procedure for each of the other dependent variables in our system—plant and equipment investment, housing construction, inventory changes, and so on. When we have a satisfactory equation for each of these, our model is set up and ready to operate.

Forecasting models may be very detailed or quite aggregative. They may deal with a few global totals or may break the economy down by industries and types of products. Finer subdivision yields greater precision but also involves more work. So where you stop is a matter of judgment, and also depends on how much money you have for statistical assistants and computer time.

One model of the American economy which is now in experimental use contains 65 variables and upward of 200 equations.[4] But for illustrative purposes we may select a simpler aggregative model contain-

---

[4] See Gary Fromm and Lawrence R. Klein, "The Brookings–S.S.R.C. Quarterly Econometric Model of the United States," *American Economic Review*, May, 1964, pp. 348–61.

ing only five equations, developed by Professor Irwin Friend and others at the University of Pennsylvania.[5]

The notation is as follows: $Y = $ GNP, $C = $ consumption, $H = $ residential construction, $HS = $ housing starts, $PE = $ plant and equipment expenditures, $PE^e = $ *expected PE* expenditures as revealed by surveys, $I = $ inventory change, $S^e = $ *expected* business sales, $G^1 = $ government expenditures plus net exports (taken as determined independently outside the system). The model is set up for 6-month periods. The symbols ΔC, ΔH, and so on refer to *changes* from one period to the next. The subscript -1, such as PE_{-1}, refers to the *level* of plant and equipment investment in the previous period. A *change* with a subscript -1, such as ΔC_{-1}, refers to the *change* between the last two periods.

The equations in the model are as follows (all figures are in billions of 1954 dollars, seasonally adjusted):

$$\Delta C = 2.18 + .37\ \Delta Y + .10\ \Delta C_{-1} \tag{1}$$
$$\Delta H = .35 + .06(\Delta Y - \Delta Y_{-1}) + .58\ \Delta HS_{-1/2} - .16\ \Delta PE^e \tag{2}$$
$$\Delta PE = -.82 + .08(\Delta Y - \Delta Y_{-1}) + .63\ \Delta PE^e \tag{3}$$
$$\Delta I = 1.51 + 0.25\ \Delta S^e - 1.15\ I_{-1} + 1.70\ \Delta PE^e \tag{4}$$
$$\Delta Y = \Delta C + \Delta H + \Delta PE + \Delta I + \Delta G^1 \tag{5}$$

The consumption equation (1) requires no comment. In the housing equation (2), the largest single influence is advance information on the number of housing starts in the recent past. There is also, however, an accelerator term $(\Delta Y - \Delta Y_{-1})$, which depends on whether the rate of GNP increase this period is *higher* than it was last period. And there is a negative (inverse) relation between housing construction and PE expenditure. The logic of this is that heavier plant and equipment expenditure means greater business borrowing and higher interest rates, and that higher mortgage rates will reduce consumer willingness to start new houses.

The plant and equipment equation (3) relies heavily on survey information about how much businessmen expect to spend on plant and equipment; but it also has an accelerator term $(\Delta Y - \Delta Y_{-1})$ for understandable reasons. The inventory equation (4) makes the change in inventory investment depend partly on sales expectations, partly on business expectations in general (PE^e being taken as an indicator of the general business outlook), and partly on the level of inventory investment in the last period. This last relation is negative—the higher was inventory investment last period, the smaller will be the expected increase in inventory investment this period.

---

[5] Irwin Friend and Paul Taubman, "A Short-term Forecasting Model," *Review of Economics and Statistics*, August, 1964, pp. 229–36. The brief account given here is necessarily rough, and those interested in techniques should consult the original source.

The last equation (5) says simply that the increase in GNP is the sum of the increases in its components.

The values of the parameters were obtained by regression analysis, using figures for the years 1953–60. The model was then used to make forecasts for the years 1961–63, i.e., years *beyond* the period on which the model was based. This, of course, is the proof of the pudding. A carefully constructed model will necessarily give a good fit to experience during the years used in constructing it—you can make it do so, by sufficient tinkering. But how well does it perform when you move out into the uncharted sea of the future? The results of this experiment for several half-year periods are summarized below:

PERIOD	ΔY PREDICTED	ACTUAL	ΔC PREDICTED	ACTUAL	ΔI PREDICTED	ACTUAL
1961 (first)	3.2	0.0	3.5	1.8	−1.6	−1.4
1961 (second)	19.7	18.1	9.7	6.5	4.9	5.9
1962 (first)	16.9	14.1	9.1	7.6	1.0	1.4
1962 (second)	5.6	7.6	5.0	6.3	−2.7	−3.3
1963 (first)	9.1	8.8	6.2	5.4	−1.3	0.9

PERIOD	ΔH PREDICTED	ACTUAL	ΔPE PREDICTED	ACTUAL
1961 (first)	0.3	− .9	−1.7	−1.8
1961 (second)	1.7	2.2	1.5	1.5
1962 (first)	0.8	−0.1	2.4	1.4
1962 (second)	0.3	1.3	1.4	1.7
1963 (first)	0.9	−0.3	0.4	−0.4

These results look reasonably good, and better than most forecasters have been able to do by the impressionistic methods described earlier. There is reason to expect that, with more effort and experimentation, the precision of this and other models can be further improved. But lest the reader conclude that economists now have a surefire way of reading the future, a few cautions are in order:

(1) The accuracy of forecasting models hinges on the basic assumption that the future will resemble the past, that parameters estimated from data for past years will continue to be reliable in future. Any marked change in reactions within the economy will reduce forecasting accuracy. This difficulty can be met in part by reestimating and changing the parameters at frequent intervals. Most econometric model builders do precisely this, which is why their work is never done.

(2) The forecast of GNP will be more accurate than the forecasts of its components, since errors in opposite directions will partly cancel each

other. Very often, however, it is one of the components in which we are really interested. Note the uneven performance of the Friend model in estimating residential construction—apparently an unusually tricky branch of the economy.

(3) These models are designed to make predictions for the very near future, from 3 months to 12 months ahead. If we want a long-term projection of what the economy will look like in 1980, a different apparatus is required.

(4) Like all other methods, econometric forecasting is likely to give better results during a sustained upswing or downswing than it gives at the turning points. Yet the turning points are of greatest practical interest. Such is life!

SUMMARY

1. Fluctuations in national income are concentrated in the various components of business investment.

2. The *acceleration principle* is helpful in explaining these fluctuations. As applied to plant and equipment investment, the principle states, first, that fluctuations in product sales will be magnified into larger fluctuations in investment. Second, a *decline in the rate of increase* of sales can cause an absolute decline in investment. The acceleration principle is applicable also to investment in housing and in business inventories.

3. On this and other grounds one can readily explain why, once an upswing is underway, it will build up momentum and continue for some time in the same direction. It is harder to explain the *turning points,* particularly the upper turning point. Review the section on the end of prosperity for some clues on this matter.

4. Whether a downswing will be mild or severe depends partly on whether it occurs during a rising or falling phase of the longer cycle in building construction, and partly on whether there is a large and dependable volume of autonomous investment resulting from major innovations.

5. We need never expect another downswing as severe and prolonged as that of 1929–33, but we we may well see sharper drops than those of 1946 to date.

6. A simple method of *barometric forecasting* involves the use of leading series which typically turn up or down in advance of general business. But this method is not entirely dependable; and at best it predicts only the *date* of turning points, not the *magnitude* of upward or downward movements.

7. A simple method of *analytical forecasting* involves the following steps: make an independent estimate of government spending, business investment, exports and imports; add in knowledge about the consump-

tion function to get a consistent estimate of consumer spending and GNP; cross-check this projection in various ways and, if you discover weaknesses, go through the first two steps again; when you are satisfied with the forecast of *money GNP*, convert this to a forecast of *real GNP* by estimating the probable change in the price level.

8. *Econometric forecasting*, which involves constructing a set of equations to determine the main components of GNP, can in principle yield more precise results than cruder methods. Forecasting accuracy depends, however, on the skill used in constructing the model and on the extent to which future relations among variables in the economy resemble those which have prevailed in the past.

DISCUSSION QUESTIONS

1. Which *kinds of spending* fluctuate most and which fluctuate least? What *products* show widest output fluctuations? What do these products have in common?

2. Once an upswing is under way, why does it build up momentum and continue for some time in the same direction? Can you use similar reasoning to explain why a downswing, once started, is bound to continue for some time?

3. What kinds of change in spending most commonly precipitate a downturn? In what sense, if at all, are such downturns inevitable? Couldn't they be postponed indefinitely by proper use of monetary fiscal policy?

4. Once a downturn has occurred, is there any "natural bottom" to the decline? What determines where this will be?

5. Comparing the American economy today with the period before 1940, would you say the economy is *no* more stable? *Moderately* more stable? *Much* more stable? Explain.

6. Take the most recent turning point which has occurred in the economy at the time you read this chapter. Look up each of the leading series listed in Table 3 and determine *their* turning points. How helpful would they have been in predicting the turning point in general economic activity?

7. Try your hand at a simple analytical forecast of GNP for the next four calendar quarters.

8. Another forecasting method, not discussed in the text, is the so-called "naïve method." This assumes that what has been happening in the immediate past will continue to happen in the immediate future—if GNP has been rising at 5 percent a year, it will continue to rise at this rate. What's wrong with this? Could one expect to do much better by fancier methods?

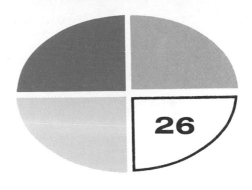

Economic Stability: Problems of

Internal Balance

> The chief difficulty Alice found at first was
> with her flamingo: . . . generally, just as she
> had got its neck straightened out, and was going
> to give the hedgehog a blow with its head, it
> *would* twist itself round and look up in her face.
> *Alice's Adventures in Wonderland*

MUST WE CONTINUE to ride the swings of the business cycle? Or would we, by sufficiently agile footwork, manage to hold the economy continuously near full capacity? In a decentralized, largely private economy, the answer seems to be no. Mild recessions of moderate duration appear to be unavoidable.

What then can we do? A realistic policy objctive might be:

a) To detect a downswing as early as possible, and to take steps which will break the force of the downswing after a short time.

b) To encourage vigorous upswings which will carry all the way to full employment. If an upswing threatens to overshoot into inflation, there should be an effort to taper it off gracefully without provoking a relapse into recession.

The available fiscal and monetary instruments were described in earlier chapters. Here we wish to consider some of the practical problems which arise in using these instruments. We need also to consider more precisely what we mean by "capacity operation" of the economy, how far there is a conflict between full employment and price stability, and what can be done to reduce the severity of this dilemma.

SETTING THE OUTPUT TARGET

It is well to begin by defining objectives. We presumably want the economy to operate at capacity. This benefits wage and salary earners, businessmen, and farmers alike. Capacity operation was written into our public policy in the Employment Act of 1946, and few policy objectives are more widely accepted.

But how do we judge the capacity of the economy? How can we determine the size of the "gap" between actual output and potential output? Probably the most widely used indicator is the level of full-time unemployment. A drop in employment of labor typically means a drop in utilization of plant capacity and other resources. From a statistical standpoint, it is easier to add units of labor than to add up plant capacity for heterogeneous products.

The unemployment yardstick, however, is not free of difficulties. First, how much of the unemployment existing at any time should we write off as *normal* or *frictional* unemployment? No figure is beyond dispute, because the level of frictional unemployment itself depends partly on the level of aggregate demand. As economic activity rises, people find jobs faster, and frictional unemployment shrinks. So the level of "unavoidable" unemployment is a policy decision. It is not simply given by the operation of labor markets.

The most frequently mentioned targets are 4 percent unemployment and 3 percent unemployment, which we may call "low full employment" and "high full employment" respectively. (If we choose the 3 percent figure, we have not had full employment since the end of the Korean War. Using the 4 percent target, we had full employment in 1957 and were approaching it again at the end of 1965.) The difference is that high full employment involves a higher level of aggregate demand, more pressure on the economy, greater likelihood of price increases. The choice of targets raises the dilemma of unemployment versus inflation discussed in Chapter 21.

Let's defer this issue temporarily by agreeing to settle for 4 percent, which has been the official position of the Kennedy and Johnson administrations. We are still not out of the woods. Suppose unemployment is currently 6 percent, and needs to be reduced by 2 percent to bring us to what we have agreed to call full employment. One might think that this requires an increase of only 2 percent in national output. But this is wrong, and would set the output target a good deal too low. Arthur Okun has estimated that "in the postwar period, on the average, each extra percentage point in the unemployment rate above 4 percent has been associated with about a 3 percent decrement in real GNP."[1] Thus to cut unemployment from 6 to 4 percent one must raise real GNP by about 6 percent. The capacity gap is substantially larger than the visible employment gap.

There are several reasons for this. First, there is considerable evidence that the labor force fluctuates in response to the level of aggregate demand. As the economy goes into recession and jobs become harder to find, many people who are near the margin of decision as to whether to work or not decide that the game is not worth the candle. Since they are no longer looking for work, they are not counted in the labor force and so cannot be considered unemployed.[2] True, during a recession, unemployment of the household head may force the wife or some other family member to go to work, and thus add to the labor force. But the number of such "additional workers" seems to be swamped by the number of "discouraged workers." Dernburg and Strand found that "over the period 1947–1962, a fall in employment of 100 is, on balance, associated with withdrawal from the labor force of 38 workers. The recorded increase in unemployment of 62 therefore understates the increase in unemployed manpower by 38."[3]

We even know a good deal about *whose* participation in the labor force fluctuates with employment opportunities. There is little variation among men in the prime working years, almost all of whom are in the labor force continuously. But a rise in the unemployment rate has a marked discouraging effect on both single and married women and an even stronger effect on boys 14 to 19 and men 65 and over.[4] These last two groups pop into and out of the labor force in large numbers as employment opportunities vary.

When the economy is operating below capacity, then, there are many people not currently in the labor force who would be available for work if the demand for labor were higher. The reservoir of available

---

[1] Arthur M. Okun, "Potential GNP: Its Measurement and Significance," *1962 Proceedings, Business and Economic Statistics Section, American Statistical Association* (reprinted as Cowles Foundation Paper 190, Yale University, 1963).

[2] Our estimates of unemployment come from a sample survey conducted monthly by the Bureau of the Census. A person is counted as in the labor force if he either has a job or is "actively seeking work." For each person in the labor force, the survey then determines whether he was working full time, working part time for one reason or another, or had no job at all. Since the "actively-seeking-work" criterion is a bit vague, the count of the labor force is not completely accurate, and so neither is the unemployment figure.

[3] Kenneth Strand and Thomas Dernburg, "Cyclical Variation in Civilian Labor Force Participation," *Review of Economics and Statistics*, November, 1964, pp. 378–91.

[4] See on this point William G. Bowen and T. A. Finegan, "Labor Force Participation and Unemployment," in Arthur M. Ross (ed.), *Employment Policy and the Labor Market* (Berkeley: University of California Press, 1965).

labor is larger than the rate of visible unemployment suggests. Dernburg and Strand tried to estimate the "low full employment labor force," i.e., the number who would be in the labor force if the unemployment rate were actually reduced to 4 percent; and also the "high full employment labor force" for a 3 percent unemployment rate. Their results for 1962 suggest the magnitudes involved. The reported civilian labor force in this year was 72.2 million, employment was 68.1 million, and unemployment 4.1 million or *5.6 percent* of the labor force. The low full employment labor force, however, was estimated at 75.3 million, yielding a "manpower gap" of over 7 million or *9.5 percent* of the labor force. With high full employment, the labor force would have been 76 million and the manpower gap *10.3 percent.*

In addition to this flexibility in numbers, the labor force is flexible in terms of man-hours worked. During years of low employment many people are forced to work shorter hours than they would prefer. In 1961, for example, in addition to almost 4.8 million wholly unemployed, there were 2.8 million reported as "working part time for economic reasons," i.e., not out of personal preference but because that was all they could find. The working hours of fully employed workers are also somewhat adjustable to the level of demand. Periods of peak output are met partly by additional overtime work, and hours are reduced again as demand falls.

Finally, there is evidence that a rise in aggregate demand brings a sharp increase in output per man-hour. "The record clearly shows that man-hour productivity is depressed by low levels of utilization, and that periods of movement toward full employment yield considerably above average productivity gains."[5] Thus a 1 percent increase in employment during an upswing produces considerably more than a 1 percent increase in output. Or, to put the point in reverse, a 1 percent rise in output can be obtained with considerably less than a 1 percent increase in labor. Eckstein and Wilson estimate that as of 1960 a rise of 1 percent in output called for only 0.52 more man-hours of labor.[6] This is partly because managerial, clerical, and other nonproduction workers are typically not laid off when business slackens. For this group, a 1 percent rise in output requires only 0.28 more man-hours. The interesting thing, however, is that even for production workers the rise in labor requirements is only 0.6 percent.

These results help to explain what happened during the 1961–65 expansion. This upswing was unusually vigorous and prolonged. Between the first quarter of 1961 and the first quarter of 1965, real GNP rose more than 20 percent. But the unemployment rate stubbornly refused to fall as fast as one might have expected. It was about 7 percent in mid-

---

[5] Okun, *op. cit.*

[6] Thomas A. Wilson and Otto Eckstein, "Short-run Productivity Behavior in U.S. Manufacturing," *Review of Economics and Statistics,* February, 1964, pp. 41–54.

1961. By mid-1965 it had fallen to only a bit under 5 percent. How could a 20 percent rise in output cut the unemployment rate only 2 percent? The answer is partly that the labor force is growing each year through population increase, partly that labor supply rises unusually fast during an upswing for the reasons already noted, and partly that labor requirements per unit of output are falling because of rapid increases in productivity.

The moral is clear: the gap between current output and potential full-employment output is much larger than appears at first glance. Starting from an unemployment rate of 6 or 7 percent, it takes a substantial push to move the economy close to full employment.

The Council of Economic Advisers maintains current estimates of potential GNP and of the gap between potential and actual output. Their estimates for 1953–64 are shown in Figure 1.[7] The potential GNP line assumes that the capacity of the economy grew at a rate of 3½ percent a year through 1962, and at a rate of 3¾ percent thereafter. It accepts a 4 percent unemployment rate as constituting full employment. Note that during the recession years 1958 and 1961 the output gap was about 10 percent. The long upswing of 1961–65 cut the gap to less than 5 percent but did not eliminate it entirely.

Unemployment or Inflation: Which Hurts Most?

If the economy continues to operate below capacity, why not just step up the pressure? Cut taxes, hold down interest rates, push private investment, use all the devices described in earlier chapters. And why settle for 4 percent unemployment? Why not push on toward 3 percent and a still larger GNP?

Here we encounter the dilemma noted in Chapter 21. Beyond a certain point, raising aggregate demand will raise prices as well as output; and the more unemployment is reduced the faster will prices rise. So where do we decide to stop? A policy decision on this point involves weighing the damage done by unemployment against that done by inflation.

The Loss from Unemployment

The people who suffer most directly from unemployment are the unemployed. Even in a mild recession, a couple of million people suddenly find themselves without work. Their income falls far below its normal level. Unemployment compensation helps, but not enough, offsetting at present only a quarter to a third of the wage loss from unemployment. If a man stays unemployed long enough to exhaust his compensation rights, his income drops some more. Another million or two

---

[7] *Annual Report of the Council of Economic Advisers* (Washington, D.C., January, 1965), p. 83.

The Output Gap and the Unemployment Rate Vary Together

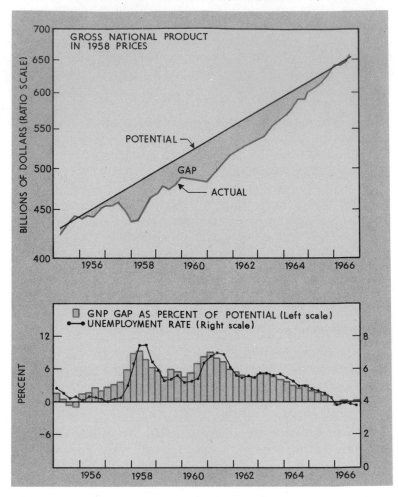

FIGURE 1. The top panel shows the gap between potential and actual GNP. The bottom panel shows this gap as a percentage of potential GNP and also shows the rate of full-time unemployment. Note the differences in the scales used. What is the significance of this? What would happen if the same scale were used?

find themselves reduced to part-time work. Still others find themselves demoted, or blocked from promotion, because of bad times.

The output loss, as we have seen, is considerably greater than the employment loss. An output gap of even 5 percent means a loss of about $35 billion a year. This is a lot of output, which might have been enjoyed by consumers or invested to raise productive capacity for the future. The consumers who do *not* get this lost GNP include not only the unemployed wage earners but businessmen whose profits fall during recession, and farmers whose prices are depressed by inadequate demand.

One must consider the indirect as well as the direct effects of unemployment. In addition to those who actually become unemployed, millions of others *fear* that they will become unemployed. This certainly reduces the pleasantness of life for the average wage earner. It leads to reluctance to change jobs and an undue preoccupation with security, deliberate slowdown on the job to spin out work as long as possible, union pressure for make-work rules, and other things which reduce economic efficiency. An economy in which people really felt assured of enough jobs to go round would be both more efficient and more satisfying to employees of all ranks.

Not the least harmful effect of unemployment is the bias which it introduces into public policy. Uneconomic proposals are urged on the ground that they will reduce unemployment. Emergency public works programs are justified on this ground, instead of being subjected to the normal test of whether the benefits are worth the cost. General reduction of working hours is urged as a work-spreading device, rather than because of any change in workers' preference for leisure. Price-fixing schemes are propounded by manufacturers, farmers, and other producer groups on the spurious ground that they will maintain aggregate demand.

Not only are dubious government programs generated by unemployment, but worthwhile programs may be frustrated. A good example is the training programs authorized under the Manpower Development and Training Act of 1962 and the Economic Opportunity Act of 1964. These are designed to raise the educational and skill level of hundreds of thousands of workers and to render them fully employable. But if jobs are not available for these people after they are trained, the program will look foolish and the people will become frustrated.

The Loss from Inflation

Unlike unemployment, inflation involves no direct loss in output. On the contrary, mild inflation is likely to go along with a continued increase of national output. But inflation does involve a redistribution of income, so that *some groups* in the economy may lose. Any group whose money income rises less rapidly than the price level suffers a loss of real income. Groups whose incomes rise faster than prices are the winners in the inflation lottery.

Who are the losers? Not business owners, who are likely to find their profits rising faster than prices because of greater physical output. Not most wage and salary earners, whose wages are usually adjusted to price changes with only a short lag. Civil servants and others whose salaries are adjusted less frequently may suffer some loss. The main losers, however, are people unable to work—the aged, the disabled, the women heads of broken homes, the people of low physical or mental capacity. These people live on pensions, relief allowances, and other transfer payments which remain fixed for considerable periods. So as the price level rises, their real income declines. (Some very high-income families living on fixed property incomes find themselves in the same boat; but about this group we need not worry unduly.)

The extent of the loss suffered by fixed-income groups depends on the rate of price increase. If consumer prices are rising 1 or 2 percent a year, the loss is barely perceptible. If they are rising 5 or 10 percent a year, the loss begins to hit home. Note also that the losses could be at least partly eliminated by policy changes. It would be quite possible to arrange that social security payments, relief scales, and other transfer payments be adjusted upward at frequent intervals as the price level rises. Only to the extent that this is not done will the poor suffer a real income loss.

There are indirect effects of inflation which must be considered. One important effect is on expectations about the future. If inflation goes on so long, or at such a rate, that it comes to be considered as normal, people will seek ways to "beat the increase." Unions, for example, may demand a wage increase large enough to offset not only last year's price rise but also the price rise expected next year. Next year's price rise will then be larger than it otherwise would have been, and there is a danger that inflation will accelerate. In order to be tolerable, inflation should be moderate and intermittent, so that people do not come to regard it as normal. It is desirable that people believe in price stability as the normal condition, even though they will be surprised from time to time.

Persistent inflation undermines the basis of long-term lending, on which much of private investment and government financing depends. If prices are rising 5 percent a year, anyone who buys a 20-year 4 percent bond is completely foolish. He will be paid off eventually in dollars which are worth less than half as much as the dollars he loaned. Instead of getting a positive rate of interest on his money, he is getting a negative rate. This is a poor bargain. If inflation continues, people will eventually catch on and stop buying bonds. They will also stop putting money into savings accounts and other assets with a fixed dollar value.

For countries heavily involved in international trade, there is another important consideration. A country which allows its prices to rise faster than those of competing export nations will lose ground in foreign markets, leading to a deterioration in its balance of payments.

The Balance of Advantage

The question "Does unemployment cause greater losses than inflation?" is not answerable in this form, because the losses on both sides are a matter of *degree*. A 4 percent unemployment rate may be acceptable, while a 10 percent unemployment rate does grave damage to the economy. Similarly, a 1 percent a year rise in prices might be ignored, but not a 10 percent rise. Beyond some point on the inflation scale, most people would agree that this is the more serious menace; but above some level of unemployment, this opinion would be reversed.

Most of the time the economy will be somewhere in the middle range of the Phillips curve, with unemployment varying between 3 and 7 percent, and the rate of price increase varying from 0 to 3 percent a year. The practical problem for policy makers is what to do within this range. Suppose the unemployment rate is 5 percent and the Wholesale Price Index is stable. Would the gain from getting the unemployment rate down to 4 percent outweigh the 1 percent a year price increase which might result?

It must be repeated that this is a matter of preference. The Board of Governors of the Federal Reserve system, the Secretary of the Treasury, and the Council of Economic Advisers will probably never agree fully on the answer.

The Best of Both Worlds?

It would be best if one could persuade union and business officials to exercise restraint on price and wage increases during periods of high employment. It might thus be possible to hit a higher employment target without running into inflation. This would amount to changing the shape of the Phillips curve, so that a zero rate of price increase became compatible with, say, a 3 percent unemployment rate instead of a 5 percent rate.

The federal administration has tried to exercise persuasion in this direction by announcing "guidelines" for proper wage and price behavior. The most recent restatement of these is as follows:

1. *The general guide for wages is that the percentage increase in total employee compensation per man-hour be equal to the national trend rate of increase in output per man-hour.*

If each industry follows this guidepost, unit labor costs in the overall economy will maintain a constant average.

2. *The general guide for prices calls for stable prices in industries enjoying the same productivity growth as the average for the economy; rising prices in industries with smaller than average productivity gains; and declining prices in industries with greater than average productivity gains.*

If each industry follows this guidepost, prices in the economy will maintain a constant average.[8]

The Council estimates that output per man-hour for the economy as a whole is presently rising at 3.2 percent a year. This would warrant an average annual increase of 3.2 percent in total employee compensation,

---

[8] *Annual Report of the Council of Economic Advisers* (Washington, D.C., January, 1965), p. 108.

i.e., hourly wage rates plus fringe benefits. It should be emphasized, however, that this is only an economy-wide average, and that individual industries may need to deviate from the average for good cause.

Wage increases above the guidepost level may be necessary where an industry is unable to attract sufficient labor to meet the demand for its products, where wages are particularly low, and where changes in work rules create large gains in productivity and substantial human costs requiring special adjustment of compensation. . . . Wages should rise less than the guidepost rate where an industry suffers from above-average unemployment and where wages are exceptionally high for that type of work.[9]

A similar flexibility is necessary on the price side. The formula would presumably lead to falling prices in agriculture, public utilities, and many branches of manufacturing. But it would warrant rising prices in some branches of manufacturing and in most of the service industries, in which productivity gains are typically subnormal.

A number of objections have been raised to the guideline idea. The theoretical basis for the proposed wage formula is rather dubious. (You might try, as an exercise, to see how the formula compares with the marginal productivity principle for wage determination outlined in Chapter 11.) The guideline approach assumes that wages and prices are in fact subject to monopoly or oligopoly control, which is true for less than half the economy. The pricing formula is essentially a cost-plus formula and does not take explicit account of demand movements. There is disagreement on the appropriate measures of man-hour productivity, unit labor costs, and profit margins. It is also argued that government intervention in wage and price decisions is inappropriate in a private enterprise economy.

The economists who devised and support the guidelines would probably answer that it is better to have crude principles than no principles at all; and that those who do not like the proposed yardsticks should try to devise something better.

The main practical difficulty is that there are no sanctions behind the guidelines except the vague sanction of public opinion. But Presidential coaxing and scolding are not completely ineffective. In 1962 the administration persuaded the United Steelworkers to accept a wage settlement lower than had been customary in previous years (with, it was thought, an implicit commitment by the companies not to raise prices). When leading steel companies nonetheless announced a price increase, President Kennedy took a strong public position against the increase and it was withdrawn.

Again, in 1965, President Johnson took an active part in steel wage negotiations, with a view to holding wage increases within bounds which would not disturb the price level. Because steel wage increases are

---

[9] *Ibid.*, p. 108.

watched closely by the Auto Workers and other key unions, and because steel prices are an important cost element for automobiles, machinery, and other steel-using industries, steel is a focal point of any effort to influence wage-price behavior. It is not more sinful than other industries, but it is more strategic. In late 1965, the administration persuaded aluminum and copper producers to rescind proposed price increases, partly by releasing substantial amounts of these metals from government stockpiles.

Whether because of the guidelines or not, the large 1961–65 expansion was well-behaved from a wage-price point of view. Employee compensation per man-hour rose at almost exactly the same rate as output per man-hour. At the end of 1964, unit labor costs in the private economy were at almost exactly the same level as in 1960, and the Wholesale Price Index was also virtually identical. In 1965, however, as unemployment fell toward 4 percent, the Wholesale Price Index did begin to edge upward.

In support of the idea that prices should behave differently in different industries, depending on the behavior of productivity and costs, there is good evidence that they do behave this way. Figure 2 shows

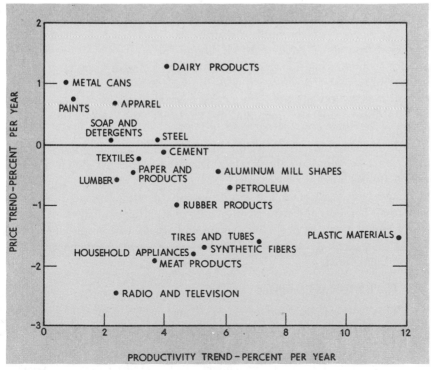

FIGURE 2. Price and productivity trends in 19 manufacturing industries, 1959–64.

price and productivity movements in 19 manufacturing industries over the years 1959–64.[10] (Note that the scales on the two axes measure average percentage change *per year*. Thus an industry located at −2 on the price axis has experienced a price reduction of *12 percent* over the 6 years.) The strong inverse relation is evident from the diagram. Industries with unusually large productivity gains show a relative decline in prices.

STRENGTHENING THE BUILT-IN STABILIZERS

So far we have been talking about target setting, about price and output objectives and their compatibility. Now we must talk about methods. Suppose we want to check an economic downswing or accelerate an upswing, how do we go about doing it?

The instruments available fall into two categories:

1. *Built-in stabilizers,* which operate automatically to check the momentum of upswings and downswings. The built-in stability of the economy can be increased by tax legislation and other measures.

2. *Discretionary actions,* taken on an *ad hoc* basis after a downswing (or an undesirably strong upswing) has been detected. These actions may be either fiscal or monetary. There is often a question as to which should be used or in what proportions the two should be combined. This is the problem of the *policy mix.*

We begin with the built-in stabilizers. They have the great advantage that you don't have to think about them. It is not necessary to predict a downswing, in which case you may be wrong, or to wait until you are sure that a downswing is underway, in which case you may be several months too late. As soon as there is any drop in national income, the stabilizers operate immediately to brake the momentum of the decline.

It is important to underline that the stabilizers *operate in both directions.* We applaud them when they serve to slow down a downswing. But we must not forget that they also act as brakes on an upswing and may stop it short of full employment. Starting from a position of underemployment, and with strong built-in stabilizers at work, it takes a larger initial push to propel the economy up to full employment than would be necessary otherwise. The system is more sluggish upward as well as downward.

The Budget as Stabilizer

This subject was explored in Chapter 22, and we need only underline the main points made there. A large public sector increases the stability of the economy for several reasons:

---

[10] This chart is from the 1965 *Annual Report of the Council of Economic Advisers,* p. 58.

1. The existence of taxes means that disposable income rises less rapidly than national income during an upswing and falls less rapidly during a downswing. Taxation reduces the value of the multiplier and thus makes the economy less responsive to any autonomous change in spending. This is true particularly of income taxes, but it is also true in lesser measure of sales taxes, excises, and most other taxes. Only a tax such as the poll tax, whose yield is independent of income, would fail to have any stabilizing effect.

2. Government purchases of goods and services are inherently stable. They do not respond appreciably to short-term fluctuations in national income. Thus the government budget has a stabilizing effect on the expenditure side as well as the tax side.

3. Transfer payments fluctuate in a stabilizing fashion over the cycle. Payments for unemployment compensation, pensions, relief, farm price supports, and the like typically rise in recession and fall in prosperity, thus helping to offset swings in personal income.

One should not conclude that unemployment compensation rates should be raised, or that the level of public services should be higher, or that income taxation should be substituted increasingly for sales taxation *just* because these changes would increase economic stability. But one can say that the effect on economic stability is a *relevant consideration* in judging a proposed tax or expenditure change. A proposal which will increase stability should receive some bonus points on this score.

The changes which have occurred in federal taxes and expenditures since 1940 have been in a strongly stabilizing direction. Some interesting calculations on this point have been made by Duesenberry, Eckstein, and Fromm.[11] They work with a simulated model of the economy; but the model is designed to be close to reality. One of their illustrations assumes a moderate recession, set off by a drop of about $9 billion in autonomous demand (business plant and equipment expenditures, construction, and government purchases). This produces a drop of $7 billion in the rate of inventory investment. Total investment falls by $16 billion. By the usual multiplier reasoning, one might expect a substantial drop in GNP. It turns out, however, that GNP falls only about $20 billion. Even more striking, personal consumption falls by only $4 billion, or a bit more than 1 percent.

What takes up the slack? The detailed calculations are shown in Table 1. The three most important stabilizers turn out to be: (1) a drop of $4.5 billion in corporate income taxes, following from the sharp drop in corporate profits which typically occurs during recession; (2) a drop of $3.3 billion in business saving. This follows from the practice of holding dividend rates fairly stable through good years and bad, so that a drop in profit after taxes shows up almost entirely as a drop in retained earnings;

---

[11] James S. Duesenberry, Otto Eckstein, and Gary Fromm, "A Simulation of the United States Economy in Recession," *Econometrica*, October, 1960, pp. 749–810.

TABLE 1

Hypothetical Behavior of the U.S. Economy in Mild Recession
(Billions of Dollars)

	PEAK QUARTER OF UPSWING	LOW QUARTER OF DOWNSWING
1. GNP	440.0	419.7
minus		
2. Depreciation	37.4	39.3
3. Indirect business taxes	37.1	37.1
4. Subsidies and statistical discrepancy	1.7	0.5
5. Corporate income taxes	20.9	16.4
6. Retained corporate earnings	7.4	4.1
7. Contributions to social insurance	14.6	13.8
plus		
8. Transfers	26.0	29.7
equals		
9. Personal income	346.9	338.2
minus		
10. Personal taxes	43.6	42.0
equals		
11. Disposable income	303.3	296.2
minus		
12. Personal saving	19.7	16.6
equals		
13. Consumption	283.6	279.6
plus		
14. Inventory change	plus 2.3	minus 5.3
plus		
15. Autonomous demand	154.1	145.4
equals		
16. GNP	440.0	419.7

(3) a rise of $3.7 billion in transfer payments, which adds to personal income.

The personal income tax also has a stabilizing effect, tax payments falling by $1.6 billion; but this is smaller than the three effects just listed. Why is this? It is because the three other stabilizers do such a good job that there is only a moderate drop in personal income. Most of the stabilizing effect, in other words, has occurred before one hits the safety net of the personal income tax. But if the drop of personal income were larger, the stabilizing effect of the income tax would be greater.

Strengthening the Budget Stabilizers

The most promising area for further progress on this front is probably the state unemployment compensation systems. In particular, it seems desirable to:

1. Raise the average level of benefit rates. The system was designed in the 1930's to offset half of the earnings lost by a worker during unemployment. Since that time wage levels have risen greatly and benefit rates have failed to keep pace. In many states at present the benefit payments offset 40 percent or less of the earnings loss. A general increase of benefit scales is desirable to restore at least the original 50 percent proportion.

2. Provide for a temporary lengthening of the benefit period during cycle downswings. In most states a worker can draw benefits for no more than 26 weeks. During both the 1957–58 and 1960–61 downswings, the federal government advanced money to the states to help them extend the period to 39 weeks for the duration of the recession. This was regarded as an emergency action, however, and required special legislation. It seems preferable to have standing legislation which would extend the benefit period automatically when unemployment reaches a certain level, and then reduce it again as unemployment shrinks.

These steps, in addition to their direct benefit to the unemployed, would put more money into circulation on the downswing and thus work in a stabilizing direction.

Greater Stability of Business Investment

Business investment is one of the less stable elements in the economy at present. Discussions of stabilization policy often accept wide swings of business investment as inevitable and concentrate solely on ways of offsetting them. But we should not give up this easily. If ways could be found to reduce the instability of private investment, this would strike directly at the heart of the business cycle.

It is not useful to exhort business executives to regularize their investment for the sake of economic stability, if by so doing they would make less money for their companies. An effective program must make it *worthwhile* for companies to behave in a way which contributes to overall stability.

It might be possible to change the corporate income tax laws so as to do one or both of the following things:

1. *Smooth out the present wide fluctuations of profits after taxes.* This would even out companies' *ability* to invest, which might lead to greater stability in their investment spending.

One possibility would be a liberal provision for *carry back of losses.* Suppose a company suffers a net loss in 1966 but had profits in the previous 5 years and paid full tax on them. The company could be allowed to reopen its tax returns for previous years, deduct the 1966 loss from the earlier profits, recalculate its tax liabilities, and claim a refund from the government. This procedure would raise companies' incomes and increase their ability to invest in poor years.

A second possibility would be systematic variation of the period over which companies are allowed to depreciate their plant and equipment. These periods are already closely controlled by rulings of the Internal Revenue Service, and these rulings could be altered according to the stage of the business cycle. During depression, depreciation periods could be shortened. This would raise the annual depreciation charge, which would reduce a company's calculated profits and its income tax liabilities, which would leave the company with more cash in hand. This should have a stimulating effect on investment. During periods of high prosperity, the Internal Revenue Service could be authorized to move in the opposite direction. It could lengthen depreciation periods, which would force companies to pay higher income taxes and leave them with less cash for investment.

This would actually be a clumsy way of varying the corporate income tax, raising it on the upswing and lowering it on the downswing. But it might be politically more palatable than a direct variation of the tax rate, because it seems more mysterious. Moreover, such a system would have greatest leverage on industries with large amounts of plant and equipment. These are presumably the best prospects for future investment in plant and equipment and hence are the industries one wants to affect.

2. *Provide a direct inducement for companies to spread their investment more evenly over good years and bad.* One system, which is used in Sweden, permits companies to carry over part of their earnings in good years for investment during depression. The Swedish system provides that a company can earmark its profits, up to a specified maximum, as a special reserve for future investment. The incentive is that profits put into the reserve are exempt from corporate income tax. When unemployment figures reveal that a recession is on, the government announces that companies can take money from these reserves and invest it in plant and equipment. This policy is continued for as long as the recession continues. If a company does not use its reserve within a certain period of years, or if it uses it for purposes other than investment, it becomes liable for income tax on the amount involved.

DISCRETIONARY ACTION

The proposals made to this point would probably not be regarded as stabilization policy by the man in the street. If prices are rising too fast or unemployment is too high many people begin to ask, "Why doesn't the government do something?" By "doing something" they mean specific, *ad hoc* actions to check and reverse undesirable movements in the economy. The main measures which can be used are monetary controls, tax changes, and changes in government expenditure.

The weakness of discretionary action is that it requires discretion. Someone must detect an undesirable degree of inflation or deflation, figure out what might be done about it, and then try to do it. This raises problems of the *timing* of action and the *strength* of action.

The timing of action. If economic forecasting were an accurate science, it might be possible to diagnose potential trouble well in advance and have corrective measures waiting at the right time. But forecasting is not very accurate, and we are normally in the position of locking the barn door after the horse is some distance down the road.

There is loss of time for three reasons. First, it takes time to make sure that a turning point in the economy has actually occurred. Second, after trouble has been diagnosed, it takes time to work out corrective policies and get approval for them from the administration and from Congress. Third, discretionary actions require time to have their full impact on the economy.

There is thus an *information lag*, a *decision lag*, and an *impact lag*. The total of these can scarcely be less than a year. Considering the speed of economic events, this makes discretionary action a blunt instrument against the cycle. There is the awkward possibility that action taken at one stage of the cycle will come to fruition at a later stage when its effects will be in the wrong direction.

The strength of stabilizing action. Monetary and fiscal medicine can be given in larger or smaller doses. How does one decide what dosage is required at a particular time?

It might seem that one need look only at how far the economy is away from the desired target position. If the unemployment rate is 8 percent, one should take stronger action than if it is 6 percent. This is correct as far as it goes, but two other things must also be considered. One must look at *how long the disequilibrium has persisted*. Stronger action is necessary if 8 percent unemployment has existed for a year than if it has existed only 3 months. One must also consider the *direction of movement* in the economy. If the unemployment level is 8 percent and *falling*, this will indicate different actions than would be appropriate if unemployment were 8 percent and *rising*.

These considerations must be weighed together in determining how strong an expansionist or contractionist line the government should take.[12] Moreover, since each of these indicators is constantly changing, policy must be under constant review and should be adjusted at frequent

---

[12] For an interesting discussion of this problem in terms of engineering control systems, see A. C. L. Day and S. T. Beza, *Money and Income* (New York: Oxford University Press, 1960), chap. xxvii.

intervals. This argues in favor of measures which can be altered quickly and by small degrees and against measures which take a long time to initiate.

The Merit of Monetary Policy

Very often the same result might be obtained, at least in principle, by monetary action alone, or by fiscal action alone, or by various combinations of the two. This raises the question of the proper policy mix in various circumstances. Here economists are not fully agreed; but they usually have preferences, and so do public officials.

It is hard to distinguish between a preference for monetary instruments per se and a preference for the policy outlook of the Federal Reserve System. It is no secret that the Fed worries more about inflation than any other group in government and is inclined to cry wolf and apply the brakes at an earlier stage of expansion. Those who share this policy outlook would naturally like to see the Fed play a large role in decision making.

But there are economic advantages also in monetary policy. It has the virtue of being applicable in small doses. Credit can be tightened gradually through open market sales and interest rate increases. Carried far enough, credit tightening can always compel a reduction of bank lending and of investment. It can be argued also that monetary policy is neutral in the sense of not discriminating by name against specific borrowers or investment projects.

But monetary policy does not operate as promptly as is sometimes supposed. Changes in monetary policy are usually made some time *after* a turning point in economic activity. The new policy of credit ease or restriction is usually applied by small steps over a period of 6 to 12 months. And it takes considerable time for a change in credit terms to affect the volume of investment activity. In the case of credit loosening, it takes time for borrowers to react to the change in rates, time for new projects to be planned and initiated, and time for activity on these projects to reach peak proportions.[13]

The length of these lags is disconcerting. In the "12-month recessions" which have characterized the American economy since 1945, monetary policy can scarcely act fast enough to have much effect until *after* the tide has turned. In a 2- to 3-year expansion, monetary policy becomes effective mainly during the last half of the upswing. But there is danger that the restrictive effect exercised at this time will spill over into the subsequent recession when it is no longer appropriate.

The neutrality of monetary policy has also been questioned. Credit

---

[13] Thomas Mayer, "The Inflexibility of Monetary Policy," *Review of Economics and Statistics,* Vol. XL, No. 4 (November, 1958), pp. 358–74. See, however, the critique of this article by Lloyd D. Orr, *Review of Economics and Statistics,* Vol. XLII, No. 3, Part I (August, 1960), pp. 329–31.

restriction bears harder on industries which depend on borrowing than on those which can use internal financing. It hits housing and state and local construction more heavily than manufacturing, and it hits small, young companies harder than well-established concerns. Is it desirable that these particular activities, rather than others, be curtailed because total demand is too high? Complaints in Congress against "tight money" as a method of economic control may be partially misinformed, but they cannot be considered altogether unreasonable.

There is another long-range consideration. Monetary policy operates mainly by imposing periodic checks on private investment. In order to control total demand, the investment component of demand is restricted. Many people are concerned, however, that the growth rate of the American economy since World War II has been considerably lower than that of Western Europe and Japan. This is attributed partly to a lower level of business investment in the United States. If we need more investment over the long run, should we rely heavily on a policy instrument which operates by restricting investment? Might it not be a good idea to stimulate investment continuously through low interest rates and use fiscal policy to drain off any excess of demand at cycle peaks?

Fiscal Policy: General Comments

The most important effect of the federal budget, its stabilizing action, has already been discussed. We turn now to the question whether this automatic stabilizing effect of the budget can usefully be reinforced at times by deliberate action to adjust tax rates, expenditure levels, or both.

Fiscal policy can be accused of operating even more sluggishly than monetary policy. The federal budget is drafted by the Bureau of the Budget far in advance of the fiscal year to which it will apply. Congress, jealous of its control over taxes and appropriations, then reviews the President's proposals at a leisurely pace. Moreover, revenues are considered by one committee, expenditures by a host of subcommittees dealing with various agencies. Congress does not consider the budget as a whole or reach decisions about the overall surplus or deficit.

Until recently it could be said also that the central principle of modern fiscal policy—that the budget should be used as an instrument for regulating aggregate demand—had little following either in the Executive Branch or in Congress. Economists had been expounding this idea to their classes for a generation, but no one else seemed to be listening. The idea that the budget should be balanced each year, regardless of economic circumstances, remained deeply entrenched.

The first president to adopt the modern approach was President Kennedy. Even he was apparently not of this mind when first elected, but was gradually persuaded by the Council of Economic Advisers, and particularly by its then chairman, Professor Walter Heller. The tax-cut recommendations of 1963 were the first deliberate application of modern fiscal policy. The new approach was continued by President Johnson, who pushed major tax reduction programs through Congress in 1964 and 1965. How far leaders of Congress have really been persuaded, and how amenable they will prove in future years, remains to be seen.

Fiscal action is probably too slow to do much about checking the short recessions which we have experienced since 1945. Here main reliance must be placed on the automatic stabilizers. Discretionary action is useful mainly in sustaining an expansion, or in accelerating an expansion which is moving too slowly toward full employment. If it appears that aggregate demand needs to be raised, this can be done by cutting taxes, increasing public expenditures, or some combination. What are the relative merits of these lines of action?

Varying Public Expenditures

Government is involved year in and year out in spending on schools, hospitals, public buildings, streets and sewers, highways, irrigation and flood control projects, soil conservation and reforestation, slum control and urban redevelopment, atomic energy installations, and military facilities. These items add up to many billions each year—money which is going to be spent anyway, at one time or another. Could we not use this large volume of spending as a stabilizing influence, speeding it up during recession when private demand is low and cutting it back as the private economy recovers?

This seems like a sensible thing to do wherever feasible. In addition to its stabilizing effect, it might save the government money by bunching expenditures in slump periods when costs are relatively low. But one should not be overoptimistic about how much can actually be done. There are several difficulties:

1. Postponing work of high social priority during prosperity will cause a good deal of inconvenience. A nice type of depression project would be repairing pot holes in streets and highways. This is necessary work and uses a good deal of labor. It can be started up and tapered off rapidly, thus meeting the test of flexible timing. If one leaves all pot holes to be filled in the next depression, however, there will soon be a lot of broken springs and a great public outcry. Or consider the rapid increase in the need for school buildings since World War II. If we were willing to wait for a depression, many of the unemployed could usefully be put to work building schools. But meanwhile children would be sitting on each others' knees.

2. It takes time to get large construction projects in motion. Even after funds have been approved, sites must be acquired, specifications drawn, bids requested and contracts let, and the contractor must assemble the necessary work force and materials. On some projects one will get no expenditures during the first 6 months or even the first 12

months. It has been calculated that for public construction as a whole, only 32 percent of expenditures occur during the first year after authorization of the project, while subsequent expenditures may linger on for 3 or 4 years. Thus there is danger that projects initiated to check depression will get going just in time to add to inflation during the next boom.[14]

3. Countercyclical timing of public works requires budgets running beyond a single year. One needs an approved capital budget for several years ahead, with actual expenditures to be timed in the light of economic conditions. Congress has usually been reluctant to relax its year-to-year control over expenditures. Long-range approval was given, however, for the federal-state superhighway program, which involves a prospective expenditure of more than $30 billion over a 15-year period. This made it possible to speed up highway construction during the slack years 1958 and 1961.

In addition to what can be done with normal public expenditures, there is sometimes pressure during recession to start extraordinary works programs. These include projects which are not of high priority by normal standards, but which will put people to work, get money in circulation, and yield some social benefit from resources presently unemployed. It seems unwise to undertake such projects for cyclical reasons alone, unless they are also considered to be worthwhile on a long-term basis. This is not the only way or the best way of getting unemployed resources back to work.

Varying Tax Rates

One can make a strong case that fiscal policy should rely *mainly* on tax changes rather than expenditure changes. This would mean lowering tax rates in periods of insufficient demand and raising rates when demand threatens to become excessive.

There are two reasons for preferring to rely mainly on tax changes. First, the tax structure is inherently more flexible. A change in personal income tax rates affects disposable income immediately because of the withholding system. A change in corporate income taxes affect income with only a short lag. Most of the expenditure budget, on the other hand, is quite rigid. Military expenditures, the regular government payroll, and interest payments on the national debt cannot be raised or lowered each time there is a turn in the business cycle. Even where expenditures can be varied, as on construction projects, it may take a year or more to produce a substantial change.

In addition to this argument of convenience, there is an argument of principle. The proper level of public services should be determined by

---

[14] Robert A. Dahl and Charles E. Lindblom, "Variation in Public Expenditure," in Max F. Millikan (ed.), *Income Stabilization for a Developing Democracy* (New Haven, Conn.: Yale University Press, 1953), pp. 347–96.

long-run priorities, as explained in Chapter 17. If the decision has been made correctly, it will be little influenced by changing phases of the business cycle.

A depression involves a drop in private incomes, private spending, and consumer living standards. There is no reason to think that this makes people want a sudden increase in government services. What they mainly want is more money in their pockets so they can buy more of the things they were able to buy at the peak of prosperity. This desire can be met by reducing tax schedules, leaving people with more money to spend, and letting them spend it as they will.

The opposite policy of offsetting recessions by raising public expenditures contains obvious dangers. There is a danger of putting manpower and materials into things which the public does not particularly want, when by tax reductions the same resources could be channeled into things which people do want. There is also a danger of bringing about permanent increases in the scope of government activity accidentally rather than through deliberate choice. It is notoriously easier to expand government activities than to curtail them, and so decisions on this front should be based on long-run rather than cyclical considerations.

The prime candidate for a policy of tax variation is the personal income tax, which contributes such a high percentage of federal revenues. Fiscal experts have frequently advocated that the President be given power to vary income tax rates within prescribed limits, somewhat as the Federal Reserve System varies the discount rate. These changes could be geared to some indicator of economic activity. One could provide, for example, that for each 1 percent increase in the unemployment rate, the basic rate on the first bracket of taxable income would be reduced by 1 percent. Duesenberry, Eckstein, and Fromm[15] suggest a formula based on the percentage decline in GNP rather than the rise in the unemployment rate. They present illustrative calculations showing that this would have a substantial braking effect during recession. Alternatively, adjustments within the prescribed limits could be left to the discretion of the President.

Concrete proposals of this sort have been submitted to Congress more than once. But Congress, jealous of its taxing power and anxious to receive credit for any tax reductions, has shown little willingness to approve such proposals.

SUMMARY

1. While the unemployment rate is a convenient indicator of economic activity, it understates the gap between actual and capacity output of the economy. A drop of 1 percent in the unemployment rate

---

[15] *Op. cit.*

corresponds to a rise of about 3 percent in GNP. The reason is that labor force participation, average hours of work, and man-hour productivity all rise during an upswing.

2. Choice of an output target involves weighing the economic loss from unemployment against the economic loss from inflation. Unemployment means a loss of national income which falls both on the unemployed and on others in the economy; and it generates pressure for harmful economic policies, private and public. Inflation redistributes income so that people living on fixed money incomes find their real incomes reduced, while other groups in the economy benefit. Persistent and immoderate inflation undermine people's expectation of price stability and hence the basis for long-term lending.

3. In the present American economy, there is no reason to expect either heavy unemployment or serious inflation. Policy choices will involve a limited range in the center of the "Phillips curve."

4. The present location of the Phillips curve is not immutable. It may be possible to encourage greater wage and price restraint during boom periods, so that we can reach a high level of employment with less inflationary pressure. The wage-price "guidelines" drafted by the Council of Economic Advisers are an experiment in this direction.

5. The built-in stabilizing effect of government budgets could be strengthened by an increase in benefit levels under the state unemployment compensation systems, and by automatic lengthening of the benefit period at times of severe unemployment.

6. The corporate income tax system could be modified to reduce the present wide fluctuation of post-tax profits, and to give companies a financial inducement to spread their investment more evenly over good and bad years.

7. Monetary policy is effective mainly in controlling unduly strong upswings. But since it operates by checking investment, which may be considered undesirable from a growth standpoint, fiscal policy is usually preferable even in boom periods. During recession main reliance must be placed on fiscal policy.

8. Fiscal policy should operate mainly through varying tax rates rather than varying public expenditures. This is partly because taxes can be changed more quickly, partly because decisions about the level of public services should be based on long-run rather than cyclical considerations. One possibility is to authorize the President to vary first-bracket personal income tax rates within prescribed limits, either according to a set formula or on a discretionary basis.

DISCUSSION QUESTIONS

1. Check on the movement of GNP, the rate of full-time unemployment, the Wholesale Price Index, and the Consumer Price Index over the past 12

months. From this evidence, do you conclude that steps should be taken to raise aggregate demand or to lower it?

2. Suppose you know two points on the Phillips curve. One involves 5 percent unemployment and stable prices, the other 4 percent unemployment with prices rising 2 percent a year. Which would you choose, and why?

3. "In a private enterprise economy, wage and price decisions should be left to the parties directly concerned. Government efforts to impose guidelines from above are an unwarranted encroachment on private initiative." Discuss.

4. If you consider the guidelines approach legitimate, can you think of any ways of making it more effective?

5. It is sometimes argued that monetary policy should be consistently expansionary, to encourage investment and long-term growth, while short swings in aggregate demand should be countered mainly by fiscal policy. What do you think of this argument?

6. Suppose a recession is under way and the federal government wants to stimulate recovery. There is a choice among raising federal purchases of goods and services, raising transfer payments, and cutting taxes. Which instrument, or combination of instruments, would you recommend?

7. Would you favor authorizing the President to vary the first-bracket rate of personal income taxation on the basis of some index of output or employment?

External Balance and the World

Monetary System

. . . it is difficult to envision in this regard
any other criterion, any other standard than gold.
Yes, gold, which does not change in nature,
which can be made either into bars, ingots or
coins, which has no nationality, which is considered, in all places and at all times, the immutable and fiduciary value par excellence.

CHARLES DE GAULLE, Paris, 1965

Gold we have, but we save it. Why? I don't
really know. Lenin said the day would come
when gold would serve to coat the walls and
floors of public toilets. When the Communist
society is built, we must certainly accomplish
Lenin's wish.

NIKITA S. KHRUSHCHEV, Paris, 1960

IF THE UNITED STATES were the only economy on earth, we would have
come to the end of our story. But we are involved in a network of trade
and financial relations with more than a hundred other countries. Our
flow of payments to and from these countries must remain in reasonable
balance. To meet this test while also meeting the requirements for
internal balance is no easy task.

It is common knowledge that since about 1958 the United States has been experiencing a "balance-of-payments problem." What does this mean, and why is it a problem? What has been done about it to date, and what other remedial measures have been suggested?

There is a second and related problem. Foreign governments, central banks, and private parties hold some $25 billion of checking accounts and other short-term dollar assets in New York, which they can legally convert into gold on very short notice. But the United States doesn't have that much gold. Monetary gold reserves in the United States total only about $15 billion. So, if there really were a scramble to turn dollars into gold, the international monetary system might come tumbling down. How serious is this danger? What steps have already been taken to avert it, and what additional steps might be taken?

Before going on to these policy issues, however, we must look into the mechanics of international finance. How does the money of one country get converted into that of another? What are the various reasons why people in one country may have to make payments to people in other countries? How is the price of one currency in terms of another determined, and to what extent can it be controlled by government action?

THE MECHANISM OF INTERNATIONAL PAYMENTS

How do buyers of goods in one country manage to pay the sellers of goods in other countries? How do dollars get converted into pounds, lira, francs, and other currencies?

Consider an American importer who buys bicycles from a British exporter. The importer sells these to customers in the United States and receives dollars in return. But the British exporter, who bought the bicycles from a British manufacturer, has to pay for them in pounds. How is the importer, who has dollars, going to pay the exporter, who needs pounds?

The answer is that there are other people in these countries who are in the opposite situation. There are importers in Britain who have pounds, which they need to change into dollars to pay exporters in the United States. Suppose a British importer has bought raw cotton from an American exporter, and suppose that the value of the cotton happens to equal that of the bicycles. Then the four parties could get together and work out the clearing arrangement shown in Figure 1. The American exporter can receive pounds from his British customer, trade these for dollars to the American importer, who then uses them to pay off the British exporter. (Or the clearing could be done in Britain with dollars crossing the ocean instead of pounds.) Now everyone has been paid off, and everyone is happy. American exports have paid for American imports, almost as though the cotton had been traded off against the bicycles in a single deal.

It would be awkward if each time an American importer needed a

Direct Clearing of International Payments

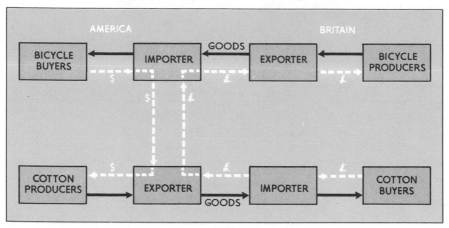

FIGURE 1

thousand pounds he had to hunt up an exporter who had exactly a thousand pounds. Foreign transactions occur at different times and in varying amounts. The logical solution is to set up a clearinghouse which will undertake to buy or sell dollars or pounds in any amount to all comers. The nature of such a clearinghouse is shown in Figure 2. As in the previous diagram, solid lines indicate movements of goods, broken lines show movements of money. The clearinghouse trades pounds for dollars at the top of the diagram, and dollars for pounds at the bottom. As long as the two flows remain in balance, they cancel out and the system works smoothly. Actually, there will be difference in the flows from day to day, and the clearinghouse needs some pounds and dollars of its own to tide over short periods of imbalance.

Note that it does not matter whether it is the American importer or his colleague the British exporter who buys pounds in exchange for dollars. They share a common interest. They are on the *same side* of the foreign exchange market. The American importer and the American exporter, on the other hand, are on *opposite* sides of the market, one selling dollars and the other buying them. The requirement for balance in the market is that American exports and imports should be equal in value, in which case they cancel out or "pay for each other."

In practice, there is no single clearinghouse for foreign exchange. The main dealers in foreign exchange are banks, chiefly banks in leading financial centers such as New York and London. The large New York banks keep checking accounts (in pounds) at the principal London banks. (The London banks have similar dollar accounts in New York, but it will be clearest to look at the process from the American end.) When a New York bank "sells pounds," it gives the customer a claim of so many pounds on its London checking account, taking his dollars in return. When it "buys pounds," these are added to its balance in London, and it

A Clearinghouse for International Payments

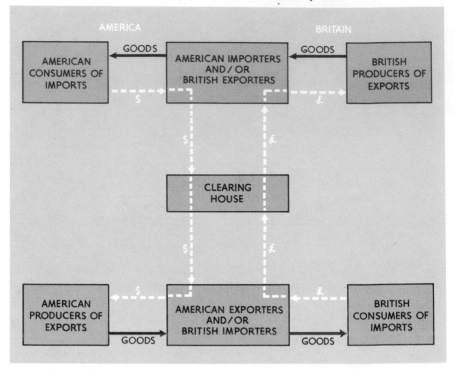

FIGURE 2.

pays off by increasing the seller's dollar checking account in New York. It is checks rather than actual currency which shuttle back and forth across the Atlantic.

How does this work out? Suppose a New York bank finds that it has more customers wanting to buy pounds than to sell them. As a result, the bank's checking account in London will decline. Up to a point, the bank may simply let this happen. But if the account becomes dangerously low, the bank will have to replenish it by buying pounds somewhere. It may buy from another American or British bank. Or it may go to the Federal Reserve Bank of New York, where it has a checking account. The Federal Reserve has an account at the British central bank, the Bank of England. It can sell the New York bank pounds from this account, deducting the dollar cost from the bank's account with it. If the Federal Reserve's own account at the Bank of England falls too low, it can replenish it by shipping gold to London and getting credit in pounds on the Bank's books.[1] Although gold is no longer used as currency by private parties, it

---

[1] Actually, the gold will probably not leave the Federal Reserve vaults at all. The Fed will simply hang a tag on it saying "property of Bank of England." The central banks of other countries trust us to watch the gold.

remains the ultimate method of settling differences between a country's receipts and payments.

The foreign exchange market, in short, is an interconnected network of private and central banks, which have checking accounts with each other and can shift funds back and forth as needed. The mechanism is basically the same as that through which checks are cleared between different regions of the United States.

Thus far we have considered only exchange dealings between Britain and the United States. But the clearinghouse principle which works for two countries can be extended to cover a larger group of trading nations. In this case it is no longer necessary for United States imports from a particular country to be balanced by exports *to the same country*. It is sufficient if U.S. exports to *all countries* equal its imports from all

TABLE 1

A Simple Export-Import System

		IMPORTS			
		A	B	C	TOTAL EXPORTS
EXPORTS	A		100		100
	B			100	100
	C	100			100
	TOTAL IMPORTS	100	100	100	300

countries. If this is true for each country in the group, the system is in balance and the clearinghouse mechanism will work. An extreme case is shown in Table 1. Country A exports only to B, B only to C, and C only to A. No country is in balance with any other single country, but each is in overall balance, with its exports equal to its imports. This recalls the famous "triangular trade" of the eighteenth century, in which the British West Indies shipped sugar to New England, which shipped rum to Britain, which shipped cloth to the West Indies.

THE BALANCE OF PAYMENTS

Now what determines how many pounds I can get for an American dollar? An exchange rate is a price, and so it is influenced by supply and demand. An import of goods to the United States, for which we must make payment in dollars, creates a *supply* of dollars available for conversion into foreign currency. Conversely, an export from the United States creates a *demand* for dollars, since the foreign buyer must get dollars to pay for the goods. Thus an increase in U.S. exports raises the demand for dollars, while an increase in U.S. imports raises the supply. In a free exchange market, the first development would raise the price of dollars in terms of other currencies, while the second would lower it.

Exports and imports are only one type of international dealing. Other transactions also affect the demand for and supply of dollars. Any transaction which obligates someone in the United States (an individual, business concern, or government agency) to make payment to someone abroad creates a *supply* of dollars. Conversely, anything which obligates foreigners to make payment to Americans creates a *demand* for dollars.

The main kinds of transaction which create a *supply* of dollars are:

1. *U.S. imports of merchandise.*

2. *U.S. imports of services.* The main items under this heading are U.S. tourist expenditures abroad and payments to foreign ship lines for shipping services.

3. *U.S. military expenditures abroad.* These include expenditures by U.S. military personnel stationed abroad, purchases by our armed forces for their own use, and "offshore procurement" (purchase of equipment abroad for delivery to other countries under military assistance programs).

4. *Interest and dividend payments* to foreign owners of U.S. securities.

5. *Unilateral transfers and gifts* by Americans to other countries. It has long been customary for immigrants to the United States to send back money to relatives and others in their home countries. But today the largest item under this heading is U.S. government grants to other countries under our international aid programs.

6. *Long-term loans and investments* by Americans to other countries. This includes U.S. government loans to other countries. On the private side, it includes purchase of plants and facilities abroad by U.S. businesses and purchase of foreign securities by Americans. These transactions are sometimes summed up as *capital exports.* (It seems odd at first that a capital export has the same effect on the foreign exchange market as a merchandise import. One way to remember this is to realize that an *export* of capital funds is an *import* of securities or titles of ownership, for which we are obliged to pay foreigners in dollars.)

7. *Net short-term investment or lending* abroad by Americans. If a U.S. bank makes a loan to a foreign company, or for that matter to a foreign subsidiary of a U.S. company, this increases the supply of dollars. So does a decision by a company or individual to shift part of his bank balance from New York to London or Paris.

8. *Inflow of monetary gold.* The foreign country shipping the gold receives a corresponding dollar credit on the books of the Federal Reserve Bank of New York. Thus the supply of dollars is increased.

If any of these transactions seems mysterious or difficult, look at it carefully. You will find that it meets the original test of obligating someone in the United States to pay dollars to someone abroad.

Each of these items has its counterpart on the other side of the balance sheet. The *demand* for dollars is increased by United States exports of goods or services, by foreign long-term investments in the United States, and by any other transactions which obligate foreigners to make payment to us.

TABLE 2

Balance of Payments of the United States, 1964
(Millions of Dollars)

ITEM	U.S. RECEIPTS (Demand for Dollars)	U.S. PAYMENTS (Supply of Dollars)	NET BALANCE
1. **Current account**	**37,017**	**29,296**	**7,721**
Merchandise (excluding military)	25,288	18,619	6,669
Transportation	2,317	2,464	− 147
Tourist expenditures	1,095	2,216	−1,121
Military expenditures	762	2,824	−2,062
Immigrant remittances and pensions		839	− 839
Interest and dividends	5,457	1,404	4,053
Other current items	2,098	930	1,168
2. **Official capital**		**3,674**	**−3,674**
3. **Private capital**	**2,024**	**7,623**	**−5,599**
Long-term	110	4,351	−4,241
Short-term	1,914	2,111	− 197
Errors and omissions		1,161	−1,161
4. **Official settlements (1 + 2 + 3)**			**−1,552**
Foreign prepayments			− 344
Gold			− 125
Increase in liabilities to foreign monetary authorities			−1,083

Source: U.S. Department of Commerce, *Survey of Current Business*, September, 1965.

Putting the two sides of the picture together, we get a statement known as the *balance of payments*. The U.S. balance of payments for 1964 is summarized in Table 2. Look first at item 1, the balance on current account, which summarizes all transactions other than international loans and investments. The United States normally has a positive current account balance, and in 1964 the balance was almost $8 billion. We exported almost $7 billion more goods than we imported. We also had net interest and dividend receipts of about $4 billion, resulting from the large investments by American companies in other countries. These two items more than offset the negative balance on tourist expenditures, military expenditures, and other minor items.

On current account, then, foreigners owed us close to $8 billion. Where did they find the $8 billion? The answer must be that we were providing dollars to the rest of the world on a large scale. And so we were. U.S. government loans and grants to other countries (item 2) totaled about $3.7 billion. There was more than $4 billion of private long-term investment. Some of this was purchase of foreign securities by Americans, termed "portfolio investment." But most of it was "direct investment," i.e., purchase or construction of plant and equipment abroad by U.S. business concerns. There was more than $1 billion of capital outflow which the records failed to catch and which appears in the "errors and omissions" item.

When our negative balance on capital account (items 2 and 3) is combined with our positive current account balance, we ended the year with an overall payments deficit of $1,552 million (item 4).[2] How did we meet this obligation? First we persuaded some of the European countries to prepay $344 million of debts to the United States for Marshall Plan aid and military exports. This left a debt to foreign central banks of $1,208 million, of which they chose to draw $125 million in gold. The end result was an increase of $1,083 in our obligations to foreign central banks. To this extent, we were operating on credit.

The items "below the line" in Table 2 are thus balancing items. When they are included, the final column of the table must total to zero. But the fact that a bookkeeping statement balances does not mean that the balance shown is satisfactory. A company's yearly profit and loss statement always balances, but the balancing item may be a large loss. Similarly, a payments statement such as Table 2 may reveal a "balance-of-

---

[2] The balance-of-payments deficit may be defined in various ways. The approach used here is that favored by a number of authorities, including Professor Robert Triffin and Dr. Edward Bernstein, and differs from the "official" tables published by the U.S. Department of Commerce.

The difference involves mainly the short-term private capital receipts item, which in 1964 was $1,914 million. This item shows the increase of foreign private dollar deposits in New York, by foreign private banks (the largest holders), other foreign business concerns, and individuals. Under the official view, this item would be *added* to our balance-of-payments deficit (which would thus have been about $3.5 billion in 1964) on the ground that it increases our obligation to make payments to foreigners on demand. At the same time, the $1,914 million is regarded as a method of *financing* or offsetting part of the deficit. We have "overspent" by $3.5 billion; but foreigners have accommodated us by being willing to hold $1.9 billion more dollars than before—in a sense, they have relent us these dollars.

The Triffin-Bernstein view is based on the fact that the deficit facing our monetary authorities is the combined result of all other transactions in the economy, including capital movements so long as these are not undertaken for the specific purpose of helping us finance the deficit. Since this is obviously not the purpose of private dollar holders, their operations should appear above rather than below the line, that is, as determining the size of our deficit rather than as a source of financing for it.

payments problem." This would be true if our gold stock were shrinking rapidly or if our obligations to foreign central banks were rising at an inordinate rate.

THE RATE OF EXCHANGE

Supply, Demand, and the Equilibrium Rate

Having seen what determines supply and demand for foreign exchange, we now ask how these forces influence the price of one currency in terms of another—say, the price of a dollar in deutsche marks. Figure 3 shows supply and demand for dollars in Germany. As usual, the

Demand and Supply for Dollars in Germany

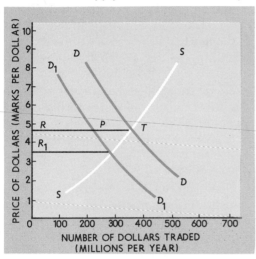

FIGURE 3. As dollars become more expensive in terms of marks, Germans will demand fewer dollars to pay for imports from the United States, while Americans will supply more dollars by importing more goods from Germany. So DD and SS have the usual shapes and determine an equilibrium exchange rate OR. If demand for dollars falls, say to D_1D_1, the equilibrium exchange rate will fall to OR_1.

vertical axis is a price axis, showing the number of marks required to buy a dollar. The horizontal axis is a quantity axis, showing the number of dollars exchanged per year.

What do the demand and supply curves mean, and why do they look as shown? Look first at DD. Why will Germans demand fewer dollars as the price of the dollar rises? The reason is that a rise in the price of the dollar raises the price *in marks* of all our export products. Take a machine which sells in the United States for $1,000. If a dollar can be bought for 4 marks, then this machine will sell for 4,000 marks in Germany (overlooking transport costs and other minor items). But if the dollar rises to 5 marks, the German price of the machine will rise to 5,000 marks.

The German buyers, who must pay in marks, will buy fewer machines as their price in marks increases. As they buy fewer machines, they will demand fewer dollars to pay for them, since the *dollar* price of machines has remained unchanged at $1,000. So we can be sure that the demand curve for dollars will slope upward to the left.

Why might we expect the supply curve of dollars to slope upward to the right? The key fact is that, as the price of the dollar rises, German goods become cheaper in the United States. If a Volkswagen costs 5,000 marks in Germany, and if the dollar is worth only 2 marks, the American price of the Volkswagen will be $2,500. But if the dollar rises to 5 marks, the American price will be only $1,000. As the price in the United States falls, more Volkswagens will be bought.

We can still not be certain that the *number of dollars* spent on Volkswagens, which determines the supply of dollars in the foreign exchange market, will also increase. True, the *number* of Volkswagens imported will rise; but each requires fewer dollars than before. The result depends on the elasticity of American demand for Volkswagens. If elasticity is greater than 1, a price decrease will increase the dollars spent on Volkswagens, and the supply curve of dollars will slope up to the right like SS. If elasticity is precisely 1, the dollar supply curve will be vertical; and if it is less than 1, SS will tilt back to the left. We shall assume, however, that SS is forward-rising.

If DD and SS represent the market situation at a particular time, the equilibrium exchange rate will be OR, or about 4½ marks to the dollar. At this price, the number of dollars offered in the market will just equal the number demanded. There is *balance of payments equilibrium*.

Adjustment to Demand-Supply Changes

Suppose now that there is a change in the demand-supply situation. Because of decreased German demand for our exports or for some other reason, the demand for dollars falls to D_1D_1. If the exchange rate remains at OR, only RP dollars will be demanded in the market while RT will be supplied. There is *balance of payments disequilibrium*.

What will happen? Suppose first that there is no government intervention in the foreign exchange market. Then the price of the dollar (in marks) will fall to OR_1, at which level demand and supply are once more in balance. This would be a *depreciation* of the dollar in terms of marks. Conversely, a rise in demand (or fall in supply), leading to a higher price for dollars, would produce an *appreciation* of the dollar.

If national currencies are freely interchangeable, a depreciation of the dollar in terms of marks must mean a corresponding depreciation in terms of British pounds, French francs, and the rest. Start from a situation in which 1 dollar = 5 marks, and 1 dollar = 5 francs. Then, since things equal to the same thing are equal to one another, 1 mark = 1 franc. Now, suppose the dollar depreciates to 1 dollar = 3 marks. Can the franc price of the dollar remain unchanged? If it did, foreign exchange dealers could make large profits by the following route: change 1 dollar into 5 francs, then change the 5 francs into 5 marks, then change the 5 marks back into 1⅔ dollars.

This kind of operation is termed *arbitrage*. Because of the possibility of arbitrage, a currency which is appreciating or depreciating must do so equally in terms of *all other currencies*. In this case, the franc exchange rate would quickly adjust to 1 dollar = 3 francs; and similarly for the pound, lira, yen, and so on.

For convenience in international trade and for other practical reasons, most countries prefer not to have the value of their currency fluctuating from day to day. So government, in fact, intervenes in the exchange market to iron out short-term fluctuations in demand and supply, and to maintain currency values at some specified level. Suppose in the present case that the United States wants to maintain the mark price of the dollar at OR. When demand falls to D_1D_1, but the exchange rate stays unchanged at OR, there is an *excess supply of dollars* equal to PT. Since an offer of dollars amounts to a demand for marks, we can equally well say that there is an *excess demand for marks* of this amount. To hold the exchange rate steady, the Federal Reserve System will have to enter the market and sell marks in exchange for dollars. Because of the interrelation among currencies already noted, it will probably find itself also selling pounds, francs, and other currencies.

But suppose the adverse balance of payments continues quarter after quarter, and even year after year. Then the Federal Reserve will find its supplies of foreign currencies and of gold shrinking, and this cannot continue indefinitely. So the monetary authorities cannot follow a purely passive policy of adjusting to the balance-of-payments situation. They must take active steps to alter the situation. In the present case, they must try to shift D_1D_1 to the right and SS to the left so that they will once more intersect at the fixed exchange rate OR.

The orthodox prescription for doing this is to restrict aggregate demand in the domestic economy through a tight monetary-fiscal policy. Raise interest rates, restrict credit, raise taxes, or reduce government expenditures. Such measures will reduce demand for imports along with other things, and will make for price stability, which will help to keep our exports competitive in foreign markets. Moreover, our exporters, finding demand reduced at home, may cultivate foreign markets more intensively. The rise in interest rates will attract short-term funds from other financial centers. All these developments will help to close the balance-of-payments gap.

This is not a very palatable course of action, however, since it may mean holding aggregate demand below the full-employment level. There may be a direct conflict between internal and external considerations. A recession at home may indicate expansionist monetary-fiscal policies, but these policies may worsen the balance of payments position.

One school of thought argues that we bring this dilemma on ourselves by the effort to maintain fixed exchange rates. Why not go over to a system of free or "floating" exchange rates? The advantages of doing this, it is argued, are similar to the advantages of any other free market.

Floating exchange rates reveal the true value of one currency in terms of another. Shifts in supply or demand for a currency are quickly reflected in its price, and the market remains in balance. The need for government intervention disappears.

One practical disadvantage of such a system is that exchange rate fluctuations may be exaggerated by speculative activity. If the price of dollars in terms of marks begins to fall, this may be taken as a sign that it will fall farther, and that one can make money by selling dollars now and buying them back later. This intensifies the excess supply of dollars and ensures that their price *will* fall farther. Thus the price fluctuations which occur in any free market may be intensified, increasing the uncertainty of all international transactions. So proposals for floating exchange rates, while they have some support among academic economists, are almost unanimously opposed by central bankers and businessmen.

What other possibilities remain open? A country has an adverse balance of payments. It is committed to maintaining a fixed exchange rate. Restrictive monetary-fiscal measures are considered undesirable for domestic reasons, or may prove inadequate to close the payments gap as rapidly as is desired. The next line of defense is direct restriction of international transactions. This might include tariff or quota restrictions on imports, restrictions on tourist expenditures abroad, and restrictions on foreign lending and other capital movements.

In many of the less developed countries, which suffer from chronic balance-of-payments deficits, restriction takes the form of comprehensive *exchange control.* All exporters and other recipients of foreign exchange are required to turn it over to the government, and are paid in local currency at a specified rate. The available foreign exchange is then rationed among would-be importers. In principle, rationing is based on some judgment of national needs. A country bent on industrialization, for example, may give priority to imports of machinery and raw materials, while discriminatory against consumer goods and particularly against luxury products. In practice, however, exchange control systems are often tinged with favoritism and bribery.

A country which does not want to engage in direct regulation of international transactions, and whose balance-of-payments difficulties appear to be chronic rather than transitory, always has the option of marking down the value of its currency to a lower level. As compared with the gradual *depreciation* which may occur with a floating exchange rate, a sudden move from one fixed exchange rate to a lower fixed exchange rate is termed *devaluation.* In the opposite (not very common) case in which a country decides to raise the price of its currency, this is termed an *upward revaluation.*

Members of the International Monetary Fund, a central monetary organization established in 1944, commit themselves to maintain fixed exchange rates and to avoid any restrictions on purchase and sale of their currencies for current transactions. An IMF member has the right, after consulting the Fund, to alter the value of its currency by as much as 10 percent. Any change larger than this may be made only to correct a "fundamental disequilibrium" in the country's balance of payments, and requires the approval of the Fund. This provision, however, does not really restrict the actions of major Fund members. At the time of the large British devaluation in 1949, the Chancellor of the Exchequer telephoned the Managing Director of the Fund and said, in effect: "This evening the Prime Minister will announce a devaluation of the pound to $2.80. We would appreciate it if at the same time we could announce your approval." Any advance discussion or publicity would have unleashed an intolerable wave of speculation against the pound.

The IMF system, which provides the possibility of altering exchange rates from time to time, is often called the system of "the adjustable peg." But the pegs have been adjusted only rarely since 1945. In 1949, the pound and the major European currencies were devalued substantially relative to the U.S. dollar. The French franc was devalued again in 1957, and in 1961 the German mark and the Dutch guilder were revalued upward by a few percent. Otherwise, relations among the major currencies have remained stable.

THE U.S. PAYMENTS POSITION

Over the recent past the United States has typically had a sizable balance-of-payment deficit. The record from 1958 through 1964 is summarized in Table 3. Item 4, the deficit which must be covered by official settlements, is the sum of the first three items. Over these seven years, our total deficit was about $19 billion.

This situation does not arise from any weakness in our export position. On the contrary, our current account balance has risen substantially over the years. But there has also been a marked rise in our negative balance on capital account, and a particularly sharp rise in private long-term investment abroad. The overall deficit, while lower than a few years ago, is still substantial.

This means that each year we owe a lot of dollars to foreign monetary authorities. They can choose either to withdraw these dollars in gold or to increase their holdings of demand deposits and securities in New York. They usually do some of both. Over the years shown in Table 3, gold withdrawals totaled about $7.4 billion, most of which went to European central banks. Over the same period our obligations to foreign monetary authorities—our I.O.U.'s, if you like—rose by $8.3 billion.

With our gold reserves shrinking and our liabilities rising, our reserve position has obviously been weakening. At the end of 1957, we had monetary reserves of $24.8 billion to set against liabilities to foreign

TABLE 3

The U.S. Balance of Payments, 1958–64
(Millions of Dollars)

ITEM	1958	1959	1960	1961	1962	1963	1964
1. Current account	1,484	− 657	3,179	4,881	4,325	4,859	7,721
2. Official capital	−2,304	−2,278	−2,443	−2,990	−3,340	−4,022	−3,674
3. Private capital							
Long term	−2,552	−1,589	−2,107	−2,177	−2,609	−3,244	−4,241
Short term*	345	1,805	−2,258	−1,703	−1,763	260	−1,358
* Including errors and omissions.							
4. Official settlements	−3,027	−2,719	−3,629	−1,988	−3,392	−2,667	−1,552
Foreign prepayments	...	− 435	− 37	− 701	−1,151	− 660	− 344
Gold	−2,275	−1,075	−1,702	− 857	− 890	− 461	− 125
Increase in liabilities to foreign monetary authorities	− 752	−1,209	−1,890	− 440	−1,351	−1,546	−1,083

central banks and the IMF of only $8.9 billion. By the end of 1964, our monetary reserves had fallen to $16.7 billion, and our obligations had risen to $16.4 billion. If the foreign central banks decided tomorrow to convert all their dollar holdings into gold, our gold supply would be wiped out. If, in addition, foreign business concerns and private individuals, who in 1964 held about $11 billion of short-term dollar assets, began demanding gold or foreign currencies, our reserves would obviously be inadequate.

The United States is not insolvent in any basic sense. On the contrary, our holdings of foreign assets far exceed our total liabilities to foreigners; and our favorable investment balance has been growing over the years (Table 4). It should be noted that these are *net* figures, representing the *difference* between our holdings of foreign assets and foreigners' holdings of U.S. assets. Thus at the end of 1964, private American investors held $20.4 billion of foreign securities (portfolio investment), while foreigners held $16.6 of long-term U.S. securities, yielding a net surplus of $3.8 billion. At the same time, U.S. companies owned $44.3 billion of plant and equipment abroad (direct investment), while foreign companies had $8.4 of assets in the United States, for a U.S. surplus of $36.0 billion. There has been a sensational rise in U.S. direct investment abroad since 1945, mainly in Canada, Britain, and Western Europe.

Most of these assets, however, are long term, and most of them are private, so that they cannot be mobilized quickly to meet claims against us. The U.S. government cannot even tap short-term assets held by U.S.

TABLE 4

The International Investment Position of the United States
(Billions of Dollars, at Year End)

	1939	1949	1959	1964
1. Net monetary reserves	17.0	22.7	10.6	0.3
2. Net short-term assets	−1.9	−3.5	−5.1	−1.5
3. Net long-term assets	4.5	19.2	36.6	58.5
U.S. government assets	...	10.7	13.5	18.8
Private portfolio investment (net)	−0.5	0.8	−0.1	3.8
Private direct investment (net)	5.0	7.8	23.2	36.0
4. Total Net U.S. Assets (1 + 2 + 3)	19.6	38.3	42.2	57.3

Source: This table rests on unpublished calculations kindly provided me by Professor Robert Triffin. Current information on the U.S. investment position is published once a year in the *Survey of Current Business.*

citizens and businesses abroad. It can depend only on its own reserve of gold and foreign currencies; and this is the figure which has been shrinking in recent years.

The United States has now assumed the position of world banker long occupied by Great Britain. Foreign governments and central banks hold their reserves partly in gold, partly in what are considered safe currencies; and among these the dollar is preponderant. To other countries, their dollar balances in New York are a valuable asset and a major prop of the world monetary system. But from our standpoint this is "hot" money, which can be withdrawn at any moment if a foreign government decides it would rather hold gold or pounds or francs instead of dollars. The private foreign balances in New York can also be shifted to other countries on short notice in response to higher interest rates there.

The accumulation of foreign balances which we are obligated to pay off in gold on demand, while at the same time our gold reserve is shrinking, naturally creates nervousness in financial circles. If all foreign depositors actually demanded gold, there would obviously not be enough to go round. In this sense we are in the position of a bank in pre-Federal Reserve days, the deposits of which typically exceeded its cash reserves, and which could always be broken by a "run" of depositors demanding payment. A "run on the dollar" is, of course, unlikely, but it is not unthinkable. The mere possibility could at some future date cause speculators to sell dollars, hoard gold, and bring on a payments crisis.

The vulnerability of the dollar also affects our international political position. We have been spending heavily abroad for military purposes, for foreign aid, and to establish (or buy up) private business concerns in Canada, Europe, and elsewhere. The total of this spending is considerably greater than our export surpluses. We have been able to live beyond our means in this way only because other countries, mainly the West European countries, have extended credit to us by holding larger and larger dollar balances. But creditors have a way of wanting a voice in borrowers' decisions. Suppose that France, Germany, or whoever, says "We don't really agree with your foreign policy, and we're not sure we want to finance it any longer. Perhaps you should take our views a bit more seriously. Otherwise, we might demand gold for some of our dollars." Indeed, President De Gaulle of France did say essentially this in 1965.

What has been done, and what more might be done, to reduce the deficit in our basic balance of payments (that is, in the items "above the line" in Table 2)? For the most part, we have relied on the monetary-fiscal approach described in an earlier section. While our policy stance since 1960 has been expansionist, it has not been as expansionist as it might have been in the absence of balance-of-payments considerations. Interest rates have probably been higher than would have been desirable on purely domestic grounds. There has been a determined effort to stabilize the U.S. price level, perhaps with a private hope that other countries would continue to inflate, thus improving our competitive position in export markets.

In addition to these overall measures, there has been action on specific fronts. The amount of goods which tourists may bring home free of duty has been cut from $500 at wholesale value to $100 at retail value. U.S. government travel has been limited to U.S. carriers, and private citizens have also been urged to use U.S. ships and airlines.

Foreign aid and military activities have been reviewed, and expenditure patterns altered so as to impose less strain on the balance of payments. In the military field, supplies can be shipped from the United States instead of being procured locally. The number of civilian dependents living abroad can be cut. Soldiers can be encouraged to spend less on local products and to put more into U.S. savings accounts or savings bonds. Loans and grants under the foreign aid program can be tied to purchase of American products. If the tying is fully effective (a matter to be considered in Chapter 33), the loan is offset by an equivalent rise in U.S. exports, and the balance of payments is not affected. In these and other ways, the balance-of-payments drain from military and aid activities was cut from $3.8 billion in 1960 to $2.8 billion in 1964; and effort on this front is continuing.

There has also been an effort to influence private capital movements. The outflow of private capital from the United States is large and has been rising rapidly in recent years. It was $3.5 billion in 1960, over $5 billion in 1964. The outflow takes three main forms: (a) Direct investment abroad by American companies. This can mean either building new plants or buying up existing foreign companies. There has recently been a strong incentive to set up subsidiary companies in the Common Market area, so as to produce behind their tariff wall instead of being forced to export over it. There is also substantial U.S. direct investment in Canada, Britain, and parts of Latin America. (*b*) Purchase of foreign securities by American investors. Foreign governments and companies often decide to float a security issue in New York rather than at home, because the New York market is efficiently organized and U.S. interest rates have been relatively low. (*c*) Short-term lending by U.S. commercial banks to foreign companies and to U.S. foreign subsidiaries. Our efficient banking organization and relatively low interest rates have encouraged many companies to borrow in New York rather than at home.

One way of reducing both short-term and long-term borrowing by foreigners is to raise American interest rates, and we have done this in a halfhearted way. Our interest rates have continued below those in most other countries, but probably above what they would have been in the absence of balance-of-payments considerations. Monetary policy has compromised between domestic employment objectives and balance-of-payments objectives. Another interesting device is the Interest Equalization Tax of 1964, designed to reduce the attractiveness of foreign portfolio investment to American investors by taxing the difference in yield between foreign and U.S. securities.

So far, we have not set up legal restrictions on private capital movements. Many other countries do have such controls. But U.S. business concerns are opposed to them for obvious reasons. They also run counter to our general belief in private enterprise, and they would reduce capital flows which are in the long-run interest of the United States as well as the recipient countries. Our past investments abroad bring back a large flow of interest and dividends, amounting to about $5.5 billion in 1964. Indeed, the dividend flow is typically larger than the flow of new private long-term investment. It remains true, however, that we could reduce new investment, continue to draw the returns on old investment, and thus improve our balance-of-payments position.

In 1965 the Johnson administration asked U.S. banks, manufacturers, and other concerns operating abroad to restrict their foreign loans and investments voluntarily. Each company was asked to draw up its own balance-of-payments statement and to show some improvement quarter by quarter. The response, while not really cheerful, was that voluntary restraint by business is at least preferable to legal regulation by government; and there was some reduction in the outflow of private capital. It remains to be seen how effective this approach will prove over the longer run.

This review does not exhaust the devices which have been invented to cope with the balance-of-payments problem. We have encouraged some countries which are now in a strong reserve position, such as France, to speed up repayment of debts to the United States. We have persuaded foreign institutions to buy new types of nonmarketable federal security, which turns "hot money" into frozen (or at least sticky) money. We have made limited use of our power to borrow from the IMF, to which for many years we used to lend. In these and other ways the problem has gradually been whittled down, but it is too early to say that it has been eliminated.

THE WORLD MONETARY SYSTEM

The major trading countries are committed to currency convertibility. This term can be defined in a variety of ways. We use it here in the IMF sense of free purchase and sale of foreign exchange for current transactions, at stable rates of exchange.

Currency convertibility is usually considered desirable, but has been rather rare over the past half century. It was destroyed by World War I, restored somewhat precariously by 1925, but broke down again in 1931 under the onslaught of the Great Depression. World War II brought further dislocations, and convertibility of the major Western currencies was not fully restored until 1958. So we have had only about a decade of experience with convertibility under late twentieth-century conditions.

Why is convertibility so hard to maintain? Partly because of the commitment to *fixed exchange rates*. Each country specifies the value of its currency in gold, which also fixes its value relative to each of the other currencies. Maintenance of fixed rates requires, as we have seen, that the central bank stand ready to intervene in the exchange market, buying or selling foreign currencies in whatever quantity is needed to hold exchange rates stable. The bank's ability to do this depends on its possessing an adequate amount of *international reserves*.

The Role of Reserves

What are international reserves? Before 1914 they consisted almost entirely of precious metals, primarily gold. Total monetary reserves in 1913 have been estimated at $10.8 billion, of which $7.3 billion was gold and the remainder silver.[3] In those days, gold coin still circulated as money within each country; and movement of gold coin and bullion among countries was the accepted method of settling international accounts.

Gold still constitutes about two thirds of the total reserves of the world's central banks. (Silver is no longer important.) But because of the undependability of new gold supplies and for other reasons, most countries now hold part of their reserve in key currencies, which are considered "as good as gold," and which can be converted into gold on demand. During the 1920's, the British pound was the main key currency. In 1928, the world's central banks held about $10 billion in gold and about $2.5 billion in pounds. With the emergence of the United States as the major financial power after World War II, and with the abundant

---

[3] Robert Triffin, *The Evolution of the International Monetary System: Historical Reappraisal and Future Perspectives* (Princeton, N.J.: Princeton Studies in International Finance, No. 12, 1964), p. 57. Other estimates in this section are from the same source, unless otherwise noted.

supply of dollars provided by our overseas programs, the dollar became the leading key currency. The pound continues to be important, especially in the "sterling area" countries which have close trading and financial relations with Britain. In 1965, world monetary reserves included some $43 billion of gold, $15 billion of dollars, and $6 billion of pounds. Because the system rests ultimately on the convertibility of the key currencies into gold, it is usually called a *gold exchange standard*.

A third type of international reserve, which is growing in relative importance, arises from the existence of the International Monetary Fund. Each member country contributes a quota to the Fund, of which one quarter must be in gold and the remainder in the country's own currency. (The gold portion of a country's contribution goes by the exotic name of *gold tranche*.) The quotas have been increased several times since the organization of the IMF in 1944 and now total some $16 billion. These gold and currency holdings give the IMF substantial lending power.[4]

On the other side, any member can request loans from the Fund to cover a payments deficit. A member can borrow without question up to the amount of its gold tranche plus the amount of its currency which the Fund has lent to other countries. Loans above that level require negotiation with IMF officials. As the size of the loan increases, the Fund looks more carefully into the reasons for the country's adverse payments position; and a loan is often conditional on the country's taking specified remedial measures. The ceiling on loans to any one country is set at double the amount of its Fund quota.

How far these borrowing privileges at the Fund should be counted as part of a country's international reserves is debatable. The present custom is to count only the unlimited borrowing rights, since only these can be used without asking anyone's consent. But the fact that there is a further "line of credit" open to a country after consultation with Fund officials does strengthen its reserve position.

In mid-1965, then, world monetary reserves (in millions of U.S. dollars) were approximately as follows:

Gold (outside IMF)	41.3
Reserve currencies	
U.S. dollars	14.6
Pounds sterling	6.5
Other	0.6
IMF gold tranches	5.3
Total	68.3

---

[4] The IMF's lending power at any time depends on its holdings of gold and currencies in active demand, which at present means mainly certain European currencies. The IMF's effective lending power in 1965 was of the order of $5 billion.

How large a reserve does a country need? For the key currency countries, Britain and the United States, the answer is paradoxical. If confidence in a key currency is so high that foreign countries will accept and hold any amount of it without question, then the country can get along with very small reserves. On the other hand, if there is widespread belief that a currency will be devalued, leading to heavy speculative selling in the foreign exchange market, no feasible volume of reserves will suffice to save it. This happened to the pound in 1931 and again in 1949. The whole system rests on faith in the intentions of the governments responsible for the key currencies. Reserves are important mainly as a visible sign of those intentions.

The conventional answer for nonkey currency countries is that the necessary level of reserves depends, first, on the size of the country's foreign trade and, second, on the vulnerability of this trade to cyclical or other fluctuations. This also leads to paradoxical conclusions. The less developed countries are most subject to wide swings in export receipts, because the primary products which they export have large variations in both price and output. So these countries should carry larger reserves, relative to their exports, than do the developed countries. But being poor, they cannot, or at any rate will not, accumulate reserves of adequate size. They tend rather to meet balance-of-payments deficits by exchange control and other devices.

Even among the developed countries, there is considerable variation in reserve ratios. The United States, whose imports are small relative to GNP, has gross reserves equal to about a year's imports. Britain, with a higher trade ratio and long financial experience, gets along with reserves of about a quarter of its annual imports. For 11 major trading nations, gross reserves at the end of 1962 were 56 percent of 1962 imports.

The ownership of world reserves in 1949 and in 1962 is summarized in Table 5. This brings out the remarkable economic and financial recovery of Western Europe since 1949. The Common Market countries, in particular, have had a surplus with the rest of the world in recent years, and their reserves have grown rapidly. Most of the $9 billion of gold which moved out of the United States during this period went to the E.E.C. countries, primarily France and Germany. Britain, Canada, Japan, and the other developed countries also increased their reserves substantially. The underdeveloped countries' share of world reserves fell considerably, and the reserves of the Latin American countries fell in absolute terms.

PROBLEMS IN THE SYSTEM'S OPERATION

There is widespread discontent with the present system of international payments. Academic critics have criticized it as jerry-built and precarious and have warned that we are living on the edge of a financial

TABLE 5

Distribution of Gross International Monetary Reserves,
1949 and 1962

	1949		1962	
COUNTRY	RESERVES (Billions of U.S. Dollars)	PERCENT OF WORLD TOTAL	RESERVES (Billions of U.S. Dollars)	PERCENT OF WORLD TOTAL
United States	26.0	55.5	17.2	26.3
United Kingdom	1.8	3.7	3.3	5.0
European Economic Community	2.8	5.9	18.4	28.0
Other developed countries	5.1	10.9	13.2	20.2
Latin America	2.8	5.9	2.4	3.6
Other underdeveloped countries	8.4	18.0	11.1	16.9
Total	46.9	100.0	65.6	100.0

debâcle.[5] Central bankers and IMF officials have also expressed qualms and have come forward with reform proposals.

The criticisms stem from the fact that the system relies heavily on *national currencies* as a component of an *international* reserve system. It is argued that under this system the volume of world reserves may not rise at an adequate rate; that the system puts undue pressure on the domestic policies of the key currency countries; and that there is continuing danger of runs on the pound and the dollar which could bring the whole system tumbling down.

The Growth Rate of International Reserves

A good way to visualize this problem is to start from the monetary system of a single country. If one looks at U.S. monetary statistics over a long period, one sees that the assets of the Federal Reserve System have been rising, member bank reserves have been rising, and so have demand deposits and total money supply. A growing money supply is required to circulate the rising output of goods and services. If one ignores

---

[5] The debate was touched off in good measure by Professor Robert Triffin's *Gold and the Dollar Crisis* (New Haven, Conn.: Yale University Press, 1960). For subsequent statements by Triffin and others, see Herbert G. Grubel (ed.), *World Monetary Reform: Plans and Issues* (Stanford, Calif.: Stanford University Press, 1963); *Guidelines for International Monetary Reform* (Hearings of the Subcommittee on International Exchange and Payments of the Joint Economic Committee [Washington, D.C.: Government Printing Office, 1965]); Robert Triffin, *The World Money Maze: National Currencies in International Payments* (New Haven, Conn.: Yale University Press, 1966); Robert V. Roosa, *Monetary Reform for the World Economy* (New York: Harper & Row, 1965).

economies in the use of money which affect its velocity of circulation, and if one sets price stability as an objective, money supply should increase in rough proportion to physical output. The monetary system must provide the economy with adequate *liquidity*.

There is a similar need for adequate liquidity in the world economy. Between 1950 and 1964, world imports rose at 6.8 percent per year. The volume of bank loans and other financial transactions across national borders has increased correspondingly. This means, first, that private bankers and businessmen need larger balances of generally acceptable currencies to conduct their international dealings. The dollar is now pre-eminent as a key currency. This is why private parties have been not merely willing but anxious to increase their dollar holdings over the years.

Second, since a country's balance-of-payments risks are related to its payments volume, a rising level of international transactions requires larger reserve holdings by the world's central banks. One cannot say that reserves must rise at precisely the same rate as world trade. But there is *some* required rate of increase—3 percent a year, 4 percent, or whatever —below which countries will become nervous about their reserve level and will restrict domestic expansion to improve their payments position and accumulate reserves. The actual rate of increase in world monetary reserves from 1950 to 1964 was only 2.8 percent per year.

The rate at which new reserves are created has nothing to do with world needs. It results from a whimsical series of accidents. Take gold itself. The amount mined each year in South Africa and elsewhere depends on calculations of private profit. About 60 percent of this disappears into private hands, including industrial uses and speculative hoarding. The amount remaining in official hands for monetary use is determined with no reference to the needs of the world economy. A substantial but sporadic supplier of gold is the U.S.S.R. In years when the U.S.S.R. needs to make unusually large purchases of wheat or other supplies from the West, considerable amounts of gold are sold on Western markets. This again has nothing to do with the reserve needs of the Western countries.

Over the years 1950–62, monetary gold reserves increased as follows:

	MILLIONS OF U.S. DOLLARS
Gold production from Western sources	13,080
Less private absorption	−8,440
	4,640
Plus U.S.S.R. gold sales	1,790
Increase in monetary gold reserves	6,430

Even more significant, the main increase in monetary reserves during this period did not come from gold at all, but rather from *increased holdings of key currencies.* While gold holdings increased by $6.4 billion, holdings of U.S. dollars rose by $9.7 billion, and holdings of pounds and other currencies by $1.1 billion. American dollars alone provided more than half of the $18.7 billion increase in reserves over these years.

How could the central banks of other countries increase their holdings of U.S. dollars at this rate? Only because of the continuing deficit in our balance of payments, by which we provided each year many more dollars than we received in return. So what appears as a problem to us is a major source of liquidity to the world monetary system. If we make a determined and successful effort to close the payments gap, this source of liquidity will dry up. The rate of increase in reserves, dependent on the vagaries of gold alone, may well become inadequate. But if we do not make such an effort and if other countries' claims against us mount while our gold stocks decline, faith in the continued convertibility of the dollar may dwindle. Thus we, and the world monetary system with us, appear to be caught in a cleft stick.

Constraints on Domestic Economic Policy

The present system imposes special burdens on the key-currency countries, Britain and the United States. While any country must watch its balance-of-payments position, these countries must be especially on guard. They must keep sufficient gold to reassure everyone of their ability to pay off in gold on demand. This may force them to take steps which are undesirable from a domestic standpoint.

What should Britain or the U.S. do if reserves are declining? The conventional answer is: restrict the growth of aggregate demand. In addition to its directly favorable effects on the balance of payments, a deflationary policy is considered the "right" thing by the conservative central bankers who manage the world monetary system. It is taken as a sign that the country recognizes its problem, is willing to take strong measures to meet the problem, and deserves the support which the banks of high-reserve countries can choose to provide—or not to provide.

But while the world's central bankers may approve such a course, one's own citizens may take a different view. It is not pleasant to keep the economy limping along below full employment. Britain's high unemployment rate during the 1920's arose partly from this source. The same constraint has hampered British economic policy since World War II. Each time a strong expansion has gotten underway, there has been a drain on reserves and government has responded by slamming on the brakes. This is one reason why Britain's rate of GNP increase since 1950 has been well below that of Germany, France, and most other industrial countries.

The United States has been similarly hampered over the past decade. With the economy operating at most times below full capacity, the domestic need has been for expansionist monetary-fiscal policies. But the balance-of-payments deficits and the continuing gold drain have indicated higher interest rates and a generally cautious policy. The resulting compromises have not satisfied anyone. The performance of the economy has certainly been below what would have been possible without the ever present balance-of-payments threat.

We are also vulnerable, as noted earlier, to pressures on the political side. Suppose the president of one of our European allies decides that he no longer approves of our overseas activities, and threatens to convert his country's dollar holdings into gold. We might reply, "You are threatening the basis of the world monetary system. We are all in the same boat. If you choose to sink the boat, you will drown along with us." We may even feel fairly sure that he would not actually sink the boat. But he might try to push us just as far as possible, and this financial brinksmanship could have unfortunate results.

So it is an open question whether any advantage which we may enjoy as a key-currency country is not more than offset by the resulting limitations on our freedom of action.

The Possibility of Collapse

Nervousness about the long-run future of the gold exchange standard stems partly from memories of 1931. During the twenties some of the European central banks developed the custom of holding part of their reserves in British pounds. The Bank of England encouraged this tendency and, so long as general confidence continued, was able to get along with small gold reserves. At the end of 1928, the Bank of England held some $750 million of gold. Outstanding against this was about $2,500 million of sterling balances held by foreign central banks, plus a large volume of foreign private deposits.

The world depression which began in 1929 brought bank failures in many countries, a sharp drop in world trade, and a general increase in economic uncertainty. The central banks, particularly the Bank of France, began to convert their pounds into gold. As doubts grew about the Bank of England's ability to pay off, private parties also rushed to convert their pounds. Finally, in 1931, the Bank was forced to abandon its promise to pay gold for pounds at a fixed rate. The nonconvertible pound dropped to a sharp discount from its official par value; and convertibility among the major currencies vanished for a generation.

The pound has continued in a precarious position since World War II. The Bank of England's reserve ratio has been higher than it used to be in the twenties. At the end of 1962, the Bank had gold and dollar reserves of $3,310 million against foreigners' pound holdings of $6,220 million. But financial nervousness seems also to be greater. Each time Britain's balance of payments has deteriorated, leading to a loss of reserves, there has been heavy speculative selling of the pound in hopes of a possible devaluation; and it has taken large loans from other central banks to prevent a collapse of the pound. During the most recent crisis, in the fall of 1964, the U.S. Federal Reserve, in cooperation with the leading European banks, mobilized $3 billion of emergency loans to the Bank of England.

At present, the pound is guaranteed by the dollar. But who will guarantee the dollar? Do we have sufficient monetary reserves[6] to meet our potential obligations? The thing which gives cause for concern is not so much the level of reserves as the direction of movement. Our reserves have fallen considerably since 1950, while our liabilities have greatly increased. Our present gold stock is insufficient even to pay off our obligations to foreign central banks, let alone the large volume of private dollar holdings.

Is this a dangerous situation? Who can say? It is no different from the position of any bank, whose reserves are usually only a small percentage of its deposit liabilities. (But remember that behind a U.S. bank stand the great resources of the Federal Reserve system. There is no world central bank to stand behind the Federal Reserve.) It is no different from the position of the British pound, which has rarely had more than a 50 percent coverage against outstanding liabilities. Confidence depends on custom and expectation rather than mathematical percentages. Foreign central banks would presumably come to the support of the dollar in crisis—by agreeing not to call for gold themselves, and by lending francs, marks, and so on to meet private withdrawal of dollars—rather than see the whole system come apart.

On the other hand, the trends of the past 15 years can scarcely continue indefinitely. Our gold stock cannot shrink toward zero while our liabilities mount to the sky. At some point along this path the situation would become explosive. And somewhere before this point other governments would urge us, even more forcibly than they now do, to eliminate our balance-of-payments deficit and stop the gold drain. The restraints on our freedom of action described a moment ago would become more and more severe.

THE FUTURE OF INTERNATIONAL FINANCE: REFORM OR RECONSTRUCTION?

It is much easier to point out the inconveniences of the present system than to suggest lines of improvement. The intensive debates of

---

[6] One possible source of confusion should be clarified. We saw in Chapter 24 that the Federal Reserve is required to hold gold equal to 25 percent of total Federal Reserve notes plus member bank reserves. So in principle, this amount of gold is earmarked against Federal Reserve liabilities, and only the surplus of "free gold" (negligible at present) is available to meet international obligations. The domestic gold backing requirement, however, is an anachronism which serves no function in our monetary system and could be repealed at any time by Congress without loss. For present purposes, therefore, we count the whole gold stock as part of our international reserves.

recent years have not yet produced anything like agreement among experts. A few things have been done. Many other things have been suggested. A word first on two popular proposals which are unlikely to be adopted: raising the price of gold, and shifting from fixed to flexible exchange rates.

The possibility of *raising the price of gold* is frequently mentioned. Private hoarders of gold obviously expect that this will be done eventually. It is argued that gold producers have been penalized by having their price fixed for 30 years at $35 an ounce, while most other prices have risen substantially. A higher gold price would stimulate mining and hence the rate of increase in international reserves. It would also increase the adequacy of present reserves in the key-currency countries. If the price of gold were doubled, U.S. gold reserves would rise overnight from $16 billion to $32 billion. If all other countries doubled the price of gold in their currencies, so that exchange rates were not altered, no one would have been cheated by the change.

The hoarders of gold would receive their long-hoped-for bonus; and one dislikes rewarding those who, by taking gold out of circulation, have helped to weaken the present system. Many also dislike the prospect of enriching the gold-mining countries, among which South Africa and the U.S.S.R. are preeminent. The main argument against a change, however, is that it would be unsettling. The dollar price of gold is the fulcrum of the world moneatry system. If this were raised (which would have to be done unilaterally by the United States and in utmost secrecy), there is no certainty that other countries would raise their gold price by the same percentage. There might be a competitive scramble to alter relative currency values. Moreover, if gold is revalued this year, what is to prevent it's being done again and again in the future? All very unsettling. So a change in the price of gold is quite unlikely.

Some economists favor shifting over to a regime of *flexible exchange rates*. Countries with a balance-of-payments deficit would then find the value of their currencies sinking, which would tend to reduce the deficit. In recent years the dollar and pound would have been falling in value, the French franc and the deutsche mark rising. This would greatly reduce the usefulness of pounds and dollars as international reserves, since they would no longer be convertible into gold at a fixed rate. Proponents of flexible exchange rates argue, however, that the need for international reserves would also be much reduced. Countries need large international reserves only because they adhere stubbornly to fixed exchange rates despite fluctuations in the equilibrium value of their currencies.

Theoretical discussion of this proposal has focused mainly on the issue of whether speculation on the foreign exchange markets would have a stabilizing or a destabilizing effect. Neither side has yet established its position beyond doubt. In any event, the central bankers have the last word, and they believe strongly that the present system is more orderly and workable. So the major trading nations are unlikely to experiment with floating rates.

If these things are not going to be done, what is going to be done? A number of things already have been done. The U.S. balance-of-payments position has been brought under firmer control. This was necessary to strengthen confidence in the long-run stability of the dollar. The lending capacity of the IMF has been considerably enlarged by increases in the members' quotas, and the United States has recently begun to use this source of credit for the first time. Foreign central banks have been willing to accept a considerable volume of special nonmarketable U.S. securities in place of dollar bank balances, which reduces our liquid liabilities to other countries.

Within the inner circle of "the Ten" (the six Common Market countries plus Britain, Canada, the United States, and Japan) there is now close consultation among Treasury and central bank officials. This goes on at the IMF governors' meetings in Washington, the quarterly Paris meetings of OECD working party number 3 on monetary and payments problems, the monthly dinners of central bank governors in Switzerland, and in frequent telephone discussions during periods of monetary unrest. This process of almost continuous consultation has come to be known as "mutual surveillance." An important part of it is informal "swap agreements" under which one central bank can borrow foreign currencies from the others up to an agreed limit on very short notice. Within a half hour of President Kennedy's assassination, the New York Federal Reserve posted an offer to supply any amount of foreign currencies in exchange for dollars at established rates. This checked possible speculation against the dollar, and little foreign currency was actually called for. In the most recent sterling crisis, several billion dollars was made available overnight to the Bank of England by a few telephone calls.

Despite these advances, there is a widespread feeling among both scholars and practitioners that more needs to be done. The U.S. Treasury in 1965 lent its powerful support to this view, and Secretary Fowler endorsed the idea of a full-scale international conference on monetary reform. Such a conference, which would be the first since 1944, may quite possibly be held within the next year or two.

The proposals for monetary reconstruction are too varied and too technical to be discussed in detail. Most of them center on creation of a new kind of international reserve asset, which we shall call simply "IMF money." Whether units of this money were called "bancors," as Lord Keynes proposed in 1944, or were given some other exotic name does not really matter. The idea is that each country would hold part of its reserves in the form of deposits, designated in units of IMF money, on the books of the IMF. Country A could draw a check against its IMF deposit and use this to make payments to country B. No gold, dollars, or anything else need change hands. This is, of course, the way in which one U.S. bank meets its net obligations to another through transfers on the books of the Federal Reserve System. So the proposal is that the IMF should become, at least to a limited extent, a central bank *for* central banks, a "world central bank."

IMF money would be convertible into national currencies or into gold at fixed rates. Even so, it would take time for national central banks to consider this new kind of asset "as good as gold." But they might gradually become willing to hold a growing proportion of their reserves in this form and a smaller proportion in gold and key currencies. They could increase their IMF deposits at any time by depositing gold with the Fund. The Fund might encourage this by paying interest on deposits, whereas gold holdings yield no return. Over the years, then, the world's monetary gold might be concentrated increasingly in the Fund rather than in national hands.

The more ambitious plans visualize the Fund as engaging in open market operations in the various member countries. It might, for example, buy British securities in London, paying for them by a check drawn on itself. This check, when deposited with the Bank of England and redeposited with the Fund, would raise the Bank of England's international reserves. Thus both the total quantity and the distribution of international reserves could be adjusted deliberately to the needs of a growing world economy. A variant of this idea is that new IMF money might be put into circulation by the Fund buying bonds from the World Bank, which would use the funds for loans to the less developed countries. The money would trickle back quite rapidly in payments to the developed countries, who would redeposit with the Fund and strengthen their own reserves; but meanwhile the "first-round spending" would have contributed to economic development.

The advantage of establishing IMF money as a new reserve asset is, first, that it would relieve pressure on the pound and the dollar. The dollar would doubtless continue as the main key currency, and foreign private holdings of dollars would continue to rise over time; but its role as a reserve currency would be reduced. Both for this reason and because the IMF's lending capacity would be greater, the danger of a run on the dollar would diminish. This would permit the United States to give greater weight to domestic economic objectives and to worry less about short-term fluctuations in the balance of payments.

Second, the rate at which new IMF money is created could be adjusted to meet the need for rising international reserves. World liquidity would no longer be dependent on the vagaries of the gold industry plus the vicissitudes of the U.S. balance of payments. The desirable rate of increase in monetary reserves could not be determined by any automatic formula. Experimentation and judgment would be necessary. But the central bank governors who control the IMF have been making such judgments in their respective countries for a long time, and could doubtless learn new tricks at the international level.

While there is widespread support for movement in this direction, there is disagreement over such practical questions as: (1) How should IMF money come into existence at the outset? Should part of the IMF members' past contributions of gold and national currencies be converted into this form? Should they be asked to make new contributions, receiving IMF deposits in return? (2) Who will control the rate at which additional IMF money is created in the future? The members of "the Ten" will doubtless want to keep this key power under their control. But shall action be based on unanimity, or a two-thirds vote, or what? (3) Once the rate of new reserve creation is decided, how shall the funds be put into circulation? Through open market operations in the developed countries? Through World Bank loans to the less developed countries? Or in some other way?

Much technical discussion is in prospect before any decisions are taken; but it would not be surprising to see action on this front within the next few years. Even so, the strengthened IMF will scarcely amount to a "world central bank." The Bank of England, the Bank of France, and the Federal Reserve System have a national political authority behind them, and there is some consensus on national economic objectives. But there is no world political authority and no clear consensus on world economic objectives. Decisions by a reformed IMF will continue to depend on consensus and compromise among national monetary authorities, in whom real power resides and who are bound to consider mainly how any change will affect their own economy.

SUMMARY

1. International trading and financial relations require a *foreign exchange market*, in which the currency of one country can be converted into that of another. The chief operators in this market are large private banks and central (government) banks. An *exchange rate* is the price of one currency in terms of another.

2. A country's foreign transactions are summarized in its *balance of payments*. When changes in gold holdings and in obligations to foreign monetary authorities are included as balancing items, receipts and payments must always be equal. But the fact that the statement balances says nothing about whether the balance is satisfactory.

3. In a free exchange market, the price of (say) pounds in terms of dollars would be determined by supply and demand in the usual way and would vary from day to day. But since frequent variation is inconvenient, governments usually undertake to *stabilize* the price of their currency. They do this just as the U.S. government stabilizes the price of wheat—by a standing offer to buy or sell at a fixed price.

4. During the fifties and early sixties the United States has had sizable deficits in its "basic balance" of payments. The dollar holdings of foreign central banks and business concerns have risen steadily, and some countries have chosen to convert part of their dollars into gold, leading to an outflow of gold from U.S. reserves. By the end of 1964, we had about $16 billion of gold against $25 billion of dollar obligations to foreigners.

5. This has produced efforts to reduce the U.S. balance-of-payments deficit including: reduction of the outflow of dollars associated with foreign aid and military activities; maintenance of higher U.S. interest rates than would have prevailed otherwise; an Interest Equalization Tax to reduce the income advantage of buying foreign securities; and efforts to persuade U.S. banks and other companies to reduce their lending and investment abroad.

6. The major national currencies are convertible into each other and into gold at fixed rates. To be certain of making good on this obligation, each central bank must maintain substantial reserves. At present, about two thirds of world monetary reserves are in gold, one third in pounds and dollars. Because the supply of monetary gold rises slowly and erratically, the proportion of reserves held in key currencies has been increasing.

7. The existing system has been criticized on the ground that the rate of increase in world monetary reserves is entirely accidental and bears no relation to the needs of a growing volume of world trade and finance. It requires, in a sense, continuing payments deficits in the United States and the United Kingdom to increase the supply of dollars and pounds; yet at the same time these deficits are considered a sign of weakness. The necessity of limiting them acts as a constraint on domestic economic policies in Britain and the United States. There is also the background possibility of heavy gold withdrawals from the United States, which might collapse the whole system as happened in 1931.

8. Steps have already been taken to reduce this danger, through "swap agreements" among the leading central banks and through increases in the lending capacity of the IMF. Proposals for further action center on creation of a new type of reserve asset, checking accounts on the books of the IMF, or "IMF money." This would have a fixed gold value, be transferable from country to country in settlement of international balances, and would supplement gold and dollars in central bank reserves.

DISCUSSION QUESTIONS

1. What is an *exchange rate?* What is the *foreign exchange market?* Who are the main demanders and suppliers in this market?

2. What are the main kinds of transaction which create a *demand* for dollars by people in other countries? What transactions create a *supply* of dollars to other countries?

3. If the balance-of-payments statement always balances, how can a country have a balance-of-payments problem?

4. Around 1950 there was much talk about a permanent "dollar shortage" in the world. By 1960 there was talk of a "dollar surplus" or "dollar glut." What do these terms mean? Why was there such a change between 1950 and 1960?

5. Some economists believe that exchange rates should be determined in a free market and should fluctuate with demand and supply changes. What would be the advantages and disadvantages of such an arrangement?

6. If a government tries to maintain the official value of its currency above the free market value, what controls become necessary? What are the economic consequences?

7. Different people have blamed different items in the U.S. balance-of-payments statement for our continuing deficits. Are any of these items particularly open to criticism or blame?

8. There has recently been a drive to induce U.S. companies voluntarily to reduce their direct investment abroad. Is this a desirable line of policy?

9. "From an international standpoint, it is quite undesirable for the United States to reduce its balance-of-payments deficit. This would dry up the supply of dollars which have recently supplied most of the increased liquidity for the world economy." Discuss.

10. "It is ridiculous that the price of gold should be the one price in the world which has not risen since 1933. A doubling of the dollar price of gold would immediately double the world's monetary reserves and solve the whole liquidity problem." Do you agree? Explain.

11. What would be the practical effects of adopting the proposal for "IMF money" as a new kind of reserve asset?

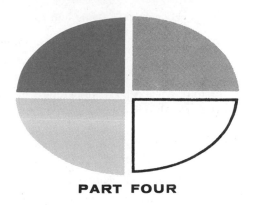

PART FOUR

THE ECONOMICS OF

GROWTH

There's nothing constant in the universe
All ebb and flow, and every shape that's born
Bears in its womb the seeds of change.

OVID, *Metamorphoses*

Yet all experience is an arch wherethrough
Gleams that untraveled world, whose margin
fades
For ever and for ever, as we move.

ALFRED, LORD TENNYSON

ONE OF THE great themes of economics concerns the growth of national output over the long run. This problem has been termed "the nature and causes of the wealth of nations" (Adam Smith), "the theory of economic development" (Joseph Schumpeter), "the conditions of economic progress" (Colin Clark). It is both more and less than the problem of economic history: more in that it strives for general principles, while the historian usually concentrates on the unique and particular; less in that it focuses on a few economic relationships and does not profess to explain the wealth of concrete experience.

If economic growth is so important, why have we left it to the end of the book? Partly because analysis of growth requires all the principles

765

of microeconomics and macroeconomics developed in earlier chapters; and partly because it is a frontier problem of modern economics. Since one purpose of an introductory course is to carry students beyond the bounds of accepted knowledge into areas of uncertainty and debate, the growth problem forms a fitting climax to our discussion.

What is economic growth? It might be defined as the rate of increase in GNP. But if one is interested in the welfare of the population, it is more significant to look at changes in output *per capita*. Rising output per capita is the distinctive feature of modern economic progress; and the term economic growth will be used hereafter in this sense.

Economists do not assert that economic growth is "good" or that it makes people happier. It is quite possible that the average American of 1860 was happier than the average American of 1960. In this area, as in others, the role of economics is strictly instrumental. We do not consider whether a nation *should* aim at rapid material development. We focus rather on the question: *If* a nation chooses this as an objective, what is the best way to go about it? What conditions are favorable to economic progress and what are the main obstacles to be overcome?

Nor are economists simpleminded enough to suppose that the rate of growth depends only on economic considerations. True, in the following chapters we shall concentrate on economic quantities, because they can be defined, measured, and reasoned about in a precise way. But this should not be misinterpreted as meaning that other things are unimportant. The political organization of a country, the system of property ownership, the relations among social classes, the pattern of family organization and child rearing, the values to which individuals are attached and the incentives to which they respond—all these have important consequences. But for most of these things we still have no satisfactory scheme of analysis; and in any event economists have no special competence in these areas.

Analysis of economic growth starts from the macroeconomic concepts of Part Three. We use the same apparatus of total demand, total supply, consumption and investment schedules, and so on. The national income approach provides an overall framework for measuring and analyzing economic change. But there is one fundamental difference. Until now we have taken the determinants of productive capacity as given—the labor supply, the stock of capital, the state of technical knowledge, forms of business organization, and so on. But as we shift to a telescopic view of change over decades and generations, all these things become variables. Labor supply is growing, the capital stock is increasing, the distribution of capital and labor among sectors of the economy is changing, technical change is producing drastic revision of products and methods of production. These things, instead of being taken for granted, must now be explained. This is what makes growth analysis both difficult and endlessly fascinating.

We do not at present have principles of economic growth applicable at all times and places. A few ideas have quite general usefulness (Chapter 28). But beyond these the growth problem looks quite different in the industrial capitalist countries (Chapter 29), the communist countries (Chapter 30), and the poorer agricultural countries (Chapters 31–32). The poor countries are given more space than the other two groups partly because there are more of them, partly because their efforts to shake off age-old poverty have attracted worldwide interest. The contributions that the richer countries are making to economic development, and the question of what the United States should do in this direction, are examined in Chapter 33.

In the Western industrial countries, economic growth can be taken for granted. Some of these economies have been expanding continuously for two centuries or more. Thus the main question becomes the *rate* at which growth will occur. National economies show substantial differences in growth rates, whether one looks backward for a century or whether one looks simply at experience since 1945. What are the reasons for these differences? Could the slowly growing countries accelerate their growth rate by changes in economic policy?

The growth rate of the same country also varies from time to time. Oak trees grow more slowly as they grow older. So do dogs, horses, and humans. What about national economies? It is sometimes asserted that the growth rate of a "mature economy" is bound to slow down gradually. On this basis it would be natural for the United States and the United Kingdom to be growing currently at a less rapid rate than more recently industrialized countries such as Italy or Japan. But is the mature economy hypothesis correct? Does it rest on solid economic reasoning or merely on a poetic analogy with biological processes?

In the communist countries, economic growth does not just happen through a myriad of independent decisions. The state planning commission sets output targets and imposes a program to achieve these targets. Communist leaders argue that this makes it possible to achieve higher growth rates than those prevailing in the capitalist world, and to do this consistently year after year.

For the U.S.S.R. there are production records reaching from 1928, when central planning was first applied, to the present time. These statistics have been thoroughly examined, revised, and analyzed by Western scholars. Thus we can usefully raise such questions as: What has been the rate of economic growth in the U.S.S.R., and how has it varied from time to time? What accounts for the relatively high Soviet growth rate? Does it really demonstrate the superior efficiency of central economic planning? Is the same rate of growth likely to be maintained in the future?

The poor countries of Asia, Africa, and Latin America present a third dimension of the growth problem. In most of these countries the institutional prerequisites for economic growth are not yet firmly established. Output per head is stationary or rising slowly and precariously. In many countries hard-won increases in output threaten to be swamped by an even more rapid increase in population. The central problem is how to *initiate* a process of sustained growth rather than how to sustain or accelerate a well-established growth pattern.

Suppose a country is able to establish institutional conditions favorable to economic growth. What next? Strategic issues of development policy must be resolved in one direction or another. How severely should government squeeze consumers' living standards in order to raise the level of investment? Is industrialization the main key to economic progress? If so, what types of industry should be given priority? Can agriculture be taken for granted meanwhile or is agricultural improvement an essential part of the development process? In countries with a large surplus of underemployed labor, how can this labor best be drawn into productive uses?

The wealthier capitalist and communist countries stand ready with advice and assistance. Each group urges the poor countries to choose its own path—the path of economic decentralization and limited government or the path of one-party government and central economic planning. Each group provides a growing amount of loans and gifts to the poor countries, intended partly to influence them in its direction. This politico-economic competition is now the central fact in international relations. One must expect over the next half century a slow, inexorable, eventually decisive struggle of East and West for the allegiance of the countries of the South.

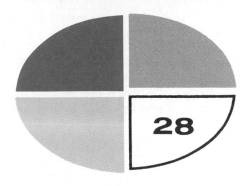

Theories of Economic Growth

The rule is, jam tomorrow and jam yesterday—but never jam today.
Through the Looking Glass

"I wish you wouldn't squeeze so," said the Dormouse. "I can hardly breathe."
"I can't help it," said Alice, very meekly: "I'm growing."
Alice's Adventures in Wonderland

WHY DO WE SAY *theories* instead of *the theory?* Because at the moment no one theory of growth commands universal acceptance. The growth problem takes different forms in different parts of the world—the industrial capitalist countries, the communist countries, the less developed countries. A great variety of ideas has been advanced, aimed at answering a considerable variety of questions. The time for a grand synthesis may arrive eventually; but that day is not yet.

Economic growth is a very old problem in economics. It was the central concern of the English classical economists. Ricardo in particular had a well-developed theory of why growth occurs and of why it must end in the stagnation of the "stationary state." Marx, who learned his economics largely from Ricardo, had a different growth theory, also predicting catastrophe but by another route. We must examine his ideas, both because of their intellectual interest and because of the wide influence they exert throughout the world.

Modern growth theory for developed countries subdivides into two branches. The "neoclassical" or supply-oriented branch is concerned with the growth of output capacity. Key names here are Hicks, Meade, Phelps, Solow. The "neo-Keynesian" or demand-oriented branch is concerned with the conditions under which this expanding capacity will be fully utilized, i.e., with the problem of full employment over time. Harrod, Domar, Duesenberry, and Fellner are among those who have taken an interest in this problem.

Growth theory relevant to the less developed countries is still in its infancy. But Lewis, Ranis, Fei, and others have contributed ideas about the development of a "surplus labor" economy in which the key problem is to absorb unused labor in an expanding industrial sector. This work is "classical" in the sense of considering problems which were familiar to Smith, Ricardo, and Mill and also in drawing heavily on their ideas.

The chapter will try, in short, to illustrate both the variety and the elements of continuity in thinking about growth over the past century and a half.

CLASSICAL GROWTH THEORY: THE ''MAGNIFICENT DYNAMICS''

Adam Smith called his great work the *wealth* of nations. By this he meant what we would now call the *income* of nations. The book is about the increase of national income over time, which is to say that it is about economic growth.

Almost 200 years after publication, this book reads like a modern treatise. It defines GNP and NNP much as we would do today. It has a complete theory of how labor and capital supplies increase over time. The explanation of rising national output is quite modern, except that Smith attached little weight to technical progress. And there is shrewd analysis of precisely the policy issues being discussed today in the less developed countries: how capital should be allocated among different branches of industry; the basic role of agriculture; the importance of transportation, education and other things which we would now call "infrastructure investment"; the role of foreign trade in broadening a country's markets; and the way in which growing production to serve an expanding market can reduce unit production costs.

Classical reasoning reached its fullest and most precise expression 40 years later, with the publication in 1817 of David Ricardo's *Principles of Political Economy and Taxation.* By a skillful simplification of the actual British economy, Ricardo divided the population into landowners, manufacturers, and workers, who supply land, capital, and labor for production. The key question is how the returns to the three factors, and consequently the incomes of their owners, will change over time in a growing economy.

The answer turns on two pillars of the Ricardian system: the law of *value* or *prices;* and the principle of *rent,* which derives from diminishing returns in agriculture. Ricardo held a cost of production theory of value. The price of a good, relative to other goods, is governed by the amount of labor required for its production. This labor is both direct and indirect, since it includes the labor embodied in machinery and other capital goods used in making the product. Differing kinds of labor were taken care of by providing that labor must be summed up in some homogeneous unit—say, hours of unskilled labor equivalent. Ricardo also recognized interest as a legitimate cost. He argued, however, that the amount of capital required, and hence the interest charges, in each line of production would be proportionate to the amount of labor used.[1] So the total cost of each good, and the price which must be charged for it, would still be *proportional* to its labor cost.

The Ricardian concept of rent was described in Chapter 11. The central idea is that agriculture is subject to diminishing returns or *increasing costs*. As population grows, the demand for food rises and more food must be produced. But this can be done only by bringing poorer land into cultivation or working existing land more intensively. In either case, if we assume no technical progress in agriculture, the amount of (say) wheat produced by a unit of labor and capital will fall. Or, putting this in reverse, the cost of producing a bushel of wheat will rise. But since the price of wheat depends on its cost of production, the price of wheat must also rise, and landowners' incomes will rise along with it.

In Figure 1, SS is a long-run supply curve for wheat. When production is at OQ, the production cost and price of a bushel of wheat is OP. Suppose now that because of population growth, wheat production is pushed up to OQ_1. Then the price of wheat rises to OP_1. In the first situation, total rent received by landowners is the triangular area SPR (total proceeds from wheat sales of $OPRQ$, minus production costs of $OSRQ$). At the higher production level OQ_1, landlords' incomes rise to SP_1R_1. Economic growth, unaccompanied by technical progress in agriculture, means a continuing enrichment of the landowning class. This prospect depressed Smith and Ricardo, who viewed the landlords largely as drones—given to luxury consumption, with a low propensity to save, and little interest in improving agricultural methods. The denunciations of landlordism in less developed countries today might have been lifted directly from English classics.

Now what will happen to wages in a growing economy? Ricardo distinguished the *natural rate* of wages from the *market rate*. The *natural rate* is a minimum level of subsistence. It can be interpreted also as the rate which would hold population and labor force constant. This natural

---

[1] This is not really as odd as it may sound. In an age of relatively simple and inexpensive machinery, the classical writers regarded capital as consisting mainly of the circulating capital required to finance the wage bill (crudely, stored-up food handed over to the workers engaged in making textiles or some other product). This clearly will be proportionate to the amount of labor used.

rate of wages depends on the cost of necessities, i.e., on the amount of labor required to produce enough food to keep a worker alive.

The market rate of wages, on the other hand, is regulated by labor supply and demand. Its movement over time depends on the relative rate of increase in labor and capital supplies. Under favorable conditions, as in a new country with plenty of fertile land, the market rate of wages can rise above the natural rate and stay above it for a long time. Following Malthus, however, Ricardo argued that workers would respond to these abnormally high wages by having more children, and more of these children would be able to survive to maturity. This accelerated increase

Growing Population Means Rising Food Prices and Higher Rents for Landowners

FIGURE 1. The food supply curve SS rises because of diminishing returns in agriculture. As population increases, food production is pushed up from, say OQ to OQ$_1$. The production cost of the last unit of food, and hence the necessary level of food prices, rises from OP to OP$_1$. Landlords' total rent increases from SRP to SR$_1$P$_1$. And this is a one-way street. Output is always moving to the right, landlords are always getting richer.

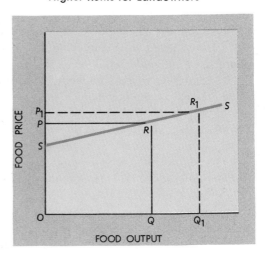

FOOD OUTPUT

in labor supply would force the market wage rate back toward the natural or subsistence level. This gloomy prognosis was dubbed "the iron law of wages," and it did much to earn economics its label of "the dismal science."

The most basic proposition, however, is that the *natural rate of wages will itself be rising over the course of time.* Because of diminishing returns in agriculture, the price of a bushel of wheat is rising steadily. Hence the value of labor, which depends on the cost of producing and sustaining a laborer, must also be rising. So the wage rate per unit of labor must rise over the long run.

What is happening to the manufacturers and to the return on their capital, which the classical writers called "profit"? The price of manufactured products has not risen, because there has been no change in the amount of labor required per unit of product. The manufacturers, then, are squeezed between a constant price level and a rising wage level, and the rate of profit must fall steadily. It could conceivably fall to zero. But somewhere before this, the classics argued, the incentive to saving would have vanished and capital accumulation would cease. The capital stock would remain constant, and the interest rate would remain constant at a low but positive level.

Thus we arrive at the stationary state. Capital supply no longer increases because the interest incentive is inadequate. Labor supply does not increase because wages are at the subsistence level which just suffices to maintain a stable population. Land cannot increase by definition. So there we are, with the economy stagnating for the rest of eternity.

Before asking what went wrong with this prognosis, let's look at the special twist which Marx gave to the doctrine a generation later.

CLASSICAL PESSIMISM: THE MARXIAN VERSION

Marx was a classical economist, in the sense that he adopted much of Ricardo's theoretical system, and in the sense that he was interested mainly in long-term growth. But in other ways he was quite different from his predecessors. He focused on *industry,* with agriculture very much in the background. He discarded the main props of classical pessimism: Malthusian population theory, which he labeled "a slander on mankind"; and diminishing returns from agriculture, which by 1850 was being rendered obsolete through cheap food from overseas. Yet he managed to reach thoroughly pessimistic conclusions by a different route.

Marx was concerned also with some modern problems scarcely mentioned in the classical literature. He denied the necessity of full employment and emphasized the importance of business cycles. He even noted that these seemed to run about 10 years in length, and speculated that this might have something to do with the average life of textile machinery. He was concerned with the organization of industry, which he thought would tend toward ever greater concentration in a few giant concerns. And his economic analysis was embedded in a much broader theory of historical evolution.

Marx's theory of wages and prices comes directly from Ricardo. Labor, like all other commodities, is valued at its cost of production. The value of labor, i.e., the wage rate, depends on the labor time required to produce the worker's subsistence.

The price of any product can be broken down into three parts: (a) the direct labor used in its production, valued at the subsistence wage; (b) the indirect labor embodied in its production, consisting of raw materials plus depreciation of the capital equipment used; (c) an extra amount, the classical "profit," which Marx termed "surplus value." Unlike Ricardo, however, Marx did not consider this a legitimate or necessary cost of production. It is a pure surplus extracted from the worker by the capitalist.

Put a bit crudely, the surplus arises in this way: suppose that in 4 hours a cotton-mill worker produces a net value product (after deducting materials, depreciation, etc.) equal to his subsistence wage. In actuality, however, he works 10 hours. His product during the last 6 hours is "surplus value." Note that the worker is not being cheated by his employer. He is being paid the subsistence wage, which is all that the market entitles him to receive. He is being exploited, not by the avarice of the individual capitalist, but by the mechanism of the system.

Each capitalist is interested, however, in raising surplus value as much as possible. How can this be done? One way would be to work people for longer hours; but there are physical limits to doing this. The other possibility is to increase each worker's productive power by providing him with more equipment. Hence the drive toward mechanization, which plays a key role in Marx's system. This mechanization is financed by saving and reinvesting profits. Marx believed that capitalists were driven by an intense, almost blind, zeal for capital accumulation.

Mechanization tends to produce increased industrial concentration —"the large capitals drive out the small." Marx's reasoning implies that optimum scale in many branches of manufacturing is very large, and that concerns which expand fastest toward this optimum can squeeze out smaller, higher-cost competitors. The end result must be monopoly or oligopoly. (As noted earlier, this is one respect in which Soviet economic planners seem really to follow Marx. They seem to believe that the long-run average cost curve never turns upward, which leads to a policy of "giantism" in both agriculture and industry.)

Mechanization also displaces labor and builds up the "reserve army of the unemployed." Unemployment plays the role of the Malthusian population theory which Marx rejects. Competition of unemployed workers for jobs maintains a constant downward pressure on the wage level and leads to growing "immiserization of labor." This is a bit puzzling. If workers' wages are already at subsistence level when the curtain rises, how can they fall any further? Some writers have maintained, indeed, that Marx meant only that labor's *share of national income* would fall over time. But such authorities as Schumpeter and Fellner agree that Marx committed himself to a declining level of real wages. This tendency could be postponed, however, by a flow of capital abroad to exploit colonial areas (leading to the Marxist theory of imperialist struggles for foreign territory).

The most puzzling feature of Marx's system is the assertion that the rate of profit will also fall over time. As a matter of arithmetic, this is certainly possible. *Total* profit in the system is rising. But the amount of capital in use is also rising. So, depending on which rises fastest, the rate of profit on capital *could* fall. But why *must* it fall? Note that the classical reasons—land scarcity, rising food prices, and rising wages—are not present in Marx's system. Borrowing modern concepts, one might argue that, if the marginal productivity curve of capital remains constant, a rising capital stock means moving farther and farther down on this curve with a consequent decline in the rate of return. But this would be to ignore technical progress and economies of scale, in which Marx apparently believed.

In any event, Marx did conclude that the rate of profit must fall. Now the capitalists become really frantic. To keep *total* profit rising, they must accumulate capital even faster than before. So more reinvestment, mechanization, concentration of industry, displacement of labor, unemployment, and falling wages in an endless circle leading to disaster—or to liberation. The millions of miserable, propertyless workers eventually rise up and overthrow the tiny minority of capitalists, who have become too few to defend themselves. "The expropriators are expropriated."

It is platitudinous to observe that this sort of Marxian revolution has not occurred, and very likely never will occur, in an advanced industrial country. The appeal of modern Marxism lies mainly in underdeveloped agricultural countries, so different from the Britain in which Marx lived and wrote. But in any oligarchic society, the apocalyptic vision of the masses rising to overthrow their oppressors retains strong popular appeal.

INTERMISSION: ONE CENTURY

Historical hindsight always has twenty-twenty vision. The pessimism of early nineteenth-century writers now appears quite myopic. The classical food bottleneck did not materialize, partly because of the inflow of food from overseas, but also because of agricultural progress at home. Real wages did rise, but technical progress was also raising productivity, so profit margins did not suffer. The new industrial system was racked by recurrent depressions, but there was no tendency toward a long-run increase in unemployment. Rising living standards brought a gradual spread of birth control methods, and the Malthusian spectre disappeared.

By the late nineteenth century, then, economics had become the cheerful science. Marshall's *Principles of Economics* (First Edition, 1890) is suffused with an optimistic faith in built-in progress. Saving, resulting mainly from "family affection," can be counted on to produce a rapid growth in the capital stock. The quality of the labor force is being raised steadily by education, technical training, and industrial experience. Manufacturing, now the largest sector in the economy, is generally subject to increasing returns. Even in agriculture, decreasing returns can be largely or wholly offset by technical progress. So on the whole, Marshall concluded, "an increase in numbers is generally accompanied by a more than proportionate increase of collective efficiency."

With this cheerful conclusion the whole subject of economic growth was laid on the shelf. There was, in fact, no major book on the subject between 1870 and 1950. Schumpeter's *Theorie der Wirtschaftlichen Entwicklung* (*Theory of Economic Development*, 1911) was misnamed. Its content is better indicated by the subtitle, "An inquiry into profits, capital, credit, interest, and the business cycle." It is essentially a business cycle theory, and while Schumpeter's concepts of the entrepreneur and of innovation have settled into the literature of economics, the book is not really about economic development in either the classical or modern sense.

The revival of interest in growth after 1945 was casual and in a sense accidental. It came about as an offshoot of post-Keynesian reasoning about economic equilibrium. As we saw in Part Three, the levels of saving and investment are closely linked. For the economy to operate at full employment, the amount that people wish to save from their full-employment incomes must be offset by intended investment. If this condition is met, the economy will be in equilibrium at full capacity. All is well for the time being.

But the story takes a new turn when we ask what is necessary for capacity operation to continue in the future. We must consider that *investment this year means greater capacity next year*. So next year's output must be larger than this year's if full employment is to be maintained. How much larger? What are the necessary conditions for smooth expansion of an economy over time? Pursuit of these questions led to intensive work on growth theory during the 1950's and 1960's.

GROWTH THEORY FOR THE DEVELOPED ECONOMY

Most of the recent theorizing about growth relates to the United States and other developed countries. The problem is not to turn a stagnant economy into a growing economy. Growth is already underway, and the only problem is to determine how fast it will be. It is usually assumed that pure competition prevails in all product and factor markets, so that each factor is paid its marginal product and earns the same return in all uses. This assumption is not so unrealistic for the American economy as it would be in a less developed country.

Our concern here is with *supply-oriented* theories, which try to explain the growth of an economy's productive capacity. If this capacity is to be fully utilized, aggregate demand must also grow at an appropriate rate. But that is another story, a story which we touched on in Chapter 26. We shall now assume that, with monetary and fiscal policy tools at our command, reasonably full employment can be maintained most of the time. So if capacity grows at a certain rate, output will grow at about the same rate over any extended period. And the concern here is with *long periods* rather than with year-to-year change.

What determines how fast capacity grows? This depends partly on the rate of increase in the factors of production and partly on how the factors cooperate in production. Here there are two main possibilities— fixed factor proportions and flexible factor proportions—which lead to two different kinds of theory.

Fixed Factor Proportions

The simplest kind of theory, associated with the names of Professor Evsey Domar of M.I.T. and Sir Roy Harrod of Oxford, assumes that there is a constant relation between the amount of capital in an economy and its output capacity. Call capital K, output Y, and the constant capital-output ratio β. Then $K = \beta Y$. If in a particular case β is 3, then each addition of $3 to the capital stock will raise output capacity by $1. If we indicate *increases* in capital and output by ΔK and ΔY, it follows that

$$\Delta K = \beta \Delta Y .$$

Now how fast will the economy grow? The increase in capital stock each year is simply the amount of net investment during the year; and if the economy is in equilibrium, this must be equal to the amount of saving. If we use s to indicate the proportion of national income saved each year, then:

$$\Delta K = I = sY .$$

From these relations we see that

$$\beta \Delta Y = sY$$

or
$$\frac{\beta \Delta Y}{Y} = s \quad \text{or} \quad \frac{\Delta Y}{Y} = \frac{s}{\beta}.$$

But $\frac{\Delta Y}{Y}$ is simply the rate of increase in output, or the growth rate. So we conclude that the growth rate depends on the savings rate divided by the capital-output ratio. For example, if s is 12 percent and β is 3, the growth rate will be 4 percent per year.

This simple arithmetic for a time had quite an intoxicating effect on development planners in the less developed countries. Suppose the population of Ruritania is growing at 3 percent a year. The government decides that to avoid discontent and give convincing evidence of progress, per capita income must rise by 2 percent a year. So the rate of increase in GNP must be 5 percent. How much investment will be necessary each year to hit the target? Pulling out of the air a magic figure, say 3, for the value of β, and applying our formula, we conclude that $s = 15$. The economy must save and invest 15 percent of its output each year if the growth target is to be attained.

Life is of course not that simple. The capital-output ratio can and does vary considerably from country to country and time to time, depending on the sectors of the economy to which capital is directed and the skill with which it is used. Taken at face value, the Harrod-Domar formula would imply that *only* capital is productive and that other factors—specifically, labor—make no contribution to output. This does not seem very plausible.

There is one way, however, by which the formula might be made more plausible. Suppose labor is viewed as productive, but that labor is always needed in *fixed proportion* to capital. An extra $100 of factory equipment always requires one additional worker—no more, no less—to operate it. Suppose also that there is surplus labor available in the economy, which is often held to be true in the less developed countries. Then as more capital is built, more of this surplus labor can be brought into employment. If capital increases by 5 percent a year, employment will rise 5 percent a year; and if we assume that the economy yields constant returns to scale, output will rise 5 percent a year.

This can go on, however, only as long as surplus labor is available. When all the surplus labor has been absorbed, employment can rise only as fast as the labor force. If population and labor force are rising at, say, 2 percent a year, K and Y cannot rise any faster than this. Investment will have to slow down. This is not a cheerful prospect, because it would mean no rise in per capita output, no possibility of higher living standards.

We can get out of this box, however, by bringing in two considerations which have been omitted so far: flexible factor proportions and the possibility of technical progress.

Flexible Factor Proportions, No Technical Change

Let us examine the first of these, continuing for the moment to assume that technology is given and constant. There are no improvements in products, methods of production, power sources, or anything else. The same products are produced in the same old way, year after year.

Under these conditions, output can grow only through addition of labor and capital inputs. Note that, in this modern schema, land has disappeared as a separate factor. In statistical analyses of economic growth, land is usually lumped with capital. The de-emphasis of land reflects the fact that in the advanced countries agriculture now provides only a small fraction of output and employment; and that technical progress in agriculture has been rapid enough to remove any fear of land scarcity. In the United States we actually have land surplus, in the sense that the total cultivated area has been shrinking for several decades, while we continue to produce more agricultural products than we can readily market.

The relation between labor and capital inputs and the resulting output is shown by the *production function* for the economy:

$$Y = f(K, L) .$$

This is usually written in the form

$$Y = V K^a L^b ,$$

where Y, K, and L have the usual meanings, V is a constant, and a and b are constant fractions.

This kind of production function has several characteristics:

1. The fraction a shows the effect on output of a small increase in the amount of capital used. If K increases by r percent, then Y will increase by ar percent. Similarly, if the quantity of labor L increases by r percent, Y will rise by br percent.

Suppose both K and L increase by, say, 1 percent. What will happen to Y? The answer depends on the values of a and b. One simple and convenient case is that in which it is assumed that $a + b = 1$. Then a 1 percent increase in both factors will produce a 1 percent increase in output. The economy shows *constant returns to scale*. This is the Cobb-Douglas case referred to in Chapter 10, and it is the case we shall consider here.

2. If, as we shall also assume, labor and capital markets are purely competitive, so that the price of each factor corresponds to its marginal product, then a and b have another interesting characteristic: *a is the capital share of national income, while b is the share of labor.*[2] Since $a + b = 1$, the two shares precisely exhaust the available income.

3. Labor and capital, instead of being required in fixed proportions, are now substitutable for each other. Labor can increase faster than capital, or vice versa. Capital is "putty with which any number can play."

---

[2] The proof is as follows: for the Cobb-Douglas case, the production function can be written $Y = V K^a L^{1-a}$. Differentiating this with respect to K yields the marginal product of K,

$$MP_K = \frac{dY}{dK} = V a K^{a-1} L^{1-a} .$$

The total return to capital is its price, which must equal its marginal productivity, times the amount of capital in use, i.e., $MP_K \cdot K$. And capital's share of national income is $\dfrac{MP_K \cdot K}{Y}$. Substituting the values of MP_K and Y, we find that capital's share is

$$\frac{MP_K \cdot K}{Y} = \frac{V a K^{a-1} L^{1-a} \cdot K}{V K^a L^{1-a}}$$
$$= \frac{V a K^a L^{1-a}}{V K^a L^{1-a}}$$
$$= a .$$

This stamps the present theory as a long-run theory, since only in the long run is it plausible to treat capital as fully malleable.

While labor and capital are substitutable, they are not perfectly substitutable (in which case they would be a single factor). The ease with which one can be substituted for the other is expressed in the *elasticity of substitution*. The Cobb-Douglas function assumes that this elasticity is constant for all combinations of L and K, and that it has the value of 1. In common-sense terms, this means that, if the ratio $\frac{K}{L}$ rises by 1 percent, the ratio $\frac{MP_K}{MP_L}$ falls by 1 percent. A *relative increase* of capital as compared to labor (the standard case in a wealthy industrial country) will be precisely offset by a *relative decline* in the marginal productivity (and hence the market price) of capital. It follows that *capital's share of national income* will remain unchanged. In fact, whatever the relative rates of increase in factor supplies, the shares of the factors in national income will never vary. Both a and b are constants.

Let's go back now to the function:

$$Y = V K^a L^b .$$

We are interested in the rate of increase in Y which will result from specified rates of increase in the factors. Let's call these rates of increase y, k, and l respectively. By some simple transformations which you can take on faith, it can be shown that

$$y = a \cdot k + b \cdot l . \tag{1}$$

This seems reasonable enough. The growth rate of output, y, depends on the rates of increase in labor and capital. But it does not depend *equally* on the two factors. Each factor is weighted by its relative importance in production, as indicated by the share of national income it receives.

Suppose, for example, that in the American economy labor receives three quarters of national output and capital one quarter; and suppose labor supply is growing 1 percent a year and capital supply 3 percent. Then our equation tells us that the rate of increase of output:

$$
\begin{aligned}
y &= .25\,(3.0) + .75\,(1.0) \\
&= .75 + .75 \\
&= 1.5 \text{ percent per year} .
\end{aligned}
$$

Suppose we are interested instead in the rate of increase of *output per worker*, which is the basis for improvement of real wages and living standards. This is shown, for small intervals, by $y - l$. Going back to equation (1) and subtracting l from both sides, we find that

$$
\begin{aligned}
y - l &= a \cdot k + b \cdot l - l \\
&= a \cdot k - (1 - b)l .
\end{aligned}
$$

And since a + b = 1,

$$y - l = a \cdot k - a \cdot l$$
$$\text{or } y - l = a(k - l) . \qquad (2)$$

But $k - l$, the rate of capital increase minus the rate of labor increase, is simply the rate of increase of *capital per worker*. The result tells us that capital per worker must increase in order for output per worker to increase. This seems sensible, and capital per worker has been increasing quite fast in the developed countries. Note, however, that the rise in labor productivity is only a fraction of the increase in capital per worker, a fraction set by the value of a. With the illustrative figures used above, an increase of 2 percent a year in capital per worker gives us an increase of only .25 (2.0) = .5 percent a year in output per worker.

Even this simple apparatus has interesting practical uses. For example, the annual increase in the U.S. labor force in the years 1950–60 was abnormally small because of low birth rates during the great depression of the thirties. The rate of labor force increase in the years 1965–75 will be much higher because of the postwar baby boom. Suppose we manage to keep aggregate demand at a level which will absorb these people into employment. What will be the effect on the growth of output and of output per worker?

Look back to equations (1) and (2). Suppose that l rises from 1 to 2 percent per year, while k remains the same as before. Then

$$y = \ .25 \ (3.0) + .75 \ (2.0)$$
$$= \textbf{2.25 percent, instead of the previous 1.5 percent .}$$
$$y - l = \ .25 \ (3.0 - 2.0)$$
$$= \textbf{.25 percent instead of the previous .5 percent .}$$

Total output will rise *more* rapidly than before, but output per worker will rise *less* rapidly. Granted all the differences between the real economy and the simplified economy we are considering here, these results are probably in the right direction. The second result arises from the fact that, with labor growing more rapidly than before but with no change in the investment rate, capital per worker must grow less rapidly. An interesting implication is that the real wage level may rise less rapidly during the next 10 years than it has over the past 20 (unless, of course, there should be an offsetting rise in the rate of technical progress, which we have so far excluded).

There is another interesting conclusion. It appears from equation (1) that output can never rise faster than *the most rapidly growing input*. The value of y must be somewhere *between* k and l. Now in an advanced industrial country, k is almost invariably growing most rapidly. But if k is greater than y, then the ratio of capital to output must be rising, which means that the marginal productivity of capital is falling.

We saw in Chapter 10 that, if the supply of one factor increases with no increase in other factors, its marginal productivity will fall. By the same token, if one factor increases *faster* than other factors, its marginal productivity will likewise fall. So its price, which under competition reflects its marginal productivity, will also fall relative to those of other factors.

In the richer countries, capital typically increases considerably faster than labor. So it is capital which faces the problem of a decline in its marginal productivity and rate of return. With no technical progress, continued accumulation of capital must lower the rate of interest. Falling interest rates accompanied by rising wage rates will encourage substitution of capital for labor; but since substitution possibilities are limited, this cannot entirely relieve the downward pressure.

Suppose this continues decade after decade. What will happen? Will the interest rate fall eventually to a level at which there is no longer any inducement to saving? Were the classical economists right after all, and will we end up in a rich but stationary state? It is time to bring technical change to the rescue.

Technical Progress: The "Residual"

Suppose that, in addition to mere increase of productive resources, there are forces which raise the productivity of these resources over time. The same bundle of inputs produces more output next year than this year. Sheer increase of labor and capital would raise output 2 percent a year, but output actually grows at 4 percent. In this case the improvement factor has a value of 2 percent.

This improvement factor is often termed "technical progress." This is not an especially apt label, since technical progress in the ordinary sense of scientific discovery and invention is only one of the forces at work, and perhaps not the most important. The term is in fact a catchall for *all sources of output growth other than increased labor and capital supplies.* So some theorists and statisticians have come to call it simply "the residual."

Let's designate the rate of technical progress as r. And assume for the moment that this progress is *neutral* as between the factors. It raises the marginal productivity of capital precisely as much as that of labor.

Our basic growth equation now becomes

$$y = a \cdot k + b \cdot l + r. \tag{3}$$

Technical progress appears as an extra term added to the effect of rising labor and capital inputs.

By the same transformation as before, the growth rate of *output per worker* becomes

$$y - l = a(k - l) + r. \tag{4}$$

There are now two factors pushing up the productivity of labor. The first is increased capital equipment per worker, or "capital deepening." The second is the new element in the situation, the residual.

This suggests the question, Which element is more important in practice? Kendrick, Solow, and others have tried to answer this question. Their methods and results will be described in the next chapter. But there is no need to hold back the main conclusion: technical progress is admittedly the more important factor. It explains more than half—some writers would say as much as 80 to 90 percent—of the growth in labor productivity in the United States since 1890.

Considering the extent to which economists have traditionally stressed mechanization and capital supply, these results are quite startling. Surely capital formation cannot be such an unimportant part of the growth picture. So several economists have proceeded to point out that capital formation is required to *embody* technical progress, which cannot otherwise be applied in production. New equipment is more productive than older equipment. This has led to "vintage capital" models, in which each part of the nation's capital stock is dated by its year of origin, and it is assumed that each year's capital is x percent more productive than that of the year before. (Note that this is the reverse of vintage wines, where the newest is least good!) When you sum up the national's capital stock on this basis, you get a faster rate of increase over time—a higher k—than you would get otherwise. This higher k contributes more to the growth of y than is the case in nonvintage models.

This is undoubtedly not the last stage in the discussion. Whatever the outcome, one can scarcely doubt the great importance of "the residual." But in saying this, we are really making a confession of ignorance. For under this term we lump a variety of things, about the relative importance of which we know very little.

What are some of the things hidden within the residual, and which may account for its heavy weight in output growth?

1. Technical change in the strict sense is undoubtedly important. This consists partly of improved methods of producing existing products. But even more important is the rise of new industries as a result of technical discoveries. One can list a long series of these over the past century—telephone and telegraph communication, oil refining, electric power, automobiles and trucks, radio and television, petrochemicals, plastics and other synthetics, electronics, and so on. The productivity of labor and capital in these new industries is typically higher than the previous average for the economy. So as these "high-powered industries" appear, and a larger share of the nation's resources is diverted into them, the average level of productivity rises.

While in principle one can distinguish the effect of an increasing *amount of capital* from the effect of *technical change*, this distinction is rather artificial in practice. For through technical change the growing capital stock takes on new and more productive forms. Further, it is only because of the profit opportunities opened up by technical change that capital accumulation proceeds as rapidly as it does. So scientific and technical discoveries are really responsible for much of the increase in national output which seems, in a superficial or statistical sense, to be due to increased capital supplies.

2. Labor and capital are not the only inputs to production. Part of the rise in their productivity, therefore, may come from using larger quantities of other resources. The amount of agricultural land in use in 1890 was considerably smaller than it is today. Our great oil fields, and many important mineral deposits, were unknown at that time. The potential of our rivers had not been harnessed for power production.

If we count organization and management as a separate factor of production, we can point to major improvements in this area. In 1890 management methods were still casual and traditional. The scientific management movement after 1900 brought major advances in production management. Developments in administrative organization have improved the overall coordination of large enterprises. More recently, mathematical methods have been applied with increasing success in management decision making.

3. Productivity calculations usually assume that labor and capital consist of identical units. A million man-hours worked in 1890 is taken as the equivalent of a million man-hours in 1960. This is clearly inaccurate. Americans of 1960 are better fed, healthier, larger, stronger than their grandfathers. They have on the average more than twice as much education. The level of skill and experience has risen. A much larger proportion of the labor force today consists of skilled craftsmen, white-collar workers, executives, and professional people.

There is an anomaly in our national income accounting on this point. We *define* investment as use of current resources to secure higher output in the future. But we *count* as investment only money spent on buildings, machines, and other forms of physical capital. Expenditures on health, education, vocational training, and other things which raise the productive capacity of human beings are not counted. This procedure is doubly unfortunate. It understates the level of investment in the economy, and it creates a bias in favor of material investment as against investment in human beings.

4. There is progress in machines as well as men. When a machine bought for $25,000 wears out and is replaced by another machine costing the same amount, we say that the country's capital stock has not increased. This is unrealistic. The new machine can usually do more work than the old. So the effectiveness of capital equipment rises faster than one would judge from the net capital formation figures alone.

5. The fact that the American economy increased tenfold in *economic size* between 1890 and 1960 must have had a favorable effect on productivity. The advantages of increasing size were underlined in Part One. It enables individual industries to build plants of optimum scale. It enables the country to support a diversified array of industries which reinforce each other, improvements in one industry reducing the

costs of others. It enables the overhead cost of the nation's transport and communication network to be spread over an ever larger volume of output. This reduces unit production costs independently of other favorable developments. All this amounts to saying that the assumption of constant returns to scale, which we made in setting up our simplified economy, is not really warranted. For the economy as a whole, increasing returns to scale seems to be the general rule. Marshall was saying this as long ago as 1890, and he seems to have been right.

Is Technical Change Neutral?

When we first brought technical change into the picture, we assumed that it was neutral as between the factors of production, i.e., that it had no effect on their *relative* marginal productivities. But there is no reason why this need be the case in practice. It is quite possible that technical change may raise the marginal productivities of the two factors *at different rates*. It may be of such a character as to raise the marginal productivity of labor more than that of capital, or vice versa. This property we may term the *factor bias of innovation*.

Here some definitions are in order. A *laborsaving innovation* is one which raises the marginal productivity of capital more than that of labor. *It acts like an increase in labor supply*. It provides opportunities to use additional capital without depressing its productivity. Mechanization and automation in manufacturing provide an abundance of illustrations.

A *capital-saving innovation* is one which raises the marginal productivity of labor more than that of capital. *It acts like an increase in capital supply*. Transmission of messages by radio instead of telegraph wires is an example of this sort. Another is the jet airplane, which can carry more transatlantic passengers per week than a large steamship, while costing considerably less to build.

A *neutral innovation* is the borderline case between these two.

Depending on which kind of innovation predominates at a particular time and place, one can say that technical change has a *laborsaving bias* or a *capital-saving bias*.

What kind of technical progress is preferable? The answer depends on the supplies of labor and capital, and the rate of increase in these supplies, in the country in question. In a poor country with surplus labor, the problem is to stretch the limited supply of capital as far as possible. Here capital-saving innovations are in order. This case will be examined in our discussion of growth in the less developed countries.

At the moment, however, we are concerned with the richer industrial countries. A few pages ago we left these countries hanging onto the edge of the cliff—capital increasing faster than labor, marginal productivity of capital and the rate of interest falling, economic stagnation in the offing. To rescue them from this predicament we need a *laborsaving bias* in the process of technical change. If we can get this, the effect will be the same *as if the labor supply had risen faster than it actually did*. Technical change can serve as at least a partial corrective to the relative shortage of labor and abundance of capital which marks the growth process in the developed countries. It can prevent the marginal productivity of capital from falling as rapidly as it otherwise would and thus stave off the day of doom foretold by the classical economists.

Has technical change in the industrial countries actually had a laborsaving bias over the past century? There are two reasons for an affirmative answer. First, there has been a strong incentive to laborsaving improvements. With labor becoming steadily more expensive, the problem of economizing labor has forced itself constantly on businessmen. It would be surprising if this were not reflected in the activities of inventors, engineers, and production managers. Some technical changes simply drop out of the blue as a by-product of basic scientific work; and there is no reason to expect that these *autonomous* inventions will have a bias in one direction or the other. But to the extent that inventions are *induced* by an effort to lower production costs, one would expect them to have a laborsaving bias.

The second piece of evidence is the behavior of profit and interest rates in the capitalist countries. True, these rates have fallen considerably relative to wage rates. The interest rate in the United States may even have fallen absolutely over the past century, though the evidence is not conclusive. The main point, however, is that rates of return on capital *have not fallen as much as one would have expected* in view of the rapid increase of capital supply. What has sustained the yield on capital and prevented it from falling to a discouraging level? The most plausible explanation is a vigorous process of technical improvement with a marked laborsaving bias.

A major uncertainty about the future of the industrial economies is whether this will continue to be true in the decades ahead. Who will forge ahead in the race between invention and capital accumulation? Will investment opportunities be exhausted faster than they can be restored by technical discoveries? Will the return on capital drop sharply after all? If so, the outlook is discouraging. But one can hope for a more favorable outcome; and there are even some things which can be done about it.

GROWTH THEORY FOR THE LESS DEVELOPED ECONOMY

In contrast to the large literature on growth in mature industrial economies, analysis of the less developed countries is scanty. There has been little useful theorizing, and this is limited mainly to one type of economy, the so-called "surplus labor economy." Important contributors to this line of theorizing have been Sir Arthur Lewis, Gustav Ranis, and

John C. H. Fei. There has been little systematic analysis of other types of economy—for example, those in which land rather than labor is the surplus factor, as is true in some countries of Africa and South America. We do not even know how to classify less developed countries effectively, how many types there will turn out to be, or how many species of theory we shall need to explain them.

We can, however, outline some of the ideas which have been developed about the surplus labor economy. This is also often termed a *dualistic economy*, because it is split into two distinct sectors: (1) A *traditional* sector, including not only subsistence agriculture but petty trade and service activities. The peasant in his rice field, the trader in his tiny market stall, the rickshaw puller on the street corner, are engaged in the traditional sector. It is the dominant sector in the sense of including 80 percent or more of the labor force. (2) A *modern* sector, including factory industry, mining, public utility enterprises, plantation agriculture, large-scale construction, and at least part of government employment. This is a small, but productive and (hopefully) growing part of the economy.

The main characteristic of the traditional sector is overpopulation and underemployment. There are too many rice farmers, small traders, and rickshaw pullers. Each person gets less than a full day's work, leading to low output per worker and a low level of living. In addition to underemployment, some countries have a good deal of open, visible unemployment. Surplus labor has drained in from the countryside to the cities, where it can find nothing to do. The traditional sector is characterized by limited use of capital and a stagnant technology. Farmers keep on farming as their fathers and grandfathers did before them.

The modern sector is concentrated in the towns and cities. Workers are employed in relatively large production units, using modern technology and substantial amounts of capital, and are paid a money wage. This wage must be higher than the level of incomes in agriculture, partly to offset higher urban living costs and partly to provide a continuing inducement for people to move from country to city.

In Figure 2, OS is the level of real income per worker in the traditional sector, while OW is the real wage in the modern sector. We assume that the wage gap SW is adequate to keep labor flowing into modern employment as needed. The supply curve of labor to the modern sector is the horizontal line WW, a situation which Lewis has labeled "economic development with unlimited supplies of labor." The demand curve for labor in the modern sector when the curtain rises is the marginal productivity schedule N_1N_1.[3] The employers, being up-to-date profit maximizers, hire labor up to the point at which the marginal

---

[3] Note that this does not answer the critical questions of where the modern sector comes from and how it gets started. It simply assumes that a beachhead has already been established and goes on from there.

productivity of labor equals the wage rate. So employment is OE_1 and output is $ON_1Q_1E_I$. Out of this the workers get OWQ_1E_I (number of workers employed $\times$ the wage rate), while the employers retain WN_1Q_1 as profit.

Now suppose the employers are frugal people and put this profit back into plant and equipment. Workers have more equipment to work with, so their marginal productivity rises to N_2N_2. (We may also, if we wish, admit technical progress as an additional factor raising the productivity curve over the course of time.) Now OE_2 workers are

Economic Development with Unlimited Supplies of Labor

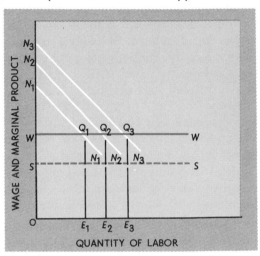

FIGURE 2. Industrial employers can hire as much labor as they wish at the wage OW. The marginal productivity of labor at the beginning is N_1N_1. So employment is OE_1, total wages are OE_1Q_1W, and profits are N_1Q_1W. These profits are reinvested in plant and equipment, which raises the marginal productivity of labor to N_2N_2. The result is employment of OE_2 and still larger profits, reinvestment of which raises marginal productivity to N_3N_3; and so on.

employed, and profits are shown by the larger area WN_2Q_2. Reinvestment of these profits raises labor productivity to N_3N_3, and so on in a cumulative process. Note that employment in the modern sector expands at a *constant real wage level, OW*. So long as surplus labor is available from the traditional sector, there is no reason for wages to rise.

In this view, the essence of economic development is the transfer of surplus labor from the traditional to the modern sector of the economy. Why is this transfer desirable? First, since the marginal productivity of labor in the modern sector is above that in the traditional sector, each transferred worker produces more than before and raises national output. Second, rising profit in the modern sector increases the rate of capital formation, which means still higher employment in the future. Third, modern employment and higher income tends to improve the skill, energy, and motivation of the labor force. To the extent that health and educational facilities are better in town than in the country, the workers' children share in the benefits.

This approach also yields a quantitative test of success for a country's development effort. The test turns on the rate of increase of employment in the modern sector. It is important here that the reservoir of surplus labor is being continuously replenished by population growth. So the rate of increase in "modern" employment *must exceed the rate of increase in the labor force.* If it does, the percentage of the labor force employed in the modern sector will be rising. The "center of gravity" of the economy will be shifting toward the modern sector. But if the opposite happens, and the percentage employed in the modern sector declines, the economy must receive a failing grade.

An arithmetical illustration will clarify this point. The first column of Table 1 shows the 1965 distribution of Ruritania's labor force, which is

TABLE 1

Employment in Ruritania, 1965–80

	1965 (1)	1980 (S) (2)	1980 (F) (3)
Total labor force	1,000,000	1,400,000	1,400,000
Employed in traditional sector	800,000	1,050,000	1,148,000
Employed in modern sector	200,000	350,000	252,000
Percent of labor force in			
Traditional sector	80	75	82
Modern sector	20	25	18
Percent increase, 1965–80			
Labor force		40	40
Traditional employment		31	44
Modern employment		87	26

assumed to total one million. With a high rate of population growth, the labor force in 1980 is estimated at 1,400,000. The last two columns of the table show two hypothetical distributions of this labor force.

In column (2), employment in the traditional sector has risen 31 percent since 1965. In the early stages of development, and with a high rate of population growth, it is virtually impossible to avoid an *absolute* increase of numbers in the traditional sector. The significant thing, however, is that modern employment has risen by 87 percent, well above the rate of increase in the labor force, so that the *proportion* of employment in the modern sector has risen from 20 to 25 percent. This path of development would be rated a success. In column (3), on the other hand, modern employment has risen less rapidly than labor force and its proportion has declined from 20 to 18 percent. This case would have to be considered a failure.

If the rate of increase of modern employment is the measure of success, on what does this rate depend? What determines whether an economy will or will not get over the hump? Four factors are of key importance: the rate of population increase, the rate of capital formation, the rate and factor bias of technical change, and the behavior of the real wage level in industry.

Population increase.   The importance of this factor is self-evident. Suppose a country, with all the resources it can muster, is able to raise employment in the modern sector by no more than 2 percent a year. If the labor force is rising 3 percent a year, the economy will be slipping backward. The percentage employed in the modern sector will be falling. But if the labor force were rising only 1 percent a year, the economy would be on the road to success. The lower the rate of labor force increase, the smaller the development effort required to shift the economy's center of gravity.

There is no doubt that rapid population growth is the greatest single obstacle to economic development. In many countries, one cannot expect any rise in per capita income unless population growth can be retarded. If we say little in later chapters about population policy, this is not because the problem is unimportant, but because it is largely noneconomic. Nor is it any longer a technical problem, for a wide array of effective techniques are known to population scientists. The problem is essentially educational, cultural, and political.

Rate of capital formation.   A distinctive feature of the modern sector is that men usually work with substantial amounts of equipment. The higher the rate of capital formation, therefore, the higher is likely to be the rate of increase of employment. Crudely, factories create jobs.

This line of reasoning, however, must be used with some caution. Early in the chapter we noted that, in very simple theorizing about growth, it is sometimes assumed that employment and output will rise in direct proportion to the amount of capital, i.e., that the output-capital ratio is constant. But this is unlikely to be so in practice.

The output from a certain amount of capital depends very much on the *kind of industry* to which the capital is devoted. The capital-output ratio may be 10:1 in housing, 5:1 in electric power production, 1:1 in textile mills, and 0.5:1 in agriculture. The overall result, then, will depend very much on the allocation of new capital among industries. Moreover, new equipment may be installed and operated with varying degrees of efficiency. It is quite possible for capital to be wasted and for the output result to be zero.

If the relation of output to capital is quite variable, so also is the relation of employment to capital. A given amount of capital may be combined with more or less labor, depending on the method of production.

The intensity and bias of technical change.   We saw earlier that, in the advanced countries, one cannot explain the rise of output per worker simply by increasing capital per worker. On the contrary, most of the increase is due to the things covered by the label of technical change.

Prima facie, technical change should be even more important in the poorer countries, which are starting from a lower technical level. The labor force is less skilled, management is less experienced, scientific and engineering knowledge is less widely disseminated, markets and other economic institutions are less developed. This technical backwardness reduces output at the present time. But by the same token it offers greater scope for improvement over the course of time, partly through research and training at home, partly through importing education and technology from more advanced countries.

In terms of Figure 2, labor's marginal productivity schedule does not rise only because of capital formation. It shifts upward also because of technical progress; and as it rises, the level of employment in the modern sector also rises.

In addition to the *intensity* of innovation, the *factor bias* of innovation is important. In a poor country with little capital, it is desirable that innovations have a *capital-saving (which means a labor-using) bias*—just the opposite of the rich country case.

Because Americans live in a country where capital is relatively abundant, we think of progress in terms of giving each man more equipment to work with, of *capital deepening*. But where labor is relatively abundant and capital scarce, one needs rather a process of *capital shallowing*, which spreads the available capital more thinly over a larger number of workers. Up to a point, this will raise national output as well as provide more jobs. Such a shallowing seems actually to have occurred in Japan, one of the most successful recent cases of economic development, over the period 1880–1920.[4]

It is sometimes argued that labor-capital proportions are rigidly fixed by technology. But except for extreme cases, such as oil refining and certain chemical processes, this does not seem to be true. One can use more labor relative to capital in a variety of ways: working the same machinery two or three shifts instead of one shift; using labor instead of conveyor belts and forklift trucks for moving materials and finished products; applying more labor for maintenance and repair of older equipment; and subcontracting parts and components to smaller workshops, as has been done extensively in Japan.

The behavior of real wages.   In Figure 2 we showed employment expanding at a constant real wage. Labor benefits from development through more jobs but not through a rising wage level. If this seems austere, one can point out that workers are already earning more in

---

[4] See on this point John C. H. Fei and Gustav Ranis, *Development of the Labor Surplus Economy: Theory and Policy* (Homewood, Ill.: Richard D. Irwin, Inc., 1964).

industry than they were in the traditional sector and that it is desirable to increase the number of "modern" jobs as rapidly as possible.

This line of argument, however, is less acceptable today than it may have been in the nineteenth century. In the less developed countries, there is usually strong pressure to raise the industrial wage level through union agreements, minimum wage legislation, or government arbitration awards. Government sometimes takes the lead by setting high wages for civil servants, which private employers then feel obliged to emulate. Managers coming in from more advanced countries are frequently shocked by the low wage levels they find, and voluntarily raise wages above the market level.

Higher real wages in industry benefit the workers already employed there. But they retard the expansion of employment by reducing the incentive to use labor instead of capital. One sees the strange phenomenon of employers busily substituting capital for "expensive" labor, amidst a large surplus of workers clamoring for employment. High urban wages also attract people to the cities more rapidly than they can be absorbed, so that workers who were partially unemployed in the country become wholly unemployed in town.

In some developing countries, then, one sees this combination of events: a substantial investment in modern industry and an encouraging rise in industrial output; a substantial rise in the industrial wage level, which pulls farther and farther above the rural level; but only a moderate increase in industrial employment, accompanied by rising unemployment in the cities and continued piling up of surplus labor in the countryside. Good output results are accompanied by poor employment results.[5] This cannot be blamed entirely on the wage level, but wage behavior certainly contributes to the outcome.

To sum up: a rapid shift of the economy's center of gravity from traditional to modern activities is facilitated by a moderate rate of population growth, a high rate of capital accumulation, a high rate of technical progress with a capital-saving bias, and a stable level of real wages in industry. To the extent that opposite tendencies develop in practice, the economy's chances are impaired.

The Role of Agricultural Expansion

This model of early economic growth emphasizes the suction of labor into the modern sector and the expansion of output and employment there. But what is happening meanwhile in the traditional sector, and particularly in agriculture? This is not a matter of indifference. On the contrary, it is crucial to smooth expansion of the economy.

---

[5] The writer has documented this in some detail for the case of Puerto Rico. See his "Wages and Employment in a Labor Surplus Economy," *American Economic Review*, March, 1965. A good deal of similar evidence is available from other countries.

Suppose, first, that the withdrawal of workers from agriculture leaves agricultural output unchanged. Tasks are rearranged, and each of the people remaining works more hours per day and per year. Thus while the number of *workers* in agriculture is smaller, the number of *man-hours of labor* used in agriculture is unchanged, and so is total output.

While in this case there is no *production* problem, there is a *transfer* problem. The workers who have moved to the city must have food to eat there. They must, as it were, carry a food supply along on their backs. This means, first, that the people remaining in the country must be prevented from eating up everything they grow, as undernourished people might reasonably wish to do. Second, they must be given an incentive to sell a growing proportion of their produce in town to supply the growing urban population. In addition to roads and marketing facilities, this requires reasonable prices and a backflow of manufactured consumer goods which the country people can buy with their cash incomes.

But simply to redistribute an unchanged production total is not enough. The new industrial workers in the city have higher incomes than before. So do workers in agriculture, since an unchanged output is now divided among fewer people. What will people do with these larger incomes? One thing they will certainly want to do is eat better. Total food demand will rise and, if supply remains unchanged, food prices will rise steadily.

This lands us back in the Ricardian dilemma. Food prices are rising. So industrial employers must raise money wages in order to give workers the same real wage as before. But the prices of manufactured products have not risen (their supply being supposedly expansible at constant cost). So employers find their profits squeezed, the incentive and the funds for new investment are reduced, and economic growth is choked off.

To avoid the classical food bottleneck, agricultural output must increase over time. At what rate? As a first approximation, one can say at a rate which leaves the relative price of foodstuffs and industrial products unchanged. What changes in traditional agriculture are needed to keep food output growing at the required rate? This is a large subject, to be explored further in Chapter 32. We are concerned here only to point out that the problem must be faced at the outset of the development process. To push industry while consigning agriculture to its traditional stagnation is not a viable policy for sustained growth.

Suppose an economy meets this test. And suppose it also meets the test of shifting the center of gravity toward the modern sector. The proportion of the labor force engaged in agriculture falls from 60 percent to 50 to 40. At what stage can one say that the economy has "arrived," that it has passed out of the less developed category? Fei and Ranis would reply: When the labor surplus is exhausted. This means that the people remaining in agriculture and other traditional activities are (except for seasonal slack periods) fully employed; and that the marginal productivity of workers in these activities has reached a level comparable with that of workers in the modern sector. Labor has then become a scarce factor, and all branches of the economy must bid for it at market wage rates.

The "equal marginal productivity" test, to be sure, must not be applied too strictly. Even in mature economies the marginal productivity of labor in agriculture typically remains below that in industry, and this is reflected in relative wage levels. In the United States, for example, the hourly wage of agricultural workers has rarely been more than half that of factory workers. One can scarcely expect the less developed countries to do better than the advanced countries. But one can expect a reduction of the abnormally wide productivity gap which exists in the early stages of development.

SUMMARY

1. Among classical writers, Ricardo developed the most systematic theory of long-term growth. He argued that, because of diminishing returns in agriculture, the price of food (and hence the wage necessary to assure the worker's subsistence) must rise relative to other prices. This will reduce profit rates until the incentive for further saving and investment disappears. The result must be a stationary state, with constant population, capital stock, and output.

2. Marx reached pessimistic conclusions by a different route. His argument leans heavily on a supposed effort by employers to increase their profits through mechanization. This leads to a growing army of unemployed, a falling level of real wages, and eventual revolution.

3. Most of modern growth theory relates to a developed economy, in which one does not ask how growth gets started, but simply how fast it will continue. The theories considered here are supply-oriented and attempt to explain the rate of increase in *productive capacity*.

4. In a simplified economy using only labor and capital, with flexible factor proportions, no technical change, constant returns to scale, and competitive factor pricing, one can show that

$$y = a \cdot k + b \cdot l$$
$$\text{and, } y - l = a(k - l) .$$

The rate of growth of output depends on the growth rate of labor and capital, each weighted by its share of national income. *Output per worker* can increase only if *capital per worker* is also increasing, that is, if $k > l$.

5. If we add technical progress, indicating its annual rate of increase by r, the growth equation becomes

$$y = a \cdot k + b \cdot l + r$$
$$\text{and } y - l = a(k - l) + r .$$

Statistical analyses have indicated that technical progress, or "the residual," has been the most important factor raising output per worker, and that capital per worker is less important. But this overlooks the possibility that capital formation may be necessary to embody at least some kinds of technical progress.

6. The residual, r, includes not only technical progress in the narrow sense but also improvements in the education and skill of the labor force, better management, improvements in overall economic organization, and possible economies of scale in a growing economy.

7. Technical change, also termed *innovation*, may be biased toward either labor or capital. A *laborsaving* (which is equivalent to a *capital-using*) innovation raises the marginal productivity of capital more than that of labor. It therefore raises the demand for capital, and the rate of return to capital, relative to that of labor. A *capital-saving* (or *labor-using*) innovation has precisely opposite effects.

8. In an economy where capital is growing faster than labor, as is typically true in the developed countries, it is desirable that technical change have a capital-using bias. This will help to avert a falling interest rate which could, by reducing the incentive to invest, usher in economic stagnation à la Ricardo. From the fact that the interest rate has not fallen appreciably in the developed countries on an absolute basis, we can infer that technical change has in fact had a capital-using bias.

9. In a less developed economy with surplus labor, development hinges on transferring labor from the low-productivity "traditional" sector of the economy to "modern" activities with higher productivity. If labor can be transferred faster than the labor force is being increased by population growth, the economy's center of gravity will shift gradually toward the modern sector.

10. Success in this effort will be facilitated by a modern rate of population growth, a rising capital formation rate, a high rate of technical progress with a labor-using (or capital-saving) bias, and a stable level of real wages.

11. Successful development normally involves also an expansion of agricultural production to avert the Ricardian food bottlenecks.

DISCUSSION QUESTIONS

1. What were the grounds for Ricardo's predictions of the economic future? Why did the actual development of the British economy differ from these predictions?

2. The future did not turn out as Marx had predicted either. Why not?

3. "Modern growth theory focuses on the relation of output to factor inputs. Statistical analysis has shown, however, that most of the increase in output is an unexplained residual which cannot be attributed to factor inputs at all. So the theory does not help much in explaining economic growth." Discuss.

4. Is this kind of growth theory applicable equally to the developed and the less developed economies? Why or why not?

5. Consider an industrial economy, with capital supply rising faster than labor supply, and with no technical progress. What difficulties might such an economy experience over the long run?

6. What are the main things hidden under the label of technical progress, or "the residual"? Which would you consider quantitatively most important?

7. Explain clearly the meaning of *laborsaving* and *capital-saving* innovations, giving some examples.

8. Why is it often said that, in the United States and other advanced industrial countries, innovations should have a laborsaving bias? How would you go about testing whether innovations in the United States over the past century have actually had such a bias?

9. Some economists argue that, in an underdeveloped economy with surplus labor, innovations should have a capital-saving bias. Do you agree? What concrete steps might be taken in this direction?

10. What kind of behavior by workers and employers is implied in the Lewis model of economic growth? Is the model applicable equally to capitalist and socialist economies?

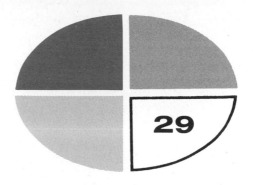

29

Growth in the West:

The United States and Its Neighbors

He was found by the Bureau of Statistics to be
One against whom there was no official complaint,
And all the reports on his conduct agree
That, in the modern sense of an old-fashioned word, he was a
   saint . . .
Both Producers Research and High-Grade Living declare
He was fully sensible to the advantages of the Installment
   Plan
And had everything necessary to the Modern Man,
A phonograph, a radio, a car and a frigidaire.
Our researchers into Public Opinion are content
That he held the proper opinions for the time of year;
When there was peace, he was for peace; when there was
   war, he went . . .
Was he free? Was he happy? The question is absurd;
Had anything been wrong, we should certainly have heard.
                           W. H. Auden

It is impossible in a few pages to do justice to the long-term growth of the American economy. But we can sketch in the broad features of this growth and draw some comparisons with the experience of other Western industrial countries.

797

THE ACCELERATION OF GROWTH: 1830–60

It is a truism that any country which embarks successfully on the path of economic development goes through a period in which its growth rate increases. If at one time GNP is rising 1 percent a year, and at a later time it is rising 4 percent a year, there must have been a phase of acceleration in between.

The best evidence for the United States locates this phase at about 1830 to 1860. The indications are that output *per capita* rose little from 1800 to 1830, and some scholars doubt that there was any increase.[1] Beginning in the 1830's, however, the economic indexes move upward more rapidly. Shipments of goods by land more than doubled between 1830 and 1840, while shipments by water almost doubled. The first overall estimates of production date from 1839. Professor Gallman has estimated the increase of total commodity output as follows:[2]

TABLE 1

Annual Rates of Change
(Percent)

PERIOD	OUTPUT	POPULATION	OUTPUT PER CAPITA
1839–49	4.3	3.1	1.0
1849–54	5.4	3.1	2.2
1854–59	5.0	3.1	1.8
1859–69	2.1	2.4	−0.4
1869–79	5.0	2.3	2.6

Thus the annual increase in output during the 1840's was about 4½ percent, and the increase in per capita output was about 1 percent. The rate of growth accelerated further during the 1850's. The devastation of the Civil War brought a setback, and per capita output in 1869 was a bit below 1859. During the 1870's, however, the economy bounced back and the growth rate returned to the level of the 1850's. The economy was firmly embarked on an upward course.

There were several reasons for the acceleration of growth during these decades.

---

[1] Some of the evidence is appraised in William N. Parker and Franklee Whartenby, "The Growth of Output Before 1840," in *Trends in the American Economy in the Nineteenth Century* (Princeton, N.J.: Princeton University Press, National Bureau of Economic Research, 1960), pp. 191–212. This source is referred to hereafter as *Trends*.

[2] *Trends*, p. 16.

1. Settlement of Western lands. In 1830 the frontier ran roughly from Detroit to western Louisiana. By 1860 it had moved west of the Mississippi, and ran from northern Minnesota through Nebraska, Kansas, and Texas to the Rio Grande. Settlement involved substantial costs for clearing the land, building fences and farm buildings, and developing roads and schools. This was mainly a direct investment of labor by the settlers. The returns did not come immediately, since the market for farm products was still limited by transportation. But this land was so rich that there was great potential for expansion of production in later decades.

2. Rapid growth of population. The rate of population increase from 1830 to 1860 was higher than it has ever been since that time, running at more than 3 percent per year. This rate means a doubling of population in about 22 years. Population grew through heavy immigration from Europe as well as through a high rate of natural increase.

Considering that the United States in 1830 was thinly populated relative to its resource potential, the rapid growth of population was an advantage. Germans, Scandinavians, and other immigrant groups played a prominent role in Western settlement. Immigrants built the railroads in the West and flooded into the factories of the East. Rapid population growth also fed the belief in the irresistible momentum of America. It became an article of faith that everything would be "bigger and better" a few years ahead. This outlook is favorable to personal initiative and business investment.

3. Railroading and the broadening of internal markets. For a long time the only cheap transportation in the United States was coastwise shipping. East-West traffic had to move by wagon or pack animals at much higher cost. This slowed the pace of Western settlement, prevented the settlers from sending their produce East to market, and hampered economic unification of the country. Industry and population remained concentrated in Boston, New York, Philadelphia, Baltimore, and other coastal cities which were in touch with each other by water.

The canal-building movement after 1810 did not solve the problem. Between 1810 and 1860 about $200 million, an enormous sum for those days, was spent on canals. About 70 percent of this came from government sources, primarily from state governments.[3] The Erie Canal and a few others made an economic contribution and were financial successes. (The Erie reduced freight costs between Buffalo and New York from 20 cents per ton-mile to 2 cents.) But the geographical obstacles to canal building proved greater in the United States than in Britain or Europe, and most of the canals did not pay off.

A real solution of the transportation problem had to await the steam locomotive and the railroad. This development began in 1830, and by

---

[3] Carter Goodrich, *Government Promotion of American Canals and Railroads, 1800–1890* (New York: Columbia University Press, 1960).

1860, thirty thousand miles of track had already been constructed. Detroit, Chicago, St. Louis, New Orleans, and Memphis were linked with each other and with the east coast. The impact of cheap mass transportation on the economy can scarcely be overstated. It opened to the western farmers both the markets of the east coast and export markets abroad. Eastern manufacturers, who could now distribute their products throughout the country, reaped economies of large-scale production. Mobility of labor was greatly increased. The rail network provided an indispensable framework for rapid economic growth.

While the railroads were particularly crucial during this early period, they continued throughout the nineteenth century to open up new areas of settlement, reduce transportation costs, knit together the internal market, and provide a major outlet for investment. Between 1870 and 1890 alone, 110,000 miles of new railroad track were built. No other industry has ever provided such a major source of investment demand over so long a period.

4. The first agricultural revolution.   During the first half of the last century, agricultural production managed to keep pace with population growth, but only by bringing new land under cultivation. Output per acre and per farm worker was probably not much higher in 1850 than it had been in 1800. But meanwhile a burst of technical development was setting the stage for a rapid rise in productivity after 1850.

The steel plow, essential for the heavy prairie soils, began to be used in the 1830's. Harrows and seed drills came into use in the 1840's, corn planters and cultivators in the 1850's. Cyrus McCormick patented his mechanical reaper in 1834, sold 50 machines in 1844, and a thousand in 1851. A practical threshing machine was used by the late 1840's. The first guano fertilizer from South America was put on sale in 1843, and the first chemical fertilizer in 1849.[4]

Farmers were given an incentive to take advantage of these improvements by two developments. During the 1850's there was a sharp increase in foreign demand for our farm products, following Britain's repeal of its import duty on wheat in 1846. During the 1860's the Civil War brought a sharp increase in domestic demand for food, accompanied by a severe shortage of manpower, which made mechanization profitable. In 1870 the quantity of machinery and fertilizers purchased by American farmers was *five times* as large as in 1850. Thus the agricultural sector set off on a path of rising productivity which has continued ever since.

5. The "American system" of manufacturing.   While the manufacturing sector was small before the Civil War, its rate of growth was high. Professor Gallman estimates that manufacturing production increased by *15 percent per year* from 1839 to 1849, and 10 percent per year from 1849

---

[4] For a review of these and other developments, see Marvin W. Towne and Wayne D. Rasmussen, "Farm Gross Product and Investment in the Nineteenth Century," *Trends,* pp. 255–315.

to 1859. In 1839 manufacturing provided only 17 percent of total commodity output. By 1859 this had risen to 32 percent.[5]

The rapid growth of population provided an insatiable market for consumer goods. The appearance of the stationary steam engine, which freed industry from dependence on "the old mill stream," was a major development. Another was the railroad, which made it economical to ship manufactured goods over much greater distances. High protective tariffs prevented the "infant industries" of the United States from being swamped by imports from Britain and elsewhere. Profit rates, high by modern standards, provided both the incentive and the funds for expansion. Mass immigration provided a ready source of labor.

Another important development was standardized and interchangable parts, pioneered by Eli Whitney and others. This was such a revolutionary idea at the time that European visitors referred to it as "the American system" of manufacturing. Workers and tools could be made more productive by specializing on one part of a product instead of tailor-making the product as a whole. These early machine shops in the Connecticut Valley were the ancestors of the modern assembly line.

6. **Increased capital formation.** The higher rate of increase in national output after 1830 was accompanied by, and partly depended on, a higher level of saving and investment. There are no direct measures of saving during this period, but there are indirect indications in the production level of capital goods. Gallman estimates that capital goods production, as a percentage of total commodity output, rose from about 23 percent in 1839 to 27 percent in 1859 and 33 percent in 1869.[6] It then leveled off and fluctuated in the range of 30–33 percent for the remainder of the century. This conforms to the general observation that capital formation rates in the Western industrial countries have not continued to rise indefinitely. After an initial phase of acceleration, they seem to level off and move along on a plateau.

7. **The inflow of foreign capital.** Domestic savings were supplemented during this critical period by heavy foreign borrowing, particularly from Britain. The rapid inflow of foreign capital after 1830 confirms the increased rate of economic development. In 1830 our private and public indebtedness to foreigners was only $75 million, about the same as it had been in 1790. Between 1830 and 1840, however, our foreign indebtedness more than *tripled* to a level of $266 million. The figure dropped during the 1840's but shot up again during the 1850's rising from $222 million in 1850 to $379 million in 1860.   ·

During these years we were importing a good deal more than we were exporting. A large proportion of the rails, railroad rolling stock, industrial tools and machinery, and other things needed for our industrial

---

[5] *Trends,* pp. 24–26.

[6] *Trends,* p. 38.

buildup came from abroad. Not until after 1870 did we begin to approach self-sufficiency in capital goods production. We also imported substantial quantities of consumer goods while our own manufacturing industries were rising toward maturity.

How did we pay for these imports? Partly through exports of grain and other materials. Partly through the earnings of our merchant marine, which was then a large factor in world commerce. After the 1849 gold strike in California, we were able to ship large amounts of gold abroad. But all this was not enough, and so we balanced our accounts by borrowing. This process of running up debt continued throughout the nineteenth century.

We sometimes look skeptically at today's poor countries when they say that their own resources are inadequate and that they need loans to get them started on the path of development. We should remember that it is normal for countries to borrow in the early stages of building up their own industries. The United States itself was once a debtor and remained so for many decades.

A CENTURY OF PROGRESS: 1870 TO DATE

After the Civil War the United States entered a period of sustained growth which has now lasted for about a century. Thanks to progress in national income measurement, we can speak with some confidence about what has happened over this period. The bare bones of the record are set out in Table 2 and Figure 1. Note that the figures represent *decade averages* rather than single years. Thus the 1903 figure is an average for 1899–1908, the 1923 figure is an average for 1919–28, and so on. This procedure is intended to eliminate the short swings of the business cycle and throw long-term trends into sharper relief.

Growth has been well sustained over this whole period, with no sharp break except for the Great Depression of the 1930's. At the same time, the pace of growth has been very gradual. The typical rate of increase in per capita output has been about 2 percent a year. But even a low rate of compound interest works wonders if you can keep it up long enough. A quantity growing at 2 percent a year will in a century have increased to six times its original value. And our GNP figures suggest that, as regards material consumption, the average American today is about six times as well off as his ancestor in 1870.

The rate of growth has varied considerably. In addition to the short business cycles analyzed in Chapter 25, there are longer and slower tides of economic activity—a period of 10 to 15 years in which growth is faster than usual, followed by an extended period of subnormal growth. These long swings have been investigated particularly by Abramovitz and Kuznets, and are often termed *Kuznets cycles*. They show up in the wavy shape of the trend lines in Figure 1.

Because of this irregularity of growth, it is unwise to draw sweeping conclusions about the economy from short periods of time. Popular writers are very subject to this myopia, and economists are not immune. A period of rapid growth (1921–29, 1946–57) sets up the cry of "permanent prosperity." A period of subnormal growth, such as 1929–39,

TABLE 2

Real GNP and GNP per Capita, United States, 1869–1962
(1929 Prices)

DECADE CENTERED ON*	TOTAL GNP		GNP PER CAPITA	
	DECADE AVERAGE (Billions)	ANNUAL RATE OF CHANGE FROM PRECEDING DECADE (Percent)	DECADE AVERAGE (Dollars)	ANNUAL RATE OF CHANGE FROM PRECEDING DECADE (Percent)
1873	11.46	n.a.	263	n.a.
1883	21.05	6.3	384	3.9
1893	29.32	3.4	433	1.2
1898	36.28	n.a.	487	n.a.
1903	45.60	4.6	559	2.6
1908	54.51	4.2	607	2.2
1913	62.38	3.2	636	1.3
1918	70.93	2.7	673	1.0
1923	85.18	3.2	752	1.7
1928	90.53	2.5	752	1.1
1933	90.70	0.6	720	−0.4
1938	116.02	2.5	886	1.7
1943	154.30	5.5	1135	4.7
1948	181.76	4.6	1244	3.4
1953	208.68	3.1	1298	1.3
1958	246.45	3.1	1399	1.1

* Actually, decades are centered on the end point of the year named. Thus, the first decade is 1869–78, which centers on December 31, 1873; and so on.
n.a. = not available.
Source: Basic data from John W. Kendrick, *Productivity Trends in the United States* (Princeton, N.J.: Princeton University Press, 1961). Per capita figures are obtained by dividing GNP by "Total Population Residing in the United States," appearing in *Historical Statistics of the United States, Colonial Times to 1957,* p. 7, and *Statistical Abstract of the U.S.,* 1959, p. 5.

leads to predictions of economic stagnation. With the benefit of hindsight, these extremes of optimism and pessimism turn out to have been unwarranted.

We saw in Chapter 28 that there are two sources of output growth: an increase in the quantity of inputs used; and improvement in the productivity of these inputs, often dubbed "technical progress." What has been the relative importance of these two elements in the United States?

The most ambitious statistical investigations have been carried out by John Kendrick at the National Bureau of Economic Research. His technique is to calculate an index of the amount of labor used in production and an index of physical capital including land. These are then combined, weighting each by the respective shares of labor and capital in national income, to yield an index of total factor input. This is divided into the index of national output to yield a measure of *total*

Real GNP and GNP Per Capita, United States, 1869–1965
(1929 Prices)

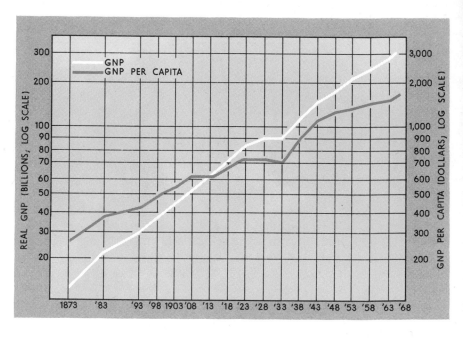

FIGURE 1

factor productivity.[7] The rate at which total factor productivity rises indicates the rate of technical progress.

[7] The basic relation used is

$$\frac{Y}{Y_o} = C\left(a\frac{L}{L_o} + b\frac{K}{K_o} \right),$$

where the subscript o indicates base period quantities, a and b are the labor and capital shares of national income, and C is the measure of total factor productivity. See John W. Kendrick, *Productivity Trends in the United States* (Princeton, N.J.: Princeton University Press, 1961), and the review article by Evsey D. Domar, "On Total Productivity and All That," *Journal of Political Economy*, December, 1962, pp. 597–608. For a different set of calculations, see Robert M. Solow, "Technical Change and the Aggregate Production Function," *Review of Economics and Statistics*, August, 1957.

Kendrick's results may be summarized as follows:

	ANNUAL PERCENTAGE INCREASE IN		
	GNP	TOTAL FACTOR INPUTS	TOTAL FACTOR PRODUCTIVITY
1889–1919	3.9	2.6	1.3
1919–1957	3.2	1.1	2.1

In the period 1889–1919, about two thirds of the annual increase in GNP can be attributed to larger factor inputs, though productivity also rose at 1.3 percent a year.

Since 1919, however, the relative contribution of these two elements in growth has been reversed. The growth of inputs has slowed down, while productivity has speeded up. Total factor inputs rose only 1.1 percent per year between 1919 and 1957. As regards labor, this reflects cessation of mass immigration, a lower rate of natural increase, and a marked shortening of the work week and work year. As regards capital, it reflects the drop in capital formation during the Great Depression and World War II. The amount of capital in use in 1945 was virtually the same as in 1929. Factor productivity, however, rose by 2.1 percent a year from 1919 to 1957, considerably faster than it had done earlier. Over these 40 years, it accounted for about two thirds of the growth of output, with increased factor inputs contributing only one third. The accelerated rate of technical progress almost succeeded in offsetting the slower growth of inputs.

FUTURE GROWTH AND GROWTH POLICY

What of the future? Are these signs that the growth of the American economy is slowing down? Is there need for special steps to sustain or increase our growth rate?

Has the Growth Rate Decreased?

The answer to the first question depends on the measure one uses. There has been a slight slowdown in the growth of *income per capita*. This was typically above 2 percent a year before 1914 but has been below that level for most of the time since. The main explanation is that productive inputs per capita have fallen. In particular, we are not putting in as much labor per head as we did a half century ago.

In 1914 the 10-hour day and the 6-day week were standard practice except for a few groups of skilled craftsmen. By the mid-thirties the 5-day, 40-hour week was firmly established. Since then, hours worked per year have fallen further through the spread of paid holidays and longer vacations. The overall result is striking. Between 1910 and 1960 the number of people in the U.S. labor force doubled, but the man-hours used in production rose by only one third. Thus we should not be surprised that output per head isn't rising as fast as it used to. Except for the acceleration of productivity, the slowdown of output would be even more noticeable.

Leisure time has value in itself. The decline in working hours represents partly a choice of greater leisure over larger incomes. So we may still be getting "better off" as fast as we did in the palmy days before World War I. But in recent decades more of our rising welfare has taken the form of leisure, and less has appeared as increased material consumption, than was true at an earlier time.

Our level of capital formation has also been quite low in recent decades. There was no net capital formation between 1929 and 1945. Since then, gross private investment as a proportion of GNP has moved in the range of 11 to 14 percent. After allowing for depreciation, net private investment has been 6 to 8 percent. This is below the level of most European countries and much below the level of Japan and the U.S.S.R.

If, on the other hand, one looks at *total factor productivity,* the figures are encouraging. Technical progress has been accelerating, and has been more rapid since 1945 than ever before. The slower growth of inputs has been largely offset by the growing productivity of these inputs.

In any event, one must look at long periods to draw significant conclusions. From 1957 to 1961 the growth of national output was certainly disappointing. There was a recession in 1957–58, a sluggish recovery from 1958 to 1960, and renewed recession in 1960–61. Between 1957 and 1961, GNP rose only 2.4 percent per year, and GNP per capita only 0.6 percent per year. This led to widespread speculation about a permanent slowdown in the economy and a serious "growth problem." In mid-1961, however, the economy took off on the longest peacetime upswing in our recorded history. From 1961 to 1965, real GNP rose at about 4.6 percent per year.

The Outlook for Growth

As we look ahead to the seventies and beyond, what is it reasonable to expect? Will the future look more like 1961–65 or more like 1957–61?

One favorable factor is the accelerated growth of the labor force. During the 1950's the labor force grew at only about 1 percent a year, because of unusually low birth rates during the depressed thirties. As postwar babies enter the labor force en masse, this will rise to about 1.7 percent a year from 1965 to 1975. In absolute terms, there will be a net addition to the labor force each year, after deducting those who are retiring, of about 1,500,000 workers.[8] The economy will need to generate this number of new jobs annually to maintain full employment. Popular writers sometimes use this as a basis for predictions of mass unemployment and economic disaster. Those who argue that we must cut hours to create jobs for more people are reasoning in this way. But there is no reason to suppose that total demand for labor is pegged at its present level. Population growth produces more mouths as well as more hands and raises aggregate consumer demand. True, smooth absorption of a growing labor force requires good monetary-fiscal management and an adequate level of private investment, but there seems no reason why this should be more difficult in the future than in the past.

Higher labor force growth is favorable to output growth in two ways—directly, because it raises l in the growth equation, and indirectly, because it strengthens investment incentives and thus tends to raise k as well. Much new investment consists of *capital widening*, providing each new worker with as much capital as previous workers. The faster new workers are appearing on the scene, the greater the scope for this kind of investment. To put the same point differently: increases in labor supply raise capital's marginal productivity schedule and help to ward off the classical menace of declining returns to capital.

There are additional benefits of rapid labor force growth. Each generation of new workers is better educated and more highly skilled than the generation before it. So there is an effect comparable to the "vintage capital" effect noted in last chapter. The higher the rate of new entrants to the labor force, the faster will the *average quality* of the labor force increase over time. Moreover, in a growing economy, the labor force has to adapt itself to shifts in the composition of labor demand—by industries, occupational levels, localities. Workers just entering the labor force are more mobile and adaptable than older workers and more readily attracted to the growth points of the economy. A high rate of new entrants means more lubricating oil for the economic machine and less danger that the machine may "seize up" because of labor shortages at critical points.

One implication of faster labor force growth, however, should not be overlooked. Price theory tells us that there must be effects on the return to labor and capital. If l accelerates, while k continues unchanged, the real wage level will move upward more slowly than before. Efforts to counteract this tendency by union action or wage legislation—say, to raise real wages at 4 percent a year when factor supplies indicate a rate of 3 percent—are bound to be largely unavailing. Missing their intended mark, such efforts will serve mainly to put upward pressure on the price level.

---

[8] *Manpower Report of the President* (Washington, D.C., March, 1965), pp. 46–47.

Apart from labor force growth, the future growth of U.S. GNP will be affected by what government does or fails to do. Since GNP summarizes the whole performance of the economy, almost everything government does will affect it in one direction or the other. These reactions should be recognized and studied. It is not so much that we need a new and distinct "growth policy." Rather, effects on the growth rate should be recognized as an important consequence of *existing* government policies, along with the effects on efficiency of resource use, equity of income distribution, and level of employment explored in earlier parts of this book. If a particular government action tends to raise the growth rate, it should be given some additional points on this account.

Government Action and the Growth Rate

While everything government does affects growth, some things affect it more than others. We may single out particularly full-employment policy, educational and research policy, and policy toward private investment.

Full use of present capacity makes for a faster rate of increase in future capacity because of its favorable effect on factor inputs. An economic climate in which businessmen expect total demand to grow steadily at, say, 4 percent a year is clearly more favorable to investment than one in which slow growth and frequent recessions are expected. Moreover, capacity operation means high profits out of which new investment can be financed. Over long periods, private capital formation forms a reasonably constant proportion of GNP. So higher output makes for higher investment and a larger k in the growth equation.

Full employment also reduces the pressure to cut working hours as a work-sharing measure. The sharp drop in annual hours worked over the past half century no doubt reflects partly a conscious income-leisure choice by employees. But the trend has been accelerated by chronic fears of job scarcity. This has also led to strong pressure for early retirement and other ways of shrinking the labor force, with needless hardship on the groups concerned.

Working hours should, so far as possible, correspond with what workers would choose freely in accordance with their income-leisure preferences. To cut hours below this level, or forcibly to shrink the labor force, reduces economic welfare and is quite unnecessary. The remedy for unemployment is not to work less but to raise aggregate demand for labor through fiscal and other measures.

Adequate *educational* policy can discover and develop productive talents which would otherwise lie latent and unused. This raises the quality of the labor force and accelerates economic growth. Training for the higher technical, professional, and managerial occupations is especially important. Despite the great educational expansion since World

War II, there are indications that we are still undereducating in many of these fields. Scarcity of teachers at all levels, of scientists and engineers, and of other highly skilled groups must be restricting our present growth rate.

Scientific and technological research presents both opportunities and problems. At first glance, the expenditure levels of recent years seem encouraging. Total spending on research and development almost tripled between 1953 and 1960, rising from $5 billion to $15 billion. Most of this money ($10.5 billion) was *used* by business concerns, while most of it ($9.2 billion) was *supplied* by the federal government. But note that two thirds of the industrial research expenditure was concentrated in three industries: aircraft and space vehicles, electrical equipment and communication, and chemicals. Research was heavily oriented toward military objectives. And basic or "impractical" research, which produces most of the important discoveries, got only 9 percent of the amount spent.

Government might well provide more support for basic research, which is done mainly in universities and government laboratories rather than in industry. There is also need for effort to break the bottleneck in the supply of research workers. Research spending rose between 1953 and 1960 at the rate of 25 percent per year. Meanwhile, the number of available scientists and engineers was rising only 6 percent per year. This means that people were being pulled out of teaching and other important activities to staff new research teams. The result has been to undermine the educational process on which the future supply of teachers and researchers depends. We need to increase greatly the number of scientists, engineers, and technicians being trained year by year. This means money for fellowships, for adequate teaching salaries, for buildings and laboratory equipment.

A variety of steps might be taken to *stimulate private business investment.* First, it is doubtful whether high investment and rapid economic growth have been given adequate weight in the framing of *federal tax policy.* A rethinking of policy with these objectives in mind might suggest important changes. It should give one pause that the tax policies of West Germany, Sweden, Japan, and most other capitalist countries are more favorable to investment than is the case in the United States.

The trick is partly to find devices which encourage high investment by business concerns but which do not permit unduly wide differences in personal income. We want to favor profits which are *reinvested,* rather than profits which go into luxury consumption. The tax changes initiated by the Kennedy administration in 1962 work in this direction. There was a general shortening of the depreciation periods allowed by the Internal Revenue Service, so that buildings and equipment can be written off more rapidly. This raises the tax-free amount which a company can set aside in depreciation allowances, and thus encourages replacement of obsolete equipment with the "latest model." This raises productivity as well as the level of investment.

A second change permits businesses to deduct 7 percent of any investment in eligible machinery and equipment from their income tax bill. This is a direct investment subsidy. It raises the prospective yield on new investment without permitting larger profits on old investment.

Making high investment a major objective also changes one's thinking about *control of cyclical fluctuations*. For example, it argues against heavy reliance on monetary policy to check an excessive upswing. Such an upswing typically involves a high level of planned investment which, when added to consumer and government spending plans, yields an excessive level of demand. Somebody's demand has to be reduced. Monetary policy operates to cut investment plans by raising interest rates and restricting credit. This may be undesirable in terms of long-run growth.

Suppose, instead, that government raised personal income tax rates to restrict consumer demand and produce a budget surplus. The money would be used to retire government securities and would become available through the capital market to finance private investment. Business concerns would be able to carry out their investment plans, and the burden of restriction would fall mainly on consumption.

Thus the conclusion of Chapter 26 that monetary policy is the natural way to control a strong upswing needs to be modified when growth objectives are brought into the picture.

A device which is used increasingly in Europe is *business-government consultation on investment levels*. This is the essence of the "economic plans" of France, Sweden, and a number of other countries. Once a year each industry canvasses its members to determine their investment plans for the year ahead. Leaders of the major industries then sit down with economic officials of the government to see how this will work out for the economy as a whole. Suppose it appears that total demand will be excessive. Several things can be done: government can reduce its own investment plans; or government can move to restrict consumer demand; or government may check private investment by raising interest rates and restricting credit, at the same time making clear to the business community why such action is necessary. In the opposite situation, where demand threatens to be insufficient, government can prepare and discuss with industry a package of proposals designed to raise demand to the full-employment level.

The essence of this procedure is *advance* consultation to ensure that business investment plans and government fiscal plans are consistent with each other and with the capacity limits of the economy. It has the advantage of reassuring business that the economy will operate near full capacity, and that they can safely make investment plans on this assumption. The nervousness which characterizes business investment decisions in the United States arises partly from the fact that business and government planners operate at arm's length, or even in an atmosphere of mutual distrust.

Efforts to stimulate private investment should be accompanied by a vigorous program of *public investment*. Without taking sides in the controversy over whether government has been "overinvesting" or "underinvesting" in the past, one can point to large areas of investment opportunity in highways, airports, navigation, and local transport; slum clearance, urban redevelopment, and low-income housing; construction of educational facilities at all levels from grade schools through medical schools; improvement of hospitals and other health facilities; funds for scholarships, fellowships, and basic scientific research; and natural resource conservation and development.

The "growth problem" can now be restated: suppose that effective action is being taken along the lines suggested above, and suppose that this results in a 4 percent annual increase in GNP over the next decade. (The Council of Economic Advisers estimated in 1965 that the nation's productive capacity was then growing at 3¾ percent a year.[9] Considering the accelerated increase of the labor force and the possible further acceleration of factor productivity, a 4 percent performance over the next decade or two seems quite plausible.) Is this figure high enough? Or should we make a drive to raise it still higher?

This probably *could* be done, if we wanted to. The strategy would be to restrain the rise of private consumption through heavier taxation and to accumulate a federal budget surplus. Part of this surplus could be used for heavier public investment, and part could be fed into the securities markets through federal debt retirement and thus made available for private investment. Long-term interest rates would be held continuously at a low level to strengthen investment incentives. With skillful management, the outcome could be a changed composition of GNP, with the investment share larger than it is at present.[10] It might be possible in this way to raise the GNP growth rate by perhaps half a percentage point—say, from 4.0 percent to 4.5 percent a year.[11]

Assuming that this could be done, *should* it be done? The most

---

[9] *Economic Report of the President*, January, 1965, pp. 80–82.

[10] For an argument supporting this kind of strategy, see an article by James Tobin reprinted in Edmund S. Phelps (ed.), *The Goal of Economic Growth* (New York: W. W. Norton & Co., Inc., 1962), pp. 88–93.

[11] Gross private investment as a percentage of GNP has been running in the neighborhood of 12 percent. It seems unlikely that even with vigorous effort this could be raised by more than one third, say to 16 percent. This would raise the rate of increase of capital stock—k in the growth equation—by one third, say from 3 percent to 4 percent a year. Because of the small share of capital in national income, however, k has a weight of only about 0.3 in the growth equation. So an increase of 1 percent a year in k raises the GNP growth rate by only 0.3 percent. By adding a dash of faith in vintage capital, one might revise this upward to 0.5 percent.

common argument in favor of forcibly boosting our growth rate is that other countries have been doing better. Japan, West Germany, the U.S.S.R., and a number of other countries have been raising their GNP at rates of 5 to 8 percent a year. How can we hold up our heads in international society unless we are doing something comparable? The cogency of this noneconomic argument everyone must judge for himself. One economic side comment: it may be *natural* for a rich country to have a lower growth rate than considerably poorer countries. In a rich country, a considerably higher percentage of consumption takes the form of services rather than commodities. These services, being largely hand-produced, offer less scope for capital investment and technical progress. It seems quite possible that, as other countries approach our present income level, they will also find their percentage growth rate declining.

A COMPARATIVE VIEW: TYPICAL GROWTH RATES IN THE WEST

What is the long-term record of other industrialized capitalist countries? What constitutes par in growth rates?

For most of the industrial nations we now have national income estimates covering approximately the past century. Information on 14 of these countries is summarized in Table 3.[12] The "total product" column indicates that the rate of GNP increase has varied from about 2 percent a year in the slowest-growing countries to about 4 percent a year at the top. The second column reveals that the variation in output growth is due partly to differences in the rate of population increase. The "areas of new settlement"—Australia, Canada, the United States—have had population growth of around 2 percent a year over the long run. Most of the European countries have had population increases of less than 1 percent a year. So it is not surprising that GNP has risen faster in the former group.

The last column of the table, showing rates of increase in *output per capita,* is particularly significant as indicating the rate of improvement in living standards. Note, first, that the rate of improvement has been gradual—between 1 and 2 percent a year in most countries. It is the steady and sustained character of the growth, rather than its speed, which has brought these countries to their present high level of output. The U.S. record compares well with that of other industrial countries over the long run. But we have not been the fastest-growing country, as we are sometimes prone to think. Several other countries, notably Japan, Russia, and Sweden, have outdone us in this respect.

It is interesting that the rate of increase in output per capita shows no relation to the rate of population growth. Some countries with high

[12] Simon Kuznets, *Modern Economic Growth: Rate, Structure, and Spread* (New Haven, Conn.: Yale University Press, 1966), chap. ii.

population growth stand well up in the table, but others stand near the bottom. Some of the European countries with low population increase had high growth rates (Sweden, Norway, Denmark), but others had much slower growth (Switzerland, United Kingdom). The implication is that more rapid population growth has not been a handicap *to nations*

TABLE 3

Long-Term Growth of Population, Output, and Output per Capita, Selected Countries (Ranked in Order of Growth in Output per Capita)

COUNTRY	INITIAL PERIOD	TERMINAL PERIOD	DURATION OF PERIOD (Years)	RATE OF GROWTH PER DECADE (Percent)		
				TOTAL PRODUCT	POPULA-TION	PRODUCT PER CAPITA
1. Sweden	1861–65	1960–62	98.0	36.9	6.7	28.3
2. European Russia-U.S.S.R	1913	1958	45.0	35.7	6.4	27.4
3. Japan	1879–81	1959–61	80.0	42.0	12.3	26.4
4. Denmark	1870–74	1960–62	89.0	31.8	10.4	19.4
5. Norway	1865–74	1960–62	91.5	29.0	8.4	19.0
6. Italy	1898–1902	1960–62	61.0	26.8	6.8	18.7
7. Canada	1870–74	1960–62	89.0	40.7	19.1	18.1
8. France	1841–50	1960–62	105.5	20.8	2.5	17.9
9. Germany-West Germany	1871–75	1960–62	88.0	31.1	11.2	17.9
10. United States	1839	1960–62	122.0	42.5	21.6	17.2
11. Switzerland	1890–99	1957–59	63.5	25.7	8.3	16.1
12. United Kingdom	1855–59	1957–59	101.0	21.1	6.1	14.1
13. Netherlands	1900–04	1960–62	59.0	29.7	14.3	13.5
14. Australia	1861–65	1959/60–1961/62	97.5	34.1	24.2	8.0

whose institutions and resources were favorable to economic growth. But it would be unsafe to extend this conclusion to the less developed countries, many of which are in a decidedly less favorable position.

Is there any tendency for the growth rate of industrial countries to slow down over the long run? Professor Simon Kuznets concludes that there is. He has divided the growth record of each country into a pre-1914 and a post-1914 period.[13] Some of the younger industrial countries

[13] Simon Kuznets, *Six Lectures on Economic Growth* (Glencoe, Ill.: Free Press, 1959), Lecture II.

(Sweden, Japan, Italy, Russia) show an acceleration of growth since 1914. In most countries, however, per capita output has risen less rapidly since 1914 than it did before. For the European countries, which suffered widespread devastation in two world wars, this is perhaps not surprising. It is more surprising for the United States, Canada, and other overseas areas.

Kuznets concludes that countries pass through three phases: a phase in which the growth rate accelerates markedly, a phase of more or less constant growth, and finally a phase of retarded growth. He finds the reason for the eventual retardation on the side of demand rather than supply:

. . . there are no inherently *compelling* reasons for the rate of growth of per capita product to decline . . . technological and other limitations on the *supply* side can hardly be viewed as an important factor. The major reason would therefore lie on the demand side. A long-term rise in real income per capita would make leisure an increasingly preferred good, as is clearly evidenced by the marked reduction in the working week in freely organized, nonauthoritarian advanced countries. One could argue that after a high level of per capita income is attained, the pressure on the demand side for further increases is likely to slacken.[14]

Recent Growth Experience

One is cautioned against premature generalization, however, by the fact that most of these countries have experienced a remarkable spurt of growth since World War II. Since 1950, Japan has raised its GNP at about 10 percent a year. The average for the European Common Market area has been above 6 percent. The record of 14 countries over the period 1948–63 is summarized in Table 4. The high growth rates of Japan, West Germany, and several other European countries stand out clearly. Britain, Canada, and the United States, on the other hand, stand near the bottom of the list.

How far was the output growth of the fast-growing countries due to more rapid increase of factor inputs, and how far was it due to a faster rise in productivity? Professor Evsey Domar and several colleagues have tried to answer this question for five countries during the 1950's.[15] Their results are summarized in Table 5. It turns out that West Germany and Japan had a substantially higher rate of increase in factor inputs than the other three countries. West Germany was absorbing large numbers of refugees from the East Zone into its labor force. Japan benefited from a

---

[14] *Ibid.*, p. 38.

[15] Evsey D. Domar, Scott M. Eddie, Bruce M. Herrick, Paul Hohenberg, Michael D. Intriligator, and Ichizo Mujamoto, "Economic Growth in the United States, Canada, United Kingdom, Germany, and Japan in the Post-War Period," *Review of Economics and Statistics*, February, 1964, pp. 33–40. The methodology is similar to that used by Kendrick for the United States. The reader interested in techniques and in interpretation of the findings should consult the original source.

TABLE 4

Annual Percentage Increase in Total and Per Capita Output
Selected Countries, 1948–63

COUNTRY	POPULATION	GROSS NATIONAL PRODUCT	GNP PER CAPITA
Japan	1.2	10.0	8.8
West Germany	1.2	7.0	5.8
Italy	0.7	6.0	5.3
France	1.0	5.3	4.3
Switzerland	1.6	5.1	3.5
Netherlands	1.4	4.8	3.4
Sweden	0.7	3.8	3.1
Denmark	1.1	4.1	3.0
United Kingdom	0.5	3.0	2.5
Norway	0.9	3.4	2.5
Australia	2.3	4.8	2.5
South Africa	2.4	4.8	2.4
Canada	2.3	4.3	2.0
United States	1.7	3.6	1.9

Source: Raymond Goldsmith, *The Determinants of Financial Structure* (Paris OECD Development Center, Studies No. 2, 1965). For more recent years, see U.N. *Yearbook of National Account Statistics*, issued annually.

high rate of past population growth and considerable surplus labor in 1950. Germany and Japan also had exceptionally high rates of capital investment, which in Japan exceeded 30 percent of GNP in some years.

In addition, however, West Germany and Japan had a much higher rate of increase in factor productivity, which Domar and his colleagues prefer to call simply "the residual," to emphasize that it includes more than

TABLE 5

Elements in Postwar Growth, Selected Countries

COUNTRY AND PERIOD	ANNUAL PERCENTAGE RATE OF GROWTH OF				PERCENTAGE OF OUTPUT GROWTH ATTRIBUTABLE TO "THE RESIDUAL"
	OUTPUT	LABOR INPUT (Man-Hours)	CAPITAL INPUT (Constant Prices)	"THE RESIDUAL"	
United States, 1948–60	3.4	0.8	3.6†	1.4†	47*
Canada, 1949–60	4.0	1.2	5.5	1.2	30
United Kingdom, 1949–59	2.4	1.0	3.5	0.6	25
West Germany, 1950–59	7.4	1.7	6.8	3.6	50
Japan, 1951–59	8.4	2.7	8.8	3.7	44

* Gross domestic product at constant market prices.
† Private economy; total economy not available.

technical progress in the usual sense. The rate of productivity increase was three times as high in Germany and Japan as in Canada or the United States, and six times as high as in Britain. This must have been due partly to the rapid modernization of productive equipment associated with a high rate of investment.

It is too early to say whether the high growth rates of the industrial capitalist countries since 1950 will persist into the future or whether there will be a tapering off at some point. But the fact that economic growth is a continually unfolding, never finished detective story makes it an interesting subject.

GROWTH AND CHANGE: THE USES OF NATIONAL OUTPUT

So far we have been concerned with measuring and explaining the growth of total output. For the rest of the chapter we shall be concerned with what goes into the output basket and with who gets the output.

It seems platitudinous to say that a growing economy must also be a changing economy. But we can say a good deal more than this. We can explain *why* certain structural changes must occur and can predict their general course. Moreover, the discussion is relevant, not only to countries with a long growth record, but (potentially) to the less developed countries as well.

A striking feature of a poor country is the high ratio of private consumption to national output. Something like 85 percent of GNP goes directly into consumption, with gross investment forming perhaps 10 percent of the total and government production only about 5 percent. Growth brings a marked rise in the investment share and the government share. Private consumption, while increasing greatly on an absolute basis, shrinks as a proportion of national output to 60–65 percent. The size of the private consumption share, and the rate at which it is declining over time, is perhaps the best single indicator of a country's economic progress.

Does this contradict the notion that a capitalist economy is consumer-oriented? Not at all. People are interested in consumption next year as well as this year. Devoting a high proportion of this year's output to investment helps to keep output growing rapidly in the future. As for government, the services it produces are presumably responsive to public demand and add to consumer welfare.

The structural changes in some of the leading industrial economies are shown in Table 6.[16] The upper part of the table shows the distribution of output in an "early" period, which for most countries is roughly 1860–80. Note the predominance of private consumption and the small-

---

[16] Data are from Simon Kuznets, *Modern Economic Growth,* chap. v.

ness of the two other components. The bottom part of the table shows the situation in these same countries as of 1950–59. Private consumption has now fallen to 60–65 percent of GNP in most countries, government consumption has risen to 14–16 percent, and gross capital formation to 20–30 percent. The U.S.S.R. is distinguished from the capitalist countries by an unusually high investment rate and an unusually high level of

TABLE 6

Distribution of Gross National Product by Final Use, Selected Countries
(Based on Totals in Current Prices)

	SHARE IN GNP (Percent)		
COUNTRY	PRIVATE CONSUMPTION	GOVERNMENT CONSUMPTION	GROSS NATIONAL CAPITAL FORMATION
Early Periods			
United Kingdom, 1860–79	82.7	4.8	12.5
Germany, 1851–70	81.6	4.0	14.4
Italy, 1861–80	87.3	4.2	8.5
Sweden, 1861–80	85.3	4.4	10.3
United States, 1869–88	76.7	3.6	19.7
Canada, 1870 and 1890	86.5	5.6	7.9
Australia, 1861–80	88.8		11.2
Japan, 1887–1906	92.0		8.0
U.S.S.R., 1928	84.1	3.4	12.5
Recent Periods			
United Kingdom, 1950–58	66.9	16.9	16.2
West Germany, 1950–59	58.7	14.4	26.8
Italy, 1950–59	68.2	12.0	19.8
Sweden, 1950–59	61.9	16.8	21.4
United States, 1950–59	63.7	16.8	21.4
Canada, 1950–59	63.5	14.1	22.4
Australia, 1950/51–1959/60	63.9	9.9	26.4
Japan, 1950–59	59.5	10.3	30.2
U.S.S.R., 1960	47.1	20.3	32.6

government consumption, with a correspondingly lower proportion of private consumption.

What are the economic reasons for these tendencies? As regards government, we can simply recall what was said in Chapter 17. The shift from agriculture to industry means growing urbanization of the population. This means larger per capita expenditures on streets, sewage and sanitation, water supply, police and fire protection, urban transportation, and other facilities. Next, certain government services, notably education, have a high income elasticity of demand. As national income rises, people choose to devote a larger proportion of this income to education. Finally, the twentieth century has seen many countries devoting a substantial part of GNP to military purposes, and this accentuates the uptrend in the government share.

The rate of capital formation also typically accelerates during the early phases of economic growth. More rapid growth of output *requires* more capital and also *permits* a higher level of saving and capital formation. To detect this acceleration in the older industrial countries one has to go far back in history, before 1800 in the case of Great Britain and before 1850 in the United States. But where rapid growth is more recent, we can get some indication from national income statistics. In Sweden GCF/GNP averaged 9.2 percent in 1861–70, 14.2 percent in 1911–20, and 20.5 percent in 1952–58. In Italy, the rate rose from 7.5 percent in 1861–70 to 15.2 percent in 1906–15 to 19.4 percent in 1952–58. In Japan, gross capital formation rose from 10.6 percent in 1892–1901 to 16.4 percent in 1922–31 and to 28.8 percent in 1952–58.[17]

The acceleration of investment is not a sharp spurt limited to a few decades. It is a gradual speed-up over two or three generations.

But acceleration does not continue indefinitely. The capital formation rate eventually levels off and moves along on a plateau. Sweden reached the 20 percent level in the 1920's and has remained near that level ever since. Britain had a gross capital formation rate of 13.6 percent in 1870–79 and has since not risen much above that level. The United States reached a rate of 20 percent soon after the Civil War and has never gone much above that.

Indeed, recent decades show some drop in the gross capital formation rate in both Britain and the United States; and there has been a substantial drop in the rate of net capital formation because of the large amount of depreciation on a relatively old capital stock. This tendency has not yet appeared in the younger industrial nations of the West. But it may turn out to be a systematic feature of an aging economy.

This leveling off, and possible eventual decline, of the capital formation rate is surprising. Rich people save more than poor people. So as a country grows richer, why doesn't its savings rate keep on rising?

This is an intriguing question, to which we do not know the answer. But we can make some guesses about the United States. Farmers and small businessmen, who are heavy savers, have declined in relative importance over the past century. Wage and salary earners, who are less noted for thriftiness, have increased greatly in importance. The distribution of household incomes has become more equal, which may have

---

[17] Simon Kuznets, "Quantitative Aspects of the Economic Growth of Nations: VI. Long-term Trends in Capital Formation Proportions," *Economic Development and Cultural Change*, Vol. IX, No. 4, Part II, July, 1961.

reduced saving. The constant struggle to keep up with the Joneses, intensified by the vigor of American advertising, has kept the consumption schedule moving upward. The great increase in military expenditures since 1940, financed largely from income taxes, has reduced the possibilities of private saving. Finally, as we emphasized in Part Three, the level of saving depends on demand as well as supply. It depends on availability of investment opportunities as well as on the desire to save. There have been periods in this century when the investment outlook was not attractive, which reduced the level of national income and therefore of saving.

COMPOSITION OF OUTPUT: SOME SOURCES OF CHANGE

What happens to the kinds of goods produced as income rises in a growing economy? The discussion in the preceding section implies that certain things will happen. Government output consists largely of services, so a growing government share in GNP implies a shift toward service production. A higher rate of capital formation implies greater demand for cement, steel, lumber, machinery, and other capital goods. So the output of heavy manufacturing should rise faster than that of light manufacturing.

But there is more to the story than this. What about the 50 to 60 percent of output going into private consumption? There are a number of reasons why the makeup of consumption also changes over the course of time.

1. Changes in the pattern of consumer expenditure. When peoples' incomes rise, they spend more on almost every kind of good. But there are differences in the *income elasticity of demand* for different products. Remember that income elasticity measures the relation between a small increase in consumer incomes and the resulting increase in consumer purchases. If, when consumer income rises 5 percent, purchases of men's shoes also rise 5 percent, the income elasticity of demand for shoes is 1.

In a poor country where most people are undernourished, the income elasticity of demand for food may be close to 1. But as the country becomes richer, this figure will fall. People can eat only so much. In the United States, income elasticity of demand for farm products has been estimated at only 0.25. Income elasticity of demand for housing is higher than for food, but still typically below 1. For clothing, income elasticity in most countries lies between 1.0 and 1.5. This does not necessarily mean that people buy disproportionately *more* clothing as their incomes rise. But the kinds of clothing they buy are more varied, elaborate, and expensive. The items with highest income elasticity are services of a semiluxury character: travel, entertainment, education, beauty care, and other personal services.[18]

Professor Kuznets has prepared estimates for various types of consumer expenditures in the United States. From his longer listing we have selected some items with quite low, and some with quite high, income elasticities of demand (Table 7).[19]

Take a period, then, over which people's real incomes have doubled. This will *not* mean doubling of their consumption of every good and service. Food expenditure may have gone up 50 percent, clothing expenditure 150 percent, and spending on recreation and personal services 200 percent. The result is a shift in the makeup of family

TABLE 7

PRODUCT GROUP	INCOME ELASTICITY OF DEMAND, UNITED STATES, 1950
Tobacco	0.22
Fuel, light, water	0.30
Food and nonalcoholic beverages	0.59
Housing (rent)	0.60
Recreation and reading	1.56
Clothing and related products	1.70
Autos and other vehicles	1.82
House operation (domestic service, etc.)	1.86
Alcoholic beverages	1.94
Other (including private education)	2.38

budgets. The dimensions of this shift in the United States between 1900 and 1963 are suggested by Table 8. Note the sharp drop in percentages spent on food and housing and the sharp rise in the "sundries" category. "Transportation" means mainly the automobile, which has gotten its nose ever further into the tent and now takes about as much income as is spent on housing.

In a market economy, industry turns out what people are willing to buy. The changed distribution of consumer expenditures is reflected in the pattern of production. This accounts for the relative decline of manufacturing industries producing staple foods and clothing, the

---

[18] For an excellent review of the statistical evidence, see H. S. Houthakker, "An International Comparison of Household Expenditure Patterns," *Econometrica,* Vol. XXV, 1957, pp. 532–51.

[19] Simon Kuznets, *Modern Economic Growth,* chap. v. Strictly, these are *expenditure* elasticities based on cross-section data from family budget studies. It should be remembered also that they are as of a certain date, 1950, and that income elasticities may change considerably over the course of time.

expansion of industries concerned with automobiles, gasoline, radios, and television, and the even more rapid expansion of the entertainment and service industries.

2. Differing productivity trends. The average rate of productivity increase in the economy conceals wide variations in particular sectors. Research workers at the National Bureau of Economic Research have calculated that, in the United States from 1889 to 1953, the productivity of labor and capital combined rose only 77 percent in the lumber

TABLE 8

Distribution of Consumer Expenditures, U. S. A., 1901, 1950, and 1963

ITEM	PERCENT OF TOTAL EXPENDITURE IN:		
	1901 (1)	1950 (2)	1963 (3)
Total	100.0	100.0	100.0
Food and beverages	43.1	32.5	23.2
Housing	18.1	10.6	13.0
Fuel, light, refrigeration	5.7	4.2	3.9
Clothing	13.0	11.5	9.9
Sundries*	20.1	41.2	50.0
Transportation	2.9	13.8	12.6
House furnishings and household operations	6.8	11.0	10.0
Recreation, reading, education	3.4	5.8	7.6
Tobacco	1.2	2.0	2.2
Medical care	4.3	5.1	6.8
Personal care	0.9	2.3	1.7
Other	0.6	1.2	9.0

Sources: U.S. Department of Labor, *How American Buying Habits Change,* chap. ii, Tables 2–6, for 1901 and 1950; *Survey of Current Business,* July, 1964, p. 16, for 1963.
* Detailed distribution of the sundries item in column 1 is for 1917–19; comparable figures for 1901 are not available. The sundries total of 20.1 per cent, however, is correct for 1901. There seems to have been little change in the sundries percentage between 1890 and 1920. The increase has come almost entirely since 1920.

industry; but it rose 259 percent in paper production and 778 percent in rubber goods. In the utilities group, productivity rose 207 percent in telephone service, but 1,664 percent in electric light and power.

Why should these differences lead to changes in the pattern of production? In a competitive market economy, product prices are closely related to production costs. If productivity is rising unusually fast in industry A, its unit cost of production will be falling unusually rapidly. This will be reflected in prices, and the products of industry A will become cheaper relative to other products. This will encourage consumers to buy more of A's products than before, and less of other things. The pattern of consumption thus tends to shift *toward* products where productivity is rising very fast and away from products where it is rising only slowly. The relative cheapening of electric power, for example, certainly has something to do with the phenomenal increase in power use since 1900.

3. **New product development.**   Technical progress creates new products, which attract patronage by drawing demand away from older products. If a new product is a direct substitute for an older one, and if it is markedly superior or cheaper, the old product may vanish entirely. Horseshoes and carriages are virtually extinct in the United States. Demand shifts toward sectors of the economy in which new product development is particularly rapid and away from those in which it is lagging.

This helps to explain a phenomenon which stands out in the industrial statistics. A new industry grows gradually in its experimental years, then enters a period of rapid growth which may last for several decades. This is the period during which the benefits of large-scale production are being reaped, costs and prices are being (relatively) reduced, and the new product is winning acceptance as a substitute for older goods. In time, however, the product achieves maximum penetration of its potential market. Meanwhile, still newer products have appeared, which tend to displace this one. So growth tapers off and moves along on a plateau. The product may even "go over the hill" and head downward toward extinction.[20]

Yet despite this tapering off of individual industries, a country's *total* output can continue to grow at about the same rate decade after decade. The explanation lies in the continued appearance of new products which grow by partial displacement of older ones. Each new industry gives the economy a booster shot toward higher levels of total output.

What does a broker mean when he advises you to buy stock in a "growth industry"? What *is* a growth industry? It is an industry which has most or all of the following characteristics: the product is relatively new; productivity in the industry is rising faster than the national average; both price and income elasticity of demand for the product are high; and no dangerous competitors or substitutes are yet in sight. This is why you would have done well in 1920 by buying Du Pont, General Motors, I.B.M., or A.T.&T.

4. **Changing comparative advantage.**   We emphasized in Chapter 18 that a country need not produce everything for itself. It will do best by concentrating on products in which it has a *comparative advantage*. But comparative advantage is not a static thing. It changes with resource

---

[20] For confirmation of this as regards the United States, see the classic study by Arthur F. Burns, *Production Trends in the United States Since 1870* (New York: National Bureau of Economic Research, 1934).

discoveries and technical developments. It changes also with *increases in the size of the economy.* In some industries the optimum scale of plant is very large. It is not feasible to build a pocket-size steel mill, or auto assembly plant, or aircraft factory. So in an economy with a GNP of $1 billion per year, it will not be sensible to produce these things.

But suppose the economy's output rises to $5 billion a year, then to $10 billion, and so on. The growth of the domestic market makes it feasible to introduce more and more types of manufacturing. First to appear will be industries in which the efficient scale of plant is relatively small, such as textiles, clothing, food processing, and other light consumer goods. As the economy continues to grow, it will become efficient to introduce more and more branches of heavy industry, until eventually the country may become largely self-sufficient in manufacturing. This process, usually called *import substitution,* has been important in the development of the United States, Canada, Japan, and other industrial countries. It will presumably be important also in the countries now embarking on the early stages of industrialization.

The nature of the process, however, must be properly understood. Economic planners in some of the poor countries seem to reason this way: "rich countries produce a great deal of steel, automobiles, and machinery. So let us begin immediately to produce steel, automobiles, and machinery. Then we too will be rich." This reverses the causal sequence. The truth is that, *as a country becomes richer* (in ways which we have still to explore), the growth of large-scale industries becomes feasible. It is a result, or an accompanying characteristic, rather than a basic cause of economic development.

THE OVERALL RESULT: THE CHANGING PATTERN OF PRODUCTION

For all these reasons, the makeup of GNP changes in a systematic way as economic growth proceeds. As explained earlier, this can be tested either by time-series analysis for individual countries or by cross-section analysis for a large number of countries.

Look first at changes in the pattern of American output since 1870, as shown in Table 9. The main trends are familiar to any reader of American history. Note first the decline in the relative importance of agriculture, from a quarter of national output in 1870 to less than 5 percent today. Farm production has continued to grow in absolute terms, otherwise we should all be on short rations. But GNP has grown so much faster that agriculture's share has fallen drastically.

The reverse of the coin is the rise of manufacturing from 15 percent of production in 1870 to around 30 percent at present. The manufacturing share has been leveling off, however, and seems unlikely to increase much further.

The trade sector shows surprising stability over the long run. True, *employment* in trade has risen relative to other sectors. But in terms of *value added,* trade has fluctuated between 15 and 17 percent with no upward trend.

Government production has risen from 5 percent of GNP at the turn of the century to more than 14 percent at the present time. The reasons for this were analyzed in Chapter 17. A major factor is the much higher level of military expenditure.

TABLE 9

Distribution of National Income by Industrial Origin, United States, 1869–1964
(Percent)

	AGRI-CULTURE*	MANUFAC-TURING AND MINING†	CON-STRUC-TION	TRADE	FINANCE, INSUR-ANCE, REAL ESTATE, AND OTHER‡	TRANSPOR-TATION, COMMU-NICATION, AND PUBLIC UTILITIES	SERVICES	GOVERN-MENT AND REST OF WORLD
1869	23.1	16.8	5.9	15.8	8.0	11.3	14.8	4.1
1879	19.9	16.1	5.2	16.9	8.4	13.5	15.9	4.1
1889	15.1	22.4	6.3	17.9	8.3	11.9	13.3	4.8
1899	19.9	21.2	4.4	17.5	8.2	10.8	11.8	6.5
1909	21.0	22.5	4.6	17.0	8.8	11.1	10.0	5.1
1919	21.0	26.9	2.7	15.1	7.9	10.7	7.4	8.3
1929	11.6	27.2	4.3	15.2	10.5	11.8	11.2	8.3
1929	9.4	27.2	4.3	15.2	14.5	10.9	11.8	6.7
1939	8.2	26.7	3.2	17.1	10.9	10.3	11.4	12.1
1949	7.8	30.8	4.8	18.6	9.2	8.5	9.8	10.6
1959	4.2	31.3	5.4	16.7	10.1	8.2	11.3	12.7
1964	3.4	31.3	5.1	15.2	11.1	8.3	11.2	14.3

* Figures for 1929–64 include forestry and fisheries.
† Figures for 1869–1929 include quarrying.
‡ Figures for 1869–1929 are sum of "Finance" and unallocated "Other." Figures for 1929–59 are for "Finance, Insurance and Real Estate."
Sources: 1869–1929: NICB, *Enterprise and Social Progress,* 1939, pp. 84, 95. 1929–64; *U.S. Income and Output,* 1958, p. 130; and *Survey of Current Business,* July, 1960, and April, 1965.

There has been no appreciable change since 1900 in the relative importance of the service industries. But this is misleading because the figures include domestic service, which is a sharply declining industry. (The disappearance of servants is recognized throughout the world as one of the best indicators of economic development!) If this were separated out, production of services outside the home would show a considerable increase.

The sectors used in Table 9 are very broad. If we dig more deeply into any of them, we find more detailed crosscurrents. The makeup of the manufacturing sector, for example, has changed a great deal. A few important gainers and losers may be found in Table 10.

These trends are not surprising. In a capital-using economy, it is natural that production of capital goods should grow in importance. In addition to our own requirements, we export substantial amounts of chemicals, metals, machinery, automobiles, trucks, and tractors to other countries. In consumer goods we are dependent mainly on home demand; and some of these industries, notably textiles, are being invaded by foreign producers who have a comparative advantage in light manufacturing.

TABLE 10

INDUSTRY	PERCENTAGE OF MANUFACTURING OUTPUT 1919	1963
Decreases		
Lumber and furniture products	7.0	4.1
Food products	9.8	8.1
Textiles	8.2	3.5
Clothing	5.8	4.1
Leather and leather products	2.8	1.2
Increases		
Automobiles and automobile equipment	4.3	7.9
Transportation equipment except automobiles	1.4	5.5
Electrical machinery	4.8	8.5
Machinery, except electrical	8.6	10.8
Chemicals	5.2	7.7

How far will past trends continue in the future? If we could extend Table 9 to the year 2000, what would it look like? Some of the past trends will doubtless slow down. The percentage of GNP coming from agriculture is already so low that it cannot fall much further. The manufacturing percentage will rise little if any. Overall, one can predict that the industries concerned with *physical production* will shrink gradually in terms of the percentage of GNP which they produce and the proportion of the labor force which they employ. The industries producing *intangible services* (trade, finance, the service industries, and government) will grow in relative importance. These industries already provide more than half the employment in the economy. This figure may rise above 60 percent by the end of the century.

There are two reasons why this is a safe prediction: income elasticity of demand for services is typically higher than for commodities, and production of services is less susceptible to mechanization. So, as consumers demand more and more services, this is bound to mean more employment. In manufacturing, on the other hand, it is often possible to meet rising demand with fewer workers through continued progress in mechanization and automation.

This is not to the credit of the service industries—rather the reverse. If more and more people are employed in these industries, and if the possibility of raising their productivity through mechanization is slight, this will slow down the overall rate of productivity increase in the economy.

Now for a cross-sectional view of output proportions. Kuznets has assembled information on about 40 countries and his results are summarized in Table 11. Category 1 includes North America, Australia and New

TABLE 11

Industrial Structure of the Labor Force,
Countries Grouped by Product per Capita

CATEGORY	1	2	3
Number of countries	13	10	15
Average percentage of labor force engaged in:			
Agriculture, forestry, fisheries	18.6	39.5	56.4
Manufacturing, mining, construction	37.8	25.5	17.6
Transportation and communication	8.1	5.2	3.4
Trade, banking, and finance	13.4	9.7	6.5
Other services (professional, personal, government)	22.2	20.1	16.1
Total	100.0	100.0	100.0

Source: Simon Kuznets, "Quantitative Aspects of the Economic Growth of Nations: II. Industrial Distribution of National Product and Labor Force," *Economic Development and Cultural Change*, Supp. to Vol. V, No. 4 (July, 1957). For most countries, the data relate to the early 1950's.

Zealand, Britain, and the more prosperous countries of Western Europe. Those in category 2 are "middle-income" countries, including Japan, several from Latin America, and several from Southern Europe. Category 3 consists of underdeveloped countries at the bottom of the income scale.

Note what happens as we go from the poorest countries to the richest. The proportion of the labor force engaged in *agriculture* drops sharply. In the poorest countries this proportion may run as high as 70 to 80 percent. In the richer countries, it drops to between 10 and 20 percent. This is partly because of low income elasticity of demand for food. But another reason is major advances in agricultural productivity in the richer countries. In 1870 each farm family in the United States produced enough food for *two* families. Today, each farm family grows enough for *twelve* families. Rising productivity in agriculture is in fact a necessary condition for sustained economic growth.

The proportion of the labor force in *manufacturing* increases sharply with economic growth. In the poorer countries, the figure rarely exceeds 10 percent, and most of these are artisans rather than factory workers. In the industrialized countries, manufacturing typically employs around 30 percent of the labor force. When mining, construction, and public utilities are added, the figure rises to between 40 and 50 percent. This growth of urban industrial activities is in fact so characteristic that one is apt to see in it the prime mover of economic progress.

Table 11 indicates the changes through which the industrialized nations have passed and are still passing; for the underlying forces of change continue to operate, even at high income levels. And it foreshadows the structural changes which will occur in the poorer nations as they get started on a sustained path of economic growth.

SUMMARY

1. The U.S. growth rate accelerated materially in the period 1830–60. This was associated with westward expansion, very rapid population increase, establishment of a railroad network, marked technical developments in both agriculture and industry, a rise in the rate of domestic saving, and large-scale borrowing from abroad.

2. Over the years since 1870, U.S. output per capita has advanced at an average rate of about 2 percent a year. The rate of growth has been uneven, however, and there was one major setback during the 1930's. *Total output* has grown more slowly since 1914 than before 1914, due mainly to slower growth of population. The growth of *output per capita* has also slowed down a bit in recent decades, mainly because of a marked drop in hours worked per year by members of the labor force. If leisure were counted as part of national output, one might conclude that the rate of progress has not declined.

3. About two thirds of the increase in output since 1919 can be attributed to rising factor productivity, with increased factor inputs contributing only one third.

4. Looking to the future, we may expect to benefit from a faster growth of the labor force and a continued high rate of productivity increase. Government can contribute to economic growth through full-employment policies, support of education and scientific research, and measures to stimulate private investment. It seems reasonable to expect GNP to grow at about 4 percent a year, and GNP per capita at better than 2 percent a year, over the next couple of decades.

5. Data for other advanced industrial countries indicate that the typical rate of increase in output per capita over the past century has been 1.5 to 2.0 percent per year. There is no apparent relation between rate of population growth and rate of increase in output per capita. In most countries, growth has been somewhat slower since 1914 than before

1914, partly because of a trend toward increased leisure like that observed in the United States.

6. Economic growth brings a gradual decline in the share of national output going to private consumption, from a level of 80–85 percent at the outset to about 60–65 percent in the wealthier countries today. Government production of current services rises from about 5 to about 15 percent of GNP, while gross capital formation also rises to 20 percent or better.

7. The composition of private consumption changes markedly over the course of time because of differing income elasticities of demand, differing rates of technical progress and cost reduction, and the continuous introduction of new products.

8. These tendencies gradually change a country's output pattern. Broadly, agricultural and other primary products fall greatly as a percentage of GNP. Manufacturing expands rapidly and stabilizes at a high level; and most service industries also increase as a percentage of GNP.

DISCUSSION QUESTIONS

1. What kinds of figures do you need to
   a) *Measure* the rate of economic growth in the United States?
   b) *Interpret* or *explain* the growth which has occurred?
2. In American history and other courses you have doubtless encountered a variety of explanations of the rapid growth of the American economy. How far do those explanations agree (or disagree) with the interpretation advanced here?
3. Suppose it were established that output per capita in the United States has risen less rapidly since 1914 than it did before 1914. Is this necessarily deplorable?
4. Should government undertake to raise the U.S. growth rate substantially above its present (and prospective) level? Why, or why not?
5. If you answered "Yes" to the previous question, what specific measures would you advocate?
6. Several other countries have had considerably higher growth rates than the United States. Why?
7. One might expect a high rate of population growth in a country to drag down the rate of increase in output per capita. In the advanced industrial nations, however, there is no apparent relation between these two things. How do you explain this?
8. The composition of GNP in rich countries differs markedly from that in poor countries. Suppose you are the President of a poor country, and are familiar with all these statistics. What lessons, if any, could you draw from them?

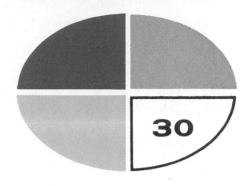

The Soviet Experience:

A Growth Race?

The Dodo suddenly called out, "The race is over!" and they all crowded around it, panting, and asking "But who has won?"

This question the Dodo could not answer without a great deal of thought, and it sat for a long time with one finger pressed upon its forehead (the position in which you usually see Shakespeare in the pictures of him), while the rest waited in silence. At last the Dodo said, "*Everybody* has won, and all must have prizes."

Alice's Adventures in Wonderland

FROM THE EIGHTEENTH CENTURY until World War I, there was only one proven prescription for economic growth. Britain, the United States, Germany, and other capitalist countries showed the way; and it was assumed that any other industrializing country would follow the same pattern.

But since 1917 a second prescription has been abroad in the world. Soviet economists maintain that this prescription is inherently superior. Under central planning, it is said, growth does not just happen. A planned economy can decide how fast it wants to grow. By setting the target high enough, it is possible to outdo anything that has been accomplished in the capitalist countries.

It is argued also that the Soviet prescription is preferable for the poor countries of Asia, Africa, and Latin America. Soviet bloc leaders say, "Of course it is possible for a poor country to lift itself by its bootstraps. We know how to do it. In fact we have done it in one country after another. The requirements are government operation of all means of production, a national economic plan which emphasizes investment and restricts consumption, and rigid political discipline through a one-party system."

So it is important to ask what the Soviet system has actually accomplished over the past half century. How rapid has been the growth in national output? How have the results been accomplished? Is the pattern of growth basically different from that in capitalist countries? Will growth continue at the same rate in the future, and will the U.S.S.R. eventually surpass the production levels of the U.S.A. and Western Europe?

The Measurement Problem

The student of Soviet growth is faced at the outset with a formidable problem of measurement. This is not due mainly to inadequacy of data on individual products. In the post-Stalin era, at least, Soviet economic statistics have been comprehensive and open to examination by Western scholars. While concepts and definitions differ somewhat from those used in the West, and while there may be some optimistic bias in the production totals, there is no reason to suspect extensive falsification.

The main problem is that the growth rate for individual products varies enormously. Output of power, metals, machinery, and other capital goods has risen very fast. Most consumer goods show much lower rates of growth. The increase in some types of agricultural output has been quite disappointing. So in calculating an overall growth rate for the economy, everything depends on how much *weight* one gives to each line of production. And since heterogeneous products can be added up only in value terms, this raises the question of the proper *price* to be attached to each product.

The characteristics of the Soviet pricing system were pointed out in Part One. Prices of capital goods are relatively low by U.S. standards, while prices of consumer goods are relatively high. The whole price structure has been revised on several occasions. So it makes considerable difference whether one makes comparisons in terms of 1937 prices, or 1950 prices, or 1965 prices. And if one valued Soviet production at U.S. prices, the result would again be different.

Fortunately, while calculations on various bases differ considerably, the outlines of the story remain much the same. In what follows, I have tried to use the most plausible estimates by leading authorities, but anyone interested in the niceties of measurement should consult the original sources.[1]

The Vagaries of History

Another important consideration is that Soviet history has been punctuated by war and invasion, and so economic progress has been jerky and discontinuous. From 1914 to 1928 the economy was ravaged by foreign war followed by civil war, and then recovered gradually under a regime which was still largely one of private ownership. From necessity rather than conviction, Soviet leaders left the peasants in control of the land while private trade and handicrafts flourished in the cities. Only factory industries were fully nationalized. Central economic planning was not yet born.

The year 1928 marks a decisive turning point. By this time Stalin had triumphed over Trotsky and other political rivals, and was in a position to shape the course of Soviet development. He announced a policy of rapid industrialization and complete socialization, applied both to industry and agriculture. The peasants were forced into collective farms amidst bloodshed and disorganization of production. Guidelines for the economy were laid down in a Five-Year Plan for 1928–32, followed by a second plan for 1933–37, and so on. There was a rapid buildup of industrial capacity, particularly of industries producing capital goods and armaments. By the mid-thirties, World War II was already visible on the horizon, and Soviet leaders were racing against time to achieve self-sufficiency in military production.

The storm broke in 1941. The most productive part of the country was invaded and occupied. Despite efforts to shift production to safe areas behind the Urals, Soviet output fell considerably, and the population suffered severe hardships. But with the remaining production, and with massive aid from the West, Russia managed eventually to roll back the invading armies. When Talleyrand was asked what he had been doing during the French Revolution, he replied "I survived." Stalin might have given the same answer in 1945 in justification of his iron policies.

For several years after 1945, the U.S.S.R. was engaged in rebuilding the devastated areas, shifting population and production back to prewar locations, and replacing wartime losses of machinery and equipment. In 1948 the average Soviet consumer was probably no better off than he had been in 1928, perhaps no better off than the average Russian of 1913. One

---

[1] See in particular Abram Bergson, *The Real National Income of Soviet Russia Since 1928* (Cambridge, Mass.: Harvard University Press, 1961); and Abram Bergson and Simon Kuznets (eds.), *Economic Trends in the Soviet Union* (Cambridge, Mass.: Harvard University Press, 1963). These sources are referred to hereafter as *Real National Income* and *Economic Trends* respectively.

could well ask, "What has the common man gained from the sacrifices and pressures imposed on him by the Soviet regime?"

Since the late 1940's, however, the picture has brightened considerably. Industrial and agricultural production have risen substantially, and consumers have begun to share in this larger output. Living standards are already well above 1950 levels, and the advance is continuing. It is this recent record which leads Soviet officials to proclaim optimistically that they will soon surpass the capitalist countries in per capita output.

Because of this roller-coaster pattern of economic growth, it is not very meaningful to discuss trends over the whole period since 1917. It is better to concentrate on periods of *peacetime development within the present institutional framework*. This means focusing on: (1) the years 1928–40, during which the institutional framework assumed its present shape, and the first great burst of industrial development was carried through; and (2) the period since 1950, which has been one of continued industrial development, accompanied for the first time by significant progress in agriculture.

THE PERIOD 1928–40: GREAT EFFORT, LOW EFFICIENCY

The story of these years is soon told. There was great effort to increase the productive resources of the economy—to enlarge the labor force, to bring more land under cultivation, to build factories and

TABLE 1

Annual Percentage Rates of Change, 1928–40

	TOTAL ECONOMY	INDUSTRY	AGRICULTURE
Output	4.2	9.8	0.3
Factor inputs	4.2	7.7	1.8
Labor input	3.7	6.6	1.1
Capital input	9.8	14.9	−0.4
Land input	. . .	. . .	2.3
Factor productivity	0.1	2.1	−1.4

Source: Data for this table and for the later Table 2, covering the years 1950–58 are drawn from essays by Raymond P. Powell (industry), D. Gale Johnson (agriculture), and Abram Bergson (total economy), in *Economic Trends*.

machinery. Total output rose at better than 4 percent a year. The striking thing, however, is that output rose at only about the same rate as resource inputs. There seems to have been virtually no gain in productivity over the period.

Another feature of this period was the divergence between the performance of industry and agriculture. Industrial output rose rapidly and productivity rose moderately, but agricultural production stagnated and productivity declined. This cleavage in the economy has persisted to the present day.

Looking first at industry, the industrial labor force doubled between 1928 and 1940. This vast transfer from country to city was accomplished partly by economic incentives. Skilled workers in industry, and production workers who were willing to work hard at piece rates, were relatively well paid. Meanwhile, government paid the collective farmers such low prices for their produce that there were strong economic incentives to leave agriculture. These incentives were reinforced by massive propaganda in favor of industrial employment. Women as well as men were urged to enlist in the labor force, and occupations from top to bottom of the economy were opened to women on an unprecedented scale.

The buildup of industrial capital also proceeded rapidly. From 1928 to 1940, capital in use rose about 15 percent per year, or fourfold over the period. This was accomplished through the industrial targets laid down in the five-year plans. The economy was deliberately oriented away from consumer goods production and toward coal, oil, electric power, steel, machinery, and other capital goods. Gross investment was raised from 12.5 percent of GNP in 1928 to 26 percent in 1937. Most of this investment went into heavy industry, power, and transport. Housing, agriculture, light industry, and other sectors were relatively neglected.

In view of this massive effort, it is not surprising that industrial production rose 10 percent a year. Yet productivity rose only 2 percent a year, and accounted for only one fifth of the increase in output. How can this be explained? During these years the U.S.S.R. was borrowing technical know-how from the West on a large scale. Western engineers helped build factories and power plants. Much foreign machinery was imported and later copied in Russian models. The growth of Soviet industry should also have produced economies of scale plus external economies which would show up as a rise in productivity.

Against this must be set the fact that industrial workers and factory managers were new and inexperienced. Many mistakes were made, and much effort went into training rather than production. Methods of central planning were new and primitive, leading to strategic errors and to the kinds of routine inefficiency described in Chapter 12. Other negative factors were the secret police activity and the bloody purges which marked the Stalin era. Fear of a Siberian labor camp or the firing squad did not prove a good stimulus to managerial efficiency.

While industry was advancing, agriculture lagged behind. During the collectivization drive, hundreds of thousands of the more prosperous and efficient peasants were shot or deported. Many peasants decided to eat their farm animals rather than turn them over to the collectives, and livestock numbers dropped sharply. Government policy toward the new collectives was discouraging to production. They were obliged to sell most of their produce to government agencies at artificially low prices. City workers enjoyed low food costs at the expense of the farmers. The amount of capital allocated to farm machinery, fertilizers, and other forms of agricultural investment was small compared to the heavy investment in industry.

The results stand out plainly in the production statistics. Between 1928 and 1940, crop production rose by one quarter, but livestock production fell by one sixth. Total farm output increased less than 5 percent, well below the 15 percent increase in population. Agricultural efficiency, measured by outputs per unit of input, fell by about 15 percent.[2]

Despite the lag of agriculture, *total* Soviet output rose from 1928 to 1940 at more than 4 percent per year. This is a respectable, if not a sensational, rate of economic growth. Where did the additional output go? Primarily, to capital formation and military production. Private consumption per capita in 1940 was probably at about the level of 1928.

It would not be fair to conclude that the Soviet consumer had gained nothing by 1940. Community consumption had risen substantially, amounting to 10.3 percent of GNP in 1940 compared with 4.6 percent in 1928. Educational facilities had been greatly expanded and were free of charge. Medical and hospital facilities were much enlarged and were also free. Greater attention was being paid to parks, cultural centers, recreational facilities, and vacation resorts. Low-rent housing developments benefited the small percentage of families lucky enough to get into them.

Even so, the average citizen in 1940 might well have concluded that the industrialization drive had not paid off in direct benefits to him. The promised era of abundance was still a mirage.

THE POSTWAR YEARS: RAPID GROWTH FOLLOWED BY SLOWDOWN

The postwar years fall into three periods. The late forties were devoted to repairing war damage and recovering the 1940 production level. The years 1950–58 were years of very rapid growth, the most rapid in Soviet history, leading to predictions that the U.S.S.R. would soon surpass the production and consumption levels of the Western industrial countries. In 1959 the pace of growth began to slacken and has remained lower through the most recent year (1963) for which data are available at this writing.

---

[2] For a more detailed analysis and a critique of the statistical sources, see D. Gale Johnson, "Soviet Agriculture," in *Economic Trends.*

The Production Upsurge of 1950–58

The performance of the Soviet economy during this period was remarkable by any standards. GNP rose at a rate of more than 7 percent per year. Almost half of this increase came from greater productivity, indicating that the economy was gaining momentum on this front. The rise in productivity extended to agriculture as well as industry. And consumers got enough of the increased output to permit a rapid rise of living standards.

The U.S.S.R. lost many millions of men during World War II and emerged with a seriously unbalanced population and labor force. In 1959, women constituted 48 percent of the working population. Women formed 39 percent of the workers in industry, 54 percent in agriculture, 61 percent in trade, service, and government administration, and 71 percent in education, science, and health. The low birth rates and heavy casualties of the war years have also meant a slow increase in the labor force since the war. During the 1950's the rate of increase was only 1.4 percent per year.

The capital stock has continued to increase at about its prewar rate. Emphasis on capital formation has not diminished. On the contrary, the investment rate has edged up to the neighborhood of 30 percent of GNP. The amount of land under cultivation also rose 3 percent a year during the 1950's through the settlement of large new areas in Kazakhstan and other eastern regions.

Since labor is still the main input, and since its rate of increase has been low, total factor inputs have increased less rapidly than before the war. Yet output rose faster. This must have been due to substantial improvements in productivity. For the economy as a whole, productivity rose at about 3 percent a year. This is not an unprecedented rate of productivity increase, but it is on the high side. Japan is the only other industrial country which has approached this rate over a long period of time. Some of the Western industrial nations have approached it for 10 to 20 years during spurts of unusually rapid growth.

Since industry has consistently been given top priority, it is not surprising that output and productivity rose faster in industry than in the economy as a whole. Factors contributing to higher productivity included: the large amounts of industrial equipment contributed by the Western allies during the war, or seized by the U.S.S.R. as reparations from occupied territories after the war; heavy Soviet investment in scientific research and education, with its payoff in technical progress; the fact that management and the industrial labor force were more experienced and better educated than during the 1930's; continuing improvement in economic organization and planning; and easing of political repression after the death of Stalin in 1953.

There were also substantial productivity increases in agriculture.

Throughout the Stalin era, agriculture stumbled along, undersupported and underrewarded, with output rising little and productivity stagnant. Livestock and dairy production fell far short of keeping up with population growth, so that the Soviet diet became increasingly dependent on cereals and potatoes. During the fifties these trends were arrested and reversed. The Khrushchev regime was strongly proagriculture. The collective farms were given greater latitude in planning and managing production. The hateful supervision of the machine tractor stations was removed. Farm prices and earnings were increased. Agriculture began for the first time to receive something like its share of the available investment funds. There was intensive development of hybrid corn and of other improved crop and livestock strains.

TABLE 2

Annual Percentage Rates of Change, 1950–58

	TOTAL ECONOMY	INDUSTRY	AGRICULTURE (Period 1950–59)
Output	7.2	10.5	4.9
Factor inputs	4.1	6.2	1.6
Labor input	1.4	3.8	−1.6
Capital input	11.2	11.5	7.9
Land input	...	...	2.9
Factor productivity	3.0	4.0	3.3

Source: Data from Bergson essay in *Economic Trends.*

These policies had a marked effect on production. Farm output rose about 5 percent a year, and most of this was due to higher productivity. The number of workers engaged in agriculture leveled off in the mid-fifties and then began to drop. The proportion of the labor force engaged in agriculture, which had previously hovered around 50 percent, fell below 40 percent. This was a major turning point, for it meant that agriculture was now able to release more labor to industry, construction, and other sectors. Without this the Soviet economy would be hampered by a severe manpower bottleneck.

Soviet agriculture is still considerably below U.S. agriculture in yields per acre, and much below American agriculture in output per farm worker. It is doubtful, indeed, that the collective form of agricultural organization can ever be as efficient as the family farm. But the trend in the U.S.S.R. seems now to be upward.

Another notable development of the 1950's is that the Soviet system has finally begun to pay off in higher living standards. Tables 3 and 4 are interesting in this connection. Table 3 shows the distribution of Soviet

TABLE 3

Relative Shares of Final Uses in Gross National Product, U.S.S.R., 1928–55
(Percent)

OUTLAY CATEGORY	1928	1937	1940	1950	1955
Household consumption outlays	79.5	52.5	49.4	45.7	48.0
Communal services	4.6	10.5	10.3	10.2	8.7
Gross investment	12.5	25.9	19.1	26.9	28.1
Government administration, including NKVD	2.1	3.2	3.9	4.3	2.1
Defense (as recorded in budget)	1.3	7.9	17.3	12.9	13.1
Gross National Product	100.0	100.0	100.0	100.0	100.0

Source: *Real National Income*, p. 237.
Calculations are in terms of 1937 ruble factor cost.

GNP by final uses at various points of time. Note the sharp cutback in the share of household consumption between 1928 and 1937, and the sharp increase in communal services and in investment. The share of household consumption is still low, not very different from the 1937 level. But with GNP increasing so rapidly, an unchanged share means that consumption is also rising at about the same rate.

This impression is confirmed by Table 4, which shows the annual rate of increase in each component of GNP over various periods of time. Note that consumption per head fell slightly from 1928 to 1940 and fell sharply during World War II. From 1950 to 1955, however, household consumption rose almost 7 percent a year; and there has been continued improvement since that time. Both the statistics and the impressions of

TABLE 4

Average Annual Rates of Growth of Per Capita GNP by Use, U.S.S.R., 1928–55
(Percent per annum)

OUTLAY CATEGORY	1928–37	1937–40	1940–44	1944–50	1950–55
Gross national product	4.5	1.0	−0.3	5.1	5.8
Household consumption outlays	−0.2	−1.0	−8.1	9.5	6.8
Communal services	14.6	0.4	−3.8	7.4	2.4
Gross investment	13.3	−8.8	−6.5	16.2	6.7
Government administration including NKVD	9.5	7.3	−3.2	9.2	−8.2
Defense (as recorded in budget)	27.9	31.1	29.8	−16.0	6.0

Source: *Real National Income*, p. 226.
Calculations are in terms of 1937 ruble factor cost. GNP figures for 1940–44 and 1944–50 refer to GNP exclusive of Lend-Lease.

Western visitors confirm that living standards are well above those of 1950.

The pattern of consumption looks unbalanced to Western eyes. Food is adequate in calories but not nearly as varied as in the West. Clothing is adequate, though rather standardized and unstylish. Health, education, and other public services are well provided for. Stores, restaurants, repair shops, and personal services are quite deficient. Housing is still scarce and crowded, and even with the present high rate of construction it will take many years to make up the deficit. Small consumer items such as radios, bicycles, and wrist watches are now available in volume. Washing machines, refrigerators, stoves, and other large consumer durables are still in short supply. Production of private automobiles is kept low as a matter of policy, partly to avoid the heavy expenditure on roads and highways which the automobile has necessitated in other countries.

The Soviet consumer, almost completely insulated from the outside world, cannot compare his living conditions with those prevailing in other countries. To him, as to most of us, the important thing is whether his position is improving year by year. In these terms, he is making substantial progress and can expect more of the same. Remember also that the Russians have the highest standard of living in the vast section of the earth stretching from Berlin eastward to Peking. To a visitor from Chicago, the U.S.S.R. may seem a rather poor country. But to a visitor from Djakarta or Calcutta, it seems very prosperous.

The Slowdown of the Early 'Sixties

Just when things looked brightest, the growth rate of the Soviet economy began to decelerate. Official Soviet statistics, which show national income rising at an average annual rate of 10.9 percent from 1950 through 1958, show a growth rate of only 8 percent for 1959 and 1960, 7 percent in 1961, 6 percent in 1962, and 4.5 percent in 1963. Western revised estimates, which typically run lower than the official figures, suggest that the actual 1963 growth rate may have been below 3 percent. This may have contributed to the sudden removal of Premier Khrushchev from power in late 1964.

The anatomy of the slowdown is suggested by Table 5. The first two columns compare the 1958–62 performance with the record of 1950–58. Note that capital accumulation continued as rapidly as before. Inputs of labor time fell slightly, however, due mainly to a general reduction of working hours. Total factor inputs thus grew at a somewhat lower rate. The most notable development, however, was a sharp drop in the rate of productivity growth. GNP per unit of factor inputs, which rose at 3.3 percent a year from 1950 through 1958, grew only 1.7 percent a year from 1958 through 1962.

This does not tell us *why* the rate of productivity growth declined.

Since a global productivity measure depends on everything happening in the economy, the reasons for the decline are undoubtedly complex. There are indications, however, that the Soviet economy is running into diminishing returns as regards both land and capital. The vast new acreage of semiarid land in Kazakhstan which was planted to grain in the mid-'fifties yielded only moderately well even at the beginning. By the early sixties, yields had dropped a third or more. As regards capital, theory suggests that a rapid increase in capital supply will lower the marginal productivity of capital. Note that even in 1950–58, output per unit of capital was falling, and that it fell even more sharply from 1958 through 1962.[3]

TABLE 5

Average Annual Rates of Growth
(Percent)

	TOTAL ECONOMY		INDUSTRY 1958–62	AGRICULTURE 1958–62
	1950–58	1958–62		
Output (GNP)	7.2	4.6	7.0	0.35
Factor inputs	3.8	2.8		
Labor input	1.2	−0.1	1.8	−2.63
Capital input	10.1	10.1		
GNP per worker	6.0	4.5	5.1	3.1
GNP per unit of capital	−2.6	−5.0		
GNP per unit of factor inputs	3.3	1.7		

Source: Unpublished estimates by Abram Bergson, which should be considered provisional. Nonfarm labor input is adjusted for changes in working hours. Capital input includes only reproducible fixed capital.

The fragmentary data in the last two columns of Table 5 reveal agriculture as once more the laggard sector of the economy. The performance of industry, while not as spectacular as from 1950 through 1958 was still quite good. Farm output per worker, however, grew only half as fast as in the earlier period, and total farm output rose scarcely at all.

SOME ELEMENTS IN SOVIET GROWTH

Even allowing for the recent slowdown, the growth rate of the Soviet economy since 1928 is impressive. Japan is the only other industrial country with a comparable record for recent decades. This

---

[3] This is confirmed by a study by Richard Moorsteen and Raymond P. Powell, *The Soviet Capital Stock, 1928–1962* (Homewood, Ill.: Richard D. Irwin, Inc., 1966). This study shows *both* the average and marginal capital-output ratios rising substantially between 1950 and 1962.

suggests two questions: First, what are the main reasons for the rapid growth of Soviet output? Second, what is likely to happen over the next decade or two? Will the U.S.S.R. be able to regain the high growth rates of 1950–58, or does the recent slowdown indicate that the economy will grow hereafter at a more moderate pace?

To the first question Soviet economists have a pat answer: "Our production grows rapidly because we have a *socialist economy*. Socialist systems grow rapidly, while capitalist economies grow slowly." This answer does not explain very much. Why are some of the Soviet bloc countries growing faster than others? Why has the U.S.S.R. growth rate varied from time to time? Central economic planning obviously does not ensure any *one* rate of economic growth. Some of the capitalist countries are growing faster than others, and faster than some of the socialist countries. Why is this? A simple ideological answer does not tell us.

Nor is it sufficient to say that Soviet output grows rapidly because of *central economic planning*. We concluded in Chapter 12 that the degree of economic centralization prevailing in the U.S.S.R. is per se unfavorable to efficient use of resources. If the U.S.S.R. has grown rapidly, it has been *in spite of* the effort to run the whole economy as a giant corporation. There is, nevertheless, one element of truth in this explanation. Central planning makes it easier to organize a high rate of investment, which has been an important element in Soviet growth.

As one digs beneath these superficial explanations, one encounters more solid reasons for the rapid growth of Soviet output. It is important to sort these out, because some will continue to operate in the future while others may taper off or disappear. Thus our analysis of the past has a bearing on the outlook for the future.

1. It is important that Soviet leaders take the increase of material production as a major national objective. While Western countries attach importance to a high rate of economic growth, they do not pursue this goal with such single-minded attention. Moreover, the Soviet economic structure removes some of the restraints on maximum production which exist in capitalist countries. There is no problem of adequate total demand, since demand can readily be manipulated through the state budget and the state bank. The inflation problem is not eliminated, but it is more manageable because wage rates and prices are prescribed by government. An adverse balance of payments cannot lead to uncontrolled gold outflows, since foreign trade is handled by government organizations, and imports can be tailored to prospective exports.

2. In line with this objective of maximum production, there has been an effort to stretch the supply of productive resources to the utmost. The basic resource, and the ultimate check on expansion of production, is the supply of labor. There has been a particular effort to bring women into the labor force, partly by eliminating sex discrimination throughout the whole range of occupations, partly by setting up nurseries and

canteens to reduce the burden of cooking and child care. The low level of Soviet wages provides a powerful incentive for the wife to contribute to the support of the household. While employment of women in Russia may strike us as being beyond the optimum, it helps to stretch the production potential of the economy.

3. The determined effort to build up capital resources has already been noted. Gross investment, adjusted to Western definitions, typically ranges from 25 to 30 percent of GNP; and since the Soviet capital stock is new and depreciation relatively low, most of this also constitutes *net* investment. The only capitalist country with such a high investment rate is Japan.

The importance of high investment is obvious. If one continues to build power plants, oil wells, steel mills, electrical equipment, industrial machinery, and other capital goods at a high rate, this will add materially to future production.

4. In addition to the large volume of Soviet investment, the *productivity* of investment seems to have been unusually high. Kuznets estimates[4] that, in the U.S.S.R. from 1950 through 1958, each new unit of capital added 0.33 units to national output. Only Japan and West Germany had equally high rates. By contrast, the yield of a unit of new capital during this period was 0.25 in France, 0.20 in the United States, 0.15 in the United Kingdom, 0.14 in Sweden, and 0.10 in Norway.

One reason for the unusually high yield of investment in the U.S.S.R. may be that Soviet industry is young and the capital stock is relatively small. The amount of capital per worker is well below that of the older industrial countries. The U.S.S.R., in short, is operating higher up on the marginal productivity curve of capital. The allocation of investment is also important. Two thirds of Soviet investment goes into industry and agriculture, which have high yields per unit of capital— usually more than 1 in agriculture, and close to 1 for many branches of manufacturing. In the United States, on the other hand, only about 30 per cent of investment goes in these directions. We allocate considerably more to housing, stores, and office buildings which have a long life and a low annual yield.

5. The U.S.S.R. allocates substantial resources to higher education, scientific research, and technological development. While the productivity payoff from these expenditures is hard to estimate, it is probably substantial. Indeed, the transformation in the knowledge and skills of the Soviet population over the past 40 years may have been as important as the accumulation of physical capital.

Large resources have been put into higher education, and the orientation of the educational system is strongly vocational. Russian universities turn out few philosophers, literary critics, and other human-

---

[4] In his essay in *Economic Trends*.

ists. They do turn out large numbers of natural scientists, medical scientists, engineers, agriculturalists, teachers, accountants, and technicians of every sort. Moreover, graduates seem to be sorted out carefully for placement on the basis of their academic records. An outstanding engineer may be recommended to a key factory in central Russia, while a poor student may find himself headed toward Irkutsk.

Scientific research is organized through the Academy of Sciences of the U.S.S.R. in Moscow and through similar academies in each of the republics. Within the Academy are specialized institutes for each branch of study. The research workers are full-time scholars, without teaching or other duties. They are well paid and are among the elite of Soviet society. They are relatively free from the political nagging and pressure to which most Soviet citizens are subject. It is not surprising that scientific careers are attractive and that they draw many of the best minds in the younger generation.

At a more applied level, each industry has one or more research institutes devoted to solving production problems of that industry. The number of people engaged in such activities probably compares well with the number of research and development people in American industry. Thus one can expect that the U.S.S.R., which for a long time was mainly a borrower of technical knowledge from the West, will in the future become increasingly a contributor.

6. The U.S.S.R. started from a relatively low level of managerial efficiency. In Chapter 12 we emphasized the inefficiencies in central planning and in the grass-roots management of Soviet enterprise. This line of argument cuts in two directions. The more badly you are doing at the moment, the more room you have for improvement in the future. There is doubtless a continuing advance in management efficiency and overall economic coordination, which may account for some of the observed rise in productivity.

In sum: There is no reason to be puzzled or overimpressed by the recent Soviet growth rate. There is nothing magical about it. It can be analyzed and understood on economic grounds. While we cannot weigh the exact importance of each contributing factor, taken together they provide an adequate explanation of what has occurred.

WHAT OF THE FUTURE?

Will the Soviet economy continue to grow rapidly during the decades ahead? The answer is of great political importance. In the past, shifts in the productive capacity of nations have been accompanied by gradual shifts in the world balance of power. In the eighteenth century, the fact that the Industrial Revolution occurred in Britain rather than France enabled the former to emerge triumphant from their long rivalry. The preponderance of German power in Europe after 1870 was associated with rapid industrialization. The emergence of the U.S.A. as the greatest power of the twentieth century was certainly connected with our production accomplishments. The world position of the U.S.S.R. in the year 2000 will depend very much on how its economy functions in the meantime.

There seems no logical reason why the Soviet growth rate *must* decline. True, the expansion rate of individual industries always slows down eventually. This may happen also for an entire sector, such as manufacturing. It does not follow that it must happen for output as a whole.

One can nevertheless think of reasons why Soviet growth *might* slow down within the next decade or two:

1. As capital accumulation continues, the marginal productivity of capital will fall, unless this tendency is offset by rapid technical progress. The race between invention and accumulation is a basic fact for any economy, including a planned economy.

2. The rate of increase in other factors of production is likely to fall. The agricultural frontier will eventually be reached. The Soviet labor force can scarcely increase in the future as rapidly as in the past. The rate of population growth has now fallen to about the U.S. level. The possibilities of urging more women into the labor force must be nearly exhausted. The U.S.S.R. also seems about to emulate the United States by going in heavily for leisure. The work week in industry has been cut to around 40 hours, and there is talk of going to a 35-hour or even a 30-hour week. If this is done, it will slow down the rise of per capita output.

3. The rate of transfer of labor from agriculture to industry will also slow down eventually. Why is this important? Because output per worker in Soviet agriculture is only about one third as high as in industry. As a matter of arithmetic, then, moving a worker from agriculture to industry raises *average* productivity in the economy. As the agricultural sector shrinks, however, this source of productivity increase becomes less important.

4. Soviet leaders may eventually reduce their concentration on commodity production and become receptive to expansion of the service industries. As the income of Soviet citizens rises, their consumption preferences will certainly tend in this direction. So the question is really whether Soviet leaders will become more responsive to consumer preferences in the future. This would get them good marks in terms of consumer satisfaction, but it would cost something on the productivity side. The service industries are not very susceptible to mechanization, and their rate of productivity increase is low. Hence a dilemma: Giving consumers what they want may imply a lower rate of increase in the amount you can give them.

5. Productivity improvement in the past has depended a good deal on borrowing technical know-how from the Western countries. To the

extent that Russia catches up and forges ahead in science and technology, the possibilities in this direction will diminish. The possibilities of improvement in economic organization and management methods will also diminish gradually. One can keep on improving forever, but it is hard to keep on improving *at the same rate.*

By giving heavy weight to these factors, one can make a case that Soviet output can't possibly keep on rising at the present rate. But the case is not conclusive. At least two things must be set on the other side. One is the continued heavy investment of resources in scientific research and technical development. The practical result of these activities is unpredictable. But it would be unwise to sell science short. It is conceivable that technical progress might be fast enough to offset all the unfavorable factors listed above.

Another important consideration is the flexibility of the Soviet investment rate. The economy is now rich enough that it can invest more heavily *and* continue to raise consumption levels. If the marginal productivity of capital should fall in the future, this might be offset by increasing investment to 30 or even 35 percent of GNP.

The division of GNP between consumption and investment is *the* political issue in communist countries. The government group typically contains some people favoring a "hard line" (a high investment ratio) and others favoring a "soft line" (less investment and more emphasis on immediate consumption). Depending on who wins out in the power struggle, decisions may veer in one direction or the other. The unpredictability of political developments in the U.S.S.R. makes economic prediction hazardous. Economics and politics, always inseparable, are particularly so in the communist setting.

There are other imponderables in the situation. What will happen to defense expenditures? Success in disarmament negotiations would release additional resources for consumption or investment. Will there be further reductions in working hours, which would reduce the rate of increase in labor inputs? Will the present experiments with greater initiative for plant managers contribute substantially to productivity? Will government be willing to invest enough resources in agriculture, offer sufficient income incentives to farmers, and permit enough local initiative in production planning to make a real dent in the agricultural problem?

In view of such major uncertainties, any flat prediction would be foolish. The range of possibilities, however, can be illustrated by a little arithmetic. Suppose labor inputs continue to grow at their recent rate of 1.2 percent a year. Then, on optimistic assumptions—capital stock continuing to grow at 10 percent and total factor productivity rising 3 percent a year—Soviet GNP would increase at about 7 percent a year. But on pessimistic assumptions—productivity rising at only 1.5 percent and capital stock growing at only 6 percent—the rate of GNP increase works out at 4.2 percent. The outcome may well be intermediate, say of the order of 6 percent a year. This would be better than in the early sixties, but lower than from 1950 through 1958. It would be higher than the prospective U.S. growth rate, but not sensationally higher.

RUSSIA AND THE UNDERDEVELOPED COUNTRIES

Russian growth is relevant to the less developed countries in two ways. First, the U.S.S.R. now has sufficient resources to extend large-scale economic aid to these countries. This will be examined in connection with our discussion of U.S. aid strategy in Chapter 33.

Second, Soviet leaders maintain that their system provides a model of effective economic development and that the poor countries need only follow this model to succeed. This contention requires a word of comment.

We may note first that Russia in 1914 was already a richer and more developed country than are most of the underdeveloped countries today. The foundations of an industrial state had already been laid. There was extensive development of food processing, textiles, clothing, and other branches of light manufacturing. There was a rail network. Agriculture was sufficiently productive that Russia before 1914 was a large exporter of grain to the West. There was a long tradition of national patriotism and centralized government. So the task confronting Soviet leaders in the 1920's was considerably easier than that now confronting the new nations of Asia and Africa.

One can say further that Soviet planning methods, which involve prescribed targets for end products and centralized control of material flows, are not directly applicable to the less developed countries. They assume a framework of complete public ownership, while the underdeveloped countries are typically "mixed economies" with the private sector predominating. The kind of development planning required by these countries is quite different from Soviet planning, as will appear in Chapter 32. The skills needed for development planning, such as macroeconomic theory, interindustry economics, linear programming, and methods of project evaluation, have been developed mainly in the West. Soviet planners probably have little in the way of special expertise which is not known in other countries.

In most countries agriculture is by all odds the leading industry, and agricultural progress is a key requirement for economic development. But in this sector the U.S.S.R. has had only limited success, and some of the other communist countries have been spectacularly unsuccessful. It has yet to be demonstrated that collective farming can be combined with agricultural efficiency. On this front the poor countries can learn a good deal more from the West than from the East.

What, then, does Soviet experience show? It shows that, if a population can be persuaded to tighten its belts for 20 or 30 years and to work hard meanwhile, it can achieve a rapid buildup of industrial capacity. People must consume less, or at least refrain from consuming more, while effort is channeled heavily into capital goods production. There is nothing mysterious about this, and the moral is not confined to communist systems. But it is a discouraging lesson, and one which is not easy to apply in a poor country.

RUSSIA AND THE WEST: A GROWTH RACE?

Russian output during the 1950's rose considerably faster than in most of the capitalist countries. While Soviet GNP was rising at better than 7 percent a year, most of the Western countries fell in the range of 3 to 5 percent. The only industrial countries which matched the Soviet growth rate were West Germany and Japan, with growth rates of almost 8 percent.

The U.S.S.R., like any young industrial nation on the make, has been preoccupied with the rate at which it may hope to overtake the older industrial countries, particularly the United States. Exhortations to "overtake and surpass the United States" appear on factories and billboards throughout the country. Predictions that this goal will be achieved by a specific date are used for propaganda effect at home and abroad.

As nearly as one can capture things in figures, Soviet GNP was about half of U.S. GNP in 1960. It is obvious that, if Soviet output continues to grow faster than U.S. output, the two output curves must eventually cross. For example, if our GNP should grow at 3 percent and Soviet GNP at 6 percent, by 1975 their output would be three quarters of ours. By 1985, the output of the two economies would be roughly the same. Since the Soviet population is about one fifth larger, however, they would not equal our output per capita until sometime in the 1990's. Meanwhile, enough other things might happen to throw off these calculations entirely.

It may be better anyway to consider particular products or industries rather than total output. The emphasis of Soviet economic expansion is different from our own. In the products to which they attach highest priority—coal, steel, machinery, electric power—they may exceed our production level within the next 10 or 15 years. In fairness, one should add to this list health services, education, scientific work, and ballet performances. It will be much longer before they reach our per capita production of meat, fresh fruits and vegetables, housing space, furniture, and kitchen equipment. It is doubtful that they will ever reach our per capita output of automobiles, tires, gasoline, communication services, travel, retailing and repair services, and personal services. This is simply to say that the patterns of life will remain different in the two countries—so different that aggregative comparisons do not mean very much.

It is doubtful that Americans need get very excited about all this. There is no military issue involved, since each country already has the capacity to annihilate the other. The United States is rich enough to match anything the U.S.S.R. might choose to do in scientific development, space exploration, economic aid to other countries, and so on. The U.S.S.R. might eventually gain a propaganda advantage by being able to say that its GNP was larger than ours, but even this is doubtful. Going around the poor countries of the world boasting about how rich you are isn't the best way to win friends and influence people. If and when the Russians do become as rich as we are, they may become equally unpopular.

It would be interesting to conclude with a survey of growth rates in the other communist countries; but the evidence on this is still fragmentary. The evidence suggests that the rate of GNP increase in the East European countries since 1950 has been high, probably as high as in Western Europe. The Eastern countries are more heavily agricultural and are starting from a considerably lower GNP level; but they are struggling hard to narrow the gap. In at least one case, Yugoslavia, the rate of GNP increase seems to have been higher than in the U.S.S.R.

China remains the great enigma. The Chinese government has released no economic statistics since 1959, and only journalistic accounts and scraps of statistical information trickle out to the West. These accounts give the impression of an early Stalinist pattern of development: intense concentration on transportation, defense, and heavy industry; severe restriction of consumption levels; and a lagging agricultural sector. When the curtain lifts, it may turn out that China has laid the basis for a powerful, modern industrial state; but the curtain is still thick.

SUMMARY

1. Soviet growth is difficult to summarize, because it has been very uneven by sectors of the economy and also by time periods.

2. The year 1928 saw the initiation of central planning and a marked reallocation of resources toward capital goods production. From 1928 through 1940, GNP rose at about 4 percent a year. This seems to have been due almost entirely to larger labor and capital inputs. And progress was confined to the industrial sector, while agriculture stagnated and food consumption per capita fell.

3. Output fell considerably during World War II and recovered during the late 1940's. The period 1950–58 was one of substantial progress. GNP rose between 7 and 8 percent a year, and GNP per capita at almost 6 percent. Agricultural output rose substantially, though not as

fast as industrial output. And for the first time, there was a sustained rise in consumer goods output and living standards.

4. The Soviet growth rate declined considerably from 1959 through 1963. Labor inputs did not rise, the rate of increase in factor productivity was only half as high as in 1950–58, and agricultural output stagnated.

5. Important factors in recent Soviet growth include a continued high rate of capital goods production, heavy allocation of capital goods toward directly productive uses in industry and agriculture, heavy investment in education and research, and improvements in economic planning and management making for greater efficiency.

6. There are a number of reasons for expecting that the Soviet growth rate will decline somewhat as the economy matures. But this is by no means certain, and the growth rate will remain high relative to most other countries.

7. During the 1950's, Japan and West Germany had growth rates above the Soviet level. But most other capitalist countries, including the United States, were considerably below.

8. If present growth trends continue, Soviet GNP per capita may reach the United States level before the end of this century. But this aggregate comparison is of doubtful significance. The uses of national output, the pattern of production, and the style of consumption will remain quite different in the two countries.

DISCUSSION QUESTIONS

1. The rate of increase in Soviet agricultural output has lagged consistently behind that of industrial output. Why is this? Is this situation readily correctable, and is it likely to be corrected in the near future?

2. If you had to select the three most important reasons for the high rate of increase in Soviet GNP during the fifties, which would you choose?

3. How do you reconcile the rapid Soviet growth rate with the efficiency problems of central planning noted in Chapter 12?

4. It is sometimes argued that, if you start from a low base, a small *absolute* increase in output will look large in percentage terms; and that the rapid percentage growth of Soviet output is readily explainable on this ground. How would you appraise this argument?

5. What would you estimate as the most probable rate of increase in Soviet GNP from 1965 through 1980? Explain the basis for your estimate.

6. The slogan of "overtake and surpass the United States" is held constantly before Soviet workers. What different quantitative interpretations might be given to this slogan? To what extent, or in what sense, do you think they will be able to accomplish this objective?

7. Suppose you are an Indian non-Communist politician. The Communist members of Parliament constantly criticize the low growth rate of the Indian economy, and maintain that this rate could be greatly increased by adopting the Soviet pattern of economic organization. What would you say in reply?

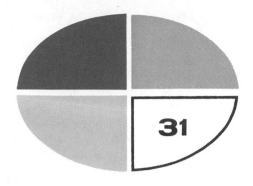

The Less Developed Countries

It is not the scarcity of money, but the scarcity of men and talents, which makes a state weak.

VOLTAIRE

In the infancy of societies it is the chiefs of the state who shape its institutions, and later it is the institutions that form the chiefs of the state.

MONTESQUIEU

MODERN INDUSTRIAL GROWTH had its origin in Britain and the adjacent areas of Western Europe. From this focal point it spread during the nineteenth century throughout western and northern Europe, the areas of new settlement overseas—the United States, Canada, Australia, New Zealand, South Africa—and eventually Japan. During the twentieth century most of southern and eastern Europe was swept into the current, though here the development remains incomplete. Portugal, Spain, southern Italy, Greece, and several of the Balkan countries remain largely agricultural, with an income level well below that of their northern neighbors.

The British classical economists were inclined to argue that "what's good for Britain is good for the world." Through universal free trade, the prosperity of the industrial countries would be spread to the farthest corners of the earth. "Pockets of development" did appear here and there, usually tied to one of the European nations by trade relations and colonial domination. But the great bulk of the populations of Africa, Asia, and Latin America remained tied to traditional activities and experienced little rise in per capita income. The gap between the have and have-not nations widened, and is continuing to widen today.

What shall we call the have-not countries? "Underdeveloped countries" is fashionable but has little meaning—every country is underdeveloped relative to its economic potential. "Developing countries" is flattering but inaccurate, for many countries in the group are not developing. The French have coined *le tiers monde* (the third world), to distinguish this group from the industrial capitalist countries and the communist countries. One might speak of "countries of the South," since they lie generally to the south of the industrial nations. Since it is clear what we mean, the label does not matter greatly. We shall use "less developed countries," occasionally shortening this for convenience to LDC's.

Interest in these countries has quickened since 1945 for several reasons. Most parts of Africa and many parts of Asia have attained national independence for the first time and are able to take a hand in their economic destiny. There is strong competition among the more powerful nations for political and economic influence in the LDC's. East competes with West, China competes with the U.S.S.R., France competes with Britain and the United States. Jet transport and improved communications have shrunk the world and made more people aware of the great income gap among nations. There is a widespread feeling that such wide and growing income differences are not healthy for the international community.

We shall discuss these countries in three stages. In this chapter we shall analyze how their economies operate and why they turn out so little product per head. This is basic, for understanding must precede improvement. The next chapter will explore what the LDC's can do, and in some cases are doing, to help themselves. What are the key problems to which a growth-oriented government should address itself? Finally, we shall consider the possibilities and limitations of assistance from the richer countries, including the United States. How much can we do, and what do we stand to gain by doing it?

SOME DIFFERENCES AMONG THE LESS DEVELOPED COUNTRIES

While it is convenient to group the 70 or so less developed countries, this has the danger of implying that they are similar. They are, in fact, a very heterogeneous assortment. Uganda and Brazil are much more different than Switzerland and Italy. So it is advisable at the outset to emphasize the main points of difference. This will warn us against undue generalization, against supposing that all LDC's have the same problems and can follow the same policies.

Size.   The estimated populations of some of the largest and smallest LDC's is shown in Table 1. The larger countries range from 50 million to more than half a billion people. Many of the smaller countries have 1 to 2 million, or the population of a good-sized American city. Not only is population small, but *economic size* is very small. A country of 10 million with per capita output of $100 per year has a GNP of only $1 billion.

The economic significance of these differences is obvious. Countries such as India or Brazil can expect to become diversified and largely self-sufficient industrial economies. But this pattern of development is not feasible for Laos or Libya. Their domestic market is too small to support a full array of manufacturing industries. They must grow mainly by developing export specialties and by participating in international trade.

TABLE 1

Estimated Population, Selected Countries, 1963
(000's)

Mainland China	686,400	Ceylon	10,625
India	460,490	Malaysia	7,607
Indonesia	100,045	Jamaica	3,375
Pakistan	98,612	Somalia	2,500
Brazil	76,409	Laos	1,882
Nigeria	55,620	Libya	1,451

Source: U.N. *World Demographic Survey*, 1963. Estimate for mainland China is for 1960.

Resource base. The Congo basin has great mineral wealth. Thus far there is no indication of equivalent deposits in Morocco or Burma. Oil is found in some areas and not in others. The land area of some countries is 90 percent desert and mountains, while other countries are fertile and have plenty of water. Some climates are more favorable than others to health and productive activity. So there are permanent differences in the *economic potential* of countries. All of them can hope to become richer than they are now. But they will not necessarily reach the same income level even in the long run.

Population pressure. One sometimes thinks of all poor countries as overpopulated. This impression comes mainly from looking at India, Pakistan, and a few other Asian countries. In most parts of Africa, population pressure is not yet severe, and this is true also of Latin America. Some Latin American countries still have an open frontier, with free land which requires only the effort of developing it.

It is hard to get an objective measure of population pressure, since this depends on the resource base and on the pattern of economic activity. Britain, Belgium, or Japan would be heavily overpopulated if they had to depend mainly on agriculture; but by development of manufacturing and other industries they can support a dense population at a rising standard of living.

For countries which are still primarily agricultural, the ratio of labor to farmland is significant. Table 2 suggests that serious population pressure is found mainly in Egypt, the Indian subcontinent, China, and southwest Asia. In southeast Asia, Africa, and Latin America the ratio of

TABLE 2

Males Engaged in Agriculture per Square Kilometer
of Standard Farmland

REGION	MALE FARM WORKERS PER SQUARE KILOMETER
Egypt	73.1
India and Pakistan	31.2
China	24.5
Southwest Asia (excluding India-Pakistan)	24.5
Philippines	7.5
Southeast Asia (excluding Philippines)	6.5
Africa: British areas	6.3
Indonesia	5.7
Central America and Caribbean	4.4
Africa: non-British areas	2.2
Argentina	1.8
Brazil	1.0
South America (excluding Argentina-Brazil)	0.8
U.S.S.R.	3.1
Canada	1.7
U.S.A.	1.2

Source: Colin Clark, *The Conditions of Economic Progress* (3d ed.; London: Macmillan & Co., Ltd., 1957), Table XXXIII, p. 308. A kilometer is roughly five eighths of a mile; thus a square kilometer is about 250 acres.

labor to land is not excessive. Low output per farm worker in these latter countries is due mainly to primitive agricultural methods and inadequate equipment.

Even when population pressure is not yet severe, the rate of population increase is often alarming. Most of the poor countries now have populations growing at 2 to 3 percent a year. Some are still below 2 percent, including Argentina (1.6), Uruguay (1.4), Puerto Rico (1.7), Tunisia (1.4), Iraq (1.6), Ethiopia (1.6), and Nigeria (1.9). But a number of countries have climbed above the 3 percent level, including Malaya (3.2), Philippines (3.2), Mexico (3.1), Venezuela (3.4), and

Brazil (3.4).[1] These high rates of population increase mean that a country must run fast simply to prevent a fall in per capita income.

Income level. Some countries are much poorer than others. GNP per capita, converted to approximate dollar equivalents, ranges from less than $60 at the bottom of the list to 10 times that amount at the top (Table 3). Note that the level of incomes in Latin America is considerably higher than in Africa or Asia. The leading Latin American countries are "middle class" rather than really poor. The world's poorest countries are found in south and southeast Asia and in tropical Africa. For purposes of comparison, most Western European countries now have

TABLE 3

National Output per Capita, U.S. Dollars,
Selected Countries, 1961–62

Venezuela	701	Ceylon	137
Argentina	462	Philippines	125
Chile	422	Thailand	106
Mexico	361	Nigeria	86
Colombia	285	Kenya	85
Turkey	272	Pakistan	74
Algeria	229	India	73
Malaya	207	Indonesia	73
Ghana	187	Afghanistan	61
Peru	173	Uganda	60
Egypt	156	Burma	57
Iran	153	Ethiopia	51

Source: U.N. *Yearbook of National Account Statistics,* 1963, pp. 327–30. Figures are gross domestic product at factor cost, per capita, converted to U.S. dollars at estimated parity rates rather than at official exchange rates. Data relate to 1961 for about half the countries, to 1962 for the remainder, and are in each case the most recent available at the time.

GNP's in the range of $1,500 to $2,000 per capita, while the U.S. figure is around $3,000.

These comparisons should not be taken too seriously. National income estimates for the LDC's are still crude. Most of the national output is subsistence production, produced and consumed within the household and passing through no outside market. Valuation of such output is notoriously difficult. How much is the Indonesian peasant's daily rice diet worth in dollars? Does such a question have much meaning? In some cases, too, the figures are distorted by high output in a small sector of the economy—oil in Venezuela and Iran, tin and rubber in Malaya. The bulk of the population does not share in this output. The

[1] Data are for the period 1958–62 and are from the U.N. *Statistical Yearbook,* 1963, pp. 23–41.

average Venezuelan is certainly not better off than the average Chilean, nor are the Malayans richer than Thais.

The national income accounts exaggerate international differences in living standards. One can safely conclude that the difference between Argentina and Burma is a *large* difference. The difference between Argentina and the United States is also a *large* difference. But it is an exaggeration to say that Americans are 50 times as well off as Burmese— indeed, it is doubtful that such a statement has any meaning.

Growth rate.   By growth we mean a sustained rise in *per capita output*. To determine a country's growth rate we would need accurate population data and output data, year after year. But estimates even of population growth are often rough. Output figures are also crude and often have an optimistic bias. So while one can find tables showing the supposed growth rates of almost all the LDC's, these estimates are not yet accurate enough to be worth listing here.

At best, one can make a rough separation of LDC's into three groups: those in which per capita output is almost certainly rising, those in which it is remaining roughly constant, and those in which it is declining. There are growing, stagnant, and deteriorating economies within the less developed group.

Some countries have made appreciable gains in per capita output over the past 20 years. In this group one could certainly include Mexico, Brazil, Israel, and Taiwan; and probably also Colombia, Venezuela, Egypt, Malaya, and the Philippines.

In many other countries the apparent change in per capita output is so slight that one cannot be sure that growth is occurring. Output is probably about holding its own in the race with population. In this category one would have to place most of the new nations of Africa; most of the Middle East, and of south and southeast Asia; and some Latin American countries, such as Argentina and Chile, which have a history of past growth but whose growth has slowed down in recent decades.

There are probably several countries in which per capita income is actually declining. For example, this is probably true in Indonesia and the Republic of the Congo.

This wide divergence in national performance poses the key questions of the next three chapters. What is it about the growing economies that accounts for their economic success? What would the stagnant economies have to do to launch themselves on the path of successful development?

Transition: Some "Family Resemblances"

So much for differences. But these countries also have common features which, in varying degree, are found throughout the less developed world. In describing these characteristics we are also, in a sense, describing the reasons for low income and the main barriers to economic progress. The main features which deserve emphasis are:

1. Limitations of political leadership and public administration.
2. Fragmentation of the economy.
3. Limited development of a market mechanism.
4. The dominance of traditional, low-income agriculture.
5. Dependence on primary exports.
6. Inadequate tax systems and a low level of public expenditure.
7. Weak educational systems, leading to a shortage of professional and and technical skills.

POLITICAL LEADERSHIP AND PUBLIC ADMINISTRATION

As we observe the difficult economic problems of the less developed countries, we are tempted constantly to exclaim, "Government should do something." When we say this, we are assuming that the country *has* a government like that in Washington or Ottawa or London, which is responsive to popular wishes and capable of administering agreed-upon policies throughout the country. But many countries do not yet have such a government; and this is the heart of their problem.

The social structure of these countries is not hospitable to political democracy. The rise of democracy in the West was *accompanied or preceded* by widespread public education, economic diversification, the growth of a middle class, and a sharp increase in occupational and social mobility. But in most of the poor countries, these things have not yet occurred. So even when the forms of democracy have been established, the system remains ineffective in operation. Government is dominated by a small clique of the "right people"; and if power changes hands, it changes to another group not very different from the first. Most of the population remains illiterate, ignorant of public issues, skeptical of government activity, and with no feeling of participation in political life.

Some countries are, of course, closer than others to being function-ing democracies. Mexico has well-established democratic institutions, with an active electorate which does influence the complexion and policies of the national government. (But remember that Mexico had a popular revolution in the 1910's, sweeping land reforms in the 1930's, and vigorous industrial development from 1940 to the present.) Two or three other Latin American countries may be approaching this degree of political sophistication and stability. At the opposite pole, Saudi Arabia is a feudal kingdom with no popular participation. Most LDC's are still closer to Saudi Arabia than to Mexico.

One can scarcely maintain that a country must have a broadly based democratic government to embark on successful development. After all, England had a rather aristocratic government during the eighteenth century, and so did Germany, Russia, Japan, and other countries whose growth accelerated in the nineteenth century. The political democratization of the presently developed countries was in good measure a *consequence* of, or at least contemporaneous with, their increasing affluence.

What, then, are the minimum prerequisites for accelerated development in a poor country? First, the political leaders, even if not popularly elected, must have widespread *popular acceptance.* Successful development normally requires heavier taxation and other belt-tightening measures. Without widespread confidence in the political leadership, these measures will not be accepted. It may be said that people can be forced to accept economic austerity by political terrorism and coercion. But coercion has its limits, and even under dictatorial rule it must be supplemented by a good measure of consent.

Second, the political leadership must be *stable.* Economic development is a long haul, requiring sustained effort and reasonable consistency of policy over a period of decades. Where political control changes hands every year or two, and where this involves (as it often does in these countries) a wholesale overturn of administrative officials, sustained development becomes impossible. There are cases such as Brazil, which manages mysteriously to grow despite a turbulent political life. But it would be unsafe to count on disorder leading to progress as a general rule.

Third, the political leadership must be *growth-oriented.* In many countries, however, it is not so oriented. It may seem natural to economists that government should attach high priority to economic growth. But there are other policy objectives which the leaders may consider of overriding importance. In a newly independent country, nation-building activities may absorb most of the leadership's time and thought: developing legislative and judicial systems, staffing the government service, improving communication and transport facilities, conveying some sense of national unity to a variety of racial or tribal groups, suppressing violence and disorder, representing the nation effectively abroad, winning friends and allies on the world stage. In some countries measures of military defense or aggrandizement have high priority. This has recently been a heavy drain on the resources of Indonesia, India, Pakistan, Israel, and Egypt. So it is all very well for economists to advise: "Put development first." Other considerations may cause a government to ignore this advice in whole or in part.

One must also remember that in these countries, government is typically dominated by the "haves" rather than the "have-nots." The "haves" may be uninterested in, or even opposed to, economic development. Why should the large landowners of Chile or Iran favor economic change? They are doing well as it is, and modernization of the economy will probably be to their disadvantage. Enlightened self-interest should perhaps lead them to cooperate in moderate reforms, which might ward off potential revolution, but this argument has rarely proven persuasive with ruling classes.

Established business concerns will also resist economic changes which might bring increased competition and erosion of monopoly profits. Religious leaders, tribal chieftains, and other guardians of the traditional culture will usually oppose economic innovation. To override these sources of opposition, and to mobilize the progressive elements in the community behind a serious development effort, takes unusual political skill. It may require a single charismatic leader—a Nasser, or Nehru, or Nkrumah—who is able to retain power over a long period and to carry the nation forward on his back.

Turning from politics to public administration, government is usually weakly staffed. But the situation varies considerably from country to country. The British encouraged higher education in their colonies, sent many students to Britain for training, and drew the best university graduates into a civil service patterned on British lines. Particularly in India and Pakistan, and to a lesser extent in other ex-British areas, strong civil service staffs have been carried over from the colonial period.

The Belgians, Dutch, and Portuguese, on the other hand, followed a policy of not providing university education in their colonies. Natives of the Belgian Congo were not allowed to go abroad for training, and university training in the Congo was begun only in the last 2 or 3 years of Belgian rule. Indonesian students could work toward a degree in medicine but not in other subjects. This barred local people from administrative positions, which were filled entirely by men from the mother country. When these men were withdrawn after independence, they left an administrative vacuum. The disorganization of economic administration in Indonesia stems directly from this source. Even more dramatic is the case of the Congo, which in 1960 was left completely stripped of trained leadership.

Even in areas which have long been independent, such as Latin America, one usually does not find a career civil service. Government jobs are frankly political, and it is taken for granted that they will change hands if the government changes. The main qualification for office is family and connections; and the upper administrative group is drawn from the educated, well-to-do elite of the country. Many of these people are able and conscientious. But their training and background bears little relation to the jobs they are supposed to be doing. Government appointments are in fact scarcely regarded as jobs. They are political perquisites, to which a man is entitled by belonging to a certain group. Under these conditions one cannot expect the continuity, efficiency, and professional spirit which marks the public services of the developed countries.

In many countries, one finds key offices manned by an able administrator surrounded by a group of low-skilled clerks. There is a great lack of second- and third-line personnel to whom work can be delegated. (This same lack of "middle management" is found also in private industry in these countries.) The result is that top officials are over burdened and at the same time unable to accomplish much.

This has serious implications for economic development. Carrying out a development program is a skilled and technical undertaking. It requires people with specialized education and administrative experience. In most less developed countries there are only a handful of such people. This is why one often finds impressive development plans and policy pronouncements emanating from the capital city, which have no practical effect, because there is no administrative apparatus behind them.

Weak government staffing also has adverse effects on private business. Private industry in the less developed countries is typically overregulated, in the sense of being subjected both to more controls than are really necessary and to more controls than the government can execute effectively. The great number of requests and reports which businesses must submit to government, and the lack of enough staff to process these papers quickly, leads to delay, confusion, and uncertainty. In some countries, bribery of government officials has become the standard way of cutting through the maze of paper work and getting something done. The low level of civil servants' salaries puts them under severe temptation to accept bribes. It is not necessarily cynical to argue that, at this stage of development, a certain measure of official corruption can promote economic efficiency.

FRAGMENTATION OF THE ECONOMY

The most significant thing that can be said about these economies is that they are not economies in the proper sense. What is a national economy? It is an area within which products and factors of production can move easily. There are no legal or other impediments to producers setting up in any part of the country and shipping products to any other part. Labor can move about geographically and can also climb the ladder of higher occupations. Under these conditions one can regard the economy as an integrated network of markets and prices, with growth in one industry or region helping to lift the whole economy forward.

In the less developed countries, however, sharp lines of cleavage run through the economy. These cleavages are of several sorts, and crisscross each other in complicated ways. Their effect is to fragment the economy into semi-isolated areas and sectors. We can no longer assume that impulses are transmitted from one sector to another, and much of the analysis which we ordinarily apply to an integrated economy breaks down.

The most obvious and striking cleavage is between the money economy and the subsistence economy. This is largely, though not entirely, an urban-rural cleavage. In the capital cities of Latin America, one feels oneself in a sophisticated, Europeanized, and prosperous environment. Fifty miles away, one is in a world of rural poverty and primitive superstition, a world which seems to have no point of contact with the first.

Most people in these countries live on the land. They sell little to the outside world and buy little from it. The nearest city may be far away, and roads may be poor or nonexistent. This reduces the incentive to grow more than one can consume or to work on improving productivity. The country people are largely illiterate and politically inert and ineffective.

A different kind of cleavage is common in colonial and ex-colonial areas. Consider the tea industry of Ceylon. This was established in the nineteenth century by British owners, who got control of large tracts of land and set up tea plantations. Capital was imported from England, and labor from southern India. The product was exported, largely to England, and profits also flowed back to the home country. The British colonial government in Ceylon levied property and export taxes on the tea planters, which were used to provide roads and other facilities for the plantations and to maintain law and order. But all this had little influence on the traditional economy of the Ceylonese. These people continued to grow and consume their rice, selling little and buying little, and largely walled off from the thriving export sector. Ceylonese exports doubled and redoubled between 1850 and 1940, but rapid development in this sector did not spill over and stimulate growth in the indigenous sector of the economy.

This kind of situation is often termed an "export enclave." The export sector is an extension of the economy of the mother country, to which it is tied by trade and financial relations. Its interaction with the local economy is minimal, consisting mainly of hiring low-skilled local labor which uses its wages to buy a few imported consumer goods. Nor is this situation confined to colonial areas. Some aspects of it appear in the American petroleum industry of Venezuela or the American copper-mining industry in Chile. Since these are independent countries with political bargaining power, however, they can levy substantial taxes on the foreign companies; and this money can be used (though it may not actually be used) for development activities within the country.

Topography and distance may fragment the economy. An extreme case is that of East and West Pakistan, separated by a thousand miles of Indian territory, and linked only by sea and air routes. In Colombia, mountain ranges split the country into distinct valleys, which are almost separate regional economies. Peru is split into the coastal plain, the altiplano of the high Andes, and the tropical forests of the Amazon basin. All the way from Mexico to Chile, the Andes have this disintegrating effect. The ex-Belgian Congo is divided by major rivers, crossed only at certain points by small and precarious ferries. So difficult is transport that most of the Congo's mineral output is shipped south through Angola to the coast.

Natural barriers apart, sheer distance is a major problem in large countries like Nigeria, Brazil, or India. Hard-surfaced roads fade out rapidly as one moves toward the interior, improved dirt roads disappear next, and one comes down finally to mule tracks and footpaths. To knit these countries together in a way even approaching that of the industrial countries will take a major construction effort lasting for decades.

We may note next the barriers arising from racial, linguistic, and religious differences. The Indian case, in which certain occupations are traditionally reserved for certain castes, and in which the lowest caste of "untouchables" is expected to have minimum contact with higher-caste people, is well known. There are also more than a hundred languages used in different parts of India. Under British rule, English served as a lingua franca; but English is now being de-emphasized as a relic of colonialism, and the babel of tongues is returning. Many of the new African nations include numerous tribes, differing in customs and language, and at bottom still hostile to each other beneath the veneer of unity imposed originally by the colonial powers. This poses barriers to ready communication, to economic relations, and to political stability.

In some countries, business has been dominated by groups which, while nationals of the country, are still regarded as "foreign." The Chinese have been the traders, bankers, and artisans throughout southeast Asia. Indians have performed these functions in Burma, East Africa, and Central Africa. This situation creates strong tensions. The majority group in the country resents the strategic position and higher incomes of the "outsiders," and there is political pressure to get rid of them. The Indonesian effort to oust the local Chinese businessmen is a case in point. But since members of the majority group are inexperienced in business management, the immediate result is a setback on economic development.

This issue often underlies the debate over private enterprise versus government enterprise. Consider the case of Burma. Following the British tradition, educated and well-born Burmese typically go from the university into government service. Thus anything operated by government is managed by Burmese. Private enterprise, on the other hand, is usually in the hands of Indians or Chinese. Thus when a Burmese politician proposes government operation of industry, he is not necessarily arguing from socialist conviction. He is mainly arguing for Burmese control as against what he considers foreign control.

Even where racial and religious differences are not serious, there is often a rigid class structure which limits personal mobility. Many of the less developed countries have a hereditary aristocracy, often associated with large landholdings. Below this comes an upper middle class of businessmen, professional people, military men, and high government officials. Families in this group are strongly intermarried; and entrance into these occupations depends mainly on family origin rather than personal merit.

At the bottom of the social pyramid are the bulk of the population, who are economically poor, socially unimportant, and politically passive. Movement from this group to the higher levels occurs in a slow trickle. The social mobility and blurring of class lines which one finds in an industrialized society has not yet occurred. The social structure is closer to that of feudal Europe than of twentieth-century Europe or America.

LIMITATIONS OF THE MARKET MECHANISM

What we have said about fragmentation of the economy implies that factor and product markets are imperfect. But since the concept of a market mechanism plays such a central role in economics, this point deserves additional emphasis.

Take first the market for labor. Most workers live in the country and are largely outside the money economy. They earn perhaps one quarter to one half the wage of a city worker. There is every incentive to leave the land, and many do leave, particularly the younger people. Rarely does one hear of a shortage of recruits for urban industries.

These recruits, however, are untrained in job skills and industrial discipline. Malnutrition has weakened their physical stamina, and they may be suffering from a variety of diseases. Their initial productivity is low and has to be raised gradually by better feeding, health care, training, and supervision on the job. To take each person's work capacity as given, as we customarily do in economics, can be highly misleading.

City labor is typically overpriced compared to wages in the countryside and compared to the wage necessary to attract industrial recruits. Where the market wage rate is so low, there is strong political pressure to raise wages above their natural level. There is also pressure to create as much employment as possible. Many countries have legislation which makes it impossible or very expensive to lay off a worker once he has been employed.

Along with an abundance of untrained labor, there are typically shortages of skilled craftsmen and of the technical, professional, and administrative skills. This is associated with educational systems in which few people receive college or even high-school training, and which may also be biased toward traditional "prestige subjects" of low economic usefulness. For example, there is often an overproduction of lawyers, along with underproduction of scientists, engineers, teachers, and business managers.

White-collar and professional salaries, as a multiple of the common laborer's wage, are *much* higher in these countries than in the industrial countries. This arises partly from the limited supply of the higher skills. But it also reflects conventional status differences, a feeling that the higher groups are entitled to earn more, so that they can live in the style to which they have become accustomed. This salary structure, plus high business profits and large incomes from landholding, makes for greater income inequality in the LDC's than in the industrial countries. The low income of the mass of the population limits the market for consumer goods and the incentive to establish new industries.

Turning to capital, the network of financial institutions to which we are accustomed—commercial banks, savings banks, investment banks, insurance companies, stock exchanges—is imperfectly developed even in Mexico and Brazil, and is almost absent in many of the poorer countries. This makes it hard to stimulate domestic saving and to transfer savings to the points of greatest demand. Savings do not flow readily into the expanding areas of the economy.

Interest rates vary more widely than they do in a developed economy. There is often a legal ceiling on bank lending rates, leading to excess demand for loans. The banks then ration their credit within a small circle of established customers. Other would-be borrowers must resort to the unorganized capital market, operating outside the control system, where they pay much higher rates. This makes it harder for newcomers to set up in competition with established industries. The farmers up country are typically left to the village moneylender, whose exorbitant interest rates discourage borrowing for any but the most urgent consumption needs. At 10 percent interest it might pay to invest in improved seed, or livestock, or fertilizer. At 200 percent it is out of the question.

Product markets are characterized by monopoly or oligopoly. The main reason is small size of the local market. But even where it would be technically feasible to have more competitors, it is hard for them to get started. The established concerns naturally view competition as undesirable and use their political and financial influence to bar newcomers. If assumptions of pure competition are somewhat unrealistic even for the United States, they are wildly unrealistic in most of the less developed countries.

Unit production costs of manufactured products are often considerably higher than in the United States or Europe. Much of a company's raw materials, machinery, spare parts, and other inputs may be imported from industrial countries which are several weeks shipping time away. This involves greater risk of unexpected shortages and makes it necessary to carry substantially larger inventories. The small domestic market means that large machines (which may be the only ones available from the industrial countries) stand idle a good deal of the time. Changes in product run are more frequent in a small-market country, and these changes are expensive. Labor is usually less productive than in the developed countries. This disadvantage can be reduced in time by training and good personnel management. But management itself often shows a low level of ability and effort. The business is usually a family business. A man becomes an executive by being a member of the owning family, rather than through demonstrated ability. Management is a prerogative to be enjoyed, not a job to be worked at.

Another important market is the market for *foreign exchange*. The LDC's depend heavily on imports for the machinery, industrial raw materials, and other requisites of industrial development. Very often the foreign exchange earned through exports falls short of the amount needed to pay for imports. This tends to raise the price of foreign exchange (= a depreciation of the country's own currency). But the country may see disadvantages in this and may try to prevent it through the exchange control measures described in Chapter 27. Essentially, this involves pegging the price of foreign currencies at an artificially low level (= pegging the price of the country's own currency at an unduly high or overvalued level).

Such a system means that a dollar's worth of exports yields less in local currency to the exporter than it would otherwise, so exports are discouraged. And imports are encouraged, because the low price of foreign exchange makes them appear cheap. These tendencies are just the opposite of what would be needed to bring the country's external payments into balance. Moreover, exchange control requires rationing the limited supply of foreign exchange among an excess of would-be importers. This opens up possibilities of economic error, favoritism, and corruption which can be quite disorganizing to the economy.

To sum up: market imperfections in these countries are much more serious than in the developed countries. These imperfections lead to grave distortion of factor and product prices. And price distortion leads in turn to distortions in resource allocation and resource rise.

This observation can lead to two quite different conclusions. One school of thought argues that, in the LDC's, the market mechanism is so imperfect and price relations are so odd that they provide no clue to the proper directions of development for a country. One cannot trust private enterprise and private markets to generate economic growth. Only government can look far enough ahead, make the necessary corrections for existing price distortions, and take action on a sufficient scale to move the economy forward. This implies a national economic plan and a substantial public sector.

Those who are more favorable to private enterprise say two things in reply: first, some of the existing price distortions are a result of unwise government action. If government would get out of the way and let wage rates, interest rates, and foreign exchange rates find their own level, economic efficiency would be improved. Second, bad as markets may be at present, they can be improved by systematic effort. Financial institutions can be created, supplies of trained labor enlarged, monopoly positions in product markets eroded. Rather than trying to supersede the market, government should spend its energies on improving the institutional structure to the point at which private initiative can play a constructive role in economic development.

THE DOMINANCE OF LOW-INCOME AGRICULTURE

In the less developed countries, agriculture has been the dominant occupation from time immemorial. Agriculture employs 60 to 80 percent of the labor force. It produces half to two thirds of national output.

An agricultural country does not have to be poor. Denmark and New Zealand testify to the contrary. The less developed countries are poor, not just because they are agricultural, but because the productivity of their agriculture is so low.

The reasons for agricultural inefficiency vary from country to country, because systems of land ownership and management vary so widely. In many countries most of the land is held by large landowners, who supply the equipment and working capital. The tenants provide labor power and receive part of the crop in return. The tenants' share is rarely more than one half and may be as low as one third. This pattern of landholding is particularly characteristic of Central and South America. In some of these countries 1 percent of the landowners control two thirds or more of the agricultural land. This pattern also prevails in most countries of the Near East.

Under a landlord-tenant system, the tenant has little economic incentive. If he produces more, most of it will go to the landlord. Buildings, fences, drainage, and other improvements on the land belong to the landlord and not to him. So why should he put extra time into these things? He also has little choice of products or methods of production.

Any impetus toward greater efficiency must come from the landlord. But the landlord may not be interested. Landowners in these countries are not "maximizing men" on the pattern of the Western capitalist. They are often absentee owners who live in the city, where they engage in a business or profession. They cling to their land for security and prestige but take little interest in its management. So long as it yields the customary income, they will not bother to squeeze out more production. They need enough for the town house in Caracas, the annual trip to Europe, the foreign education of their children. Why bother about more?

In other parts of the world, including most of south and southeast Asia, peasant agriculture is the dominant system. The peasant producer, who owns his land and receives the whole output, has greater incentive to behave economically. Peasant farmers generally are systematic and rational in using their land and labor resources, *within limits set by their needs and by known methods of production*. But by adding these qualifications we have given away a good deal.

The basic *need* is for family consumption. Unless there are roads over which produce can be moved to market, an urban demand for foodstuffs, and something which the peasant can buy with money income, he has no incentive to produce more than this. Effort and output will be increased only under pressure of more mouths to be fed.

Now consider *techniques*. Peasants may be quite diligent in using the agricultural methods they know. But they don't know very much. The rural population of these countries is dominated by a traditional culture little affected by events in the outside world. The South Indian villager knows nothing of the economic plans and pronouncements emanating from New Delhi. The Peruvian Indian in the high Andes scarcely believes in the existence of Lima. Rural children may go to school for a few years, but quickly slip back into the age-long illiteracy which surrounds them. Agricultural methods are handed down from father to son, and suggestions for change are resisted rather than welcomed.

The very poverty of the people acts as a barrier to change. Living close to the margin of subsistence, they are chronically in debt to the landlord or the local moneylender. Surplus income from a good crop year is immediately swallowed up in debt repayment. Their meager resources do not permit even small capital outlays for tools, fertilizer, or livestock. They dare not risk new crops or methods because, if the experiment should fail, they would be left destitute. Thus poverty perpetuates itself in a way which has been familiar in these countries for centuries.

If a country's land is all settled and the rural population continues to increase, as is true over large areas of Asia, land fragmentation becomes a problem. If the legal system requires family property to be divided among the surviving heirs, landholdings are split finer and finer with each successive generation. In some Asian countries, farms average only 1 or 2 acres. Even this small area may be divided into a number of separate pieces, as was true in medieval Europe. This wastes the time of the farm operator and uses valuable land for boundaries and footpaths.

In this situation one usually finds heavy rural underemployment (termed also "disguised unemployment," "surplus labor," "redundant labor"). This differs from open unemployment in that everyone on the farm is doing something. The work is spread around among whatever number of hands is available. But each person may be working much less than a full day and week. Suppose 10 people on a farm average 4 hours work per day. If five of these people were withdrawn, and if the remaining five could be persuaded to work 8 hours a day, the same output might be obtained from half the existing labor force.

Underemployment is difficult to measure precisely;[2] but in many countries it is estimated at 20 to 40 percent of the agricultural labor force. From one standpoint this is discouraging, since it reduces output per capita. But on the other hand this idle labor time provides a reserve of human resources which can conceivably be mobilized for industry and other nonfarm employments.

While agriculture is dominant in the less developed countries, it is not the only activity. The people not working in agriculture are engaged mainly in three things: (1) Handicraft production. In thousands of tiny shops, men sit cross-legged on earth or stone floors weaving and dyeing cloth, cutting out and sewing garments, beating out kitchen utensils by hand, producing pottery jugs and plates, and so on through the list of simple consumer goods. (2) Retail trade, which means mainly petty trade, involving great expenditure of time for a very small sales volume. (3) Service activities of every sort—barbers and beauticians, priests and scribes, messengers and porters, rickshaw and pedicab drivers, and the host of domestic servants whose ready availability is perhaps the surest index of underdevelopment.

These activities are characterized also by heavy underemployment and low per capita output. People who leave farming for city life must find subsistence somehow. Some remain openly unemployed and beg, steal, or sponge a living. But the majority crowd into every nook and cranny of the trade and service industries, getting at most a few hours' work per day and forcing down the earnings of everyone in these industries to a bare subsistence.

What does this leave for the "modern" sector of the economy? Factory industry, usually very limited in extent; transportation, power, and other public utilities; wholesale and export-import trade; banking; and government service. Rarely does this modern sector produce more than 20 percent of the country's GNP. Consider the implications for the arithmetic of economic growth. Suppose a country wants to raise its GNP by 5 percent a year. It proves impossible to do anything about output in

---

[2] One difficulty is the marked seasonality of many agricultural operations. The minimum number of people needed in agriculture has to be defined as the number which, if working a full day, would be sufficient to meet labor requirements at the sesonal peak. This will necessarily involve some underemployment in the off season. An interesting problem in the less developed countries is to find ways of utilizing this seasonal slack for nonfarm production.

agriculture and other traditional activities. Then if the modern sector is producing 20 percent of GNP, output in this sector would have to grow initially by 25 *percent per year* to attain the overall target.[3] This rate of increase seems very unlikely, quite apart from the difficulties which would arise from raising urban incomes rapidly in the face of a stagnant supply of foodstuffs.

These economies, in short, are starting from a very small base of modern economic activity. To attain an adequate overall growth rate they must get *both* a high rate of expansion in this base *and* a moderate expansion of agriculture and other traditional activities.

SPECIALIZATION AND EXPORT DEPENDENCE

In the less developed countries, exports typically form a high percentage of GNP (Table 4). Many countries export 10 to 20 percent of

TABLE 4

Exports as a Percentage of GNP, Selected Countries, 1961

British Guiana	51	Ghana	21
Malaya	45	Burma	17
Rhodesia and Nyasaland	39	Chile	10
Venezuela	33	Argentina	9
Ceylon	27	Brazil	7
Jamaica	25	Mexico	6
Peru	24	Turkey	6

Source: U.N. *Yearbook of National Account Statistics,* 1962 and 1963.

their output, and in very small countries the proportion may run to one half or more. Exports consist mainly of oil, minerals, foodstuffs, and industrial raw materials. Many countries get more than half their export revenue from a single product: rubber in Malaya and Liberia, rice in Burma, sugar in the Philippines, jute in Pakistan, oil in Venezuela and Iraq, copper in Chile and Zambia, bananas in Central America, coffee in Colombia, cocoa in Ghana, cotton in Egypt and the Sudan.

This dependence on specialized exports raises both short-run and long-run problems. In the short run, it leads to serious economic instability. The demand for primary products fluctuates with economic activity in the industrial countries, particularly the United States. A recession in the United States lowers demand for a wide range of raw

---

[3] On this basis, of course, the modern sector would be providing a larger share of GNP year after year, and as this happens its *percentage* rate of increase can slow down gradually. When the modern sector reaches one third of GNP, for example, a 15 percent rate of expansion in this sector will mean 5 percent for the economy.

materials. World output of agricultural products fluctuates considerably for climatic and other reasons. These shifts in demand and supply produce wide swings in the prices of primary products, much wider than in the case of manufactured goods.

Any of these countries, then, may suddenly experience a sharp drop in the value of its exports. If its foreign trade was previously in balance, it now has a balance-of-payments deficit. Unless this can be covered from reserves or borrowing, imports will have to be cut. This is unpleasant. Cuts in imports of consumer goods mean higher prices, speculation and profiteering, higher living costs and aggressive wage demands, and political unrest. Cuts in imports of capital goods may mean abandonment of important development projects.

Moreover, since these governments usually depend heavily on export and import taxes, a drop in exports means a drop in tax revenue. The government must then either cut its spending, including its development activities; or it must cover the budget deficit by borrowing from the central bank.

There is a characteristic difference between business cycles in industrial and nonindustrial countries. In the industrial countries, cycles occur mainly because of fluctuations in domestic investment. In the primary producing countries the impetus typically comes from the outside, from fluctuations in export revenues.

Over the long run, dependence on primary exports raises a different kind of problem. Suppose a country launches a development program designed to raise GNP 5 percent a year. Its import requirements will probably rise even faster, perhaps 7 or 8 percent a year. Most of the machinery, building materials, and other goods needed for industrialization will have to come from abroad. There will also be increased needs for fuel and materials to feed the new factories. As incomes in the country rise, there will be heavier demand for manufactured consumer goods; and import of many of these items cannot be resisted.

What are the chances that these import requirements can be covered by an equivalent increase in exports? World demand for primary products depends mainly on the rate of growth in the advanced countries. Suppose real GNP in these countries is rising 5 percent per year. Then their imports of primary products will probably rise by something less than 5 percent. Foodstuffs, which constitute a large share of primary exports, have a low income elasticity of demand. Demand for many nonfood products is also being reduced by new inventions— synthetic fibers instead of natural fibers, synthetic rubber instead of natural rubber, and so on.

It is also often argued that *price* trends are likely to be adverse to primary products over the long run. Prices of manufactured goods are often controlled by monopoly arrangements. Improvements in production methods are reflected in higher wages and profits rather than in lower product prices. Supply is adjusted to demand at a fixed price. It is much harder to control the world supply and price of rubber, coffee, or cotton. With uncontrolled supply and a slowly growing demand, there is chronic downward pressure on primary product prices. So the poor countries are likely to find the prices of their export products falling relative to the prices of the manufactured goods which they import.

A developing country, then, can find itself in a situation in which its import needs are rising 8 percent a year but it can increase exports only 3 percent a year. Something has to give. One possibility is to close the gap by loans or grants from abroad. This is a major reason why rapidly developing countries need foreign capital. Another avenue of adjustment is to reduce the need for imports by forced draft development of local manufacturing industries. This is termed *import substitution*. The strategy of successful import substitution will be examined in the next chapter.

TAX SOURCES AND GOVERNMENT EXPENDITURE

Many of the things necessary for development must be done by government. This takes money. So it is pertinent to ask where government revenues come from in these countries.

Most countries rely heavily on excise or sales taxes and on export and import taxes (Table 5). These taxes are normally *regressive*. Moreover, indirect taxes are typically inflexible, that is, their yield rises less rapidly than national income. But if government is to meet its development responsibilities, it needs a tax system under which revenues will rise *more* rapidly than national income..

The industrial countries have such a revenue source in the personal and corporate income taxes, the yield of which rises more than proportionately to increases in GNP. But the less developed countries draw little revenue from these sources. The politically powerful landowners largely escape taxation. High-income groups in the cities also pay little. There may be a stiff income tax on the books, but the rates are not enforced. In some countries it is said that only two groups pay the personal income tax: foreign businessmen, who are fair game, and civil servants, whose incomes are a matter of public record. Much the same is true of taxes on business income. Large foreign concerns pay the full tax. Large local concerns may pay the tax, in whole or in part. Smaller local businesses typically do not pay. The revenue yield is small and falls mainly on the most progressive businesses.

The difficulty of collecting taxes hampers the financing of development programs. In the industrial countries, government expenditures usually form 20 to 30 percent of GNP. Yet in the poor countries, where the economic tasks of government are even more critical, government

TABLE 5

Sources of Tax Revenue, Selected Countries, 1960–61

COUNTRY	GOVERNMENT EXPENDITURE AS PERCENT OF GNP	PERCENT OF TAX REVENUE DERIVED FROM			
		DIRECT TAXES ON INCOME AND WEALTH	EXPORT AND IMPORT TAXES	EXCISES, SALES, AND OTHER TAXES ON CON-SUMPTION	OTHER SOURCES
Asia:					
Burma	16.2	30.8	33.7	23.5	12.0
Ceylon	15.3	27.3	57.0	10.4	5.3
India	n.a.	30.2	13.0	23.4	33.4
Iran	n.a.	8.7	26.2	———→	65.1
Malaya	12.6	22.0	66.2	3.2	8.6
Pakistan	n.a.	23.4	35.2	39.7	1.7
Philippines	8.7	16.5	40.8	17.2	25.5
Thailand	8.6	10.0	38.8	29.3	21.9
Latin America:					
Argentina	13.0	28.4	42.3	———→	29.3
Brazil	11.3	20.1	7.4	———→	72.5
Chile	9.3	34.8	20.2	———→	45.0
Colombia	6.3	55.0	36.8	———→	8.2
Ecuador	12.6	18.0	51.0	———→	51.0
Mexico	6.1	39.9	24.9	12.4	22.8
Peru	11.9	53.6	12.5	———→	33.9
Venezuela	21.1	55.1	31.2	———→	13.7
Africa:					
Egypt	n.a.	29.6	——————————→		70.4
Ghana	10.2	17.5	76.5	———→	6.0
Kenya	n.a.	42.2	37.1	———→	20.7
Rhodesia and Nyasaland	11.8	59.4	26.6	———→	14.0
Tanganyika	10.2	36.0	43.6	20.3	0.1
Uganda	n.a.	20.3	56.4	———→	23.3

Data do not cover precisely the same time period for all countries. In most cases, however, they refer to fiscal 1959–60, calendar 1960, or fiscal 1960–61.

n.a. = not available.

———→ = combined total shown in right-hand column.

Sources: U.N. *Economic Survey of Asia and the Far East*, 1961.

U.N. *Economic Survey of Latin America*, 1961.

U.N. *Statistical Yearbook*.

U.N. *Yearbook of National Accounts Statistics*.

expenditures are typically in the neighborhood of 10 percent. Professor Arthur Lewis has argued cogently that a country must raise its tax collections to around 20 percent of GNP if it is serious about economic development.

With tax sources restricted, and with heavy pressure for expenditure, many of these countries have large budget deficits. A little money can be raised by selling government bonds to the public. But the main way of closing the deficit is to borrow from the central bank. In some countries, the main function of the central bank is to finance deficits of the national government. The higher level of spending, instead of raising production, mainly pushes up the price level. Brazil, Chile, and several other Latin American countries have suffered from inflation for decades. This is true also of some of the Asian and African countries in the period since independence.

Some economists believe that mild inflation can be helpful in the early stages of economic development. But there would be little disagreement that inflation of 25 or 50 percent a year has a disorganizing effect on the economy.

EDUCATION AND THE SHORTAGE OF SKILLS

Most of these countries have very inadequate educational systems. On the economic side, this limits the skill and productivity of the labor force. On the political side, an illiterate electorate provides a poor foundation for stable democratic government.

In Iran, at the time of the most recent census, 85 percent of the population was illiterate. The corresponding percentages were 82 in India, 75 in Egypt, 65 in Turkey, 62 in Malaya, 51 in Brazil and Venezuela, and around 45 percent in Thailand, Burma, and Ceylon.[4]

In many countries only a minority of children ever attend school. In the late 1950's the percentage of children of primary school age who were enrolled in school was 65 in Ceylon, 63 in the Philippines, and 56 in Thailand. But it fell as low as 38 in Egypt, 33 in Brazil, 25 in Burma, and 18 in Iran. Moreover, most pupils drop out so early that school leaves no lasting imprint. The proportion of children of high-school age enrolled in high schools is typically only 10 to 20 percent.[5]

Educational facilities are particularly inadequate in the rural areas. There are few teachers, because of a shortage of teachers' colleges, and these teachers usually prefer to live in the city rather than in isolated rural areas. The outlook of the country people is usually indifferent or even hostile to book learning.

Only a small percentage of young people get the prerequisites for college training, and facilities for higher education are pathetically inadequate. The vast Republic of the Congo has one university, admitting a few hundred students a year. Indonesia, with its hundred million people, has two universities. Universities are badly understaffed, and faculty salaries are usually so low that they must be supplemented from outside sources. In Latin America, college teaching is almost always a sideline occupation for people whose main job is in government, law practice,

---

[4] It should be added that some of these censuses are several years in the past, and that in most countries the situation is gradually improving.

[5] UNESCO, *Basic Facts and Figures, 1960* (Paris, 1961), pp. 22–24.

or business. Since most college students in Latin America also hold jobs and are studying on the side, their training is not very intensive.

The training provided in the universities often bears little relation to the needs of the economy. The ex-British colonies, notably India, have a surplus of liberal arts graduates, who remain unemployed in the larger cities. At the same time, there are crying shortages of engineers, scientists, doctors, and business executives.

Almost all these countries have severe shortages of the professional skills needed in a modern economy. There are far too few educated people fitted for business administration and government service. There are far too few engineers, architects, agronomists, teachers, economists, statisticians, medical technicians, scientific research workers. The gap can be only partially closed by sending students to Europe or the United States for training. At some stage, there must be a massive effort to build up educational facilities within these countries.

Transition: The Prospects of Development

The list of defects in the less developed economies appears long and bleak. A country suffering in full measure from all these deficiencies would have no prospect of economic development. Fortunately, each of these things is a matter of *degree*. Government is better in some countries than others, and so is education, agricultural technology, and the rest. A country which is badly off on one front may be better off on another.

The moral is not that economic development is impossible but that it will be slow and difficult. Development requires a major national effort, involving more work and saving, and also a transformation of economic institutions. The transformation may be peaceful or violent, gradual or sudden, but it must come. The main impetus must come from *within* the developing country. Outside capital and advice may be helpful, but they cannot play a decisive role.

Even under favorable circumstances it takes decades before one can be sure that a nation has embarked on self-sustained growth. Politicians in both developed and less developed countries often paint rosy pictures of rapid growth, propelled by a brief burst of foreign aid which can be quickly withdrawn. These pictures are largely illusory. The growth of a country's productive resources and the reshaping of its institutions are bound to be slow. And any richer country which wishes to aid in the process had better be prepared for a long period of support.

Transition: The Usefulness of "Western Economics"

In the next chapter we turn to measures for stimulating growth in a poor country. Here an American adviser is tempted to say, "Do as we do. Study economic principles, which you can find in any textbook. Then apply them in your policy making." To this the local official may well reply, "Unfortunately, your economic principles were developed for your kind of economy. Our economy operates quite differently, and your economics doesn't help us."

There is a good deal to this. Take first the theory of pricing and resource allocation. We learned in Part One that, in a purely competitive economy, each product will sell at a uniform price throughout the market, this price will tend toward the minimum necessary production cost, the price of each factor will also be uniform throughout the market, and each factor will be allocated so that its marginal productivity is the same in all uses. But do things happen this way in Ecuador or Iran? They certainly do not. Immobility and misallocation of resources, serious distortion of factor prices, and monopolistic pricing of commodities are the general rule. At most, one can claim that price theory suggests directions of institutional reform for a country which chooses to develop by the market route.

In Part Three we learned that unemployment arises from insufficient aggregate demand. The remedy for unemployment is to raise the level of spending by monetary-fiscal measures. Production will respond, and output will rise toward capacity. But suppose India attempted to remedy its massive unemployment by running a large government deficit. This increased money demand could do little to raise the level of production. Agricultural output is limited by traditional systems of landholding and cultivation. Industrial output is limited by the small amount of plant and equipment available. A sudden increase in spending will raise ths price level but will have little effect on output or employment.

The theory of international trade suggests that a country should specialize in products for which it has a comparative advantage. Nigeria presently has a comparative advantage in cocoa and palm oil. But suppose world demand for these things fluctuates violently, so that an economy tied to them moves like a crow's nest in a typhoon. And suppose world demand for these products is growing very slowly or that competition from other supply sources is increasing. Might it not be better to diversify the economy by moving into lines where Nigeria might develop a comparative advantage 20 or 30 years from now? Can the *static* theory of international trade provide much guidance for the *dynamic* development of an economy over time?

Even the modern theory of economic growth outlined in Chapter 28 has little to say about growth in the less developed countries. The standard models assume that growth is already under way and that the only question is whether it will be faster or slower. Increased inputs of labor and capital appear magically year after year. There is also a substantial annual increase in factor productivity, which can be counted on even if it cannot be explained. All this is tailored to the circumstances of the developed countries. But in a less developed country the main problem may be to *initiate* growth after a long period of stagnation.

Increased labor supplies can be counted on, but increased capital certainly cannot. Productivity improvement is something to be struggled for rather than assumed.

Western economic analysis, in short, addresses itself to questions which are not the most important questions facing the less developed countries. Our theory takes *resource supplies, production technology,* and the *institutional framework* as given. The economic problem then reduces to how resources can be deployed most effectively within this framework.

This does not come to grips with the development problem. The things we take as given are precisely the things which the less developed countries must change if they are to move forward. Resources must be enlarged, technology improved, institutions transformed. The problem is to accelerate the rate of increase of national output over a long period in the future. This is quite different from the problem of extracting greatest output from given resources at a moment of time.

In good measure, then, policy makers in the less developed countries have to work with their bare hands. They cannot just lift tested economic principles off the shelf. They have to construct both principles and policy as they go along. This makes their task at once more difficult and more challenging.

SUMMARY

1. The less developed countries differ in many important respects. Some have a long experience of political independence, while others are just emerging from colonial rule. Some are considerably richer than others. Some are experiencing rising per capita income, while others are stagnating. They differ widely in size, resource base, and degree of population pressure. There are, nevertheless, common characteristics which appear in some measure in all of them.

2. Political leadership is often unstable or not oriented toward economic growth. Government service is usually weakly staffed, which hampers efficiency both in government and in private industry.

3. There is typically a sharp cleavage between city and country, between the money economy and the subsistence economy. The economy is often fragmented also by geographical barriers, and by racial, religious, and caste divisions within the population.

4. Markets for commodities, capital, labor, and foreign exchange are quite imperfect, and price relations are seriously distorted. One cannot rely on the existing market mechanism to achieve efficient allocation and use of productive resources.

5. Most people are engaged in agriculture, and productivity in agriculture is typically low. In some countries this is traceable partly to landlordism; but independent peasant agriculture can also be very

inefficient. The nonagricultural population is engaged mainly in low-productivity handicraft, trade, and service activities.

6. Exports often constitute 10 to 20 percent of GNP, and are usually concentrated in one or two primary products. Fluctuations in export sales have the same unsettling effect on these economies that fluctuations in investment have in the industrial countries. Over the long run, low income and price elasticity of demand for primary products poses a problem of how to increase exports fast enough to pay for the imports needed for economic development.

7. Tax revenue is typically only 10 percent or so of GNP, and comes mainly from commodity taxes rather than income taxes. Hence revenue may rise less than proportionately to increases in national income, seriously hampering development expenditures.

8. Educational facilities are increasingly inadequate as one proceeds from the primary to the university level. There are severe shortages of training capacity for the technical and professional skills needed in a modern industrial economy.

9. Income distribution is more unequal than in the industrial countries, and the high incomes of the rich tend to go into luxury consumption or hoarding rather than into industrial investment.

10. There is a serious deficiency of business leadership. In some countries most businessmen belong to foreign ethnic groups, which places them at a political disadvantage. Where there is a local business group, as in the Latin American countries, it is typically traditional and monopolistic rather than innovative.

11. Not every country suffers in equal measure from these handicaps. Some are making progress. But progress is bound to be very gradual, as indeed it was in the older developed countries.

DISCUSSION QUESTIONS

1. It is often said that the economic principles which we study and apply to the American economy are not very useful in the less developed countries. Do you agree? Why, or why not?

2. The market mechanism analyzed in Part One is imperfectly developed in these countries. Does it follow that the main aim of government should be to improve the market mechanism, or rather that government must supersede the market and make the key economic decisions itself?

3. Peasant farmers seem to be quite shrewd and "economic" in their behavior, yet they produce much less than farmers in the advanced industrial countries. Why is this? What would be needed to get them to produce more?

4. Agriculture in many less developed countries is said to be characterized by "surplus labor," that is, labor whose marginal productivity is zero. How might one test whether this is so and try to estimate the amount of surplus labor?

5. Do the less developed countries have economic fluctuations? What sets them off, and how do they differ from business cycles in the industrial countries?

6. What problems arise from heavy dependence on exports of primary products? Can you think of ways of eliminating or mitigating these problems?

7. Economists usually urge governments in the less developed countries to tax more heavily, so that they can invest more in development projects. What kinds of tax would be most useful in raising additional revenue?

8. Suppose the Agency for International Development sends you out to a less developed country to appraise its development prospects over the next 20 years. What kinds of information would you collect, and how would you organize your report?

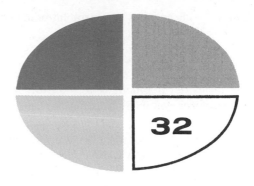

Policies for Economic Development

> If to do were as easy as to know what to
> do, chapels had been churches, and poor men's
> cottages princes' palaces.
> WILLIAM SHAKESPEARE, *The Merchant of Venice*

> Whoever makes two blades of grass to
> grow where only one grew before renders a serv-
> ice to the State.
> VOLTAIRE

PLACE YOURSELF in the position of the President of a poor country striving for economic development. You are beset by all the problems described in the last chapter. The country lacks virtually everything. Where do you begin? What do you set as high-priority objectives? How do you lay hands on the resources to work toward these objectives? Can you learn anything from the history of countries which have had a long and successful growth experience?

SOME HISTORICAL EVIDENCE

Evidence from the West

Rapid economic growth began in the West. Starting from England in the period 1750–1800, modern industry spread during the nineteenth century to the United States, Western Europe, and the British Commonwealth. It is natural to look first at the record of growth in these countries. What was their situation at the beginning of the modern era?

How did growth get underway? What was the sequence of events during the crucial early stages?

Conditions in the Western countries at the beginning of *their* period of rapid development were more favorable than those now prevailing in the poorer countries. Income per capita was considerably higher. It has been estimated that average income in Britain in 1800 was about at the level of Argentina or Chile today, which would place it well above most of Asia, Africa, and Latin America. So there was more margin for saving and capital accumulation and also a wider market for manufactured consumer goods.

Population growth in Western Europe from 1750–1850 was typically less than 1 percent a year. At a later stage these countries experienced a "population explosion," because of rapid reduction of death rates. But they had entered a period of sustained economic growth *before* there was a rapid increase in population. The reverse is true in most of the poorer nations today. Modern medical science has arrived there in advance of any increase in economic productivity. The population of many countries is rising at between 2 and 3 percent a year. This requires considerable effort just to keep per capita income from falling.

The Western nations had other advantages in the early stages: political unification, which in some cases had existed for centuries; economic unification through a road network, to be followed in the nineteenth century by a rapid development of canals, railroads, and steamships; stable government, including guarantees for private property and business enterprise; and a sizable business class, which was to grow rapidly in social prestige and political power. Most poor countries today are less well off in these respects.

Starting from this advantageous position, the growth rates of the Western nations were not spectacular. Growth began gradually, and it was often a half century before one could be sure that a permanent acceleration had occurred. Even in more recent times, annual growth rates have not been high. Kuznets' calculations for the past century indicate that even in the fastest-growing industrial nations, GNP has typically risen by 3 to 4 percent a year. In some countries (Britain, France, Holland, Australia) the average annual increase has been 2 percent or less.

The development plans of the poorer countries today often aim to increase GNP at 4 to 6 percent a year, i.e., more rapidly than the wealthier nations have done over the long run. This does not prove that the targets are unattainable. But to attain them will require a larger national effort than was made in the industrial countries at a corresponding stage.

As regards the *pattern* of growth in the Western countries, we may note first the existence of a progressive agricultural sector. In most countries there were important advances in agricultural productivity *before* there was much development of factory industry. The agricultural revolution typically led the industrial revolution. This was true not only in the West but in Russia, which had developed a large export surplus of grain before 1914. Without this initial cushion, the U.S.S.R. could scarcely have survived the shock of collectivization and the long neglect of agriculture during the 1930's and 1940's. In Japan, too, agriculture led the march of the economy into the modern era.

Second, growth was associated in many countries with increased opportunities for international trade. Ocean transportation became cheaper throughout the eighteenth and nineteenth centuries; improved roads, canals, and railroads lowered the cost of getting goods from the interior to port cities; tariffs and other trade restrictions among the advanced countries fell considerably; and colonization of many parts of the world by Europeans opened up trade opportunities in those areas. The countries which grew rapidly were typically countries which had something to sell abroad; textiles from England, timber from Sweden, foodstuffs from Denmark, grain from Russia and the United States, silk from Japan. Trade was an engine of growth.

Some economists argue that primary producing nations today do not have the favorable export opportunities which existed at an earlier time and that it is particularly hard for them to break into the world market for manufactures. There is doubtless something to this. But the prominent role of trade in economic growth over the past two centuries suggests that one should not reject the possibilities of trade without careful examination.

Third, we may note the complex and pervasive nature of economic growth, the diffusion of pioneer activity throughout all branches of the economy. Economic historians tend to simplify the picture by focusing on major inventions or on new industries which were growing with particular speed—the "coal and iron age," the "railroad era," and so on. This overlooks the great amount of "follow-up investment" by innumerable small men in subsidiary lines of activity whose growth is necessary to support that of the major industries. It neglects also the gradual spillover of talent and capital from the leading sectors into other lines of industry.

Fourth, government played an important role in developing transport and communication facilities. Government took main responsibility for the network of roads and canals, the postal system, and other means of communication. It subsidized and protected merchant shipping in various ways. Railroads were a government monopoly from the beginning in most countries, and so was electric power at a later stage. Education and public health, so closely linked with the improvement of human resources, were mainly a government responsibility. It is thus inaccurate to picture Western economic growth as arising solely from private initiative with government playing a passive role. The blend of private and public activity naturally varied from country to country, depending on national institutions and traditions. Government initiative was more important in Japan than in Europe, and more important on the Continent than in Britain or the United States.

Finally, we may look at the financing of private capital formation. The main source of finance in most countries was reinvestment of business profits, often termed the *classical process of capital accumulation*. The way in which this process operated in the Western countries (and in Japan after 1868) is well known. Inventions and improvements were raising productivity in both agriculture and industry. But real wages rose only slightly. This lag of wages behind the increase of productivity yielded large business profits. Rates of return on capital during the nineteenth century were substantially higher than they are today.

Most capitalists of this era were conscientious men, who lived well but not wildly, and who put most of their profits into business expansion. Hence, a cumulative process: profits were reinvested in plant and equipment, to make still larger profits in the future, leading to more reinvestment, and so on and on. With profits forming an increasing share of national income, and with most of these profits reinvested, it followed that capital formation must also form a rising share of national income. The rise in capital formation rates was one of the striking features of nineteenth-century economic growth.

Why was the increase in national output not swallowed up immediately by wage increases and thus channeled into consumption rather than investment? There were several reasons. In some countries, agricultural progress was creating a surplus of landless workers who could be drawn into urban industries at low wages. So long as this surplus continued, there was no need to raise city wages substantially. Another reason was the limited development of effective trade unions. Great Britain did not have large-scale unionism until the 1890's, the United States not until the 1930's, and Japan is only now reaching this stage. There seems to have been a lag of about a century between the beginnings of large-scale industry and the development of strong union organizations.

Nineteenth-century wage earners took little part in politics and had little influence on government policy. During the period of rapid industrial buildup, there was no unemployment compensation, or old-age pensions, or family allowances, or medical and hospital insurance, or other appurtenances of the "welfare state." Nor was there a progressive income tax to reduce inequalities of income.

For a considerable time, then, the laboring class enjoyed only limited participation in the benefits of economic growth. The welfare of the average British worker seems to have risen only moderately between 1780 and 1840. But while the common man benefited little at the time, the high rate of capital formation made possible larger output and higher living standards at a later stage. Without exploitation of labor in the nineteenth century, there would have been less product for the welfare state to redistribute in the twentieth. One difficulty in the poor countries today is that there is political pressure to legislate a wide range of welfare measures immediately, before productive capacity has risen to the point at which the economy can "afford" the promised increases in living standards.

These features of early industrialism in the West provide a useful background for our later discussion of development strategy. This is not to say that the future must repeat the past. But it would be surprising if the future were entirely *unlike* the past and if the rules of economic growth had changed completely since 1945.

It is worth noting that the classical process of capital accumulation has operated in the U.S.S.R. somewhat as it operated in the Western countries at an earlier stage. Productivity is raised through investment and technology, while wages and living standards are held back. The result is a large profit gap, which in this case shows up mainly as tax receipts by the central government. A large share of these receipts is plowed back into industrial investment, leading to larger output and profits on the next round. This process operated so successfully from 1928 to 1950 that it has now become possible to relax the austerity of the Stalin era and to permit workers to share in the rise of productivity. The moral for the less developed countries is not so much that growth occurs through planning as that growth occurs through belt-tightening over a prolonged period.

Evidence from Japan

A nation embarking on economic development might well make a careful study of Japanese experience. A century ago Japan was a very poor country, with a feudal political structure and a substantial population confined in a small land area. Beginning with the Meiji Restoration in 1868, Japan proceeded to become a major industrial nation, which in recent years has had one of the highest growth rates in the world. How did they do it? Several points may be underlined:

1. While there is a widespread impression that Japan developed rapidly after 1868, early growth was in fact quite gradual. Industrialization did not really get underway until the 1890's, 25 years after the Restoration. Even then, industry meant mainly textiles. As late as 1930, Japan was not self-sufficient in steel, and far from it in machinery. Metals, machinery, and chemicals did not begin to rival textiles until the armament program of the 1930's and did not outshine textiles until the 1950's. The sequence was from a primarily agricultural development (1868–90), to textiles and other light industries (1890–1930), and finally to heavy industry (1930 to date).

2. Early Japanese growth was marked by a sharp rise in agricultural output. Between 1878 and 1908, land under cultivation increased by

35 percent and output per acre by 80 percent, so that total output more than doubled. How was this accomplished? There was a basic land reform early in the period, under which government paid off the feudal landowners with government bonds and resold the land to the cultivators, who had a more direct interest in raising productivity. There was also considerable public investment in irrigation, drainage, and land reclamation.

Within this framework, productivity rose through a multitude of small improvements: increased use of fertilizers, better varieties of seeds, weed control, double-cropping of rice, better layout of plots, improved methods of cultivation. Government research and agricultural extension activities, which relative to Japanese national income have been even larger than in the United States, were important in promoting these improvements. Improved agricultural credit facilities, and efforts to raise the literacy of the rural population, were important. Farm incomes also benefited from sideline activities: a wide diffusion of handicraft production throughout the countryside and the introduction of silkworms, which gave Japan a major export product.

The government taxed away much of the increase in farmers' incomes to finance capital formation elsewhere in the economy. From 1878 to 1912 about two thirds of total tax collections came from agricultural sources. The tax burden on agriculture, as a percentage of agricultural income, was about three times as heavy as on other sectors of the economy. Thus the agricultural sector provided food for the growing population, a major source of exports, the main source of tax revenues, and a growing market for domestic manufactures. What more could one ask?

3. The influence of government on economic development was important but indirect. While the government started many model factories in the early stages of industrialization, most of these were sold in 1882 to private concerns. The government continued to operate only such things as railroads, the tobacco monopoly (for revenue purposes), and steel and munitions (for strategic reasons). The main thing government did was to create a unified internal market through improved transport and communications, an atmosphere of political stability, an enforceable tax system, corporation laws, and other prerequisites for the successful operation of private enterprise. The point has been well put by Patrick:

Flexibility in the utilization of factors was greatly enhanced by clearing away the legal and political obstacles to freedom of ownership of land, occupation, and movement for labor, and by institutional reforms in law, taxation, currency, banking and other areas. Consumption and saving relationships were altered, especially in the redistribution of income away from the *daimyo* lords and their retainers. A start was made at bringing in foreign knowledge and at disseminating it, both through a government drive at general basic literacy, and emphasis on a wide variety of technical skills through vocational schools, the hiring of foreign technicians, sending missions and students abroad, importing machinery, and so on.

By and large the state used the private market mechanism to allocate resources and to obtain its objectives generally, exerting its influence through the market (via tariffs, subsidies, differential tax rates, purchases, and the like), rather than replacing the market through government planning or production . . . except at the very beginning the government was not important as an industrial producer and its contribution to the growth of the economy did not lie in State-owned enterprise.[1]

4. The early Japanese entrepreneurs were mainly of rural origin— sons of country merchants, rich peasants, or landlords. "They were restless young men, with considerable education and early practical experience, who in a sense broke with the past, had great faith in Western methods, and who moved as young men to one of the large urban centers, in the quest of progress and personal advancement."[2]

Pursuit of private profit was fused with service to the Emperor and development of national power. It was taken for granted that "what is good for Mitsubishi is good for Japan," and vice versa. Development of large industrial enterprises was considered a national service. How pleasant to become rich and patriotic at the same time! The social structure of the country remained oligarchic, with close interlocking by marriage among the top business, political, and military families. This new ruling class rapidly assumed the position held by the feudal landlords before 1868.

5. Alongside the growth of factory industry, the small workshop has continued to play an important role in the Japanese economy. As recently as 1955, three quarters of manufacturing employment was in shops with fewer than 300 workers, and 40 percent was in shops with less than 30 workers. How have the small shops managed to survive instead of being squeezed out by mass-production enterprises? There appear to be several reasons. First, the surplus of labor and scarcity of capital in Japan favors labor-intensive methods, which usually means smaller production units. Second, small shops pay considerably lower wages than large ones. In 1954, manufacturing plants with 100 to 500 workers paid wages only 70 percent as high as plants with 1,000 workers or more. Plants with 10 to 30 workers paid only 55 percent as much as the largest establishments. Thus low wages serve as an offset to the lower productivity of the small shops.[3]

---

[1] Hugh T. Patrick, "Lessons for Underdeveloped Countries from the Japanese Experience of Economic Development," *Indian Economic Journal,* October, 1961, pp. 150–66. Excerpts from p. 151 and p. 157.

[2] *Ibid.,* p. 162.

[3] How are the small shops able to get by with these lower wage rates? Partly because of the chronic labor surplus in the economy, but also because the small plants are largely unaffected by union organization, which has been a strong factor in large-scale industry since World War II.

Third, small plants are not necessarily in competition with large plants. On the contrary, large factories often subcontract a good deal of their work to low-cost small producers. In assembly industries such as bicycles, sewing machines, radios, and electronics, the parts are often made in small shops and then brought to the central factory for final assembly. There may be lessons in this for some of the newly developing countries, which are apt to think of industrialization as synonymous with large-scale production.

6. Foreign trade was important in Japanese development. Before World War II, Japan typically exported about 20 percent of her national product. But the character of this trade changed as Japanese manufacturing grew in diversity and competitive power. In 1880, Japan was exporting raw materials and importing both capital goods and manufactured consumer goods. By 1940 she was exporting primarily manufacturers, while importing raw materials and even some foodstuffs.

Unlike the United States and many other countries, Japan did *not* depend heavily on foreign borrowing in the early stages of development. Capital formation came almost entirely from domestic sources: increased government tax revenues, reinvestment of business profits, and personal savings of the frugal Japanese people. It is interesting that the capital formation rate was not high in the crucial early decades. Gross investment seems to have been 10 to 11 percent, and net investment perhaps 6 or 7 percent, of national product from 1889 to 1914. The growth of national output seems to have been due mainly to technical progress and institutional changes, rather than to investment per se.

We should reemphasize in conclusion the tentative character of early economic growth. The acceleration of output and investment is gradual and long drawn out. It may be interrupted for shorter or longer periods. Only after several decades of expansion can one safely conclude that the economy is going to "make it."

This period of tentative and precarious growth has been given various names. Ranis terms it the *breakout period*. Rostow has labeled it the *takeoff period*.[4] This term may be misleading, however, since it suggests a rate of acceleration faster than usually occurs in practice, and suggests also that movement is always in one direction. As a Burmese economist commented, "When we looked at our statistics for the early fifties, we concluded that we had taken off. Unfortunately, a short time later we landed again." There may be several such landings in the early years of growth. One is inclined to agree with the remark of a Yugoslav economist at a recent international conference: "Nations do not take off. They *creep over the threshold* of economic development."

---

[4] W. W. Rostow, "The Take-off into Self-sustained Growth," *Economic Journal*, Vol. LXVI, March, 1956.

THE DEVELOPMENT PROBLEM TODAY

We can say of economic history, as Keynes said of economic theory, that it "does not furnish a body of settled conclusions immediately applicable to policy." It is useful to know something about early growth in the older industrial countries. But the world economy of 1970 is not that of 1850 or 1750. Today's developing countries cannot be merely imitative but must respond creatively to the situation in which they find themselves.

There is not yet any "standard model" for economic development. There probably never will be, because of the wide variation among countries emphasized in the preceding chapter. But certain characteristics of the development process are *broadly applicable* to *many* countries. A brief review of these will set the stage for the remainder of this chapter.

While the less developed countries have many handicaps, most of them have one substantial asset: a large reserve of unutilized labor time. This reserve army of the underemployed is found in agriculture, in petty trade and service activities, in open unemployment in the cities. The trick of development, as suggested in Chapter 28, is partly to transfer this surplus labor to manufacturing and other "modern" activities. Moreover, this transfer must be at a rate greater than the rate of increase in the labor force, so that the *proportion* of the labor force employed in the modern sector is rising and the "center of gravity" of the economy is shifting in the right direction.

The necessary rate of increase in "modern" employment is thus closely linked to the rate of population growth. The importance of the population problem cannot be overemphasized. A country which can cut its population growth rate from 3 percent to, say, 1½ percent per year has taken the largest single step toward raising per capita output. Apart from this, it is not very clear what economics has to say. The history of the richer countries suggests that if a country can somehow attain a rising per capita income, this will itself bring down birth rates over the long run. But this is rather cold comfort; and today's poor countries can scarcely afford to wait several generations for this "natural" solution to the population problem.

Many things are needed for rapid enlargement of the modern economic sector. There must be *entrepreneurs* to initiate and manage the new industries. There must be adequate *incentives* for entrepreneurs and workers. Government must provide an *institutional framework* favorable to private economic initiative. But the most tangible need, and the one easiest to fit into an economic analysis, is that for *physical capital* with which new workers can collaborate in production.

The rate of physical capital formation can be stepped up in several ways: by using unemployed labor directly to create new capital goods; by importing capital goods from abroad; by raising the rate of voluntary saving by businesses and households; and by compulsory saving enforced through the fiscal system. So the first thing we shall do in this chapter is to explore the possibilities and limitations of each of these methods.

No matter how successful the drive to increase capital formation, capital will remain very scarce relative to its possible uses. Capital must be *allocated* appropriately among the demands of agriculture, manufacturing, public utilities, and other public services. Within the growing manufacturing sector, those industries should be pushed which will contribute most to future economic growth. We shall argue that in this sphere government should aim mainly to create a market structure and a price system which will draw forth correct responses from a multitude of private producers.

A special aspect of the allocation problem is foreign trade policy. Many of the goods and services produced in a country are national goods, which by their nature cannot be exported or imported. Transport, communications, and most other services are of this character. But there are also many internationally traded goods, which can either be produced at home or imported from abroad. Here cost considerations are relevant. If the quantity of resources needed to produce and export enough coffee to import a ton of steel is less than the quantity needed to produce the steel at home, then the import alternative seems preferable. But there are numerous qualifications to this argument. Moreover, the price of foreign exchange is a vital element in these calculations, which will lead us into some discussion of exchange rates and exchange control systems.

In most of the less developed countries, government provides basic public services such as health and education, plus transportation, power, and communications. Agriculture, most of manufacturing, commerce, and the service industries—altogether, 80 to 90 percent of national output —remains in private hands. But the fact that most production is private production does not mean that government can be inactive. We have seen that government played an important role in the early growth of the older industrial countries. The burden falling on government in today's poor countries is even heavier. This is partly because these countries are starting from a lower level in terms of education, communications, and other public services; partly because private economic institutions are less fully developed than they were in Europe and America even in 1800; and partly because of a different political climate, in which government responsibility for the functioning of the economy is more widely accepted than it was in earlier times.

In addition to specific lines of government activity, most governments in the LDC's are concerned with setting overall targets and priorities for the economy. They have *development plans* looking 5, 10, or more years into the future. Indeed, private enterprise America has recently insisted that any less developed country requesting an Agency for International Development loan or grant *must* come in with a comprehensive development program. Since the framework of these economies is largely private, these are obviously not Soviet-style plans. So what are they? What does development planning accomplish which could not be accomplished without it?

These considerations explain the sequence of topics in this chapter. We begin with a review of sources of capital formation, proceed to the problem of allocating capital among its main alternative uses, consider the special problems which arise in the foreign trade sector, and conclude with a brief analysis of development planning. It should be emphasized that this is a highly *selective* treatment of a few key policy issues. To do more than this would quickly run us out of space, and perhaps even out of ideas.

SOURCES OF CAPITAL FORMATION

Simple growth theories often turn entirely on the rate of investment. It is simply assumed that the *marginal capital-output ratio,* that is, the relation between dollars of new investment and dollars of additional output, is say 3:1, and that this ratio remains unchanged over time. Then if the economy invests 9 percent of GNP each year, output will grow at 3 percent. If investment can be raised to 12 percent, the growth rate will rise to 4 percent; and so on.

This is clearly too simple. In the underdeveloped economy, characterized by underemployment, traditional techniques, and poor organization of production, it may be possible to raise output substantially with little increase in capital. On the other hand, new capital may be wasted by being invested in unwise directions or in poorly managed enterprises. But with this qualification, there would be general agreement that capital is important. Capital formation rose substantially in the older industrial countries during their early development; and one would expect this to be true also of today's developing countries.

It is convenient to divide the sources of capital into two groups: first, those which appear to be *costless* in the sense of involving no reduction of current consumption. This group includes mobilization of presently unutilized resources, principally labor; and imports of capital goods from abroad. Second, there are sources which do involve reduction of current consumption and which pose the usual choice of present *versus* future. In this group are voluntary saving by businesses and households, taxation, and inflation. An energetic development program will probably involve effort in all these directions at once. Let us review the possibilities.

Mobilizing Idle Resources

Investment in agriculture often requires mainly the farmer's own labor. Fencing, ditching, drainage, tree planting, and additions to farm buildings are usually done in this way. One reason for giving farm operators security of tenure, and preferably outright ownership, is to provide maximum incentive for these types of improvement.

Road building and other public works can also be carried out on a nonmonetary basis. Until quite recently this was common practice in rural American communities. The town assessed taxes each year against the farmers. But each year also the country roads needed mending. So a farmer would turn out with his horses and equipment to grade the road, repair potholes, and spread gravel, receiving credit for each hour worked. Mysteriously, the farmer's credits were usually about equal to his tax bill. Little money changed hands, but the work got done. The farmer had been taxed in time rather than in money.

This is not very different from the system used in parts of Africa in colonial times. A small poll tax was placed on each man in a village. The man had no money to pay. So he was offered a chance to earn money by working on roads and other local improvements. When he had worked enough to earn his tax, he was free to quit.

The late Professor Nurkse argued that this principle could be widely extended in underdeveloped countries. His argument starts from the observation that many countries have redundant labor in agriculture. Suppose these people are withdrawn from agriculture and put to work somewhere else. The opportunity cost of doing this is zero, since output in agriculture will not fall. So if these previously useless people are put to work on roads, dams, irrigation ditches, schools, and other local improvements, whatever they produce is a net gain.

True, some money financing is required. The people transferred from agriculture were previously paid nothing. When they are employed on public works they must be paid a wage. Isn't this an added cost to society? A money cost, perhaps; but not a real cost. Remember that there are now fewer people left to be fed in agriculture, but just as much farm production as before. If the excess food—the food which used to be consumed on the farm by the people who have now been withdrawn— can be transferred and made available to these people in their new location, everything balances out.

One might do it this way: Put a tax on the people remaining in agriculture. They get the money to pay the tax by selling surplus food in town. The public works employees are paid from the proceeds of the tax, and then go to the store and buy the food which has been shipped in from the country. The flows of money and food just balance.

This is not quite as easy as it sounds. It will be hard to prevent the people who remain in the country from eating more, so it may be impossible to extract the full food "surplus" from them. The people who have moved are now doing hard physical work, so will need to eat more than they did when sitting around the farm. The country's total food requirements will probably rise. Moreover, the people employed on public works cannot work with their bare hands. There will have to be some investment in tools and building materials. So capital formation by the Nurkse route is not really *free*. But it is a very *low-cost* method, requiring mainly leadership and organization.

Capital Imports

Many of the physical components of early economic growth must come from abroad. An industrialization program requires machinery and building materials for the factories, generators and electric cable for the power projects, rails and rolling stock for the railroads. Operation of the new factories requires increased imports of fuels and materials. As industry becomes established, these import needs may gradually taper off. But in the first few decades of industrialization they are likely to grow at a staggering rate.

How are these imports to be paid for? The country might conceivably be able to raise its exports fast enough to balance the rising import requirements. But in this event resources are being devoted to export production which could otherwise be used to produce goods for home consumption. So the imports are not costless. A reduction of current consumption is involved.

Suppose that the countries supplying the capital goods are willing to finance the transfer through loans or grants. An outright grant might be regarded as costless to the receiving country, and this is probably *almost* correct. There is the possibility, however, that the availability of foreign grants may cause a country to relax efforts to raise its own savings rate, so that the net gain in capital formation is less than it appears. But the main practical consideration is that grants are hard to come by. France and Britain have made direct grants to some of their former colonies, mainly in Africa. The United States has made substantial grants to South Korea, South Vietnam, and Taiwan. But most of the financing available from the developed countries is loan financing, requiring repayment of principal and interest.

Capital imports financed by borrowed money are costless for the moment, but obviously not forever. At some point in the future, the country's repayment obligations will rise above its new borrowings. By this time it must have raised its exports to the point where it has an export surplus sufficient to earn the foreign exchange needed for loan repayment. So an LDC must practice careful "debtmanship." It must ensure that, during the period in which it is accumulating debt, it is also raising its GNP and its export capacity. Its future repayment obligations must bear a reasonable relation to its projected exports. It is usually thought that if debt servicing comes to absorb more than 25 percent or so of normal export earnings, the country is in a precarious position.

Raising Voluntary Saving

When a country has done what it can to mobilize unused resources, and when it has borrowed all that it safely can from abroad, its total supply of goods is fixed; and we come back to the usual problem of capital goods *versus* consumer goods. If more resources are to be devoted to capital goods production, they must be withdrawn from consumer goods production. The population must save more, in real terms.

Voluntary private saving by businesses and households is typically low, in the range of 0 to 5 percent of national income. If the problem were to raise this percentage out of a static national income, which would mean an actual reduction of current consumption, the prospect would certainly be bleak. But if the economy is inching forward in the sense that per capita income is rising, one may hope to capture a good share of this *additional* income. The objective is to raise the *marginal* savings ratio substantially above the *average* savings ratio; and if this can be done, the average ratio will gradually rise. The development plans of most countries aim at a marginal savings ratio in the range of 0.2–0.3, that is, 20 to 30 cents of additional saving out of each additional income dollar. In some of the LDC's, actual marginal savings rates over the last decade are within this range.

Part of this step-up in saving must be accomplished through taxation, to which we turn in a moment. But to the extent that people can be persuaded to save voluntarily, the pressure on the tax collector is reduced. The argument that "people are too poor to save" can scarcely be accepted. Even in very poor countries, people do not in fact use all their income for current consumption. They spend substantial amounts on elaborate marriage and funeral ceremonies. They accumulate resources in the form of jewelry and precious metals, which serve both as personal ornament and as a rainy-day reserve. The problem is partly to create *savings institutions* and *new types of asset* which people will find as acceptable as the old. They must be persuaded that a postal savings account or a government bond is as safe a reserve as a gold bracelet. In India and some other countries, government is now able to raise substantial amounts from small savers throughout the economy.

Business concerns in the modern sector of the economy may be expected to save a good part of their profits for reinvestment; and as the modern sector expands, this source of saving becomes more and more important. The most important policy issues in this area relate to business taxation. To a government in urgent need of more revenue, business profits are naturally a tempting and politically popular target. Yet if government digs too heavily into this source, both the incentive for private investment and the funds to finance it will be reduced. A possible approach here is to give favorable tax treatment to *reinvested earnings,* with a stiffer tax on profits withdrawn for dividend payment.

Taxation and Public Saving

The amount which people can be persuaded to save voluntarily typically falls short of the amount needed to raise GNP at a desirable rate. How far is government justified in enforcing a higher rate of saving through the tax system? As we have already noted in discussing the centrally planned economies, economics at present is not able to say much about this. There are certainly outside limits of feasibility. Governments outside the communist orbit rarely propose a savings rate which would actually *reduce* present levels of consumption. This would be quite unpopular; so the savings rate which would hold per capita consumption unchanged as output rises can be taken as a practical maximum. Moreover, an even lower maximum may be set by the fact that the output capacity of the economy at any moment is frozen in a certain pattern. The amount of resources devoted to capital goods production, or which can be quickly diverted to capital goods production, is limited. If it is not physically feasible in the near future for capital goods to form more than, say, 15 percent of total output, there is no point in enforcing an average saving rate of 20 percent. This would mean cutting demand for consumer goods below what the economy is geared to producing and would cause needless hardship to the population.

Within these limits, government must decide how far to sacrifice present to future and must choose a particular rate of saving. It may rationalize this by saying that it is choosing what the citizens of the country *would* choose if they were sufficiently informed and farsighted. In any event, someone must decide. The decision is highly important, and quite variable from country to country. There are "hard" or "austerity" programs of development in some countries, considerably "softer" programs in others.

The technique of raising the national savings rate through government is two-sided. Government must tax *and* it must save. Expenditure on current services must be held down so that funds can be devoted to capital projects.

Tax rates usually need to be raised. But *which* tax rates? The problem, noted already in Chapter 17, is that raising revenue is only one objective of a tax system. One would like at the same time to improve the distribution of income in the country, or at any rate not worsen it. Moreover, people's incomes provide the primary incentive to greater effort and output. If this incentive is too much reduced through taxation, the whole effort to raise output may falter.

The higher ranges of personal income could doubtless be taxed more effectively than at present. It is hard to condone spectacular luxury consumption in the higher income brackets, while most people are very poor and the country is starved for development capital. Many countries have a graduated personal income tax on the books, but it is usually not enforced. If income tax enforcement is considered too difficult, one could try a general tax on *expenditures*. Luxury expenditures can also be reached to some extent by high commodity taxes—import duties in the case of imported items, excise taxes in the case of domestic products. In one way or another the upper-income groups should be compelled to make a greater contribution than they typically make at present.

But "soaking the rich" is not enough. There aren't enough of them. A serious development effort requires "soaking the poor" as well. This may mean substantial sales or excise taxes on all but the most basic necessities. Something like the Russian policy in this respect may be essential for any country which wishes to force the pace of development. This policy is, of course, much harder politically with an "open" government, which must reveal what it is doing, than in the U.S.S.R., where turnover tax rates are virtually a state secret.

A serious problem in most countries is that farmers use their political leverage to avoid their share of the tax burden. If incomes in agriculture are low and static, it is hard to squeeze out much tax revenue. It becomes easier if agricultural incomes are being raised through technical progress, so that government is simply siphoning off part of the annual increase. The success of the Japanese government with this strategy during the nineteenth century has already been noted. Unless a country is able to step up agricultural output substantially, and then tax away a good part of the proceeds, the pace of development will be reduced.

For farm products sold on the export market, it is possible to siphon off part of the income either through an export tax or through a government marketing agency which buys the produce at one price from farmers and sells it at a higher price on world markets. But here again there is a conflict between revenue considerations and incentive considerations. If export crops are taxed more heavily than other crops, farmers may be discouraged from producing them. Exports may fall off, depriving the nation of foreign exchange which is needed to import capital goods and other materials for development. The system of agricultural taxation should be so devised that, at a minimum, it does not tip the scales against export products, and it should perhaps give them positive encouragement.

Government must not only raise more revenue, but must conserve this revenue for high-priority uses. If extra revenue is swallowed up immediately by the army and the police, the economy may be worse off than before. The procedures for making the annual budget allocation are centered traditionally in the Ministry of Finance. The Minister of Finance, who actually collects the taxes, is always a powerful figure. He is apt to regard the revenue inflow as his money, and the doling out of this money among the spending departments as his prerogative. At any rate, the spending departments normally submit their budget requests to the Ministry of Finance, and a group of Finance officials sit down with representatives of each department to whittle down their requests and hammer out a recommended amount. The basis for departmental requests is often very flimsy. The amount requested is heavily influenced by what the department has received in the past, and by the aggressiveness and political standing of the Minister in question. The criteria used by Finance officials in screening and cutting these requests are equally unsatisfactory; and a powerful Minister will often bypass the whole procedure by going directly to the Prime Minister.

To install an effective budgetary procedure, which promotes rational allocation of public funds, is a slow and complicated process. It involves better grass-roots preparation of program proposals within each department; a central budget agency responsible directly to the President or Prime Minister; and setting each year's budget decisions within the framework of a multiyear development plan. We shall argue later that this is the greatest single contribution which planning organizations can make in the LDC's.

Inflation

Another possible source of capital formation is bank loans or note issues, extended to finance construction by private industry or to cover a government budget deficit. This increases the supply of money. So an initial question is how fast money supply can be increased without putting pressure on the price level.

If output is rising, and if money supply is increased no faster than output, prices can still remain stable. This consideration may permit monetary expansion at the rate of 3 or 4 percent a year. One can even be a bit more venturesome. One feature of a developing economy is a gradual increase in the public's use of money. Goods which used to be produced and consumed at home now pass through the market. Barter transactions are replaced by money transactions. People in remote villages become used to the sight of money and put some of it away under mattresses. So the demand for money rises, and an increase in money supply which simply matches this increase in demand creates no problem. Lewis estimates this possibility at perhaps 1 percent of national income per year during the early stages of development.

At some point, however, the price level will begin to rise. What are the consequences? Can inflation itself be a source of capital formation and economic growth? Or is it harmful to economic development?

Framed in this way, the question is probably meaningless. The reason is that inflation has many sources, many forms, many rates. One can certainly define a kind of inflation which would contribute nothing to growth. But one can also specify conditions under which inflation might be helpful.

Suppose inflation originates in note issues by the central bank to cover a government deficit. The funds are used for current government expenditures and do not add to capital formation. Suppose also that inflation has been going on so long that the major economic interests have developed ways of protecting themselves against it. Workers have wage escalator arrangements under which cost of living increases are followed promptly by wage increases. Oligopolistic industries mark up prices to cover higher costs; and so on. Under these conditions one can have a high rate of inflation, which continues year after year, but the effect of which on growth is almost certainly negative.

Consider, on the other hand, the process visualized in Schumpeter's growth theory. After a period of price stability, there is a substantial injection of bank credit into the system. The new money goes into the hands of entrepreneurs, who use it for capital formation. As these people bid resources away from consumer goods industries, the output of consumer goods falls and prices rise. This comes as a surprise to consumers, who have not developed ways of protecting themselves against it. They take a cut in real income, and it is this "forced saving" which makes possible a higher rate of capital formation. But after a time —determined by the gestation period of the new capital goods—the new industries begin to pour out a larger stream of consumer goods, and prices begin to fall toward their previous level. The inflation is extinguished.

This model is useful in bringing out the conditions under which inflation can contribute to capital formation: the inflation should be moderate, preferably intermittent, and at all times under control by the monetary authorities. The new funds should be directed toward people who will use them for capital formation and should lead within a reasonable period to an increased flow of consumer goods, which will itself dampen the rate of inflation. And the economy should be as free as possible of automatic escalator devices capable of turning the initial price increase into a perpetual upward spiral. People must *not* be capable of protecting themselves against inflation if it is to work constructively.

USING RESOURCES EFFECTIVELY

Let's return now to the problem of the President of Chile or Pakistan. His government has limited resources of administrative talent as well as money. How should these resources be deployed for development purposes?

This may be viewed from one standpoint as a problem of *balance*. How can the growth of various sectors of the economy be made consistent and mutually supporting? From another standpoint it is a problem of *time sequence*. What activities, if started first, will be most conducive to later growth of other activities?

One is involved in a variety of issues: the balance between investment in direct production and in social overhead capital; the balance between agricultural and nonagricultural activities; the choice of industries for development; and the degree of emphasis which should be placed on foreign trade and development of export markets. On each of these matters there is considerable disagreement even among experts. This is one reason why economic development is an unusually lively area of economic study and practice. While we cannot resolve all disagreements in this area, we can at least try to clarify what the argument is about.

Developing Economic Infrastructure

Industries may be divided into two broad groups:

1. Those which provide basic services required for the development of other industries. This includes electric power production; road, rail, air, and water transport; postal, telephone, telegraph, and radio communication; and technical education, scientific research, and extension services. The familiar term *public utilities* covers most of these industries. They are also sometimes called *economic infrastructure*, a military term which denotes the communications and supply network needed to support an army in the field. Another common term is *social overhead capital* (SOC), which one wit has defined as "anything for which the World Bank will lend money."

2. Agriculture, mining, manufacturing, and the like are usually termed *directly productive activities* (DPA). This does not put the matter quite correctly, for public utilities are also productive. But the DPA industries are in a sense built on top of and serviced by the SOC facilities.

The development of social overhead capital is in most countries considered a function of government. Well-conceived projects can usually be financed by borrowing from the World Bank or other foreign sources, since they yield a cash revenue from which to pay interest and principal. But one cannot equate the economic return from a railroad or power project with the revenue from sale of its services. The benefit to the economy will usually be considerably larger than the cash revenue. This is because of the beneficial effects on other lines of production. If cheaper transport lowers costs and prices of manufactured goods, this means higher real incomes for the population and a larger national output of manufactures.

To go back to the terminology of Chapter 12, an SOC project yields *external economies*. Its *social product* is typically a good deal larger than the *private product* which can be appropriated as profit by the operators of the project. So it is usually desirable from a national standpoint to invest *more* in such projects than one would do if the objective were to maximize private profit. This is one reason why decisions about the level of social overhead investment should be made by public authorities rather than private investors.

It seems sensible that SOC investment should proceed in step with development of manufacturing and other DPA industries. But precise balance cannot be attained at each moment of time. In addition to the usual difficulties of forecasting demand, many SOC investments are large and time-consuming. A major hydro project can easily take 10 years from conception to completion. This raises a problem of strategy: is it better for social overhead investment to be somewhat *ahead* of investment in directly productive activities, or somewhat *behind* it? This question has been posed particularly by Hirschman,[5] who terms the former course *development via excess capacity* (of SOC), and the latter *development by shortages*.

The first strategy involves building railroads, highways, port facilities, and power plants ahead of immediate demand, in the hope that availability of these services will call forth investment in DPA industries. This is a safe strategy in the sense that *eventually* the country will grow sufficiently to use these overhead investments. The difficulty is that this excess capacity has only a *permissive* rather than a *compulsive* effect. One cannot be sure how quickly DPA investment will be forthcoming. If the lag is long, facilities may deteriorate for lack of use, and some of the premature investment will be wasted.

The opposite course is to push ahead as fast as possible with DPA investment, which will raise the demand for public utility services. Then, as shortages of these services become apparent, go ahead with SOC investment to overcome the shortages. The advantage of this *compulsive* sequence is that, if the first step is taken successfully, the second can be counted on to follow. As transport lines and power output become inadequate, there will be political pressure to do something about it, and the necessary steps will be taken almost automatically. The disadvantage is that, since SOC investment takes so long, an expansion undertaken only *after* shortages are visible means that these shortages will continue for several years. The existence of these bottlenecks will have a discouraging effect on further productive investment.

Despite these difficulties, Hirschman concludes that the second strategy is generally preferable:

. . . if we endow an underdeveloped country with a first-class highway network, with extensive hydroelectric and perhaps irrigation facilities, can we be certain that industrial and agricultural activity will expand in the wake of

---

[5] Albert Hirschman, *The Strategy of Economic Development* (New Haven, Conn.: Yale University Press, 1958), chap. 5.

these improvements? Would it not be less risky and more economical first to make sure of such activity . . . and then let the ensuing pressures determine the appropriate outlays for social overhead capital and its location? As examples of this type of sequence, one may cite the development of Japan, Turkey, and, to a considerable extent, of the U.S.S.R.[6]

Closely related to investment in physical overhead capital is expenditure on public health, education, technical training, and other things which improve the quality of the labor force. This is usually classified as current expenditure in government budgets and is regarded as an addition to consumption; but it contains an important investment element. Giving people stronger physiques, more knowledge, and greater technical skill raises their productive capacity just as surely as giving them more elaborate tools and equipment.

The parallels between investment in social overhead capital and investment in human beings are in fact quite striking. Most countries regard both as normal functions of government. Both have widespread beneficial effects throughout the economy and encourage the growth of other industries. In both cases the social product of the investment is substantially greater than the private gain. There is consequently a danger of underinvestment, which can be averted only by farsighted government action.

Human investment raises two questions. First, *how much* should government spend in this direction? One can safely answer, "More than usually is spent." Even in the United States, with its elaborate educational system, the yield on investment in education is still high. One would expect it to be considerably higher in countries where educational facilities are severely limited. It seems likely that in most countries there is (relative) overinvestment in material capital and underinvestment in raising personal productive capacity.

While the less developed countries differ in degree of educational advancement, the typical situation is as follows: most children get through a few grades of elementary school, but learn so little that they quickly relapse into illiteracy. The number finishing elementary school is much smaller than the number who start. The high-school population is tiny and constitutes an educational aristocracy, as was true in the Western countries a century ago. The percentage of young people reaching college is insignificant and is drawn largely from the upper economic groups.

To widen the upper levels of this educational pyramid is a formidable task. The main barrier to expansion is a physical shortage of teachers at each level. There are not enough high-school graduates to expand the supply of primary-school teachers rapidly, not enough college graduates to feed back into high-school teaching. The bottleneck in high-

---

[6] *Ibid.*, pp. 93–94.

school training capacity is especially serious. In some countries just to expand primary education at a desirable rate would absorb all of each year's high-school graduates. Yet these graduates are also in demand for white-collar employments and as potential college students, so that only a small proportion in fact go into teaching.

The physical bottlenecks to expansion show up also as financial constraints. Some four fifths of educational costs in these countries are teacher salary costs. Since teachers are scarce, their salaries are higher relative to the general wage level than is true in the developed countries. This limits the number of teachers who can be hired with the available government budget. If the push for educational expansion is successful, however, the financing problem diminishes over time. As the flow of high-school and college graduates increases, this rise in the supply of teachers will gradually reduce their relative salaries and allow more teachers to be hired from a given budget. Employment of more teachers still further increases the flow of graduates, and so on in a "virtuous circle."

In addition to the problem of increasing educational resources, there are important questions of how these resources should be allocated. A basic issue is how far—or how quickly—one should move toward universal literacy for all children of primary-school age as against more prolonged high-school and college education for a smaller number. There is also the issue of liberal versus technical education. In terms of political enlightenment and personal culture, one might wish to put as many people as possible through academic high schools and liberal arts colleges. But in terms of maximum productivity gain, one might argue for more school training in manual and clerical skills, and more technical and professional training in college. These issues are important even in wealthy countries. In the poor countries they are very important, because the total resources available for education are so limited.

Raising Output in Agriculture

Is it feasible for an economy to grow simply through industrial development, while agriculture continues in its traditional stagnation? Both history and theory suggest a negative answer. In the older industrial countries a transformation of agriculture typically accompanied, or even preceded, the rise of factory industry. We can also suggest logical reasons why rising agricultural output *must* accompany any sustained economic growth.

Industrial development means among other things a transfer of manpower from country to city, the formation of an urban wage-earning class. How are these people to be fed? It may be said that, since they have simply moved in from the country, the food which they formerly consumed on the farm is now "surplus." All one needs is some way of capturing this surplus and shipping it to the city to be consumed there.

But this is not very realistic. As the number of mouths to be fed from each farm plot declines, the people remaining on the land will probably eat more than before. Conceivably, they may eat up all of the hypothetical surplus. Moreover, the people who move to the city are now working harder and earning money wages, so their demand for food will be higher than before. Thus the amount of food available must increase if the economy is to remain in balance.

If domestic food production does not rise sufficiently, the increased demand will spill over into foreign markets. Food imports will rise and this, given a limited supply of foreign exchange, will reduce the country's ability to import capital goods for development. Alternatively, if imports are restricted, food *prices* will rise, and this will act as a brake on industrial development. Industrial wages will have to be raised to cover the higher food costs, which will cut into profit margins and into the funds available for reinvestment.

Rising domestic demand for food, then, is a basic reason why farm output must rise as development proceeds. But there are other reasons as well. First, agriculture produces not only food but also wool, cotton, flax, hides, oilseeds, and other raw materials. Unless production of these things is increased, the processing industries which depend on them either cannot develop or must use imported materials. Second, agriculture is normally the main source of the increased exports so desperately needed to finance imports of industrial goods. Third, rising farm output and income is needed to provide a rising demand for consumer goods from the country's manufacturing industries. If these industries must depend only on taking in each other's washing within the limited urban population, their growth will be slow and stunted. Finally, industrialization leads eventually to a shortage of labor. At this point improvements in agricultural productivity become necessary to release additional labor for urban employment.

Many less developed countries presently have surplus labor in agriculture. But if agricultural workers can be drawn off into industrial employment faster than new workers are being added by population growth, the amount of surplus labor will gradually fall. Eventually one reaches a point at which pulling more labor off the land will significantly reduce agricultural output *unless*, at the same time, steps are being taken to raise output per farm worker. In some of the more thinly populated countries, labor is a scarce factor from the outset. In these countries, to transfer labor out of agriculture, while at the same time raising agricultural output, requires a substantial rate of productivity increase.

It is much easier to demonstrate the need for agricultural progress than to devise ways of getting it. Basic organizational changes may be needed, such as buying out absentee landlords and breaking up large landholdings into efficient-sized family farms. The point of this is not mainly to penalize the landlord or to redistribute income. The point is rather to establish a system in which the farm operator who makes the production decisions also receives the financial reward, so that economic incentives have a chance to operate effectively.

Given an effective institutional framework, the proper prescription for raising output depends mainly on the labor-land ratio. After the point of labor shortage has been reached, it makes sense to replace farm labor by machinery. But up to that point, mechanization is inappropriate. What one wants in the early stages is not *laborsaving improvements* but *land-saving improvements,* i.e., measures which increase output per acre while requiring as much or more labor than before. This means fertilizers, irrigation, improved seeds and breeds of animal, improved cultivation methods, use of insecticides and pesticides, double-cropping where climate permits, systematic crop rotation, and the like.

A puzzling thing about agriculture in the less developed countries is that the techniques in use are so far behind those already known to agricultural scientists. In India, experts say that it would be possible to raise farm output 30 to 50 percent by using only known techniques and with no increase in the cultivated area. This would stave off the food problem for a generation and give the country an invaluable breathing space. Yet the potential gains in output are not being realized. Why not? What might be done to reduce the gap between the known techniques and the actual techniques?

One necessity is an effective agricultural extension service. The best agricultural methods are known mainly to scientists and other experts in the cities. If these methods are to become effective, they must be applied by millions of farmers in the rural areas. There is often an almost total lack of communication between the two groups. The job of the extension service is to break this impasse and to establish effective two-way communication.

This requires extension workers who are willing to dirty their hands working with the farmer. Too often the agricultural agent, having some education and being a government official, considers himself several steps above the peasant. He will pass out literature or issue instructions, but he will not get out in the field and use his hands. Thus effective communication is not established. The United States, with its long and successful record of extension activity, has a good deal to teach on this front.

Raising the level of agriculture also requires new rural institutions —land banks and credit cooperatives, purchasing and marketing associations, and so on. It is not enough to set the small farmer up on his land and urge him to produce. Particularly where he has been used to getting capital and instructions from the landlord, he is apt to flounder when left on his own. Efficient family farming requires that the farmer be surrounded by a network of servicing institutions organized on a larger scale, as is true in the United States and other advanced agricultural countries.

Investment is needed in several directions: new fertilizer factories; adequate roads from farm to market; warehousing, refrigeration, and processing facilities; agricultural colleges and experiment stations. The prime necessity, however, is organization and education. If this is done effectively, a small amount of capital put into agriculture may yield large returns.

Industrial Development

Factory industry is a small sector in most of the less developed countries, contributing only a few percent of national output. But it is, or at least is expected to be, a rapidly expanding sector whose contribution to GNP will rise substantially over time. Indeed, establishment of manufacturing industries is often considered the hallmark of economic development.

Since everything cannot be done at once, the initial question is *which* industries are most appropriate at a particular time and place? How does one decide whether to encourage textile mills or shipyards, radio plants or steel works?

Why can't we get the answer by following the usual business procedures for determining the worthwhileness of an investment? Estimate future sales revenues from the proposed enterprise, deduct production costs, and get the stream of expected future profits. Reduce this to a percentage rate of return on the initial investment. Then compare with the going rate of interest. If the prospective rate of return is above the rate of interest, go ahead with the project. If not, drop it.

This kind of calculation should certainly be made for any proposed project. But the results are not necessarily conclusive. The problem is more complicated than appears at first glance. First, the *factor and product prices* used in the calculation should, as nearly as possible, reflect the true cost of resources and the true value of output to the economy. For reasons explained in the last chapter, existing market prices may not give an accurate indication of costs and benefits and may need to be adjusted upward or downward.

Second, one must consider the interrelation of various industries which are expanding simultaneously in a growing economy. New investment in one industry may be profitable if, and only if, certain related industries are also expanding at appropriate rates. Expansion of industry A may confer indirect benefits on industries B, C, and D. These are valuable to the national economy even though they do not add to industry A's profits.

From a national standpoint, then, one can scarcely calculate the profitability of each act of investment in isolation. It is more useful to calculate the joint profitability of alternative "bundles" of interdependent projects. At the extreme, one can regard all the industrial investment which is expected to be undertaken during the next several years as constituting a single "bundle" and compare the total yield with the total cost. One can then tinker with the bundle by adding and subtracting projects to see whether it is possible to get greater returns for the same cost.

Third, planning industrial development does not involve merely sorting out alternative investment projects *at a point of time*. It involves also determining the *sequence of events over time*. The decision is not just to accept or reject a particular project. An acceptable project can be started immediately, or it can be postponed. It is impossible to do everything at once, and this raises what Hirschman calls the problem of *efficient sequences* of investment.

An efficient sequence, in Hirschman's view, is one in which the early investments encourage and stimulate later investments. This may happen because of *backward or forward linkages* between industries. Building a plant to produce a raw material will encourage the development of industries using this material. This is forward linkage. Conversely, a factory producing finished goods and buying materials will stimulate the growth of plants to produce those materials. This is backward linkage, which is perhaps the more dependable of the two. A finishing industry *must* have materials to work with and, as it becomes large enough to use the output of an efficient-sized material producing plant within the country, this plant will be established quite naturally. Forward linkage, on the other hand, is permissive rather than compelling.

The commonest case of forward linkage in developing countries is the processing of agricultural raw materials by flour mills, sugar refineries, breweries, cotton gins, coffee roasting plants, and the like. Backward linkage often takes the form of a gradual substitution of home production for imports. A country has been importing, say, women's rayon and nylon clothing. As a first step, a clothing industry may be established which continues to use cloth imported from abroad. Next, cloth mills may be set up using imported yarn. Later, facilities for producing the synthetic yarn may be constructed, still using imported chemicals. Eventually the chemicals may be produced at home, and substitution is complete. This "nibbling away" at a sequence of related industries, starting with the finished goods end and working back toward basic materials, may prove quite efficient.

Given these complications, *who* is to decide that certain industries shall be expanded and others not? At one extreme, a group of government planners might sit down and lay out an expansion program for the industrial sector. At the other extreme, investment decisions might be left entirely to private businessmen. And there are many intermediate combinations of private initiative and public control.

It is often said that government must dominate the expansion process, because only government can mobilize capital on a sufficient scale. Further, it is argued that, because of the defects already noted in the market mechanism, private investment decisions will be wrong from a national standpoint and will misallocate resources. Finally, it is said that potential businessmen are very scarce in these countries. It is no use appealing to private entrepreneurship, because it isn't there.

This last proposition seems quite dubious. True, in many of these countries, landowning, the civil service, and the professions carry greatest prestige, and business is no fit occupation for a gentleman. But there are usually some people around—merchants, native bankers, small operators in the handicraft and service industries—who are quite keen to turn small profits into larger ones. These people may not be highly visible, but inconspicuousness is a hallmark of the budding entrepreneur. You learn of his existence only after he has appeared and cashed in on some profitable opportunity. A favorable government attitude can probably uncover sizable supplies of business talent, often uncouth and poorly educated, but shrewd and adept in responding to economic incentives.

The main argument for relying heavily on private initiative is simply that government is not staffed to do the job. The small nucleus of good administrators is spread very thin; and there are many things they must do. They must raise taxes, maintain law and order, provide basic public services, develop economic infrastructure, formulate and apply a wide variety of economic policies. If in addition they try to move heavily into management of manufacturing, trade, and service enterprises, the rate at which new enterprises are actually started is likely to be slow, and these enterprises are likely to be badly managed and inefficient. If, on the other hand, the government administrators are willing to encourage private initiative in these areas, they may be able to increase substantially the *total* supply of administrative talent, or what Hirschman has called "decision-making ability." Moreover, this approach can raise the rate of capital formation. In the private sector, instead of money being saved in *vacuo* and then looking around for investment opportunities, the sequence is very often reversed. It is the perception of an investment opportunity which then *leads* to saving by the entrepreneur and his associates, and also to reinvestment of business profits.

The process of encouraging small enterprises to grow into larger ones is, of course, not feasible in most branches of heavy manufacturing; but these industries come late in the development sequence anyway, because their large optimum scale requires a large market. And it is a slow process, which appears distasteful to those who dream of a rapid leap into industrial affluence. But is there any realistic alternative? Is not actual economic growth bound to be gradual, as it has been even in the richer and older industrial economies?

Development by the market route is quite compatible with, indeed it requires, a wide array of complementary activities by government. Provision of physical infrastructure, plus education and technical training, has already been mentioned. In addition, where the optimum scale of plant is large, government may have to take the lead in mobilizing capital for manufacturing investment. Many countries now have development banks which are authorized to buy stock in or make long-term loans to industrial enterprises. One of the best-known examples is the National Financera in Mexico. This organization raises money by selling its own bonds, which have a good credit rating, in the financial market. It then uses the funds to acquire part ownership in a wide variety of private businesses. Except for the fact that National Financera is publicly owned, the operation is similar to that of the private investment banks in older industrial countries.

Another technique is for government to launch and finance a new enterprise completely, with a view to selling it off later to private owners. The Japanese government did this extensively during the 1880's and 1890's, and some of the less developed countries are doing it today. The Pakistan Industrial Development Corporation is a good illustration. A Canadian company, say, is called in to construct a paper mill in West Pakistan. P.I.D.C., a government-owned corporation, puts up the initial capital. It also negotiates a management contract under which the Canadian company agrees to operate the mill for the first few years, meanwhile training Pakistani managers to take over. With this breathing space, P.I.D.C. scouts around Karachi to see whether some wealthy families may be willing to buy into the paper company. A sizable number of new industries have already been transferred to private operation in this way, freeing the P.I.D.C. funds to start additional industries.

Apart from financial support, the main policies bearing on industrial expansion are tax policy, trade policy, and wage policy. We have already noted the desirability of light taxes on business profits, or at least on reinvested profits. A common device is a "tax holiday" for new industries during the first 5 or 10 years of operation. This device has been used with great success in Puerto Rico where, in combination with an ample labor supply and relatively low wage rates, it has produced a massive inflow of capital from the mainland United States. As regards trade policy, the usual infant-industry argument applies, though it should be applied only to industries which show some real prospect of growing up. In addition to tariff protection against competing imports, manufacturers can be allowed to import their own machinery and materials free of duty. Government can also provide a variety of technical services: market surveys to determine the prospects for a new product, technical training courses for prospective workers, help with plant design and construction.

The importance of wage policy arises from the fact that, where labor is in excess supply and capital is scarce, one wants to encourage relatively labor-intensive types of industry. And within each industry, one wants to encourage simple, labor-intensive production methods rather than highly mechanized techniques. Applying more labor to each unit of capital will, up to a point, raise the average productivity of the available capital stock (the average output: capital ratio), and will thus maximize national output. At the same time it serves the desirable social purpose of reducing the unrest arising from unemployment.

This conclusion has sometimes been disputed. It is argued that capital-intensive plants have numerous indirect benefits. Investment in highly mechanized factories will mean substantial profits for the factory owners; and on the premise that capitalists save while workers do not this will increase the funds available for reinvestment. Introduction of the most modern technology into a backward economy will also have important educational effects on managers, technicians, and workers. On these grounds some economists have argued that the limited amount of capital available for industrialization should be concentrated in plants of the most modern type, which will become demonstration centers for the remainder of the economy.

But need one go this far? Indirect as well as direct effects of a proposed investment should certainly be considered in estimating its yield. But after having done this, the choice among products or methods of production should be made on the usual productivity grounds. This will not necessarily lead to use of the most capital-intensive methods available.

At a factual level, it is argued that factor proportions are rigidly fixed by technology and that there is little scope to substitute capital for labor or vice versa. There is some truth in this. But even where the central production operations are automatic, there is usually room to use more or less labor in subsidiary operations, such as getting raw materials and parts to the points where they are needed, removing finished products, overhauling and repairing equipment, packing, and warehousing. Russian steel plants use more labor in these subsidiary operations than do American plants, and Indian steel mills use still more. This is partly a rational response to relative factor supplies in the three countries.

There are also industries in which the main production operations can be done in a variety of ways. Cotton cloth can be woven on anything from the simplest hand looms to fully automatic power looms. A. K. Sen has made some interesting calculations[7] on the relative efficiency of these various methods in India, using actual output figures and experimenting with various "accounting prices" for labor and capital. It turns out that the most efficient technique is usually *neither* the simplest (which has very low output) nor the most highly automatic (which has high capital costs), but something in between; and the choice is influenced by the prices assigned to labor and capital.

Another way of using additional labor is by subcontracting the manufacture of parts to small shops using simple hand methods. The

---

[7] A. K. Sen, *The Choice of Techniques* (Oxford, England: Blackwell, Ltd., 1902), Appendix C.

parts are then brought together into a larger factory for final assembly. This "putting-out system" was important in the early stages of the Industrial Revolution in England, and it has also been used very successfully in Japan. Large plants using modern equipment are not necessarily an *alternative* to small handicraft shops. The two can often be combined to reinforce each other. Fei and Ranis have demonstrated that in Japan from about 1880 to 1920, a crucial period in the country's development, there was a process of *capital shallowing* rather than *capital deepening*. The amount of capital used by each worker declined or, the same thing, the amount of labor applied to each unit of capital rose.

How can government encourage capital shallowing and use of labor-intensive techniques? Certainly not by overpricing labor. We noted in Chapter 31 that, in surplus-labor economies, the market wage for industrial labor is usually much above its social or opportunity cost as measured by marginal productivity in agriculture and services. Capital, on the other hand, is probably somewhat underpriced. So businessmen, who must respond to market prices, will choose production methods which use too much capital and too little labor from a national standpoint. It has been suggested that government might try to offset this bias in factor pricing and factor use by a tax-and-subsidy system. A subsidy based on quantity of labor used would reduce the money cost of labor to something closer to the opportunity cost. Such a system would be hard to administer and subject to abuse, which is perhaps why it has been little used. But in principle it would seem to offer distinct advantages.

EXTERNAL ECONOMIC RELATIONS

A basic problem of the less developed countries is the tendency for import requirements to rise faster than export earnings. And acceleration of a country's growth rate does not solve this problem. On the contrary, since growth depends heavily on imports of capital goods and industrial materials, more rapid growth will in the short run make the problem worse rather than better. So there is need for special effort to increase exports on one hand, and on the other to reduce import needs by developing domestic production.

Exports here means mainly exports of primary products—temperate zone foodstuffs, tropical foodstuffs, agricultural raw materials, minerals, and oil. It has been fashionable recently to take a dim view of the long-run future for such exports, to assert that world demand is growing only slowly and that prices of primary products are likely to decline relative to those of manufactured goods. Note that this is precisely contrary to the prediction of the classical economists, who believed that population growth would outrun food production, that food would become relatively more expensive, and that this would bring both population expansion and economic progress to an end. It is probably too early to say that the classical writers were wrong and that the recent theories of "raw material abundance" are a better guide to the future.

In any event, there seems no reason for indiscriminate pessimism. It does not make much sense to say that the market outlook for *all* primary products is poor, while that for *all* manufactures is good. The demand prospects for coffee, bananas, and crude rubber may indeed be poor, while the prospects for copper, wood pulp, and oil may be much brighter. A country should be alert to changing market prospects and energetic in shifting resources from products whose prospects are poor toward those for which the outlook is promising.

A country may find its share of the world market for a particular product declining because it has not kept up with technical progress and has allowed its production costs to rise above those of rival producing nations. Puerto Rican sugar production has declined to the point where it cannot meet its permissible export quota to the U.S. market. Argentina has lost ground in wheat and meat exports. Malaysia, on the other hand, has managed to keep crude rubber production costs at a level where the product can compete effectively with synthetic rubber, and producers can earn good returns. So primary producing countries can do much to help themselves within the orbit of their traditional export products.

What can be done about the wide variation in export earnings which results from fluctuating world prices for primary products? Brazil's coffee receipts, or Nigeria's cocoa earnings, can easily drop 25 percent in a year. This is upsetting to farmers' incomes, to government export tax receipts, and to the nation's supply of foreign exchange. The most drastic remedy is an agreement among countries producing a particular commodity to control their marketings and hold the world price at a desired level. If the target price of coffee beans, say, is 50 cents a pound, and if it is estimated that world demand at this price will be 600 million bags, producing countries can be assigned quotas totaling up to this figure.

It is hard to reach and enforce such agreements, however, and few have survived for very long. It is hard to get agreement among countries over their "fair" share of the world market. If a country's productive capacity is above its assigned quota, there must be some system of production control within the country to prevent accumulation of unsold surpluses. If the pegged price is attractive, new countries may start producing the product, and this uncontrolled increase in supply can eventually break the price. The consuming nations usually suspect that the whole scheme is a monopolistic arrangement to *raise* the price in addition to *stabilizing* it, and their opposition can be a powerful factor preventing agreement. The United States, however, has recently agreed to support a world coffee agreement. And there is a long-standing wheat agreement supported by both exporting and importing nations.

Where the world price cannot be stabilized, the returns to domestic producers can be divorced from the world price through a government marketing board. The board buys the whole crop from the farmers, sells it on the world market, and pays farmers a price which, if not completely stable, at least varies less than the world price. While such a scheme appears simple, there are several practical problems. Is the object to stabilize the farmer's *price* or his *income* (price × quantity marketed)? The two objectives will require different price policies. Will the board, on the average over the years, return to farmers the full value of their crops or something less than this? A government which is in serious need of revenue will be tempted to underpay farmers and thus use the marketing board as a taxation device. This in turn reduces the incentive to grow the crop. Any price is an *incentive* as well as a *source of income,* and both aspects must be kept in mind in framing policy.

Turning from exports to imports, what can be done to hold down import requirements and thus ease the balance-of-payments problem? As development proceeds, one can expect gradually to replace imports of many manufactured goods through development of local industries, a process termed *import substitution.* The question is whether it is feasible or wise to push this process faster than it would go under spontaneous private initiative.

The answer has already been given in our discussion of industrialization. To determine whether it pays to introduce a new industry from a national standpoint requires something different from the profit calculation of a private producer. Factor prices and the rate of exchange should be taken at their true scarcity value rather than at current market prices; the indirect benefits which this industry will confer on others (and the prospective cost reductions which it may secure from simultaneous expansion of other industries) should be taken into account; and the favorable effect on the balance of payments should be given proper weight.

Having said this, it remains true that one should encourage only those industries which appear nationally profitable or which can be expected to become so within a reasonable period. Indiscriminate industrialization under the guise of import substitution is unwise. What not to do is well illustrated by the experience of Argentina during the forties and fifties. The Perón regime established a variety of heavy industries with production costs much above the world level, meanwhile discouraging agricultural production which had been the mainstay of the country's exports. Argentina's dependence on world trade declined; but economic efficiency and the country's growth rate also declined. It would have been more sensible to encourage wheat and meat production, in which Argentina has long had a comparative advantage, and to concentrate industrial protection on those industries in which Argentina could reasonably expect to become a low-cost producer

The decisive factor in all this is the size of the domestic market. A very small country can do little in the way of import substitution and economic diversification. It can do little, at least, unless it is willing to merge its market with those of neighboring countries through a customs union or "common market." The countries of Central America put a common market program into effect some years ago. There has been intensive discussion of a Latin American Free Trade Area (LAFTA) including most of the South American countries. At one stage Malaya, Thailand, and the Philippines took gingerly steps in this direction through an Association of Southeast Asia (ASA).

A serious obstacle is that the less developed countries themselves stand at different stages of industrialization; and the least industrialized want protection against their somewhat more industrial brethren. Peru does not want its infant industries killed off by imports from Brazil and Chile. Uganda and Tanzania want to build up local industries in competition with the older established industries of Kenya; and the common market which prevailed for these countries in the British period seems in danger of disintegration. Nationalism and xenophobia are powerful forces, especially when combined with local business interests. The East European countries, without private business pressure and supposedly linked by a common ideology, have failed signally to work out efficient specialization and trade arrangements.

A serious obstacle to rational trade policy in some countries is incorrect pricing of foreign exchange. To illustrate this, consider only two countries, the United States and Arcadia, whose currency unit is the bolo. The present rate of exchange is 100 bolos = 1 dollar. This amount which Arcadia is able to export to the United States at this rate, plus the amount we are willing to lend the Arcadian government, falls considerably short of the amount which Arcadians would like to import. There is a "dollar shortage." In a free exchange market this would cause the price of dollars to rise, say to 200 bolos = 1 dollar. But the Arcadian government does not wish to permit this and insists on maintaining the present rate.

With the price of dollars fixed below the equilibrium level, the shortage of dollars will continue and the available supplies must be rationed. The Arcadian government requires exporters to turn in all the dollars they earn to the central bank of Arcadia, which pays them off in bolos at 100 to 1. The bank then resells the dollars to would-be importers, either at the same price or at a higher price. The government could charge anything up to the equilibrium price of 200 to 1, thus making a profit on its exchange dealings; and this revenue possibility is one reason for the persistence of exchange-control systems.

Such a system has several disadvantages. Producers of exports receive fewer bolos for their goods than they would in a free market, and so export production is discouraged. Imports, on the other hand, are made to appear artificially cheap, and this may discourage production of import substitutes which would actually be worthwhile for Arcadia. The government's power to decide who shall get dollars with which to import machinery and raw materials enables it to control in detail what industries may be established and how rapidly each may expand. This power could conceivably be used with perfect wisdom to further an optimum pattern of economic development. But assuming·that government is not all-wise, and that reasonable scope should be left for private initiative, it might be better to let each business concern figure out the maximum it can afford to pay for dollars, and then let them compete for the dollars in a free market.

A few countries, notably the Philippines, have recently moved to revalue their currencies at a rate near the supply-demand equilibrium and to allow free dealings in foreign exchange for exports and imports. The International Monetary Fund has encouraged this tendency by supplying reserves of dollars and other key currencies which the government can use for its exchange operations.

THE SUCCESSFULLY DEVELOPING ECONOMY

The problems analyzed above may be attacked through a variety of strategies and institutional devices. In this sense there are many roads to economic development. But looking at economic results rather than at tactics, there are certain things one should observe in any economy which is experiencing sustained growth. For example:

1. Agricultural output should be rising faster than population growth.

2. Government tax receipts should be rising faster than national income.

3. A rising proportion of government expenditure should be going into physical and human investment.

4. Private saving (household and business) should be rising as a percentage of private income.

5. The percentage of the labor force engaged in agriculture should be falling, while the percentage employed in manufacturing, construction, and public utilities should be rising.

6. It is perhaps too much to require that surplus labor should be decreasing during the early stages of growth; but until it does begin to decrease, one can scarcely consider the economy successful. The capital-labor ratio in nonagricultural industries is a significant indicator of progress. This ratio should preferably be falling ("capital shallowing") in order to absorb surplus labor more rapidly.

7. Exports should be keeping pace with the rise of GNP. Imports will probably be rising faster than this, and the trade gap will be widening both absolutely and relatively. The implied accumulation of

foreign debt is normal in the early stages of growth and is no reason for concern *provided* the economy is raising output at a good rate.

8. There are several aspects of price behavior which, while they cannot be specified as essential, are almost certainly helpful in the growth process: absence of sharp and prolonged inflationary movements; absence of sharp shifts in the terms of trade between agriculture and industry; stability of the real wage level in manufacturing and other urban employments; and realistic pricing of foreign exchange.

9. A declining rate of population increase, while again not essential, is decidedly helpful.

Efforts to appraise the performance of the less developed countries focus unduly on a single magic number—the estimated rate of increase in GNP. But this figure is subject to a sizable margin of error. The reason is that most of the output of these economies comes from sectors in which output measurement is very imprecise: nonmarketed agricultural output, small-scale trade and handicrafts, and the whole range of service industries. The wiser course, then, is to rely on the kinds of detailed evidence just suggested.

How many of the less developed countries could presently get a good score in terms of these criteria? Probably not more than 10 to 15. But many others are trying. We can hope that they may succeed, and we can even contribute to the outcome in ways suggested in the next chapter.

SUMMARY

1. The early stages of economic growth in the Western industrial nations and in Japan had several significant characteristics: the gradualness of the rise in per capita income; the importance of improvements in agriculture; the importance of foreign trade; the role of government in financing infrastructure investment; the growth of an influential class of business enterprisers; and the importance of profits as a source of finance for business investment.

2. A major problem in today's developing countries is to raise the rate of capital formation. Much capital formation in agriculture and public works can be carried out at low social cost by mobilizing reserves of unused labor. Capital can also be obtained from abroad on a grant or loan basis; but if loans are used, the country must be sure that its repayment capacity is rising at an adequate rate.

3. Voluntary saving by businesses and households can be encouraged by developing financial institutions, through tax policy, and in other ways. It is also necessary, however, for government to tax more heavily in order to accumulate funds for investment in the public sector and for loans to the private sector. Overall, the economy's *marginal* rate of saving should exceed the *average* rate.

4. Rapid, uncontrolled inflation, which perpetuates itself through a cost-price spiral, is harmful to economic growth. But moderate, controlled, and temporary inflation can raise the level of investment.

5. A major use for new capital is in transport, communications, power, and other types of *economic infrastructure*. It is wasteful, however, to push capacity in these industries much ahead of demand for their services. Investment in education, technical and professional training, industrial research, and other things which raise *factor productivity* may also be as important as investment in physical structures.

6. Increases in agricultural output are needed to provide food for a rising population at higher income levels, to supply industrial raw materials, and possibly to provide additional exports.

7. Private operation of enterprises in the manufacturing, trade, and service sectors will usually be more efficient than public operation. Government action is needed, however, to mobilize initial capital for large new enterprises, to provide encouragement and protection through tax policy and tariff policy, and to correct biases in the market prices of labor and capital.

8. Developing countries have a chronic tendency toward balance-of-payments deficits. It is important, therefore, to push exports, which may require shifting resources from less promising to more promising export products. Import requirements can be reduced gradually by developing home production as the home market grows; but indiscriminate import substitution can lead to serious inefficiency.

DISCUSSION QUESTIONS

1. "Today's less developed countries are operating under conditions which are quite different from, and generally less favorable than, those faced by the older industrial countries in their early growth period. It follows that economic history can tell us little about proper development strategy under present circumstances." Do you agree or disagree? Explain.

2. What did Japan do to initiate rapid growth in the period 1868–1914? To what extent is this experience transferable to today's less developed countries?

3. A central issue in any economy is the proper balance between government action and private initiative. What division of labor between the public and private sectors would you consider desirable in the typical less developed country? Does your answer involve a role for government which is larger or smaller than:
   a) The role which government played in the older industrial countries during their early growth period?
   b) The role which government plays in these countries today?

4. What practical difficulties are involved in withdrawing surplus labor from agriculture and putting it to work on capital improvements? Is such a program costless from a social standpoint?

5. "The best investment a poor country can make is in training its officials to solicit foreign aid. If it is good enough at this, it doesn't need to worry much about domestic saving." Do you agree?

6. You are the Minister of Finance in an LDC, and the Prime Minister has assigned you the task of raising tax collections from 10 percent to 15 percent of national income. Where would you look for extra revenue?

7. You are the Minister of Finance, and a Federal Reserve delegation from Washington advises you that the best thing you can do is hold your country's price level stable. In fact, if you don't do this, the country's growth rate will be reduced. What would you say to this?

8. Is Hirschman right in arguing that development *via* shortage of social overhead capital is preferable to development via excess capacity of SOC?

9. In a country where education is deficient at all levels, how would you allocate a limited educational budget for maximum economic effect?

10. It is usually said that a rise in agricultural output is a necessary condition for sustained economic growth. Are there any circumstances under which this would *not* be true?

11. What determines the desirable rate of increase in total agricultural output, and in output per farm worker? What will happen if this rate of increase is not attained?

12. Why may calculation of the prospective profit from a new investment fail to reflect accurately the advantage of this investment to the national economy? What practical conclusions do you draw from this?

13. You are Minister of Commerce in an LDC, and are asked to recommend whether a proposed new manufacturing industry should be given protection against imports from abroad. What information would you ask your staff to provide as a basis for decision? Would the grounds for your decision be identical with those which would be appropriate in a developed industrial country?

APPENDIX: PLANNING FOR ECONOMIC DEVELOPMENT

Almost every country, developed and underdeveloped, engages to some extent in national economic planning. But "planning" is a slippery term, which can mean quite different things. Working up from milder to stronger versions, we can distinguish:

1. Forecasts or projections of future economic developments, with no control mechanism beyond the usual tools of the central bank and the government budget. The Japanese Planning Bureau is in essentially this position.

2. Systematic budgeting of government finances over a period of years ahead. The Puerto Rican Planning Board, for example, projects government revenues and expenditures for 5 years in the future. As each fiscal year is completed, another year is added at the far end of the plan, to maintain a 5-year moving horizon.

3. The next step beyond this involves setting aggregate targets for the private economy, particularly private investment. This normally includes consultation with private industrialists to discover and perhaps influence their investment programs; and it involves systematic manipulation of monetary-fiscal instruments to hit the desired targets. This may be termed "French planning" or "Tinbergen planning," after a noted Dutch economist who has spelled out the technique in a number of books.[8]

4. A further step is to establish direct controls over private investment, with a view to determining its composition as well as its level. These controls may differ considerably in inclusiveness, technique, and firmness of enforcement. They may constitute random interventionism or may add up to a carefully designed and consistent program. There is some degree of direct investment control in most less developed countries, whether or not they have a formal economic plan. Yugoslav economic planning is of this character. Enterprises make up their own investment plan, which they finance partly from reinvested profits; but to the extent that they come to the state bank for financing, government can encourage expansion in certain directions and restrain others.

5. Most comprehensive and detailed is Soviet-style planning, which was described in Chapter 3 and needs no further discussion here.

The less developed countries stand somewhere in the middle of this spectrum. Their plans are intended to be more than mere projections; but since the economy of these countries is predominantly private, Soviet planning methods have little usefulness. The heart of an economic development plan is a program for mobilizing and using resources within the public sector. There is usually an effort also to influence the course of events in the private sector. But this may be more or less comprehensive, more or less well administered, and may have considerable effect or close to zero effect.

Many countries, unfortunately, have impressive plans on paper about which little is actually being done. Any group of bright economists can whip together a *plan document*. It is much harder to put together an effective *planning organization*. This requires a sizable technical staff, a location at some prestigious point in the government (preferably the office of the President or Prime Minister), strong support from top political leaders, and effective coordination with the regular government departments who actually raise and spend money. Only a handful of countries have this kind of planning machinery at present. The list includes India, Pakistan, Malaysia, Egypt, Ghana, Venezuela, and Chile. The following discussion rests mainly on the experience of these countries.

---

[8] See particularly Jan Tinbergen, *Economic Policy: Principles and Design* (Amsterdam: North Holland Publishing Co., 1956); and Jan Tinbergen, *Economic Planning* (New Haven, Conn.: Yale University Press, 1964).

The main elements of a development plan are:

1. **A projection of the grand aggregates of the economy.** This usually runs for 5 years ahead, and covers total output, the distribution of output by major sectors, private consumption, private saving, government receipts and expenditures, exports and imports, and so on. A serious limitation is that most countries are short on reliable economic statistics. This makes it hard to determine what has happened in the past, and hence what it is reasonable to expect in future.

But the figures are not just a mechanical projection of past trends. They contain also an element of intention and target setting. The output and investment targets are typically set higher than the economy has been doing in the recent past. Just how high it is wise to set them is a key political decision. Up to a point, higher targets may be helpful in mobilizing local effort and soliciting foreign aid. But they should not be so high that actual performance falls much below them; otherwise the government will lose credibility both at home and abroad.

In addition to being plausible, the projections must be internally consistent. Savings and investment must balance; planned government expenditures must be financed from taxation or borrowing; import requirements must be covered by export proceeds plus foreign grants and loans. The consistency problem can be framed in mathematical terms and solved by solving a set of simultaneous equations. In practice, planning boards normally use more primitive methods of "cutting and fitting." If prospective saving falls short of investment requirements on the first round of estimates, there is a search for additional sources of saving, and some figures on that side of the balance may be raised. If there is still a shortfall, some of the investment items must be cut. Similarly for the balance of government revenue and expenditure and other key pieces of the jigsaw.

2. **Targets for private investment and production.** Development plans normally profess to be comprehensive plans, covering events in the private as well as the public sector. In the official tabulations, the targets for private output and investment look just as firm as those for public expenditure. But in practice they are not equally firm. What happens in the private sector depends on decisions by a multitude of farmers, manufacturers, and other businessmen. While government may be able to influence these decisions, it cannot control them in detail; and so the course of events may differ quite widely from that envisaged in the plan.

In manufacturing, the plan usually expresses a hope that new plants will be set up in specific industries. But inviting private industry to enter certain areas does not necessarily get the plants constructed. For large undertakings, government may have to recruit the entrepreneurs and provide a good share of the initial capital. Unless there is an effective program for doing this, the investment targets will be underfulfilled. In industries where optimum scale is small, greater reliance can be placed on spontaneous private initiative. Given a favorable government attitude, private enterprise often does better than anyone expected.

It is easier to project the expansion of existing industries. The Indian Planning Commission regularly surveys the investment intentions of each major industry and takes these into account in preparing the plan figures. In turn, the Planning Commission's calculations of the rate at which the national market will grow in the future encourages each industry to set its investment targets higher than it would do in an atmosphere of complete uncertainty. The general technique is somewhat the same as in French indicative planning.

Agriculture is, of course, the largest sector and the largest problem. Here the planning exercise serves to dramatize the dimensions of the problem and to create a sense of urgency. If GNP is expected to grow at, say, 5 percent a year, this implies a marked rise in demand for foodstuffs. And as a matter of arithmetic, GNP cannot grow this fast unless the massive agricultural sector is also growing. Agriculture is notoriously hard to influence, however, and output plans are subject to the vagaries of weather. So the divergence between planned and actual output is apt to be unusually wide in this sector.

3. A plan for raising and using funds in the public sector.   This is the heart of the plan for practical purposes, since it covers the things which are under direct government control. Much of the estimating for the private sector is a mixture of guesswork, hope, and window dressing. But government should be able to come close to realizing its own budget plans. If it does so, the planning exercise can reasonably be considered a success. It is necessary, of course, to have more than a nice table of expected revenues and expenditures. One needs effective budgeting machinery within the government, and we have already noted that this is not easy to establish.

The most important practical contribution which a planning body can make is to improve the allocation and use of public funds. A strong planning organization can persuade government departments and public corporations to look ahead several years rather than one year, to make better cost-benefit calculations for proposed investment projects, and to coordinate their plans with those of related departments and agencies. It can provide the head of government with an independent judgment on how best to divide the budget pie. It can make follow-up checks to see how far the programs approved in this year's budget were actually carried out, how actual costs compared with estimated costs, and so on. All this may seem obvious; but the obvious is often not done.

Space does not permit illustration of these points from actual development plans. But if your college library contains one or more such plans, you will find it a useful exercise to glance through them and try to sort out the meat of the plan from the window dressing.

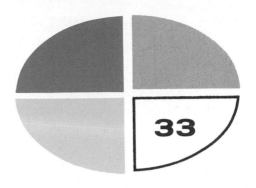

33

Economic Development and

the American Interest

> Now it is not good for the Christian's health to
>   hustle the Aryan brown,
> For the Christian riles, and the Aryan smiles, and
>   it weareth the Christian down;
> And the end of the fight is a tombstone white,
>   with the name of the late deceased,
> And the epitaph drear, "A fool lies here, who
>   tried to hustle the East."
>
> RUDYARD KIPLING

MOST OF THE RESOURCES for economic development come from inside the developing countries, but a critical proportion must come from outside. A country with little industry must import tools and machinery in the first instance. Industrial development also means increased imports of fuel and raw materials. As development proceeds and personal incomes rise, part of this will spill over into demand for imported consumer goods.

These imports must be paid for. The poor countries must somehow acquire dollars, pounds, marks, and so on to finance the inflow of goods. What are the main sources of foreign currency at present? Are these sources adequate to the need?

SOURCES OF FOREIGN FUNDS

The less developed countries earn some $25 billion a year from exports. The problem of expanding and stabilizing these export earnings is highly important. But most less developed countries wish to import beyond their export capacity, and to do this they must depend on loans and grants from the developed world. Total foreign assistance in 1964 from Western sources was of the order of $10 billion dollars (Table 1). If one could get an accurate estimate of aid from mainland China, the U.S.S.R., and Eastern Europe, this might add another billion to the total.

TABLE 1

Loans, Grants, and Technical Assistance
to the Less Developed Countries, 1964

SOURCE	AMOUNT (Millions of Dollars)
Private net long-term investment	2,581
Government loans and grants:	
From U.S.A.	3,308
From other Western countries	2,452
Multilateral organizations:	
UN	200
IBRD	1,023
IDA	309
IFC	25
Total	9,898

Source: These estimates, which are only approximations, were compiled mainly from *Development Assistance Efforts and Policies, 1965 Review* (Paris: OECD, 1965), and from the 1964–65 Annual Reports of the International Bank of Reconstruction and Development and its affiliates, the International Development Association, and the International Finance Corporation. Data are usually for 1964; but the IBRD, IDA, and IFC totals are for their fiscal year 1964–65; and 1963 figures were used in one or two cases where 1964 data were not yet available.

The estimates are on a net basis, after deducting repayments. In some cases they represent new commitments, which may not have been fully drawn upon during the year. The estimates do not include aid from mainland China, the U.S.S.R., and Eastern Europe, or IMF lending, or short-term credits of less than 5 years' duration.

We may comment briefly on the major sources and types of foreign capital:

1. **Private investment.** This was the main way in which Britain and Europe contributed during the nineteenth century to economic development in the U.S.A., Canada, and Australasia. While private investment still contributes substantial amounts, its relative importance has diminished. In some of the poor countries, political instability is a serious deterrent to private investment. Others do not welcome private capital because it carries overtones of colonialism and foreign domination.

2. **Government loans and grants: The U.S.A.** During the years 1948–53 the United States made massive loans and grants to Western

Europe for postwar reconstruction under the Marshall Plan. Since that time our activities have shifted mainly to Asia, Latin America, and Africa. We operate at three levels:

a) *Hard Loans.* These are loans on a straight business basis, at rates of 4 to 6 percent, repayable in dollars, and usually for projects which yield a cash return. The Export-Import Bank and the Inter-American Development Bank are the main vehicles for this type of lending. In addition, we supply about one third of the capital for the International Bank for Reconstruction and Development, which is also a hard-loan agency.

b) *Soft Loans.* These are loans for longer periods and at lower interest rates; and they are sometimes repayable in the currency of the borrowing country, which is much easier than repayment in dollars. While they are sometimes tied to specific projects, they may also provide general support for a development program. They are made principally by the Agency for International Development (AID).

c) *Grants.* These are used mainly in countries where there is no realistic prospect of repayment in the near future. They are used also for sending U.S. experts abroad and for other forms of technical assistance. Over the years, grants have diminished and soft loans have risen as a percentage of our aid activity. Grants are handled largely by AID.

The total of these activities is less than popularly supposed. The figure that runs in one's mind from congressional debates is $4 to $5 billion a year. A large part of this, however, has consisted of military supplies to allied nations plus semimilitary assistance which goes largely to South Korea, South Vietnam, and Taiwan. Loans and grants for development purposes have typically been between $2 and $3 billion a year.

3. Government loans and grants: Britain, West Europe, Japan. Most of these countries are gradually increasing their lending to the less developed countries. They are under pressure to do so from their business communities, which want export markets in these countries but can find them only if someone will provide the necessary financing. This commercial motivation has not been absent in the United States. The Export-Import bank was established specifically to promote American exports, and the dollars loaned or granted by AID are usually tied to purchase of American products. Loans by the other Western countries and Japan are typically hard loans.

4. Government loans and grants: The Soviet bloc. Since the mid-1950's, the Soviet bloc countries have stepped up their lending activities. The total now exceeds a billion dollars a year and is still rising. More than three quarters of this comes from the U.S.S.R., but several of the East European countries make sizable contributions.

The Soviet bloc lending program has several distinctive characteristics. First, it is a concentrated program. More than three quarters of the money has gone to India, United Arab Republic, Indonesia, Afghanistan, Iraq, and Cuba, though there have been smaller loans to about 15 other Asian and African countries. The program aims at maximum leverage in a few countries which are considered especially susceptible to Soviet political influence.

Second, the program consists almost entirely of soft loans. Grants are avoided, except for an occasional showpiece project. The loan terms are liberal. Loans usually run from 10 to 30 years. The interest rate is typically 2½ percent, but has sometimes been as low as 1 percent. And the loans are normally repayable in local currency or local products. These are essentially barter transactions in which the donor supplies industrial materials and equipment, technical assistance, and sometimes military assistance, receiving mainly agricultural products in return.

The inefficiency of agriculture in the U.S.S.R. gives it a certain advantage over the U.S.A. Since the U.S.S.R. is short of foods and fibers, it needs just those things which the borrower countries can most readily supply—wheat, rice, cotton, sugar, and the like. One can imagine the outcry in Congress if the United States began to import these things in repayment of our foreign loans.

Finally, Soviet bloc loans are typically made for particular projects, such as the Aswan dam in Egypt or a steel mill in India. And Soviet officials appear to accept the priorities of the borrower countries without question. If a country says, "This is what we need most," the U.S.S.R. agrees. United States aid officials, on the other hand, usually try to form an independent judgment of the country's needs.

5. International organizations. The largest international lending organization is the International Bank for Reconstruction and Development (IBRD), usually called the World Bank. Its capital has been raised by stages to $10 billion, of which the United States has provided about one third and West Europe most of the remainder. The Soviet bloc countries do not participate. The Bank has authority to raise additional money by selling its own bonds in the leading money markets and has done this on a substantial scale. Its loans to mid-1965 were about $9 billion, and were widely distributed around the world.

The World Bank is a hard-loan agency, and normally lends for completion of a particular project. It has a strong preference for revenue-yielding projects such as power developments, railroads, telephone systems, and manufacturing plants. Two thirds of its funds have gone into transportation and electric power. The loan is normally limited to the amount of foreign exchange required to import machinery and other components for the project. The borrowing country is expected to finance local currency costs from its own resources. Loans usually run from 15 to 25 years, carry interest of 4½ to 5 percent, and are repayable in the currency borrowed.

Some countries are not able to take on additional debt commitments, and some projects do not meet banking standards of low risk and assured yield. So there has been pressure to set up a soft-loan organization operating parallel to the IBRD. In 1960, the International Development Association (IDA) was established. It can make loans for as long as 50 years, with a grace period of up to 10 years before repayment begins, and can charge interest or not as it sees fit. While its activities are still small relative to those of the IBRD, they have already reached the billion-dollar mark.

The United Nations is important mainly in the area of technical assistance, where it operates through a variety of agencies including the regular technical assistance program, the Special Fund for Economic Development, the World Health Organization, the Food and Agriculture Organization, and the regional economic commissions. Through these agencies the United Nations maintains training and research centers in the less developed countries, sends nationals of these countries abroad for technical training, and supplies thousands of experts and advisers from the more developed countries. The cost of these activities is not large relative to the other items in Table 1, but they are often of key importance.

What does this list of sources boil down to, from the standpoint of the recipient countries? A country which is able and willing to assume the obligations of a hard loan has many possibilities open to it. It can go to the World Bank, or the United States Export-Import Bank, or the governments of France, Britain, West Germany, Japan, or a dozen other countries. If it wants a soft loan, the possibilities are more limited. Only the U.S.A. and the U.S.S.R. are in this business on a substantial scale. And only the U.S.A. provides much money in outright grants.

There is no international agency for overall review and coordination of aid programs, but there is some degree of coordination among the Western powers. The Organization for Economic Cooperation and Development, which includes the United States and Canada along with Britain and the West European countries, maintains a standing Development Advisory Committee (DAC) at its Paris headquarters. DAC is now a focal point for discussing the capital requirements of the less developed countries. The other focal point is the IBRD. Where there is a well-developed economic program requiring large foreign resources (the Indian Fourth Five-Year Plan, the Pakistan Third Five-Year Plan, the Indus River Valley Project), the World Bank often takes the lead in organizing a consortium of lending countries. In the three cases mentioned, the U.S.A., Britain, West Germany, several other countries, and the Bank agreed to share the total loan required.

There has been much discussion of whether the volume of government loans and grants now flowing toward the less developed countries is adequate to their needs. The core of the problem is the present capacity of these countries to use foreign capital productively, sometimes referred to as *absorptive capacity*. On this there is wide disagreement. A study by Professors Millikan and Rostow in 1957 set the figure at $6.5 billion a year.[1] A more recent analysis by Professor Rosenstein-Rodan came up with a total of $5.7 billion.[2] Several U.N. studies, on the other hand, have arrived at estimates in the range of $15 to $20 billion a year. But these studies tend to assume that all the poor countries are ready to embark on economic growth, that capital is the sole bottleneck, and that additional investment will yield proportionate returns in output. These assumptions are questionable, and the estimates flowing from them seem considerably exaggerated.

The question cannot really be answered without some specification of the *terms* on which funds are to be made available. If one thinks of hard loans, at high interest and repayable in hard currencies, the poor countries are probably already getting as much as they can prudently borrow. The lending capacity of the IBRD and other hard-loan agencies is far from exhausted. On a soft-loan or grant basis, the borrower countries doubtless could use more funds to advantage. So how "soft" does one want to get? And what order of risk are the lending countries willing to accept? In many countries it is an open question whether the country will or will not move ahead economically. How far are we willing to gamble? The answer could make a difference of several billion dollars in the estimate of absorptive capacity.

THE POSSIBILITIES OF PRIVATE INVESTMENT

Loans and grants are only one way for the poor countries to get hold of foreign funds. Another important way is to increase exports. But there is not too much that the developed countries can do about this directly. They can try to keep their own economies growing rapidly, thus providing a growing market for primary products. They can reduce tariffs and other barriers to imports. They can take a sympathetic interest in efforts to iron out the wide price fluctuations for primary products, which wreak such havoc at present. But the main effort must come from the poor countries themselves, through development of their productive capacity in export industries.

In the area of private investment, the developed countries can perhaps take more initiative. We shall speak here particularly about American investment, which provides about one third of the private capital flowing to the less developed countries. American private investment in the less developed countries is almost entirely direct rather than portfolio investment. The present distribution of U.S. direct investment

[1] M. F. Millikan and W. W. Rostow, *A Proposal: Key to an Effective Foreign Policy* (New York: Harper & Bros., 1957).

[2] P. N. Rosenstein-Rodan, "International Aid for Underdeveloped Countries," *Review of Economics and Statistics*, May, 1961, pp. 107–38.

is shown in Table 2. Most of our funds have gone to the economically advanced and politically stable areas of Canada, Britain, and Western Europe. Sizable amounts have gone to Latin America, relatively little as yet to Asia or Africa. In the less developed areas, our investments have been strongly oriented toward primary production.

There are economic reasons for this distribution of investment. Capital will move abroad only if the prospective return, adjusted for risk, is at least equal to what can be earned at home. This argues for Canada and Western Europe, where domestic markets are growing rapidly, property is secure, and there are adequate supplies of trained labor and

TABLE 2

U.S. Direct Investment Abroad, 1963
(Millions of Dollars)

GEOGRAPHIC AREA	TOTAL	MINING AND SMELTING	PETROLEUM	MANU- FACTURING	PUBLIC UTILITIES	TRADE	OTHER
Total, All Areas	40,645	3,350	13,698	14,890	2,051	3,305	3,351
Canada	13,016	1,540	3,133	5,746	460	747	1,390
Latin America	9,875	1,303	3,627	2,211	758	963	1,014
Europe	10,351	55	2,828	5,610	40	1,234	585
Africa	1,423	351	701	176	9	81	105
Asia	2,784	31	1,925	420	38	200	170
Other	3,195	70	1,484	728	746	81	88

Source: *Survey of Current Business*, August, 1964, p. 10.

management. Investment in the less developed countries is inherently more risky. Where an American concern goes in to exploit oil or mineral resources, the risk is limited by the fact that the size of the resources is known and the product can be sold on the world market. To set up a manufacturing concern in Colombia or Thailand producing for the *domestic* market is quite another matter. The rate at which the domestic market will grow in the future, and possible difficulties with labor supply, local management, and government regulation, are hard to estimate in advance. Thus the venture will be undertaken only if there is a possibility of extraordinarily high returns, say 20 to 30 percent a year on invested capital instead of the 6 or 8 percent which might be considered adequate at home.

Another factor conditioning private investment is the attitude of governments in the recipient countries. Many of these countries have recently won political independence and are strongly nationalist in outlook. They are suspicious of U.S. private investment in their countries, not so much because it is *private* as because it is *foreign*. They view it as a kind of "economic colonialism" which may retard development of locally owned industries and even threaten their political independence. Antipathy to foreign control is stronger in some areas of investment than in others. It is strongest in transportation, communications, power, and other public utilities. There is also growing opposition to foreign exploitation of oil fields, mineral deposits, and other national resources. These views may be shortsighted and unwise, but they are deeply held. And so foreign control of public utilities and natural resource industries can probably not continue over the long run, except in places like the "oil sheikdoms" which make no pretense of economic independence.

Even if these areas are gradually closed off, U.S. private investment can make an important contribution in less sensitive sectors, and particularly in manufacturing. The contribution of private investment in this area is not so much that it provides capital, but rather that it provides technology and management. If the United States government lends money to the government of Ceylon to start a cement industry, Ceylon still has the problem of getting the plants built, staffed, and into operation. But if an American company comes in, *it* takes responsibility for getting the plants built and for providing experienced management until local executives can be trained to take over. The training of managers as well as workers, and the establishment of modern production and personnel methods, are probably the main contributions of American private enterprise abroad.

There are several things which the United States government can do to help realize the potentialities of American private investment. The most obvious is providing information about investment opportunities. This is one function of the economic staffs of our embassies and AID country missions. The government can also use AID funds to pay for technical surveys of the feasibility and cost of proposed investment projects.

Our government can negotiate with foreign governments over the treatment of American investors in their countries. If a country decides to admit foreign capital to certain areas of the economy, it should provide fair and nondiscriminatory treatment. U.S. companies should not be subjected to special taxes, penalties, or regulations beyond those imposed on locally owned enterprises. There should be security against arbitrary seizure of property. And there should be provision for converting a reasonable share of local profits into hard currencies for transfer to the parent company.

There are other ways of reducing the risks of foreign investment. AID now operates an insurance system under which an American company operating abroad can, by paying a modest premium, insure itself against losses from expropriation, property damage arising from war or insurrection, and inconvertibility of its foreign earnings into dollars. This comes close to eliminating all but the normal commercial risks of overseas operation, and should make it worthwhile for American capital to go abroad at lower expected profit rates.

AID is contributing increasingly to the financing of development banks and other intermediate credit institutions in the less developed countries. The main function of these banks is to finance locally owned business concerns. But they can also lend to American-owned subsidiaries in the country, or to joint ventures combining American and local capital. The United States also owns large amounts of local currency in some countries, arising mainly from sale of our surplus agricultural products. Our foreign aid legislation provides that up to 25 percent of any currency acquired in this way may be used by AID for loans to American business concerns operating in the country. This is a useful source of supplementary finance.

There is general agreement that we should do what can be done along these lines, and that American private investment will continue to make an important contribution to economic development. But it is equally clear that it cannot do the whole job. There are certain kinds of industry to which American private capital will not be admitted. Nor can private capital be used to finance government programs of education, public health, agricultural development, and the like. Needs of these types require government-to-government loans or grants.

UNITED STATES GOVERNMENT PROGRAMS

Our main foreign aid agency has had a long and alphabetical history. Originating in Marshall Plan days as the Economic Cooperation Administration (ECA), it became successively the Mutual Security Administration (MSA), Foreign Operations Administration (FOA), International Cooperation Administration (ICA), and most recently (1961) the Agency for International Development (AID). After some experiments with independent status, it has settled down as an arm of the State Department, under an AID Administrator who ranks as an Under Secretary of State. The AID mission chief in each country operates under the American Ambassador, though he also reports directly to AID headquarters in Washington.

Several other agencies also operate in this area. The Export-Import Bank operates independently, though in close cooperation with AID. The Department of Agriculture manages the supply side of our surplus disposal operations, though decisions about amounts of agricultural produce to be sent to recipient countries are handled by AID. The Department of Defense handles transfers of military equipment but coordinates with AID on the economic implications of these transfers. The Peace Corps operates a separate program of technical assistance.

At the height of the Marshall Plan in 1950, foreign economic aid was about $5 billion a year. It declined after that, and in recent years has rarely exceeded $3 billion. There have also been important changes in geographic emphasis. As European activities tapered off, emphasis shifted to the Near East and south Asia, which now receive about half the funds. India and Pakistan alone absorb close to $1 billion a year, and significant amounts go to Greece, Turkey, the U.A.R., and Iran. Latin America was relatively neglected before 1960. Since then activity has increased considerably and Latin America now receives close to $1 billion a year through AID, the Export-Import Bank, the Inter-American Development Bank, and other sources. Little aid money has gone to Africa, though a beginning is now being made in Nigeria, Tunisia, and the Sudan. Opportunities for effective use of capital in Africa will undoubtedly grow as the new governments of that continent become more firmly established.

U.S. Loans and Grants for Economic Development
Fiscal Year 1964
(Millions of Dollars)

Loans: AID	1,315
Grants: AID	297
Agricultural surplus disposal	1,223
Supporting assistance	360
Contributions to international organizations	116
Contingency fund	107
Total*	3,418

* Exclusive of Export-Import Bank loans.

Aid expenditures in fiscal year 1964, by type of activity, were as shown in Table 3.

Let us see what is involved in each of these activities.

Hard Loans: The Ex-Im Bank

Partly because of congressional objection to "giveaway programs," partly on grounds of economic policy, aid activities have shifted increasingly from grants to loans. Much the greater part of our aid is now repayable in one form or another.

The Export-Import Bank makes business-style loans to American or foreign private companies, or to foreign governments and their agencies. In recent years it has made net new loans of around half a billion a year, and its total accumulated loans are above $10 billion. It lends mainly for industrial and public utility projects requiring machinery and equipment from the United States. The loan usually finances only the foreign exchange cost of the project, though AID sometimes cooperates in financing local costs. Loan periods are typically 8 to 12 years for industrial projects, but as much as 16 to 20 years for hydroelectric projects. Interest charges cannot be more than 2 percent above the cost of money to the U.S. Treasury, with a ceiling of 5¾ percent. Most loans in recent years have been at the ceiling figure. Loans are repayable in dollars.

Semisoft Loans: AID

These differ from Ex-Im or World Bank loans in two ways. First, loan terms are more liberal. For countries with low repayment capacity, AID can lend for as long as 40 years, with a 10-year grace period before repayment begins, and with interest as low as ¾ of 1 percent. For countries in a stronger position, AID usually sets terms of 15 to 25 years, with perhaps a 5-year grace period, and interest of 3½ to 5 percent. These loans are repayable in dollars, and so can be considered semisoft rather than really soft.

Second, the purposes for which loans can be used are broader. AID loans are sometimes made for specific projects. But they may also provide support for an overall development program, as has typically been the case in India and Pakistan. AID loans are not limited to meeting the direct foreign exchange cost of the investment program, but may exceed this amount. This flexibility is necessary because an active development program raises local purchasing power, which in turn generates pressure for larger imports. While this pressure can be partially contained by import quotas and exchange controls, it may not be wise to cut it off entirely. So the borrower country may need dollars for general import purposes in addition to those needed to buy equipment for specific projects.

AID loans can be made to tide over balance-of-payments crises, provided the country is meanwhile taking steps to bring its accounts into balance. Loans can be made for social as well as directly economic purposes—for schools, hospitals, housing, adult education, or community development. Many of these purposes could not be financed from the Ex-Im Bank or the IBRD.

Where a country needs a loan for a specific industrial or utility project, it is expected to canvass the Ex-Im Bank and the IBRD first to see whether they will support it. Only if the proposal fails to interest the banks can it get consideration from AID. Anyone who criticizes AID loans as being of dubious profitability should remember that this is their purpose. AID provides a second line of defense for countries whose immediate repayment capacity does not warrant taking on heavy interest obligations and for projects whose benefits are so diffused throughout the economy that they are not bankable by ordinary standards.

Really Soft Loans: The Agricultural Surplus Program

An act of 1954, usually referred to as Public Law 480, authorized several methods for disposing of surplus agricultural products abroad.

Food may be donated free for famine relief or for distribution by private American relief agencies. Produce may be sold for dollars under long-term supply contracts. Most important, however, is the provision for sale of agricultural products in exchange for local currency. This involves no dollar financing, and hence no foreign exchange problem for the recipient country.

The United States turns over several million tons of wheat, say, to the Indian government, which sells the wheat for rupees in the Indian market. What happens to the rupees after that? Some may be used to meet expenses of United States government agencies operating in India, and some may be set aside for lending to subsidiaries or affiliates of American business concerns. As much as 50 percent of the proceeds of each sale can be set aside for these purposes. The actual percentage is usually considerably lower, since United States need for rupees is limited. Rupees not used for these purposes may be reloaned to the Indian government for development activities on a long-term, low-interest basis, repayable eventually in rupees rather than dollars. Outright grants may also be made where this seems preferable.

It is an interesting question how far the United States will ever be able to use the local currency which other countries owe us under this program. What can we do with large amounts of Indian or Iranian or Brazilian currency? A good deal of this may eventually be written off, and some loans will turn out to have been grants.

Activities under P. L. 480 have in recent years amounted to between $1 billion and $1½ billion a year. The great bulk of this represents wheat shipments, though there have also been sizable transfers of cotton and feed grains.

How do these food shipments aid economic development in the recipient countries? We saw in Chapter 32 that a vigorous development program raises the demand for food. If there is no outside aid, and if local agriculture cannot produce enough extra food to match the increase in demand, food prices will rise. This will cause social unrest, force up the money wage level, and hinder the development program. Food imports under P. L. 480 can prevent these undesirable tendencies by closing the gaps between local food production and the rising demand for food. They permit a country to go ahead with industrial development *without* the prior progress in agriculture which is a normal prerequisite.

The limitations of the program are also apparent from this description. Since the U.S. imports are sold through normal commercial channels, they affect the price level of agricultural products in the recipient countries. Unless sales are carefully managed, they may depress prices to a degree which discourages local production. Moreover, if a country can meet its food deficit in this way year after year, it may continue to neglect the problem of raising agricultural output within the country. At some point the agricultural problem must be faced if development is to continue, and it should be faced sooner rather than later. Another very common criticism is that P. L. 480 reduces the market for wheat exports from Canada, Australia, Argentina, and other producers. True, P. L. 480 provides that we will ship food only in addition to what the recipient country would normally buy on a commercial basis. But this line is hard to draw, and our program doubtless does reduce commercial exports. This is a continuing source of friction between us and other agricultural exporters.

Development Grants

Development grants are mainly a way of financing technical assistance to countries which are at such an early stage of development that it would not be realistic to expect repayment. Technical assistance means providing support in such areas as general and technical education, health and sanitation, agricultural research and development, public administration, development planning, and industrial technology. It includes the cost of sending American experts to work in the country; building schools, hospitals, research facilities, and other physical structures; training local personnel within the country; and sending people to the United States for specialized education. The interchange of personnel under this program is substantial. Thousands of foreign nationals are in the United States each year for advanced training, and thousands of American experts are out working in the poor countries.

This is a program of human and institutional development. It is intended to establish the preconditions for economic growth and to move more countries to the point at which they can absorb increasing amounts of physical capital.

In addition to AID, the Peace Corps is an important channel of technical assistance. Young Americans are now being sent at the rate of more than ten thousand a year to work abroad as teachers, agriculturalists, engineers, technicians, and craftsmen. The United States also contributes about 40 percent of the amount spent on technical assistance by the United Nations. The U.N. program is mainly a two-way exchange of personnel: teachers and technicians, mainly from the developed countries, going out to work in the less developed, while students and trainees from the less developed countries go abroad for advanced training.

Supporting Assistance

Under this label about half a billion dollars a year has been going to South Korea, South Vietnam, and Taiwan.[3] These countries have become military and economic dependencies of the United States. We give them

---

[3] In 1965, however, it was announced that Taiwan, whose GNP has risen rapidly in recent years, had reached a stage of self-sufficiency and no longer required U.S. economic assistance. AID organized a "graduation ceremony" in Washington with considerable fanfare—the first of its kind, but hopefully not the last.

large quantities of military hardware and supplies. They maintain standing armies considerably larger than they could support from their own resources. So we bolster their economies with dollar grants which allow them to supplement their domestic production by importing fuel, food, and consumer goods from the United States. There may be an incidental contribution to economic development, but the primary purpose is to maintain the present governments in power. With careful planning, our aid could probably contribute more to economic growth than it presently does; and policy toward these countries is under frequent review with this object in mind.

Contingency Fund

This is a fund which can be drawn on to meet special emergencies. Our ambassador to Ruritania cables Washington that the country is in dire straits. The prices of its export products are falling. It has a balance-of-payments deficit. Food stocks are low. Social unrest is growing. Local communist groups are active. "Do something!" he urges. The something often turns out to be a dollar grant, large enough to tide over the immediate crisis, but unrelated to any broader development program. Some countries have managed to draw on the United States in this way fairly heavily, without showing much progress toward better economic management or sustained growth. Whatever the justification of these grants in terms of international politics, they can scarcely be classified as development assistance.

Even this brief review indicates the diverse content and rationale of our foreign economic activities. They range all the way from orthodox bank loans to emergency political handouts. And the emphasis is different in each country with which we deal. It is too simple to ask: Are we spending too much or too little on foreign aid? It is more meaningful to ask whether we are putting too much into certain types of program and perhaps too little into others, and whether the allocation of aid by countries is correct.

THE ECONOMICS OF FOREIGN AID

What is the point of foreign loans and grants? What do they cost the donor country? How do they benefit the recipient country? Can we calculate the productivity of foreign aid as we calculate the productivity of investment in the United States?

Effects on the U.S. Economy

We shall not distinguish initially between loans and grants, because their immediate impact is the same. The United States lends or grants a certain amount of money. What the recipient country wants, however, is an increase in its supply of foreign goods. So we must ask how the money transaction is converted into a goods transaction. International trade theorists call this "the transfer problem."

How the process operates depends on several things. First, are we considering a two-country world in which money and goods move only between the two countries concerned? Or are we thinking of a many-country world with multiple trade relations?

Second, what is the state of the economy in the donor country when the loan is made? If the economy is fully employed, a transfer of goods abroad will have to be at the expense of consumption or investment at home; but if there is underemployment, this need not be so. It also makes a difference whether the funds loaned are raised by taxation or credit creation.

Third, what does the government of the recipient country do with the funds? It will probably deposit the dollars in its central bank in return for local currency, which is then available for expenditure on government projects. The central bank will resell the dollars to would-be importers, probably through a control system under which capital goods and other things needed for development are given priority. The resulting imports may come from the donor country or, in a multicountry setting, they may come partly from other countries.

Instead of exploring all possible combinations of these conditions, we shall concentrate on the conditions under which the U.S. aid program has typically operated.

For much of the U.S. aid program, notably military equipment and P. L. 480 shipments, there is no transfer problem, because the grant is a *direct grant of goods* from the start. The cost of these grants to the American economy is less than the money figures which appear in the federal budget. The military equipment which we send abroad is usually obsolete from the standpoint of our own forces. For bookkeeping purposes, it is usually valued at its original purchase price; but the actual cost of giving it away is close to zero. Similarly, surplus agricultural commodities are valued in the aid budget at what the government paid for them. But since we have no other use for them, and they are in fact clogging up granaries needed for next year's surplus, their real cost is mainly the cost of transporting them to the recipient country.

The remainder of the aid budget is presently of the order of $3 billion per year. Suppose this is used entirely to buy goods from the United States, which is not far from the fact. The impact depends on whether our economy is or is not operating at full capacity. If we are at capacity, production of more goods for shipment abroad must mean a corresponding reduction of consumption and investment at home.

This is not, however, the usual situation. Over the past 10 years the American economy has typically been operating 5 to 10 percent below capacity. Under these conditions, adding some aid demand to the other demands on the economy raises the aggregate expenditure schedule and the equilibrium level of output. It can be argued that the resources used to produce the aid exports still cost us something because, with a correct monetary-fiscal policy, they might have been mobilized to produce goods for domestic use. Even with this qualification, however, the real cost of aid to the economy is probably less than the dollar figures appearing in the federal budget.

How does aid affect our balance-of-payments position? What happens when we lend or grant a million dollars? This appears as a negative item in the payments statement, since it gives other nations a claim against us. If the funds are spent entirely on American products, our exports rise by a million dollars. This appears as a plus item in the payments statement, and the balance of payments is unaffected.

But suppose the recipient country is free to spend the dollars anywhere and decides to buy machinery from Britain or Sweden. In this case our exports will not necessarily rise, and our balance-of-payments position may be worsened. (Britain or Sweden may, of course, use the dollars to increase their purchases from the United States; but they may also withdraw gold or accumulate dollar balances.)

Suppose we want to minimize adverse effects on our balance of payments. There are two main approaches. One is to "tie" our foreign aid by requiring aid recipients to spend the money only on American products. The borrower countries do not like this, since they could often obtain goods more cheaply from some other country. Tying reduces the value of aid to the recipient. But from our standpoint, it reduces the balance-of-payments impact, and so most of our aid is now on a tied basis. This applies not only to military and P. L. 480 shipments, where tying is automatic, but to most of the general aid budget. The amount of untied aid is only about half a billion dollars per year.

But there is a loophole in this arithmetic. The underdeveloped countries earn several billion dollars each year by exporting to us; and most of these dollars are normally used to purchase American goods. So when we furnish tied aid dollars which can be used only in the United States, the recipient may finance more of its U.S. imports with aid money and switch its "free dollars" to purchases from other countries. *Example:* Country A exports $200 million of goods a year to the United States. In return it imports $100 million of goods from the United States and $100 million from Europe. Now we furnish A with $100 million a year of tied aid. It continues to import $100 million a year from the United States, paying for this with aid money; and it now has $200 million available to spend in Europe. This would be an extreme case; and it is difficult to estimate how far tied aid does lead to diversion of "free dollars" to other suppliers. But this loophole is probably quite important.

A second approach is to urge the other Western industrial nations to engage in aid programs which, relative to their GNP, are as large as the U.S. program, and to give this aid on an untied basis. We could then feel safe in untying our own aid. The flow of dollars going to the underdeveloped countries and respent on foreign goods would be offset by the flow of pounds, francs, marks, yen, and so on, going to the underdeveloped countries and respent on American products. Things would balance out, provided our export prices remain competitive with those of other countries.

There has been active discussion of "fair sharing" of the aid burden within the Development Advisory Committee of OECD; and the flow of aid from other nations has been increasing. The French aid program, relative to French GNP, is larger than ours, and the British program is of comparable size. In 1964, OECD estimates of net official capital movements, as a percentage of national income, from some of the principal lending nations were as follows: France 1.26, United States 0.70, United Kingdom 0.67, Belgium 0.67, West Germany 0.58, Canada 0.39, and Japan 0.33.[4]

Most of this is tied aid, however, and it goes mainly to countries which have been traditional customers of the donor country—French aid to the ex-French colonies, British aid to ex-British colonies, Japanese aid to southeast Asia. Businessmen and political leaders in these countries are naturally interested in financing their own exports rather than someone else's exports. So while a general untying of aid might be feasible in principle, the prospect of action is not bright.

While loans and grants are similar in their immediate effect, there is a difference when repayment time rolls around. If we make a hard loan at normal U.S. interest rates, and if the interest and principal payments are met, we have not really provided "aid." This is a normal international capital movement. If the loan is on softer terms—say, 2 percent when the normal interest rate would be 5 percent—we have provided aid to the extent of the interest subsidy. The longer the grace period before interest payments begin, the longer the repayment period, and the lower the interest rate charged, the larger is the aid element in the transaction. Only in the case of a grant, or a soft loan which turns out to have been a grant, have we provided aid to the full extent of the transaction; and even here, as we saw earlier, the goods provided should be valued at their opportunity cost rather than their original purchase price.[5]

The Impact on the Recipient

A million dollars of U.S. aid will add more to national output in some countries than in others. There would be general agreement that

---

[4] *Development Assistance Efforts and Policies, 1965 Review* (Paris. OECD, 1965), p. 55.

[5] See in this connection John A. Pincus, "The Cost of Foreign Aid," *Review of Economics and Statistics*, November, 1963, pp. 360–67. Pincus estimates that actual U.S. aid in 1961 was less than two thirds of the nominal value. The other developed countries appear also to overvalue their aid by at least as much as we do.

the prospective productivity of aid should be given heavy weight in allocating the aid budget among countries. Aid officials spend much of their time trying to make judgments about prospective productivity.

What determines the productivity of aid at a particular place and time? It is helpful to think of economic growth in a poor country as being subject to three kinds of constraint: (a) a bottleneck in supplies of imported capital goods and other materials; (b) a shortage of domestic saving relative to the desired level of investment; and (c) a shortage of skilled workers, business managers, public administrators, and other human agents needed to make capital fully productive. The productivity of aid depends heavily on which of these is the actual limiting factor in a particular situation.[6]

Very often the third factor is decisive. The government of the country is poorly led and poorly administered. The educational system is weak. The supply of technical and administrative talent is small. Under these conditions the marginal productivity of capital may be close to zero. This is often expressed by saying that such a country has little "absorptive capacity" for capital goods. This does not mean that nothing can be done. It means rather that the appropriate form of aid is technical assistance, particularly in the field of education, which will gradually enlarge the supply of human skills and raise the country's absorptive capacity.

Consider now a country which has the human skills and institutional organization required for economic growth. The savings rate is low but positive, say 5 percent of GNP. But investment requires imports of capital goods and other material inputs—to make a clear case, let us say that *all* the materials needed for investment must be imported. The country's export proceeds, however, are so low that it can actually import capital goods amounting to only 3 percent of GNP. In this case, investment cannot reach the 5 percent level, and part of the country's potential saving capacity runs to waste. The foreign exchange bottleneck is the effective constraint on the country's growth.

In this situation the function of aid is to relax the foreign exchange constraint, to permit importation of larger qualities of machinery and materials. The productivity of aid here is unusually high, since the imported materials are essential to domestic capital formation.

If the aid is used effectively, one may expect that the export capacity of the economy will grow along with total output; and as the industrial base expands, more goods which were formerly imported can be produced at home. At some point the quantity of capital goods which can be pro-

---

[6] For an elegant development of this approach, see H. B. Chenery and M. Bruno, "Development Alternatives in an Open Economy: The Case of Israel," *Economic Journal*, March, 1962, pp. 79–103. For a lucid exposition at a less technical level, see Ronald I. McKinnon, "Foreign Exchange Constraints in Economic Development and Efficient Aid Allocation," *Economic Journal*, June, 1964, pp. 388–409.

duced domestically plus what can be imported, measured as a percentage of GNP, will rise above the level of domestic savings. From this point on, the savings constraint becomes operative. The country's investment level can rise only as rapidly as savings can be expanded.

Is foreign aid still useful? Yes, it is, but its function has changed. Its function now is to *supplement domestic saving.* In money terms, domestic saving *plus* foreign finance can be set equal to the investment level permitted by the physical availability of capital goods. In physical terms, foreign aid enlarges the total goods supply available to the economy, so that more goods can be devoted to investment with a smaller cut in consumption than would be necessary otherwise.

The productivity of foreign aid, in short, depends on the function which aid is performing. Where aid is supplying imported capital goods which are essential for domestic capital formation, its productivity is unusually high. Where it is raising the aggregate rate of saving and investment, its productivity is roughly that of new capital goods in general. Where the effective constraint on growth is human skills and organization, only a limited amount of aid can be used and this mainly in the form of education and technical assistance.

The usefulness of aid must be appraised also in a time dimension. Supporters of aid usually argue that it need be only temporary. Foreign finance for a limited period will "prime the pump" and lift the economy to a level from which it can grow under its own power. What determines how rapidly this point will be reached, or whether it will be reached at all?

Progress toward self-sufficiency depends mainly on three things: the *marginal export ratio,* the *marginal savings ratio,* and the *marginal output-capital ratio.* The marginal export ratio is the relation between a (small) percentage increase in GNP and the associated percentage increase in export earnings. For example, if exports rise at the same rate as GNP, the marginal export ratio is 1.0. The higher the marginal export ratio, the more rapidly will the economy escape from the foreign exchange constraint.

Especially strategic is the marginal savings rate. In a poor economy, the average savings rate is low and, unless it can be raised substantially over the years, self-sustained growth is impossible. A necessary condition for a rise in the average rate is that the *marginal rate must be above the average.* If the average savings rate is 0.05 but the marginal rate is 0.10, the average rate will increase as income rises. If the marginal rate is 0.20, the average rate will increase still faster. So aid officials look closely at marginal savings rates in their client countries. The higher the marginal savings rate, the sooner the country's own savings will be adequate to finance further expansion.

The size of the marginal savings rate depends on whether industrialization has progressed to the point at which business saving is important, on the adequacy of incentives and institutions for household saving, on whether government is able to accumulate savings through the fiscal system. In some countries the marginal savings rate is well above the average rate, and to this extent their long-term outlook is hopeful.

The marginal output-capital ratio shows the addition to GNP resulting from an additional unit of capital. If an extra dollar of capital adds 50 cents worth of output, the marginal Y/K ratio is $1:2$. The ratio is a shorthand expression for everything affecting the productivity of capital in the economy: effectiveness of capital allocation among industries and sectors, managerial skill, supplies of land and other cooperating factors, external economies, technical progress. Raising the yield of capital has the same favorable growth effects as raising the rate of saving and helps to advance the date of economic independence.

It is easy enough to calculate what will happen in an economy over time, given a certain level of foreign aid, and given certain values of the three marginal ratios. If these ratios are too low, the economy will never get off the ground. Aid would have to continue forever. But if they are above a certain level, the need for aid will eventually taper off. Indeed, if the marginal ratios are high enough, putting in larger amounts of aid in the early years will reduce the *total* aid needed to lift the economy to self-sufficiency.

SOME ISSUES OF AID POLICY

Several issues arise repeatedly in discussions of aid policy. Perhaps they recur because there is no final answer to them. Why are we in the aid business anyway? What standards can be applied in allocating aid among countries? To what extent should loans be based on specific projects, to what extent on the needs of an overall development program? What kind of economic strings should be attached to American aid?

The Rationale of Aid Policy

Aid might be justified on several grounds, some more convincing than others. One could argue the case on grounds of charity. Just as a rich man should give some of his income to the poor, so should a rich nation. It is doubtful, however, whether this argument would persuade a majority of Congress to vote for aid year after year.

Some Washington officials look on aid mainly as a weapon in the game of international politics; and it has been widely advertised on this basis to the general public. Dipping into the moneybag will help to keep friendly governments in power or unfriendly ones out of power. It will win friends and votes in the U.N. and other international forums. It will induce more of the neutral nations to be "neutral on our side."

Unfortunately, there is probably not very much to this line of argument. Any Tammany politician knows that people who are bought don't necessarily stay bought. The young nations of the less developed world are intensely nationalistic, sensitive, suspicious of outsiders. Any suggestion of pressure or hidden political motives is likely to backfire. It is proverbial that the feeding hand shall be bitten. And this applies to the Russians or the Chinese as well as ourselves.

If aid is not a way to win international popularity contests, what is it? A persuasive rationale must be largely economic, based on the productivity considerations outlined above. The argument is that in some of the less developed countries, doubtless only a minority at this stage, conditions are basically favorable to economic growth, but growth is constrained by the foreign exchange bottleneck. Providing foreign capital for a limited period can accelerate the country's growth rate and increase its capacity to invest from internal resources so that foreign aid can eventually cease. ("Eventually," however, may mean 20 or 30 years in the future.) If in a particular country this is not true, and if foreign funds will merely go down the drain (or into the back pockets of enterprising local politicians!) the case for aid is weak.

Granted that aid during a transitional period can lift some countries to the point of self-sustained growth, there is still the question of what this does for the United States. Here we must recognize frankly that the potential benefits are long-range, indirect, and conjectural. On the economic side, one can argue that raising the national income of other countries makes them better customers and better suppliers, with whom we can carry on increased trade to our mutual advantage. On the political side, it is plausible to argue that nations which are advancing economically stand the best chance of maintaining political stability and independence. Widely diffused economic progress should contribute to a stable and peaceable community of nations, the kind of community in which Americans would prefer to live.

This cannot be demonstrated conclusively; and so aid is to some extent a gamble. Even if the gamble pays off, in whole or in part, we shall never be able to calculate a percentage rate of return on our aid expenditures.

Multilateral versus Unilateral Aid

Suppose we decide to gamble so many billions a year on aid activities. Why do we insist on going it alone? Why not pool our resources with those of other like-minded nations and operate through international lending organizations? Professor Benjamin Higgins advocated this approach some years ago.[7] More recently, Senator William Fulbright, chairman of the Senate Foreign Relations Committee, has proposed that direct U.S. aid be confined to technical assistance and that all loan money be channeled through multilateral bodies.

---

[7] Benjamin Higgins, *United Nations and U.S. Foreign Economic Policy* (Homewood, Ill.: Richard D. Irwin, Inc., 1962).

If we wanted to move in this direction, the most appropriate organization would be the three corporations of the "World Bank group." In addition to the World Bank itself, which specializes in hard loans, the group includes the International Development Association (IDA), which makes loans on considerably softer terms; and the International Finance Corporation (IFC), which specializes in making funds available for private investment. The IFC can make loans directly to private companies in the less developed countries, or provide equity capital by buying stock in such companies, or participate in financing local development banks which in turn advance funds to private enterprises.

The members of the group share a common governing board, common management, and a common physical headquarters. They amount to three "windows" in the same shop, to which different kinds of loan application can be taken. The United States puts up about 30 percent of their total capital and has a corresponding number of votes on the governing board. The board is controlled by the leading creditor nations, and so is not subject to the difficulties of the United Nations, where the debtors can outvote the creditors. The Bank is competently staffed and managed, and seems to steer a reasonable course between cold-eyed bankerishness and warm-hearted generosity.

The less developed countries prefer to deal with multilateral organizations, which are less suspect of political motives and hidden strings. To U.S. government officials who view aid as a short-run political instrument, this is precisely the point. Channeling aid funds through the World Bank or other international bodies would deprive us of the opportunity to manipulate these funds for our supposed political advantage. So they prefer independent national action.

There is the further difficulty that, even if we were willing to channel our funds through multilateral agencies, Britain, France, Japan, and other major lenders might not be willing to do so. They have their own political interests and their traditional ties with certain regions of the world. So most aid money will probably continue to flow through national channels, with the loose coordination provided by discussions at OECD and the World Bank.

The Problem of Aid Criteria

Suppose Congress next year appropriates $3 billion for the aid program. How should this be divided among the dozens of underdeveloped nations of the world? What standards can be used as a guide to proper allocation?

There seems to be increasing agreement inside and outside AID that the main test should be a *productivity* test. Aid should go where it will be most effective in raising national output. Another standard frequently mentioned in Washington, the test of "self-help," is not very different. Aid should go mainly to countries which are making a successful effort to help themselves, as measured by marginal savings rates, marginal export rates, and other indicators. These will typically not be the poorest countries, but they are the countries which can make best use of additional capital.

One result of this approach is an increasing concentration of aid on a dozen or so sizable countries with good growth prospects. The "scatteration" which was evident in the program a decade ago is diminishing. Even in stagnant economies where the prospect of growth is slight, AID often makes token grants. Small amounts of educational and other technical assistance can be useful in almost any situation. But activities in the 40 or 50 countries outside the core group take only a small part of the total aid budget.

When one applies the productivity test, it is clear that the more outside capital is put into a country per year, the lower will be its marginal yield. So one must set a standard of expected marginal yield, and one can argue that this standard should be uniform for all borrower countries. If we provide Brazil with capital up to the point at which its marginal yield falls to 5 percent, we should do the same for India or Nigeria. This is the principle which applies to capital allocation among industries within the United States, where it serves the same purpose of maximizing total expected return.

Judgments about the prospective yield of aid are difficult to make, but they are unavoidable. Any decision that so many million dollars of aid should go to Nigeria this year *implies* a judgment about yield. So the judgment should be made consciously, with as much documentation as possible, rather than casually and intuitively.

It is well within our economic capacity to saturate the less developed world with capital, to the point where its marginal yield falls to zero. But Congress will certainly not be this generous. Appropriations will be small enough relative to world needs that AID officials will have to apply a positive rate of expected return. The smaller the appropriation, the higher the standard which must be imposed. The point of having a standard is to provide a basis for rationing capital among countries, *not* to assess interest charges against the borrowers. What interest rate should be charged in each case is a separate problem, with no bearing on the allocation decision.

Project Support versus Program Support

The productivity test can be applied in various ways. One can ask the borrowing country for a list of proposed investment projects, each of which can be reviewed on its merits. Or one can ask the country to come in with an overall development program, specifying the resources which it expects to have available from domestic and foreign sources, and the way in which these will be allocated among sectors of the economy. AID can then review the total program, analyze its foreign exchange implications, and decide how much dollar support should be made available.

In the past there has been heavy reliance on the project approach, partly because few governments have had the capacity to draft and administer an overall program. AID officials have often preferred the project approach because it gives them something concrete to work with. It is easier to appraise the cost and yield of a new textile mill than to say whether the Second Five-year Plan of Pakistan makes sense. It is also argued that the project approach gives the United States greater leverage over the use of its funds. AID can urge that some projects be stricken from the list and others added, and so influence the shape of the development program.

But there are serious limitations to this approach. Granted that most countries are not yet able to draft overall development programs, it is not certain that they are further advanced in the art of defining feasible projects. Estimates of project costs and time schedules have often proven wide of the mark, and in some countries U.S. officials have virtually had to compile the project list, because the country itself was unable to do so. Moreover, the yield of a particular project cannot be judged in isolation. It depends partly on what is going on elsewhere in the economy. A list of isolated projects may not add up to a consistent and optimal development program. It is doubtful also whether the project approach really gives us much control over a country's development activities. Rarely does our support amount to more than 5 or 10 percent of the country's investment program. If we insist that our funds be used only for certain projects, the government will withdraw other resources from those projects and shift them to the uses which *it* prefers. So we may be deceiving ourselves about the extent of our influence.

In recent years we have urged the countries with which we deal to draft comprehensive development programs, in the belief that systematic planning makes for better use of resources. It gives AID officials a picture of where the country thinks it is going, and a better basis for estimating the dollar resources required for success of the plan. For reasons already explained, the foreign exchange requirements of a plan are typically *greater* than the direct cost of the machinery and other capital goods which must be imported for specific investment projects.

While the program approach seems generally preferable, it also has limitations which make it unwise to rely on it exclusively. There is always a danger of leading countries to expect a certain level of U.S. aid, year in and year out, which then becomes difficult to reduce. The danger is less if aid is tied to projects with a definite completion date. Support for specific projects is easier to dramatize to the American public and to Congress. It is also easier for the United States to get credit abroad for having financed identifiable projects, instead of simply contributing dollars which get lost in a general resource pool. The U.S.S.R. finances almost exclusively projects which can be dramatized effectively in the recipient countries.

For these reasons we shall probably continue a mixed policy of furnishing some aid linked to major projects, plus some funds intended to close the foreign exchange gap in an overall development program.

A Word of Caution

The foreign aid program is important and would seem to merit continuation. But it should not be sold under false pretenses. Proponents of foreign aid sometimes speak as though it will yield rapid results and will be all over in a decade or two. We need only prime the pump for a short time, after which the poor countries will be able to go ahead under their own power. Since many Americans seem to believe this, it is only natural that the borrowing countries should sing the same tune. One development plan after another asserts that the country will be independent of further aid in 10 or 15 years.

This is quite unrealistic. As a country's growth begins to accelerate, its ability to absorb capital rises sharply. Its capacity for saving also increases, but less rapidly. So the gap remaining to be filled from foreign sources increases instead of diminishing. Remember that the United States, where development occurred under unusually favorable circumstances, remained a large net borrower for about 70 years. It would be unreasonable to expect today's poor countries, starting from a lower level and with many handicaps, to work their way to economic independence in a decade or two.

There is every prospect that we shall be in the foreign aid business for many decades to come. This is not surprising, since the task is nothing less than equipping two thirds of the people on earth with the knowledge, skills, and equipment of modern industry. The prospect should be challenging rather than alarming. But the long-run nature of the effort should be recognized, lest the program collapse in disillusionment because we have not set the world right by next year.

SUMMARY

1. The early stages of economic development typically require imports of capital goods and other materials beyond what can be paid for from the country's export earnings. The gap can be financed by private long-term investment, governmental loans or grants from more developed countries, and loans from international organizations such as the World Bank.

2. Private investment can make a valuable contribution to economic development, especially in manufacturing. The U.S. government can encourage American private investment in the less developed countries

by providing information on investment opportunities, negotiating with foreign countries for nondiscriminatory treatment of our investors, granting concessions as regards U.S. taxation of foreign earnings, lending local currency through AID to American companies operating abroad, and insuring them against expropriation and other special risks.

3. The U.S. foreign aid program embraces a wide spectrum of activities: normal business loans through the Export-Import Bank; dollar loans on more liberal terms through AID; shipments of surplus agricultural products, which are paid for largely in local currency; outright grants, mainly for technical assistance; special assistance to countries such as South Korea, South Vietnam, and Taiwan, for politico-military purposes; and emergency handouts to tide over economic or political crises. Each activity has somewhat different objectives and rationale.

4. The impact of foreign aid on the donor country depends on whether the grant is tied to purchase of goods from the donor, whether the goods are newly produced or taken from stockpiles, and whether the economy of the donor country is or is not operating at capacity. The true economic cost of the U.S aid program is considerably below the official budget figures.

5. From the standpoint of the recipient country, the purpose of aid is to raise investment and the rate of economic growth by relaxing the foreign exchange constraint or the domestic savings constraint. If, however, the effective constraint on growth is limited human skills and organizing capacity, the amount of aid which can be used is small.

6. Whether temporary aid can lift a country to self-sustaining growth, and how rapidly this can be done, depends on the marginal export ratio, the marginal savings ratio, and the marginal output-capital ratio.

7. Administration of foreign aid raises numerous policy issues. What are the main objectives of the program, and in what ways can the United States expect to benefit from it? What criteria should be used in allocating the aid budget among individual countries? Should aid be extended on the basis of specific investment projects or as general support for a comprehensive development program?

8. We should beware of expecting large and quick returns from the aid program. Even where aid is well used, it may be 20 or 30 years before one sees a substantial payoff in terms of economic growth.

DISCUSSION QUESTIONS

1. It is sometimes argued that it would be better for the recipient countries if all foreign aid were channeled through the UN and other international agencies instead of each donor country operating its own program. What advantages and difficulties do you see in this suggestion?

2. Are the aid programs of the United States and other Western countries competitive with those of the communist countries? In what way?

3. Suppose you are asked to estimate the true cost of U.S. aid to the American economy during the present fiscal year. What information would you collect, and how would you evaluate it?

4. "Government loans and grants to the less developed countries are often simply a waste of funds. Business concerns are likely to be more hard-headed about investment decisions, and we would do best to limit ourselves to encouraging U.S. private investment abroad." Discuss.

5. What is the difference between hard loans, soft loans, and grants? Under what circumstances may an outright grant be justifiable?

6. Country X has applied to AID for a $50 million loan. As an official of AID, you are asked to recommend whether to lend this amount, some smaller amount, or nothing. What information would you assemble as a basis for decision?

7. Is it good policy to require countries applying to us for loans or grants to present a comprehensive development program? If the program is satisfactory, should we extend aid without requiring an itemization of specific projects?

8. Does our foreign aid program contribute to the long-run interests of the United States? If so, in what way?

9. Assuming that you consider some kind of aid program desirable, how would you alter the existing program to increase its effectiveness?

INDEX

Index

The text type in this book is 10 point Caledonia designed for the Linotype by W. A. Dwiggins. Text headings are 10 point News Gothic and News Gothic Bold and chapter openings have been typeset by hand in 14 and 18 point Venus Bold Extended.